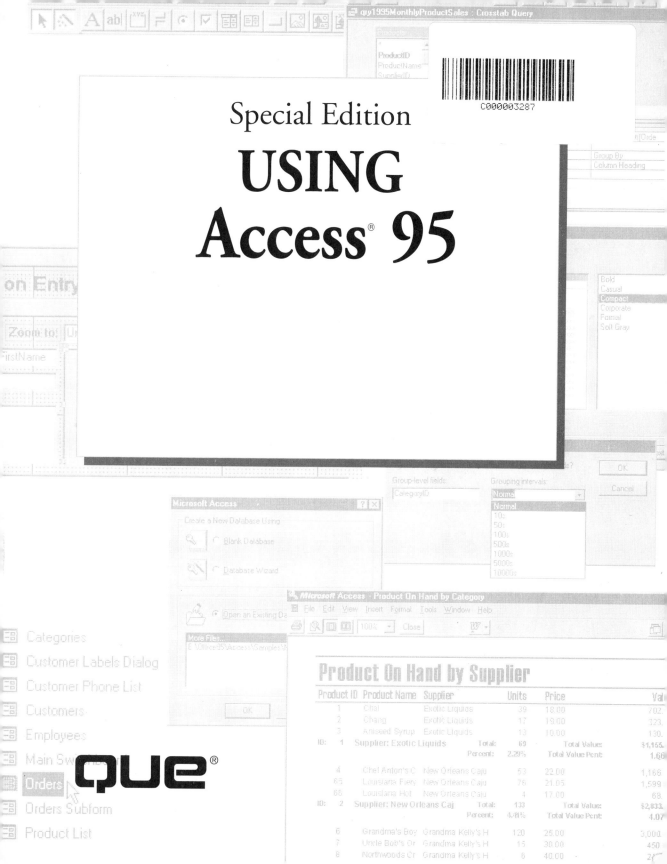

Special Edition
USING
Access® 95

C000003287

QUE®

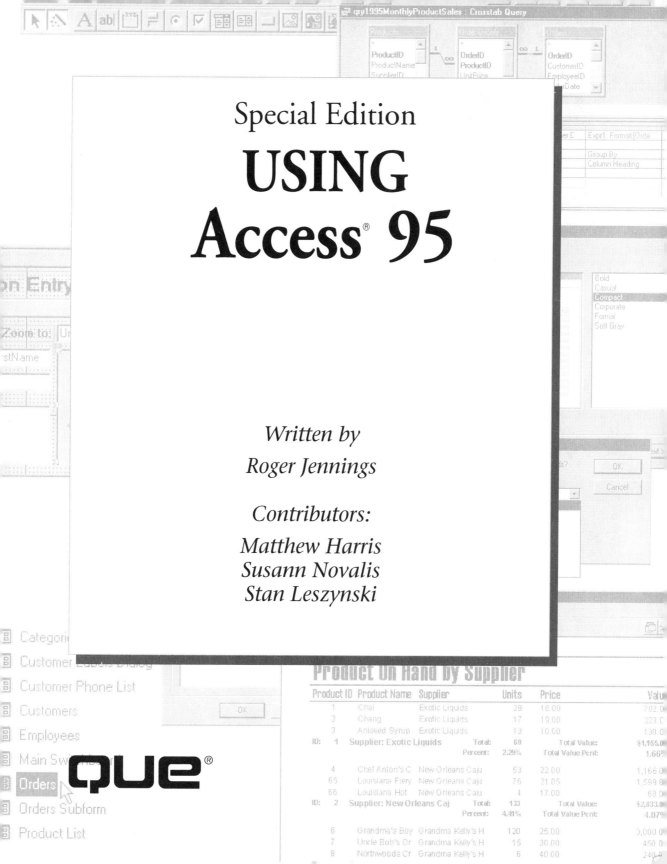

Special Edition
USING
Access ® 95

Written by

Roger Jennings

Contributors:

Matthew Harris
Susann Novalis
Stan Leszynski

que®

Special Edition Using Access 95

Composed in *Stone Serif* and *MCPdigital* by Que Corporation

Credits

President and Publisher
Roland Elgey

Associate Publisher
Joseph B. Wikert

Editorial Services Director
Elizabeth Keaffaber

Managing Editor
Sandy Doell

Director of Marketing
Lynn E. Zingraf

Senior Series Editor
Chris Nelson

Publishing Manager
Joseph B. Wikert

Acquisitions Editor
Fred Slone

Product Director
Nancy D. Price

Production Editor
Susan Ross Moore

Editors
Tom Cirtin
Don Eamon
Noelle Gasco
C. Kazim Haidri
Andy Saff
Heather Stith

Assistant Product Marketing Manager
Kim Margolius

Technical Editors
Brian Blackman
Joseph Risse
Robert L. Tackett

Acquisitions Coordinator
Angela C. Kozlowski

Operations Coordinator
Patricia J. Brooks

Editorial Assistant
Michelle R. Newcomb

Book Designers
Ruth Harvey
Kim Scott

Cover Designer
Dan Armstrong

Production Team
Steve Adams
Angela D. Bannan
Brian Buschkill
Jason Carr
Anne Dickerson
Bryan Flores
Trey Frank
Stephanie Layton
Bobbi Satterfield
Michael Thomas
Scott Tullis
Kelly Warner
Jody York

Indexer
Carol Sheehan

This book is dedicated to my wife, Alexandra.

About the Author

Roger Jennings is a consultant specializing in Windows database and multi-media applications. He was a member of the Microsoft beta-test team for Microsoft Access 1.0, 1.1, 2.0, and 95, Project 4.0 and 4.1, Windows 3.1, Windows for Workgroups 3.1 and 3.11, Windows 95, Windows NT 3.5 and 3.51, Video for Windows 1.0 and 1.1, Visual Basic for DOS, Visual Basic 2.0, 3.0, and 4.0 for Windows, and Microsoft SQL Server 6.0. He is the author of Que Corporation's *Unveiling Windows 95*, *Using Windows Desktop Video, Special Edition, Discover Windows 3.1 Multimedia* and *Access for Windows Hot Tips*, and is a contributing author to Que's *Special Edition Using Windows 95, The Official VBPJ Guide to Visual Basic, Excel Professional Techniques, Killer Windows Utilities*, and *Using Visual Basic 3*. He has written two other books about creating database applications with Access and Visual Basic, co-authored a book on using Microsoft Visual C++ for database development, is a contributing editor of *Visual Basic Programmer's Journal*, and has written articles for the Microsoft Developer Network News and the MSDN CD-ROMs.

Roger has more than 25 years of computer-related experience and has presented technical papers on computer hardware and software to the Academy of Sciences of the former USSR, the Society of Automotive Engineers, the American Chemical Society, and a wide range of other scientific and technical organizations. He is a principal of OakLeaf Systems, a Northern California software development and consulting firm; you may contact him via CompuServe (ID 70233,2161), the Internet (70233.2161@compuserve.com) or the Microsoft Network (Roger_Jennings).

Acknowledgments

Matthew Harris, a consultant and author living in Oakland, California, updated Chapters 2 through 7 and 12 through 15. Matthew has been involved with the microcomputer industry since 1980. He has provided programming, technical support, training, and consulting services to the 6th International Conference on AIDS, the University of California at San Fransisco, and many private firms. Matthew began programming applications for IBM PCs and compatibles in 1983 and has written commercially distributed applications and in-house applications for a variety of clients. He also has taught classes on using MS-DOS and on programming in BASIC and Pascal. Matthew is the author of *The Disk Compression Book*, and the co-author of *Using FileMaker Pro 2.0 for Windows* (both published by Que Books). He was a contributing author for Que Corporation's *Using Word for Windows 6, Using Excel 5, Excel Professional Techniques, Using Paradox 4.5 for DOS, Using Paradox for Windows 5.0, The Paradox Developer's Guide, Using MS-DOS 6*, and *Unveiling Windows 95*. Matthew helped launch Pinnacle Publishing's *Windows 95 Transition Report* newsletter. Reach Matthew on CompuServe at 74017,766.

Susann Novalis, PhD, who updated Part IV, "Powering Access with Macros," of this edition is a Professor of Mathematics and Associate Dean of the College of Science and Engineering at San Fransisco State University. With degrees in mechanical engineering and aeronautical science, she has more than twenty years experience teaching applied mathematics at all university levels. Her administrative work has provided a dozen years experience with computer database management systems. The release of Microsoft Access at the end of 1992 was the beginning of her intense involvement in application development and computer training with Access. While maintaining a full-time administrative position, Susann teaches and creates training materials for Access classes at the university and has published articles in *Access/Visual Basic Advisor*. She is the author of a book on automating Access databases using macros. You may contact her via CompuServe (ID 73312,3437) or the Internet (novalis@sfsu.edu).

Stan Leszynski is the author of the *Leszynski Naming Conventions for Microsoft Access*, an abridged version of which appears in Appendix B, "Naming Conventions for Access Objects and Variables." He also is the author of *Access Expert Solutions* published by Que Books. Stan founded Leszynski Company, Inc., in 1982 to create custom PC database applications, and since that time the firm has created solutions for hundreds of clients, including Microsoft. The company has also written retail products sold by Microsoft, Microrim, Qualitas, and Kwery with a user base of over two million people. Successful products include the OLE Calendar controls shipped with Access 2 and Access 95, the 386MAX memory manager, and four R:BASE developer tools. The company currently specializes in Access, Visual Basic, SQL Server, and Visual C++ applications. Stan's second company, Kwery Corporation, shipped the first Access add-in, Access To Word, and the first OLE Controls for Access 2.0, Kwery Control Pak 1. Stan is a monthly columnist on developer issues for *Access/Visual Basic Advisor* magazine and speaks regularly at Access conferences in the U.S., Canada, and Europe. You contact Stan on CompuServe (71151,1114).

Thanks to Monte Slichter, Roger Harui, Jim Sturms, Michael Mee, and all of the other members of the Microsoft Corporation's Product Support Staff (PSS) and development teams for Access 95 and the Jet 3.0 database engine during their beta-testing period. The PSS staff's prompt replies to questions concerning the prerelease versions of Access are especially appreciated. David Risher, the Access Product Unit Manager who represented the Microsoft Access management team in the beta forum, provided valuable insight on Microsoft Corporation's marketing strategy for Access 95 and the Access Distribution Toolkit (ADT). The contributions of the Access Insiders and other members of the Access 95 beta program to this book are gratefully acknowledged.

Nancy D. Price, product director, provided valuable insight and suggestions for the development of this book's content and organization. Fred Slone, acquisitons editor, made sure that I did not fall too far behind the manuscript submission schedule. Susan Moore, production editor, put in long hours to add last-minute changes incorporated in the final release candidate of Access 95 and still met a tight publication schedule. Technical editing was done by Brian Blackman, Joseph Risse, and Robert L. Tackett, each of whom is an Access expert. Their contributions to this book are gratefully acknowledged. The responsibility for any errors or omissions, however, rests solely on my shoulders.

Trademarks

All terms mentioned in this book that are known to be trademarks or service marks have been appropriately capitalized. Que cannot attest to the accuracy of this information. Use of a term in this book should not be regarded as affecting the validity of any trademark or service mark.

IBM and OS/2 are registered trademarks of International Business Machines Corporation.

Lotus and 1-2-3 are registered trademarks of Lotus Development Corporation.

Microsoft, Microsoft Word, Microsoft Word for Windows, and MS-DOS are registered trademarks of Microsoft Corporation.

FoxPro, Microsoft Access for Windows, Windows, Windows for Workgroups, and Windows NT are trademarks of Microsoft Corporation.

WordPerfect is a registered trademark of Novell Corporation.

We'd Like to Hear from You!

As part of our continuing effort to produce books of the highest possible quality, Que would like to hear your comments. To stay competitive, we *really* want you, as a computer book reader and user, to let us know what you like or dislike most about this book or other Que products.

You can mail comments, ideas, or suggestions for improving future editions to the address below, or send us a fax at (317) 581-4663. For the online inclined, Macmillan Computer Publishing has a forum on CompuServe (type **GO QUEBOOKS** at any prompt) through which our staff and authors are available for questions and comments. The address of our Internet site is **http://www.mcp.com** (World Wide Web).

In addition to exploring our forum, please feel free to contact me personally to discuss your opinions of this book: I'm 75767,2543 on CompuServe, and I'm **nprice@que.mcp.com** on the Internet.

Thanks in advance—your comments will help us to continue publishing the best books available on computer topics in today's market.

Nancy D. Price
Product Development Specialist
Que Corporation
201 W. 103rd Street
Indianapolis, Indiana 46290
USA

Contents at a Glance

Learning Access

Specific Information

Forms and Reports

Access with Macros

Integrating Access

Advanced Techniques

Contents

2 Up and Running with Access Tables 55

3 Navigating within Access 71

II Querying for Specific Information   257

8 Using Query by Example   259

9 Understanding Operators and Expressions in Access   285

V Integrating Access with Other Office 95 Applications — 701

19 Using 32-Bit OLE 2.1 — 703

20 Adding Graphics to Forms and Reports — 729

21 Using Access with Microsoft Excel 765

22 Using Access with Microsoft Word and Mail Merge 803

25 Securing Multiuser Network Applications   903

VII Programming with Visual Basic for Applications 993

VIII   Completing an Access Application   1115

31 Using the Access Developer's Toolkit   1117

32 Adding Online Help for Users   1133

Introduction

Microsoft Access for Windows 95 Version 7, called Access 95 in this book, is a powerful and robust 32-bit relational database management system (RDBMS) for creating desktop and client/server database applications that run under Windows 95 and Windows NT 3.5+. As a component of the Professional Edition of the Microsoft Office 95 suite, Access 95 has an upgraded user interface that is consistent with Microsoft Excel 95 and Word 95, as well as the new Windows 95 common controls, such as Explorer-style file open dialogs. Access 95 is designed to take maximum advantage of 32-bit protected-mode (PM) operation and 32-bit OLE 2.0. Unlike many newly-introduced Windows 95 versions of Windows 3.1 applications, Access 95 uses threads to accommodate preemptive multitasking under Windows 95 and Windows NT 3.5+. The Access operating environment and Visual Basic for Applications (VBA) each have their own thread of execution and Jet 3.0 is multithreaded. Access 95 is the first desktop database development tool to gain the "Designed for Windows 95" logo.

If you're a new Access user, a brief history of Microsoft Access is useful to put Access 95 in perspective. Version 1.0 of Access revolutionized the Windows database market and achieved a new record for sales of a Windows application—Microsoft Corporation received orders for more than 750,000 copies of Access 1.0 between its release data in mid-November 1992, and January 31, 1993. Access 1.1, introduced in May 1993, solved some of the shortcomings in Access 1.0, and the Access 1.1 Distribution Kit (ADK) gave developers the ability to release royalty-free, run-time versions of their Access applications. Access 2.0, released about a year after Access 1.1, added OLE 2.0 client capability and was the first Microsoft application to use OLE Controls, prepackaged objects that extend the already rich set of control objects of Access. Access 2.0 is a member of the Professional Edition of the phenomenally successful Microsoft Office 4.x software suite. When this edition was written, Microsoft reported that total sales of all versions of Access exceeded four million copies.

One of the primary reasons for Access's initial success is that Access duplicates on the PC desktop most of the capabilities of client/server relational database systems, also called *SQL databases*. Client/server RDBMSs are leading the way in transferring database applications from mini-computers and mainframes to networked PCs—a process called *downsizing*. Despite Access's power, the system is easy for nonprogrammers to use. Buttons on upgraded multiple toolbars offer shortcuts for menu commands and an extensive collection of wizards and add-ins handle most of the mundane chores involved in creating and modifying tables, queries, forms, graphs, and reports. Builders aid you in creating complex controls on forms and reports, as well as in writing expressions.

Microsoft Access 1.0 introduced a new approach to writing macros that automate repetitive database operations. Access's 40+ macro instructions are remarkably powerful; you can create quite sophisticated database applications using only Access macros. For programmers, version 7.0 brings 32-bit Visual Basic for Applications to Access. VBA's syntax is easy to learn, yet VBA provides a vocabulary rich enough to satisfy veteran xBase and Paradox application developers. Microsoft Excel 5.0 and Project 4.0 use 16-bit VBA as their programming language; Excel 95 and Project 95 offer 32-bit VBA. Visual Basic 4.0 lets you program in either 16-bit or 32-bit VBA. VBA is Microsoft's *lingua franca* for developing *business solutions* with Excel 95, Project 95, and Visual Basic 4.0. Word remains the only mainstream Microsoft productivity application that hasn't adopted VBA.

Access 95 now supports 32-bit Object Linking and Embedding (OLE) 2.0 as both a container (client) and an OLE Automation server application, giving you the benefits of in-place activation of objects, such as Excel 95 worksheets and Word 95 documents stored in Access databases. (Access 2.0 was an OLE 2.0 container application only.) Conversely, you can activate an Access form or other Access object within an Excel 95, Project 95, or 32-bit Visual Basic 4.0 application. Access 95 also lets you manipulate OLE Automation objects created with Visual Basic 4.0. LOBjects (Line of Business Objects) built with Visual Basic 4.0 and shared with other VBA-enabled applications promise to make a major change in the methodology of creating enterprise-scale database applications. Access 95 and Visual Basic 4.0 share the ability to take advantage of the new OLE 2.0 Custom Controls that Microsoft, third-party add-in software publishers, and you create with Microsoft Visual C++, the Microsoft Foundation Class Libraries, and the new OLE 2.0 Control Development Kit (CDK). (Access 2.0 predated the final OLE Control specification, so its initial support for OLE Controls was limited.) OLE Controls provide Access 95 with the extensibility that VBX custom controls brought to Visual Basic. Access 95 can accommodate almost every 32-bit OLE Control included with the Professional and Enterprise editions of Visual Basic 4.0.

Access is specifically designed for creating multiuser applications where database files are shared on networks, and Access incorporates a sophisticated security system to prevent unauthorized persons from viewing or modifying the databases you create. Access's security system is modeled on that of Microsoft SQL Server 4+. Access 2.0 simplified the labyrinthine security model employed by versions 1.x and made creating secure Access applications much easier. No substantial changes have been made to the Access security system in version 95, but the new User-Level Security Wizard makes secure applications easier to implement.

Access has a unique database structure that is capable of combining all related data tables and their indexes, forms, reports, macros, and Access Basic code within a single .mbd database file. It is now a generally-accepted database design practice (GADBDP) to use separate .mdb files to contain data and application objects; your application .mbd *links* tables contained in the data .mbd. (The term *link* replaces *attach* in Access 95.) Access has the capability to import data from and export data to the more popular PC database and spreadsheet files, as well as text files. Access also can attach dBASE, FoxPro, Paradox, and Btrieve table files to databases and manipulate these files in their native formats. You also can use Access on workstations that act as clients of networked file and database servers in client/server database systems. Access, therefore, fulfills all the requirements of a professional relational database management system, as well as a front-end development tool for use with client/server databases. Microsoft has made many improvements to these features in Access 95. The most important new features of Access 95 are discussed in Chapter 1, "Access 95 for Access 2.0 Users—What's New."

The contributors to this book are seasoned users of database management systems and Windows. The author, Roger Jennings, has more than 10 years of experience in developing database systems for personal computers and is the author of several other books about Windows 95, Access, and Windows database development. Contributor Susann Novalis, who updated Part IV of this edition, "Powering Access with Macros," is a mathemetician, an administrator of a university school of engineering, and an Access training instructor. Matthew Harris updated Chapters 2 through 7 of Part I, "Learning Access Fundamentals," and all of Part III, "Creating Forms and Reports." Matthew is a professional database developer, the author of a book on Visual Basic for Applications, and a contributor to a variety of books published by Macmillan Computer Publishing. This book, therefore, isn't just a recompilation of the manuals that are shrink-wrapped with Access 95's installation CD-ROM or diskettes. *Special Edition Using Access 95* makes comparisons between Access and other popular database management applications when such comparisons are appropriate. This feature makes the book a useful tool in determining whether Access 95 is the appropriate database manager for you or the organization for which you work.

This book provides extensive coverage on using your existing database files in their native formats—alone or with those in Access's own file structure. Many readers have used the dBASE dot prompt and programming language, FoxPro, Paradox macros and PAL (the Paradox Application Language, including Object PAL), or all three of these desktop database management systems. References to both xBase (the name applied to applications that use dialects of the dBASE programming language) and PAL appear throughout this book. If you aren't an xBase or Paradox user, just skip these references. You don't need experience in using a relational database management program, however, in order to create useful, even complex, database applications with what you learn in this book.

Several chapters of this book are devoted to using Access 95 with other 32-bit Windows applications, such as Microsoft Excel 95 and Microsoft Word 95, and the applets supplied with Windows 95, Access 95, and Word 95: Paint, Microsoft Graph 5, and WordArt. Applets are small but useful applications supplied as components of major applications; Paint, for example, is an OLE 2.0 applet. Using the multimedia features found in Windows 95 with Access 95 also is covered.

Who Should Read This Book?

Special Edition Using Access 95 takes an approach that is different from most books about database management applications. This book doesn't begin with the creation of a database for Widgets, Inc., nor does it require you to type a list of fictional customers for their new Widget II product line to learn the basics of Access. Instead, this book makes the following basic assumptions about your interest in Microsoft's relational database management system:

- You have one or more PCs operating in a business, professional, institutional, or government agency setting.

- You are using or have decided to use Microsoft Windows 95 or Windows NT 3.5+ as the operating environment for at least some, if not all, of your PCs. (Applications you create with Access 95 run only under Windows 95 or Windows NT 3.5+.)

- You are able to navigate Microsoft Windows 95 using the mouse and keyboard. Books about DOS database managers no longer attempt to teach you DOS, nor does *Special Edition Using Access 95* try to teach you Windows fundamentals.

- You aren't starting from "ground zero." You now have or will have access via your PC to data that you want to process with a Windows database manager. You already may have acquired Access and want to learn to use it more quickly and effectively. Or you may be considering using Access as the database manager for yourself, your department or division, or your entire organization.

- Your existing data is in the form of one or more database, spreadsheet, or even plain text files that you want to manipulate with a relational database management system. Access can process the most common varieties of all three types of files.

- If your data is on a mini- or mainframe computer, you are connected to that computer by a local area network and a database gateway or through terminal emulation software and an adapter card. Otherwise, you are able to obtain the data on PC-compatible disks; some people call this method *SneakerNet* or *FootWare*.

If some or all of your data is in the form of ASCII or ANSI text files, or files from a spreadsheet application, you need to know how to create an Access database from the beginning and import the data into Access's own .MDB file structure. If your data is in the form of dBASE, FoxPro, Paradox, or Btrieve files, you can link the files as tables and continue to use them in the format native to your prior database manager. Access 95 lets you link Excel and text files to Access databases. (Access 2.0 required the Microsoft ODBC Desktop Database Driver kit to attach Excel and text files.) The capability to link files in their native format is an important advantage to have during conversion from one database management system to another. Each of these subjects receives thorough coverage in this book.

Special Edition Using Access 95 is designed to accommodate readers who are new to database management; who are occasional or frequent users of dBASE, FoxPro, or Paradox for

DOS or Windows; or who are seasoned Windows database application developers who are migrating to Microsoft Access.

How This Book Is Organized

Special Edition Using Access 95 is divided into eight parts that are arranged in increasing levels of detail and complexity. Each division after Part I draws on the knowledge and experience you have gained in the prior parts, so use of the book in a linear, front-to-back manner through Part IV, "Powering Access with Macros," is recommended during the initial learning process. After you have absorbed the basics, *Special Edition Using Access 95* becomes a valuable reference tool for the advanced topics.

As you progress through the chapters in this book, you create a model of an Access application called Personnel Actions. In Chapter 4, "Working with Access Databases and Tables," you create the Personnel Actions table. In the following chapters, you add new features to the Personnel Actions application until, when you reach Chapter 18, "Taking Advantage of Advanced Macro Features," you have a complete, automated method of adding and editing Personnel Actions data. When you are learning Access, therefore, it is important that you read this book in a sequential manner, at least through Chapter 18. Make sure to perform the example exercises for the Personnel Actions application each time you encounter them, because succeeding examples build on your prior work.

The eight parts of *Special Edition Using Access 95*, and the topics they cover are described in the following sections.

Part I. Part I, "Learning Access Fundamentals," introduces you to Access and many of the unique features that make Access the easiest to use of all database managers. The chapters in Part I deal almost exclusively with tables, the basic elements of Access databases.

Chapter 1, "Access 95 for Access 2.0 Users—What's New?" provides a summary of the most important new features of Access 95 and a detailed description of each of these additions and improvements. Much of the content of this chapter is of interest primarily to readers who now use Access 1.x and 2.0, but readers new to Access will benefit from the explanations of why many of these features are significant in everyday use of Access 95.

In Chapter 2, "Up and Running with Access Tables," you learn how to open an Access database, view a table, use a typical query, add a few new data items, view the results of your work, and finally print a formatted report. Chapter 2 shows you how to use the new Database Wizard to create a database from the standard database templates included with Access 95.

Chapter 3, "Navigating within Access," shows you how to navigate Access by explaining its toolbar and menu choices and how they relate to the structure of Access.

Chapter 4, "Working with Access Databases and Tables," delves into the details of Access tables, how to create tables, and how to choose the optimum data types from the many new types Access offers.

Chapter 5, "Entering, Editing, and Validating Data in Tables," shows you how to arrange the data in tables to suit your needs and limit the data displayed to only that information you want. Finding and replacing data in the fields of tables also is covered here.

Chapter 6, "Sorting, Finding, and Filtering Data in Tables," describes how to add new records to tables, enter data in the new records, and edit data in existing records. Chapter 6 describes how to make best use of the new Filter by Form and Filter by Selection features of Access 95.

Chapter 7, "Linking, Importing, and Exporting Tables," explains how you import and export files of other database managers, spreadsheet applications, and even ASCII files you may download from the Internet or information utilities such as The Microsoft Network, CompuServe, America Online, Dow Jones News Service, or government-sponsored databases. Chapter 7 explains the new Table Analyzer Wizard that aids in creating a relational database structure from "flat files" in ASCII and spreadsheet formats.

Part II. Part II, "Querying for Specific Information," explains how to create Access queries to select the way you view data contained in tables and how you take advantage of Access's relational database structure to link multiple tables with joins.

Chapter 8, "Using Query by Example," starts you off with simple queries created with Access's graphic query-by-example (QBE) design window. You learn how to choose the fields of the tables that are included in your query and return query result sets from these tables. Chapter 8 shows you how to use the new Select Query Wizard to simplify the QBE process.

Chapter 9, "Understanding Operators and Expressions in Access," introduces you to the operators and expressions that you need to create queries that provide a meaningful result. You use the new Debug Window of the Visual Basic for Applications code editor to evaluate the expressions you write.

In Chapter 10, "Creating Multitable and Crosstab Queries," you create relations between tables, called *joins*, and learn how to add criteria to queries so that the query result set includes only those records you want. Chapter 10 also takes you through the process of designing powerful crosstab queries to summarize data and to present information in a format similar to that of worksheets.

Chapter 11, "Using Action Queries," shows you how to develop action queries that update the tables underlying append, delete, update, and make-table queries. Chapter 11 also covers Access 95's referential integrity features, including cascading updates and cascading deletions.

Part III. Part III, "Creating Forms and Reports," is your introduction to the primary application objects of Access. (Tables and queries are considered database objects.) Forms make your Access applications come alive with the control objects you add using Access

95's toolbox. Access's full-featured report generator lets you print fully formatted reports or save reports to files that you can process in Excel or Word.

Chapter 12, "Creating and Using Forms," shows you how to use Access's Form Wizards to create simple forms and subforms that you can modify to suit your particular needs. Chapter 12 introduces you to the new Subform Builder Wizard that uses drag-and-drop techniques to automatically create subforms for you.

Chapter 13, "Designing Custom Multitable Forms," shows you how to design custom forms for viewing and entering your own data with Access's advanced form design tools.

Chapter 14, "Printing Basic Reports and Mailing Labels," describes how to design and print simple reports with Access's Report Wizard and how to print preformatted mailing labels using the Mailing Label Wizard.

Chapter 15, "Preparing Advanced Reports," describes how to use more sophisticated sorting and grouping techniques, as well as subreports, to obtain a result that exactly meets your detail and summary data reporting requirements.

Part IV. Part IV, "Powering Access with Macros," is your introduction to the first level of programming provided by Access 95.

Chapter 16, "Understanding Access Macros and Events" is an introduction to Access macros and the events that cause macro execution. This chapter shows you how to use the Macro Editor window to write simple macros.

Chapter 17, "Using Macros with Forms and Reports," explains how you write the macros that automate the forms and reports of your Access applications, and gives you examples of combining Access 95's standard macro actions into macro objects for tasks such as opening a form, changing a form's size, adding and deleting records, and printing a form.

Chapter 18, "Taking Advantage of Advanced Macro Features," gives you specific examples of useful macros that you can use to control how your application starts, to create custom menus and toolbars, and to automatically import ASCII data into an Access database.

Part V. Part V, "Integrating Access with Other Office 95 Applications," shows you how to use the new 32-bit Object Linking and Embedding (OLE) 2.0 features of Access 95 with Microsoft Graph 5.0, plus OfficeLinks to Excel 95 and Word 95.

Chapter 19, "Using 32-Bit OLE 2.1," explains Object Linking and Embedding, the principles that make OLE 2.1 a major advance in Windows application development, how these principles apply to your Access database applications, and how you use 32-bit OLE 2.1 server applications and OLE Controls with Access 95. Chapter 19 also explains Windows 95's Registry that replaces the registration database (REG.DAT) and .INI files of Windows 3.x.

Chapter 20, "Adding Graphics to Forms and Reports," describes how to take best advantage of Access OLE Object field data type and bound object frames to display graphics and play multimedia objects stored in your Access tables. Adding static graphics to forms and reports with unbound object frames also is covered.

Chapter 21, "Using Access with Microsoft Excel," gives you detailed examples of exchanging data between Access and Excel 95 workbooks by using Access as an OLE 2.0 client and server, without the need to write VBA code. The new "Analyze It With MS Excel" OfficeLink feature of Access 95 also is covered, as is the use of Access DDE functions for dynamic data exchange with Excel 95.

Chapter 22, "Using Access with Microsoft Word and Mail Merge," shows you how to store documents in OLE Object fields, explains the OfficeLink "Publish It with MS Word" option for database publishing, and how to use Access 95's "Merge It" OfficeLink feature to interactively create form letters and envelopes addressed with data from your Access applications.

Part VI. Part VI, "Using Advanced Access Techniques," covers the theoretical and practical aspects of relational database design and Structured Query Language (SQL), and then goes on to describe how to set up and use secure Access applications on a local area network. Part VI also describes how you use the Open Database Connectivity (ODBC) Application Programming Interface (API) to create Access front-ends for client/server databases.

Chapter 23, "Exploring Relational Database Design and Implementation," describes the process you use to create relational database tables from real-world data—a technique called normalizing the database structure. This chapter explains how to use the Database Documentor add-in included with Access to create a data dictionary that fully identifies each object in your database.

Chapter 24, "Working with Structured Query Language," explains how Access uses its particular dialect of SQL to create queries and how you write your own SQL statements. Special emphasis is given to the newer Access SQL extensions, such as UNION queries and subqueries, as well as Access's implementation of SQL's Data Definition Language (DDL).

Chapter 25, "Securing Multiuser Network Applications," explains how to set up Access to share database files on a network and how to use the security features of Access to prevent unauthorized viewing of or tampering with your database files.

Chapter 26, "Connecting to Client/Server Databases," introduces you to the 32-bit ODBC 2.5 API and shows you how to create ODBC data sources from client/server databases, as well as the basics of designing Access front-ends for client/server databases.

Chapter 27, "Replicating Access Briefcases," shows you how to create independent replicas of Access databases on network servers or diskettes. Users update the replica databases, and the updated replicas later are merged with the design master database.

Part VII. Part VII, "Programming with Visual Basic for Applications," assumes that you have no programming experience in any language. Part VI explains the principles of writing programming code in object-enabled VBA and applies these principles to using OLE Automation to exchange data with an Excel 95 worksheet.

Chapter 28, "Writing Visual Basic for Applications Code," describes how to use VBA to create user-defined functions stored in modules and to write simple procedures that you activate with macros or directly from events. Access's Code Behind Forms (CBF) feature that lets you store event-handling code in Form and Report objects is also described.

Chapter 29, "Understanding the Data Access Object Class," shows you how to declare and use members of the Access database engine's object collections, such as TableDefs, to create new tables and modify the properties of tables with VBA code.

Chapter 30, "Exchanging Data with OLE Automation and DDE," gives you a complete, working application that uses VBA and OLE Automation to transfer data to and from an Excel 95 worksheet. Use of Access as a DDE client and server also is covered in this chapter.

Part VIII. Part VIII, "Completing an Access Application," is oriented toward adding the finishing touches to applications you create for others to use and converting your existing Access 1.x and 2.0 database applications to Access 95 standards.

Chapter 31, "Using the Access Developer's Toolkit," describes the content of the ADT, the distributable 32-bit OLE controls included in the ADT, and how to design applications for use under run-time Access 95.

Chapter 32, "Adding Online Help for Users," outlines the techniques you use to create applications for others to use, including how to write Windows 95-style help files to answer users' questions about how the application works. This chapter also describes how you use the new Windows help compiler (Hcw.exe) included with the ADT.

Chapter 33, "Migrating Access 2.0 Applications to Access 95," tells you what changes you need to make when you convert your current Access 1.x and 2.0 database applications to 32-bit Access 95.

Appendixes. Appendix A, the "Glossary," presents a glossary of the terms, abbreviations, and acronyms used in this book that may not be familiar to you and cannot be found in commonly used dictionaries.

Appendix B, "Naming Conventions for Access Objects and Variables," incorporates the most commonly used set of standardized rules for naming Access objects and Access VBA variables, the *Leszynski Naming Conventions for Microsoft Access*.

Appendix C, "Data Dictionary for the Personnel Actions Table," shows you how to implement the Personnel Actions table that is used for many of the examples in this book.

How This Book Is Designed

The following special features are included in this book to assist readers:

- Readers who have never used a database management application are provided with quick-start examples to gain confidence and experience while using Access with the Northwind Traders demonstration data set. Like Access, this book uses the *tabula rasa* approach: each major topic begins with the assumption that the reader has no experience with the subject. Therefore, when a button from the toolbar or control object toolbox is used, its icon is displayed in the margin.

- Users of the DOS and Windows versions of xBase and Paradox will find marginal icons that identify important points of similarity with or departures from xBase and Paradox methodologies. These icons are accompanied by brief explanations and, where necessary and possible, short workarounds (methods of implementing the equivalent of xBase and Paradox commands not available in Access). Many of these icons also apply to other RDBMSs that have related macro or programming languages.

- Notes offer advice to aid you in using Access, describe differences between Access 2 and 1.x, and explain the few remaining anomalies you find in version 2.0 of Access. In a few instances, notes explain similarities or differences between Access and other database management applications.

- Tips describe shortcuts and alternative approaches to gaining an objective. These tips are based on the experience the authors gained during more than two years of testing successive alpha and beta versions of Access and the Access Distribution Kit.

- Cautions are provided when an action can lead to an unexpected or unpredictable result, including loss of data; the text provides an explanation of how you can avoid such a result.

- Features that are new or have been modified in Access 95 are indicated by the version 95 icon in the margin, unless the change is only cosmetic. Where the changes are extensive and apply to an entire section of a chapter, the icon appears to the left or right of the section head.

- Tips, techniques, and cautions that apply to the design of applications you plan to distribute to use with run-time Access, are indicated by the ADT 95 marginal icon. You may need to change the design of your Access applications to obtain a satisfactory result under run-time Access.

- All sample databases and associated queries, forms, reports, and the like, used in this book are posted to the Macmillan Computer Publishing Forum (GO QUEBOOKS) on CompuServe and the Macmillan Superlibrary on the Internet (**http://www.mcp.com**). GO QUEBOOKS while online with CompuServe and browse the Libraries with the keywords USING ACCESS 95. In the Superlibrary, go to the Que page, then to Databases.

Most software manuals require you to wade through all the details relating to a particular function of an application in a single chapter or part, before you progress to the next topic. In contrast, *Special Edition Using Access 95* first takes you through the most frequently used steps to manipulate database tables and then concentrates on using your existing files with Access. Advanced features and nuances of Access are covered in later chapters. This type of structure requires cross-referencing so that you can easily locate more detailed or advanced coverage of the topic. Cross-references to specific sections in other chapters occur in the margins next to the material they pertain to, such as in the sample reference next to this paragraph.

Typographic Conventions Used in This Book

This book uses various typesetting styles to distinguish between explanatory and instructional text, text you enter in dialogs, and text you enter in code-editing windows.

Typefaces and Fonts

Terms employed by the graphics profession are used in this book to designate typefaces and fonts used in forms and reports. The terms typeface and face are substituted interchangeably for the term font when referring to multiple sizes of the same typeface. Font is used to indicate type in a single size, such as Courier New 12, indicating the Courier New (TrueType) family, 12-point size, roman (regular) style. A typeface *family* includes all available styles of a face: black, bold, normal, light, condensed, expanded, italic, oblique, and so on.

The term *font* is used by printers to mean a collection of characters of a single typeface, style, and size. In the days of metal type, these characters were stored in trays with compartments of varying sizes proportional to the frequency of use of the character. When Hewlett-Packard introduced its first LaserJet series of laser printers, the term font was properly applied to the choices offered because each was a bitmap of a specific family, style, and size, like Courier 10 Italic. Printers using the Adobe PostScript page description language, which introduced scalable typefaces, used *font* instead of *typeface* or *face* to describe the outline used to create typefaces. This transgression was perpetuated by the Microsoft/Apple TrueType products designed to compete with PostScript.

Key Combinations and Menu Choices

Key combinations that you use to perform Windows operations are indicated by joining the keys with a plus sign: Alt+F4, for example. This indicates that you press and hold the Alt key while pressing the function key F4. In the rare cases when you must press and release a control key, and *then* enter another key, the keys are separated by a comma without an intervening space: Alt,F4, for example. Key combinations that perform menu operations that require more than one keystroke are called *shortcut keys*. An example of such a shortcut is the Windows 95 key combination, Ctrl+C, which substitutes for the Copy choice of the Edit menu in almost all Windows applications.

To select a menu option with the keyboard instead of the mouse, you press the letter that appears in boldface type in the menu option. Sequences of individual menu items are separated by a comma: <u>E</u>dit, Cu<u>t</u>, for example. The Alt key required to activate a choice from the main menu is assumed and not shown.

Successive entries in dialogs follow the tab order of the dialog. *Tab order* is the sequence in which the caret moves when you press the Tab key to move from one entry or control option to another, a process known as *changing the focus*. The entry or control option that has the focus is the one that receives keystrokes or mouse clicks. Command buttons, option buttons, and check box choices are treated similarly to menu choices, but their access key letters aren't set in bold type. Text box entries for choosing files sometimes are shown with the menu choices that precede them, as in the example <u>F</u>ile, <u>O</u>pen *Database*.mdb.

When, for example, you must substitute a name of your own making for a text box entry, italic type is used for the substitutable portion, as in the example <u>F</u>ile, Save <u>A</u>s *Filename*.mdb. Here, you substitute the name of your file for *Filename*, but the .mdb extension is required because it is in a roman (standard) face. File and folder names are initial-letter-capitalized in the text and headings of this book, in conformity to Windows 95 file naming conventions.

SQL Statements and Keywords in Other Languages

SQL statements and code examples, including macro commands, are set in a monospace font. Keywords of SQL statements, such as `SELECT`, are set in all uppercase, as are the keywords of foreign database programming languages when they are used in comparative examples, such as xBase's `DO WHILE ... ENDDO` structure. Ellipses indicate intervening programming code that isn't shown in the text or examples.

Square brackets in `monospace boldface` type (`[]`) that appear within Access Basic SQL statements don't indicate optional items as they do in syntax descriptions. In this case, the square brackets are used in lieu of quotation marks to frame a literal string or to allow use of a table and field names, such as `[Personnel Actions]`, that include embedded spaces or special punctuation, or field names that are identical to reserved words in VBA.

Typographic Conventions Used for Access Basic

This book uses a special set of typographic conventions for references to Visual Basic for Applications keywords in the presentation of VBA examples:

- Monospace (MCPdigital) type is used for all examples of VBA code, as in the following statement:

  ```
  Dim NewArray ( ) As Long
  ReDim NewArray (9, 9, 9)
  ```

- Monospace type also is used when referring to names of properties of Access database objects, such as `FormName.Width`. The captions for text boxes and drop-down lists in which you enter values of properties, such as Source Connect String, are set in the proportionally spaced font (Stone Serif) of this book.

■ **Bold monospace** type is used for all VBA reserved words and type-declaration symbols (which are seldom used in the code examples in this book), as shown in the preceding example. Standard function names in VBA also are set in bold type so that reserved words, standard function names, and reserved symbols stand out from variable and function names and values you assign to variables.

■ *Italic monospace* type indicates a replaceable item. For example,

    `Dim DataItem As String`

■ ***Bold italic monospace*** type indicates a replaceable reserved word, such as a data type, as in

    `Dim DataItem As DataType`

  DataType is replaced by a keyword corresponding to the desired VBA data type, such as **String** or **Variant**.

■ An ellipsis (...) substitutes for code not shown in syntax and code examples, as in
    `If...Then...Else...End If.`

■ French braces ({}) surrounding two or more identifiers separated by the pipe symbol (|) indicate that you must choose one of these identifiers, as in

    `Do {While|Until}...Loop`

  In this case, you must use either the **While** or the **Until** reserved word in your statement.

■ Square brackets ([], not in bold type) surrounding an identifier indicate that the identifier is optional, as in

    `Set tblName = dbName.OpenTable(strTableName[, fExclusive])`

  Here, the fExclusive flag, if set **True**, opens the table specified by strTableName for exclusive use. fExclusive is an optional argument.

System Requirements for Access

Access 95 is a very resource-intensive application. Access must be installed on an 80386DX33 or better PC running Windows 95 or Windows NT 3.5+. You will find execution of Access on computers using the 80386-series CPUs to be very slow, and operation may be glacial with large tables. Although the documentation accompanying Access 1.1 said that you could use Access 1.1 on a computer with only 4M of RAM, a bare minimum of 6M to 8M was required for Access 2.0. Access 95 requires 12M of RAM for adequate performance under Windows 95. If you plan to use Access 95 for extensive handling of graphic images or run it often with other applications using object linking and embedding (OLE), 16M to 20M of RAM should be installed for use under Windows 95 and 24M of RAM or more for Windows NT 3.5+. Using OLE 2.0 to manipulate complex objects, such as large bitmaps, requires substantial amounts of memory. As a rule, adding more RAM is more cost-effective than increasing processor speed or power if you're using an 80486DX-based PC.

A complete installation of Access 95 requires a total of about 50M of free disk space, and you should reserve at least 10M to store the new databases you create. (The incremental disk space requirement of Access 95 is somewhat less if you've already installed Office 95; Access 95 and the other members of Office 95 share a variety of files.) You also should have at least 25M of space available for a Windows 95 swap file or a dedicated Windows NT swap file of at least 50M. Access also makes use of numerous temporary files when processing large client/server database tables or storing large amounts of data returned from queries against client/server databases. Plan on reserving 20M for the Access 95 Developers Toolkit if you plan to distribute applications that operate with run-time Access. Access 95 and Windows 95 have been tested under Microsoft's DriveSpace 3.0 disk data compression system included with Microsoft Plus! for Windows 95. DriveSpace 3.0 reduces the physical fixed disk space required to install Access 95 by a factor of about 1.5 to 1.7. Bear in mind that DriveSpace compression is not compatible with the file compression system included with Windows NT 3.51, so you cannot share compressed disk volumes between Windows 95 and Windows NT 3.51 in 32-bit dual-boot mode.

> **Note**
>
> Fixed disk compression utilities such as DriveSpace do not compress encrypted Access .mdb files. Compression utilities rely on creating tokens that represent repeating groups of bytes in files. The utility stores the tokens and a single copy of the translation of each token. Encryption removes most, if not all, of the repeating groups of bytes in the file. More forceful compression techniques, such as those employed by PKWare's PKZIP utility, can achieve some (but usually not worthwhile) compression.

A mouse or trackball isn't a requirement for using the Access applications you create, but you need one of these two pointing devices to select and size the objects that you add to forms and reports using Access's toolbox. Because a pointing device is required to create Access applications, this book dispenses with the traditional "Here's how you do it with the mouse..." and "If you want to use the keyboard..." duplicate methodology in step-by-step examples. Designing your Access applications with shortcut keys to eliminate mouse operations speeds keyboard-oriented data entry by enabling the operator to keep his or her fingers on the keyboard during the entire process. Users accustomed to mouseless DOS database applications will appreciate your thoughtfulness.

Chapters 21 and 30 use data from a large worksheet of stock prices created by Ideas Unlimited that is available for downloading from CompuServe Information Services. The name of the file is STOCK.ZIP, and it's located in Library 3 (Excel for the PC) of CompuServe's Microsoft Excel Forum (GO MSEXCEL). STOCK.ZIP is compressed with PKWare's shareware archiving program, PKZIP.EXE. You need a modem, communication software, and a CompuServe account to obtain the data and a copy of PK204G.EXE that contains PKUNZIP.EXE to decompress STOCK.ZIP. Information on obtaining a CompuServe account is provided in a section later in this introduction. If you don't have a modem, now is the time to install one. An external 14,400-bps or 28,800-bps modem is recommended for users who are new to PC telecommunications because the light-emitting diodes let you know what is happening (or not happening), and external modems don't occupy a valuable adapter card slot. External 28,800-bps fax modems now are available in the $150–$200 range.

Other Sources of Information for Access

SQL and relational database design, which are discussed in Chapters 19 and 20, are the subject of myriad guides and texts covering one or both of these topics. Articles in database-related periodicals and files you download from online information utilities, such as CompuServe, provide up-to-date assistance in using Access 95. The following sections provide a bibliography of database-related books and periodicals, as well as a brief description of the CompuServe forums of interest to Access users.

Bibliography

Introduction to Databases, by James J. Townsend, gives a thorough explanation of personal computer databases and their design. This book is especially recommended if the subject of PC databases is new to you. (Indianapolis, 1993, Que Corporation, ISBN 0-88022-840-7.)

Using SQL, by Dr. George T. Chou, provides a detailed description of SQL, concentrating on the dialects used by dBASE IV and ORACLE databases, and explains the essentials of the design of relational database systems. (Indianapolis, 1990, Que Corporation, ISBN 0-88022-507-6.)

Understanding the New SQL: A Complete Guide, by Jim Melton and Alan R. Simpson, describes the history and implementation of the American National Standards Institute's X3.135.1-1992 standard for the latest official version of Structured Query Language, SQL-92. Jim Melton of Digital Equipment Corp. was the editor of the ANSI SQL-92 standard, which consists of more than 500 pages of fine print. (San Mateo, CA, 1993, Morgan Kaufmann Publishers, ISBN 1-55860-245-3.)

American National Standards Institute (ANSI) supplies copies of its standards and those originating from the International Standards Organization (ISO), headquartered at the United Nations facility in Geneva. You can get copies of ANSI Standard X3.135.1-1992 by writing to the following address:

> American National Standards Institute
> 11 West 42nd Street
> New York, NY 10036
> (212) 642-4900 (Sales Department)

SQL Access Group (SAG) is a consortium of users and vendors of SQL database management systems. SAG publishes a number of standards that supplement ANSI X3.135. The Open Database Connectivity (ODBC) API developed by Microsoft Corporation is derived from SAG's Call-Level Interface (CLI) standard.

> SQL Access Group
> 1010 El Camino Real, Suite 380
> Menlo Park, CA 94025
> (415) 323-7992 x221

Periodicals

The following are a few of the magazines and newsletters that cover Access exclusively or in which articles on Microsoft Access appear on a regular basis:

- *Access/Visual Basic Advisor,* published by Advisor Communications International, Inc., is a full-color, bi-monthly magazine intended to serve Access users and developers. You can supplement your subscription with an accompanying diskette that includes sample databases, utilities, and other software tools for Access.

- *Data Based Advisor* is published by Data Based Solutions, Inc., a firm related to the publishers of Access Advisor. *Data Based Advisor* covers the gamut of desktop databases, with emphasis on xBase products, but Access receives its share of coverage, too.

- *DBMS* magazine, published by M&T, a Miller-Freeman company, is devoted to database technology as a whole, but *DBMS* concentrates on the growing field of client/server RDBMS. *DBMS* covers subjects, such as SQL and relational database design, that are of interest to all developers, not just those who use Access.

- *Inside Microsoft Access* is a monthly newsletter of Access tips and techniques of the Cobb Group, which publishes a variety of newsletters on products such as Visual Basic and Paradox.

- *Smart Access* is a monthly newsletter of Pinnacle Publishing, Inc., which publishes several other database-related newsletters. *Smart Access* is directed primarily to developers and Access power users. This newsletter tends toward advanced topics, such as creating libraries and using the Windows API with VBA. A diskette is included with each issue. Like other publications directed to Access users, much of the content of *Smart Access* is of equal interest to Visual Basic database developers.

- *Visual Basic Programmer's Journal* is a monthly magazine from Fawcett Technical Publications that covers all of the dialects of VBA. *Visual Basic Programmer's Journal* has a monthly column devoted to database topics of interest to Access and Visual Basic developers.

Online Sources

Your modem-equipped PC enables you to tap the resources of online commercial and government databases, as well as special-interest lectronic bulletin board systems (BBSs) run by individuals and organizations.

CompuServe. When this edition was written, CompuServe was the primary source of online technical support for all Microsoft products. Microsoft provides technical support of Access and the ADT in the Microsoft Access forum (GO MSACCESS) on CompuServe Information Services. The MSACCESS forum is one of the most active application forums on CompuServe, and a substantial number of Microsoft Product Support Specialists are available to answer technical questions on Access topics. Many authors of books about

Access and contributors to publications that feature Access, as well as professional Access developers, participate regularly in this forum. A variety of useful utility and sample applications written by Microsoft staff members and third-party developers also are available for no charge other than the cost of connection time to CompuServe. For information on joining CompuServe, call (800) 848-8199.

The Microsoft Knowledge Base (GO MSKB) contains text files of technical tips, workarounds for bugs, and other useful information about Microsoft applications. Use "Access" as the search term, but remember to turn on your communication software's capture-to-file feature because the information is in the form of messages that scroll down your screen, not in the form files. You also can search the Knowledge Base on America Online; use the keyword "Microsoft."

The Windows Users Group Network (GO WUGNET) is in charge of the CompuServe WINNEWS forum that's devoted to Windows 95. WUGNET members provide a valuable technical support resource and you can obtain the latest news about new drivers and third-party add-ons for Windows 95 in the WINNEWS forum.

Support for Windows 95 is provided in the WinSupport 95 forum (GO WIN95) and users of Windows NT obtain support from the Windows NT forum (GO WINNT). The ODBC Library (Lib 10) of the Windows Extensions forum (GO WINEXT) provides technical assistance in using the ODBC API.

Fawcette Technical Publications operates the Visual Basic Programmers Journal and Discussion forum (GO VBPJFO) and two Windows Components forums (GO COMPA and GO COMPB). VBPJFO offers message and library sections devoted to OLE, VBA/Office, Database, and Client/Server topics. Now that Access 95 has adopted the VBA programming language and shares 32-bit OLE controls with Visual Basic 4.0, Access and Visual Basic developers have many areas of common interest. Vendors of Visual Basic custom controls (.VBXs, Visual Basic eXtensions) are represented in the Components forums. As publishers of .VBX custom controls migrate their products to 16-bit and 32-bit OLE Controls, you'll find the Windows Components forums to be an excellent source of information and product support for extensions to Access 95. Data Based Advisor magazine operates a forum on CompuServe (GO DBA) that covers a wide range of database topics, including client/server systems. One section of the DBA forum is devoted to Microsoft Access. DBMS magazine also has its own forum (GO DBMS) on CompuServe. All of these forums cover a variety of Access database development topics.

The Internet. The Internet is a dynamic environment, so new Internet World Wide Web sites that specialize in Microsoft Access content pop up almost weekly. Use Carnegie-Mellon University's Lycos (**http://lycos.cs.cmu.edu**) or a similar Internet search engine with the search term "microsoft adj access" to find these Web sites. Lycos is included with Microsoft's Windows 95 Web browser. The Access UseNet address, sometimes called the Access NewsGroup, is **comp.databases.ms-access** and is one of the most active software-related usenet locations on the Internet.

The Microsoft Network. Use the Go word "msaccess" to reach the Microsoft Access 95 Forum or "Windows" to find the Microsoft Windows 95 Forum on The Microsoft Network (MSN). Get to Windows NT Workstation support with the Go word "MSNTW" and to the Microsoft SQL Server 6.0 Forum with "mssql." These forums were "under construction" when this edition was written, but you can expect Microsoft to shift their product support emphasis from CompuServe to MSN as Microsoft's new online service gains momentum.

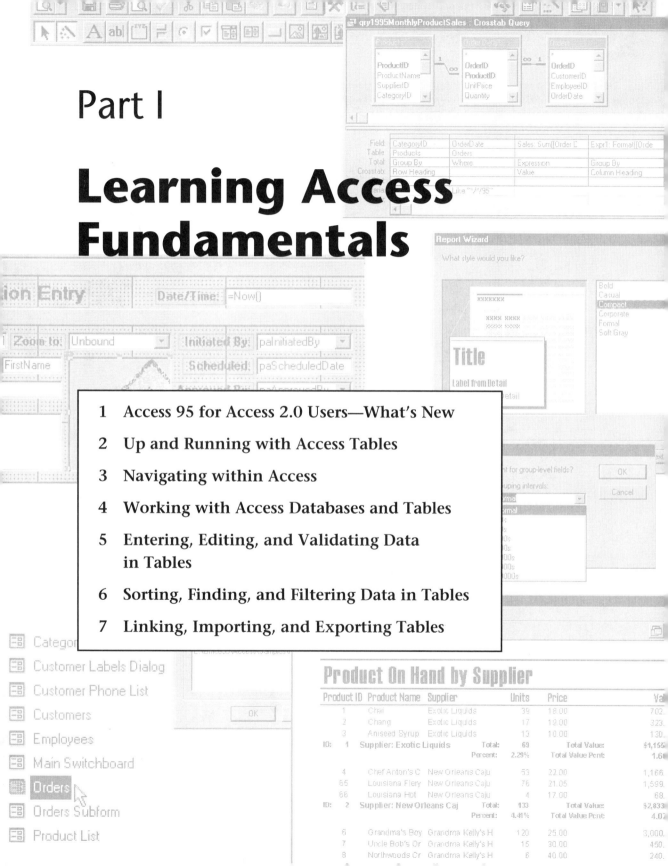

Part I

Learning Access Fundamentals

Chapter 1

Access 95 for Access 2.0 Users—What's New

Microsoft Access for Windows 95 Version 7.0, called Access 95 in this book, is the first desktop database application to carry Microsoft's "Designed for Windows 95" logo. Access 95 is a 32-bit Windows application that runs *only* under Windows 95 or Windows NT 3.5+. Thus the commercial success of Access 95 depends upon the widespread adoption of Windows 95 or Windows NT by existing users of Windows 3.1+. Access 2.0 database applications perform quite well under Windows 95 and Windows NT, so the short-term acceptance of Access 95 also depends on users' perception of the value of the new features offered by Access 95. In the long term, however, the success of Access 95 and/or its successors is assured because there is no future 16-bit upgrade path for *any* 16-bit Microsoft productivity software. This book defines *productivity software* to include the three categories of mainstream Windows products— word processing, spreadsheet, and desktop database applications—plus project management software.

Access 95 is a member of the Microsoft Office 95 Professional software suite that consists of 32-bit versions of Microsoft Word, Excel, PowerPoint, and Schedule+. Most users will acquire Access 95 by upgrading from Office 4.x or through purchase of Office 95 Professional licenses. The Office 95 feature enhancements to Word 95 and Excel 95 primarily involve accommodating the Windows 95 user interface (UI) guidelines. Access 95, however, is a major upgrade from Access 2.0 and involves yet another (the third) major modification of the Access .mdb file structure. Word 95 .doc files and Excel 95 .xls files are fully compatible with 16-bit Word 6.0 and Excel 5.0 files, respectively. Access 95's .mdb file structure, however, is not backwardly compatible with Access 2.0. You can open an Access 1.x or 2.0 database in Access 95, but you cannot open an Access 95 database in Access 2.0. You cannot change in Access 95 the properties of database objects created with prior versions of Access. Fortunately, you can *link* (Access 95's new term for *attach*) Access 1.x and 2.0 tables to Access 95 applications. Thus you can accommodate simultaneous links to tables in Access 1.x and 2.0 .mdb files by database applications created with Access 95 *and* its predecessors.

Some of the main topics in this chapter are

- The new user interface

- New add-ins and wizards

- Improved data import/export

- Automatic Lookup fields

- Filter by Selection and by Form

- Briefcase replication

- Access as an OLE Automation server

- The Access Developer's Toolkit

This chapter begins with a categorized summary of what's new in Access 95; it also includes a detailed description of each of the most important new features and improvements found in Access 95, and why these new elements are significant. Microsoft has made about 100 additions and changes in the transition from Access 2.0 to Access 95; the changes are about evenly divided between features designed to aid new Access users and elements designed to accommodate the extensive Access developer community. In all of the following chapters of this book, the "New in Access 95" icon, shown here in the margin, indicates a new or altered feature. Because this chapter is devoted entirely to the new features of and improvements to Access 95, the icon only appears once in this chapter.

Note

This chapter assumes familiarity with Access 2.0. If you're a new Access user, consider skimming or skipping this chapter. After you've worked your way through the first four parts of this book (Chapters 2 through 18), you're likely to find most of the "What's New" information presented here to be much more meaningful.

Summarizing Access 95's New Features and Improvements

Access 95's new features and improvements fall into the ten categories of the following list:

- *User interface* (UI) modifications make Access 95 conform to the "look and feel" of the other members of Microsoft Office 95, Excel 95, Word 95, and PowerPoint 95. The primary changes to the Access 95 UI include a tabbed Database window that features the Explorer look, new File Open common dialogs that also support import and link operations, and many relocated menu commands. Access 95's toolbars conform to the Office 95 model. Tabbed dialogs used to set Access 95's operating environment options and set database file properties emulate Windows 95's property sheets. Windows 95 proportional scroll bars size the scroll button to indicate the percentage of the data being displayed. When you click the scroll button, Access displays a "scroll tip" with the current record number and the total number of records.

- *Multithreaded preemptive multitasking* improves the performance of large Access 95 applications. Access and Visual Basic for Applications (VBA) each have their own thread of execution and the new Jet 3.0 Data Access Object is multithreaded. The Windows 95 Process Viewer (Pvw95.exe) indicates that Access 95 spawns 5 threads of the following priorities: one of normal (8), three above-normal (9), and one time-critical (23). Very large Access 95 applications can take advantage of Windows 3.5+'s Symmetrical Multiprocessing (SMP) when running on a Windows NT workstation having two or more Intel processors. It's likely that Microsoft will make available versions of Access 95 recompiled for use under Windows NT with RISC (Reduced Instruction Set Computing) processors such as Digital Equipment

Corporation's 64-bit Alpha product line and the 32-bit IBM/Apple PowerPC processors.

■ *New and improved add-ins and wizards* aid Access users by automating a wider variety of tasks. The new Database Splitter add-in automates the process of separating data objects and application objects into individual .mdb files. The Table Analyzer Wizard finds repeated data in tables imported from flat ASCII or spreadsheet files and automatically creates a related lookup table to eliminate the redundancy. The Performance Analyzer Wizard makes suggestions for improving your application's operating speed. The new User-Level Security Wizard automatically creates a new secure database file from a conventional, unsecured database.

■ *Data import and export* operations are enhanced. The Import/Export Wizard makes setting up import and export specifications a snap. Exporting reports to other applications in .XLS, .RTF, and .TXT file formats now include data in subreports. Access copies data to the Clipboard in BIFF format so data pasted into Excel worksheets includes formatting. Dragging selected data from an Access datasheet into an Excel worksheet also preserves formatting.

■ *Lookup fields* let you make selections in table datasheets from a drop-down combo box or list box populated by a field of a related table or from a list of fixed values. Lookup fields are likely to generate controversy among relational database purists because the foreign key value stored in a column of the Lookup data type is replaced in datasheet view by a column returned from another table or by the result set of an Access SQL query.

■ *Filter by Form and Filter by Selection* speed searches for the data you want. Filter by Form lets you enter a value in a control of a form or a field of a datasheet then limit by applying the filter the underlying data set to records that match the entered value. Filter by Selection lets you select a value in a form or datasheet and limit the underlying data set to records containing the selected value.

■ *Startup properties* eliminate the need for AutoExec macros and let you assign an opening form, customize the titlebar caption, and control a variety of other application properties without writing macros or Access VBA code.

■ *Briefcase replication* makes easy the process of synchronizing changes to Access tables by users without network access to shared databases. You also can distribute updated versions of your application .mdbs with Windows 95 Briefcases.

■ *Full support for 32-bit OLE 2.1* lets you extend your repertoire of Access control objects with 32-bit OLE Controls (.ocxs) included with Visual Basic 4.0 and from third-party OLE Control publishers. (OLE is an acronym for Object Linking and Embedding.) Unlike Access 2.0, which was an OLE 2.0 client only, Access 95 is an OLE Automation client and server. (Unlike Excel 95 and Word 95, Access 95 is not an OLE local server.)

■ *Developer features* focus on bringing Access 95 into the fold of Microsoft's VBA-enabled productivity applications. Visual Basic for Applications truly has become the *lingua franca* of applications programming, now that VBA is supported by current versions of Microsoft Access, Visual Basic, Excel, and Project. Word 95 is the sole remaining Microsoft productivity application that has not adopted VBA. (Microsoft promises that the next version of Word will be VBA-compliant.)

The sections that follow describe the new and improved features of Access 95 in detail and place these features in perspective for users of Access 2.0.

Improvements to the User Interface

One of the principle benefits that accrue to purchasers of Windows application suites is a consistent user interface for each of the applications included. The major cost of adopting new Windows applications in large organizations is the training of prospective users; a consistent UI shortens the learning curve for each application. Although Windows 95's new UI is easier for new users to comprehend, those accustomed to Windows 3.1+ may need re-training to adapt to the Windows 95 model. Microsoft's goal in the redesign of the UI of Office 95 Professional is to closely integrate its member applications with the Windows 95 operating environment. By incorporating or emulating Windows 95 features in the Office 95 applications, the cost of training new users and retraining the current workforce is minimized. The sections that follow describe the changes you see in the new user interface of Access 95.

Opening Databases

Relational database management systems (RDBMSs) are the least familiar and the most complex of all mainstream Windows applications. The blank page metaphor of word processing applications and the grid-like windows of spreadsheets have physical manifestations in everyday life. Almost everyone with a PC has had at least some experience using one or more word processing and spreadsheet applications. The container for your data appears when you launch the word processing or spreadsheet application, and you can start typing on the empty page or enter data in the blank cells without knowing a great deal about how the application works. This is not the case with RDBMSs; you must create the container(s) for your data (tables in a database) before the RDBMS becomes a useful application. Thus users who are new to RDBMSs need more assistance in getting started than word processing or spreadsheet users.

 When you launch Access 95, a dialog appears and offers you the choices of creating a new empty (blank) database, using the Database Wizard to create a new database based on one of a series of templates, or opening an existing database (see fig. 1.1). If you double-click the More Files item in the list box of the Open an Existing Database frame, the Open dialog (an Office 95 common dialog contained in Office.dll) appears with My Documents as the default folder. Clicking the Commands and Settings button and choosing Search Subfolders from the menu automatically searches all folders and subfolders for Access .mdb files, starting from the drive or folder specified in the Look In drop-down list (see fig. 1.2).

Fig. 1.1 The dialog that enables you to choose the database to open appears when you launch Access 95.

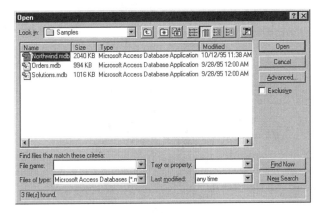

Fig. 1.2 The Open dialog automatically searches folders for Access .mdb database files.

All of the members of the Microsoft Office 95 suite share a common properties sheet for identifying and commenting documents. (*Document* is the official OLE 2.1 term for files that contain information.) The entries you make in the Summary properties page are used by the Find feature of Windows 95 to locate a document based on the value of the document's properties. Document properties are the key to the object file system of the next version of Windows NT, code-named Cairo. Figure 1.3 shows Summary property entries for an example database, 23_PFEL.mdb, for Chapter 23, "Exploring Relational Database Design and Implementation." If you click the Properties button of the Open dialog, the property values of the file you select in the Name list appear in a frame to the right of the Name list (see fig. 1.4).

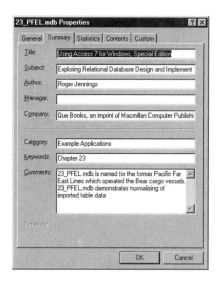

Fig. 1.3 These are typical entries for the Summary properties of an Access 95 database document (file).

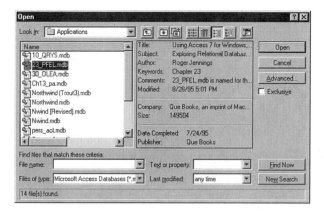

Fig. 1.4 You click the Properties button of the Open dialog to display the property values of the document.

Access 95 Toolbars, Menus, and Options

Access 95's toolbars and menubar choices are reorganized to conform to the Office 95 model. Figure 1.5 shows, from top to bottom, the menubar and first row of buttons of Windows 95 versions of Microsoft Access, Word, Excel, and Project. Eight of the leftmost 10 toolbar buttons perform identical functions in all four applications. With minor exceptions, the name and sequence of menubar choices are identical across the Office 95 and Project 95 applications. Consistent toolbars and menubars minimize user indecision when making the transition from one Office 95 application to another. It is this type of attention to human factors (a synonym for *usability*) that, to a great extent, determines the ultimate commercial success of Windows productivity software suites.

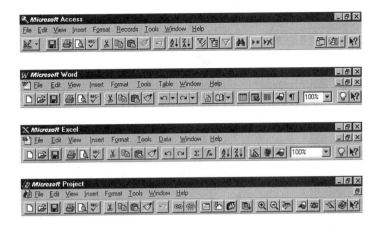

Fig. 1.5   This is a comparison of the menubar choices and toolbar buttons of the Windows 95 versions of Microsoft Access, Word, Excel, and Project.

Microsoft also has standardized the method of setting environmental options for the members of Office 95. Choosing Tools, Options opens a tabbed dialog that is similar across all of the Office 95 products. Figure 1.6 shows the dialog page for setting the options for Access VBA modules. All Microsoft applications that support VBA have a similar options page.

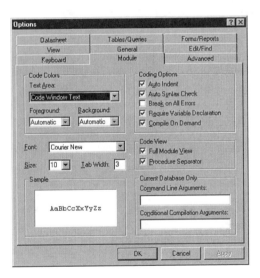

Fig. 1.6   The Module Options page enables you to customize the environment of VBA modules.

> **Warning**
>
> Do not mark the Break On All Errors check box of the Module Options page unless you have a very specific reason to do so. Marking the Break On All Errors check box defeats the VBA **On Error Resume Next** command, which many programmers use for conditional processing of runtime errors. If you mark the Break On All Errors check box, the majority of the Access Wizards *will not operate.*

Tabbed Properties Windows

Tabbed Properties windows make viewing and setting property values of form and control objects faster. Figure 1.7 shows four of the five tab pages of the Properties window for the CustomerID combo box of Northwind.mdb's Orders form. There has been a marked increase in the popularity of tabbed dialogs in Access and Visual Basic applications. You can add tabbed dialogs to your Access 95 applications with the Sheridan Tabbed Dialog Control (Tabdlg32.ocx), a 32-bit OLE Control included with the Professional and Enterprise editions of Visual Basic 4.0.

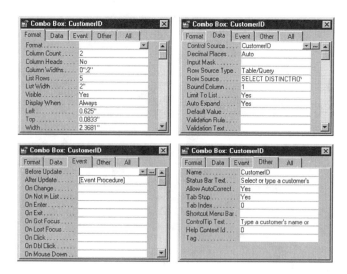

Fig. 1.7   The Format, Data, Event, and Other pages of the tabbed Properties window for a combo box make finding properties easier.

New or Improved Access 2.0 Add-Ins and Wizards

Access 2.0 introduced a variety of new add-ins and wizards to aid new users in the creation of forms, reports, and queries. Several of the Access 2.0 add-ins, such as the Attachment Manager, also made life easier for Access developers. Access 95 continues the Access wizard tradition with the new or improved wizards and add-ins described in the following sections. Some wizards that are associated with other new features of Access 95 are described later in the chapter.

The Database Wizard and Switchboard Manager Add-In

The Database Wizard provides 22 templates for creating the most common types of user databases for applications such as customer contact management, maintaining lists of recipes, and organizing your collection of audio CDs or videotapes. When you click the New Database toolbar button, the New database dialog appears. Clicking the Small Icons button displays the entire list of template choices shown in figure 1.8. Double-clicking a template item starts the Database Wizard, which opens a standard Save dialog. After you choose a folder for your new database, the Wizard presents a series of dialogs that enable you to customize objects in the database. As an example, you can add optional fields to the standard tables included in the Contact Management database in the second Database Wizard dialog shown in figure 1.9.

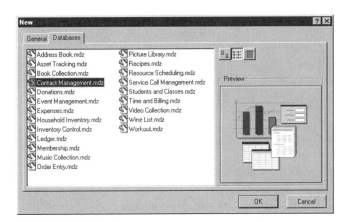

Fig. 1.8 The New dialog enables you to create a new Access 95 database from one of 22 standard templates.

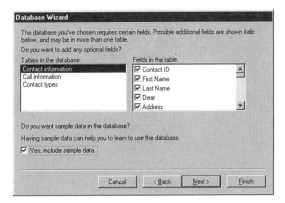

Fig. 1.9 The Database Wizard enables you to add optional fields to the tables created by the template.

The ability to add bitmap backgrounds is a new feature of Access 95 forms. The Database Wizard lets you select one of seven standard background bitmaps or the Windows 95 look, a simple gray background. When you select a background, you get a preview of the form's appearance; figure 1.10 shows the preview of the International bitmap, a pastel image of an elliptical globe. You also can select between several formats for pre-defined printed reports, as shown in figure 1.11.

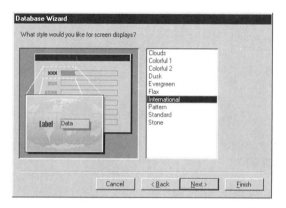

Fig. 1.10   You can select a background bitmap for your new database's forms.

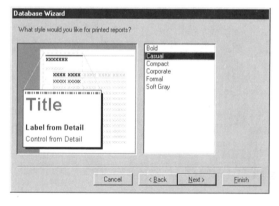

Fig. 1.11   You can select a style for the template's standard set of printed reports.

When you get to the last Database Wizard dialog and click the Finish button, the Wizard creates the objects for the new database. In addition to the basic tables, queries, forms, and reports of the template database, the Database Wizard uses the new Switchboard Manager add-in to create a standard Switchboard form to open forms or reports, customize the Switchboard, or exit the database (see fig. 1.12). Clicking the Customize button opens the Switchboard Manager add-in to reduce the number of buttons or alter the captions for the buttons of the Switchboard form. When you click the Enter or look at Contacts button, the Contacts form with the International background bitmap appears (see fig. 1.13).

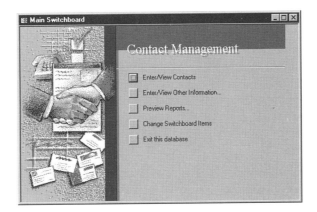

Fig. 1.12 The Database Wizard adds the standard Switchboard form.

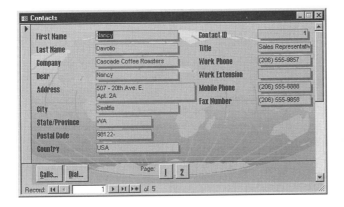

Fig. 1.13 The Database Wizard creates the final Contacts form of the Contact Management database.

The Database Splitter Add-In

One of the most interesting features of Microsoft Access is the ability to store all related database objects within a single document. It has become *de rigeur*, however, among Access database developers to create two separate .mdb files for Access applications; one .mdb file contains the data objects (tables), and the other .mdb file contains application objects, such as queries, forms, reports, macros, and modules. You link (attach) the tables in the data .mdb file to your application .mdb file. Following are the two primary advantages to the two-container approach:

■ *In a single-user environment,* you can update the application objects without affecting existing data stored in tables by replacing the application .mdb file. The alternatives, such as importing updated application objects, are more cumbersome and error-prone than simply replacing the application .mdb file with the updated version.

■ *In a multiuser environment,* each user opens his or her local copy of the application .mdb file, but shares the same data .mdb file that is located on a networked file server. Using a local copy of the Access 95 application .mdb file, rather than a copy shared on a file server, is recommended to improve application performance and reduce network traffic. (Running multiple copies of Access 95 from an application server with shared application .mdb files is definitely not recommended.)

Note

An exception to the rule of maintaining all tables in a separate database occurs when you use local tables to store application information that is not subject to change or that changes only when you update application objects. (Examples are tables of two-letter state abbreviations, application object names, and the like.) Local tables that store per-user application preferences, such as SQL statements for saved queries, should be stored in a second local .mdb file and attached to the application .mdb in order to prevent loss of preference information when updating application objects.

To split a database, such as Northwind.mdb, into data and application container .mdbs, you create a backup copy of your single .mdb file, then choose Tools, Add-Ins, Database Splitter to display the Database Splitter's single opening dialog (see fig. 1.14). When you click the Split Database button, the Save dialog appears so you can assign a file name to the data .mdb, Northwind (Data).mdb in this example. After the Database Splitter exports the structure and data of the tables to the new data .mdb, the tables in your application .mdb are deleted and the Database Splitter creates links (attachments) to the tables. You can verify the definition of the links by choosing Tools, Add-Ins, Linked Table Manager to display the table names and database name for the links, as shown in figure 1.15. The redesigned Linked Table Manager replaces Access 2.0's Attachment Manager add-in.

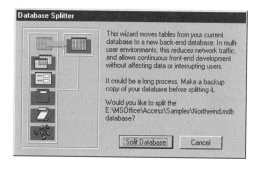

Fig. 1.14 The Database Splitter add-in has only one dialog.

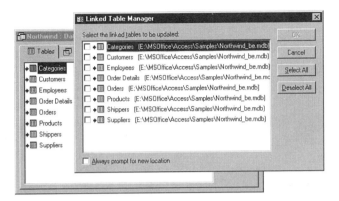

Fig. 1.15 You verify the links to the tables in the newly created data .mdb with the Linked Table Manager add-in.

Note

The Database Splitter is an add-in, not a wizard, because the process is a single-step event. To qualify as a wizard, the add-in must lead you through two or more steps to accomplish a task.

The Performance Analyzer Add-In

The new Performance Analyzer add-in checks selected objects in your database and makes suggestions to improve the speed of execution of your Access application. Choosing Tools, Analyze, Performance opens the Performance Analyzer's dialog in which you select the database objects to analyze (see fig. 1.16.) After some serious disk activity, the recommendations appear in the Performance Analyzer's main dialog. Figure 1.17 shows a few of the recommendations made by Performance Analyzer for the Northwind.mdb sample database. You can select individual recommendations or all of the recommendations, then click the Optimize button for automatic processing of the selected recommendations. (Make a backup of your database before you run the optimizing process in case you don't like the result.)

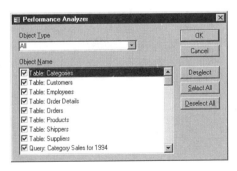

Fig. 1.16 You choose the database objects to test with the Performance Analyzer add-in.

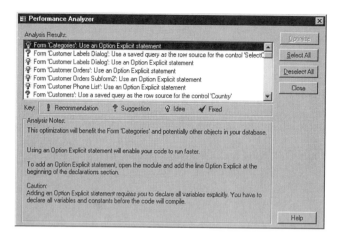

Fig. 1.17   A few of Performance Analyzer's recommendations to improve the operating speed of Northwind.mdb are shown.

Note

The Performance Analyzer omits some important recommendations; for example, it doesn't recommend the use of linked tables when data tables are included with application objects in the same .mdb. Even better would be a system check which recommends that you upgrade your PC to 16M or more of RAM and change to a Pentium processor if your PC is of the 80486DX or lesser variety.

The Macro to VBA Code Converter

The Performance Analyzer recommends that you convert all macros, except menu macros, to VBA code stored in Access modules. Andrew Miller, a member of the Access testing team, wrote an Access 1.1 add-in library, FIRSTLIB.MDA, that included a macro-to-module converter, a menu builder, and a control alignment tool. Microsoft incorporated the menu builder and control alignment features of FIRSTLIB.MDA into Access 2.0. Access 95 now gains Miller's macro-to-module converter, renamed the Macro to VBA Code Converter.

To convert a macro to VBA code, you open the macro in design mode, then choose File, Save As to open the macro version of the Save As dialog (see fig. 1.18). Click the Save As Visual Basic Module option button, then click OK to open a dialog that lets you add standard error handling to your macro functions and include macro comments as VBA code comments. When the process completes, your converted macro appears as a VBA function similar to that shown in figure 1.19. You must manually change the reference to the original macro to the new VBA function in the event "property" that calls the macro. The Macro to VBA Code Converter creates a separate global module for each macro rather than adding the macro's VBA equivalent to a form or report module, which is the customary location for event-handling code in Access 2.0+ applications. The `With CodeContextObject ... End With` VBA structure is required to act on the form, report, or control object that triggered the event; `CodeContextObject` is a pointer to the active form, report, or control object.

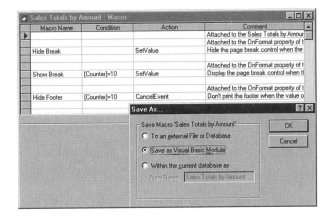

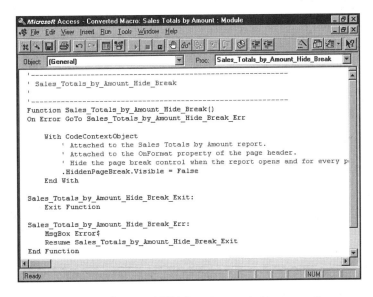

Fig. 1.18 The File Save As dialog for macro objects offers conversion to VBA code as an option.

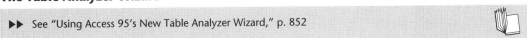

Fig. 1.19 This is an example of a typical VBA function created by converting a macro.

The Table Analyzer Wizard

▶▶ See "Using Access 95's New Table Analyzer Wizard," p. 852

The Table Analyzer Wizard, which you open with the Tools, Analyze, Table command, is designed for users who transfer data from flat files to Access tables. Most flat files, whether downloaded from mainframe computers or imported from spreadsheet files contain duplicated data. The classic example of duplicated data is inclusion of customer name and address information in tables containing invoice data. The Table Analyzer Wizard tests each column of imported flat files for duplicate cells. If duplicate cells are found, the Wizard proposes to split the flat-file table into base and lookup tables with a many-to-one relationship. The base table consists of the original table without the fields containing duplicate data; the lookup table consists of the fields that contained duplicate data, with duplications removed. Figure 1.20, the Table Analyzer Wizard's second explanatory dialog, provides a graphic illustration of the table division process.

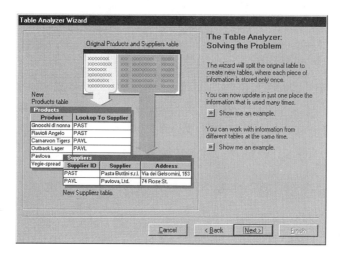

Fig. 1.20   The second dialog of the Table Analyzer Wizard explains the process of removing duplicate data from flat files.

If the Table Analyzer Wizard can't identify a primary key field for the lookup table, the Wizard proposes to create a primary key using an AutoNumber (formerly Counter) field and to add a corresponding foreign key field (a *Lookup* field) to the base table. Access 95's new Lookup field is described in the "Automated Lookup Fields" section, later in this chapter. In the final step, the Wizard renames the base table and creates a query having the name of the original table. Substituting an identically-named query for the original table eliminates the need to change application object (form, report, and control) references to the original table.

Substituting the Registry for MSACC*.INI

 ▶▶ See "The Windows 95 Registry," p. 720

Prior versions of Access determined the availability of wizards and add-ins to Access users through entries in the [Libraries] and [Menu Add-Ins] sections of MSACC*.INI files. Access 95, like other well-behaved "Designed for Windows 95" applications, substitutes Registry entries for *APPNAME*.INI files. Access 95 uses entries in the Windows 95 or Windows NT Registry to specify the library files used by wizards and builders, and to add items to the Tools, Add-Ins menu. Unlike Access 2.0, Access 95 does not automatically load wizard libraries on startup. The registry key for wizard libraries is \HKEY_LOCAL_MACHINE\SOFTWARE\Microsoft\Access\7.0\Wizards. Figure 1.21 shows the Registry Editor, RegEdit.EXE, displaying the a list of the wizards implemented by the Wzlib70.mda, Wzlib70.mda, Wzmain70.mda, and Wzcnf70.mda wizard libraries, plus the Wzdat70.mdt data library. The Form Wizards key is expanded to list the individual types of Form Wizards available in Access 95. The entry for the Chart Wizard shown in figure 1.21 is typical of of the Registry data required to specify the library file and the function (entry point, `cw_WizardEntry`) to call when initiating the chosen wizard.

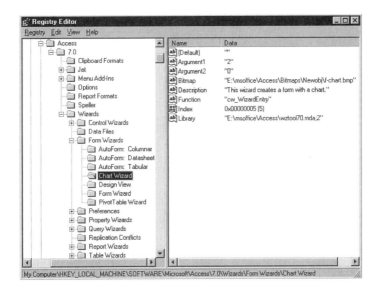

Fig. 1.21   Windows 95's Registry Editor (REGEDIT.EXE) displays the Registry keys for Access 7.0 wizard libraries.

Note

By default, the Windows 95 Registry Editor does not appear in the Start, Programs, Accessories, System Tools menu or elsewhere in the Start menu hierarchy. To make RegEdit.exe, which is located in your \Windows folder, easily available, create a desktop shortcut to RegEdit.exe or add a shortcut to RegEdit.exe to your \Windows\Start Menu\Programs\Accessories\System Tools folder. You can see a list of all of the Access 95 wizards by expanding the `Wizards` hive (section) of the Registry. To find the `Wizards` hive quickly, launch REGEDIT, choose Edit, Find, type **Form Wizards** in the Find What text box, and click the Find Next button.

The registry key for Add-Ins menu items is `\HKEY_LOCAL_MACHINE\SOFTWARE\Microsoft \Access\7.0\Wizards\MenuAdd-Ins\MenuName` (see fig. 1.22) The `Expression` value is the name of the entry point function preceded by =. Entries for Add-Ins menu items are similar to those in Access 2.0's MSACC20.INI `[Menu Add-Ins]` section. The Add-In Manager automatically adds required entries to the Registry when you add a new wizard or add-in and deletes the entries when you uninstall a wizard or add-in. Thus in the ordinary course of Access application development, you don't need to use the Registry Editor.

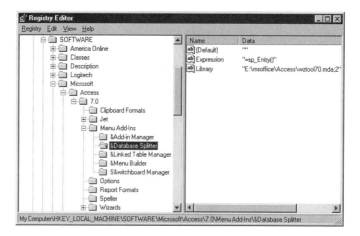

Fig. 1.22 REGEDIT displays the Registry keys for adding items to the Add-Ins menu.

New File Import and Export Features

Improved interoperability was one of Microsoft's primary objectives when upgrading the members of Microsoft Office to the 32-bit Office 95 version. Interoperability of a desktop RDBMS with data exported by mainframe database systems requires quick and easy import of text files. Access 95 also provides improved interoperability with other members of the Office 95 software suite. The following sections describe Access 95's new file import and export features.

The Text Import and Export Wizards

The Text Import Wizard is a boon to users importing text files, especially fixed-width text files. Choosing File, Get External Data, Import opens the Import dialog in which you choose a file to import to a new or to an existing Access table. You select the class of file to import in the Files of Type drop-down list and Import displays all files with extensions corresponding to your selection in the Explorer-type list (see fig. 1.23). Select the file you want to import, then click the Import button. If you pick a text file, the first dialog of the Text Import Wizard offers a preview of the file in the format the Wizard has detected, either delimited or fixed-width. Clicking the Next button displays the proposed field breaks for fixed-width files, as shown in figure 1.24 for Wildfeed.txt. (Wildfeed.txt is a flat file listing unscheduled satellite TV programming.) You can modify the position of the field breaks and add or delete field breaks as necessary.

If you plan multiple imports of files with the same format, you click the Advanced button to create a file import specification (see fig. 1.25). The Filename ImportSpec dialog lets you change the field names from the default Field# names and alter field data types as necessary. (The Wizard automatically detects most date and numeric formats.) When your import specification is complete, click the Save As button and assign your import specification a name. You can reuse the import specification the next time you need to import the text file. When you click the Finish button, the Wizard creates a new table or adds the records to an existing table. (The Wizard gratuitously adds an ID column with a field of the AutoNumber type that you can delete in Table Design mode.)

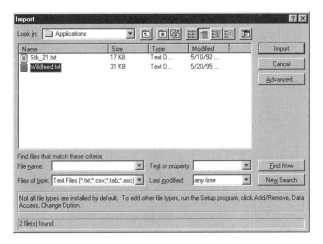

Fig. 1.23 The Import dialog enables you to select a file of a supported type for import to an Access table.

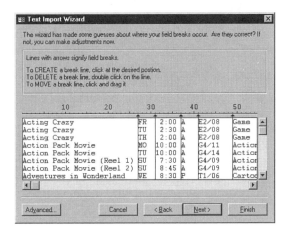

Fig. 1.24 The second dialog of the Text Import Wizard verifies field breaks in a fixed-width text file.

The Text Export Wizard performs the reverse operation of the Text Import Wizard. When you choose File, Save As/Export, select To an External Database, specify Text Files in the Save Table dialog, and click OK, the first dialog of the Text Export Wizard appears (see fig. 1.26). The default for saving text files is the standard delimited format (.SDF, commas separate fields, string values are enclosed with quotes) used by dBASE and many other desktop database applications, but you also can export fixed width text files.

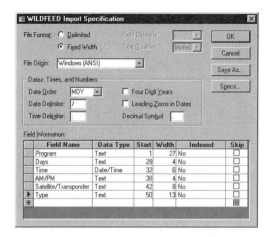

Fig. 1.25 You create an import specification for repeated importing of fixed-width text files.

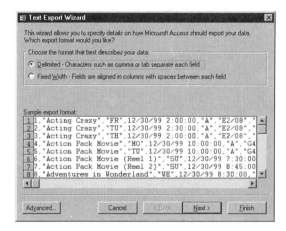

Fig. 1.26 The first dialog of the Text Export Wizard enables you to export data to delimited or fixed-width text files.

Note

The 12/30/99 date preceding the time values results from importing data with time values that do not have corresponding dates. Although you can apply the Short Time format to fields of the Date/Time data type, the format is not applied when data is exported. To eliminate the spurious date, use a make-table query to convert Date/Time fields to Text fields with the Format([*FieldName*], "hh:nn") function before exporting.

Exporting Data to Microsoft Word and Excel

 The Office Links button replaces the Output to Word and Output to Excel buttons and the Mail Merge Wizard of Access 2.0. The Office Links button offers you the following three options:

- *Merge-it* uses DDE (Dynamic Data Exchange) to execute a mail merge operation with Microsoft Word documents. Other than the means by which you start the Microsoft Word Mail Merge Wizard, mail merge operations are the same as those of Access 2.0.

- *Publish It with MS Word* creates an *ObjectName*.rtf file from a table, query, form, or report and opens Word to display the file. Files created from tables, queries, and forms appear as Word tables; reports appear as formatted for printing by Access 95.

- *Analyze It with MS Excel* creates an *ObjectName*.xls file opens Excel to display the file. Figure 1.27 shows Excel 95 displaying Northwind.mdb's Alphabetical List of Products report exported as an Excel worksheet.

	A	B	C	D	E
1	12-Oct-95				
2	FirstLetterofName	ProductName	CategoryName	QuantityPerUnit	UnitsInStock
3	A				
4		Aniseed Syrup	Condiments	12 - 550 ml bottles	13
5	B				
6		Boston Crab Meat	Seafood	24 - 4 oz tins	123
7	C				
8		Camembert Pierrot	Dairy Products	15 - 300 g rounds	19
9		Carnarvon Tigers	Seafood	16 kg pkg.	42
10		Chai	Beverages	10 boxes x 20 bags	39
11		Chang	Beverages	24 - 12 oz bottles	17
12		Chartreuse verte	Beverages	750 cc per bottle	69
13		Chef Anton's Cajun Seasoning	Condiments	48 - 6 oz jars	53
14		Chocolade	Confections	10 pkgs.	15
15		Côte de Blaye	Beverages	12 - 75 cl bottles	17
16	E				
17		Escargots de Bourgogne	Seafood	24 pieces	62
18	F				
19		Filo Mix	Grains/Cereals	16 - 2 kg boxes	38

Fig. 1.27 Excel 95 displays an exported Access 95 report.

▶▶ See "Access's Integrated Data Dictionary System," p. 859

Access 95 now includes data in subforms and subreports when exporting to .rtf and .xls files. This feature allows Access 95's Data Documentor add-in to export the full version of its data dictionary to Microsoft Word or Excel. When you copy data to the Clipboard and paste the data to Excel, Access now uses the BIFF format to transfer Access text formatting to the Excel worksheet.

Attaching Data to Microsoft Exchange Messages

Windows 95 alters the action of the File, Send command of all Office 95 applications because the Microsoft Exchange client substitutes for the Microsoft Word 3.x client of Windows for Workgroups 3.1+. You can attach the data contained in an Access object to a message in Microsoft Excel, rich text, or MS-DOS text format. Figure 1.28 illustrates finding the address of the recipient for a message to be sent via The Microsoft Network.

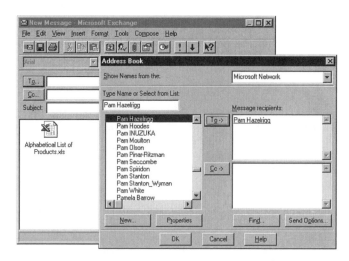

Fig. 1.28   You set the address of an Exchange message recipient who is a member of The Microsoft Network.

Lookup Fields in Access Tables and the Lookup Wizard

▶▶ See "Using Lookup Fields in Tables," p. 328
▶▶ See "Using Access 95's New Table Analyzer Wizard," p. 852

Many Access application developers create forms or subforms that include bound combo boxes populated by data from a table, a query, or a list of fixed values. Access 95 now provides the equivalent functionality in table datasheets with the Lookup property for fields that contain foreign key values. If you specify as an SQL SELECT statement the Lookup property for a field containing foreign key values, such as the CustomerID field of Northwind.mdb's Orders table, you can substitute the value of a field from a lookup table, such as the CompanyName field of the Customers table. Figure 1.29 shows the Orders table in Table Design view with the CustomerID field selected. The full SQL statement for the Record Source property of the Lookup field that binds the Company Name field of the Customers table is:

```
SELECT DISTINCTROW Customers.CustomerID,
      Customers.CompanyName
   FROM Customers
   ORDER BY Customers.CompanyName;
```

When in Table Datasheet view you place the caret in a Lookup field, the cell changes from the equivalent of a text box to a drop-down list (combo box). When you open the list, as shown in figure 1.30, you can select from any of the items in the list, in this example any CompanyName value in the Customers table. (By default, the Limit To List property of the combo box is **True**.)

Orders : Table
Field Name
Data Type
Description
OrderID
AutoNumber
Unique order number.
CustomerID
Text
Same entry as in Customers table.
EmployeeID
Number
Same entry as in Employees table.
OrderDate
Date/Time
RequiredDate
Date/Time
ShippedDate
Date/Time
ShipVia
Number
Same as Shipper ID in Shippers table.
Freight
Currency
Field Properties
General
Lookup
Display Control
Combo Box
Row Source Type
Table/Query
Row Source
SELECT DISTINCTROW [CustomerID],[C
Bound Column
1
Column Count
2
Column Heads
No
Column Widths
0"
List Rows
8
List Width
Auto
Limit To List
Yes
Source of control's data

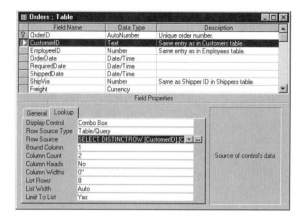

Fig. 1.29 The Lookup properties page for the CustomerID field of Northwind.mdb's Orders table.

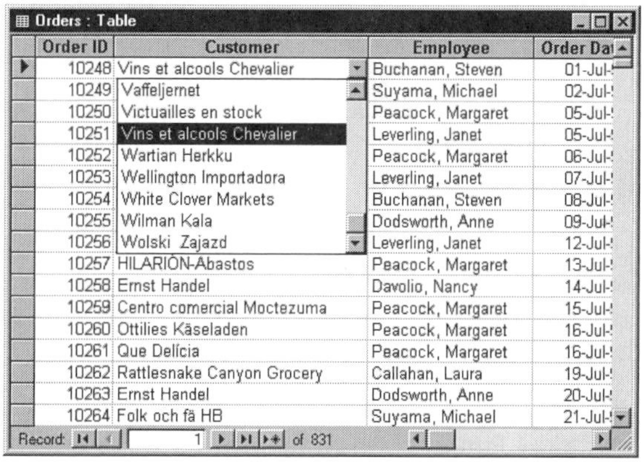

Orders : Table
Order ID
Customer
Employee
Order Da
10248 Vins et alcools Chevalier Buchanan, Steven 01-Jul-
10249 Vaffeljernet Suyama, Michael 02-Jul-
10250 Victuailles en stock Peacock, Margaret 05-Jul-
10251 Vins et alcools Chevalier Leverling, Janet 05-Jul-
10252 Wartian Herkku Peacock, Margaret 06-Jul-
10253 Wellington Importadora Leverling, Janet 07-Jul-
10254 White Clover Markets Buchanan, Steven 08-Jul-
10255 Wilman Kala Dodsworth, Anne 09-Jul-
10256 Wolski Zajazd Leverling, Janet 12-Jul-
10257 HILARIÓN-Abastos Peacock, Margaret 13-Jul-
10258 Ernst Handel Davolio, Nancy 14-Jul-
10259 Centro comercial Moctezuma Peacock, Margaret 15-Jul-
10260 Ottilies Käseladen Peacock, Margaret 16-Jul-
10261 Que Delícia Peacock, Margaret 16-Jul-
10262 Rattlesnake Canyon Grocery Callahan, Laura 19-Jul-
10263 Ernst Handel Dodsworth, Anne 20-Jul-
10264 Folk och fä HB Suyama, Michael 21-Jul-
Record: 1 of 831

Fig. 1.30 Opening the drop-down list in the CustomerID column (aliased as Customer) of the Orders list lets you choose from any value in the CompanyName field of the Customers table.

To change a field from a conventional field data type to a Lookup field, you choose Lookup Wizard in the Data Type list for the foreign key field to launch the Lookup Wizard. The lookup Wizard is one of the subjects of Chapter 13, "Designing Custom Multitable Forms," and Chapter 23, "Exploring Relational Database Design and Implementation."

Filtering by Form and by Selection

▸▸ See "Filtering Table Data," p. 185

Access 95 makes finding the specific records you want in Table Datasheet and Form view with the new Filter by Form and Filter by Selection features. With a table or query open in Datasheet view, clicking the Filter by Form button of the toolbar displays a single row into which you type a filter criterion or, if a Lookup field, from which you choose a filter value (see fig. 1.31 top). If you click the Or tab at the bottom of the form, you can enter an additional filter criterion. When you click the Apply Filter button, only records that match your filter criterion appear in the datasheet (see fig. 1.31 bottom).

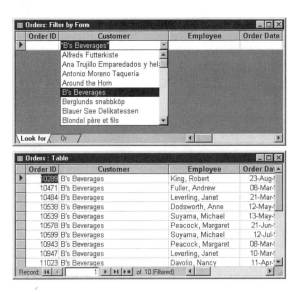

Fig. 1.31 Clicking the Filter by Form button in Table Datasheet view opens a single form in which you enter a filter criterion (top); clicking the Apply Filter button restricts the Datasheet view to the filter criterion (bottom).

 To use Filter by Selection, you select a value for the filter in one of the fields of your table (see fig. 1.32 top). Clicking the Filter by Selection button displays only those records meeting the filter criteria (see fig. 1.32 bottom). When using Filter by Selection, you don't need to click the Apply Filter button.

Both Filter by Form and Filter by Selection also work in Form view. Filter by Form empties all bound controls on your form; you enter a value in one of the bound controls and click the Filter by Form button to set the filter criteria (see fig. 1.33). Similarly, you select a bound control and click the Filter by Selection button to limit the record source of your form to those records that meet the filter criteria. In both cases, the total number of records that appears to the right of the record navigation buttons changes to reflect the number of records in the filtered set followed by "(Filtered)," as shown at the bottom of figure 1.34.

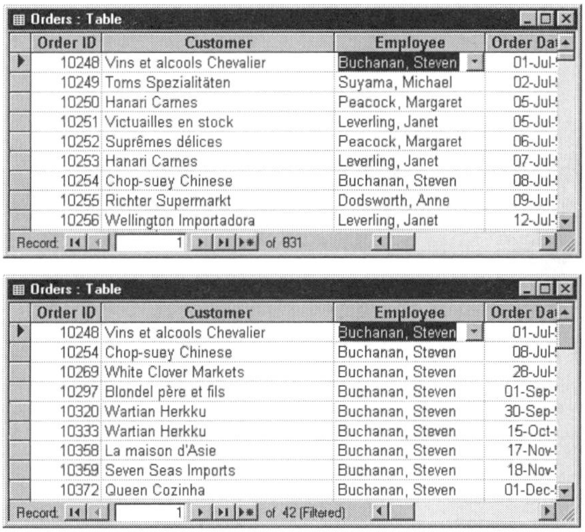

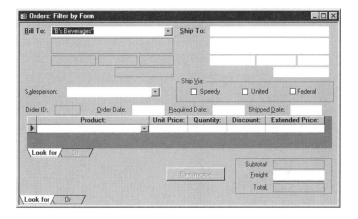

Fig. 1.32 Selecting a filter criterion in Table Datasheet view (top) and clicking the Filter by Selection button displays only those records meeting the filter criterion.

Fig. 1.33 Filter by Form empties the values of bound controls when applied in Form view.

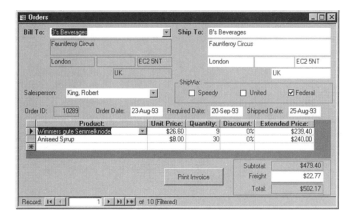

Fig. 1.34 The total number of records in the filtered set appears to the right of the record navigation buttons.

Opening a Database with Startup Properties

Access 2.0 required you to write an AutoExec macro to control the startup of your database application. Typically, AutoExec macros included actions to maximize Access, hide the Database window, and open the main form of your application. Choosing Tools, Startup opens the new Startup dialog that, in most cases, can take the place of an AutoExec macro. Clicking the Advanced button of the basic Startup dialog exposes additional property value settings shown below the dividing line in figure 1.35. You can enter a toolbar caption for your application in the Application Title text box, specify an application icon (.ico file), create a menubar with the Menu Builder, and create your own startup shortcut menu. (The new ShortcutMenuBar property lets you define your own shortcut menu for forms and controls.) You also can specify the menus and toolbars to which users of your application have access. The Startup menu does not include a maximize option, but Windows 95 shortcuts let you determine whether Access launches in a normal, maximized, or minimized state.

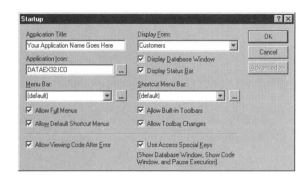

Fig. 1.35 The new Startup dialog displays advanced options.

Replicating Access Databases

Window 95's Briefcase feature is designed for management of multiple document updates by users who are unable to share a networked document file. As an example, if you have a home computer that you also use for business purposes, but you cannot take advantage of RAS (Remote Access Services, called Remote Networking by Windows 95) to connect to the office network, Briefcase replication lets you update documents from replica copies stored on diskette. Another example is updating documents on a laptop computer that you only periodically connect to a network. The basic principal of replication, which also is used by Lotus Notes, Microsoft SQL Server 6.0, and Microsoft Exchange Server, is propagating only the changes to a master document.

Access 95 lets you create Windows 95 Briefcase replicas of Access databases and to keep the replicas synchronized. (Briefcase replication with Windows NT 3.51+ Workstation won't be possible until Windows NT gains the Windows 95 user interface.) Access Briefcase replication depends on the creation of an Access *replica set*. A replica set consists of one (and only one) *replica master*, but may include more than one database replica. To create a replica set, you drag the database file from My Computer or Explorer and drop it onto the My Briefcase desktop icon. (You cannot convert an open database to a replica.) Figure 1.36 shows the first set of messages you receive prior to the conversion process. Jet 3.0 offers to create a backup copy of the original database, then converts the database into a replica and creates a Briefcase replica set. During the conversion process, you can specify if design changes are allowed only to the original database or only to the Briefcase replica.

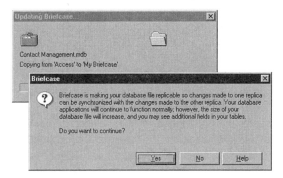

Fig. 1.36 Two of the messages you receive while converting an Access 95 database to a replica master and creating a Briefcase replica set.

Figure 1.37 shows the Briefcase window and the Update Status properties page for a replica of the Contact Management database created by the Database wizard. You can make multiple replicas of your database by dragging the desktop database replica into different Briefcases. To create multiple Briefcases, use the Windows Explorer to create a new folder, if necessary, then choose New, Briefcase. If you create a briefcase on a network server, multiple users can drag the replica database into the Briefcase on their computer; it's not necessary for the server to be running Windows 95. Alternatively, you can create a Briefcase on diskette and drag the replica database onto the diskette briefcase. Diskettes must include the Briefcase and the replica database for changes to propagate to the replica master. Chapter 27, "Replicating Access Databases," describes the objectives of and methods for creating and distributing Briefcase replicas of Access databases.

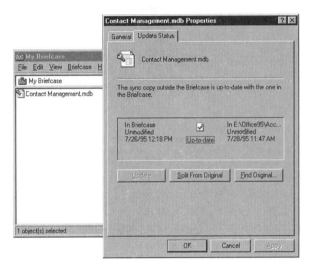

Fig. 1.37 You can check the update status of an Access database replica.

Note

The primary application for Briefcase replicas of Access database is updating data. Thus it is most common to replicate .mdb files of "split" Access applications that contain only data objects. You can automatically distribute updated application .mdb files by creating a separate application replica set.

Upgrading To 32-Bit OLE 2.1

One of the primary incentives for upgrading to Office 95 is to take advantage of 32-bit OLE 2.1's enhanced performance and integrity features. 32-bit OLE 2.1 provides an interapplication data path that's twice as wide as conventional 16-bit OLE 2.0. Windows 95 and Windows NT assign 32-bit applications participating in OLE 2.1 operations their own protected memory space. Windows NT 3.51 includes multithreaded OLE 2.1 to further improve performance on servers and workstations with multiple processors. Chapter 19, "Using 32-Bit OLE 2.1," describes Access 95's new OLE features in detail. The following sections provide a brief summary of the most important new OLE 2.1 elements of Access 95.

Extending Access 95 with 32-bit OLE Controls

Access 2.0 was the first Microsoft product to support OLE Controls (also called OCXs, OLE Control eXtensions), which are designed to supplant Visual Basic's VBX custom controls. Microsoft released Access 2.0 before finalizing the OLE Control specification and completing Visual C++'s Control Wizard, which developers need to write OCXs.

Subsequently, Microsoft distributed an interim upgrade to Access 2.0, the Microsoft Access 2.0 Service Pack, that upgraded Access 2.0 to the OLE 2.02 standard, replaced the Jet 2.0 Data Access Object (DAO) to version 2.5, and provided replacements for the Paradox and Btrieve ISAM (Indexed Sequential Access Method) drivers included with Access 2.0. Access 2.0 acts as a container for 16-bit OLE Controls only.

Access 95 is a fully-compliant OLE 2.1 container for standard 32-bit OLE Controls. The retail version of Access 95 contains two 32-bit OLE Controls, Calendar and Data Outline. Figure 1.38 shows Access 95's enhanced Calendar control (Msacal70.ocx) added to a form in Design mode. Msacal70.ocx now is a bound control that you can bind to a Date/Time field of a table or query; the Calendar in Form view displays the date field value of the current record and you can change the date value with the control.

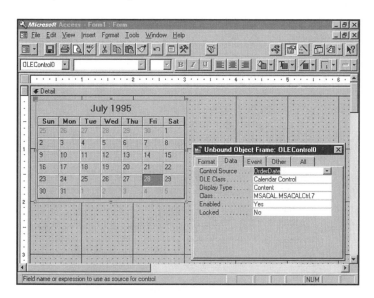

Fig. 1.38   Adding Access 95's enhanced Calendar OLE Control is bound to the Order Date field of Northwind.mdb's Orders table.

The Access Developer's Toolkit includes a number of additional 32-bit OLE Controls drawn from the collection supplied with the Professional Edition of Visual Basic 4.0. If you have a license for Visual Basic 4.0, you can use most of the 32-bit OLE Controls included with Visual Basic 4.0 in your Access applications. Access 95 does not support Visual Basic 4.0's Data control or the Remote Data control of the Visual Basic 4.0 Enterprise Edition, so you can't use Visual Basic 4.0's bound data controls in your Access applications. This is not a significant limitation because Access's built-in control objects provide all of the features of Visual Basic 4.0's data-aware controls (except the Remote Data control). You can use Visual Basic's 32-bit Remote Data object, however, to speed Access 95 queries against client/server databases.

OLE Automation and Workflow Applications

As noted earlier in this chapter, Microsoft Corporation's strategy for its mainstream Windows applications is to maximize interoperability of the 32-bit Office 95 applications. The goal is to let you create large-scale workgroup and workflow applications using Microsoft Access, Excel, Word, Project, and Visual Basic 4.0 as building blocks. Workflow applications are designed to automate business processes by providing a means for participants in a particular activity (the workgroup) to contribute their input electronically. Creating workflow applications is one of the elements of business re-engineering. Part of the plan is to use the Microsoft Exchange client as the communication link between participants in the workflow process. The mainstay of workflow applications, however, is OLE Automation's ability to manipulate objects exposed by OLE 2.0 server applications. Like its predecessor, Access 95 is an OLE Automation client that can manipulate objects exposed by any OLE Automation server.

Now that Access 95 is an OLE Automation server, you can take advantage of Access's unique capabilities, particularly its flexible reporting features, from within other VBA-enabled applications, such as Visual Basic 4.0 or Excel 95. As an example, to manipulate Access 95 objects with Microsoft Excel 95 VBA, you create in an Excel module a reference to Microsoft Access 95. You then can view the objects exposed by Access 95 in Excel's Object Browser and check the properties of and the methods applicable to each object (see fig. 1.39). VBA code in Excel modules can manipulate any object exposed by Access 95.

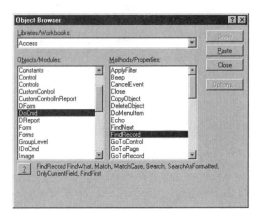

Fig. 1.39   You can browse Excel 95 objects exposed by creating a reference to Microsoft Access 95.

Using OLE Servers and DLLs Created with Visual Basic 4.0

You can create with Visual Basic 4.0 custom out-of-process OLE 2.0 server applications (.exe files), as well as in-process OLE Automation servers (.dll files.) Out-of-process servers use LRPCs (Lightweight Remote Procedure Calls) for communication between the OLE client and server. In-process servers share the address space of the client application; this makes in-process OLE servers perform faster than the out-of-process variety because of reduced interprocess communication overhead. Creating both types of OLE servers with Visual Basic 4.0 is a much simpler process than writing the Visual C++ code to accomplish the same objective.

Traditionally, developers use Access add-ins to provide standard library services, such as a collection of utility functions, for use with multiple Access applications. The problem with Access add-ins is that .mda files are useful only with Access. The advantage of a custom OLE Automation server is that all OLE Automation clients can use the same .exe or .dll file. As an example, you can create an OLE Automation server object that uses the Visual Basic 4.0 Enterprise Edition's Remote Data Object (RDO) to expedite processing of queries against client-server databases. Your Microsoft Access, Visual Basic, Excel, and Project applications can use the RDO OLE Automation server object.

New Features for Access Developers

Everyone who creates an Access application automatically becomes an Access developer. This book, however, uses the term developer in a more restrictive sense; developers are persons who design and develop database applications as independent consultants or entrepreneurs, or who specifically have been assigned database application development responsibility by their employer. The sections that follow describe some new features of Access 95 that are of interest primarily to Access 2.0 developers and those users who have made regular use of Access Basic code in their Access 2.0 applications.

Visual Basic for Applications

The most important change for Access developers is the migration of Access 95 from Access Basic to Visual Basic for Applications. Microsoft designed VBA to be the *lingua franca* of application programming (also called *scripting*) languages. A common programming language, code editor, and debugging methodology for Microsoft productivity applications plus Visual Basic makes it far easier for developers to create automated cross-application business solutions for the desktop. Even the tools for developing content for The Microsoft Network, code-named Blackbird, are slated to be VBA-enabled in 1996. When Microsoft Word gains VBA, Bill Gate's goal to develop a "common macro language," announced in late 1989, finally will be realized.

Although the reserved words of VBA are common to all implementations of VBA, each application adds its own VBA "flavor" by virtue of a standard set of application-specific objects that each VBA-enabled application references by default. Thus you'll see the term *Access VBA* used throughout this book, plus references to *Excel VBA* and even *Project VBA*. For a quick introduction to Access VBA code and the new code editing window of Access 95, open Northwind.mdb, then open the Switchboard form in Design view. Click the Code button to open the VBA code editor (Module) window and page down to the DisplayDatabaseWindows procedure (see fig. 1.40). One of the changes between Access 2.0 Basic and Access 95 VBA involves DoCmd, which is now an Access application-specific object. In Access VBA, macro actions are methods of the Access DoCmd object, so now you use *Object.Method* syntax to invoke an Access macro action. By default VBA reserved words appear in blue and comments in green, improving readability.

Converting Access 2.0 Applications to Access 95

In the majority of cases, converting Access 2.0 applications to Access 95 is automatic. As an example, DoCmd *MacroAction* statements automatically take the DoCmd.*MacroAction* form. You may need to change dot (.) to bang (!) separators where you reference members of collections other than the default member. If your Access 2.0 application uses Windows API calls, however, you'll need to rewrite your function prototype declarations to conform to the 32-bit Windows API (Win32) standards. Any Windows API functions that have arguments of the **String** data type must take into account use of Unicode in both Windows 95 and Windows NT. In most cases, you simply alias the function to the ANSI version (suffix A). The general case is:

```
Declare Function "Win16Name" Lib "Win32Lib" Alias "Win32NameA" _
(ByVal Arguments As Datatype) As Datatype
```

Many values returned by the Win32 functions, such as Window handles (hWnd) are of the **Long** instead of the **Integer** data type, so you may need to make additional alterations to your code. Access 95 has returned to use of the CurrentDB() function (in place of Databases(0)(0)) to refer to the open application database. Access 1+ object data types, such as Snapshot and Dynaset, continue to be supported by referencing the Microsoft DAO 2.5/3.0 Compatibility Library. When converting and upgrading your code to Access 95, use of Jet 3.0 DAO Object types (Recordset objects of the Snapshot or Dynaset type, for example) is recommended because there is no guarantee that obsolete object types will be supported in future versions of Access.

The Access Developer's Toolkit

Most Access 2.0 applications created by developers were distributed as runtime versions that used MSARN110.EXE, instead of MSACCESS.EXE for execution. Access 95 uses the retail version of MSACCESS.EXE with a run-time flag set to prevent recipients of runtime applications from using Access 95 in design mode. The Access Development Toolkit includes the following components:

- Msaccess.exe, the executable file for Access 95, plus other distributable (licensed) files that you supply with your run-time applications, including the run-time version of Microsoft Graph 5.

- The Microsoft Help Compiler and the *Help Compiler Guide*, which shows you how to use the new Windows 95 help compiler, HCW.EXE, with .rtf files you create with Microsoft Word.

- A greatly improved Setup Wizard for creating distribution disks for your run-time applications.

- Distributable 32-bit OLE Controls: Common dialogs, nine Windows 95 common controls, and 19 of the 32-bit OLE Controls included with the Professional Edition of Visual Basic 4.0.

- The Replication Manager application for managing replicated Access databases.

- The Office Compatible Basic Toolkit for creating applications that comply with the requirements for the "Microsoft Office Compatible" logo.

- The *Access VBA Language Reference*, which is not included as a component of the Access 95 documentation. You can purchase the *Language Reference* manual directly from Microsoft Corporation if you want to experiment with Access VBAS but don't want to purchase the ADT.

- A book that describes how to design Access applications for the run-time environment, as well as how to use the components of the ADT.

The ADT is a necessity for those who develop Access 95 applications on a regular basis, whether these applications run under the retail version or the run-time version of Access. Chapter 31, "Using the Access Developer's Toolkit" describes the ADT in detail.

From Here...

This chapter has given you an overview of the new and improved features that Microsoft incorporated in Access 95, and why these upgrades to Access 2.0 are significant to both new and seasoned users of Microsoft Access. There is little question that Access 2.0 has been the undisputed victor in the Windows database war that has raged since the introduction of Access 1.0 in November, 1992. Access 95 promises to extend Access 2.0's dominance to the 32-bit Windows 95 and Windows NT environment. It remains to be seen whether promised 32-bit versions of competitive desktop database products can come close to matching Access 95's combination of ease of use and remarkably flexible programmability.

- Chapter 2, "Up and Running with Access Tables," gives you a quick introduction to the use of Access 95's `Database` and `Table` objects so that you become accustomed to Access's user interface and obtain a foundation in handling the primary objects of relational databases: tables.

- Chapter 8, "Using Query by Example," describes how to create queries in Access's graphical QBE window, and shows how Access translates the query design into Access SQL.

- Chapter 12, "Creating and Using Forms," introduces you to Access's form design environment to create the graphical user interface for Access applications.

- Chapter 19, "Using 32-Bit OLE 2.1," is an overview of how Access 2.0's implementation of in-place activation and OLE Automation makes integrating OLE 2.0 servers with database applications a reality.

- Chapter 27, "Replicating Access Databases," explains the new briefcase replication method that synchronizes individual copies of Access databases.

- Chapter 29, "Understanding the Data Access Object Class," defines the structure of the Jet 3.0 DAO, describes new DAO properties, and shows you how to manipulate the members of the DAO class with Access Basic code.

Chapter 2

Up and Running with Access Tables

This chapter is designed to give you an overview of Access's two most important database objects: databases and tables. Even if you're well acquainted with Access 1.x or 2.0, you might want to browse this chapter for the Access 95 icon in the margin that indicates a description of a new feature or an improvement over version 2.0. You see the Access 95 icon at each location in this book where a new or improved feature is discussed except in Chapter 1, which is devoted to the novel elements of Access 95. The examples in this chapter, like most other examples in this book, use the Northwind Traders sample database, Northwind.mdb, that is supplied with Access. *Northwind Traders* is a fictitious wholesaler of specialty food products whose accounting system is an Access database application created by Microsoft. The sample database includes tables, forms, and reports that a small firm might use to automate its invoicing, inventory control, ordering, and personnel operations. The remainder of Part I (Chapters 3 through 7) expands on the subjects you learn in this chapter using Northwind.mdb and describes in detail how you create and use Access database tables.

In this chapter, you learn to

- Launch Access and open the Northwind Traders database

- Open a table and view its contents

- Select records and edit the data they contain

- Use design mode to view the properties of a table and its fields

- Print the contents of a table

Note

This chapter assumes that you have already installed Access. If you haven't installed Access, refer to your Access documentation for instructions on setting up Access on your fixed disk.

Starting Access and Opening Databases

Before you can open any database in Access, you must start Access itself. You can open a database at the same time you start Access, or you can open a database any time after you've started Access. You also can run multiple instances of Access, if you have enough system resources. Access allows you to have only one database per instance open at a time, however.

The next two sets of instructions first explain how to open a database at the same time you start Access 95, and then explain how to open a database after Access is already running.

Opening a Database During Access Startup

 To simultaneously start Access and open the Northwind Traders database, Northwind.mdb, perform the following steps:

1. Choose Microsoft Access from Windows 95's Start, Programs menu. (Access is installed on this menu by default.)

    As Access is loading, a copyright notice (called a *splash screen*) appears with the name and organization that was entered at the time Access was installed. After Access has loaded, it displays the database opening dialog shown in figure 2.1.

    Notice the list of previously opened databases at the bottom of the dialog—if this is the first time you've ever run Access, this list is empty, except for the More Files choice.

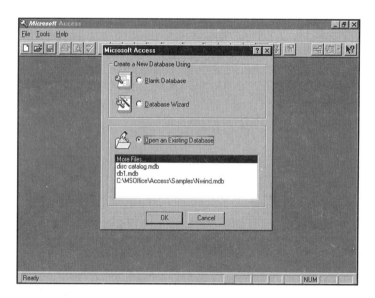

Fig. 2.1   On startup, Access 95 displays this dialog to open a database.

2. Select the Open an Existing Database option.

3. Select the More Files choice in the list at the bottom of the dialog, and then click OK. Access displays a standard Windows 95 Open dialog, shown in figure 2.2.

4. Select the \MSOffice\Access\Samples folder in the Open dialog. (The Northwind.mdb files are located in the Samples subfolder of whatever folder in which you installed Access 95; the default location is \MSOffice\Access.) Figure 2.2 shows the Open dialog with the contents of the Samples folder displayed.

Fig. 2.2   Use Access's Open dialog to open a database.

5. Double-click Northwind.mdb to open the Northwind Traders sample database.
Access opens the Northwind Traders database.

If this is the first time you've opened the Northwind Traders sample database, the
Access Basic program code in the sample database displays a special splash screen
for the Northwind Traders database (see fig. 2.3). If you don't want to see this
splash screen again, mark the Don't Show This Screen Again checkbox.

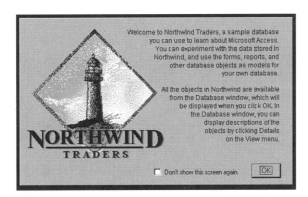

Fig. 2.3   The first time you open the Northwind Traders sample database, it displays this special
splash screen.

6. Click OK to close the Northwind Traders splash screen. After closing the
Northwind Traders splash screen, Access displays the Database Window shown in
figure 2.4.

Learning Access

Fig. 2.4 The Database Window is Access's "home base."

> **Note**
>
> You can use several other methods to open a database in the common Open dialog. You can click Northwind.mdb to place it in the File name text box and then click OK. Or you can type **nwind** in the File Name text box and click OK. Access adds the default .mdb extension for you. However, double-clicking is the fastest and most mistake-proof method of opening a file.

Opening a Database When Access is Already Running

As you'd expect, it's also possible to open a database after you start Access. You can have only one database open at a time in an instance of Access, so opening a database causes Access to close any currently open database, and replaces the contents of the Database Window with the newly opened database's information. (The Datababase Window is explained in the next section of this chapter.)

To open the Northwind Traders database, Northwind.mdb, when Access is already running, follow these steps:

 1. Click the Open Database button of the toolbar, or choose File from the main menubar. If you use the menu to open a database, the File menu appears (see fig. 2.5); if you use the Open Database toolbar button, the file Open dialog appears immediately.

   If you have run Access previously, the file names of up to four Access database files you have opened may appear above Exit.

2. Choose File, Open Database to display the Open dialog (refer to fig. 2.2).

3. Finish opening the Northwind Traders database by following the procedures in steps 4 through 6 of the preceding section ("Opening a Database During Access Startup").

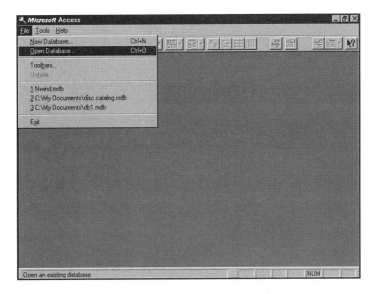

Fig. 2.5   The Access File menu, with the Open Database command selected, lets you open another .mdb file.

Note

Access's toolbar buttons provide *ToolTips*. ToolTips are small captions that appear under a button after the mouse pointer has rested on a button for more than about 0.5 seconds. If you find ToolTips to be distracting, you can turn off this feature by choosing View, Toolbars View menu to display the Toolbars dialog. Click the Show ToolTips check box to remove the check mark and then click the Close button. If you're using SVGA mode (800×600 pixels) or UVGA mode (1,024×768 pixels), you may want to try clicking the Large Buttons check box of the Toolbars dialog. The icons of larger buttons are easier to discern in SVGA mode and especially UVGA mode.

Note

You can close any open database by clicking the close button at the top right corner of the Database Window, or by choosing File, Close. When there is no open database, Access displays an empty window, only the New Database and Open Database toolbar buttons are enabled and the File, Close command does not appear.

Understanding the Database Window

The Database window is your "home base" for all operations with the sample database or databases you create. Almost every operation you perform with Access begins with a choice you make from the Database window.

After you open a database file, the 20 buttons to the right of the New Database and Open Database buttons of the Database toolbar (under the main menu bar) are enabled or disabled, depending on Access 95's current status. *Toolbar buttons*, a common feature of new Windows applications (and of Windows 95 itself), are shortcuts for menu choices.

Any operation you can perform by clicking a toolbar button can be performed by making two or more menu choices. Access 95 has 19 standard toolbars; Access displays the appropriate toolbar for the database object in the active window. You can customize the standard toolbars or create your own special-purpose toolbars. Using the toolbar buttons is much quicker and, once you learn what the symbols mean, more intuitive than using the standard menu structure. Chapter 3, "Navigating within Access," describes the use of Access 95's new toolbars in detail.

▶▶ See "The Toolbar in Table View," p. 79

▶▶ See "Customizable Toolbars," p. 447

Using Database Tables

This chapter is devoted to exploring tables, which are the basic elements of all databases and the portion of the Access database file where data is stored.

▶▶ See "Understanding Access's Table Display," p. 75

Viewing Data in Tables

To display the contents of the Categories table, which describes the types of products in which Northwind trades, double-click Categories in the Database window's list of tables. The Categories table appears, as shown in figure 2.6.

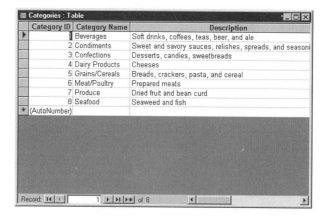

Fig. 2.6 The Datasheet display of the records in the Categories table.

Tip

You also can display the Categories table by clicking Categories and then clicking the Open button or pressing Enter. The double-clicking method is quicker, however.

The normal method of displaying the information contained in relational database tables is the familiar row-column technique used by spreadsheet applications. Every widely used PC RDBMS (relational database management system) uses row-column presentation for data contained in tables. The rows of a table are known as *records*, and the columns are referred to as *fields*. A record contains information on a single object, such as one class of product or a particular invoice. A field contains the same type of information, such as a product code, for all records in a table. In this book, the intersection between a row and a column—a single field of a single record—is called a *data cell*. A data cell contains a single piece of information. The terms *data item* and *data entity* often are used as synonyms for *data cell*.

Figure 2.6 shows the data in the Categories table in what Access calls *Datasheet View*—the default method of displaying a table. You select the Datasheet View, if another type of view is active, by clicking the Datasheet button, which resembles a spreadsheet, on the toolbar (the Datasheet button only appears when the table is *not* in Datasheet View). You also can choose View, Datasheet. Datasheet View also is the default for viewing the results of queries; you can see a Datasheet View of the table or query when you are creating an Access form.

Selecting and Editing Data Records

To change the data contained in any cell of the table (other than in OLE Object fields that are used to display pictures), select the cell by clicking it with the mouse or by using the arrow keys. Selected content is indicated by the white on black (reverse) appearance of the cell. The default selected cell is the first field of the first record of the table. All contents of that cell are selected when you first display the table.

> **Caution**
>
> If you type a character into a cell when its entire content is selected, the character you type replaces what was in that cell. You can recover from an accidental replacement by pressing Esc; this action restores the original content, but *only* if you have not yet selected a different cell. When you make a change in a data cell and then move to a new data cell, the change is made to the content of the table. Click the selected data cell to deselect the entire contents of the cell. You can choose Edit, Undo Saved Record or press Ctrl+Z to reverse the changes you made after saving a record.

> **Note**
>
> See Chapter 5, "Entering, Editing, and Validating Data in Tables," for detailed information on editing data records.

You can select any cell to edit by positioning the mouse pointer at the point within a cell where you want to make the change and then clicking your left mouse button. The mouse pointer resembles an I-beam when it is located within the contents of data cells. The editing cursor, a thin vertical line called the *caret* by Windows and this book, often referred to as the *insertion point* in other texts, appears.

The conventional text-editing functions of Windows applications apply to Access. At this point, you shouldn't change the data, called *values*, of the data cells. Changes to values may affect the appearance of examples in later chapters. If you do make a change, a pencil symbol appears in the gray box at the left of the window corresponding to the record whose value you have changed. You can return to the original value by pressing Esc. If you click an OLE Object field, the cell has a thick, gray border and the caret does not appear. (The Categories table contains an OLE Object field, although it isn't visible in figure 2.6; the field stores a bitmap picture, and contains the words "Paintbrush Picture" to let you know that this is an OLE object field containing picture data.) You cannot edit the text of an OLE Object field.

 You use the empty record at the bottom of the table, indicated by the asterisk (*) in the selection button column for the record, to add a new record to the table. If you enter any data into a cell of this record, a new record containing the data you entered is added to the table. If you accidentally add data in this *tentative append* record, click the Record Selection button to select the record, and then press Delete. A dialog appears, requesting confirmation of your deletion. Click OK.

 If you use the arrow keys to select a data cell, all contents of the cell are selected. You cannot click the corner of a cell and drag the mouse pointer to a cell in the opposite corner of an imaginary rectangle to select a group of cells, as you do with Excel. You can, however, select an entire record by clicking the selection button for that record, or you can select a group of records by dragging the mouse down the selection button column. Records and groups of records most often are selected to copy the records to the Windows Clipboard. Notice that when you select a cell with the keyboard or the mouse, the triangular arrow moves to the selected record. The button with the triangular arrow is called the *current record pointer*, or sometimes the *active record pointer*.

 You use the left set of buttons in the bar at the bottom of the datasheet window to position the current record pointer within the bounds of the table. Click the left-arrow button to position the current record pointer at the first record in the table, and click the right-arrow button to move to the last or bottom record of the table. The left- and right-arrow buttons move the pointer one record at a time in the direction indicated. You can enter a record number in the Record text box or use the vertical scroll bar to position the active record pointer. The vertical scroll bar appears only if more records are present than can fit in the vertical dimension of the Datasheet window.

 The horizontal scroll bar enables you to view fields that lie to the right of the far right visible field. Use the left and right arrows for small movements, or use the scroll box to make large moves to the left or right. You also can traverse several fields by clicking the region of the scroll bar between the scroll box and the arrow. If you click the right scroll arrow in the Categories table two or three times, you'll be able to see the column for the Picture field, which is an OLE object field containing Windows Paintbrush bitmap pictures.

 To select all data cells in a field column, click the button containing the field name at the top of the datasheet. When the mouse pointer is over a field name, the pointer changes to a down arrow. You can search for cells within the selected field that contain a particular group of characters by clicking the toolbar's Find button—a pair of binoculars. The Find dialog appears (see fig. 2.7).

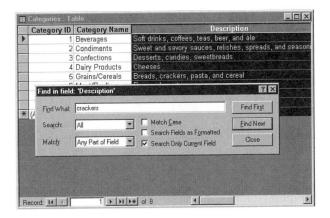

Fig. 2.7 Use the Find dialog to locate fields that contain particular words or phrases.

Enter the characters you want to find in the Find What text box. Then open the Match drop-down list box by clicking the down arrow, and select Any Part of Field. You can search up, down, or in both directions from the position of the current record by selecting Up, Down, or All in the Search drop-down list box. If you select All, Access searches down from the current record until it reaches the end of the database, and then continues from the beginning until the current record position is reached. When searching Up or Down, Access searches in the specified direction and stops when it reaches the beginning or end of the database records. Click the Find First button to search for the first occurrence of a match, and then click the Find Next button to locate other matches. After you find all matching records or no matching records, a dialog appears stating that you have reached the end of the table. Click the Close button to return to the Table window.

Viewing and Editing Graphics

One of the reasons for choosing the Categories table for this chapter is that it includes bitmapped graphic images stored in an OLE Object field. If you double-click one of the Bitmap Image data cells, Windows 95's Paint window appears with the bitmapped image displayed, as shown in figure 2.8. (You may need to scroll to the right to make the Picture field column visible in the window.) You can use Paint to display the image or to edit it. Because Windows 95's Paint is an OLE server, all of Paint's bitmapped image display and editing capabilities are available to you while you are using Access. (In-place editing isn't suitable in Datasheet View, so Access invokes Paint in a separate window if you edit a Bitmap Image field when the table is in Datasheet View.)

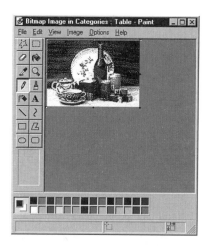

Fig. 2.8   A bitmapped image displayed using Windows 95 Paint.

 When you're finished viewing an image, click the Close Window button in the upper-right corner of Paintbrush's window to close the image. You also can exit an OLE server by choosing File, Exit & Return. If you have made any changes to the image, a dialog appears asking whether you want to update the Access table. In this case, click No to retain the original image.

Using Design Mode

 Design mode for tables displays the characteristics of each field in the table in a grid format similar to a spreadsheet. To view the design of the Categories table, click the Design View button, which appears as an architect's triangle and pencil, at the left end of the toolbar. Design mode appears, as shown in figure 2.9. Alternatively, you can choose View, Table Design or select the table name in the Database window and click the Design button.

 ▶▶ See "Defining Access Operating Modes," p. 74

 You can view and edit the properties that apply to the table object as a whole in the Table Properties window, as shown in figure 2.10. Click the Properties button on the toolbar (a hand pointing to a window) or choose View, Properties to display the Table Properties window. The Table Properties window enables you to enter a text description of the table and assign a value to the Validation Rule property of the table. Table-level validation rules can contain a rule that applies to more than one field in a table. The Validation Text text property is the message that appears if you attempt to violate the validation rule.

 ▶▶ See "Validating Data Entry," p. 168

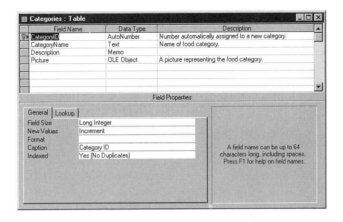

Fig. 2.9 The Design View of the Categories table displays Field Name, Data Type, and Description properties.

Fig. 2.10 The Table Properties window lets you add validation rules and messages that appear when the rules are violated.

Click the Indexes button or choose <u>V</u>iew, <u>I</u>ndexes to display the Indexes window. The Indexes window, shown in figure 2.11, displays each of the fields of the table and identifies the *primary-key field*, which is the field with the symbol of the key in its selection button column. The primary-key field is the field or combination of fields that is used to uniquely identify each record in the table. Most tables are indexed on a single primary-key field, and primary-key field indexes do not permit duplicate keys. *Indexes* are internal tables that speed the creation of query result tables by simulating the sorting of the table on the value of the key field. Key fields establish the relations by which multiple tables of a database are linked when you create a query. The term *relational database* indicates database management applications that are capable of linking tables by key fields.

▶▶ See "Using Access Indexes," p. 862

Each field in a table requires a unique name and must be assigned a field data type. Field names, data types, and an optional text description of the field are entered in the design grid. (Click the Indexes button or click the Close Window button of the Indexes window to close it so that the entire design grid is visible. Do the same to close the Properties window.) Text is the most common type of data in tables; therefore, Text is the default data type. Many other field data types are available in Access; you already have been introduced to the OLE Object field data type. Click one of the Data Type cells, and then click the down arrow to open the Data Type drop-down list box to display the Data Type choices offered by Access. Click the arrow again to close the list. Field data types in Access include various numeric formats, date and time, and other types that you learn about in later chapters of this book. Now click the Datasheet View button to display the Datasheet View of the Categories table in run mode.

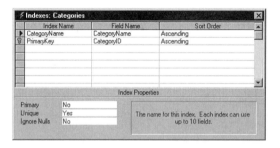

Fig. 2.11 The Indexes window displays the Index Name, Field Name, and Sort Order for each index of a table.

Printing the Contents of a Table

Access enables you to print the contents of your table without creating a fully formatted report. You may want to print raw table data to proofread the new records you have created or the old ones you have edited. The Print Preview window is much like the one offered by Microsoft Word and Excel. The Print Preview window enables you to see how tables, forms, and reports will appear if printed.

To see how the Categories table will appear if printed, click the toolbar's Preview button (the page symbol with the magnifying glass). The Print Preview window appears, as shown in figure 2.12. The title bar of the Print Preview window reflects what you're preparing to print. In this example, the title bar shows Categories:Table. You also can choose File, Print Preview to display the Print Preview window.

To see a magnified view of how the printed version of your table will appear, click the surface of the simulated sheet of paper in the Print Preview window. When the mouse pointer is on the paper, the pointer turns into the shape of a magnifying glass, as shown in figure 2.12. Place the magnifying glass over the image; otherwise, when the window is magnified, the view is of a blank page and you wonder where the table went. Figure 2.13 shows the magnified (zoomed) view of the Categories table. Click again to restore the original, unreadable version of the report. The Zoom button has an effect similar to clicking the mouse on the surface of the preview image.

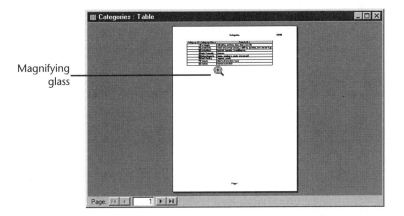

Magnifying glass

Fig. 2.12   The Print Preview window for the Categories table displays the eight records in the table.

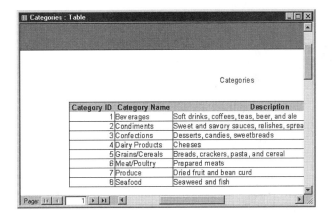

Fig. 2.13   Click the print preview image to show a magnified view of the Categories table.

When you are ready to print, click the Print button (with the symbol of a printer) on the toolbar—Access immediately begins printing the table, using the current printer settings for your computer.

To print in landscape mode with your laser printer or to otherwise change your printer's settings, you must choose File, Print to display the Print dialog, shown in figure 2.14. To change the printer settings, click the Properties button and make the appropriate changes in the Properties dialog for your printer, as shown in figure 2.15 (the exact appearance of your printer's Properties dialog depends on your specific printer). Click the OK button to close the Print dialog and begin printing the table.

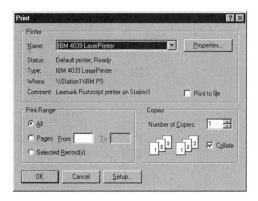

Fig. 2.14 The Print dialog.

Fig. 2.15 The options that appear in the Printer Options dialog depend on the driver for your printer.

 If you want to change the printing margins, choose File, Page Setup to display the Page Setup dialog shown in figure 2.16. Click the Margins tab to display the page margin settings, and change the print margins by entering different values in the Margins text boxes. Click OK to close the Page Setup dialog and return to the Print Preview windows. Click the Print button on the toolbar to print the table with the new margin settings.

Tip

You can also change the page orientation (portrait or landscape) on the Page sheet of the Page Setup dialog. If you only want to change printing margins or the page orientation, using the Page Setup dialog is easiest.

Fig. 2.16 Use the Margins tab of the Page Setup dialog box to change the printing margins; use the Page tab to change the printing orientation.

Now that you have run the gamut of the basic operations available for Access tables, double-click the Document Control menu box to close the Print Preview window and return to the Database window. Now, you may open one or more of the other tables that comprise the Northwind Traders database to learn a bit more about their contents. The Employees table includes scanned images of photographs of the fictional staff of Northwind Traders. The Suppliers table lists an eclectic group of food-processing firms from many points on the globe. You can see most of the international characters, such as umlauts and tildes, in Windows' ANSI character set in the supplier name and address fields. Both Access 95 and Windows 95 are available in a wide range of languages in addition to British, Canadian, and U.S. English. Access 95 replaces 8-bit ANSI with 16-bit Unicode characters to accommodate Asian and other languages that use more than the about 200 characters accommodated by ANSI. Use of Unicode in Access 95 is transparent to the user, but requires modification of specific string operations performed with Access VBA.

To see a brief description of each table listed in the Database window, click the Details button on the toolbar. Access displays the text entered in the Description text box of the table's Table Properties dialog to the right of the table's name, along with date and time the table was last modified, and the date and time of the table's creation. You can display the contents of the Database window in any of the viewing formats available in any Windows 95 folder window: large icons, small icons, list, and details.

From Here...

This chapter gave you a feel for the methods you can use to view and manipulate the data contained in tables. The basic operations you learned in this chapter are applicable, in general, to all other functions of Access, as should be the case with any well-designed Windows application.

Your next step is to learn more about the overall plan that Microsoft drew up for the user interface of Access. The plan was implemented by changing toolbar buttons and menu choices depending on whether you are viewing or creating tables, queries, forms, reports, macros, or modules.

- Chapter 3, "Navigating within Access," describes how Access is organized, as well as how you manage multiple document windows, keyboard commands, and Access's context-sensitive help system.

- Chapter 4, "Working with Access Databases and Tables," has you begin to apply what you learned in this chapter in order to work with Access tables. The majority of the examples in Chapter 4 continue to use the Northwind Traders database, but you add your own tables to expand its capabilities.

- Chapter 5, "Entering, Editing, and Validating Data in Tables," shows you how to add records to tables, edit data in the records, and add validation rules to your tables to ensure that data values fall within accepted limits.

- Chapter 6, "Sorting, Finding, and Filtering Data in Tables," describes how to use Access's built-in sorting, search, search and replace, and filters to locate records meeting criteria you set, and how to make bulk changes to field data.

- Chapter 7, "Linking, Importing, and Exporting Tables," explains how to import data from your existing database tables, worksheets, or text files, and how to export table data in a variety of useful formats.

- Chapter 20, "Adding Graphics to Forms and Reports," shows you how to display and print OLE objects contained in OLE Object fields of Access tables and in OLE control objects you place on forms and reports.

Chapter 3

Navigating within Access

Learning Access

This chapter describes how Microsoft has structured and organized Access to expedite the design and use of the database objects that it offers. A substantial portion of this chapter consists of tables that list the functions of window Control-menu boxes, toolbar buttons, and an array of function-key combinations. Many function and key assignments derive from other Microsoft applications, such as Excel (F2 for editing) and Word for Windows (Shift+F4 to find the next occurrence of a match). These assignments don't duplicate those key assignments to which you might have become accustomed when using dBASE, xBase, or Paradox.

This chapter is a reference to which you can return when you conclude that a keystroke combination might be a better choice for an action than a mouse click, but you cannot remember the required combination. (Refer to Chapter 5, "Entering, Editing, and Validating Data in Tables," for details of the key combinations that you use to edit data in tables and queries.) This chapter also explains the structure and content of Access's Help system.

In this chapter, you learn how to do the following

- Use Access 95's toolbars with tables

- Use global function keys to perform common operations

- Set your own default options for Access 95

- Use the Access Help system

- Compact and repair Access 95 databases

Understanding Access's Functions and Modes

Access, unlike word processing and spreadsheet applications, is a truly multifunctional program. Although word processing applications, for example, have many sophisticated capabilities, their basic purpose is to support text entry, page layout, and formatted printing. All a word processing application's primary functions and supporting features are directed to these ends. You perform all word processing operations using views that represent a sheet of paper—usually 8 1/2 inches by 11 inches. Most spreadsheet applications use the row-column metaphor for all their functions—even for writing highly sophisticated programs in the applications' macro languages. The sections that follow describe Access's basic functions and operating modes.

Defining Access Functions

To qualify as a full-fledged relational database management system, an application must perform the following four basic but distinct functions, each with its own presentation (or *view*) to the user:

- *Data organization* involves creating and manipulating tables that contain data in conventional tabular (row-column or spreadsheet) format, called *Datasheet View* by Access.

- *Table linking and data extraction* links multiple tables by data relationships to create temporary tables, stored in your computer's memory or temporary disk files, that contain the data that you choose. Access uses *queries* to link tables and to choose the data to be stored in a temporary table called a Recordset object. (For backward compatibility, Access 95 supports Access 1.x's Dynaset and Snapshot objects, which are both Recordset objects.) A Recordset object consists of the data that results from running the query; Recordset objects are called *virtual tables* because they are stored in your computer's memory rather than in database files. The capability to link tables by relations distinguishes relational database systems from simple list-processing applications, called *flat-file managers*. Data extraction limits the presentation of Dynasets to specific groups of data that meet criteria that you establish. *Expressions* are used to calculate values from data (for example, you can calculate an extended amount by multiplying unit price and quantity), and to display the calculated values as if they were a field in one of the tables.

- *Data entry and editing* require design and implementation of data viewing, entry, and editing forms as an alternative to tabular presentation. A form enables *you*, rather than the *application*, to control how the data is presented. For most users, forms are much easier to use for data entry than are Recordsets in tabular format, especially when many fields are involved. The capability to print forms, such as sales orders and invoices, is definitely a benefit to the user.

- *Data presentation* requires the creation of reports that can summarize the information in Recordsets that you can view and print (this is the last step in the process). The capability to provide meaningful reports is the ultimate purpose of any database management application. Also, the management of an enterprise usually lends more credence to reports that are attractively formatted and contain charts or graphs. Charts and graphs summarize the data for those officials who take the "broad brush" approach.

The four basic functions of Access that are implemented as views are organized into the application structure shown in figure 3.1. If you are creating a new database, you use the basic functions of Access in the top-down sequence shown in figure 3.1. You choose a function by clicking a button in the Datasheet window, except for security and printing operations, which are menu choices. In most views, you can display the Print Preview window that leads to printing operations by clicking the Print Preview button of the toolbar.

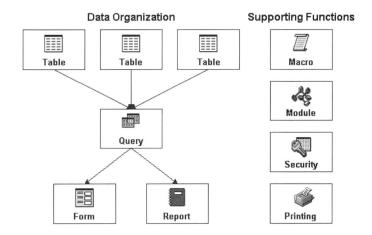

Fig. 3.1 The basic and supporting functions of Access.

Four supporting functions apply to all the basic functions of Access:

- *Macros* are sequences of actions that automate repetitive database operations. You create a macro in Access by choosing from a list of available actions, in the order in which you want Access to perform them. You can use a macro, for example, to open a report, print the report, and then close the report. Later this section defines *open* and *close* as they are used in Access terminology.

- *Modules* are functions and procedures written in Access's dialect of the Visual Basic for Applications (VBA) programming language. (Access's dialect of VBA was formerly known as Access Basic, and is still frequently referred to by that name.) You use Access VBA functions to make calculations that are more complex than those that can be expressed easily by a series of conventional mathematical symbols, or to make calculations that require decisions to be made. Access VBA procedures are written to perform operations that exceed the capabilities of standard macro actions. You run Access VBA procedures by invoking them with the macro action RunCode or by attaching the procedure to particular events, such as clicking a command button with the mouse, that occur when a form or report is the active object.

- *Security* consists of functions available as menu choices only. With security functions in a multiuser environment, you can let other people use your database. You can grant access to user groups and individuals, and you can restrict their ability to view or modify all or a portion of the tables in the database.

- *Printing* enables you to print virtually anything you can view in Access's run mode. From the toolbar, you can print your Access VBA code, but not the macros that you write. (You can use the Database Document add-in to print the content of your macros.)

The terms *open* and *close* have the same basic usage in Access as in other Windows applications, but usually involve more than one basic function:

■ Opening a database makes its content available to the application through the Database window described in Chapter 2, "Up and Running with Access Tables." You can open only one database at a time during ordinary use of Access. Writing Access VBA code enables you to operate with tables from more than one database. You can achieve the equivalent of multiple open Access databases by *linking* (Access 95's new term for *attaching*) tables from other databases.

■ Opening a table displays a Datasheet View of its contents.

■ Opening a query opens the tables involved but does not display them. Access then runs the query on these tables to create a tabular `Recordset`. Changes made to data in the `Recordset` cause corresponding changes to be made to the data in the tables associated with the query, if the `Recordset` is updatable. (Access 1.x's `Table` and `Dynaset` objects usually are updatable, but `Snapshot` objects are never updatable. The same rules apply to `Recordset` objects of the `Table`, `Dynaset`, and `Snapshot` type.)

■ Opening a form or report automatically opens the table or query with which it is associated. Both forms and reports usually are associated with queries, but a query also can employ a single table.

■ Closing a query closes the associated tables.

■ Closing a form or report closes the associated query and its tables.

Defining Access Operating Modes

Access has three basic operating modes:

■ *Startup* mode enables you to compress, convert, encrypt, decrypt, and repair a database by choosing commands from the <u>T</u>ools, Database <u>U</u>tilities and <u>T</u>ools, Security menu before opening a database. These commands, some of which are discussed at the end of this chapter, are available only when you *don't* have a database open.

■ *Design* mode enables you to create and modify the structure of tables and queries, develop forms to display and edit your data, and format reports for printing. Access calls design mode *Design View*.

■ *Run* mode displays your table, form, and report designs in individual document windows (run is the default mode). You execute macros by choosing one and then selecting run mode. Run mode does not apply to Access VBA modules, because functions are executed when encountered as elements of queries, forms, and reports. Procedures in modules are run by macro commands, or directly from events of forms and reports. Run mode is called *Datasheet View* for tables and queries, *Form View* for forms, and *Print Preview* for reports.

You can select design or run mode by choosing command buttons in the Datasheet window, buttons on the toolbar, or commands from the <u>V</u>iew menu.

You can change the default conditions under which Access displays and prints your tables, queries, forms, and reports by choosing Tools, Options. The section, "Setting Default Options," near the end of this chapter, describes options that apply to Access as a whole and those that apply only to tables.

Understanding Access's Table Display

You're probably familiar with the basic terms for many of the components that comprise the basic window in which all conventional Windows 95 applications run (these controls, although similar in function, have a somewhat different appearance and location than those used in Windows 3.x). The presentation of Access windows differs with each of the basic functions that Access performs. Because Part I of this book deals almost exclusively with tables, the examples that follow use Table View. Figure 3.2 shows Access for Windows's basic display for operations with tables. Table 3.1 describes the window's individual components.

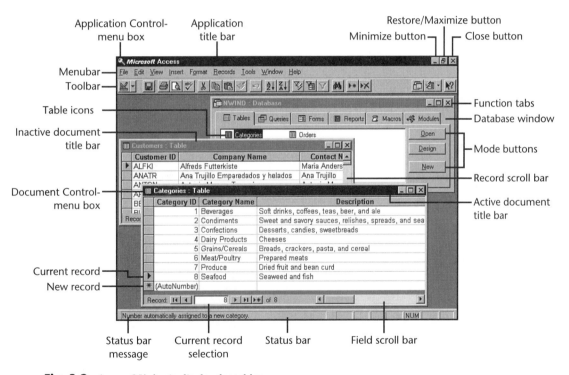

Fig. 3.2 Access 95's basic display for tables.

Learning Access

Table 3.1 Components of the Access Display for Tables

Term	Description
Active window	The window to which all mouse and keyboard actions are directed. When an application or document is active, its title bar appears in color (dark blue, unless you have changed your Windows color scheme). If both the application title bar and a document title bar are active, the document title bar receives the mouse and keyboard actions.
Application Control-menu box	The icon for the Application Control menu that controls the presentation of the Application window. You display the Application Control menu by clicking the box or pressing Alt+space bar.
Application title bar	A bar at the top of the application's window that displays its name. You can move the entire application, if it isn't maximized, by clicking the application title bar and dragging it to a new position.
Application window	The window within which Windows displays Access. Each application that you launch runs within its own application window.
Caret	A vertical flashing line that indicates the insertion point for keyboard entry in areas of a window that accept text.
Current Record button	A button that indicates a single selected record in the table. When you are editing the current record, the button icon becomes a pencil rather than a triangular arrow. The Current Record button also is called the *record pointer*.
Current Record selection	Buttons that position the record pointer to the first, next, preceding, and last record number in the table. If you specify a key field, the current record number is not that which corresponds to the sequence of its addition to the database (as is the case with xBase and Paradox), but the sequence of the record in the primary key's sorting order.
Database window	The window that controls the operating mode of Access and selects the active document window's current function. From the database components displayed in the Database window, you select the component (such as a particular table) to display in the document window.
Document Control-menu box	The icon for the Document Control menu that controls a document window's presentation. To access the Document Control menu, click the box or press Alt+- (hyphen).
Document title bar	At the top of each document's window, a bar that displays the document's name. You can move the document, if it isn't maximized, by clicking the application title bar and dragging the document to a new position.
Document window	The window that displays an Access database component. Tables, queries, forms, reports, macros, and modules are referred to as *documents* in Windows terminology. You can have multiple Access documents of any type open simultaneously. These windows are called *multiple document interface (MDI) child windows*, because the Access application window is their *parent*.

Term	Description
Field scroll bar	The scroll bar that enables you to view fields of tables that are outside the bounds of the document window. Record scroll bars provide access to records located outside the document window.
Function buttons	Six buttons with which you can choose whether the active document window displays tables, queries, forms, reports, macros, or modules.
Inactive window	A window in the background, usually with a grayed title bar. Clicking the surface of an inactive window makes it the active window and brings it to the front. If an inactive window is not visible because other windows obscure it, you can make the window active by choosing the window's name from the Window menu.
Maximize button	Clicking the *application's* Maximize button causes Access to occupy your entire display. Clicking the *document's* Maximize button causes the document to take over the entire display. When a window is maximized, this button's icon changes to the Restore button. Figure 3.3 shows a maximized table document.
Menubar	A horizontal bar containing the main menu choices. These choices remain constant, but the choices in the drop-down menus corresponding to the main menu selections change, depending on Access's status.
Minimize button	A button that enables you to collapse the application or document window to an icon at the bottom of your display.
Mode buttons	Three buttons that determine the operating mode of Access. *Open* places Access in run mode. *New* or *Design* puts Access in design mode, where you can create or edit tables.
New record	A button with an asterisk that indicates the location of the next record to be added to a table. Entering data in the new record appends the record to the table and creates another new record.
Restore button	A double set of boxes that, when clicked, returns the window from full display to its normal size, with moveable borders. When displayed, the Restore button takes the place of the Maximize button in the window's upper-right corner.
Status bar	A bar, located at the bottom of the application window, that displays prompts and indicators, such as the status of the Num Lock key.
Toolbar	A bar containing command buttons that duplicate the more commonly used menu choices. The number and type of toolbar buttons change depending on which basic function of Access you are using.

Maximized Document Windows

Access uses a windowing technique that you should know about; otherwise, you might accidentally minimize or close Access when you intended to minimize or close a maximized document. After you click a document window's Maximize button, the document window takes the place of the application window and occupies the entire display, except for the menubar and toolbar (see fig. 3.3). Most other Windows applications that display multiple documents, such as Word for Windows and Excel, have a similar capability to expand a document to occupy the entire window.

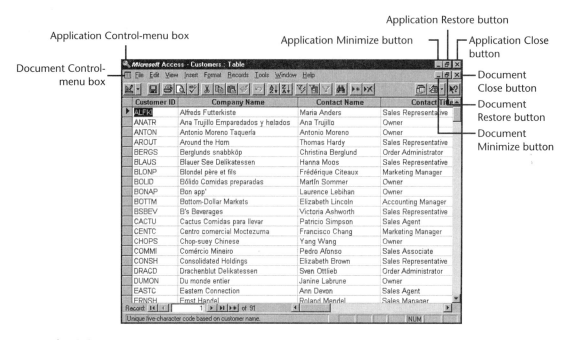

Fig. 3.3 An Access table in a maximized document window.

The Document Control-menu box and the Document Minimize, Restore, and Close buttons move to the menubar's extreme left and right, respectively. The title of the document is added to the application title in the title bar at the top of the display. To return the document window to its original size, established when the application window was first active, click the Document Restore button; alternatively, click the Document Control-menu box and then choose Restore from the Document Control menu. You can close the document window by clicking the Document Close button, or by double-clicking the Document Control-menu box. If you accidentally click the Application Close button (or double-click the Application Control-menu box just above the Document Control-menu box), however, you close Access 95. You receive no warning that you are about to exit Access unless you have changed the design of an object.

Document Windows Minimized to Icons

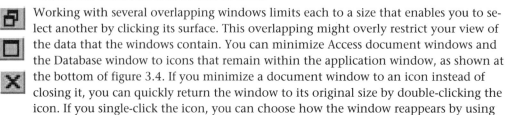

Working with several overlapping windows limits each to a size that enables you to select another by clicking its surface. This overlapping might overly restrict your view of the data that the windows contain. You can minimize Access document windows and the Database window to icons that remain within the application window, as shown at the bottom of figure 3.4. If you minimize a document window to an icon instead of closing it, you can quickly return the window to its original size by double-clicking the icon. If you single-click the icon, you can choose how the window reappears by using the Document Control menu, as shown for the Database window in figure 3.4. You can also restore, maximize, or close a minimized icon by clicking the corresponding button within the icon.

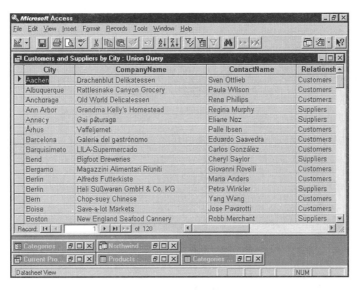

Fig. 3.4   Tables, a query, a form, and the Database window minimized to icons within the application window.

If you choose to display your document window in maximized form by choosing Maximize from the Document Control menu that appears when you click the icon, the document hides the icons at the bottom of the application window. In this case, open the Window menu and choose the document that you want. If you size your document windows (like the window in fig. 3.4) by dragging their borders, you can avoid the substantial mouse movement and two-step menu-selection process to select the active document.

The Toolbars in Table View

The buttons that appear in Access's toolbar, and the number of toolbars displayed, changes according to the function that Access is currently performing. When you are working with tables in run mode, Access 95 displays the Table Datasheet and the Datasheet Formatting toolbars, shown in figures 3.5 and 3.6, respectively. The next two sections of this chapter describe the toolbars that appear in table run mode (Datasheet View).

Note

Even if you have some experience with previous versions of Access, you should note tables 3.2 and 3.3. Access 95 adds many new shortcut buttons to the toolbars and has also moved several menu commands to new locations. For example, the Save Record command has moved from the File menu to the Records menu—a location that is more intuitive for users.

The Table Datasheet Toolbar. The Table Datasheet toolbar appears whenever you open an Access table in Datasheet View. Figure 3.5 shows the Table Datasheet toolbar, and table 3.2 describes the buttons that appear on the toolbar.

> **Note**
>
> Toolbar buttons provide shortcuts to traditional selection methods, such as choosing menu commands or choosing command or option buttons in a particular sequence. The Alternate Method columns of tables 3.2 and 3.3 list how you can achieve the same effect as clicking a toolbar button by using the menus or the command buttons in the Database window.

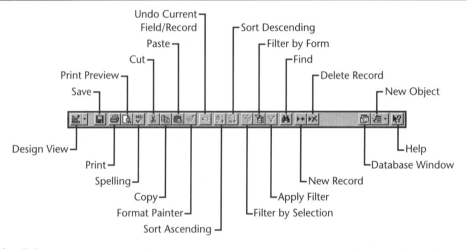

Fig. 3.5   Access displays the Table Datasheet toolbar when you have a table opened in Datasheet View.

Table 3.2   Appearance and Functions of Buttons and Other Elements of the Table Datasheet Toolbar

Icon	Button	Alternate Method	Function
	Design View	View, Table Design	Changes the table display to design mode. In design mode, you specify the properties of each field of the table.
	Datasheet View	View, Datasheet	Returns the table display to run mode (Datasheet View) from design mode. (You cannot see this button in figure 3.5; it appears only when the table is in Design View.)
	Save	File, Save	Saves the database.
	Print	File, Print	Prints the table.
	Print Preview	File, Print Preview	Displays the contents of a table in report format and enables you to print the table's contents.
	Spelling	Tools, Spelling	Starts the spelling checker.

Icon	Button	Alternate Method	Function
	Cut	Edit, Cut	Cuts the selected information and puts it in the Windows Clipboard.
	Copy	Edit, Copy	Copies selected information to the Windows Clipboard.
	Paste	Edit, Paste	Pastes information from the Windows Clipboard into Access at the current location of the caret.
	Format Painter		Copies a control's format to another control. Used only in Design View; it is enabled only when you select a control.
	Undo	Edit, Undo	Returns you to the status immediately preceding the last action that you took. The Undo button is inactive if there is no action to undo. Access provides a single-level Undo feature that repeals only one action.
	Sort Ascending	Records, Sort, Ascending	Sorts the records in ascending order, based on the current field.
	Sort Descending	Records, Sort, Descending	Sorts the records in descending order, based on the current field.
	Filter by Selection	Records, Filter, Filter by Selection	Filters records based on the selected text in a field.
	Filter by Form	Records, Filter, Filter by Form	Enables you to enter criteria in table datasheet to establish how records are filtered.
	Apply/ Remove Filter	Records, Apply Filter/Sort	Applies or removes a filter.
	Find	Edit, Find	Displays the Find dialog that locates records with specific characters in a single field or all fields.
	New Record	Edit, Go To, New	Selects the tentative append record.
	Delete Record	Edit, Delete Record	Deletes the active record.
	Database Window	Window, 1	Displays the Database window.
	New Object		Displays a drop-down list from which you choose the type of new object that you want to create: tables, forms, reports, queries, macros, or modules.
	Help	Shift+F1	Turns the mouse pointer into a ? symbol with a pointer. Placing the pointer on a toolbar button and clicking the mouse button displays the Help window for the button or the corresponding menu choice.

The Datasheet Formatting Toolbar. In addition to presenting the Table Datasheet toolbar, you can display the Datasheet Formatting toolbar whenever you view a table in Datasheet View. Choose View, Toolbars to open the Toolbars dialog, mark the Formatting (Datasheet) check box, then click Close to add the toolbar (see Fig.3.7). The buttons in the Datasheet Formatting toolbar provide shortcuts to various text-formatting commands. Figure 3.6 shows the Datasheet Formatting toolbar, and table 3.3 summarizes the action of each button on the toolbar.

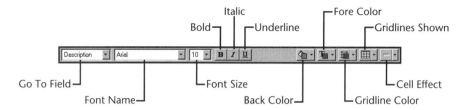

Fig. 3.6 Access also displays the Datasheet Formatting toolbar whenever you view a table in Datasheet View.

Icon	Button	Alternate Method	Function
Table 3.3 Appearance and Functions of Buttons and Other Elements of the Datasheet Formatting Toolbar			
ShipName	Go To Field		Displays a drop-down list from which you can jump quickly to any field in the table.
MS Sans Serif	Font Name	Format, Font	Enables you to select the font (typeface) for text in a table.
8	Font Size	Format, Font	Enables you to select the size of the text in a table.
B	Bold	Format, Font	Turns bold text formatting on and off for the text in a table.
I	Italic	Format, Font	Turns italic text formatting on and off for text in a table.
U	Underline	Format, Font	Turns underlining on and off for text in a table.
(back color icon)	Back Color	Format, Cells	Displays a palette of colors from which to choose the background color for the table's data cells.
(fore color icon)	Fore Color	Format, Font	Displays a palette of colors from which to choose the color of the text in the table.
(gridline color icon)	Gridline Color	Format, Cells	Displays a color palette from which to choose the color of the gridlines that indicate rows and columns in the table.
(gridlines shown icon)	Gridlines Shown	Format, Cells	Displays four buttons that enable you to choose which gridlines are shown: horizontal and vertical, vertical only, horizontal only, or none.
(cell effect icon)	Cell Effect	Format, Cells	Displays three buttons that enable you to choose the cell display style: flat, raised, or sunken.

Manipulating Access's Toolbars

Access 95 uses the resizable, customizable, floating toolbars that have become standard in Microsoft applications such as Excel and Microsoft Word. Access 95's View, Toolbars menu choice opens the Toolbars dialog (see fig. 3.7) that lets you display as many toolbars at once as will fit in your display—or hide toolbars that Access would otherwise display automatically. To display a toolbar, click the box to the left of the toolbar name in the Toolbars dialog so that the check box is selected. To hide a toolbar, click the box again to clear the check box selection.

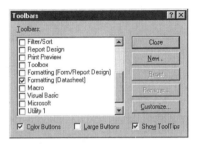

Fig. 3.7 Use Access 95's Toolbars dialog to display or hide toolbars.

Note

When an Access toolbar is in its docked position, it has a fixed width, anchored at its left edge. If you reduce the width of Access's application window by dragging either vertical border inward, the buttons at the docked toolbar's extreme right begin to disappear beyond the application window's right edge. Operating Access in a maximized window with docked toolbars is usually best, because you can then easily access all the toolbar buttons when you use the default in-line horizontal toolbar.

In addition to displaying multiple toolbars, you can reshape the toolbars to suit your own taste. Click a blank area of the toolbar and hold down the left mouse button to drag the toolbar to a new location. The toolbar turns into a *popup* floating toolbar, similar to the toolbox that you use to add control objects to forms and reports. Popup toolbars always appear on top of any other windows open in your application.

Figure 3.8 shows two floating toolbars: the Table Datasheet toolbar and the Formatting Datasheet toolbar. (These are the same toolbars—discussed in the preceding section of this chapter—that Access displays in Datasheet View mode.) Toolbars in their fixed position are called *docked* toolbars, while toolbars in their popup window are referred to as *floating* toolbars. After you change a toolbar to a floating toolbar (or dock it), Access always displays the toolbar in that location until you again reposition the toolbar.

Tip

You can also dock toolbars at the bottom of the Access application window, or at either the left or right edge of the application window.

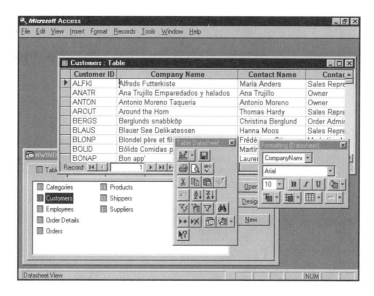

Fig. 3.8 Access's Table Datasheet and Datasheet Formatting toolbars dragged from their default positions below the menubar.

Right Mouse Button Shortcut Menus

Another feature that Access 95 shares with other Microsoft applications, and Windows 95 itself, is the shortcut menu that appears when you right-click the surface of an Access database object. Shortcut menus (also called *popup* or *context menus*) present choices that vary depending on the type of object that you click. Figure 3.9 shows the shortcut menu for a field of a table selected by clicking the field name header. If you select a single data cell, the shortcut menu lets you display the data in the Zoom dialog, copy the selection to the Clipboard, or obtain help on editing data in tables.

Tip

Shortcut menus are quite useful, and provide shortcuts to many common tasks. If you're not sure what you can do with an object on-screen, try right-clicking it to see what shortcut menu commands are available.

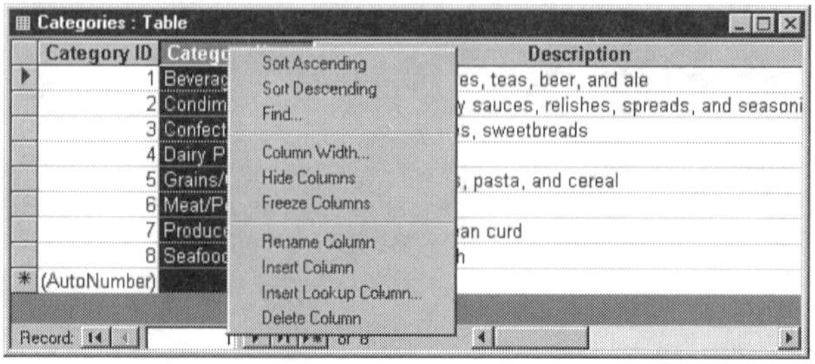

Fig. 3.9 The shortcut menu for selected field of a table.

Using the Function Keys

Access assigns specific purposes to all 12 function keys of the 101-key extended keyboard. Some keys, such as Shift+F4 (which you press to find the next occurrence of a match with the Find dialog), derive from other Microsoft applications—in this case, Word for Windows. You use function keys with the Shift, Alt, and Ctrl keys to enable users to perform as many as 96 functions with the 12 function keys.

Global Function Keys

Windows, rather than Access, uses global function-key assignments, except for F11 and Alt+F1, to perform functions that are identical in all Windows applications. Table 3.4 lists the global function-key assignments.

Table 3.4 Global Function-Key Assignments	
Key	**Function**
F1	Displays context-sensitive help related to the present basic function and status of Access. If a context-sensitive help topic isn't available, F1 starts the Access Answer Wizard (described in the next section of this chapter).
Shift+F1	Adds a question mark to the mouse pointer. Place the mouse pointer with the question mark over an object on-screen for which you want help and then click.
Ctrl+F4	Closes the active window.
Alt+F4	Exits Access or closes a dialog if one is open.
Ctrl+F6	Selects each open window in sequence as the active window.
F11 or Alt+F1	Selects the Database window as the active window.
F12 or Alt+F2	Opens the File Save As dialog.
Shift+F12 or Alt+Shift+F2	Saves your open database; the equivalent of the File, Save menu choice.

Function-Key Assignments for Fields, Grids, and Text Boxes

▶▶   See "Using Keyboard Operations for Entering and Editing Data," p. 160

Access assigns function-key combinations that aren't reserved for global operations to actions that are specific to the basic function that you are performing at the moment. Table 3.5 lists the function-key combinations that apply to fields, grids, and text boxes. (To present complete information, this table repeats some information that appears in the previous tables.)

	Table 3.5 Function Keys for Fields, Grids, and Text Boxes
Key	**Function**
F2	Toggles between displaying the caret for editing and selecting the entire field.
Shift+F2	Opens the Zoom box for entering expressions and other text.
F4	Opens a drop-down combo list or list box.
Shift+F4	Finds the next occurrence of a match of the text entered in the Find or Replace dialog, if the dialog is closed.
F5	Moves the caret to the record-number box. Enter the number of the record that you want to display and press Enter.
F6	In Design View, cycles between upper and lower parts of the window. In Datasheet View and Form View, cycles through the header, body (detail section), and footer.
Shift+F6	In Datasheet View and Form View, cycles through the footer, body (detail section), and header, moving backward.
F7	Starts the spelling checker.
F8	Turns on extend mode. Press F8 again to extend the selection to a word, the entire field, the whole record, and then all records.
Shift+F8	Reverses the F8 selection process.
Ctrl+F	Opens the Find dialog.
Ctrl+H	Opens the Replace dialog.
Ctrl++ (Plus sign)	Adds a new record to the database.
Ctrl +- (Minus sign)	Deletes the current record.
Shift+Enter	Saves changes to the active record in the database.
Esc	Undoes changes in the current record or field. By pressing Esc twice, you can undo changes in both the current field and record. Also cancels extend mode.

Function Keys in the Module Window

▶▶ See "Exploring the Module Window," p. 1024

You use the Module window when writing Access VBA code, which is the subject of this book's Part VII, "Programming with Visual Basic for Applications." Table 3.6 lists the purposes of the Module window's function keys. The Module window shares many of the characteristics of Windows's Notepad applet, including the F3 key, which you use for searching.

	Table 3.6 Function Keys in the Module Window
Key	**Function**
F1	Displays context-sensitive help about the currently selected Access VBA keyword, dialog, or menu command.
F2	Opens the Object Browser dialog (a new feature in Access 95), which enables you to view Access objects and move among them and other applications that support VBA, including the applications' properties, controls, procedures, and methods.

Key	Function
Shift+F2	Goes to the procedure selected in the Module window.
F3	Finds the next occurrence of text specified in the Find or Replace dialog.
Shift+F3	Finds the preceding occurrence of text specified in the Find or Replace dialog.
F5	Continues executing code after a break condition.
Shift+F5	Resets the VBA interpreter, utilizing all variables.
F6	Cycles between upper and lower panes (if you have split the window).
F8	Traces execution one step at a time (single step or Step Into mode).
Shift+F8	Traces execution by procedure (procedure step or Step Over mode).
F9	Toggles a breakpoint at the selected line.
Shift+F9	Creates an Instant Watch for the selected variable or expression.
Ctrl+Shift+F9	Clears all breakpoints.
Ctrl+F	Opens the Find dialog.
Ctrl+G	Displays the Debug window.
Ctrl+H	Opens the Replace dialog.
Ctrl+L	Displays the Calls dialog.
Ctrl+M	Indents selected lines.
Ctrl+Shift+M	Removes indentation.
Ctrl+Y	Cuts the current line and copies it to the Clipboard.
Ctrl+Break	Halts macro execution.
Ctrl+↑	Displays the previous procedure.
Ctrl+↓	Displays the next procedure.

Setting Default Options

You can set about 100 options that establish the default settings for the system as a whole, and also those for the six functions defined by the Database window's buttons. You aren't likely to change default options until you are more familiar with Access. However, because this book is a reference as well as a tutorial guide, and options are a basic element of Access's overall structure, this section explains how to change these settings.

You set defaults by choosing <u>T</u>ools, <u>O</u>ptions. The Options dialog appears as shown in figure 3.10. View, General, Keyboard, and Edit/Find category options apply to the system as a whole. Datasheet, Tables/Queries, and Forms/Reports options all apply to table views in Datasheet View, forms, and queries. The remainder of the option categories are specific to other basic functions.

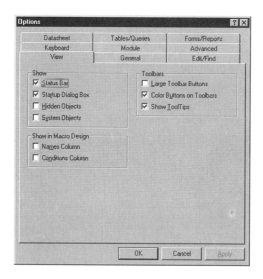

Fig. 3.10   The Options dialog displaying the View Options sheet.

You select an Options category by clicking the tab near the top of the Options dialog. When you change a category, the dialog displays the Options sheet for that category. Most of the settings are option buttons and check boxes, although many other items require multiple-choice entries that you select from drop-down lists. In some cases, you must enter a specific value from the keyboard. After you complete your changes, click OK to close the dialog. If you decide not to implement your changes, click Cancel to exit the Options dialog without making any changes. The next few sections and their tables summarize options that affect Access as a whole, and those options that affect viewing and printing data in Datasheet View.

System Defaults

   ▶▶   See "Sharing Your Access Database Files with Other Users," p. 906

Access uses a special Access database, System.mdw, to store all default properties for displaying and printing the contents of tables, queries, forms, reports, and modules for each user of Access. The .mdw extension for workgroup system files is new with Access 95, replacing the .MDA extension shared by libraries, wizards, and SYSTEM.MDA in Access 1.x and 2.0. Access stores user default properties in system tables, along with other tables that determine the behavior of Access, in System.mdw. System.mdw also stores user names and passwords when you secure your Access database or use Access in a multiuser (workgroup) environment.

> **Note**
>
> System.mdw is vital to the proper operation of Access. You should keep a backup copy of System.mdw on a diskette. If you make changes to any options or implement Access's security features, you should create an updated backup after completing your changes or additions.

View Options. The View options, as described in table 3.7, enable you to customize the appearance of Access's application window, and to control how Access displays toolbars.

Table 3.7   View Options for the Access System

Option	Group	Function
Status Bar	Show	If checked, displays the status bar at the bottom of the Access application window.
Startup Dialog Box	Show	If checked, displays the startup dialog whenever you start Access. This dialog prompts you to open an existing database or to create a new one.
Hidden Objects	Show	When checked, displays hidden objects in the Database window.
System Objects	Show	If checked, displays system objects in the Database window.
Names Column	Macro Design	If checked, displays the Names column in new macros.
Conditions Column Conditions	Macro Design	If checked, displays the column in new macros.
Large Toolbar Buttons	Toolbars	When checked, displays large buttons on its toolbars. Use this option if you use SVGA screen resolution and want to see the buttons more easily.
Color Buttons on Toolbars	Toolbars	When checked, displays color buttons on the toolbars. Leave this option on for color monitors; turn it off to see the toolbar icons on a monochrome screen better.
Show ToolTips	Toolbars	Controls whether Access displays the ToolTips hints on the mouse cursor for toolbar buttons.

General Options. General options, described in table 3.8, apply to Access as a whole. The settings that you make in the General options apply to any new objects that you create (tables, forms, and reports), but don't retroactively affect existing objects. For example, changing the print margins in General options affects only any reports that you create subsequently, but not any existing reports. To change the print margins of existing objects, you must change each object's individual printing settings in Design View.

Margins usually are expressed in inches. If you are using an international version of Access, margin settings are in centimeters. You also can specify margin settings in *twips*, the default measurement of Windows. A twip is 1/20 of a printer's point. A point is 1/72 inch, so a twip is 1/1,440 inch.

The one-inch default margins are arbitrary; you might want to reset them to your preference before creating any forms or reports of your own. If you are using a laser printer, refer to its manual to determine the maximum printable area. The printable area determines the minimum margins that you can use.

Apart from the printing margins, the General option you're most likely to want to change is the default database directory. When you create your own databases, you should store them in a folder dedicated to databases, to simplify backup operations. A dedicated database folder also is a good place to keep a backup copy of System.mdw.

Table 3.8 General Options for the Access System		
Option	**Group**	**Function**
Left Margin	Print Margins	Establishes the default left margin.
Top Margin	Print Margins	Establishes the default top margin.
Right Margin	Print Margins	Establishes the default right margin.
Bottom Margin	Print Margins	Establishes the default bottom margin.
Default Database		Changes the default folder for the Open Database dialog. The default Folder folder is the Access working folder, indicated by a period.
New Database Sort Order		Sets the alphabetical sort order used for new databases. You can change the sort order for an existing database by selecting a different sort-order setting and then compacting the database by choosing Tools, Database Utilities, Compact Database.

Edit/Find Options. The Edit/Find options all affect the behavior of Access Find feature for both tables in a Form or Datasheet View and when working with Access VBA code in a module. Table 3.9 summarizes the Edit/Find options and their effects. The options in the Default Find/Replace group all determine the default searching method for the Edit, Find and Edit, Replace commands. Options in the Confirm group all determine which actions that Access asks the user to confirm. The final option group in the Find/Replace options sheet is the Filter by Form Defaults for the current database. These options don't actually affect Access itself, but affect the defaults for the particular database that is open.

Table 3.9 Edit/Find Options for the Access System		
Option	**Group**	**Function**
Fast Search	Default Find/Replace	Sets the default search method to search in the current field, and to match the whole field.
General Search	Default Find/Replace	Sets the default search method to search in all fields, and matches any part of a field.
Start of Field Search	Default Find/Replace	Causes the default search method to search the current field, matching only the beginning of the field.
Record Changes	Confirm	Causes Access to confirm any changes that you make to a record.
Document Deletions	Confirm	Causes Access to confirm document (table, form, or report) deletions.
Action Queries	Confirm	Causes Access to confirm an action query (such as adding or deleting records) before carrying out the query.
Local Indexed Fields	Filter by Form Defaults	Includes local indexed fields in the list of values that you can use when entering filter criteria.

Option	Group	Function
Local Non-Indexed Fields	Filter by Form Defaults	Includes nonindexed fields in the list of values that you can use when entering filter criteria.
Remote Defaults	Filter by Form	Includes fields from remote tables in the lists of values that you can use when entering filter criteria.
Don't display lists where more than this number of rows read		Prohibits the display of filter values whenever the number of items in the list exceeds the specified number.

Keyboard Options

▶▶   See "Using Data Entry and Editing Keys," p. 161

▶▶   See "Running a Macro from a Shortcut Key," p. 608

Keyboard options, listed in table 3.10, are especially important if you are accustomed to a particular type of arrow-key behavior. You probably will want to change keyboard options more than any of the other categories. For example, you can make the arrow keys behave as if you are editing xBase fields, instead of using the keys' default behavior, which duplicates that of Excel. The options in the Move After Enter group affect what Access does when you press Enter after editing or entering data. The options in the Arrow Key Behavior group affect how the left- and right-arrow keys work, while the options in the Behavior Entering Field group determine what happens when the caret enters a field.

Table 3.10   Keyboard Options for the Access System

Option	Group	Function
Don't Move	Move After Enter	When selected, the caret remains in the current field when you press Enter.
Next Field	Move After Enter	When selected, the caret moves to the next or previous field when you press Enter. This is the Move After Enter group's default option.
Next Record	Move After Enter	When selected, the caret moves down the column to the next or previous record when you press Enter.
Next Field	Arrow Key Behavior	If selected, pressing the right- or left-arrow keys moves the caret to the next or previous field. This is the Arrow Key Behavior group's default option.
Next Character	Arrow Key Behavior	If selected, pressing the right- or left-arrow keys moves the caret to the next or previous character in the same field.
Select Entire Field	Behavior Entering Field	When this option is selected, the entire field's contents are selected when you use the arrow keys to move the caret into the field. This is the Behavior Entering Field group's default option.
Go to Start of Field	Behavior Entering Field	If selected, causes the caret to move to the beginning of the field when you use the arrow keys to move the caret into the field.

(continues)

Learning Access

	Table 3.10 Continued	
Option	**Group**	**Function**
Go to End of Field	Behavior Entering Field	If selected, causes the caret to move to the end of the field when you use the arrow keys to move the caret into the field.
Cursor Stops at First/Last Field		If selected, keeps the caret from moving to another record when the left- or right-arrow keys are pressed, and the caret is in the first or last field of the record.

Advanced Options. Access has several advanced system options that affect multiuser operations, OLE updates, DDE linking and updating, and tables attached by the Open Database Connectivity (ODBC) feature of the Jet 3.0 database engine. Table 3.11 describes the Advanced options that you can set. Options in the Default Record Locking group affect how Access locks records in a multiuser environment, and the Default Open Mode option group controls whether Access shares opened databases. The DDE Operations options group controls how Access handles DDE requests from other applications; other options control OLE updating and query updating. Usually you won't need to change the Advanced options much, unless you're working in a multiuser environment with several users sharing the same database.

	Table 3.11 Advanced Options for the Access System	
Option	**Group**	**Function**
No Locks	Default Record Locking	When selected, leaves all records unlocked in the open database tables, so that other networked users can update the records. This is the group's default option.
All Records	Default Record Locking	When selected, locks all records in the open database tables. No other networked users can update the records.
Edited Records	Default Record Locking	When selected, locks only edited records. When the changes to the record are saved, Access unlocks the record.
Ignore DDE Requests	DDE Operations	If enabled, ignores all Dynamic Data Exchange (DDE) requests from other Windows applications.
Enable DDE Refresh	DDE Operations	If enabled, lets Access dynamically update linked DDE data. This is the group's default option.
OLE/DDE Timeout (sec)		Specifies how long Access waits for a response from a DDE or OLE server. If the specified interval passes without a response, Access reports an error. Access's default value for this option is 30 seconds.
Shared	Default Open Mode	When selected, enables other networked users to use the open database simultaneously. This is the group's default option.
Exclusive	Default Open Mode	When selected, opens the database in an exclusive mode so so that other network users cannot open the database.
Number of Update Retries		Specifies how many times that Access tries to update a query, OLE object, or DDE link before giving up. The default number of tries is 2.
ODBC Refresh Interval (sec)		Specifies how many seconds that Access waits before refreshing records that you view through an ODBC connection. The default interval is 1,500 seconds.

Option	Group	Function
Refresh Interval (sec)		Specifies how many seconds that Access waits before refreshing remote data. The default Refresh Interval is 60 seconds.
Update Retry Interval (msec)		Specifies how many milliseconds (thousandths of a second) that Access waits in between attempts at updating an OLE, DDE, ODBC, or other link. The default is 250 milliseconds.

Defaults for Datasheet View

You use Datasheet View options to customize the display of all query datasheets and new table and form datasheets (see table 3.12). As with printing options, to change the display format of existing table and form datasheets, you must edit the appropriate properties of the table or form in Design View. The Datasheet View options that you set don't apply to forms and reports created with Access wizards. Each wizard has its own set of default values. The options in the Default Colors group set the background and foreground colors for text displayed in Datasheet View, while the Default Font group's options determine the typeface and text size. The Default Gridlines Showing options determine which gridlines (if any) Access displays in Datasheet View. Finally, the Default Cell Effect options enable you to select a default style for datasheet cells.

Table 3.12   Options for Datasheet Views

Option	Group	Function
Font	Default Colors	Displays a drop-down list from which you can select the color of the text in new tables, queries, and forms. Access's default Font color selection is black.
Background	Default Colors	Enables you to select the background color of cells in Datasheet View. Access's default Background color is white.
Gridlines	Default Colors	Enables you to select the color of the gridlines displayed in Datasheet View. Access's default gridline color is silver.
Font	Default Font	Displays a drop-down list from which you can select the typeface that Access uses to display text in Datasheet View. Access's default font is Arial.
Weight	Default Font	Displays a drop-down list from which you can select the weight of the text characters displayed in Datasheet View. You can select Normal (the default), Thin, Extra Light, Medium, Semi-bold, Bold, Extra Bold, or Heavy.
Size	Default Font	Enables you to select the default font size, in points. Access's default font size is 10 points.
Italic	Default Font	If selected, displays all datasheet text in italics.
Underline	Default Font	If selected, displays all datasheet text with a single underline.
Horizontal	Default Gridlines Showing	If selected, displays horizontal gridlines (that is, gridlines between rows) in Datasheet View. By default, this option and the Vertical gridlines option are turned off.

(continues)

Table 3.12	Continued	
Option	**Group**	**Function**
Vertical	Default Gridlines Showing	If selected, displays vertical gridlines (that is, gridlines between columns) in Datasheet View. You can display both vertical and horizontal gridlines by combining Veritical gridlines option with Horizontal gridlines option.
Default Column Width		Specifies the default column width in inches. Access's default value for this text box setting is one inch.
Flat	Default Cell Effect	When selected, displays a data cell as a "flat" cell—that is, the cell has no special shading. This is the group's default option.
Raised	Default Cell Effect	When selected, adds shadow effects to each data cell so that the cell appears to be raised above the surface of the screen, like a command button on a toolbar.
Sunken	Default Cell Effect	When selected, adds shadow effects to each data cell so that the cell appears to be sunken below the surface of the screen.
Show Animations		If selected, displays animated cursors and other animation effects (like the moving circular arrow in the Answer Wizard). If you have a slow computer, you'll probably want to turn off this option to improve Access's operating speed slightly.

Note

The remaining option categories—Tables/Queries, Forms/Reports, and Module—are discussed in the chapter(s) of this book that cover the subject of the particular option category. Also, options related to multiuser, DDE, and ODBC features are described in more detail in the chapter(s) devoted to those special topics.

Using Access Help

 The Access help system is extensive and easy to use. All the new help functions incorporated in Windows 95's 32-bit WinHelp engine are used by Access's Help system.

This section discusses methods of getting help with specific functions and objects of Access. Chapter 32, "Adding Online Help for Users," describes how you can aid users of your applications by writing help files of your own to accompany your Access applications.

Context-Sensitive Help

Context-sensitive help tries to anticipate your need for information by displaying help windows related to the operating mode, function, and operation in which you are involved or attempting to perform. You can get context-sensitive help in any of the following ways:

- By using the help mouse pointer that appears after you click the What's This button (located near the top-right corner of the dialog window) in the active dialog. Move the help mouse pointer over the dialog option for which you want help, and click again to display a popup help window with information about that dialog option.

- By using the help mouse pointer that appears after you press Shift+F1 or click the Help button on the toolbar. Move the help mouse pointer over the item for which you want help, and click again to display a popup help window.

- By pressing the F1 key. Access displays a help window with information about the active area (dialog control, window, menu command, and so on), or displays the Answer Wizard dialog, described later in this section.

- By clicking the Help button in a dialog. Use this method, or press the F1 key, for dialogs that don't have a What's This button.

To get context-sensitive help in an open dialog, click the What's This button; the mouse pointer changes to a question mark. Move the help mouse pointer over the dialog control that you want help with, and click. You can also get context-sensitive help on the active dialog control by pressing F1 or clicking the control with the right mouse button. For example, you might want more information about the effects of the Find dialog's Match Case option. To find such information, click the What's This button, and then click the Find dialog's Match Case option. Figure 3.11 shows the resulting popup help window explaining the Match Case option.

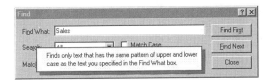

Fig. 3.11   The context-sensitive help for the Find dialog's Match Case option.

Another method for getting context-sensitive help is to click the Help button on the toolbar (or press Shift+F1) and then place the mouse pointer with the question mark on the item with which you need help. When you click the mouse button, the topic related to the object appears. Figure 3.12 shows an example that explains the purpose of the Table Datasheet toolbar's Find button.

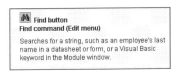

Fig. 3.12   The popup help window explaining the purpose of the toolbar's Find button.

The Help Menu

Access's <u>H</u>elp menu provides an alternative to using context-sensitive help. Table 3.13 lists the options that the <u>H</u>elp menu presents.

Table 3.13 Access's Help Menu Options	
Option	**Function**
Microsoft Access <u>H</u>elp Topics	Displays the Help Topics dialog, which enables you to select or search for help topics either through a table of contents, an index, a Find utility, or the Answer Wizard.
Answer <u>W</u>izard	Displays the Help Topics dialog with the Answer Wizard tab active. (The Answer Wizard is described in detail later in this chapter.)
<u>A</u>bout Microsoft Access	Displays the copyright notice for Microsoft Access, and the name and organization that you entered during setup. The About dialog also contains two command buttons: one that displays sources of technical support for Access in North America and throughout the world, and another that displays information about your computer system, such as how much memory you have installed, whether you have a math coprocessor, and the amount of remaining disk space.

Using the Help Topics Dialog

You can get a more general form of help by choosing <u>H</u>elp, Microsoft Access <u>H</u>elp Topics. In this case, you always start from square one—the Help Topics dialog for the entire help system, shown in figure 3.13. The Help Topics dialog contains four tabbed sheets: Contents, Index, Find, and Answer Wizard. The first three options in the Help Topics dialog are described next; the Answer Wizard is described in a separate, subsequent section.

The Contents Tab. Figure 3.13 shows the Help Topics Contents tab (you might have to click the Contents tab to bring the table of contents to the front of the dialog). The Contents tab is like the table of contents in a book; it shows the structure of the topics in the Help system, based on the topic's title.

Each table of contents entry that has subheadings is indicated by a book icon to its left. To see subheadings for a topic, double-click the closed book icon. The Help system expands the topic list and changes the icon to an open book. (To hide the list of subheadings, double-click the open book icon; this hides the expanded subheading branch and changes the icon back to a closed book.)

Table of contents headings that lack subheadings have to their left an icon resembling a sheet of paper with a question mark on it. Figure 3.13 shows the "Finding and Sorting Data" heading expanded to show its subheadings; the "Sorting Data in Tables, Queries, and Forms" subheading, in turn, has been expanded, revealing a list of three help topics. To display a topic, double-click it. Figure 3.14 shows the displayed help topic for "Sort records in a table, query, form, or subform."

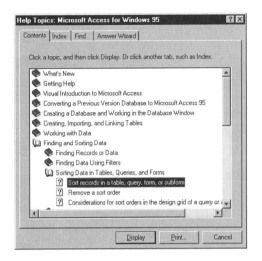

Fig. 3.13 The Contents tab of the Help Topics dialog, showing expanded headings and subheadings.

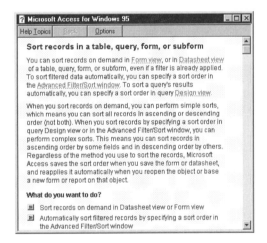

Fig. 3.14 You display a help topic by double-clicking a topic in the Help Topics dialog's Contents list.

Understanding the Help Window

Tip

You can copy text from any help window. Simply drag the mouse over the text that you want to copy to select it, and then press Ctrl+C or choose Edit, Copy. You can then paste the copied help text into any Windows application from the Clipboard.

You can reposition and resize the help window by dragging its borders with your mouse. To reposition the help window, click and drag the help title bar. If the help file on the topic that you selected has more information than can fit in the window, a vertical scroll bar appears at the right of the window. Drag the scroll box down to display additional text.

Most of Access's help windows include *hot spots* that provide additional information about a topic. Hot spots with dotted underlines, such as "Form view" and "Datasheet view" in figure 3.14, display popup windows that usually contain a definition of the term or contain more detailed information about that topic. Figure 3.15 shows the window that pops up when you click the "Datasheet view" hot spot. To close the popup window, click anywhere on the screen outside the popup window.

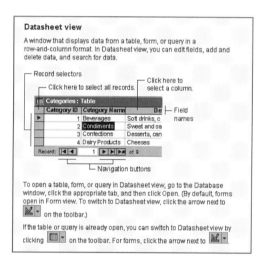

Fig. 3.15   The popup window displayed by the "Datasheet view" hot spot.

Note

When you click hot-spot text, which usually is highlighted in green, you receive an explanation of the hot-spot topic. Hot spots in green, underlined, and bold text are links to additional windows in the help file related to the hot spot's topic.

Some hot spots lead to additional help topics. These hot spots are usually shown in bold text with a solid underline (like all hot spots, they're typically displayed in green text). You click the hot spot that represents the subject about which you want to learn. This action causes a jump to the subject's first help window, which often provides several additional choices for more detailed help on a specific topic.

> **Tip**
>
> You can return to the Help Topics dialog at any time by clicking the Help Topics button in the help window.

Most help windows, in addition to providing information about a particular topic, also have tutorial, step-by-step instructions for the task about which you are inquiring. In figure 3.14, notice that the help topic has a section titled "What do you want to do?" (visible near the bottom of the window). This section lists a variety of tasks that you might be trying to accomplish if you're looking for help on sorting records (the list extends beyond the bottom edge of the dialog in figure 3.14). Each item in the list has a button to its left. After you click this button, Access displays a help screen with step-by-step instructions for accomplishing the indicated task.

For example, figure 3.16 shows the step-by-step tutorial help window that Access displays if you click the button next to "Sort records on demand in Datasheet view or Form view" at the bottom of the dialog in figure 3.14.

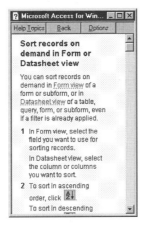

Fig. 3.16   To display this step-by-step help window, you click the first button in the "What do you want to do?" list from the Sort records help topic shown in figure 3.14.

> **Tip**
>
> To return to the previously displayed topic, choose the Back button in the help window. To move backward through more than one topic, choose the same button repeatedly. When there are no previous topics to return to, Access disables the Back button.

Notice the icon near the bottom of the step-by-step help window shown in figure 3.16. This icon, which depicts the Sort Ascending toolbar button described earlier in this chapter, is also a hot spot. Clicking this hot spot displays a popup window describing the action of the Sort Ascending toolbar button. Many help topics throughout the Access Help system contain graphic hot spots like this one.

> ### Tip
>
> Whenever you place the mouse pointer over a help hot spot, the pointer turns into a pointing-hand shape.

The Index Tab. You can also look up help topics in an index much like that which is at the end of this book. Click the Index tab in the Help Topics dialog to bring the Index sheet to the front of the dialog. Figure 3.17 shows the Index sheet as it appears after you type the topic **help** in the text box.

Fig. 3.17   The Index sheet of the Help Topics dialog.

Using the Help Topics Index is simple—just type in the text box at the top of the dialog the name of the topic on which you want help. As you type, the Help system adjusts the topic list in the bottom of the dialog to show the topic that most closely matches the text that you've typed so far. In figure 3.17, the user has typed **help** in the text box at the top of the dialog, and the help topics list shows the first matching entry: "Help files." To display a topic from the list, double-click it (or click once to select it and then choose the Display button). If you want, you can also use the scroll bar to view the list of available help topics.

The Find Tab. The Help Topics Index is only an alphabetical listing of the help topics available. The Find tab provides you with a way to search quickly through the actual text in the available help topics so that you can quickly find topics even if you don't know the name of the topic.

Click the Find tab in the Help Topics dialog to display the Find sheet. Figure 3.18 shows the Find sheet, after searching for the words "getting help."

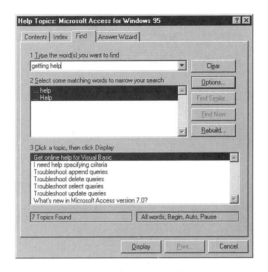

Fig. 3.18   The Find tab of the Help Topics dialog.

> **Note**
>
> The first time that you use the Help Topics Find option, the Windows 95 WinHelp engine must build a word list to use for searching. The Help system needs to build this word list only once; thereafter, the system loads that list each time that you display the Find sheet.

The Help Topics Find sheet works essentially the same as the Index sheet. In the text box at the top of the dialog, you type words related to the topics that you want help on. Find uses its word list to locate all the topics that contain the words that you type. The list in the center of the dialog displays additional matching words, and a list at the bottom of the dialog displays matching help topics. Unfortunately, explaining all the options available in the Find tab is beyond the scope of this book. For most searches, the default settings work just fine. To get more help about the specific controls in the Find sheet, click the What's This button.

The Help Window Options. The Help system provides you with several options that you can take advantage of to print, copy, or annotate the displayed help topic, or that enable you to change the help window's style or appearance. To display a menu of options, click the help window's Options button or right-click the dialog. Table 3.14 summarizes each menu choice and its effect.

Table 3.14	Options for Datasheet Views
Option	**Function**
Annotate	Enables you to add your own comments to the current help topic.
Copy	Copies selected text from the help window to the Windows Clipboard.
Print Topic	Prints the currently visible help topic on your printer.
Font	Enables you to select one of three predetermined font sizes for text displayed in the help window: Small, Normal, and Large.
Keep Help on Top	Enables you to choose whether the help window always displays on top of other windows, never displays on top of other windows, or displays with the default setting. (The Help system determines whether the window should be on top or not.)
Use System Colors	Tells the Help system to use the window border and background colors defined for the Windows 95 system as a whole. By default, the Help system uses its own color scheme for its windows.
Version	Displays the copyright notice for the current version of the WinHelp engine in use.

Using the Answer Wizard

An important new feature in Access help is the Answer Wizard. You can start the Answer Wizard by choosing Help, Answer Wizard, or by clicking the Answer Wizard tab in the Help Topics dialog. Access also starts the Answer Wizard if you press F1 for context-sensitive help, but Access can't determine the precise context in which you're working. Use the Answer Wizard to search for help on any topic.

Figure 3.19 shows the Answer Wizard sheet after searching for help topics that answer the question "How do I find text in a field?" To use the Answer Wizard, type a request in the text box at the top of the dialog and then choose the Search button. The Answer Wizard displays a list of topics that answer your request, arranged into sections such as the "How Do I" and "Tell Me About" lists visible in figure 3.19. Typically, the help topics in the "How Do I" list lead to step-by-step tutorial help windows, and the "Tell Me About" help topics lead to popup windows that contain definitions and explanations. To display the help topic, double-click the topic in the list, or select the topic and choose the Display button.

Tip

If you can't find help any other way, use the Answer Wizard. It provides the best way to find help for specific tasks.

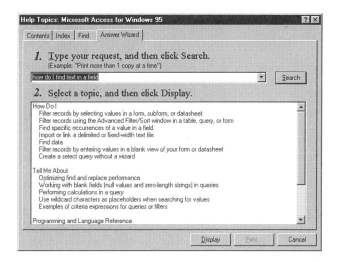

Fig. 3.19 Use the Answer Wizard to get answers to specific requests for information.

Using the Database Utilities

Access has three functions that you can perform only when no database is open. You access these database functions from the Tools, Database Utilities menu. If you have a large database, these operations take a considerable amount of time. Each of the operations described in the following sections involves two dialogs. In the first dialog, you select the database in which Access is to perform the operation; in the second dialog, you enter the name of the file that the operation is to create. Default file names for new files are DB#.MDB, where # is a sequential number, beginning with 1, assigned by Access.

Compacting Databases

After you make numerous additions and changes to objects within a database file, especially additions and deletions of data in tables, the database file can become disorganized. As with xBase files, when you delete a record, you don't automatically regain the space in the file that the deleted data occupied. You must compact the database, using the equivalent of xBase's PACK command, to optimize both its file size and the organization of data within the tables that the file contains. When you pack an Access file, however, you regain space only in 32K increments, not in the fixed disk cluster increments (usually 2K) that you regain by packing xBase files.

To compact a database, perform the following steps:

   1. Choose Tools, Database Utilities, Compact Database. The Database to Compact From dialog appears, as shown in figure 3.20.

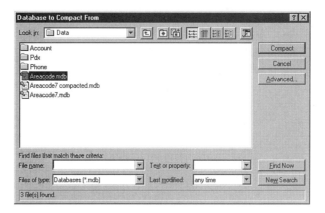

Fig. 3.20   The Database to Compact From dialog.

2. Double-click the name of the database file that you want to compact, or click the name and then click OK. The Compact Database Into dialog appears, as shown in figure 3.21.

Fig. 3.21   The Compact Database Into dialog.

3. In the File Name text box, enter the name of the new file that is to result from the compaction process. If you choose to replace the existing file with the compacted version, you see a message box requesting that you confirm your choice. Click Save.

> **Caution**
>
> If the compaction process fails, your database might be damaged. Databases damaged in the compaction process are unlikely to be repairable (see the "Repairing Databases" section that follows). Thus, you should not compact the database into a new database with the same name. Do so only after backing up your database with a different name, in a different directory, or on a floppy disk.

Access then creates a compacted version of the file. The progress of the compaction is shown in a blue bar in the status bar. If you decide to use the same file name, the new file replaces the preceding file after compaction.

Periodically compacting files usually is the duty of the database administrator in a multiuser environment, usually in relation to backup operations. You should back up your existing file on disk or tape before creating a compacted version. When you're developing an Access 95 database, you should compact the database frequently. Uncompacted Access 95 databases grow in size much more rapidly during modification than with prior verisons of Access.

Converting Databases to Access 95 Format

To convert Access .MDB database files and .MDA library files created with Access 1.x or Access 2.0 to the new database format of Access 95, choose Tools, Database Utilities, Convert Database. The process of converting database files from earlier versions of Access database formats to that of Access 95 is almost identical to the file-compaction process described in the preceding section. The only difference that you'll notice is that the names of the dialogs are Database to Convert From and Database to Convert Into. (Chapter 33, "Migrating Access 2.0 Applications to Access 95," covers this conversion process in detail.)

Caution

Although you can convert databases created with earlier versions of Access into Access 95 format, Access 95 does not enable you to convert the databases back from Access 95 format to a prior Access database format. If you attempt to open an Access 95 database or library file with the Convert Database menu choice, you receive the following message: "The database you tried to convert was either created in or was already converted to the current version of Microsoft Access." Thus, if you want to support users of Access database applications who do not have Access 95, you must maintain two separate sets of database files. Therefore, you must have the retail versions of any earlier Access versions and Access 95 available to maintain your application. You also need both versions of the Access Developer's Toolkit if your applications use run-time Access.

Repairing Databases

A database can become corrupted as the result of the following problems:

- Hardware problems in writing to your database file, either locally or on a network server

- Accidental restarting of the computer while Access databases are open

- A power failure that occurs after you have made modifications to an Access object, but have not saved the object

Access includes a database repair facility that you can use to recover a usable database file from the majority of files corrupted by one of the preceding causes. The process is the same as that for creating compacted and encrypted versions of the file.

Occasionally, a file might become corrupted without Access detecting the problem. This lack of detection occurs most frequently with corrupted indexes. If Access or your application behaves strangely when you open an existing database and display its contents, try repairing the database. Choose Tools, Database Utilities, Repair Database, and then follow the same steps as described for compacting the database.

From Here...

This chapter explained the structure of Access 95 for Windows, the shortcut keys, and the terminology and appearance of your display. You learned about the table functions and about the options for establishing the default methodology for Access as a whole. The chapter explained Access's extensive, context-sensitive Help system, which enables users to take full advantage of the new features of the Windows 95 WinHelp engine.

Refer to the following chapters for more information related to the topics covered in this chapter:

- Chapter 4, "Working with Access Databases and Tables," has you begin to apply what you learned in this chapter to work with Access tables. Most of Chapter 4's examples continue to use the Northwind Traders database, but you add your own tables to expand the database's capabilities.

- Chapter 5, "Entering, Editing, and Validating Data in Tables," and Chapter 6, "Sorting, Finding, and Filtering Data in Tables," show you how to manipulate data contained in tables.

- Chapter 7, "Linking, Importing, and Exporting Tables," starts you working with tables created from your existing database or spreadsheet applications by using Access 95's Import and Link functions.

Chapter 4

Working with Access Databases and Tables

The traditional definition of a database is *a collection of related data items that are stored in an organized manner.* Access is unique among desktop database development applications for the PC because of its all-encompassing database file structure. Unlike conventional desktop databases, such as dBASE, FoxPro, and Paradox, a single Access .mdb file can contain data objects—tables, indexes, and queries—as well as application objects—forms, reports, macros, and Access Visual Basic for Applications (VBA) code modules. Thus, you can create a complete Access database application stored in a single .mdb file. Most Access developers use two .mdb files: one to contain data objects and the other to hold application objects. This chapter and Chapter 25, "Securing Multiuser Network Applications," explain why developers use two .mdb files. Regardless of the approach that you choose, Access's all-encompassing .mdb file structure makes creating and distributing database applications simpler.

Defining the Elements of Access Databases

Access databases include the following elements in a single .mdb database file:

■ *Tables* store data items in a row-column format similar to that used by spreadsheet applications. An Access database can include as many as 32,768 tables, and as many as 254 tables can be open at one time if you have sufficient resources available. You can import tables from other database applications (such as xBase and Paradox), client/server databases (such as Microsoft SQL Server), and spreadsheet applications (such as Microsoft Excel and Lotus 1-2-3). In addition, you can link to Access databases other types of database tables (dBASE, FoxPro, and Paradox tables, for example), formatted files (Excel worksheet and ASCII text), and other Access databases. Chapter 7 discusses linking, importing, and exporting tables.

In this chapter, you learn about the following

■ Recognizing the elements of Access database files

■ Creating new databases

■ Adding tables to a database

■ Creating default relations among database tables

■ Enforcing referential integrity rules

■ Copying and pasting tables

■ *Queries* display selected data contained in as many as 16 tables. With queries, you can specify how to present data by choosing the tables that comprise the query and as many as 255 specific fields (columns) of the chosen tables. You determine the records (rows) to display by specifying the criteria that the data items in the query data must meet to be included in the display. Part II, "Querying for Specific Information," explains how to create queries.

 ■ *Forms* display data contained in tables or queries and enable you to add new data and update or delete existing data. You can incorporate pictures and graphs in your forms, and, if you have a sound card, include narration and music in your form. You learn how to create forms in Chapters 12 and 13, and you learn how to add graphics to forms in Chapter 20. Access 95 forms also can incorporate Access VBA code, a feature called Code Behind Forms (CBF), to provide event-handling subprocedures for forms and the controls that appear on forms.

 ■ *Reports* print data from tables or queries in virtually any format that you want. Access enables you to add graphics to your reports so that you can print a complete, illustrated catalog of products from an Access database. Access's report capabilities are much more flexible than those of most other relational database management applications, including those designed for mini- and mainframe computers. You can include Access VBA event-handling subprocedures, like forms, in Access 95 reports. Chapters 14 and 15 cover creating reports.

 ■ *Macros* automate Access operations. Access macros take the place of the programming code required by other database applications, such as xBase, to perform specific actions in response to user-initiated events, such as clicking a command button. In most cases, you can create a fully functional database application without writing any programming code at all. Chapters 16 through 18 discuss macros.

 ■ *Modules* contain Access VBA code that you write to perform operations that the standard collection of macros included in Access does not support. Chapter 28 describes how to write Access VBA code stored in modules or behind forms and reports.

▶▶ See "Defining the Client/Server Environment," p. 950

A better definition of an Access database is *a collection of related data items and, optionally, the methods necessary to select, display, update, and report the data*. This definition emphasizes an important distinction between Access and other database management applications. Even client/server database systems, such as Microsoft SQL Server, that include all related tables within a single database do not include the equivalent of forms and reports within the database. You must use another application, called a *front-end*, to display, edit, and report data stored in client/server databases. You can use Access to create front-ends for client/server databases by linking tables from the client/server database to your Access database. Creating front-ends for client/server databases is one of the major applications for Access in medium- to large-sized firms.

> **Note**
>
> As previous chapters mentioned, it is a good database application development practice to main-
> tain tables that store your application's data in one Access database (.mdb) file and the remainder
> of your application's objects, such as forms and reports, in a separate .mdb file. This chapter uses
> the Northwind Traders sample database, which is a self-contained application with a single .mdb
> file. Chapter 7, "Linking, Importing, and Exporting Tables," describes how to use or create sepa-
> rate .mdb files to store data and application objects.

This chapter introduces you to Access databases and tables—the fundamental elements
of an Access application. You will see many references in this book to the term *Access application*. An Access application is an Access database that has the following characteristics:

- It contains the queries, forms, reports, and macros necessary to display the data in
  a meaningful way and to update the data as necessary. This book calls these elements *application objects*. A self-contained (single-user) Access application includes
  tables in the application database. Multiuser Access applications usually consist of
  two .mdb files, one containing the tables shared by users (*database objects*) and the
  other consisting of the Access application that manipulates the data. (Most Access
  developers use separate application and data .mdb files even for single-user applications.) If you are creating a front-end application, you usually link tables from the
  client/server database. Some front-end applications, however, also use local tables
  stored in the application database file.

- It does not require the database's users to know how to design any of its elements.
  All elements of the database are fully predefined during the application's design
  stage. In most cases, you want to restrict other users from intentionally or uninten-
  tionally changing the application's design.

- It is automated by Access macros or Access VBA code so that users make choices
  from command buttons or custom-designed menus rather than from the lists in
  the Database window that you used in Chapter 2, "Up and Running with Access
  Tables."

As you progress through the chapters in this book, you create a model of an Access application called *Personnel Actions*. Later in this chapter, you create the Personnel Actions
table. In the following chapters, you add new features to the Personnel Actions application until, when you reach Chapter 18, "Taking Advantage of Advanced Macro Features,"
you have a complete, automated method of adding and editing Personnel Actions data.
Therefore, you should read this book sequentially, at least to Chapter 18. Make sure to
perform the example exercises for the Personnel Actions application each time that you
encounter them, because succeeding examples build on your prior work.

Understanding Relational Databases

All desktop database managers enable you to enter, edit, view, and print information
contained in one or more tables divided into rows and columns. At this point, the
definition of a database manager doesn't differ from that of a spreadsheet application—

most spreadsheets can emulate database functions. Three principal characteristics distinguish relational database management systems (RDBMSs) from spreadsheet applications:

- All RDBMSs are designed to deal efficiently with very large amounts of data—much more than spreadsheets can handle conveniently.

- RDBMSs easily link two or more tables so that they appear to the user as if they are one table. This process is difficult or impossible to accomplish with spreadsheets.

- RDBMSs minimize information duplication by requiring repetition of only those data items, such as product or customer codes, by which multiple tables are linked.

Database managers that cannot link multiple tables are called *flat-file managers* and are used primarily to compile simple lists such as names, addresses, and telephone numbers.

Because relational databases eliminate most duplicate information, they minimize data storage and application memory requirements. Figure 4.1 shows a typical relational database that a manufacturing or distributing firm might use. This database structure is similar to that of the Northwind Traders sample database provided with Access.

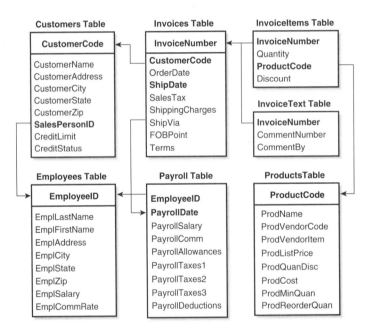

Fig. 4.1 A portion of a typical database for a manufacturing or distributing firm.

▶▶ See "The Process of Database Design," p. 829

If your job is to create an invoice-entry database, you don't need to enter a customer's name and address more than once. Just assign each customer a unique number or code and add to the Customers table a record containing this information. Similarly, you don't need to enter the names and prices of the standard products for each invoice. You assign unique codes to products, and then add records for them to the Products table. When you want to create a new invoice for an existing customer, you enter the customer code and type the codes and quantities for the products ordered. This process adds one record (identified by an automatically assigned sequential numeric code) to the Invoices table and one record for each different item purchased to the InvoiceItems table.

▶▶ See "Joining Tables to Create Multitable Queries," p. 318

Each table is related to the other by the customer, invoice, and product codes and numbers, shown by the connecting lines between the tables in figure 4.1. The codes and numbers shown in boxes are unique; only one customer corresponds to a particular code, and one invoice or product corresponds to a given number. When you display or print an invoice, the Invoices table is linked (called a *join*) with both the Customers and InvoiceItems tables by their codes. In turn, the InvoiceItems table is joined with the Products table by the common value of a ProductCode in the InvoiceItems table and a ProductNumber in the Products table. Your query (view) of the desired sales orders displays the appropriate customer, invoice, items, and product information from the linked records. (The following section explains queries.) You can calculate quantity-price extensions, including discounts, by multiplying the appropriate values stored in the tables. You can add the extended items, sales taxes, and freight charges; you also can calculate the total invoice amount. These calculated values need not be included (and in a properly designed database never are included) in the database tables.

Using Access Database Files and Tables

Access has its own database file structure, similar to that used by client/server RDBMSs, and uses the .mdb extension. As discussed in this chapter's introduction, Access differs from traditional PC databases in that a single file contains all the related tables, indexes, forms, and report definitions. The .mdb file even includes the programming code that you write in Access VBA. You don't need to be concerned with the intricacies of the .mdb file structure because Access handles all the details of file management for you.

All the field data types familiar to xBase and Paradox users are available in Access, as well as some new and useful field data types, such as Currency for monetary transactions. dBASE users need to learn to use the term *table* for file and *database* to indicate a group of related tables or files, the equivalent of dBASE's CATALOG. *Records* commonly are called *rows*, and *fields* often are called *columns*. This book uses the terms *records* and *fields* when referring to database tables, rows, and columns for sets of records returned by queries. Users with Paradox, Excel, or 1-2-3 experience should find the terminology of Access quite familiar. Paradox and FoxPro users will appreciate dealing with only one .mdb file rather than the myriad files that make up a multitable Paradox or FoxPro database.

The Access System Database

◀◀ See "Setting Default Options," p. 87

In addition to including database files with the .mdb extension, Access includes a master database file, called a *workgroup* file, named System.mdw. (System.mdw is the equivalent of Access 2.0's SYSTEM.MDA.) This file contains information about the following:

- Names of users and groups of users who can open Access

- User passwords and a unique binary code, called a System ID (SID), that identifies the current user to Access

- Operating preferences that you establish by choosing <u>T</u>ools, <u>O</u>ptions

- Definitions of customized Access 95 toolbars that each user creates

Chapter 25, "Securing Networked Multiuser Applications," covers sharing database files and granting permission for others to use the files.

Access Library Databases

 ▶▶ See "Creating a Transaction-Processing Form with the Form Wizard," p. 397
▶▶ See "Access's Integrated Data Dictionary System," p. 859

 Another category of Access database files is *add-ins*, also called *libraries*. Add-ins are Access library databases, usually with an .mda extension to distinguish them from user databases, that you can link to Access by choosing <u>T</u>ools, <u>R</u>eferences in the Module window, or through the Add-in Manager (which you can access by choosing <u>T</u>ools, Add-<u>i</u>ns).

When you link an Access library, all the elements of the library database are available to you after you open Access. The Access 95 wizards—which you use to create forms, reports, and graphs—are stored in a series of Access library database files: Wzlib70.mda, Wztool.mda, and Wzmain.mda. Another wizard enables you to create data dictionaries for Access databases. A *data dictionary* is a detailed written description of each of a database's elements. Add-in library databases are an important and unique feature of Access. Microsoft and other third-party firms provide a wide range of Access libraries to add new features and capabilities to Access.

Creating a New Database

If you have experience with relational database management systems, you might want to start building your own database as you progress through this book. In this case, you need to create a new database file at this point. If database management systems are new to you, however, you should instead explore the sample databases supplied with Access as you progress through the chapters of this book, and design your first database using the principles outlined in Chapter 23, "Exploring Relational Database Design and Implementation." Then return to this section and create your new database file.

To create a new database, follow these steps:

1. If you aren't already running Access, launch it and skip to step 3.

2. If Access is running and the Database window is visible, click its title bar to make the Database window the active window. If the Database window is not visible, click the Show Database Window button of the toolbar, choose <u>W</u>indow, <u>1</u> Database, or press the F11 key.

This action is called giving the Database window the *focus*. When a window has the focus, the background of its title bar is usually blue; when a window does not have the focus, it is inactive and its title bar is usually gray. If you have changed from the default Windows color scheme by altering the Windows 95 desktop's properties, these colors are different.

3. Click the New Database button of the toolbar, or choose <u>F</u>ile, <u>N</u>ew Database. For the Database toolbar to be visible and the New Database and other database file options to be present when you open the <u>F</u>ile menu, the Access application window must be empty or the Database window must be active. The New dialog appears as shown in figure 4.2.

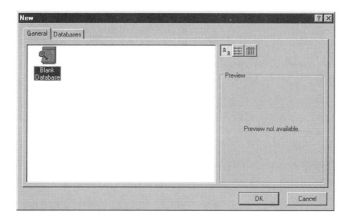

Fig. 4.2   The New dialog enables you to select the type of new database that you want to create: a blank database or one of several predefined database templates.

The General page of the New dialog enables you to choose to create a blank database, and the Database page lets you use any one of 22 new database templates. Access 95 comes with database templates for asset tracking, book and video collections, contact management, and many other typical business and personal database uses. You choose a template that suits the purpose for which you want to create the database.

4. For this example, click the General tab, select Blank Database, and then click OK to display the File New Database dialog shown in figure 4.3.

Access supplies the default filename, db1.mdb, for new databases. (If you have previously saved a database file as db1.mdb, Access proposes db2.mdb as the default.)

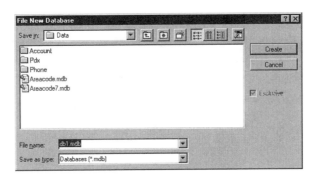

Fig. 4.3 In the File New Database dialog, you enter the new database's name and select the folder in which to store it.

   5. In the File Name text box, enter a filename for the new database. Use conventional Windows 95 file-naming rules (you can use spaces and punctuation in the name). Don't include an extension in the filename; Access automatically supplies the .mdb extension.

   6. Click Create to create the new database.

   If a database was open when you created the new database, Access closes any windows associated with the database and the Database window. During the process of creating the database, the following message appears in the status bar:

```
Verifying system objects
```

   Whenever you open a new or existing database, Access checks whether all the database's elements are intact. Access's main window and the Database window for the new database (named new.mdb for this example) appear as shown in figure 4.4.

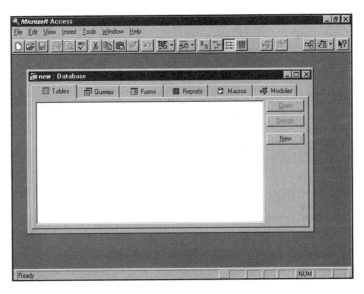

Fig. 4.4 Access displays its main window and the Database window for a newly created database.

Each new database occupies approximately 80K of disk space when you create it. Most of the 80K is space consumed by hidden system tables for adding the information necessary to specify the names and locations of other database elements that the database file contains. Because of the way that data is stored in Access tables, what appears to be an excessive amount of reserved space quickly is compensated for by Access's more efficient data storage methods.

Understanding the Properties of Tables and Fields

Before you add a table to a database that you have created, or to one of the sample databases supplied with Access, you need to know the terms and conventions that Access uses to describe the structure of a table and the fields that contain the data items that comprise the information stored in the table. With Access, you specify properties of tables and fields.

▶▶ See "Working with Data Dictionaries," p. 857

Properties of Access tables apply to the table as a whole. Entering table properties is optional. You enter properties of tables in text boxes of the Table Properties window (see fig. 4.5), which you display by clicking the toolbar's Properties button in Table Design View. The five basic properties of Access tables follow:

- *Description.* An optional explanation of the table's purpose. If you choose <u>V</u>iew, <u>D</u>etails, the Database window displays this description. This description also is useful with a data dictionary. You use data dictionaries to document databases and database applications.

- *Validation Rule.* An optional Validation Rule property value that lets you establish domain integrity rules with expressions that refer to more than one field of the table. The validation rule that you enter here applies to the table as a whole, rather than to a single field.

- *Validation Text.* An optional Validation Text property value that specifies the text of the message box that appears if you violate a table's Validation Rule expression.

- *Filter.* An optional property value that specifies a filter to apply to the table whenever it is opened. Chapter 6, "Sorting, Finding, and Filtering Data in Tables," discusses filters.

- *Order By.* An optional property value that specifies a sorting order to apply to the table whenever it is opened. Chapter 6 also explains sorting orders.

▶▶ See "Using Access Indexes," p. 862

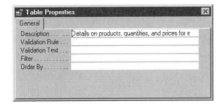

Fig. 4.5 The Table Properties window for the Northwind Traders sample database's Order Details table.

Access 1.x used the Properties window to define the table's primary-key fields and composite indexes on table fields. Access 2.0 and Access 95 provide a separate Indexes window to specify the primary key and all table indexes. The section "Adding Indexes to Tables," later in this chapter, describes how to use the Indexes window.

 You assign each field of an Access table a set of properties. The first three field properties are assigned within the *Table Design grid*, the upper pane of the Table Design window shown in figure 4.6. To assign the Primary Key property, select the field and click the Primary Key button on the toolbar (the Order Details table shown in fig. 4.6 has two primary keys). You set the remaining property values in the Table Design window's lower pane, Field Properties.

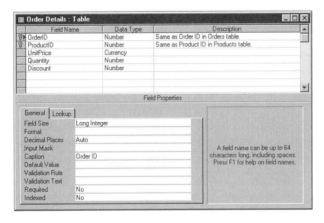

Fig. 4.6 The Table Design window for the Northwind Traders sample database's Order Details table.

The following list summarizes the properties that you set in the Table Design grid:

- *Field Name.* You enter the name of the field in the Table Design grid's first column. Field names can be as long as 64 characters and can include embedded (but not leading) spaces and punctuation—except periods (.), exclamation marks (!), and square brackets ([ ]). Field names are mandatory, and you cannot assign the same field name to more than one field. It is a good database programming practice not to include spaces in field names. (Substitute an underscore (_) for spaces or use upper- and lowercase letters to improve the readability of field names.) Minimizing the length of field names conserves resources and saves typing when you refer to the field name in macros or Access VBA code.

- *Data Type.* You select data types from a drop-down list in the Table Design grid's second column. Data types include Text, Memo, Number, Date/Time, Currency, AutoNumber, Yes/No, OLE Object, and Lookup Wizard. (AutoNumber replaces the Counter data type of Access 1.x and 2.0.) Choosing a data type is the subject of the next section of this chapter.

- *Description.* You can enter an optional description of the field in the text box in the Table Design grid's third column. If you add a description, it appears in the status bar at the lower left of Access's window when you select the field for data entry or editing.

- *Primary Key.* To choose a field as the primary-key field, select the field by clicking the field-selection button to the left of the Field Name column, and then click the Primary Key button on the toolbar. The Order Details table has a composite primary key, consisting of the OrderID and ProductID fields. (See "Selecting a Primary Key," later in this chapter, for instructions on how to create a composite primary key.)

Depending on the specific data type that you choose for a field, there are additional properties that you can set for a table field. You set these additional properties in the General tab of the Table Design window's Field Properties pane by selecting from drop-down or combo lists or by typing values in text boxes. (You use the Field Properties pane's Lookup tab to set the control type for lookup fields on forms—list box, combo list, and so on. Chapter 13, "Designing Custom Multitable Forms," describes how to use lookup fields.) The following list summarizes the General field properties:

- *Field Size.* You enter the field size for the Text data type in this text box. (See "Text Fields," later in this chapter, to learn how to choose a text field size.) For Numeric data types, you choose the field size by selecting from a drop-down list. Field size does not apply to the Date/Time, Yes/No, Currency, Memo, or OLE Object data type.

- *Format.* You can select a standard, predefined format in which to display the values in the field from the drop-down combo list applicable to the data type that you chose (except Text). Alternatively, you can enter a custom format in the text box (see "Custom Display Formats" later in this chapter). The Format property does not affect the data values; it affects only how these values are displayed. The Format property does not apply to OLE Object fields.

- *Decimal Places.* You can select Auto or a specific number of decimal places from the drop-down combo list, or you can enter a number in the text box. The Decimal Places property applies only to Number and Currency fields. Like the Format property, the Decimal Places property affects only the display, not the data values, of the field.

- *Input Mask.* Input masks are character strings, similar to the character strings used for the Format property, that determine how to display data during data entry and editing. If you click the Ellipsis button for a field of the Text, Currency, Number, or Date/Time field data type, the Input Mask Wizard appears to provide you with a predetermined selection of standard input masks, such as telephone numbers with optional area codes.

- *Caption.* If you want a name (other than the field name) to appear in the field name header button in Table Datasheet View, you can enter in the Caption list box an alias for the field name. The restrictions on punctuation symbols do not apply to the Caption property. (You can use periods, exclamation points, and square brackets.)

- *Default Value.* By entering a value in the Default Value text box, you specify a default value that Access automatically enters in the field when a new record is added to the table. The current date is a common default value for a Date/Time field. (See "Setting Default Values of Fields," later in this chapter, for more information.) Default values do not apply to fields with AutoNumber or OLE Object field data types.

- *Validation Rule.* Validation rules test the value entered in a field against criteria that you supply in the form of an Access expression. Chapter 9, "Understanding Operators and Expressions in Access," explains expressions. The Validation Rule property is not available for fields with AutoNumber, Memo, or OLE Object field data types. Adding validation rules to table fields is one of the subjects of the next chapter, "Entering, Editing, and Validating Data in Tables."

- *Validation Text.* You enter the text that is to appear in the status bar if the value entered does not meet the Validation Rule criteria.

- *Required.* If you set the value of the Required property to Yes, you must enter a value in the field. Setting the Required property to Yes is the equivalent of typing **Is Not Null** as a field validation rule. (You do not need to set the value of the Required property to Yes for fields included in the primary key because Access does not permit **Null** values in primary-key fields.)

- *Allow Zero Length.* If you set the value of the Allow Zero Length property to Yes, and the Required property is also Yes, the field must contain at least one character. The Allow Zero Length property applies to the Text and Memo field data types only. A zero-length string ("") and the **Null** value are not the same.

- *Indexed.* From the drop-down list, you can select between an index that allows duplicate values or one that requires each value of the field to be unique. You remove an existing index (except from a field that is a single primary-key field) by choosing No. The Indexed property is not available for Memo or OLE Object fields. (See "Adding Indexes to Tables," later in this chapter, for more information on indexes.)

- *New Values.* This property applies only to AutoNumber fields. You select either Increment or Random from a drop-down list. If you set the New Values property to Increment, Access generates new values for the AutoNumber field by adding 1 to the highest existing AutoNumber field value. If you set the property to Random,

Access generates new values for the AutoNumber field by producing a random long integer. Typically, Access uses randomly generated AutoNumber values for replicated databases, to ensure that it assigns unique values to records in the database replicas.

To add your first table, Personnel Actions, to the Northwind Traders database, you must choose appropriate data types, sizes, and formats for your table's fields.

Choosing Field Data Types, Sizes, and Formats

You must assign a field data type to each field of a table, unless you want to use the Text data type that Access assigns as the default. One of the principles of relational database design is that all the data in a single field consists of one type of data. Access provides a much wider variety of data types and formats from which to choose than most PC database managers. Besides setting the data type, you can set other field properties that determine the format, size, and other characteristics of the data that affect its appearance and the accuracy with which numerical values are stored. Table 4.1 lists the field data types that you can select for data contained in Access tables.

Table 4.1 Field Data Types Available in Access		
Information	**Data Type**	**Description of Data Type**
Characters	Text	Text fields are most common, so Access assigns Text as the default data type. A Text field can contain as many as 255 characters, and you can designate a maximum length less than or equal to 255. Access assigns a default length of 50 characters. A fixed-length Text data type is similar to xBase's Character field and Paradox's Alphanumeric field.
	Memo	Memo fields can contain as many as 64,000 characters. You use them to provide descriptive comments. Memo fields are similar to those of xBase, except that the Memo field's data is included in the table rather than in a separate file. Access displays the contents of Memo fields in Datasheet View. A Memo field cannot be a key field, and you cannot index a Memo field.
Numeric Values	Number	A variety of numeric data subtypes are available. You choose the appropriate data subtype by selecting one of the Field Size property settings listed in table 4.2. You specify how to display the number by setting its Format property to one of the formats listed in table 4.4.
	AutoNumber	An AutoNumber field is a numeric (Long Integer) value that Access automatically fills in for each new record that you add to a table. Access can increment the AutoNumber field by one for each new record, or fill in the field with a randomly generated number, depending on the New Values property setting that you choose. An AutoNumber field creates a value similar to xBase's and Paradox's record number. The maximum number of records in a table that can use the AutoNumber field is slightly more than 2 billion.

(continues)

Table 4.1	Continued	
Information	**Data Type**	**Description of Data Type**
	Yes/No	Logical (Boolean) fields in Access use (Logical numeric (integer) values: –1 for Yes fields) (**True**) and 0 for No (**False**). You use the Format property to display Yes/No fields as Yes or No, True or False, On or Off, or -1 or 0. (You also can use any nonzero number to represent **True**.) Logical fields cannot be key fields, but they can be indexed.
	Currency	Currency is a special fixed format with four decimal places designed to prevent rounding errors that would affect accounting operations where the value must match to the penny (similar to the Paradox Currency data type).
Dates and Times	Date/Time	Dates and times are stored in a special fixed format. The date is represented by the whole number portion of the Date/Time value, and the time is represented by its decimal fraction. You control how Access displays dates by selecting one of the Date/Time Format properties listed in table 4.4.
Large Objects	OLE Object (BLOBs, binary large objects)	Includes bitmapped graphics, vector-type drawings, waveform audio files, and other types of data that can be created by an OLE server application, some of which are listed in table 4.3. You cannot assign an OLE object as a key field, and you cannot include an OLE field in an index.

Regardless of the length that you set for Text fields in Access, the database file stores them in variable-length records. All trailing spaces are removed. This technique conserves the space wasted in xBase files, for example, which store text in fixed-length character fields. Fixed-length character fields in conventional PC RDBMSs waste the bytes used to pad short text entries in long fields.

Choosing Field Sizes for Numeric and Text Data

The Field Size property of a field determines which data type a Number field uses or how many characters fixed-length text fields can accept. Field Size properties are called *subtypes* to distinguish them from the *data types* listed in table 4.2. For numbers, you select a Field Size property value from the Field Size drop-down list in the Table Design window's lower pane, Field Properties (refer to fig. 4.6).

Subtypes for Numeric Data. The Number data type of table 4.2 isn't a fully specified data type. You must select one of the subtypes from those listed in table 4.3 for the Field Size property to define the numeric data type properly. To select a data subtype for a Number field, follow these steps:

1. Select the Data Type cell of the Number field for which you want to select the subtype.

2. Click the Field Size text box in the Field Properties window. You also can press F6 to switch windows, and then use the arrow keys to position the caret within the Field Size text box.

 3. Click the drop-down arrow to open the list of choices shown in figure 4.7. You can also press the F4 key to open the list.

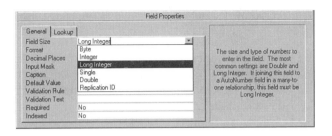

Fig. 4.7 Selecting from the Field Size list a subtype for the Number data type.

4. Select the data subtype. Table 4.3 describes data subtypes. When you make a selection, the list closes.

After you select a Field Size property, you select a Format property from those listed in table 4.4 to determine how to display the data. Table 4.4 includes the Currency data type because it also can be considered a subtype of the Numeric data type.

Regardless of how you format your data for display, the number of decimal digits, the range, and the storage requirement remains that specified by the Field Size property. Except for the Byte and Boolean data types, these data types are available in most dialects of BASIC, including Visual Basic for Applications and Visual Basic 4.0. Access VBA includes all the data types listed in table 4.2 as reserved words. You cannot use a reserved data type word for any purpose in Access VBA functions and procedures other than to specify a data type.

Table 4.2 Subtypes of the Number Data Type Determined by the Field Size Property					
Field Size	**Decimals**	**Range of Values**	**Bytes**	**xBase**	**Paradox**
Double	15 places	$-1.797 \cdot 10^{308}$ to $+1.797 \cdot 10^{308}$	8	Numeric	Numeric
Single	7 places	$-3.4 \cdot 10^{38}$ to $+3.4 \cdot 10^{38}$	4	N/A	N/A
Long Integer	None	$-2,147,483,648$ to $+2,147,483,647$	4	N/A	N/A
Integer	None	$-32,768$ to $32,767$	2	N/A	Short Number
Byte	None	0 to 255	1	N/A	N/A
Currency (a data type, not a subtype)	4 places	-922337203685477.5808 to $+922337203685477.5808$	4	N/A	N/A

Table 4.2's xBase and Paradox columns indicate the Access data types that correspond to data types commonly used with these two types of Windows and DOS RDBMSs.

Both xBase RDBMSs and Paradox store numbers with 15 significant-digit precision. Neither xBase nor Paradox, however, offers the full range of values of numbers having Access's Double Field Size property. All references to Paradox in this book apply to DOS version 4.5 and Paradox for Windows version 5. Access is compatible only with Paradox 3.5 (and later) tables.

As a rule, you select the Field Size property that results in the smallest number of bytes that encompasses the range of values you expect and that expresses the value in sufficient precision for your needs. Mathematical operations with Integer and Long Integer proceed more quickly than those with Single and Double data types (called *floating-point* numbers) or the Currency and Date/Time data types (*fixed-point* numbers).

Fixed-Width Text Fields. You can create a fixed-width Text field by setting the value of the Field Size property. By default, Access creates a 50-character-wide Text field. Enter the number, from 1 to 255, in the Field Size cell corresponding to the fixed length that you want. If you import to the field data that is longer than the selected field size, Access truncates the data; thus, you lose the far right characters that exceed your specified limit. You therefore enter a field length value that accommodates the maximum number of characters that you expect to enter in the field. Fixed-width Text fields behave identically to the Character and Alphanumeric field data types of xBase and Paradox applications.

Note

The terms *fixed-width* and *fixed-length* have two different meanings in Access. Even if you specify a fixed-width for a field of the Text field data type, Access stores the data in the field in variable-length format.

Subtypes for the OLE Object Data Type. Fields that have data types other than characters and numbers must use the OLE (object linking and embedding) Object data type. Chapter 19, "Using 32-Bit OLE 2.1," describes object linking and embedding, and Chapter 20, "Adding Graphics to Forms and Reports," explains the OLE field data type. Because many subtypes of OLE data exist, this data type enables you to violate the rule of database design that requires all data in a field to be of a single data type. Table 4.3 lists typical OLE Object subtypes. To avoid breaking the rule, you should create separate OLE Object fields for different OLE data subtypes.

Table 4.3   Subtypes of the OLE Object Data Type and the OLE Servers That Create Them

OLE Subtype	File Format	OLE Server(s) That Create the Subtype
Bitmapped graphics	.BMP, .DIB, .TIF	Windows 95 Paint, Adobe Photoshop
Vector-based drawings	.WMF	Microsoft Draw, CorelDRAW!, PowerPoint
Formatted text	.RTF	Windows 95 Wordpad, Word for Windows 95, Lotus Word Pro
Unformatted text	.TXT	Object Packager (with Windows Notepad as the application); Memo fields are a better choice
Spreadsheet	.XLS, .DIF	Microsoft Excel 3.0 and later

OLE Subtype	File Format	OLE Server(s) That Create the Subtype
Waveform Audio	.WAV	Windows 95 Sound Recorder, Windows 95 Media Player, Media Vision Pocket Recorder
MIDI Music	.MID	Media Player
Digital Video	.AVI	Media Player

In the case of OLE Object fields, the data subtype is determined by the OLE server used to create the data, rather than by an entry in a text box or a selection from a list box. Windows 95's Object Packager OLE server enables you to embed files created by applications that aren't OLE servers. You can, for example, embed .TXT files and .MID files with Object Packager.

Selecting a Display Format

You establish the Format property for the data types that you select so that Access displays them appropriately for your application. You select a format by selecting the field and then clicking the Format text box in the Field Properties window. Figure 4.8 shows the choices that Access offers for formatting the Long Integer data type. You format Number, Date/Time, and Yes/No data types by selecting a standard format or creating your own custom format. The following sections describe these two methods.

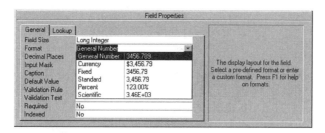

Fig. 4.8   Assigning one of the standard formats to a Long Integer field from the Format list.

Standard Formats for Number, Date/Time, and Yes/No Data Types. Access provides 17 standard formats that apply to the numeric values in fields of the Number, Date/Time, and Yes/No data types. The standard formats shown in table 4.4 probably will meet most of your needs.

Table 4.4   Standard Display Formats for Access Number, Date/Time, and Yes/No Data Types

Data Type	Format	Appearance
Number	General Number	1234.5
	Currency	$1,234.50
	Fixed	12345
	Standard	1,234.50
	Percent	0.1234 = 12.34%
	Scientific	1.23E+03

(continues)

Learning Access

Table 4.4 Continued		
Data Type	**Format**	**Appearance**
Date/Time	General Date	10/1/92 4:00:00 PM
	Long Date	Thursday, October 1, 1992
	Medium Date	1-Oct-92
	Short Date	10/1/92
	Long Time	4:00:00 PM
	Medium Time	04:00 PM
	Short Time	16:00
Yes/No	Yes/No	Yes or No
	True/False	True or False
	On/Off	On or Off
	None	−1 or 0

xBase

PDOX

The Short Date format is similar to the Date data type in xBase and Paradox, except that leading zeros for months and days having a value less than 10 aren't displayed. The four date formats are included in the 11 date formats offered by Paradox; you can create the other Paradox formats by using custom formats described in the next section. The Short Time format is equivalent to what you obtain from an xBase SUBSTR(TIME(),5) expression. A Double data type with Currency format appears identical to Paradox's Currency data type.

The Null Value in Access Tables. Fields in Access tables can have a special value, **Null**, which is a new term for most users of PC-based database management systems. The **Null** value indicates that the field contains no data at all. **Null** isn't the same as a numeric value of zero, nor is it equivalent to blank text that consists of one or more spaces. **Null** is similar but not equivalent to an empty string (a string of zero length, often called a *null string*). For now, the best synonym for **Null** is *no entry*. (**Null** is set in monospace bold type because it is a reserved word in Access VBA.)

The **Null** value is useful for determining whether a value has been entered in a field, especially a numeric field in which zero values are valid. Until the advent of Access, the capability to use **Null** values in database managers running on PCs was limited to fields in the tables of client/server database systems, such as Microsoft SQL Server. Later in this chapter, the sections "Custom Display Formats" and "Setting Default Values of Fields" use the **Null** value.

Custom Display Formats. To duplicate precisely the format of xBase's Date data type or one of the date formats offered by Paradox that is not a standard format in Access, you must create a custom format. You do so by creating an image of the format using combinations of a special set of characters called *placeholders*, listed in table 4.5. Figure 4.9 shows an example of a custom format for date and time. If you enter **mmmm dd",** **"yyyy - hh:nn** as the format, the date 03/01/95 displays as March 1, 1995 - 00:00.

Except as noted, the example numeric value that table 4.5 uses is 1234.5. Bold type distinguishes the placeholders that you type from the surrounding text. The resulting display is shown in monospace type.

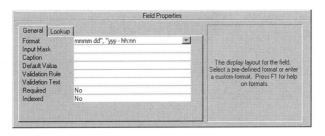

Fig. 4.9 Creating a custom date and time format from entries in the Format text box.

Table 4.5 Placeholders for Creating Custom Display Formats	
Placeholder	**Function**
Empty string	Displays the number with no formatting. Enter an empty string by deleting the value in the Format Text field of the Field Properties window.
0	Displays a digit if one exists in the position, or a zero if not. You can use the *0* placeholder to display leading zeros for whole numbers and trailing zeros in decimal fractions. **00000.000** displays 01234.500.
#	Displays a digit, if one exists in the position; otherwise, displays zeros. The # placeholder is equivalent to 0, except that leading and trailing zeros aren't displayed. **#####.###** displays 1234.5.
$	Displays a dollar sign in the position. **$###,###.00** displays $1,234.50.
.	Displays a decimal point at the indicated position in a string of 0 and # placeholders. **##.##** displays 1234.5.
%	Multiplies the value by 100 and adds a percent sign in the position shown with 0 and # placeholders. **#0.00%** displays 0.12345 as 12.35% (12.345 is rounded to 12.35).
, (comma)	Adds commas as thousands separators in strings of 0 and # placeholders. **###,###,###.00** displays 1,234.50.
E– e–	Displays values in scientific format with the sign of exponent for negative values only. **#.###E–00** displays 1.2345E03. **0.12345** displays 1.2345E–01.
E+ e+	Displays values in scientific format with the sign of exponent for positive and negative values. **#.###E–00** displays 1.2345E+03.
/	Separates the day, month, and year to format date values. **mm/dd/yy** displays 06/06/92. You can substitute hyphens to display 06-06-92.
m	Specifies how to display months for dates. **m** displays 1, **mm** displays 01, **mmm** displays Jan, and **mmmm** displays January.
d	Specifies how to display days for dates. **d** displays 1, **dd** displays 01, **ddd** displays Mon, and **dddd** displays Monday.
y	Specifies how to display years for dates. **yy** displays 95, and **yyyy** displays 1995.
: (colon)	Separates hours, minutes, and seconds in format time values. **hh:mm:ss** displays 02:02:02.
h	Specifies how to display hours for time. **h** displays 2, and **hh** displays 02. If you use an AM/PM placeholder, **h** or **hh** displays 4 PM for 1,600 hours.
n	Minutes placeholder for time. **n** displays 1, and **nn** displays 01. **hhnn "hours"** displays 1600 hours.
s	Seconds placeholder for time. **s** displays 1, and **ss** displays 01.

(continues)

Table 4.5 Continued	
Placeholder	**Function**
AM/PM	Displays time in 12-hour time with AM or PM appended. **h:nn AM/PM** displays 4:00 PM. Alternative formats include am/pm, A/P, and a/p.
@	Indicates that a character is required in the position in a Text or Memo field. You can use @ to format telephone numbers in a Text field, as in @@@-@@@-@@@@ or **(@@@) @@@-@@@@**.
&	Indicates that a character in a Text or Memo field is optional.
>	Changes all text characters in the field to uppercase.
<	Changes all text characters in the field to lowercase.
*	Displays the character following the asterisk as a fill character for empty spaces in a field. **"ABCD"*x** in an eight-character field appears as ABCDxxxx.

The Format drop-down combo list is one of the few examples in Access where you can select from a list of options or type your own entry. Format is a true drop-down combo list; lists that only enable you to select from the listed options are *drop-down lists*. You don't need to enter the quotation marks shown in figure 4.9 surrounding the comma and space in the Format text box (**mmmm dd", "yyyy - hh:nn**) because Access does this for you. The comma is a nonstandard formatting symbol for dates (but is standard for number fields). When you create nonstandard formatting characters in the Field Properties window, Access automatically encloses them in double quotation marks.

When you change Format or any other property of a field, and then change to Datasheet View in run mode to view the result of your work, you first must save the updated table design. The confirmation dialog shown in figure 4.10 asks you to confirm any design changes.

Fig. 4.10 The confirmation dialog for changes to a field's format.

If you apply the custom format string **mmmm dd", "yyyy - hh:nn** (refer to fig. 4.9) to the Birth Date field of the Employees table, the Birth Date field entries appear as shown in figure 4.11. For example, Nancy Davolio's birth date appears as December 08, 1948 - 00:00. The original format of the Birth Date field was Medium Date, the format also used for the Hire Date field.

You need to expand the width of the Birth Date field to accommodate the additional characters in the Long Date format. You increase the field's width by dragging the field name header's right vertical bar to the right to display the entire field. Access right-justifies date fields.

Access displays the time of birth as 00:00 because the decimal fraction that determines time is 0 for all entries in the Birth Date field.

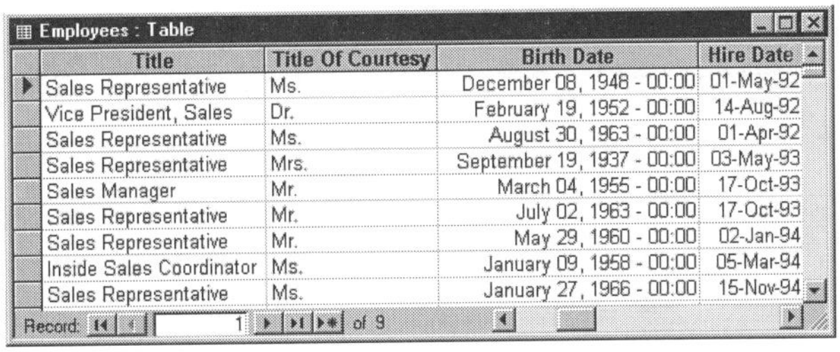
Employees : Table

Title	Title Of Courtesy	Birth Date	Hire Date
Sales Representative	Ms.	December 08, 1948 - 00:00	01-May-92
Vice President, Sales	Dr.	February 19, 1952 - 00:00	14-Aug-92
Sales Representative	Ms.	August 30, 1963 - 00:00	01-Apr-92
Sales Representative	Mrs.	September 19, 1937 - 00:00	03-May-93
Sales Manager	Mr.	March 04, 1955 - 00:00	17-Oct-93
Sales Representative	Mr.	July 02, 1963 - 00:00	17-Oct-93
Sales Representative	Mr.	May 29, 1960 - 00:00	02-Jan-94
Inside Sales Coordinator	Ms.	January 09, 1958 - 00:00	05-Mar-94
Sales Representative	Ms.	January 27, 1966 - 00:00	15-Nov-94

Record: 1 of 9

Fig. 4.11 Comparing Long Date and Medium Date formats.

The following is an example that formats negative numbers enclosed in parentheses and replaces a **Null** entry with text:

```
$###,###,##0.00;$(###,###,##0.00);0.00;"No Entry Here"
```

The entries 1234567.89, –1234567.89, 0, and a **Null** default value appear as follows:

```
$1,234,567.89
$(1,234,567.89)
0.00
No Entry Here
```

Using Input Masks

Access 95 enables you to restrict entries in Text fields to numbers or to otherwise control the formatting of entered data. Access 95's Input Mask property closely resembles xBase's `PICT[URE]` expression, which is used to format telephone numbers, social security numbers, ZIP codes, and similar data. Access's Input Mask property is based on Visual Basic 3.0's Masked Edit custom control, but the Input Mask property accommodates **Null** values and offers several improvements over Visual Basic 3.0's quirky Masked Edit control.

Table 4.6 lists the placeholders that you can use in character strings for input masks in fields of the Text field data type.

Table 4.6 Placeholders for Creating Input Masks

Placeholder	Function
Empty string	No input mask.
0	Number (0–9) or sign (+/–) required.
9	Number (0–9) optional (a space if nothing is entered).
#	Number (0–9) or space optional (a space if nothing is entered).
L	Letter (A–z) required.
?	Letter (A–z) not required (a space if nothing is entered).
A	Letter (A–z) or number (0–9) required.
a	Letter (A–z) or number (0–9) optional.
&	Any character or a space required.
C	Any character or a space optional.
. , : ; / ( )	Literal decimal, thousands, date, time, and special separators.
>	All characters to the right are converted to uppercase.

(continues)

Table 4.6 Continued	
Placeholder	**Function**
<	All characters to the right are converted to lowercase.
!	Fills the mask from right to left.
\	Precedes the other placeholders to include the literal character in a format string.

For example, typing **\(000") "000\-0000** as the value of the Input Mask property causes results in the appearance of (___) ___-____ for a blank telephone number cell of a table. Typing **000\-00\-000** creates a mask for Social Security numbers, ___-__-____. When you type the telephone number or Social Security number, the digits that you type replace the underscores.

> **Note**
>
> The \ characters (often called *escape* characters) that precede parentheses and hyphens specify that the character that follows is a literal, not a formatting character. If the format includes spaces, enclose the spaces and adjacent literal characters in double quotation marks.

Access 95 includes an Input Mask Wizard that appears when you place the cursor in the Input Mask text box for a field of the Text or Date/Time field data type and click the Ellipsis button at the extreme right of the text box. Figure 4.12 shows the opening dialog of the Input Mask Wizard, which provides 10 common input mask formats from which you can choose.

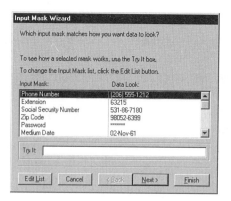

Fig. 4.12   The Input Mask Wizard for Text and Date/Time field data types.

Using the Northwind Traders Sample Database

One of the fundamental problems with books about database management applications is the usual method of demonstrating how to create a "typical" database. You are asked to type fictitious names, addresses, and telephone numbers into a Customers table. Next, you must create additional tables that relate these fictitious customers to their purchases of various widgets in assorted sizes and quantities. This process is unrewarding for readers and authors, and few readers ever complete the exercises.

Therefore, this book takes a different tack. Access includes a comprehensive and interesting sample database, Northwind Traders. Instead of creating a new database at this point, you create a new table as an addition to the Northwind Traders database. Adding a new table minimizes the amount of typing required and requires just a few entries to make the table functional. The new Personnel Actions table demonstrates many of the elements of relational database design. Before you proceed to create the Personnel Actions table, try the quick example of adding a new table to the Northwind Traders sample database that is given in the following section.

Using the Table Wizard to Create New Tables

Access includes a variety of wizards that provide services that simplify the creation of new database objects. Wizards lead you through a predetermined set of steps that determine the characteristics of the object that you want to create. Access 95 includes a Table Wizard that you can use to create new tables based on prefabricated designs for 77 business-oriented and 44 personal-type tables. Many of the business-oriented table designs are based on tables contained in Northwind.mdb.

The Table Wizard serves as an excellent introduction to the use of Access wizards in general. Follow these steps to create a new Access table that catalogs a video collection:

1. If the Employees table is open, close it by clicking the Close Window button to make the Database window active. Alternatively, click the Show Database Window button of the toolbar.

2. Click the Table button of the Database window, if it isn't selected, and then click the New button to display the New Table dialog shown in figure 4.13.

Fig. 4.13   The New Table dialog lets you elect to use the Table Wizard for table design.

3. Select Table Wizard in the list, and click OK to display the opening dialog of the Table Wizard. (If you select Datasheet View, Access creates a blank table with default fields; Design View creates a blank table and displays it in design mode ready for you to add fields. The Import Table Wizard and Link Table Wizard import databases and link external tables to a database, respectively.)

4. Click the Personal option button to display a list of tables for personal use in the Sample Tables list, and then use the vertical scroll bar to display the Video Collection entry in the list.

5. In the Sample Tables list, click the Video Collection entry to display the predetermined set of field names for the new table in the Sample Fields list.

6. Click the >> button to add all the fields from the Sample Fields list to the Fields in My New Table list. (The > button adds a single selected field from the Sample Fields list, the < button removes a single selected field from the My New Table list, and the << button deletes all the fields in the My New Table list.) The Table Wizard's dialog now appears as in figure 4.14.

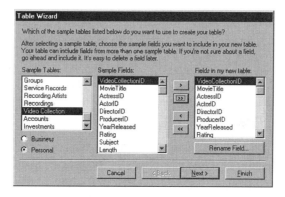

Fig. 4.14   Adding fields to the new Video Collection table.

7. Choose the Next button to display the second Table Wizard dialog in which you select the name for your new table, and select how to determine the table's primary-key field. Accept the default table name or enter a name of your choice, and then click the option button No, I'll Set the Primary Key. The Table Wizard's second dialog now appears (see fig. 4.15).

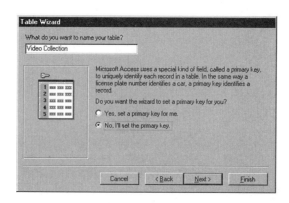

Fig. 4.15   Choosing a table name and how to determine the table's primary key.

8. Choose the Next button to display the dialog shown in figure 4.16. This dialog enables you to select the primary-key field and its data type. The Video Collection ID field is the logical choice for a primary key, and the AutoNumber field data type, which automatically creates a sequential number for the Collection ID, is appropriate in this case. (The Table Wizard's option Consecutive Numbers Microsoft Access Assigns Automatically to New Records creates an AutoNumber type field.) Thus, you can accept the default values determined by the Table Wizard.

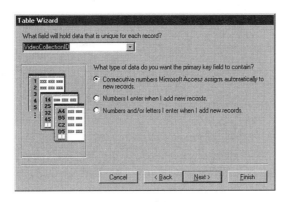

Fig. 4.16   The Table Wizard's primary-key dialog.

9. Choose the Next button to continue with the next stage of the table design definition process. The Table Wizard's relationships dialog (see fig. 4.17) appears only if other tables already exist in the database in which you're creating the new table. Because almost every database consists of two or more related tables, the Table Wizard gives you an opportunity to define the relationships between tables. By default, the new table has no relationships to other tables in the database. In this exercise, you don't add any table relationships to the new Video Collection table.

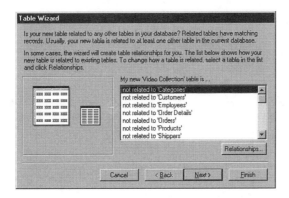

Fig. 4.17   The Table Wizard gives you an opportunity to specify the relationships between fields in the new table and other tables in the database.

10. Choose the Next button to finish designing the table. Access displays the final step of the Table Wizard, shown in figure 4.18.

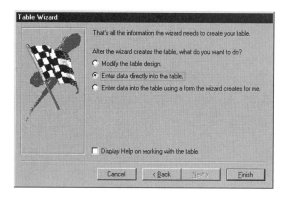

Fig. 4.18 The last Table Wizard dialog.

11. Click the Modify the Table Design option, and then choose the Finish button to display your new table in design mode, as shown in figure 4.19.

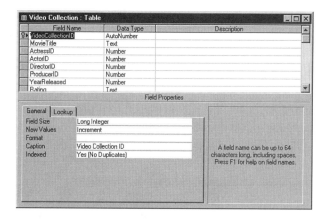

Fig. 4.19 The new Video Collection table in design mode.

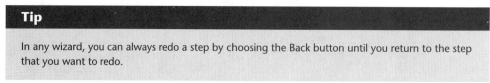

Tip

In any wizard, you can always redo a step by choosing the Back button until you return to the step that you want to redo.

If you want to delete the Video Collection table from Northwind.mdb, click the Show Database Window button of the toolbar, click the Table button if the Tables list is not open, and then click the Video Collection entry in the Table list to select (highlight) it. Press Delete, and click OK when the message box asks you to confirm the deletion. (You must close a table before you can delete it.)

> **Note**
>
> Creating tables based on the sample tables provided by the Table Wizard has limited usefulness in real-life business applications. In most cases, you import data from another database or spreadsheet application to create your Access tables. If you can't import the data, you probably need to define the fields of the tables to suit particular business needs. Thus, in the remainder of this chapter, you design a new database table by using the traditional method of manually adding fields to a blank table design and then specifying the properties of each field.

Adding a New Table to an Existing Database

The Northwind Traders database includes an Employees table that provides most of the information about the employees of the firm that is typical of personnel tables. This chapter explains how to add a table called Personnel Actions to the database. The Personnel Actions table is a record of hire date, salary, commission rate, bonuses, performance reviews, and other compensation-related events for employees. Because Personnel Actions is based on information in the Employees table, the first step of this process is to review the structure of the Employees table to see how you can use it with your new table. The structure of tables is displayed in design mode. In the next chapter, "Entering, Editing, and Validating Data in Tables," you add validation rules to the Personnel Actions table and enter records in the table.

To open the Employees table in design mode, follow these steps:

1. Close any Access document windows that you have open, and then click the Table button in the Database window to display the list of tables in the Northwind.mdb database.

2. Click Employees in the Database window, and then click the Design button. You also can open the Employees table by double-clicking the Database window entry and then clicking the Tables toolbar's Design View button.

3. The Design grid for the Employees table appears. Maximize the document window to the size of your Access window by clicking the document's Maximize button.

4. Close the Properties window, if it appears, by clicking its Close Window button. Alternatively, you can choose <u>V</u>iew, <u>P</u>roperties.

   The <u>V</u>iew, <u>P</u>roperties command toggles the visibility of the Table Properties window. A check mark next to the <u>P</u>roperties menu choice indicates that the window is always visible in Table Design View.

At this point, your display resembles that shown in figure 4.20.

The Table Design window displays the field names and the field data types and provides a third column for an optional description of each field in the table. This display is called a *grid* rather than a *datasheet* because the display doesn't contain data from a table. A scroll bar is provided, regardless of whether more fields exist in the table than the window can display. The Field Properties pane enables you to set additional properties of individual fields and briefly describes the purpose of each column of the grid and of the Field Properties entries as you select them. You cannot resize this pane.

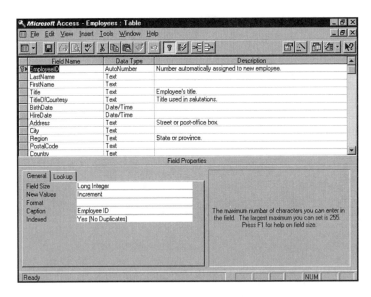

Fig. 4.20 The Employees table of the Northwind Traders database in Table Design View.

One field is conspicuous by its absence: the social security number that most firms use in databases to identify their personnel. The Employee ID field is an adequate substitute for the social security number for an example table because a unique sequential number (the AutoNumber field data type) is assigned to each employee. Click the Datasheet View button to display the data in the Employee ID field, and then return to design mode by clicking the Design View button.

Designing the Personnel Actions Table

Instead of adding fields for entries (such as salary, commission rate, and bonuses) to the Employees table, you should place employee remuneration data in a table of its own, for the following reasons:

■ Multiple personnel actions are taken for individual employees over time. If you add these actions to records in the Employees table, you have to create many additional fields to hold an arbitrary number of personnel actions. If, for example, quarterly performance reviews are entered, you have to add a new field for every quarter to hold the review information. In this situation, flat-file managers encounter difficulties.

■ You can categorize personnel actions by type so that any action taken can use a common set of field names and field data types. This feature makes the design of the Personnel Actions table simple.

■ You can identify employees uniquely by their Employee ID numbers. Therefore, records for entries of personnel actions can be related to the Employees table by an Employee ID field. This feature eliminates the necessity of adding employee names and other information to the records in the Personnel Action table. You link the Employees table to the Personnel table by the Employee ID field, and the two tables are joined; they act as if they are a single table. Minimizing information duplication to only what is required to link the tables is your reward for choosing a relational, rather than a flat-file, database management system. (In an actual business's employee database, you would probably use the employee's Social Security number as the unique identifier for each employee, and as the link to the Personnel Actions table.)

- Personnel actions usually are considered confidential information and are made accessible only to a limited number of people. Although Access enables you to grant permission for others to view specific fields, restricting permission to view an entire table is simpler.

The next step is to design the Personnel Actions table. Chapter 23, "Exploring Relational Database Design and Implementation," discusses the theory of database design and the tables that make up databases. Because the Personnel Actions table has an easily discernible relationship to the Employees table, the theoretical background isn't necessary for this example.

Determining What Information the Table Should Include. Designing a table requires that you identify the type of information that the table should contain. Information associated with typical personnel actions might consist of the following items:

- *Important dates.* The date of hire and termination, if applicable, are important dates, but so are the dates when the employer adjusts salaries, changes commission rates, and grants bonuses. You should accompany each action with the date when it was scheduled to occur and the date when it actually occurred.

- *Types of actions.* Less typing is required if personnel actions are identified by a code character rather than a full-text description of the action. This feature saves valuable disk space, too. First-letter abbreviations used as codes, such as *H* for *hired*, *T* for *terminated*, and *Q* for *quarterly review*, are easy to remember.

- *Initiation and approval of actions.* As a rule, the employee's supervisor initiates a personnel action, and the supervisor's manager approves it. Therefore, the table should include the supervisor's and manager's Employee ID number.

- *Amounts involved.* Salaries are assumed to be based on monthly payment, bonuses are paid quarterly with quarterly performance reviews, and commissions are paid on a percentage of sales made by the employee.

- *Performance rating.* Rating employee performance by a numerical value is a universal, but somewhat arbitrary, practice. Scales of 1 to 9 are common, with exceptional performance ranked as 9 and candidacy for termination as 1.

- *Summaries and comments.* The table should provide for a summary of performance, explanation of exceptionally high or low ratings, and reasons for adjusting salaries or bonuses.

If you are involved in personnel management, you probably can think of additional information that the table might include, such as accruable sick leave and vacation hours per pay period. The Personnel Actions table is just an example; it isn't meant to add full-scale human resources development capabilities to the database. The limited amount of data described serves to demonstrate several uses of the new table in this and subsequent chapters.

Assigning Information to Fields. After you determine the types of information, called *data entities* or *entities*, to include in the table, you must assign each data entity to a field of the table. This process involves choosing a field name that must be unique within the table. Table 4.7 lists the candidate fields for the Personnel Actions table. *Candidate fields* are written descriptions of the fields proposed for the table. Data types have been assigned from those listed in table 4.8 in the following section.

> **Note**
>
> Although the table name contains a space, the field names of the Personnel Actions table do not contain spaces (as shown in table 4.8). As mentioned earlier in this book, including spaces in table names or field names is not a good database design practice. In this case, the table names include a space to demonstrate the special rule (enclosing the name within square brackets) that you must observe when referring to object names that include spaces. The Northwind Traders sample database includes spaces in many of its table names, so the use of spaces here is consistent with the other tables in the database.

Table 4.7   Candidate Fields for the Personnel Actions Table

Field Name	Data Type	Description
paID	Number	The employee to whom the action applies. paID numbers are assigned based on the EmployeeID field of the Employee table (to which the Personnel Actions table is linked).
paType	Text	Code for the type of action taken: H = hired, C = commission rate adjustment, Q = quarterly review, Y = yearly review, S = salary adjustment, B = bonus adjustment, and T = terminated.
paInitiatedBy	Number	The EmployeeID number of the supervisor who initiates or is responsible for recommending the action.
paScheduledDate	Date/Time	The date when the action is scheduled to occur.
paApprovedBy	Number	The EmployeeID number of the manager who approves the action proposed by the supervisor.
paEffectiveDate	Date/Time	The date when the action occurred. The effective date remains blank if the action has not occurred.
paRating	Number	Performance on a scale of 1 to 9, with higher numbers indicating better performance. A blank indicates no rating; 0 is reserved for terminated employees.
paAmount	Currency	The salary per month, the bonus per quarter, or commission rate as a percent of the amount of the order, expressed as a decimal fraction.
paComments	Memo	Abstracts of performance reviews and comments on actions proposed or taken. The comments can be of unlimited length. The supervisor and manager can contribute to the comments.

> **Note**
>
> Use distinctive names for each field. This example precedes each field name with the abbreviation *pa* to identify the field with the Personnel Actions table. When developers design xBase databases, for example, a common practice is to use the same name for fields that contain identical data but are located in different tables. Because of the way that Access uses these names in expressions for validating data entry and calculating field values (discussed later in this chapter and in Chapter 9, "Understanding Operators and Expressions in Access"), a better practice is to assign related, but distinctive, names to such fields.

Creating the Personnel Actions Table

Now you can put to work what you have learned about field names, data types, and formats by adding the Personnel Actions table to the Northwind Traders database. Table 4.8 shows the field names, taken from table 4.7, and the set of properties that you assign to the fields. The text in the Caption property column substitutes for the Field Name property that is otherwise displayed in the field header buttons.

Table 4.8	Field Properties for the Personnel Actions Table			
Field Name	**Caption**	**Data Type**	**Field Size**	**Format**
paID	ID	Number	Long Integer	General Number
paType	Type	Text	1	@> (all uppercase)
paInitiatedBy	Initiated By	Number	Integer	General Number
paScheduledDate	Scheduled	Date/Time	N/A	Short Date
paApprovedBy	Approved By	Number	Integer	General Number
paEffectiveDate	Effective	Date/Time	N/A	Short Date
paRating	Rating	Number	Integer	General Number
paAmount	Amount	Currency	N/A	#,##0.00#
paComments	Comments	Memo	N/A	(None)

You must set the paID field's Field Size property to the Long Integer data type, although you might not expect Northwind Traders to have more than the 32,767 employees that an integer allows. You must use the Long Integer data type because the AutoNumber field data type of the Employees table's EmployeeID field is a Long Integer. The section "Enforcing Referential Integrity," later in this chapter, explains why paID's data type must match thatof the Employees table's EmployeeID number field.

To add the new Personnel Actions table to the Northwind Traders database, complete the following steps:

1. Close the Employees table, if it is open, by clicking the Close Window button to make the Database window active.

2. Click the Table button of the Database window, if it isn't selected, and then click the New button. Select Design View in the New Table dialog and click OK. Access enters design mode and opens a blank grid where you enter field names, data types, and optional comments. By default, Access selects the grid's first cell.

3. Enter **paID** as the first field name. Press Enter to accept the field name. The caret moves to the Data Type column; Access adds the default field type, Text.

4. Press F4 to open the Data Type list. You use the function keys rather than the mouse because your entries are from the keyboard.

5. Use the arrow keys to select the Number data type, and press Enter to accept your selection (see fig. 4.21).

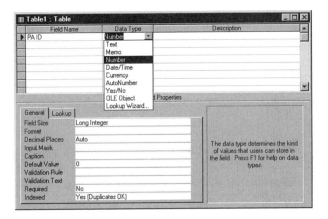

Fig. 4.21 Entering the field data type for the paID field in the Personnel Actions table.

6. Press F6 to move to the Field Properties window's Field Size text box. Access has already entered Long Integer as the value of the default Field Size property. To learn more about the Field Size property, press F1 for help.

   Whenever you create a new Number type field, Access enters Long Integer in the `Field Size` property as the default. Because the paID field should be a Long Integer, you don't need to set the Field Size property for this field, and can skip to step 8; continue with step 7 when you enter the other fields from table 4.8.

7. For Number data types, press F4 to open the Field Size list. Select from the list the appropriate field size value for the field, and press Enter.

8. Press the down arrow to select the Format text box. You can press F1 for context-sensitive help on the Format property.

9. Press F4 to open the Format list, select General Number from the list, and press Enter (see fig. 4.22).

10. Press the down-arrow key three times, bypassing the Decimal Places and Iput Mask properties, and select the Caption text box. You skip the Decimal Places property; Long Integers cannot have decimal fractions, so Decimal Places can remain set to Auto. You skip the Input Mask property because this field doesn't need an input mask.

11. Enter **ID** as the caption and press Enter. ID is used as the Caption property to minimize the column width necessary to display the paID number.

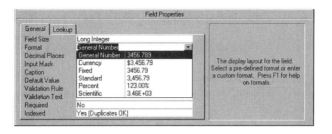

Fig. 4.22 Assigning the General Number format to the paID field.

12. Press F6 to return to the Table Design grid. The caret is located in the Description column. You complete the remaining properties for each field after completing the basic properties shown in table 4.8.

13. You use descriptions to create prompts that appear in the status bar when you are adding or editing records in run mode's Datasheet View. Although descriptions are optional, a good database design practice is to enter the field's purpose if its use isn't obvious from its Field Name or Caption property. You can skip the Caption property entries for now. After completing the basic steps described here, you can refer to table 4.8 and enter the captions as a group.

14. Press the down-arrow key to select the next row of the grid.

15. Repeat steps 3 through 13, entering the values shown in table 4.8 for each of the eight remaining fields of the Personnel Action table. N/A (not applicable) means that the entry in table 4.8 doesn't apply to the field's data type.

Your Table Design grid should now look similar to the one shown in figure 4.23. You can double-check your properties entries by selecting each field name with the arrow keys and reading the values shown in the properties text boxes of the Field Properties window.

Field Name	Data Type	Description
paID	Number	
paType	Text	
paInitiatedBy	Number	
paScheduledDate	Date/Time	
paApprovedBy	Number	
paEffectiveDate	Date/Time	
paRating	Number	
paAmount	Currency	
paComments	Memo	

Fig. 4.23 The initial design of the Personnel Actions table.

Click the Datasheet toolbar button to return to Datasheet View in run mode to view the results of your work. You receive the "Must save table first. Save now?" message. Click OK, and a Save As dialog appears requesting that you give your table a name and suggesting the default table name, Table1. Type **Personnel Actions**, as shown in figure 4.24, and press Enter or click OK.

Fig. 4.24   The Save As dialog for naming the Personnel Actions table.

At this point, Access displays a dialog informing you that the new table does not have a primary key. You'll add primary keys to the Personnel Actions table later in this chapter, so click No in this dialog.

Your table appears in Datasheet View, with its first default record. To view all the fields of your new table, narrow the field name header buttons by dragging to the left the right vertical bar that separates each of the headers. When you finish adjusting your fields' display widths, the Personnel Actions table appears in Datasheet View as shown in figure 4.25. Only the empty tentative append record (a new record that Access will add to your table if you enter values in the cells) is present. You have more property values to add to your Personnel Actions table, so don't enter data in the tentative append record at this point.

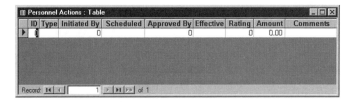

Fig. 4.25   The tentative append record of the Personnel Actions table.

Setting Default Values of Fields

 Access 1.x assigned your fields' default values, such as 0 for Number and Currency fields and No for Yes/No fields. Access 2.0 did not assign default values to Number and Yes/No fields automatically. Access 95 covers the middle ground by assigning Number and Currency fields a default value of 0; all other field types are empty by default. (Notice that the tentative append record in figure 4.25 has zeros entered in all the Number and Currency fields.) In all versions of Access, Text, Memo, and Date fields are empty by default. You can save data-entry time by establishing your own default values for fields; in some cases, Access 95's default values for Number and Currency fields may be inappropriate, and you'll need to change them. Table 4.9 lists the default values for the Personnel Actions tables' fields.

Table 4.9 Default Field Values for the Personnel Actions Table		
Field Name	**Default Value**	**Comments**
paID	No entry	0 is not a valid Employee ID number, so you should remove Access's default.
paType	Q	Quarterly performance reviews are the most common personnel action.

Field Name	Default Value	Comments
paInitiatedBy	No entry	0 is not a valid Employee ID number.
paScheduledDate	Date( )	The expression to enter today's (DOS) date.
paApprovedBy	No entry	0 is not a valid Employee ID.
paEffectiveDate	Date( )+28	Today's (DOS) date plus 28 days.
paRating	No entry	In many cases, a rating does not apply. A 0 rating is reserved for terminated employees.
paAmount	No entry	If a salary, bonus, or commission has no change, no entry should appear. 0 would indicate no salary, for example.
paComments	No change	For now, Access's default is adequate.

If you don't enter anything in the Default Value text box, you create a `Null` default value. You can use `Null` values for testing whether a value has been entered into a field. Such a test can ensure that the user has entered required data. (The following section discusses this subject.) The Date+28 default is an *expression* that returns the DOS date plus four weeks. You use expressions to enter values in fields, make calculations, and perform other useful duties, such as validating data entries. Expressions are discussed briefly in the next section and in greater detail in Chapter 9, "Understanding Operators and Expressions in Access." Expressions that establish default values always are preceded by an equal sign.

To assign the new default values from those of table 4.9 to the fields of the Personnel Actions table, complete these steps:

1. Change to design mode by choosing <u>V</u>iew, Table <u>D</u>esign. Select the paID field.

2. Press F6 to switch to the Field Properties window, and then move the caret to the Default Value text box. Press Delete to clear the text box.

3. Press F6 to switch back to the Table Design grid. Move to the next field and press F6 again.

4. Create the default values for the eight remaining fields from the entries shown in table 4.9, repeating steps 2 through 4. For example, after selecting the Default Value text box for the paType field, you would type **Q** to set the default value. Enter **=Date( )** for the paScheduledDate field and **=Date( )+28** for the paEffectiveDate Date field. Delete any default values that might appear in the other fields that call for no entry in table 4.9.

5. After completing your default entries, choose <u>V</u>iew, Data<u>s</u>heet to return to run mode. A dialog appears requesting that you confirm your changes. Click OK. The Personnel Actions table now appears in Datasheet View with the new default entries that you have assigned, as shown in figure 4.26.

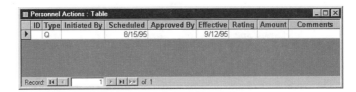

Fig. 4.26 The first record of the Personnel Actions table with the new default values.

Working with Relations, Key Fields, and Indexes

Your final tasks before adding records to the Personnel Actions table are to determine the relationship between Personnel Actions and an existing table in the database, assign a primary-key field, and add indexes to your table.

Establishing Relationships between Tables

Relationships between existing tables and your new table determine the field used as the new table's primary key. The following four possibilities exist for relationships between tables:

- *One-to-one* relationships require that the key field's value in only one record in your new table matches a corresponding value of the related field in the existing table. In this case, the key field in your new table must be unique; duplicate values aren't allowed in the key field. A one-to-one relationship is the equivalent of a table that contains all the fields of the existing table and the new table. Tables with one-to-one relationships are uncommon.

- *Many-to-one* relationships allow your new table to have more than one value in the key field corresponding to a single value in the related field of the existing table. In this case, duplicate key field values are allowed. Many-to-one relationships are the most common type; the capability to create many-to-one relationships is the principal reason for choosing a relational system, rather than a flat-file application, to manage your databases.

- *One-to-many* relationships require that your new table's key field be unique, but the values in the key field of the new table can match many entries in the related field of the existing database. In this case, the related field of the existing database has a many-to-one relationship with the key field of the new database.

- *Many-to-many* relationships are free-for-alls in which no unique relationship exists between the key fields in the existing table or the new table, and both of the tables' key fields contain duplicate values.

 ▶▶ See "Types of Relationships," p. 847

Keep in mind that the many-to-one and one-to-many relationships apply to how your new table relates to an existing table. When viewed from the existing table's standpoint, the relationships to your new table are one-to-many and many-to-one, respectively. Chapter 23, "Exploring Relational Database Design and Implementation," explains the four types of relations more comprehensively.

Many entries in the Personnel Actions table may apply to a single employee whose record appears in the Employees table. A record is created in Personnel Actions when the employee is hired, and a record is created for each quarterly and yearly performance review. Also, any changes made to bonuses or commissions other than as the result of a performance review are entered, and employees may be terminated. Over time, the number of records in the Personnel Actions table is likely to be greater by a factor of 10 or more than the number of records in the Employees table. Thus, the records in the new Personnel table have a many-to-one relationship with the records in the Employees table. Establishing the relationships between the new and existing tables when you create the new table enables Access to reestablish the relationship automatically when you use the tables in queries, forms, and reports.

Access requires that the two fields participating in the relationship have exactly the same data type. In the case of the Number field data type, the Field Size property of the two fields must be identical. You cannot, for example, create a relationship between an AutoNumber type field (which uses a Long Integer data type) and a field containing Byte, Integer, Single, Double, or Currency data. On the other hand, Access enables you to relate two tables by text fields of different lengths. Such a relationship, if created, can lead to strange behavior when you create queries, which is the subject of Part II, "Querying for Specific Information." As a rule, the relationships between text fields should use fields of the same length.

Access 95 uses a graphical Relationships window to display and create the relationships among tables in a database. To establish the relationships between two tables using Access's Relationships dialog, follow these steps:

1. Close the Personnel Actions table by clicking the Close Window button. If the Employees table is open, close it. You cannot create or modify relationships between open tables.

2. If the Database window isn't the active window (indicated by a colored title bar), click the Database window, click the Show Database Window button of the toolbar, or choose <u>W</u>indows, <u>1</u> Database. As many as nine of the windows for database objects that you have opened appear as numbered choices in the <u>W</u>indows menu. (The Database window is always number 1.) Before you can establish relationships, the Database window must be active.

3. Click the Relationships button of the toolbar or choose <u>T</u>ools, <u>R</u>elationships. The Relationships window for the Northwind Traders database appears (see fig. 4.27). This window displays all the tables for which relationships are defined.

4. Click the Show Table button of the toolbar or choose <u>R</u>elationships, <u>S</u>how Table. The Show Table dialog shown in figure 4.28 appears.

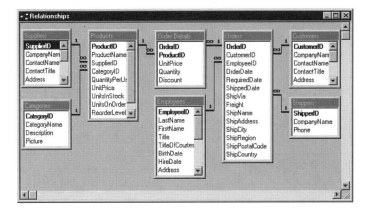

Fig. 4.27 The Relationships window shows all the relationships that have been defined for a database.

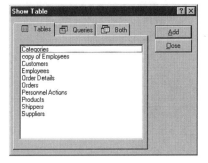

Fig. 4.28 Adding a new table to the Relationships window.

5. Add the Personnel Actions table to the Relationships window by double-clicking the Personnel Actions entry in the Tables list or by clicking the entry to select it and then choosing the Add button. Choose the Close button to close the Show Table dialog.

6. The relationship of the Personnel Actions table with the Employees table is based on the Personnel Actions table's paID field and the Employees table's EmployeeID field. Click the Employees table's EmployeeID field and, holding the left mouse button down, drag the field to the Personnel Actions table's paID field. Release the left mouse button to drop the field symbol on the paID field. When you drag and drop a new relationship, the Relationships dialog appears (see fig. 4.29).

Note

The sequence of the drag-and-drop operation to create a new relationship is important. Drag the field from the *one* side of a one-to-many relationship and drop it on the *many* side. This sequence ensures that the primary (or base) table for the *one* side of the relationship appears in the Table/Query list and that the table for the *many* side appears in the Related Table/Query list. If you

(continues)

(continued)

reverse the relationships (creating a many-to-one relationship) and attempt to enforce referential integrity, you receive an error message in the final step of the process when you attempt to create the relationship.

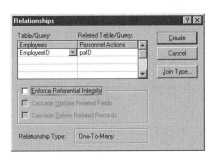

Fig. 4.29 Defining a relationship with the Relationships dialog.

7. Choose the Join Type button to display the Join Properties dialog shown in figure 4.30. You want to create a one-to-many join between the Employees table's EmployeeID field (the *one* side) and the Personnel Actions table's paID field (the *many* side). Thus, you want to include *all* Personnel Actions records for a single employee. To do so, choose option 3 in the Join Properties dialog. Click OK to close the dialog and return to the Relationships dialog.

Fig. 4.30 Choosing the type of join for the Personnel Actions and Employees tables.

8. The Relationships dialog offers the Enforce Referential Integrity check box so that you can specify that Access perform validation testing and accept entries in the paID field that correspond to values for the Employees table's EmployeeID field. This process is called *enforcing* (or maintaining) referential integrity. The following section discusses referential integrity. The relationship between these two tables requires enforced referential integrity, so make sure that you select this check box. The Relationships dialog now appears as shown in figure 4.31.

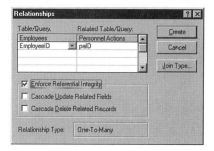

Fig. 4.31 The Relationships dialog entries for a one-to-many relationship with referential integrity enforced.

Note

You can specify that Access 95 automatically maintains referential integrity of tables by providing check boxes that you can select to cause cascading updates to and cascade deletions of related records when the primary table changes. The following section discusses cascading updates and deletions. Access enables the cascade check boxes only if you elect to enforce referential integrity.

---

9. Click the Create button to accept the new relationship and display it in the Relationships window as shown in figure 4.32.

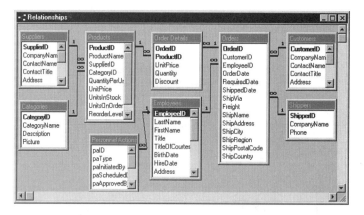

Fig. 4.32 The Relationships window with the new Personnel Actions relationship added.

 10. Click the Close Window button to close the Relationships window and return to the Database window. Click Yes when asked to confirm that you want to save the layout changes to the Relationships diagram.

Access uses the relationship that you have created when you create queries and design forms and reports that require data in the Personnel Actions table.

The relationship is equivalent to that created by the following xBase statements:

```
SELECT 1
USE employee INDEX emp_idno
```

```
SELECT 2
USE pers_act
SELECT employee
SET RELATION TO emp_idno INTO employee
```

The difference between Access and xBase relationships is that the related table in xBase, pers_act, must be indexed on the key expression of the primary table, EmployeeID. Access does not require that the related table be indexed.

Enforcing Referential Integrity

The capability to enforce referential integrity automatically is an important feature of Access; few other PC relational database managers include this feature. Referential integrity prevents the creation of "orphan records" that have no connection to a primary table. An example of an orphan record is a record for a personnel action for paID 10 when you have records in the Employees file for employees numbered only 1 through 9. You could not know who employee 10 is until you enter the next employee hired. Then the orphan record, intended for some other employee, is linked, improperly, to the new employee's record.

How Referential Integrity Is Enforced. Referential integrity enforcement prevents you from deleting or modifying values of a primary table's record on which related records depend. If you terminate an employee and then try to delete the employee's record from the Employees table, Access prevents you from doing so. Access displays a message box informing you that you must delete all records related to the primary table's record before you can delete the primary record. You can't change a value in the Employees table's Employee ID field because the field data type is AutoNumber. If the data types are such that you can change the value of an Employee ID on which related records depend, however, Access also displays a warning message.

Similarly, if you attempt to change an employee ID value in the paID field of the Personnel Actions table to a value that does not exist in the Employees table's EmployeeID field, you also incur an error message. Thus, enforcing referential integrity eliminates the need to validate entries in the paID field using the Validation Rule property. With referential integrity enforced, Access automatically ensures that the value you enter corresponds to a valid EmployeeID value when you save the new or edited record.

Cascading Updates and Deletions. Prior to Access 2.0, you had to write macros or Access Basic code to implement the series of actions required to maintain referential integrity. For example, to delete a record in the Employees table, you had to run a test to determine whether related records existed in any other table that depended on the Employee ID field, and then delete the dependent records. If you wanted to change the Customer ID of a record in the Customers table, the situation became more complex: You couldn't change the related records to a new Customer ID that wasn't yet in the table, nor could you change the Customer ID in the primary table because it had dependent records. You could resolve this dichotomy by a variety of methods, none of which were simple.

With Access 95's cascading deletion and cascading update options for tables with enforced referential integrity, maintaining referential integrity is a simple process: Just check the Cascade Update Related Fields and Cascade Delete Related Records check boxes. Access 95 does all the work for you.

> **Note**
>
> Automatically enforcing referential integrity is usually, but not always, a good database design practice. An example of where you would not want to employ cascade deletions is between the EmployeeID fields of the Orders and Employee tables. If you terminate an employee and then attempt to delete the employee's record, you might accidentally choose to delete the dependent records in the Orders table. Deleting records in the Orders table could have serious consequences from a marketing and accounting standpoint. (In the real world, however, you probably would not delete a terminated employee's record.)

Selecting a Primary Key

You do not need to designate a primary-key field for a table that is never used as a primary table. A *primary table* contains information representing a real-world object, such as a person or an invoice, and only one record uniquely associated with that object. The Personnel Actions table can qualify as a primary table because it identifies an object—in this case, the equivalent of a paper form representing the outcome of two actions: initiation and approval. Personnel Actions, however, probably would not be used as a primary table in a relationship with another table.

Using a key field is a simple method of preventing the duplication of records in a table. Access requires that you specify a primary key if you want to create a one-to-one relationship or to update two or more tables at the same time. Chapter 10, "Creating Multitable and Crosstab Queries," covers this subject.

The primary table participating in relations that you set with the Relationships dialog must have a primary key. Access considers a table without a primary-key field to be an oddity; therefore, when you make changes to the table and return to Design View, you often will see a message stating that you haven't created a key field. (Access 95 asks you only once whether you want to add a primary-key field.) Related tables can have primary-key fields and often do. A primary-key field is useful to prevent the accidental addition of duplicate records.

You can create primary keys on more than one field. In the case of the Personnel Actions table, a primary key that prevents duplicate records must consist of more than one field, because more than one personnel action for an employee can be scheduled or approved on the same date. If you establish the rule that no more than one type of personnel action for an employee can be scheduled for the same date, you can create a primary key that consists of the paID, paType, and paScheduledDate fields. When you create a primary key, Access creates an index based on the primary key. The next section and Chapter 23, "Exploring Relational Database Design and Implementation," discuss indexes in detail.

To create a multiple-field primary key and index for the Personnel Actions table, follow these steps:

1. Open the Personnel Actions table from the Database window in design mode.

2. Click the selection button for the paID field.

3. Hold down the Ctrl key and click the selection button for the paType field. In most instances, when you hold down Ctrl and click a selection button, you can make multiple selections.

4. Hold down Ctrl and click the selection button for the paScheduledDate field.

   If you accidentally select one of the other fields, click the field's selection button again to deselect it.

5. Click the Primary Key button on the toolbar. Symbols of keys appear in each of the selected fields, indicating their inclusion in the primary key (see fig. 4.33).

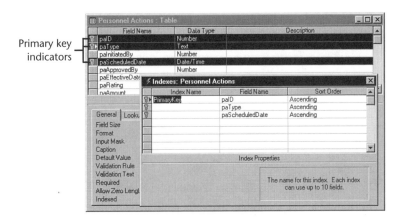

Fig. 4.33 Setting a multiple-field primary key for the Personnel Actions table.

6. To determine the sequence of the fields in the primary key, click the toolbar's Index button to display the Indexes window as shown in figure 4.33.

   In Access, you can create multiple-field primary keys and indexes with fields of different data types, without resorting to xBase-type changing functions. The entry in the Primary Key text box is the equivalent of the following xBase statement:

```
INDEX ON STRZERO(pa_id,2) + pa_type + DTOS(pa_sced)
TO whatever
```

   The capability to concatenate different data types to form an index instruction or a string is the result of Access's Variant data type, which Chapter 28, "Writing Visual Basic for Applications Code," discusses.

You now have a multiple-field primary key and a corresponding index to the Personnel Actions table that precludes the addition of records that duplicate records with the same primary key.

Adding Indexes to Tables

Although Access creates an index on the primary key, you might want to create an index on some other field or fields in the table. Indexes speed searches for records that contain specific types of data. You might want to find all personnel actions that occurred in a given period and all quarterly reviews for all employees in paScheduledDate sequence, for example. If you have many records in the table, an index speeds up the searching process. A disadvantage of multiple indexes is that data-entry operations are slowed by the time that it takes to update the additional indexes. You can create as many as 32 indexes for each Access table, and five of those can be of the multiple-field type. Each multiple-field index can include as many as 10 fields.

To create a single-field index for the Personnel Actions table based on the paEffectiveDate field, and a multiple-field index based on the paType and the paScheduledDate fields, follow these steps:

1. Select the paEffectiveDate field by clicking its selection button.

2. Select the Indexed text box in the Field Properties window.

3. Open the Indexed drop-down list by clicking the arrow button or pressing F4. The list appears as shown in figure 4.34.

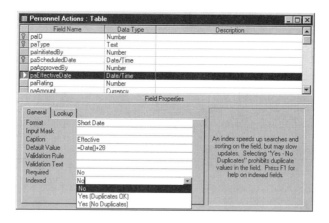

Fig. 4.34 Creating a single-field index on the paEffectiveDate field.

4. In this case, duplicate entries are acceptable, so click Yes (Duplicates OK) and close the list. You can create only a single-field index by using this method.

5. Click the Indexes button if the Indexes window is not open. The Primary Key and paEffectiveDate indexes already created appear in the list boxes. Enter **pa Type/ Date** as the name of the composite index, and then select paType and paScheduledDate from the Field Name drop-down list to create a multiple-field index on these two fields, as shown in figure 4.35.

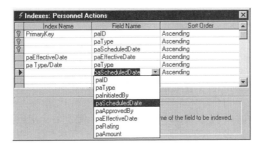

Fig. 4.35 Creating a multiple-field index on the paType and paScheduled Date fields.

6. Click the Datasheet View button to return to run mode. Click OK when the message box asks whether you want to save your design changes. A message in the status bar indicates that Access is creating the new indexes as you leave design mode.

You now have three indexes for the Primary Key table: the index automatically created for the primary key, the single-key index on paEffectiveDate, and the multiple-key index on paType and paScheduledDate.

Altering Fields and Relationships

When you are designing your own database, you often discover that you must alter the original choices that you made for the sequence of fields in a table, data types, or relationships between tables. One of the reasons for adding substantial numbers of records to tables during the testing process is to discover any changes that are necessary before putting the database into daily use.

You can change formats, change validation rules and text, change lengths of Text fields, and make other minor modifications to the table by changing to design mode, selecting the field to modify, and making the changes in the properties boxes. Changing data types can cause a loss of data, however, so be sure to read the section "Changing Field Data Types and Sizes," later in this chapter, before you attempt to make such changes. Changing relationships between tables is considered a drastic action if you have entered a substantial amount of data, so this subject also is covered in a later section, "Changing Relationships between Tables."

> **Note**
>
> Avoid changing a field name if you have created data-entry forms or reports that use the data in the field. Although Access performs many operations automatically, it does not change the field names that you have assigned to text boxes and other objects in forms or to the groups in reports. The time to finalize field names is while creating your tables; a bit of extra thought at this point saves hours of modification after you are well into creation of a complex application.

Rearranging the Sequence of Fields in a Table

If you are manually entering historical data in Datasheet View, you might find that the sequence of entries isn't optimum. You might, for example, be entering data from a printed form with a top-to-bottom, left-to-right sequence that doesn't correspond to the left-to-right sequence of the corresponding fields in your table. Access makes rearranging the order of fields in tables a matter of dragging and dropping fields where you want them. You can choose whether to make the revised layout temporary or permanent when you close the table.

To rearrange the fields of the Personnel Actions table, follow these steps:

1. Click the Datasheet View button. This is the only table design change that you can implement in Access's Datasheet View.

2. Click the field name button of the field that you want to move. This action selects the field name button and all the field's data cells.

3. Hold down the left mouse button while over the field name button. The mouse pointer turns into the drag-and-drop symbol, and a heavy vertical bar marks the field's far-left position. Figure 4.36 shows the paScheduledDate field being moved to a position immediately to the left of the paEffectiveDate field.

ID	Type	Initiated B	Schedule	Approved B	Effective	Rating	New Amou	Commen
1	H	1	4/1/87		4/1/87		2,000.00	Hired
2	H	1	7/15/87		7/15/87		3,500.00	Hired
3	H	2	3/1/88	2	3/1/88		2,250.00	Hired
4	H	2	4/1/88	2	4/1/88		2,250.00	Hired
5	H	2	9/15/89	2	9/15/89		2,500.00	Hired
5	Q	2	1/15/90	2	1/15/90	8	2,750.00	First quarte
5	Y	2	1/15/91	2	1/15/91	7	3,000.00	Steven cou
5	Y	2	1/15/92	2	1/15/92	8	3,500.00	Steven's sa
5	Y	2	1/15/93	2	1/15/93	8	4,000.00	Steven con
5	Y	7	1/15/94	7	1/15/94	9	4,250.00	Despite St
6	H	5	9/15/89	2	9/15/89	8	4,000.00	Hired
7	H	5	12/1/89	2	12/1/89		3,000.00	Hired
8	H	2	2/1/90	2	2/1/90		2,500.00	Hired
9	H	5	10/15/91	2	10/15/91		3,000.00	Hired
*	Q		8/15/95		9/12/95			

Fig. 4.36 Dragging a field to a new position in run mode.

4. Move the mouse pointer and vertical bar combination to the new position for the selected field and release the mouse button. The field assumes the new position shown in figure 4.37.

5. When you close the Personnel Actions table, you see the familiar Save Changes message box. To make the modification permanent, click OK; otherwise, click No.

Dragging and dropping fields to a new location is a much simpler process than the MODIFY STRUCTURE operations required by xBase to achieve the same result. You can reposition fields in design mode by clicking the select button of the row of the field that you want to move and then dragging the row vertically to a new location. Changing the position of a table's field doesn't change any of the field's other properties.

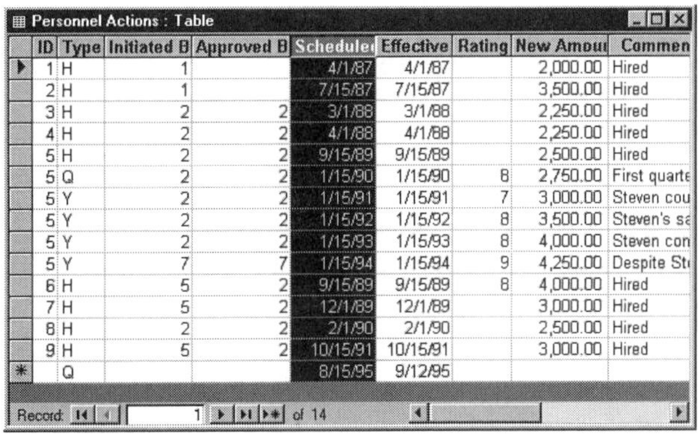

Fig. 4.37 The paScheduledDate field dropped into a new position in Datasheet View.

Changing Field Data Types and Sizes

You might have to change a field data type as the design of your database develops or if you import tables from another database, a spreadsheet, or a text file. If you import tables, the data type automatically chosen by Access during the importation process probably won't be what you want, especially with Number fields. Chapter 7, "Linking, Importing, and Exporting Tables," discusses importing and exporting tables and data from other applications. Another example of altering field properties is changing the number of characters in fixed-length Text fields to accommodate entries that are longer than expected, or converting variable-length Text fields to fixed-length fields.

Caution

Before making changes to the field data types of a table that contains substantial amounts of data, back up the table by copying or exporting it to a backup Access database. If you accidentally lose parts of the data contained in the table, such as decimal fractions, while changing the field data type, you can import the backup table to your current database. Chapter 7, "Linking, Importing, and Exporting Tables," covers the simple and quick process of exporting Access tables. After creating a backup database file, you can copy a table to Windows Clipboard and then paste the table to the backup database. The section "Copying and Pasting Tables," later in this chapter, discusses copying and pasting tables to and from the Clipboard.

Numeric Fields. Changing a data type to one that requires more bytes of storage is, in almost all circumstances, safe. You do not sacrifice your data's accuracy. Changing a numeric data type from Byte to Integer to Long Integer to Single and, finally, to Double does not affect your data's value because each change, except for Long Integer to Single, requires more bytes of storage for a data value. Changing from Long Integer to Single and Single to Currency involves the same number of bytes and decreases the accuracy of the data only in exceptional circumstances. The exceptions can occur when you are using very high numbers or extremely small decimal fractions, such as in some scientific and engineering calculations.

On the other hand, if you change to a data type with fewer data bytes required to store it, Access might truncate your data. If you change from a fixed-point format (Currency) or floating-point format (Single or Double) to Byte, Integer, or Long Integer, any decimal fractions in your data are truncated. *Truncation* means reducing the number of digits in a number to fit the new Field Size property that you choose. If you change a numeric data type from Single to Currency, for example, you might lose your Single data in the fifth, sixth, and seventh decimal places (if any exists) because Single provides as many as seven decimal places and Currency provides only four.

You cannot convert any type of field to an AutoNumber-type field. You can use the AutoNumber field only as a record counter; the only way that you can enter the field is by appending new records. You cannot edit a record number field. When you delete a record in Access, the AutoNumber values of the higher-numbered records are not reduced by 1. Access record numbers are assigned to records in the order of the primary key, not in the order in which the records were entered. If your table doesn't have a primary key, the record numbers represent the order in which the records were created.

Text Fields. You can convert Text fields to Memo fields without Access truncating your text. Converting a Memo field to a Text field, however, truncates characters beyond the 255 limit of Text fields. Similarly, if you convert a variable-length Text field to a fixed-length field, and some records contain character strings that exceed the length that you chose, Access truncates these strings.

Conversion between Number, Date, and Text Field Data Types. Access makes many conversions between Number, Date, and Text field data types for you. Conversion from Number or Date to Text field data types does not follow the Format property that you assigned to the original data type. Numbers are converted using the General Number format, and dates use the Short Date format. Access is quite intelligent in the methods it uses to convert suitable Text fields to Number data types. For example, it accepts dollar signs, commas, and decimals during the conversion, but ignores trailing spaces. Access converts dates and times in the following Text formats to internal Date/Time values that you then can format the way that you want:

```
1/4/96 10:00 AM
04-Jan-96
January 4
10:00
10:00:00
```

Changing Relationships between Tables

Adding new relationships between tables is a straightforward process, but changing relationships might require you to change data types so that the related fields have the same data type. To change a relationship between two tables, complete the following steps:

1. Close the tables that are involved in the relationship.

2. If the Database window is not active, click it and then click the Show Database Window button, or choose <u>W</u>indows, <u>1</u> Database.

3. Display the Relationships window by clicking the Relationships button of the toolbar or choosing <u>T</u>ools, <u>R</u>elationships.

4. Click the join line that connects to the field whose data type you want to change. When you select the join line, the line becomes darker (wider) as shown in figure 4.38.

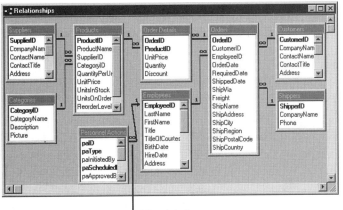

Join line selected for deletion

Fig. 4.38 Deleting a relationship before changing a data type in a related field.

5. Press Delete to clear the existing relationship. Click Yes when the message box asks you to confirm your deletion.

6. If you are changing the data type of a field that constitutes or is a member field of the primary table's primary key, delete all other relationships that exist between the primary table and every other table to which it is related.

7. Change the data types of the fields in the tables so that the data types match in the new relationships.

8. Re-create the relationships, using the procedure described in the earlier section, "Establishing Relationships between Tables."

Copying and Pasting Tables

You can copy a complete table or records of a table to the Windows Clipboard by using the same methods that apply to most other Windows applications. (Using the Clipboard to paste individual records or sets of records into a table is one of the subjects of the next chapter.) You use Clipboard operations extensively when you reach Part V of this book, "Integrating Access with Other Applications." You can copy tables into other databases, such as a general-purpose backup database, by using the Clipboard; however, exporting a table to a temporary database file, described in Chapter 7, "Linking, Importing, and Exporting Tables," is a more expeditious method.

To copy a table to another Access database, a destination database must exist. To create a backup database and copy the contents of the Personnel Actions table to the database, follow these steps:

1. Make the Database window active by clicking it, if it is accessible, or by choosing Windows, 1 Database.

2. Click the Table button, if necessary, to display the list of tables.

3. Select the table that you want to copy to the new database.

4. Click the Copy button on the toolbar, press Ctrl+C, or choose Edit, Copy.

   If you plan to copy the table to your current database, skip to step 7.

5. If you have created a destination backup database, choose File, Open Database to open the database; then skip to step 7.

6. To create a backup database, choose File, New Database; choose a blank database and name it **backup.mdb** or another appropriate filename. Access creates your Backup.mdb database, which occupies 80K without any tables (this is called 80K of overhead). Your new database is now active.

7. Click the Paste button on the toolbar, press Ctrl+V, or choose Edit, Paste. The Paste Table As dialog shown in figure 4.39 appears.

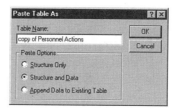

Fig. 4.39   The Paste Table As dialog used to create a backup table.

8. You have three options for pasting the backup table to the destination database. You can create a new table or replace the data in a table of the name that you enter in the Table Name text box by selecting Structure and Data. This is the most common choice. You also can paste the structure only and then append data to the table later by selecting Structure Only, or append the records to an existing table of the name that you enter. For this example, accept the default: Structure and Data.

9. Your current or backup database now has a copy of the table that you selected, and the name that you entered appears in the backup's Database window. You can save multiple copies of the same table under different names if you are making a series of changes to the table that might affect the integrity of the data that it contains.

To delete a table from a database, select the table name in the Database window and then press Delete. A confirmation message box appears. Click Yes to delete the table forever. You cannot choose Edit, Undo after deleting a table.

From Here...

Tables are the core elements of the databases that you create. The capability to segregate data of different types into individual tables and then relate the tables by common fields or combinations of fields is central to the concept of relational databases.

The techniques that you used in this chapter to add the Personnel Actions table to the Northwind Traders database are typical of those techniques that you use when you create databases from the information that you have stored in other types of databases, spreadsheets, or text files, or from information that you or others enter manually.

For information related to the topics discussed in this chapter, refer to the following chapters:

■ Chapter 5, "Entering, Editing, and Validating Data in Tables," shows you how to add records to tables, edit data in the records, and add validation rules to your tables to ensure that data values fall within accepted limits.

■ Chapter 6, "Sorting, Finding, and Filtering Data in Tables," shows you how to sort data in tables and how to apply filters to display or print records that meet the criteria you enter in the Filter window. Filters are queries in disguise; when you add a filter to a table, you actually create a SELECT query that Access calls a filter.

■ Chapter 23, "Exploring Relational Database Design and Implementation," gives you an in-depth description of how you design tables that conform to the rules of relational databases. This chapter also explains how Access and other database indexes work.

Learning Access

Chapter 5

Entering, Editing, and Validating Data in Tables

Ease of data entry is a primary criterion for an effective database development environment. Most of your Access database applications probably use forms for data entry. In many instances, however, entering data in Table Datasheet View is more expeditious than using a form, especially during the database development cycle. For example, it is a good idea to test your proposed database structure before you commit to designing the forms and reports because changing table and field names or altering relationships between tables after you create a collection of forms and reports involves a substantial amount of work. In order to test the database design, you often need to enter test data. In this instance, using Table Datasheet View to enter data makes more sense than using a form. Even if you import data from another database type or from a worksheet, you will likely need to edit the data to make it compatible with your new application. The first part of this chapter concentrates on data entry and editing methods.

Another important factor in a database development environment is the capability to maintain the domain integrity of your data. Domain integrity rules limit the values you enter in fields to a range or set of values you specify. Domain integrity rules complement the referential integrity rules described in Chapter 4. As mentioned in Chapter 1, "Access 95 for Access 2 Users—What's New," Access 95 enables you to enforce domain integrity rules (often called *business rules*) at the field and table levels. You enforce domain integrity by entering expressions as the value of the Validation Rule property of fields and tables. This chapter teaches you how to use simple expressions for domain integrity validation rules. After you master Access operators and expressions (the subject of Chapter 9, "Understanding Operators and Expressions in Access"), you can write complex validation rules that minimize the possibility of erroneous data in your tables.

In this chapter, you learn how to

- Use shortcut keys to enter repetitive data

- Change the default behavior of data entry keys

- Add new records to a table

- Edit the data in new and existing records

- Add validation rules to enforce domain integrity

- Test your validation rules to make sure that they work

Using Keyboard Operations for Entering and Editing Data

Although Access is oriented to using a mouse to make selections, keyboard equivalents are provided for the most common actions. One reason for providing keyboard commands is that many data entry operators aren't accustomed to using a mouse, trackball, or other pointing device. Constant shifting of the hand from a keyboard to mouse and back can reduce data entry rates by more than half. Shifting between a keyboard and mouse also can lead to or aggravate repetitive stress injury (RSI), of which the most common type is carpal tunnel syndrome (CTS).

Data entry operators are likely to expect the data entry screens of your Windows database applications to behave identically to the DOS data entry screens of the xBase or Paradox applications to which they are accustomed. Keyboard operations, therefore, are as important in a data entry environment as they are in word processing applications. Consequently, the information concerning key combinations for data entry appears here rather than being relegated to fine print in an appendix. The data entry procedures you learn in the sections that follow prove quite useful when you come to the "Entering Personnel Actions Table Data and Testing Validation Rules" section near the end of the chapter.

Creating an Experimental Copy of Northwind.mdb

Tip

If you're short on fixed disk space, open a new database and copy the Northwind.mdb Customers and Orders tables to your new database as described in the "Copying and Pasting Tables" section of Chapter 4, "Working with Access Databases and Tables."

If you want to experiment with the various keyboard operations described in the following sections, you are wise to work with a copy of the Northwind.mdb database. When you use a copy, you don't need to worry about making changes that affect the sample database. Experimenting also gives you the opportunity to try the Access database-compacting operation described in Chapter 3, "Navigating within Access."

To compact Northwind.mdb to a new copy of Northwind.mdb, follow these steps:

1. Close all open document windows. You can leave the Database window open.

2. Choose File, Close Database, or click the Close Window button. Access reverts to a blank window.

3. Choose Tools, Database Utilities, Compact Database to open the Database to Compact From dialog. In this case, the file is compacted to make a copy of the Northwind.mdb file.

4. Double-click the Northwind.mdb item in the Database to Compact From dialog's list box. The Compact Into dialog appears.

5. You can accept the default filename, db1.mdb, in the Filename text box, or you can enter a more creative name, such as **Illwind.mdb**, in the Filename text box, then click Save. Compacting a database file with a new name creates a new, compacted database that you can use for testing.

6. Choose File, Open Database, and double-click db1.mdb or the name of your file from step 5.

7. Open the Customers table by double-clicking its entry in the Database window.

Using Data Entry and Editing Keys

> **Note**
>
> Most keyboard operations described in this section apply to tables and updatable queries in Datasheet View, the new Datasheet View for table creation, text boxes on forms, and text boxes used for entering property values in Properties windows and in the Field Properties grid of Table Design View. In the examples in this section, the Arrow Key Behavior property is set to the Next Character value rather than the Next Field value (the default). See the "Setting Data Entry Options" section that follows for instructions on how to change the value of the Arrow Key Behavior property. When the Arrow Key Behavior property is set to Next Field, the arrow keys move the caret from field to field. Data entry operators accustomed to DOS or mainframe database applications usually prefer the Next Character approach.

Arrow keys and key combinations in Access are, for the most part, identical to those used in other Windows applications. Little resemblance exists between these combinations and the key combinations used by DOS database managers, however. The F2 key, used for editing cell contents in Excel, has a different function in Access—it toggles between editing and select mode. *Toggle* means to alternate between two states. In the editing state, the caret indicates that the insertion point in the field and the key combinations shown in table 5.1 are active. If the field is selected (indicated by a black background with white type), the editing keys behave as indicated in table 5.2.

> **Note**
>
> In the tables that follow, the term *field* is used in place of the more specific description, *data cell* or *cell*, to maintain consistency with Access' documentation and the Help windows. A *field*, in conventional database terminology, indicates the collection of data consisting of the contents of a certain category of information in every record of the table.
>
> The term *grid* in the tables that follow indicates a display in tabular form that doesn't represent fields and records. The list of fields and their descriptions in table design mode is an example of a grid.

Table 5.1	Keys for Editing Fields, Grids, and Text Boxes
Key	**Function**
F2	Toggles between displaying the caret for editing and selecting the entire field. The field must be deselected (black type on a white background), and the caret must be visible for the keys in this table to operate as described.
→	Moves the caret right one character until you reach the last character in the line
Ctrl+→	Moves the caret right one word until you reach the last word in the line
End	Moves the caret to the end of the line
Ctrl+End	Moves the caret to the end of a multiple-line field
←	Moves the caret one character to the left until you reach the first character in the line
Ctrl+←	Moves the caret one word to the left until you reach the first word in the line
Home	Moves the caret to the beginning of the line
Ctrl+Home	Moves the caret to the beginning of the field in multiple-line fields
Backspace	Deletes the entire selection or the character to the left of the caret
Delete	Deletes the entire selection or the character to the right of the caret
Ctrl+Z	Undoes typing, a replace operation, or any other change to the record since the last time it was saved. An edited record is saved to the database when you move to a new record or close the editing window.
Alt+Backspace	Same as Ctrl+Z
Esc	Undoes changes to the current field. Press Esc twice to undo changes to the current field and to the entire current record, if you edited other fields.

Operations that select the entire field or a portion of the field, as listed in table 5.2, generally are used with the Windows Clipboard operations described in table 5.3. Selecting an entire field and then pressing Delete or typing a character is a quick way of ridding the field of its original contents.

Table 5.2	Keys for Selecting Text in Fields, Grids, and Text Boxes	
Selection	**Key**	**Function**
Text within a field	F2	Toggles between displaying the caret for editing and selecting the entire field. The field must be selected (white type on a black background) for the keys in this table to operate as described.
	Shift+→	Selects or deselects one character to the right
	Ctrl+Shift+→	Selects or deselects one word to the right
	Shift+←	Selects or deselects one character to the left
	Ctrl+Shift+←	Selects or deselects one word to the left
Next field	Tab or Enter	Selects the next field. The "Setting Default Data Entry Options" section later in this chapter tells you how to change the effect of the Enter key.
Record	Shift+space bar	Selects or deselects the entire current record
	↑	Selects the preceding record when a record is selected
	↓	Selects the next record when a record is selected

Selection	Key	Function
Column	Ctrl+space bar	Toggles selection of the current column
	→	Selects the column to the right (if a column is selected and there is a column to the right)
	←	Selects the column to the left (if a column is selected and there is a column to the left)
Fields and records	F8	Turns on extend mode. You see EXT in the status bar. In extend mode, pressing F8 extends the selection to the word, field, record, and all records.
	Shift+F8	Reverses the last F8
	Esc	Cancels extend mode

Using Key Combinations for Windows Clipboard Operations

In Table Datasheet View, the Windows Clipboard is used primarily for transferring Access data between applications. However, you also can use the Clipboard for repetitive data entry. Access 95 enables you to select a rectangular block of data cells in a table and copy the block to the Clipboard. To select a block of cells, follow these steps:

1. Position the mouse pointer at the left edge of the top left cell of the block you want to select. The mouse pointer (shaped like an I-beam until this point) turns into a cross similar to the mouse pointer for Excel worksheets.

2. Hold the left mouse button down and drag the mouse pointer to the left edge of the bottom right cell of the desired block.

3. The selected block appears in reverse video (white on black). Release the left mouse button when the selection meets your requirement.

A selected block of data in the Customers table appears in figure 5.1. You can copy data blocks but cannot cut them.

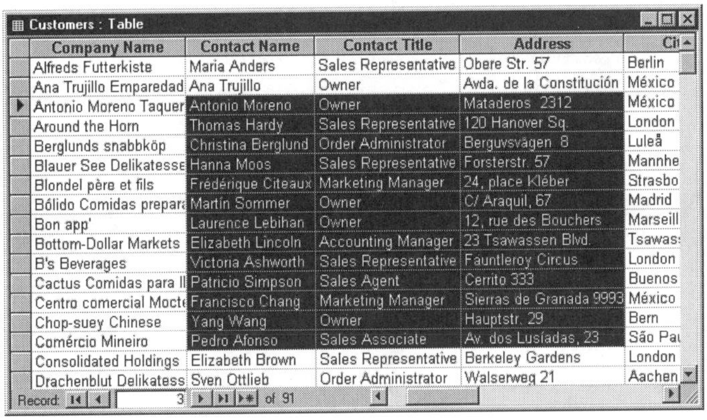

Customers : Table

Company Name	Contact Name	Contact Title	Address	Ci
Alfreds Futterkiste	Maria Anders	Sales Representative	Obere Str. 57	Berlin
Ana Trujillo Emparedad	Ana Trujillo	Owner	Avda. de la Constitución	México
Antonio Moreno Taquer	Antonio Moreno	Owner	Mataderos 2312	México
Around the Horn	Thomas Hardy	Sales Representative	120 Hanover Sq.	London
Berglunds snabbköp	Christina Berglund	Order Administrator	Berguvsvägen 8	Luleå
Blauer See Delikatesse	Hanna Moos	Sales Representative	Forsterstr. 57	Mannhe
Blondel père et fils	Frédérique Citeaux	Marketing Manager	24, place Kléber	Strasbo
Bólido Comidas prepar	Martín Sommer	Owner	C/ Araquil, 67	Madrid
Bon app'	Laurence Lebihan	Owner	12, rue des Bouchers	Marseill
Bottom-Dollar Markets	Elizabeth Lincoln	Accounting Manager	23 Tsawassen Blvd.	Tsawas
B's Beverages	Victoria Ashworth	Sales Representative	Fauntleroy Circus	London
Cactus Comidas para ll	Patricio Simpson	Sales Agent	Cerrito 333	Buenos
Centro comercial Moct	Francisco Chang	Marketing Manager	Sierras de Granada 9993	México
Chop-suey Chinese	Yang Wang	Owner	Hauptstr. 29	Bern
Comércio Mineiro	Pedro Afonso	Sales Associate	Av. dos Lusíadas, 23	São Pa
Consolidated Holdings	Elizabeth Brown	Sales Representative	Berkeley Gardens	London
Drachenblut Delikatess	Sven Ottlieb	Order Administrator	Walserweg 21	Aachen

Record: 3 of 91

Fig. 5.1 Selecting a rectangular data block in Table Datasheet View.

Table 5.3 lists the key combinations for copying or cutting data to and pasting data from the Clipboard. When you paste data from the Clipboard, all the data in the Clipboard is pasted to a single cell if the Clipboard data is of the correct data type and fits within the size of the field. You also can use the Cut, Copy, and Paste buttons on the toolbar as a substitute for the key combinations. Another alternative is to choose Edit, Cut, Copy, or Paste.

Table 5.3 Key Combinations for Windows Clipboard Operations	
Key	**Function**
Ctrl+C	Copies the selection to the Clipboard
Ctrl+Insert	Copies the selection to the Clipboard
Ctrl+V	Pastes the contents of the Clipboard at the location of the caret
Shift+Insert	Pastes the contents of the Clipboard at the location of the caret
Ctrl+X	Copies the selection to the Clipboard, and then deletes it. This operation also is called a *cut*. You can cut only the content of a single cell you select with the caret
Shift+Delete	Copies the selection to the Clipboard, and then deletes it. This operation also is called a *cut*. You can cut only the content of a single cell you select with the caret
Ctrl+Z	Undoes your last Cut, Delete, or Paste operation
Alt+Backspace	Undoes your last Cut, Delete, or Paste operation

> **Note**
>
> If you attempt to paste a rectangular block into a cell, you receive a `Data too long for field` error message. Access then creates a Paste Errors table that contains the contents of the rectangular block. This is a quick way of creating a new table from a block selection.

Using Shortcut Keys for Fields and Text Boxes

You use shortcut keys to minimize the number of keystrokes required to accomplish common data entry tasks. Most shortcut key combinations use the Ctrl key with other keys. Ctrl+C, Ctrl+V, and Ctrl+X for Clipboard operations are examples of global shortcut keys in Windows 95. Table 5.4 lists shortcut keys applicable to field and text box entries.

Table 5.4 Shortcut Keys for Text Boxes and Fields in Tables	
Key	**Function**
Ctrl+; (semicolon)	Inserts the current date
Ctrl+: (colon)	Inserts the current time
Ctrl+' (apostrophe) or Ctrl+" (quote)	Inserts the value from the same field in the preceding record
Ctrl+Enter	Inserts a newline character (carriage return plus line feed) in a text box
Ctrl++ (plus)	Adds a new record to the table
Ctrl+– (minus)	Deletes the current record from the table
Shift+Enter	Saves all changes to the current record

Setting Data Entry Options

> **Tip**
>
> Emulating the data entry key behavior of DOS RDBMs can make a major difference in the acceptance of your database applications by data entry operators who have years of experience with DOS database applications.

You can modify the behavior of the arrow keys and the Tab and Enter keys by choosing Tools, Options and clicking the Keyboard tab to display the keyboard options settings. Table 5.5 lists the available options with the default values shown in bold type. (This table also appears in Chapter 3, "Navigating within Access.") These keyboard options enable you to make the behavior of the data entry keys similar to that of DOS database managers, such as dBASE and Paradox.

Table 5.5   Keyboard Options for the Access System

Option	Group	Function
Don't Move	Move After Enter	When this option is selected, the caret remains in the current field when you press Enter.
Next Field	Move After Enter	When this option is selected, the caret moves to the next field when you press Enter. Use this setting to duplicate xBase behavior.
Next Record	Move After Enter	When this option is selected, the caret moves down the column to the next record when you press Enter.
Next Field	Arrow Key Behavior	If this option is selected, pressing the right or left arrow keys moves the caret to the next field.
Next Character	Arrow Key Behavior	If this option is selected, pressing the right or left arrow keys moves the caret to the previous or next character in the same field. Use this setting if you want to duplicate the behavior of xBase.
Select Entire Field	Behavior Entering Field	When this option is selected, the entire field's contents are selected when you use the arrow keys to move the caret into the field.
Go to Start of Field	Behavior Entering Field	Selecting this option causes the caret to move to the beginning of the field when you use the arrow keys to move the caret into the field.
Go to End of Field	Behavior Entering Field	Selecting this option causes the caret to move to the end of the field when you use the arrow keys to move the caret into the field. Use this setting to duplicate xBase behavior.
Cursor Stops at First/Last Field	None	If this option is selected, it keeps the caret from moving to another record when the left or right arrow keys are pressed, and the caret is in the first or last field of the record.

Adding Records to a Table

Tip

To go to the tentative append record quickly, click the New Record button on the toolbar.

When you create a new table in Datasheet View, it contains 30 empty records with an asterisk (*) in the record selection button of the last (31st) row. Record selection buttons are the gray buttons in the leftmost column of Table Datasheet View. A similar blank record also appears at the end of an existing table if the table is *updatable*. If you open a database for read-only access by marking the Exclusive check box of the Open dialog, this blank record does not appear. Tables attached from other databases also can be read-only; the updatability of attached tables is discussed in Chapter 7, "Linking, Importing, and Exporting Tables."

This book refers to the blank record as the *tentative append* record. The term *tentative* is used because the record is appended to the table only after you enter data in one of the fields and then save the changes you make to the record. You can save changes to a record by moving the record pointer to a different record or by choosing Records, Save Record. The location of the record pointer is indicated by an arrow symbol in the record selection button. The record with the arrow symbol is called the *selected record*.

◄◄ See "Using Input Masks," p. 127

When you place the caret in a field of the tentative append record, the record selection button's asterisk symbol turns into the selected record symbol. When you add data to a field of the selected tentative append record, the selected record symbol changes to the edit symbol (a pencil), and a new tentative append record appears in the row after your addition. Figure 5.2 shows a new record in the process of being added to the Customers table. The Customer ID field has an input mask that requires you to enter five letters, which are capitalized automatically as you enter them. The input mask changes the caret from an I-beam to a reverse-video block.

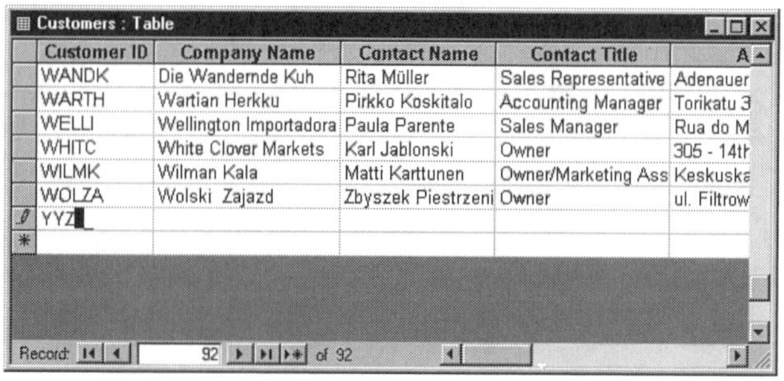

Customer ID	Company Name	Contact Name	Contact Title	A
WANDK	Die Wandernde Kuh	Rita Müller	Sales Representative	Adenauer
WARTH	Wartian Herkku	Pirkko Koskitalo	Accounting Manager	Torikatu 3
WELLI	Wellington Importadora	Paula Parente	Sales Manager	Rua do M
WHITC	White Clover Markets	Karl Jablonski	Owner	305 - 14th
WILMK	Wilman Kala	Matti Karttunen	Owner/Marketing Ass	Keskuska
WOLZA	Wolski Zajazd	Zbyszek Piestrzeni	Owner	ul. Filtrow
YYZ				

Record: ◄◄ ◄ 92 ► ►◄ ►* of 92

Fig. 5.2 Adding a new record to the Customer table.

You can cancel the addition of a new record by deleting all the entries you made in the record before moving the record pointer. If you edited only the first field and did not move the record pointer, you can press the Esc button to cancel the addition.

Selecting, Appending, Replacing, and Deleting Table Records

You can select a single record or a group of records to copy or cut to the Clipboard, or to delete from the table, by the following methods:

- To select a single record, click its record selection button.

- To select a contiguous group of records, click the first record's selection button and then drag the mouse pointer along the record selection buttons to the last record of the group.

- Alternatively, to select a group of records, click the first record's selection button, hold down the Shift key, and then click the last record to include in the group. Alternatively, you can hold down the Shift key and press the down arrow to select a group of records.

> **Note**
>
> You can cut *groups of records* to the Clipboard, deleting them from the table, but you cannot cut *data blocks*. A group of records includes all fields of one or more selected records. A *data block* consists of a selection in a table datasheet that does not include all fields of the selected rows. The Edit, Cut menu choice is enabled for groups of records and disabled for data blocks.

You can cut or copy and append duplicate records to the same table (if appending the duplicate records does not cause a primary-key violation) or to another table. You cannot cut records from a primary table that have dependent records in a related table if you enforce referential integrity. The following methods are applicable to appending or replacing the content of records with records stored in the Clipboard:

- To append records from the Clipboard to a table, choose Edit, Paste Append. (No shortcut key exists for Paste Append.)

- To replace the content of a record(s) with data from the Clipboard, select the record(s) whose content you want to replace and then press Ctrl+V or choose Edit, Paste. Only the number of records you select or the number of records stored in the Clipboard, whichever is fewer, is replaced.

To delete one or more records, select the records you want to delete and press Delete. If deletion is allowed, a message box asks you to confirm your deletion. You cannot undo deletions of records.

Validating Data Entry

The data entered in tables must be accurate if the database is to be valuable to you or your organization. Even the most experienced data entry operators occasionally enter incorrect information. You can add simple tests for the reasonableness of entries by adding short expressions to the Validation Rule text box. If the data entered fails to conform to your validation rule, a message box informs the operator that a violation occurred. Validating data maintains the domain integrity of your tables.

Expressions are the core element of computer programming. Access enables you to create expressions without requiring that you be a programmer, although some familiarity with a programming language is helpful. Expressions are statements used to calculate values using the familiar arithmetic symbols, **+**, **-**, ***** (multiply), and **/** (divide). These symbols are called *operators* because they operate on (use) the values that precede and follow them. The symbols are printed in bold monospace type because they are reserved symbols in Access VBA. The values operated on by operators are called *operands*.

You can also use operators to compare two values; the **<** (less than) and **>** (greater than) symbols are examples of *comparison operators*. **And**, **Or**, **Is**, **Not**, Between, and Like are called *logical operators*. Comparison and logical operators return only **True**, **False**, and unknown (the **Null** value). The **&** operator combines two text entries (character strings or just strings) into a single string; **&** is the equivalent of the **+** used to join (concatenate) character strings in xBase, Excel, and other related applications. (You can use **+** in Access to concatenate strings, but **&** is the preferred symbol because the **&** symbol allows you to concatenate strings, numbers, and dates.) To qualify as an expression, at least one operator must be included. You can construct complex expressions by combining the different operators according to rules that apply to each of the operators involved. The collection of these rules is called *operator syntax*.

    ▶▶ See "Understanding the Elements in Expressions," p. 285

Data validation rules use expressions that result in one of two values: **True** or **False**. Entries in a data cell are accepted if the result of the validation is true and rejected if it is false. If the data is rejected by the validation rule, the text you enter in the Validation Text text box appears in a message box. Chapter 9, "Understanding Operators and Expressions in Access," explains the syntax of Access validation expressions.

Adding Field-Level Validation Rules

Validation rules that restrict the values entered in a field based on only one field are called *field-level validation rules*. Table 5.6 lists the simple field-level validation rules used for some of the fields of the Personnel Actions table you created in Chapter 4, "Working with Access Databases and Tables."

Table 5.6	**Validation Criteria for the Fields of the Personnel Actions Table**	
Field Name	**Validation Rule**	**Validation Text**
paID	>0	Please enter a valid employee ID number.
paType	"H" **Or** "S" **Or** "Q" **Or** "Y" **Or** "B" **Or** "C"	Only H, S, Q, Y, B, and C codes can be entered.
paInitiated By	>0	Please enter a valid supervisor ID number.
paScheduledDate	Between **Date**() -3650 **And** **Date**() +365	Scheduled dates cannot be more than 10 years ago or more than one year from now.
paApprovedBy	>0 **Or Is Null**	Enter a valid manager ID number or leave blank if not approved.
paRating	Between 0 **And** 9 **Or Is Null**	Rating range is 0 for terminated employees, 1 to 9, or blank.
paAmount	No rule	No text
paComments	No rule	No text

The validation rules for fields that require employee ID numbers are not, in their present form, capable of ensuring that a valid ID number is entered. You could enter a number greater than the total number of employees in the firm. The validation rule for the paID field tests the EmployeeID number field of the Employees table to determine whether the paID number is present. You don't need to create this test because the rules of referential integrity, discussed in the "Enforcing Referential Integrity" section in Chapter 4, "Working with Access Databases and Tables," perform this validation for you. Validation rules for paInitiatedBy and paApprovedBy require tests based on entries in the Employees table.

To add the validation rules to the Personnel Actions table, follow these steps:

1. Open the Personnel Actions table, if it isn't already open, by double-clicking the table name in the Database window.

2. Return to design mode by clicking the Design View button. The paID field is selected.

3. Press F6 to switch to the Field Properties window, and then move to the Validation Rule text box.

4. Enter **>0**. Press Enter to accept the entry and move to the Validation Text text box.

5. Type **Please enter a valid employee ID number** in the Validation Text text box. The text scrolls to the left when it becomes longer than can be displayed in the text box. To display the beginning of the text, press Home. Press End to position the caret at the last character. Press Enter to complete the operation.

6. Move to the Required text box and enter **Yes**, or open the drop-down list and click Yes. Figure 5.3 shows your entries in the Field Properties text boxes.

7. Press F6 to switch back to the Table Design grid. Move to the next field, and press F6.

8. Enter the validation rule and validation text for the six remaining fields listed in table 5.6 that use data entry validation, repeating steps 2 through 5. Square brackets ([ ]) enclose field names that include punctuation or spaces. Enter **Yes** in the Required text box for the paType, paInitiatedBy, and paScheduledDate fields.

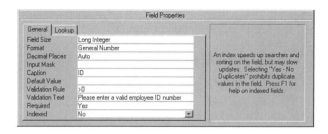

Fig. 5.3 The Field Properties text boxes showing your first validation entries.

You test your validation rule entries in the "Entering Personnel Actions Table Data and Testing Validation Rules" section later in this chapter.

Adding Table-Level Validation Rules and Using the Expression Builder

One of the fields, paEffectiveDate, requires a validation rule that depends on the value of paScheduledDate. The effective date of the personnel department's action should not be prior to the scheduled date for the review that results in the action. Access 1.x enabled you to refer to one or more field names when creating a field-level validation rule expression. Like Access 2.0, however, you cannot refer to other field names in a validation rule expression in Access 95; instead, you enter the validation rule in the Table Properties dialog. Validation rules in which the value of one field depends on a previously entered value in another field of the current record are called *table-level validation rules*.

The following steps create a table-level validation rule for the paEffectiveDate field:

1. Click the Properties button on the toolbar to display the Table Properties dialog (see fig. 5.4).

2. Enter **Personnel Department Actions** in the Description text box, as shown in figure 5.4.

3. Move the caret to the Validation Rule text box. Click the ellipsis button that appears to right of the Validation Rule text box (see fig. 5.5) to display the Expression Builder dialog. The current table, Personnel Actions, is selected in the left list, and the fields of the table appear in the center list.

4. Double-click **paEffectiveDate** entry in the center list to place **[paEffectiveDate]** in the expression text box at the top of the dialog.

5. Enter **>=** in the expression text box and double-click **paScheduledDate** in the center list to add **[paScheduledDate]** to the expression.

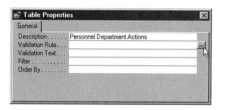

Fig. 5.4   Adding a table description in the Table Properties dialog.

6. You also want to accept a blank entry if the effective date of the personnel action is not scheduled, so add **Or [paEffectiveDate] Is Null** to the expression. Your expression appears as shown in figure 5.5.

7. Click OK to add the table-level validation rule and close the Expression Builder dialog.

8. Move to the Validation Text text box and enter **Effective date must be on or after scheduled date**. Your Table Properties dialog appears as shown in figure 5.6.

9. Click the Close Window button of the Table Properties dialog or click the Properties button on the toolbar to close the dialog.

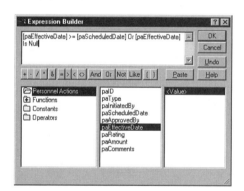

Fig. 5.5   Creating a validation rule with the Expression Builder.

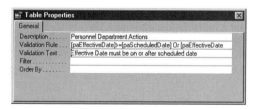

Fig. 5.6   Adding Validation Text to a table-level validation rule.

> **Note**
>
> You can create more than one table-level validation rule by using the And reserved word and then adding another expression that involves the relationship between other fields of the table. However, Access only provides a single Validation Text message that appears when you violate any of the table-level validation rules.

Adding Records to the Personnel Actions Table

Now you have a chance to test your work in creating the Personnel Actions table and to check whether Access is enforcing referential integrity. The initial entries for each of the nine employees of Northwind Trading are shown in table 5.7. The entries for paScheduledDate and paEffectiveDate are taken from the HireDate field of the Employees table. The HireDate field of the Employees table now is superfluous because it duplicates the data in the Personnel Actions table. You delete the HireDate field in a later chapter. Feel free to be as generous or as parsimonious as you want with the monthly salaries shown in the paAmount field.

Table 5.7   First Nine Entries for the Personnel Actions Table

ID	Type	Initiated By	Scheduled	Approved By	Effective Date	New Amount	Comments
1	H	1	01-May-92		01-May-92	2,000	Hired
2	H	1	14-Aug-92		14-Aug-92	3,500	Hired
3	H	1	01-Apr-92		01-Apr-92	2,250	Hired
4	H	2	03-May-93	2	03-May-93	2,250	Hired
5	H	2	17-Oct-93	2	17-Oct-93	2,500	Hired
6	H	5	17-Oct-93	2	17-Oct-93	4,000	Hired
7	H	5	02-Jan-94	2	02-Jan-94	3,000	Hired
8	H	2	05-Mar-94	2	05-Mar-94	2,500	Hired
9	H	5	15-Nov-94	2	15-Nov-94	3,000	Hired

Entering historical information in a table in Datasheet View is a relatively fast process for an experienced data entry operator. This process also gives you a chance to test your default entries and Format properties for each field. You can enter bogus values that don't comply with your validation rules to verify that your rules are operational. To add the first nine historical records to the Personnel Actions table using the data from table 5.7, follow these steps:

1. Click the Datasheet button on the toolbar to return to Datasheet View in run mode, if necessary. The caret is positioned in the paID field of the default first record.

2. Enter the paID of the employee. Press Enter, Tab, or the right-arrow key to move to the next field. When you do this, a new default blank record is added to the view but not to the content of the table. A new record is added to the table only when a value is entered in one of the fields of the default blank record.

3. Type the numeric value for the paInitiatedBy field. (You need a value in this field for each employee because of the field's validation rule.) Press Enter, Tab, or the right-arrow key to move to the next field.

4. Type the paScheduledDate entry. You don't need to delete the default date value. When you type a new date, it replaces the default value. Then press Enter, Tab, or the right-arrow key.

5. If a value is in the table for paApprovedBy, type the value. Then press Enter, Tab, or the right-arrow key.

6. Type the paEffectiveDate entry. Press Enter, Tab, or the right-arrow key twice to skip the Rating field, which is inapplicable to newly hired employees.

7. Enter the paAmount of the monthly salary at the time of hiring. Press Enter, Tab, or the right-arrow key.

8. Type Hired in the paComments field, or any other comment you care to make. Press Enter, Tab, or the right-arrow key. The caret moves to the paID field of the next default blank record.

9. Repeat steps 2 through 9 for eight more employees in table 5.7. (You can add similar records for employees 10 through 15 if you want.)

When you complete your entries, your table appears as shown in figure 5.7.

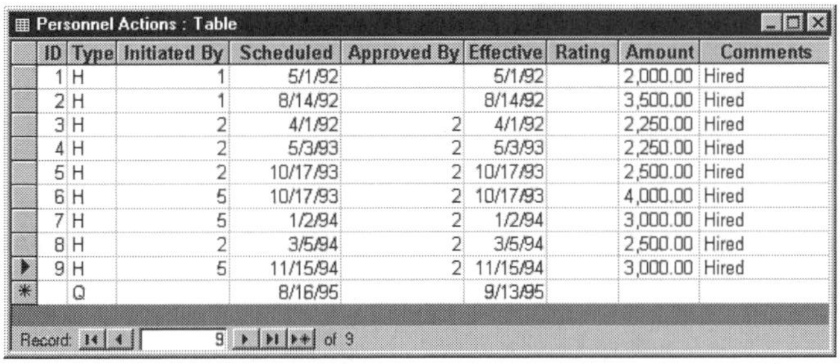

ID	Type	Initiated By	Scheduled	Approved By	Effective	Rating	Amount	Comments
1	H	1	5/1/92		5/1/92		2,000.00	Hired
2	H	1	8/14/92		8/14/92		3,500.00	Hired
3	H	2	4/1/92	2	4/1/92		2,250.00	Hired
4	H	2	5/3/93	2	5/3/93		2,250.00	Hired
5	H	2	10/17/93	2	10/17/93		2,500.00	Hired
6	H	5	10/17/93	2	10/17/93		4,000.00	Hired
7	H	5	1/2/94	2	1/2/94		3,000.00	Hired
8	H	2	3/5/94	2	3/5/94		2,500.00	Hired
9	H	5	11/15/94	2	11/15/94		3,000.00	Hired
*	Q		8/16/95		9/13/95			

Record: 9 of 9

Fig. 5.7   The first nine records of the Personnel Actions table.

Troubleshooting

Error messages appear when I attempt to enter data in fields with validation rules.

Edit or reenter the data to conform to the data types and validation rules for the field. Error messages that appear when you enter the data correctly indicate that something is amiss with your validation rules. In this case, change to design mode and review your validation rules for the offending fields against those listed in table 5.6. You may want to remove the validation rule temporarily by selecting the entire expression and cutting the rule to the Clipboard. (You can paste the expression back into the text box later.) Return to run mode to continue with your entries.

Entering Personnel Actions Table Data and Testing Validation Rules

You can experiment with entering table data and testing your validation rules at the same time. Testing database applications often requires much more time and effort than creating them. The following basic tests are required to confirm your validation rules:

■ *Referential integrity.* Type **25** in the paID field and **2** in the paInitiatedBy field of the default blank record, record number 10, and then press the up-arrow key. Pressing the up-arrow key tells Access that you are finished with the current record and to move up to the preceding record with the caret in the same field. Access then tests the primary-key integrity before enabling you to leave the current record. The message box shown in figure 5.8 appears. Click OK, or press Enter.

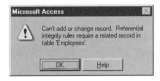

Fig. 5.8   The message box indicating that an entry violates referential integrity rules.

■ *No duplicates restriction for primary key.* In the record just added, attempt to duplicate exactly the entries for record number 9, and then press the up-arrow key. You see the message box shown in figure 5.9. Click OK, or press Enter.

Fig. 5.9   The message box that appears when a record with a duplicate key is added to a field indexed with the No Duplicates option.

- paType *validation.* Type **x** and press the right-arrow key to display the message box with the validation text you entered for the paType field, shown in figure 5.10. Click OK, or press Enter.

Fig. 5.10   A message box created by an entry that violates a validation rule.

Type **q**, and move to the paInitiatedBy field. When the caret leaves the paType field, the **q** changes to Q because of the > format character used. Type **0** (an invalid employee ID number), and press the right-arrow key to display the message box shown in figure 5.11. Click OK, or press Enter.

Fig. 5.11   The message box that appears in response to an invalid employee ID number entry.

Continue with the testing. Type a date, such as 1/1/80, for the paScheduled Date, and type the same date for the paEffective Date to display the error message boxes with the validation text you entered. Enter a valid date after the test. To edit a field rather than retype it, press F2 to deselect the entire field and display the caret for editing. F2 toggles selection and editing operations.

When you finish your testing, click the selection button of the last field you added, and then press Delete. The confirmation message box shown in figure 5.12 appears.

Fig. 5.12   The confirmation box for deletion of one or more records.

From Here...

This chapter outlined the various key combinations you can use to make keyboard-oriented data entry more efficient. The basic procedures for selecting, adding, editing, and deleting records also were covered in detail. The methods are applicable not only to tables but also to updatable queries in Datasheet View and text box controls you add to forms. You learned how to use the Windows Clipboard to cut, copy, and paste fields and entire records or groups of records. Adding and testing validation rules for data entry completed the chapter.

See the following chapters for information related to the topics covered in this chapter:

■ Chapter 6, "Sorting, Finding, and Filtering Data in Tables," describes how to use Access's built-in sort feature, search feature, search and replace feature, and filters to locate records that meet the criteria you set. This chapter also describes how to make bulk changes to field data.

■ Chapter 7, "Linking, Importing, and Exporting Tables," explains how to import data from your existing database tables, worksheets, or text files, and how to export table data in a variety of useful formats.

Chapter 6

Sorting, Finding, and Filtering Data in Tables

Microsoft Access provides a variety of sorting and filtering features that make customizing the display data in Table Datasheet View a quick and simple process. Sorting and filtering records in tables is quite useful when you use data in a table to create a mailing list or print a particular set of records.

Access also includes versatile search (find) and replace facilities that enable you to locate every record that matches a value you specify, and then, optionally, change that value. If you have a large table, Access's find facility enables you to quickly locate the needles in the haystacks. Search and replace often is needed when you import data from another database or a worksheet, which is the subject of the next chapter.

The sorting, filtering, searching, and replacing features of Access actually are implemented by behind-the-scenes queries that Access creates for you. When you reach Part II of this book, which deals exclusively with queries, you'll probably choose to implement these features with Access's graphical query-by-example (QBE) methods. Learning the fundamentals of these operations with tables, however, makes understanding queries easier. You also can apply filters to query result sets, use the find feature with queries in Datasheet View, and use search and replace on the result sets of updatable queries. For readers who are xBase users or know SQL, statements in these two languages equivalent to the operation being performed are given where applicable.

Sorting Table Data

A fundamental requirement of a database development environment is the capability to sort records quickly so that they appear in the desired sequence. Early desktop database managers, such as dBASE II and III/III+, required that you create a new copy of a table if you wanted physically to sort the table's records in a new order. Creating and specifying an index on a field table enabled you to display or print the table in the order of the index. If you wanted to sort the data by two or more fields, however, you either had to create a composite index on the fields, or pre-sort the data in the order of one or more fields, and then apply the single-field index.

In this chapter, you learn to

- Sort tables on one or more fields
- Show and hide columns of tables
- Find records matching values you enter
- Search for and replace data in table fields
- Apply filters so that only certain records appear
- Customize your Table Datasheet View
- Export sorted and filtered data to a file

Modern desktop database development systems, such as Access, never require that you physically sort the table. Instead, the physical location of the records in the file is the order in which the records were entered. By default, Access displays records in the order of the primary key. This behavior is similar to that of Borland's Paradox. If your table doesn't have a primary key, the records display in the order you enter them. Unlike dBASE and its clones, you cannot choose a specific Access index to alter the order in which the records display in Table Datasheet View of the user interface (UI). You can, however, specify an index to order records of tables you manipulate with Access VBA code. Access uses sorting methods to display records in the desired order. If an index exists on the field in which you sort the records, the sorting process is much quicker. Access automatically uses indexes, if indexes exist, to speed the sort. This process is called *query optimization*. Access's indexes and query optimization methods are discussed in Chapter 23, "Exploring Relational Database Design and Implementation."

The following sections show you how to use Access's sorting methods to display records in the sequence you want. The Customers table of Northwind.mdb is used for the majority of the examples in this chapter because it is typical of a table whose data you can use for a variety of purposes.

Freezing Display of a Table Field

If the table you are sorting contains more fields than you can display in Access's Table Datasheet View, you can freeze one or more fields to make viewing the sorted data easier. Freezing a field makes the field visible at all times, regardless of which other fields you display by manipulating the horizontal scroll bar. To freeze the Customer ID and Company Name fields of the Customers table, follow these steps:

1. Open the Customers table in Datasheet View.

2. Click the field header button of the Customer ID field to select the first column.

3. Hold the Shift key down and click the Company Name field header button. Alternatively, you can drag the mouse from the Customer ID field to the Company Name field to select the first and second columns.

4. Choose F__o__rmat, Free__z__e Columns.

When you scroll to fields to the right of the frozen columns, your Datasheet View of the Customers table appears as illustrated in figure 6.1. A solid vertical line replaces the half-tone grid line between the frozen and thawed (selectable) field columns.

> **Note**
>
> If you frequently freeze columns, you can add the Freeze Columns button from the Datasheet collection to your Datasheet toolbar. See Chapter 13, "Designing Custom Multitable Forms," for how to customize your toolbars.

Customers : Table						
Customer ID	Company Name	Region	Postal Code	Country		
BERGS	Berglunds snabbköp		S-958 22	Sweden	0	
BLAUS	Blauer See Delikatessen		68306	Germany	0	
BLONP	Blondel père et fils		67000	France	8	
BOLID	Bólido Comidas preparadas		28023	Spain	(S	
BONAP	Bon app'		13008	France	9	
BOTTM	Bottom-Dollar Markets	BC	T2F 8M4	Canada	(6	
BSBEV	B's Beverages		EC2 5NT	UK	(	
CACTU	Cactus Comidas para llevar		1010	Argentina	(1	
CENTC	Centro comercial Moctezuma		05022	Mexico	(5	
CHOPS	Chop-suey Chinese		3012	Switzerland	0	
COMMI	Comércio Mineiro	SP	05432-043	Brazil	(1	
CONSH	Consolidated Holdings		WX1 6LT	UK	(	
DRACD	Drachenblut Delikatessen		52066	Germany	0	

Record: 2 of 91

Fig. 6.1 The Customers table of Northwind.mdb with the Customer ID and Company Names fields frozen.

Sorting Data on a Single Field

When creating a mailing list, a standard practice in the United States is to sort the records in ascending ZIP Code order. This practice often is observed in other countries that use postal codes. To sort the Customers table in the order of the Postal Code field, follow these steps:

1. Select the Postal Code field by clicking the field header button of the Postal Code field.

2. Click the Sort Ascending (A-Z) button of the toolbar or choose Records, Sort, Ascending.

▶▶ See "Writing Select Queries in SQL," p. 885

Your Customers table quickly is sorted into the order shown in figure 6.2. Sorting a table is equivalent to specifying the selected field as the table name of the ORDER BY clause of an SQL statement, as in

```
SELECT * FROM Customers ORDER BY [Postal Code]
```

To perform the same operation with xBase, use the following statements at the command line:

```
USE customer INDEX cust_zip
{LIST|BROWSE}
```

Sorting Data on Multiple Fields

Although the sort operation in the preceding section accomplishes exactly what you specify, the result is less than useful because of the vagaries of postal code formats used in different countries. What's needed here is a multiple-field sort on the Country field first and then the Postal Code field. Thus, you might select both the Country and the Postal Code fields to perform the multi-column sort. The Quick Sort technique, however, automatically applies the sorting priority to the leftmost field you select, Postal Code. Access offers two methods of handling this problem: Reorder the field display or specify the sort order in a Filter window. Filters are discussed in the "Filtering Table Data" section, later in this chapter, so follow these steps to use the reordering process:

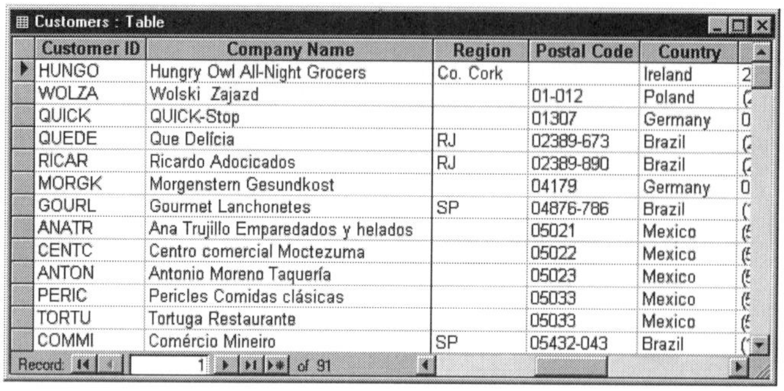

Customer ID	Company Name	Region	Postal Code	Country	
▶ HUNGO	Hungry Owl All-Night Grocers	Co. Cork		Ireland	2
WOLZA	Wolski Zajazd		01-012	Poland	G
QUICK	QUICK-Stop		01307	Germany	0
QUEDE	Que Delícia	RJ	02389-673	Brazil	G
RICAR	Ricardo Adocicados	RJ	02389-890	Brazil	G
MORGK	Morgenstern Gesundkost		04179	Germany	0
GOURL	Gourmet Lanchonetes	SP	04876-786	Brazil	(
ANATR	Ana Trujillo Emparedados y helados		05021	Mexico	(
CENTC	Centro comercial Moctezuma		05022	Mexico	(
ANTON	Antonio Moreno Taquería		05023	Mexico	(
PERIC	Pericles Comidas clásicas		05033	Mexico	(
TORTU	Tortuga Restaurante		05033	Mexico	(
COMMI	Comércio Mineiro	SP	05432-043	Brazil	(

Record: ◀◀ ◀ 1 ▶ ▶◀ ▶* of 91

Fig. 6.2 Applying an ascending sort order to the Postal Code field of the Customers table.

1. Select the Country field by clicking its field header button.

2. Hold the left mouse button down and drag the Country field to the left of the Postal Code field. Release the left mouse button to drop the field in its new location.

3. Press the Shift key and click the header button of the Postal Code field to select both the Country and Postal Code columns.

4. Click the Sort Ascending button of the toolbar or choose Records, Sort, Ascending.

The sorted table, shown in figure 6.3, now makes much more sense. Applying a multi-field sort on a table (sometimes called a *composite sort*) is the equivalent of the following SQL statement:

```
SELECT * FROM Customers ORDER BY Country, [Postal Code]
```

If you had a composite xBase index derived from the country and post_code fields, the statements in xBase to achieve the same result are the same as those in the preceding section.

Customer ID	Company Name	Region	Country	Postal Code	
▶ RANCH	Rancho grande		Argentina	1010	(
OCEAN	Océano Atlántico Ltda.		Argentina	1010	(
CACTU	Cactus Comidas para llevar		Argentina	1010	(
PICCO	Piccolo und mehr		Austria	5020	6
ERNSH	Ernst Handel		Austria	8010	7
MAISD	Maison Dewey		Belgium	B-1180	((
SUPRD	Suprêmes délices		Belgium	B-6000	((
QUEDE	Que Delícia	RJ	Brazil	02389-673	G
RICAR	Ricardo Adocicados	RJ	Brazil	02389-890	G
GOURL	Gourmet Lanchonetes	SP	Brazil	04876-786	(
COMMI	Comércio Mineiro	SP	Brazil	05432-043	(
FAMIA	Família Arquibaldo	SP	Brazil	05442-030	(
HANAR	Hanari Carnes	RJ	Brazil	05454-876	G

Record: ◀◀ ◀ 1 ▶ ▶◀ ▶* of 91

Fig. 6.3 The effect of a multiple-field sort on the Country and Postal Code fields of the Customers table.

Removing a Table Sort Order and Thawing Columns

After you freeze columns and apply sort orders to a table, you might want to return the table to its original condition. To do so, Access offers you the following choices:

- To return to the Datasheet View of an Access table with a primary key to its original sort order, select the field(s) that comprise the primary key (in the order of the primary key fields).

- To return to the original order when the table has no primary key field, close, save the changes, and reopen the table.

- To thaw your frozen columns, choose Format, Unfreeze All Columns.

- To return the sequence of fields to its original state, either drag the fields you moved back to their prior position or close the table without saving your changes.

If you make substantial changes to the layout of the table and apply a sort order, it usually is quicker to close and reopen the table. (Don't save your changes to the table layout.)

Removing the sort order from a field is the equivalent of issuing the following SQL statement:

```
SELECT * FROM Customers
```

Finding Matching Records in a Table

To search for and select records with field values that match (or partially match) a particular value, use Access's Find feature. To find Luleå—a relatively large city in northern Sweden close to the Arctic Circle—in the City field, follow these steps:

1. Select the field—City—you want to search. You can select the City field by either clicking the header button or placing the caret in the field.

2. Click the Find button of the toolbar or choose Edit, Find to display the Find in field dialog shown in figure 6.4.

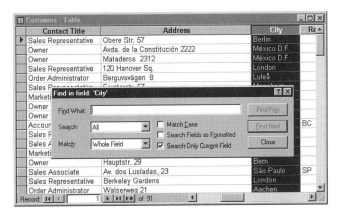

Fig. 6.4 Opening the Find in field dialog with the City field selected.

3. Type the name of the city, **Lulea**, in the Find What text box (see fig. 6.5). When you make an entry in the Find What text box, the Find First and Find Next command buttons are enabled.

4. Select Whole Field from the Match drop-down list. (The other choices, Start of Field and Any Part of Field, are just as effective in this case.)

5. The default value of the Search option button is satisfactory, and matching case or format is not important here.

6. Click the Find First button. If you do not have a Scandinavian keyboard, Access displays the "finished searching" message box shown in figure 6.6.

Fig. 6.5 Attempting to find Luleå in the City field.

Fig. 6.6 The message box that appears when Access cannot find a match to the content of the Find What text box.

The "finished searching" message indicates that the Find feature did not locate a match between the present position of the record pointer and the last record of the table. The reason Access missed your entry is that the Scandinavian diacritical "°" is missing over the *a* in *Lulea*. In the ANSI character set, "a" has a value of 97, and "å" has a value of 229.

Note

You can enter international (extended) characters in the Find What text box by typing the English letters and then using Windows 95's Character Map (Charmap.exe) applet to find and copy the extended character to the Clipboard. (Don't worry about choosing the correct font.) Paste the character into the Find What text box at the appropriate location.

If the letters preceding an extended character are sufficient to define your search parameter, follow this set of steps to find Luleå:

1. Type **Lule**, or delete the *a* from *Lulea*, in the Find What text box.

2. Select Start of Field from the Where drop-down list.

3. Click the Find First button. Access finds and highlights *Luleå* in the City field, as shown in figure 6.7.

You also can find entries in any part of the field. If you type **ule** in the Find What text box and choose Any Part of Field from the drop-down list, you get a match on *Luleå*. However, you also match *Thule*, the location of the Bluie West One airfield (AKA Thule AFB) in Greenland.

Fig. 6.7 Finding a record that contains a special character.

Note

Searching all fields for an entry is usually much slower than searching a single field, especially if you have an index on the field being searched. Unless you specify the Any Part of Field option, Access uses the index to speed the searching operation.

Following is a list of the options available in the Find in Field dialog:

- To specify a case-sensitive search, mark the Match Case check box.

- To search using the field's format, mark the Search Fields as Formatted check box. This enables you to enter a search term that matches the formatted appearance of the field rather than the native (unformatted) value if you applied a Format property value to the field. Using the Search Fields as Formatted option slows the search operation; indexes are not used.

- To find additional matches, if any, click the Find Next button. If the Search option is set to Down, then clicking the Find First button starts the search at the first record in the table, regardless of the current position of the record pointer. If the Search option is set to All, then clicking the Find First button starts the search at the current record pointer.

- To start the search at the last record of the table, select Up in the Search drop-down list.

SQL has no direct equivalent to a Find First or Find Next operation. SQL is a set-oriented language, so the following SQL statement:

```
SELECT * FROM Customers WHERE City = "Luleå"
```

returns the set of all records that meet the criterion. The SQL CURSOR construct enables you to move between records of a set, but the CURSOR reserved word is not supported in Access SQL and its use is beyond the scope of the SQL discussion in this chapter.

The following statements in xBase find the first and second records meeting the criteria:

```
LOCATE FOR city = "Luleå"
CONTINUE
```

Neither xBase's FIND or SEEK commands, both of which require an index on the field, provide the Find Next function. FIND and SEEK only duplicate the effect of the Find First button.

Replacing Matched Field Values Automatically

A variation on the Find in field dialog's theme—the Replace in field dialog—enables you to replace values selectively in fields that match the entry in the Find What text box. To display the Replace in file dialog, choose Edit, Replace. (No button on the standard Table Datasheet toolbar exists for the search and replace feature.) The derivation of the short-cut key combination for Edit, Replace—Ctrl+H—is a mystery.

The entries to search for *Luleå* and replace with *Lulea* appear in figure 6.8. To replace entries selectively, click the Find Next button, and then click the Replace button for those records in which you want to replace the value. You can do a bulk replace in all matching records by clicking the Replace All button.

Fig. 6.8 The Replace in field dialog.

▶▶ See "Updating Values of Multiple Records in a Table," p. 379

In SQL, the statement to replace all occurrences of *Luleå* with *Lulea* is as follows:

```
UPDATE Customers SET City = 'Lulea' WHERE City = 'Luleå'
```

▶▶ See "Specifying Action Query Syntax," p. 896

The xBase dot prompt command to replace the first or all instances of *Luleå*—if you have the appropriate Scandinavian code page loaded in DOS—is as follows:

```
REPLACE [ALL] city WITH 'Lulea' FOR city = 'Luleå'
```

Filtering Table Data

Access enables you to apply a filter to specify the records that appear in the Datasheet View of a table or a query result set. For example, if you wanted to view only those customers located in Germany, you would use a filter to limit the displayed records to only those whose Country field contains the text "Germany." Access gives you three different ways to apply filters to the data in a table:

- *Filter by Selection*. This is the fastest and simplest way to apply a filter. In a filter by selection, you establish the filter criteria by selecting all or part of the data in one of the table's fields; Access displays only records that match the selected sample. You can only filter records based on criteria in a single field of the table with a filter by selection.

- *Filter by Form*. This is the second fastest way to apply a filter. In a filter by form, you enter the filter criteria into a blank datasheet form of the table; Access displays records that match the combined criteria in each field. Use a filter by form to quickly filter records based on criteria in more than one field.

- *Advanced Filter/Sort*. This is the most powerful, and also the most difficult type of filter to use. With an advanced filter/sort you can make an Access filter do double-duty because you also can add a sort order on one or more fields.

Each of the three available types of filters is described in the next few sections. Filter by Selection and Filter by Form are new features of Access 95.

Filtering by Selection

Creating a filter by selection is as easy as selecting (highlighting) text in a field. When you apply the filter, Access uses the selected text to determine which records to display. Table 6.1 summarizes what records are displayed, depending on how you select text in the field. In all cases, Access applies the filter criteria only to the field in which you have selected text. Filter by selection only allows you to establish filter criteria for a single field at one time.

Table 6.1 How Selected Text Affects Filter by Selection	
Selected Text	**Filter Effect**
Entire field	Displays only records whose fields contain exactly matching values.
Beginning of field	Displays records where the text at the beginning of the field matches the selected text.
End of field	Displays records where the text at the end of the field matches the selected text.
Characters anywhere in field, except beginning or end	Displays records where any part of the field matches anywhere in the selected text.

To create a Filter by Selection on the Customers table (displaying only those customers located in Germany), follow these steps:

1. If necessary, open the Customers table in Datasheet View, and use the scroll bars to make the Country field column visible in the table window.

2. Click the First Record button to make the first record in the table the active record.

3. Select all of the text in the Country field of the first record in the Customers table. (This should be **Germany**.)

4. Click the Filter by Selection button on the toolbar, or choose <u>R</u>ecords, <u>F</u>ilter, Filter by <u>S</u>election. Access applies the filter, as shown in figure 6.9.

Notice that the Apply Filter button on the toolbar is now displayed in a "down" position, indicating that a filter is being applied to the table and the tooltip changes to "Remove Filter." The legend "(Filtered)" is also added to the record selection and information bar at the bottom of the table window.

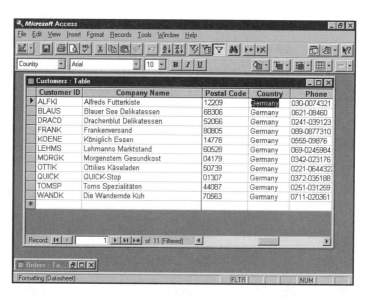

Fig. 6.9 A Filter by Selection applied to the Customers Table to display only those customers in Germany. (The Customer ID and Company Name columns have been frozen.)

> **Tip**
>
> Use the Find dialog to quickly locate the first record of a group you're interested in filtering, and then apply a filter by selection.

As mentioned previously, you can also apply a filter by selection based on partially selected text in a field. Figure 6.10 shows the Customers table with a different filter by selection applied—this time, only the letters **er** in the Country field were selected.

Fig. 6.10   The Customers table, this time filtered by selecting the letters "er" in the Country field.

> **Note**
>
> To remove a filter, click the Remove Filter button on the toolbar. This is really the same as the Apply Filter button—the button is "down" whenever a filter is in effect, and "up" otherwise.

Filtering by Form

Filtering by form is slightly more complex than filtering by selection, but allows you to filter records based on criteria in more than one field at a time. For example, you saw in the preceding section how to use a filter by selection to view only those customers located in Germany. To further limit the displayed records to those customers located in Berlin, Germany, use a filter by form.

▶▶ See "Understanding the Elements in Expressions," p. 285
▶▶ See "Creating Access Expressions," p. 307
▶▶ See "Expressions for Query Criteria," p. 308

In a filter by form, Access presents you with a blank form for the table (see fig. 6.11). This window is called a *form* to distinguish it from the table design grid and the table datasheet windows, although it is not the same as the data-entry forms discussed later in this book. You can use any query expression you want in the fields of the filter by form window. Query expressions are described Chapter 9, "Understanding Operators and Expressions in Access." You can combine criteria in a filter by form with either a logical Or condition or a logical And condition. For example, you can filter the Customers table to display only those customers in the United States or in Canada. As another example, you could filter the Customers table to display only those customers in the United States and in zip codes beginning with the digit 9 (such as 94609 or 90807).

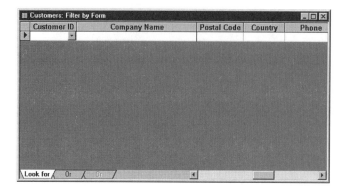

Fig. 6.11   An empty Filter by Form window for the Customers table.

To create a Filter by Form on the Customers table (displaying only those customers located in the United States or Canada), follow these steps:

1. If necessary, open the Customers table in Datasheet View, and use the scroll bars to make the Country field column visible in the table window.

 2. Click the Filter by Form button on the toolbar, or choose Records, Filter, Filter by Form. Access displays the Filter by Form window (refer to fig. 6.11).

3. Use the scroll bars to make the Country field visible in the Filter by Form window, if necessary. (The Customer ID and Company Name columns in the figures have been frozen, as described previously in this chapter.)

 4. Click inside the Country field to move the caret to that field, and then click the arrow to open the Country list box, or press F4. The drop-down list contains a list of all the unique values in the Country list box (see fig. 6.12).

5. Select **Canada** in the list box, as shown in figure 6.12. Access automatically adds the quotation marks around the value you select, and enters it into the Country field form box.

6. Click the Or tab at the bottom of the Filter by Form window. Access combines criteria that you enter on separate tabs in the Filter by Form window with a logical Or condition.

 7. Click the arrow to open the Country list box, or press F4, and select **USA** from the drop-down list (see fig. 6.13).

 8. Click the Apply Filter button, or choose Filter, Apply Filter/Sort. Access applies the new filter to the table, displaying the records shown in figure 6.14.

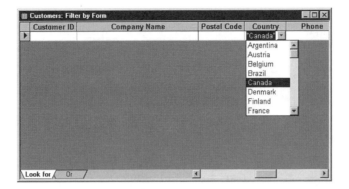

Fig. 6.12   Selecting the first country to filter for in the Customers table.

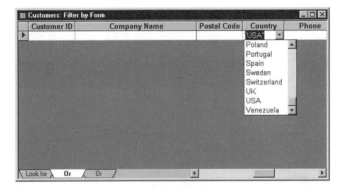

Fig. 6.13   Selecting the Or condition for the Filter by Form in the Customers table.

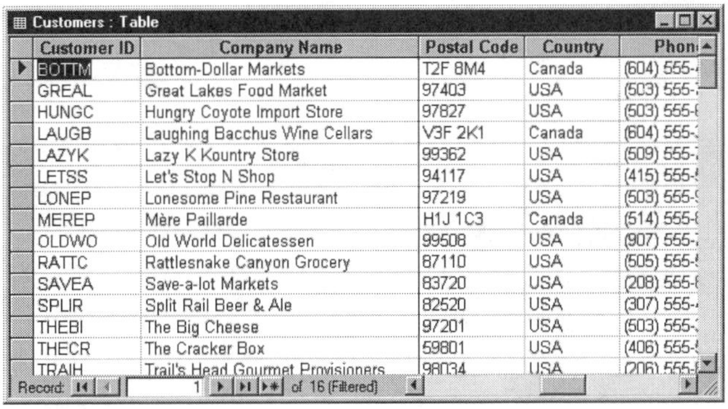

Customer ID	Company Name	Postal Code	Country	Phone
BOTTM	Bottom-Dollar Markets	T2F 8M4	Canada	(604) 555-
GREAL	Great Lakes Food Market	97403	USA	(503) 555-
HUNGC	Hungry Coyote Import Store	97827	USA	(503) 555-
LAUGB	Laughing Bacchus Wine Cellars	V3F 2K1	Canada	(604) 555-
LAZYK	Lazy K Kountry Store	99362	USA	(509) 555-
LETSS	Let's Stop N Shop	94117	USA	(415) 555-
LONEP	Lonesome Pine Restaurant	97219	USA	(503) 555-
MEREP	Mère Paillarde	H1J 1C3	Canada	(514) 555-
OLDWO	Old World Delicatessen	99508	USA	(907) 555-
RATTC	Rattlesnake Canyon Grocery	87110	USA	(505) 555-
SAVEA	Save-a-lot Markets	83720	USA	(208) 555-
SPLIR	Split Rail Beer & Ale	82520	USA	(307) 555-
THEBI	The Big Cheese	97201	USA	(503) 555-
THECR	The Cracker Box	59801	USA	(406) 555-
TRAIH	Trail's Head Gourmet Provisioners	98034	USA	(206) 555-

Fig. 6.14   The result of the Filter by Form, displaying only those records for customers in Canada or the USA.

You can also combine filter criteria in a logical And condition by entering criteria in more than one field on the same tab of the form window. For example, say you wanted to filter the Orders table to find all orders handled by Nancy Davolio and shipped to France. You could easily use a Filter by Form to do so, as the following example shows:

1. Open the Orders table, if necessary, and freeze the Order ID, Customer, and Employee columns, then use the field scroll bars to position the Ship Country field so that it is visible in the window (see fig. 6.15). (Freezing the columns isn't an essential step, but it makes setting up the filter and viewing the filtered data easier.)

2. Click the Filter by Form button on the toolbar, or choose <u>R</u>ecords, <u>F</u>ilter, <u>F</u>ilter by Form. Access displays the Filter by Form window.

3. Click the Clear Grid button on the toolbar, or choose <u>E</u>dit, Cl<u>e</u>ar Filter to clear any previous filter criteria from the Filter by Form grid.

4. Use the drop-down list in the Employee field to select **Davolio, Nancy** and then use the drop-down list in the Ship Country field to select **France** (see fig. 6.16).

5. Click the Apply Filter button, or choose Filte<u>r</u>, <u>A</u>pply Filter/Sort. Access applies the new filter to the table, displaying the records shown in figure 6.17.

This filter only shows those records for orders that were both handled by Nancy Davolio and were shipped to France.

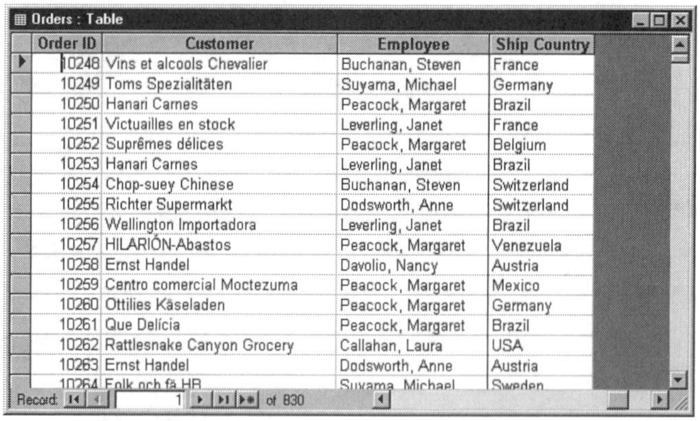

Order ID	Customer	Employee	Ship Country
10248	Vins et alcools Chevalier	Buchanan, Steven	France
10249	Toms Spezialitäten	Suyama, Michael	Germany
10250	Hanari Carnes	Peacock, Margaret	Brazil
10251	Victuailles en stock	Leverling, Janet	France
10252	Suprêmes délices	Peacock, Margaret	Belgium
10253	Hanari Carnes	Leverling, Janet	Brazil
10254	Chop-suey Chinese	Buchanan, Steven	Switzerland
10255	Richter Supermarkt	Dodsworth, Anne	Switzerland
10256	Wellington Importadora	Leverling, Janet	Brazil
10257	HILARIÓN-Abastos	Peacock, Margaret	Venezuela
10258	Ernst Handel	Davolio, Nancy	Austria
10259	Centro comercial Moctezuma	Peacock, Margaret	Mexico
10260	Ottilies Käseladen	Peacock, Margaret	Germany
10261	Que Delícia	Peacock, Margaret	Brazil
10262	Rattlesnake Canyon Grocery	Callahan, Laura	USA
10263	Ernst Handel	Dodsworth, Anne	Austria
10264	Folk och fä HB	Suyama, Michael	Sweden

Record: 14 ◄ 1 ► ►I ►* of 830

Fig. 6.15   The Orders table with the Order ID, Customer, and Employee columns frozen, and the Ship Country scrolled into visibility.

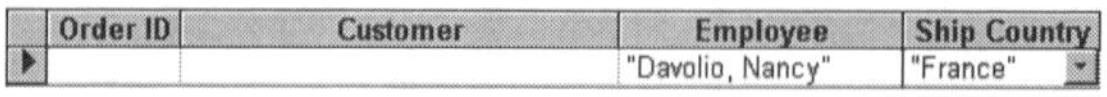

Order ID	Customer	Employee	Ship Country
		"Davolio, Nancy"	"France"

Fig. 6.16   This Filter by Form combines the criteria in two fields in a logical *And* condition because the criteria are entered on the same form tab.

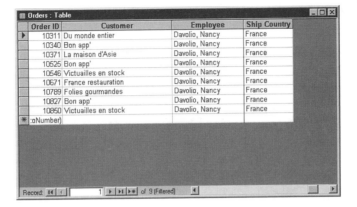

Fig. 6.17 The Filter by Form shown in figure 6.16 displays these records when applied to the Orders table.

Troubleshooting

My Filter by Form filters don't produce the records I expect. I'm seeing either too few records, or records extraneous to the filter I've selected.

Access keeps your last filter settings for a table until you close the table. If you've applied a different filter, whether through Filter by Selection or Filter by Form earlier in your current work session, Access may be applying additional filter criteria that you're not expecting. Use the Clear Grid button or choose Edit, Clear Filter in Filter by Form to clear all previous filter criteria and ensure that the new filter criteria you enter are the only ones in effect.

Advanced Filters and Sorts

Filters in Access, as mentioned previously, are queries in disguise. Creating an Advanced Filter/Sort is very much like creating a query, with some basic differences. The basic differences between the Filter design window and the Query design window are as follows:

- The Show Table dialog does not appear.

- The SQL button is missing from the toolbar, so you can't display the underlying SQL statement.

- The Show row is missing from the Filter Design grid.

Filters are limited to using one table or query that Access automatically specifies when you enter the filter design mode. You can save a filter you create as a query, but Access has no provision for saving a filter as a filter. The sections that follow describe how to add criteria to filter records and to add a sort order in the Filter Design window.

Adding a Multi-Field Sort and Compound Filter Criteria

There is no toolbar button for the Advanced Filter/Sort operation; you can only start this operation by choosing Records, Filter, Advanced Filter/Sort. To create a filter on the

Orders table, which provides more records to filter than the Customers table, follow these steps:

1. Open the Orders table in Datasheet View.

2. Choose Records, Filter, Advanced Filter/Sort to display the Filter window. The Filter window appears as shown in figure 6.18. The default filter name, Filter1, is concatenated with the table name to create the default name of the first filter, OrdersFilter1. The field list window for the Orders table appears in the upper pane of the Filter window.

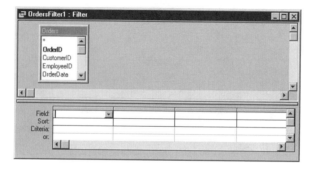

Fig. 6.18 The Filter design window opened by choosing Records, Filter, Advanced Filter/Sort.

3. One of the fields that you might want to sort or limit displayed records is OrderID. Click the OrderID field in the Orders field list window in the upper pane and drag the field to the first column of the Fields row of the filter design grid in the lower pane and drop it. (When your mouse pointer reaches the lower pane, it turns into a field symbol.)

4. Repeat step 3 for other fields on which you want to sort or establish criteria. Candidates are CustomerID, ShipCompany, ShipCountry, ShipPostalCode, OrderDate, and ShippedDate fields.

5. Add an ascending sort to the ShipCountry and ShipPostalCode fields to check the sorting capabilities of your first filter. Your Filter design window appears as shown in figure 6.19.

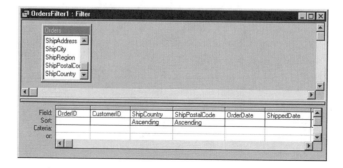

Fig. 6.19 Adding fields and sort orders to the Filter design window.

6. Click the Apply Filter button of the toolbar, or choose Filter, Apply Filter/Sort.

7. Use the horizontal scroll bar of the datasheet to reveal the ShipCountry and ShipPostalCode fields. Your sorted table appears as shown in figure 6.20.

Ship Address	Ship City	Ship Region	Ship Postal Code	Ship Country
Ing. Gustavo Moncada 8585	Buenos Aires		1010	Argentina
Av. del Libertador 900	Buenos Aires		1010	Argentina
Ing. Gustavo Moncada 8585	Buenos Aires		1010	Argentina
Ing. Gustavo Moncada 8585	Buenos Aires		1010	Argentina
Cerrito 333	Buenos Aires		1010	Argentina
Av. del Libertador 900	Buenos Aires		1010	Argentina
Ing. Gustavo Moncada 8585	Buenos Aires		1010	Argentina
Av. del Libertador 900	Buenos Aires		1010	Argentina
Cerrito 333	Buenos Aires		1010	Argentina
Cerrito 333	Buenos Aires		1010	Argentina
Av. del Libertador 900	Buenos Aires		1010	Argentina
Av. del Libertador 900	Buenos Aires		1010	Argentina
Cerrito 333	Buenos Aires		1010	Argentina
Cerrito 333	Buenos Aires		1010	Argentina
Cerrito 333	Buenos Aires		1010	Argentina
Ing. Gustavo Moncada 8585	Buenos Aires		1010	Argentina
Geisweg 14	Salzburg		5020	Austria
Geisweg 14	Salzburg		5020	Austria
Geisweg 14	Salzburg		5020	Austria

Record: 1 of 830 (Filtered)

Fig. 6.20   The Orders table ordered by the ShipCountry and ShipPostalCode fields.

8. Choose Records, Filter, Advanced Filter/Sort to display the Filter design window so you can edit the filter criteria. Access displays the Filter design window with all of the criteria from the preceding filter already entered.

9. Type **USA** in the Criteria row of the ShipCountry column to limit records to those orders shipped to an address in the United States. Access automatically adds double-quotes (") around "USA", indicating that the entry is text, not a number.

10. Click the Apply Filter button of the toolbar or choose Filter, Apply Filter/Sort and scroll to display the sorted fields. Only records with destinations in the United States appear, as shown in figure 6.21. (The width of the fields to the left of the Ship Country field have been reduced so that the Ship Country field appears as in figure 6.21.)

Ship Name	Ship Address	Ship City	Ship Region	Ship Postal Code	Ship Country
The Cracker Box	55 Grizzly Peak Rd.	Butte	MT	59801	USA
The Cracker Box	55 Grizzly Peak Rd.	Butte	MT	59801	USA
The Cracker Box	55 Grizzly Peak Rd.	Butte	MT	59801	USA
Split Rail Beer & Ale	P.O. Box 555	Lander	WY	82520	USA
Split Rail Beer & Ale	P.O. Box 555	Lander	WY	82520	USA
Split Rail Beer & Ale	P.O. Box 555	Lander	WY	82520	USA
Split Rail Beer & Ale	P.O. Box 555	Lander	WY	82520	USA
Split Rail Beer & Ale	P.O. Box 555	Lander	WY	82520	USA
Split Rail Beer & Ale	P.O. Box 555	Lander	WY	82520	USA
Split Rail Beer & Ale	P.O. Box 555	Lander	WY	82520	USA
Split Rail Beer & Ale	P.O. Box 555	Lander	WY	82520	USA
Save-a-lot Markets	187 Suffolk Ln.	Boise	ID	83720	USA
Save-a-lot Markets	187 Suffolk Ln.	Boise	ID	83720	USA
Save-a-lot Markets	187 Suffolk Ln.	Boise	ID	83720	USA
Save-a-lot Markets	187 Suffolk Ln.	Boise	ID	83720	USA
Save-a-lot Markets	187 Suffolk Ln.	Boise	ID	83720	USA
Save-a-lot Markets	187 Suffolk Ln.	Boise	ID	83720	USA
Save-a-lot Markets	187 Suffolk Ln.	Boise	ID	83720	USA

Record: 1 of 122 (Filtered)

Fig. 6.21   The result of applying a "USA" criterion to the Ship Country field.

Using Composite Criteria

You can apply composite criteria to expand or further limit the records that display. Composite criteria are applied to more than one field. To display all orders received on or after 1/1/94 with destinations in North America, try the following:

1. Choose Records, Filter, Advanced Filter/Sort to display the Filter design window.

2. Type **Canada** in the second criteria line of the ShipCountry column and **Mexico** in the third line, and then move the caret to a different cell. When you add criteria under one another, the effect is to make the criteria alternative—that is, combined in a logical Or condition. (Adding criteria in successive rows is the equivalent of using the OR operator in SQL.)

3. Type **>=#1/1/95#** in the first criteria line of the OrderDate field. When you add criteria on the same line as another criterion, the criteria is additive (a logical And condition); that is, orders for the United States placed on or after 1/1/94. (Adding criteria in the same row is the equivalent of using the SQL AND operator.) The # symbols indicate to Access that the enclosed value is of the Date/Time data type.

4. Press F2 to select the entry of step 2, and then press Ctrl+C to copy the expression to the Clipboard. Position the caret in the second row of the Order Date column, and press Ctrl+V to add the same expression for Canada. Repeat this process to add the date criterion for Mexican orders. Your Filter Design grid now appears as shown in figure 6.22. You need to repeat the date criterion for each country criterion because of a limitation in constructing SQL statements from QBE grids, which is discussed shortly.

 5. Click the Apply Filter button to display your newly filtered datasheet (see fig. 6.23).

Fig. 6.22   The Filter grid with composite criteria added.

The SQL statement equivalent to this filter/sort combination is as follows:

```
SELECT * FROM Orders
WHERE ([Ship Country] = 'USA' AND [Order Date] >= #1/1/94#)
OR ([Ship Country] = 'Canada' AND [Order Date] >= #1/1/94#)
OR ([Ship Country] = 'Mexico' AND [Order Date] >= #1/1/94#)
ORDER BY [Ship Country], [Ship Postal Code]
```

The following is a more efficient SQL statement that accomplishes the same objective:

```
SELECT * FROM Orders
WHERE ([Ship Country] = 'USA'
OR [Ship Country] = 'Canada'
OR [Ship Country] = 'Mexico')
AND [Order Date] >= #1/1/94#
ORDER BY [Ship Country], [Ship Postal Code]
```

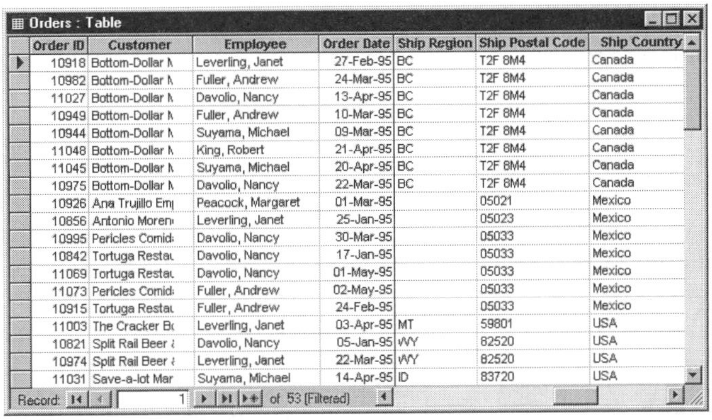

Orders : Table

Order ID	Customer	Employee	Order Date	Ship Region	Ship Postal Code	Ship Country
10918	Bottom-Dollar N	Leverling, Janet	27-Feb-95	BC	T2F 8M4	Canada
10982	Bottom-Dollar N	Fuller, Andrew	24-Mar-95	BC	T2F 8M4	Canada
11027	Bottom-Dollar N	Davolio, Nancy	13-Apr-95	BC	T2F 8M4	Canada
10949	Bottom-Dollar N	Fuller, Andrew	10-Mar-95	BC	T2F 8M4	Canada
10944	Bottom-Dollar N	Suyama, Michael	09-Mar-95	BC	T2F 8M4	Canada
11048	Bottom-Dollar N	King, Robert	21-Apr-95	BC	T2F 8M4	Canada
11045	Bottom-Dollar N	Suyama, Michael	20-Apr-95	BC	T2F 8M4	Canada
10975	Bottom-Dollar N	Davolio, Nancy	22-Mar-95	BC	T2F 8M4	Canada
10926	Ana Trujillo Em	Peacock, Margaret	01-Mar-95		05021	Mexico
10856	Antonio Moren	Leverling, Janet	25-Jan-95		05023	Mexico
10995	Pericles Comid	Davolio, Nancy	30-Mar-95		05033	Mexico
10842	Tortuga Restau	Davolio, Nancy	17-Jan-95		05033	Mexico
11069	Tortuga Restau	Davolio, Nancy	01-May-95		05033	Mexico
11073	Pericles Comid	Fuller, Andrew	02-May-95		05033	Mexico
10915	Tortuga Restau	Fuller, Andrew	24-Feb-95		05033	Mexico
11003	The Cracker B	Leverling, Janet	03-Apr-95	MT	59801	USA
10821	Split Rail Beer	Davolio, Nancy	05-Jan-95	WY	82520	USA
10974	Split Rail Beer	Leverling, Janet	22-Mar-95	WY	82520	USA
11031	Save-a-lot Mar	Suyama, Michael	14-Apr-95	ID	83720	USA

Record: 1 of 53 (Filtered)

Fig. 6.23 The result of the filter of figure 6.22 applied to the Orders datasheet.

A statement using the SQL `IN` predicate is even simpler:

```
SELECT * FROM Orders
WHERE [Ship Country] IN('USA', 'Canada', 'Mexico')
AND [Order Date] >= #1/1/94#
ORDER BY [Ship Country], [Ship Postal Code]
```

You can't generate either of the more efficient forms of the SQL statement with QBE because Access has to take into consideration that you might want a different range of order dates for each country.

The xBase equivalent of the preceding SQL statement is as follows:

```
USE orders INDEX ctry_zip
LIST FOR AT(country, 'USACanadaMexico') > 0 .AND.;
ord_date >= _CTOD('01/01/94')
```

Alternatively, you can use xBase's `SET FILTER TO` command to apply the filter, and then `LIST` the records.

Saving Your Filter as a Query and Loading a Filter

Access does not have a persistent Filter object. A *persistent* database object is an object you create that is stored as a component of your database's .MDB file. All persistent database objects appear as items in one of the list boxes of the Database window. A *filter* is the equivalent of a single-table query, so Access lets you save your filter as a QueryDef object. Access saves the names of the filters associated with each table in the system tables of your database when you save a filter as a query. This is the principal advantage of using a filter rather than a query when only a single table is involved.

To save your filter and remove the filter from the Orders table, follow these steps:

1. Choose Records, Filter, Advanced Filter/Sort to display the Filter design window, if it is not already displayed.

2. Choose File, Save As Query to display the Save As Query dialog.

3. Enter a descriptive name for your filter in the Query Name text box. Using the **flt** prefix distinguishes the filters you save from conventional queries (see fig. 6.24).

Fig. 6.24   Naming the QueryDef object that contains a filter.

4. Click OK to save the filter.

5. Click the Close Window button to close the Filter window.

6. Click the Remove Filter of the toolbar or choose Records, Remove Filter/Sort to remove the filter from the Orders datasheet.

7. A filter remains in memory while the table to which it applies is open. To close the filter, click the Close Window button to close the Orders table.

Re-creating a filter from the filter you saved as a query requires the following steps:

1. Reopen the Orders table in Datasheet View.

2. Choose Records, Filter, Advanced Filter/Sort to open the Filters window with an empty filter.

3. Choose File, Load from Query to display the Applicable Filter dialog, shown in figure 6.25.

Fig. 6.25   A saved filter listed in the Applicable Filters dialog.

4. Double-click the **fltOrdersNorthAmerica** filter to load the saved query into the Filter window.

5. Click the Apply Filter button on the toolbar to display the resulting filter set in the Orders datasheet.

You can save the preceding steps by simply executing the saved query. You execute a query the same way you open a table:

1. Close the Orders table.

2. Click the Query tab of the Database window to list the saved queries.

3. Double-click the **fltOrdersNorthAmerica** item. The datasheet of the fltOrdersNorthAmerica : Select Query window that appears is identical to the datasheet you created in step 5 of the preceding operation.

4. Click the Design View button of the toolbar to display the query design, shown in figure 6.26. Notice that the columns of your original filter, in which no criteria were entered, are empty.

5. Choose View, SQL to display the SQL statement behind the query, illustrated by figure 6.27.

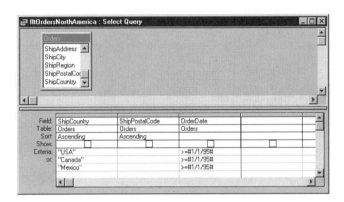

Fig. 6.26   The Query Design View of a saved filter.

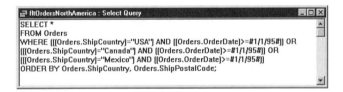

Fig. 6.27   Displaying the SQL statement for a filter saved as a query.

Access adds a multitude of parentheses, plus table name qualifiers, to the field names of the statements created from QBE grids. Most of the parentheses are superfluous. (They are present to help the Q Jet engine's query parser execute more complex queries.) Table name qualifiers are not necessary in a SQL statement when only one table is included in the FROM clause.

Customizing Datasheet View

You can customize the appearance of the Datasheet View by hiding the fields you don't want to appear in your datasheet, changing the height of the record rows, eliminating the grid lines, and selecting a different font for your display. The following list describes each of the options for customizing Table and Query Datasheet View:

■ To hide a field, select the field by clicking the field header or placing the caret in the column for the field and then choose F_ormat, _Hide Columns. Alternatively, you can use the Unhide Columns method described in the next option.

■ To show a hidden field, choose F_ormat, _Unhide Columns to display the Unhide Columns dialog shown in figure 6.28. Columns that appear in Datasheet View are indicated by a check mark next to the field name in the Column list. Click the box to the left of the field name to toggle between hiding and showing the column.

Fig. 6.28   The Unhide Columns dialog that lets you show and hide datasheet fields.

■ To change the font used to display and print the datasheet, use the Font Name drop-down list on the toolbar, or choose F_ormat, _Font to display the Font dialog, shown in figure 6.29. (The Font dialog is one of the common dialogs of Windows 95. Other common dialogs include the Open and Save dialogs.)

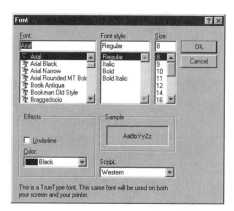

Fig. 6.29   Choosing a display and printing font for datasheets.

■ To remove grid lines from the display and printed versions of the datasheet, click the Gridlines Shown drop-down list button on the toolbar, or choose F_ormat, Cells. If you choose the Gridlines Shown drop-down list, Access displays a palette of four gridline display choices: Both, Horizontal, Vertical, and None; click the button corresponding to the gridline display you want. If you choose Format, Cells, Access displays the Cells Effects dialog, which contains checkboxes for the horizontal and vertical gridlines; select or clear the checkboxes to obtain the desired gridline display.

■ To change the height of the rows as displayed and printed, position the mouse pointer at the bottom edge of one of the record selector buttons. The mouse pointer turns into a double-headed arrow, as shown in figure 6.30. Drag the bottom edge of the button to adjust the height of all the rows. Alternatively, choose Format, Row Height and set the height in points in the Row Height dialog. (Multiply the size of your font by about 1.25 to obtain normal row spacing; printers call 10-point type with 12-point spacing *10 on 12.*)

■ To change the width of the columns to accommodate a larger font, choose Format, Column Width and then click the Best Fit button to let Access determine the size of your columns. You might need to adjust individual column widths by dragging the right edge of the field header with the mouse.

Figure 6.30 shows the Orders datasheet with several columns hidden, grid lines off, 10-point Century Schoolbook TrueType font, and the height of the rows adjusted to accommodate the larger font.

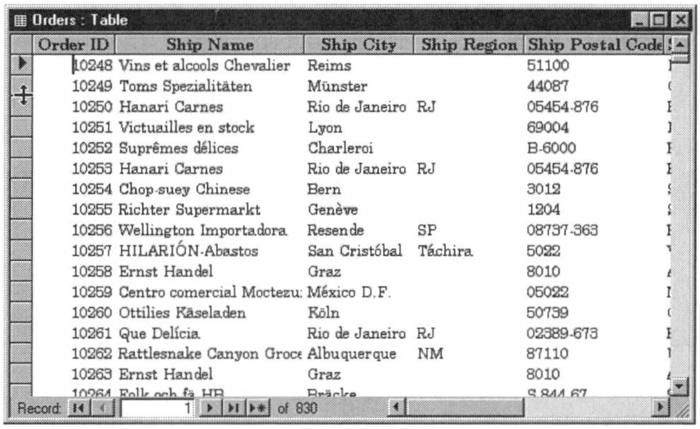

Fig. 6.30 The Orders datasheet in a customized view.

> **Tip**
>
> For the greatest printing speed, choose a typeface family native to your printer, such as Helvetica for PostScript or Swiss for LaserJet printers. (Native fonts are indicated by a printer and page symbol next to the typeface family name in the Font list.) Alternatively, choose a TrueType face, such as the default Arial, for both display and printing.

Copying, Exporting, and Mailing Sorted and Filtered Data

A primary use for filters and customized datasheets is so that you can export the filtered records to another application, such as Microsoft Excel or Word. A variety of methods for exporting filtered and custom-formatted records is available, each of which is described in the following list:

▶▶ See "Exporting Data from Access Tables," p. 252

- Copy the entire datasheet to the Clipboard, and then paste it into the other application. Hidden columns don't appear, but formatting (font, font attributes, and row height) is preserved.

- Use the Save As/Export feature to export the datasheet to an Excel worksheet (.XLS) or a rich text format (.RTF) file for Word or other Windows word processing applications. (Choose File, Save As/Export, select To an external File or Database in the Save As dialog, and then select the file type you want in the Save as type drop-down list of the Save Table In dialog.) Save As/Export preserves the attributes you use to customize the filtered and sorted data when you choose Excel format. Hidden columns, however, appear when you open the resulting file in any version of Excel.

- Click the Analyze It with MS Excel or Publish It with MS Word button. (If these buttons do not appear in your Table Datasheet View toolbar, you need to customize your Table Datasheet menu and add the two buttons.)

- Click the Merge It button to create form letters with Microsoft Word. (You may need to customize your Table Datasheet toolbar by adding the Output To Mail Merge button.) Using Mail Merge with Microsoft Word is discussed in Chapter 22, "Using Access with Microsoft Word and Mail Merge."

- Send the file as an attachment to a Microsoft Mail or Exchange message. Hidden columns don't appear, but formatting is not preserved in Microsoft Mail messages. (The attached file is in Excel BIFF format.)

If you make the Database window the active window and choose File, Save As/Export, the entire content of the table is exported without regard to the filter you added.

Troubleshooting

When attempting to use the Mail Merge with Word feature, a "Must save object first" or "Name not found in this collection" message box appears.

You applied a filter or created a query for your Mail Merge operation that you did not save before clicking the Merge It button. The filter or query object (filters are saved as QueryDef objects) must be a member of a the QueryDefs collection before the DDE conversation between Access and Word commences. Save the filter or the query, and then try clicking the Merge It button again. Chapter 29, "Understanding the Data Access Object Class," provides detailed information on database objects and object collections.

From Here...

Microsoft provided table sorting and filtering features so that Access can duplicate the functions of other less-powerful desktop database managers, such as dBASE. Some of the examples give you insight into the simple SQL statements used to create filters/queries. The find and the search and replace features of Access also are offered as macro actions, and you execute these macro actions from Access VBA code.

- Chapter 8, "Using Query by Example," shows you how to use Access's graphical QBE design window to create queries that can act as filters.

- Chapter 16, "Understanding Access Macros and Events," describes how to use Access macro actions to apply filters and execute queries.

- Chapters 21 and 22, "Using Access with Microsoft Excel" and "Using Access with Microsoft Word and Mail Merge," describe how your Access 95 applications can interact with these two popular members of the Microsoft Office 95 software suite.

- Chapter 24, "Working with Structured Query Language," provides an in-depth analysis of Access SQL's SELECT query syntax.

Chapter 7

Linking, Importing, and Exporting Tables

Undoubtedly, more than 90 percent of personal computer users have data that can be processed by database management techniques. Any data a computer can arrange in tabular form, even tables in word-processing files, can be converted to database tables. The strength of a relational database management system (RDBMS) lies in its capability to handle large numbers of individual pieces of data stored in tables and to relate the pieces of data in a meaningful way.

PC users acquire RDBMSs when the amount of data created exceeds the application's capability to manipulate the data effectively. A common example of this situation is a large mailing list created in a word-processing application. As the number of names in the list increases, using the word processor to make selective mailings and maintain histories of responses to mailings becomes increasingly difficult. A PC RDBMS is the most effective type of application for manipulating large lists.

One Access strong point is its capability to transform existing database table, spreadsheet, and text files created by other DOS and Windows applications into the Access .MDB format—a process known as *importing* a file. Access can *export* (create) table files in any format in which it can import the files. Most PC RDBMSs share this capability, but Access can import and export Borland Paradox files—many other systems cannot. Most client/server RDBMSs can import and export only text-type files.

Access can link a database table file created by Access or another RDBMS to your current Access database; Access then acts as a database front end. Because Access has a linking capability, it can use a file created by another RDBMS in its native form. This capability is far less common in other PC and client/server RDBMSs. When you link a database table from a different RDBMS, you can display and update the linked table as if it were an Access table contained in your .mdb file. If the file that contains the table is shared on a network, other users can employ the file with their applications, while it is linked to your database. This capability to link files is an important feature

---

In this chapter, you learn to perform the following actions with Microsoft Access

- Link tables from Access and other desktop databases

- Use the Linked Table Manager add-in to alter where Access looks for linked files

- Link Excel worksheets, using the Microsoft ODBC Desktop Database Drivers

- Import and export files from worksheet, text, and database files in other formats

for two reasons—you can have only one Access database open at a time, and you can create new applications in Access that can coexist with applications created by other database managers.

This chapter deals primarily with what are known as desktop database-development applications—a term used to distinguish them from client/server RDBMSs, such as Microsoft and Sybase SQL Server, ORACLE, Informix, and Ingres databases. (Client/server RDBMSs are designed specifically for use with networked PCs and—except for Microsoft SQL Server for Windows NT—require you to set aside a PC for use as a database application and file server to run the RDBMS and store the database files.) Desktop RDBMSs, such as dBASE, FoxPro, and Paradox, are more widely used than client/server systems. The majority of desktop RDBMSs can share files on a network, but several publishers of desktop RDBMSs require that you purchase a special multiuser version of the RDBMS to do so. Multiuser desktop RDBMSs, while accommodating the workstation-server configuration required by conventional networks such as Novell NetWare, Windows NT Server, or IBM LAN Server are especially well-suited to the peer-to-peer networks discussed in Chapter 25, "Securing Multiuser Network Applications," such as Windows 95 peer networking, NetWare Lite, and LANtastic. Chapter 25 explains how to use Access with shared database files in general, and Chapter 26, "Connecting to Client/Server Databases," deals with client/server databases in particular.

Learning How Access Handles Tables in other Database File Formats

Conventional desktop database development applications maintain each table in an individual file. Each file contains a header followed by the data. A *header* is a group of bytes that provides information on the structure of the file, such as the names and types of fields, the number of records in the table, and the length of the file. When you create a table file in dBASE, FoxPro, or Paradox, for example, the file contains only a header. As you add records to the file, the file grows by the number of bytes required for one record, and the header is updated to reflect the new file size and record count. Novell Btrieve files differ slightly from the files created by dBASE and Paradox because Btrieve files use variable-width records for storing text data.

Desktop RDBMSs create a variety of supplemental files, which are shown in the following list—some of which are required to import, link, or export RDBMSs:

- Paradox stores information about the primary-key index file (.PX) in the associated table (.DB) file; the .PX file for the .DB file must be available for Access to open a Paradox .DB file for updating. Access links the .PX file automatically if it exists.

- dBASE and FoxPro store memo-type data in a separate .DBT file. If a dBASE table file contains a memo field, the .DBT file must be available. If the .DBT file is missing, you cannot import or link dBASE or FoxPro tables that contain a memo field.

- Use of .NDX (dBASE III), .MDX (dBASE IV), or .IDX or .CDX (FoxPro) index files is optional. You always should use index files when you have them. If you don't link the index files when you link an indexed .DBF table file, modifications you make to the linked tables aren't reflected in the index, which causes errors to occur when you try to use the indexed tables with dBASE or FoxPro.

■ Opening Btrieve files requires having File.ddf and Field.ddf data dictionary files for the database that contains the table file. You need a copy of Btrieve's Wbtrcall.dll in your \Windows\System folder to open or create a Btrieve table. Wbtrcall.dll isn't supplied with Access 95. (You can purchase a license for Wbtrcall.dll from Btrieve, Inc. Wbtrcall.dll usually is included with third-party Btrieve utilities.)

> **Note**
>
> The 32-bit Btrieve driver for the Jet 3.0 database engine was not available in time for the retail release of Access 95. When the Btrieve driver for Access 95 is available, it will be posted in the MSACCESS forum of CompuServe and will be available for downloading by FTP from **http://www.microsoft.com**.

All supplemental files must be in the same folder as the related database file to be used by Access.

The header of an Access 95 .mdb file differs from conventional PC RDBMS files in that an .mdb header consists of a collection of system tables that contain information on all the tables, indexes, macros, and Access VBA functions and procedures stored in a single Access file. The Access system tables also contain information on the location and characteristics of other PC RDBMS files that you linked to your Access database. Access's system tables are similar to the tables used in client/server databases that maintain information on the content of database devices (files), plus the databases and tables contained in the devices.

> **Note**
>
> You can view the Access 95 system tables by choosing Tools, Options. Select the View tab and under the Show dialog, select System Objects. Never modify anything in these tables (most of them are read-only). Some database developers have used the data and values in these tables to aid in referencing items in the database. This is not a good practice as the design of these tables is not guaranteed to remain consistent from version to version and could result in substantial rework to convert a database to a new version.

Identifying PC Database File Formats

Access can import, link, and export the following types of database table files used by the most common PC database managers:

■ *dBASE .DBF table and .DBT memo files, and dBASE III .NDX and dBASE IV .MDX index files.* dBASE III and IV files and indexes are the standard language of the PC RDBMS industry. The majority of PC RDBMSs, and also all common spreadsheet applications, can import and export .DBF files. Most of these RDBMSs can update existing .NDX and .MDX index files, and some RDBMSs can create these index files.

The .DBF file structure is native to other Xbase clone applications such as FoxPro, but not all these RDBMSs create fully compatible dBASE file structures. Compilers like CA-Clipper have their own native index-file structures, but they can use .NDX indexes when necessary. The capability to use .MDX multiple-index files is less widespread.

Access can link and create .NDX and .MDX files. Access updates both types of dBASE index files when you edit or add records to a linked .DBF file. "Setting Primary Keys and Using Index Files," a following section of this chapter, discusses index files in linked tables. When you export an Access table with a memo field, a .DBT memo file with the same name you assign to the dBASE file is created.

- *FoxPro 2+ .DBF table files.* You can import, export, and link FoxPro 2+ .DBF files and files created by earlier versions of FoxPro. The procedures for handling FoxPro 2+ .DBF files are the same as the procedures used for dBASE III and IV. Access maintains the currency of FoxPro 2+ .IDX (single) and .CDX (multiple) index files.

- *Paradox 3.x, 4.x, and 5.0 .DB table and .PX primary key files.* You can link Paradox for DOS 3.x and 4.x table and index files; and those files created by Paradox for Windows 5.0. The following section presents the specific limitations applicable to Paradox files.

- *Btrieve table and .DDF data definition files.* The Btrieve file structure is one of the first RDBMSs used by PC applications written in the C language. The Btrieve table file contains the indexes; they aren't in separate files. A number of PC-based accounting applications use Btrieve files but do not advertise this fact. If the application you are using creates databases and the files aren't dBASE or Paradox files, they may be Btrieve files. If the folder that contains the database files includes a .DDF file, you probably can link the tables to an Access database. If the folder doesn't contain a .DDF file, you can contact the publisher of the application to determine whether the files are in Btrieve format and whether a data definition file with a disguised extension exists.

The majority of applications that use table and index files also use the standard file extensions presented in the preceding paragraphs. The dBASE memo file, for example, requires a standard extension, .DBT. Using the standard extensions for all types of files, however, is not a requirement. Some developers of Xbase applications disguise their files by using arbitrary extensions. You may have to do some detective work to determine which files contain data and which are indexes.

> **Note**
>
> If you work in a multiuser environment, you must have exclusive access to the file you intend to import. No other user can have this file open when you initiate the importing process, and other users are denied access to the file until you close the Import dialog.

> **Caution**
>
> Make sure that you work on a backup, not on the original copy of the linked file until you are certain that your updates to the data in the linked table are valid for the existing database application.

Linking and Importing External Tables

To link or import an Xbase, Paradox, or Btrieve file as a table in an open Access database, such as Northwind.mdb, follow these steps:

> **Note**
>
> *Linking* an external file to an Access database was referred to as *attaching* a table in earlier versions of Access. Don't confuse linking an external file to an Access database with OLE links; when you link an external file, you just give Access information about the external file so it knows how to open, read, and modify the data in that file.

1. Click the Show Database Window button on the toolbar or choose Window, 1 Database. Access doesn't require that all open tables are closed before you link or import a table.

2. If you have a test database that you can use for this procedure, click the Open Database button of the toolbar or choose File, Open Database; then select the test database, open it, and skip to step 5.

3. If you don't have a test database, create a sample to use throughout this chapter. Click the New Database button of the toolbar or choose File, New Database to display the New dialog.

4. Double-click the Blank Database icon in the New dialog; Access displays the File New Database dialog. Type a name, such as **Mdb Test.mdb**, in the File name text box and click Create. You must wait while Access creates and tests the new database.

5. In this example, you link an external table to the database. Choose File, Get External Data, Link Tables. The Link dialog appears (see fig. 7.1); the Link dialog is a variation of the common Windows 95 Open dialog. If you choose File, Get External Data, Import, the Import dialog appears.

6. Use the Files of type drop-down list to select the type of file you want to link. (If you have a suitable Paradox table to link, select Paradox. Otherwise, select dBASE III, dBASE IV, or Btrieve as appropriate to the format of your table file.)

7. Double-click the name of the table you want to link or import (or click the name to select it, and then click the Link button). Access supplies the standard extensions for dBASE, FoxPro, and Paradox table files and the .DDF extension for Btrieve data definition files.

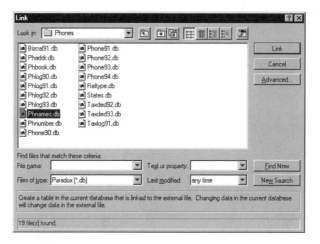

Fig. 7.1 Selecting an external file to link to an Access database in the Link dialog.

> **Note**
>
> You can link Access 1.x and Access 2.0 files to an Access 95 database. Linking Access 1.x and 2.0 files solves the problem of not being able to convert an Access 95 .mdb file to any previous Access version .MDB format for backward compatibility, which is another reason to always use one .mdb file for tables and another .mdb file for your application database objects.

If you are linking a Btrieve file, the Link Tables dialog appears. Select the table to link, and then click the Link button.

8. If the file you choose is encrypted (coded) and requires a password to decrypt it, the Password Required dialog appears. Type the password in the box and press Enter.

9. After you successfully link or import the file, a dialog appears, confirming this operation (see fig. 7.2). If you link more than one table with the same name, Access automatically appends a sequential digit to the table name.

The Link (or Import) dialog remains open; if you have additional external tables you want to link or import to this database—most Paradox and xBase databases consist of several separate table files—repeat steps 6 through 9 for all the files you wish to link or import. If you are linking external Access tables you may select all the tables you wish to link at once by simply clicking on each one.

Fig. 7.2   Access displays this message after successfully linking an external table to a database.

10. In the Link dialog, click Close. The table(s) you linked or imported now are listed in the Database window. If you linked a file, Access adds an icon that indicates the type of database table and an arrow that indicates that the table is linked (see fig. 7.3).

11. Select the table you linked, and then click the Open button to display the records in Table Datasheet View (see fig. 7.4). Alternatively, you can double-click the table name.

Fig. 7.3   The Database window displays special icons to indicate the type of linked table.

Fig. 7.4   The Datasheet View of a Paradox file linked to a test database is identical to Access tables.

After you link an external file as a table, you can use it almost as if it were a table in your own database. The only general limitation is that you cannot change the structure of a linked table: field names, field data types, or the Field Size properties. In linked Paradox files, Access prevents you from changing a table's primary-key field that previously was defined because this property determines the contents of the associated .PX index file.

> **Note**
>
> Although you cannot change field properties for linked tables, you can change the name of the attached table, *within this database only*. Choose Edit, Rename and type the new name for the table. The name for the table (called an *alias*) is changed only in the current Access database and not in the native database.

Solving Problems with Importing or Linking Files

Access detects problems with linked or imported tables that may cause errors when you try to use the tables with Access. The following sections describe these problems and how to overcome most of them.

The Incorrect Password Dialog. If you enter a wrong password or just press Enter, Access informs you that it cannot decrypt the file. You do, however, get another opportunity to enter the password or to click Cancel to terminate the attempt (see fig. 7.5).

Fig. 7.5   This dialog results from an incorrect password entry to a Paradox 4.x table.

The Null Value in Index Dialog. Occasionally, older Paradox .PX index files don't have an index value for a record; when this situation occurs, you see a warning dialog with the message, "Can't have Null value in Index." Usually, you can disregard the message and continue linking or importing the file. The offending record, however, may not appear in the table; fixing the file in Paradox and starting over is better than ignoring the message.

The Missing Memo File Dialog. Both dBASE and Paradox use additional memo files to store the data from memo fields in a particular table. dBASE memo files have the .DBT file type, and Paradox memo files have the .MB file type. Access correctly decides that it can't import or link an external table if it can't open the table's associated memo file—either because the memo file doesn't exist, isn't in the same folder as the table with which it is associated, or contains nontext data.

If the table you're trying to link or import is a dBASE table, Access displays the error dialog shown in figure 7.6. If the table you're trying to link is a Paradox table, however, you receive the less informative error message shown in figure 7.7. For assistance in solving the problem, click the Help button. To close the error dialog, click OK; Access then cancels the linking or importation.

The Graphics Field Type Restriction. If the successful-link dialog doesn't appear, your table or its accompanying dBASE or Paradox memo file probably contains a graphics field type. The following section discusses how to modify files with graphics content so that you can link or import them as Access tables.

Fig. 7.6 Access displays this error dialog if it cannot open a required dBASE memo file.

Fig. 7.7 Access displays this error dialog if it cannot open a required Paradox memo file.

Dealing with Graphics in External Files

Most database managers designed for Windows include some form of graphics field data type. Superbase, Paradox 4.0, and Paradox for Windows provide a special field data type for graphics. Although dBASE IV lacks a field data type for graphics, third-party software firms publish applications that enable you to store graphic images in dBASE memo fields. A variety of add-on applications enables CA-Clipper programmers to display and edit graphic images. The images usually are in individual files but a few third-party applications place images in memo files. CA-dbFast, for example, can display—but not edit—images stored in Windows bitmap (.BMP) files. CA-dbFast doesn't add a graphics field type to store bit-mapped data within tables.

When you try to import or link Paradox 4.x, Paradox for Windows files, or dBASE .DBT files that contain images or other binary data, you may receive an error message that the memo file is corrupted or a message that you cannot import the .DB or .DBF file that contains the offending memo or graphics field. In rare cases, usually involving tiny images, you can import the .DBF and .DBT files, but you see random characters in the Access memo field. With Paradox tables, the graphic or binary fields simply disappear from the table.

If a dialog appears, reporting a problem during importing or linking a file, the linking or importing process is canceled.

The following recommendations can help you deal with graphic images processed with other RDBMSs and add-on applications:

- Use add-on applications for Xbase clones and compilers that operate with the original graphics files in their native format, such as .TIF, .PCX, .GIF, or .TGA. In nearly all cases, the original graphics file is on your computer's fixed disk or on a file server. You can link or embed the graphics file in an Access OLE Object field by using the techniques described in Chapter 20, "Adding Graphics to Forms and Reports."

- Do not use add-on applications that incorporate graphics in .DBT files. If you are committed to this approach, use the method that follows to place the offending memo file in a new file.

- If you use Paradox 4.x or Paradox for Windows with application development in Access, maintain files with graphics fields (as well as any OLE fields in Paradox for Windows tables) separate from files containing conventional data types.

- Use an OLE server that can process the graphics file type of the original image. Windows Paint is limited to Windows bitmap files (.BMP and .DIB) and only can read, not save, .PCX files. To display the image in a form or report, you can create a reduced-size, 16-color or 256-color, Windows bitmap file to be displayed as a bound object. Chapter 20 discusses methods of handling images in this way.

To link or import an Xbase file that contains a memo field or a Paradox file that contains graphics fields, you must be familiar with file-restructuring methods for dBASE or Paradox. To restructure an Xbase file with a memo file that contains graphic images, follow these steps:

1. Make a copy of the file and give it a new name.

2. Modify the structure of the original file by deleting all but the related fields and the memo or graphics field of the original file. Modifying the new file with Modify Structure creates a backup of the original file with a .BAK extension.

3. Modify the structure of the new file by deleting the memo or graphics field.

4. Add a field for the path and file name of the original graphics file, if it isn't already included. Access then can use the location of the original graphics file to pass the file name to an OLE server. You must write some Access VBA code, however, to handle this process. See Chapter 27, "Replicating Access Databases," for examples of writing Access VBA code.

5. Modify the source code of your original application, establishing a one-to-one relationship between the new files.

Converting Field Data Types to Access Data Types

When you import or link a file, Access reads the header of the file and converts the field data types to Access data types. Access usually is quite successful in this conversion; Access offers a greater variety of data types than most of the other widely used PC RDBMSs. Table 7.1 shows the correspondence of field data types between dBASE, Paradox, Btrieve, and Access files.

| **Table 7.1   Field Data Type Conversion between Access and other RDBMSs** | | | |
dBASE III/IV	**Paradox** **3.x, 4.x, 5.0**	**Btrieve**	**Access**
Character	Alphanumeric	String, lstring, zstring	Text (Specify Size property)
Numeric, Float*	Number, Money, BCD*	Float or bfloat (8-byte)	Number (Double)
		Float or bfloat (4-byte)	Number (Single)
		Integer (1-byte)	Number (Byte)
	Short Number	Integer (2-byte)	Number (Integer)
	Long Number	Integer (4-byte)	Number (Long)
	AutoIncrement	AutoNumber	
Logical	Logical		Yes/No
Date	Date, Time, Timestamp*		Date/Time
Memo	Memo, Formatted Memo, Binary*		Memo
	OLE		OLE

Sometimes two types of field data, separated by commas, are shown within a single column in table 7.1. When Access exports a table that contains a data type that corresponds with one of the two field data types, the first of the two data types is assigned to the field in the exported table. The Float data type is available only in dBASE IV.

◄◄ See "Choosing Field Data Types, Sizes, and Formats," p. 119
◄◄ See "Adding Indexes to Tables," p. 150

If you are importing tables, you can change the field data type and the Field Size property to make them more suitable to the type of information contained in the field. When you change a data type or Field Size, however, follow the precautions noted in Chapter 4, "Working with Access Databases and Tables." Remember that you cannot change the field data type or Field Size property of linked tables. You can, however, use the Format property with imported or linked tables to display the data in any format compatible with the field data type of imported or linked files. You can change any remaining properties applicable to the field data type, such as validation rules and text. Using the Caption property, you can give the field a new and more descriptive name.

Setting Primary Keys and Using Index Files

Methods of setting primary keys and creating indexes differ according to the type of file you use to link a table. Tables based on Paradox, Btrieve, and client/server RDBMS files usually have predefined primary-key fields and are indexed on the key fields. Files based on dBASE structures, however, don't have fields specified as primary-key fields and use separate index files. The following two sections discuss the effects these differences have on the tables you create.

Establishing Key Fields in Linked Paradox and Btrieve Tables. When you link or import a Paradox or Btrieve table that has a primary-key index, Access establishes this primary key as the primary key for the new table. To verify that Access establishes a primary key for a linked Paradox or Btrieve table, click the Design View button on the toolbar. A dialog states that you cannot modify some properties of the table and asks if you want to open the table anyway (see fig. 7.8). Click Yes.

Fig. 7.8   This dialog reminds you that, when you enter table design mode, a table is linked.

 The table appears in design mode. The primary key of the linked table is shown with the key icon next to the field name, as with primary keys for Access tables you create yourself.

When you link a Paradox .DB table file that has a primary key, Access uses the Paradox .PX file to establish the primary key. (With Btrieve, Access uses the .DDF and database files.) If you modify the values in a key field, the .DB and .PX files simultaneously reflect this modification.

Linking dBASE Index Files. Key-field indexing is not automatic with dBASE files linked as tables; dBASE file headers do not include data about the indexes used by the application that has the .DBF file. The first time you link the .DBF file as an Access table, you must manually link the index files associated with a dBASE file. Then, when you open the Access database with the linked table again, Access links the indexes you specify.

Note

Access cannot open or update index files in proprietary formats of Xbase clones and compilers. You cannot, for example, link CA-Clipper .NTX files. CA-Clipper (5+), however, can create and maintain .NDX files as an addition to, or a substitute for, their original index structures. Access cannot use secondary indexes of Paradox tables. If you create or commission custom database applications that use nonstandard or secondary indexes and you plan to use Access to update these files while they are linked, you must modify your applications so that they use only .NDX or .PX indexes. You probably don't need to make a major revision of the source code, but you may find that your present applications run more slowly with .NDX indexes.

When you link a dBASE file as a table in your database and select the file name for the table, Access displays a Select Index Files dialog (see fig. 7.9). When you import a dBASE file, this dialog doesn't appear.

If you select a dBASE III source file, Access supplies the default .NDX file extension in the Select Index Files dialog. Your dBASE III file may have one or more .NDX index files associated with it. The five indexes that appear in figure 7.9 are for the Customer.dbf table (a dBASE III file, created by exporting the Customer table from the Northwind.mdb sample database).

Fig. 7.9   This dialog selects dBASE II, III, IV, and 5 index files.

dBASE IV and 5 can create a multiple-index (.MDX) file that includes all the indexes associated with the .DBF file. The .MDX file usually has the same file name as the .DBF file. Access supplies both .MDX and .NDX as default index-file extensions when you select a dBASE IV or 5 file.

To link index files to tables created from dBASE files, follow these steps:

1. From the file list in the Select Index Files dialog, select the index file name, and then click Select. Access adds the index, and displays a message dialog, confirming that the index was added (see fig. 7.10).

Fig. 7.10   Access displays this dialog to confirm the addition of a dBASE index to a linked table.

Caution

Access does not test to determine whether the table's .NDX or .MDX index file matches the structure of its associated Access .DBF file. If the index file doesn't match the Access file, Access doesn't update the index file. Unfortunately, Access does not advise you that it is ignoring the nonconforming index. If you add records to the table in Access, and then attempt to use the table with an Xbase application that uses the proper index, you receive the error message, "Index does not match database." You then must re-index the .DBF file.

> **Caution**
>
> When you link a dBASE file that is used by another application, you must select *all* indexes associated with this file if your Access application modifies fields in the index expressions of each index file. If you do not update all the associated index files while updating the .DBF file with Access, the other application may display the error message, "Index does not match file." Worse, the application may produce erroneous or unpredictable results. If the message or errors occur, you must re-index the file in the other application.

2. If more than one index file is associated with the dBASE.DBF file, you must repeat step 1 for each .NDX file until you add the names of all the indexes needed for your Access table, and then click Close in the Select Index Files dialog. Access displays the Select Unique Record Identifier dialog (see fig. 7.11).

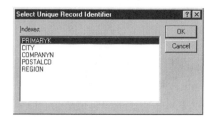

Fig. 7.11   Access displays this dialog to enable you to select a unique index for a linked dBASE file.

3. If you want Access to use one of the linked dBASE indexes to ensure that records have a unique value in the indexed field (that is, to use the dBASE index as a primary key in the table), double-click this index's name in the Indexes list of the Select Unique Record Identifier dialog.

4. Click the Close button in the Select File dialog.

5. Click the Design button in the Database window to display the structure of your linked dBASE table.

6. If the Indexes window is not visible, click the Indexes button on the toolbar or choose Indexes from the View menu. The field names that are the basis for any linked single- or multiple-field indexes appear in the Index Name text boxes of the Indexes window (see fig. 7.12).

> **Caution**
>
> Access does not distinguish between dBASE indexes created with **SET UNIQUE ON** and **SET UNIQUE OFF**. If there are multiple identical entries in the field you select as the primary key, Access will reject your choice of that field in the Select Unique Record Identifier dialog. You must copy the dBASE file with SET UNIQUE ON to another file, reindex the file, and then repeat the attachment process.

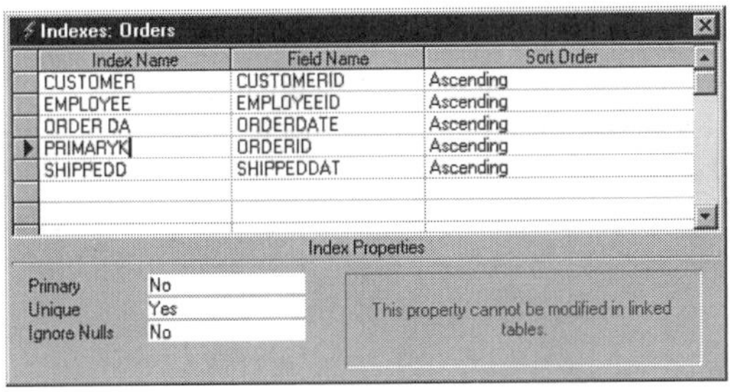

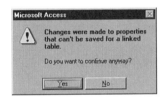

Fig. 7.12 The Indexes window displays the index name and field name for each index.

If you try to modify the primary-key field or change the data type or the Field Size property of a linked table, and then click the Datasheet button in run mode, Access displays a dialog (see fig. 7.13). Click Yes. (Clicking No restores the original values.) Access doesn't change the properties in the linked file, nor do the Design and Datasheet windows display the changes.

Fig. 7.13 Access displays this dialog to remind you that design changes to linked tables are not permitted.

Creating Access .INF Files for dBASE Indexes. When you link one or more indexes to a table created from a dBASE file, Access creates a file with the same file name as the .DBF file but with an .inf extension. The *Filename*.inf file is a text file that contains the path and the file name of the index you linked, in the following format (the following .inf file is for the Orders dBASE III indexes shown in figure 7.12):

```
[dBase III]
NDX1=D:\TESTDATA\dbase3\orders\CUSTOMER.NDX
NDX2=D:\TESTDATA\dbase3\orders\EMPLOYEE.NDX
NDX3=D:\TESTDATA\dbase3\orders\ORDER DA.NDX
NDX4=D:\TESTDATA\dbase3\orders\PRIMARYK.NDX
NDX5=D:\TESTDATA\dbase3\orders\SHIPPEDD.NDX

[UIDX1 PRIMARYK]
NDX5=D:\TESTDATA\dbase3\orders\SHIPPEDD.NDX
```

The .INF file is located in the same folder as the .DBF file you are linking. If you create an invalid .inf file or if one or more of the indexes listed in the .inf file isn't found in the specified location, Access terminates the current link operation, and you must link the dBASE file again. Figure 7.14 shows the error message you see if Access can't find an index specified in the .inf file. When you relink the dBASE file to correct a prior error, a message box indicates that an .inf file already exists (see fig. 7.15). If the indexes changed or you moved the indexes, click Yes to create a new .inf file.

> **Note**
>
> If you try to find an .inf file by selecting the folder in which it should be located, the .inf extension may be missing. This is because .inf files are registered by their type, which is Setup Information.

Fig. 7.14 Access warns that a linked index for a dBASE file wasn't found, and then terminates the operation with the linked dBASE file.

Fig. 7.15 Access displays this dialog to inform you that an .INF file for a linked dBASE file already exists.

Linking Tables from other Access Databases

The procedure for linking a table from one Access database to another Access database is like the procedure for linking other tables. To link a table from Northwind.mdb to your test database, for example, follow these steps:

1. Choose File, Get External Data, Link tables, select Northwind.mdb in the Link dialog and click the Link button. The Link Tables dialog appears (see fig. 7.16).

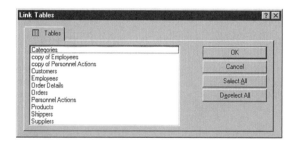

Fig. 7.16 The Link Tables dialog displays the tables in the external .mdb file.

2. Select the name of the table to link from the Tables list that displays the names of tables in the other Access database. You can select more than one table in this list; just click each table in the list you want to link, or click Select All to link all the tables.

3. Click OK. Access adds the linked table(s) and closes all dialogs. The name(s) of your linked Access table(s) appears in the Database window.

Access maintains a record of the drive and folder containing the files responsible for your linked tables. If you rename or change the location of a file that you linked as a table, Access no longer can find the file and displays an error dialog (see fig. 7.17).

Fig. 7.17 This dialog indicates that Access cannot find a linked file.

Using the Linked Table Manager Add-In to Relink Tables

Before Access 2.0, if you moved a file that was linked to or contained objects linked to an Access database, you had to delete the linked tables, and then relink the tables from their new location. Access 95 provides an add-in assistant known as the Linked Table Manager, which simplifies relinking tables. (The Linked Table Manager was known as the Attachment Manager in Access 2.0.) If you move an Access, dBASE, FoxPro, or Paradox file that provides a table linked to an Access 95 database, choose Tools, Add-Ins, Linked Table Manager. The Linked Table Manager's window lists all the linked tables (except linked Btrieve and ODBC tables). Access also displays the path to the .mdb file with the linked tables at the time the link is created. You also can view the path to the .mdb for a linked table by opening the linked table in Design View and and opening the Table Properties window. Click the checkbox of the file(s) whose location(s) changed (see fig. 7.18).

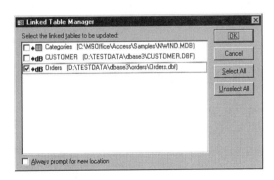

Fig. 7.18 Use the Linked Table Manager add-in to refresh links to an external table that has been moved.

Click OK to display the Select New Location of *TableName* dialog shown in figure 7.19. Select the folder and file where the table is located, and then click Open to change the link reference and close the dialog. If Access successfully refreshes the table links, it displays a dialog saying so; click OK to close the success message dialog. Click the Close button of the Linked Table Manager to close the add-in.

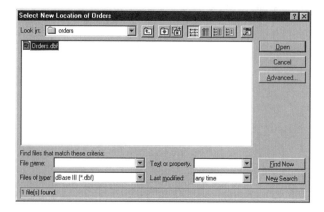

Fig. 7.19 Changing the location of a table with the Linked Table Manager add-in.

Note

The Linked Table Manager is capable of only refreshing links for tables that have been moved to another disk or folder—the table must have the same name. If the linked table's file was renamed, you must delete the table link from your Access database and relink the table under its new name.

Importing Versus Linking Database Files as Tables

The preceding examples demonstrate the differences between the behavior of Access with linked and imported database files. You should link tables contained in another database file if any of the following conditions exist:

- You share the file with other users who are allowed to update the file, or you make updates of the file available to other users.

- You use another RDBMS to modify the file in any way.

- The file is resident on another computer, such as a server, and its size is larger than fits comfortably on your fixed disk.

- You observe the recommended database application development practice of maintaining separate .MDB files for tables and your application's objects.

You should import a table when one of the following conditions exists:

- You are developing an application and want to use data types or Field Size properties different from those chosen for you by Access.

- You or the users of your application do not have online access to the required database files and cannot link them.

- You want to use a key field different from the field specified in a Paradox, Btrieve, or client/server table. This situation can occur when the structure of one or more of the files you plan to use seriously violates one or more of the normalization rules described in Chapter 23, "Exploring Relational Database Design and Implementation."

- You need Access to allow duplicate values in your table when a primary-key field precludes duplicate values.

If you decide to use a temporarily imported table in an application that, when completed, also will use a linked table, make sure that you do not change any field names, field data types, or Field Size properties after you import the table. If you change Field Name properties, you may have to make many changes to forms, reports, macros, and Access VBA code when you change to a linked table. If your application involves Paradox, Btrieve, and client/server database tables, do not change the primary-key fields of these tables. With dBASE tables, make sure that the indexes you create correspond to the indexes of the associated .NDX or .MDX files.

Importing and Linking Spreadsheet Files

Access can import files created by spreadsheet and related applications, such as project management systems, in the following formats:

- Excel 2.x, 3.0, 4.0, 5.0, and 95 .XLS files and task and resource files created by Microsoft Project in .XLS format.

- Lotus 1-2-3 .WKS (Release 1 and Symphony), .WK1 (Release 2), and .WK3 (Release 3 and later) files. Most spreadsheet applications can export files to at least one of these Lotus formats.

You can use OLE to embed or link charts created by Microsoft Excel that are stored in files with an .XLC extension. Copy the contents of the file to the Windows Clipboard from Excel. Then choose Edit, Paste to embed or link (via OLE) the chart in fields of the OLE object type, and display the chart on a form or print it on a report as an unbound object. Similarly, you can embed or link views displayed in Project for Windows 3.0 or 4.0, which also uses the Microsoft Chart applet, except task and resource forms and the Task PERT chart. Chapters 19 through 22 describe OLE linking and embedding techniques.

Creating a Table by Importing an Excel Worksheet

Figure 7.20 illustrates the preferred format for exporting data from Excel and other spreadsheet applications to Access tables. Most spreadsheet applications refer to the format as a *database*. The names of the fields entered in the first row and the remainder of the database range consist of data. The type of data in each column must be consistent within the database range you select.

Caution

All the cells that comprise the range of the worksheet to be imported into an Access table must have *frozen values*. Frozen values substitute numeric results for the Excel expressions used to create the values. When cells include formulas, Access imports the cells as blank data cells. Freezing values causes Access to overwrite the formulas in the spreadsheet with the frozen values. If the range to import includes formulas, save a copy of your .XLS file with a new name. Using the worksheet window with the new file name, select the range to import and freeze the values by choosing Edit, Copy, or by pressing Ctrl+C. Choose Edit, Paste Special, select the Values option, and click OK. Save the new spreadsheet by its new name and use this file to import the data. The "Using the Clipboard to Import Data" section that follows in this chapter presents an alternative to this procedure.

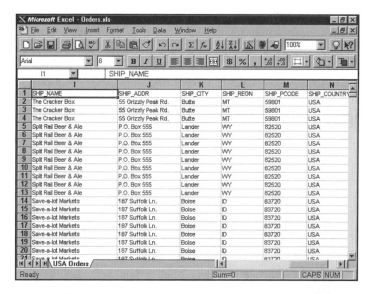

Fig. 7.20   Orders data in a Microsoft Excel 95 worksheet.

Tip

You get an opportunity to assign field names to the columns in the worksheet during the importation process, although it's easier if you add field names as column headings first.

To prepare the data in an Excel spreadsheet for importation into an Access table, follow these steps:

1. Launch Excel, and then open the .XLS file that contains the data you want to import.

2. Add field names above the first row of the data you plan to export (if you haven't done so). Field names cannot include periods (.), exclamation points (!), or square brackets ([ ]). You cannot have duplicate field names. If you include improper characters in field names or use duplicate field names, you see an error message when you attempt to import the worksheet.

3. If your worksheet contains cells with data you don't want to include in the imported table, select the range that contains the field names row and all the rows of data needed for the table. In Excel, choose Insert, Name, Define and name the range.

4. If the worksheet cells include expressions, freeze the values as described in the caution that precedes these steps.

5. Save the Excel file (using a different file name if you froze values), and exit Excel to conserve Windows resources for Access if your computer has less than 8M of memory.

Now you are ready to import worksheets from the Excel workbook file.

To import the prepared data from an Excel spreadsheet into an Access table, follow these steps:

1. Launch Access, if it's not running, and open the database to which you want to add the new table. The Database window must be active (with a dark title bar, usually blue) before you can import a file.

2. Choose File, Get External Data, Import in Access. The Import dialog appears (see fig. 7.21). The Files of type drop-down list provides several more formats for importing tables than it provides for linking files.

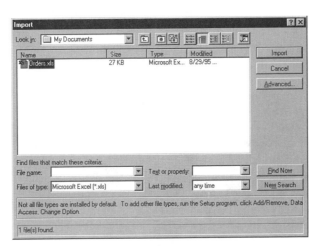

Fig. 7.21   Use the Import dialog to import Excel and Lotus 1-2-3 spreadsheets.

3. Select Microsoft Excel (*.xls) in the Files of type drop-down list, and then double-click the name of the Excel workbook that contains the spreadsheet you want to import (you also can click the file name to select it, and then click Import).

Access now invokes the Import Spreadsheet Wizard, which displays the dialog shown in figure 7.22.

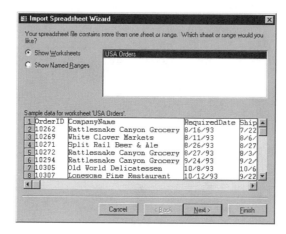

Fig. 7.22   When you import a spreadsheet, Access invokes the Import Spreadsheet Wizard.

4. If you're importing an entire worksheet, select the Show Worksheets option; if you're importing a named range, select the Show Named Ranges option. The Import Spreadsheet Wizard lists the worksheets or named data ranges, depending on the option you select in the list box in the upper right corner of the wizard's opening dialog (refer to fig. 7.22).

5. Select the worksheet or the named data range that you want to import in the list box. The Import Spreadsheet Wizard shows a sample view of the data in the worksheet or named range in the scrollable area at the bottom of the dialog.

6. Click the Next button to move to the next step of the Spreadsheet Import Wizard. The wizard displays the dialog shown in figure 7.23.

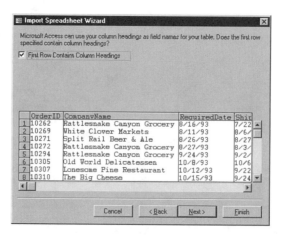

Fig. 7.23   The second step in the Import Spreadsheet Wizard is to select whether the first row contains field names.

7. If the first row of your spreadsheet data contains the field names for the imported table, select the Include Field Names on First Row checkbox. Click Next to continue with the third step; the Import Spreadsheet Wizard displays the dialog shown in figure 7.24.

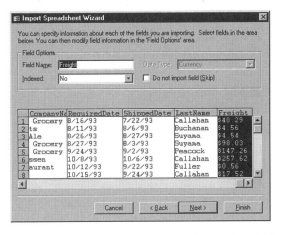

Fig. 7.24 The third step in the Spreadsheet Import Wizard is to select field names, indexes, and the data type.

8. If you want to exclude this column from the imported database, select the Do not import field (Skip) checkbox, and skip to step 12.

9. The Import Spreadsheet Wizard enables you to edit or add the field names for the spreadsheet columns; click the column whose name you want to edit or add, and then type the name in the Field Name text box.

10. If you want Access to index this field, choose the appropriate index type in the Indexed list box; you may choose No index, Yes (Duplicates OK), or Yes (No Duplicates).

11. If the data in the spreadsheet column is unformatted or is formatted as text, Access enables you to select the data type for the field in the Data Type drop-down list. The Data Type control is disabled in figure 7.24 because the cells in the selected column of the Excel worksheet have a currency format; Access recognizes the currency format, and automatically selects a Currency data type for this field.

12. Repeat steps 8 through 11 for each column in the worksheet or data range that you import. When you are satisfied with your options for each column, click Next to move to the next dialog in the Import Spreadsheet Wizard (see fig. 7.25).

Tip

Use an existing field column in the worksheet for a primary key field if the column contains unique values only. In figure 7.25, the OrderID field is known to contain unique values.

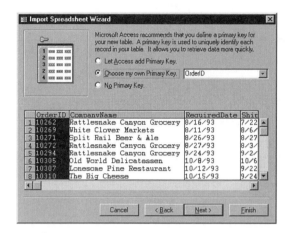

Fig. 7.25 The Import Spreadsheet Wizard prompts you to select a primary key for the new table.

13. Select the Let Access add Primary Key option to have Access add an AutoNumber field to the imported table; Access fills in a unique number for each existing row in the worksheet that you're importing. Select the Choose my own Primary Key option and select the primary key field in the drop-down list if you know there is a column in the worksheet or data range that you can use as a primary key for the imported table. If this imported table doesn't need a primary key, select the No Primary Key option.

▶▶ See "Using Access 95's New TableAnalyzer Wizard," p. 852

14. Click Next to move to the final dialog of the Import Spreadsheet Wizard (see fig. 7.26). Type the name of the new table in the Import to Table text box; Access uses the name of the worksheet or data range as the default table name. If you want to use the Table Analyzer Wizard to split the imported table into two or more related tables, select the checkbox labeled, I would like the wizard to analyze the structure of my table after it finishes importing the data. (You can use the Table Analyzer Wizard at any time, on any table by choosing Tools, Analyze, Table.)

15. Click Finish to complete the importing process. Access closes the Import Spreadsheet Wizard and imports the data. When Access completes the import process without errors, it displays the dialog shown in figure 7.27.

Access analyzes, approximately, the first 20 rows of the spreadsheet you are importing, and assigns data types to the imported fields based on this analysis. If every cell in a column has a numeric or date value, the columns convert to Number and Date/Time field data types, respectively. If a column contains mixed text and numbers, Access converts the column as a text field. If, however, a column contains numeric data in the first 20 rows (the rows that Access analyzes), and then has one or more text entries, Access does not convert these rows.

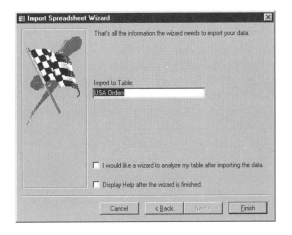

Fig. 7.26   The final step in the Import Spreadsheet Wizard is to give the new table a name.

Fig. 7.27   After successfully importing a spreadsheet, the Import Spreadsheet Wizard displays this message.

If Access encounters cell values that it cannot convert to the data type that it assigned to the imported field, Access creates an ImportErrors table with one record for each error (see fig. 7.28; the errors shown here are the result of a spreadsheet that contains duplicate column headings every 20 rows). You can review this table, select the records in which the errors are reported, and fix them. A better approach, however, is to correct the cells in the spreadsheet, resave the file, and import the corrected data.

Error	Field	Row
Type Conversion Failure	ORDER_ID	21
Type Conversion Failure	EMP_ID	21
Type Conversion Failure	ORD_DATE	21
Type Conversion Failure	REQ_DATE	21
Type Conversion Failure	SHIP_DATE	21
Type Conversion Failure	SHIP_VIA	21
Type Conversion Failure	FREIGHT	21
Type Conversion Failure	ORDER_ID	41
Type Conversion Failure	EMP_ID	41
Type Conversion Failure	ORD_DATE	41
Type Conversion Failure	REQ_DATE	41
Type Conversion Failure	SHIP_DATE	41
Type Conversion Failure	SHIP_VIA	41
Type Conversion Failure	FREIGHT	41
Type Conversion Failure	ORDER_ID	61
Type Conversion Failure	EMP_ID	61
Type Conversion Failure	ORD_DATE	61
Type Conversion Failure	REQ_DATE	61
Type Conversion Failure	SHIP_DATE	61

Record: |◄| ◄ | 1 | ► | ►| | ►* | of 42

Fig. 7.28   Access creates an ImportErrors table when inconsistent field data types occur in the imported data.

> **Note**
>
> The Import Spreadsheet Wizard doesn't display an error message when it encounters inconsistent field data types; it just creates the ImportErrors table. You must look in the Database window to see if the ImportErrors table is present. After you resolve the import errors, make sure that you delete the ImportErrors table so that you can more easily tell whether or not there are errors the next time you import a spreadsheet or other external file.

The Database window now contains a new table with the name you entered in the final step of the Import Spreadsheet Wizard. If you import another file with the same name as your spreadsheet file name, Access adds the number 1 to the file name.

To verify that you obtained the desired result, double-click the name of the imported table in the Database window to display the new table in Datasheet View. Figure 7.29 illustrates a portion of the Access table created from the USA Orders worksheet in the Orders.xls spreadsheet file of figure 7.20.

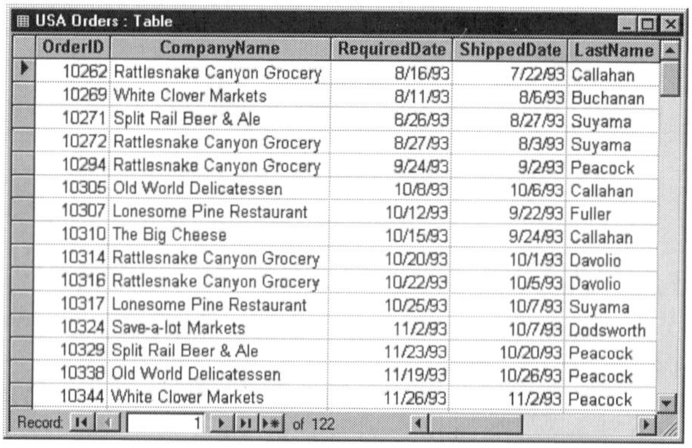
USA Orders : Table

OrderID	CompanyName	RequiredDate	ShippedDate	LastName
10262	Rattlesnake Canyon Grocery	8/16/93	7/22/93	Callahan
10269	White Clover Markets	8/11/93	8/6/93	Buchanan
10271	Split Rail Beer & Ale	8/26/93	8/27/93	Suyama
10272	Rattlesnake Canyon Grocery	8/27/93	8/3/93	Suyama
10294	Rattlesnake Canyon Grocery	9/24/93	9/2/93	Peacock
10305	Old World Delicatessen	10/8/93	10/6/93	Callahan
10307	Lonesome Pine Restaurant	10/12/93	9/22/93	Fuller
10310	The Big Cheese	10/15/93	9/24/93	Callahan
10314	Rattlesnake Canyon Grocery	10/20/93	10/1/93	Davolio
10316	Rattlesnake Canyon Grocery	10/22/93	10/5/93	Davolio
10317	Lonesome Pine Restaurant	10/25/93	10/7/93	Suyama
10324	Save-a-lot Markets	11/2/93	10/7/93	Dodsworth
10329	Split Rail Beer & Ale	11/23/93	10/20/93	Peacock
10338	Old World Delicatessen	11/19/93	10/26/93	Peacock
10344	White Clover Markets	11/26/93	11/2/93	Peacock

Record: 1 of 122

Fig. 7.29 Access imports the Excel worksheet data to the USA Orders table.

To display the .xls file data types that Access chose, click the Design View button on the toolbar. Figure 7.30 shows the structure of the new USA Orders table.

After you successfully import the table, you may want to change the properties of the fields. Unlike the procedure with linked files, Access places no restrictions on altering the field properties of imported files. The section, "Modifying Linked and Imported Tables," that follows in this chapter discusses how to change the default field data types of tables created by imported files.

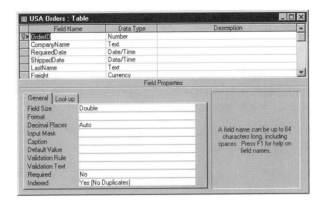

Fig. 7.30 The structure of the imported USA Orders table uses Excel data types.

Linking an Excel Worksheet by Using the ODBC API

▶▶ See "Understanding ODBC Drivers," p. 953

Access 95 comes with ODBC drivers for Microsoft SQL Server; a 32-bit Oracle ODBC driver is available from Microsoft. Access 95 also installs Excel, FoxPro, Paradox, Access, dBASE, Btrieve, and Text file ODBC drivers. ODBC and the ODBC drivers are installed if you choose a Complete Microsoft Office 95 or Access 95 setup. If you don't have the ODBC drivers on your system, you can rerun Access Setup to install them. Additional ODBC drivers are available from various third-party vendors.

You can use the ODBC drivers provided with Office 95 to link Excel worksheets to your Access databases. Linking an Excel worksheet has the advantage of providing up-to-date information if the data in the worksheet is subject to periodic updates. You can use the ODBC Manager application supplied with Access 95 (and installed into the Windows 95 Control Panel) to create an ODBC data source from your Excel worksheet. You also can link Excel worksheets directly to a database by using ODBC directly from Access. *Data source* is a synonym for database when you use the ODBC API to link tables. (In Windows NT, the ODBC Manager is referred to as the ODBC Administrator.)

> **Note**
>
> To link data in an Excel worksheet, you *must* create a named data range for the worksheet data you want to link. Usually, you should make sure that the worksheet you link via ODBC meets all the requirements for a worksheet that you intend to import, as described in the preceding section of this chapter. That is, make sure that the data in the worksheet is laid out in a tabular format. You don't, however, have to freeze values for an ODBC linked worksheet.

Linking an Excel worksheet via ODBC is similar to the spreadsheet importing and linking you learned about previously in this chapter. Assuming that you installed the ODBC Manager and ODBC drivers, follow these steps to link an Excel worksheet to an Access database via ODBC:

   1. Launch Access and open a database, if necessary. Choose File, Get External Data, Link Table to display the Link dialog (refer to fig. 7.1).

   2. Select ODBC Databases in the Files of type drop-down list. Access closes the Link dialog and displays the SQL Data Sources dialog (see fig. 7.31).

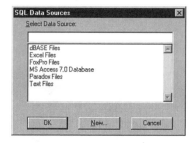

Fig. 7.31   Access displays this dialog to enable you to select an ODBC data source.

   3. If you previously defined an ODBC data source for the worksheet you want to link, select its name in the Select Data Source list. Otherwise, select Excel Files from the list. Click OK; Access displays the Select Workbook dialog (see fig. 7.32).

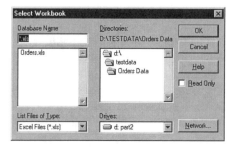

Fig. 7.32   The Select Workbook dialog enables you to select the workbook to link to your database.

   4. Select Workbook is a Windows 3.x-style file opening dialog. If needed, use the Drives and Directories list to navigate to the correct folder in which your workbook is stored and select its name in the Database Name list. Click OK; Access closes the Select Workbook dialog and opens the Link Tables dialog (see fig. 7.33).

   5. The Link Tables dialog lists only the named data ranges in the workbook. Click a worksheet or range name to select it. After you select all the worksheets or ranges that you want to link, click OK. Access closes the Link Tables dialog, and displays the Select Unique Record Identifier dialog (see fig. 7.34).

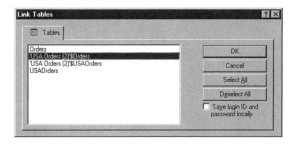

Fig. 7.33 Select the specific worksheet you want to link in the Link Tables dialog.

Fig. 7.34 You must select one or more fields to create a unique key for each record if you intend to update data in the linked worksheet.

6. If you want to be able to update the data in the ODBC-linked worksheet, you must select a field (or combination of fields) that creates a unique record identification for each row in the worksheet—essentially, you create a primary key for the linked table. To select a field, click it with the mouse.

7. After you are satisfied with your key field selection, click OK. At this point, Access formulates the SQL query to establish indexes for the linked worksheet and analyzes the data in the worksheet. Depending on the outcome of this analysis, Access either immediately links the worksheet, or invokes the Link Spreadsheet Wizard.

   Using the Link Spreadsheet Wizard is the same as using the Import Spreadsheet Wizard described in the preceding section of this chapter, except that Access doesn't allow you to edit the field names it assigns to the linked data.

8. Your linked worksheet table appears in the Database window (with the ODBC globe turned to display Africa), as shown in figure 7.35.

Click the Open button of the Database window to display your linked worksheet. The look of the worksheet as a linked table is identical to a table imported from a worksheet with one major difference—you cannot update a linked worksheet. When you link a table to an Access database by using the ODBC API and the Microsoft ODBC drivers, you can update the table only if the table has a designated primary-key field. (The imported table is represented by a read-only Recordset object of the Snapshot type.)

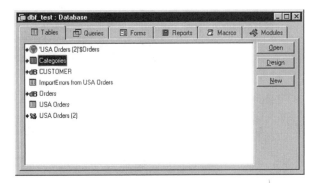

Fig. 7.35 Access's Database window uses a globe icon to identify tables linked with ODBC drivers.

> **Note**
>
> Some third-party ODBC drivers, such as the Intersolve ODBC drivers in the ODBC Driver Pack, have an option that enables you to edit Excel worksheet and text files that you link to Access tables. For more information, see Chapter 26, "Connecting to Client/Server Databases."

Importing Text Files

If the data you want to import into an Access table was developed in a word processor, database, or other application that cannot export the data as a .DBF, .WK?, or .XLS file, you need to create a *text file* in one of the text formats supported by Access. (A text file is a file with data consisting of characters that you can read with a text editor, such as Windows Notepad or the DOS Edit.com text editor.) Most DOS- and Windows-compatible data files created from data in mainframe computers and files converted from nine-track magnetic tapes are text files, and Access imports these files in various formats.

Access refers to the characters that separate fields as *delimiters* or *separators*. In this book, the term *delimiter* refers to characters that identify the end of a field; the term *text identifiers* refers to the single and double quotation marks that you can use to distinguish text from numeric data.

> **Note**
>
> EBCDIC (Extended Binary-Coded-Decimal Interchange Code) is a proprietary format used by IBM to encode data stored on nine-track tape and other data interchange media. EBCDIC is similar to the ANSI (American National Standards Institute) and ASCII (American Standard Code for Information Interchange) codes. You need to convert EBCDIC-encoded data to ANSI or ASCII code before you can import the data into an Access table. Nine-track tape drives designed for PC applications and service bureaus who provide tape-to-disk conversion services handle the EBCDIC-ASCII conversion. The printable (text) characters with values 32 through 127 are the same in ANSI and ASCII, so conversion from ASCII to ANSI, the character set used by Windows and Access, is seldom necessary.

Table 7.2 details the formats that Access supports.

Table 7.2 Text File Formats Supported by Access 95	
Format	**Description**
Comma-delimited text files (also called CSV [Comma-Separated Value] files)	Commas separate (delimit) fields. The *newline pair*, carriage return (ASCII character 13), and line feed (ASCII character 10) separate records. Some applications enclose all values within double quotation marks; this format often is called mail-merge format. Other applications enclose only text (strings) in quotation marks to differentiate between text and numeric values, the standard format for files created by the Xbase command, COPY TO *FILENAME* DELIMITED.
Tab-delimited text files (also called ASCII files)	These files treat all values as text and separate fields with tabs. Records are separated by newline pairs. Most word-processing applications use this format to export tabular text.
Space-delimited files	Access can use spaces to separate fields in a line of text. The use of spaces as delimiter characters is uncommon because it can cause what should be single fields, such as names and addresses, to be divided inconsistently into different fields.
Fixed-width text files	Access separates (parses) the individual records into fields based on the position of the data items in a line of text. Newline pairs separate records; every record must have exactly the same length. Spaces pad the fields to a specified fixed width. Using spaces to specify field width is the most common format for data exported by mainframes and minicomputers on nine-track tape.

Using the Text Import Wizard

To import any of the text file types listed in table 7.2, you follow a procedure similar to the procedure for importing any external data into Access. To import a text file, follow these steps:

1. Open the database into which you want to import the text file and make the Database window active, if necessary.

2. Choose File, Get External Data, Import. Access displays the Import dialog.

3. In the Import dialog, select Text Files (*.txt, *.csv, *.tab, *.asc) in the Files of type drop-down list. Use the Look in drop-down list to select the folder that contains the text file you want to import, and double-click the text file's name. Access now starts the Text Import Wizard (see fig. 7.36).

4. Select the Delimited option to import a delimited text file, or select the Fixed Width option to import a fixed-width text file. The Text Import Wizard displays a sample of the text file's contents in the lower portion of the dialog to help you determine the correct file type. Figure 7.36 shows a comma-delimited text file being imported. Click Next to proceed to the next step in the Text Import Wizard. If you selected Delimited as the file type, the Text Import Wizard displays the dialog shown in figure 7.37; if you selected the Fixed Width option, the wizard displays the dialog in figure 7.38.

Next >

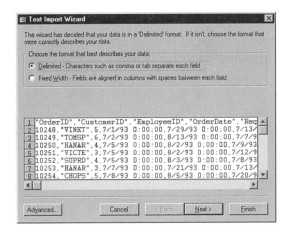

Fig. 7.36 In the first step of the Text Import Wizard, choose whether the text file you're importing is a delimited or a fixed-width text file.

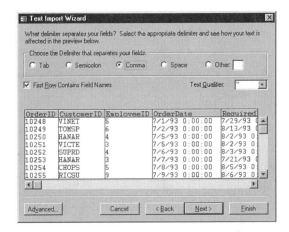

Fig. 7.37 The Text Import Wizard displays this dialog as the second step for delimited text files.

> **Note**
>
> In almost every case, you will select the Delimited option. Use the Delimited option for comma-delimited, tab-delimited, and all other types of delimited text files. Use fixed-width for space-delimited text files and also text files actually formatted as fixed-width.

5. If you're importing a fixed-width text file, skip to step 6. Otherwise, select the delimiter character that separates fields in the table (most delimited files use the default comma separator.) If the text file you're importing uses a text qualifier other than the double quote, enter it in the Text Qualifier text box. If the first line in the text file contains field names (such as the column headings in a spreadsheet file), select the First Row Contains Field Names checkbox. Click Next to move to the next step of the Text Import Wizard.

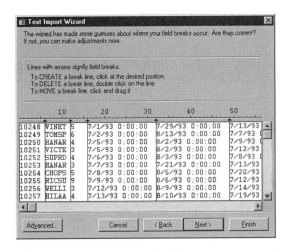

Fig. 7.38 The Text Import Wizard displays this dialog as the second step for fixed-width text files.

6. If you're importing a delimited text file, skip to step 7. In a fixed-width text file, the Text Import Wizard analyzes the columns and makes an approximation about where the field breaks lie. Scan through the sample data at the bottom of the dialog; if the field breaks aren't in the right place, there are too many field breaks, or there aren't enough field breaks, you can add, delete, or move the field breaks that the Text Import Wizard suggests. To move a field break, drag it with the mouse. To remove a field break, double-click it. To add a field break, click at the location where you want the field break added. When you're satisfied with the field break arrangement, click Next to continue with the Text Import Wizard.

7. The Text Import Wizard now displays the dialog shown in figure 7.39. Choose the In a New Table option to create a new Access table for the imported text file. Choose the In an Existing Table option to add the data in the text file to an existing database table, then select the table to which you want the data added in the accompanying drop-down list. Click Next to continue with the next step in the Text Import Wizard. (If you selected the In an Existing Table option, the Text Import Wizard skips directly to its final step, step 10 of this procedure.)

Caution

Access matches fields from left to right when you import a text file into an existing table. You must make sure that the data types of the fields in the imported text file match those in the Access table, otherwise the added data values aren't inserted into the correct fields; in most cases, you end up with many import errors in the ImportErrors table. If you're not absolutely certain that the format of your input data matches the format of the desired table exactly, you can choose the In a New Table option, and then place your data in the existing table with an append query, as discussed in Chapter 11, "Using Action Queries."

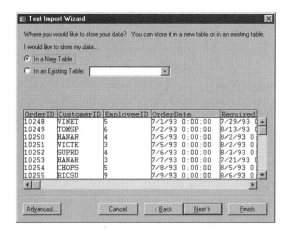

Fig. 7.39 The Text Import Wizard lets you choose to create a new table for the imported text data or to add the data to an existing table.

8. The Text Import Wizard now displays the dialog shown in figure 7.40. The Text Import Wizard enables you to edit field names, choose whether and what kind of index to use for each field, and to adjust each field's data type. To set the options for each field, click the field column at the bottom of the dialog to select it; you then may edit the field name, select an index method in the Indexed drop-down list, and select the data type for the field in the Data Type drop-down list. Select the Do not import field (Skip) checkbox if you don't want to import the select field column. When you're satisfied with your field settings, click Next.

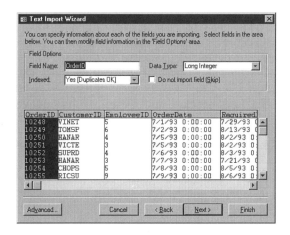

Fig. 7.40 The Text Import Wizard lets you edit the field name, select an index type and data type for the field, or even skip importing the field.

9. Now the Text Import Wizard displays the dialog in figure 7.41. Choose the appropriate option for the primary keys you want—whether to allow Access to add a new field with an automatically generated primary key, select an existing field to use as a primary key, or import the table without a primary key. After selecting the primary key options, click Next.

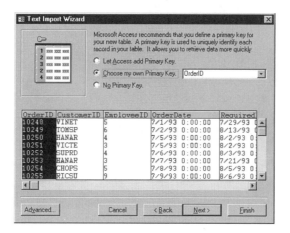

Fig. 7.41   As with Access' other import operations, the Text Import Wizard asks you to select options for the table's primary key.

10. The Text Import Wizard now displays its final dialog, shown in figure 7.42. You now must enter the name for the new imported table. The Text Import Wizard displays this dialog even if you chose to import the text file into an existing table. Access enters either a default table name that is the same as the original name of the text file or the table name you selected for importing the data into. Edit the table name, or type a different table name, if you want. Click Finish to import the text file.

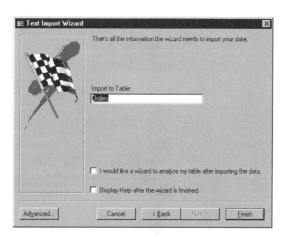

Fig. 7.42   The final step in the Text Import Wizard is to give the new table a name.

The Text Import Wizard imports the text file, and displays a success message. As with other import operations, Access creates an ImportErrors table to document any errors that occurred during the import process.

The specific values you should select for field delimiters and text qualifiers are described in following sections, along with some tips on importing fixed-width text files.

The Text Import Wizard Advanced Options

Occasionally, you may find that you import text data from the same text file more than once, or that you have several text files that all have the same format. A typical situation in many corporations is that data from the company's mainframe computer system is provided to desktop computer users in the form of a text file report. Frequently, reports are delivered over the network to users in a text file, using the same name for the text file each time. You can use the Text Import Wizard's advanced options to configure Access to import a text file, and save these options so that you don't have to go through every step in the wizard every time you import the text file.

Every step of the Text Import Wizard has an Advanced button. Clicking this button displays a special dialog that shows all the Text Import Wizard settings in a single dialog and allows you to select a few options, such as date formatting, that don't appear in the regular Text Import Wizard dialogs. If you select the Delimited option, the Advanced dialog has the options and field grid shown in figure 7.43. If you select the Fixed-width option, the Advanced dialog has the options and field grid shown in figure 7.44.

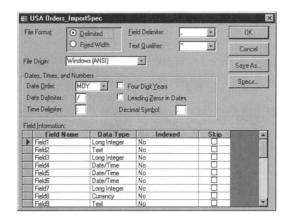

Fig. 7.43 Use the Advanced options of the Text Import Wizard to create import specifications for files you import repeatedly.

> **Tip**
>
> For text files you intend to import only once, it's much easier to import the file by going step-by-step through the Text Import Wizard.

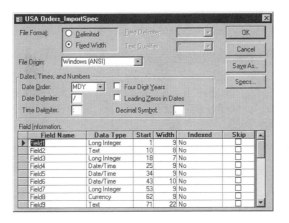

Fig. 7.44 The Advanced options for importing a fixed-width text file differ from options for delimited text.

The following list summarizes the options you can select in the Advanced dialog:

- *File Format.* Use these option buttons to choose which type of text file format you're importing: Delimited, or Fixed Width. Depending on the file format you select, the specific options available to you change.

- *Field Delimiter.* Use this drop-down list to select the symbol that delimits fields in the text file. This option is disabled for fixed-width text files.

- *Text Qualifier.* Use this drop-down list to select the symbol that marks the beginning and end of text strings in the text file. This option is disabled for fixed-width text files.

- *File Origin.* Select the character set used for the text file in this drop-down list. If you're importing a text file that originated on a Macintosh computer, for example, select Macintosh in this list.

- *Date Order.* If the data in the text file uses a European or other date format that differs from the month-day-year format typical in the United States, select the appropriate date order in the Date Order drop-down list.

- *Date Delimiter and Time Delimiter.* Type the symbol used to separate the month, day, and year in a date in the Date Delimiter text box, and type the symbol used to separate hours, minutes, and seconds in the Time Delimiter text box. For example, in the United States, the Date Delimiter is the slash (/) character, and the Time Delimiter is the colon (:).

- *Four Digit Years.* Mark this checkbox if the dates in the text file use four digits for the year, such as 8/28/1995.

- *Leading Zeroes in Dates.* Mark this checkbox if the dates in the text file have leading zeroes, such as 08/09/95.

■ *Decimal Symbol.* Type the symbol used for the decimal separator in numeric values in the text box. In the United States, the decimal symbol is the period (.), but many European nations use a comma (,).

■ *Field Information.* The appearance of this grid varies, depending on the file format that you select. For a delimited text file, the Field Information grid allows you to edit field names, select the field's data type and indexing, and specify whether to skip the field in importing (refer to fig. 7.43). For a fixed-width text file, the Field Information grid allows you to perform the same operations, but adds specifications for the starting column and width of each field (refer to fig. 7.44).

■ *Save As.* Click this button to display the Save Import/Export Specification dialog. By entering a name for the specification and clicking OK, you can save the file import settings for later use.

■ *Specs.* Click this button to display the Load Import/Export Specification dialog. Select a previously saved specification and click OK to use import settings that you defined previously.

The following sections on using delimited and fixed-width text files discuss the application of some of these Advanced options in greater detail.

Using Delimited Text Files

Delimited files can accept a wide variety of field- and record-delimiting characters. The native format (used by files created within WordPerfect) of WordPerfect secondary merge files, for example, uses control characters to separate fields and records. Access provides commas, tabs, and spaces as standard field delimiters. You can type any printable character, such as an asterisk or a dollar sign, in the text box as a delimiter (refer to fig. 7.37). Because spaces and other special-character delimiting are seldom used, only comma-delimited (.csv) and tab-delimited files are presented in this chapter.

Word-processing applications use both commas and tabs as delimiters in the mail-merge files that they or other applications create for personalized documents. The newline pair is universally used to indicate the end of a record in mail-merge files; a record always consists of a single line of text.

Comma-Delimited Text Files without Text-Identifier Characters. Comma-delimited files come in two styles—with or without quotation marks surrounding text fields. The quotation marks, usually the standard double quotation marks ("), identify the fields within them as having the Text data type. Fields without quotation marks are processed as numeric values if they contain numbers only. Not all applications offer this capability; .CSV files, for example, exported by Excel don't enclose text within quotation marks. Figure 7.45 shows a typical Excel .csv file opened in the Windows Notepad applet.

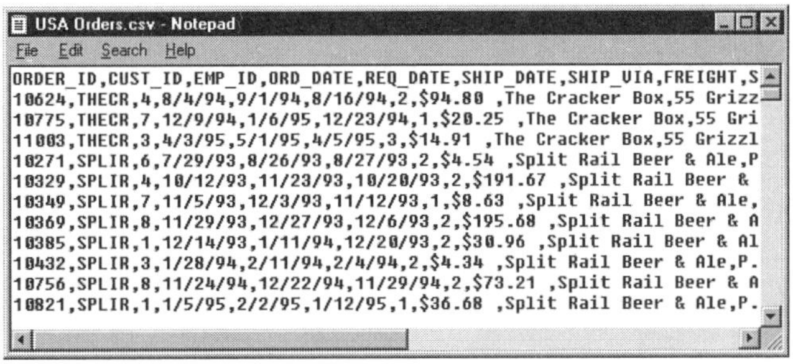

Fig. 7.45 Use Windows Notepad or Wordpad applet to determine the type of field delimeter.

Note

Using Notepad to view files that fit within its 60K file size limitation is a quick way to determine the type of text file with which you are dealing. If the file is longer than 60K, you can use Windows WordPad to view the file. Make sure, however, that you do not save the file as a .DOC file after you view or edit it. If you used WordPad to edit the file, choose File, Save As and specify a .TXT file.

Caution

If you export the Orders table from Northwind.mdb to Excel, and then use Excel to create an Orders.csv file and import the file into an Access table, you may receive an extraordinary number of errors. Most of these errors are due to a mixture of numeric values for United States ZIP codes and alphanumeric values used for Canadian, U.K., and European postal codes. The first data cell in the Postal Code column is a number, so the Access import procedure determines that the field should have the Number field data type. Therefore, mixed value fields (letters and numbers) cause import errors. A wise policy is to not import delimited text files without text-identification characters to Access tables.

Comma-Delimited Text Files with Text-Identifier Characters. The default delimited text file type of dBASE, named .SDF for Standard Data Format, created by the COPY TO *FILENAME* DELIMITED command, creates comma-delimited files with text fields surrounded by double quotation marks. (Date and Numeric field types do not have quotation marks.) This type of delimited file is standard in many other database systems, as well as project and personal information management applications. Figure 7.46 shows an example of a delimited text file that contains text qualifiers.

Note

When you create a DOS dBASE III+ file from an Access file, Access translates characters with ANSI values 128 through 255 to the PC-8 character set used by character-based DOS and OS/2 applications. Letters with diacriticals and special characters of Scandinavian and romanized Slavic languages do not have the same values in the PC-8. These letters and characters appear on-screen as black rectangles because the PC-8 values do not correspond to printable ANSI values. For text files that don't use the Windows ANSI character set, use the Text Import Wizard's advanced options to select the appropriate character set.

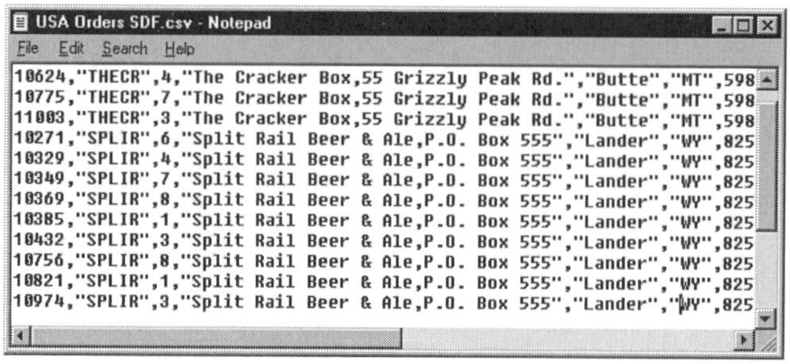

Fig. 7.46 A dBASE .SDF file displayed in Windows Notepad.

Tab-Delimited Text Files. Word-processing applications often use tab characters to separate fields in mail-merge files. These tab characters usually define the fields of tables when you convert conventional text to tabular format (and *vice versa*) in word processors such as Word 95. Tab-delimited text files rarely use text qualifier characters. When exporting tab delimited text files (described in a following section of this chapter), Access adds double quotation marks as text-identifier characters so that Word doesn't interpret embedded newline pairs (carriage return and line feed, or CR/LF) in text fields as the end of the record. (Allowing embedded newline pairs in text fields isn't a recommended database design practice.)

Many organizations acquire RDBMSs because the amount of their data is too large for their word-processing application to maintain mailing lists for direct-mail advertising and other promotional and fundraising purposes. RDBMSs also enable you to create specialized merge data files for specific types of customers, ranges of ZIP codes, and other parameters you select.

Fortunately, Access has a simple process for converting the merge data files used by most word processors to text files that can be imported and maintained by an Access database application. In Word 95, for example, you simply open the merge data file in whatever format you use (usually the native .DOC) and save the document in Text Only (.TXT) format under a different file name. WordPerfect 5+ (using CONVERT.EXE) and WordPerfect for Windows offer a variety of export formats for their secondary merge files. Unless you have a specific file type in mind, select the tab-delimited format for these files.

Handling Fixed-Width Text Files

If you have a choice of text file formats for the data you plan to import into Access, avoid using fixed-width text files by choosing a delimited file format. If you are importing data created by a mainframe or minicomputer, however, the data probably is in fixed-width format. In a fixed-width text file, you must name the fields, rather than relying on the first line of the text file to provide names for you. Fixed-width text files seldom come with a field name header in the first line.

A fixed-width text file resembles the file in figure 7.47. Fixed-width text files often contain more spaces than data characters. In a tab-delimited file, the spaces between fields aren't included in the file itself, but are added by the text editor when tab characters (ASCII or ANSI character 9) are encountered. In a fixed-width file, each space is represented by ASCII or ANSI character 32.

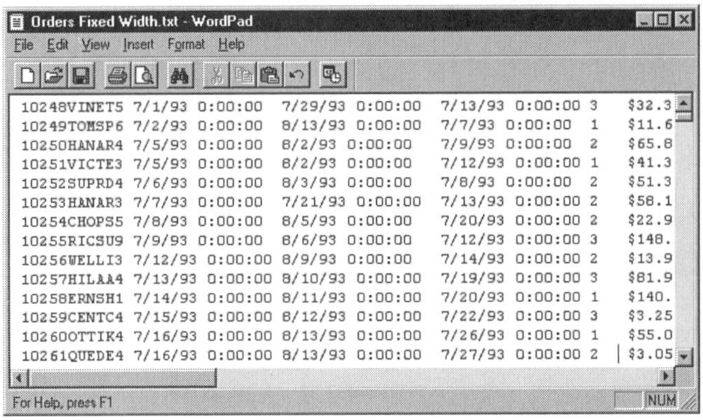

Fig. 7.47 A fixed-width text file pads fields to the same length with spaces.

Note

The fields of fixed-width text files often run together; the first four fields of the Orders Fixed Width.txt file shown in figure 7.47 are Order ID (five digits), Customer ID (four letters), Employee ID (one digit), and Order Date (16 characters). The Order Date field is padded with spaces to a width of 16 characters. The appearance of the data in figure 7.47 is typical of COBOL "text dumps" from mainframe and minicomputer tables. If you have the COBOL file description for the fixed-width table, it's far easier to complete the import specification.

Troubleshooting

When importing tables created from fixed-width text files, a large number of errors occur.

You probably miscalculated one or more of the starting positions of a field. Locate the first field name with a problem; the names following it usually have problems, too. Close all open tables. From the Database window, select the table you imported and press the Delete key. If you have an ImportErrors table, delete it, too. You cannot delete an open table. Perform the importation process again, and reposition the field breaks in the Text Import Wizard. Remember that Access only analyzes the first 20 lines of the text file, so its guesses about where to position the field breaks may be incorrect, and may not allow enough room for the actual width of a field.

Appending Text Data to an Existing Table

If the data you import is provided on a floppy disk, you may need several disks to store the data. Fixed-width text files usually require more floppy disks because in most cases, they are derived from data on mini- and mainframe computers, and the fixed-width format is quite inefficient. If you ever imported multiple-disk data into dBASE files, for example, you probably learned that you must concatenate all the files on your hard disk into one large text file. You concatenate files by using the DOS **COPY file1+file2 file3** command or by appending each file to a separate dBASE file and then appending the remaining dBASE files to the file created from the first disk. This process is very tedious.

Access enables you to append data from text files to an existing table. Besides simplifying the process described in the preceding paragraph, you can update an imported file with new text data by appending it directly from the source text file—rather than by creating a new Access table—and then appending the new table to the existing one.

You can append a text file to an existing table by following these steps:

1. Make a backup copy of your table in the same database or another database, in case an error occurs during the importing operation.

2. Choose File, Get External Data, Import, and select a text file as though you are going to import it to a new table.

3. Make sure that you select the In an Existing Table option and specify a table name in step 3 of the Text Import Wizard (refer to fig. 7.39).

4. If you used the Advanced button to create and save an import specification, click Advanced to display the advanced options dialog, and then click Specs to load the previously saved import specification.

5. Proceed with the importation process as you would for any other text file.

At the end of the appending process, a message box appears. The ImportErrors table displays any errors made.

Note

Maintaining a backup copy of the table to which you are appending files is important. If you have a problem with field delimiters or field lengths, or accidentally select the wrong import specification for the file, you can end up with one error for each appended record. Then, if you do not have a backup file, you must delete the appended records and start over. To use a backup table file, close and delete the damaged table. Then choose Edit, Rename to change the name of the backup table to the name of the damaged table.

Using the Clipboard to Import Data

If another Windows application generates the data you want to import, you can use the Windows Clipboard to transfer the data without creating a file. This technique is useful for making corrections to a single record with many fields or for appending new records to a table. This process requires a table with the proper field structure so that you can paste the data copied to the Clipboard into the other application. Pasting rows from an Excel spreadsheet, for example, requires a table with fields containing data types that correspond to those of each column that you copy to the Clipboard. Other Windows applications that can copy tabular data to the Clipboard use similar techniques.

Pasting New Records to a Table

To import data from the Clipboard, and then append the data to an existing table or table structure, use the following procedure:

1. Open the application you are using to copy the data to the Clipboard—in this case, Microsoft Excel. Then open the file that contains the data.

2. Select the range to be appended to the table (see fig. 7.48). The Excel columns you select must start with the column that corresponds to the first field of your Access table. You do not, however, need to copy all the columns that correspond to fields in your table. Access supplies blank values in the columns of your appended records that are not included in your Excel range. Remember that, if any of the columns you select contain formulas, the values must be frozen.

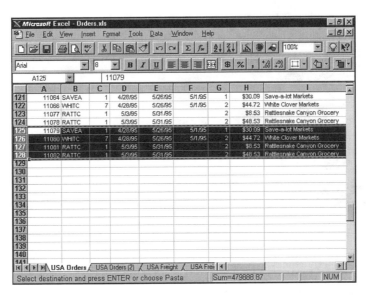

Fig. 7.48   Select cells in Excel to be appended to an Access table by copying to the Clipboard.

3. To copy the selected cells to the Clipboard, press Ctrl+C or choose Edit, Copy.

4. Launch Access (if necessary), and open the table to which you are appending the records in Datasheet View.

5. Choose Edit, Paste Append in Access. If no errors occur during the pasting process, a message box reports how many new records you are about to add (see fig. 7.49). Click Yes. The records are appended to the bottom of your Access table (see fig. 7.50). Choose Records, Remove Filter/Sort to place the appended records in the correct order.

Fig. 7.49 This message appears when Access can successfully append records you paste from the Clipboard.

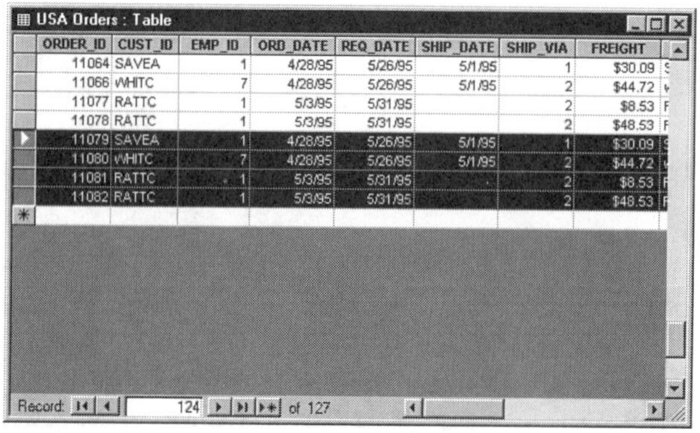

Fig. 7.50 The paste operation appends records to an Access table.

Troubleshooting

Paste errors occur when pasting spreadsheet cells into a table.

Errors usually occur during the Paste/Append process for one of two reasons—the data types in the Excel cells don't match those in the corresponding fields of your Access table, or you attempted to paste records with data that duplicates information in key fields of the table. Both types of errors result in Access creating a PasteErrors table that contains information on the records with the errors. The Paste Errors table for field-type mismatches is similar in purpose and appearance to the ImportErrors table described previously in this chapter.

Errors caused by duplicate primary-key violations result in the following series of cascading message boxes:

1. Figure 7.51 shows the first message you receive that indicates a primary-key violation. Access does not offer a Cancel option; therefore, you must click OK.

2. Next, a message box appears enabling you to suppress further error messages (see fig. 7.52). To cancel the append operation, click Cancel. Otherwise, click Yes to try to paste the remaining records without reporting further errors. If you want to see which errors occur as they are encountered, click No.

Fig. 7.51 This dialog indicates that an attempt was made to paste a record with a duplicate key value.

Fig. 7.52 This message lets you continue pasting records without reporting more errors.

3. Finally, a message box reports where the records that couldn't be pasted were placed (see fig. 7.53). Click OK.

Fig. 7.53 This message reports that some records could not be pasted.

Figure 7.54 illustrates the result of this Pandora's box of messages. The set of four records copied to the Clipboard from Excel had all been previously pasted into the Access table; all four records duplicated key-field values in the existing table. Access pasted records without problems into the table and inserted the four records with duplicate key values into a PasteErrors table.

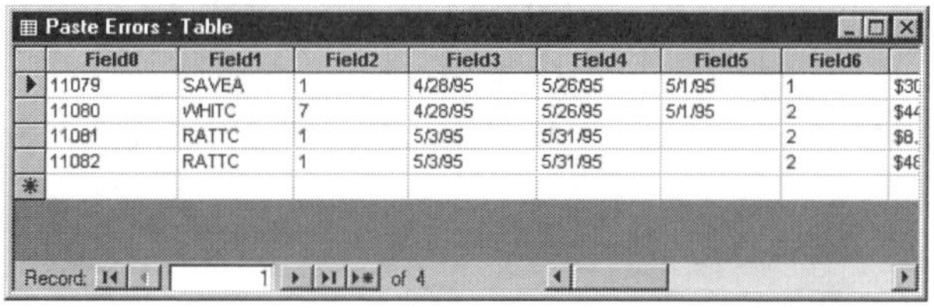

	Field0	Field1	Field2	Field3	Field4	Field5	Field6	
▶	11079	SAVEA	1	4/28/95	5/26/95	5/1/95	1	$30
	11080	WHITC	7	4/28/95	5/26/95	5/1/95	2	$44
	11081	RATTC	1	5/3/95	5/31/95		2	$8.
	11082	RATTC	1	5/3/95	5/31/95		2	$48

Fig. 7.54 Access puts all records that it could not paste from the Clipboard into the PasteErrors table.

If you specified one or more primary-key fields for your table, records that duplicate key field values are not appended. Tables without primary-key fields do not preclude adding duplicate records. The capability to index a nonkey field with the condition, "no duplicates allowed," is useful when you make new entries into a spreadsheet or word-processing document and you want to append the new entries as records to a table. You preserve the uniqueness of the records by preventing the addition of records that duplicate records already in your table.

Note

When pasting or importing large numbers of records to a table, you must specify primary-key fields or a no-duplicates-allowed index for fields that later may become the primary key before you import any data. If you import the data before you create the primary-key fields index, you may find many duplicate records in the table. Then, when Access tries to create a no-duplicates index on the key fields, you see the message, "Can't have duplicate key." You must manually review all the added records for duplicates because Access doesn't create an Errors table in this case. If, however, the data you are importing contains redundant information that you ultimately will remove to one or more secondary tables, you must import every record. Do not assign key fields or no-duplicates indexes in this case. The section, "Deleting Redundant Fields in Imported Tables," that follows in this chapter, discusses the requirement to import every record when records contain one-to-many relations.

Tip

If you do encounter the "Can't have duplicate key." error message when trying to establish a primary key, there is a quick way to find the duplicates. Open a new query and select the Find Duplicates Query Wizard. This Wizard creates a query that you can use to quickly find exactly where the duplicates are, without having to search record-by-record through your data.

Replacing Records by Pasting from the Clipboard

You can replace existing records in an Access table by pasting data in the Clipboard over the records. This process is useful when you are updating records with data from another Windows application. The data you paste must have a one-to-one column-to-field correspondence and must begin with the first field of the table. You need not, however, paste new data in all the fields. If no data is pasted in a field that is not included in the copied data's range, that field retains its original values.

To use data in the Clipboard to replace existing records in a table, follow this procedure:

1. Select and copy the data from the other application that you want to paste to the Clipboard, using the method previously described for appending records from Clipboard data.

 If you choose more than one row of data in Excel, for example, the rows must have a one-to-one correspondence with the records to be replaced in the Access table. The one-to-one correspondence is likely to occur only if the table is indexed and the source data you are copying is sorted in the same order as the index. You can paste only contiguous rows from Excel.

2. Open your Access table. To select the records to be replaced by the Clipboard data, click the selection button for a single record or drag the mouse across the buttons for multiple records.

If you are replacing multiple records, the number of records you select must be equal to or exceed the number of rows you copied to the Clipboard. If the number of records selected is less than the number of rows, the remaining rows are ignored.

If you are replacing records in a table with key fields or a no-duplicates index, the columns of the replacement data corresponding to the key or indexed fields of the table must match exactly the key fields of the selected records. Otherwise, you see the key duplication error message sequence.

3. Choose Edit, Paste in Access. In this case, rather than appending the records, the contents of the existing records are overwritten, and you see a dialog that tells you how many records will be replaced.

When you use Paste for a replacement record rather than Paste Append for a new record with an identical key field value, Access suppresses the key violation error messages.

> **Note**
>
> If you do not select one or more records to be replaced by the Pasting operation, and the caret is located within a data cell of one of your records or a data cell is selected, Access attempts to paste all the data in the Clipboard to this one cell, rather than to the records. If the data doesn't create a mismatch type error or exceed 255 characters (if the caret is in a Text field), you do not receive a warning message. If you notice unexpected data values in the cell, Access pasted all the data to a single cell. Press Esc before selecting another record; Access restores the original value of the data cell.

Modifying Linked and Imported Tables

Access provides a great deal of flexibility in the presentation of the Datasheet View of tables. You can rearrange the sequence of fields in Datasheet View without changing the underlying structure of the database. You also can alter the Caption property of the fields to change the names of the field name buttons. Although you cannot modify the field names, field data types, or Field Length properties of linked tables, you can use the Format property to display the data in linked or imported tables in various ways, as described in the sections that follow.

Restructuring the Presentation of Tables

The basic structure of the tables you link or import is controlled by the structure of the files from which the table was created. The original structure, unfortunately, may not be in the sequence you want to use for data entry. Database design, for example, often displays the key fields in a left-to-right sequence, starting with the first field. This sequence may not be the best sequence for entering data. You can change the order of the fields displayed by dragging and dropping the field name buttons of linked or imported tables to new locations, using the method described in Chapter 5, "Entering, Editing, and Validating Data in Tables."

Adding Fields to Tables with Imported Data

You can add fields to tables that use imported data. During the development of your database application, you may need to repeatedly import data into your table. Therefore, you should append new fields to the end of the field list in Design View rather than insert them between existing fields. The imported data fills the fields in the sequence of the rows in the field list, and the added fields contain null values. You then can rearrange the display position of the new fields in Design View, as described in the preceding section.

Changing Field Data Types of Imported Files

Access converts all numeric data within imported files to the Double data type. The only exception is Btrieve files, where Access assigns Byte, Integer, Long Integer, and Single data types when you link or import Btrieve files that include these data types. The following list contains recommendations for field data type changes for data imported from any type of source file:

■ Use *Integer* or *Long Integer* field data types for numeric fields that do not require decimal values. Your database files consume less disk space, and your applications run faster.

■ Change the data type of values that represent money to the data type, *Currency*, to eliminate rounding errors.

■ Assign Field Length property values to text-type fields. You should assign Field Length values no greater than the longest text entry you expect to make. If you assign a Field Length value less than the number of characters in the field, characters in positions beyond the Field Length value are lost irretrievably.

Because Paradox versions prior to Paradox 4.x do not provide a memo field data type, you often can find comments in large, fixed-width alphanumeric fields. If you import Paradox files that contain fields of comments, you should convert the fields to memo fields unless you plan to export the data back to a Paradox 3.x file. (You cannot export a table that contains a memo-type field to Paradox 3.x files, although you can export tables with memo fields to Paradox 4.x and Paradox for Windows 5.) The same recommendation applies to comments in variable-length string fields of Btrieve files.

Adding or Modifying other Field Properties

The following table includes properties of both linked and imported tables that you can change:

Property	Description
Caption	Use to change the caption of the field name buttons when using linked files. You can assign any FieldName property to imported tables.
Decimal Places	Use to specify the number of decimal places to be displayed for numeric values other than Byte, Integer, and Long Integer.

Property	Description
Default Value	Default values are substituted for data elements missing in the imported or linked file. The default values, however, do not replace zeros and blank strings that represent "no entry" in the fields of most PC database files.
Format	Use to create custom formats to display the data in the most readable form.
Validation Rule	Validation rules do not affect importing data; they affect only editing the data or appending new records in Access. You cannot use a validation rule to filter imported records. Filtering, in this case, means importing only records that meet the validation rule.
Validation Text	Prompts created from validation text assist data entry operators when they begin using a new table.

Deleting Redundant Fields in Imported Tables

The purpose of a relational database is to eliminate redundant data in tables. If you design a database that doesn't use data imported or linked from existing databases, you can eliminate data redundancy by following the normalization rules of relational database design described in Chapter 23, "Exploring Relational Database Design and Implementation." When you link files, however, you are at the mercy of the database designer who originally created the files. Any redundant data the linked file contains is likely to remain a permanent characteristic of the file. Existing database structures are substantially inert; developers of applications that work usually are reluctant to make changes. Changes may introduce new problems that can later return to haunt the developers.

If you import table data from a file or append records by pasting from the Clipboard, you can eliminate data redundancy by restructuring the resulting tables. An Invoice table, for example, may contain one record for each invoice. When a customer makes more than one purchase, the customer information is duplicated in the invoice file for each purchase. In this situation, you need to create separate tables for customers and invoices. The Customer table should contain one record per customer, with name and address information. The Invoice table should contain one record per customer with date, amount, and other information specific to the transaction.

Removing redundancy from existing tables by dividing them into two or more related tables is not a simple task, even if you use the Table Analyzer Wizard (accessed by choosing Tools, Analyze, Table). You must either manually (or with the help of the table analyzer) create a query that establishes the relationship between two tables that contain one record for each invoice based on a new primary-key field. Then you delete the duplicate records from the Customer table. Fortunately, the ImportErrors table can do much of the work; import the data into a new table with primary-key fields or a no-duplicate index on the customer name and address.

Another type of redundancy is the presence of fields in tables that have values calculated from other fields, either within the table or in the fields of related tables. Any field with values derived from combinations of values within the table or accessible in any other related table within the database or linked to the database contains redundant data. In this case, just remove the redundant field and perform the calculation with a query. Do not remove redundant fields, however, until you verify that your calculated values match those in the redundant field to be replaced.

You need to learn about queries and joining tables—the subject of the next four chapters—to know how to eliminate redundancy in imported tables. The point of this discussion is to let you know that you can perform much of the restructuring by using specialized Access operations and to caution you not to try to remove duplicate data from imported tables prematurely.

Exporting Data from Access Tables

▶▶ See "Joining Tables to Create Multitable Queries," p. 318

You can export data contained in Access tables in any format you can use to import data. The most common export operation with PC RDBMSs is the creation of mail-merge files, used with word-processing applications and spreadsheet files, for data analysis. In most cases, you may want to export the result of a query, enabling you to select specific records to export rather than the entire contents of a file. Exporting tables created from action queries is discussed in Chapter 11, "Using Action Queries."

Exporting Data through the Windows Clipboard

If a Windows application is to use your exported data, the simplest method to export data is to copy the records you want to export to the Windows Clipboard, and then paste the data into the other application. You can copy specific groups of contiguous records to the Clipboard by using the techniques described in Chapter 5, "Entering, Editing, and Validating Data in Tables."

To create a merge data file from the Customers table of the Northwind sample database for use with Word, follow these steps:

1. Open the Northwind.mdb database.

2. Open the Customers table from the table list.

3. Select the records to copy by selecting the upper left corner of the block with the F2 key, and then holding down the Shift key and using the arrow keys to define the records you want to copy to the Clipboard. Alternatively, you can select the area to copy by placing the cursor at the upper left corner of the block you want to copy; the cursor turns into a big plus symbol. Hold down the left mouse button and drag to the lower right corner of the block. The Datasheet View should look like the window in figure 7.55. (If you want to select all fields of all records in the table, choose Edit, Select All Records.)

4. Press Ctrl+C or choose Edit, Copy to copy the selected records to the Clipboard.

5. Open Word and choose File, New to create a new document for your merge data file.

6. Press Ctrl+V or choose Edit, Paste to paste the records from the Clipboard into your new document. Access 95 pastes the records as a fully-formatted table in Word, as illustrated by figure 7.56. The column widths you select in Access are used to define the column widths of the Word table.

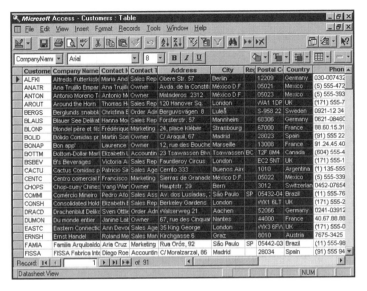

Fig. 7.55 Select the records to copy to the Clipboard.

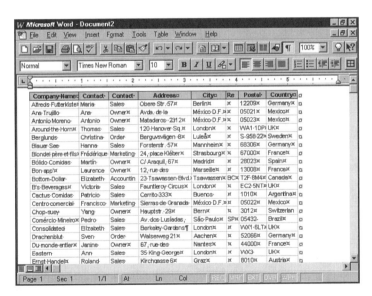

Fig. 7.56 Data imports into a Word document as a formatted table.

When you copy Access records to the Clipboard, the first line contains field names, no matter what group of records you select. If you append individual records or groups of records to those already pasted to a document in another application, you must manually remove the duplicated field names.

> **Note**
>
> The field names pasted into Word documents contain spaces. Spaces, however, are not allowed in the first (field names) row for merge data documents. Delete the spaces or replace them with underscores so that Word accepts the names. If you do not remove the spaces, you receive an error message when you try to use the document during the Merge operation.

Exporting Data as a Text File

Exporting a table involves a sequence of operations similar to importing a file with the same format. To export a table as a comma-delimited file that you can use as a merge file with a wide variety of word-processing applications, complete these steps:

1. Activate the Database window.

2. Choose <u>F</u>ile, Save <u>A</u>s/Export. The Save As dialog appears (see fig. 7.57). Select the To an external File or Database option, and then click OK.

Fig. 7.57 The Save As dialog lets you select saving a table as an external file.

3. Access now displays the Save Table *Filename* As dialog (see fig. 7.58). Select Text Files in the Save as type drop-down list. Use the Save in drop-down list to select the drive and folder in which you want to store the exported file, enter a name for the exported file in the File name text box, and then click Export.

4. Access starts the Text Export Wizard. Using the Text Export Wizard, including its advanced options, is the same as using the Text Import Wizard described previously, except that the end result is an external file instead of an Access table. (When exporting a text file, the Text Export Wizard doesn't have a step to edit field names, or select field data types; these options aren't relevant when exporting data.) To finish exporting the text file, follow the procedures as if you were importing a text file. Figure 7.59 shows the exported Customers table from the Northwind.mdb database displayed by Windows Notepad.

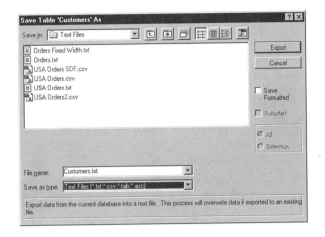

Fig. 7.58   To start the Text Export Wizard, use the Save Table As dialog.

Fig. 7.59   You can use Windows Notepad or Wordpad to view the comma-delimited text file.

Note

The two highlighted lines in figure 7.59 are a single record from the Access table that was split into two text records during the export process. A newline pair is included in the Address field of the record for Consolidated Holdings. The purpose of the newline pair is to separate a single field into two lines, Berkeley Gardens and 12 Brewery. Use of newline pairs within fields causes many problems with exported files. As mentioned previously in this chapter, use of embedded newline pairs in text fields isn't good database design practice. Use two address fields if you need secondary address lines.

The records in files created by Access are exported in the order of the primary key. Any other order you may have created is ignored. If you do not assign primary-key fields, the records are exported in the sequence that you entered them into the table.

Exporting Data in other File Formats

In addition to text files, you can export data to any other file format that Access can import. Access supports export to Excel .XLS files (in formats for versions 2.0 through 95), Lotus 1-2-3 and Symphony .WK? format, rich-text format (.RTF) files for Microsoft Word and other Windows word-processing applications, Btrieve, Paradox for DOS 3.x, 4.x and 5.0 formats, FoxPro 2.x, and 3.0 formats, dBASE III/III+, IV and 5 formats, or through an ODBC driver.

> **Note**
>
> When you export a dBASE file in Access 95, Access creates .NDX files that correspond to the primary key and any additional indexes you may have created in Access. Exporting a Paradox .DB file, however, does *not* create an associated .PX file to accompany it. You must use Paradox to re-create any index files required for your application.

From Here...

Importing data created by other applications is one of the most important subjects when explaining how to use an RDBMS with a new and, for PC RDBMSs, unusual file structure. Fortunately, with Access you can link dBASE, Paradox, and even Btrieve files; Btrieve file compatibility is uncommon in PC RDBMSs. After you create your database applications by using Access forms, reports, and macros and change over to Access as your primary RDBMS, you probably will choose to import all your files into the Access native .MDB structure.

The following four chapters deal with queries—the method used by Access to enable you to select the specific data you need from one or more tables:

- Chapter 8, "Using Query by Example," introduces you to Access's graphical QBE design window.

- Chapter 9, "Understanding Operators and Expressions in Access," shows how to create expressions that you use to add criteria to your queries.

- Chapter 10, "Creating Multitable and Crosstab Queries," explains how to join two or more tables based on primary- and foreign-key fields, and how to rearrange your query result set into a spreadsheet-like format.

- Chapter 11, "Using Action Queries," describes how to create queries that alter the data in tables or create new tables from a query result set.

A few of these chapters are extensive; you don't have to remember all the nuances of these chapters. You do need to remember where the instructions for performing specific types of operations are presented, so that you can return to that point in the book when you create your initial database applications.

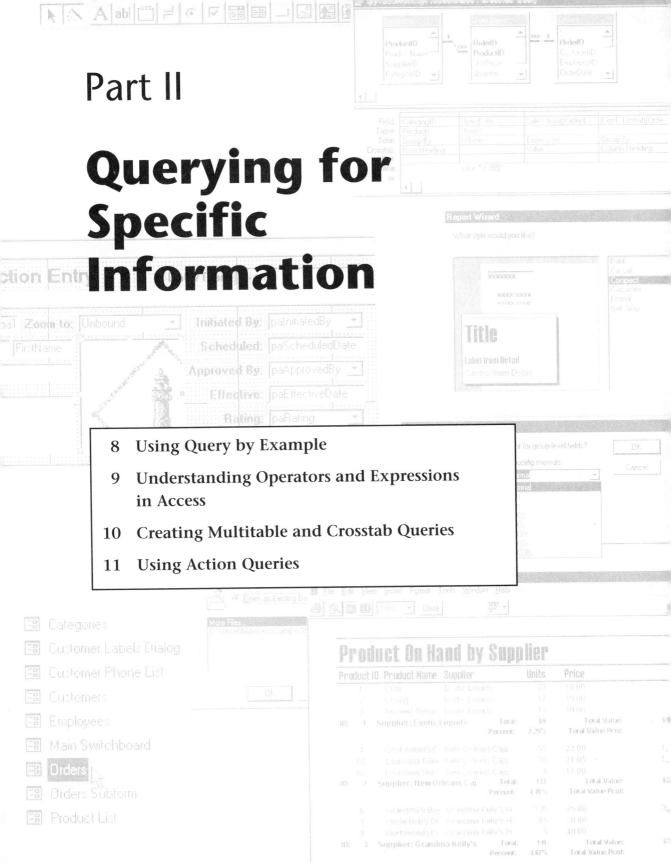

Part II

Querying for Specific Information

Chapter 8

Using Query by Example

Query by Example, usually abbreviated QBE, was originally developed to enable users of mainframe-computer database applications to find and display pieces of data (or collections of data) without having to know a computer language. Many database management systems eventually came to use QBE in one form or another. (In fact, dBASE, the first commercially successful PC database manager, uses a variant of QBE for its dot-prompt commands.)

At a command prompt, for example, QBE users enter such statements as this:

```
LIST ALL lastnames LIKE Lin* WITH state IL IN us_hist
```

These are known as *give me an example of* statements. The QBE application program then searched the `lastnames` field of the `us_hist` table file for all names beginning with `Lin`. The program disregarded the remaining characters in the names and displayed only those records that have a state field containing the value `IL`.

As computer display terminals became more sophisticated, *graphical QBE* developed as the preferred method of creating queries. Graphical QBE displays the field names of one or more database tables as headers of a column. Users can type partial example statements, or *expressions*, in these columns to create a query. Because terminals capable of displaying actual graphics were a rarity when graphical QBE was developed, the standard 80-character by 25-line text mode was used. The term *graphical* is a misnomer, therefore, in today's world of truly graphical user environments like Windows. In the original version of graphical QBE, the preceding example statement might resemble the following display:

```
LASTNAME FIRSTNAME ADDRESS CITY STATE
Like LIN*                         IL
```

Fields corresponding to the columns in which no expressions are entered are not checked for compliance with the query.

After checking the designated fields and finding all matches within the searched file, the application displays those addresses containing matching

In this chapter, you learn to

- Create a simple select query for a single table

- Print your query as a report

- Create a simple make-table action query

- Add user-entered parameters to queries

- Understand simple SQL statements

II

Specific Information

values. The parts of each address appear in their respective columns, as in the following example:

```
LASTNAME    FIRSTNAME   ADDRESS         CITY          STATE
Lincoln     Abraham     123 Elm St.     Springfield   IL
Lincoln     Mary Todd   123 Elm St.     Springfield   IL
```

Learning to type query expressions in graphical QBE columns proved easier for most computer users than typing QBE expressions at a prompt. The user had to know the syntax of only a few expressions to create relatively complex queries. The use of graphical QBE was one feature that made Ansa Software's original Paradox RDBMS a success in the PC desktop RDBMS market, dominated at the time by dBASE II and dBASE III.

Microsoft Windows introduced a graphical user environment ideally suited to a truly graphical QBE database management system. Microsoft has taken full advantage of the wide range of graphical features incorporated in Windows 95, as you see when you create your first true Access query.

Creating Your First Real Query

Chapter 6, "Sorting, Finding, and Filtering Data in Tables," introduced the concepts of creating queries. You applied a sort order to tables and added record selection criteria to filters for data contained in tables. Access's Query Design window, however, gives you greater flexibility than the Filter window because it lets you choose the fields that appear in the query result set. You also can create more complex queries by joining primary and related tables.

This chapter explains the basics of QBE. You learn to create multitable queries in Chapter 10, "Creating Multitable and Crosstab Queries," after you learn the details of how to use operators and create expressions in Chapter 9, "Understanding Operators and Expressions in Access." Expressions often are used as criteria for more complex queries.

To devise a simple query that enables you to customize mailing lists for selected customers of Northwind Traders, for example, follow these steps:

1. Open the Northwind Traders database (filename Northwind.mdb in the \MSOffice\Access\Samples folder. The Northwind Database window appears.

2. Click the arrow adjacent to the New Object button in the toolbar and choose New Query from the drop-down menu; alternatively, click the Query tab in the Database window and then click the New button. The New Query dialog appears (see fig. 8.1). This dialog lets you select between creating a query yourself (Design View) or using one of the the Query Wizard's button to design specialized queries. Select the New Query item and click OK to display the Query Design window.

3. The Show Table dialog is superimposed on the Query Design window, as shown in figure 8.2. The tabbed lists in the Show Table dialog box let you select from all existing tables, all queries, or a combination of all tables and queries. You can base a new query on one or more previously entered tables or queries. (The tables and

queries listed in the Show Table list come with Access as samples for the Northwind Traders database.)

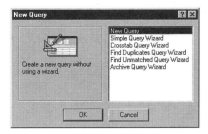

Fig. 8.1 The New Query dialog lets you choose between Query Wizards and Design View to create your own query design.

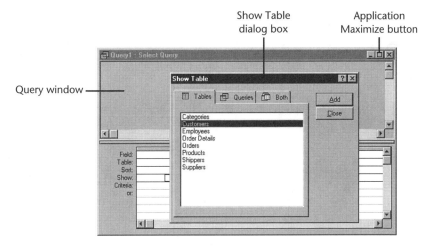

Fig. 8.2 You begin the design of a new query with the Show Table dialog.

4. This example uses only tables in the query, so accept the default selection of Tables. Click (or use the down-arrow key to select) Customers in the Show Table list to select the Customers table, and then choose the Add button. Alternatively, double-click Customers to add a table to the query. You can use more than one table in a query by choosing another table name from the list and choosing Add again. This example, however, uses only one table. After selecting the tables that you want to use, choose Close. The Show Table dialog disappears.

5. The Field list for the Customers table appears at the left in the upper pane of the Query Design window, and a blank Query Design grid appears in the lower pane, as shown in figure 8.3. The Field list displays all the names of the fields listed in the Customers table.

Upper pane

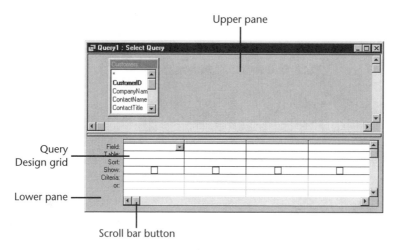

Query Design grid

Lower pane

Scroll bar button

Fig. 8.3 The Field list box of the Customers table in a Query Design window.

By clicking the Query and New buttons in the Database window, you enter Access's Query Design view. By default, you create SELECT queries that return selected data from tables or the result set of other SELECT queries. Access assigns a default name, Query1, to the first query that you create (but have not yet saved) in this mode. You assign your own names to queries when you save them. If you create additional queries without saving the first query, Access assigns them the default names Query2, Query3, and so on, in sequence.

Choosing Fields for Your Query

After you choose a table from the Show Table dialog, the next step is to decide which of the table's fields to include in your query. Because you plan to use this query to create a customer mailing list, you must include the fields that make up a personalized mailing address.

As this chapter's introduction explained, the first row of any graphical QBE query contains the names of each field involved in the query. (These field names also are called *field headers*.) The sample query that you are creating, therefore, must include in its first row the names of all the fields that constitute a mailing address.

To choose the fields that you want to include in the Query Design grid, follow these steps:

1. When you open the Query Design window, the insertion point (called the *caret* in this book) is located in the Field row of the first column. Click the List Box button that appears in the right corner of the first column, or press F4, to open the Field Name list (see fig. 8.4).

2. Click the ContactName field to choose it as the first field header of the query, or use the down-arrow key to highlight the name and press Enter. The Field list in the lower pane closes.

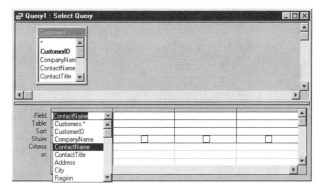

Fig. 8.4   The first step in creating a query design is to add a field name.

3. Move the caret to the second column by using the right-arrow or Tab key. (Notice that the List Box button moves to the second column along with the caret.) Double-click CompanyName in the Customers field list in the upper pane to add CompanyName as the second field of your query. Double-clicking entries in the upper pane's list is the second method that Access provides to add fields to a query.

Access offers a third method of adding fields to your query: the *drag-and-drop* method. You can add the Address, City, and Region fields to columns 3 through 5, respectively, in one step by using the drag-and-drop method (see steps 4 and 5).

4. To use the drag-and-drop method of adding fields, you must first select the fields. In the Customers field list of the upper pane's Query Design window, click Address and hold the Shift or Ctrl key as you click City and Region. Alternatively, select Address with the down-arrow key, hold the Shift or Ctrl key, and press the down-arrow key twice more. You have selected the Address, City, and Region fields, as shown in figure 8.5.

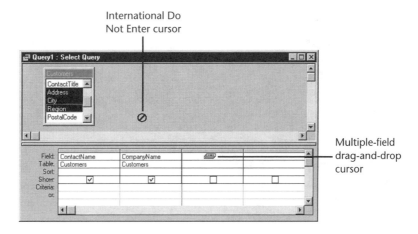

Fig. 8.5   Select multiple fields and use the drag-and-drop method to add the fields to the query.

5. Position the mouse pointer over the selected fields and click the left mouse button. Your mouse pointer turns into a symbol representing the three selected field names. Drag the symbol for the three fields to the third column of your query's Field row, as shown in figure 8.5, and release the left mouse button.

Access adds the three fields to your query, in sequence, starting with the column in which you drop the symbol. When the mouse pointer is in an area where you cannot drop the fields, it becomes the international Do Not Enter symbol shown in the upper pane of the Query Design window.

6. The Query Design grid in the lower pane displays four columns (in the default width) in a normal Query Design window. This query uses seven fields, so you need to drag the edges of the Query Design window to increase the width of the grid's display to expose two additional empty fields. You can reduce the columns' width by dragging the divider of the grid's header bars to the left. Click the scroll-right button (on the horizontal scroll bar at the bottom of the window) twice to display two blank fields, or drag the scroll bar slider button to the right to expose empty fields as necessary.

7. Click the scroll-down button in the Customers field list to display the PostalCode and Country fields. Hold the Shift or Ctrl key and select PostalCode and Country. Drag the symbol for these two fields to the first empty field cell (column 6), and drop the two fields there. Your Query Design window appears similar to the one shown in figure 8.6. (Notice that the check boxes in the Show row for the columns that contain a field name now are marked.)

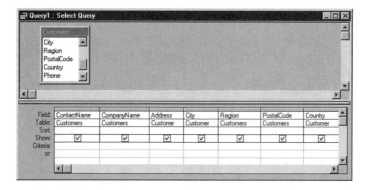

Fig. 8.6 The seven field names included in the new query.

Note

Most of the figures in this book are created with windows in *Normal* style, which occupies a portion of the display, rather than *Maximized* style, which occupies all the display. Normal style is used so that figures can be reproduced on a larger scale, which improves legibility.

8. Click the Query View button on the toolbar to enter run mode. Expect a brief waiting period while Access processes your query on the Customers table. Alternatively, click the Run button on the toolbar to run your query against the Customers table.

Because you have not yet entered any selection criteria in the Criteria row of the Query Design grid, your query results in the Customers table displaying all records. These records appear in the order of the primary key index on the CustomerID field because you have not specified a sorting order in the Sort row of the design. (The values in the CustomerID field are alphabetic codes derived from the Company Name field.) Figure 8.7 shows the result of your first query.

Contact Name	Company Name	Address
Maria Anders	Alfreds Futterkiste	Obere Str. 57
Ana Trujillo	Ana Trujillo Emparedados y helados	Avda. de la Constitución 2222
Antonio Moreno	Antonio Moreno Taquería	Mataderos 2312
Thomas Hardy	Around the Horn	120 Hanover Sq.
Christina Berglund	Berglunds snabbköp	Berguvsvägen 8
Hanna Moos	Blauer See Delikatessen	Forsterstr. 57
Frédérique Citeaux	Blondel père et fils	24, place Kléber
Martín Sommer	Bólido Comidas preparadas	C/ Araquil, 67
Laurence Lebihan	Bon app'	12, rue des Bouchers
Elizabeth Lincoln	Bottom-Dollar Markets	23 Tsawassen Blvd.
Victoria Ashworth	B's Beverages	Fauntleroy Circus
Patricio Simpson	Cactus Comidas para llevar	Cerrito 333
Francisco Chang	Centro comercial Moctezuma	Sierras de Granada 9993
Yang Wang	Chop-suey Chinese	Hauptstr. 29
Pedro Afonso	Comércio Mineiro	Av. dos Lusíadas, 23

Record: 1 of 91

Fig. 8.7 A list of all records contained in the table.

> **Note**
>
> Many field names of tables in Access 2.0's NWIND.MDB sample database contained spaces. Most RDBMSs don't permit spaces in field names or table names. Field names in Access 95's Northwind.mdb no longer include spaces. Access 95's Northwind.mdb uses the `Caption` property of table fields to alter (alias) the field headers of tables to add spaces where appropriate. For example, to alias the Customers table's CompanyName field, you set the `Caption` property's value to Company Name.

Selecting Records by Criteria and Sorting the Display

◄◄ See "Working with Relations, Key Fields, and Indexes," p. 142

The mailing for which you are creating a list with your sample query is to be sent to U.S. customers only, so you want to include in your query only those records that have USA in their Country fields. Selecting records based on the values of fields—that is, establishing the criteria for the records to be returned (displayed) by the query—is the very heart of the query process.

Perform the following steps to establish criteria for selecting the records to comprise your mailing list:

1. Click the Design View button on the toolbar to return to design mode. The partially filled Query Design grid replaces the mailing list on-screen.

2. To restrict the result of your query to firms in the United States, type the expression **USA** in the Criteria row of the Country column. Entering a criterion's value without preceding the value with an operator indicates that the value of the field must match the value of the expression *USA*. You do not need to add quotation marks to the expression; Access adds them for you (see the Country column in fig. 8.8).

3. Click the Show check box in the Country column to remove the check mark that appeared when you named the column. After you deactivate the Show check box, the Country field does not display when you run your query. (You do not need to include the Country column in your mailing list address if you are mailing from a U.S. location to other U.S. locations.) If you do not deactivate a Show check box, that field in the query displays by default.

4. Move the caret to the PostalCode column's Sort row and press F4 to display the sorting options for that field: Ascending, Descending, and (not sorted). Choose the Ascending option to sort the query by PostalCode from low codes to high.

   At this point, the Query Design grid appears as shown in figure 8.8.

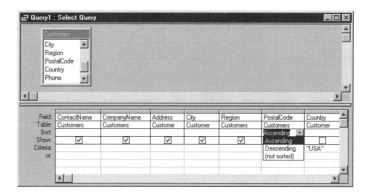

Fig. 8.8 Adding the Ascending sort order to the PostalCode field.

5. Click the Query View or Run button on the toolbar to display the result of your criterion and sorting order. Use the horizontal scroll bar to display additional fields.

Figure 8.9 displays the query result table (also called a *query result set*) that Access refers to as an updatable Recordset (a Recordset object of the Dynaset type, to be more precise). A Recordset object is a temporary table stored in your computer's memory; it is not a permanent component of the database file. A Recordset object differs from the conventional view of an object created by the SQL VIEW reserved word because you can update the data in a Recordset object of the Dynaset type. After you save the query, the Northwind.mbd file saves only the design specifications of the query, not the values that the query contains. The query design specification is called a `QueryDef` object.

Fig. 8.9 Sorting the query in numeric order by Postal Code values.

Creating More Complex Queries

To limit your mailing to customers in a particular state or group of states, you can add a Criteria expression to the Region or PostalCode field. To restrict the mailing to customers in California, Oregon, and Washington, for example, you can specify that the value of the PostalCode field must be equal to or greater than 90000. Alternatively, you can specify that Region values must be CA, OR, and WA.

Follow these steps to restrict your mailing to customers in California, Oregon, and Washington:

1. Click the Design View button on the toolbar to return to design mode.

2. Use the right-arrow or Tab key to move the caret to the Region column. If the Region column is not on-screen, click the scroll-right button until that column appears.

3. Type **CA** in the first criteria row of the Region column. Access adds the quotation marks around CA (as it did when you restricted your mailing to U.S. locations with the USA criterion).

4. Press the down-arrow key to move to the next criteria row in the Region column. Type **OR**, and then move to the third criteria row and type **WA**. Your query design now appears as shown in figure 8.10. Access adds the required quotation marks to these criteria also.

5. Click the Query Datasheet View or Run button on the toolbar to return to run mode. The query result set appears as shown in figure 8.11.

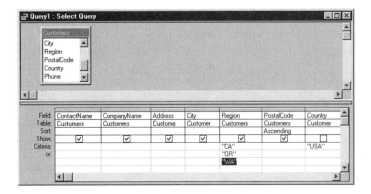

Fig. 8.10 Adding criteria to the Region field of the Query Design grid.

> **Note**
>
> After you type a criterion on the same line as a previously entered criterion in another field, only those records that meet *both* criteria are selected for display. In the preceding example, therefore, only those records with Region values equal to CA *and* Country values equal to USA are displayed. To be displayed, records for Region values OR and WA need not have Country values equal to USA because the USA criterion is missing from the OR and WA rows. This omission does not really affect the selection of records in this case because all OR and WA records are also USA records. To eliminate possible ambiguity, however, USA should appear in each criterion row that contains a state code.
>
> (Note that the remaining criteria rows in the different columns on the Query Design grid enable you to enter additional criteria to qualify further which records to display. In the current example, you need no additional criteria, so Access leaves these cells blank.)

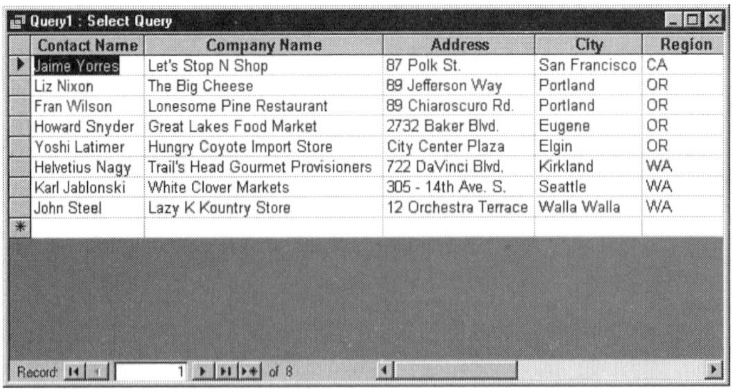

	Contact Name	Company Name	Address	City	Region
▶	Jaime Yorres	Let's Stop N Shop	87 Polk St.	San Francisco	CA
	Liz Nixon	The Big Cheese	89 Jefferson Way	Portland	OR
	Fran Wilson	Lonesome Pine Restaurant	89 Chiaroscuro Rd.	Portland	OR
	Howard Snyder	Great Lakes Food Market	2732 Baker Blvd.	Eugene	OR
	Yoshi Latimer	Hungry Coyote Import Store	City Center Plaza	Elgin	OR
	Helvetius Nagy	Trail's Head Gourmet Provisioners	722 DaVinci Blvd.	Kirkland	WA
	Karl Jablonski	White Clover Markets	305 - 14th Ave. S.	Seattle	WA
	John Steel	Lazy K Kountry Store	12 Orchestra Terrace	Walla Walla	WA
*					

Record: ◀◀ ◀ 1 ▶ ▶▶ ▶* of 8

Fig. 8.11 The query result set for customers in California, Oregon, and Washington.

Editing Table Data in Query View

You can edit the data in any visible fields of the table in the query display. Any table that underlies the Recordset reflects the changes that you make to data cells in an updatable Recordset object of the Dynaset type. To edit an entry in a query and then verify the change to the corresponding record in the underlying table, perform these steps:

1. Use the right-arrow or Tab key to move the caret to the first row of the Company Name column (Let's Stop N Shop).

2. Press F2 to deselect the field and to enter edit mode.

3. Use the arrow keys to position the cursor to immediately before the *N* and add an apostrophe to change the Company Name value to Let's Stop 'N Shop.

4. Press Enter or move the caret down another line to make the change to Let's Stop 'N Shop permanent. (Data in the underlying table does not change until you press Enter or move to a different record.)

> **Note**
>
> Unlike edits made to values in indexed fields in dBASE's browse mode, changes made to sorted fields in Access do not actually move the edited records to their correct locations in the query tables until you press Shift+F9 to rerun the query.

5. Click the Database Window button of the toolbar, or choose <u>W</u>indow, <u>1</u> Database and then click the Table tab of the Database window.

6. Double-click the Customers table to display the table in Datasheet View. Scroll down to verify that the underlying Customers table reflects your update to the query data (see fig. 8.12).

Customer ID	Company Name	Contact Name	Contact Title
LEHMS	Lehmanns Marktstand	Renate Messner	Sales Representative
LETSS	Let's Stop 'N Shop	Jaime Yorres	Owner
LILAS	LILA-Supermercado	Carlos González	Accounting Manager
LINOD	LINO-Delicateses	Felipe Izquierdo	Owner
LONEP	Lonesome Pine Restaurant	Fran Wilson	Sales Manager
MAGAA	Magazzini Alimentari Riuniti	Giovanni Rovelli	Marketing Manager
MAISD	Maison Dewey	Catherine Dewey	Sales Agent
MEREP	Mère Paillarde	Jean Fresnière	Marketing Assistant
MORGK	Morgenstern Gesundkost	Alexander Feuer	Marketing Assistant
NORTS	North/South	Simon Crowther	Sales Associate
OCEAN	Océano Atlántico Ltda.	Yvonne Moncada	Sales Agent
OLDWO	Old World Delicatessen	Rene Phillips	Sales Representative
OTTIK	Ottilies Käseladen	Henriette Pfalzheim	Owner
PARIS	Paris spécialités	Marie Bertrand	Owner
PERIC	Pericles Comidas clásicas	Guillermo Fernández	Sales Representative
PICCO	Piccolo und mehr	Georg Pipps	Sales Manager

Record: 45 of 91

Fig. 8.12   Rerunning the query displays the correction to the record's Company Name.

Changing the Names of Query Column Headers

You can substitute a query's field header names with column header names of your choice, a process called *aliasing*, but only if the header name has not been changed by an entry in the field Caption property of the table. If you are a U.S. firm, for example, you might want to change Region to State and PostalCode to ZIP. (Canadian firms might want to change only Region to Province.) As demonstrated in the following example, you cannot make the change to the PostalCode field for queries based on the Customers table because the PostalCode field previously has been changed (aliased) to Postal Code by the Caption property for the field. You can, however, make the change to the Region field because this field is not aliased at the table level.

> ### Tip
>
> If you already have a main document for the merge operation, substitute the main merge document's merge field names for the table's field header names in your query.

> ### Note
>
> The inability to alias field names in queries that have been altered by use of the Caption property in the source table is a good reason not to use the Caption property of table fields. If you want to display different field headers, use a query for this purpose. In a client/server RDBMS, such a query is called an SQL VIEW. Aliasing field names in tables, rather than queries, is not considered a generally-accepted database design practice.

To attempt to change the query column header names, perform the following steps:

1. Switch to design mode by clicking the toolbar's Design View button. Then use the right-arrow or Tab key to move the caret to the Field column containing the field header name that you want to change—in this case, the Region column.

2. Press F2 to deselect the field; then press Home to move the caret to the first character position.

3. Type the new name for the column and follow the name with a colon (with no spaces):

   State:

   The colon separates the new column name that you type from the existing table field name, which shifts to the right to make room for your addition. The result, in this example, is State:Region (see fig. 8.13).

4. Use the arrow key to move to the PostalCode field and repeat steps 2 and 3, typing **ZIP:** as that header's new name. The result, as shown in figure 8.13, is ZIP:PostalCode.

5. Change the column header for the ContactName field to Contact; change the column header for the CompanyName field to Company (refer to steps 2, 3, and 4).

6. Delete the CA, OR, and WA criteria from the State:Region column so that all records for the U.S. appear.

7. Click the toolbar's Query View or Run button to return to run mode and execute the query. Observe that only the Region column header is changed to State; the other columns are unaffected by the alias entry (see fig. 8.14).

Query1 : Select Query
Customers
City
Region
PostalCode
Country
Phone
Field: Company: CompanyName | Address | City | State: Region | ZIP: PostalCode | Country
Table: Customers | Custome | Custome | Customers | Customers | Customer
Sort: Ascending
Show:
Criteria: "USA"
or:

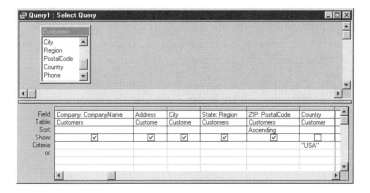

Fig. 8.13 Changing the names of the Region and Postal Code column headers.

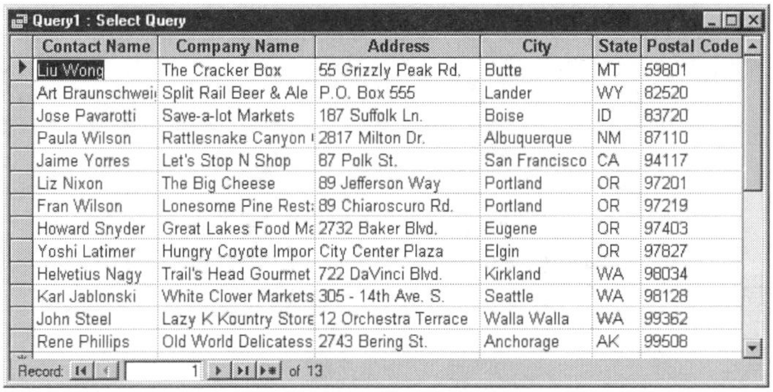

Query1 : Select Query
Contact Name | Company Name | Address | City | State | Postal Code
Liu Wong | The Cracker Box | 55 Grizzly Peak Rd. | Butte | MT | 59801
Art Braunschwei | Split Rail Beer & Ale | P.O. Box 555 | Lander | WY | 82520
Jose Pavarotti | Save-a-lot Markets | 187 Suffolk Ln. | Boise | ID | 83720
Paula Wilson | Rattlesnake Canyon | 2817 Milton Dr. | Albuquerque | NM | 87110
Jaime Yorres | Let's Stop N Shop | 87 Polk St. | San Francisco | CA | 94117
Liz Nixon | The Big Cheese | 89 Jefferson Way | Portland | OR | 97201
Fran Wilson | Lonesome Pine Rest | 89 Chiaroscuro Rd. | Portland | OR | 97219
Howard Snyder | Great Lakes Food M | 2732 Baker Blvd. | Eugene | OR | 97403
Yoshi Latimer | Hungry Coyote Impor | City Center Plaza | Elgin | OR | 97827
Helvetius Nagy | Trail's Head Gourmet | 722 DaVinci Blvd. | Kirkland | WA | 98034
Karl Jablonski | White Clover Markets | 305 - 14th Ave. S. | Seattle | WA | 98128
John Steel | Lazy K Kountry Store | 12 Orchestra Terrace | Walla Walla | WA | 99362
Rene Phillips | Old World Delicatess | 2743 Bering St. | Anchorage | AK | 99508
Record: 1 of 13

Fig. 8.14 The query result set appears with only one new column header.

> **Note**
>
> To make field aliasing in queries operable, delete the entries in the Caption field for each of the aliased fields of the table. In the sections that follow, the entries in the Caption property of the ContactName, CompanyName, and PostalCode fields of the Customers table have been deleted. Deleting these entries makes the aliases you entered in the preceding example work as expected.

Printing Your Query as a Report

Queries are often used to print quick, *ad hoc* reports. Access 95 lets you print your report to a Word for Windows .rtf (rich-text format) file, Excel worksheet .xls file, or a DOS .TXT (text) file, or as an attachment to an Exchange message. Chapter 14, "Printing Basic Reports and Mailing Labels," describes how to print reports to .rtf and .xls files and as attachments to Microsoft Mail messages.

Previewing your query table's appearance to see how the table will appear when printed is usually a good idea. After you determine from the preview that everything in the table is correct, you can print the finished query result set in a variety of formats.

To preview a query result set before printing it, follow these steps:

1. In Query View, click the Print Preview button on the toolbar. A miniature version of the query table appears in report preview mode.

2. Position the *Zoom mouse pointer* (the magnifying glass cursor) at the upper-left corner of the miniature table and click the left mouse button or the Zoom button above the window to view the report at approximately the scale at which it will print.

3. Use the vertical and horizontal scroll bar buttons to position the preview in the window (see fig. 8.15).

Fig. 8.15 Preview the Mailing List query table at zoomed scale.

> **Note**
>
> Field width in the query table is based on the column width that you last established in run mode. You might have to drag the right edge of the field header buttons to the right to increase the columns' width so that the printed report does not truncate the data. If the query data's width exceeds the available printing width (the paper width minus the width of the left and right margins), Access prints two or more sheets for each page of the report.

4. Click the Close button and then alter the width of the columns in run mode so that all seven columns of the query fit on one sheet of paper when you print it. Return to report preview mode after you finish this process.

> **Note**
>
> Adjust the displayed width of query fields the same way that you adjusted table fields (as described in Chapters 4, "Working with Access Databases and Tables," and 6, "Sorting, Finding, and Filtering Data in Tables"). Access stores query column widths as properties of the query.

To print to the default printer a query table after previewing it and determining that all the data is correct, simply click the Print button of the toolbar. To change the default printing margins of one inch on all sides of the sheet (or any revised defaults that you might have set earlier by choosing Tools, Options and entering new values in the Print Options text boxes of the General page), or to print only data (but not field header names), follow these steps:

1. Choose File, Page Setup to open the Page Setup dialog shown in figure 8.16. If necessary, click the Margins tab to display the Margins page.

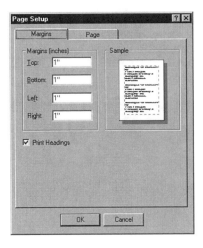

Fig. 8.16   The Page Setup dialog.

2. Enter any changes that you want to make to the margins; mark the Print Headings check box if you want to print the field header names. Click the Page tab to change the print orientation, paper size or source, or printer. Then click OK to return to print preview mode.

3. Click the Print button of the toolbar to print your query data.

Using the Data from Your Query

Occasionally, you might want to use data from your query as part of a different Windows application without printing the data in a report. The simplest technique for transferring data in your query to another Windows application is to use the Clipboard. Clipboard operations for data in query tables are identical to those operations for tables described in Chapter 7, "Linking, Importing, and Exporting Tables."

Access 95 includes a Merge It choice when you click the arrow adjacent to the Office Links button on the toolbar. Merge It automatically creates a Word mail merge document. Performing automated operations manually, however, gives you insight into how

Access 95 implements Office Links. To create manually a merge data file for Word directly from a query, for example, follow these steps:

1. In Query View, choose <u>E</u>dit, Select <u>A</u>ll Records.

> ### Tip
>
> For a partial mailing, such as to firms in California only, you can choose the individual records by dragging the mouse over the records' selection buttons.

2. Press Ctrl+C or choose <u>E</u>dit, <u>C</u>opy to copy the selected records to the Clipboard.

3. Run Word and, if necessary, choose <u>F</u>ile, <u>N</u>ew to open a new window.

4. Press Ctrl+V or choose <u>E</u>dit, <u>P</u>aste. Your Access mailing records are added as a table to the Word document (see fig. 8.17).

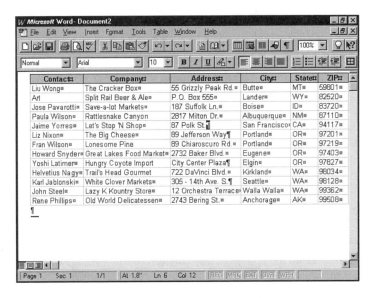

Fig. 8.17 The query result set copied to a Word for Windows document.

5. Convert the table to the tab-delimited format necessary for Word merge data files. Place the caret in one of the cells of the table and choose T<u>a</u>ble, Select T<u>a</u>ble to select all the rows and columns of the table.

6. Choose T<u>a</u>ble, Con<u>v</u>ert Table to Text to display the dialog that lets you choose the field-delimiter character. Accept the default Tab selection in the Convert Table to Text dialog and click OK. Your merge data file appears as shown in figure 8.18.

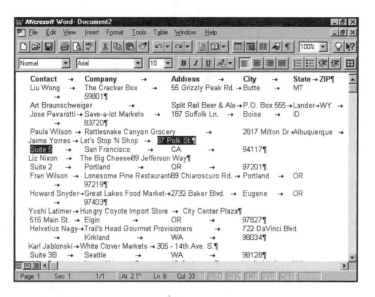

Fig. 8.18 A Microsoft Word merge data file with extra newline pairs embedded.

> **Note**
>
> Some of the records of this query also contain *newline pairs* (paragraph marks) embedded in fields that result in premature ends of these records. An example of a spurious newline pair in the Address field is highlighted for the Let's Stop 'N Shop record in figures 8.17 and 8.18. Replace the extra newline pairs with commas and spaces, and delete the quotation marks that enclose fields containing extra headline pairs before using the document in a merge operation.

If you use a DOS word processor and want to import query data into a merge data file, save the query in the form of a table and export the table as a file in a format compatible with that of your word processor. This process requires that you create an action query to create a table. Then export the table's data in a compatible format, as described in Chapter 7, "Linking, Importing, and Exporting Tables." Action queries are discussed briefly in the section "Creating and Using a Simple Make Table Action Query," later in this chapter, and in Chapter 11, "Using Action Queries."

Saving and Naming Your Query

After completing your query, save it as an element of your database file, giving the query its own descriptive name.

Follow these steps to save and name your query:

1. Close your query by clicking the close window button. Access prompts you with a message box to save the new or modified query, as shown in figure 8.19.

Fig. 8.19   A message reminds you to save a newly created or modified query.

   2. Click the message box's Yes button to save your query. Because Access has already assigned a default name to your query, the Save As dialog appears (see fig. 8.20). If you click Cancel or press Esc, Access does not save your query.

Fig. 8.20   The Save As dialog.

   3. Type in the Query Name text box a descriptive name for your query, in this case **qryUSMailList**, and then press Enter or click OK. Your query now is saved under the name that you assigned it rather than under the default name.

Note

Prefixes, called tags, commonly are used to identify types of Access objects you create. Tags are one of the subjects of Appendix B, "Naming Conventions for Access Objects and Variables."

Alternatively, you can save your query by choosing File, Save As.

To rename a saved query, follow these steps:

   1. Close the query by clicking the close window box. (You cannot rename an open query.)

   2. In the Queries page of the Database window, select the query that you want to rename.

   3. Choose Edit, Rename. Alternatively, right-click the selected icon and choose Rename from the popup menu.

   4. Type in the text box a new name to replace the caption adjacent to the query's icon.

   5. Press Enter to accept the change. Access saves your query with the new name that you assigned.

Creating Other Types of Queries

Access enables you to create the following four basic types of queries to achieve different objectives:

- *Select* queries extract data from one or more tables and display the data in tabular form.

- *Crosstab* queries summarize data from one or more tables in the form of a spreadsheet. Such queries are useful for analyzing data and creating graphs or charts based on the sum of the numeric field values of many records.

- *Action* queries create new database tables from query tables or make major alterations to a table. Such queries enable you to add or delete records from a table or to make changes to records based on expressions that you enter in a query design.

- *Parameter* queries repeatedly use a query and make only simple changes to its criteria. The mailing list query that you created earlier in this chapter is an excellent candidate for a parameter query because you can change the criterion of the Region field for mailings to different groups of customers. When you run a parameter query, Access displays a dialog to prompt you for the new criterion. Parameter queries are not actually a separate query type because you can add the parameter function to select, crosstab, and action queries.

Chapters 10, "Creating Multitable and Crosstab Queries," and 11, "Using Action Queries," explain how to create each of the four query types. Creating a table from the mailing list query to export to a mail merge file is an example of an action query. (In fact, this is the simplest example of an action query and also the safest because make-table queries do not modify data in existing tables.)

Creating and Using a Simple Make-Table Action Query

To create a table from your mailing list query, you first must convert the query from a select to an action query. Follow these steps to make this change:

1. Open your mailing list query in design mode by selecting the name that you gave the query in the Database window and clicking the Design button.

2. Choose Query, Make Table. (You can access the Query menu only in query design mode.) Alternatively, click the Query Type button on the toolbar and select Make Table. The Make Table dialog appears, as shown in figure 8.21.

Fig. 8.21   The Make Table dialog.

3. In the Table Name text box, type a descriptive table name for your query table, such as **tblUSMailList**.

   The Make Table dialog enables you to define your query table's properties further in several ways. You can add the table to the Northwind Traders database by choosing the Current Database option (the default). You also can choose the Another Database option to add the table to a different database that you specify in the File Name text box.

4. Click OK. Access converts your select query to the make-table type of action query.

5. Close your query by clicking the close window box. Your query name in the Database window now is prefixed by an exclamation point, as shown in figure 8.22. An exclamation point indicates that the query is an action query.

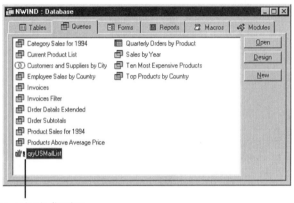

Exclamation point indicating
an action query

Fig. 8.22 A highlighted action query in the list of queries.

Now that you have converted your query from a select query to an action query, you can create a new U.S. mailing list table. To create the table, follow these steps:

1. Run the newly converted action query table to create your mailing list by double-clicking its name in the Queries page of the Database window (see fig. 8.22).

   When you open an action query table, it performs the desired action—in this case, creating the tblUSMailList table—instead of simply displaying a select query result set. Before Access carries out the action, however, a message (see fig. 8.23) appears and warns you that the query will modify the data in the tblUSMailList table (despite the fact that you haven't yet created the table).

2. Click Yes to dismiss the message box and continue the operation. A second message, shown in figure 8.24, appears to tell you what happens after you execute the action query.

3. Click Yes. Because you have not run this action query before, running it now creates the new tblUSMailList table.

4. Click the Table tab in the Database window. Access adds the new tblUSMailList table to the list of tables in the Northwind database, as shown in figure 8.25.

Fig. 8.23 The message box that appears after you open an action query.

Fig. 8.24 A second message indicates the effects of running the action query.

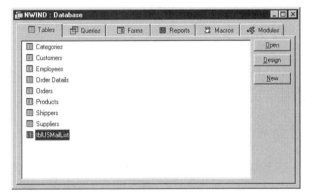

Fig. 8.25 The new table added to the Northwind database's table list.

5. Double-click the tblUSMailList icon to open the table. Its contents, which are identical to the contents of the Datasheet View of the make-table query, appear as shown in figure 8.26.

After you create the new table, you can export its data to any of the other file formats supported by Access. To do so, use the methods described in Chapter 7, "Linking, Importing, and Exporting Tables."

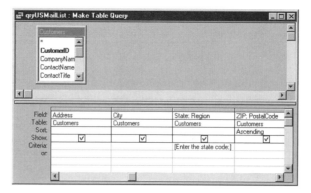

Fig. 8.26   Running a Datasheet View of the records in the new table.

Adding a Parameter to Your Make-Table Query

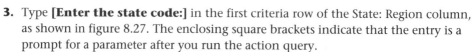

◀◀   See "Setting Default Options," p. 87

A simple modification to your mailing list query enables you to enter a selection criterion, called a *parameter*, from a prompt created by Access. Follow these steps:

1. Close the tblUSMailList table by double-clicking the close window button; then click the Query tab in the Database window.

2. Choose the qryUSMailList query that you created earlier in the chapter, and then choose the Design button to display your make-table action query in design mode.

3. Type **[Enter the state code:]** in the first criteria row of the State: Region column, as shown in figure 8.27. The enclosing square brackets indicate that the entry is a prompt for a parameter after you run the action query.

Fig. 8.27   Entering a parameter prompt as a criterion in Query Design View.

4. Close and save changes to the action query, select the qryUSMailList query, and choose File, Edit, Rename.

5. Rename your query by typing **qryStateMailList** in the text box and pressing Enter.

6. Select the renamed qryStateMailList query from the list in the Database window, and then click the Open button. Alternatively, double-click the qryStateMailList icon. You see the message indicating that data will be modified (refer to fig. 8.23).

Open

7. Choose Yes. Another message appears, warning that you are about to overwrite the data in the table created by the last execution of your query (see fig. 8.28).

Fig. 8.28   The message warning that you are about to overwrite data.

8. Choose Yes. Access displays the Enter Parameter Value dialog. This dialog contains a prompt for you to enter the state criterion, as shown in figure 8.29.

Fig. 8.29   The text box for entering a parameter to be used as a select criterion.

9. Type **WA**, and press Enter or choose OK. (You do not need to type an equal sign before the state code because Access enters the equal sign for you.)

   Another message appears, similar to the one in figure 8.24, indicating the number of records in the new version of the tblUSMailList table that have a value in the Regions field that matches your state parameter entry.

10. Choose Yes to close the message box and execute the make-table query.

11. Click the Table tab in the Database window, and select tblUSMailList. Choose the Open button. Records only for customers in Washington appear in the table.

You can delete the new table from the Northwind Traders database by closing the table, selecting the tblUSMailList table in the Database window, and then pressing the Delete key. (Access requests that you confirm your deletion. Click OK and Access removes the table from the database.)

II

Specific Information

Translating Graphical QBE to Structured Query Language

Structured Query Language, or SQL, is a standard set of English words used to describe a query. Access translates the QBE expressions that you type in the Query Design grid into a series of statements in Structured Query Language. Access then carries out these instructions on any tables that contain fields matching those specified in your query.

Access's use of SQL is important when you are dealing with client/server databases that process SQL statements on the server's computer. After processing the query, the server sends the data for the query result table to your Access client application for further processing.

To display the SQL statements created from your mailing list query, perform the following steps:

1. Open the mailing list query in design mode by selecting the name you gave the query in the Database window and choosing the Design button.

2. Click the Query View button of the toolbar and choose SQL from the menu, or choose View, SQL.

3. The SQL window, which acts as a multiline text box, appears, as shown in figure 8.30.

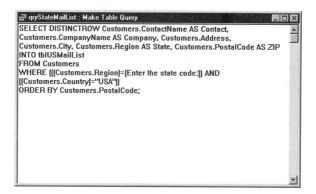

```
qryStateMailList : Make Table Query
SELECT DISTINCTROW Customers.ContactName AS Contact,
Customers.CompanyName AS Company, Customers.Address,
Customers.City, Customers.Region AS State, Customers.PostalCode AS ZIP
INTO tblUSMailList
FROM Customers
WHERE (((Customers.Region)=[Enter the state code:]) AND
((Customers.Country)="USA"))
ORDER BY Customers.PostalCode;
```

Fig. 8.30   Graphical QBE expressions translated by Access into SQL.

SQL *reserved words* are displayed in uppercase letters. SQL reserved words are the instructions or the actions that the query is to perform. The names of the objects in your query appear in uppercase and lowercase letters. The following list explains the meanings of the reserved words used in your query:

■ SELECT is usually the first reserved word in a SQL statement that returns records to a query result set. The expressions that follow specify the fields involved in the query. Fields are identified by the table's name followed by a period and the field's name.

- DISTINCTROW causes only unique records to be included in the query result table. DISTINCTROW is an Access SQL (and Transact-SQL) reserved word and is not included in ANSI SQL-92.

- AS establishes the alias for the field name preceding the alias. ZIP, for example, is the *alias* for the PostalCode field. The alias is the caption that appears in the field header for the PostalCode field.

- INTO specifies the name of the table into which the results of the query are to be placed. INTO applies only to action queries.

- FROM is the name of the table in which the fields are located.

- WHERE identifies the expressions that follow as the query's selection criteria.

- AND is a logical operator that results in records that meet both the criterion that precedes the AND *and* the criterion that follows the AND.

- ORDER BY specifies the field or fields by which the query result table is to be sorted.

When you finish viewing the SQL statements, close the SQL window.

▶▶ See "What Is Structured Query Language," p. 876

This chapter and Chapter 6, "Sorting, Finding, and Filtering Data in Tables," provide only a brief glimpse of SQL, and this example uses only a small cross-section of SQl's reserved words. Chapter 24, "Working with Structured Query Language," explains in detail the syntax that you use to edit and create SQL statements.

From Here...

This introduction to Query by Example gave you insight into the methods that Access uses to choose data from tables and to organize the selected data into query result sets (which Access 95 calls Recordset objects of the Dynaset and Snapshot type). Even when you are not concerned with creating Access forms and reports, you can use queries to display data in tabular form for analysis or to export data to other Windows and DOS applications.

To learn more about related topics, see the following chapters:

- Chapter 10, "Creating Multitable and Crosstab Queries," expands on the query designs described in this chapter to create query result sets based on more than one table and to rearrange your data into a format similar to that associated with spreadsheets.

- Chapter 12, "Creating and Using Forms," and Chapter 13, "Designing Custom Multitable Forms," show you how to use queries as the RecordSource property value for forms.

- Chapter 24, "Working with Structured Query Language," describes Access 95's dialect of SQL.

To create more sophisticated queries than those covered in this chapter, you must learn more about the syntax of the expressions that you need to choose records. As you become increasingly specific in the selection of records for your queries, the complexity of these expressions will increase. For this reason, the next chapter, "Understanding Operators and Expressions in Access," precedes the chapter in which you actually learn the detailed procedures for creating queries based on more than one table and optimizing your queries.

Chapter 9

Understanding Operators and Expressions in Access

Chapter 5, "Entering, Editing, and Validating Data in Tables," briefly introduced you to operators and the expressions that use them when you added validation rules to table fields. Chapter 8, "Using Query by Example," touched on expressions again when you devised selection criteria for the query that you created. You must use expressions with the forms (Chapters 12 and 13), reports (Chapters 14 and 15), and macros (Chapters 16 through 18) that you combine when creating custom Access applications; furthermore, you use expressions extensively when programming with Access VBA (Chapters 28 through 30). To work effectively with Access, therefore, you must know how to create simple expressions that use Access's group of functions and operators.

If you use spreadsheet applications, such as Microsoft Excel or Lotus 1-2-3, you might be familiar with using operators to create expressions. In spreadsheet applications, expressions are called *formulas*. As discussed in Chapter 4, "Working with Access Databases and Tables," the syntax for expressions that create default values, such as **=Date**() + 28, is similar to formula entries in Excel. Conditional expressions that use the =IF() function in Excel use the **IIf**() function in Access.

Much of this chapter is devoted to describing the functions available in Access for manipulating data of the Numeric and Text field data type. Functions play important roles in every element of Access, from validation rules for tables and fields of tables to the control of program flow in Access VBA. You use functions when creating queries, forms, reports, and macros. To use Access effectively, you must know what functions are available to you.

Understanding the Elements in Expressions

An *expression* is a statement of intent. If you want an action to occur after meeting a specific condition, your expression must specify that condition. To select records in a query that contains ZIP field values of 90000 or higher, for

In this chapter, you learn how to do the following

- Distinguish among the elements of expressions

- Use operators, literals, and identifiers to create expressions

- Create expressions for default values and validating data

- Write expressions for query criteria

- Use expressions to create calculated query columns

II

Specific Information

example, you type the expression **ZIP>=90000**. You can use expressions in arithmetic calculations also. If you need an Extended Amount field in a query, for example, you type **[Extended Amount]: Quantity * [Unit Price]** as the expression to create calculated values in the data cells of the Extended Amount column.

> **Note**
>
> Square bracket pairs ([ ]) must surround object names, such as field names that contain spaces or punctuation other than the underscore character. You also use square bracket pairs to identify field names in expressions for validating data. The Northwind Traders sample database in prior versions of Access used field names that included spaces; in Access 95, the field names of tables in Northwind.Mdb do not contain spaces, but table names include spaces. It is a Good Database Design Practice (GDBDP) never to use spaces in object names of any type. If you want to make object names more readable, separate words with the underscore character (_). In most cases, using upper- and lowercase object names provides adequate readability.

To qualify as an expression, a statement must have at least one operator and at least one literal, identifier, or function. The following list describes these elements:

- *Operators* include the familiar arithmetic symbols +, -, * (multiply), and / (divide), as well as many other symbols and abbreviations. Most other operators available in Access are equivalent to those operators found in traditional programming languages, such as BASIC, but some are specific to Access or SQL, such as the Between, In, Is, and Like operators.

- *Literals* consist of values that you type, such as **12345** or **ABCDE**. Literals are used most often to create default values and, in combination with field identifiers, to compare values in table fields.

- *Identifiers* are the names of objects in Access (such as fields in tables) that return distinct numeric or text values. The term *return*, when used with expressions, means that the present value of the identifier is substituted for its name in the expression. For example, the field name identifier [Company Name] in an expression returns the value (a name) of the Company Name field for the currently selected record. Access has five predefined named constants that also serve as identifiers: **True**, **False**, **Yes**, **No**, and **Null**. Named constants and variables that you create in Access VBA also are identifiers.

- *Functions*, such as **Date**() and **Format$**(), which are used in the examples in Chapter 5, "Entering, Editing, and Validating Data in Tables," return a value in place of the function name in the expression. Unlike identifiers, most functions require that you supply with parentheses an identifier or value as an argument. Later in this chapter, the "Functions" section explains functions and their arguments.

When literals, identifiers, or functions are used with operators, these combinations are called *operands*. The following sections explain these four elements of expressions more thoroughly.

> **Note**
>
> Expressions in this book appear in monospace type to distinguish expressions from the explanatory text of the book. Operators, including symbolic operators, built-in functions, and other reserved words and symbols of VBA, are set in **monospace bold type**. (VBA reserved words appear in blue color in the code-editing window of modules.) SQL operators and names of Access objects are set in monospace type.

Operators

Access provides six categories of operators that you can use to create expressions:

- *Arithmetic* operators perform addition, subtraction, multiplication, and division.

- *Assignment* and *comparison* operators set values and compare values.

- *Logical* operators deal with values that can only be true or false.

- *Concatenation* operators combine strings of characters.

- *Identifier* operators create unambiguous names for database objects so that you can assign the same field name, for example, in several tables and queries.

- Other operators simplify the creation of expressions for selecting records with queries.

Operators in the first four categories are available in almost all programming languages, including Xbase and PAL. Identifier operators are specific to Access; the other operators of the last category are provided only in relational database management systems (RDBMSs) that create queries using Query by Example (QBE) or Structured Query Language (SQL). The following sections explain how to use each of the operators in these categories.

Arithmetic Operators. Arithmetic operators operate only on numeric values and must have two numeric operands, with the following exceptions:

- When the minus sign (-) changes the sign (negates the value) of an operand. In this case, the minus sign is called the *unary minus*.

- When the equal sign (=) assigns a value to an Access object or an Access Basic variable identifier.

Table 9.1 lists the arithmetic operators that you can use in Access expressions.

Table 9.1	Arithmetic Operators	
Operator	**Description**	**Example**
+	Adds two operands	`[Subtotal] + [Tax]`
-	Subtracts two operands	`Date() - 30`
- (unary)	Changes the sign of an operand	`-12345`

(continues)

Table 9.1	Continued	
Operator	**Description**	**Example**
*	Multiplies two operands	`[Units] * [Unit Price]`
/	Divides one operand by another	`[Quantity] / 12.55`
\	Divides one integer operand by another	`[Units] \ 2`
Mod	Returns the remainder of division by an integer	`[Units] Mod 12`
^	Raises an operand to a power (exponent)	`[Value] ^ [Exponent]`

Access operators are identical to operators used in Microsoft QuickBASIC, QBasic (supplied with DOS 5.0 and later), and Visual Basic. If you aren't familiar with BASIC programming, the following operators need further explanation:

\   The integer division symbol is the equivalent of *goes into*, as used in the litany of elementary school arithmetic: *Three goes into 13 four times, with one left over.* When you use integer division, operators with decimal fractions are rounded to integers, but any decimal fraction in the result is truncated.

Mod   An abbreviation for *modulus*, this operator returns the *left over* value of integer division. Therefore, 13 **Mod** 4, for example, returns 1.

^   The exponentiation operator raises the first operand to the power of the second. For example, 2 ^ 4, or two to the fourth power, returns 16 (2*2*2*2).

These three operators seldom are used in business applications but often are used in Access Basic program code.

Assignment and Comparison Operators. Table 9.1 omits the equal sign associated with arithmetic expressions because in Access you use it in two ways—neither of which falls under the arithmetic category. The most common use of the equal sign is as an *assignment operator*; = assigns the value of a single operand to an Access object or to a variable or constant. When you use the expression = "Q" to assign a default value to a field, the equal sign acts as an assignment value. Otherwise, = is a comparison operator that determines whether one of two operands is equal to the other.

Comparison operators compare the values of two operands and return logical values (**True** or **False**) depending on the relationship between the two operands and the operator. An exception is when one of the operands has the **Null** value. In this case, any comparison returns a value of **Null**; because **Null** represents an unknown value, you cannot compare an unknown value with a known value and come to a valid **True** or **False** conclusion. The **Null** value is an important concept in database application, but few desktop RDBMSs support **Null** values.

Table 9.2 lists the comparison operators available in Access.

Table 9.2	Comparison Operators		
Operator	**Description**	**Example**	**Result**
<	Less than	`123 < 1000`	**True**
<=	Less than or equal to	`15 <= 15`	**True**

Operator	Description	Example	Result
=	Equal to	2 = 4	False
>=	Greater than or equal to	1234 >= 456	True
>	Greater than	123 > 123	False
<>	Not equal	123 <> 456	True

The principal uses of comparison operators are to create validation rules, to establish criteria for selecting records in queries, to determine actions taken by macros, and to control program flow in Access VBA.

Logical Operators. *Logical operators* (also called *Boolean operators*) are used most often to combine the results of two or more comparison expressions into a single result. Logical operators can combine only expressions that return the logical values `True`, `False`, or `Null`. With the exception of `Not`, which is the logical equivalent of the unary minus, logical operators always require two operands.

Table 9.3 lists the Access logical operators.

Table 9.3	Logical Operators		
Operator	**Description**	**Example 1** **Example 2**	**Result 1** **Result 2**
And	Logical and	True And True True And False	True False
Or	Inclusive or	True Or False False Or False	True False
Not	Logical not	Not True Not False	False True
Xor	Exclusive or	True Xor False True Xor True	True False

The logical operators `And`, `Or`, and `Not` are used extensively in Access expressions. `Xor` is seldom used in Access. `Eqv` (equivalent) and `Imp` (implication) are rarely seen, even in programming code, so table 9.3 omits these two operators.

Concatenation Operators. *Concatenation operators* combine two text values into a single string of characters. If you concatenate ABC with DEF, for example, the result is ABCDEF. The ampersand (`&`) is the preferred concatenation operator in Access because the character is SQL's standard concatenation symbol. Although you can use the + operator to link two strings of characters as in BASIC, using the + operator for concatenation can lead to ambiguities because the operator's primary purpose is to add two numeric operands.

Identifier Operators. The *identifier operators,* ! (the exclamation point, often called the *bang operator*) and . (the period, called the *dot operator* in Access), are separators and perform the following operations:

- Combine the names of object classes and object names to select a specific object or property of an object. For example, the following expression identifies the Personnel Actions form:

  ```
  Forms![Personnel Actions]
  ```

  This identification is necessary because you might also have a table called Personnel Actions.

- Distinguish object names from property names. Consider the following expression:

  ```
  TextBox1.FontSize = 8
  ```

  TextBox1 is a control object and FontSize is a property.

- Identify specific fields in tables, as in the following expression, which specifies the Company Name field of the Customers table:

  ```
  Customers![Company Name]
  ```

You use the ! character to separate object references; the general syntax is *ObjectClass!ObjectName*. The . character separates objects and their properties or methods, as in *ObjectClass!Object.Property* or *ObjectClass!ObjectName.Method()*.

Other Operators. The remaining Access operators are related to the comparison operators. These operators return **True** or **False**, depending on whether the value in a field meets the chosen operator's specification. A **True** value causes a record to be included in a query; a **False** value rejects the record. When you use these operators in validation rules, entries are accepted or rejected based on the logical value returned by the expression.

Table 9.4 lists the four other operators used in Access.

Table 9.4	Other Operators	
Operator	**Description**	**Example**
Is	Used with **Null** to determine whether a value is **Null** or **Not Null**	Is **Null** Is **Not Null**
Like	Determines whether a string value begins with one or more characters (for Like to work properly, you must add a wild card, *, or one or more ?s)	Like "Jon*" Like "FILE????"
In	Determines whether a string value is a member of a list of values	In("CA", "OR", "WA")
Between	Determines whether a numeric value lies within a specified range of values	Between 1 **And** 5

You use the wild-card characters * and ? with the Like operator the same way that you use them in DOS. The * (often called *star* or *splat*) takes the place of any number of characters. The ? takes the place of a single character. For example, Like "Jon*" returns **True** for values such as *Jones* or *Jonathan*. Like "*on*" returns **True** for any value that contains *on*. Like "FILE????" returns **True** for *FILENAME*, but not *FILE000* or *FILENUMBER*.

Wildcard characters can precede the characters that you want to make, as in `Like "*son"` or `Like "????NAME"`.

Except for `Is`, the operators in this other category are equivalent to the SQL reserved words `LIKE`, `IN`, and `BETWEEN`. Access includes these operators to promote compatibility with SQL. You can create each of these operators by combining other Access operators or functions. `Like "Jon*"` is the equivalent of Access VBA's `InStr(Left$(FieldName, 3), "Jon")`; `In("CA", "OR", "WA")` is similar to `InStr("CAORWA", FieldName)`, except that no matches occur for the ambiguous *AO* and *RW*. `Between 1 And 5` is the equivalent of `>= 1 And <= 5`.

Literals

Access provides three types of literals that you can combine with operators to create expressions. The following list describes these types of literals:

- *Numeric* literals are typed as a series of digits, including the arithmetic sign and decimal point, if applicable. You don't have to prefix positive numbers with the plus sign; Access assumes positive values unless the minus sign is present. Numeric literals can include `E` or `e` and the sign of the exponent to indicate an exponent in scientific notation—for example, `-1.23E-02`.

- *Text* (or *string*) literals can include any printable character, plus unprintable characters returned by the `Chr$()` function. The `Chr$()` function returns the characters specified by a numeric value from the ANSI character table (similar to the ASCII character table) that Windows uses. For example, `Chr$(9)` returns the Tab character. Printable characters include the letters A through Z, numbers 1 through 0, punctuation symbols, and other special keyboard symbols such as the tilde (~). Access expressions require that you enclose string literals within double quotation marks (`""`). Combinations of printable and unprintable characters are concatenated with the ampersand. For example, the following expression separates two strings with a newline pair.

    ```
    "First line" & Chr$(13) & Chr$(10) & "Second line"
    ```

    `Chr$(13)` is the carriage return (CR), and `Chr$(10)` is the line-feed (LF) character; together they form the *newline pair*.

    When you enter string literals in the cells of tables and Query Design grids, Access adds the quotation marks for you. In other places, you must enter the quotation marks yourself.

- *Date/time* literals are enclosed within number or pound signs (#), as in the expressions `#1-Jan-80#` or `#10:20:30#`. Access adds the enclosing pound signs if the program detects that you are typing into a Design grid a date or time in one of the standard Access date/time formats.

Numeric and string literals have exact equivalents in BASIC, xBase, and PAL, but Access defines the date/time literal data type.

Identifiers

An *identifier* is usually the name of an object; databases, tables, fields, queries, forms, and reports are objects in Access. Each object has a name that uniquely identifies that object. Sometimes, to identify a subobject, an identifier name consists of a *family name* (object class) separated from a *given name* (object name) by a bang symbol or a period (an identifier operator). The family name of the identifier comes first, followed by the separator and then the given name. SQL uses the period as an object separator. An example of an identifier in an SQL statement is as follows:

```
Customers.Address
```

In this example, the identifier for the Address field object is contained in the Customers table object. *Customers* is the family name of the object (the table), and *Address* is the given name of the subobject (the field). In Access, however, you use the ! symbol to separate table names and field names. (The period separates objects and their properties.) If an identifier contains a space or other punctuation, enclose the identifier within square brackets, as in this example:

```
[Personnel Actions]![PA ID]
```

You cannot include periods or exclamation points within the names of identifiers; `[PA!ID]`, for example, is not allowed.

In simple queries that use only one table, identifiers are usually the name of a field. You use identifiers to return the values of fields in form and report objects. Chapters 12 through 15 cover the specific method of identifying objects within forms and reports.

Functions

> ▶▶ See "Using DDE Links with Excel," p. 799
> ▶▶ See "Modules, Functions, and Subprocedures," p. 999

Functions return values to their names; functions can take the place of identifiers in expressions. One of the most common functions used in Access expressions is **Now()**, which returns to its name the date and time from your computer's internal clock. (The empty parentheses are optional for the **Now** function.) If you type **Now()** as the DefaultValue property of a table's Date/Time field, for example, 5/95 9:00 appears in the field when you change to Datasheet View (at 9:00 A.M. on March 15, 1995).

Access and VBA define about 140 individual functions. The following list groups functions by purpose:

- *Date and time* functions manipulate date/time values in fields or date/time values that you enter as literals. You can extract parts of dates (such as the year or day of the month) and parts of times (such as hours and minutes) with date and time functions.

- *Text-manipulation* functions are used for working with strings of characters.

- *Data-type conversion* functions enable you to specify the data type of values in Numeric fields instead of depending on Access to pick the most appropriate data type.

- *Mathematic and trigonometric* functions perform on numeric values operations that are beyond the capability of the standard Access arithmetic operators. You can use simple trigonometric functions, for example, to calculate the length of the sides of a right triangle (if you know the length of one side and the included angle).

- *Financial* functions are similar to functions provided by Lotus 1-2-3 and Microsoft Excel. They calculate depreciation, values of annuities, and rates of return on investments. To determine the present value of a lottery prize paid out in 25 equal yearly installments, for example, you can use the PV() function.

- *General-purpose* functions don't fit any of the preceding classifications; you use these functions to create Access queries, forms, and reports.

- Other functions include those that perform dynamic data exchange (DDE) with other Windows applications, domain aggregate functions, SQL aggregate functions, and functions used primarily in Access Basic programming.

The following sections describe these functions more fully.

You can create user-defined functions by defining them with Access VBA programming code. Chapter 28, "Writing Visual Basic for Applications Code," describes how to create user-defined functions.

Using the Debug Window. When you write Access VBA programming code in a module, the Debug window, which replaces Access 2.0's Immediate window, is available to assist you in debugging your code. You also can use the module's Debug window to demonstrate the use and syntax of functions.

To experiment with some of the functions described in the following sections, perform these steps:

1. Click the Modules tab in the Database window.

2. Choose the New button to create a temporary module. Access assigns the default name Module1 to the temporary module.

3. Click the Debug Window button of the toolbar or choose <u>V</u>iew, <u>D</u>ebug Window. The Debug window appears, as shown in figure 9.1. The entries shown in figure 9.1 aren't visible at this point. You can create similar entries by using the functions for date and time described later in this chapter.

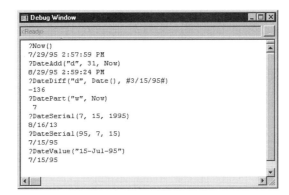

Fig. 9.1   Using the Debug window of a temporary module to experiment with functions.

4. Type **?Now()** and press Enter. The date and time from your computer's clock appear on the next line. The ? is shorthand for the VBA Print statement (which displays the value of a function or variable) and must be added to the Now() function to display the function's value.

   If you neglected to precede the function entry with ? or Print, an error message appears, indicating that Access expected you to type a statement or an equal sign. Click OK and type ? before the function name in the Debug window. Press End to return the caret to the end of the line and then Enter to retry the test.

The following sections describe and provide the correct syntax for the various functions available to Access users. This information should help you get acquainted with using functions with queries, forms, and reports. These descriptions and syntax examples are brief compared to the information available from the Access online Help system and in the *Microsoft Access Language Reference*.

One way to learn more about functions is to choose Help, Microsoft Access Help Topics, click the Index tab, and type in the Index dialog's text box the name of the function on which you want more information. For a faster method to learn more about a particular function, however, follow these steps:

1. In the Debug window, press Enter to move the caret to the beginning of a new line.

2. Type the name of the function; select the name by clicking it or by pressing Shift+left arrow (as shown for the Format function in fig. 9.2). Alternatively, you can press Home to place the cursor in front of the function name's first character.

3. Press F1. The Help window opens. If a function and a property or event share the same name, as is the case with Format, an intermediate Context Help On window appears that enables you to choose the function, the event, or the property (see fig. 9.2). Double-click VBA. The Format Function Help window appears (see fig. 9.3).

4. Click the See Also hotspot. Related Help topics appear in a Topics Found dialog (see fig. 9.4). Select a related topic and choose Display to display the associated Help window, or click Cancel to close the dialog.

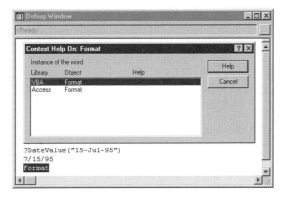

Fig. 9.2 Choosing between help for the VBA or Access version of a keyword for a function or an event.

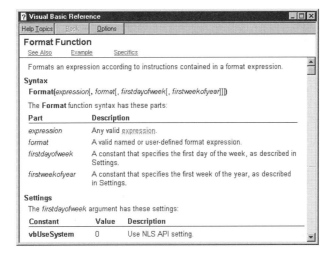

Fig. 9.3 The Format Function Help window.

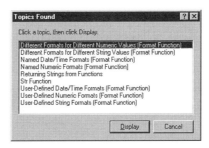

Fig. 9.4 You open the Topics Found dialog by clicking the See Also hotspot.

II

Specific Information

5. After reviewing the syntax and other information concerning the function, close the Help window by double-clicking its close window box.

Help windows for functions have a standard format, as shown in figure 9.3. If you click the Example hotspot in any function Help window, another window displays an example of the function used in Access VBA code. These examples show the syntax of the functions and appropriate arguments.

The Variant Data Type in Access. **Variant** is a special data type unique to Microsoft Object Basic dialects. No equivalent of the **Variant** data type exists in xBase, Paradox 3+, or other BASIC dialects. The **Variant** data type enables you to concatenate values that ordinarily have different data types, such as an integer and a character string. The capability to concatenate different data types is called *turning off data-type checking*. **Variant** values are related to the **As Any** data type that Access VBA uses to turn off data-type checking when declaring external functions contained in Windows Dynamic Link Libraries (DLLs).

The **Variant** data type enables you to concatenate field values of tables and queries that have dissimilar data types without using BASIC's data-type conversion functions such as **Str$()** or xBase's **DTOC()**. (**Str$()** converts numeric values to the **String** data type; DTOC() converts xBase date values to the character, or string, data type.) The **Variant** data type also simplifies expressions that combine field values to create concatenated indexes. Specifying a composite (concatenated) index on customer number (**Long** integer) and date (Date/Time) in Access 95's Indexes window, for example, is much simpler than using the expression STRZERO (Cust_Num,6) + DTOC(Order_Date) required to create a similar index in xBase. The **Variant** data type also enables you to use the **&** symbol to concatenate values of different data types. Structured Query Language *requires* you to use the ampersand for such concatenation.

▶▶ See "Access Intrinsic Constants," p. 1013

Table 9.5 lists the 16 subtypes of the **Variant** data type of Access VBA along with the names of the intrinsic Visual Basic constants, vbConstant, corresponding to the **Variant** subtype value. Access 2.0 defined only **Variant** subtypes 0 through 8. In addition to the Access intrinsic constants that Access 2.0 originally defined, VBA provides its own set of intrinsic constants, which are prefixed with vb. Access intrinsic constants are prefixed with ac. Intrinsic constants, which you use primarily when writing Access VBA code, are one of the subjects of Chapter 29, "Understanding the Data Access Object Class."

Table 9.5 Subtypes of the Variant Data Type			
Subtype	**Constant**	**Corresponds to**	**Stored as**
0	(None)	Empty (uninitialized)	Not applicable
1	vbNull	**Null** (no valid data)	Not applicable

Subtype	Constant	Corresponds to	Stored as
2	vbInteger	**Integer**	2-byte integer
3	vbLong	**Long**	4-byte long integer
4	vbSingle	**Single**	4-byte single-precision floating point
5	vbDouble	**Double**	8-byte double-precision floating point
6	vbCurrency	**Currency**	4-byte fixed point
7	vbDate	Date/Time	8-byte double-precision floating point
8	vbString	**String**	Conventional string variable
9	vbObject	**Object**	OLE Automation object
10	vbError	**Error**	**Error** data type (error number)
11	vbBoolean	**Boolean**	**True** or **False** values only
12	vbVariant	**Variant**	Used with **Variant** arrays
13	vbDataObject	Special	Non-OLE Automation object
17	vbByte	**Byte**	Numeric value from 0 to 255
8192	vbArray	**Array**	Used with **Variant** arrays

You can concatenate **Variant** values with **Variant** subtypes 1 through 8 listed in table 9.5. You can concatenate a subtype 8 **Variant** (**String**) with a subtype 5 **Variant** (**Double**), for example, without receiving from Access the Type Mismatch error message that you receive if you attempt this concatenation with conventional **String** (text) and **Double** data types. Access returns a value with the **Variant** subtype corresponding to the highest subtype number of the concatenated values. This example, therefore, returns a subtype 8 (**String**) **Variant** because 8 is greater than 5, the subtype number for the **Double** value. If you concatenate a subtype 2 (**Integer**) value with a subtype 3 (**Long**) value, Access returns subtype 3 **Variant** data.

Distinguishing between the Empty and **Null Variant** subtypes is important. Empty indicates that a variable that you created with Access Basic code has a name but doesn't have an initial value. Empty applies only to Access VBA variables (see Chapter 28, "Writing Visual Basic for Applications Code"), but Empty is not a reserved word or a keyword in Access Basic. **Null** indicates that a data cell doesn't contain an entry. You can assign the **Null** value to a variable, in which case the variable is initialized to the **Null** value, **Variant** subtype 1.

You can experiment with **Variant** subtypes in the Debug window to become more familiar with using the **Variant** data type. VBA provides a function, **VarType**(), that returns the integer value of its argument's subtype. Figure 9.5 shows the data subtype values that **VarType**() returns for four variables (A to D) and the result of the concatenation of these variables (E).

II

Specific Information

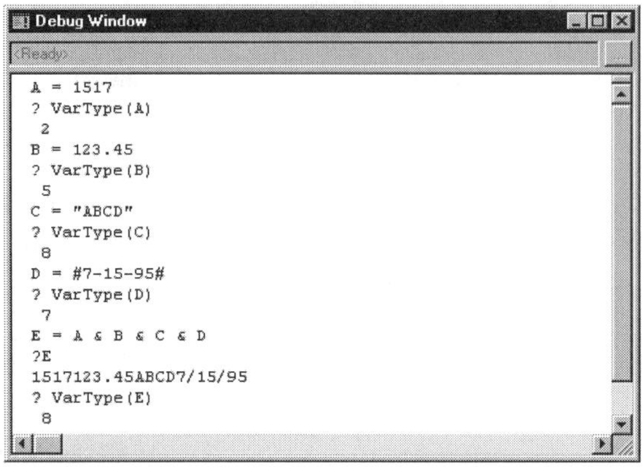

```
Debug Window                                    _□×
<Ready>
A = 1517
? VarType(A)
 2
B = 123.45
? VarType(B)
 5
C = "ABCD"
? VarType(C)
 8
D = #7-15-95#
? VarType(D)
 7
E = A & B & C & D
?E
1517123.45ABCD7/15/95
? VarType(E)
 8
```

Fig. 9.5 The **Variant** subtypes return values for four variables and the result of the concatenation.

◄◄ See "Choosing Field Data Types, Sizes, and Formats," p. 114
◄◄ See "Adding Indexes to Tables," p. 150

Functions for Date and Time. Access offers a variety of functions for dealing with dates and times. If you have used Visual Basic, you probably recognize most of the functions applicable to the Date/Time field data types shown in table 9.6. VBA has several Date/Time functions, such as **DateAdd()** and **DateDiff()**, to simplify the calculation of date values.

All Date/Time values are stored as double-precision values but are returned as **Variant** subtype 7 unless you use the function's **String** form. The **String** form is identified by the **String** data type identification character, $, appended to the end of the function name. Both ? **VarType(Date$())** and ? **VarType(Time$())** return a subtype 8 (**String**) **Variant**.

> **Note**
>
> The Debug window in figure 9.1 shows a few of the entries used to test the syntax examples of table 9.6.

Table 9.6 Access Functions for Date and Time

Function	Description	Example	Returns
Date(), **Date$()**	Returns the current system date and time as a subtype 7 date **Variant** or a standard date **String** subtype 8	**Date()**	7/15/95 07-15-95
DateAdd()	Returns a subtype 7 date with a specified number of days, weeks ("ww"), months ("m"), or years ("y") added to the date	**DateAdd**	8/15/95 ("d",31,#7/15/95#)

Function	Description	Example	Returns
DateDiff()	Returns an **Integer** representing the difference between two dates using the d/w/m/y specification	DateDiff ("d",**Date**(), #4/15/95#)	-91 (assuming **Date**() = 7/15/95)
DatePart()	Returns the specified part of a date such as day, month, year, day of week ("w"), and so on, as an **Integer**	DatePart ("w",#7/ 15/95#)	7 (Saturday)
DateSerial()	Returns a subtype 7 **Variant** from year, month, and day arguments	DateSerial (95,7,15)	7/15/95
DateValue()	Returns a subtype 7 **Variant** that corresponds to a date argument in a character format	DateValue ("15-Jul-95")	7/15/95
Day()	Returns an **Integer** between 1 and 31 (inclusive) that represents a day of the month from a Date/Time value	Day(**Date**())	15 (assuming that the date is the 15th of the month)
Hour()	Returns an **Integer** between 0 and 23 (inclusive) that represents the hour of the Date/Time value	Hour(#2:30 PM#)	14
Minute()	Returns an **Integer** between 0 and 59 (inclusive) that represents the minute of a Date/Time value	Minute (#2:30 PM#)	30
Month()	Returns an **Integer** between 1 and 12 (inclusive) that represents the month of a Date/Time value	Month(#15- Jul-95#)	7
Now()	Returns the date and time of a computer's system clock as a **Variant** of subtype 7	Now()	7/15/95 11:57:28 AM
Second()	Returns an **Integer** between 0 and 59 (inclusive) that represents the second of a Date/Time value	Second (**Now**())	28
Time(), Time$()	Returns the Time portion of a Date/Time value from the system clock	Time() (returns subtype 7) Time$() (returns **String**)	11:57:20 AM
TimeSerial()	Returns the time serial value of the time expressed in integer hours, minutes, and seconds	TimeSerial (11,57,20)	11:57:20 AM
TimeValue()	Returns the time serial value of the time (entered as the **String** value) as a subtype 7 **Variant**	TimeValue ("11:57")	11:57
Weekday()	Returns day of the week (Sunday = 1) corresponding to the date as an **Integer**	Weekday (#7/15/95#)	7
Year()	Returns the year of a Date/Time value as an **Integer**	Year (#7/15/95#)	1994

Text-Manipulation Functions. Table 9.7 lists the functions that deal with the Text field data type, corresponding to the **String** data type or **Variant** subtype 8. Most of these functions are modeled on BASIC string functions and have similarly named equivalents in xBase and PAL.

Table 9.7   Functions for String and Subtype 8 Variant Data Types

Function	Description	Example	Returns
Asc()	Returns ANSI numeric value of character as an **Integer**	Asc("C")	67
Chr(), Chr$()	Returns character corresponding to the numeric ANSI value as a string	Chr(67) Chr$(10)	C (line feed)
Format(), Format$()	Formats an expression in accordance with appropriate format strings	Format(Date(), "dd-mmm-yy")	15-Jul-95
InStr()	Returns the position of one string within another	InStr("ABCD","C")	3
LCase(), LCase$()	Returns the lowercase version of a string	LCase("ABCD")	abcd
Left(), Left$()	Returns the leftmost characters of a string	Left("ABCDEF",3)	ABC
Len()	Returns the number of characters in a string as a **Long**	Len("ABCDE")	5
LTrim(), LTrim$()	Removes leading spaces from string	LTrim(" ABC")	ABC
Mid(), Mid$()	Returns a portion of a string	Mid("ABCDE",2,3)	BCD
Right(), Right$()	Returns the rightmost characters of a string	Right("ABCDEF",3)	DEF
RTrim(), RTrim$()	Removes trailing spaces from a string	RTrim("ABC ")	ABC
Space(), Space$()	Returns a string consisting of a specified number of spaces	Space(5)	
Str(), Str$()	Converts the numeric value of any data type to a string	Str(123.45)	123.45
StrComp()	Compares two strings for equivalence and returns the integer result of the comparison	StrComp("ABC", "abc")	0
String(), String$()	Returns a string consisting of specified repeated characters	String(5, "A")	AAAAA
Trim(), Trim$()	Removes leading and trailing spaces from a string	Trim(" ABC ")	ABC
UCase(), UCase$()	Returns the uppercase version of a string	UCase("abc")	ABC
Val()	Returns the numeric value of a string in a data type appropriate to the argument's format	Val("123.45")	123.45

> **Note**
>
> There are two different types of **String** variables: variable-length and fixed-length. Access 95 table fields of the Text data type are variable-length (**Variant** subtype 8) and can range from 0 to 255 characters. In Access VBA, variable-length strings can contain up to about two billion (2 ^ 31) characters. (Access 2.0 Basic limited variable-length strings to about 64K characters.) Fixed-length strings, which you declare in VBA with the syntax **Dim** str*Variable* **As String *** lng*Length*, can range from 1 to about 64K (2 ^ 16) characters. Access 95 Memo fields remain limited to a maximum of 64K characters.

Table 9.7 shows two versions of most of the functions—one with, and one without, a string-identifier character (**$**). In these cases, the function without **$** returns a **Variant** subtype 8 (String); the function with $ returns the Text field data type (String in VBA). Figure 9.6 shows tests of a few of the string functions in the Debug Window.

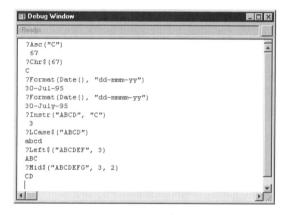

Fig. 9.6   Testing the string-manipulation functions.

Access's **Format()** and **Format$()** functions are identical to the **Format()** and **Format$()** functions of Visual Basic 3.0 and VBA (see Chapter 4, "Working with Access Databases and Tables," for the arguments of these functions). Table 9.7 doesn't include the **Tab()** and **Spc()** functions because these functions are used primarily to format the printing of text strings, which Access's built-in report-generation feature handles.

> **Note**
>
> Access 95 stores **String** and **Variant** subtype 8 values in 32-bit Windows' *Unicode* format, which requires two bytes to define a single character. Unicode has the advantage of providing two-byte codes for both alphabetic characters and the pictographic characters used in Asian languages. Access 95's string-manipulation functions count characters, not bytes. The FieldSize property of fields of Access 95 Recordset objects, however, is measured in bytes. Thus, values returned by the FieldSize property of a Recordset are twice those returned by the **Len()** function. The difference between characters and bytes is significant in VBA programming that uses the GetChunk and AppendChunk methods, but not in the ordinary use of Access 95.

Numeric, Logical, Date/Time, and String Data-Type Conversion Functions. You can assign a particular data type to a numeric value with any of the data-type conversion functions. After you *freeze* (or *coerce*) a data type with one of the numeric data-type conversion functions, you cannot concatenate that data type with the **String** data type or data **Variant** subtype 7. Table 9.8 lists the 11 numeric data-type conversion functions of Access 95. Access 95 introduces VBA's **Boolean**, **Byte**, and **Error** data types. The *NumValue* argument in the Syntax column can be any numeric or **String** value. However, if you use a **String** value as the argument of a numeric-type conversion function, the first character of the argument's value must be a digit, a dollar sign, a plus symbol, or a minus symbol.

Table 9.8   Data-Type Conversion Functions for Numeric, Time/Date, and String Values

Function	Description	Syntax
CBool()	Converts a numeric value to a **Boolean** (**True** or **False**) data type	CBool(*NumValue*)
Cbyte()	Converts a numeric value to a **Byte** (0–255) data type	CByte(*NumValue*)
CCur()	Converts a numeric value to a **Currency** data type	CCur(*NumValue*)
CDbl()	Converts a numeric value to a **Double**-precision data type	CDbl(*NumValue*)
CInt()	Converts a numeric value to an **Integer** data type	CInt(*NumValue*)
CLng()	Converts a numeric value to a **Long** integer data type	CLng(*NumValue*)
CSng()	Converts a numeric value to a **Single**-precision data type	CSng(*NumValue*)
CStr()	Converts a numeric value to a **String** data type	CStr(*NumValue*)
CVar()	Converts a numeric value to a **Variant** data type	CVar(*NumValue*)
CVDate()	Converts a numeric value to a **Variant** subtype 7	CVDate(*NumValue*)
CVErr()	Converts a valid error number to create user-defined errors	CVErr(*NumValue*)

Mathematic and Trigonometric Functions. Access provides a sufficient number of mathematic and trigonometric functions to meet most scientific and engineering requirements. You can create additional trigonometric functions with more complex expressions. If you are interested in more obscure transcendental functions, such as cosecants or hyperbolic functions, choose <u>H</u>elp, Microsoft Access <u>H</u>elp Topics, click the Index tab, enter **math functions** in the text box, and then click Derived Math Functions in the Topics Found dialog. Table 9.9 lists the mathematic and trigonometric functions available directly in Access.

Table 9.9   Mathematic and Trigonometric Functions

Function	Description	Example	Returns
Abs()	Returns the absolute value of a numeric value	Abs(-1234.5)	1234.5
Atn()	Returns the arctangent of a numeric value, in radians	Atn(1)	.7853982
Cos()	Returns the cosine of the angle represented by a numeric value, in radians	Cos(p/4)	.707106719949

Function	Description	Example	Returns
Exp()	Returns the exponential (antilog) of the numeric value	Exp(2.302585)	9.9999990700 (rounding errors)
Fix()	Identical to Int(), except for negative numbers	Fix(-13.5)	13
Int()	Returns a numeric value with the decimal fraction truncated; the data type isn't changed unless the argument is a string	Int(13.5) Int(-13.5)	13 14
Log()	Returns natural (Napierian) logarithm of a numeric value	Log(10)	2.302585
Rnd()	Creates a random single-precision number between 0 and 1 when no argument is supplied	Rnd() (varies)	.533424
Sgn()	Returns the sign of a numeric value: 0 if positive, -1 if negative	Sgn(-13.5)	-1
Sin()	Returns the sine of a numeric value, in radians	Sin(π/4)	.707106842423
Sqr()	Returns the square root of a numeric value	Sqr(144)	12
Tan()	Returns the tangent of a numeric value, in radians	Tan(π/4)	1.0000001732 (fraction because of rounding)

The angles returned by the trigonometric functions are expressed in radians, as is the argument of the arctangent (**Atn()**) function shown in the table. To obtain the values shown in table 9.9's examples, you type the expression **Pi = 3.141593** in the Debug window before entering the syntax example expressions. The returned values of the trigonometric functions are for an angle of approximately 45 degrees, corresponding to $\pi/4$ radians.

Note

Because a 360-degree circle contains 2π radians, you convert radians to degrees with the expression radians * 360/2π. Because Pi is a rounded value of π and the trigonometric functions round results, you usually obtain values with rounding errors. The cosine of 45 degrees, for example, is 0.7070707... but Access returns 0.7071067.... These rounding errors are not significant in most applications.

Int() and **Fix()** differ in the following way: **Fix()** returns the first negative integer *less than or equal to* the argument; **Int()** returns the first negative integer *greater than or equal to* the argument. **Int()** and **Fix()**, unlike other mathematic and trigonometric functions, return the integer value of a string variable but not the value of a literal string argument. Entering **? Int("13.5")**, for example, returns a data-type error message; however, if you type **A = 13.5** and then **? Int(A)**, Access returns 13.

Financial Functions. You might be interested in the financial functions of Access because you have used similar functions in Microsoft Excel or Lotus 1-2-3 spreadsheets. The financial functions of Access (supplied by VBA and listed in table 9.10) are identical to their capitalized counterparts in Excel and employ the same arguments. If you have a table of fixed asset records, for example, you can use the depreciation functions to calculate monthly, quarterly, or yearly depreciation for each asset and then summarize the depreciation schedule in an Access report.

> **Note**
>
> A full description of the use and syntax of these functions is beyond the scope of this book. If you are interested in more details about these functions, choose Help, Microsoft Access Help Topics, click the Index tab and enter the function name in the text box.

Table 9.10   Financial Functions for Calculating Depreciation and Annuities

Function	Description
DDB()	Returns the depreciation of a fixed asset over a specified period by using the double-declining balance method
FV()	Returns the future value of an investment based on a series of constant periodic payments and a fixed rate of interest
IPmt()	Returns the amount of interest for an installment payment on a fixed-rate loan or annuity
IRR()	Returns the internal rate of return for an investment consisting of a series of periodic incomes and expenses
MIRR()	Returns the modified internal rate of return for an investment consisting of a series of periodic incomes and expenses
NPer()	Returns the number of payments of a given amount required to create an annuity or to retire a loan
NPV()	Returns the net present value of an annuity paid in equal periodic installments
Pmt()	Returns the amount of the periodic payment that must be made to create an annuity or to retire a loan
PPmt()	Returns the amount of principal in an installment payment on a fixed-rate loan or annuity
PV()	Returns the present value of an annuity paid in equal periodic installments
Rate()	Returns the interest rate of a loan or annuity based on a constant interest rate and equal periodic payments
SLN()	Returns the depreciation of a fixed asset over a specified period by using the straight-line method
SYD()	Returns the depreciation of a fixed asset over a specified period by the sum-of-the-years'-digits method

Miscellaneous Functions. Access provides several functions that don't fit in any of the preceding categories but that you can use for creating queries and validating data entries, or with forms, reports, and macros. Table 9.11 lists these general-purpose functions.

Table 9.11   Miscellaneous Access Functions

Function	Description	Syntax
Choose()	Returns a value from a list of values, based on the value's position in the list	Choose([Unit of Measure], "Each", "Dozen", "Gross")

Function	Description	Syntax
`IIf()`	Returns one value if the result of an expression is **True**, another if the result is **False**	`IIf([Order Quantity] Mod 12 = 0, "Dozen", "Each")`
`IsArray()`	Returns **True** if the argument is an array; otherwise, returns **False**	**IsArray**(var*Name*)
`IsDate()`	Returns **True** if the argument is the Date/Time field data type; otherwise, returns **False**	`IsDate(`*FieldName*`)`
`IsEmpty()`	Returns **True** if the argument is a noninitialized variable; otherwise, returns **False**	`IsEmpty(`var*Name*`)`
`IsError()`	Returns **True** if the argument is an **Error** object; otherwise, returns **False**	`IsError(`var*Name*`)`
`IsMissing()`	Returns **True** if an optional argument has not been passed to a procedure; otherwise, returns **False**	`IsMissing(`arg*Optional*`)`
`IsNull()`	Returns **True** if the argument is **Null**; otherwise, returns **False**	`IsNull(`*FieldName*`)`
`IsNumeric()`	Returns **True** if the argument is one of the Number field data types; otherwise, returns **False**	`IsNumeric(`*FieldName*`)`
`IsObject()`	Returns **True** if the argument refers to a valid OLE Automation object; otherwise, returns **False**	**IsObject**(obj*Name*)
`Partition()`	Returns a **String** value indicating the number of occurrences of a value within a range of values	`Partition (`*Number*`, `*Start*`, `*Stop*`, `*Interval*`)`
`Switch()`	Returns the value associated with the first of a series of expressions evaluating to **True**	`Switch([Unit of Measure], "Each", 1, "Dozen", 12, "Gross", 144)`
`TypeName()`	Returns the **String** value representing the name of the **Variant** data type; for instance, "`Byte`"	`TypeName(`var*Name*`)`

Choose() creates a lookup table that returns a value corresponding to a position from a list of values that you create. **Choose**() is related closely to the **Switch**() function, which returns a value associated with the first of a series of expressions evaluating to **True**. In table 9.11's **Choose**() example, if the value of the Unit of Measure field is 1, the function returns Each; if the value is 2, **Choose**() returns Dozen; and if the value is 3, the function returns Gross. Otherwise, the function returns #Null#.

The **Switch**() example returns a divisor value for an order. If the value of the Unit of Measure field is Each, **Switch**() returns 1. If Unit of Measure is Dozen, the function returns 12; if Unit of Measure is Gross, **Switch**() returns 144. The function returns #Null# for no matching value. **Choose**() and **Switch**() have similarities to the **Select Case** statement in VBA and other BASIC dialects (**Null** is the **Case Else** value).

The **IIf**() function is called *in-line If* because it substitutes for the multiline **If...Then...Else...End If** structure of the VBA conditional expression. In the example shown in table 9.11, the **IIf**() function returns Dozen if the quantity ordered is evenly divisible by 12; otherwise, the function returns Each.

The **Partition**() function creates histograms. A *histogram* is a series of values (usually displayed as a bar chart) representing the frequency of events that can be grouped within specific ranges. A familiar histogram is a distribution of school examination grades, indicating the number of students who received grades A, B, C, D, and F. The grades might be based on a range of test scores from 90 to 100, 80 to 89, 70 to 79, 60 to 69, and less than 60. You establish the upper and lower limits of the data and then add the partition value.

Effective use of the **Partition**() function requires typing or editing an SQL statement; the result of the query is most useful if presented in graphical form. Adding a histogram chart to a form is much easier than using the **Partition**() function.

The eight *IsDataType*() functions, four of which are new in Access 95, determine the type or value of data. You can use **IsNull**() in validation rules and query criteria of one field to determine whether another field—whose field name is used as the argument—contains a valid entry. Although *FieldName* is the argument in the example syntax in table 9.11, you can substitute an Access VBA variable name.

Other Functions. The chapters that cover other aspects of Access 95 describe and provide the syntax for the following special-purpose functions:

- *SQL aggregate functions* are described in Chapter 10, "Creating Multitable and Crosstab Queries." You use these functions most often with multiple-table queries that provide the data source forms. SQL aggregate functions return statistical data on the records selected by a query. You cannot use these functions in macros or call them from Access Basic modules, except within quoted strings used to create SQL statements to populate Recordset objects.

- *Domain aggregate functions* perform the same functions as the SQL aggregate functions, but on calculated values rather than the values contained in query fields. Chapter 12, "Creating and Using Forms," covers these functions. One domain aggregate function, DCount(), is useful in validating entries in tables; this function is explained later in this chapter in the section "Expressions for Validating Data."

- The two dynamic data exchange functions, **DDE**() and **DDESend**(), are used to transfer data from and to other applications, respectively. In most cases, you use DDE functions with applications that don't support OLE Automation, the preferred method of interapplication data exchange. Chapter 21, "Using Access with Microsoft Excel," covers the use of **DDE**() and **DDESend**().

- The remaining Access functions are used exclusively or almost exclusively in Access VBA modules, and are described in Part VII of this book, "Programming with Visual Basic for Applications."

Intrinsic and Named Constants

As noted earlier in this chapter, VBA and Access have many predefined intrinsic constants. The names of these constants are considered *keywords* because you cannot use these names for any purpose other than returning the value represented by the names, such as –1 for **True** and Yes, 0 for **False** and No. (**True** and Yes are synonyms, as are **False** and No, so you can use these pairs of values interchangeably.) As mentioned earlier in the chapter, **Null** indicates a field with no valid entry. **True**, **False**, and **Null** are the most commonly used VBA intrinsic constants.

Named constants, which you define, return a single, predetermined value for the entire Access session. You can create named constants for use with forms and reports by defining them in the declarations section of an Access Basic module. Chapter 28, "Writing Visual Basic for Applications Code," describes how to create and use named constants such as Pi (used in the examples of trigonometric functions).

Creating Access Expressions

Chapter 4, "Working with Access Databases and Tables," uses several functions to validate data entry for most fields in the Personnel Actions table. Chapter 7, "Linking, Importing, and Exporting Tables," uses an expression to select the states to be included in a mailing list query. These examples provide the foundation on which to build more complex expressions that can define more precisely the validation rules and query criteria for real-life database applications.

The topics that follow provide a few examples of typical expressions for creating default values for fields, validating data entry, creating query criteria, and calculating field values. The examples demonstrate the similarity of syntax for expressions with different purposes. Part III of this book, "Creating Forms and Reports," provides additional examples of expressions designed for use in forms and reports; Part IV, "Powering Access with Macros," explains the use of expressions with macros.

Expressions for Creating Default Values

Expressions that create default field values can speed the entry of new records. Assigning values ordinarily requires you to use the assignment operator (=). When entering a default value in the Properties pane for a table in design mode, however, you can enter a simple literal. An example is the Q default value assigned to the paType field in Chapter 4, "Working with Access Databases and Tables." In this case, Access infers the = assignment operator and the quotation marks surrounding the Q. To adhere to the rules of creating expressions, the default value entry must be = "Q". You often can use shorthand techniques when typing expressions because Access infers the missing characters. If you enter = "Q", you achieve the same result; Access doesn't infer the extra characters.

You can use complex expressions for default values if the result of the expression conforms to or can be converted by Access to the proper field data type. You can enter = **1** as the default value for the paType field, for example, although 1 is a Numeric field data type and paType is a Text type field.

Expressions for Validating Data

The Personnel Actions table uses several expressions to validate data entry. The validation rule for the paID field is > 0; the rule for the paType field is "S" **Or** "Q" **Or** "Y" **Or** "B" **Or** "C"; the rule for the paApprovedBy field is > 0 **Or Is Null**. The validation rule for the paID field is equivalent to the following imaginary in-line **IIf**() function:

```
IIf(DataEntry > 0, paID = DataEntry,
    MsgBox("Please enter a valid employee ID number."))
```

Access tests *DataEntry* in the validation rule expression. If the validation expression returns **True**, the value of *DataEntry* replaces the value in the current record's field. If the expression returns **False**, a message box displays the validation text that you typed. **MsgBox**() is a function used in VBA programming to display a message box on-screen. You cannot type the imaginary validation rule just described; Access infers the equivalent of the imaginary **IIf**() expression after you add the ValidationRule and ValidationText properties with entries in the two text boxes for the paID field.

You might change the expression "S" **Or** "Q" **Or** "Y" **Or** "B" **Or** "C", which you use to test the paType field, to a function. The **In**() function provides a simpler expression that accomplishes the same objective:

```
In("S", "Q", "Y", "B", "C")
```

Alternatively, you can use the following table-level validation expression:

```
InStr("SQYBC",[paID]) > 0
```

Both expressions give the same result, but you can use **InStr**() only for table-level validation because one of its arguments refers to a field name. Thus, the **In**() function provides the better solution.

Expressions for Query Criteria

 ◀◀ "Creating More Complex Queries," p. 267

When creating Chapter 8's qryUSMailingList query to select records from the states of California, Oregon, and Washington, you enter ="CA", ="OR", and ="WA" on separate lines. A better expression is **In**("CA", "OR", "WA"), entered on the same line as the ="USA" criterion for the Country field. This expression corrects the failure to test the Country field for a value equal to USA for the OR and WA entries.

You can use a wide range of other functions to select specific records to be returned to a query table. Table 9.12 shows some typical functions used as query criteria applicable to the Northwind Traders tables.

Table 9.12	Typical Expressions Used as Query Criteria		
Table	**Field**	**Expression**	**Records Returned**
Customers	Country	**Not** "USA" **And** **Not** "Canada"	Firms other than those in the U.S. and Canada
Customers	Country	**Not** ("USA" **Or** "Canada")	Firms other than those in the U.S. and Canada; the parentheses apply the condition to both literals
Customers	CompanyName	Like "[N–Z]*"	Firms with names beginning with *N* through *Z*, outside the U.S.
Customers	CompanyName	Like S* **Or** Like V*	Firms with names beginning with *S* or *V* (Access adds Like and quotation marks)

Table	Field	Expression	Records Returned
Customers	CompanyName	`Like "*shop*"`	Firms with *shop*, *Shop*, *Shoppe*, or *SHOPPING* in the firm name
Customers	PostalCode	`>=90000`	Firms with postal codes greater than or equal to 90000
Orders	OrderDate	`Year([OrderDate]) = 1995`	Orders received to date, beginning with 1/1/1995
Orders	OrderDate	`Like "*/*/95"`	Orders received to date, beginning with 1/1/1995; using wild cards simplifies expressions
Orders	OrderDate	`Like "1/*/95"`	Orders received in the month of January 1995
Orders	OrderDate	`Like "1/?/95"`	Orders received from the 1st to the 9th of January 1995
Orders	OrderDate	`Year([OrderDate] = 1995 And DatePart("q", [OrderDate]) = 1`	Orders received in the first quarter of 1995
Orders	OrderDate	`Between #1/1/95# And #3/31/95#`	Orders received in the first quarter of 1995
Orders	OrderDate	`Year([OrderDate] = 1995 And DatePart("ww", [OrderDate]) = 10`	Orders received in the 10th week of 1995
Orders	OrderDate	`>= DateValue ("1/15/95")`	Orders received on or after 1/15/95
Orders	Shipped Date	`Is Null`	Orders not yet shipped
Orders	Order Amount	`>= 5000`	Orders with values greater than or equal to $5,000
Orders	Order Amount	`Between 5000 And 10000`	Orders with values greater than or equal to $5,000 and less than or equal to $10,000
Orders	Order Amount	`< 1000`	Orders less than $1,000

The wild-card characters used in `Like` expressions simplify the creation of criteria for selecting names and dates. As in DOS, the asterisk (*) substitutes for any legal number of characters and the question mark (?) substitutes for a single character. When a wild-card character prefixes or appends a string, the matching process loses its default case-sensitivity. If you want to match a string without regard to case, use the following expression:

`UCase$(FieldName) = "MATCH STRING"`

> **Note**
>
> The Orders table of the Northwind Traders sample database supplied with Access 1.0 and 1.1 included an Order Amount field. The value in the Order Amount field was set equal to the sum of
>
> *(continues)*

(continued)

the products of the Quantity and Unit Price fields, less the Discount percentage, of the records in the Order Details table. Including the Order Amount field violates the rule of relational databases that requires that all data in the fields of primary tables (Orders is a primary table) be dependent on the primary key and independent of other fields, either in the table or in other tables. The Order Amount field's value depends on the entries in the Order Details table.

Entering a Query Criterion. To experiment with query criteria expressions, follow these steps:

1. Click the Queries tab of the Database window, click the New button to open a new query, then click OK when the New Query dialog appears.

2. Select the Customers table from the Tables list of the Show Table dialog, and click the Add button. Repeat this process for the Orders and Order Details table. (Alternatively, you can add a table from the Show Table dialog by double-clicking the table.) Click the Close button to close the Add Table dialog. The CustomerID fields of the Customers and Orders tables and the OrderID fields of the Orders and Order Details tables are joined; *joins* are indicated by a line between the fields of the two tables. (The next chapter covers joining multiple tables.)

3. Add the CompanyName, PostalCode, and Country fields of the Customers table to the query. You can add fields by selecting them from the field drop-down list in the Query Design grid, by clicking a field in the Customers field list above the grid and dragging the field to the desired Field cell in the grid, or by double-clicking a field in the Customers field list above the grid.

4. Add to the query the OrderID, Order Date, Shipped Date, and Freight fields of the Orders table. Use the horizontal scroll bar slider under the Query Design grid to expose additional field columns as necessary. Click the Table Names button of the toolbar or choose View, Table Names to display the table names in the Tables row of the Query Design grid, if necessary. Place the caret in the Sort row of the OrderID field, press F4 to open the Sort list box, and select Ascending Sort.

5. Click the Totals button of the toolbar or choose View, Totals to add the Total row to the Query Design grid. The default value, Group By, is added to the Total cell for each field of your query.

6. Scroll the grid so that the Freight column appears. Click the selection bar above the Field row to select the Freight column and press the Insert key to add a new column.

7. Type **Amount: CCur([UnitPrice]*[Quantity]*(1–[Discount]))** in the new column's Field cell (see fig. 9.7). This expression calculates the net amount of each line item in the Order Details table and formats the column as if the field data type were Currency. The next section discusses how to use expressions to create calculated fields.

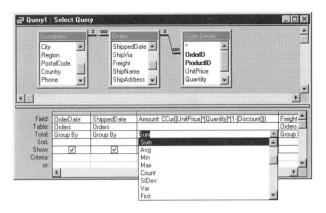

Fig. 9.7 The query design for testing the use of expressions to select records with values that meet criteria.

8. Move the caret to the Total row of the new column and press F4 to open the drop-down list. Choose Sum from the list (see fig. 9.7). The Sum option totals the net amount for all the line items of each order in the Orders table. In the next chapter, you learn the details of how to create queries that group data.

The Total row for all the other columns of the query shows Group By. Make sure that you mark the Show check box so that your new query column appears when you run the query. (Do not make an entry in the Table row of your new query column; if you do, you receive an error message when you run the query.)

9. Click the Run or Datasheet View button of the toolbar to run your new query. Your query appears as shown in figure 9.8. The Amount column contains the total amount of the order, and the net of discounts, if any.

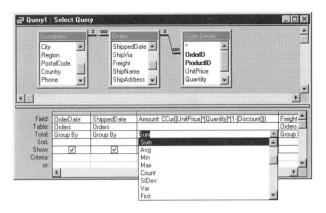

Fig. 9.8 The query result set for the query design shown in figure 9.7.

Using the Expression Builder to Add Query Criteria. After creating and testing your query, you can apply criteria to limit the number of records that the query returns. You can use Access's Expression Builder to simplify the process of adding record-selection criteria to your query. To test some of the expressions listed in table 9.12, follow these steps:

1. Click the Design View button of the toolbar to change to query design mode.

2. Place the caret in the Criteria row of the field for which you want to establish a record-section criterion.

3. Click the Builder button of the toolbar to display the Expression Builder's window. Alternatively, you can right-click in the Criteria row, then choose Build from the popup menu.

4. In the expression text box at the top of Expression Builder's window, type one of the expressions from table 9.12. Figure 9.9 shows the sample expression Like "*shop*" that applies to the Criteria row of the Company Name column. You can use the Like button under the expression text box as a shortcut for entering Like.

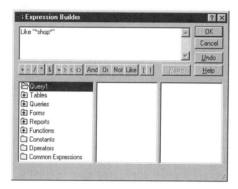

Fig. 9.9   Entering a criterion in the Expression Builder to create a criterion to match *shop*.

5. Click OK to return to the Query Design grid. In the field where the caret is located, the Expression Builder places the expression that you built (see fig. 9.10).

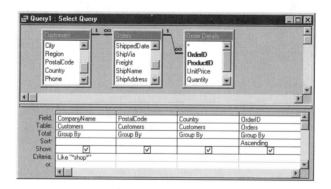

Fig. 9.10   The Query Design grid with the expression that you created in the Expression Builder.

6. Click the Run button of the toolbar to test the expression. The query result for the example in figure 9.10 appears as shown in figure 9.11.

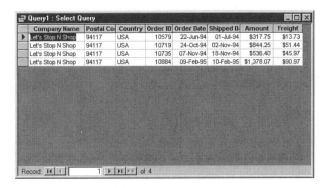

Fig. 9.11 The query result set resulting from adding the Like "*shop*" criteria to the Company Name field.

7. Return to query design mode, then select and delete the expression by pressing the Delete key.

8. Repeat steps 2 through 7 for each expression that you want to test. When you test expressions using Date/Time functions, sort the OrderDate field in ascending order. Similarly, sort on the Amount field when queries are based on amount criteria. You can alter the expressions and try combinations with the implied **And** condition by entering criteria for other fields in the same row. Access warns you with an error message if you make a mistake in an expression's syntax.

9. After you finish experimenting, save your query with a descriptive name, such as **qryOrderAmount**.

Expressions for Calculating Query Field Values

The preceding section demonstrated that you can use expressions to create new, calculated fields in query tables. Calculated fields display data computed based on the values of other fields in the same row of the query table. Table 9.13 shows some representative expressions that you can use to create calculated query fields.

Table 9.13 Typical Expressions to Create Calculated Query Fields		
Column Name	**Expression**	**Values Calculated**
TotalAmount	`[Amount] + [Freight]`	Sum of the Order Amount and Freight fields
FreightPercent	`100 * [Freight]/[Amount]`	Freight charges as a percentage of the order amount
FreightPct	**Format**(`[Freight]/[Amount]`, `"Percent"`)	Freight charges as a percentage of the order amount, but with formatting applied
SalesTax	**Format**(`[Amount] * 0.05`, `"$#,###.00"`)	Sales tax of 5 percent of the amount of the order added with a display similar to the Currency data type

To create a query containing calculated fields, follow these steps:

1. In Query Design view, move to the first blank column of the query that you created in the preceding section. Type the column name shown in table 9.13, followed by a colon and then the expression. (Click the Builder button of the toolbar to use the Expression Builder to enter the expression, as shown in figure 9.12, or press Shift+F2 to use the Zoom box to enter the expression.) The expression for the example in figure 9.12 is FreightPct: **Format**([Freight]/[Amount],"Percent"). If you don't type the field name and colon, Access provides the default Expr1 as the calculated field name.

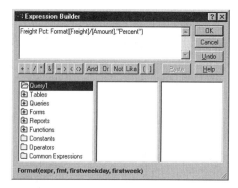

Fig. 9.12   Entering an expression in the Expression Builder to create a calculated field in a query.

2. Place the caret in the Total cell of the calculated field and select Expression from the drop-down list, as shown in figure 9.13. (If you don't select Expression, your query opens a Parameters dialog or returns an error message when you attempt to execute it.)

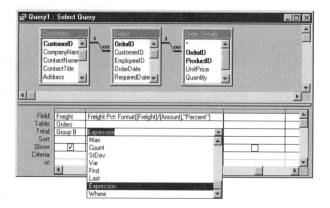

Fig. 9.13   The query design for two of the calculated fields of table 9.13.

3. Run the query. The result set for the query with the calculated field appears as shown in figure 9.14.

Query1 : Select Query

Company Name	Postal Co	Country	Order	Order Da	Shipped	Amount	Freight	Freight Pct
Vins et alcools Chev	51100	France	10248	01-Jul-93	13-Jul-93	$440.00	$32.38	7.36%
Toms Spezialitäten	44087	Germany	10249	02-Jul-93	07-Jul-93	$1,863.40	$11.61	0.62%
Hanari Carnes	05454-876	Brazil	10250	05-Jul-93	09-Jul-93	$1,552.60	$65.83	4.24%
Victuailles en stock	69004	France	10251	05-Jul-93	12-Jul-93	$654.06	$41.34	6.32%
Suprêmes délices	B-6000	Belgium	10252	06-Jul-93	08-Jul-93	$3,597.90	$51.30	1.43%
Hanari Carnes	05454-876	Brazil	10253	07-Jul-93	13-Jul-93	$1,444.80	$58.17	4.03%
Chop-suey Chinese	3012	Switzerlar	10254	08-Jul-93	20-Jul-93	$556.62	$22.98	4.13%
Richter Supermarkt	1203	Switzerlar	10255	09-Jul-93	12-Jul-93	$2,490.50	$148.33	5.96%
Wellington Importado	08737-363	Brazil	10256	12-Jul-93	14-Jul-93	$517.80	$13.97	2.70%
HILARIÓN-Abastos	5022	Venezuela	10257	13-Jul-93	19-Jul-93	$1,119.90	$81.91	7.31%
Ernst Handel	8010	Austria	10258	14-Jul-93	20-Jul-93	$1,614.88	$140.51	8.70%
Centro comercial Mo	05022	Mexico	10259	15-Jul-93	22-Jul-93	$100.80	$3.25	3.22%
Ottilies Käseladen	50739	Germany	10260	16-Jul-93	26-Jul-93	$1,504.65	$55.09	3.66%
Que Delícia	02389-673	Brazil	10261	16-Jul-93	27-Jul-93	$448.00	$3.05	0.68%
Rattlesnake Canyon	87110	USA	10262	19-Jul-93	22-Jul-93	$584.00	$48.29	8.27%
Ernst Handel	8010	Austria	10263	20-Jul-93	28-Jul-93	$1,873.80	$146.06	7.79%

Record: 1 of 830

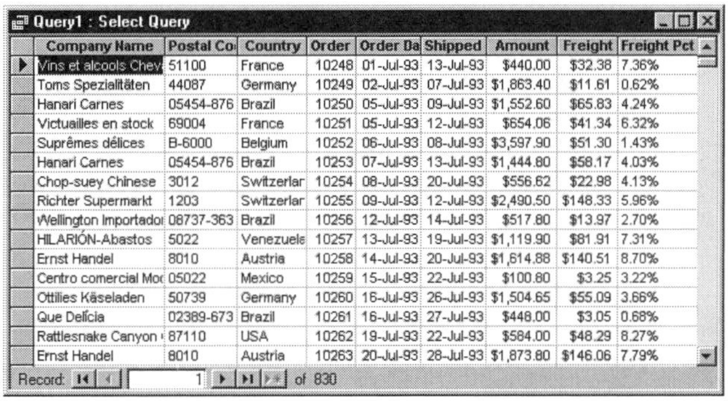

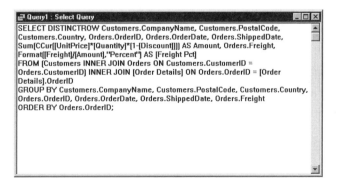

Fig. 9.14 The query result set displaying the order total and freight charges as a percent of the order amount.

4. Repeat steps 1, 2, and 3 for each of the four examples in table 9.13.

You use the **`Format()`** function with your expression as its first argument to display the calculated values in a more readable form. When you add the percent symbol (`%`) to a format expression or specify `"Percent"` as the format, the value of the expression argument multiplies by 100, and the percent symbol preceded by a space appends to the displayed value. (Access 2.0 introduced `"Percent"` as a new format specifier equivalent to entering `"0.00%"`.)

Figure 9.15 shows the rather complex SQL statement that creates the query with three calculated fields in Access's SQL window. (Choose View, SQL or right-click in a blank area of the upper pane and choose View SQL from the popup menu to display the SQL window.) Note that you cannot include periods to indicate abbreviations in field names. Periods and exclamation points are identifier operators, and you cannot include them within identifiers.

Query1 : Select Query

```
SELECT DISTINCTROW Customers.CompanyName, Customers.PostalCode,
Customers.Country, Orders.OrderID, Orders.OrderDate, Orders.ShippedDate,
Sum(CCur([UnitPrice]*[Quantity]*(1-[Discount]))) AS Amount, Orders.Freight,
Format([Freight]/[Amount],"Percent") AS [Freight Pct]
FROM (Customers INNER JOIN Orders ON Customers.CustomerID =
Orders.CustomerID) INNER JOIN [Order Details] ON Orders.OrderID = [Order
Details].OrderID
GROUP BY Customers.CompanyName, Customers.PostalCode, Customers.Country,
Orders.OrderID, Orders.OrderDate, Orders.ShippedDate, Orders.Freight
ORDER BY Orders.OrderID;
```

Fig. 9.15 The SQL statement used to create a query with three calculated fields.

Troubleshooting

When attempting to execute a query that contains an expression, a "Can't evaluate expression" or "Wrong data type" message box appears.

The "Can't evaluate expression" message usually indicates a typographic error in naming a function or an object. Depending on the use of the function, an Enter Parameter Value dialog might appear if the named object does not exist. The "Wrong data type" message is most likely to occur as a result of attempting to use mathematic or trigonometric operators with values of the Text or Date/Time field data types. If your expression refers to a control contained in a Form or Report object, the form or report must be open when you execute the function.

Other Uses for Expressions

You can use expressions with update queries, as conditions for the execution of a macro action, or as an argument for an action such as RunMacro (see Chapter 16, "Understanding Access Macros and Events"). SQL SELECT statements use expressions as in the following fragment:

```
WHERE [Birth Date] >= #1/1/60#
```

See Chapter 24, "Working with Structured Query Language," for more information. Access VBA code also uses expressions extensively to control program flow and structure. The chapters focusing on macros, SQL, and Access VBA programming (Parts IV, VI, and VII) describe these uses for expressions.

From Here...

Expressions that you create with Access operators, identifiers, constants, and functions—and the literals that you supply—are used in every aspect of an Access database application. Although this chapter's emphasis is on using expressions to validate data entry in tables and creating query tables, expressions also are basic elements of forms, reports, macros, and modules.

To learn more about related topics, see the following chapters:

■ Chapter 10, "Creating Multitable and Crosstab Queries," teaches you how to join tables in one-to-many relationships using Access's Query Design window.

■ Chapter 11, "Using Action Queries," deals with queries that update data in tables, delete and add table records, and create new tables.

■ Chapter 24, "Working with Structured Query Language," shows you how to use expressions in WHERE clauses that serve as query criteria and to create joins between tables.

Chapter 10

Creating Multitable and Crosstab Queries

Your purpose in acquiring Access is undoubtedly to take advantage of this application's relational database management capabilities. To do so, you have to be able to link related tables based on key fields that have values in common, a process known as a *join* in database terms. Chapters 8, "Using Query by Example," and 9, "Understanding Operators and Expressions in Access," showed you how to create simple queries based on a single table. If you tried the examples in Chapter 9, you saw a glimpse of a multiple-table query when you joined the Order Details table to the Orders table that you then joined to the Customers table to create the query for testing expressions. The first part of this chapter deals exclusively with queries created from multiple tables related through joins.

This chapter provides examples of queries that use each of the four basic types of joins that you can create in Access's Query Design View: *equi-joins*, *outer joins*, *self-joins*, and *theta joins*. Two of the three new query features introduced by Access 2.0, subqueries and UNION queries, cannot be used in the queries that you design in Access's graphic Query by Example (QBE) window. You can implement these two new query features only by writing SQL statements, the subject of Chapter 24, "Working with Structured Query Language." Some of the example queries in this chapter use the Personnel Actions table that you created in Chapter 4, "Working with Access Databases and Tables." If you didn't create the Personnel Actions table, refer to the "Creating the Personnel Actions Table" section of Chapter 4 or to Appendix C, "Data Dictionary for the Personnel Actions Table," for instructions to build this table. Other example queries build on queries that you create in preceding sections. You will find, therefore, that reading this chapter and creating the example queries sequentially, as the queries appear in text, is more efficient than taking the random approach.

▶▶ See "Implementing Subqueries," p. 895
▶▶ See "Using UNION Queries," p. 894

In this chapter, you learn to how to do the following

- Join tables with queries

- Design queries that establish indirect relationships between tables

- Create Lookup fields in tables with the Lookup Wizard

- Format the data in query result sets

- Summarize data with crosstab queries

- Design parameter queries

II

Specific Information

This chapter also includes descriptions and examples of four of the five categories of queries that you can create with Access: *select*, *summary*, *parameter*, and *crosstab* queries. Four types of action queries exist that you can use to create or modify data in tables: *make-table*, *append*, *delete*, and *update*. The next chapter, "Using Action Queries," presents typical applications for and examples of each type of action query.

Joining Tables to Create Multitable Queries

Before you can create joins between tables, you must know the contents of the tables' fields and which fields are related by common values. As mentioned in Chapter 4, "Working with Access Databases and Tables," assigning identical names to primary- and foreign-key fields in different tables that contain related data is a common practice. This approach, which Microsoft used when creating the Northwind Traders sample database, makes determining relationships and creating joins among tables easier. The Customers table's CustomerID field and the Orders table's CustomerID field, for example, are used to join orders with customers. Figure 10.1 shows the structure of the Northwind Traders database, together with a graphical display of the joins among the tables. Access query designs indicate joins with lines between field names of different tables. Bold type indicates primary-key fields. Each join usually involves at least one primary-key field.

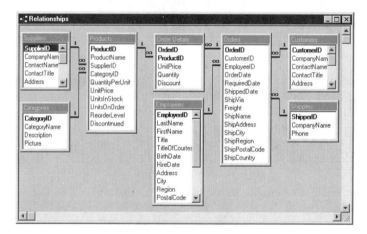

Fig. 10.1   The joins among the tables of the Northwind Traders sample database.

You can display the structure of the joins among the tables in Access 95's Northwind Traders database by giving the Database window the focus (click the Database Window button of the toolbar) and then clicking the Relationship button of the toolbar or choosing Tools, Relationships. The 1 above the line that shows the join between two tables in figure 10.1 indicates the "one" side of a one-to-many relationship; the infinity symbol ( ) indicates the "many" side.

> **Note**
>
> Access 95 lets you choose between displaying only the direct relationships for a single table (the Show Direct Relationships button on the toolbar) or all relationships for all tables in a database (the Show All Relationships button). All the tables of Northwind.mdb appear by default when you open the Relationships window of the Northwind sample database. In this case, clicking the Show Direct Relationships button has no effect. To show relationships for only one table, click the toolbar's Clear Layout button, click the Show Table button to display the Show Table dialog, select the table to display in the Tables list, then click Add and Close. Click the Show Direct Relationships button to display the relationships for the selected table. Clearing the layout of the Relationships windows does not affect the underlying relationships between the tables. The Show Direct Relationships feature is useful primarily with databases that contain many related tables.

Access supports four types of joins in the graphical QBE design mode:

- *Equi-joins* (also called *inner joins*) are the most common join for creating select queries. Equi-joins display in one table all the records that have corresponding records in another table. The correspondence between records is determined by identical values (WHERE *field1 = field2* in SQL) in the fields that join the tables. In most cases, joins are based on a unique primary-key field in one table and a foreign-key field in the other table, in a one-to-many relationship. If none of the table's records that act as the *many* side of the relationship has a field value that corresponds to a record in the table of the *one* side, the corresponding records in the *one* side don't appear in the query result.

  Access automatically creates the joins between tables if the tables share a common field name that is a primary key of one of the tables or if you previously specified the relationships between the tables in the Relationships window.

- *Outer joins* are used in database maintenance to remove orphan records and to remove duplicate data from tables by creating new tables that contain records with unique values. Outer joins display records in one member of the join, regardless of whether corresponding records exist on the other side of the join.

- *Self-joins* relate data within a single table. You create a self-join in Access by adding to the query a duplicate of the table (Access provides an alias for the duplicate) and then creating joins between the fields of the copies.

- *Theta joins* relate data by using comparison operators other than =. Theta joins include *not-equal joins* (<>) used in queries designed to return records that lack a particular relationship. You implement theta joins by WHERE criteria rather than by the SQL JOIN reserved word. The Query Design window does not indicate theta joins by drawing lines between field names, nor do theta joins appear in the Relationships window.

Specific Information

II

Creating Conventional Single-Column Equi-Joins

 ◄◄ See "Establishing Relationships between Tables," p. 142

Joins based on one column in each table are known as *single-column equi-joins*. Most relational databases are designed to employ single-column equi-joins only in one-to-many relationships. The following list details the basic rules for creating a database that enables you to use simple, single-column equi-joins for all queries:

- Each table on the *one* side of the relationship must have a primary key with a No Duplicates index to maintain referential integrity. Access automatically creates a No Duplicates index on the primary-key field or fields of a table.

- Many-to-many relationships, such as the relationship of Orders to Products, are implemented by an intermediary table (in this case, Order Details) having a one-to-many relationship (Orders to Order Details) with one table and a many-to-one relationship (Order Details to Products) with another.

 - Duplicated data in tables, where applicable, is extracted to a new table that has a primary-key, no-duplicates, one-to-many relationship with the table from which the duplicate data is extracted. Using a multicolumn primary key to identify extracted data uniquely often is necessary because individual key fields might contain duplicate data. The combination (also known as *concatenation*) of the values of the key fields, however, must be unique. Access 95's new Table Analyzer Wizard locates and extracts most duplicate data automatically. The "Creating New Tables with Make-Table Queries" section in Chapter 11, "Using Action Queries," describes how to extract extracting duplicate data from tables manually.

All the joins in the Northwind Traders database, shown by the lines that connect field names of adjacent tables in figure 10.1, are single-column equi-joins between tables with one-to-many relationships. Access uses the ANSI SQL-92 reserved words INNER JOIN to identify conventional equi-joins, and LEFT JOIN or RIGHT JOIN to specify outer joins.

Among the most common uses for queries based on equi-joins is to match customer names and addresses with orders received. You might want to create a simple report, for example, that lists the customer name, order number, order date, and amount. To create a conventional one-to-many, single-column equi-join query that relates Northwind's customers to the orders that the customers place, sorted by company and order date, follow these steps:

 1. If Northwind.mdb is open, close all windows except the Database window by double-clicking the windows' close box. Otherwise, open Access's File menu and choose 1 Northwind.mdb to open the Northwind Traders database.

 2. Click the Queries tab of the Database window and then choose New to create a new query. The New Query dialog appears. With the New Query item selected, click OK. Access displays the Show Table dialog superimposed on an empty Query Design window.

3. Select the Customers table from the Show Table list and click the Add button. Alternatively, you can double-click the Customers table name to add the table to the query. Access adds to the Query Design window the Field Names list for Customers.

4. Double-click the Orders table in the Show Table list, and then click the Close button. Access adds to the window the Field Names list for Orders, plus a line that indicates a join between the CustomerID fields of the two tables, as shown in figure 10.2. Access creates the join automatically because CustomerID is the Customers table's key field and Access found a field with the same field name (a foreign key) in the Orders table.

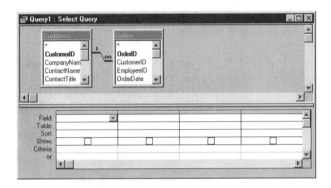

Fig. 10.2 A join between fields of two tables with a common field name, created automatically by Access.

5. To identify each order with the customer's name, select the CompanyName field of the Customers table and drag the field symbol to the Field row of the Query Design grid's first column.

6. Select the OrderID field of the Orders table and drag the field symbol to the second column's Field row. Drag the OrderDate field to the third column. Your query design appears as shown in figure 10.3.

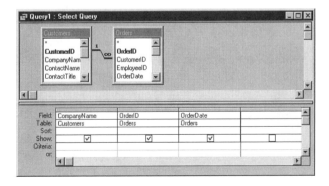

Fig. 10.3 Designing a query to display orders placed by customers, sorted by company name and order date.

7. Click the Run or Query View button to display the result of the query, the `Recordset` shown in figure 10.4. Note that the field headers of the query result set show the captions for the table fields, which include spaces, rather than the actual field names, which don't have spaces.

Company Name	Order ID	Order Date
Alfreds Futterkiste	10643	22-Aug-94
Alfreds Futterkiste	10692	30-Sep-94
Alfreds Futterkiste	10702	10-Oct-94
Alfreds Futterkiste	10835	12-Jan-95
Alfreds Futterkiste	10952	13-Mar-95
Alfreds Futterkiste	11011	06-Apr-95
Ana Trujillo Emparedados y helados	10308	15-Sep-93
Ana Trujillo Emparedados y helados	10625	05-Aug-94
Ana Trujillo Emparedados y helados	10759	25-Nov-94
Ana Trujillo Emparedados y helados	10926	01-Mar-95
Antonio Moreno Taquería	10365	24-Nov-93
Antonio Moreno Taquería	10507	12-Apr-94
Antonio Moreno Taquería	10535	10-May-94
Antonio Moreno Taquería	10573	16-Jun-94

Fig. 10.4   The result of the query design of figure 10.3 that joins the Customers and Orders tables.

Specifying a Sort Order for the Query Result Set

◀◀ See "Adding Indexes to Tables," p. 150

Access displays query result sets in the order of the index on the primary-key field. If more than one column represents a primary-key field, Access sorts the query result set in left-to-right key-field column precedence. Because Company Name is the farthest left primary-key field, the query result set displays all orders for a single company in order-number sequence. You can override the primary-key display order by adding a sort order. For example, if you want to see the latest orders first, you can specify a descending sort by order date. To add this sort sequence to your query, follow these steps:

1. Click the Design View button to return to query design mode.

2. Place the caret in the Sort row of the Order Date column of the Query Design grid and press F4 to open the drop-down list.

3. Select Descending from the drop-down list to specify a descending sort on date— latest orders first (see fig. 10.5).

4. Click the Run button or the Query View button to display the query result set with the new sort order (see fig. 10.6).

Creating Queries from Tables with Indirect Relationships

You can create queries that return indirectly related records, such as the categories of products purchased by each customer. You must include in the query each table that serves as a link in the chain of joins. If you are creating queries to return the categories of products purchased by each customer, for example, include each of the tables that link the chain of joins between the Customers and Categories tables. This chain includes the Customers, Orders, Order Details, Products, and Categories tables. You don't need to add any fields, however, from the intermediate tables to the Query Design grid; the CompanyName and the CategoryName fields suffice.

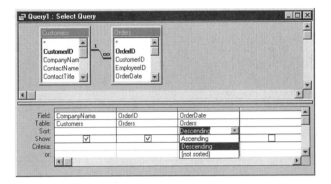

Fig. 10.5 Adding a special sort order to the query.

Fig. 10.6 The result of adding to the query a descending sort on Order Date.

To modify your customers and orders query so that you create a query that displays fields of indirectly related records, follow these steps:

1. In Query Design view, delete the OrderIDcolumn of the query by clicking the thin bar above the Field row to select (highlight) the entire column, then press Delete. Perform the same action for the OrderDate columns so that only the CompanyName column appears in the query.

2. Click the Show Table button of the toolbar or choose Query, Show Table and add the Order Details, Products, and Categories tables to the query, in sequence, then click the Close button of the Add Table dialog. The upper pane of figure 10.7 shows the chain of joins that Access automatically creates between Customers and Categories based on the primary-key field of each intervening table and the identically named foreign-key field in the adjacent table.

   As you add tables to the Query Design window, the table field lists might not appear in the upper pane. Use the upper pane's vertical scroll bar to display the "hidden" tables. You can drag the table field lists to the top of the upper pane and then rearrange the field lists to match the appearance of figure 10.7.

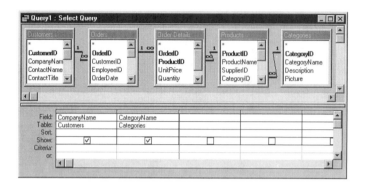

Fig. 10.7 The chain of joins required to create queries from tables that have an indirect relationship.

3. Drag the CategoryName from the Categories field list to the Field row of the grid's second column. Alternatively, you can double-click the field name to add it to the next empty column of the grid.

4. If you want to see the SQL statement that Access uses to create the query, choose View, SQL to display Access 2.0's new SQL window, shown in figure 10.8. The table's joins appear as INNER JOIN...ON... clauses. Cascaded joins use the INNER JOIN...ON...ON... syntax, which is explained in Chapter 24, "Working with Structured Query Language."

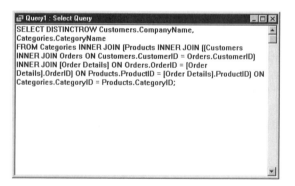

Fig. 10.8 The SQL statement that creates the query to determine which customers purchased specific categories of products.

5. Click the toolbar's Query Design View button to close the SQL window. Then click the Run button on the toolbar. The query result set shown in figure 10.9 appears.

6. Close the query by clicking the window close box. This query is only an example, so you don't need to save it.

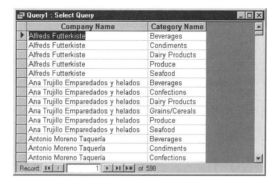

Fig. 10.9 The Customers-Categories Recordset, resulting from the query of figure 10.7.

Queries made on indirectly related tables are common, especially when you want to analyze the data with SQL aggregate functions or Access's crosstab queries. For more information, see the sections "Using the SQL Aggregate Functions" and "Creating Crosstab Queries" in this chapter.

Creating Multicolumn Equi-Joins and Selecting Unique Values

You can have more than one join between a pair of tables. You might, for example, want to create a query that returns the names of customers for which the billing and shipping addresses are the same. The billing address is the Customers table's Address field, and the shipping address is the Orders table's ShipAddress field. Therefore, you need to match the Customer ID fields in the two tables and Customers.Address with Orders.ShipAddress. This task requires a *multicolumn equi-join*.

To create this example of an address-matching multicolumn equi-join, follow these steps:

1. Create a new query by giving the Database window the focus, clicking the Queries tab (if necessary), and then choosing the New button. With Design View selected in the New Query dialog, click OK.

2. Add the Customers and Orders tables to the query by selecting each table in the Show Table dialog and clicking the Add button. Click Close.

3. Click and drag the Address field of the Customers table's Field List box to the ShipAddress field of the Orders table's Field List box. This creates another join, indicated by the new line between Address and ShipAddress (see fig. 10.10). The new line in the graphical QBE window has dots at both ends, indicating that the join is between a pair of fields that do not have a specified relationship, the same field name, or a primary-key index.

4. Drag the Customer table's CompanyName and Address fields to the Field row of the first and second query columns and drop the fields. Drag the Orders table's ShipAddress field to the query's third column and drop the field in the Field row.

5. Add an ascending sort to the CompanyName column.

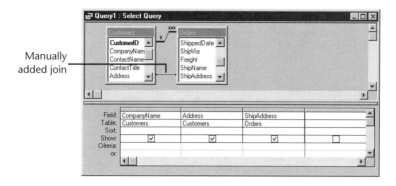

Manually
added join

Fig. 10.10 Creating a multicolumn equi-join by dragging one field name to a field in another table.

6. Click the Run button on the toolbar. Figure 10.11 shows the query's result.

Fig. 10.11 A query result set of orders for customers who have the same billing and shipping addresses.

7. To eliminate the duplicate rows, you must use the Unique Values option of Access's Query Properties sheet. To display the Query Properties sheet, which is shown in figure 10.12, click the Design View button, and then click the toolbar's Properties button or double-click an empty area in the Query Design window's upper pane. If the Properties window's title bar displays Field Properties or Field List, click an empty area in the Query Design window's upper pane so that the title bar displays Query Properties. Alternatively, right-click an empty region of the upper pane and select Properties from the popup menu.

8. The UniqueRecords query property is set **True** (Yes) and the UniqueValues property is set **False** (No) by default. The default settings add the Access SQL DISTINCTROW keyword to the SQL statement that creates the query (refer to fig. 10.8). Place the caret in the Unique Values text box and press F4 to open the drop-down list. Select Yes and close the list. Setting the UniqueValues property **True** substitutes the ANSI SQL reserved word DISTINCT for Access's DISTINCTROW. Click the Properties button again to close the Properties window.

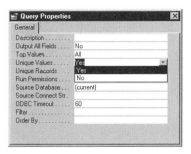

Fig. 10.12 Using the Query Properties sheet to display only rows with unique values.

9. Click the Run button of the toolbar. The result set no longer contains duplicate rows, as shown in figure 10.13.

Company Name	Address	Ship Address
Alfreds Futterkiste	Obere Str. 57	Obere Str. 57
Ana Trujillo Emparedados	Avda. de la Constitución 2222	Avda. de la Constitución 2222
Antonio Moreno Taquería	Mataderos 2312	Mataderos 2312
B's Beverages	Fauntleroy Circus	Fauntleroy Circus
Berglunds snabbköp	Berguvsvägen 8	Berguvsvägen 8
Blauer See Delikatessen	Forsterstr. 57	Forsterstr. 57
Blondel père et fils	24, place Kléber	24, place Kléber
Bólido Comidas preparada	C/ Araquil, 67	C/ Araquil, 67
Bon app'	12, rue des Bouchers	12, rue des Bouchers
Bottom-Dollar Markets	23 Tsawassen Blvd.	23 Tsawassen Blvd.
Cactus Comidas para lleva	Cerrito 333	Cerrito 333
Centro comercial Moctezu	Sierras de Granada 9993	Sierras de Granada 9993
Comércio Mineiro	Av. dos Lusíadas, 23	Av. dos Lusíadas, 23
Consolidated Holdings	Berkeley Gardens	Berkeley Gardens

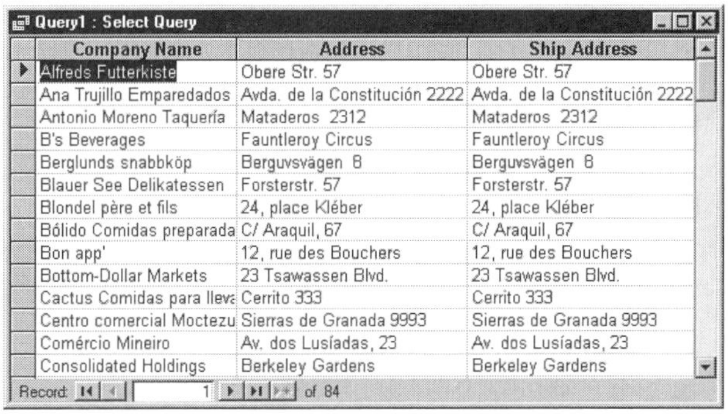

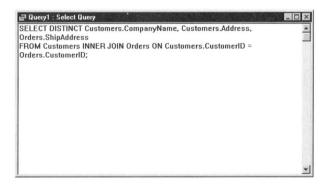

Fig. 10.13 The query result set after you remove duplicate rows.

10. Choose View, SQL to display the SQL statement (see fig. 10.14). The `DISTINCT` modifier of the `SELECT` statement causes the query to display only those records whose field values that *are included in the query* differ.

Fig. 10.14 The SQL statement that results in the query result set of figure 10.13.

11. Click the Close Window button to close the query without saving it. You then avoid cluttering the Database window's Queries list with obsolete query examples.

Because most of the orders have the same billing and shipping addresses, a more useful query is to find the orders for which the customer's billing and shipping addresses differ. You cannot create this query with a multicolumn equi-join, however, because the INNER JOIN reserved word in Access SQL doesn't accept the <> operator. Adding a not-equal join uses a criterion rather than a multicolumn join, as explained in the "Creating Not-Equal Theta Joins with Criteria" section later in this chapter.

Troubleshooting

When I run my query, an Enter Parameter Value dialog appears that asks me to enter a value. I hadn't specified a parameter for the query.

The Enter Parameter Value dialog appears when the Jet engine's query parser cannot identify an object specified in the query or evaluate an expression. Usually, the Enter Parameter Value dialog appears because of a typographic error. Intentionally creating parameter queries is the subject of the "Designing Parameter Queries" section, later in this chapter.

Using Lookup Fields in Tables

Access 95's new lookup feature for table fields lets you substitute combo (drop-down list) boxes or list boxes for conventional field text boxes. The lookup feature lets you provide a list of acceptable values for a particular field. When you select the value from the list, the value automatically is entered in the field of the current record. You can specify either of the following two types of lookup field:

- In a field that contain a foreign key values, a list of values from one or more fields of a related base table. As an example, the Orders table of Northwind.mdb has two foreign key fields: CustomerID and EmployeeID. The lookup feature of the CustomerID field displays in a combo box the CompanyName field value from the Customers table and the EmployeeID displays the LastName and FirstName fields of the Employees table, separated by a comma and space (see fig. 10.15). The foreign key lookup feature is implemented by a simple Access SQL select query, SELECT DISTINCTROW [CustomerID],[CompanyName] FROM [Customers] ORDER BY [CompanyName];, in the case of the CustomerID field.

- With any field except a single primary key field, a list of fixed values from which to select.

Note

Lookup is a feature of a field, not a field data type. The field data type is that of the content of the field, such as Number (Long Integer) for the EmployeeID field of the Orders table. The lookup feature is implemented by a special set of Access-specific properties stored with the common (Data Access Object or DAO) field properties of the table. (Lookup properties are included in the Properties collection of the Field object of the TableDef object for the table. These objects are described in Chapter 29, "Understanding the Data Access Object Class".)

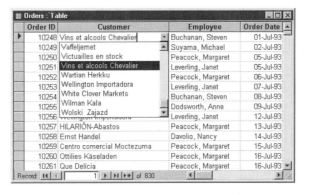

Fig. 10.15   Placing the caret in a lookup field causes the control to change to combo box; opening the combo box displays a list of acceptable field values.

You can add a new lookup field in either Design View or Table Datasheet View; however, you only can add the lookup feature to an existing field in Design View. In Datasheet View, only the combo box control is displayed, even if you specify a list box control. You can display a combo box or a list box on a form that is bound to a table with lookup fields. In practice, the drop-down list (a combo box with the Limit to List property set to Yes) is the most common type of lookup field control. The following sections describe how to add foreign key and fixed list lookup features to table fields.

Adding a Foreign Key Drop-Down List with the Lookup Wizard

The Personnel Actions table you created in earlier chapters of this book is a candidate for a lookup field that uses a foreign key drop-down list. Follow these steps to use the Lookup Wizard to change the paID field of the Personnel Actions table to a lookup field:

1. In the Database window, select the Personnel Actions table, press Ctrl+C to copy the table to the Clipboard.

2. Press Ctrl+V to display the Paste Table As dialog. Enter a name for the copy, such as tblLookup, and click the OK button to create the copy.

3. Open the table copy in Design View and select the paInitiatedBy field. Click the Lookup tab to display the current lookup properties; a text box control has no lookup properties. Open the Data Type drop-down list and select Lookup Wizard (see fig. 10.16). The first dialog of the Lookup Wizard appears.

4. You want the field to look up values in another table (Employees), so accept the first (default) option (see fig. 10.17). Click the Next > button to display the Lookup Wizard's second dialog.

5. With the View Tables option enabled, select the Employees base table to which the paInitiatedBy field is related (see fig. 10.18). Click Next > to display the third dialog.

6. Click the > button three times to add the EmployeeID, LastName, and FirstName fields to your lookup list (see fig. 10.19). You must include the base table key field that is related to your foreign key field. Click the Next > for the fourth dialog.

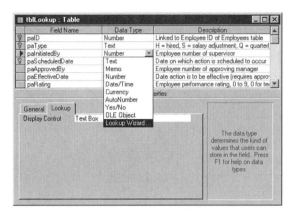

Fig. 10.16 Selecting the Lookup Wizard to add the lookup feature to a field.

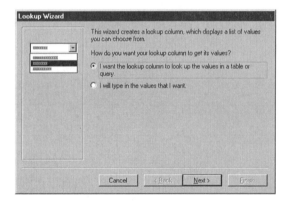

Fig. 10.17 Selecting between a foreign-key and fixed-list lookup in the first dialog of the Lookup Wizard.

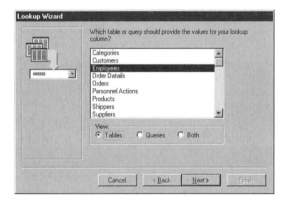

Fig. 10.18 Selecting between a foreign-key and fixed-list lookup in the second dialog of the Lookup Wizard.

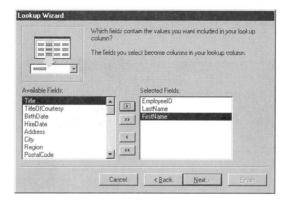

Fig. 10.19 Selecting the fields to include in your lookup list.

7. Adjust the widths of the columns to display the first and last names without excessive trailing "white space." (Double-clicking the right edge of the column, as recommended by the wizard, does not give the optimum result.) The wizard determines that EmployeeID is the key column and recommends hiding the key column (see fig. 10.20). Click Next > to display the fifth and final dialog.

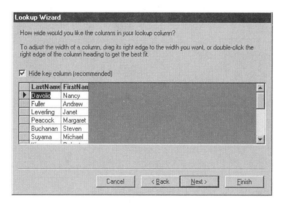

Fig. 10.20 Adjusting column widths of the lookup list and hiding the key column.

8. Accept the default "label" for the lookup field in the text box (see fig. 10.21). (If you change the default value, you change the field name, not the caption.)

9. Click the Finish button to complete the Wizard's work. Click OK when the Wizard asks if you'd like to save the table design. Your new lookup field properties appear as shown in figure 10.22. The Access SQL statement created by the Wizard is SELECT DISTINCTROW [Employees].[EmployeeID], [Employees].[LastName], [Employees].[FirstName] FROM [Employees];.

10. Click the Table View button to display the table datasheet. Only the first visible column of the list appears in the Initiated By column. Adjust the width of the Initiated By column to the width of the drop-down list, about 1.5 inches. With the caret in the Initiated By column, open the drop-down list to display the wizard's work (see fig. 10.23).

Fig. 10.21 Specifying the caption for the lookup field.

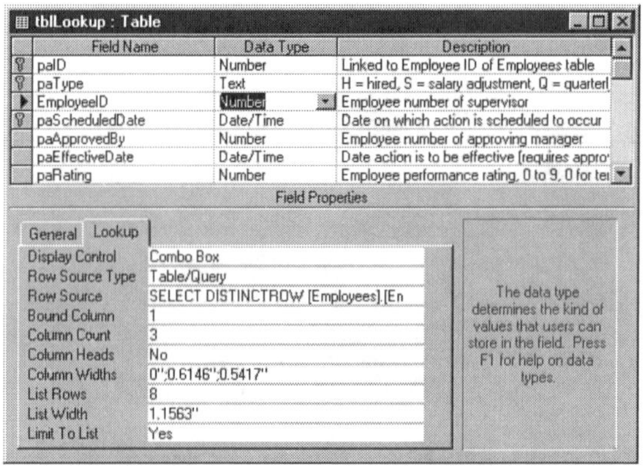

Fig. 10.22 Lookup properties are added to the paInitiatedBy field.

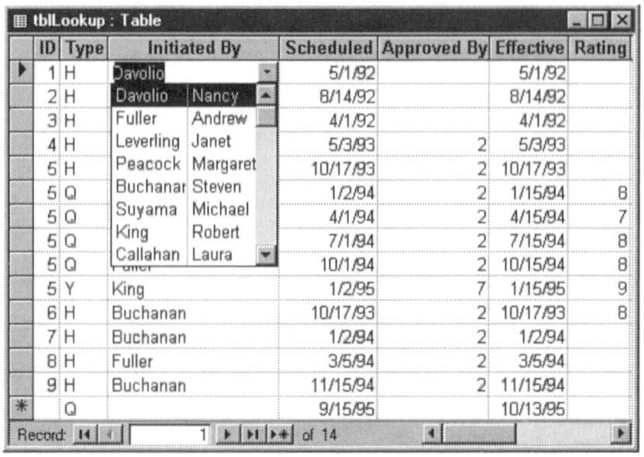

Fig. 10.23 The drop-down lookup list created by the wizard.

11. Return to Design View, select the Row Source property of the paInitiatedBy field and click the Builder button to display the Row Source SQL statement in Query Design View (see fig. 10.24), then close the Query Design window.

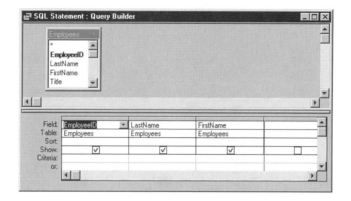

Fig. 10.24   The Query Design view of the SQL statement of the Row Source property in Query Design View.

Note

The properties of the combo box control created by the wizard are described in the "Using List Boxes and Combo Boxes" section of Chapter 13, "Designing Custom Multitable Forms." You can alter the lookup properties of a field to customize the basic work done for you by the wizard. The wizard's entries are quite adequate for most Access applications.

Adding a Fixed Value Lookup List to a Table

You add the alternative lookup feature, a fixed list of values, using the Lookup Wizard in much the same way as you created the foreign-key lookup list in the preceding section. To add a fixed-list lookup feature to the paType field of your copy of the Personnel Actions table, follow these steps:

1. Select the paType field, open the Data Type list and select Lookup Wizard to launch the Wizard.

2. In the first Lookup Wizard dialog, select the I Will Type in the Values That I Want option and click the Next > button.

3. In the second Lookup Wizard dialog, type 2 in the Number of Columns text box and press the Tab key to create the second list column.

4. Enter H, Hired; Q, Quarterly Review; Y, Yearly Review; and S, Salary Adjustment in the Col1 and Col2 columns of four rows. Adjust the width of the columns to suit the entries (see fig. 10.25). Click the Next > button to display the Wizard's third dialog.

5. The paType field uses single-character abbreviations for the type of personnel actions, so select Col1 as the "field that uniquely identifies the row," as shown in figure 10.26. (The paType field does not uniquely identify the row; Col1 contains

the single-character value that you want to insert into the field.) Click the Next > button to display the fourth and final Wizard dialog.

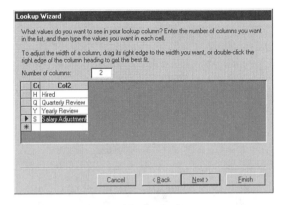

Fig. 10.25   Adding the lookup list values in the Lookup Wizard's second dialog.

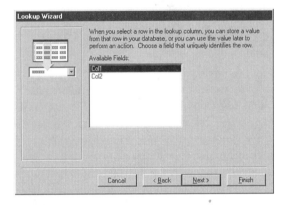

Fig. 10.26   Selecting the column that contains the value to insert into the field.

6. Accept the default "label" for your column and click the Finish button. The lookup properties for the paType field appear as shown in figure 10.27. The Row Source Type is Value List and the Row Source contains the values: "H";"Hired";"Q";"Quarterly Review";"Y";"Yearly Review";"S";"Salary Adjustment".

7. Click the Table View button and save the changes to your table. Increase the width of the Type column to about 1.5 inches, place the caret in the Type column and open the fixed value list to check the Wizard's work (see fig. 10.28).

8. If you don't want the abbreviation to appear in the drop-down list, change the first entry of the Column Widths property value to **0**.

9. If you want to remove the lookup feature from a field, select the field, click the Lookup tab, and choose Text Box from the drop-down Display Control list.

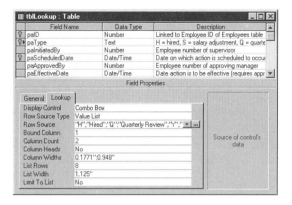

Fig. 10.27   Selecting the column that contains the value to insert into the field.

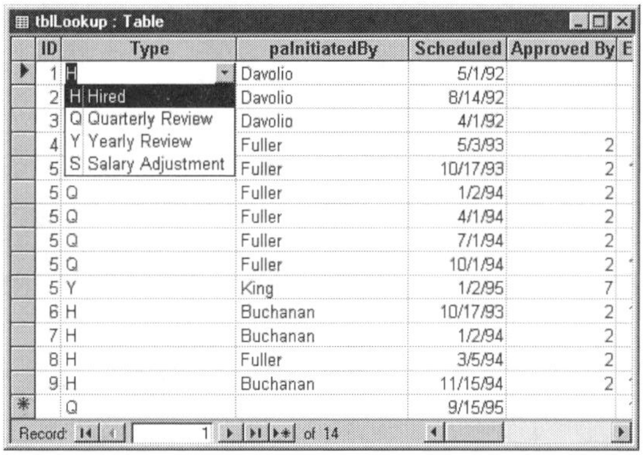

Fig. 10.28   The fixed value list created by the Lookup Wizard.

> **Note**
>
> The lookup feature has generated controversy among seasoned database developers. Relational database purists object to the principle of modifying the properties of tables with embedded queries. Another objection to the use of foreign-key drop-down lists is that it is easy for uninitiated users to inadvertently change data in a table after opening the list. Access 95's lookup feature, however, is a useful tool, especially for new database users.

Outer, Self, and Theta Joins

The preceding sections of this chapter described the equi-join or, in the parlance of SQL-92, an inner join. Inner joins are the most common type of join in database applications. Access also lets you create three other joins: outer, self, and theta. The following sections describe these three less common types of joins.

Creating Outer Joins

Outer joins enable you to display fields of all the records in a table participating in a query, regardless of whether corresponding records exist in the joined table. With Access, you can choose between left and right outer joins.

When diagramming database structures (a subject of Chapter 23, "Exploring Relational Database Design and Implementation"), you traditionally would draw the primary *one* table to the left of the secondary *many* table. A left outer join (LEFT JOIN or *= in SQL) query in Access, therefore, displays all the records in the table with the unique primary key, regardless of whether matching records exist in the *many* table. Conversely, a right outer join (RIGHT JOIN or =*) query displays all the records in the *many* table, regardless of the existence of a record in the primary table. Records in the *many* table without corresponding records in the *one* table usually, but not necessarily, are orphan records; these kinds of records may have a many-to-one relationship to another table.

To practice creating a left outer join, follow these steps to detect whether records are missing for an employee in the Personnel Actions table:

1. Open a new query and add the Employees and Personnel Actions tables.

2. Drag the EmployeeID field symbol to the paID field of Personnel Actions to create an equi-join between these fields if Access didn't create the join. (Access automatically creates the join if you established a relationship between these two fields when you created the Personnel Actions table in Chapter 4, "Working with Access Databases and Tables.")

3. Select and drag the Employees table's LastName and FirstName fields to columns 1 and 2 of the Query Design grid. Select and drag the Personnel Actions table's paType and paScheduledDate fields to columns 3 and 4.

4. Click the *line* joining EmployeeID with paID to select it, as shown in figure 10.29. The thickness of the line's center part increases to indicate the selection. (In fig. 10.29, the two Field List boxes are separated so that the thin section of the join line is apparent.)

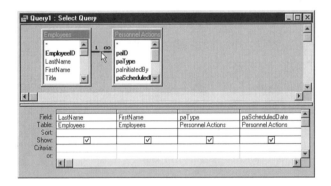

Fig. 10.29 Selecting a join to change its property from an inner to a left or right outer join.

5. Choose <u>V</u>iew, <u>J</u>oin Properties. (The Join Properties command is active only after you select an individual join with a mouse click.) You also can double-click the *thin section* of the join line. (Double-clicking either of the line's thick sections displays the Query Properties sheet.) The Join Properties dialog in figure 10.30 appears. Type <u>1</u> is a conventional inner join, type <u>2</u> is a left join, and type <u>3</u> is a right join.

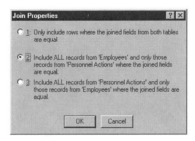

Fig. 10.30   The Join Properties dialog for choosing inner, left, or right joins.

6. Select a type <u>2</u> join—a left join—by choosing <u>2</u>. Click OK to close the dialog.

Note that Access adds an arrowhead to the line that joins EmployeeID and paID. The direction of the arrow, left to right, indicates that you have created a left join between the tables.

7. Click the Run button of the toolbar to display the result of the left join query. In figure 10.31, three employees without a record in the Personnel Actions table appear in the result table's last rows. Your query result set may differ, depending on the number of entries that you made when creating the Personnel Actions table. (If all employees show a personnel action, open the Personnel Actions table and delete the entries for a few employees, then rerun the query.)

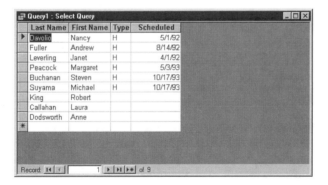

Fig. 10.31   The result of creating a left join between the ID fields of the Employees and Personnel Actions tables.

8. Close, but don't save, the query.

If you could add a personnel action for a nonexistent EmployeeID (the validation rule that you added in Chapter 9, "Understanding Operators and Expressions in Access," prevents you from doing so), a right join would show the invalid entry with blank employee name fields.

Creating Self-Joins

Self-joins relate values in a single table. Creating a self-join requires that you add to the query a copy of the table and then add a join between the related fields. An example of the use of a self-join is to determine whether supervisors have approved personnel actions that they initiated, which is prohibited by the imaginary personnel manual for Northwind Traders.

To create this kind of self-join for the Personnel Actions table, follow these steps:

1. Open a new query and add the Personnel Actions table.

2. Add to the query another copy of the Personnel Actions table by clicking the Add button again. Access names the copy Personnel Actions_1. Close the Show Tables dialog.

3. Drag the original table's paInitiatedBy field to the copied table's paApprovedBy field. The join appears as shown in the upper pane of figure 10.32.

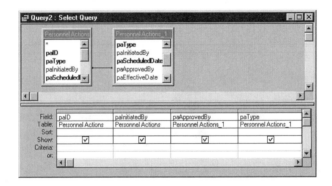

Fig. 10.32   Designing the query for a self-join on the Personnel Actions table.

4. Drag the paID and paInitiatedBy fields of the original table, and the paApprovedBy and paType fields of the copy of the Personnel Actions table, to the Field row of columns 1 through 4, respectively, of the Query Design grid.

5. With self-joins, you must specify that only unique values are included. Click the Properties button on the toolbar or double-click an empty area in the Query Design window's upper pane, and set the value of the Query Properties sheet's UniqueValues property to Yes. Click the Properties button again to close the Query Properties sheet.

6. Click the Run button of the toolbar to display the records in which the same employee initiated and approved a personnel action, as shown in figure 10.33. In this case, EmployeeID 2 (Mr. Fuller) is a vice president and can override personnel policy. (Your results may differ, depending on the number of entries that you made in the Personnel Actions table.)

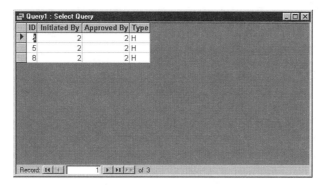

Fig. 10.33 The result of a self-join that tests for supervisors approving personnel actions that they initiated.

In this example, you can add the Employees table to the query to display the employee name. Adding the Employees table creates an additional join between the original Personnel Actions table's paID field and the Employees table's EmployeeID field. You then must drag the LastName field to the Query Design grid's fifth column. Because this join includes a primary-key field, EmployeeID, the default DISTINCTROW process yields unique values. To verify that the values are unique, click the Properties button of the toolbar or double-click an empty area in the Query Design window's upper pane, set the value of the UniqueValues property to Yes and then rerun the query.

▶▶ See "Validating Data Entry," p. 649
▶▶ See "Maintaining Referential Integrity," p. 872

Full-fledged relational database applications seldom use self-joins because validation criteria and enforcement of referential integrity can (and should) eliminate the types of problems that self-joins can detect.

Creating Not-Equal Theta Joins with Criteria

Most joins are based on fields with equal values, but sometimes you need to create a join on unequal fields. Joins that you create with graphical QBE in Access are restricted to conventional equi-joins and outer joins. You can create the equivalent of a not-equal theta join by applying a criterion to one of the two fields you want to test for not-equal values.

Finding customers that have different billing and shipping addresses, as mentioned previously, is an example in which a not-equal theta join is useful. To create the equivalent of this join, follow these steps:

1. Create a new query and add the Customers and Orders tables.

2. Select the Customers table's CompanyName and Address fields and the Orders table's ShipAddress field, and drag them to the Query Design grid's first three columns, respectively.

3. Type **<> Customers.Address** in the Criteria row of the ShipAddress column. (Access automatically adds square brackets surrounding table and field names regardless of whether the names include spaces or other punctuation.) The Query Design window appears as shown in figure 10.34. This criterion adds the WHERE Orders.ShipAddress <> [Customers.Address] clause to the SQL SELECT statement shown in figure 10.35.

Typing **<> Orders. ShipAddress** in the Address column gives an equivalent result. This criterion adds a WHERE Customers.Address <> Orders.[ShipAddress] clause to the SQL SELECT statement.

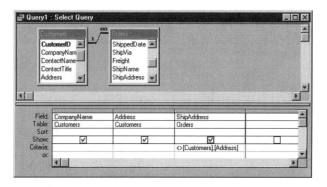

Fig. 10.34   Designing the query for a not-equal theta join.

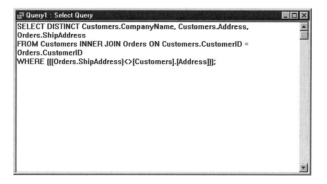

Fig. 10.35   The SQL statement for a not-equal theta join.

4. Click the toolbar's Properties button or double-click an empty area in the Query Design window's upper pane to open the Query Properties sheet and set the value of the Unique Values property to Yes.

5. Run the query. Only the records for customers that placed orders with different billing and shipping addresses appear, as shown in figure 10.36.

6. Click the Close Window button and save your query, if desired.

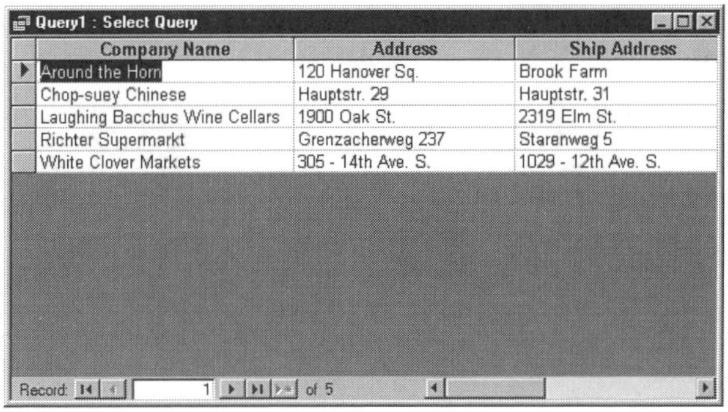

Company Name	Address	Ship Address
Around the Horn	120 Hanover Sq.	Brook Farm
Chop-suey Chinese	Hauptstr. 29	Hauptstr. 31
Laughing Bacchus Wine Cellars	1900 Oak St.	2319 Elm St.
Richter Supermarkt	Grenzacherweg 237	Starenweg 5
White Clover Markets	305 - 14th Ave. S.	1029 - 12th Ave. S.

Fig. 10.36 The result of a not-equal theta join designed to identify different billing and shipping addresses.

Updating Table Data with Queries

Many of the queries that you create with the Unique Records property set to Yes are updatable because you use Access SQL's `DISTINCTROW` modifier to create them. These queries create `Recordset` objects of the updatable `Dynaset` type. You cannot update a query unless you see the tentative (blank) append record (with the asterisk in the select button) at the end of the query result table. Queries that you create with the Unique Values property set to `Yes` create `Recordset` objects of the `Snapshot` type by substituting ANSI SQL's `DISTINCT` modifier. You cannot edit, add new records to, or otherwise update a `Recordset` object of the `Snapshot` type. The next few sections describe the conditions under which you can update a record of a table included in a query and how to use the Output Field Properties window to format a query data display and edits.

> **Note**
>
> `Dynaset` and `Snapshot` are types of Access 95's `Recordset` object. Microsoft states that the reserved words `Dynaset` and `Snapshot` as object names are included in Access 95 only for compatibility with Access 1.x. Although thedistinctive terminology of `Dynaset` and `Snapshot` makes it unlikely that these two terms will disappear from common use among Access developers, future versions of Access might not support `Dynaset` and `Snapshot` objects and might instead *require* you to specify `Recordset` objects of different types in Access VBA.

Characteristics That Determine Whether You Can Update a Query

Adding new records to tables or updating existing data in tables included in a query is a definite advantage in some circumstances. Correcting data errors that appear when you run the query is especially tempting. Unfortunately, you cannot append or update records in most of the queries that you create. The following properties of a query *prevent* you from appending and updating records:

- Unique values are set with a check box in the Query Properties sheet.
- Self-joins are used in the query.

- SQL aggregate functions, such as Sum(), are employed in the query. Crosstab queries, for example, use SQL aggregate functions.

- No primary-key fields with a unique (No Duplicates) index exist for the *one* table in a one-to-many relationship.

When designing a query to use as the basis of a form for data entry or editing, make sure that none of the preceding properties applies to the query.

If none of the preceding properties applies to the query or to all tables within the query, you can append records to and update fields of queries in the following:

- A single-table query

- Both tables in a one-to-one relationship

- The *many* table in a one-to-many relationship

- The *one* table in a one-to-many relationship if none of the fields of the *many* table appears in the query

Updating the *one* table in a one-to-many query is a special case in Access. To enable updates to this table, follow these steps:

1. Add to the query the primary-key field or fields of the *one* table and additional fields to update.

2. Add the field or fields of the *many* table that correspond to the key field or fields of the *one* table; this is required to select the appropriate records for updating.

3. Add the criteria to select the records for updating to the fields chosen in step 2.

4. Click the Show box so that the *many* table field or fields don't appear in the query.

After following these steps, you can edit the *nonkey* fields of the *one* table. You cannot, however, alter the values of key fields that have relationships with records in the *many* table. Such a modification violates referential integrity. You also cannot update a calculated column of a query; tables cannot include calculated values.

Note

By adding Lookup fields to tables, you often can avoid having to write one-to-many queries and precisely following the preceding rules to make such queries updatable. For example, the Orders table, which includes three Lookup fields (CustomerID, EmployeeID, and ShipVia), is updatable. If you want to allow updates in Datasheet View (called *browse updating*), using Lookup fields is a better approach than creating an updatable query. Most database developers consider simple browse updating to be a poor practice because of the potential for inadvertent data-entry errors.

Formatting Data with the Output Field Properties Window

The display format of data in queries is inherited from the format of the data in the tables that underlie the query. You can override the table format by using the Format(*ColumnName*, *FormatString*) function described in Chapter 9, "Understanding Operators and Expressions in Access," to create a calculated field.

Access 95 provides an easier method: it adds a Field Properties window that you can use to format the display of query data. You also can create an input mask to aid in updating the query data. To open the Field Properties window, place the caret in the Field cell of the query column that you want to format and then click the Properties button of the toolbar or double-click an empty area in the Query Design window's upper pane. Figure 10.37 shows the Field Properties window for the Order Date column of a simple one-to-many query created from the Customers and Orders tables.

> **Note**
>
> The Format drop-down list of the Field Properties sheet shown in figure 10.37 does not appear until you execute the query at least once. If you have not executed the query, an empty drop-down list appears. To add a Format property, execute the query without formatting the field, then return to Query Design View and add the formatting. Alternatively, you can type a valid format name, such as **Medium Date**, into the drop-down list's text box before executing the query.

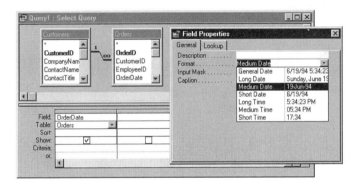

Fig. 10.37   Changing the display format for a query column of the Date/Time field data type.

The Field Properties window displays the following subset of the properties that apply to a table's fields:

- *Description* enables you to enter the text to appear in the status bar when the user selects the field in Datasheet View.

- *Format* enables you to control the appearance of the data in Datasheet View, such as Medium Date.

- *Input Mask* enables you to establish the format for entering data, such as 90/90/00. (To create an input mask appropriate for the field data type, double-click the ellipsis button to open the Input Mask Wizard.)

- *Caption* enables you to change the query column heading, such as Received for the Order Date column.

Each of the preceding query properties follows the rules described in Chapter 4, "Working with Access Databases and Tables," for setting table field properties. Adding a value (Received) for the Caption property is the equivalent of adding a column alias by typing

Received: as a prefix in the Order Date column's Field cell. The value of the Input Mask property need not correspond to the value of the Format property. For example, the Received (OrderDate) field in figure 10.38, which shows the effect of setting the property values shown in the preceding list, has a Medium Date display format and an input mask for updating in Short Date format.

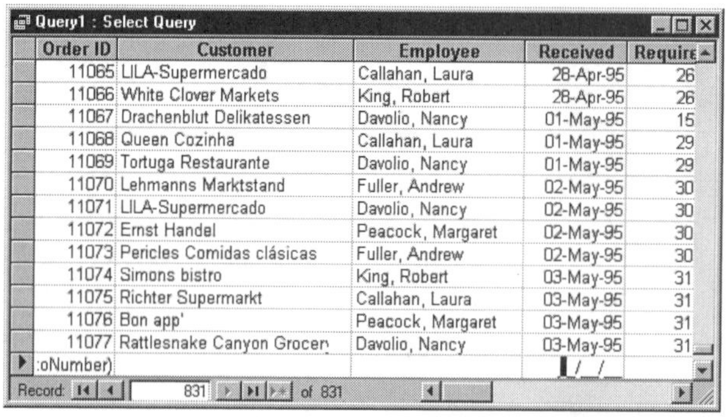

Fig. 10.38 Adding a new order record with an Order Date input mask.

Troubleshooting

I can't create an updatable one-to-many query with my attached dBASE tables, despite only displaying fields from the many side of the relationship.

You must specify (or create) primary-key indexes for each dBASE table that participates in the query. The field or fields that you choose must uniquely identify a record; the index doesn't allow duplicate values. Delete the attachment to the dBASE tables, and then reattach the table with the primary-key indexes. Make sure that you specify which index is the primary-key index in the Select Unique Record Identifier dialog that appears after you attach each table.

Also, make sure that you don't include the field of the *many-side* table on which the join is created in the query. If you add the joined field to the field list, your query is not updatable.

Making All Fields of Tables Accessible

Most queries that you create include only the fields you specifically choose. To choose these fields, you either select them from or type them into the drop-down combo list in the Query Design grid's Field row, or drag the field names from the field lists to the appropriate cells in the Field row. You can, however, include in a query all the fields of a table. Access provides three methods, which are covered in the following sections.

Using the Field List Title Bar to Add All Fields of a Table

One way to include all the fields of a table in a query is to use the field list title bar or asterisk. To use this method in your query to include all fields, together with their field name headers, follow these steps:

1. Open a new query and add the required tables.

2. Double-click the title bar of the field list of the table for which you want to include all fields. This selects all the fields in the field list.

3. Click and drag a field name to the Query Design grid's Field cell and drop the field name where you want the first field to appear. Figure 10.39 shows an example of the result of the preceding steps for the Customers table.

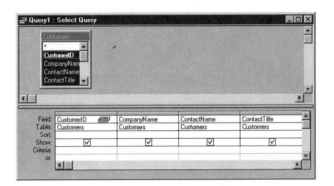

Fig. 10.39   Adding all fields of the Customers table to a query by double-clicking the Customers field list's header and dragging the fields to the Query Design grid.

Adding all the fields to the table by this method creates an SQL statement equivalent to the following:

```
SELECT DISTINCTROW TableName.FirstField,
      TableName.SecondField, ... TableName.LastField
   FROM TableName
```

Using the Asterisk to Add All Fields without Field Names

To include in the query all fields of the table without displaying their field names, click and drag the asterisk to the first Field cell of the Query Design grid and drop the asterisk where you want all the fields to appear in the query result table. The asterisk column is equal to the Access SQL statement SELECT DISTINCTROW * FROM TableName.

You cannot sort on a column with an asterisk in its Field cell, nor can you establish criteria on such a column. If you choose the asterisk approach, you can sort or apply criteria to one or more fields in the table by following this technique:

1. After you add the asterisk to the Field cell, drag the name of the field that you want to sort or to which you want to apply a criterion, and drop that field name to the adjacent column's Field row.

2. Add the sort specification to the Sort cell or the criterion to the Criteria cell.

3. Click the Show box, which removes the check mark, so that the field doesn't appear twice in the query. Figure 10.40 shows the resulting query design with the Customers table.

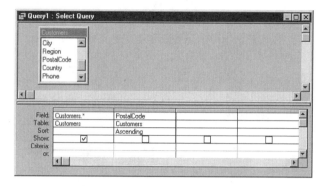

Fig. 10.40   Adding all fields of the Customers table with the asterisk field and providing a hidden column for sorting by PostalCode.

You can use this method to add to the query as many columns from the asterisk table as you need. The field on which you sort the data is added to the SQL statement as an ORDER BY *TableName.FieldName* clause, and a criterion is added in a WHERE *CriterionExpression* clause.

Selecting All Fields with the Output All Fields Property

Usually, only the fields whose names appear in the query are available for updating in forms or including in reports. All other fields are excluded from the result set. You can make all the fields in every table used in the query available to the forms and reports that you create—even though the query design does not include the fields by name—by setting the Output All Fields property to Yes. To use the Output All Fields property to make all table fields available, follow these steps:

1. Open a new query and add the table(s) that participate in the query.

2. Click the Properties button of the toolbar or double-click an empty area in the Query Design window's upper pane to display the Query Properties window.

3. In the Query Properties window, place the caret in the Output All Fields text box, press F4 to open the drop-down list, and change the default value, No, to Yes.

4. If the Unique Values Only text box displays Yes, you cannot update fields.

5. Click the Properties button to close the Query Properties sheet.

Turning off the Restrict Available Fields option adds an all-fields asterisk to the list of specified fields in the SQL statement, as in the following example:

```
SELECT DISTINCTROW Customers.[CompanyName],
       Categories.[CategoryName], *
```

When you include all fields in your queries, you might find that running the query takes longer, especially with queries that create many rows in the result set.

Making Calculations on Multiple Records

One of QBE's most powerful capabilities is that of obtaining summary information almost instantly from specified sets of records in tables. Summarized information from databases is the basis for virtually all management information systems (MIS). Such systems usually answer questions, such as "What are our sales to date for this month?" or "How did last month's sales compare with the same month last year?" To answer these questions, you must create queries that make calculations on field values from all or selected sets of records in a table. To make calculations on table values, you must create a query that uses the table and employ Access's SQL aggregate functions to perform the calculations.

Using the SQL Aggregate Functions

Summary calculations on fields of tables included in query result tables use the SQL aggregate functions listed in table 10.1. These are called *aggregate functions* because they apply to groups (aggregations) of data cells. The SQL aggregate functions satisfy the requirements of most queries needed for business applications. You can write special user-defined functions with Access VBA code to apply more sophisticated statistical, scientific, or engineering aggregate functions to your data.

Table 10.1	SQL Aggregate Functions	
Function	**Description**	**Field Types**
Avg()	Average of values in a field	All types except Text, Memo, and OLE Object
Count()	Number of Not Null values in a field	All field types
First()	Value of a field of the first record	All field types
Last()	Value of a field of the last record	All field types
Max()	Greatest value in a field	All types except Text, Memo, and OLE Object
Min()	Least value in a field	All types except Text, Memo, and OLE Object
StDev(), StDevP()	Statistical standard deviation of values in a field	All types except Text, Memo, and OLE Object
Sum()	Total of values in a field	All types except Text, Memo, and OLE Object
Var(), VarP()	Statistical variation of values in a field	All types except Text, Memo, and OLE Object

StDev() and Var() evaluate population samples. You can choose these functions from the drop-down list in the Query Design grid's Total row. (The Total row appears when you click the Sum button of the toolbar or choose View, Totals.) StDevP() and VarP() evaluate populations and must be entered as expressions. If you're familiar with statistical principles, you recognize the difference in the calculation methods of standard deviation and variance for populations and samples of populations. The following section explains the method of choosing the SQL aggregate function for the column of a query.

> **Note**
>
> ANSI SQL and most SQL (client/server) databases support the equivalent of Access SQL's Avg(), Count(), First(), Last(), Max(), Min(), and Sum() aggregate functions as AVG(), COUNT(), FIRST(), LAST(), MAX(), MIN(), and SUM(), respectively. ANSI SQL and few, if any, SQL databases provide equivalents of the StdDev(), StdDevP(), Var(), and VarP() functions.

Making Calculations Based on All Records of a Table

Managers, especially sales and marketing managers, are most often concerned with information about orders received and shipments made during specific periods of time. Financial managers are interested in calculated values, such as the total amount of unpaid invoices and the average number of days between the invoice and payment dates. Occasionally, you might want to make calculations on all the records of a table, such as finding the historical average value of all invoices issued by a firm. Usually, however, you apply criteria to the query to select specific records that you want to total.

 Access considers all SQL aggregate functions to be members of the Totals class of functions. You create queries that return any or all SQL aggregate functions by clicking the Totals button (with the Greek sigma, Σ, which represents summation) on the toolbar.

The Orders table of Access 95's Northwind.mdb sample database does not include an OrderAmount field that represents the total amount of the order, less freight. (The "Entering a Query Criterion" section of Chapter 9, "Understanding Operators and Expressions in Access," used a simplified version of this example to demonstrate the use of functions to calculate field values.) To create a sample query that uses the SQL aggregate functions to display the total number of orders, total sales, and the average, minimum, and maximum order values, you need a field that contains the total amount of each order. Follow these steps to create a new table that includes an additional field with a computed Order Amount:

1. Create a new query, and add the Orders and Order Details tables to it.

2. Drag the Orders table's OrderID field to the Query Design grid's first column, and then drag the OrderDate field to the second column.

3. Type **Order Amount: Sum([Quantity]*[UnitPrice]*(1-[Discount]))** in the Field row of the third (empty) column. This expression sums the net amount of all line items for each order. With the caret in the Order Amount column, click the Properties button of the toolbar to open the Field Properties sheet and type **Currency** in the text box for the Format property to format your new column.

 4. Click the Totals button on the toolbar. A new row, Total, is added to the Query Design grid. Access adds Group By, the default action, to each cell in the Totals row. The following section discusses the use of Group By.

5. Move to the third column's Total row and press F4 to display the drop-down list of SQL aggregate functions. Select Expression from the list. Your Query Design grid appears as shown in figure 10.41.

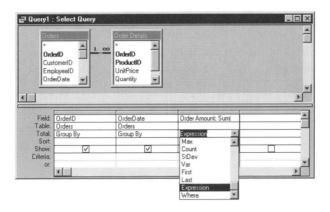

Fig. 10.41 The Query Design grid to create a calculated field with the Sum() function.

6. Click the Run button of the toolbar to test your initial entries. Your query in Datasheet View appears as in figure 10.42.

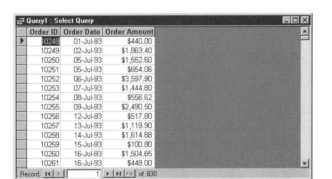

Fig. 10.42 Running the query design shown in figure 10.41.

7. Close and save your query with the name **Order Totals**.

Note

When you apply the **Format** property to the Order Amount column by selecting or typing **Currency** in the Field Properties window, successive queries that you create do not inherit the value of the **Format** property (instead, the default **Format** value, **Double** is applied). If you type **Order Amount: CCur(Sum([Quantity]*[Unit Price]*(1-[Discount])))** in the Order Amount column's Field row, however, the **Format** property of the Order Amount fields of successive queries that you create is set to **Currency**. The **CCur()** function *coerces* the field's data type to **Currency**.

Follow these steps to apply the SQL aggregate functions to the Order Amounts field of the query result set of the Order Totals query:

1. Open a new query, and add the Order Totals query. (To base a query on a prior saved query, drag the OrderID field to the first column and then drag the Order Amount column four times to the adjacent column to create four Order Amount columns.)

2. Choose View, Totals to add the Totals row to your Query Design grid. Alternatively, right-click in the grid region and choose Totals from the popup menu.

3. Move to the Total row of the OrderID column and press F4 to display the drop-down list of SQL aggregate functions. Choose Count as the function for the Order ID, as shown in figure 10.42.

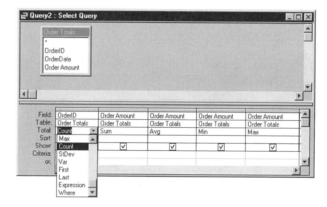

Fig. 10.43 Choosing the SQL aggregate function for calculations based on multiple records in a table.

4. Move to the first Order Amount column, open the list, and choose Sum from the Total drop-down list. Repeat the process, choosing Avg for the second Order Amount column, Min for the third, and Max for the fourth.

5. Place the caret in the Count field, and click the Properties button of the toolbar (or right-click in the Count field and then click Properties in the popup menu) to display the Field Properties window. Type **Count** as the value of the Caption property.

6. Repeat step 4 for the four Order Amount columns, typing **Currency** for the **Format** property and typing **Sum**, **Average**, **Minimum**, and **Maximum** as the values of the Caption property for the four columns, respectively. (You don't need to set the **Format** property if you used the **CCur**( ) function in the Order Totals query.)

7. Click the Run button of the toolbar to display the query's result. You haven't specified criteria for the fields, so the result shown in figure 10.44 is for the whole table. Notice that each field name button caption is prefixed with the name of the function employed. (The values in the result may differ from the values in figure 10.44 because of records that Microsoft might add to the sample database after this book is written.)

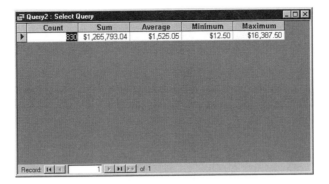

Fig. 10.44   The result of the all-records query shown in figure 10.43.

8. Save your query with a descriptive name, such as **qrySQLAggregates**, because you use this query in the two sections that follow.

Note

When you run qrySQLAggregates, the Jet database engine determines that Order Totals is a query (QueryDef object) rather than a table (TableDef object). Thus Jet executes the Order Totals query before executing the qrySQLAggregates query. One of the most important features of Access is that you can execute queries against the query result sets (Recordset objects) of other queries, a process called *nesting* queries. In theory, at least, there is no limit to the depth to which you can nest Access queries. As you increase the number of queries in the chain, however, execution slows for the last query in the nested sequence.

Making Calculations Based on Selected Records of a Table

The preceding example query performed calculations on all orders received by Northwind Traders that were entered in the Orders table. Usually, you are interested in a specific set of records—a range of dates, for example—from which to calculate aggregate values. To restrict the calculation to orders that Northwind Traders received in March 1995, follow these steps:

1. Click the Query View button on the toolbar to return to design mode so that you can add criteria to select a specific group of records based on the date of the order.

2. Drag the OrderDate field to the OrderID column to add OrderDate as the first column of the query. You need the OrderDate field to restrict the data to a range of dates.

3. Open the Total drop-down list in the Order Date column, and choose Where to Replace the Default Group By. Access deselects the Show box of the OrderDate column. (If you attempt to show a column that provides the SQL WHERE restriction, you receive an error message when you run your query.)

4. In the Order Date column's Criteria row, type **Like "3/*/95"** to restrict the totals to orders received in the month of March 1995 (see fig. 10.45). When you use the Like criterion, Access adds the quotation marks if you forget to type them.

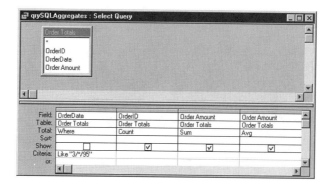

Fig. 10.45 Adding a Where criterion to restrict the totals to a range of records.

5. Choose <u>V</u>iew, SQL to display your query's SQL statement. The Where criterion in the Total row adds a WHERE clause to the SQL statement—in this case, WHERE ((([Order Totals.OrderDate Like "3/*/94")))—to restrict the totaled records to the records for the specified date range. (The Access query parser tends to add extra sets of parentheses to expressions.) If you don't add the Where instruction to the Total row, the query result consists of rows with the totals of orders for each day of March 1995, not for the entire month.

 6. Click the Run button on the toolbar to display the result: the count, total, and average value of orders received during the month of March 1995 (see fig. 10.46).

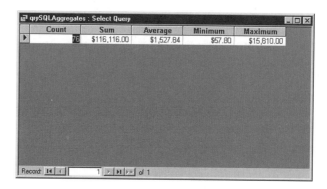

Fig. 10.46 The result of adding the Where criterion to the query.

You can create a more useful grouping of records by replacing the field name with an expression. For example, you can group aggregates by the year and month (or year and quarter) by grouping on the value of an expression created with the **Format**() function. The following steps produce a sales summary record for each month of 1994, the latest year for which 12 months of data are available in the Orders table:

1. Click the Query View button of the toolbar, and then click the header bar of the query's OrderDate column to select the first column. Press the Insert key to add a new, empty column to the query.

2. Type **Month: Format([Order Date],"yy-mm")** in the the first (empty) column's Field row. (You use the "yy-mm" format so that the records sort in date order. For a single year, you also can use "m" or "mm", but not "mmm" because it sorts in alphabetic sequence starting with *Apr.*)

3. Change the Where criterion of the Order Date column to **Like "*/*/94"**. Your query design appears as shown in figure 10.47.

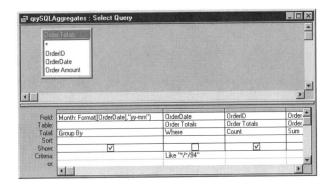

Fig. 10.47   Designing a query for a yearly sales summary by month.

4. Click the toolbar's Run button to display the result of your query (see fig. 10.48). The query creates sales summary data for each month of 1994.

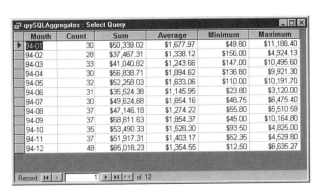

Fig. 10.48   The result set of the query design shown in figure 10.33.

5. Choose <u>V</u>iew, SQL to display the SQL statement that created the query result set. The SQL statement in the SQL window of figure 10.49 has been reformatted for clarity. (Formatting an SQL statement with spaces and newline pairs does not affect the statement's execution.)

6. Choose <u>F</u>ile, Save <u>A</u>s and save the query under a different name, such as **qryMonthlySales**, because you modify the query in the next section.

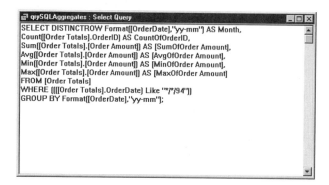

Fig. 10.49 The SQL statement for a yearly sales summary by month.

Designing Parameter Queries

If you expect to run a summary or another type of query repeatedly with changes to the criteria, you can convert the query to a *parameter query*. Parameter queries—which Chapter 8, "Using Query by Example," explained briefly—enable you to enter criteria with the Enter Parameter Value dialog. You are prompted for each parameter required. For the example qryMonthlySales query that you created previously in this chapter, the only parameter likely to change is the range of dates for which you want to generate the product sales data. The two sections that follow show you how to add a parameter to a query and how to specify the data type of the parameter.

Adding a Parameter to the Monthly Sales Query

To convert the qryMonthlySales summary query to a parameter query, you first create prompts for the Enter Parameter Value dialog that appears when the query runs. You create parameter queries by substituting the text with which to prompt, enclosed within square brackets, for actual values. Follow these steps:

1. Open in design mode the qryMonthlySales query that you created in the preceding section.

2. With the caret in the Month column's Field row, press F2 to select the expression in the Field cell. Then press Ctrl+C to copy the expression to the Clipboard.

3. Move the caret to the OrderDate column's Field row, and press F2 to select OrderDate. Then press Ctrl+V to replace Order Date with the expression used for the first column.

4. Move to the Order Date column's Criteria cell and replace Like "*/*/94" with **[Enter the year and month in YY-MM format:]** (see fig. 10.50).

5. Click the Run button of the toolbar. The Enter Parameter Value dialog appears with the label that you assigned as the value of the criterion in step 4.

6. Type **95-04** in the text box to display the data for April 1995, as shown in figure 10.51.

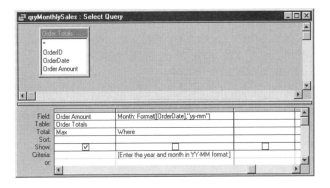

Fig. 10.50 The expression to create the Enter Parameter Value dialog with boxes for the year and month.

Fig. 10.51 The Enter Parameter Value dialog for entering the year and month.

7. Click OK to run the query. The result appears as shown in figure 10.52.

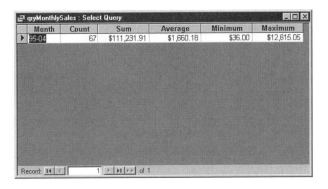

Fig. 10.52 The query result for the 95-04 parameter.

Specifying the Parameter's Data Type

The default field data type for parameters of Access queries is Text. If the parameter creates a criterion for a query column of the Date/Time or Number field data type, you must assign a data type to each entry that is made through an Enter Parameter Value dialog. Data types for values entered as parameters are established in the Query Parameters dialog. Follow these steps to add an optional data type specification to your parameter:

1. Use the mouse to select Enter the Year and Month in YY-MM Format: in the Month column's Criteria cell (omit the square brackets) and copy the text of the prompt to the Clipboard by pressing Ctrl+C.

2. Choose Query, Parameters to display the Query Parameters dialog.

3. To insert the prompt in the Parameter column of the dialog, place the caret in the column and press Ctrl+V. The prompt entry in the Parameter column must match the prompt entry in the Criteria field exactly; copying and pasting the prompt text ensures an exact match. Do not include the square brackets in the Parameter column.

4. Press Tab to move to the Data Type column, press F4 to open the Data Type drop-down list, and choose Text (see fig. 10.53). Click OK to close the dialog.

Fig. 10.53   The Query Parameters dialog for assigning data types to user-entered parameters.

Note

Complete your query design and testing before you convert any type of query to a parameter query. Using fixed criteria with the query maintains consistency during the testing process, and you can make repeated changes between design and run mode more quickly if you don't have to enter one or more parameters in the process. After you finish testing the query, edit the criteria to add the Enter Parameter Value dialog.

The parameter-conversion process described in this section applies to all types of queries that you create, if one or more of the query columns includes a criterion expression. The advantage of the parameter query is that you or a user of the database can run a query for any range of values, in this case dates, such as the current month to date, a particular fiscal quarter, or an entire fiscal year.

Creating Crosstab Queries

Crosstab queries are summary queries that enable you to determine exactly how the summary data appears on-screen. Crosstab queries display summarized data in the traditional row-column form of spreadsheets. Crosstab queries use the Access SQL TRANSFORM keyword to indicate that the statements that follow the keyword are for a crosstab query. (TRANSFORM is not an ANSI SQL keyword.) With crosstab queries, you can perform the following processes:

■ Specify the field that creates labels (headings) for rows by using the Group By instruction.

- Determine the field or fields that create column headers and the criteria that determine the values appearing under the headers.

- Assign calculated data values to the cells of the resulting row-column grid.

The following list details the advantages of using crosstab queries:

- You can display a substantial amount of summary data in a compact format familiar to anyone who uses a spreadsheet application or a columnar accounting form.

- The summary data is presented in a format ideally suited for creating graphs and charts automatically with the Access GraphWizard.

- Designing queries to create multiple levels of detail is quick and easy. Queries with identical columns but fewer rows can represent increasingly summarized data. Highly summarized queries are ideal to begin a drill-down procedure by instructing the user, for example, to click the Details button to display sales by product.

Using crosstab queries imposes only one restriction: You cannot sort your result table on calculated values in columns. You cannot, therefore, create a query that ranks products by sales volume. Columns are likely to have values that cause conflicts in the sorting order of the row. You can choose an ascending sort, a descending sort, or no sort on the row label values in the first column.

One of Access 95's Query Wizards is designed to help you create crosstab queries. However, the Crosstab Query Wizard is limited to creating crosstab queries for a single table or query. If your database follows the rules of relational database design, a usable crosstab query is far more likely to be based on at least two tables. Using the Crosstab Query Wizard requires you to create a query that includes the tables needed for the crosstab query. Thus, you create the examples of crosstab queries in the next two sections with help from this book, instead of from the Crosstab Query Wizard.

Creating a Monthly Product Sales Crosstab Query

To create a typical crosstab query that displays products in rows and the monthly sales volume for each product in the corresponding columns, follow these steps:

1. Open a new query and add the Products, Order Details, and Orders tables to it.

2. Drag the ProductID and ProductName fields from the Products table to the first query's two columns, and then drag the OrderDate field of the Orders table to the third column.

3. Choose Query, Crosstab. The title bar of the query changes from *Select Query: Query1* to *Crosstab Query: Query1*, and another row, Crosstab, is added to the Query Design grid.

4. Open the drop-down list of the ProductID column's Crosstab row and select Row Heading. Repeat this process for the ProductName column. These two columns provide the required row headings for your crosstab.

5. Open the Total drop-down list of the OrderDate column and select Where. Type **Like "*/*/94"** in this column's Criteria row to restrict the crosstab to orders received in 1994, the latest year for which 12 months of data are available.

6. Move to the next (empty) column's Field row and type the following:

Sales: Sum([Order Details].[Quantity]*

[Order Details].[UnitPrice])

Move to the Total row, choose Expression from the drop-down list, and then choose Value from the Crosstab row. The expression calculates the gross amount of the orders received for each product that populates your crosstab query's data cells. (You need to specify the Orders Detail table name; if you don't, you receive an "Ambiguous field reference" error message.)

7. In the next (empty) column's Field row, type **Format([OrderDate], "mmm")**. Access adds a default field name, Expr1:. Accept the default because the `Format()` function that you added creates the column names, the three-letter abbreviation for the months of the year (`"mmm"` format), when you run the query. The months of the year, Jan through Dec, are your column headings, so move to the Crosstab row and choose Column Heading from the drop-down list. The design of your crosstab query appears as shown in figure 10.54.

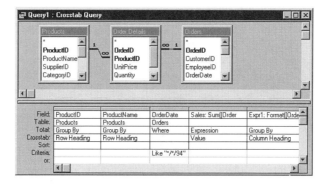

Fig. 10.54   The design of a crosstab query for monthly sales of products.

8. Click the Run button on the toolbar to execute the query. A period of disk activity occurs, followed by display of the crosstab query's result, shown in figure 10.55.

Notice that the crosstab query result contains a major defect: The columns are arranged alphabetically by month name rather than in calendar order. You can solve this problem by using fixed column headings, which you learn about in the following section.

Product ID	Product Name	Apr	Aug	Dec	↑
1	Chai	$720.00	$720.00		
2	Chang	$228.00	$1,900.00	$1,615.00	$8
3	Aniseed Syrup				
4	Chef Anton's Cajun Seasoning	$1,100.00	$1,034.00		
5	Chef Anton's Gumbo Mix		$320.25		
6	Grandma's Boysenberry Spread				
7	Uncle Bob's Organic Dried Pears	$1,500.00	$1,050.00	$1,140.00	$3
8	Northwoods Cranberry Sauce	$1,360.00		$1,200.00	
9	Mishi Kobe Niku	$1,552.00			
10	Ikura	$558.00	$558.00	$1,612.00	$8
11	Queso Cabrales		$210.00	$1,785.00	$8
12	Queso Manchego La Pastora		$1,368.00		$4
13	Konbu	$60.00	$78.00	$162.00	
14	Tofu	$1,627.50	$558.00	$348.75	↓

Record: ◄ ◄ 1 ► ►► ►* of 77

Fig. 10.55 The first result set from the crosstab query design shown in figure 10.54.

Using Fixed Column Headings with Crosstab Queries

◄◄ See "Functions for Date and Time," p. 298

Access uses an alphabetical or numerical sort on row and column headings to establish the sequence of appearance in the crosstab query result table. For this reason, if you use short or full names for months, the sequence is in alphabetic rather than calendar order. You can correct this problem by assigning fixed column headings to the crosstab query. Follow these steps to modify and rerun the query:

1. Return to query design mode and click the Properties button of the toolbar, or double-click an empty area in the Query Design window's upper pane. The Query Properties window has an option that appears only for crosstab queries: Column Headings.

2. In the Column Headings text box, type the three-letter abbreviations of all 12 months of the year (see fig. 10.56). You must spell the abbreviations of the months correctly; data for months with spelling mistakes do not appear. You can separate entries with commas or semicolons, and you don't need to type quotation marks because Access adds them. Spaces are unnecessary and undesirable between the Column Headings values. After you complete all 12 entries, close the Query Properties window.

3. Click the Run button of the toolbar. Now the result table, shown in figure 10.57, includes columns for all 12 months, although you can see only January through April in figure 10.57. (Scroll to the right to see the remaining months.) If the crosstab appears differently, check whether you entered the fixed column headings in the Query Properties window properly. A misspelled month causes Access to omit the month from the query result set.

4. Choose File, Save As and save the query with an appropriate name, such as **qry1994MonthlyProductSales**.

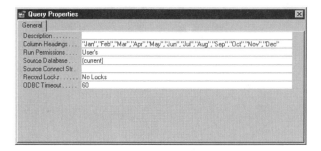

Fig. 10.56 Entering fixed column headings in the crosstab Query Properties window.

Fig. 10.57 The result table from the crosstab query design with fixed column headings and a date-limiting criterion.

You can produce a printed report quickly from the query by clicking the Print Preview button on the toolbar and then clicking the Print button.

> **Note**
>
> You might want to use fixed column headings if you use the Group By instruction with country names. U.S. users will probably place *USA* first, and Canadian firms will undoubtedly choose *Canada* as the first entry. If you add a record with a new country, you must remember to update the list of fixed column headings with the new country value. Fixed column headings have another, hidden benefit: they usually make crosstab queries operate more quickly.

Decreasing the Level of Detail in Crosstab Queries

The result table created by the preceding example query has a row for every product for which Northwind Traders received an order in each month of 1993. Higher-level management usually wants information in the form of a graph or chart to use to analyze trends in the data. Therefore, you must reduce the number of rows and columns so that you can create a readable graph from the values in the query result table.

To create a summary query that reports quarterly gross sales of products by category (rather than by ProductID), follow these steps:

1. Choose <u>F</u>ile, Save <u>A</u>s and save a copy of the query that you created in the preceding section with a descriptive name, such as **qry1994QuarterlyCategorySales**.

2. In Query Design View, click the Show Table button on the toolbar and add the Categories table to the query.

3. To make the relationships among the tables more clear, click the title bar of each of the field lists in the upper pane and drag the field lists to the positions shown in figure 10.58.

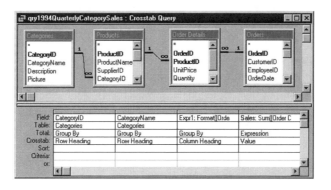

Fig. 10.58   The design of a summary query for quarterly sales by product category.

4. Drag and drop the Categories table's CategoryID and CategoryName fields to the first column's Field cell, which contains ProductID. New CategoryID and CategoryName columns are added to the query. Move down to the Crosstab cell and choose Row Heading from the drop-down list for both new columns.

5. Click the selection bar above the third column's ProductID cell, and then press Delete to delete this column. Repeat this process for the EnglishName column. The Crosstab Query Design grid then appears as shown in figure 10.58.

6. Edit Expr1:, which creates the column headings, so that the expression appears as **Format([OrderDate],"""Quarter ""q")**. This results in column headings of Quarter 1 through Quarter 4. (The multiple quotation marks are necessary to specify Quarter and a space as literals and q as a formatting character.)

7. Double-click an empty area in the Query Design window's upper pane to open the Query Properties window. Delete the Column Headings entries for the month abbreviations, then close the Query Properties window. (If you don't delete the fixed column headings, your query can't return any rows. To make your query run more quickly, you can add the four Quarter # headings, separated by commas or semicolons, as the value of the Column Heading property in the Query Properties window.)

8. Click the Run button on the toolbar. The query result set appears as shown in figure 10.59.

qry1994QuarterlyCategorySales : Crosstab Query

Category I	Category Name	Quarter 1	Quarter 2	Quarter 3	Quarter 4
1	Beverages	$37,838.00	$26,993.50	$23,542.25	$22,521.25
2	Condiments	$12,045.60	$13,338.65	$16,524.20	$15,413.05
3	Confections	$18,279.80	$21,864.43	$24,222.35	$20,356.29
4	Dairy Products	$24,588.40	$27,358.20	$32,999.60	$39,524.60
5	Grains/Cereals	$11,163.60	$16,209.60	$15,397.00	$15,770.75
6	Meat/Poultry	$17,411.30	$15,400.59	$27,204.08	$25,526.06
7	Produce	$9,270.60	$15,849.30	$11,728.25	$20,870.40
8	Seafood	$7,718.60	$16,712.70	$24,996.83	$22,113.92

Record: 1 of 8

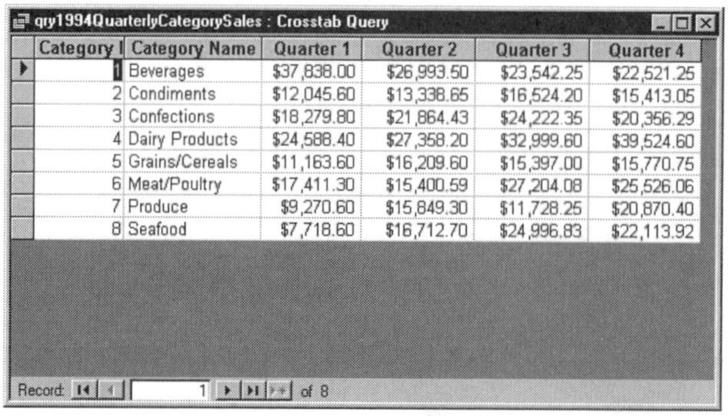

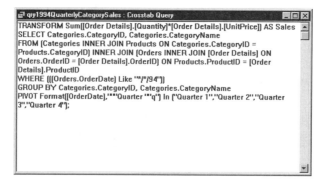

Fig. 10.59 The result set of the query design for the quarterly sales by product category.

9. Choose View, SQL to view the SQL statement that creates the crosstab query (see fig. 10.60). The Access SQL `TRANSFORM` clause, which corresponds to the Values crosstab property, defines the values that appear in the data cells. The `PIVOT` statement defines the column headings. (The `IN` predicate following the `PIVOT` statement specifies the fixed column headings, if any.) `TRANSFORM` and `PIVOT` are not reserved words of ANSI SQL. Access crosstab queries and conventional SQL `SELECT` queries interpret the ANSI SQL `IN` predicate differently.

qry1994QuarterlyCategorySales : Crosstab Query

```
TRANSFORM Sum([Order Details].[Quantity]*[Order Details].[UnitPrice]) AS Sales
SELECT Categories.CategoryID, Categories.CategoryName
FROM (Categories INNER JOIN Products ON Categories.CategoryID =
Products.CategoryID) INNER JOIN (Orders INNER JOIN [Order Details] ON
Orders.OrderID = [Order Details].OrderID) ON Products.ProductID = [Order
Details].ProductID
WHERE (((Orders.OrderDate) Like "*/*/94"))
GROUP BY Categories.CategoryID, Categories.CategoryName
PIVOT Format([OrderDate],"""Quarter ""q") In ("Quarter 1","Quarter 2","Quarter
3","Quarter 4");
```

Fig. 10.60 The SQL statement that creates the quarterly-sales-by-product query.

10. Choose File, Save to save your query. The qry1994QuarterlyCategorySales query is used for many different purposes in later chapters of this book.

Crosstab queries that display time-series data, such as monthly and quarterly sales for products or categories of products, often are used as the basis for graphs. Chapter 20, "Adding Graphics to Forms and Reports," uses the qry1994QuarterlyCategorySales query to create two types of Access graphs.

Creating Queries from Tables in Other Databases

Access's Query Properties window includes two properties that let you create a query based on tables contained in a database other than the current database. Access calls the database that you open after you launch Access the *current* database. Databases other than the current database commonly are called *external* databases. The use of these two new properties is as follows:

- The value of the Source Database property for desktop databases is the path to the external database and, for Access databases, the name of the database file. To run a query against tables contained in the Solutions.mdb sample database, replace (current) in the Source Database text box with the following, as shown in figure 10.61:

  `c:\msoffice\access\samples\solutions.mdb`

  To run a query against a set of Paradox tables in the *D*:\PARADOX folder, you type the path only (***d*:\paradox**, where *d*: is the logical drive letter). If you're using the ODBC API to connect to a client/server database, you leave the Source Database text box empty.

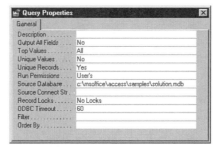

Fig. 10.61 Setting the Source Database property for a query against an external database.

- The value of the Source Connect Str property also depends on the type of external database. If your external Access database is not secure, you leave the Source Connect Str text box empty; otherwise, you type **UID=*UserID*;PWD=*Password*** to specify the user ID and password needed to open the external database. For other desktop databases, you type the product name, such as **Paradox 3.5** or **dBASE IV**. ODBC data sources require the complete ODBC connect string. Using ODBC databases is one of the subjects of Chapter 25, "Securing Multiuser Network Applications."

Running a query against an external database is related to running a query against attached tables. When you attach tables, the data in the tables is available at any time that your application is running. When you run a query against an external database, the connection to the external database is open only while your query is open in design or run mode. There is a slight performance penalty for running queries against an external database; each time that you run the query, Access must make a connection to open the database. The connection is closed when you close the query.

Figure 10.62 shows a query design based on tables contained in the SOLUTION.MDB sample database that accompanies Access 2.0. In this case, Access 95's Northwind.mdb is the current database. Figure 10.63 shows the result of executing the query design of figure 10.62 against the Example Objects, Examples, and Example Topics tables of SOLUTION.MDB.

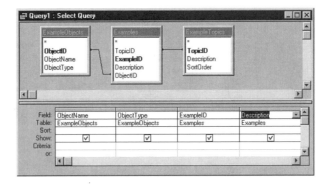

Fig. 10.62 A query design based on tables in an external Access database.

ObjectName	ObjectType	ExampleID	Descrip
EditProducts	Form	1	Limit the contents of one list based
EditProducts	Form	7	Create a form in which you can edit
EditProducts	Form	17	Update a list to show current data.
EditProducts	Form	21	Create a custom menu bar for a forr
EditProducts	Form	62	Change the color of a control based
EditProducts	Form	66	Update a list after you change its cc
EditProducts	Form	71	Find a record based on a value you
EditProducts	Form	74	EditProducts
EditProducts	Form	105	Limit the contents of one list based
EnterOrEditProducts	Form	8	Create a form in which you can ente
EnterOrEditProducts	Form	18	Create a toolbar that has custom bu
EnterOrEditProducts	Form	23	Change toolbars in response to evei
EnterOrEditProducts	Form	59	Add a new record to a list.
EnterOrEditProducts	Form	61	Change the color of a section and c

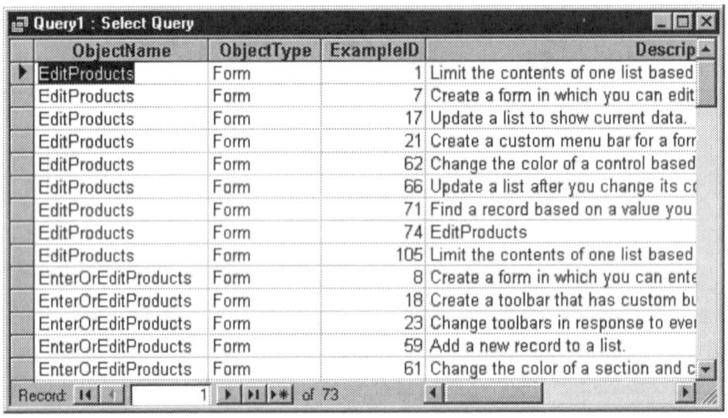

Fig. 10.63 The query result set of the query design shown in figure 10.62.

From Here...

Queries are the foundation on which you build most of the forms and reports that you design to create full-scale applications in Access. One of the principal features of Access, however, is its capability to select, display, and print both detailed and summary information without requiring the design of forms or reports. In many cases, a simple query can answer *ad hoc* requests for status reports. The query's printed output does not have a slick format, but the data is what counts.

The section of this chapter on crosstab queries, for example, demonstrates that you can design a query to display and print a time-series area chart for trend analysis in less than five minutes. In this regard, Access shines in comparison to conventional spreadsheet applications; with Access, you can select and process the data required to produce a time-series chart in a tenth or so of the time required to produce the equivalent spreadsheet. Although the Pivot feature of Microsoft Excel makes creating crosstab worksheets easier, Access still wins hands down when you have many records to process.

To learn more about related topics, see the following chapters:

- Chapter 9, "Understanding Operators and Expressions in Access," provides a complete description of the functions and operators that you can use in creating queries.

- Chapter 11, "Using Action Queries," describes how you use action queries to update, append, and delete table records. Action queries also let you create new tables from query result sets.

- Chapter 24, "Working with Structured Query Language," delves deeper into the use of SQL and how to write queries in the SQL window instead of using Access's Query by Example method.

Chapter 11

Using Action Queries

Action queries create new tables or modify the data in existing tables. Four types of action queries are available in Access:

- *Make-table* queries create new tables from the data contained in query result sets. One of the most common applications for make-table queries is to create tables that other applications can export. A make-table query provides a convenient way to copy a table to another database. In some cases, you can use make-table queries to speed the generation of multiple forms and reports based on a single, complex query.

- *Append* queries add new records to tables with data that the queries create.

- *Delete* queries delete records from tables that correspond to the rows that you delete from the query result set.

- *Update* queries change the values of existing fields of table records corresponding to rows of the query result set.

This chapter shows you how to create each of the four types of action queries and how to try Access's cascading deletions and cascading updates of related records. It also shows you how to use the Archive Query Wizard to copy query result sets to a new archive table and to remove the copied records from the original table. This chapter covers cascading deletions and cascading updates because these features are related to delete and update action queries, respectively.

In this chapter, you learn how to do the following

- Design queries that create new tables

- Append records to existing tables with queries

- Delete selected records from tables with queries

- Update values in tables with queries

- Use the Query Wizard to create archive queries

Specific Information

Creating New Tables with Make-Table Queries

▶▶ See "Using Access 95's New TableAnalyzer Wizard," p. 852

In the following sections, you learn how to use a make-table query to create a new table, Shipping Address, for customers that have different shipping and billing addresses. This process enables the deletion of the shipping address data that, in most of the records in the Orders table, duplicates the address data in the Customers table. Removing duplicated data to new tables is an important step when you are converting data contained in a flat (nonrelational) database to a relational database structure. You can use the Table Analyzer Wizard, described in Chapter 23, "Exploring Relational Database Design and Implementation," to perform an operation similar to that described in the following sections. Removing duplicated data manually, however, is one of the best methods of demonstrating how to design make-table queries.

Caution

Always make a backup copy of a table that you are going to modify with an action query. Changes made to table data with action queries are permanent; an error can render a table useless. Invalid changes made to a table with an action query containing a design error often are difficult to detect.

 ◄◄ See "Creating Not-Equal Theta Joins with Criteria," p. 339

The example that you create in the following sections extracts data from the Orders table based on data in the Customers table and creates a new table, tblShipAddresses. A modification of the query that you created in the "Creating Not-Equal Theta Joins with Criteria" section of Chapter 10 generates the data for the new table. Make-table queries are useful in converting flat-file tables that contain duplicated data, including tables created by spreadsheet applications, to relational form.

Designing and Testing the Select Query

To create the new shipping addresses table from the data in the Orders table, you first must build a select query. To build a select query, follow these steps:

1. Create a new query and add the Customers and Orders tables to it.

2. Drag the CustomerID field from the Customers table and drop it in the query's first column. The CustomerID field links the Shipping Address table to the Orders table.

3. Drag the ShipName, ShipAddress, ShipCity, ShipRegion, ShipPostalCode, and ShipCountry fields and drop them in columns 2 through 7, respectively. You use these fields, in addition to CustomerID, to create the new Shipping Address table.

   Next, you want to add only the records of the Orders table for which the ShipName doesn't match the CompanyName or the ShipAddress doesn't match the Customers table's address.

4. In the ShipName column's first Criteria row, type the following:

   < >[Customers].[CompanyName]

5. In the next row of the ShipAddress column, type the following:

< >[Customers].[Address]

This entry must be in a different Criteria row than the CompanyName criterion so that the 0r operator is applied to the two criteria. The Query Design grid appears as shown in figure 11.1.

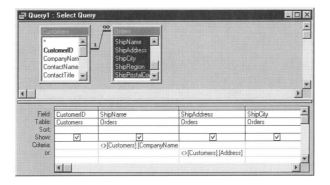

Fig. 11.1 Creating the select query for the new Shipping Address table.

> **Note**
>
> A more precise approach is to add additional 0r criteria to test for not-equal cities, regions, postal codes, and countries. A customer having exactly the same address in two different cities, however, is highly improbable.

6. Double-click an empty area in the Query Design window's upper pane to open the Query Properties sheet. Open the Unique Values drop-down list and select Yes.

7. Click the toolbar's Run button to run the select query. Data for customers that placed orders with different billing and shipping addresses appears, as shown in figure 11.2.

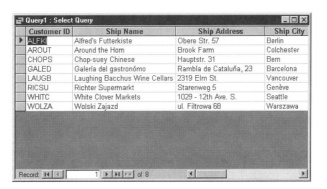

Fig. 11.2 The data to add to the new Shipping Address table.

Converting the Select Query to a Make-Table Query

Now that you have tested the select query to make sure that it creates the necessary data, you can create the table from the query. To create the table, follow these steps:

1. Choose Query, Make Table. The Make Table dialog, which is a variation of the Query Properties dialog, appears. Type the name of the table, **tblShipAddresses**, in the Table Name text box (see fig. 11.3). Click OK.

Fig. 11.3 The Make Table dialog for make-table queries.

2. Click the Run button on the toolbar. A message confirms the number of records that you are adding to the new table (see fig. 11.4). Choose Yes to create the new tblShippingAddresses table.

Fig. 11.4 The confirmation message box that precedes the creation of the new table.

3. Click the toolbar's Database Window button to activate the Database window, click the Table tab, and open the new tblShippingAddresses table. The entries appear as shown in figure 11.5.

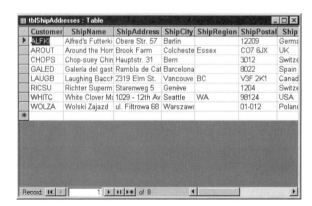

Fig. 11.5 The tblShippingAddresses table created from the make-table query.

Now complete the design of the new tblShippingAddresses table by following these steps:

1. Click the Design View button of the toolbar. The table's basic design is inherited from the properties of the fields of the tables used to create the new table. The tblShippingAddresses table does not, however, inherit the primary-key assignment from the Customers table's CustomerID field.

2. Click the toolbar's Properties button to display the Table Properties sheet. In the Table Properties sheet's Description text box, type **Shipping addresses different from billing addresses**, as shown in figure 11.6.

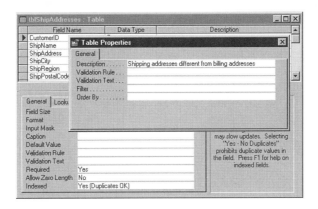

Fig. 11.6 The design of the newly created Shipping Address table.

3. The tblShippingAddresses table presently has a partial one-to-one relationship with the Customers table because only one shipping address record exists for each customer that has different shipping and billing addresses. A customer might have many different shipping addresses, however, so the relationship of Customers to Shipping Address is one-to-many, and you must allow duplicate values in the CustomerID field of tblShippingAddresses. You cannot, therefore, create a primary key for the tblShippingAddresses table unless you include three fields—CustomerID, ShipName, and ShipAddress—to make multiple entries for one customer unique. This particular example doesn't use a primary key. Choose the CustomerID field, open the Indexed property drop-down list, and choose the Yes (Duplicates OK) value. Indexing improves the performance of queries when you have many different shipping addresses for customers.

4. The CustomerID, ShipName, ShipAddress, ShipCity, and ShipCountry fields are required, so set the value for each of these fields' Required property to Yes. (Many countries do not have values for the ShipRegion field, and a few countries do not use postal codes.)

Establishing Relationships for the New Table

Now you need to complete the process of adding the new table to your database by establishing default relationships and enforcing referential integrity so that all records in the tblShipAddress table have a corresponding record in the Customers table. Access 95's new graphical Relationships window makes this process simple and intuitive. To establish the relationship of tblShipAddress and the Customers table, follow these steps:

1. Close the tblShipAddress table and click the toolbar's Database Window button to make the Database window active.

2. Click the Relationships button of the toolbar or choose <u>T</u>ools, <u>R</u>elationships to open the Relationships window that establishes the default relationships between tables. Click the toolbar's Show Table button and double-click the tblShipAddresses table to add the table to the Relationships window; then click the Close button. Move the field list to the position shown in figure 11.7. (Drag up the bottom of the Orders field list to make room for the tblShipAddress field list.)

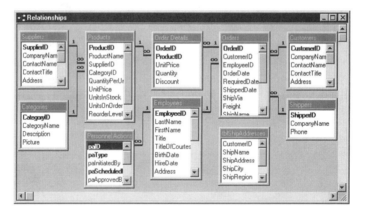

Fig. 11.7 Adding the tblShipAddresses table to the Relationships window.

3. Click the Customers table's CustomerID field, drag the field symbol to the tblShipAddresses table's CustomerID field and drop the symbol. This example emphasizes the table names, so the direction in which you drag the field is important. The Relationships dialog appears (see fig. 11.8). The field that you select to drag appears in the Table/Query list (the *one* side of the relationship), and the field on which you drop the dragged field appears in the Related Table/Query list (the *many* side of the relationship).

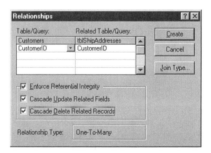

Fig. 11.8 The Relationships dialog for the new shipping addresses table.

4. Select the Enforce Referential Integrity check box. Access sets the default relation type, one to many, which is the correct choice for this relation. Access also establishes a conventional equi-join as the default join type, so in this case you don't need to click the Join Type button to display the Join Properties window. Select the Cascade Update Related Fields and the Cascade Delete Related Records check boxes to maintain referential integrity automatically.

5. Choose the Create button of the Relationships dialog to close it. Your Relationships window appears as shown in figure 11.9.

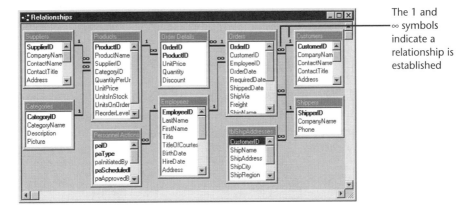

The 1 and ∞ symbols indicate a relationship is established

Fig. 11.9 The Relationships window showing a relationship established for the new table.

6. Close the Relationships window and click OK to save your changes. Save your make-table query with an appropriate name, such as **qryMakeShippingAddresses**.

Using the New tblShipAddresses Table

After creating a new table from a make-table query, you must take care of several "housekeeping" chores before you can take advantage of your new table. The purpose of creating the new shipping addresses table is to eliminate the data in the Orders table that duplicates information in the Customers table. The additional steps that you must take to use the new table include the following:

■ You need a new Number (Integer) field, ShipID, for the tblShipAddresses and Orders tables. In the Orders table's ShipID field, you can have a 0 value indicate that the shipping and billing addresses are the same. You then assign a sequential number to each shipping address for each customer. (In the present case, the value of the ShipID field is 1 for all records in tblShipAddresses.) By adding the ShipID field to the tblShipAddresses table, you can create a composite primary key on the CustomerID and ShipID fields. The no-duplicates index on the composite primary key prevents accidental duplication of a ShipID value for a customer.

■ Do not delete fields that contain duplicate data extracted to a new table until you confirm that the extracted data is correct and modify all the queries, forms, and reports that use the table. You use the update query described later in this chapter to assign the correct ShipID field value for each record in the Orders table. After you verify that you have assigned the correct value of the ShipID field, you can delete the duplicate fields.

■ Add the new table to any queries, forms, reports, macros, and modules that require the extracted information.

■ Change references to fields in the original table in all database objects that refer to fields in the new table.

During this process, you have the opportunity to test the modification before deleting the duplicated fields from the original table. Making a backup copy of the table before you delete the fields also is a low-cost insurance policy.

Creating Action Queries to Append Records to a Table

A make-table query creates the new table structure from the structure of the records that underlie the query. Only the fields of the records that appear in the query are added to the new table's structure. If you design and save a Shipping Address table before extracting the duplicated data from the Orders table, you can use an append query to add the extracted data to the new table.

Another situation in which append queries are useful is when removing duplicate data from a table currently in use. In this case, you use make-table queries to create the related tables and then change them to append queries. You change the type of query by opening the Query menu and choosing Select, Crosstab, Make Table, Append, or Delete, or by clicking the Query Type button of the toolbar while in design mode and choosing the type of query from the menu.

An append query also differs from a make-table query because an append query can have fewer fields than the table to which the query is appending the data. Otherwise, the make-table and append processes are basically identical. To append records to the tblShipAddress table, for example, follow these steps:

1. Open the tblShipAddresses table in Datasheet View, choose Edit, Select All Records, and then press the Delete key to delete all the records from the table. Click Yes when asked to confirm the deletion, and then close the table.

2. Open your make-table query, qryMakeShippingAddresses, from the Database window in design mode (or choose the query from the Window menu if it is open). If you double-click qryMakeShippingAddresses or open qryMakeShippingAddresses in Datasheet View, you run the make-table query.

3. Choose Query, Append. The Append variant of the Query Properties dialog appears with tblShipAddresses as the default value in the Table Name drop-down list, as shown in figure 11.10. Click the OK button to close the Query Properties dialog.

Fig. 11.10   The Query Properties dialog for an append query.

> **Note**
>
> To append data to a table, the field names of the query and of the table to which you are appending the records must be identical, or you must specify the field of the table to which the append query column applies. Access does not append data to fields in which the field name differs by even a single space character. The Query Design grid for append queries has an additional row, Append To (shown in fig. 11.11), that Access attempts to match by comparing field names of the query and the table. Default values appear in the Append To row of columns for which a match occurs. If a match does not occur, open the Append To row's drop-down list and select the table's field.

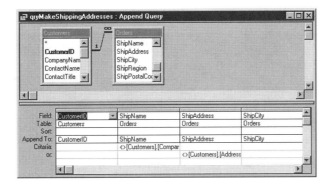

Fig. 11.11   The Append Query Design grid with the Append To row added.

   4. Click the toolbar's Run button to execute the append query. A message box displays the number of records that the query will append to the table (see fig. 11.12). Choose Yes to append the records.

Fig. 11.12   The message box that announces an impending append.

5. Open the tblShipAddresses table to verify that you have added the records.

Troubleshooting

After appending records to an existing table, I can't create a primary key on the table.

The Unique Values Only test that you specify in the Query Properties dialog applies only to the query, not to the table to which you are appending the records. If you want to preclude the possibility of appending duplicate records to the tblShipAddress table, you must first create the composite primary key, discussed in the preceding section, which creates a No Duplicates index on the primary key, and then append the records.

You cannot append records that contain values that duplicate those of the key fields in existing records. If you try to do so, you see a message box that indicates the number of records that cause key-field violations. Unlike the Paste Append operation described in previous chapters, however, Access does not create a Paste Errors table that contains the unappended records.

Deleting Records from a Table with an Action Query

Tip

It's a good practice to run a select query to display the records that you are about to delete and then convert the select query to a delete query.

Often, you might have to delete records from a table. For example, you might want to delete records for canceled orders, or records for customers that have made no purchases for several years. Deleting records from a table with a delete query is the reverse of the append process. You create a select query with all fields (using the * choice from the field list) and then add the individual fields to be used to specify the criteria for deleting specific records. If you don't specify any criteria, Access deletes all the table's records when you convert the select query into a delete query and run it against the table.

To give you some practice at deleting records—you stop short of actual deletion in this case, however—suppose that Northwind Traders' credit manager has advised you that Austrian authorities have declared Ernst Handel (CustomerID ERNSH) insolvent and that you are to cancel and delete any orders from Ernst Handel not yet shipped. To design the query that selects all of Ernst Handel's open orders, follow these steps:

1. Open a new query and add the Orders table to it.

2. Drag the * (all fields) item from the field list to the Field cell of the query's first column.

3. Drag the CustomerID field to the second column's Field cell. You need this field to 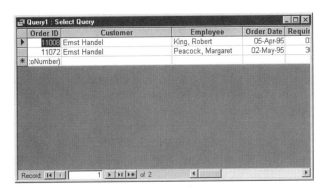 select a specific customer's record. The fields that comprise the query must be exactly those of the Orders table, so click the Show box to hide the CustomerID field. This field is included in the first column's * (all fields) indicator.

4. In the CustomerID field's Criteria cell, type **ERNSH** to represent Ernst Handel's ID.

5. A **Null** value in the ShippedDate field indicates orders that have not shipped. Drag 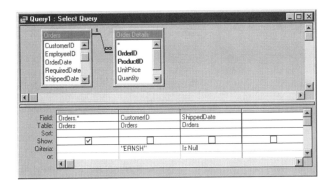 the ShippedDate field from the field list to the third column's Field cell. Click the Show box to hide the ShippedDate field because the first column also includes that field.

6. In the ShippedDate field's Criteria cell, type **Is Null.** To ensure that you delete only records for Ernst Handel *and* those that have not been shipped, you must place this criterion on the same line as that for the CustomerID field. The select query design for the delete query appears as shown in figure 11.13.

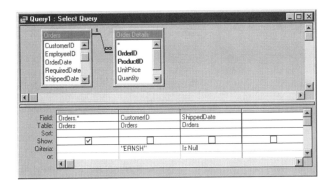

Fig. 11.13   The select query design for a delete query.

7. Run the select query to display the records to delete when the delete query runs. Figure 11.14 shows the query result set.

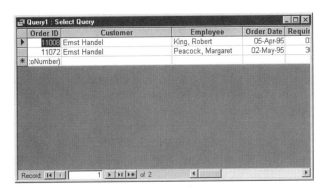

Fig. 11.14   The unshipped orders for Ernst Handel to be deleted from the Orders table.

To proceed with the simulated deletion, follow these steps:

1. Click the toolbar's Database Window button to activate the Database window, then click the Table button to display the table list. Create a copy of the Orders table by clicking the Orders table entry and pressing Ctrl+C to copy the table to the Clipboard. Press Ctrl+V. The Paste Table As dialog appears. Type **tblOrders** as the name of the new table copy and press Enter. Repeat this process for the Order Details table, naming it **tblOrderDetails**. These two tables are backup tables in case you actually delete the two records for Ernst Handel.

2. Activate your select query and click the toolbar's Design button to return to design mode. Choose Query, Delete. Access then replaces the Select Query grid's Sort and Show rows with the Delete row, as shown in figure 11.15. The From value in the Delete row's first column, Orders, indicates that Access will delete records that match the Field specification from the Orders table. The Where values in the remaining two cells indicate fields that specify the deletion criteria.

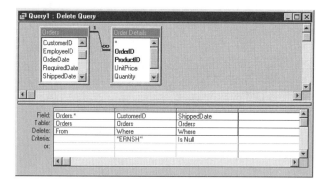

Fig. 11.15 The delete query design created from the select query of figure 11.13.

3. Click the Run Query button. The message box shown in figure 11.16 appears, asking you to confirm the deletion of the rows. Click No to prevent the deletion.

Fig. 11.16 The deletion confirmation message box.

> **Note**
>
> Deleting records in a *one* table when records corresponding to the deleted records exist in a related *many* table violates the rules of referential integrity; the records in the *many* table would be made orphans. In this situation, referential integrity is enforced between the Order Details and Orders table, preventing the creation of orphan Order Details records for the two records of the Orders table that you want to delete. To delete the two records of the Orders table, you must use a process called *cascading deletion*. First you delete the Order Details records, then you delete the Orders records. Northwind.mdb's one-to-many relationship between Orders and Order details includes cascading deletions. If you clear the Relationships dialog's Cascade Delete Related Records check box, attempting to delete the two open Orders records for Ernst Handel results in the message shown in figure 11.17.

Fig. 11.17 The message box that indicates a violation of the rules of referential integrity.

If you accidentally delete records for Ernst Handel, reverse the process that you used to make the backup tables: Copy the backup tables, tblOrders and tblOrderDetails, to Orders and Order Details, respectively.

Updating Values of Multiple Records in a Table

Update queries change the values of data in a table. Such queries are useful when you must update field values for many records with a common expression. For example, you might need to increase or decrease the unit prices of all products or products within a particular category by a fixed percentage.

To see how an update query works, you perform some of the housekeeping chores discussed earlier in the chapter that are associated with using the tblShipAddress table. To implement this example, you must have created the tblShipAddress table, as described in the "Creating New Tables with Make-Table Queries" section earlier in this chapter. You also must modify the tblOrders and tblShipAddresses tables to include a field for the ShipID code, by following these steps:

1. Click the Tables tab in the Database window and open the tblOrders table in design mode. If you didn't create the tblOrders table as a backup table for the example of the preceding section, do so now.

2. Select the ShipName field by clicking the selection button, and press Insert to add a new field between Employee ID and ShipName. (Access inserts fields in tables above the selected field.)

3. Type **ShipID** as the field name, select Number as the field data type, and select Integer as the field's description. Set the Required property's value to Yes. The table design pane appears as in figure 11.18 (which shows the new ShipID field selected).

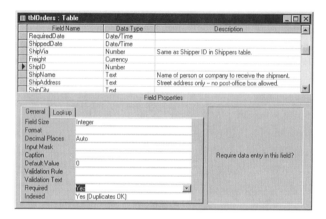

Fig. 11.18   Adding the ShipID field to the tblOrders table.

4. Close the tblOrders table and save the changes to your design. You changed the domain integrity rules when you added the Required property, so the message box in figure 11.19 appears. Choose No to avoid the test, which would fail because no values have been added to the ShipID field.

Fig. 11.19   Choosing whether to test changes to domain integrity rules.

5. Open the tblShipAddresses table in Datasheet View.

6. Click the ShipName field header and choose <u>I</u>nsert, <u>C</u>olumn to add a Field1 field between the CustomerID and the ShipName field. The capability to add new columns (fields) in Table Datasheet View is a new feature of Access 95.

7. Type **1** in the Field1 cell for each record of the tblShipAddress table.

8. Change to design mode, and change the name of Field1 to ShipID. Access 95 detects from your data entries that the field should be a Number field, but assigns LongInteger as the FieldSize property value. Change the value of the FieldSize property to Integer.

9. Select both the CustomerID and the ShipID field by clicking and dragging the mouse.

10. Click the toolbar's Primary Key button to create a composite primary key on the CustomerID and ShipID fields, and then close the tblShipAddress table. This time you test the changes that you made to the table.

Now you need to set up a query to select the orders to which you want to add a value of 1 to the ShipID field to indicate the use of data from the tblShipAddresses table. This query is quite similar to that which you used to create the tblShipAddresses table earlier in this chapter. Follow these steps to design your update query:

1. Create a new query and add the Customers and tblOrders tables to it.

2. Drag the Customers table's CompanyName and Address fields to columns 1 and 2, and the tblOrders table's ShipName and ShipAddress fields to columns 3 and 4 of the Query Design grid.

3. Type <>**[Customers].[CompanyName]** in the first Criteria row of the ShipName column and <>**[Customers].[Address]** in the second Criteria row of the Ship Address column. Your query design appears as shown in figure 11.20.

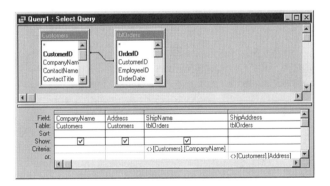

Fig. 11.20 The select query to test for orders that will require 1 as the value of ShipID.

4. Run the query to verify that you have correctly selected the set of records to be updated. If you changed the name of Let's Stop N Shop to Let's Stop 'N Shop in the "Editing Table Data in Query View" section of Chapter 8, "Using Query by Example," the five records for orders placed by this firm appear when you run the query. Using the apostrophe in the entries for Alfred's Futterkiste is inconsistent in the versions of the Customers and Orders tables that were used to write this book (see the highlighted records in fig. 11.21). Checking for errors of this type is one

reason for running the select query before you run the update query. If these records appear, however, you also have a tblShipAddress record for the firm. This is only an example, so you can proceed with the update or you can correct the errors in the query, because the query is updatable.

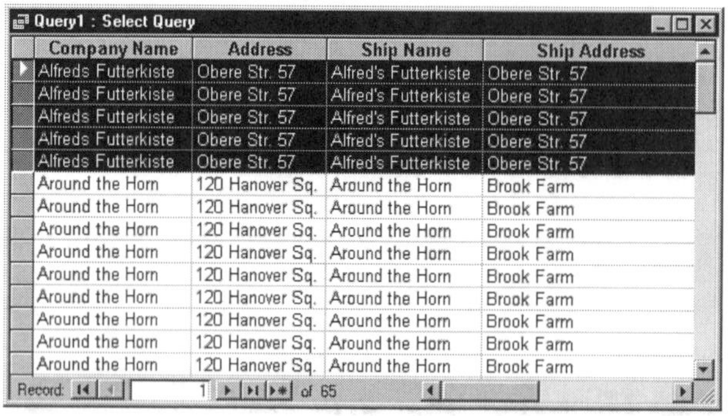

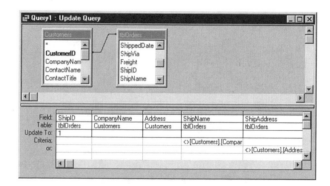

Fig. 11.21   The result of the select query used to test the records to be updated.

After ensuring that you have selected the appropriate records of the tblOrders table for updating, you are ready to convert the select query to an update query by following these steps:

1. Return to design mode and drag the tblOrders table's ShipID field to the query's first column.

2. Choose Query, Update. A new Update To row replaces the Sort and Show rows of the Select Query Design grid.

3. In the ShipID column's Update To cell, type **1** to set ShipID's value to 1 for orders that require the use of a record from the tblShipAddresses table. The Update Query Design grid appears as shown in figure 11.22. The Update To cells of the remaining fields are blank, indicating that Access is not to update values in these fields.

Fig. 11.22   The completed Update Query Design grid.

4. Run the update query. A message box such as that shown in figure 11.23 indicates the number of records that you will update. (The query might return a different number of records because of changes made to the sample database since this book was written.)

Fig. 11.23 The message box that indicates the number of records to be updated.

5. Click the Database Window button and open the tblOrders table. Check a few records to see that you correctly added the ShipID value of 1.

6. You must add 0 values to the ShipID cells of records that have the same shipping and billing addresses. Close the update query, create a new query, and add only the tblOrders table.

7. Drag the ShipID field to the query's first column and choose Query, Update.

8. Type **0** in the Update To row, and **Is Null** in the Criteria row. Then click the Run Query button to replace **Null** values in the ShipID column with 0.

After you check the tblOrders table to verify the result of your second update query, you can change to table design mode and safely delete the ShipName, ShipAddress, ShipCity, ShipRegion, ShipPostalCode, and ShipCountry fields. Later chapters in this book show you how to link the tblShipAddress table to the tblOrders table to choose shipping addresses.

Testing Cascading Deletion and Updating

Access 2.0 introduced two new features that were requested by Access 1.x users: cascading deletion and cascading updating of records having a many-to-one relationship. When you delete a record in a primary or base table on which records in a related table depend, cascading deletion automatically deletes the dependent records. Similarly, if you modify the value of a table's primary-key field and a related table has records related by the primary-key field's value, cascading updating changes the value of the related foreign-key field for the related records to the new primary-key field value.

Cascading deletions and cascading updates are special types of action queries that the Jet engine executes for you. The following three sections show you how to use Access's cascading deletion and cascading updating features with a set of test tables copied from the Orders and Order Details tables of Northwind.mdb.

Creating the Test Tables and Establishing Relationships

When experimenting with database features, you should work with test tables rather than "live" data. As mentioned in the note at the beginning of this chapter, using copied test tables is particularly advisable when the tables are participants in action queries. The remaining sections of this chapter use the two test tables, tblOrders2 and tblOrderDetails, that you create in the following steps:

1. Click the Database window's Table tab and then select the Orders table from the list.

2. Press Ctrl+C to copy to the Clipboard a reference (pointer) to the table.

3. Press Ctrl+V to display the Paste Table As dialog.

4. In the Table Name text box, type **tblOrders2**, then click OK or press Enter to create the test tblOrders2 table.

5. Repeat steps 1 through 4 for the Order Details table, naming the copy **tblOrderDetails**.

6. Open the tblOrders2 table in Table Design View and change the field data type of the OrderID field from AutoNumber to Long Integer. (This change is necessary to test cascading updates in the next section.)

Cascading deletions and updates require that you establish a default relationship between the primary and related tables, and enforce referential integrity. To add both cascading deletions and updates to the tblOrderDetails table, follow these steps:

1. Click the toolbar's Relationships button to display the Relationships window.

2. Click the Clear Layout button to clear the display of the Relationships window. A message box appears warning you that the Relationships window will be cleared. Click Yes to continue.

3. Click the toolbar's Show Table button to display the Add Table dialog. Alternatively, right-click the upper pane of the Query window and choose Show Table.

4. Double-click the tblOrders2 and tblOrderDetails items in the list, and then click the Close button to close the Show Table dialog.

5. Click the OrderID field of tblOrders2, then drag the field symbol to the tblOrderDetails table's OrderID field to establish a one-to-many join on the OrderID field. The Relationships window appears.

6. Select the Enforce Referential Integrity check box to enable the two cascade check boxes.

7. Select the Cascade Update Related Fields and Cascade Delete Related Records check boxes, as shown in figure 11.24.

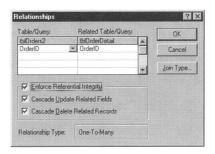

Fig. 11.24 Setting the cascading deletions option.

8. Click the Relationships dialog's OK button to make your changes to the join effective, and then double-click the close window box to close the Relationships window, saving your changes to the window's layout.

Troubleshooting

When I try to enforce referential integrity, I get a "Can't create relationship to enforce referential integrity" message.

You dragged the field symbols in the wrong direction when you created the relationship. The related table is in the Table/Query list and the primary or base table is in the Related Table/Query list. Close the Relationships dialog, click the thin area of the join line to select the join, and then press the Delete key to delete the join. Make sure that you drag the field name that you want from the primary table to the related table.

Testing Cascading Deletion
To try cascading deletion with the test tables, follow these steps:

1. Open the tblOrders2 and tblOrderDetails tables in Datasheet View.

2. Click the surface of the tblOrders2 datasheet to make it the active window, and then click a record-selection button to pick an order in tblOrders2 to delete.

3. Press the Delete key to delete tentatively the selected records and the related order's line-item records in tblOrderDetails.

4. The message shown in figure 11.25 appears requesting that you confirm the deletion. Choose Yes to delete the records.

To verify that you have deleted the related records, you can scroll to the related record or records for the order that you deleted in the tblOrderDetails table. If you opened tblOrderDetails in step 1, the data cell values for the deleted related records are replaced with #Deleted.

Fig. 11.25 Confirming the cascading deletion.

Testing Cascading Updates

Cascading updates to the foreign-key field of records that depend on a primary-key value that you want to change in a primary table is a valuable feature of Access. Performing updates of primary-key values while enforcing referential integrity is not a simple process; Chapter 4, "Working with Access Databases and Tables," briefly discusses the problems associated with performing such updates manually. To see how Access takes the complexity out of cascading updates, follow these steps:

1. With the tblOrders2 and tblOrderDetails windows open, size and position the two datasheets as shown in figure 11.26. Then click the surface of the tblOrders2 datasheet to make it the active window. Positioning the two table datasheet windows as shown in figure 11.26 enables you to see the cascading updates in the tblOrderDetails window as they occur.

2. Change the value of the OrderID cell of the first record to the order number that you deleted in the preceding section. Alternatively, change the value of the OrderID cell to a value, such as 20000, that is outside the range of the values of the test table.

3. Move the caret to another record to cause the cascading update to occur. You see the changes in the OrderID foreign-key field of the related dependent records immediately (see fig. 11.26).

Fig. 11.26 An example of a cascading update.

No confirmation message appears when you execute a cascading update, because the effect of a cascading update is reversible. If you make an erroneous entry that causes an undesired cascading update, you can simply change the entry to its original value by choosing Edit, Undo Saved Record. Alternatively, you can simply reenter the original or the correct value manually.

Creating an Archive Query with the Query Wizards

Access 95 includes five Query Wizards that you can use to create the following types of queries:

- *Simple Query.* A basic SELECT query. (The Simple Query Wizard is new in Access 95.)

- *Find Duplicates Query.* Locates records with duplicate values in a particular field. The Find Duplicates Query is most useful when you want to specify a field as the primary key, but duplicate records prevent you from doing so.

- *Find Unmatched Query.* Creates a right outer join to locate related records that do not have a corresponding primary record (orphan records).

- *Crosstab Query.* A summary crosstab query in which all the column headers represent values in table or query fields rather than months or quarters. The Crosstab Query Wizard cannot create time-series crosstabs.

- *Archive Query.* An action query that copies unneeded records to a new table and then optionally deletes the unneeded records from the source table.

The preceding two chapters discussed the types of specialty queries created by the first four of these wizards. Although the first four wizards are useful, learning to write your own versions of these types of queries is an important step in gaining familiarity with query methodology. After you learn the fundamentals of query design, you probably will not use the first four wizards.

The Archive Query Wizard creates two-stage queries that are useful in a production database environment. The purpose of an archive query is to append a specified set of obsolete records to a new or existing destination table and to delete the original records from the source table. The following steps show you how to use the Archive Query Wizard to delete records for pre-1994 orders from the tblOrders2 and tblOrderDetails test tables:

1. Click the Queries tab of the Database window, and then click the New button to display the wizard-selection dialog shown in figure 11.27.

II

Specific Information

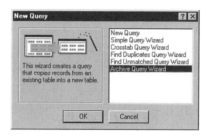

Fig. 11.27   Choosing the type of Query Wizard to employ.

2. Double-click Archive Query Wizard in the list box to display the Archive Wizard's opening dialog (see fig. 11.28).

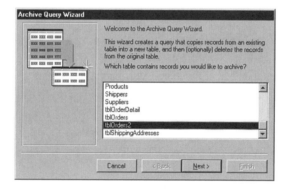

Fig. 11.28   Choosing the table that contains the records that you want to archive.

3. In the list box, select the tblOrders2 table and choose the Next button to display the criteria-entry dialog shown in figure 11.29.

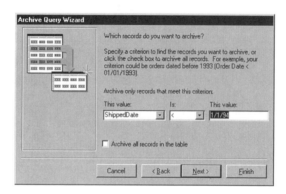

Fig. 11.29   Entering the archiving criteria.

4. Open the This Value drop-down list and select the ShippedDate field.

5. In the Is drop-down combo, type < or select the < symbol from the list.

6. In the This Value text box, type **1/1/94**. Your entries are designed to archive all orders shipped before 1994.

7. Choose the Next button to display the records to be archived in a datasheet (see fig. 11.30).

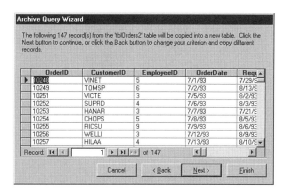

Fig. 11.30   The records to be archived in Datasheet View.

8. Choose the Next button to display the wizard's dialog shown in figure 11.31, which lets you elect to delete the original record or records. Click the Yes, I Want to Delete the Original Record(s) option button.

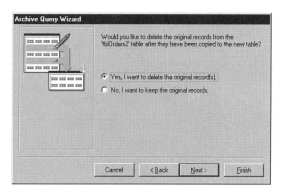

Fig. 11.31   Electing to delete the original records from the source table.

9. Choose the Next button to display the final dialog (see fig. 11.32), which lets you assign the name to the table to receive the archived records. In the drop-down combo list, type **tblOrders2Archive** to create a new archive table. If you already have an archive table for orders, you can append the records to the existing archive table by selecting the table from the combo list.

Fig. 11.32 Naming or selecting a name for the destination table.

10. Click the Archive the Records option button, and then choose the Finish button to execute the query.

11. Choose Yes to confirm that you want to copy the records to the destination table in the message box of figure 11.33.

Fig. 11.33 Confirming archiving of the records.

12. When the message box of figure 11.34 appears, click OK to confirm that you want to delete the records from the source table.

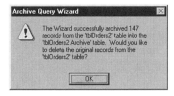

Fig. 11.34 Confirming deletion of the archived records.

13. The message box of figure 11.35 confirms that the wizard deleted archived records from the source table. Click OK to complete the archiving process.

Fig. 11.35 Final confirmation that the archiving process is completed.

The Archive Query Wizard adds two new queries to the Database window: Append to tblOrders2 Archive and Delete from tblOrders2, representing the append query and the delete query, respectively (see fig. 11.36).

Fig. 11.36 The two archive queries added to the list of queries in the Database window.

From Here...

This chapter demonstrates the power of action queries to update, append, and delete records in tables. Action queries are the foundation of Access transaction-processing applications. Access executes each of the action queries described in this chapter with the SQL Data Manipulation Language (DML) statements described in Chapter 24, "Working with Structured Query Language."

For more information related to the topics addressed in this chapter, refer to the following:

- Chapter 9, "Understanding Operators and Expressions in Access," explains how to write expressions to create criteria for action queries.

- Chapter 10, "Creating Multitable and Crosstab Queries," explains how to design select queries that you can easily convert to action queries.

- Chapter 24, "Working with Structured Query Language," shows you how to write action queries using SQL instead of employing Access's graphical Query Design window.

Part III

Creating Forms and Reports

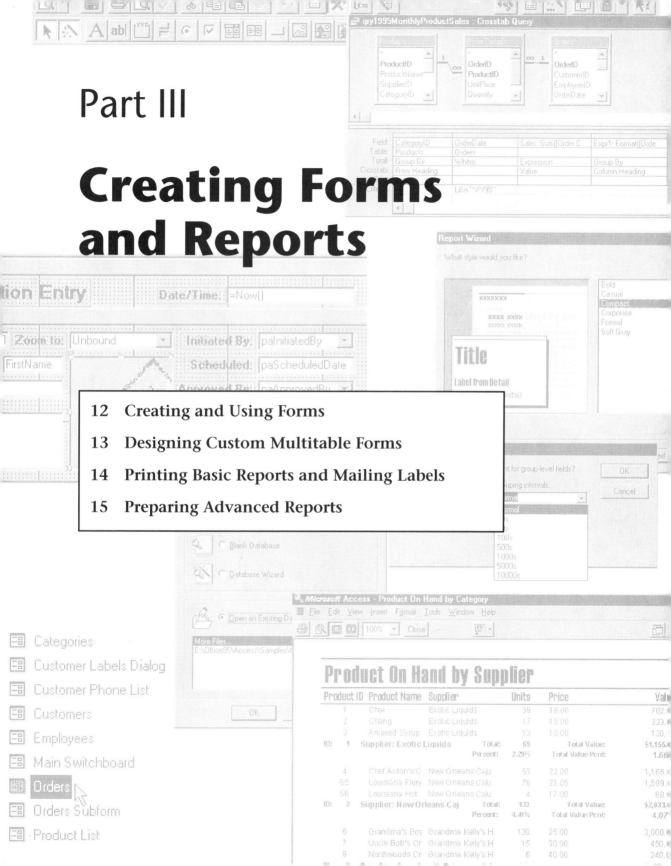

Chapter 12

Creating and Using Forms

Access *forms* create the user interface to your tables. Although you can use Table View and Query View to perform many of the same functions as forms, forms offer the advantage of presenting data in an organized and attractive manner. You can arrange the location of fields on a form so that data entry or editing operations for a single record follow a left-to-right, top-to-bottom sequence. Forms enable you to create multiple-choice selections for fields that use shorthand codes to represent a set of allowable values. A properly designed form speeds data entry and minimizes operator keying errors.

Forms are constructed from a collection of individual design elements called *controls* or *control objects*. Controls are the components you see in the windows and dialogs of Access and other Windows applications. You use *text boxes* to enter and edit data, *labels* to hold field names, and *object frames* to display graphics. A form consists of a window in which you place two types of controls: some that display the data in your tables, and others that display static data such as labels or logos.

This chapter concentrates on creating forms that consist only of text-based controls. Part V, "Integrating Access with Other Office 95 Applications," provides explanations of object linking and embedding (OLE), the method Access uses to incorporate graphs and other graphical elements in forms and reports.

Access forms are versatile; they enable you to complete tasks that you cannot complete in Table View or Query View. You can validate entries based on information contained in a table other than the one you are editing. You can create forms that incorporate other forms (a form within a form is called a *subform*). Forms can calculate values and display totals. This chapter shows you how to create a form using the Access Form Wizard and how to modify the form to speed data entry. Chapter 13, "Designing Custom Multitable Forms," explains how to use the form toolbox to add controls to forms, and how to establish default values and validation rules with forms.

In this chapter, you learn how to do the following

■ Use the Form Wizard to create a new form

■ Modify the design of a form

■ Relocate and resize controls on forms

■ Modify the foreground and background colors of controls

■ Change the formatting of text in controls

III

Forms and Reports

Identifying Types of Forms

The content and appearance of your form depend on its use in your database application. Database applications fall into three basic categories:

- *Transaction processing.* Add new records to tables, or edit existing records. Transaction-processing applications require write access to (permissions for) the tables that are linked to the form.

- *Decision support.* Supply information as graphs, tables, or individual data elements, but don't enable the user to add or edit data. Decision-support applications require only read access to the tables that are linked to the form.

- *Database maintenance.* Perform administrative functions such as creating databases or database tables, controlling database access by users, security assurance via encryption, periodic database compaction, and backup operations. Database-maintenance applications require full permissions for all the objects in the database.

Forms are key elements in transaction-processing and decision-support applications, which are described in the following sections. Common database maintenance operations don't require forms, but forms can be useful for maintaining records of maintenance activities.

Forms for Transaction Processing

Forms for transaction processing usually operate directly on tables when only one table is involved. If a single form is used for adding or editing information in more than one table, you can create a query that includes all the fields you need, then base the form on the query. Your primary form also can use a single table as its data source, but use a subform that has a related table as its data source. An example of a transaction-processing form that uses the subform approach is the Orders form of the Northwind Traders sample database (see fig. 12.1). The datasheet subform that appears below the Order ID, Order Date, Required Date, and Shipped Date text boxes is used to display and add line items on an invoice.

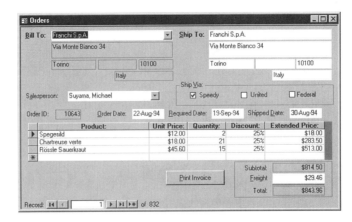

Fig. 12.1   The Orders form of the Northwind Traders database is a typical form for transaction processing.

This chapter concentrates on forms used for transaction processing, but the techniques you learn are applicable to forms used for any other purpose.

Forms for Decision Support

Forms designed only to present information fall into the category of decision support; these forms provide historical data that managers and supervisors use to determine a course of action. You can design decision-support forms for long-range planning or for short-term decisions. Short-term decisions relate to a single action, such as granting a larger credit line to a customer, or sending a sales representative to determine why the customer's purchases have declined. An example of a form to support a short-term decision is Northwind's Quarterly Orders form (see fig. 12.2).

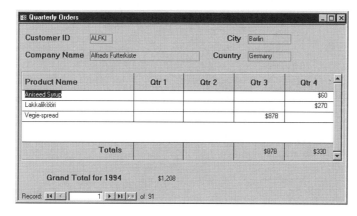

Fig. 12.2 Quarterly Orders is an example of a form used for decision support.

The Quarterly Orders form consists of a main form that displays Customer ID, Company Name, City, and Country, and a subform that displays quarterly sales of products to the customer. The main form is based on the Customers table. The subform consists of a separate form based on the Quarterly Orders by Product crosstab query. Access enables you to include subforms within forms and even subforms within subforms. (Including a subform within a subform is called *nesting*). You can have up to three levels: main form, subform, and sub-subform.

Forms that support short-term decisions often are based on crosstab queries that summarize data in a time series, such as sales to a customer totaled by month, quarter, or year. A table used to support the decision to grant additional credit to a customer might list by quarters the number of invoices issued to the customer, total purchases, and average payment times in days.

Creating a Transaction-Processing Form with the Form Wizard

The form that you create in this example is typical of the transaction-processing forms used to add new records to the many side of a one-to-many relationship. Adding line items to an invoice is an example of when a form of this kind—called a *one-to-many form*—is necessary. The object of the Personnel Actions form is to add new records to the Personnel Actions table, or enable you to edit the existing records. If you didn't add the Personnel Actions table shown in figure 12.3 to the Northwind Traders database in Chapter 4, "Working with Access Databases and Tables," or Chapter 5, "Entering, Editing, and Validating Data in Tables," do so before proceeding with this example. The structure of the Personnel Actions table is provided in Appendix C, "Data Dictionary for the Personnel Actions Table."

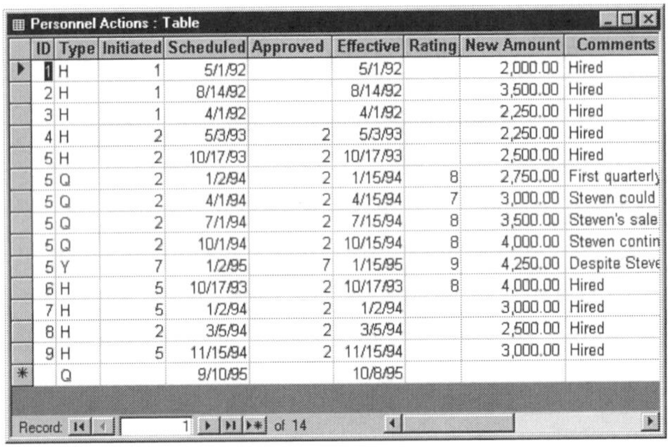

ID	Type	Initiated	Scheduled	Approved	Effective	Rating	New Amount	Comments
1	H	1	5/1/92		5/1/92		2,000.00	Hired
2	H	1	8/14/92		8/14/92		3,500.00	Hired
3	H	1	4/1/92		4/1/92		2,250.00	Hired
4	H	2	5/3/93	2	5/3/93		2,250.00	Hired
5	H	2	10/17/93	2	10/17/93		2,500.00	Hired
5	Q	2	1/2/94	2	1/15/94	8	2,750.00	First quarterly
5	Q	2	4/1/94	2	4/15/94	7	3,000.00	Steven could
5	Q	2	7/1/94	2	7/15/94	8	3,500.00	Steven's sale
5	Q	2	10/1/94	2	10/15/94	8	4,000.00	Steven contin
5	Y	7	1/2/95	7	1/15/95	9	4,250.00	Despite Steve
6	H	5	10/17/93	2	10/17/93	8	4,000.00	Hired
7	H	5	1/2/94	2	1/2/94		3,000.00	Hired
8	H	2	3/5/94	2	3/5/94		2,500.00	Hired
9	H	5	11/15/94	2	11/15/94		3,000.00	Hired
*	Q		9/10/95		10/8/95			

Record: 1 of 14

Fig. 12.3   The Personnel Actions table here contains some sample data.

If you didn't add records to the Personnel Actions table when you created it in Chapter 4, you can add them with the Personnel Actions form you're going to create now with the assistance of Access's Form Wizard.

Choosing the Form Type

The Personnel Actions form that you create in this exercise has a subform that displays all the previous personnel actions for a given employee, and enables you to add new entries to the Personnel Actions table. The majority of forms found in common database applications are one-to-many forms, and most one-to-many forms require a subform to display data from the many side of the relationship.

The Personnel Actions form is intended as both a transaction-processing form and a decision-support form. You can take two approaches to designing a form that accomplishes the objectives of the Personnel Actions form:

■ Use the Employees table as the source of the data for the main form, and use the subform to display, add, and edit records to the Personnel Actions table. This method enables you to add a new employee to the Employees table, as well as to add a new Personnel Actions record.

■ Use the Personnel Actions table as the source of data for both the main form and the subform. You cannot construct forms of this type with the Form Wizard. In this case, you could not add a new employee using this form, because the Employees table has a one-to-many relationship with the Personnel Actions table being edited. This approach is demonstrated in Chapter 13, "Designing Custom Multitable Forms."

The first approach is by far the easiest, and it's the approach we use to create this version of the Personnel Actions form.

Creating the Basic Form with the Form Wizard

The easiest way to create a form and subform is with the Access Form Wizard. The Form Wizard enables you to create forms (with or without subforms) that contain fields from one or more tables or queries. The Form Wizard creates the basic design of the form and adds text box controls to display and edit the values of data items.

To create the Personnel Actions form with the Form Wizard, follow these steps:

1. Click the Forms tab of the Database window, then click the New button. The New Form dialog appears, as shown in figure 12.4.

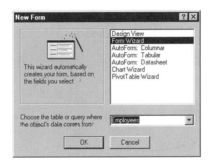

Fig. 12.4 Use the New Form dialog to start the Form Wizard, which helps you to create basic forms.

2. Select Form Wizard from the list in the New Form dialog. Access 95's Form Wizard allows you to create either a simple form without a subform, or a data form that does contain a subform. The Design View choice opens a blank form in Design mode. The various AutoForm choices automatically create forms with the specified layouts: Columnar, Tabular, and Datasheet. The Chart Wizard choice invokes the ChartWizard to add a graph or chart to your form, while the PivotTable Wizard choice helps you create a form based on Excel pivot tables.

3. The drop-down list at the bottom of the New Form dialog lists all the existing tables and queries that can serve as a source of data for a form. Click the arrow to open the drop-down list, then click to select the Employees table. Click OK, and Access displays the first dialog of the Form Wizard (see fig. 12.5).

4. Click to select the EmployeeID field in the Available Fields list, then click the > button to move the EmployeeID field from the Available Fields list to the Selected Fields list. Alternatively, you can double-click the field name to move it.

III

Forms and Reports

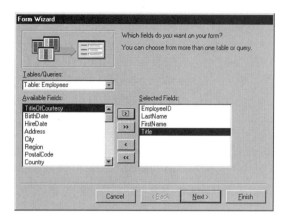

Fig. 12.5   The first step in the Form Wizard is to select the fields that you want to appear on your form.

Repeat this step for the LastName, FirstName, and Title fields of the Employees table. (Placing these fields on the form enables you to edit data from these fields in the Employees table.)

  5. Open the Tables/Queries drop-down list and select the Personnel Actions table. The Available Fields list changes to show the available fields in the Personnel Actions table.

  6. Click the >> button to copy all the fields from the Available Fields list to the Selected Fields list. (You copy all fields from the query onto this form because you need to be able to edit every field in the Personnel Actions table; copying all fields from the query also enables you to edit the FirstName and LastName fields from the Employees table.)

  7. Because the EmployeeID field from the Employees table is included in the Selected Fields list, you don't need to include the paID field from the Personnel Actions table on the form. Select the paID field in the list of Selected Fields, then click the < button to move this field out of the Selected Fields list and back to the Available Fields list. Finally, click the Next button to display the second step of the Form Wizard, shown in figure 12.6.

> **Note**
>
> If you realize you made an error—or change your mind about something—and you're on a later step of the Form Wizard, you can click the Back button to return to and modify your previous choices. You can also click Cancel at any time to abort the form creation and get back to the database window.

  8. Because the fields you have selected to appear on the form come from two different tables, the Form Wizard asks how you want to view the data. Because you want to view the data by employee, with the employee's personnel action data in a subform, click by Employees, and make sure that the Form with subform(s) option is selected (see fig. 12.6). The picture in the upper-right area of the Form Wizard dialog changes to show the fields of the master form (from the Employees table), with a sunken area containing the fields of the subform (from the Personnel Actions table). Click Next to reach the third step of the Form Wizard.

> **Note**
>
> In one-to-many forms, the subform needs to be linked to the main form so that all records displayed in the subform are related to the current record displayed in the main form. The Access 95 Form Wizard obtains the information it needs to link the main form and subform from a join in the Relationships window (in this case, between the Employees table and the Personnel Actions table). If you haven't established a relationship between the two tables in the Relationships window, the Form Wizard skips the step asking you to choose how to view the data and lay out the subform (steps 8 and 9), and goes directly to the dialog asking which style you want for the form (step 10). For this procedure to work correctly, you must establish a relationship between the two tables, as described in Chapter 4, "Working with Access Databases and Tables."

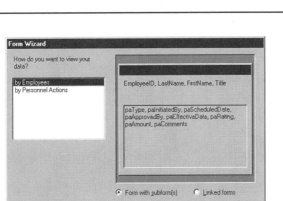

Fig. 12.6 You have to select which table is the master table in the form-subform relationship.

9. The Form Wizard now displays the dialog shown in figure 12.7, asking you to select the layout style for the subform. Select the Tabular option; this creates a subform that displays the data from the Personnel Actions table in a tabular format similar to Datasheet View, but one in which you can change the formatting (colors, column headings, and so on). Click Next to reach the fourth step in the Form Wizard.

10. The Form Wizard displays the dialog shown in figure 12.8, asking you to select a style for the new form. The Access Form Wizard has several predefined styles. Because the sample form we're creating is for use by a data-entry operator—and doesn't need special effects to highlight or decorate any fields—you can click Stan-dard, then click Next to reach the Form Wizard's final dialog, shown in figure 12.9.

III

Forms and Reports

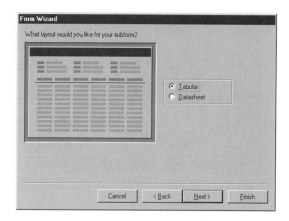

Fig. 12.7   Here, you select a tabular layout for the Personnel Actions subform.

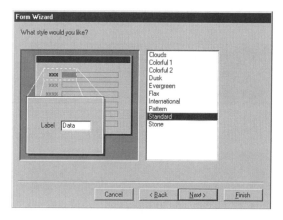

Fig. 12.8   The Form Wizard enables you to select one of several predefined form styles.

Finish

11. In this final step, the Form Wizard asks you to enter a name for the master form and any subforms, and asks you to select what you want done with the form after the Form Wizard has finished creating it. Type **frmPersonnelActions** in the Form text box and **sbfPersonnelActions** in the Subform text box. Select the Open the form to view or enter information option, then click Finish to complete your form. (If you want Access to display help for working with your completed form, select the Display Help on working with the form check box before you click Finish.)

Tip

Access suggests default names for the form and any subforms; make sure that you type in names that describe what the form really does. Also, make sure that you include the name of the main form (or an abbreviation) in the name of your subform so that the relation between the form and subform is evident.

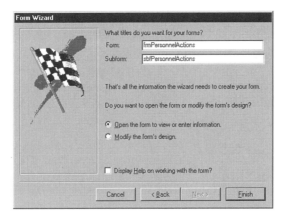

Fig. 12.9   In the final step of the Form Wizard, you enter names for the forms and subforms.

Note

In previous versions of Access, the title you entered for a form was inserted as a heading in the actual form. Instead of doing this, Access 95 uses the form title you enter in the final step of the Form Wizard as the name of the form. The title is displayed in the form window's title bar, but not as part of the actual form.

The Form Wizard creates the form and any subforms, then automatically saves them. When the Form Wizard has finished creating the forms, it displays the main form (see fig. 12.10).

Caution

If you didn't select the Open the form to view or enter information option in the final step, you'll be placed automatically into Design View to work with your new form.

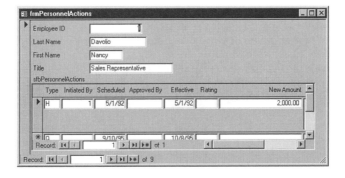

Fig. 12.10   The basic Personnel Action form created by the Form Wizard.

On the main form, the Form Wizard creates a single column of text boxes—each with an associated label—for entering or editing data values in each of the fields from the Employees table that you placed on this form. The subform contains all the fields from the Personnel Actions table (except the paID field) arranged in a tabular layout. Access uses the field names as default text box labels, and also as column headings for the tabular subform. Access uses the name that you entered for the subform as the label for the subform area.

In figure 12.10, notice that the paComments field is almost totally obscured, and scrollbars appear in the subform area. The subform is larger than the area created for it in the main form, so Access automatically adds scrollbars to let you access all the data displayed in the subform.

The basic form as created by the Form Wizard is immediately usable, but could benefit from cosmetic adjustments to the layout of both the main form and the subform. The remaining discussions and exercises in this chapter show you how to modify forms created with the Form Wizard; you can apply these form editing skills when you create your own forms from scratch, as described in the next chapter.

No matter how expert you become in the design of Access forms, using the Form Wizard to create the basic form design saves you time.

Using the Form Design Window

To modify the design of your new form, click the Design View button on the toolbar. The Form Design window appears (see fig. 12.11, where the design window has been maximized). The floating window that appears in Form Design mode contains an undocked toolbar, called the *toolbox*, which enables you to place new control elements on a form. Using the toolbox to add new control elements to the form is covered in the next chapter. For this exercise, hide the toolbox by clicking the Toolbox button on the Forms toolbar, or by clicking the Close window button at the upper-right corner of the toolbox.

Note

Access usually shows the toolbox automatically whenever you enter Form Design mode. If you've manually closed the toolbox, Access does not automatically display it the next time you open the Form Design window. To display the toolbox, click the Toolbox button on the Forms toolbar, or choose <u>V</u>iew, Tool<u>b</u>ars and then click the check box for the toolbox.

The Personnel Action Entry (frmPersonnelActions) form enables you to experiment with methods of modifying forms and their content, which are described in the following sections.

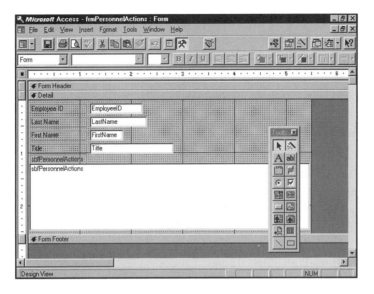

Fig. 12.11 The basic frmPersonnelActions form in Design View.

Caution

Do not save the form with the changes you make when following the instructions in this section. These changes are for demonstration purposes only. Saving these changes would permanently modify the form you created in the preceding section. If you really want to experiment, you can make a copy of the frmPersonnelActions main form and the sbfPersonnelActions subform, then work with the form copies. (Make a backup copy of a form the same way you make a backup copy of a table: choose Edit, Copy to copy the selected form, then choose Edit, Paste to paste a copy of the form.)

Elements of the Form Design Window

Forms can be divided into three sections: Form Header, Detail, and Form Footer. Headers and footers are optional. The Form Design window includes the following basic elements:

- The Form Design toolbar, which contains buttons that are shortcuts for menu selections in Form Design mode. The functions of the buttons and their equivalent menu choices are listed in tables in the next section.

- The Formatting toolbar, which contains buttons that are shortcuts for color, text, border, and various other formatting options. The functions of the formatting buttons and their equivalent menu choices are listed in tables in the next section.

- A set of vertical and horizontal rulers, calibrated in inches for the United States version of Access, and in centimeters for versions of Access supplied to countries where the metric system is used.

- A vertical line (shown to the right of the toolbox in figure 12.11) that establishes the right margin of the form. You can move this margin indicator line by clicking and dragging it to the desired location.

- A horizontal line that establishes the bottom margin of the form. You can click and drag this line to a new location. Margins are important when you are designing a subform to fit within a rectangle of predetermined size on the main form.

- Vertical and horizontal scroll bars that enable you to view portions of the form outside the boundaries of the form window.

- A Form Header bar that defines the height of the form's header section. This applies only if you choose to add a header and footer to your form. The Form Header section contains static text, graphic images, and other controls that appear at the top of form. The header only appears on the first page of a multipage form.

- A Form Detail bar that divides the Form Header from the rest of the form. Controls that display data from your tables and queries, plus static data elements such as labels and logos, are on the Form Detail bar.

- A Form Footer bar that defines the height of the form's footer section. The Form Footer section is similar in function to the Form Header section. If you print a multipage form, the Form Footer appears only at the bottom of the last page.

Note

Although the form shown in figure 12.11 has both Form Header and Form Footer sections, neither section takes up any space on the form—that's why the Form Header bar touches the Detail bar, and the Form Footer bar touches the bottom margin of the form. Even though no text or other information is in the header and footer areas, the Form Wizard adds these elements to the form automatically. When you create a new, blank form without using the Form Wizard, header and footer sections are not added automatically.

You can add Form Header and Form Footer sections to a form—or delete these sections— by choosing View, Form Header/Footer. (If the form currently contains these sections, a check mark appears to the left of the Form Header/Footer menu choice.) Clear the check marks to delete the Header and Footer sections of the form.

Note

If a header or footer section contains any text or other form controls when you try to delete it, Access displays a dialog warning that you will lose the contents of the header and footer.

Form Design Toolbar Buttons and Menu Choices

 The Form Design toolbar of Access 95 contains several buttons that apply only to the design of forms. You select color and font options from the Format toolbar, a new feature in Access 95. Table 12.1 lists the function and equivalent menu choice for each of the Form Design toolbar buttons. The buttons that relate to text and color formatting are described in the following section.

Table 12.1	**Standard Toolbar Buttons in Form Design Mode**	
Button	**Function**	**Menu Choice**
	Displays the form in Run mode (Clicking the arrow at the right of this button displays a drop-down list that enables you to select Datasheet View.).	View, Form
	Saves the current form.	File, Save
	Prints all records in the table using the on-screen form to format the printed data, and using the current printer settings.	n/a
	Selects Print Preview to display how your form appears if printed. You can print the form from the Print Preview window.	File, Print Preview
	Starts the spelling checker to check the spelling of the selected label control.	Tools, Spelling
	Cuts selected objects from the form and puts them on the Clipboard.	Edit, Cut
	Copies selected objects from the form onto the Clipboard.	Edit, Copy
	Pastes the contents of the Clipboard onto the form.	Edit, Paste
	Copies formatting from selected objects to another object of similar type.	n/a
	Undoes the last change you made to the form.	Edit, Undo
	Displays a list of the fields inthe query or table that is the data source for the main form.	View, Field List
	Displays or closes the toolbox.	View, Toolbox
	Applies your choice of several predefined form formats, including formatting for the background bitmap of a form, text fonts, and color settings.	Format, AutoFormat
	Opens the code editing window for Access VBA code contained in a module as an integral part of the form (Code Behind Forms, or CBF).	View, Code
	Displays the Properties window for one of the two sections of the form when you click the section bars, or displays the properties of a control when you select it.	View, Properties
	Displays the BuilderWizard for the selected object or property in the form. This is enabled only if Access has a builder for the selected item.	n/a
	Displays the Database window	Window, 1 Database

III

Forms and Reports

(continues)

Table 12.1 Continued		
Button	**Function**	**Menu Choice**
	Creates a new object. Click the arrow at the right of this button to see a drop-down list of the objects you can create.	n/a
	Click this button, then click an object on-screen (such as a toolbar button) to display a pop-up help window with information about that object.	n/a

The appearance of the Form Design window after clicking the Properties button is shown in figure 12.12.

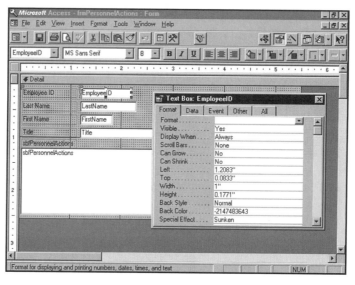

Fig. 12.12 The Form Design window with the Properties window open.

You can close the Properties window by clicking the Close window button, or by clicking the Properties button on the toolbar.

The Formatting Toolbar

 Access 95 displays in Form and Report Design View shortcut buttons and drop-down lists for all the text formatting, line, color, and cell effects options on a separate toolbar, the Formatting toolbar. When you select an object (such as a text box) on a form, Access enables the relevant Formatting toolbar buttons. Drop-down lists enable you to choose the desired typeface and type size for the text. Additional buttons on this toolbar, used to format the text, are similar to the buttons you find on the toolbar of Microsoft Word for Windows and other Windows word processing applications.

ShipName ▼ Access 95 adds a new drop-down list to the toolbar, the Select Object list. The Select Object list displays the name of the currently selected object on the form, and enables you to rapidly select another object on the form by selecting its name. In figure 12.12, the EmployeeID text box is the currently selected object.

The default typeface for forms is the same as that for tables and queries, MS Sans Serif in an 8-point font. You can select any bit-mapped or TrueType family installed on your computer from the drop-down list containing type families.

You can choose from a drop-down list of preset type sizes, or enter a size in points in the Size combo box. You apply attributes and formatting with the text buttons. Table 12.2 lists the function of each text-formatting button and its equivalent property setting.

Table 12.2   Toolbar Buttons for Text Controls in Form Design Mode

Button	Function	Property and Value
B	Sets text style to bold (the default for titles and labels).	Font Weight = Bold
I	Sets italic text style.	Font Italic = Yes
U	Sets underline text style.	Font Underline = Yes
	Left-justifies text within border.	Text Align = Left
	Centers text horizontally within border.	Text Align = Center
	Right-justifies text within border.	Text Align = Right
	Displays a color palette from which you choose the background color for the selected object.	Back Color = *number*
	Displays a color palette from which you choose the color of the text in the selected object.	Fore Color = *number*
	Displays color palette from which you choose the color for the border of the selected object.	Border Color = *number*
	Displays a drop-down list from which you choose the width of the selected object's borders. You may select a hairline width, or widths ranging from 1 to 6 points.	Border Width = *width*
	Displays a drop-down list from which you choose a special effect for how the selected object is displayed. You may choose Flat, Raised, Sunken, Etched, Shadowed, or Chiseled.	Special Effect = *name*

Default Values for Forms

You can change some of the default values used in the creation of all forms by choosing Tools, Options and then selecting the Forms/Reports tab (see fig. 12.13). You can create a form to use as a template and to replace the standard template, and you can determine how objects are displayed when chosen. The effects of these options are described in the sections that follow. The options that you or other Access users choose in the Options dialog are saved for each user ID in the MSysOptions table of the current System.mdw workgroup system file.

You can change the default values for the current form, section, or controls by choosing the object as described in the following section, and then changing the default values displayed in the Properties window for that object. You can also use the AutoFormat feature to quickly apply a predefined format to all of the controls in the form. The next section describes using AutoFormat to change a form's appearance, and subsequent sections describe ways to manually change the format of text or controls on a form.

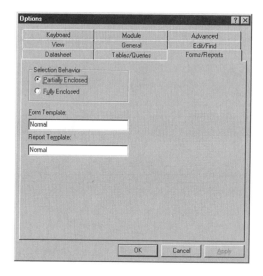

Fig. 12.13   Displaying Forms/Reports options in the Options dialog.

Using AutoFormat

 The AutoFormat feature is new to Access 95. AutoFormat enables you to apply a predefined format to an entire form with only a few mouse clicks. Access 95 comes with several predefined formats, and you also can create your own formats for use with AutoFormat.

Applying an AutoFormat. To apply a format to a form with AutoFormat, follow these steps:

1. Click the AutoFormat button on the toolbar. Access displays the AutoFormat dialog, shown in figure 12.14.

2. Click to select the format you want to use in the Form AutoFormats list; a preview of the format you select appears in the window in the center of the dialog.

3. Click OK to apply the format to the form. Figure 12.15 shows the frmPersonnelActions form after the International format has been applied.

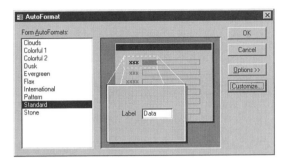

Fig. 12.14   Use the AutoFormat dialog to apply a predefined format to an entire form.

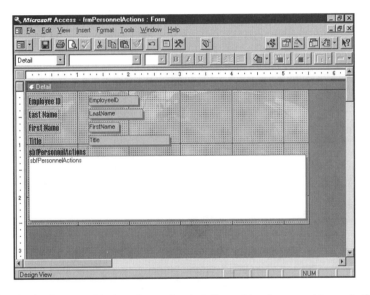

Fig. 12.15   The frmPersonnelActions form after AutoFormat has been used to apply the International format.

The AutoFormat dialog enables you to omit the application of font, color, or border style information to your form when you apply the AutoFormat. When the AutoFormat dialog is open, click the Options button; the AutoFormat dialog expands to display three additional check boxes (see fig. 12.16). Deselect the check box for the elements of the AutoFormat that you want omitted when you apply the AutoFormat to your form.

Creating, Customizing, and Deleting AutoFormats. The predefined AutoFormat styles might not suit your tastes, or you might want to create AutoFormat styles specific to your company or application.

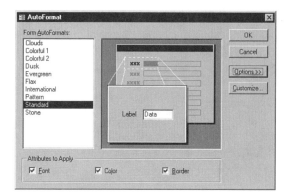

Fig. 12.16 The expanded AutoFormat dialog contains optional check boxes that enable you to control which elements are applied to your form by the AutoFormat.

To create a new AutoFormat, or customize an existing one, follow these steps:

1. Create a form and alter its appearance (using the techniques described later in this chapter) so that the form has the font, border, background picture, and other options adjusted exactly the way you want them for your new or customized AutoFormat.

2. Click the AutoFormat button to display the AutoFormat dialog. If you want to modify an existing AutoFormat, select it in the Form AutoFormats list now.

3. Click the Customize button to display the Customize AutoFormat dialog shown in figure 12.17.

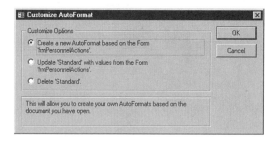

Fig. 12.17 The Customize AutoFormat dialog enables you to create, modify, or delete an AutoFormat.

4. Select the Create a new AutoFormat based on the Form *formname* option, or the Update *formatname* with values from the Form *formname* option to create or modify an AutoFormat, respectively. (We'll talk about deleting AutoFormats in a moment).

5. Click OK. If you're creating a new AutoFormat, the New Style Name dialog appears (see fig. 12.18). Type an appropriate name for your new AutoFormat, and click OK. Access now creates or updates the AutoFormat, and returns you to the AutoFormat dialog.

6. Click Close to close the AutoFormat dialog.

Fig. 12.18   Access prompts you for a name for a new AutoFormat.

If you have created your own AutoFormats, you may want to delete an AutoFormat that you no longer use. To delete an AutoFormat, follow these steps:

1. Open any form in Design View.

2. Click the AutoFormat button to display the AutoFormat dialog.

3. Click to select the AutoFormat you want to delete in the Form AutoFormats list, then click the Customize button. Access displays the Customize AutoFormat dialog.

4. Select the Delete *formname* option, and click OK. Access deletes that AutoFormat from the list.

> **Caution**
>
> Access does not ask for confirmation when you delete an AutoFormat; make sure to select the correct AutoFormat for deletion before you click OK.

5. Click Close to close the AutoFormat dialog.

Applying formatting to a form through an AutoFormat style is the easiest way by far to create standardized forms for your database application—especially since the Form Wizard uses the same format style list as the AutoFormat feature. In other words, any AutoFormats you create become available in the Form Wizard dialog, also.

The next few sections of this chapter describe how you can customize the appearance of various objects on a form.

Changing an Object's Colors

Access 95 no longer uses the Palette window that users of Access 2.0 are familiar with. Instead, you select object colors through the buttons on the Formatting toolbar, and through property settings accessible through the Properties window of the form and individual objects on the form. The following sections describe how to use the Formatting toolbar controls, and the Property dialog, to change background and foreground colors of form sections and control objects, as well as border properties of control objects.

Background Colors. The background color (Back Color property) of a form section (Header, Detail, or Footer) applies to all areas of that section except those occupied by control objects. The default background color of all sections of forms created by the Form Wizard depends on the specific form style you choose when you create the form; the Standard format scheme used to create the frmPersonnelActions form, for example, is light gray.

The default color choices on the palette displayed by the Back Color toolbar button are 16 of the standard *system colors* of Windows 95. If you are creating a form that you intend to print, a gray or deeply textured background will not only be distracting, but will also consume substantial amounts of printer toner. Data entry operators often prefer a white background rather than a gray, colored, or textured background. Colored backgrounds hinder text visibility.

To change the background color of a section of a form, follow these steps:

1. Click an empty area within the section of the form (Header, Detail, or Footer) whose background color you want to change. This selects the appropriate section.

 2. Click the Back Color button on the toolbar to display the color palette.

3. Click the box that contains the color you want to use.

Because the background color of each form section is independent, you must repeat the process if you want to change the color for other sections of your form. The Transparent button of the Back Color palette is disabled when a form section is chosen, because a transparent background color isn't applicable to forms.

You choose the background color of a control object, such as a label, just as you do for forms. In most cases, the chosen background color of labels is the same as that of the form, so click the Transparent button to allow the background color to appear. The default value of the Back Color property of text boxes is white, so that text boxes (and the data they contain) contrast with the form's background color.

 Changing the Background Bitmap. A new feature in Access 95 enables you to use a bitmap picture as the background for a form. Unlike background colors, of which you can have several, you select a single bitmap picture for the entire form. Access 95 comes with a few bitmap pictures that it uses in the AutoFormat formats—International, for example, uses the Globe.wmf graphics file (stored in the MSOffice\Access\Bitmaps\Styles folder) as the background for the form. You can use any .WMF or .BMP graphics file as a background for a form.

> **Note**
>
> Forms with bitmap graphics as a background can look dramatic, and therefore are best suited for public-access information terminals, or for decision-support forms. These forms, however, tend to be more visually complex, which might make it difficult for users to read text labels, or to identify specific fields on the form. For accurate, high-speed data-entry, you should keep your transaction-processing forms visually simple so that users can easily distinguish data fields on the form, and can easily read text labels.

You set or remove a form's background bitmap through the Properties window of the form; you can also specify several viewing and formatting properties for the background picture. Follow these steps to set the background picture properties of a form:

1. Open the form in Design View, if necessary.

2. Click the square at the upper-left corner of the form design window (where the horizontal and vertical rulers meet) to select the form as a whole. A black square appears when the form is selected (see fig. 12.19).

3. If the Properties window isn't already open, click the Properties button on the toolbar to display this window.

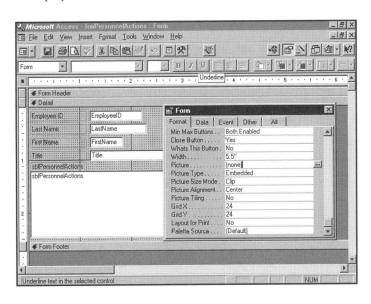

Fig. 12.19 Set the file name and formatting properties for a form's background picture in the Properties window.

4. Click the Format tab in the Properties window, and scroll down to the end of the Format properties list to view the various Picture properties: Picture, Picture Type, Picture Size Mode, Picture Alignment, and Picture Tiling. Each of these properties, and their effects, are described in the list following these numbered steps.

5. Set the various Picture properties until you are satisfied with the appearance of the form. As you change each property, results of the change become immediately visible on the form.

6. Click the Close window button in the Properties window to close this window.

The following list summarizes form properties related to the background picture, available choices for each property, and the effects of each choice.

■ *Picture.* This is the folder path and file name of the graphics file that Access uses as the form's background. You may either type the folder path and file name directly in the Picture property text box, or you may use the builder to help you select the background graphics file. To use the builder, click the Picture property field to select that field, then click the Builder button that appears next to the text box. Access displays the Insert Picture dialog shown in figure 12.20. The Insert Picture dialog is a standard Windows 95 dialog for opening files. Click the Preview button (second button from the right), if necessary, to display the background image.

When you locate the graphics file you want, click to select its name, then click OK to have Access fill in the Picture property.

Tip

To remove a background picture, simply delete the entry in the Picture text box.

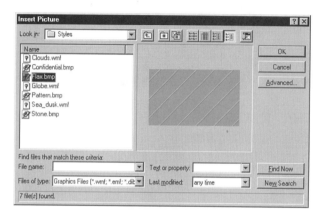

Fig. 12.20   Use the Insert Picture dialog to select a picture as a form background; this dialog is a standard Windows 95 file open dialog with the Preview option on.

- *Picture Type.* This specifies the OLE method that Access uses to attach the background picture to the form. You can select either Embedded or Linked as the picture type. You usually should use the Embedded picture type, especially if you intend to distribute your database application—the resulting form is self-contained, and doesn't rely on the presence of external files that might be moved or deleted. If you have many forms that use the same background bitmap graphic, however, linking the background picture can save some disk space.

- *Picture Size Mode.* This property controls how Access sizes the background picture. The available choices are Clip, Stretch, and Zoom. Clip causes Access to display the picture at its full size behind the form; if the picture is larger than the form, it is clipped to fit the form. If the picture is smaller than the form, the form's own background color shows in any part of the form background not covered by the picture. Stretch causes Access to stretch the picture vertically and horizontally to match the size of the form; the Stretch option permits distortions in the picture. Zoom causes Access to magnify the picture, without distortion, to fit the size of the form.

- *Picture Alignment.* This property controls where Access positions the background picture. The available choices are Top-left (aligns the upper-left corner of the picture with the upper-left corner of the form window), Top-right (aligns the upper-right corner of the picture with the upper-right corner of the form window), Center (places the picture in the center of the form window), Bottom-left (aligns the lower-left corner of the picture with the lower-left corner of the form),

Bottom-right (aligns the lower-right corner of the picture with the lower-right corner of the form), and Form Center (centers the picture on the form).

> **Tip**
>
> To ensure that a background picture is displayed relative to the form, rather than the form's window, select Form Center as the value for the Picture Alignment property.

- *Picture Tiling.* This property has two permissible values: Yes or No. *Tiling* means that the picture is repeatedly displayed to fill the entire form or form window (if the Picture Alignment property is set to Form Center, the tiling fills just the form).

Now that you know how to adjust the background picture and colors of a form, the next section describes how to adjust the foreground colors and border properties of the form and objects on the form.

Foreground Color, Border Color, and Border Style. You may set the foreground color, border color, and border width through buttons on the Formatting toolbar, or directly in the Properties window for a selected control. To set a border style (solid, or a variety of dashed-line styles), you must set the property directly in the Properties window.

Foreground color (the Fore Color property) is applicable only to control objects. (The Fore Color button on the toolbar is disabled when you select a form section.) Foreground color specifies the color for the text in labels and text boxes. The default value of the Fore Color property is black. You choose border colors for control objects that have borders by using the Border Color toolbar button.

The Special Effects button of the Formatting toolbar enables you to simulate special effects for control objects, such as a raised or sunken appearance. The Border Width button enables you to control the width of the border of controls. The Formatting toolbar buttons were listed earlier in this chapter, in Table 12.2. Table 12.3 lists the property name for each border property, and lists the specific values that each may have.

To set a control's foreground color, border width, or border color by using the Formatting toolbar buttons, first click the control whose properties you want to change, then click the arrow to the right of the toolbar button for the property you want to change. Click the color or line width you want for the control.

To set a control's foreground color, border width, border color, or border style in the Properties window, click the control whose properties you want to change to select it. If necessary, open the Properties window by clicking the Properties button on the toolbar. Click the Format tab in the Properties window, then scroll to the text box for the property you want to change. Most of the border properties are selected from drop-down lists; color properties require you to enter a number representing the desired color in Windows 95 color notation. (Windows 95 color notation is too complex to explain here; the easiest way to enter color values is with the toolbar buttons, or by using the color builder described in the following section of this chapter.)

Table 12.3 Border Style Properties and Values		
Property Name	**Function**	**Values**
Border Style	Determines the line style of the border.	Transparent, Solid, Dashes, Short Dashes, Dots, Sparse Dots, Dash Dot, Dash Dot Dot
Border Color	Sets the color of the border.	Depends on the color
Border Width	Determines the width of the border.	Hairline, or any whole point size from 1 to 6

Creating Custom Colors with the Color Builder. If you aren't satisfied with one of the 16 Windows system colors for your form sections or control objects, you can create your own custom colors by following these steps:

1. Place the caret in the Back Color, Fore Color, or Border Color text box of the Properties window for a control.

2. Click the ellipsis button to display the Color dialog. The basic form of this dialog enables you to choose from a set of 48 colors. If one of these colors suits your taste, click the color square and then click OK to assign that color as the value of the property and close the dialog. If you want a custom color, proceed to step 3.

3. Click the Define Custom Colors button to expand the Color dialog to include the Hue/Saturation and Luminance windows, as shown in figure 12.21.

4. Click and drag the cursor within the square Hue/Saturation area to choose the color you want.

5. Click and drag the arrow at the right of the rectangular luminance area while observing the Color block; release the mouse button when the Color block has the luminance (brightness) value you want.

6. Click Add to Custom Colors to add your new color to the first of the 16 custom color blocks.

7. Click the new custom color block to select it; click OK to add this color value to the property and close the Color dialog.

Many PCs used for data entry and editing applications run in 16-color VGA mode because this mode is slightly faster than the standard 256-color mode used by most of today's PCs. In 16-color VGA mode, any colors you choose or create, other than the standard Windows system colors, are simulated by a *dithering* process. Dithering alternates pixels of differing colors to create the usually imperfect illusion of a solid color. Thus, it is good programming practice to stick with the 16 Windows system colors unless you have a very good reason to do otherwise.

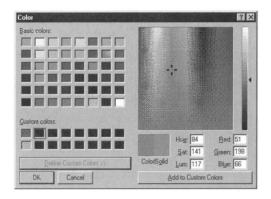

Fig. 12.21 This is the Color dialog after it has been expanded to display the custom color selection controls.

Selecting, Editing, and Moving Form Elements and Controls

The properties that apply to the entire form, to the five sections of the form, and to each control object on the form are determined by the values shown in the Properties window. To view the Properties window for a control, select the control by clicking anywhere on its surface; then click the Properties button on the toolbar. The sections of an Access form are shown in figure 12.22.

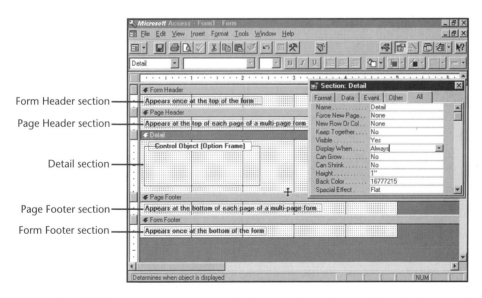

Fig. 12.22 Five sections are contained on this Access form, and the Detail section is currently selected.

The following list describes how to choose and display the properties of the entire form, its sections, and its control objects:

■ *Form.* Click the area of the form to the right of the right-margin indicator line; click the square where the ruler lines meet; or choose Edit, Select Form. (If the Properties window isn't open, you must double-click the square where the ruler lines meet.) Selecting the form enables you to set properties for the form as a whole by entering values from the properties listed in the Properties window.

■ *Header section only.* Click the Form Header or Page Header bar. The set of properties you work with applies only to the Form Header or Page Header section. A Form Header and Footer appear when you choose View, Form Header/Footer. A Page Header and Footer appear when you choose View, Page Header/Footer from the Layout menu. Page Headers and Footers primarily are used in conjunction with printing forms. You delete headers and footers by choosing View, Form Header/ Footer or View, Page Header/Footer a second time.

■ *Detail section only.* Click the Detail bar. You get a set of properties similar to those of the Form Header section, but all of these apply to the Detail section.

■ *Footer section only.* Click the Form Footer or Page Footer bar. A set of properties identical to the header properties is available for the footer sections. A Form Footer appears only if a Form Header has been added. The same applies to Page Headers and Footers.

■ *Control object* (or both elements of a control with an associated label). Click the surface of the control. Each type of control has its own set of properties. Displaying the properties of multiple control objects is the subject of a later section.

Changing the Size of the Form Header and Form Footer

You can change the height of a form section by dragging the Form Header, Page Header, Detail, Page Footer, or Form Footer bar vertically with the mouse. When you position the mouse pointer at the top edge of a section divider bar, it turns into a line with two vertical arrows (refer to fig. 12.22). You drag the pointer with the mouse to adjust the size of the section above the mouse pointer.

The height of the Detail section is determined by the vertical dimension of the window in which the form is displayed, less the combined heights of all the header and footer sections that are fixed in position. When you adjust the vertical scroll bar, only the Detail section scrolls.

Selecting, Moving, and Sizing a Single Control

When you select a control object by clicking its surface, the object is enclosed by a shadow line with an anchor rectangle at its upper-left corner and five smaller, rectangular sizing handles (see fig. 12.23).

Note

Text boxes, combo boxes, check boxes, and option buttons have associated (attached) labels. When you select one of these objects, the label and the object are selected as a unit.

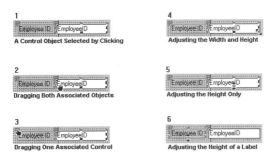

Fig. 12.23 The appearance of a control object selected for relocation and resizing.

The following choices are available for moving or changing the size of a control object (the numbered choices correspond with the numbers in fig. 12.23):

1. *To select a control (and its associated label, if any),* click anywhere on its surface.

2. *To move the control (and its associated label, if any) to a new position,* move the mouse pointer within the outline of the object at any point other than the small resizing handles or the confines of a text box (where the cursor can become an editing caret). The mouse pointer becomes a hand symbol when it's on an area that you can use to move the entire control. Press and hold down the left mouse button while dragging the hand symbol to the new location for the control. An outline of the control indicates its position as you move the mouse. When the control is where you want it to be, release the mouse button to drop the control in its new position.

> **Tip**
>
> If the control doesn't have an associated label, you can drag the control's anchor handle at the upper-left corner to move the control.

3. *To separately move the elements of a control that has an associated label,* position the mouse pointer on the anchor handle in the upper-left corner of the control you want to move. The mouse pointer becomes a hand with an extended finger. Click and drag the individual element to its new position, then release the mouse button.

4. *To simultaneously adjust the width and height of a control,* click the small sizing handle at any of the three corners of the outline of the control. The mouse pointer becomes a diagonal two-headed arrow. Click and drag this arrow to a new position, then release the mouse button.

5. *To adjust only the height of the control,* click the sizing handle on one of the horizontal surfaces of the outline. The mouse pointer becomes a vertical two-headed arrow. Click and drag this arrow to a new position, then release the mouse button.

Selecting and deselecting controls is a *toggling* process. Toggling means repeating an action with the effect of alternating between On and Off conditions. The Properties, Field List, and Toolbox buttons on the toolbar—as well as their corresponding menu choices—are toggles. The Properties dialog, for example, appears and disappears if you repeatedly click the Properties button.

Aligning Controls to the Grid

The Form Design window includes a grid consisting of one-pixel dots with a default spacing of 10 to the inch horizontally and 12 to the inch vertically. When the grid is visible, you can use the grid dots to assist in maintaining the horizontal and vertical alignment of rows and columns of controls. Even if the grid isn't visible, you can cause controls to "snap to the grid" by choosing Format, Snap to Grid. This menu command is a toggle, and when Snap to Grid is active, the menu choice is checked. Whenever you move a control while Snap to Grid is active, the upper-left corner of the object jumps to the closest grid dot.

You can cause the size of control objects to conform to grid spacing by choosing Format, Size to Grid. You also can make the size of the control fit its content by choosing Format, Size, to Fit.

> **Tip**
>
> If Snap to Grid is on and you want to locate or size a control without reference to the grid, press and hold the Ctrl key while you move or resize the control.

Toggling the View, Grid menu command controls the visibility of the grid; by default, the grid is visible for all new forms. If the grid spacing is set to more than 24 per inch or 10 per centimeter, the dots aren't visible. To change the grid spacing for a form, follow these steps:

1. Choose Edit, Select Form.

2. Click the Properties button on the toolbar to make the form properties appear.

3. Click the Format tab in the Properties window to display the formatting properties, and scroll through the list until the Grid X and Grid Y properties are visible.

4. Change the value of Grid X to 10 dots per inch (dpi) and Grid Y to 12 dpi, or change both values to 16 (if you want controls to align with inch ruler ticks). Users with metric rulers are likely to prefer a value of 10 for both Grid X and Grid Y.

Tip

The default values of grid spacing of Access 95 is 24 dots per inch. Better values are 10 for Grid X and 12 for Grid Y. This grid dot spacing is optimum for text controls that use the default 8-point MS Sans Serif font. The Form Wizards also use 24 dpi horizontally and vertically.

Selecting and Moving a Group of Controls

You can select and move more than one object at a time by using one of the following methods:

- Enclose the objects with a rectangle. Begin by clicking the surface of the form outside the outline of a control object. Press and hold down the mouse button while dragging the mouse pointer to create an enclosing rectangle that includes each of the objects you want to select (see fig. 12.24). Release the mouse button. You may now move the group of objects by clicking and dragging the anchor handle of any one of them.

- Click to select one object; hold down Shift while you click to select the next object. (You can repeat this as many times as is necessary to select all the objects you want.)

- Delete a selected object from a group by clicking its anchor with the mouse to deselect it. To deselect an entire group, click any inactive area of the form. An inactive area is an area outside the outline of a control.

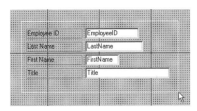

Fig. 12.24   A collection of control objects enclosed with a selection rectangle.

If you select or deselect a control with an associated label, the label is selected or deselected along with the control.

Note

The selection rectangle selects a control if any part of the control is included within the rectangle. This behavior is unlike many drawing applications in which the entire object must be enclosed to be selected. You can change the behavior of Access's selection rectangle to require full enclosure of the object by choosing Tools, Options, then selecting the Forms/Reports tab, and changing the value of the Selection Behavior option from Partially Enclosed to Fully Enclosed.

III

Forms and Reports

Aligning a Group of Controls

You can align selected individual controls, or groups of controls, to the grid or to each other by choosing F<u>o</u>rmat, A<u>l</u>ign and completing the following actions:

- To align a selected control (or group of controls) to the grid, choose To Grid from the submenu.

- To adjust the positions of controls within a selected columnar group so that their left edges fall into vertical alignment with the far-left control, choose Left from the submenu.

- To adjust the positions of controls within a selected columnar group so that their right edges fall into vertical alignment with the right edge of the far-right control, choose Right from the submenu.

- To align rows of controls at their top edges, choose Top from the submenu.

- To align rows of controls at their bottom edges, choose Bottom from the submenu.

Your forms have a more professional appearance if you take the time to align groups of controls vertically and horizontally.

Using the Windows Clipboard and Deleting Controls

All the conventional Windows Clipboard commands apply to control objects. You can cut or copy a selected control or group of controls to the Clipboard. After that, you can paste the control or group to the form using <u>E</u>dit menu commands, and then relocate the pasted control or group as desired. Access uses the Windows 95 keyboard shortcut keys: Ctrl+X to cut and Ctrl+C to copy selected controls to the Clipboard, and Ctrl+V to paste the Clipboard contents. The traditional Shift+Del, Ctrl+Ins, and Shift+Ins commands perform the same operations.

You can delete a control by selecting it, then pressing Del. If you accidentally delete a label associated with a control, do the following: select another label, copy it to the Clipboard, select the control with which the label needs to be associated, and paste the label to the control.

Changing the Color and Border Style of a Control

As mentioned earlier in this chapter, the default color for the text and borders of controls is black. Borders are one pixel wide (called *hairline* width); some objects, such as text boxes, have default borders. Labels have a gray background color by default, but a better choice for the default label color would have been transparent. Transparent means that the background color appears within the control except in areas occupied by text or pictures.

You control the color and border widths of a control from the Border Color and Border Width buttons on the Formatting toolbar; you must select a border style directly in the Properties window.

To change the color or border width of a selected control or group of controls, follow these steps:

1. Select the control(s) whose color or border width you want to change.

2. Click the arrow of the Back Color toolbar button to open the color palette popup window. Click the color square you want, or click the Transparent button to make the background transparent.

3. Click the arrow of the Border Color toolbar button to open the color palette popup window, where you change the border color for any selected control that has borders.

4. Click the arrow of the Border Width toolbar button to open the border width popup window, where you change the thickness of the border for any selected control whose borders are enabled.

5. Click the arrow of the Fore Color toolbar button to open the color palette popup window, where you change the color of the text of selected controls.

Note

The general practice for Windows database entry forms is to indicate editable elements with borders and clear backgrounds. Still, some popular software (most notably, the DOS versions of dBASE and Paradox) uses reverse video as the default to indicate editable text. You can create the effect of reverse video by choosing black or another dark color for the fill of a text box control, and a light color for its text. If you decide to implement reverse text, remember that it's more difficult to read than normal text, and consider using a larger font and adding the bold attribute to ensure legibility.

To set the border style, you must select the Border Style property directly in the Properties window, as explained earlier in this chapter.

Changing the Content of Text Controls

You can edit the content of text controls using conventional Windows text-editing techniques. When you place the mouse pointer within the confines of a text control and click the mouse button, the mouse pointer becomes the Windows text-editing caret that you use to insert or delete text. You can select text by holding down Shift and moving the caret with the mouse; all Windows Clipboard operations are applicable to text within controls. Keyboard text selection and editing techniques using the arrow keys in combination with Shift are available, also.

If you change the name of a field in a text box and make an error naming the field, you receive a #Name? error message in the offending text box when you select Run mode. Following is a better method of changing a text box with an associated label:

1. Delete the existing field control by clicking to select it, then pressing Delete.

2. Click the Field List button in the Properties bar to display the Field List dialog.

3. Scroll through the entries in the list until you find the field name you want.

4. Click the field name; click and drag the field name to the location of the deleted control. Release the mouse button to drop the new name.

5. Close the Field List dialog when you are finished.

You can relocate and resize the new field caption and text box (or edit the caption) as necessary.

Using the Format Painter

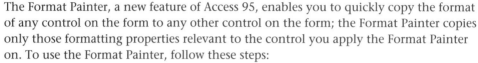

The Format Painter, a new feature of Access 95, enables you to quickly copy the format of any control on the form to any other control on the form; the Format Painter copies only those formatting properties relevant to the control you apply the Format Painter on. To use the Format Painter, follow these steps:

1. Select the control that has the formatting you want to copy.

2. Click or double-click the Format Painter button on the toolbar; the mouse cursor changes to a pointing arrow with a paintbrush icon attached to it. (Double-clicking "locks" the Format Painter on; double-click the Format Painter button only if you want to copy the formatting to more than one control.)

3. Click any control that you want to copy the formatting to; the Format Painter copies all relevant formatting properties to this control. If you didn't double-click the Format Painter button, the Format Painter turns itself off after copying the formatting properties to one control.

4. If you locked the Format Painter on by double-clicking its button, you can repeat step 3 as many times as you want. Click the Format Painter button again to turn the Format Painter off.

Typically, you use the Format Painter to quickly set the formatting properties for field text labels, or in any situation where selecting several controls by dragging a selection rectangle seems undesirable. By locking the Format Painter on, it's easy to format several controls, one after another.

Rearranging the Personnel Actions Form

The objective of the following set of instructions is to rearrange the controls on the frmPersonnelActions form so that all the elements on the form (and its subform) are completely visible in the form window, and to optimize the position of the fields for data entry. After you complete the following steps, your main form appears as shown in figure 12.25, and your subform appears as shown in figure 12.26.

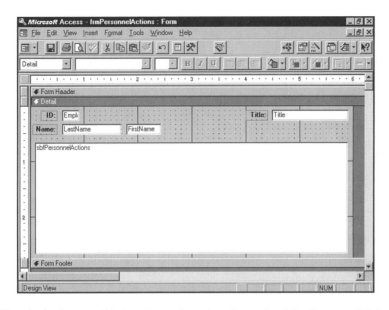

Fig. 12.25   The frmPersonnelActions form after relocating and resizing its control objects.

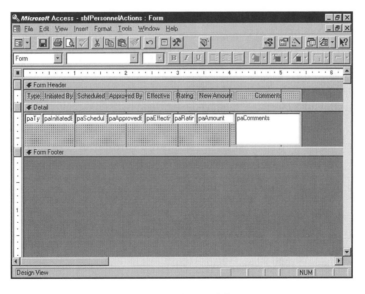

Fig. 12.26   The sbfPersonnelActions subform after modifying its appearance.

Setting Properties of the Main Form

To change the color of form objects and rearrange the controls of the frmPersonnelActions form to correspond with the positions shown in figure 12.25, follow these steps:

1. Close the frmPersonnelActions form by clicking the Close window button. Do *not* save any changes you made in the preceding section.

2. Choose frmPersonnelActions from the Forms list in the Database window, and click the Design button.

3. Click the Maximize window button to maximize the form design window, if it isn't already maximized.

4. Choose <u>E</u>dit, Select Fo<u>r</u>m, and then click the Properties button on the toolbar.

5. Click the Format tab of the Properties window, and then scroll through the properties list until you see Grid X and Grid Y. Change the Grid X property to 10 and the Grid Y property value to 12. (Metric users may prefer a 5-by-5 grid, providing 2 mm resolution.)

6. Close the Properties window by clicking the Properties button on the toolbar again.

7. Drag the right margin of the form from its present position (5.5 inches) to 6 inches.

8. Click the Title field text box to select the text box and its label.

9. Move the mouse pointer onto the selected Title field until the pointer changes to the shape of a hand, then click and drag the Title field to the right of the EmployeeID text box.

10. Delete the FirstName label (click the label, then press Del), then use the technique described in steps 8 and 9 to select the FirstName field and drag it to a position to the right of the LastName field (refer to fig. 12.25).

11. Edit the LastName label to read **Name:**, the EmployeeID label to read **ID:** and the Title label to read **Title:**.

12. Delete the sbfPersonnelActions field label (the size and content of the subform is sufficient to identify it), and drag the subform control to a position below the FirstName and LastName fields (refer to fig. 12.25).

13. Click and drag the Form Footer bar to approximately 2.7 inches. At present, the dimensions of your form are 6"×2.7".

14. Resize the sbfPersonnelActions subform control on the form so that its left, right, and bottom edges are one grid mark inside the edges of the form (this makes the sbfPersonnelActions subform control about 5.8"×1 7/8".

15. Click the text label of the EmployeeID field to select it, and then click the Bold and Align Right buttons on the Formatting toolbar to make the text label bold and right justified.

16. Double-click the Format Painter button on the toolbar (remember that this locks the Format Painter).

17. In turn, click the text labels for all the remaining controls on the form, to apply the formatting with the Format Painter.

18. Click the Format Painter button on the toolbar again to turn off the Format Painter.

19. Adjust the widths of the labels and text boxes to suit their content (refer to fig. 12.25).

20. Click the Save button on the toolbar (or choose File, Save) to save your changes to the frmPersonnelActions form.

You may need to adjust the sizes of some controls individually to make their appearance consistent with other controls. When you complete your rearrangement, click the Form View button. Your form appears as shown in figure 12.27.

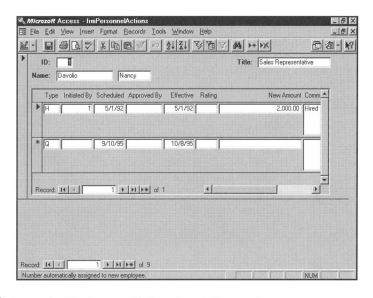

Fig. 12.27 The revised frmPersonnelActions form in Run mode.

Setting the Properties of a Subform

You can learn about modifying the properties of a subform by working with the subform used to create the history of prior Personnel Actions for an employee. In this example, editing or deleting entries using the subform is not allowed, but you can add new entries. The subform needs to be modified so that all of its columns are readable without horizontal scrolling. To change the properties of the Personnel Actions subform, follow these steps:

1. Close the frmPersonnelActions form.

2. Open the sbfPersonnelActions subform from the Database window in Design View.

3. Select the form, and use the Properties window to make sure that the Grid X and Grid Y properties are both set to 24, then close the Properties window.

4. Using the same techniques you used when working with the main form, resize the label boxes in the Form Header section of the form, so that they match what you saw in figure 12.26. Use the Format Painter to center the text in every text label in the Form Header section.

5. Adjust the field text boxes in the Detail section of the form, if necessary, to line up with the headings in the Form Header section (refer to fig. 12.26).

6. Drag the right edge of the form to the left until the form is 5 3/8" in width, then drag the Form Footer upward so that the Detail section is about 5/8" high.

7. Choose Edit, Select Form to select the form, then click the Properties button on the toolbar to display the Properties window for the subform.

8. Click the Data tab in the Properties window so that the Allow Edits, Allow Deletions, and Allow Additions properties are visible.

9. Set the Allow Edits property to No; this prevents the user from editing records displayed in this subform.

10. Set the Allow Deletions property to No; this prevents the user from deleting records displayed in this subform.

11. Set the Allow Additions property to Yes; this enables the user to add new records in this subform.

12. Close the sbfPersonnelActions subform and save your changes.

To see how the new form and subform look, open the frmPersonnelActions form; the adjusted form and subform should appear similar to figure 12.28. Notice that there's no horizontal scroll bar, and that the appearance and visibility of fields and column headings in the subform has improved. By changing the size of the subform control in the main form, and resizing the subform to fit completely within the subform control (allowing room for the vertical scrollbar) the subform now fits completely in the main form. Notice also the tentative append record visible as the second record in the subform.

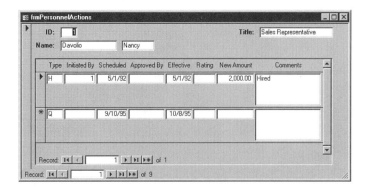

Fig. 12.28   The completed frmPersonnelActions and sbfPersonnelActions forms in Form View displayed in normal window mode.

> **Note**
>
> You can set the Data Entry property to Yes to achieve a result similar to setting the Allow Edits and Allow Deletions property to No and setting the Allow Additions property to Yes. When you set the Data Entry property to Yes, however, only the tentative new record appears—no prior entries appear in the subform.

You can change the default view of the subform to a continuous form that you can modify to display the data in another format. When displaying historical data, the Datasheet View (a tabular view) is usually the best choice because it is the easiest to implement.

Using Transaction-Processing Forms

As noted near the beginning of this chapter, the purpose of transaction-processing forms is to add new records to, delete records from, or edit data in one or more tables that underlie the form. This section describes how to add new records to the Personnel Actions table with the frmPersonnelActions form.

Toolbar Buttons in Form View

When you display your form in Run mode (Form View), the toolbar contains the command buttons listed in Table 12.4. This table lists all the buttons that appear on the toolbar, along with each one's function and the equivalent menu choice.

Table 12.4 Standard Toolbar Buttons in Form Run Mode		
Button	**Function**	**Menu Choice**
	Selects Form Design mode.	View, Form Design
	Saves the form layout.	File, Save
	Prints the form.	File, Print
	Selects Print Preview to display how your form will appear if printed. You can print the form directly from the Print Preview window.	File, Print Preview
	Starts the spelling checker to check the spelling of the current selection or field.	Tools, Spelling
	Cuts the current selection and places it on the Windows Clipboard.	Edit, Cut
	Copies the current selection to the Windows Clipboard.	Edit, Copy

(continues)

III

Forms and Reports

Table 12.4	**Continued**	
Button	**Function**	**Menu Choice**
	Pastes the current contents of the Windows Clipboard onto the form.	Edit, Paste
	Format Painter. This button is always disabled in Form View.	n/a
	Undoes the most recent change to a record.	Edit, Undo
	Sorts records in ascending order, based on the current field.	Records, Sort, Ascending
	Sorts records in descending order, based on the current field.	Records, Sort, Descending
	Filters records based on selected text in a field.	Records, Filter, Filter by Selection
	Filters records based on criteria you enter in a form's fields.	Records, Filter, Filter by Form
	Applies a filter. Click this button a second time to show all records.	Records, Apply Filter/Sort or Records, Remove Filter/Sort
	Searches for a value in the selected field or in all fields. Displays the Find dialog.	Edit, Find
	Goes to the tentative append record.	Edit, Go To, New
	Deletes the current record.	Edit, Delete Record
	Gives the Database window the focus.	Window 1 Database
	Displays a drop-down list of new database objects.	n/a
	Displays context-sensitive help for forms in Run mode.	F1 key

The Find button serves the same purpose for forms in Run mode as it does for tables and queries. You enter characters in the Find dialog—using wild cards if needed—and when you execute the search, Access displays the first record that matches your entry.

The Sort Ascending, Sort Descending, Filter by Selection, and Filter by Form buttons work the same way in Form View as they do in Datasheet View; using these filter buttons was described in Chapter 6, "Sorting, Finding, and Filtering Data in Tables." Sorting specified in the form overrides the sort criteria of the primary query used as the source of the data (if your form is based on a query, rather than based directly on one or more tables). The filter or sort criteria you specify don't take effect until you click the Apply Filter/Sort button or make the equivalent Records, Apply Filter/Sort menu choice.

Using the Personnel Actions Form

Forms you create with the Form Wizard use the standard record-selection buttons located at the bottom of the form. The record-selection buttons perform the same functions with forms as they do with tables and queries. You can select the first or last records in the table or query that's the source of data for your main form, or you can select the next or previous record. Subforms always include their own set of record-selection buttons that operate independently of the set for the main form.

Navigation between the text boxes used for entering or editing data in the form is similar to navigation in queries and tables in Datasheet View, except that the up-arrow and down-arrow keys cause the caret to move between fields rather than between records. Accept the values you've entered by pressing Enter or Tab.

To edit or append new records to a table in Form View, the Allow Editing property must be set to Yes (which is the default). You can only change this property by using the Properties window for the form in Form Design View (as you did earlier in this chapter for the subform).

Appending New Records to the Personnel Actions Table

In Datasheet View of a table or query, the last record in the datasheet is provided as a *tentative append record* (indicated by an asterisk on the record-selection button). If you enter data in this record, the data automatically is appended to the table, and Access starts a new tentative append record. Forms also provide a tentative append record, unless you have set the Allow Additions property for the form to No.

To append a new record to the Personnel Actions table and enter the required data, follow these steps:

1. Open the frmPersonnelActions form if it is not already open, or click the Form View button if you are in Design View. Data for the first record of the Employees table—with the matching data from the corresponding record(s) in the Personnel Actions table—appears in the text-box controls of your form.

   Because data from the Employees table is included in the main form, the ID number, name, and title of the employee appear in the text boxes on the main form. Access lets you edit the LastName, FirstName, and Title data, although these fields are incorporated in the table (Employees) on the one side of a one-to-many relationship. The editing capability of a form is the same as that for the underlying table or query that serves as its source, unless you change this by setting the form's Allow Editing property and other related properties.

   If you added an entry for the chosen employee ID when you created the Personnel Actions table in Chapter 4, "Working with Access Databases and Tables," the entry appears in the subform's fields. The subform's data display is linked to the data in the main form through the one-to-many relationship between the Employees table and the Personnel Actions table. The subform only displays records from the Personnel Actions table whose paID match the value of the EmployeeID field of the record currently displayed by the main form.

2. Access places the caret in the first text box of the main form, the ID text box. Our first example uses Steven Buchanan, whose employee ID is 5, so you should do the following: click the Find button on the toolbar to open the Find dialog, type **5** in the Find What text box, make sure that the Search Only Current Field option is selected, and click Find First. Access displays the Employees table data for Steven Buchanan in the main form, and his Personnel Actions records in the subform. Click Close to close the Find dialog.

3. Click in the Type field of the tentative append record in the subform. If the tentative append record in the subform isn't visible, click in any field in the subform, then click the New Record button on the toolbar to move to the tentative append record at the end of the existing Personnel Actions table entries for Steven Buchanan.

4. The controls of the tentative append record in the subform become empty, except for those fields with default values assigned to them.

5. Access places the caret in the first text box of the subform, the Type (paType field) text box. Enter a valid Personnel Action type (H, S, Q, Y, B, or C, because of the field's validation rule) in the Type text box. In this example, you bring Steven Buchanan's Personnel Actions records up-to-date by adding quarterly performance review information, so you can stick with the default value, **Q**. Press Tab or Enter to accept the Type and move the caret to the next data-entry text box, Initiated By.

6. Mr. Buchanan reports to the Vice President of Sales, Andrew Fuller, whose employee ID is 2. Enter **2** in the Initiated By text box, and press Enter.

The pencil symbol, which indicates that you are editing a record, replaces the triangle at the top of the Record Selector bar to the left of the record you're entering. The Description property you entered for the field in the table underlying this query appears in the status bar and changes as you move the caret to the next field. (To change a previous entry, press Shift+Tab, or use the up- and down-arrow keys to maneuver to whichever text box contains a value you want to change.)

7. Mr. Buchanan was hired on 10/17/93, so his first quarterly performance review should be dated about three months after that, so use a date near **1/2/94** for the Scheduled text box. Today's date is the default for the paScheduled date. Edit the date, or press F2 to select the default date, and then replace the default value with a new date.

8. Because Mr. Fuller is a vice president, he has the authority to approve salary increases. Enter Mr. Fuller's employee ID, **2**, in the Approved By text box, and press Enter to move the caret to the next field.

9. The effective date for salary adjustments for Northwind Traders is the first or fifteenth day of the month in which the performance review is scheduled. Enter the appropriate date in the Effective text box.

10. You can enter any number from **0** (terminated) to **9** (excellent) in the Rating text box, which reflects the employee's performance.

11. You can be as generous as you want with the salary increase that you enter in the New Amount text box. The value of the New Amount is a new monthly salary (or a new commission percentage), not an incremental value.

12. Add any comments you care to make concerning how generous or stingy you were with this salary increase in the Comments multiline text box to the right of the New Amount field. The multiline text box includes a scroll bar that appears when the caret is within the text box.

13. When you complete your entries, Access stores them in a memory buffer but does not add the new record to the Personnel Actions table. You can add the record to the table by doing any of the following: pressing Shift+Enter; choosing <u>R</u>ecords, Save Rec<u>o</u>rd; clicking the New Record button; or changing the position of the record pointer with the Prior or Next record selector button. If you want to cancel the addition of a record, press Esc.

14. Repeat steps 3 through 13 to add a few additional records.

Tip

If you ever click the New Record button on the toolbar (or the Next record selector button) and decide that you don't want to add any more data, simply click the Prior button to make sure this new record is not added to the table.

After you add several records, your form appears like the one shown in figure 12.29. Each record for an employee appears in the subform datasheet in the order of the primary key fields of the Personnel Actions table.

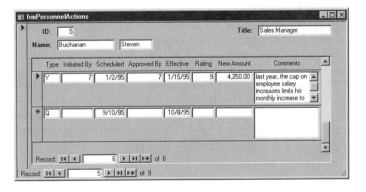

Fig. 12.29   The Personnel Actions form after appending several subform records for a single employee.

The key fields of the Personnel Actions table are paID, paType, and paScheduledDate; duplicate values of the combination of the three fields aren't allowed. If you try to enter a duplicate of another record, the message box shown in figure 12.30 appears. If you still want to add the new record, you must change the Type or Scheduled Date entry to be different from the existing record.

Fig. 12.30   The message box that results when you try to complete a duplicate entry.

Editing Existing Data

You can edit existing records the same way you add new records. Use the Next button to find the record you want to edit, and then make your changes. You can use the toolbar's Find button to locate records by employee ID, by one of the dates in the record, or by a word or phrase contained in the paComments field. If you prefer that the records be ordered by paEffective date to find all records for which an effective date hasn't been entered, use the Filter by Form button and specify an Ascending Sort on the paEffective field. Click the Apply Filter button to apply the sort to the records.

Committing and Rolling Back Changes to Tables

As with tentative append records, Access does not apply record edits to the underlying table until you move the record pointer with the record-selection buttons (or choose Records, Save Record). Either action is the equivalent of the CommitTrans instruction in transaction-processing terminology.

Rollback reverses a CommitTrans instruction. You can do the equivalent of rolling back a single transaction by clicking the Undo button on the toolbar immediately after you save the record to the table (or by choosing Edit, Undo Saved Record if that choice is available).

Deleting a Record in Form View

To delete the current record underlying the form (either the main form or a subform), click the Delete Record button on the toolbar (or choose Edit, Delete Record). Access displays the message box shown in figure 12.31, asking you to confirm the permanent removal of the record you've selected. Click Yes to delete the record.

Access also enables you to delete records by clicking the vertical record selection bar to the left of the Detail section of the form. The vertical record selection bar becomes a darker shade of gray, and the triangle used to identify a selected record appears at the top of the bar. Press Del, and the confirmation message appears. Click Yes to delete the record, or click No if you've changed your mind.

Fig. 12.31   The message box that asks you to confirm or cancel the deletion of a record.

Note

You can't use the sbfPersonnelActions form to delete records from the Personnel Actions table, because you set the Allow Deletions property to No when you modified the subform earlier in this chapter. The main form, however, will permit you to delete records from the Employees table. If you want to experiment with deleting records from the Personnel Actions table in the subform, open the sbfPersonnelActions form in Design mode, and change the Allow Deletions property (on the Data tab of the Properties window for the form) to Yes.

Modifying the Properties of a Form or Control after Testing

The entries you added and edited gave you an opportunity to test your form. Testing a form to ensure that it accomplishes the objectives you have in mind usually takes much longer than creating the form and the query that underlies it. During the testing process, you might notice that the order of the fields isn't what you want, or that records in the subform aren't displayed in an appropriate sequence. The following two sections deal with modifying the properties of the form and the subform control.

Changing the Order of Fields for Data Entry

The order in which the editing caret moves from one field to the next is determined by the Tab Order property of each control. The Form Wizard established the tab order of the controls when you first created the form. The default Tab Order property of each field is assigned, beginning with the value 0, in the sequence in which you add the fields. Because the Form Wizard created a single-column form, the order of the controls in Personnel Actions is top to bottom. The tab order originally assigned doesn't change when you relocate a control.

To change the sequence of entries—for example, to match the pattern of entries on a paper form—follow these steps:

1. Click the Design View button on the toolbar.

III

Forms and Reports

2. Choose <u>V</u>iew, Tab Ord<u>e</u>r to display the Tab Order dialog shown in figure 12.32. The order of entry is shown by the sequence of field names in the Custom Order list. (In this example, changing the sequence of the entries is unnecessary because the sequence is logical, even after moving the controls to their present locations on the Personnel Actions form.)

3. Click the Auto Order button if you want to reorder the entry sequence going left to right across each row of fields, then top to bottom.

4. Drag any control to a new location by clicking the button at the left of its name and dropping it wherever you want it to be in the sequence.

5. Click OK to implement the changes you made; click Cancel to retain the original entry sequence.

> **Note**
>
> Using the Auto Order button to change the tab order of fields on a form also changes the left-to-right order of the table fields in Datasheet View to correspond to the Auto Order field sequence.

Fig. 12.32   The Tab Order dialog is used to change the sequence of data-entry fields.

Removing Fields from the Tab Order

Access 95 enables you to set the value of the Tab Stop property to No to prevent controls from receiving the focus in the tab order. To remove a control from the tab order, select the control; open the Properties window; select Other Properties; and change the value of Tab Stop to No (see fig. 12.33). You cannot edit the EmployeeID field, so set the Tab Stop property to No for this control.

> **Note**
>
> Setting the Tab Stop property's value to No does not disable a given control, but it removes the control from the tab sequence.

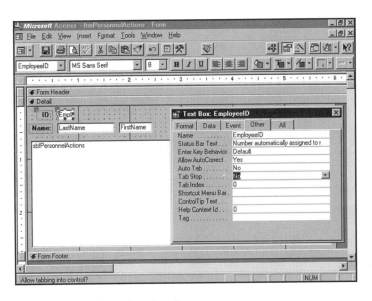

Fig. 12.33 Removing a field from the tab order.

Changing the Source of Data for the Subform and Sorting the Subform Data

The Personnel Actions table is indexed by paType and paScheduledDate, but the sequence of the records appears in the order of the primary key: paID, paType, and paScheduledDate. Because only paID is used to link the records, records for a particular employee appear in the order of the remaining key fields, paType and paScheduledDate. Eventually, the number of records for an employee can become quite large, so having the records appear in type and date order is convenient. Because only a few records can be displayed in the subform datasheet, the latest entries should appear by default. This requires a descending sort on the Personnel Actions table. You can establish a descending sort only by substituting a sorted query containing all the records of the Personnel Actions table, as described in the following two procedures.

To create a new sorted query, follow these steps:

1. Close the Personnel Action entry form, and make the Database window active.

2. Click the Queries tab of the Database window, and then click the New button to create a new query. With Design View selected in the New Query dialog, click OK.

3. In the Show Table dialog, select Personnel Actions as the table on which to base the query; click Add and then click Close.

4. Drag the * field to the Query grid, and drop it in the first column.

5. Drag the paScheduledDate field to the Query grid, and drop it in the second column.

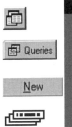

Forms and Reports

6. Click to remove the check mark from the Show box in the new paScheduledDate column, so that you don't duplicate a field name in the query. Add a descending sort to the paScheduledDate column (see fig. 12.34).

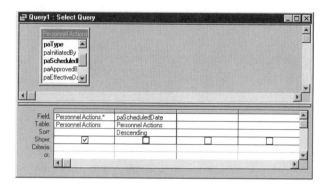

Fig. 12.34   The query design for the subform with all the personnel actions sorted in descending date sequence.

7. Click the Run Query button to check to see that the records are sorted in reverse chronological order.

8. Close your query and name it **qryPersonnelActionsSubform**.

To change the data source for the subform to the new sorted query, complete the following steps:

1. Click the Form tab in the Database window, and open the sbfPersonnelActions subform in Design mode.

2. Click the Properties button to display the Properties window, then click the Data tab.

3. Click the Record Source box, open the list, and select qryPersonnelActionsSubform as the new data source for the subform (see fig. 12.35).

4. If you want to review the design of the table or query you select as the value of the Record Source property, click the ellipsis button to display the source object in Design mode.

5. Close the Properties window, and click the Form View button on the toolbar to verify that the datasheet display is correct.

6. Close the sbfPersonnelActions subform.

7. Reopen the Personnel Actions form. Use Find in the main part of the form to locate the employee for whom you added additional records in the Personnel Actions table. The history in the subform now appears sorted, with the most recent dates first.

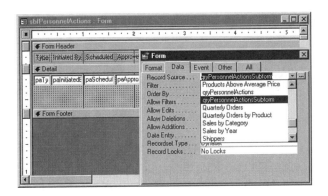

Fig. 12.35 Use the Record Source property of the subform to change the underlying data source from a table to a query.

8. To verify that the sort stays active when you add new entries, add a new record with today's date and then click the Prior button to save the new entry. Click Next to display the new entry so you can be sure the sorting is functional.

You can use the same method described in the preceding steps to change the data source of a main form. For example, you could create a query for the main form so that the records in the form are displayed alphabetically by last name, instead of in numerical order by EmployeeID.

Troubleshooting

I receive an error message in the Scheduled column of the subform datasheet every time I try to run the query.

You didn't click the Show box in step 6 of the set of instructions given earlier for creating the new query. When a field is duplicated in a query, Access doesn't know which of the two fields to use if the Show check box is marked for both fields.

Note

Pressing Shift+Enter (or choosing <u>R</u>ecords, Save Rec<u>o</u>rd) to save a record does not update the subform, and the new entry is not displayed in the subform. You must choose <u>R</u>ecords, Refres<u>h</u> to update the subform's display. The Refres<u>h</u> command doesn't requery the database, but does cause any updates that have occurred since the last automatic refreshing operation to appear. The best approach, therefore, is to use the record position buttons to commit the new or edited record. The Refresh command is discussed in Chapter 25, "Securing Multiuser Network Applications."

III

Forms and Reports

From Here...

This chapter demonstrated the capabilities of relatively simple Access forms, created by the Form Wizard, to add and edit data. You learned to relocate, resize, and edit control objects that the Form Wizard added to a form for you. The chapter also explained the basic steps involved in using a form to add, edit, and delete records. After testing your form, you made changes to the form's design to make it more effective. Database application developers use this process to create sophisticated forms that ultimately comprise a full-scale database application.

The Form Wizard uses only text-box controls with associated labels to create the basic form. The Access toolbox provides many other types of controls you can add to a form that you create without the Form Wizard's help.

■ Chapter 8, "Using Query by Example," shows you how to create queries to serve as the Record Source property of forms.

■ Chapter 13, "Designing Custom Multitable Forms," describes how to use the Access toolbox to design a form starting with a blank form.

■ Chapters 14, "Printing Basic Reports and Mailing Labels," and 15, "Preparing Advanced Reports," apply the techniques you learned in this chapter to the task of creating reports.

Chapter 13

Designing Custom Multitable Forms

The controls that the Form Wizard adds to the forms it creates are only a sampling of the 18 control functions offered by Access. Until now, you used the Form Wizard to create the labels, text boxes, and subform controls for displaying and editing data in the Personnel Actions table. These three kinds of controls are sufficient to create a conventional transaction processing form; you can duplicate a conventional dBASE or Paradox 4+ DOS data entry screen by using only Access labels and text boxes.

The remaining 15 controls, described in this chapter, enable you to take full advantage of the Windows graphical user environment. You add controls to the form by using the Access Toolbox. List boxes and combo boxes increase data entry productivity and accuracy by enabling you to choose from a list of predefined values rather than requiring you to type the value. Option buttons, toggle buttons, and check boxes supply values to Yes/No fields. If you place option buttons, toggle buttons, and check boxes in an option frame, these controls can supply the numeric values you specify. Access 95's new Image control supplements the Bound and Unbound Object Frame controls for adding pictures to your forms. Page breaks control how forms print. Command buttons enable you to execute Access macros or Access VBA procedures. OLE controls, which greatly expand the versatility of Access forms, are one of the subjects of Chapter 19, "Using 32-Bit OLE 2.1."

Understanding the Access Toolbox

The Access Toolbox was based on the Toolbox created for Microsoft Visual Basic. Essentially, the Access Toolbox is a variety of toolbar. You choose one of the 18 tools to add a control, represented by that tool's symbol, to the form. When you create a report, the Toolbox serves the same purpose—although tools that require user input, such as combo boxes, are seldom used in reports.

In this chapter, you learn to:

- Use the Access Toolbox to add control objects

- Take advantage of the Access Control Wizards

- Create a useful form from a blank form

- Add an option group to a form

- Add combo boxes to a form

- Add a linked subform to a main form

III

Forms and Reports

Control Categories

Three control object categories exist in Access forms and reports:

- *Bound controls* are associated with a field in the data source for the form or subform. The data source can be a table or query. Bound controls display and update values of the data cell in the associated field of the currently selected record. Text boxes are the most common bound control. You can display the content of graphic objects or play a waveform audio file with a bound OLE object. You can bind toggles, check boxes, and option buttons to Yes/No fields. All bound controls have associated labels that display the Caption property of the field; you can edit or delete these labels without affecting the bound control.

- *Unbound controls* display data you provide that is independent of the data source of the form or subform. You use the unbound OLE object to add a drawing or bitmapped image to a form. You can use lines and rectangles to divide a form into logical groups, or to simulate boxes used on the paper form. Unbound text boxes are used to enter data not intended to update a field in the data source but for other purposes, such as establishing a value used in an expression. Some unbound controls, such as unbound text boxes, include labels; others, such as unbound OLE objects, don't include labels.

- *Calculated controls* use expressions as their source of data. Usually, the expression includes the value of a field, but you also can use values created by unbound text boxes in calculated control expressions.

The Toolbox

 You use the Access Toolbox to add control objects to forms and reports. The Toolbox appears only in Design mode for forms and reports, and appears only if you click the Toolbox button on the toolbar or toggle the View, Toolbox menu command. When the Toolbox is visible, the Toolbox menu choice is checked; the Toolbox is shown in figure 13.1. You can choose from the 18 controls and one wizard button whose names and functions are listed in table 13.1.

Fig. 13.1 The Access 95 Toolbox in its floating window.

Table 13.1 Control Objects of the Access Toolbox

Tool	Name	Function
	Pointer	Deselects a previously selected tool and returns the mouse pointer to normal function. Pointer is the default tool when you display the Toolbox.
	Control Wizards	Turns the Control Wizards on and off. Control Wizards are a new feature of Access 2.0 that aid you in designing complex controls, such as option groups, list boxes, and combo boxes.
	Label	Creates a box that contains fixed descriptive or instructional text.
	Text Box	Creates a box to display and allow editing of text data.
	Option Group	Creates a frame of adjustable size in which you can place toggle buttons, option buttons, or check boxes. Only one of the objects within an object group frame may be selected. When you select an object within an option group, the previously selected object is deselected.
	Toggle Button	Creates a button that changes from On to Off when clicked. The On state corresponds to Yes (–1), and the Off state corresponds to No (0). When used within an option group, toggling one button On toggles a previously selected button Off. You can use toggle buttons to let the user select one value from a set of values.
	Option Button	Creates a round button (originally called a *radio button*) that behaves identically to a toggle button. Option buttons are most commonly used within option groups to select between values in a set.
	Check Box	Creates a check box that toggles On and Off. Multiple check boxes should be used outside of option groups so that you can select more than one check box at a time.
	Combo Box	Creates a combo box with an editable text box where you can enter a value, as well as a list from which you can select a value from a set of choices.
	List Box	Creates a drop-down list box from which you can select a value. A list box is simply the list portion of a combo box.
	Command Button	Creates a command button that, when clicked, triggers an event that can execute an Access macro or an Access VBA event-handling procedure.
	Image	Displays a static graphic on a form or report. This is *not* an OLE-type picture, so you can't edit it after placing it on the form.
	Unbound Object	Adds an OLE object, created by an OLE server application, such as Microsoft Graph or Microsoft Draw, to a form or report. The Custom Control object is a special version of the Unbound Object that contains OLE Controls.
	Bound Object	Displays the content of an OLE field of a record, if the field contains a graphic object. If the field contains no graphic object, the icon that represents the object appears, such as the Sound Recorder's icon for a linked or embedded .WAV file. Data-bound OLE Controls are stored in a special version of the Bound Object.

III

Forms and Reports

(continues)

Tool	Name	Function
Table 13.1	**Continued**	
	Page Break	Causes the printer to start a new page at the location of the page break on the form or report. Page breaks don't appear in form or report Run mode.
	Subform	Adds a subform or subreport to a main form or report, respectively. The subform or subreport you intend to add must exist before you use this control.
	Line	Creates a straight line that you can size and relocate. The color and width of the line can be changed by using the Formatting toolbar buttons or the Properties window.
	Rectangle	Creates a rectangle that you can size and relocate. The border color, width, and fill color of the rectangle are determined by selections from the palette.

Using controls in the design of reports is discussed in the following two chapters, which are devoted entirely to the subject of Access reports. The use of bound and unbound OLE objects is described in Chapter 20, "Adding Graphics to Forms and Reports." Using command buttons to execute macros is covered in Part IV of this book, which deals with Access macros. Writing Access VBA code to respond to command button clicks is included in Part VII. You learn how to use the remaining 15 controls on your forms in the following sections.

Access's Control Wizards, Builders, and Toolbars

Access provides a number of features to aid you in designing and using more complex forms. Three of these features—Control Wizards, Builders, and customizable toolbars—are described in the three sections that follow.

Access Control Wizards. Much of the success of Access is attributable to the Form Wizard, Report Wizard, and Graph Wizard that simplify the process of creating database objects. The first wizard appeared in Microsoft Publisher, and most of Microsoft's productivity applications now include a variety of wizards. Chapter 12, "Creating and Using Forms," introduced the Form Wizard; the Report Wizard is discussed in Chapter 14, "Printing Basic Reports and Mailing Labels;" and the Graph Wizard is described in Chapters 19, "Using 32-Bit OLE 2.1," and 20, "Adding Graphics to Forms and Reports." Developers can create custom wizards to perform a variety of duties. You can expect a wide range of wizards to become available from independent software vendors (ISVs) as Access continues to gain adherents.

Access's repertoire of wizards includes Control Wizards that lead you step-by-step through the design of more complex control objects, such as option groups, list boxes, and combo boxes. Designing and populating list and combo boxes requires several steps. In this chapter, you are introduced to a Control Wizard each time you add a control for which a wizard is available.

Access Builders. Builders are another feature that makes Access easy to use. You use the ExpressionBuilder, introduced in Chapter 4, "Working with Access Databases and Tables," to create expressions that supply values to calculated controls on a form or report. The QueryBuilder creates the SQL statements you need when you create list boxes or combo boxes whose Row Source property is an SQL statement that executes a select query. Using the QueryBuilder to insert SQL statements created by graphical QBE is much simpler than the method originally used with Access 1.x: you had to create a query, open the SQL window, copy the SQL statement to the clipboard, and then paste it to the Row Source property's text box. Using the QueryBuilder is described in the "Using the QueryBuilder to Populate a Combo Box" section, near the end of this chapter.

Customizable Toolbars. The preceding chapters demonstrated that the toolbars of Access include many shortcut buttons to expedite the design and use of Access database objects. Access 95, like most other contemporary Microsoft applications, lets you customize the toolbars to your own set of preferences. If you have experience with Access 2.0 or Excel 5.0+, you'll find Access 95's toolbar customization process to be quite familiar. Access 1.x stored toolbars as forms in UTILITY.MDA. Access 2.0 used the 16-bit common toolbar Dynamic Link Library, COMMTB.DLL, to manipulate toolbars. Access 95 uses the 32-bit version of the common toolbar Dynamic Link Library, Commtb32.dll, and (like Access 2.0) stores definitions of your customized versions of standard toolbars in the MSysToolbars table of System.mdw. The significance of storing your preferences in System.mdw is discussed in Chapter 25, "Securing Multiuser Network Applications."

You can convert conventional floating design tools, such as the Toolbox, to conventional toolbars by the drag-and-drop method. To anchor the Toolbox as a toolbar, also called *docking* the toolbar, follow these steps:

1. Press and hold down the mouse button while the mouse pointer is on the title bar of the Toolbox, then drag the Toolbox toward the top of Access's parent window.

2. When the Toolbox reaches the toolbar area, the dotted outline changes from a rectangle approximately the size of the Toolbox into a wider rectangle with only as much height as a toolbar.

3. Release the mouse button to change the Toolbox to an anchored toolbar positioned below the standard Form Design toolbar.

> **Note**
>
> You can anchor or dock a toolbar to any edge of Access's parent window. Press and hold down the mouse button on an empty area of the toolbar (not covered by a button), then drag the toolbar until its outline appears along the left, right, or bottom edge of the window. If you drop the toolbar within the confines of Access's main window, it becomes a floating toolbar.

You can add or delete buttons from toolbars with the Customize Toolbars dialog. If you are using the conventional VGA display format (640 by 480 pixels), there is very little room to add new buttons to the Form Design toolbar, and no room to add buttons to the Formatting toolbar. However, the Toolbox toolbar has room to add seven or eight additional buttons when Access's main window is maximized. To add form design utility buttons to the Toolbox toolbar (whether it's docked or floating), do the following:

1. Choose <u>V</u>iew, Tool<u>b</u>ars to display the Toolbars dialog.

2. Click Customize to display the Customize Toolbars dialog.

> **Tip**
>
> You can also open the Customize Toolbars dialog by right-clicking any part of a toolbar, and then choosing Customize on the resulting popup menu.

3. Select Form & Report Design from the Categories list. The optional buttons applicable to form design operations appear in the Buttons area, as shown in figure 13.2.

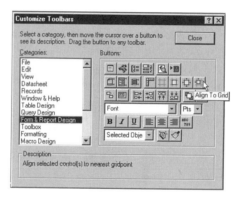

Fig. 13.2   The Toolbox docked as an anchored toolbar at the top of Access' main window, and the open Customize Toolbars dialog.

4. The most useful optional buttons for form design are control alignment and sizing buttons. Press and hold down the mouse button on the Align to Grid button, then drag this button to the Toolbox toolbar and drop it to the right of the Lock button. The right margin of the Toolbox toolbar expands to accommodate the new button (if you customize the Toolbox while it's floating, the window expands to accommodate the new button). You can drag the Snap to Grid button slightly to the right to create a gap between the new button and the Rectangle button.

5. Repeat step 4 for the Size to Fit, Size to Grid, and Align Controls Left buttons, dropping each button to the right of the preceding button. You now have four new buttons available in your Toolbox.

The Toolbars and Customize Toolbars dialogs provide the following additional capabilities:

■ To remove buttons from the toolbar, open the Customize Toolbars dialog; click and drag the buttons you don't want, and drop them in the Buttons window of the dialog.

■ To reset the toolbar to its default design, open the Toolbars dialog. In the Toolbars list, select the toolbar you want to reset, then click the Reset button. A message box asks you to confirm that you want to abandon any changes you made to the tool-bar.

■ To create a button that opens or runs a database object, open the Customize Tool-bars dialog and scroll the Categories list to display the All Objects items. When, for example, you select All Tables, the table of the current database appears in the Objects list. Select a table name, such as Employees, and drag the selected item to an empty spot on a toolbar. The ToolTip for the new button displays "Open Table 'Employees'." (If you select All Macros and drag a macro object to the toolbar, to the button you add runs the macro when clicked.)

■ To substitute text or a different image for the picture on buttons you add to a toolbar, open the Customize Toolbar dialog; then click the button you want to change with the right mouse button to display the button shortcut menu. Click Choose Button Face to display the Choose Button Face dialog. Click one of the images offered, or click the Text check box and type the text you want to display in the text box.

■ To create a new empty toolbar that you can customize with any set of the supplied buttons you want, open the Toolbars dialog and select Utility 1 or Utility 2. If there is space to the right of an existing toolbar, the empty toolbar appears in this space. Otherwise, Access creates a new toolbar row for the empty toolbar.

■ To create a custom toolbar that becomes part of your database, open the Toolbars dialog and click New. The New Toolbar dialog appears, requesting a name for the new toolbar (Toolbar1 is the default). Access creates a new floating tool window to which you add buttons from the Custom Toolbars dialog. You can anchor the cus-tom tool window to the toolbar if you want.

■ To delete a custom toolbar, open the Toolbars dialog, select the custom toolbar, and click the Delete button. You are requested to confirm the deletion. The Delete button is disabled when you select one of Access's standard toolbars in the list.

Custom toolbars to which you assign names become part of your database application, and are stored in the current database file, not in System.mda.

The Appearance of Controls in Design and Run Modes

The appearance in Form Design mode of the 16 different controls you can create with the Toolbox is shown in figure 13.3. Labels were added to the page break, image, un-bound object, bound object, line, and rectangle controls to identify them in the illustra-tion; the labels aren't actually components of the controls.

When you click the Form View button, the controls appear as shown in figure 13.4. The text box displays a #Name? error message because no value is assigned to the content of the text box. The list and combo boxes show some test values, provided only to show how a the control appears in Form View. The image field displays a bitmap copied from the International.wmf graphic with the Size Mode property set to Zoom; the contents of the image field aren't editable. The unbound object field contains the Sea_dusk.wmf graphics file; this file is an embedded OLE object. The bound object field is empty because no value for its content is assigned to it. The subform field displays a portion of the sbfPersonnelActions subform (the field is too small to display a significant portion of the subform). You can't create a subform control unless you enter the name of an existing form as the value.

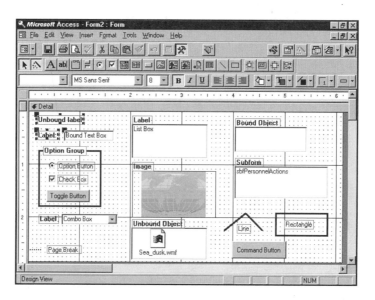

Fig. 13.3 The 16 controls you can create by using the Toolbox, shown in Design mode (with five custom buttons added to the Toolbox toolbar).

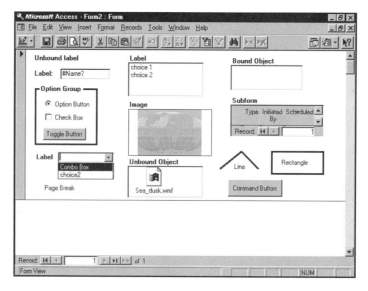

Fig. 13.4 The 16 controls you can create by using the Toolbox, shown in Form View; notice that the list in the combo box has been dropped down.

Using the Toolbox to Add Controls

◄◄ See "Creating the Personnel Actions Table," p. 137
◄◄ See "Changing the Source of Data for the Subform and Sorting the Subform Data," p. 439

Experimenting is the best way of learning how to use a new computer application. No matter how well the product's documentation—or a book such as this one—describes a process, no substitute exists for trying the methods. This axiom holds true whether you are designing a form or writing programming code. The Microsoft programmers who created Access cleverly designed the user interface for creating custom forms so that the interface is intuitive and flexible. After you complete the examples in this chapter, you probably will agree that this is true.

The examples in this chapter use the Personnel Actions table that you created in Chapter 4, "Working with Access Databases and Tables," and two queries: qryPersonnelActions (which you create in the next section of this chapter) and qryPersonnelActionsSubform (which you created in Chapter 12, "Creating and Using Forms"). The data dictionary needed to create the Personnel Actions table appears in Appendix C.

Creating the Query on Which to Base the Main Form

The Personnel Actions table identifies employees only by their ID numbers, located in the paID field. As before, you need to display the employee's name and title on the form to avoid entering records for the wrong person. To obtain the employee's name and title data for the form, you need to create a one-to-many query that joins the Employees table, which has only one entry per employee, with the Personnel Actions table, which can have many entries for one employee.

> **Note**
>
> In the form you created in Chapter 12, you used the Form Wizard to specify the tables from which you wanted to display data on the form. When you create a multitable form from scratch, you need to create a query as a data source for the form. The query joins the data from the tables into a unified source for use by the form.

To create the Personnel Actions query that serves as the data source for your main form, follow these steps:

1. Close any open forms, click the arrow to the right of the New Object button on the toolbar to open the drop-down menu, and click New Query. Next, select New Query in the list of the New Query dialog and click OK. Double-click the Personnel Actions table in the list of tables of the Show Table dialog, to add the Personnel Actions table to your query.

   Alternatively, you can bypass the Show Table dialog step by clicking the Table button of the Database window and then selecting Personnel Actions in the table list. When you click the New Query button with a table selected, the table is added automatically to the new query.

2. Double-click the Employees table in the table list, then click Close. The field list windows for the Personnel Actions and Employees tables appear in the upper pane of the Query Design window.

   If you used the alternative method to add the Personnel Actions table to the query described in step 1, you need to click the Show Table button on the toolbar to open the Show Table dialog to add the Employees table to your query.

3. Choose <u>V</u>iew, Table <u>N</u>ames to add the Tables row to your Query Design grid. (If the Table <u>N</u>ames command already has a check mark next to it, you don't need to choose it.)

4. If you defined relationships for the Personnel Action table as described in Chapter 4, "Working with Access Databases and Tables," the upper pane of the query window appears as shown in figure 13.5; the line connecting the two tables indicates that there is a many-to-one relationship between the paID field in the Personnel Action table and the EmployeeID field of the Employees table. If you didn't define any relationships, the join line won't appear, and you'll need to drag the paID field from the Personnel Actions field list to the EmployeeID field of the Employees field list to create a join between these two fields.

Fig. 13.5   The upper pane of the Query Design window for the Personnel Actions query.

5. Click the * field of the Personnel Actions table, drag it to the first column of the Query Design grid, and drop it in the Personnel Actions column. This adds all the fields to the Personnel Actions table to your query.

6. Click the LastName field of the Employees table, drag it to the Query grid, and drop it in the second column.

7. From the Employees table, click and drag the FirstName, Title, and Photo fields, and drop them in columns 3, 4, and 5 of the Query grid, respectively, as shown in figure 13.6.

Field:	Personnel Actions.*	LastName	FirstName	Title	Photo
Table:	Personnel Actions	Employees	Employees	Employees	Employees
Sort:		Ascending			
Show:	☑	☑	☑	☑	☑
Criteria:					
or:					

Fig. 13.6   The Query grid for the Personnel Actions query.

8. To simplify finding an employee, click the Sort row of the LastName column and select an Ascending sort.

9. Close the new query. Click Yes when the message box asks if you want to save the query.

10. In the Save As dialog, name the query **qryPersonnelActions** and click OK (see fig. 13.7).

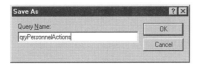

Fig. 13.7 The Save As dialog for the Personnel Actions query.

Now that you've created the query that will provide a unified record source for the main form, you're ready to begin creating your custom multitable form.

Creating a Blank Form with a Header and Footer

When you create a form without using the Form Wizard, Access provides a default blank form to which you add controls that you choose from the Toolbox. To create a blank form with which to experiment with Access controls, perform the following steps:

1. With the Database window active, click the Forms button in the Database window, and then click the New button. Access displays the New Form dialog.

2. Even an experimental form requires a data source, so choose qryPersonnelActions from the drop-down list, choose Design View from the list in the upper-right corner of the New Form dialog, and click OK.

3. Access creates a new blank form with the default title Form1. Click the Maximize button to expand the form to fill the document window.

4. If the Toolbox isn't visible, click the Toolbox button on the toolbar (or choose View, Toolbox) to display the Toolbox. Drag the Toolbox to the top or bottom of the form to anchor it there as a toolbar (do this if the Toolbox isn't already in a docked position—docking the toolbar usually makes it easier to work on a form, because the floating Toolbox window obscures the form underneath it).

5. Choose View, Form Header/Footer. The blank form appears as shown in figure 13.8. If the grid doesn't appear on the form, choose View, Grid.

The default width of blank forms is 5 inches. The default height of the Form Header and Footer sections is 0.25 inch, and the height of the Detail section is 2 inches.

6. To adjust the height of the Detail section of the form, place the mouse pointer on the top line of the Form Footer bar. The mouse pointer becomes a double-headed arrow with a line between the heads. Hold down the left mouse button and drag the bar to create a height of about 2 7/8 inches, measured by the left vertical ruler. The active surface of the form, which is gray with the default 24×24 grid dots, expands vertically as you move the Form Footer bar, as shown in figure 13.9.

Forms and Reports

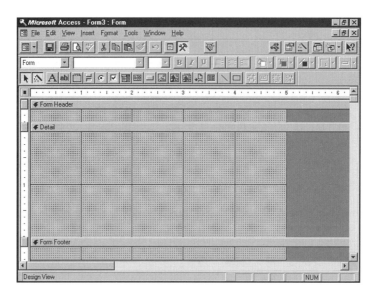

Fig. 13.8 Access's default blank form with Form Header and Form Footer sections added.

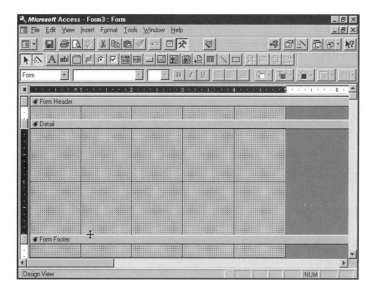

Fig. 13.9 Expanding the Detail section of the blank form.

7. Minimize the Form Footer section by dragging the bottom margin of the form to the bottom of the Form Footer bar.

8. Drag the right margin of the form to 6 inches as measured by the horizontal ruler at the top of the form.

You are using the blank form to create a form similar to the frmPersonnelActions form that you created in Chapter 12, "Creating and Using Forms."

Adding a Label to the Form Header

The label is the simplest control in the Toolbox to use. Labels are unbound and static, and they display only text you enter. *Static* means that the label retains the value you originally assigned for as long as the form is displayed. To add a label to the Form Header section, complete the following steps:

1. Click the Label button in the Toolbox. When you move the mouse pointer to the active area of the form, the pointer becomes the symbol for the Label button, combined with a crosshair to indicate position at its upper left. The center point of the crosshair defines the position of the upper-left corner of the control.

2. Locate the crosshair at the upper-left of the Form Header section. Press and hold down the left mouse button while you drag the crosshair to the position for the lower-right corner of the label (see fig. 13.10).

   As you drag the crosshair, the outline of the container for the label follows your movement. The number of lines and characters that the text box can display in the currently selected font is shown in the status bar.

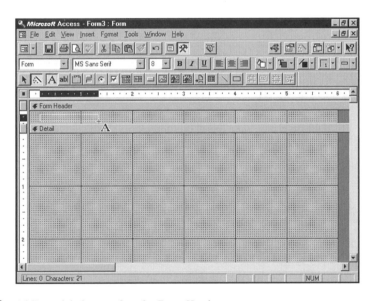

Fig. 13.10   Adding a label control to the Form Header.

3. If you move the crosshair beyond the bottom of the Form Header section, the Form Header bar expands to accommodate the size of the label. When the label is the size you want, release the mouse button.

4. The mouse pointer becomes the text editing caret inside the outline of the label. Enter **Personnel Action Entry** as the text for the label. If you don't type at least one text character in a label after creating it, the box disappears the next time you click the mouse.

◀◀ See "Selecting, Moving, and Sizing a Single Control," p. 420

 You use the basic process described in the preceding steps to add most of the other types of controls to a form. (Some Toolbox buttons, such as the graph and command buttons, launch a Control Wizard to help you create the control, if the Control Wizards button is activated.) After you add the control, you use the anchor and sizing handles described in Chapter 12, "Creating and Using Forms," to move the control to the desired position and to size the control to accommodate the content. The location of the anchor handle determines the Left (horizontal) and Top (vertical) properties of the control. The sizing handles establish the control's Width and Height properties.

Formatting Text and Adjusting Text Control Sizes

When a control is selected that accepts text as the value, the typeface and font size combo boxes appear on the toolbar. To format the text that appears in a label or text box, complete the following steps:

1. Click the Personnel Action Entry label you created in the previous section to select the label.

2. Double-click the label (or click the Properties button on the toolbar) to display the Properties window. (You don't actually need to use the Properties window to make these formatting changes; you open the Properties window to help you learn about how the changes you make to a control with toolbar buttons and menu commands affects the control's properties.)

 3. Open the Font Name list on the Formatting toolbar and select the typeface family you want. MS Sans Serif, the default, is recommended because all users of Windows 95 have this bitmapped font. (MS Sans Serif is quite similar to Linotype Company's Helvetica typeface, or the Arial TrueType typeface also supplied with Windows 95.) Sans serif faces are easier to read on forms than faces with serifs, such as MS Serif or Times New Roman. (Serif faces are easier to read when a large amount of text is involved, such as in newspapers or the body text of this book.)

4. Open the Font Size list, and select 14 points.

5. Click the Bold attribute button on the toolbar.

6. The size of the label you created isn't large enough to display the larger font. To adjust the size of the label to accommodate the content of the label, click the Size to Fit button—if you added it to the Toolbox—or choose Format, Size, To Fit. Access resizes the label's text box to display the entire label; if necessary, Access also increases the size of the Form Header section.

> **Note**
>
> The two sizing commands (Size to Grid and Size to Fit) work slightly differently, depending on whether one or more controls are selected. If one or more controls are selected when you execute one of the sizing commands, the command is applied to the selected control(s). If no controls are

selected, the chosen sizing command applies as the default to all objects you subsequently create, move, or resize.

When you change the properties of a control, the new values are reflected in the Properties window for the control, as shown in figure 13.11. If you move or resize the label, you see the label's Left, Top, Width, and Height values change in the Properties window. You usually use the Properties window to actually change the characteristics of a control only if a toolbar button or a menu choice isn't available.

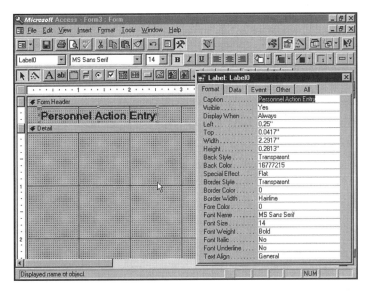

Fig. 13.11 The form title label and its Properties window.

You can choose different fonts and the bold, italic, and underline attributes (or a combination) for any label or caption for a control. You can assign the text content of list boxes and combo boxes to a typeface or size other than the default, but this practice is uncommon in Windows applications.

Creating Bound, Multiline, and Calculated Text Boxes

Access uses the following four basic kinds of text boxes:

- *Single-line text boxes* usually are bound to controls on the form or to fields in a table or query.

- *Multiline text boxes* usually are bound to Memo field types and include a vertical scroll bar to allow access to text that doesn't fit within the dimensions of the box.

- *Calculated text boxes* obtain values from expressions that begin with = (equal sign) and usually are a single line. If you include a field value, such as [paScheduledDate], in the expression for a calculated text box, the text box is bound to that field. Otherwise, calculated text boxes are unbound. You cannot edit the value of a calculated text box.

- *Unbound text boxes* that aren't calculated text boxes can be used to supply values, such as limiting dates, to macros or Access VBA procedures.

The following sections show you how to create the first three types of text boxes.

Adding a Text Box Bound to a Field. The most common text box used in Access forms is the single-line bound text box that comprises the majority of the controls of the frmPersonnelActions form you created in Chapter 12. To add a text box that is bound to a field of the form's data source with the field list window, complete the following steps:

1. Click the Field List button on the toolbar. The field list window appears.

2. Click the paID field in the field list window. Hold down the mouse button and drag the field to the upper-left of the Detail section of the form. When you move the mouse pointer to the active area of the form, the pointer becomes a field symbol but no crosshair appears. The position of the field symbol indicates the upper-left corner of the text box, not the label, so drop the symbol in the approximate position of the text box anchor handle, as shown in figure 13.12.

3. Drag the text box by the anchor handle closer to the ID label, and decrease the box's width.

4. Small type sizes outside of a field text box are more readable when you set the bold attribute on. Choose the ID label and click the Bold button.

5. Choose File, Save, then type the name **frmPersonnelActionsEntry** in the Form Name text box of the Save As dialog; click OK.

> **Note**
>
> When Access creates a text label associated with a form control, it uses the bound object's name as the value for the text label. If the form control is bound to a table object, such as a field, that has a Caption property (and the Caption property isn't blank), then Access uses the value of the Caption property as the default value for the text label of the bound form control. In Chapter 4, "Working with Access Databases and Tables," when you created the Personnel Actions table, you set the Caption property for each field name. The paID field has a Caption property set to ID, so the label for the text box bound to the paID field is also ID.

Steps 3 and 4 in the preceding example are included to show how to make minor design adjustments to controls that improve the appearance of forms. Step 5 was included because you've already spent some effort on this sample form (which you'll continue to experiment with and eventually complete in the following sections of this chapter), and it's good working practice to save your documents frequently.

Adding a Multiline Text Box with Scroll Bars. Although you can use a conventional text box to display comments or other text fields with lengthy content, you must then scroll the caret through the text box to read the content. Multiline text boxes enable you to display long strings of text as a series of lines whose width is determined by the width of the multiline text box. To create a multiline text box, perform the following steps:

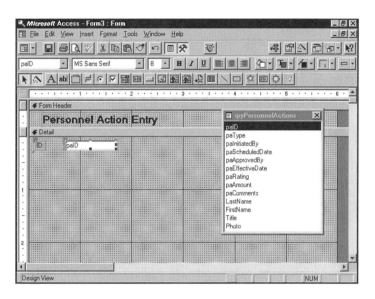

Fig. 13.12 Adding a text box control bound to the paID field.

1. Click and drag paComments from the field list window to about the middle of the Detail section, and drop it there.

2. Delete the Comments label, and size the text box as shown in figure 13.13.

3. Click the Properties button on the toolbar, and click the Format tab in the Properties window. Scroll the Format Properties list for the text box until the Scroll Bars property appears.

4. Open the drop-down list for the Scroll Bars property, and choose Vertical to add a vertical scroll bar to the Comments text box.

5. If you plan to print the form, change the Can Grow and Can Shrink properties from No to Yes, for the height of the printed version of the form to vary with the number of lines of text in the box. The Can Grow and Can Shrink properties don't affect the appearance of the form in Run mode.

> **Note**
>
> The vertical scroll bar of a multiline text box is visible only in the form's Run mode, and then only when the multiline text box has the focus (when the caret is within the text box).

Creating a Calculated Text Box. You can display the result of all valid Access expressions in a calculated text box. An expression must begin with = (equal sign) and may use Access functions to return values. As mentioned in the introduction to this section, you can use calculated text boxes to display calculations based on the values of fields. To create a calculated text box that displays the current date and time, complete the following steps:

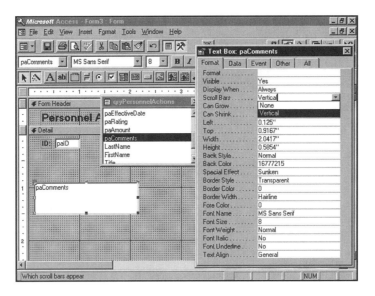

Fig. 13.13   Adding the multiline paComments text box.

    1. Close the field list and Properties windows. Click the Text Box tool in the Toolbox to add an unbound text box at the right of the Form Header section of the form.

2. Edit the label of the new text box to read **Date/Time:** and relocate the label so that it is adjacent to the text box.

3. Type **=Now( )** in the text box to display the current date and time from your computer's clock. (In Design View, the form displays the calculation formula; it displays the actual date and time only in Form View.)

4. Adjust the length of the text box to accommodate the number of characters in the default DD/MM/YY HH:MM:SS PM format used for dates and times. The entry appears as shown in the Date/Time text box of figure 13.14. You add the other two text boxes in the following section.

Formatting Values. You can use the Format property you learned about in Chapter 4 to determine how dates, times, and numbers are displayed in a text box on a form. To format a date entry, perform the following steps:

    1. Using the Text Box tool, add a second unbound text box in the Detail section of the form, under the first text box in the Form Header section. Adjust the new box's dimensions to correspond to the other text box.

2. Edit the label to read **Date:** and enter **=Date( )** in the text box.

    3. Select the text box, then display the Properties window in one of two ways: click the right mouse button to display a popup menu, and choose Properties; or click the Properties button on the toolbar. Click the Format tab in the Properties window.

4. Click the Format property and open the drop-down list. Select Long Date from the list.

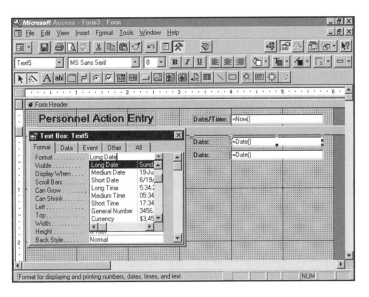

Fig. 13.14 Creating a calculated text box to display the date and time.

A Format property applied to a bound text box on a form or report overrides the format assigned to the field in the table design that supplies the value to the text box.

Note

When you display a form in Run mode, the value displayed in the Date/Time text box is the time that you open the form. To update the time, choose Records, Refresh. The refreshing process that occurs at an interval determined by the Refresh Interval property of the Multiuser Options (the default value is 15 seconds) doesn't update unbound text boxes.

Using the Clipboard with Controls. You can use the Windows Clipboard to make copies of controls and their properties easily. As an example, create a copy of one of the Date/Time controls using the Clipboard, by performing the following steps:

1. Select the bound control and its label by clicking the field text box of the second date text box you added in the preceding section. Both the label and the text box are selected, as indicated by the selection handles on both controls.

2. To copy the selected control to the Clipboard, do one of the following: press Ctrl+C, click the Copy button on the toolbar, or choose Edit, Copy.

3. To paste the copy of the control below the original version, do one of the following: press Ctrl+V, click the Paste button on the toolbar, or choose Edit, Paste.

4. Click the Format property in the Properties window for the copied control, and select Short Date from the drop-down list.

5. To display the controls you've created, click the Form View button on the toolbar, then return to Design View.

6. Delete the two Date text boxes and labels. To do so, enclose both with a selection boundary, created by dragging the mouse pointer across the text boxes from the upper-left to the lower-right, and then press the Del key. (You only need the Date/Time text box in the Form Header section for this form.)

7. Click the Form View button to view the form (see fig. 13.15).

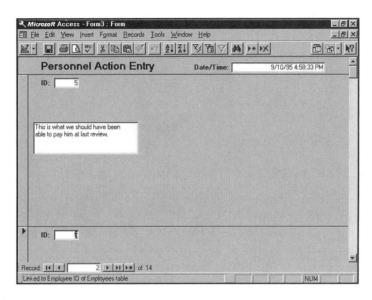

Fig. 13.15 The form title and text boxes displayed in Form View.

Text boxes (and the associated labels) are the most commonly used control objects on Access forms.

Changing the Default View and Obtaining Help for Properties

A form that fills Access's Design window might not necessarily fill the window in Run mode. Run mode may allow the beginning of a second copy of the form to appear (as you might have noticed at the bottom of fig. 13.15). The second copy is created because the Default View property has a value of Continuous Forms. (In Access 2.0, the default property value for Default View was Continuous Forms; in Access 95, the default value of Default View is Single Form—your test form won't show the second form at the bottom of the screen.) Forms have the following three Default View property values from which you can choose:

■ *Single Form* displays one record at a time in one form.

■ *Continuous Forms* displays multiple records, each record having a copy of the Detail section of the form. You can use the vertical scroll bar or the record selection buttons to select which record to display. Continuous Forms view is the default value for subforms created by the Form Wizard.

■ *Datasheet* displays the form fields arranged in rows and columns.

To change the Default View property of the form, complete the following steps:

1. Click the Design View button on the toolbar.

2. Choose Edit, Select Form.

3. Click the Properties button on the toolbar if the Properties window isn't visible. Click the Format tab in the Properties window.

4. Click the Default View property to open the list.

5. Select the value you want for this property for the current form. For this exercise, select Single Form (the default) from the list.

6. While Default View is selected, press F1. The Help window for the Default View property appears. This Help window also explains how the Default View and Views Allowed properties relate to one another.

   The vertical scroll bar disappears from the form in Run mode if a single form fits within its MDI child window.

You can verify your changes to the Default View property by clicking the Form View button to review the form's appearance.

Adding Option Groups, Binding Controls, and Using the Lock Tool

Option buttons, toggle buttons, and check boxes can return only Yes/No (–1/0 or True/False) values when used by themselves on a form. Here, their use as bound controls is limited to providing values to Yes/No fields in a table. When you place any of these controls within an option group, the buttons or check boxes can return a number you specify for the Option Value property of the control.

The capability of assigning numbers to the Option Value property enables you to use one of these three controls inside an option group frame to assign values to the paRating field of the Personnel Actions table. Option buttons are most commonly employed in Windows applications to select one value from a limited number of values.

> **Caution**
>
> Placing check boxes within option groups violates the Windows user interface design guidelines. According to the guidelines, a group of check boxes provides multiple additive choices. Thus, if you have more than one check box in a group, any or all of the check boxes can be marked. Use the shape control to create a frame around check boxes. Only option buttons and toggle buttons should be used in option groups.

By default, all the tools you add with the Toolbox are unbound controls. You can bind a control to a field by choosing the control you want to use, then clicking the field name in the Field List window to which you want the control bound. Another way of binding a control is to create an unbound control with a tool, and then type the name of a field in the Control Source property text box (reach this by clicking the Data tab in the Properties window for the control).

III

Forms and Reports

Access 95 offers two means of creating an option group: using the OptionGroup Wizard, or manually adding option buttons or toggle buttons to the option group. The following two sections describe these methods.

Using the Option Group Wizard. The Option Group Wizard is one of three Control Wizards that take you step-by-step through the creation of complex controls. To create an option group for the paRating field of the Personnel Actions table with the Option Group Wizard, follow these steps:

1. Click the Control Wizards tool to turn on the wizards, if the toggle button is not On (the default value). Toggle buttons indicate the On (True) state with a sunken appearance.

2. Click the Option Group tool, position the pointer where you want the upper-left corner of the option group, and then click the mouse button to display the first dialog of the OptionGroup Wizard.

Next >

3. Type five of the nine ratings in the Label Names datasheet: **Excellent**, **Good**, **Acceptable**, **Fair**, and **Poor**. Click the Next button to display the second dialog of the OptionGroup Wizard (see fig. 13.16).

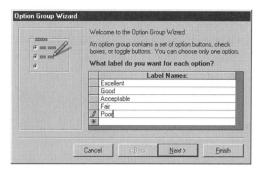

Fig. 13.16   The opening dialog of the Option Group Wizard.

> **Tip**
>
> You can create accelerator keys in the captions of your option buttons by placing an ampersand (&) before the letter to be used as an accelerator key. Thereafter, pressing Alt in combination with that letter key selects the option when your form is in Run mode.

Next >

4. The second dialog lets you set an optional default value for the option group. Select the option named Yes, the default choice is, and then open the drop-down list. Select Good, as shown in figure 13.17, and then click Next. If you need to, you can always return to the prior step by clicking Back.

Next >

5. The third dialog of the Option Group Wizard provides for the assignment of option values to each option button of the group. Type **9**, **7**, **5**, **3**, and **1** in the five text boxes, as illustrated by figure 13.18, and then click the Next button.

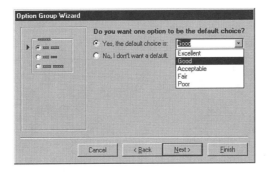

Fig. 13.17   Choosing a default value for the options group.

The domain integrity rule for the paRating field provides for nine different ratings. Nine option buttons, however, occupy too much space on a form. Thus, only five of the nine ratings are provided here. Later in the chapter, you add to this form a drop-down combo list that has all nine ratings.

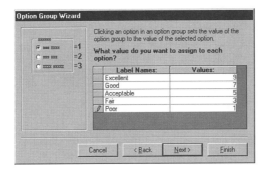

Fig. 13.18   Assigning the numeric OptionValue property to the option buttons.

6. The fourth OptionGroup Wizard dialog allows you to bind the option frame to a field of a table, or a column of a query, that acts as the Record Source of the bound form. Select the paRating column of the qryPersonnelActions query to which your form is bound (see fig. 13.19). Click Next to continue with the next stage of the wizard.

7. The fifth dialog lets you determine the style of the option group, as well as the type of controls (option buttons, check boxes, or toggle buttons) to add to the option group. You can preview the appearance of your option group and button style choices in the Sample pane. For this example, accept the defaults, Etched and Option Buttons (see fig. 13.20).

   The sunken and raised styles of option groups, option buttons, and check boxes are applicable only to control objects on forms with a Back Color property other than white. Light gray is used to aid in the three-dimensional simulation, and neither option buttons nor check boxes have a Back Color property. Thus, option buttons and check boxes with special effects are best suited for light gray backgrounds (Back Color = 12632256).

Next >

III

Forms and Reports

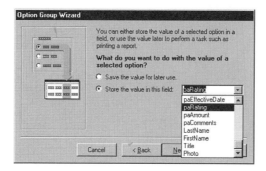

Fig. 13.19 Binding the option group to a column of the Record Source of the form.

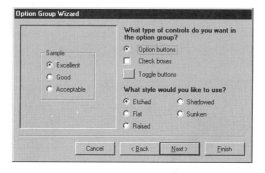

Fig. 13.20 Selecting a style for the option group and the type of button to add.

Finish

8. The last dialog provides a text box to enter the value of the Caption property of the label for the option group. Type **Rating**, as shown in figure 13.21, then click Finish to let the wizard complete its work. Your completed Rating option group appears as shown in figure 13.22.

Fig. 13.21 Assigning the value of the Caption property for the option group's label.

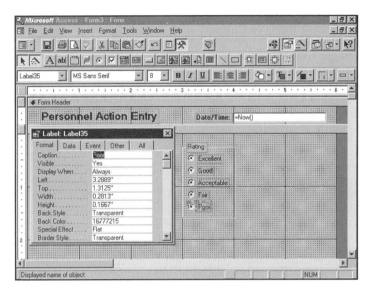

Fig. 13.22   The option group created by the OptionGroup Wizard.

To test your new bound option group, add a text box bound to the paRating column of the query that underlies the form. Figure 13.23 shows the option group in Form View with the space between the buttons closed up, the bold attribute applied to the option group label, and the Rating text box added. Click the option buttons to display the rating value in the text box.

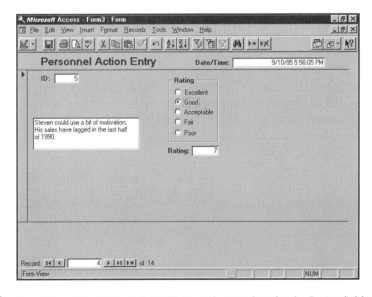

Fig. 13.23   The new option group in Form View, with a text box for the Rating field added to show the effect of selecting different options.

Creating an Option Group Manually. Although the OptionGroup Wizard does a good job of creating option groups, it's useful to know how to create a bound option group on your own. To bind an option group frame to the paRating field of the Personnel Actions query without taking advantage of the Control Wizard, complete the following steps:

1. Deactivate the Control Wizards toggle button in the Toolbox (make sure the button has a raised appearance) so you won't get any help from a wizard, and then click the Option Group tool in the Toolbox.

2. Click the Field List button on the toolbar to display the Field List window and choose the paRating column of your query.

3. Hold down the mouse button and drag the field pointer to a position to the right of the Rating option group you created in the preceding section, then release the mouse button to create an option group of the default size.

   When you create a bound option group by dragging a field from the Field List window, the option group name is assigned to the Caption property of the associated label automatically.

4. Resize the option group frame so that it is the same size as the other Rating option group. Apply the bold attribute to the option group's label.

Option buttons, toggle buttons, and check boxes within bound frames inherit many of their properties, such as Control Source, from the frame. The option frame provides the binding of these tools when they are inside a frame. Therefore, you don't use the field list with these controls. Adding multiple copies of a control is easier if you double-click the tool's button in the Toolbox to lock the tool on. (Click the tool at any time to unlock it.) To add five option buttons to assign values to the paRating field, perform the following steps:

1. Double-click the Option Button tool.

2. Using the crosshair as a reference to the upper-left corner of an imaginary rectangle that surrounds the option button, drop the option button at the appropriate location in the option group frame. When the option button symbol enters the option group frame, the button, the frame, and contents appear in reverse video as shown in figure 13.24.

3. Repeat step 2 four times to include a total of five Rating option buttons inside the Rating option group frame. The labels of the buttons are assigned numbers in the sequence in which they were added.

4. Click the Option Button tool in the Toolbox again to unlock this tool; Access automatically changes back to the pointer tool.

5. Edit the labels to read, from top to bottom: **Excellent**, **Good**, **Acceptable**, **Fair**, and **Poor**, corresponding to option values of 9, 7, 5, 3, and 1, respectively.

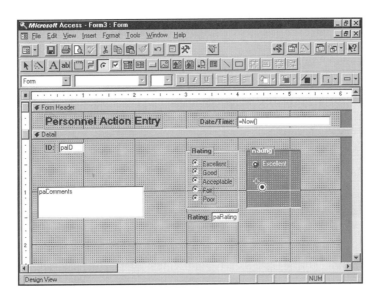

Fig. 13.24 Manually adding a second option button to an option frame.

6. Double-click the option button at the top to display its Properties window. Click the Data tab, and then replace 1 with **9** as the Option Value in the Data Properties list. A default Option Value is assigned in sequence from 1 to the number of buttons in the frame.

7. Repeat step 6 for the four remaining buttons, replacing the default values 2, 3, 4, and 5 with **7**, **5**, **3**, and **1**, respectively. No two buttons in an option frame can have the same value.

8. To test the entries, click the Run Mode button on the toolbar. The form appears as shown in figure 13.25.

9. Using the record selection buttons, choose a record to edit. If you previously assigned ratings with odd-numbered values, the option button that corresponds to the value is selected.

10. Click the option buttons in sequence to verify that the proper numeric values appear in the Rating text box.

11. Click the Design View toolbar button to return to Design View.

12. You won't need either of the Rating option group boxes currently on the form, so delete both.

The drop-down lists and combo boxes you'll learn about in the following sections of this chapter are a better control type to use than an option group for the relatively large number of choices available in the ratings field—option groups are best for choosing one of only three or four choices.

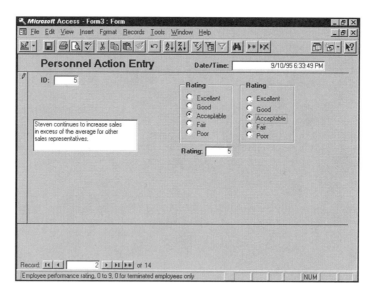

Fig. 13.25 The option group frame and option buttons, displayed in Run mode.

If you have a Yes/No field in the table, you can use a single option button bound to a field (not inside an option frame) to create the Yes/No values for the user.

> ### Note
>
> If you add a button or a check box within a frame with the Field List drag-and-drop method, the button is independently bound to the selected field, rather than to the field through the option frame. In this case, the button's Properties window doesn't include the Option Value property, and the button assigns Yes/No values to the field.
>
> An independently bound button inside an option frame doesn't follow the rules of the option frame; you can choose this button and another button simultaneously.
>
> Adding independently bound buttons within option frames results in assignment of inconsistent values to fields.

Using the Clipboard to Copy Controls to Another Form

Access's capability of copying controls and their properties to the Windows Clipboard enables you to create controls on one form and copy them to another form. If you use a standard header style, you can copy the controls in the header of a previously designed form to a new form and edit the content as necessary. The form that contains the controls to be copied need not be in the same database as the destination form in which the copy is pasted. You can create a library of standard controls in a dedicated form used only for holding standard controls.

The Time/Date calculated text box is a candidate to add to the frmPersonnelActions form you created in Chapter 12, "Creating and Using Forms." You may want to add a Time/Date text box to the Form Header or Detail section of all your transaction forms. To add the Time/Date control to the frmPersonnelActions form, perform the following steps:

1. Click the Design View button, and select the Time/Date control and its label by clicking the field text box.

2. To copy the selected control(s) to the Clipboard, do one of the following: press Ctrl+C, click the Copy button on the toolbar, or choose Edit, Copy.

3. Click the Show Database Window button on the toolbar; then open the frmPersonnelActions form from the Database window in Design mode.

4. Click the Detail section selection bar, and then do one of the following: press Ctrl+V, click the Paste button on the toolbar, or choose Edit, Paste. A copy of the control appears at the upper-left corner of the Detail section.

    Controls are pasted to the section of the form that is presently selected. You cannot drag controls between sections of a form.

5. Position the mouse pointer over the copied option group so that the pointer becomes a hand symbol.

6. Hold down the mouse button and drag the option group to the position shown in figure 13.26, then release the mouse button.

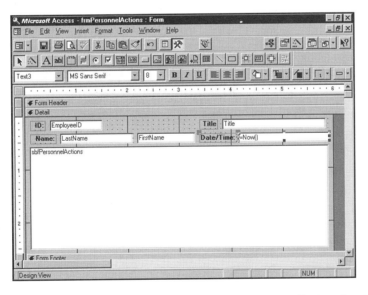

Fig. 13.26   Copying the Date/Time calculated field to the frmPersonnelActions form by using the Clipboard.

7. Click the Form View button on the toolbar. The Personnel Action Entry form appears as shown in figure 13.27.

8. Return to Design mode, click the Save button to save your changes, and then click the Close window button to close the frmPersonnelActions form.

III

Forms and Reports

Troubleshooting

I've copied a control to another form, but when I attempt to use the form, I get an error message whenever that control gets the focus.

When you copy a control to a form that uses a data source different from the one used to create the original control, you need to change the Control Source property to correspond with the field to which the new control is to be bound. Changing the Control Source property doesn't change the Status Bar Text, Validation Rule, or Validation Text properties for the new control source; you must enter the appropriate values manually.

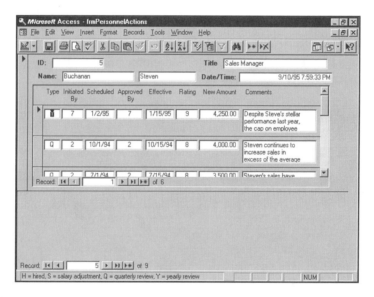

Fig. 13.27 The Date/Time text box displayed in Run mode.

Using List Boxes and Combo Boxes

List boxes and combo boxes both serve the same basic purpose by enabling you to pick a value from a list, rather than type the value in a text box. These two kinds of list boxes are especially useful when you need to enter a code that represents the name of a person, firm, or product. You don't need to refer to a paper list of the codes and names to make the entry. The differences between list boxes and combo boxes are shown in the following list:

- *List boxes* don't need to be opened to display their content; the portion of the list that fits within the size of the list box you assign is visible at all times. Your choice is limited to values included in the list.

- *Drop-down combo boxes and drop-down lists* consume less space than list boxes in the form, but you must open these controls to select a value. Combo boxes in Access are drop-down lists plus a text box, not traditional combo boxes that display the list at all times. You can allow the user to enter a value in the text box element of the drop-down combo list, or limit the selection to just the members in the drop-down list. If you limit the choice to members of the drop-down list (sometimes called a *pick list*), the user can still use the edit box to type the beginning of the list value—Access searches for a matching entry. This feature reduces the time needed to locate a choice in a long list.

Drop-down lists and combo boxes are two of the most powerful controls that Microsoft programmers developed for Access. The data source for these controls may be a table, a query, a list of values you supply, or the names of Access VBA functions. The boxes may have as many columns as you need to display the data needed to make the correct choice.

Adding a Combo Box with a Table or Query as the Data Source. In the majority of cases, you bind the drop-down list or combo box to a field so that the choice updates the value of this field. Two-column controls are the most commonly used. The first column contains the code that updates the value of the field to which the control is bound, and the second column contains the name associated with the code. An example of where a limit-to-list, multiple-column drop-down list is most useful is the assignment of supervisor and manager employee ID numbers to the paInitiatedBy and paApprovedBy fields in the frmPersonnelActionsEntry form. The ComboBox Wizard is used to add the paInitiatedBy drop-down list, and then you employ manual methods to add the paApprovedBy drop-down list in the two sections that follow.

Using the Combo Box Wizard. Designing combo boxes is a more complex process than creating an option group, so you're likely to use the ComboBox Wizard for most of the combo boxes you add to forms. Follow these steps to use the ComboBox Wizard to create the paInitiatedBy drop-down list that lets you select from a list of Northwind Traders' employees:

1. Open the frmPersonnelActionsEntry form (that you created and saved earlier in this chapter) from the Database window, in Design mode, if it is not presently open.

2. Click the Control Wizards button, if necessary, so that the wizards are turned on.

3. Click the Combo Box tool in the Toolbox. The mouse pointer turns into a combo box symbol while on the active surface of the form.

4. Click the Field List button to display the Field List window.

5. Drag the paInitiatedBy field to a position at the top and extreme right-hand edge of the Detail section of the form, opposite the paID field (look ahead to fig. 13.34). The first Combo Box Wizard dialog appears.

6. You want the combo box to look up values in the Employees table, so accept the default option button with the query and table symbols, and then click Next (see fig. 13.28). Your selection specifies Table/Query as the value of the Record Source property of the combo box. The second ComboBox Wizard dialog appears.

7. Select Employees from the list of tables in the list (see fig. 13.29). Click Next to reach the third dialog.

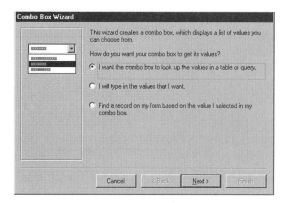

Fig. 13.28   The opening dialog of the ComboBox Wizard.

Fig. 13.29   Selecting the Record Source property of the combo box.

8. You need the EmployeeID and LastName fields of the Employees table for your combo box. EmployeeID serves as the bound field, and your combo box displays the LastName field. EmployeeID is selected in the Available Fields list by default, so click the > button to move EmployeeID to the Selected Fields list. LastName is selected automatically, so click the > button again to move LastName to the Selected Fields list. Your ComboBox Wizard dialog appears as shown in figure 13.30. This selection specifies the SQL SELECT query that serves as the value of the Row Source property and populates the combo box's list. Click Next to reach the fourth dialog.

9. The fourth dialog (see fig. 13.31) displays the value list for the combo box. Access has successfully determined that the EmployeeID field is the key field of the Employees table, and has assumed (correctly) that the EmployeeID field is the bound field for the combo box. The Hide key column check box is selected by default; this option causes Access to hide the bound column of the combo box. The result is that, although you've selected two columns for the combo box, only one column (the LastName field) is displayed in the combo box's list. The EmployeeID column is hidden, and is used only to supply the data value for the paInitiatedBy field.

Resize the LastName column by dragging the right edge of the column leftward; you want the column wide enough to display everyone's last name, but not any wider than absolutely necessary. Click Next to continue to the fifth ComboBox Wizard dialog.

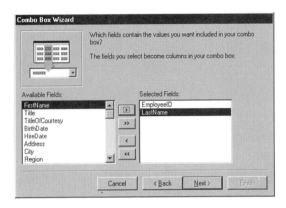

Fig. 13.30 Selecting the fields of the table with which to populate the combo box.

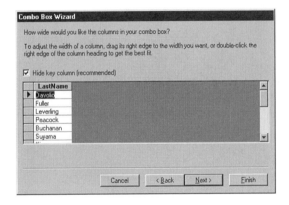

Fig. 13.31 Selecting the width of the columns for the combo box. The key field column is hidden (the default) in this figure.

10. Your combo box supplies the EmployeeID value corresponding to the name you select to the paInitiatedBy field. You previously specified that the Control Source property is paInitiatedBy when you dragged the field symbol to the form in step 5. The ComboBox Wizard uses your prior selection as the default value of the Control Source property (see fig. 13.32), so accept the default value by clicking the Next button to display the sixth and final dialog.

11. The last dialog lets you edit the label associated with the combo box (see fig. 13.33). Type **Initiated By:** and click Finish to add the combo box to your form. Your combo box in Design mode appears as shown in figure 13.34.

III

Forms and Reports

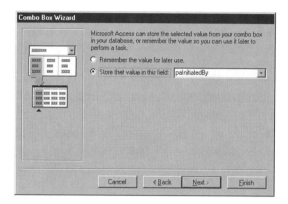

Fig. 13.32 Assigning the Control Source property value.

Fig. 13.33 The final ComboBox Wizard dialog allows you to edit the control's label.

12. Click the Form View button on the toolbar to test your combo box (see fig. 13.35). Change the Initiated By value to another person, such as Mr. Fuller, the Vice President of Sales, and then move the record pointer to make the change permanent. Return to the original record, and open the combo box to verify that the combo box is bound to the paInitiatedBy field.

Adding a Combo Box Manually. As mentioned previously in this chapter, it is good practice to create control objects manually so that you learn the properties associated with each control. To substitute a two-column combo box that you create yourself for the paApprovedBy text box in the frmPersonnelActionsEntry form, complete the following steps:

1. Open the frmPersonnelActionsEntry form from the Database window in Design mode, if it is not presently open.

2. If necessary, click the Control Wizards button in the Toolbox to disable the wizards (make sure the button is raised).

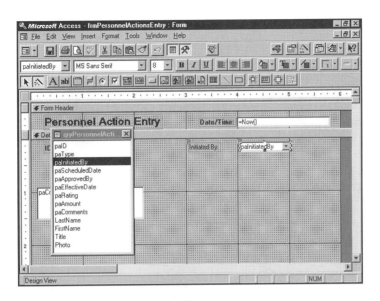

Fig. 13.34 The new combo box in Design mode.

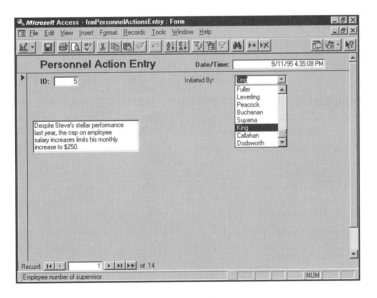

Fig. 13.35 The Initiated By combo box in Run mode.

3. Click the Field List button on the toolbar to open the Field List window, if it isn't already open.

4. Click the Combo Box tool in the Toolbox. Then click paApprovedBy in the Field List window, and drag and drop the field symbol underneath the Initiated By combo box you created previously. Size the combo box and its label to match the Initiated By combo box above it.

5. Double-click the combo box to display the Properties window, and then click the Data tab.

6. The source of the data for the combo box is the Employees table, so the default value of the Row Source Type property, Table/Query, is correct. Open the combo list and select Employees as the value of the Row Source property.

7. When you choose the name of a table or query as the Row Source property, all fields of the table or columns of the query are included automatically as combo box columns. The first two columns of the Employees table provide EmployeeID to be assigned as the value of the paApprovedBy field and LastName to identify the supervisor. Click the Format tab in the Properties window, and type **2** as the Column count to create a two-column combo box.

8. The default width of each column of the combo box is 1 inch. The EmployeeID column can be less than 1 inch wide because it consists of only one digit. Type **0.2** as the width of the first column, followed by a semicolon (or comma) separator, and type **0.8** as the width of the second column. Access adds inch units (in) for you.

9. Click the Data tab to return to the data properties. The first column of the Employees table, EmployeeID, contains the value to assign to the paApprovedBy field, so the default value of the Bound Column property, column 1, is correct. You can choose any column by its number (in left-to-right sequence) as the value to be assigned to the field to which the combo box is bound.

10. Only an employee included in the Employees table can initiate or approve a Personnel Action, so open the Limit to List drop-down list and select Yes. (If you want to allow the user to add a value not included in the list, accept the default No value. Adding a user-defined value is not applicable in this case.) The Personnel Actions form appears as shown in figure 13.36.

11. Click the Form View button on the toolbar to test the combo boxes. When you open the Approved By combo box, the display appears as shown in figure 13.37.

Notice that the EmployeeID field value appears in the text element of the combo box, rather than the LastName field value as in the Initiated By combo box. If the bound column appears in the list element, the value of the bound column appears in the text element.

12. To display only the name of the supervisor or manager in the list and text boxes, return to Design mode and change the value of the Column Widths property (on the Format tab of the Properties window) of the first column from 0.2 to **0** inches. This action causes only the second column to appear in the text box and list elements of the combo box, making the two combo boxes of your form consistent.

As an example, if the fourth column of the table or query is the column you want to display in the combo box, type three zero-width columns preceding the width you want for the column that you want to display (**0,0,0**, and **1**).

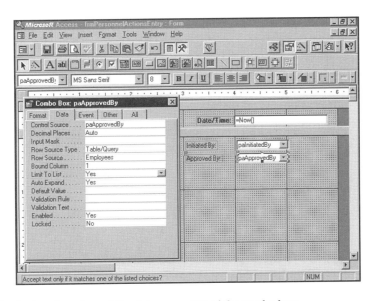

Fig. 13.36 Setting the values of the data properties of the combo box.

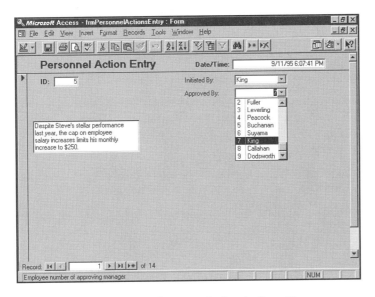

Fig. 13.37 The Approved By multiple-column combo box in Form View.

List and combo boxes are a boon to developers because Access does all the work. Users who, in early versions of Clipper or later versions of dBASE, wrote the code necessary to create a popup window that contains a drop-down list will appreciate the ease of creating a combo box in Access.

Using the Query Builder to Populate a Combo Box. If the Row Source Type property for a combo box is Table/Query, you can substitute an SQL statement for a named table or query as the value of the Row Source property. In the case of queries, the advantage of the substitution is that this process prevents the list of queries in the Database window from becoming cluttered with named queries used to create a multitude of combo boxes. For either tables or queries, you can choose only the fields or columns you want for the text box, eliminating the need to hide columns. In addition, you can specify a sort order for the list element of your combo box.

To invoke Access 95's QueryBuilder to create an SQL statement to populate the Approved By combo box, follow these steps:

1. Return to or open frmPersonnelActions in Design mode, and double-click the paApprovedBy combo box to open the Properties window. Click the Data tab of the Properties window, if necessary.

2. Select the Row Source property, and click … to launch the QueryBuilder. You previously selected the Employees table as the value of the Row Source property, so the message box shown in figure 13.38 appears. Click Yes to confirm the replacement and open the QueryBuilder window.

Fig. 13.38   Confirming you want to replace the Employees table with an SQL Statement.

3. The QueryBuilder's window is identical in most respects to the Query Design window, but its title and behavior differ. The Employees table automatically appears in the upper pane. Drag the EmployeeID and LastName fields to columns 1 and 2 of the Query Design grid.

4. You want an ascending sort on the LastName field, so select Ascending in the Sort list box. Your query design appears as shown in figure 13.39.

   When you use the QueryBuilder, you can test the results of your query by clicking the Run button on the toolbar. Access executes the query, and displays a Datasheet View of the query's results.

5. Click the Close window button to close the QueryBuilder. The message box shown in figure 13.40 appears for confirmation of your change to the Row Source property value, instead of asking if you want to save your query. Click Yes and the SQL statement derived from the graphical QBE design appears as the value of the Row Source property.

6. SQL statements, especially those created by Access, have a tendency to be lengthy. With the caret in the Row Source property text box, press Shift+F2 to display the SQL statement in the Zoom box, as shown in figure 13.41.

   In this case, the field name prefix is applied in each field reference, although it is really only necessary in the FROM clause since just one table is involved in the query.

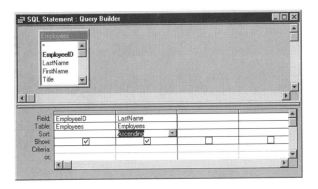

Fig. 13.39   The design of the query to create the SQL statement for the Approved By combo box.

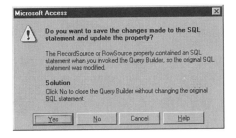

Fig. 13.40   Confirming your change to the Row Source property value.

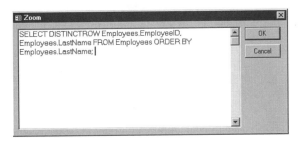

Fig. 13.41   Displaying the SQL statement in the Zoom box.

Switch to Form View to test the effect of adding the sort (the ORDER BY clause) to the query. Writing your own SQL statements to fill combo boxes with values is discussed in Chapter 24, "Working with Structured Query Language."

Creating a Combo Box with a List of Static Values. Another application for list boxes and combo boxes is picking values from a static list of options that you create. A drop-down list to choose a Rating value saves space in a form compared with the equivalent control created with option buttons within an option frame. As you design more complex forms, you find that display "real estate" becomes increasingly valuable.

The option frame you added to the frmPersonnelActionsEntry form provides a choice of only 5 of the possible 10 ratings. To add a drop-down list with the ComboBox Wizard to allow entry of all the possible values, perform the following steps:

1. Click the Design View button on the toolbar (if the form isn't already in Design View). Click the Control Wizards button in the Toolbox, if necessary, to enable the ComboBox Wizard (the button should have a sunken appearance).

2. Open the Field List window, and select paRating.

3. Click the Combo Box tool in the Toolbox. Then drag the paRating field symbol to a position underneath the Approved By combo box you added previously. The first ComboBox Wizard dialog appears.

4. Select the option named I will type in the values that I want, and then click Next to reach the second dialog.

5. The Rating combo box requires two columns—the first column contains the allowable values of paRating, 0 through 9, and the second column contains the corresponding description of each rating code. Enter **2** as the number of columns. Access assigns Row Source property values in column-row sequence; you enter each of the values for the columns in the first row, and then do the same for the remaining rows. Type **9 Excellent, 8 Very Good, 7 Good, 6 Average, 5 Acceptable, 4 Marginal, 3 Fair, 2 Sub-par, 1 Poor, 0 Terminated**, as shown in figure 13.42 (don't type the commas). Click Next to reach the third dialog.

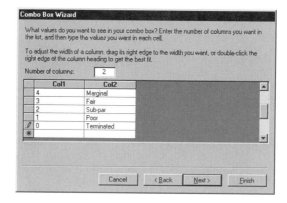

Fig. 13.42 Entering Static values in the ComboBox Wizard's datasheet.

6. Set the widths of the columns you want by dragging the edge of each column header button to the left, as shown in figure 13.43. If you don't want the rating number to appear, drag the left edge of column 1 fully to the left to reduce its width to 0. When you're done adjusting column widths, click Next to reach the fourth dialog.

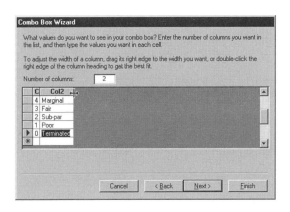

Fig. 13.43 Setting the column widths of the combo box.

7. Select Col1, the rating number code, as the bound column for your value list—that is, the column containing the value you want to store or use later (see fig. 13.44); this must be a column containing unique values. Click Next to reach the fifth dialog.

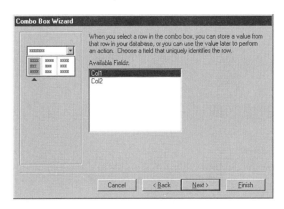

Fig. 13.44 Choosing a column to bind to a field of a table, or to a column of a query.

8. Accept the default value (the paRating field) in this dialog by clicking Next to go to the final dialog of the ComboBox Wizard.

9. Type **Rating:** as the label for the new combo box control, and click Finish to complete the combo box specification and return to Design mode.

10. Open the Properties window for the combo box, then click the Data tab in the Properties window. Set Limit to List to Yes to convert the drop-down combo to a drop-down list. The frmPersonnelActionsEntry form in Design mode appears as shown in figure 13.45. Notice that Access has added commas after the numbers and semicolons between the row entries, plus quotation marks to surround the text values. This is the format you use when you enter list values manually.

III

Forms and Reports

Fig. 13.45 The data properties for the value list combo box.

11. Click the Form View button on the toolbar to display the form. The open Rating static-value combo box appears as shown in figure 13.46.

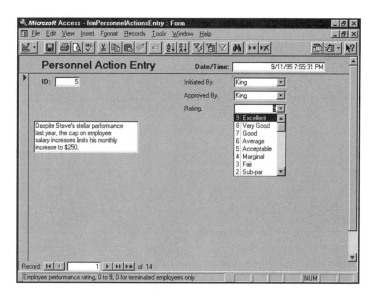

Fig. 13.46 The Rating static-value combo box opened in Run mode.

Another opportunity to use a static-value combo box is as a substitute for the Type text box. Several kinds of performance reviews exist: Quarterly, Yearly, Bonus, Salary, Commission, and so on, each represented by an initial letter code.

> **Note**
>
> You can improve the appearance of columns of labels and associated text, list, and combo boxes by right-aligning the text of the labels and left-aligning the text of the boxes. Select all the labels in a column with the mouse, and click the Right Justify button on the toolbar. Then select all the boxes, and click the Left Justify button.

Creating a Combo Box to Find Specific Records

The ComboBox Wizard in Access 95 includes a new, third type of combo list box that you can create—a combo list that locates a record on the form based on a value you select from the list. You can use this type of combo box, for example, to create a Find Last Name box on the frmPersonnelActionsEntry form that contains a drop-down list of all the last names from the Employees table, so you can quickly find Personnel Actions records for those employees.

To create a combo box that finds records on the form based on a value you select in the combo box, follow these steps:

1. Click the Design View button on the toolbar (if the form isn't already in Design View). Click the Control Wizards button in the Toolbox, if necessary, to enable the ComboBox Wizard (the button should have a sunken appearance).

2. Click the Combo Box tool in the Toolbox, and then click and drag on the surface of the Detail section of the form to create the new combo box in a position underneath the Rating drop-down box you created previously. Release the mouse, and the first ComboBox Wizard dialog appears.

3. Click the option named Find a record on my form based on the value I selected in my combo box. Click Next to reach the second dialog.

4. Scroll the Available Fields list until the LastName field is visible. Click to select this field, then click the > button to move it to the Selected Fields list. Click Next to reach the third dialog.

> **Note**
>
> When creating a combo box to find records, select only one field. The combo box won't work for finding records if you select more than one field for the combo box's lists.

5. The ComboBox Wizard now displays a list of the field values from the column you just selected. Double-click the right edge of the LastName column to get the best fit column-width for the data values in the column, then click Next to go to the fourth and final step of the wizard.

6. Type **Zoom to:** as the label for the new combo box, and then click Finish to complete the new combo box control. Your form should appear as shown in figure 13.47.

7. Click the Form View button on the toolbar to display the form. The open Zoom to: combo box appears as shown in figure 13.48.

When you create this type of combo box, the ComboBox Wizard automatically creates an Access VBA *event procedure* for the After Update property of the combo box (refer to the Property window in fig. 13.47). An event procedure is a VBA procedure that Access executes automatically whenever a particular event—in this case, updating the combo box—occurs. Chapter 28, "Writing Visual Basic for Applications Code," describes how to write Access VBA code.

III

Forms and Reports

Fig. 13.47   The new combo box that will find a record on the form based on a value selected in the combo box.

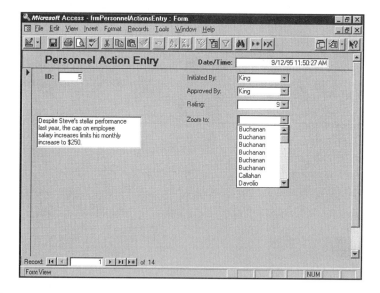

Fig. 13.48   The combo box to find a record on the form in Form View.

To view the event procedure code that the wizard created for your new combo box, open the Properties window for the Zoom to: combo box, click the Events tab in the window, select the After Update property text box, and then click .... Access opens the CodeBuilder window shown in fig. 13.49. After you've looked at the code, click the Close window button to close the CodeBuilder window and return to Design mode.

To use a combo box of this type, select a value from the list—as soon as you select the new value, Access updates the combo box's text box, which then invokes the Access VBA code for the After Update event procedure; the VBA code in the After Update procedure finds the first record in the form's record set that has a matching value, and displays it. You can only use this type of combo box to find the first matching record in a record set.

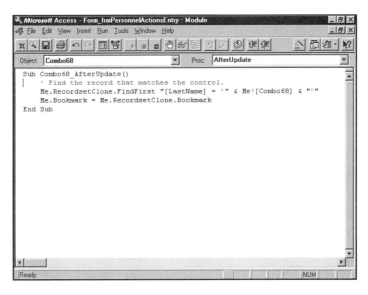

Fig. 13.49 The Module window for the After Update event property of the locating combo box.

Because the field on the form is based on the LastName column of the form's underlying query, you'll see an entry in the list for each and every last name entry in the record set produced by the qryPersonnelActions query. If there is more than one Personnel Action record for Steve Buchanan, let's say, then Buchanan appears in the combo list as many times as there are records for him. To display a unique list of last names to be located on the form, change the Row Source property to obtain the LastName field values for the combo box list through an SQL statement based on a query from the Employees table.

To change the Row Source property, follow the procedure you learned in the "Using the QueryBuilder to Populate a Combo Box" section, earlier in this chapter: open the Properties window of the Zoom to: combo box, click the Data tab, select the Row Source text box, and then open the QueryBuilder. Change the query so that it uses the Employees table, as shown in fig. 13.50. You should also change the Limit to List property value to Yes.

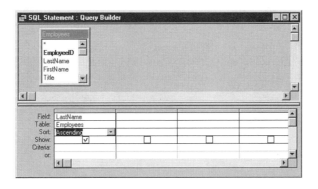

Fig. 13.50 The QueryBuilder window for the new combo box, showing the Employees table selected as the new Row Source property value for the combo box.

Changing One Control Type to Another

 In earlier versions of Access, if you made a mistake in selecting the type of control, you would have to delete the control and start over. Access 95 allows you to "morph" a control of one type to become a control of a compatible type. You can change an option button to a check box, for example, or you can change a toggle button to an option button. You can't however, change a text box to an object frame or other control with a different field data type. To change a control to a different type, follow these steps:

1. In the form's Design View, select the control whose type you want to change.

2. Choose Format, Change To to see a submenu of form control types. Only the submenu choices for control types that are compatible with the selected control are enabled.

3. Select the control type you want from the submenu. Access changes the control type.

Completing the Main Personnel Actions Entry Form

In the following sections of this chapter, you'll learn how to use the Control Wizards to help you add a subform to a form. Before you add the subform, however, you should complete the main frmPersonnelActionsEntry form. Like the form that you created with the Form Wizard in Chapter 12, the purpose of this form is to display records from the Personnel Actions table so that a user can view the history of an employee's personnel actions, and also to provide a convenient means of adding new personnel action records.

In the form you created in Chapter 12, you viewed the history of personnel records, and also added new records, in a tabular subform, while information from the Employees table was displayed only on the main form. In this custom form, you place fields from the Personnel Actions table on the main form to make adding new records to the Personnel Actions table easier, and the subform area is used to display only historic personnel action records. The frmPersonnelActionsEntry form has fields from the Personnel Actions table on both the main form and the subform, and uses the qryPersonnelActions form you created at the beginning of this chapter as the form's data source. If you were creating a full-scale human resources database application, you might choose the Employees table as the data source for the form, and design a subform for editing the Personnel Actions table with the history displayed in a subform of the subform.

> **Note**
>
> Creating a form and subform that are both based on the same underlying table—in this example, the Personnel Actions table—is a somewhat unconventional, but totally acceptable, database application design method. Most forms that employ subforms employ a base table (such as Employees) or a query whose data source is a base table as the record source of the main form. A

related table or a query based on a related table serves as the record source of the subform. Many of the forms of Northwind.mdb demonstrate the conventional form-subform design. Our form example, frmPersonnelActionsEntry, uses a common underlying table for both the form and subform, to illustrate some of the unique characteristics of this approach to one-to-many form design.

To complete the main form, follow these steps (refer to fig. 13.51 for field placement):

1. Click the Design View button on the toolbar (if the frmPersonnelActionsEntry form isn't already in Design View).

2. If necessary, click the Toolbox button to enable the Control Wizards (make sure the button has a sunken appearance), then click the Field List button on the toolbar to open the Field List dialog, if it isn't already open.

3. Drag the LastName field from the Field List to a position under the ID field text box; when you release the mouse, Access creates a text box for the field. Edit the field's label to read **Name:**.

4. Drag the FirstName field from the Field List to a position to the right of the LastName field; delete the FirstName field's label.

5. Drag the Title field from the Field List to a position on the form beneath the two name fields.

6. Repeat step 5 for the paType, paScheduledDate, paEffectiveDate, and paAmount fields (refer to fig. 13.51 for field positioning and sizing). (You'll need to move the Approved By, Rating, and Zoom to: fields that you placed on the form earlier in this chapter.)

7. Drag the Photo field onto the center of the form, and delete its label (the fact that this field displays a photo of the employee is enough to identify the field). Size and position the Photo field in the center of the form.

8. Double-click the Photo field to display its Properties window, click the Format tab, and select the Size Mode property's text box (see fig. 13.52). Select Zoom from the drop-down list to have the employee photo scaled down to fit the photo field's size.

> **Tip**
>
> Use the Format Painter to format the text labels of the fields. Using the Format Painter is described in Chapter 12, "Creating and Using Forms."

9. Use the techniques you learned in Chapter 12 to move, rearrange, and change the label formats to match the appearance of fig. 13.51. (All labels are bold and right-aligned.)

10. Test your new fields by clicking the Form View button on the toolbar. Your form appears as shown in figure 13.53.

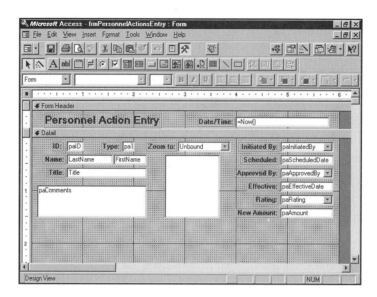

Fig. 13.51 The frmPersonnelActionsEntry form in Design View, showing the final placement and formatting of the main form fields.

Fig. 13.52 Setting the Photo field's Size Mode property so that photos are scaled to fit the size of the field on the form.

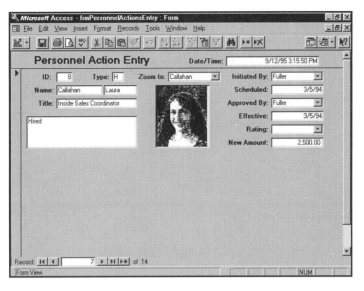

Fig. 13.53 The sbfPersonnelActions form with all fields added, in Form View.

Creating a Subform Using the Subform/Subreport Wizard

The frmPersonnelActionsEntry form needs a subform in which to view the history of personnel actions for the employee displayed in the main part of the form. Access 95's new Subform/Subreport Wizard makes it possible for you to create a new subform at the same time you add the subform field to the main form. To do so, follow these steps:

1. Click the Design View button on the toolbar (if the frmPersonnelActionsEntry form isn't already in Design View).

2. Click the Control Wizards button to enable the Control Wizards (if the button isn't already down).

3. Click the Subform button in the Toolbox, then click beneath the paComments text box in the Detail section of the form. Access displays the first dialog of the Subform/Subreport Wizard.

4. You can use this wizard either to create a new subform based on a table or query, or to insert an existing subform (see fig. 13.54). (You'll learn how to insert an existing form as a subform later in this chapter.) For this exercise, select the Table/Query option, and click Next to reach the second dialog.

5. The wizard asks you to indicate which table or query the new subform is based on, and which fields appear in the subform (see fig. 13.55). Select Query: qryPersonnelActionsSubform in the Tables and Queries drop-down list. To expedite field selection, click the >> button to copy all the fields to the Selected Fields list. Select the paComments field in the Selected Fields list, and click the < button to remove this field from the list. Click Next to reach the third dialog.

Fig. 13.54 Use the Subform/Subreport Wizard to insert a new subform based on a table or query, or to insert an existing form as a subform.

Fig. 13.55 Selecting the data source and fields for the new subform.

6. The wizard now asks you to specify the link between the main form and the subform. You may select from a list of possible relationships that Access has determined, or define your own link. Click the Define my own option, and the wizard dialog changes to show four drop-down list text boxes (see fig. 13.56).

Fig. 13.56 Selecting the fields to link the subform to the main form.

7. In the upper Form/report fields list, select paID as the linking field; in the upper Subform/subreport fields list, also select paID as the linking field. Click Next to go to the fourth and final dialog of the wizard.

8. Type **sbfTest** as the name of this new subform, and click Finish to complete the subform's specifications (see fig. 13.57). Access creates and saves the new form; it inserts the completed subform into the subform field on the main form, and sizes the subform field to accommodate the new subform (see fig. 13.58). The text you entered for the subform's name is assigned to the label for the subform; the subform itself is saved under a name made up of the name of the table or query it's based on, followed by the word "subform." In this case, the new subform's name is "qryPersonnelActionsSubform subform."

Fig. 13.57 Entering a name for your new subform. This name only affects the label of the subform field on the main form; Access gives the subform itself a name based on the table or query that is the basis for the subform.

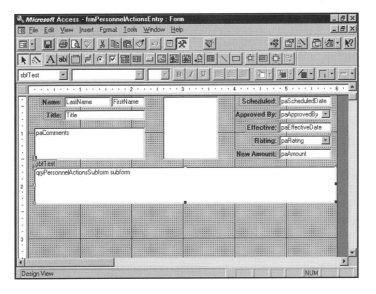

Fig. 13.58 The completed subform field in Design View.

9. Click the Form View button on the toolbar to check the appearance of the new subform. Your form appears as shown in figure 13.59.

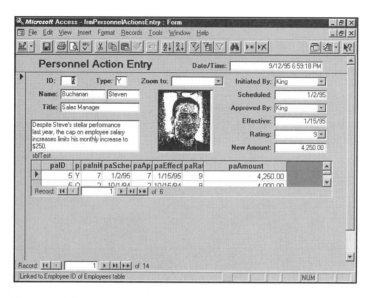

Fig. 13.59 The new subform in Form View.

As you can see from figure 13.59, the Subform/Subreport Wizard always creates new subforms with Datasheet View. In many cases, this is acceptable—or even desirable. For the frmPersonnelActionsEntry form, however, a better view of the data can be had with a tabular continuous form view of the data. The following sections of this chapter explain the advantages of a tabular continuous form, and guide you through the steps necessary to create such a form and insert it as a subform into the main form.

10. Close the frmPersonnelActionsEntry form by clicking the Close window button. Click No when Access asks if you want to save changes to the form's design.

You'll create a much more useful form in the next section.

Creating and Using Continuous Forms

Continuous forms are useful for displaying data contained in multiple records of a table or query in a format other than Datasheet View. The sbfPersonnelActions subform you created in Chapter 12, for example, is designed only to display the most recent Personnel Action records for an employee. Editing isn't allowed in the subform, so you don't need the field headers, record selection buttons, and scroll bars associated with Datasheet View. These graphic elements focus more attention on the subform than is deserved. You need a plain vanilla display of the history for the employee; this basic display requires a continuous form.

The Form Wizard offers the choice of creating a tabular continuous form, so using the Form Wizard is the quickest method of creating a plain vanilla subform. To create a tabular continuous form with the Form Wizard, perform the following steps:

1. Click the Form tab, then click New in the Database window to create a new form. Access displays the New Form dialog.

2. Select qryPersonnelActionsSubform as the source of data for the new form.

3. Select Autoform: Tabular Form Wizard from the list at the top of the New Form dialog, then click OK. Access immediately creates a tabular form based on the fields in the query qryPersonnelActionsSubform, then displays the form in Form View (see fig. 13.60).

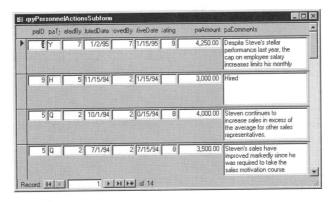

Fig. 13.60   The tabular form produced by the Form Wizard from qryPersonnelActionsSubform.

4. Click the Close window button to close the tabular form. Access displays a message dialog asking if you want to save changes to the form. Click Yes to save the new tabular form; Access displays the Save As dialog.

5. Type **frmTest** as the name of the form, and click OK.

The Form Wizard created the tabular form using the qryPersonnelActionsSubform query as the data source. To customize the form to make the size and appearance compatible with the frmPersonnelActionsEntry form, follow these steps:

1. Click the Design View button to switch the frmTest form to Design View, then maximize the form window.

2. Delete the paID and paComments fields from the Detail section of the form; delete the paID and paComments labels from the Form Header section of the form.

3. Click the Form Header bar, and use the Back Color button on the Formatting toolbar to change the background color (Back Color property) to white; change the background color of the Detail section to white, also.

4. Edit the labels in the Header Section of the form as follows: paType to **Type**; paInitiatedBy to **Initiated By**; paScheduledDate to **Scheduled**; paApprovedBy

to **Approved By**; paEffectiveDate to **Effective**; paRating to **Rating**; paAmount to **New Amount**.

5. Drag a selection box around all the labels in the Form Header section; click the Bold button on the formatting toolbar, then click the Center button.

6. Choose Format, Size, to Fit; then choose Format, Size, to Grid. This sequence of commands has the effect of making the label text boxes large enough to display their entire contents, then sizing them to the nearest regular grid mark, which makes it easier to position the labels into columns with the fields in the Detail section of the form.

7. Drag the Type label to the upper-left corner of the Form Header section; position the remaining labels along the top edge of the same section, one grid mark apart from each other (see fig. 13.61). Then drag the Detail section header bar to the bottom of the labels.

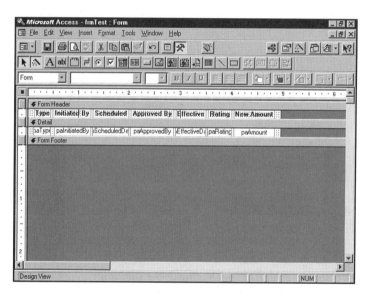

Fig. 13.61   The modified tabular form in Design View.

8. Drag the paType field to the upper-left corner of the Detail section, and resize it to match the Type label in the Form Header section. Position each of the remaining fields from left to right under the corresponding label in the Form Header section, sizing each field to match its label. Drag the Form Footer section header bar to the bottom of the text boxes.

9. Drag a selection box around all the fields in the Detail section of the form, then click the Center button on the formatting toolbar to center the data in each field. Click the Border Color button, and then click the Transparent button to make all the fields' borders transparent.

10. Choose Edit, Select Form, and then click the Properties button on the toolbar.

11. Click the Data tab, and set the value of the Allow Edits property to No, the Allow Deletions property to No, and the Allow Additions property to No. These changes prevent records displayed by this form from being edited, added to, or deleted.

12. Click the Format tab, and set the value of the Scroll Bars property to Neither, then set the Record Selectors and Navigation Buttons properties to No. The default GridX and GridY property values of 24 correspond to the grid spacing of the frmPersonnelActionsEntry form.

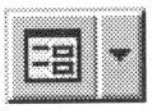

13. Close the Properties window, and drag the right edge of the form leftward until the form is just under 5 inches wide. Your form should look like the one you saw in figure 13.61.

14. Click the Form View button on the toolbar. The continuous form displays all the records in the Personnel Actions subquery, as shown in figure 13.62.

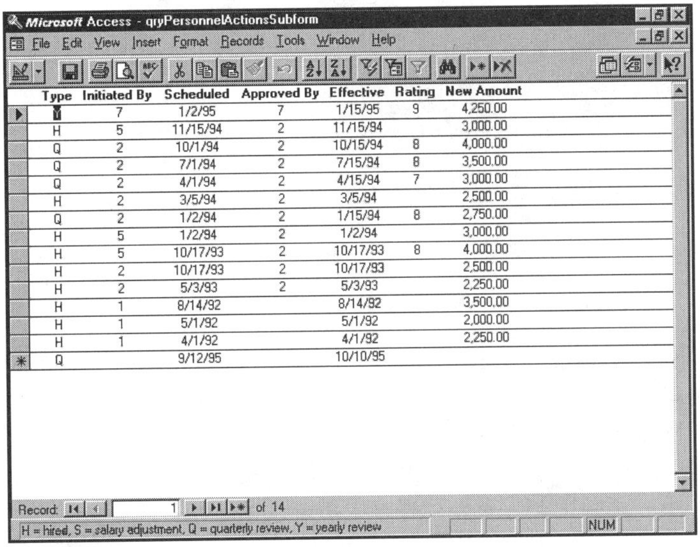

	Type	Initiated By	Scheduled	Approved By	Effective	Rating	New Amount
▶	Y	7	1/2/95	7	1/15/95	9	4,250.00
	H	5	11/15/94	2	11/15/94		3,000.00
	Q	2	10/1/94	2	10/15/94	8	4,000.00
	Q	2	7/1/94	2	7/15/94	8	3,500.00
	Q	2	4/1/94	2	4/15/94	7	3,000.00
	H	2	3/5/94	2	3/5/94		2,500.00
	Q	2	1/2/94	2	1/15/94	8	2,750.00
	H	5	1/2/94	2	1/2/94		3,000.00
	H	5	10/17/93	2	10/17/93	8	4,000.00
	H	2	10/17/93	2	10/17/93		2,500.00
	H	2	5/3/93	2	5/3/93		2,250.00
	H	1	8/14/92		8/14/92		3,500.00
	H	1	5/1/92		5/1/92		2,000.00
	H	1	4/1/92		4/1/92		2,250.00
✳	Q		9/12/95		10/10/95		

Record: ◄◄ ◄ 1 ► ►► ►✳ of 14

H = hired, S = salary adjustment, Q = quarterly review, Y = yearly review   NUM

Fig. 13.62   The appearance of the continuous form of figure 13.61 in Run mode.

15. Choose File, Save As/Export. Select the option named Within the current database as, and type **sbfPersonnelActionsTab** in the New Name text box. Click OK to save the form under its new name. Click the Close window button to close the form.

Now, you need to add the tabular form you just created as a subform in the frmPersonnelActionsEntry form. You'll use the Subform/Subreport Wizard to insert this form into your main form. To complete this procedure, perform the following steps:

1. Open the frmPersonnelActionsEntry form, and click the Design View button on the toolbar.

III

Forms and Reports

2. If necessary, click the Control Wizards button on the toolbar to enable the Control Wizards (the button position should be down).

3. Click the Subform button on the Toolbox, then click beneath the paComments text box in the Detail section of the form. Access displays the first dialog of the Subform/Subreport Wizard.

 4. To insert an existing form, select the Forms option, then select sbfPersonnelActionsTab in the drop-down list (see fig. 13.63). Click Next to reach the second dialog.

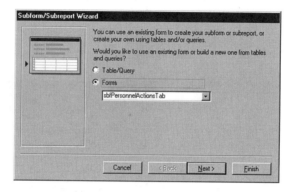

Fig. 13.63 Using the Subform/Subreport Wizard to insert an existing form as a subform.

 5. The wizard asks you to specify the link between the main form and the subform. You may select from a list of possible relationships that Access has determined, or define your own link. Click the Define my own option; select paID in the upper Form/report fields list, and select paID in the upper Subform/subreport fields list. Click Next to go to the third dialog.

6. Accept the default label name for the new subform field, and click Finish to complete the new subform field. Access now inserts the form you specified as a subform on the main form, and sizes the subform field to accommodate the new subform, as shown in figure 13.64.

7. Delete the label from the subform field, and resize the field so that it fills the width of the main form. Scroll the Form Design window downward, and resize the subform field so that the bottom of the field is at approximately the 3 3/8" mark. Drag the Form Footer upward so that the form is 3.5 inches high (see fig. 13.65).

8. Click the Form View button on the toolbar to check the appearance of the new subform. Your form appears as shown in figure 13.66. If the subform displays scroll bars or a record selector, close the Personnel Action Entry form and reopen it from the Database window to remove these features (called *adornments*).

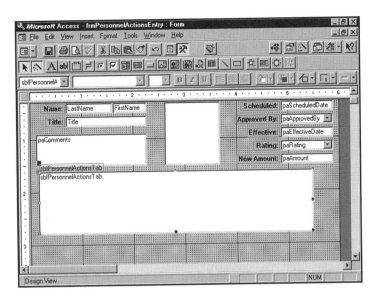

Fig. 13.64 The new subform field for the sbfPersonnelActionsTab form, inserted by the Subform/Subreport Wizard.

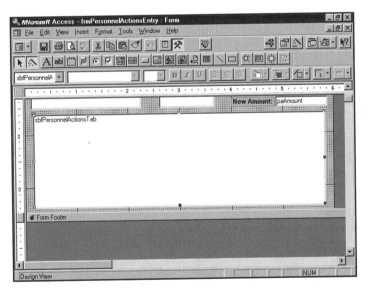

Fig. 13.65 The modified sbfPersonnelActionsTab form in Design View.

III

Forms and Reports

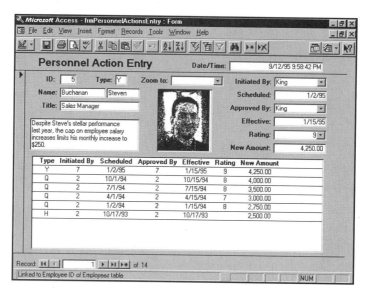

Fig. 13.66 The completed subform and main form in Form View.

> **Note**
>
> Delete the vertical scroll bar when all the control objects of the noncontinuous form fit in a maximized form window. The horizontal scroll bar need not be present when record selectors are used. You can eliminate both the horizontal scroll bar and the record selectors when you substitute command buttons for the record selectors in Part IV, "Powering Access with Macros." Unnecessary graphic elements are distracting and have a negative influence on the overall appearance of a form.

9. Choose File, Save, and then click the Close window button to close the frmPersonnelActionsEntry form.

The frmPersonnelActionsEntry form's fields and field formatting are essentially complete. In a real-world application, you would now adjust the tab order of the form, and test the form by entering and editing records—you learned to do these steps in Chapter 12, "Creating and Using Forms."

Overriding the Field Properties of Tables

Access uses the table's property values assigned to the fields as defaults. The form or subform *inherits* these properties from the table or query on which the form is based. You can override the inherited properties, except for the Validation Rule property, by assigning a different set of values in the Properties window for the control. Properties of controls bound to fields of tables or queries that are inherited from the table's field properties are shown in the following list:

- Format

- Decimal Places

- Status Bar Text

- Validation Rule

- Validation Text

- Default Value

- Typeface characteristics, such as Font Name, Font Size, Font Bold, Font Italic, and Font Underline

Values of field properties that you override with properties in a form apply only when the data is displayed and edited with the form. Here, the Format, Decimal Places, and Validation Rules you apply in forms are similar to Xbase PICTURE and VALID instructions appended to the GET command.

You can establish validation rules for controls bound to fields that differ from properties of the field established by the table, but you can only narrow the rule. The table-level validation rule for the content of the paType field, for example, limits entries to the letters H, S, Q, Y, B, and C. The validation rule you establish in a form cannot broaden the allowable entries; if you add T as a valid choice by editing the validation rule for the paType field to InStr("HSQYBCT",[PA Type])>0, you receive an error when you type **T**. However, you can narrow the range of allowable entries by substituting InStr("SQYB",[PA Type])>0. Notice that you can use expressions that refer to the field name in validation rule expressions in forms; such expressions are not permitted in table validation rule expressions in Access 95.

Adding Page Headers and Footers for Printing Forms

Access enables you to add a separate pair of sections, Page Header and Page Footer, that appear only when the form prints. You add both these sections to the form at once, by choosing View, Page Header/Footer. The following list shows the purposes of Page Headers and Footers:

- *Page Header* sections enable you to use a different title for the printed version. The depth of the Page Header can be adjusted to control the location where the Detail section of the form is printed on the page.

- *Page Footer* sections enable you to add dates and page numbers to the printed form.

Page Header and Page Footer sections appear only in the printed form, not when you display the form on-screen in Run mode. The frmPersonnelActionsEntry form in Design mode with Page Header and Page Footer sections added is shown in figure 13.67. The subform control has been deleted so that both the Form Footer and Page Footer sections appear in the window. Usually, you need to use the vertical scroll bar to display these sections in Design mode.

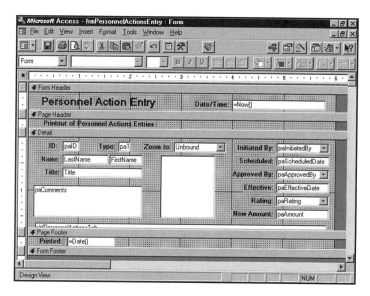

Fig. 13.67 The frmPersonnelActionsEntry form with Page Header and Page Footer sections added.

With the Display When (Format) property of the Properties window for the Form Header and Form Footer sections, you can control whether these sections appear in the printed form. In figure 13.67, the Form Header duplicates the information in the Page Header (except for the Date/Time label and text box), so you don't want to print both. To control when a section of the form prints or is displayed, perform the following steps:

1. Double-click the title bar of whichever section of the form you want to change; this opens the related Properties window. (The Page Header and Page Footer sections don't have a Display When property; these sections only appear when printing.)

2. Click the Format tab if the formatting properties aren't already showing. Click to drop down the Display When list.

3. To display, but not print, this section in Run mode, select Screen Only.

4. To print, but not display, this section, select Print Only.

From Here...

The examples presented in this chapter demonstrate the ease with which you can add productivity features to an Access form created by the Form Wizard, or else build a custom form from ground zero. The Control Wizards and their related methodology suffice to create forms that satisfy the majority of your database transaction-processing and decision-support applications.

- Chapters 14, "Printing Basic Reports and Mailing Labels," and 15, "Preparing Advanced Reports," describe how to use the Toolbox to add control objects to reports.

- Chapter 17, "Using Macros with Forms and Reports," shows you how to add command buttons to forms and attach macros to the command buttons.

- Chapter 20, "Adding Graphics to Forms and Reports," describes how you add bound and unbound object frames containing graphic images to forms.

Chapter 14

Printing Basic Reports and Mailing Labels

The final product of most database applications is a report. In Access, a *report* is a special kind of continuous form designed specifically for printing. Access combines data in tables, queries, and even forms to produce a report that you can print and distribute to people who need or request it. A printed version of a form can serve as a report, which often is the case for reports designed for decision support, one of the topics of Chapter 20, "Adding Graphics to Forms and Reports." By printing a continuous form, you can create a report that displays some or all the values of fields in a table or query.

This chapter describes how you create relatively simple reports, including multicolumn mailing labels, using the Report Wizards, and how you modify the design of the wizard's reports to suit your particular needs. The next chapter describes how you design a report from scratch, without using the Report Wizards.

Differences and Similarities between Forms and Reports

Most methods of creating transaction-processing forms, which you learned about in Chapter 11, "Using Action Queries," and Chapter 12, "Creating and Using Forms," also apply to reports. The following list details the principal differences between reports and forms:

- Reports are intended for printing only and, unlike forms, aren't designed for display in a window. When you view an 8 1/2-by-11-inch report in Print Preview, its content is not legible. In the zoomed (full-page) view, only a portion of the report is visible in the Print Preview window.

- You cannot change the value of the underlying data for a report with a control object from the toolbox, as you can with forms. With reports, Access disregards user input from option buttons, check boxes, and the like. You can use these controls, however, to indicate the status of

In this chapter, you learn how to do the following

- Create an AutoReport from a table or query

- Customize Report Wizard styles

- Use the Report Wizard to create a group-totals report

- Modify a report created by the Report Wizard

- Print multicolumn reports as mailing labels

III

Forms and Reports

Yes/No option buttons and check boxes and of fields with values derived from multiple-choice lists.

■ Reports do not provide a Datasheet View. Only Print Preview and Report Design Views are available.

■ You can create an *unbound* report that isn't linked to a source of data. Unbound reports are used as "containers" for individual subreports that use unrelated data sources.

■ The Printer Setup dialog controls the minimum left, right, top, and bottom printing margins of reports. If a report is less than the printable page width, the report's design determines the right margin. You can increase the left margin over the default setting by positioning the print fields to the right of the display's left margin.

■ In multicolumn reports, the number of columns, the column width, and the column spacing are controlled by settings in the Printer Setup dialog, not by controls that you add or properties that you set in design mode.

Access reports share many characteristics of forms, including the following:

■ *Report Wizards* can create the three basic kinds of reports: single-column, groups/totals, and mailing labels. You can modify as necessary the reports that the Report Wizard creates. The function of the Report Wizard is similar to that of the Form Wizard discussed in Chapter 12, "Creating and Using Forms," and Chapter 13, "Designing Custom Multitable Forms."

■ *Sections* include report headers and footers that appear once at the beginning and at the end of the report, and page headers and footers that print at the top and bottom of each page. The report footer often is used to print grand totals. Report sections correspond to similarly named form sections.

■ *Group sections* of reports, as a whole, comprise the equivalent of the Detail section of forms. Groups often are referred to as *bands,* and the process of grouping records is known as *banding.* You can add Group Headers that include a title for each group, and Group Footers to print group subtotals. You can place static (unbound) graphics in header and footer sections and bound graphics within group sections.

■ *Controls* are added to reports from the Access toolbox and then moved and sized with their handles.

■ *Subreports* can be incorporated into reports the same way that you add subform controls within main forms.

Types of Access Reports

Reports created by Access fall into six basic types, also called *layouts,* which the following list details:

■ *Single-column reports* list in one long column of text boxes the values of each field in each record of a table or query. A label indicates the name of a field, and a text box to the right of the label provides the values. Access 95's new AutoReport feature creates a single-column report with a single click of the toolbar's AutoReport button. Single-column reports are seldom used because the format wastes paper.

- *Tabular reports* provide a column for each field of the table or query and print the value of each field of the records in rows under the column header. If you have more columns than can fit on one page, additional pages print in sequence until all the columns are printed; then the next group of records is printed. Figure 14.1 shows in Report Preview mode a tabular report based on Northwind.mdb's Customers table.

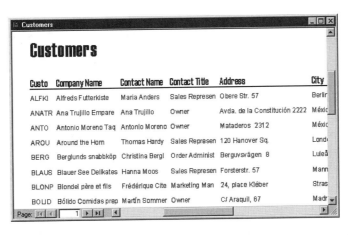

Fig. 14.1 A preview of a tabular report created from Northwind.mdb's Customers table.

- *Multicolumn reports* are created from single-column reports by using the "newspaper" or "snaking" column approach of desktop publishing and word processing applications. Information that doesn't fit in the first column flows to the top of the second column, and so on. The format of multicolumn tables wastes less paper, but has limited uses because the alignment of the columns is unlikely to correspond to how you want them.

- *Groups/totals reports* are the most common kind of report. Access groups/totals reports are similar to the reports created by other database managers, such as dBASE and Paradox. They summarize data for groups of records and then add grand totals at the end of the report.

- *Mailing labels* are a special kind of multicolumn report designed to print names and addresses (or other multifield data) in groups. Each group of fields constitutes a cell in a grid. The design of the stock adhesive label on which you are printing determines how many rows and columns are on a page.

- *Unbound reports* contain subreports based on unrelated data sources, such as tables or queries.

III

Forms and Reports

The first four types of reports use a table or query as the data source, as do forms. These kinds of reports are said to be *bound* to the data source. The main report of an unbound report is not linked to a table or a query as a data source. The subreports contained by an unbound report, however, must be bound to a data source. Unbound reports enable you to incorporate subreports bound to independent tables or queries.

Creating a Grouping Report with the Report Wizard

This section shows you how to use the Report Wizard to create a grouping report based on data in the Northwind Traders sample database's Products and Suppliers tables. (Like the Form Wizard, the Report Wizard enables you to create reports that contain data from more than one table without first creating a query.) This report displays the quantity of each specialty food product in inventory, grouped by product category.

To create an inventory report, you modify the basic report created by the Report Wizard. The process of creating a basic report with the Report Wizard is similar to the process that you used to create a form in Chapter 12, "Creating and Using Forms." An advantage of using the Report Wizard to introduce the topic of designing Access reports is that the steps for this process parallel the steps that you take when you start with a default blank report. Chapter 15, "Preparing Advanced Reports," explains how to start with a blank report and create more complex reports.

To create a Product On Hand by Category report, follow these steps:

1. Click the Reports tab in the Database window, and then click the New button. Access displays the New Report dialog (see fig. 14.2).

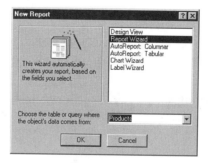

Fig. 14.2 The New Report dialog, in which you select the report's type and data source.

2. Like forms, reports require a data source, which can be a table or a query. Select the Products table from the choices offered in the New Report dialog's drop-down list (refer to fig. 14.2). Select Report Wizard in the list in the dialog's upper-right corner, and click OK. The Report Wizard displays its opening dialog.

3. The fields that you choose to display represent rows of the report. You want the report to print the product name and supplier so that users do not have to refer

to another report to associate codes with names. The fields from the Products table that you need for this report are CategoryID, ProductID, ProductName, SupplierID, and UnitsInStock. With the > button, select these fields in sequence from the Available Fields list (see fig. 14.3). As you add fields to the Selected Fields list, Access removes the field names from the Available Fields list. Alternatively, you can double-click the field name in the Available Fields list to move the field name to the Selected Fields list. The fields appear from left to right in the report, based on the top-to-bottom sequence in which the fields appear in the Selected Fields list.

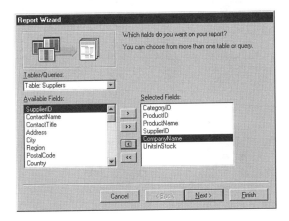

Fig. 14.3 The opening Report Wizard dialog enables you to select the fields of a report from one or more tables or queries.

4. To avoid having to look up Supplier ID numbers in a separate report, you need to add to this report the CompanyName field from the Suppliers table. Open the Tables/Queries drop-down list and select Table: Suppliers (refer to fig. 14.3).

5. Instead of presenting the supplier name as the report's last field, you want the report's CompanyName column to follow the SupplierID report column. Select the SupplierID field in the Selected Fields list. Now select the CompanyName field from the Available Fields list and click the > button. Access moves the CompanyName field from the Available Fields list and inserts the field into the Selected Fields list, after the SupplierID field and before the UnitsInStock field (refer to fig. 14.3). Choose Next to continue with the second wizard dialog, shown in figure 14.4.

> **Note**
>
> If you want to change the field order shown in the right pane of figure 14.4, use the < button to move the field back to the Available Fields list. You can retrace your steps to correct an error by clicking the Back button whenever it is activated. The Finish button accepts all defaults and jumps to to the end of the wizard, so you shouldn't use this button.

6. The Report Wizard asks you to choose how you want to view the data in the report. Notice the Show Me More Information button near the left center of the wizard

Next >

dialog. Click this button to display the first of a series of hint dialogs for the Report Wizard (see fig. 14.5). If you click the Show Me Examples option, Access displays additional hint screens. These screens use examples from the Sales Reps, Customers, and Orders tables to show you the different groupings that the Report Wizard can automatically add to the report. Click the Close button repeatedly until you return to the Report Wizard dialog shown in figure 14.4.

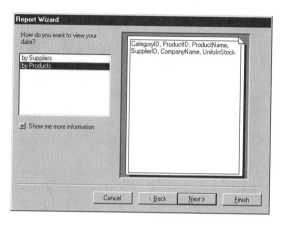

Fig. 14.4 The second step in the Report Wizard is to choose how you want to view your data.

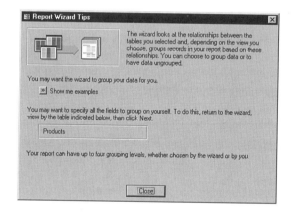

Fig. 14.5 The first Report Wizard hint screen suggests that you view the data in the Products table to set your own groupings, or offers the Show Me Examples button to show you how the wizard can group your data.

7. For this report, you select your own groupings. Select By Products in the list, and choose Next to continue with the third Report Wizard dialog.

8. The Report Wizard asks whether you want to add any grouping levels to the report. Select the CategoryID field in the list, and click the > button to establish the grouping by Products category. The Report Wizard dialog now appears as shown in figure 14.6.

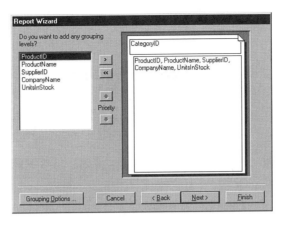

Fig. 14.6 The Report Wizard lets you select your own grouping levels; here, the CategoryID field is selected as the first grouping level.

9. Click the Grouping Options button. The Report Wizard displays the Grouping Intervals dialog shown in figure 14.7. By changing the grouping interval, you can affect how Access groups data in the report. For numeric fields, you can group items by tens, fifties, hundreds, and so on. For text fields, you can group items based on the first letter, the first three letters, and so on.

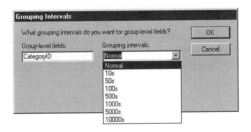

Fig. 14.7 The Report Wizard lets you select grouping intervals.

> **Note**
>
> If your application uses a text-coding scheme, such as BEVA for alcoholic beverages and BEVN for nonalcoholic beverages, you can combine all beverages in a single group by selecting 1st 3 Characters from the Grouping Intervals list. Access 95 provides this option for numeric fields and for fields of the Text data type.

10. This report doesn't require any special grouping interval, so select Normal in the Grouping Intervals list, and click OK to return to the Report Wizard's third dialog (refer to fig. 14.6). Choose Next to continue with the fourth wizard dialog.

11. You can sort the records within groups by any field that you choose (see fig. 14.8), with up to four different sorted fields. The dialog does not offer CategoryID as a choice because the records are grouped in this field. Select ProductID in the first drop-down list. By default, the sort order is ascending; if you want a descending

Next >

III

Forms and Reports

sort order, click the button to the right of the drop-down list. (This button is a toggle control; click it again to return to an ascending sort.)

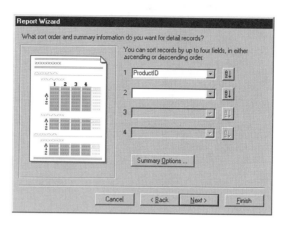

Fig. 14.8 The Report Wizard enables you to select as many as four different fields on which to sort data within a group.

12. Choose the Summary Options button to display the Summary Options dialog (see fig. 14.9). If you want to add summary information to a report column, you set the options for that column in this dialog. The Report Wizard lists all the numeric fields on the report that aren't AutoNumber fields, and offers you check boxes to select a Sum, Average, Minimum, and Maximum for that report column. Depending on the check boxes that you select, the Report Wizard adds those summary fields to the end of the report. The Show option group enables you to select whether the report shows the summary fields only or shows the full report with the summary fields added at the end of each group and at the end of the report. For this report, select the Sum and Avg check boxes, the Detail and Summary option, and the Calculate Percent of Total for Sums check box. (The Calculate Percent of Total for Sums check box displays the percentage a group's total that is of the grand total for all groups.) Click OK to return to the Report Wizard dialog.

Next >

13. Choose Next to continue with the fourth wizard dialog, shown in figure 14.10. The Report Wizard asks you to select one of six layout styles for your report. The window in the left side of the wizard dialog shows a preview of the layout style that you select. For this report, choose Stepped in the Layout option group.

Next >

14. By default, the Report Wizard selects the Adjust the Field Width So All Fields Fit on a Page check box. As a rule, you should select this option to save paper and make your report more legible. In the Orientation option group, you select the report's printing orientation. Make sure that you select the Portrait option. Choose Next to continue with the fifth Report Wizard dialog.

Next >

15. Select one of the predefined report styles for your report. The window on the left shows a preview of the selected style (see fig. 14.11). (You can customize or create your own styles for the Report Wizard to use. This activity is described in the

"Using AutoFormat and Customizing Report Styles" section, later in this chapter.) Select the Compact style, and then choose Next to continue with the sixth, and final, Report Wizard dialog.

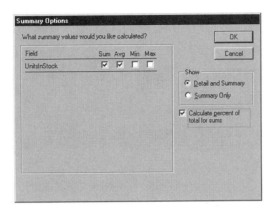

Fig. 14.9 In the Report Wizard's Summary Options dialog, select the types of summary fields that you want in your report.

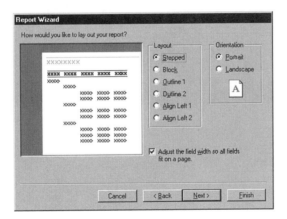

Fig. 14.10 The Report Wizard lets you choose from six standard layout formats.

16. Type **Product On Hand by Category** as the title for the new report; the Report Wizard also uses this title as the name of the saved report it creates (see fig. 14.12). Select the Preview the report option and click Finish to complete your report specification; the Report Wizard creates the report and displays it in print preview mode. (To get Help with the report, click the Do you want to display Help on working with the report? checkbox.)

Figure 14.13 shows the basic report that the Report Wizard creates. Use the vertical and horizontal scroll bars to position the preview as shown. (Leave the report in print preview mode for now because you use this report as the basis for examples in subsequent sections of this chapter.)

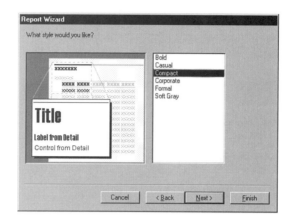

Fig. 14.11 The Report Wizard enables you to select a predefined style for your report.

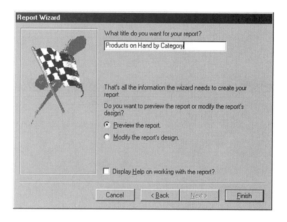

Fig. 14.12 In the final stage of the Report Wizard, you give your report a title and select how you want to view the completed report.

 ◀◀ See "Using Lookup Fields in Tables," p. 328

In figure 14.13, notice that the report appears to have duplicate columns—there is a Supplier column, which lists the name of the product's supplier, and the Company Name column, which also lists the name of the product's supplier. The reason for this duplication is twofold:

■ The Products table's SupplierID field has a Caption property set. This property establishes an alias for the field. The Report Wizard substitutes the text in the Caption property for the field name in field labels on the report.

■ The Products table's SupplierID field is defined as a lookup field. Therefore, Access automatically looks up the value corresponding to the SupplierID code in the Suppliers table, and displays that value rather than the actual code number stored in the field.

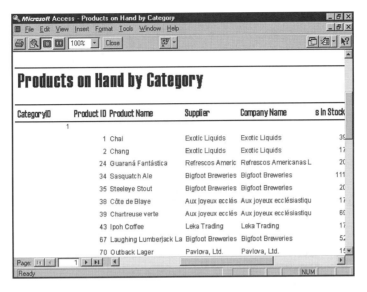

Fig. 14.13 The basic report created by the Report Wizard.

When you view the lookup field in Design View, a nonfunctional drop-down list button (see fig. 14.14 in the next section) designates lookup fields. This report doesn't need to include the Suppliers table's CompanyName field, because the SupplierID field is a lookup field.

With a few simple modifications, you can obtain a finished report with the information necessary to analyze Northwind's current inventory. (See "Modifying a Basic Report Wizard Report" later in this chapter.)

Using Access's Report Windows

The windows that you use to design and run Access reports are easier to use than those windows that you use for other basic Access functions. To open an existing Access report, click the Report tab in the Database window and then select a report name from the Database window. If you click the Design button or the New button to create a new report, the design mode toolbar appears with the buttons listed in table 14.1.

Design

New

III

Table 14.1 Standard Toolbar Buttons in Report Design Mode		
Button	**Function**	**Menu Choice**
	Selects Print Preview to display how your report appears when printed. You can print the form from the Print Preview window. (Same as the Print Preview button.)	File, Print Preview
	Saves the current report.	File, Save

(continues)

Table 14.1 Continued

Button	Function	Menu Choice
	Prints the report without displaying the Print dialog. Access prints the report using the current printer settings.	Not applicable
	Selects Print Preview to display how your report appears when printed. You can print the form from the Print Preview window.	File, Print Preview
	Starts the spelling checker to check the selected label control's spelling.	Tools, Spelling
	Cuts the selected object(s) from the report and puts them on the Clipboard.	Edit, Cut
	Copies the selected object(s) from the report onto the Clipboard.	Edit, Copy
	Pastes the Clipboard's contents onto the report.	Edit, Paste
	Copies formatting from the selected object to another object of a similar type.	Not applicable
	Undoes the last change that you made to the report.	Edit, Undo
	Displays a list of fields in the query or table that is the main report's data source.	View, Field List
	Displays or closes the toolbox.	View, Toolbox
	Displays the Sorting and Grouping dialog in which you can establish the structure of reports and the order in which the report presents the data.	View, Sorting and Grouping
	Applies your choice of several predefined report formats, including formatting for the text fonts and color settings.	Format, AutoFormat
	Opens the window in which you can edit event-handling code.	View, Code
	Displays the Properties dialog for the entire report, the sections of the report when you click the section divider bars, or the properties of a control when a control is selected.	View, Properties
	Displays a Builder Wizard for the selected object or property in the report. This button is enabled only if Access has a builder for the selected item.	Not applicable
	Displays the Database window.	Window, 1 Database
	Creates a new object. Click the arrow to the right of this button to see a drop-down list of objects that you can create.	Not applicable
	Click this button, then click an object on-screen (such as a toolbar button) to display a pop-up help window with information about that command or button.	Not applicable

The buttons not listed in table 14.1 serve the same purposes for both forms and reports. As is the case for form design mode, the Formatting toolbar's buttons for formatting text are enabled only when a control object that can contain text is selected.

If you double-click the name of an existing report, or click the Open button in the Database window, the report displays in print preview mode, which is the run mode for reports. Table 14.2 lists the toolbar's buttons in print preview mode.

Table 14.2	Standard Toolbar Buttons in Report Print Preview Mode	
Button	**Function**	**Menu Choice**
🖨	Prints the report without displaying the Print dialog. The report is printed using the current printer settings.	Not applicable
🔍	Toggles between full-page and full-size views of the report. Clicking the mouse when its pointer appears as the magnifying glass symbol produces the same effect.	View, Zoom
▣	Displays one full page.	View, Pages, 1
▣▣	Displays two full pages.	View, Pages, 2
Fit ▼	Changes the size of the view from 200 percent to 10 percent, or fits the report to the window.	View, Zoom
Close	Closes Print Preview and returns to Report Design View or to the Database window.	File, Print Preview
📇▼	Displays a drop-down list of shortcut commands for Microsoft Office Links: Merge It, Publish It with MS Word, and Analyze It with MS Excel.	Tools, OfficeLinks
📇	Opens the Database window.	Window, 1 Database
📇▼	Creates a new object. Click the arrow at the right of this button to display a drop-down list of objects that you can create.	Not applicable
▶?	Displays a pop-up help window with information about an object or button on-screen (such as a toolbar button). Click this button, then click the object or button for which you want information.	Not applicable

Chapter 22, "Using Access with Microsoft Word and Mail Merge," discusses using the Office Links button to print reports as files in rich-text format. Chapter 21, "Using Access with Microsoft Excel," discusses printing files in Excel BIFF format. Chapter 15, "Preparing Advanced Reports," describes linking files created from reports to Microsoft Mail messages.

Using AutoFormat and Customizing Report Styles

◀◀ See "Using AutoFormat," p. 410

The AutoFormat toolbar button works the same way for reports as it does for forms. Chapter 12, "Creating and Using Forms," contains a detailed, step-by-step explanation of how to use Access 95's new AutoFormat button and how to customize the predefined AutoFormat styles or create your own AutoFormat styles. Follow the instructions in the "Using AutoFormat" section of Chapter 12 to apply an AutoFormat style to a report, or to define or customize a report AutoFormat style. Access stores styles for reports and forms separately, so you'll need to create separate AutoFormat styles for your reports.

As with forms, to create an AutoFormat style for customized reports, you must first create a report that contains controls formatted the way that you want for your new style. You click the AutoFormat button on the toolbar, and then click the Customize button in the AutoFormat dialog to customize the format.

Modifying a Basic Report Wizard Report

The Report Wizard tries to create the optimum final report in the first pass. Usually, the wizard comes close enough to a finished product that you spend far less time modifying a wizard-created basic report than you spend creating a report from the default blank template.

In the following sections, you use Access's report design features to make the report easier to read and more attractive.

Deleting, Relocating, and Editing Existing Controls

The first step in modifying the wizard's report is to modify the existing controls on the report. You don't need to align the labels and text boxes precisely during the initial modification; later in this chapter, the section "Aligning Controls Horizontally and Vertically" covers control alignment. To modify the wizard's report to create space to add additional controls, follow these steps:

1. Click the Print Preview toolbar's Close button on to enter report design mode; click the Maximize Window button to maximize the design window, if necessary. The Product on Hand by Category report, as created by the Report Wizard, appears as shown in figure 14.14.

2. The SupplierID and CompanyName fields are redundant in this report because the SupplierID field is a lookup field. Select the Company Name label in the Page Header section, then hold down the Shift key and click the CompanyName field in the Detail section; press Delete to remove the field and label from the report. (Don't worry about aligning the fields and labels yet.)

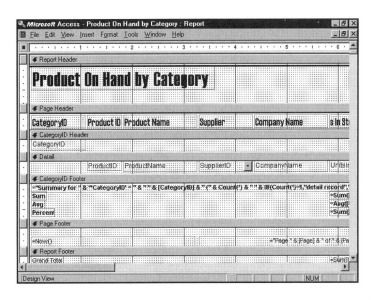

Fig. 14.14   The basic report in design mode (all toolbars have been hidden to make the entire report visible).

3. This report is more useful if you include the dollar value of both the inventory and the number of units on hand. To accommodate one or two additional columns, you must compress the fields' widths. CategoryID occupies a column, but you can display this column's content in the CategoryID footer (or header) without using the extra column space. Select and delete the CategoryID label from the Page Header section and the CategoryID text box from the CategoryID Header section. For this report, you'll put the CategoryID name in the footer section of the group, so drag the Detail section bar upward to eliminate the space occupied by the CategoryID Header. Your report appears as shown in figure 14.15.

4. All the Page Header labels, Detail text boxes, and Totals text boxes in the CategoryID Footer and Report Footer sections must move to the left as a group. Click the Product ID label to select it, and then press and hold down Shift. Click the remaining Page Header labels, each of the Detail text boxes, the three summary field text boxes in the Category ID Footer section, and the Grand Total text box in the Report Footer section, and then release Shift. (To select all the labels and text boxes, you'll need to scroll the report to the right and left, and up and down.)

5. Position the mouse pointer over the Product ID label at a location at which the pointer turns into the graphic showing the palm of a hand. Hold down the left mouse button and drag the selected fields to the left margin. Your report appears as shown in figure 14.16.

6. You can more easily edit and position the labels if you left-justify them. Click a blank area of the report to deselect the group, select all the Page Header labels, and click the Align Left button on the toolbar. Do the same for the Grand Total label in the Report Footer section.

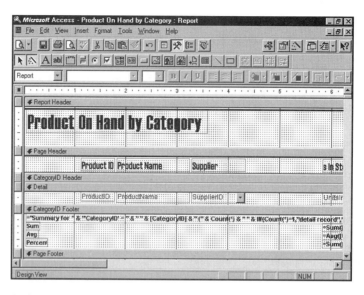

Fig. 14.15 The basic report after you delete the CategoryID label and text box and close the space for the CategoryID Header.

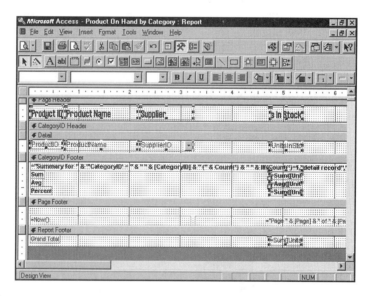

Fig. 14.16 Moving selected labels and text boxes to the report's left margin.

7. Edit the Product ID label to remove *ID*, and edit the Units In Stock label to read only *Units*. Select all the labels in the Page Header and choose F̲ormat, S̲ize, to F̲it. Resize the widths of the ProductID, SupplierID, and UnitsInStock text boxes in the Detail section to match the width of the labels in the Page Header. Relocate the labels to provide more space on the right side of the report, as shown in figure 14.17.

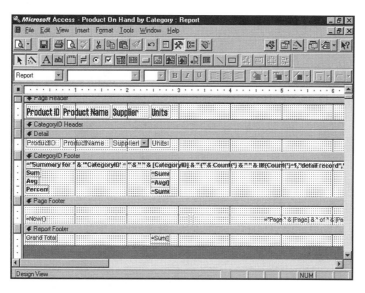

Fig. 14.17 The Product on Hand by Category report after you edit, resize, and relocate existing controls.

8. By default, the Report Wizard adds to the CategoryID Footer a calculated field (visible in fig. 14.17) that displays the group's field name (CategoryID) and value to help identify the group footer's summary fields. For example, for CategoryID 1, the calculated field displays the following:

   ```
   "Summary for 'CategoryID = 1' (12 detail records)."
   ```

   For this report, you want a more explicit description of the product category—more than just the CategoryID number. Delete this calculated field; you'll replace it in the next step.

9. You now need to add a bound text box to identify the subtotal in the CategoryID Footer section. Click the Field List button on the toolbar. Select CategoryID from the list in the Field List window.

10. Click and drag the field symbol mouse pointer to the left margin of the CategoryID Footer. Because the CategoryID field is a lookup field, it displays with a drop-down list button for the field box. When printed or displayed in Print Preview, this field shows the CategoryID name rather than the numeric code.

11. Select the label of the CategoryID field that you just placed, and use the Font and Size drop-down lists on the Formatting toolbar to set the label's font to Arial and the label's size to 8 points. Next, select the CategoryID text box, click the Bold button on the toolbar to add the bold attribute to the CategoryID text box, and also select the Arial font at a size of 8 points. Figure 14.18 shows the new bound CategoryID field in place of the calculated field that you deleted in step 8. (In the figure, the report has been scrolled upward in the window to make the Report Footer and Page Footer sections visible.)

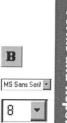

III

Forms and Reports

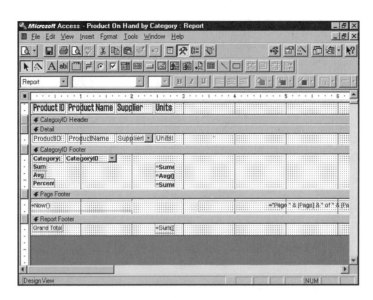

Fig. 14.18   The Product On Hand by Category report after you add the CategoryID field to the CategoryID Footer section and reduce the Page Footer section's height.

12. Drag the two calculated fields in the Page Footer section until they are one grid mark away from the top of the Page Footer section. Drag the Report Footer bar upward to reduce the Page Footer's height as shown in figure 14.18.

13. For this report, the Average field is unnecessary; delete it and its label, and then rearrange the remaining fields and labels. Click and drag the =Sum([UnitsInStock])/ [UnitsInStock Grand Total Sum] text box from its present location below the =Sum([UnitsInStock]) text box to a position at the top of the CategoryID Footer, near the page's right edge. Drag the =Sum([UnitsInStock]) field to a position at the top of the CategoryID text box and near the center of the page. Finally, move up the Page Footer divider bar to reduce the footer's depth (see fig. 14.19).

14. Click the toolbar's Save button to save your report.

Troubleshooting

When I preview or print my report, Access displays or prints a blank page after each page with data.

If a report's width becomes greater than the net printable width (the paper width minus the sum of the left and right margins), the number of report pages doubles. Columns of fields that do not fit a page's width print on a second page, similar to the printing method used by spreadsheet applications. If you set your right margin beyond the right printing margin, or if the right edge of any control on the report extends past the right printing margin, the added pages often are blank. Change the printing margins or reduce the width of your report so that it conforms to the printable page width. (See the section "Adjusting Margins and Printing Conventional Reports" later in this chapter.)

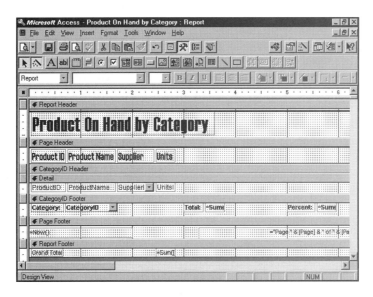

Fig. 14.19 The completely modified Product On Hand by Category report in design mode.

To check the progress of your work, periodically click the toolbar's Print Preview button to display the report prior to printing. At this point, your Product On Hand by Category report appears in print preview mode as shown in figure 14.20.

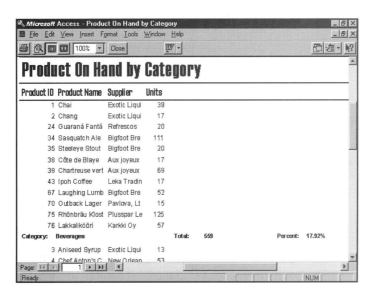

Fig. 14.20 Previewing the Product On Hand by Category report.

Using the DLookUp() Domain Aggregate Function to Print Product Category Names

As you saw in the preceding section of this chapter, lookup fields in a table are placed on a report as a limited-function combo box; you can't use the combo box to select values, but it causes a value looked up from another table to be displayed instead of the actual field value. For example, if you place the CategoryID field on the report (as you did in the preceding section), Access displays the category name in the report rather than the actual CategoryID number, because the CategoryID field in the Products table has lookup field properties assigned to it. When you place the CategoryID field on the report, Access automatically creates a combo box control with the properties needed to look up the CategoryName field from the Categories table.

Not every table that you use in your reports will have lookup fields, however, nor is it necessarily desirable to create lookup fields for all numeric code fields (such as CategoryID and SupplierID). If you want to display a looked-up value for a field that isn't defined as a lookup field, you use Access's domain aggregate function, DLookUp(), to find values from another table that correspond to a value in one of the report's fields. For example, if you want to display both the actual CategoryID number and the CategoryName in the Group Footer of the Product On Hand by Category report, you can use the DLookUp() function to display the text of the CategoryName field from the Categories table, and a bound text field to display the CategoryID number from the Products table.

To change the CategoryID combo box control to a standard text box, and to add a new Category Name field that uses the DLookUp() function to the Product On Hand by Category report's Category ID Footer section, follow these steps:

1. In report design mode, select the CategoryID combo box, and then choose Format, Change To, Text Box to convert the combo box to a regular text box field. This field will no longer display the looked-up CategoryName field, but will display the actual number stored in the CategoryID field.

2. Edit the CategoryID field label to read **ID:**, then resize the CategoryID text box so that it is approximately 3/8 of an inch wide; move both the text box and the field box closer together, near the left edge of the report's CategoryID Footer section (see fig. 14.21).

3. Click the Toolbox button to display the toolbox, if it is not already displayed.

4. Click the text box tool and add a new unbound text box to the right of the CategoryID text box with the approximate dimensions shown in figure 14.21.

5. Delete the field label for the new text box control, and give the text box itself the bold text attribute.

6. Click the new text box and type the following as the text box's value:

```
=DLookUp("[CategoryName]","Categories","[CategoryID] =
Report!CategoryID") & " Category"
```

[CategoryName] is the value that you want to return to the text box. Categories is the table that contains the CategoryName field. [CategoryID] = Report!CategoryID is the criteria that selects the record in the Categories table with a CategoryID value equal to the value in your report's CategoryID text box. The Report prefix is necessary to distinguish between the CategoryID field of the Categories table and a control object of the same name. (Report is necessary in this example because Access has automatically named the report's CategoryID text box control as CategoryID.)

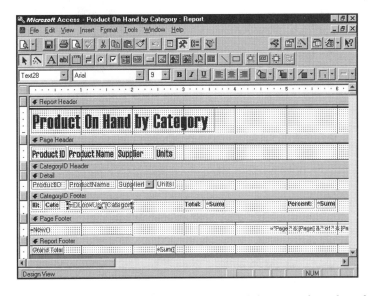

Fig. 14.21 The transformed and resized CategoryID field, and the new unbound text box containing the DLookUp() function.

7. Select the Category ID text box and verify that the name CategoryID appears in the Object Name text box (at the left side of the Formatting toolbar). If not, click the Properties button of the toolbar, select the Other tab in the Properties window, and type **CategoryID** as the value of the control's Name property (see fig. 14.22).

8. Click the Report View button of the toolbar. Your Product On Hand by Category report appears as shown in figure 14.23.

Troubleshooting

When I preview or print my report, the text box that contains the DLookUp() function displays #error or just the word Category.

Your DLookUp expression contains a typographical error, or one of the objects that you specified does not exist. Make sure that you have typed the entry in the CategoryName text box exactly as shown in the preceding step 6. If the field name in the table or query for which you are searching is the same as the control name, make sure that you add the Report! prefix to the control name. For example, you must add Report! if you assign Category Name as the name of the new control that you added in the preceding example.

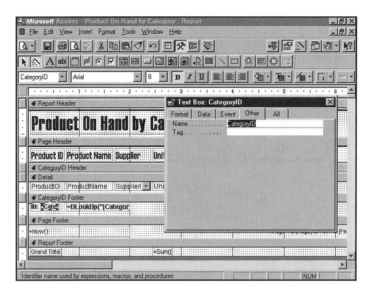

Fig. 14.22   Verifying the name of the CategoryID text box.

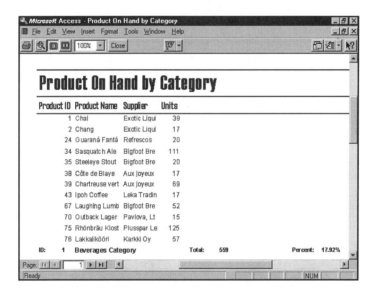

Fig. 14.23   The Product On Hand by Category report with the DLookUp() field added.

Adding Other Calculated Controls to the Report

Calculated controls, such as the DLookUp() control that you added in the preceding section, are quite useful in reports. You use calculated controls to determine extended values, such as quantity times unit price or quantity times cost. Now you have enough space at the right of the report to add a column for the UnitPrice field and a column for the extended inventory value, which is UnitPrice multiplied by UnitsInStock. To add these controls, follow the steps described in the following subsections.

Changing the Report's Record Source. You created the Product On Hand by Category report by selecting fields directly from the Products and Suppliers table in the Report Wizard. As a result, the Record Source property for the report, as a whole, is an SQL statement that selects only those fields that you chose initially in the Report Wizard. Although it's possible to add fields to the report by creating unbound text box controls and using the Expression Builder to create an expression to retrieve the desired value, it's much easier to create a query to select the fields desired for the report, and substitute the new query as the report's data source.

To create a query for use with the Product On Hand by Category report, follow these steps:

1. Click the toolbar's Database Window button to display the Database window. Click the Queries tab and then click New to create a new query.

2. In the New Query dialog, select Design View and then click OK.

3. Double-click the Products table in the Show Table dialog to add the table to the query. Then click Close to dismiss the Show Table dialog.

4. Drag the * field to the first column of the query grid to add to the query all the Products table's fields.

5. Drag the Discontinued field to the query grid's second column.

6. Clear the Show check box for the Discontinued field, and then type **=False** in the Discontinued field's first Criteria row (see fig. 14.24).

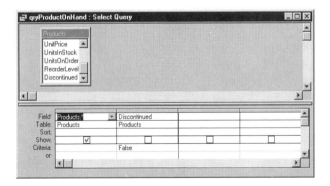

Fig. 14.24 The `qryProductOnHand` query, which contains all the fields from the Products table and excludes discontinued products, serves as the new Record Source property for the Product On Hand by Category report.

7. Click the Close Window button to close the Query window. A prompt asks whether you want to save changes to the query design. Click Yes.

8. In the Save As dialog's Query Name text box, type **qryProductOnHand**. Then click OK to save the query.

The query that you have just created contains all the fields from the Products table and excludes discontinued products from the record set. (In other words, the query includes only those records whose Discontinued field contains the False or No value.)

To change the report's Record Source property, follow these steps:

1. Open the Product On Hand by Category report in design mode.

2. Choose Edit, Select Report.

3. Click the toolbar's Properties button to open the report's Properties window. Then click the Data tab to display the report's various data properties.

4. Click the Record Source text box, and then use the drop-down list to select the qryProductOnHand query as the report's new Record Source property.

5. Click the toolbar's Save button to save the changes to the report.

Adding the Calculated Fields. Now that you've changed the report's record source, you have easy access to the UnitPrice field that you need to add the additional calculated fields to the report. To add the UnitPrice field and the Value calculated field to the report, follow these steps:

1. Display the Product On Hand by Category report in design mode, if necessary. Then click the toolbar's Toolbox button to display the Access toolbox if it isn't already displayed.

2. Click the Label tool in the toolbox and place the label to the right of the Units label in the Page Header section. Type **Price** as the label.

3. Add another label to the right of Price, and type **Value**.

4. Click the toolbar's Field List button to display the Field List dialog. Select UnitPrice and drag the field symbol to a position under the Price label in the Detail section. Drop the text box, then delete the UnitPrice field's label in the report's Detail section.

5. To create the calculated Value text box, click the Text Box button in the toolbox and add the text box to the right of the Unit Price text box.

> **Tip**
>
> Entering expressions is easier if you press Shift+F2 to open the Zoom box or double-click the text box to display the Properties dialog and then enter the expression as the Control Source property.

6. Type **=[UnitsInStock]*[UnitPrice]** as the expression for the Value text box. Delete the field label for this text box in the report's Detail section.

7. Drag the Page Footer section bar downward to increase the height of the report's CategoryID Footer section, and rearrange the text labels and fields as shown in figure 14.25.

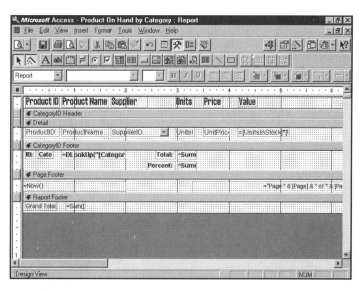

Fig. 14.25 Rearranging the CategoryID Footer section to make room for additional fields.

8. Repeat steps 5 and 6 to create the Value subtotal text box in the CategoryID Footer section, but type **=Sum([UnitsInStock]*[UnitPrice])** as the subtotal expression. Click the toolbar's Bold button to set the FontBold property to Yes. In the Properties dialog, click the Other tab and then set this text box's Name property as `txtTotalValue`.

9. Repeat step 8 to create the Value grand total box in the Report Footer section. In the Properties dialog's Other page, set this text box's Name property as `txtGrandTotalValue`.

10. Add another unbound text box underneath the `txtTotalValue` text box. Type **=[txtTotalValue]/[txtGrandTotalValue]** as the value of the Control Source property and set the Format property's value to Percent. The report design appears as shown in figure 14.26.

> ### Tip
>
> If the Parameter dialog appears, you misspelled one or more field names in the expressions. Click Cancel and check the properties that you added in steps 6 through 10.

III

Forms and Reports

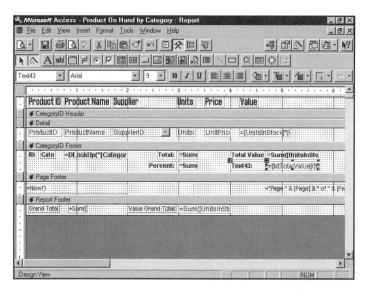

Fig. 14.26 Adding the Price, Value, Total Value, Total Value Pcnt, and Grand Total Value fields to the report.

11. Click the toolbar's Report View button to check the result of your additions. The report appears as in figure 14.27. Use the vertical scroll bar, if necessary, to display the category subtotal. The next section describes how you can correct any mis-aligned values and the spacing of the rows of the Detail section.

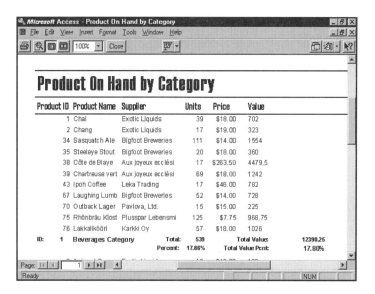

Fig. 14.27 Page 1 of the report, with calculated product values and value subtotals.

12. Click the Bottom of Report page selector button to display the grand totals for the report (see fig. 14.28). The record selector buttons become page selector buttons when you display reports in run mode.

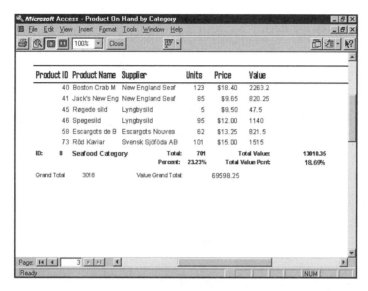

Fig. 14.28 The last page of the report, with grand totals for Units and Value.

Aligning and Formatting Controls and Adjusting Line Spacing

On reports, the exact alignment of label and text box controls is more important than alignment on forms, because in the printed report, any misalignment is obvious. Formatting the controls further improves the report's appearance and readability.

The spacing of the report's rows in the Detail section is controlled by the section's depth. Likewise, you can control the white space above and below the headers and footers by adjusting the depth of their sections and the vertical position of the controls within the sections. To create a professional-looking report, you must adjust the controls' alignment and formatting and the sections' line spacing.

Aligning Controls Horizontally and Vertically. You align controls by first selecting the rows to align and then aligning the columns. Access provides several control sizing and alignment options to make the process easier. To size and align the controls that you created, follow these steps:

1. Click the Report View toolbar's Close button to return to design mode.

2. You can adjust the height of all the text boxes simultaneously to fit the font used for their contents. Choose Edit, Select All to select all the controls in the report.

3. Choose Format, Size to Fit to adjust the height of the selected controls. Access adjusts all the controls to the proper height. To deselect all the controls, click a blank area of the report.

4. Select all the labels in the Page Header sections. Choose Format, Align, Top. This process aligns the tops of each selected label with the uppermost selected label. Click a blank area of the report to deselect the labels.

5. Select all the text boxes in the Detail section, and repeat step 4 for the text boxes.

6. Select the labels and text boxes in the CategoryID Footer and Report Footer sections and repeat step 4.

7. Select all the controls in the Units column. Choose Format, Align, Right so that Access aligns the column to the right edge of the text farthest to the right of the column. Next, click the toolbar's Align Right button to right-align the contents of the labels and text boxes. (The first part of this step aligns the controls themselves to the rightmost control, and the second part right-aligns the text or data displayed by the selected controls.)

8. Select all controls in the Price column and repeat step 7.

9. Select all controls in the Values column (except the Page Footer text box) and repeat step 7.

10. Click the toolbar's Report View button to display the report with the improved alignment of rows and columns.

Formatting Controls. As you can see in figure 14.27, you must revise the formatting of several controls. Although Product ID values are right-aligned, centering or left-justification is more appropriate for values used as codes rather than numbers to total. The repeated dollar signs in the Unit Price field detract from the report's readability, and the Value column's left-justification is inappropriate.

To change the Format property of these fields, follow these steps:

1. Click the toolbar's Close button to return to design mode.

2. Select the ProductID text box in the Detail section and click the toolbar's Center button.

3. Select and then center the CategoryID text box in the CategoryID Footer section.

4. Double-click the Unit Price text box to open its Properties dialog, then click the Properties window's Format tab.

5. In the Format text box, type **#,#00.00**. This procedure eliminates the dollar sign, but preserves the monetary formatting.

6. Repeat steps 4 and 5 for the Values text box. The Detail section doesn't require dollar signs.

> **Tip**
>
> If you select Currency formatting, instead of typing **$#,#00.00** to add a dollar sign to the value, your totals do not align. Currency formatting offsets the number to the left to provide space for the parentheses that accountants use to specify negative monetary values.

7. Select the Values subtotal in the CategoryID Footer. Click the Properties window's Format tab and type **$#,#00.00** in the Format field. Accountants use dollar signs to identify subtotals and totals in ledgers.

8. Select the Values grand total in the Report Footer and type **$#,#00.00** as the Values grand total's Format property.

9. The Values grand total in the Report Footer is the report's most important element, so click the toolbar's Border Color button and then click the black box to give this field a black border. Next, click the Border Width button and then the two-point border button. This procedure increases the thickness of the border around the grand total.

10. Click the toolbar's Report View button to check your formatting modifications. Click the Bottom of Report page selector button to display the last page of the report (see fig. 14.29).

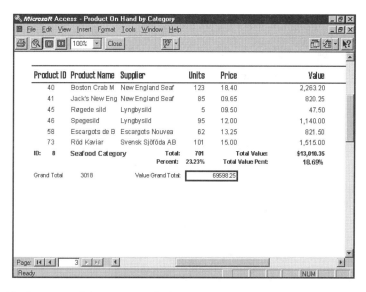

Fig. 14.29   The last page of the report, with the correct Format property assigned to the values.

Adjusting Line Spacing. In the Page Header section, shown in figure 14.27, the controls are placed further apart than is necessary, and the depth of the controls in Report Header is out of proportion to the size of the text. The line spacing of the remainder of the report's sections is satisfactory, but you can change this spacing, too. Minimizing line spacing enables you to print a report on fewer sheets of paper.

> **Tip**
>
> You might have to return to design mode and adjust the width or position of the Subtotals and Grand Totals text boxes to align these values with those for the individual products.

To change the spacing of the report's Page Header and Detail sections, follow these steps:

> **Tip**
>
> You can adjust the size of controls and the line spacing more precisely if you choose Format, Snap to Grid. This command toggles the Snap to Grid feature on and off.

1. Click the toolbar's Close button to return to design mode.

2. Select all the labels in the Page Header and move the group as close to the top of the section as possible.

3. Click the bottom line of the Page Header and move the line as close to the bottom of the text boxes as possible. (To select the line, you might have to move the CategoryID Header section downward temporarily.)

4. Click a blank area of the report and then move the CategoryID Header section to the bottom of the labels. You cannot reduce a section's depth to less than the Height property of the label that has the maximum height in the section.

5. Select all the text boxes in the Detail section and move those boxes as a group to the top of the section. Move the Category ID footer up to the bottom of the text boxes.

6. Move the line and label in the Report Header section upward to minimize the amount of white space in the Report Header.

7. Click the toolbar's Report View button to check the Page Header depth and Detail section's line spacing. The spacing shown in figure 14.30 is close to the minimum that you can achieve. You cannot reduce a section's line spacing to less than that required by the tallest text box or label by reducing the section's Height property in the Properties box, because Access rejects the entry and substitutes the prior value.

8. Click the toolbar's Zoom button to display the report in full-page view. Clicking the mouse when the pointer is the magnifying glass symbol has the same effect as

clicking the Zoom button. Alternate clicks toggle between full-size and full-page views.

9. Choose File, Save to save your changes.

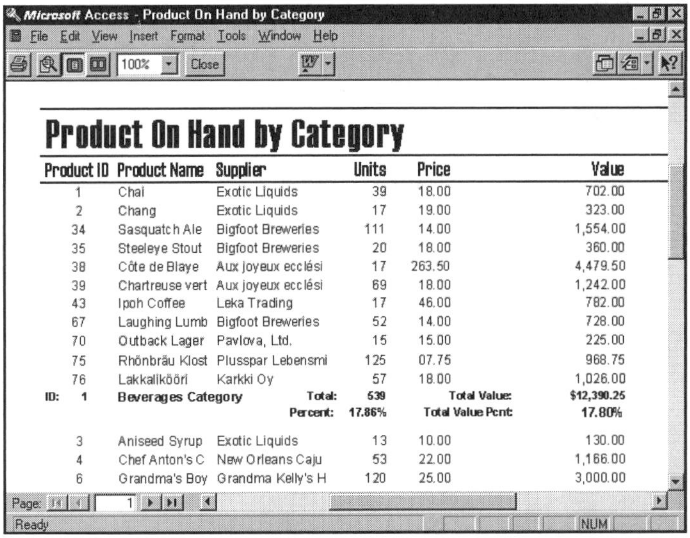

Fig. 14.30 The report in Report View after you adjust the depth of the Report Header, Page Header, and Detail sections.

Adjusting Margins and Printing Conventional Reports

The full-page Report View of the report shows the report as it would print, using Access's default printing margins of one inch on the top, bottom, and sides of the report (see fig. 14.31). In the Print Setup dialog, you can make adjustments to the printed version of the report. The procedure for printing a report also applies to printing the data contained in tables and queries, as well as single-record or continuous forms.

To change the printing margins for a report, follow these steps:

1. Choose File, Page Setup to open the Page Setup dialog (see fig. 14.32).

2. The Page Setup dialog is similar to the Print and Page Setup dialogs of other Windows applications, with a section for printing margins included. To increase the amount of information on a page, decrease the top and bottom margins. By selecting the Print Data Only check box, you can print only the data in the report; the Report and Page Headers and Footers do not print.

3. In the Left text box, type **2.0** to specify a two-inch left margin and in the Right, Top, and Bottom text boxes, type **0.75** inches. Click OK. The full-page view of the report with the revised margins appears (see fig. 14.33).

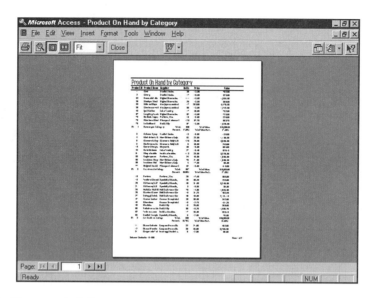

Fig. 14.31 The report in full-page view.

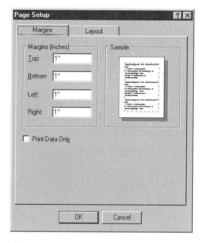

Fig. 14.32 The Page Setup dialog for printing data sheets, forms, and reports.

Tip

The printing margins that you establish for a report in the Page Setup dialog apply to the active report only; each report has a unique set of margins. When you save the report, Access saves the margin settings.

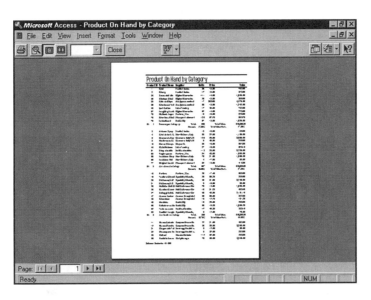

Fig. 14.33 The full-page preview of the report with new printing margins applied

4. To print the report, click the toolbar's Print button. Access immediately prints the report using the current printer options. If you want to change the selected printer, page orientation, graphics quality, or other printer options, choose File, Print. The standard Print dialog appears for the printer specified in Windows as the default printer. Figure 14.34 shows, for example, the Print dialog for a PostScript printer shared on a network.

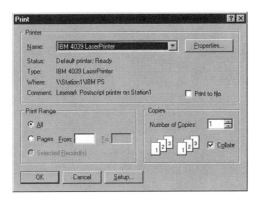

Fig. 14.34 The Print dialog controls printing of datasheets, forms, and reports.

5. You can choose to print all or part of a report, print the report to a file for later printing, and select the number of copies to print. By choosing the Properties button, you can change the parameters that apply to the printer that you are using. Click OK to print the report.

Forms and Reports

III

The Page Setup dialog includes a Layout tab that enables you to establish specifications for printing mailing labels and other multiple-column reports. The next section describes these specifications and how you set them.

Preventing Widowed Records with the Group Keep Together Property

Access includes a Keep Together property for groups that prevents widowed records from appearing at the bottom of the page. Depending on your report section depths, you might find that only a few records of the next group (called widowed records) appear at the bottom of the page. You can force a page break when an entire group does not fit on one page by following these steps:

1. With the report in Design View, click the toolbar's Sorting and Grouping button to open the Sorting and Grouping dialog.

2. Select the field with the group symbol in the selection button that corresponds to the group that you want to keep together. In this example, select CategoryID.

3. Open the Keep Together drop-down list and select Whole Group, as shown in figure 14.35.

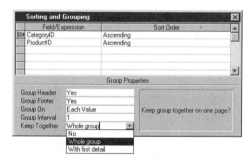

Fig. 14.35 Setting the group's Keep Together property.

4. Close the Sorting and Grouping dialog, and click the Report View button to see the result of applying the group Keep Together property.

Tip

If you want to delete or add a Group Header or Footer singly (rather than in pairs), select Yes or No in the appropriate property field of the Sorting and Grouping dialog.

The Report Wizard makes the other entries in the Sorting and Grouping dialog for you. The next chapter describes how to use the Sorting and Grouping dialog to design reports without the aid of the wizard.

Printing Multicolumn Reports as Mailing Labels

Access enables you to print multicolumn reports. You can create a single-column report with the Report Wizard, for example, and then arrange the report to print values from the Detail section in a specified number of columns across the page. The most common application of multicolumn reports is the creation of mailing labels.

You can create mailing lists with the Report Wizard, or you can start with a blank form. The Report Wizard's advantage is that it includes the dimensions of virtually every kind of adhesive label for dot-matrix or laser printers made by the Avery Commercial Products division. You select the product number of the label that you plan to use, and Access determines the number of columns and rows per page and the margins for the report's Detail section. You can also customize the Mailing Label Wizard for labels with unusual sizes or labels that other manufacturers produce.

The Northwind Traders database includes a Customer Labels report that you can modify to suit the design of any mailing label. Figure 14.36 shows the Detail section of the Customer Mailing Labels report with the font changed to Courier New in a 10-point font and the size of the label adjusted to 2.5 by 0.833 inches.

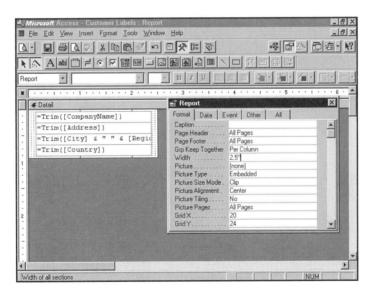

Fig. 14.36 The modified Customer Labels report in design mode.

You specify the number of columns in a row and the number of rows on a page by selecting settings in the Page Setup dialog's Layout tab, shown in figure 14.37. This dialog appears when you choose File, Page Setup in either print preview or report design mode.

III

Forms and Reports

Fig. 14.37 The Layout tab of the Page Setup dialog.

The dialog's text boxes, check boxes, and option buttons enable you to perform the following procedures:

■ The Items Across property sets the number of labels across the page. In this example, this property changes from 2 to 3.

> **Note**
>
> The Left and Top margin settings (which you set on the Margins tab of the Page Setup dialog) specify the position at which Access prints the upper-left corner of the first label on the page. For most laser and inkjet printers, these values cannot be less than about 0.25 inch. Labels designed for laser and inkjet printers are die-cut so that the marginal areas remain on the backing sheet when you remove the individual labels.

■ The Width property in the Item Size group overrides the left margin and the Height property overrides the bottom margin that you establish in Report Design View only if you don't select Same as Detail to use the margins that you set in the Detail section.

■ Column Spacing specifies the position of the left edge of columns to the right of the first column.

■ Row Spacing and the Height property determine the number of labels that fit vertically on a page and the vertical distance between successive labels. If you set Row Spacing to zero, the depth of your Detail section determines the vertical spacing of the labels.

■ The Across, then Down option causes the labels to print in columns from left to right, and then in rows from the top to the bottom of the page. This is the preferred setting for mailing labels, because it wastes less label stock for continuous-feed printers.

■ The Down, then Across option causes the labels to print in *snaking* column style, in the first column, top to bottom, and then the next column, top to bottom, and so on.

You set these properties' values for three columns of 12 labels per page. You can access the settings for all these columns and pages in the Page Setup dialog's Layout page.

After you set the dimensions of the mailing labels and click OK, the full-size view of the labels appears as shown in figure 14.38.

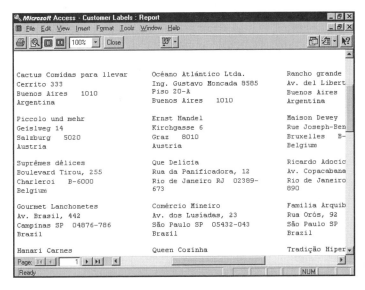

Fig. 14.38 Three-across mailing labels shown in Report View's full-size view.

Click the toolbar's Zoom button to display the full-page layout. To test the label layout properties that you set, print only the labels' first page on standard paper or a xerographic duplicate of the label template supplied with labels designed for laser printing.

You might have to make minor alignment adjustments because the position of the upper-left corner of the printer's image and the upper-left corner of the paper might not correspond exactly.

If you select the Down, then Across option, the technique for printing successive Detail rows is identical to that which word processing and page layout applications such as Aldus PageMaker use to create newspaper (*snaking*) columns. When the first column fills to the page's height, Detail rows fill the next column to the right.

> **Note**
>
> Newspaper columns are suitable for mailing labels but are difficult to format correctly when you convert other kinds of single-column reports to multiple columns. For newspaper columns to operate at all, you must set the Keep Together property of the report's Detail section to No and then set the Detail section's height so that the field data for a single record appears in a single set of rows. If the Detail data includes Memo fields with variable amounts of text in a text box with the Can Grow property set to Yes, formatting newspaper columns properly becomes almost impossible. Instead of having Access attempt to create newspaper columns, an easier approach is to lay out the Detail section with multiple columns in design mode.

From Here...

Access 95's report-generation capability is unrivaled by any other desktop database management application or client/server front-end design tool. Access's report-design capabilities are one of the principal incentives for using Access rather than Visual Basic 3.0 or 4.0 when developing database applications. This chapter introduced you to the basic elements of creating reports with the Report Wizards and demonstrated how to modify the reports that the wizards create for you.

Refer to the following chapters for related information:

- Chapter 15, "Preparing Advanced Reports," describes how to sort and group reports, create reports from a blank report, and send reports as files attached to Microsoft Mail messages.

- Chapter 17, "Using Macros for Forms and Reports," shows you how to write macros that print reports automatically.

- Chapter 20, "Adding Graphics to Forms and Reports," leads you through the methods of using object frame controls to add to reports such graphic images as logos.

Chapter 15

Preparing Advanced Reports

Access 95's Report Wizard can create reports that you can use "as is" or that you can modify to suit most of your database reporting requirements. In some cases, however, you might have to create reports that are more complex than, or that differ from, those offered by the Report Wizard. For example, you might have to apply special grouping and sorting methods to your reports. Including subreports within your reports requires that you start from a blank report form instead of using one of the Report Wizard.

To understand fully the process of designing advanced Access reports, you must be familiar with Access functions, which is one of the subjects of Chapter 9, "Understanding Operators and Expressions in Access." You also must understand the methods that you use to create and design forms, which are covered in Chapters 12 and 13. Reports use extensively Access functions like Sum() and expressions like ="Subtotal of" & [Field Name] & ":". The toolbox that you use to add controls to forms also adds controls when you create or modify reports. You assign properties of controls, such as labels and text boxes, with the methods that you use with forms. If you skipped Chapter 9 or Chapters 12 and 13, you might want to refer to the appropriate sections of those chapters whenever you encounter unfamiliar subjects or terminology in this chapter.

Grouping and Sorting Report Data

Most reports that you create require that you organize their data into groups and subgroups, in a style similar to the outline of a book. The Report Wizard lets you establish the initial grouping and sorting properties for your data, but you might want to rearrange your report's data after reviewing the Report Wizard's first draft.

The Sorting and Grouping dialog (see fig. 15.1) enables you to modify these report properties in design mode. This section uses the Product On Hand by Category report that you created in the preceding chapter. The sorting and grouping methods described here, however, apply to any report that you

In this chapter, you learn about the following

- Grouping and sorting report data

- Starting from a blank report

- Controlling report page breaks

- Printing headers and footers

- Incorporating subreports

- Sending a report as a file linked to a Microsoft Exchange message

III

Forms and Reports

create. To display the dialog, open the report in Design View and click the toolbar's Sorting and Grouping button.

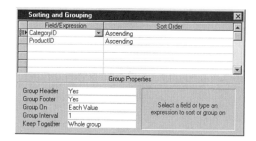

Fig. 15.1 The Sorting and Grouping dialog lets you create or alter report groups and the sort order within groups.

The Sorting and Grouping dialog enables you to determine the fields or expressions on which Access is to group the products, for a maximum of three levels. You can sort the grouped data in ascending or descending order, but you must select one or the other; "unsorted" is not an option. The Sorting and Grouping symbol in the selection button at the left of the window indicates that Access uses the field or expression in the adjacent column to group the records.

Grouping Data

The method that you use to group data depends on the data in the field by which you group. You can group by categories, in which case a unique value must represent each category. You can group data by a range of values, which usually are numeric but also can be alphabetic. You can use the data in a field to group the data, or you can substitute an expression as the basis for the grouping.

Grouping by Category. When you told the Report Wizard to use CategoryID as the field by which to group, you elected to group by category. You can alter the grouping sequence easily by using the Sorting and Grouping dialog. To group by SupplierID, for example, select SupplierID as the first group field. (When you change the group field, Access automatically renames the Group Header and Footer sections.) In the SupplierID Footer section, change the ID text box's Control Source property to the SupplierID field, and rename the text box as txtSupplierID. Next, change the title label in the Report Header to Product On Hand by Supplier, and use the DLookUp() function to change the text box's expression to the following:

```
="Supplier: " & DLookUp("[CompanyName]","Suppliers",
    "[SupplierID]=Report!SupplierID"
```

Increase the DLookUp() text box's width so that more of the supplier's name is visible in the report. The report appears as shown in figure 15.2. Choose File, Save As and save the report under the new name **Product On Hand by Supplier**.

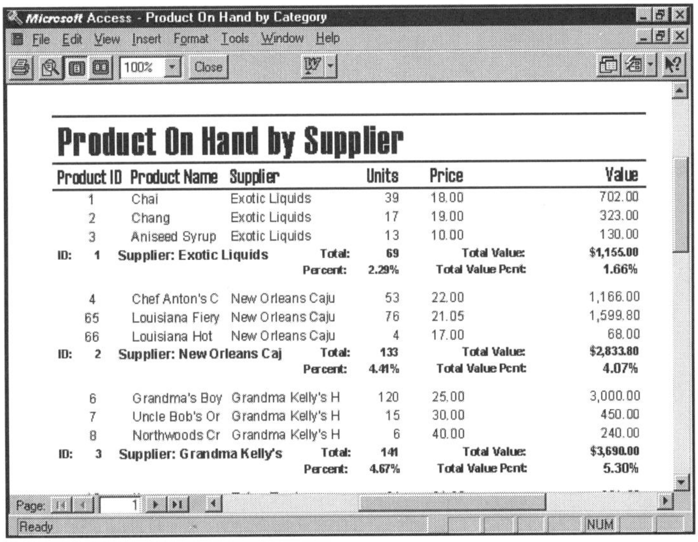

Fig. 15.2 The effect of changing the report grouping so that it displays records by SupplierID.

> **Note**
>
> You cannot let a report's properties or controls limit the number of rows of detail data that a report presents, unless you write a Top*N* or Top*N*Percent query using Access SQL. (Search the online Help for the `TopValues` property to learn more about Top*N* and Top*N*Percent queries.) All the rows of a table or query appear somewhere in the report's Detail section, if the report includes a Detail section with at least one control. To include only a selected range of dates in a report, for example, you must base the report on a query with the criteria necessary to select the Detail records. If the user is to choose the range of records to include in the report, use a parameter query as the report's data source.

◀◀ See "Text-Manipulation Functions," p. 300

If you use a systematic code for grouping, you can group by the first five or fewer characters of the code. With an expression, you can group by any set of characters within a field. To group by the second and third digits of a code, for example, use the following expression:

=**Mid**([*FieldName*],2,2).

If your table or query contains appropriate data, you can group reports by more than one level by creating subgroups. The Employee Sales by Country report (one of the Northwind Traders sample reports), for example, uses groups (Country) and subgroups (the employee's name—the actual group is an Access expression combining the FirstName and LastName fields) to organize orders received within a range of dates. Open the Employee Sales by Country report in design mode to view the additional section created by a subgroup.

Grouping by Range. You often must sort reports by ranges of values. (If you opened the Employee Sales by Country report, close this report and reopen the Product On Hand by Category report in design mode.) If you want to divide the Product On Hand by Category report into a maximum of six sections, each beginning with a five-letter group of the alphabet (A through E, F through J, and so on) based on the ProductName field, the entries in the Sorting and Grouping dialog should look like the entries in figure 15.3.

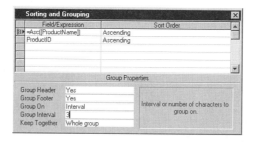

Fig. 15.3 The Sorting and Grouping criteria to group records in alphabetical intervals.

Access VBA's `=Asc(ProductName)` function returns the ASCII (numeric) value of the first character of its string argument, the ProductName field. You set the Group On specification to Interval, and then set the Group Interval to 3. This setup groups the data into names beginning with A through C, D through F, and so on (see fig. 15.4). You delete all the text boxes in the Group Footer, because subtotals by alphabetic groups are not significant. Although of limited value in this report, an alphabetic grouping often is useful for grouping long, alphabetized lists to assist readers in finding a particular record.

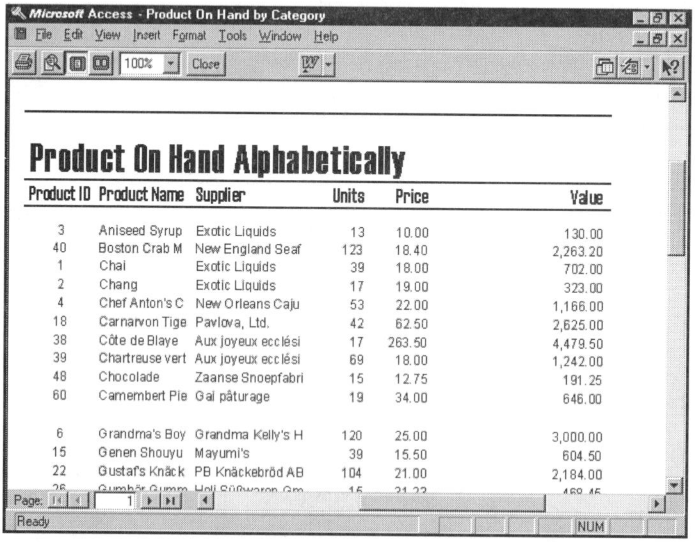

Product On Hand Alphabetically

Product ID	Product Name	Supplier	Units	Price	Value
3	Aniseed Syrup	Exotic Liquids	13	10.00	130.00
40	Boston Crab M	New England Seaf	123	18.40	2,263.20
1	Chai	Exotic Liquids	39	18.00	702.00
2	Chang	Exotic Liquids	17	19.00	323.00
4	Chef Anton's C	New Orleans Caju	53	22.00	1,166.00
18	Carnarvon Tige	Pavlova, Ltd.	42	62.50	2,625.00
38	Côte de Blaye	Aux joyeux ecclési	17	263.50	4,479.50
39	Chartreuse vert	Aux joyeux ecclési	69	18.00	1,242.00
48	Chocolade	Zaanse Snoepfabri	15	12.75	191.25
60	Camembert Pie	G al pâturage	19	34.00	646.00
6	Grandma's Boy	Grandma Kelly's H	120	25.00	3,000.00
15	Genen Shouyu	Mayumi's	39	15.50	604.50
22	Gustaf's Knäck	PB Knäckebröd AB	104	21.00	2,184.00
26	Gumbär Gumm	Heli Süßwaren Gm	15	31.23	468.45

Fig. 15.4 A report that categorizes products by three-letter alphabetic intervals.

◀◀ See "Functions for Date and Time," p. 298

If you group data on a field with a Date/Time data type, Access enables you to set the Sorting and Grouping dialog's Group On property to Year, Qtr (quarter), Month, Week, Day, Hour, or Minute. To group records so that values of the same quarter for several years print in sequence, type the following in the Sorting and Grouping dialog's Field/Expression column:

```
=DatePart("q",[FieldName])
```

Sorting Data Groups

Although most data sorting within groups is based on the values contained in a field, you also can sort by expressions. When compiling an inventory valuation list, the products with the highest inventory value are the most important, and the report's users might want these products listed first in a group. This decision requires a sort of the records within groups on the expression `=[UnitsInStock]*[UnitPrice]`, the same expression that Access uses to calculate the report's Value column. Figure 15.5 shows the required entries in the Sorting and Grouping dialog.

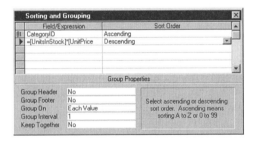

Fig. 15.5   Sorting data by each record on an expression.

The descending sort on the inventory value expression results in the report shown in figure 15.6. As expected, the products with the highest inventory value appear first in each field.

Microsoft Access - Product On Hand by Category

File Edit View Insert Format Tools Window Help

100% ▼ Close

Product On Hand by Category

Product ID	Product Name	Supplier	Units	Price	Value
38	Côte de Blaye	Aux joyeux ecclési	17	263.50	4,479.50
34	Sasquatch Ale	Bigfoot Breweries	111	14.00	1,554.00
39	Chartreuse vert	Aux joyeux ecclési	69	18.00	1,242.00
76	Lakkalikööri	Karkki Oy	57	18.00	1,026.00
75	Rhönbräu Klost	Plusspar Lebensmi	125	07.75	968.75
43	Ipoh Coffee	Leka Trading	17	46.00	782.00
67	Laughing Lumb	Bigfoot Breweries	52	14.00	728.00
1	Chai	Exotic Liquids	39	18.00	702.00
35	Steeleye Stout	Bigfoot Breweries	20	18.00	360.00
2	Chang	Exotic Liquids	17	19.00	323.00
70	Outback Lager	Pavlova, Ltd.	15	15.00	225.00

ID: 1   **Beverages Category**   **Total:** 539   **Total Value:** $12,390.25

    Percent: 17.86%   **Total Value Pcnt:** 17.80%

61	Sirop d'érable	Forêts d'érables	113	28.50	3,220.50
6	Grandma's Boy	Grandma Kelly's H	120	25.00	3,000.00
65	Louisiana Fiery	New Orleans Caju	76	21.05	1,599.80

Page: ◄◄ ◄ 1 ► ►► ◄

Ready   NUM

Fig. 15.6 The Product On Hand by Category report, with groups sorted by inventory value.

Working from a Blank Report

Usually, the fastest way to set up a report is to use the Report Wizard to create a basic report and then modify the basic report as described in Chapter 14, "Printing Basic Reports and Mailing Labels," and in the previous sections of this chapter. If you are creating a simple report, however, it could take you longer to modify a standard report style created by the Report Wizard than it would take to create a report by using the default blank report that Access provides.

The Basis for a Subreport

◄◄ See "Creating a Monthly Product Sales Crosstab Query," p. 357

To create a report to use as the Monthly Sales by Category subreport (sbr1994MonthlyCategorySales) in the following section of this chapter, follow these steps:

1. Close the Product On Hand by Category report and click the Query tab in the Database window.

2. Select the qry1994MonthlyProductSales query that you created in Chapter 10, "Creating Multitable and Crosstab Queries," and click the Design button. A slightly modified version of this crosstab query serves as the data source for the report of the same name.

3. Change the first column's field name from ProductID to CategoryID by opening the Field list and clicking the CategoryID field name. You need the CategoryID field to link with the CategoryID field in the Products On Hand query that the Product On Hand by Category report uses as its data source.

4. Delete the ProductName column. The modified query appears as shown in figure 15.7.

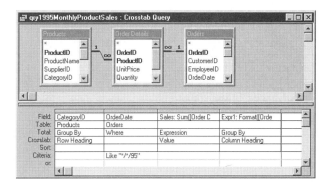

Fig. 15.7 The modified crosstab query for the Monthly Sales by Category subreport.

5. Choose File, Save As and name the modified query **qryMonthlyCategorySales**. Your query result set appears as shown in figure 15.8.

Category	Jan	Feb	Mar	Apr	May
Beverages	$45,901.00	$19,765.00	$30,512.25	$20,963.50	$4,107.00
Condiments	$4,740.45	$8,483.20	$11,615.80	$8,384.00	$1,074.00
Confections	$12,179.75	$11,170.95	$23,808.05	$9,659.78	$1,333.20
Dairy Products	$17,856.00	$12,467.00	$16,596.40	$33,656.50	$636.00
Grains/Cereals	$11,511.75	$4,267.75	$4,070.50	$5,089.25	$4,421.00
Meat/Poultry	$5,701.57	$24,226.46	$11,368.16	$18,931.38	$48.00
Produce	$1,639.00	$1,202.80	$15,223.00	$13,018.00	$1,333.05
Seafood	$16,245.20	$10,790.98	$10,278.95	$9,760.91	$1,042.80

Fig. 15.8 The result set returned by the crosstab query of figure 15.7.

6. Open the New Object drop-down list on the toolbar, and select New Report from the list. The New dialog appears.

7. Access automatically selects qryMonthlyCategorySales as the query on which to base the report. Select Design View from the list and click OK. Access creates the default blank report shown in figure 15.9.

Adding and Deleting Sections of Your Report

When you create a report from a blank template or modify a report created by the Report Wizard, you might want to add a new section to the report by using the following guidelines:

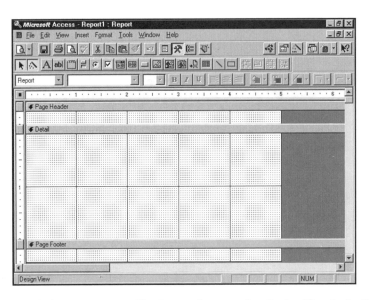

Fig. 15.9 The default report presented by Access after you select Design View in the New dialog.

- To add Report Headers and Footers as a pair, choose View, Report Header/Footer.

- To add Page Headers and Footers as a pair, choose View, Page Header/Footer.

 ■ To add a Group Header or Footer, click the toolbar's Sorting and Grouping button and set the Group Header or Group Footer property value to Yes.

Figure 15.10 shows a blank report, with the headers and footers for each section that you can include in a report.

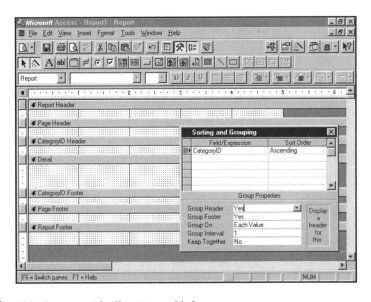

Fig. 15.10 A blank report with all sections added.

If you group the data in more than one level (group, subgroup, sub-subgroup), you can add a Group Header and Footer for each level of grouping. This action adds to your report another pair of sections for each subgroup level.

You delete sections from reports by using methods similar to those that you use to create the sections. To delete unwanted sections, use the following guidelines:

- To delete the Detail section or an individual Report Header, Report Footer, Page Header, or Page Footer section, delete all the controls from the section, and then drag up the divider bar below so that the section has no depth. To delete a report footer, drag the report's bottom margin to the Report Footer border. These actions do not actually delete the sections, but sections with no depth do not print or affect the report's layout.

- To delete Report Headers and Footers as a pair, choose <u>V</u>iew, Report <u>H</u>eader/Footer. If the Report Header or Footer includes a control, a message box warns you that you will lose the controls in the deleted sections.

- To delete Page Headers and Footers as a pair, choose <u>V</u>iew, P<u>a</u>ge Header/Footer. A warning message box appears if either section contains controls.

- To delete a Group Header or Footer, click the toolbar's Sorting and Grouping button and set the Group Header or Group Footer property's value to No.

Note

Page and Report Headers and Footers that incorporate thin lines at the header or footer's upper border can be difficult to delete individually. To make these lines visible, choose <u>E</u>dit, Select <u>A</u>ll to add sizing anchors to the lines. Hold down the Shift key and click the controls that you want to save to deselect these controls, and then press the Delete key to delete the remaining selected lines.

Controlling Page Breaks and the Printing of Page Headers and Footers

The Force New Page and Keep Together properties of the report's Group Header, Detail, and Group Footer sections control manual page breaks. To set these properties, double-click the group's section border to display the section's Properties dialog. Force New Page causes an unconditional page break immediately before printing the section. If you set the Keep Together property to Yes, and insufficient room is available on the current page to print the entire section, a page break occurs and the section prints on the next page.

To control whether Page Headers or Footers print on the first or last page of a report, choose <u>E</u>dit, Select <u>R</u>eport and then click the toolbar's Properties button. You then select a Page Headers and Page Footers printing option in the Format page of the Properties window (see fig. 15.11).

Creating the Monthly Sales by Category Report

Earlier in this chapter, you created the Monthly Sales by Category report, which is a good example of a report that you might want to create by starting with a blank report. The report includes information about total monthly sales of products by category.

Comparing the monthly sales to the inventory level of a category enables the report's user to estimate inventory turnover rates. This report serves two purposes: as a report and as a subreport within another report. You add the Monthly Sales by Category report as a subreport in the "Incorporating Subreports" section later in this chapter.

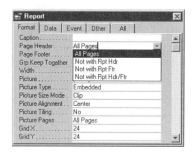

Fig. 15.11 The Properties window for a report, displaying page-section printing options.

The crosstab query that acts as the report's data source is closely related to a report, but the crosstab query doesn't include detail records (see Chapter 10, "Creating Multitable and Crosstab Queries"). Each row of the query consists of subtotals of the sales for a category for each month of the year. One row appears below the inventory value subtotal when you link the subreport to the main report, so the report needs only a Detail section. Each detail row, however, requires a *header* label to print the month. The CategoryID field is included so that you can verify that the data is linked correctly.

To create the Monthly Sales by Category report (and subreport), follow these steps:

1. Delete all sections of your blank report except the Detail section. By default, blank reports have 24 by 24 grid dots and Snap to Grid is selected.

2. Drag down the Detail section's bottom margin so that the section has an inch or two of depth. You need maneuvering room to relocate the text boxes and associated labels that you add in the following steps. Drag the Detail section's right margin to the right so that the report is 6.5 inches wide.

3. Click the toolbar's Sorting and Grouping button to display the dialog, and select CategoryID as the field to use to sort the data with a standard ascending sort. Close the Sorting and Grouping dialog.

4. Click the toolbar's Field List button, select CategoryID, and drag the field symbol to the Detail section.

5. Click the CategoryID label, and relocate the label to the Detail section's upper left so that the CategoryID combo box is directly underneath it. (CategoryID is a dummy combo box, not a text box, in report Design View because CategoryID is a Lookup field.) Adjust the depth of the label and the text box to 0.2 inches (four grid dots) and the width to 1 inch. Edit the label's text to **ID**.

6. Click and drag the field list's Jan field to the right of the CategoryID field. Move the label to the top of the section, adjacent to the right border of the field to its

left. Move the text box under the label. Adjust the label and text box depth to 4 dots, the label width to 6 dots, and the combo box width to 16 dots. Edit the label's text to delete the colon.

7. Repeat step 6 for the month fields of Feb through Jun. The report design now appears as shown in figure 15.12.

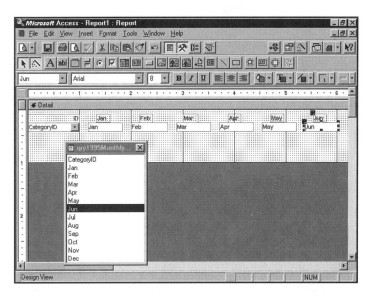

Fig. 15.12   The report with labels and text boxes added for the first six months of 1995.

8. Click each label while holding down the Shift key so that you select all the labels (but only the labels).

9. Click the toolbar's Bold button to add the bold attribute to the labels. Then click the Center button to center the labels above the text boxes.

10. Select the CategoryID text box, and click the toolbar's Bold button.

11. Choose Edit, Select All and drag the labels and text boxes so that the tops of the labels are two dots down from the top of the Detail section. Click a blank area of the report to deselect the controls.

12. If the toolbox is invisible, click the Toolbox button of the toolbar. Click the Line tool and add a line at the top edge of the labels. Drag the line's right-end handle to the right edge of the Jun text box.

13. Click the drop-down list of the Border Width button on the toolbar, and click the 2-point line-thickness button.

14. Repeat steps 12 and 13 for another identical line, but add the new line under the labels (and above the text boxes).

15. Drag the Detail section's margins to within two dots of the bottom and right edge of the controls. The report's design appears as shown in figure 15.13.

III

Forms and Reports

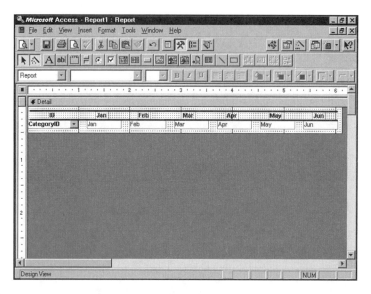

Fig. 15.13   The layout of the report's Detail section.

 16. Click the toolbar's Print Preview button to verify the design. The full-size view of the report appears (see fig. 15.14).

ID	Jan	Feb	Mar	Apr	May	Jun
Beverages	$23,979.60	$2,831.20	$11,027.20	$10,137.50	$13,130.00	$3,726.00
ID	Jan	Feb	Mar	Apr	May	Jun
Condiments	$3,081.30	$6,618.40	$2,345.90	$5,463.00	$5,728.80	$2,146.85
ID	Jan	Feb	Mar	Apr	May	Jun
Confections	$6,869.40	$7,413.50	$3,996.90	$12,257.65	$7,104.50	$2,502.28
ID	Jan	Feb	Mar	Apr	May	Jun
Dairy Products	$8,940.80	$5,515.20	$10,132.40	$6,359.00	$12,326.70	$8,672.50
ID	Jan	Feb	Mar	Apr	May	Jun
Grains/Cereals	$2,413.40	$4,343.40	$4,406.80	$5,347.60	$5,069.00	$5,793.00
ID	Jan	Feb	Mar	Apr	May	Jun
Meat/Poultry	$5,696.80	$8,442.90	$3,271.60	$7,932.99	$2,461.30	$5,006.30
ID	Jan	Feb	Mar	Apr	May	Jun
Produce	$2,895.00	$2,698.80	$3,676.80	$6,137.10	$5,238.70	$4,473.50

Fig. 15.14   The report in print preview mode.

17. Choose File, Save As and type **rptMonthlyCategorySales** as the report's name.

To add to your report the remaining months of the year, follow these steps:

1. To accommodate another row of labels and text boxes, increase the Detail section's depth by dragging the bottom margin down (about one inch).

2. Choose <u>E</u>dit, Select <u>A</u>ll.

3. Click the Copy button on the toolbar, or press Ctrl+C to copy the labels and text boxes to the Clipboard.

4. Click the Paste button on the toolbar, or press Ctrl+V to paste a copy of the labels and text boxes to the Detail section.

5. Move this copy under the original labels and text boxes, spaced two grid dots below the originals, as shown in figure 15.15.

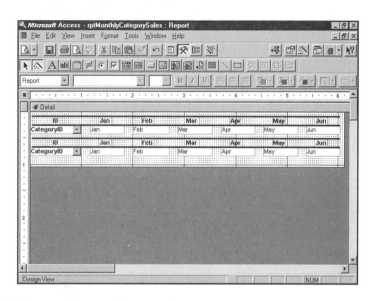

Fig. 15.15   The report design, with a copy of the labels and text boxes added.

6. Click a blank area of the report to deselect the controls, and then select the new CategoryID text box. Delete the CategoryID text box. When you delete this text box, you also delete the associated label.

7. Edit *both* the labels and text boxes to display Jul through Dec.

8. Delete the ID label in the first row, and drag the CategoryID text box to the position that its label formerly occupied.

9. Drag up the bottom margin to within two dots of the bottom of the text boxes in the second row. The final design appears in figure 15.16.

10. Click the toolbar's Print Preview button to display the double-row report (see fig. 15.17).

11. Close the rptMonthlyCategorySales report and save the changes.

The technique of copying controls to the Clipboard, pasting copies to reports, and then editing the copies is often faster than creating duplicate controls that differ from one another only in the text of labels and text boxes.

III

Forms and Reports

Microsoft Access - rptMonthlyCategorySales : Report
File Edit View Insert Format Tools Window Help
Report
Detail
CategoryID
Jan Feb Mar Apr May Jun
Jan Feb Mar Apr May Jun
Jul Aug Sep Oct Nov Dec
Jul Aug Sep Oct Nov Dec
Design View
NUM

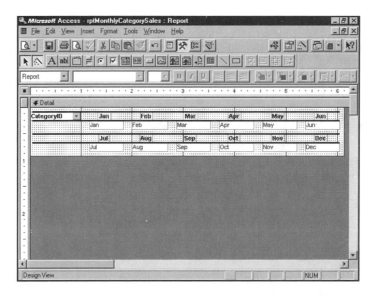

Fig. 15.16 The final design of the `rptMonthlyCategorySales` report.

Microsoft Access - rptMonthlyCategorySales : Report
File Edit View Insert Format Tools Window Help
100%
Close
Beverages
Jan Feb Mar Apr May Jun
$23,979.60 $2,831.20 $11,027.20 $10,137.50 $13,130.00 $3,726.00
Jul Aug Sep Oct Nov Dec
$7,983.50 $6,514.00 $9,044.75 $5,837.00 $8,271.50 $8,412.75
Condiments
Jan Feb Mar Apr May Jun
$3,081.30 $6,618.40 $2,345.90 $5,463.00 $5,728.80 $2,146.85
Jul Aug Sep Oct Nov Dec
$8,288.70 $3,015.80 $5,219.70 $5,595.65 $3,504.80 $6,312.60
Confections
Jan Feb Mar Apr May Jun
$6,869.40 $7,413.50 $3,996.90 $12,257.65 $7,104.50 $2,502.28
Jul Aug Sep Oct Nov Dec
$6,825.65 $8,471.70 $8,925.00 $5,685.15 $8,370.16 $6,300.98
Dairy Products
Jan Feb Mar Apr May Jun
$8,940.80 $5,515.20 $10,132.40 $6,359.00 $12,326.70 $8,672.50
Jul Aug Sep Oct Nov Dec
$13,570.10 $8,055.50 $11,374.00 $14,400.00 $12,942.10 $12,182.50
Page: 1
Ready
NUM

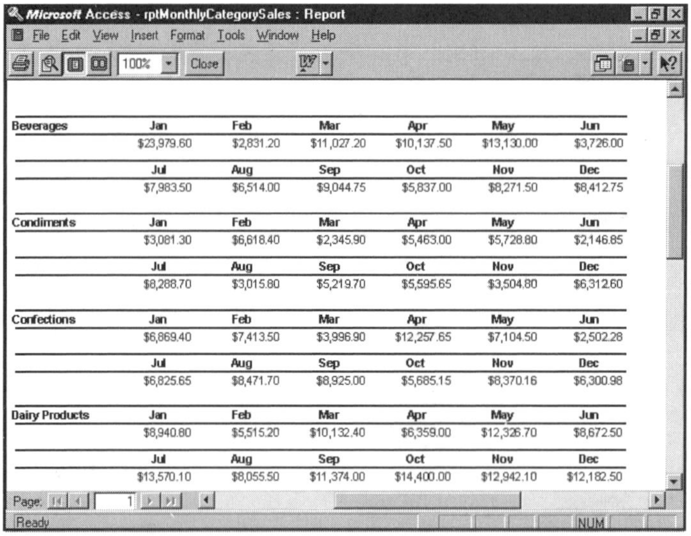

Fig. 15.17 The `rptMonthlyCategorySales` report with data for 12 months.

Incorporating Subreports

Reports, like forms, can include subreports. Unlike the Form Wizard, however, the Report Wizard offers no option of automatically creating reports that include subreports. You can add subreports to reports that you create with the Form Wizard, or you can create subreports from blank reports, as shown in the preceding section.

Adding a Linked Subreport to a Bound Report

If a main report is bound to a table or a query as a data source, and the subreport's data source can be related to the main report's data source, you can link the subreport's data to the main report's data.

To add and link the rptMonthlySalesbyCategory report as a subreport to the Product On Hand by Category report, for example, follow these steps:

1. Open the Product On Hand by Category report in design mode.

2. Drag down the top of the Page Footer border to make room for the subreport in the CategoryID Footer section.

3. Click the toolbar's Database Window button. If the Database window is maximized, click the Restore button.

4. Click and drag the small Report icon from the left of the rptMonthlyCategorySales report to a location inside the CategoryID Footer section. Drop the icon below the CategoryID text box.

5. At the point at which you drop the icon, Access creates a subreport box similar to a text box, with an associated label (see fig. 15.18). Delete the label.

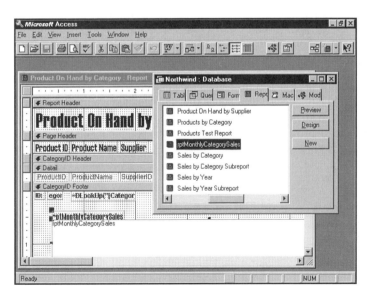

Fig. 15.18   Dragging and dropping a report as a subreport within another report.

6. Click the Maximize button to restore the Report Design window.

7. Adjust the CategoryID Footer's depth to provide about 0.1-inch margins above and below the section's controls. The report appears in Design View as shown in figure 15.19.

Forms and Reports

III

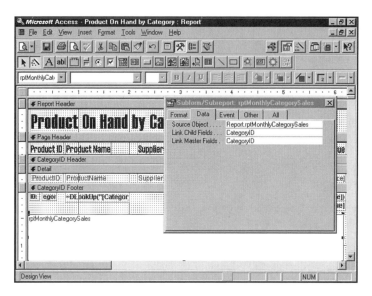

Fig. 15.19 Adding the `rptMonthlyCategorySales` report as a subreport of the Product On Hand by Category report.

 8. You need to link the data in the subreport to the data of the main report so that only the sales data that corresponds to a specific group's CategoryID value appears on-screen. Select the subreport box and click the Properties button to display the subreport's Properties window. Click the Data tab and enter **CategoryID** as the value of the Link Master Fields property and **CategoryID** as the value of the Link Child Fields property.

Access attempts to create the link. If the main report and subreports are based on tables, and a relationship is set between the tables, Access creates the link to the related fields. If the main report is grouped to a key field and the subreport's table or query contains a field of the same name and data type, Access creates the link.

 9. Click the toolbar's Print Preview button to display the report in the full-size view. The subreport appears as shown at the bottom of figure 15.20. Click the page selector buttons to view other parts of the subreport to confirm that the linkage is correct.

10. Choose File, Save to save the changes.

You can add and link several subreports to the main report if each subreport has a field in common with the main report's data source.

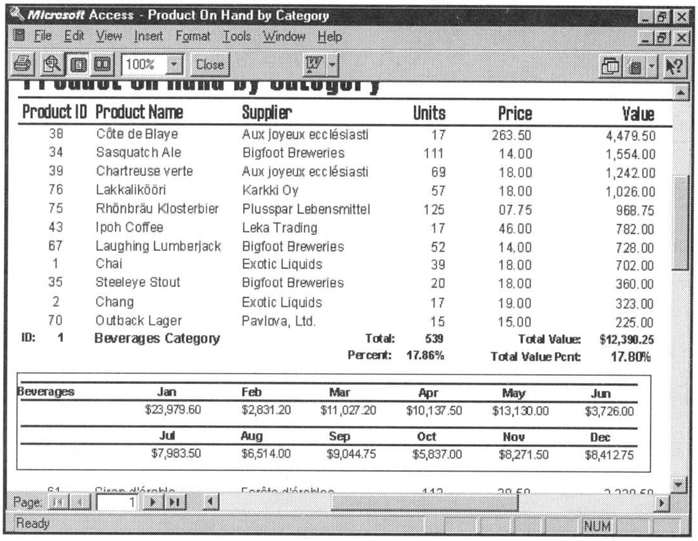

Fig. 15.20 The `rptMonthlyCategorySales` subreport linked to the Product On Hand by Category report.

Note

You can use calculated values to link main reports and subreports. Calculated values often are based on time—months, quarters, or years. To link main reports and subreports by calculated values, you must create queries for both the main report and the subreport that include the calculated value in a field, such as Month or Year. You create the calculated field in each query by using the corresponding Access date function, `Month()` or `Year()`. To group by quarters, select `Interval` for the Group On property and set the value of the Group Interval property to 3. You cannot use `Qtr` as the Group On property because the calculated value lacks the Date/Time field data type.

Troubleshooting

When I try to create a link between the main report and the subreport, I get a "Can't evaluate expression" error message.

The most likely cause is that you are trying to create a master-child (or more properly, parent-child) link with an incompatible data type. The parent-child linkage is similar to joins of queries that use the `WHERE Subreport.FieldName = Report.FieldName` criterion. As with joins, the data types of the linked fields of tables or columns of queries must be identical. You cannot, for example, link a field of the Text data type with a field of the Integer data type, even if your text field contains only numbers. If you use an expression to create the link, the data type that the expression returns must match the field value. You can use the data type conversion functions described in Chapter 9, "Understanding Operators and Expressions in Access," to change the data type that the expression returns to that of the linked field. For example, you can link a text field that contains numbers to a field of the Long Integer data type by entering `=CLng(TextField)` as the linking value.

Using Unlinked Subreports and Unbound Reports

Most reports that you create use subreports linked to the main report's data source. You can, however, insert independent subreports within main reports. In this case, you don't enter values for the Link Child Fields and Link Master Fields properties—in fact, if Access adds values, you delete those values. The subreport's data source can be related to or completely independent of the main report's data source. Figure 15.21 shows how a portion of page 2 of the `rptMonthlyCategorySales` subreport appears within the Product On Hand by Category report when you delete the CategoryID values of the Link Child Fields and Link Master Fields properties.

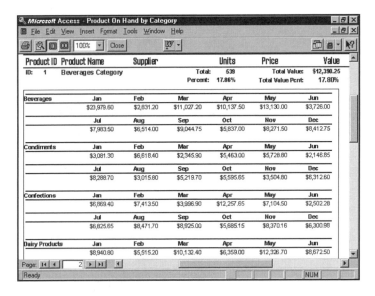

Fig. 15.21 The complete `rptMonthlyCategorySales` subreport inserted in the Product On Hand by Category report.

You can add multiple subreports to an unbound report, if all the subreports fit on one page of the report or if all the subreports fit across the page. In the latter case, you can use landscape printing orientation to increase the available page width. To create an unbound report with multiple subreports, follow these steps:

1. Click the Report tab in the Database window, and then click the New button.

2. Keep the text box for the New Report dialog's data source blank, select **Design View** in the list, and then click OK. This action creates an unbound report.

3. Click the toolbar's Database Window button to display the Database window, and drag the Report icon for the first subreport to the blank form's Detail section.

4. Drag the Report icon for the second subreport to the blank form's Detail section. If the two subreports fit vertically on one page, place the second subreport below the first subreport. If either of the two subreports requires more than a page, place the second subreport to the right of the first. In this case, you must add column labels

for the subreports in the main report's Page Header section so that each page identifies the columns.

Adding Other Controls to Reports

Access places no limit on the toolbox controls that you add to reports. So far, the controls that you have modified or added have been limited to labels, text boxes, lines, and the combo boxes that Access places automatically for fields configured as lookup fields. These four kinds of controls are likely to comprise more than 90 percent of the controls used in the reports that you create. Controls that require user interaction, such as lists and combos, can be used in a nonprinting section of the report, but practical use of these controls in reports is limited. The following list describes other controls that you might want to add to reports:

- *Bound object frames* print the contents of the OLE Object field data type. An OLE object can be a still or animated graphic, a video clip, waveform or CD audio, or even MIDI music. Reports are designed only for printing, so animated graphics, video, and sound are inappropriate for reports.

- *Unbound object frames* display OLE objects created by OLE server applications, such as Microsoft Graph 5 (included with Access), Windows Paint, Excel, or the Microsoft WordArt or Equation Editor OLE applets included with Microsoft Word. Usually, you place unbound objects in the report's Form Header or Form Footer section, but you can add a logo to the top of each page by placing the image object in the Page Header section. A graph or chart created by the Chart Wizard is a special kind of unbound OLE object.

- *Lines* and *rectangles* (also called *shapes*) create decorative elements on reports. Lines of varying widths can separate the sections of the report or emphasize a particular section.

- *Check boxes* and *option buttons* can be used to indicate the values of Yes/No fields or within group frames to indicate multiple-choice selections. Group frames, option buttons, and check boxes used in reports indicate only the value of data cells, and do not change the values. Reports seldom use toggle buttons.

- *Command buttons* execute Access macros and Access VBA procedures.

Bound and unbound object frames are the subject of Chapter 20, "Adding Graphics to Forms and Reports." Using Access macros is covered in Part V, "Integrating Access with Other Office 95 Applications," and Access VBA programming is the topic of Part VII, "Programming with Visual Basic for Applications."

Sending Reports by Microsoft Exchange

If you have installed the Microsoft Exchange client (Inbox), you can send a report to others as an attachment to a Microsoft Mail or other Microsoft Exchange message. Exchange lets you send the report output as a fax, CompuServe mail, Internet Mail, Microsoft Network mail, and any other messaging system that you have configured to work with Microsoft Exchange. (A full discussion of Microsoft Exchange is beyond the scope of

III

Forms and Reports

this book. Search the Windows 95 online Help for more information about Microsoft Exchange.) To send a report by Microsoft Exchange, follow these steps:

1. In print preview mode, open the report that you want to send. (You do not need to have Microsoft Mail or other Exchange client software running when you create the message.) You can also select the report that you want to send in the Database window's Reports tab.

2. Choose File, Send to display the Send dialog (see fig. 15.22).

Fig. 15.22   Choosing the format for the Microsoft Exchange attachment.

3. In the Select Format list box (refer to fig. 15.22), select the format in which you want to send the report file. This example sends the Product On Hand by Category report in Microsoft Excel 95 (.xls) format.

4. Click OK to create the message. A progress-reporting dialog appears while Access creates the .XLS file. When the process is complete, Microsoft Exchange's Choose Profile dialog appears (see fig. 15.23).

Fig. 15.23   Choosing the Microsoft Exchange profile for sending a report as a mail attachment.

5. In the Profile Name drop-down list box, select the profile name that you want to use for this message, and then click OK. (Refer to Exchange's online Help for information about Exchange's profiles.) The Microsoft Exchange's New Message window now appears (see fig. 15.24).

6. Enter the recipients' names, a subject, and an optional transmittal message, as shown in figure 15.24. Click the Send button (the leftmost button of the upper toolbar) to send the message with the attached report file.

You can view the attachment in a message that an application creates. If you double-click the workbook icon in the New Message window, you can view the report. The Product On Hand by Category report file shown in Excel 95 (or 5.0) has additional formatting applied (see fig. 15.25).

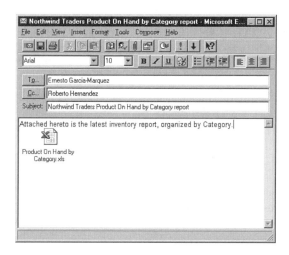

Fig. 15.24 Completing the Microsoft Exchange message.

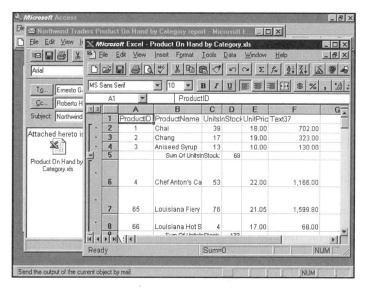

Fig. 15.25 The appearance of the report attachment in Microsoft Excel 95.

> **Note**
>
> Depending on your report's formatting, some of the field values might not appear in an Excel worksheet file. For example, the subtotals for the Values fields, as well as both percentage fields, are missing. However, you can easily reconstruct these fields in Excel. Access cannot incorporate subreports contained in reports printed to files of any of the three available formats. You must provide individual columns for subtotals and other section footers to ensure that the values appear in an .XLS file.

From Here...

This chapter completes Part III, "Creating Forms and Reports," which covered all the basic functions of Access that duplicate the capabilities of database front-ends. In Parts II and III, you learned the basic steps to create queries, forms, and reports. Although all the examples used the Northwind Traders sample database, you also can apply the queries, forms, and reports that you have created to tables linked to Access. If the Access or linked tables are on a network server rather than on the computer's fixed disk, the same procedures that you learned in the preceding eight chapters apply.

For information related to the topics discussed in this chapter, refer to the following chapters:

- Chapter 9, "Understanding Operators and Expressions in Access," describes how to use the DLookUp() domain aggregate function and how to create expressions for calculating field values and linking subreports.

- Chapter 20, "Adding Graphics to Forms and Reports," shows you how to print images contained in OLE Object fields of tables or queries and how to add to reports logos or other decorative graphics.

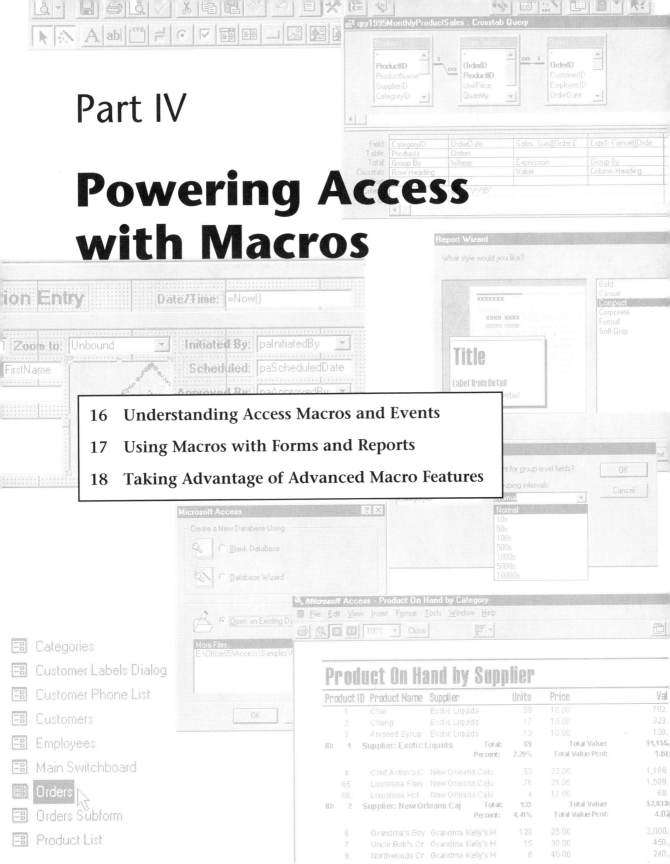

Part IV

Powering Access with Macros

Chapter 16

Understanding Access Macros and Events

In the broadest sense, *programming* is telling the computer what to do and when to do it. The Access interface has several built-in levels of programming. You've actually been learning different kinds of programming in the previous chapters. Up to this point, however, the programming has consisted of following step-by-step instructions to accomplish a specific task. In a narrower sense, programming consists of defining step-by-step operations by means of a series of statements written in a programming language. Once you save the statements, you can execute the series of statements at will. Access macros constitute a programming language, albeit with a limited vocabulary. This chapter begins with a description of programming with Access 95's options, object properties, and Wizards. The majority of the chapter is devoted to Access macros, the easiest way to automate your database applications, and the use of events to trigger execution of Access macros.

Taking Advantage of User Interface Programming

Access 95 lets you set the values of options, alter object property values, design queries, and add new objects with wizards. Programming that doesn't involve a formal programming language is called *user-interface* (UI) programming. The following sections describe how UI programming fits into the Access database application development framework.

Programming by Setting Options

When you change options and set preferences by choosing Tools, Options, you are using a kind of programming. The choices that you make in the Options dialog become the new defaults for Access itself and not just for the current database that is open when you set the options. Select a tab at the top of the Options dialog to view and make changes for a category of options (see fig. 16.1).

In this chapter, you learn about the following

- How to use macros to automate a database

- The steps to create a macro

- How to find the macro action that you want

- Nine ways to run a macro

- The timing of events

- How to control the flow of macro execution

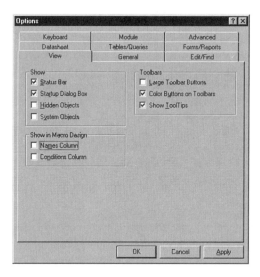

Fig. 16.1 The Options dialog.

You can set default options to specify how Access responds to keystrokes. To do so, you first click the Keyboard tab to display the Keyboard Options page. Other tabs available from the Options dialog enable you to choose which field types and sizes are defaults when you create new table fields, and whether you want to join tables automatically, display table names, and display all query fields in the query datasheet. You can specify colors, fonts and gridline appearance for datasheets, and custom form and report templates for creating new blank forms and reports. You can decide whether to display or suppress confirmation dialogs when the user deletes records or runs action queries. You can hide the status bar, suppress ToolTips, and specify how you want to resolve conflicts when two users try to edit the same record. These are some of the ways that you can program the Access environment by choosing Tools, Options.

> **Note**
>
> The placement of the Tools, Options command is a little confusing, because you can access it only when a database is open. Nevertheless, when you choose Tools, Options, you change the Access environment, not just the open database.

Other menu commands provide ways to set the environment. You can customize, hide, or show various toolbars by choosing View, Toolbars, and you can specify startup conditions by choosing Tools, Startup.

Programming by Setting Object Properties

The previous chapters introduced four of the six database objects: the tables, queries, forms, and reports and the objects contained within the database objects. Tables have fields and indexes, queries have fields, and forms and reports have sections and controls. Each object has a behavior that you can specify by setting properties in the object's property sheet. Setting an object's properties is also a kind of programming.

Many of the properties control the object's visual appearance. For a text box control on a form, you can specify the size and location, the font type, size, style, and weight, the colors displayed, and other formatting properties. Other properties control how you can interact with the data in the control. For the text box control on a form, you can set properties to test data, prevent changes in the data, and even prevent mouse clicks within the text box. You can set the control source property to specify how the text box gets its data.

Some of the objects seem intelligent because of the properties that you can set. The main form-subform linking is due to the correct setting of three properties of the subform control to specify which form to display in the control and how to link the records in the two forms. You don't have to write commands—the formal "programming" is built in to the subform control itself. The combo box control is a versatile tool that can display one value and store another value in a table. When you click the combo box's down arrow, Access automatically displays a list of values. Instead of formal "programming," you need only set three properties of the combo box control to create the link to a field in a table, to create a link to another table that provides the data for the combo box rows, and to specify which column in the list links to the underlying table.

You can set properties for the relationship between two tables so that when you make changes to the data in a table's primary-key field, Access automatically makes changes to the matching fields in the related tables. If you delete records in the parent table, Access automatically deletes the related records in all related child tables.

Programming in the Query Design Window

Queries provide still another way to "program" without writing commands. Instead of writing a formal program, you create most queries in a special query design window. You program graphically in this window by dragging tables and other queries to the window's upper pane, by drawing join lines to relate fields, and by dragging fields to the Query by Example (QBE) grid. You complete the query design by setting properties and entering criteria expressions in specific cells. With a properly designed database structure, you can easily create simple queries by using the QBE grid to select the data from among several tables, and create action queries to make changes to groups of records and to move data from one table to another.

As the questions that you ask of your database become more complex, so do the queries that you need to create. Some questions require queries that you cannot create graphically in the query design window. To create these queries, you must use Structured Query Language (SQL). When you finish designing the query by using either the QBE Design grid or SQL, you store the instructions as a query object. When you save a query, Access interprets the instructions that you have entered into the cells, analyzes the query instructions, determines the optimum strategy for executing the instructions, and stores the query. When you want to execute your query "program," you click the Run button or switch to Datasheet View.

Programming with the Wizards

The wizards provide another way to "program" without writing commands. Each wizard displays a series of dialogs that present design and behavioral choices. Screen by screen, the wizard obtains the information necessary to create the object to your specifications. A wizard doesn't do anything that you can't do yourself; it just does most of the work for you. Wizards are limited in the types of objects that they can create and are sometimes slow. Often you use a wizard to build the first draft of the object and then modify and fine-tune the design in Design View.

Whether you "program" by setting options, setting object properties, designing queries in the query design window, or using wizards, you are actually programming by using the user interface. Access is easy to work with because it enables you to program by manipulating graphical objects, setting properties in specially designed property sheets and design windows, and answering wizard questions. In a few hours you can create simple queries and attractive forms and reports that would take weeks if you had to write formal programs.

Access provides additional ways to program that enable you to transform an interactive database into a fully automated database application that others can use. The balance of this chapter is devoted to automating your Access applications.

Automating a Database

The first three parts of this book have shown you how to create an *interactive* database. In such a database, the user initiates each action that the computer takes. By selecting menu commands and toolbar buttons and by using the mouse, the user opens forms, moves and resizes windows, renames objects, prints reports, selects records, finds a specified record, imports and exports data, and so on. The user has to know the commands required to perform tasks. Many common database tasks require several steps. For example, a routine database task is to import data from a spreadsheet, manipulate the data into a suitable format, and append the formatted data into one or more tables. When such a task requires several commands, the user must know the correct order of commands to invoke.

The next step in working with Access is to learn how to shift some of your labor to the computer by automating the database. In an *automated* database, the user takes a single action—such as clicking a button or selecting a value from a combo list—and the computer responds by executing the entire set of actions required to accomplish a task. To automate a task, you must know how to tell the computer the actions to take in response to the user input.

In addition to automating a multistep task, there are other reasons for learning a new kind of programming in Access. An existing menu command might not work in just the way you want. For example, Edit, Find displays a dialog with a text box that requires the user to type the text of the value for which to search, two combo boxes, and three check boxes with choices (see fig. 16.2).

Fig. 16.2   The Find dialog.

You can improve the find operation by replacing this dialog with a combo box and telling the computer to find the record that the user selects from the list. The user simply selects a value from the combo list.

Another reason to learn the next level of programming is to replace Access's default error messages with more informative and helpful custom messages. For example, suppose that you create a new record by entering data into the all the controls displayed in a data-entry form. When you try to save the record, Access validates the value that you entered in the primary-key fields. If Access finds in the table a record with the same values, it displays the following cryptic message: "Duplicate value in index, primary key, or relationship. Changes were unsuccessful." Such a message can mystify an untrained user trying to use your database. An improvement is to have Access validate the entered values when the user tabs out of the primary-key control. Then the user doesn't have to enter data in the remaining controls. You can then replace the default message with a more clear one, like the following: "A record with this Customer ID already exists. Enter a different value." An even better solution is to display the stored record so that the user can see the record and decide what to do.

Access provides two kinds of programming to automate a database: macro programming and, new in Access 95, Visual Basic for Applications or Access VBA. These separate yet overlapping programming languages are both tools that enable you to write commands to shift the labor burden from the user to the computer.

In macro programming, you create programs called *macros* in a special macro design window analogous to the query design window. The design window's structure makes writing macros a matter of filling in the blanks by dragging objects from the Database window, selecting from combo box lists, and entering expressions in specified cells. The macro design window makes it easy to learn how to create macros. The window's structure minimizes the need to learn syntax—the spelling, grammar, and order that a programming language usually requires to write macros.

The Access macro-programming language is a reduced version of the more powerful Visual Basic for Applications programming language; compared to VBA, the macro-programming language has limited powers. Nevertheless, you can use it to automate most database tasks and create sophisticated stand-alone applications. When you need the additional power provided by a full-featured programming language, Access VBA is available.

This part of the book introduces you to macro programming, and Part VII, "Programming with Visual Basic for Applications," shows you how to program with Access VBA.

> **Note**
>
> Despite its power, Access VBA is inherently dependent on the macro-programming language because many of Access VBA's commands are actually macro commands that Access VBA calls. Although you can automate a database by using only macro programming, when you use Access VBA you must also use a part of macro programming.

What Is a Macro?

 In macro programming, you create small programs called *macros*. Each macro consists of a list of actions that you want Access to perform. To create a macro, you select actions from a list of 49 defined macro actions. Some of the macro actions duplicate menu commands, such as Print, Close, and ApplyFilter. Some macro actions substitute for mouse actions. For example, you can use the `SelectObject` action to select a database object in the same way that you select an open window by clicking it or select a database object in the Database window by clicking the object's name. Other macro actions provide capabilities not available through menu commands, such as `Beep`, which emits a beep sound, or `MsgBox`, which displays a custom message. Table 16.1 lists available macro actions grouped by task. Access 2.0 provided 47 macro actions; Access 95 adds two new actions: `Save` and `SetMenuItem`.

Table 16.1 Macro Actions Grouped by Task

Category	Task	Macro Action
Manipulating	Copy or rename a database object	CopyObject, Rename
	Delete a database object	DeleteObject
	Open a table, query, form, report, or module	OpenTable, OpenQuery, OpenForm, OpenReport, OpenModule
	Close a database object	Close
	Save a database object	Save
	Print a database object	Print, OpenForm, OpenQuery, OpenReport
	Select a database window object	SelectObject
	Copy or rename an object	CopyObject, Rename
	Update data or update the screen	RepaintObject, Requery, ShowAllRecords
	Set the value of a field, control, or property	SetValue
Executing	Carry out a menu command	DoMenuItem
	Run a query	OpenQuery, RunSQL
	Run a macro or a BASIC procedure	RunMacro, RunCode
	Run another Windows or DOS application	RunApp

Category	Task	Macro Action
	Stop execution of a macro	`StopMacro, StopAllMacros`
	Stop execution of Access	`Quit`
	Stop execution following an event	`CancelEvent`
Working with data in forms and reports	Select or sort records	`ApplyFilter`
	Find a record	`FindRecord, FindNext`
	Move to a particular location	`GoToControl, GoToRecord, GoToPage`
Importing and exporting data	Output data from a table, query, form, report, or module in .xls, .rtf or .txt formats	`OutputAs`
	Include in an e-mail message data from a table, query, form, report, or module in .xls, .rtf or .txt format	`SendObject`
	Transfer data between Access and other data formats	`TransferDatabase, TransferSpreadsheet, TransferText`
Miscellaneous	Create a custom menubar	`AddMenu, SetMenuItem`
	Sound a beep	`Beep`
	Display or hide a toolbar	`ShowToolbar`
	Send keystrokes to Access or a Windows application	`SendKeys`
	Display an hourglass	`Hourglass`
	Display or hide system information	`Echo, SetWarnings`
	Display custom messages	`MsgBox`

Most macro actions require additional information as *action arguments* to specify how the action works. For example, when you use the `OpenForm` action, you must specify the name of the form to open as the `Form Name` argument. Also, to specify whether you want to display the Form, Design, Print Preview, or Datasheet View, you must use the `View` argument; to specify whether you want to allow editing or adding new records, you must use the `Data Mode` argument; and to specify whether you want the form to be hidden, to behave like a dialog, or to be in normal mode, you must use the `Window Mode` argument.

After you create the macro, you tell Access to run it. There are several ways that you initiate a macro; most are discussed in the "Running a Macro" section, later in this chapter. Probably the most important way to initiate a macro is to ask Access to run the macro in response to an *event*.

What Is an Event?

When you interact with the computer by using the mouse or the keyboard, you cause the object that has the focus to change its state. When you click a button, you change the button's state from unclicked to clicked; when you select a form name in the Database window and double-click, the form's state changes from closed to open; if you then click back into the Database window, the form changes from activated to deactivated.

When you interact with an object by using the keyboard or the mouse, you can change the object's state. The object's state is stored with the other data about the object. Access makes some of the changes in the object's state available as opportunities to interrupt normal processing. These special changes in an object's state are called events. An *event* is a change in the state of an object at which you can interrupt normal processing and define a response.

 Not all Access objects trigger events. Forms and reports are the only database objects for which Access defines events. All forms, form sections, and controls on a form trigger events; all reports and report sections also trigger events. Access 2.0 defined 35 events; Access 95 adds four more: `Filter`, `ApplyFilter`, `NoData`, and `Page`. One way to understand events is to categorize each by the type of action that causes the event to occur. There are nine categories:

- *Mouse events* are triggered when you click form objects.

- *Keyboard events* are triggered by forms and form controls when you type or send keystrokes with the `SendKeys` action while the form object has the focus.

- *Window events* are triggered by opening or closing forms or reports.

- *Focus events* are triggered when a form or form control gains or loses the focus or when a form or report becomes active or inactive.

- *Data events* are triggered by forms and form controls when you change data in controls or records, or by forms when the focus moves from one record to another.

- *Filter events* are triggered by forms when you apply or remove filters.

- *Print events* are triggered by reports and report sections when you print or preview a report.

- *Error events* are triggered by a form or report that has the focus when an error occurs.

- *Timing events* are triggered by forms when a specified time interval passes.

Table 16.2 groups the 39 events according their cause.

Table 16.2	Events Grouped by Cause	
Category	**Cause**	**Events**
Mouse events	The user creating mouse actions	Click DblClick MouseDown MouseUp MouseMove
Keyboard events	The user typing on the keyboard or SendKeys sending keystrokes	KeyDown KeyUp KeyPress

Category	Cause	Events

Window events	Opening, closing, or resizing a window	`Open`
		`Load`
		`Unload`
		`Close`
		`Resize`

Focus events	An object losing or gaining the focus, or a form or report becoming active or inactive	`Enter`
		`GotFocus`
		`Exit`
		`LostFocus`
		`Activate`
		`Deactivate`

Data events	Making changes to a control's data, displaying records in a form, or moving the focus from one record to another in a form	`Current`
		`BeforeInsert`
		`AfterInsert`
		`Delete`
		`BeforeDelConfirm`
		`AfterDelConfirm`
		`BeforeUpdate`
		`AfterUpdate`
		`Change`
		`Updated`
		`NotInList`

Filter events	Opening or closing a filter window, or applying or removing a filter.	`Filter` `ApplyFilter`

Print events	Selecting or arranging data for printing	`Format`
		`Print`
		`Retreat`
		`NoData`
		`Page`

Error event	Generating an error	`Error`
Timing event	A specified amount of time expiring	`Timer`

Events are defined for specific objects, so you can also organize events by object. Table 16.3 lists the events for each object.

Each event that an object triggers has a corresponding *event property* listed in a separate category of the object's property sheet. Usually the corresponding event property is the event name preceded by the word On; for example, the `Click` event triggered by a command button becomes the On Click property in the button's property sheet. Figure 16.3 shows the event category for the property sheet of a text box indicating the 15 events that the text box control triggers. Notice that all event properties—except the Before Update and After Update data event properties—follow the pattern of preceding the event name with `On`.

Table 16.3   Events for Each Object

Object	Mouse	Keyboard	Window
Label	Click DblClick MouseDown MouseUp MouseMove		
Text Box	Click DblClick MouseDown MouseUp MouseMove	KeyDown KeyUp KeyPress	Enter Exit
Option Group	Click DblClick MouseDown MouseUp MouseMove		Enter Exit
Toggle Button	Click DblClick MouseDown MouseUp MouseMove	KeyDown KeyUp KeyPress	Enter Exit
Option Button	Click DblClick MouseDown MouseUp MouseMove	KeyDown KeyUp KeyPress	Enter Exit
Check Box	Click DblClick MouseDown MouseUp MouseMove	KeyDown KeyUp KeyPress	Enter Exit
Combo Box	Click DblClick MouseDown MouseUp MouseMove	KeyDown KeyUp KeyPress	Enter Exit
List Box	Click DblClick MouseDown MouseUp MouseMove	KeyDown KeyUp KeyPress	Enter Exit
Graph	Click DblClick MouseDown MouseUp MouseMove		Enter Exit
Subform/ Subreport			Enter Exit
Object Frame	Click DblClick MouseDown MouseUp MouseMove		Enter Exit

IV

Access with Macros

Focus	Data and Filter	Print	Error and Timing
GotFocus LostFocus BeforeUpdate AfterUpdate	Change		
BeforeUpdate AfterUpdate			
GotFocus LostFocus BeforeUpdate AfterUpdate			
GotFocus LostFocus BeforeUpdate AfterUpdate			
GotFocus LostFocus BeforeUpdate AfterUpdate			
GotFocus LostFocus BeforeUpdate AfterUpdate	Change NotInList		
GotFocus LostFocus BeforeUpdate AfterUpdate			
GotFocus LostFocus	Updated		
GotFocus LostFocus	Updated		

(continues)

Table 16.3 Events for Each Object

Object	Mouse	Keyboard	Window
Bound Object Frame	Click DblClick MouseDown MouseUp MouseMove	KeyDown KeyUp KeyPress	Enter Exit
Line Rectangle	Click DblClick MouseDown MouseUp MouseMove		
Page Break			
Command Button	Click DblClick MouseDown MouseUp MouseMove	KeyDown KeyUp KeyPress	Enter Exit
Form Sections	Click DblClick MouseDown MouseUp MouseMove		
Form	Click DblClick MouseDown MouseUp MouseMove	KeyDown KeyUp KeyPress	Open Load Unload Close Resize Activate Deactivate Current Delete
Report Page Header/Footer			Format Print
Group Header/ Footer			Format Print Retreat
Report Detail section			Format Print Retreat
Report			Open Close Activate Deactivate
Page			
Error			

Focus	Data and Filter	Print	Error and Timing
GotFocus LostFocus BeforeUpdate AfterUpdate	Updated		
GotFocus LostFocus			
GotFocus LostFocus BeforeUpdate AfterUpdate BeforeInsert AfterInsert BeforeDelConfirm AfterDelConfirm	Filter ApplyFilter		Error Timer
	NoData		

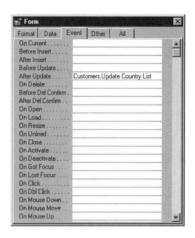

Fig. 16.3   A text box's event category.

Events occur in response to a user action. The response might be directly or indirectly related to the user's keystroke or mouse click. If you click a command button to close a form, the direct response is the Click event triggered by the button; subsequently, the form itself triggers the various events associated with the actual closing of the form in an indirect response to clicking the button.

To intercept the computer's processing of the keystroke or mouse click, you assign a macro to an event triggered by a particular object. You assign a macro to an event—or *trap* the event—by entering the macro's name in the object's event property. When the object triggers the event, the event triggers the macro—that is, Access runs the macro that you have assigned to the object's event.

When you set up an event trap by assigning a macro, you are interrupting the operations that Access would normally carry out. When you click a command button, the button triggers the Click event, then Access waits for the next user action. You can trap the Click event by assigning a macro that, for example, instructs Access to open a form before resting. When you select a new value from a combo list, the AfterUpdate event occurs as Access triggers the changed value; then Access rests. You can trap the AfterUpdate event by assigning a macro that instructs Access to find the corresponding record first before resting.

Creating macros to perform a set of actions and assigning them to events is called *event-driven programming*. By using events to trigger macros, you have greater control over when the macro runs. For example, the combo box's AfterUpdate event relies only on the user changing the value in the combo box; the event does not require a separate button click or keystroke combination to run the macro to find the specified record.

Creating Macros

You create and edit macros in a special macro design window, which this book calls the *macrosheet* (for consistency with the name *datasheet*).

Note

Most other programmable applications, including Microsoft Word and Excel, have a macro recorder that is very helpful when you are learning how to write programs. To begin creating a macro, you turn on the macro recorder; you then perform each step of a task by pressing keystrokes, using the mouse, and choosing menu commands; then when you finish the task, you turn off the recorder. Typically, you edit the recorded macro in a separate programming window that displays the recorded program as text. You edit to remove unnecessary steps and to add capabilities that you cannot record. When you work in the programming window, you are not limited to the actions that you can record, and the full functionality of the application's programming language is available.

Access does not have a recorder to record either macros or Access VBA code.

The Macrosheet and the Macro Design Toolbar

You open a new macrosheet from the Database window by clicking the Macro tab and then clicking the New button. Alternatively, click the down arrow for the toolbar's New Object button and select New Macro. The new macrosheet opens in Design View as shown in figure 16.4.

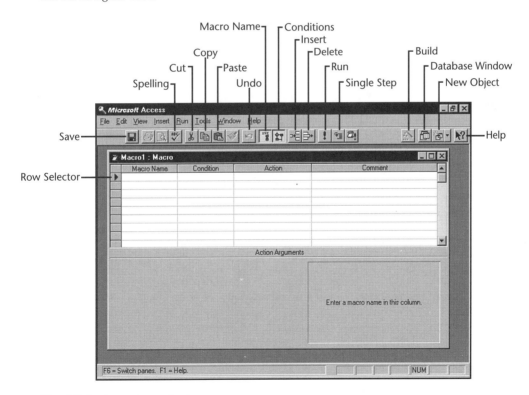

Fig. 16.4 A new macrosheet.

The macrosheet has four columns: Macro Name, Condition, Action, and Comments. You can show or hide either of the first two columns by toggling the Macro Names and Conditions buttons on the Macro Design toolbar. By default, Access displays only the Action and Comments columns. To change the default display to show all four columns, choose Tools, Option, click the View tab, and check the Names Column and the Conditions Column check boxes in the View Options sheet's Show in Macro Design group (refer to fig. 16.1). Normally, you store several macros in the same macrosheet, each with a different name entered in the Macro Name column. In the Conditions column, you enter expressions to test current values if you want to control when a portion of a macro runs.

The Macro Design toolbar displays whenever a macrosheet is active. The toolbar contains tools to help you create, run, and troubleshoot macros. These tools include editing tools to cut, copy, and paste text, undo changes, and insert and delete rows, a Build button that opens the Expression Builder dialog, a Run tool that runs the first macro in the macrosheet, and a Single Step tool that helps you troubleshoot a macro by running the macro one step at a time. Later sections of this chapter describe these tools. The toolbar tools duplicate many of the Macro Design menubar's commands.

Tip

The Run tool runs only the first macro in a macrosheet. To run any macro in the macrosheet from the toolbar, customize the Macro Design toolbar by adding the Run Macro tool from the File category in the Customize Toolbars dialog. The "Understanding the Access Toolbox" section of Chapter 13, "Designing Custom Multitable Forms," shows how to add buttons to toolbars.

You can open an existing macrosheet to review, edit, or copy existing macros or add a new macro to the sheet. To open an existing macrosheet, click the Macro tab in the Database window, select a macrosheet from the list, and click the Design button. Figure 16.5 shows a macrosheet with two macros.

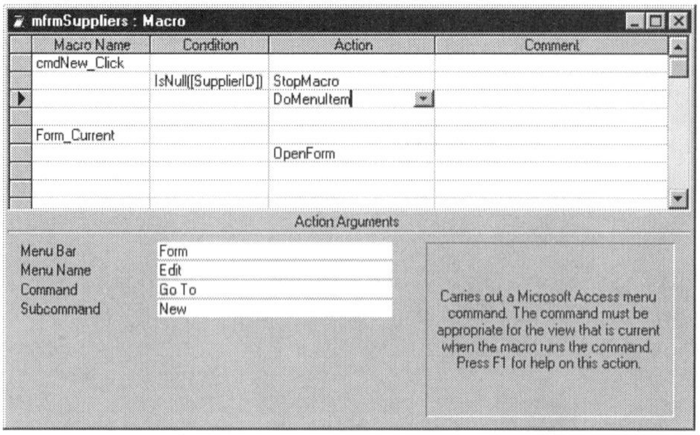

Fig. 16.5 A macrosheet with two macros.

You enter the name of the macro in the Macro Name column. To test the value of a *condition* (a logical expression that evaluates to **True** or **False**) and run part of the macro only if the condition is **True**, enter the condition in the Condition column. In the Action column, enter macro actions in the order that you want to perform them. When you select an action, the window's lower portion displays the corresponding action arguments that you can use to define the way that the macro works. In the Comments column, you enter informative messages for your own use. Access ignores the Comments column, but you shouldn't. Note that the macrosheet's design has a limitation: You can view the arguments for only one action at a time. This limitation is bothersome when you are trying to understand how the macro works. One way to overcome the limitation is to include in the Comments column information about the important arguments for each action; you can then see all the relevant information in the macro at a single glance. Chapter 18, "Taking Advantage of Advanced Macro Features," describes additional ways to document macros.

Organizing Macro Groups and Individual Macros

There are two ways to store macros. The first is to store each macro in a separate macrosheet. In this case, you store the macro as a database object that the Database window displays. The Macro Name column is not necessary because the macrosheet name is the same as that of the macro.

The second way is to store several macros on a single macrosheet. In this case, the macrosheet is the database object and the Database window displays only the name of the macrosheet. As explained in the previous section, most macros are triggered by events that are triggered by objects on forms and reports. Typically, you use several events on a form or a report to trigger macros.

A fully automated database application might include hundreds of macros. Organizing macros so that you can easily locate particular macros is essential. A particularly effective scheme is to create for each form or report a separate macrosheet to hold macros triggered by events on that form or report. A macrosheet that stores several macros is called a *macro group*. The following is the syntax for an individual macro in a macro group:

        MacroGroupName.MacroName

For example, the full name of the second macro in figure 16.5 is mfrmSuppliers.cmdNew_Click. These names are chosen to include a maximum amount of information. To use macros effectively, you should adopt a consistent naming scheme.

Naming Macro Groups and Individual Macros

▶▶ See "Using Macros Instead of VBA," p. 1237

After you start creating macros to automate a database to make it easier to work with, you can quickly accumulate dozens of short macros. The best way to keep track of macros is to use a consistent naming convention so that you can tell, at a glance, the object and the event that triggers the macro. When naming objects, this book uses the

Leszynski naming conventions, included in Appendix B, "Naming Conventions for Access Objects and Variables." This naming convention uses the following prefixes (called *tags*) in naming macrosheets:

- Use the tag *mcr* for macrosheets that are not associated with a particular form or report. For example, if you have some macros that perform common tasks that most of your database's forms require, you might store them together in a macro group named `mcrGlobal`.

- Name macrosheets that you create for a form or report by placing an *m* in front of the form or report name, as follows:

  mFormName (as in `mfrmSuppliers`)

  mReportName (as in `mrptInventorySummary`)

- Use the tag *mmnu* for macros that you create for custom menus. For example, you might name a macro to display a custom menubar for data-entry forms `mmnuDataEntry`. Each menu that appears on a custom menubar has a separate macro group that contains a macro for each of the menu commands. The Access convention is to name a menu's macro group by using the menubar name followed by an underscore and the menu name. Therefore, following the previous example, you would name the File menu's macro group `mmnuDataEntry_File`. Chapter 18, "Taking Advantage of Advanced Macro Features," discusses the creation of custom menubars.

There are two exceptions to the Leszynski naming convention for macrosheets. If you create a macro to start your application, you must name the macro AutoExec. When you open a database, Access automatically looks for and runs a macro named AutoExec. If you create a macro group to assign macros to keystrokes, you use the default name Autokeys. Chapter 18, "Taking Advantage of Advanced Macro Features," discusses how to create startup and key-assignment macros.

According to the Leszynski naming conventions, the name of an individual macro stored in a macro group reflects the event that the macro traps. The name includes the object's name followed by an underscore and the event's name. The full name of an individual macro has the following syntax:

  MacroGroupName.ObjectName_EventName

For example, if a form named `frmSuppliers` contains a command button named `cmdNew` and the `Click` event of the button triggers a macro, you store the macro in the macrosheet named `mfrmSuppliers`, and you type the name **cmdNew_Click** in the Macro Name column. The full name of the macro is `mfrmSuppliers.cmdNew_Click`. If a form or report triggers an event that in turn triggers a macro, the name of the macro in the macro group is simply Form_*EventName* or Report_*EventName*. Therefore, in the previous example, if the form's `Open` event triggers a macro, you type the name **Form_Open** in the Macro Name column, and the macro's full name is `mfrmSuppliers.Form_Open`.

Steps in Creating a Macro

To create a macro, follow these steps:

1. Decide what you want the macro to do. Simple macros require only a few actions and can be designed in your head. For more complex tasks, use a flow diagram to design the macro.

2. Decide which event will trigger the macro. Objects typically trigger more than a dozen events. Forms trigger 29 events—more than any other object.

3. Open the macro group for the form or report that contains the object whose event triggers the macro. Or, if necessary, open a new macrosheet, choose File, Save As or press F12, and enter the name of the new macro group for the form or report.

4. In the first empty row, enter the name of the new macro. Access ignores empty rows, so you can make your macro groups easier to read by skipping a row between macros.

5. Beginning with the next row, enter the macro actions in the order required to carry out the task. For each action, enter the arguments required to define how you want Access to execute the action.

> **Tip**
>
> Although you could begin entering the first action in the same row that contains the macro name, you should move to the next row. This makes it is easier to modify the macro when you need to insert another initial action, and easier to copy the macro actions if you want to use them in another macro.

6. Save the macrosheet by clicking the Save button on the toolbar, choosing File, Save, or pressing F12. Before you can run a macro, you must save it to memory.

7. Run the macro to test it. The next section details the variety of ways to run a macro.

Entering Macro Actions

The macrosheet makes it easy to enter macro actions and action arguments. When you click a cell in the Action column, a drop-down arrow appears in the right side of active cell (see fig. 16.6).

Enter an action by typing it into the action cell and pressing the Enter key. As you type characters, Access automatically fills the cell with the first macro action in the list matching the characters that you have typed. If you spell the action correctly, Access enters it in the cell and the lower pane displays the corresponding action arguments. If you misspell the action, Access displays an error message.

If you want to review the available macro actions, click the down arrow, press F4, or press Alt+down to display the combo list of the macro actions (see fig. 16.7). Scroll through the list and click an entry to select an action, or, with the list displayed, begin typing the first letter or two of the action to have Access scroll the list and fill the cell with the first action matching the typed characters. Press F1 to display the Help window for the selected action.

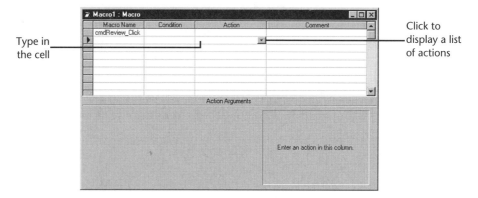

Fig. 16.6   The combo list arrow enables you to select an action from a list or to type the action.

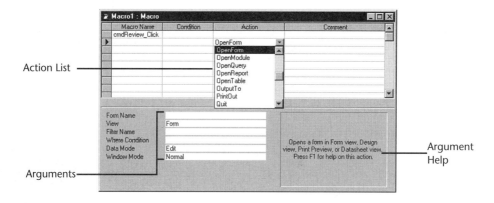

Fig. 16.7   The action list and action arguments defining how an action works.

You can enter some actions by dragging and dropping database objects. If you drag and drop a table, query, form, or report object from the Database window to an action cell, Access inserts a row above the cell over which you released the object icon and automatically enters the respective action to open the object—OpenTable, OpenQuery, OpenForm, or OpenReport. Access also automatically fills in the action argument calling for the name of the object to open. Figure 16.8 shows how you can arrange windows for entering an action with drag-and-drop, and shows the result of dropping a form object. Dragging and dropping a macro object inserts a RunMacro action with the name of the macro object entered into the MacroName argument.

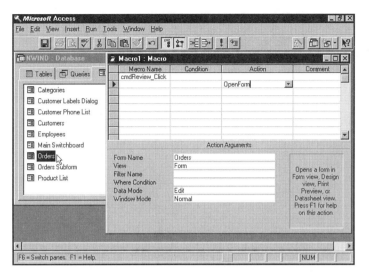

Fig. 16.8   Entering a macro action by dragging and dropping an object from the Database window.

Entering Action Arguments

Action arguments define how an action works. Each macro action has a related set of action arguments. When you first enter an action, the lower pane displays its arguments. To view the arguments of any action, click the row containing the action. Figure 16.6 shows the action arguments for the OpenForm action. After selecting an action, click the first action argument or press F6. This shifts the focus between the upper and lower panes of the Design window. You have to type some arguments, but most arguments provide a combo list that enables you to type or select the argument.

> **Tip**
>
> When arguments require the name of a database object, you can type the name directly, select it from a combo list, or drag the object from the Database window and drop the object icon on the argument's text box.

When the combo list presents a set of options, you can double-click the argument to cycle through the available options. When an argument requires an expression, the Build button appears to the right of the text box when you select the argument. Click to select a different argument, or tab from one argument to the next. A help message and a description of the selected argument appears in the Macro Design window's lower-right corner. If you need help with any argument, press F1 to display the Help window for the selected action.

Table 16.4 lists the action arguments and their entry methods for the `OpenForm` action.

Argument Name	Entry Method	Defines
Table 16.4 Arguments for the `OpenForm` Action		
Form Name	Combo list	The form that opens.
View	Combo list; cycle through properties: Form, Design, Print Preview, and Datasheet	The view in which the form opens.
Filter Name	Typing	The name of the query or filter saved as a query to restrict or sort the records to display.
Where Condition	Typing; Expression Builder is available	The expression that selects records to display; can be an SQL WHERE clause.
Data Mode	Combo list; cycle through properties: Add, Edit, Read Only	The form's data-entry mode.
Window Mode	Combo list; cycle through properties: Normal, Hidden, Icon, Dialog	The form window's mode.

Note

You can use the Zoom box to view, enter, and edit the contents of any cell in the macrosheet except action cells and to view the contents of any argument's text box. Press Shift+F2 to open the Zoom box. When you finish entering or editing the cell's contents, click OK or Cancel to return to the macrosheet. In figure 16.9, the Zoom box displays the complete `Where Condition`.

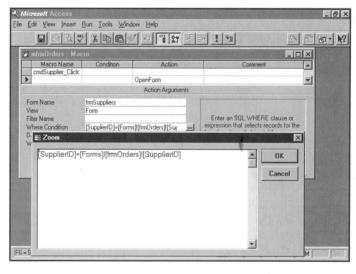

Fig. 16.9 Using the Zoom box to view the contents of an argument text box.

Entering Comments

▶▶ See "Troubleshooting Macro Errors," p. 692

Use the Comments column to document your macros with additional information that will make it easier for you and others to understand how the macro works. Comments are valuable when troubleshooting a macro that doesn't work as intended.

Because the macrosheet's structure limits the display of action arguments to a single action, you should use your comments to help document your macros by including information about the relevant arguments. The Leszynski naming conventions automatically documents the name of the object and the event that triggers the macro.

Access ignores blank rows, so you can insert rows between macros in a macro group. By inserting blank rows, you can make your macros easier to read, and by entering additional comments in inserted rows, you can make your macros easier to understand. Figure 16.10 shows how to use comments and the L-R naming standard to document macros.

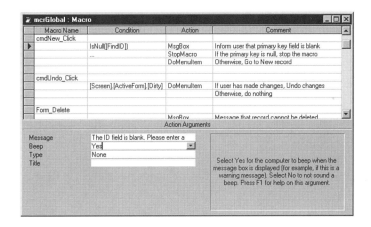

Fig. 16.10 Using comments and the Leszynski naming standard to document macros.

Understanding Macro Actions

Access 95 offers 49 macro actions from which you can choose. The following sections describe how to find the macro action that you need to perform a particular task.

Getting Online Help and Examples for Actions

Use the online help system to find in-depth information about macro actions. To see the entire list of macro actions for which help is available, follow these steps:

1. Choose Help, Microsoft Access Help Topics to view the Help Topics window.

2. Click the Contents tab.

3. Double-click the Microsoft Access Programming and Language Reference book icon then double-click the Actions book icon. The macro actions are grouped alphabetically in books.

 **4.** To learn more about a macro action displayed in the Help Topics window as shown in figure 16.11, double-click the book that contains the initial letter of the action to display a list of macro actions in the book.

5. Select the name of the action for which you want help, then choose Display.

Fig. 16.11 Selecting an action from the Help window to learn about the action and see an example.

If you already know which action you want information for, choose the Index tab when the Help Topics window first opens. Type in the top text box the name of the action. As you type, the list scrolls to match whatever characters you have typed. Choose the Display button to display subtopics in the lower list. Select one of the subtopics and then click the Go To button. Figure 16.12 shows SetValue typed in the top text box.

Another way to get help on a macro action is to select the action from the combo list in any of the macrosheet's action cells and press F1 to display context-sensitive help for the action.

Figure 16.13 shows an example of the help for the SetValue action. In the Help window, underlined words are called *hot spots* and are linked to additional help topics. You can jump to this related help topic by clicking an underlined word; alternatively, you can press Tab until you have selected the underlined word, and then press Enter. Return to the Help document from which you started by choosing the Back button or pressing Alt+B. Click the underlined word *Example* at the top of the window to see an example of the action or how to complete its arguments.

Fig. 16.12   Using the Help system to search for macro commands.

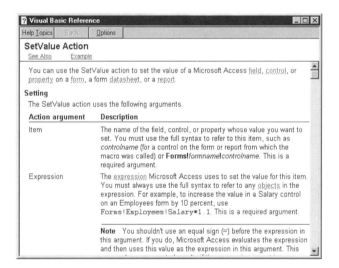

Fig. 16.13   Using Help to learn about actions and see examples.

The Access Help system is a separate Windows application (Winhelp.exe) that runs in a separate window. To close the window when you are finished, press Alt+F4 (the shortcut key for closing a Windows application), double-click the Control-menu box, or click the Cancel button at the top-right of the dialog.

Finding the Appropriate Action

Macro actions can duplicate most of the actions needed in an automated database. Before you begin to automate your work, you should read table 16.5 to understand the actions available. Macro actions satisfy most of your application programming needs. If you must perform an operation unavailable as a macro action or a set of macro actions, you can create it with Access VBA.

 For more explicit information about macro actions, their syntax, and arguments, use the Help command as described earlier to display information about an action. Chapter 17, "Using Macros with Forms and Reports," describes how to use many of the actions in actual macros. Table 16.5 is a complete list of macro actions, their arguments, and their functions. Access 2.0 provided 47 macro actions; Access 95 adds two more: Save and SetMenuItem. The updated AddMenu action of Access 95 lets you create shortcut (also called *popup* or *context*) menus to your forms, controls on forms, and reports.

Table 16.5	**Macro Actions**	
Action	**Argument**	**Function**
AddMenu	Menu Name Menu Macro Name Status Bar Text	Adds a drop-down menu to a custom menubar or adds a custom shortcut menu.
ApplyFilter	Filter Name Where Condition	Filters the data available to a form or report using a filter, query, or SQL WHERE clause.
Beep	No arguments	Produces a beep tone for use in warnings or alerts.
CancelEvent	No arguments	Cancels the normal processing that follows the event. This action is useful if a user enters invalid data in a record; then the macro can cancel the update of the database. See Help on CancelEvent for a list of applicable events.
Close	Object Type Object Name	Closes the active (default) window or a specified window.
CopyObject	Destination Database New Name	Duplicates the specified database object in another database, or in the original database by using a different name.
Delete Object	Object Type Object Name	Deletes the specified object. Leaves the arguments blank to delete the object selected in the Database Explorer.
DoMenuItem	Menu Bar Menu Name Command Subcommand	Runs any command on a built-in Access menubar if the menubar is appropriate for the view when the macro carries out the command.
Echo	Echo On Status Bar Text	Turns screen refresh on or off during macro operation. Hides results until they are complete and speeds macro operation.
FindNext	No arguments	Finds the next record specified by the FindRecord action or the Find command.

Action	Argument	Function
FindRecord	Find What Where Match Case Direction Search As Formatted Search In Find First	Finds the next record after the current record meeting the specified criteria. Searches through a `Table`, `Form`, or `Recordset` object.
GoToControl	Control Name	Moves the focus to the specified field or control in the current record of the open form, form datasheet, table datasheet, or query datasheet. To move the focus to a subform's control, use the GoToControl action twice, first to move to the subform control and then to move to the control on the subform.
GoToPage	Page Number Right Down by Tab	Selects the first field in the tab order on the designated page in a multipage form.
GoToRecord	Object Type Object Name Record Offset	Displays the specified record in an open table, form, or query datasheet.
Hourglass	Hourglass On	Displays an hourglass in place of the mouse pointer while the macro runs. Use this action while running long macros.
Maximize	No arguments	Maximizes the active window.
Minimize	No arguments	Minimizes the active window to an icon within the Access window.
MoveSize	Right Down Width Height	Moves or changes the size of the active window.
MsgBox	Message Beep Type Title	Displays a warning or informational message box and waits for the user to click the OK button.
OpenForm	Form Name View Filter Name Where Condition Data Mode Window Mode	Opens or activates a form in one of its views. You can restrict the form to data-matching criteria, different modes of editing, and whether the form acts as a modal or pop-up dialog.
OpenModule	Module Name Procedure Name	Opens the specified module and displays the specified procedure.
OpenQuery	Query Name View Data Mode	Opens a select or crosstab query or runs an action query.
OpenReport	Report Name View Filter Name Where Condition	Opens a report in the view that you specify and filters the records before printing.

(continues)

Table 16.5 Continued

Action	Argument	Function
OpenTable	Table Name View Data Mode	Opens or activates a table in the view that you specify. You can specify the data-entry or edit mode for tables in Datasheet View.
OutputTo	Object Type Object Name Output Format Output File Autostart	Copies the data in the specified object to a Microsoft Excel (.xls), rich-text format (.rtf), or DOS text (.txt) file. Autostart = Yes starts the application with the association to the extension.
Print	Print Range Page From Page To Print Quality Copies Collate Copies	Prints the active datasheet, report, or form.
Quit	Options	Closes Access, saving altered objects according to the command that you specify.
Rename	New Name	Renames the object selected in the Database window.
RepaintObject	Object Type Object Name	Forces pending recalculations and screen updates for the controls of the specified database object or the active database object if you leave the arguments blank. Does not show new, changed, or deleted records from the object's underlying source.
Requery	Control Name	Updates the data in the specified control by repeating the control's query if the control is based on a query or by displaying new, changed, or deleted records if the control is based on a table. Leave the argument blank to requery the source of the active object.
Restore	No arguments	Restores a maximized or minimized window to its previous window.
RunApp	Command Line	Runs a Windows- or an MS-DOS-based application.
RunCode	Function Name	Runs a user-defined function procedure written in Visual Basic for Applications.
RunMacro	Macro Name Repeat Count Repeat Expression	Runs the specified macro. Enter the macro name's full syntax to run an individual macro in a macro group. Use the Repeat Count and Repeat Expression arguments to specify how many times to run the macro.
RunSQL	SQL Statement	Runs an action query as specified by the SQL statement. (To run a select query, use the OpenQuery action instead.)
Save	Object Type Object Name	Saves the specified database object. Leave the arguments blank to save the active window.
SelectObject	Object Type Object Name In Database Window	Selects a specified database object.
SendKeys	Keystrokes Wait	Sends keystrokes to any active Windows application.

Action	Argument	Function
SendObject	Object Type Object Name Output Format To Cc Bcc Subject Message Text Edit Message	Sends the specified datasheet, form, report, or module in an electronic mail message. You can't send a macro. This action requires that you have a MAPI-compliant electronic mail application on your computer.
SetMenuItem	Menu Index Menu Item Menu Sub Item Flag	Sets the state of a menu item on a custom menu to check a command or to make it unavailable (grayed, or disabled).
SetValue	Item Expression	Sets the value of a field, control, or property on a form, form datasheet, or report. Cannot be used to set the value of a calculated control on forms and reports or a bound control on a report.
SetWarnings	Warnings On	Turns default warning messages on or off. Does not suppress error messages or system dialogs that require that you input text or select an option.
ShowAllRecords	No arguments	Removes any filters and requeries the active object.
StopAllMacros	No arguments	Stops all macros that are currently running.
StopMacro	No arguments	Stops the current macro.
TransferDatabase	Transfer Type Database Type Database Name Object Type Source Destination Structure Only	Imports data from another database, exports data to another database, or links a table in another database to the current database. The other database can be an Access or SQL database.
TransferSpreadsheet	Transfer Type Spreadsheet Type Table Name File Name Has Field Names Range	Imports data from a spreadsheet file or exports Access data to a spreadsheet file.
TransferText	Transfer Type Specification Name Table Name File Name Has Field Names	Imports data from a text file or exports Access data to a text file.

Duplicating a Menu Command with a Macro Action

When working with a database interactively, you tell Access what to do by entering keystrokes, moving and clicking the mouse, and selecting menu commands. To automate tasks with macros, you replace these manual interactions with macro actions. Table 16.1 groups the macro actions by task, and table 16.5 lists the actions alphabetically for easy reference. These tables include macro actions that are equivalents to operations you perform with the mouse, such as GoToControl to move the focus to a specified control and SelectObject to select a database object. This section focuses on duplicating menu commands with macro actions, and the following section explains how to enter keystrokes with a macro action.

Some of the actions listed in table 16.5 are equivalent to menu commands. For example, the Close, Save, Print, and Quit actions' are equivalent to the File menu commands Close, Save, Print, and Exit, which are available from nearly every built-in menu. Most of the menu commands are not available as separate macro actions. Instead, you duplicate menu and submenu commands by using the DoMenuItem action and setting the action arguments to specify the desired menu command. Table 16.6 shows the arguments for the DoMenuItem action.

Table 16.6 DoMenuItem **Arguments**	
Argument	**Description**
Menu Bar	Each menubar corresponds to a view. Use the combo list to select the view to use when running this command. If you use DoMenuItem when a form is active, for example, choose Form.
Menu Name	Use the combo list to select the menu heading that contains the command that you want.
Command	Use the combo list to select the command that you want.
Subcommand	If a subcommand is required, select the subcommand. On a form, for example, the Records, GoTo choice requires a subcommand such as First.

The DoMenuItem action has the same effect as selecting the specified command from a built-in menu. Access displays a specific menubar when a database object is active. You can ask Access to carry out only the menu commands on the menubar that are available when you make the request. For example, if the active database object is a form in Form View, Access can't carry out a command to hide the Database window because that command is available only on the Database menubar.

Caution

Even when the active database object's menubar lists a command, the command's availability status might change as you interact with the object. Good examples are the Undo commands that appear on the Edit menu of the menubars for Form, Table, and Query Datasheet views. The Undo command's name changes to reflect the operation that the command can reverse. When unavailable, the command is grayed. Use the Undo Typing command to reverse the most recent typing entry, cut, paste, or delete operation, or changes to the last saved record. Choose Edit, Undo Current Field/Record to reverse all changes to the current field before moving the focus to another control, or to reverse all changes to the current record after moving the focus to another control in the record.

When you first open a form in Form View, the Can't Undo command in the Edit menu is grayed and unavailable. If you make a change to a control, the Edit, Undo Typing command is available before you move to another control, and the Edit, Undo Current Field/Record command is available after you move to another control. If you save the record by pressing Shift+Enter or by selecting Records, Save Record, Edit, the Edit, Undo Saved Record is available. When you begin editing the next record, you no longer can reverse the changes that you saved to the first record, and the menubar replaces Edit, Undo Saved with Edit, Undo Typing.

A command's availability is not an issue when you work interactively with a database; you simply cannot ask Access to carry out an inappropriate or unavailable command. However, when you use the DoMenuItem action, you can specify a command that is inappropriate or unavailable at the instant that you want Access to carry it out. If Access cannot perform a macro action, it displays an error message and terminates the execution of the macro that contains the action. When the DoMenuItem action fails, Access displays the message that the command is not available, followed by a message that the macro action failed. Figure 16.14 shows the Action Failed dialog that Access displays whenever it cannot execute an action.

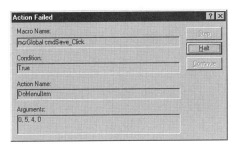

Fig. 16.14   The Action Failed dialog for the DoMenuItem action.

Sending Keystrokes with a Macro Action

The SendKeys action sends keystrokes to Access or another active Windows-based application as if you had typed them directly. When you work interactively with a database, you have the choice of using the mouse or typing keystrokes. Nearly every mouse operation in Access has a keystroke equivalent, so the SendKeys action provides the capability to duplicate nearly every mouse operation in a macro.

Use the SendKeys action to enter information required by menu commands. Many of the menu commands display a dialog that requires additional information before Access can execute the command; examples include File, Save As, the Edit, Paste Special, the Edit, Find, and the Edit, Replace. While displaying the dialog, Access suspends execution of the macro until you provide the information and close the dialog. If you don't want to interrupt the macro, use the SendKeys action to send the keystrokes to the dialog. Place the SendKeys action before the action that opens the dialog.

Table 16.7 lists the arguments for the SendKeys action.

Table 16.7	SendKeys **Action Arguments**
Argument	**Description**
Keystrokes	Can send as many as 255 characters. Replaces some keyboard characters with symbols, as described in table 16.8.
Wait	Type **Yes** to make the macro pause until the keystrokes are executed. The default is No.

Note

To send keystrokes to a dialog that `DoMenuItem` displays, put the `SendKeys` action before `DoMenuItem` and specify No for SendKeys's Wait argument. If the string of characters that you want to send exceeds the 255-character limit, use multiple `SendKeys` actions. Chapter 17, "Using Macros with Forms and Reports," provides examples of how to use `DoMenuItem` and `SendKeys` to enter information in a dialog.

To send alphanumeric characters used as text, such as *a*, *A*, *b*, or *B*, or *1*, *2*, or *3*, enclose in quotation marks the characters that you want to send, as in the following example:

```
"Denver"
```

Tip

To see interim results from SendKeys, use the Echo and StopMacro actions.

If a long macro is running and you are sending text and keystrokes to a dialog, in the middle of the macro you're likely to want to see whether the dialog accepts the characters correctly, whether the correct options are chosen, and whether any text requires quotation marks. To see the SendKeys action work, change the Echo On argument to Yes for any preceding Echo actions. Insert a StopMacro action after the DoMenuItem action that opens the dialog that is to receive the keystrokes. When you run the macro, you can see the characters as the macro enters them in the dialog.

Some keystrokes, such as Enter and Esc, have no symbol. You must represent such characters with codes. Table 16.8 lists the codes that you use to send such keystrokes as Tab, Delete, and arrow movements.

Table 16.8   SendKeys **Codes for Special Keys**

Key to Send	Code Used in a Keystroke Argument
Command Keys	
Backspace	{BACKSPACE}, {BS}, or {BKSP}
Break	{BREAK}
Caps Lock	{CAPSLOCK}
Clear	{CLEAR}
Delete	{DELETE} or {DEL}
End	{END}
Enter	{ENTER} or ~
Esc	{ESCAPE} or {ESC}
Help	{HELP}
Home	{HOME}
Insert	{INSERT}
Num Lock	{NUMLOCK}
Print Screen	{PRTSC}

Key to Send	Code Used in a Keystroke Argument
Function Keys	
F*n* (where n is one of the 16 function key numbers)	{F*n*} (*n*=1 to *n*=16)
Movement Keys	
Down arrow	{DOWN}
Left arrow	{LEFT}
Page Down	{PGDN}
Page Up	{PGUP}
Right arrow	{RIGHT}
Scroll Lock	{SCROLLLOCK}
Tab	{TAB}
Up arrow	{UP}

Many actions in Access require that you use keystroke combinations—keys used in combination with Shift, Ctrl, or Alt keys. Table 16.9 lists the codes that you must use to represent these keystrokes.

Table 16.9 SendKeys **Codes for Shift, Ctrl, and Alt**	
Key to Send	**Code Used in the Keystroke Argument**
Shift	+
Ctrl	^
Alt	%

When you press two keys in combination, such as Alt+S, use the following syntax:

    %S

To press Alt+S, followed by R (without Alt), enter the following:

    %SR

If you hold a key down while pressing two or more keys, enclose the group of following keys in parentheses. The following example is the equivalent of Alt+D+V:

    %(DV)

When you want to send the same keystroke many times, add to the keystroke a number specifying how many times to repeat. To move down three times, for example, enter the following:

    {DOWN 3}

Some characters are used as symbols for keys or are reserved for use in such programming features as dynamic data exchange (DDE). To use such characters, enclose them in French braces ({}). Table 16.10 lists these reserved characters and their codes.

Table 16.10 SendKeys **Codes for Reserved Characters**	
Key to Send	**Code Used in the Keystroke Argument**
+ (plus)	{+}
^ (caret)	{^}
% (percent)	{%}
~ (tilde)	{~}
[or] (brackets)	{[} or {]}
{ or } (braces)	{{} or {}}

Caution

Beware of using movement keys such as {Down} or {Tab} as arguments of the SendKeys action to select menu commands or dialog items. Future versions of Access might move commands to different menus or change the order of menu items, and might involve dialogs with a different structure. You are less likely to have to modify your SendKeys argument for future versions if you use an Alt+*letter* combination to choose menu commands or dialog items. If a menu command has a corresponding macro action, use the macro action rather than SendKeys.

Editing in the Macrosheet

You might have to edit a macro to change its actions or to correct an error. You also might want to copy all or part of a macro from one macrosheet to another so that you don't repeat work that you already have done. You can even copy, export, and import macros between databases.

Editing Macros

Using a mouse to edit a macro requires fewer steps than editing from the keyboard. To edit an action or argument, click the mouse pointer in a text box in which you want to edit and then use normal Windows editing actions.

If you are using a keyboard, press Tab or Enter to move right and then down through the macrosheet. Press Shift+Tab or Shift+Enter to move left and then up. You can move in any direction with the four directional arrows.

As you move between cells, you select the entire cell contents. You can type or select an item from a combo list to replace all of the selected entry. To edit, press F2 and then press the left- or right-arrow keys, Delete, or Backspace. If the contents that you are editing are too long to edit conveniently in the active column cell or the argument cell, press Shift+F2 to display the Zoom box. This box displays the entire cell contents in an edit window. Table 16.11 lists some other useful keys.

Table 16.11 **Editing Keys**	
Key	**Movement**
Esc	Cancels the edit before moving the caret out of the cell.
Home	Moves to the far-left cell in the same row.

Key	Movement
End	Moves to the far-right cell in the same row.
Ctrl+Home	Moves to the far-left cell in the top row.
Ctrl+End	Moves to the far-left cell in the last row.
Shift+←	Selects characters as the caret moves left.
Shift+→	Selects characters as the caret moves right.
Ctrl+←	Moves left one word at a time.
Ctrl+→	Moves right one word at a time.
Shift+Ctrl+←	Selects one word at a time, moving leftward.
Shift+Ctrl+→	Selects one word at a time, moving rightward.

Deleting, Inserting, or Moving Rows

You should delete rows in a macro when you no longer need the action or condition in that row. You can delete one or more rows by first selecting the rows, by clicking the row selector arrow to the left of the macrosheet. To select multiple rows, click the top row selector and drag down as many rows as you want to select. After selecting the rows, press Delete or click the toolbar's Delete Row button.

> **Tip**
>
> To undo an insertion or deletion that has just occurred, choose Edit, Undo, press Ctrl+Z, or click the toolbar's Undo button.

Insert rows in a macro when you want to insert an action between existing actions or when you want a blank space between macros to make them more readable. To insert a row, move the caret into a row. (The inserted row appears above the row containing the caret.) Click the row selector or drag across multiple row selectors and then press Insert or click the toolbar's Insert Row button.

To move one or more rows with the mouse, click the row selector or drag across multiple row selectors so that you select the rows that you want to move. Release the mouse button. Then move the mouse pointer over one of the selected row selectors and hold down the mouse button. As you hold down the button, the pointer becomes a pointer overlying a shaded, square box.

Drag the mouse pointer to the row in which you want to move the selected rows. Notice that a horizontal line appears where the moved rows will appear. Release the mouse pointer at the location in which you want to move the rows.

Copying Macros

You can copy all or a portion of a macro from one macrosheet to another. This capability can help you reuse macros or use portions of a macro more than once.

> ### Tip
>
> Copying rows from a macro and pasting them into another macro doesn't change the actions' arguments. After pasting the rows, make sure that you check that the arguments reflect what you want them to do in the new location.

To copy a single cell, such as an action, select all the characters in the cell and press Ctrl+C or click the toolbar's Copy button. To cut a cell's contents, select the characters and press Ctrl+X or click the toolbar's Cut button. Move the caret to the location at which you want to paste, then press Ctrl+V or click the toolbar's Paste button. When you copy an action cell's contents and paste them to another action cell, the action arguments are not pasted to the new location.

To copy entire rows or an entire macro, click the row selector arrows to select the rows that you want to copy and then press Ctrl+C or click the Copy button. Open a new or existing macro. Select the cell in which you want to paste the copied data and then press Ctrl+V or click the Paste button.

To copy a macro from one database to another, copy the macro rows that you want to move by using one of the copy methods described. Choose File, Open while the Database window is active, and open the database in which you want to move the macro. Open an existing or new macrosheet in this database. Select the cell in which you want to paste the first macro cell and paste by using one of the paste methods described. Save the new macro.

You can import or export an entire macro group to another Access database in the same way that you import or export any database object.

Running a Macro

There are nine ways that you can run (or execute) a macro:

- From the Macro Design window
- From any active window
- From the Database window
- From another macro
- From a custom toolbar button
- From a custom menu command
- From a shortcut key
- At startup
- By trapping an event on a form or report

IV

Access with Macros

If you are creating macros for your immediate use or if you are testing macros, the first three methods are useful. You use the remaining methods to automate individual tasks and to create a fully automated application.

> **Tip**
>
> If you run or reference a macro group, but identify only the macro group name and not the name of a macro within it, the first macro within the group runs.

Running a Macro from the Macro Design Window

You can run a macro from the active macrosheet that contains the macro that you want to run. This capability is useful when you want to test a macro. If the macrosheet contains only one macro or if you want to run the first macro in a macro group, you can run the macro by clicking the Run button on the toolbar or by choosing Run, Start. Figure 16.15 shows the mouse pointer poised over the Run button on the toolbar. Clicking the Run button runs the first macro in the active macro window, cmdReview_Click.

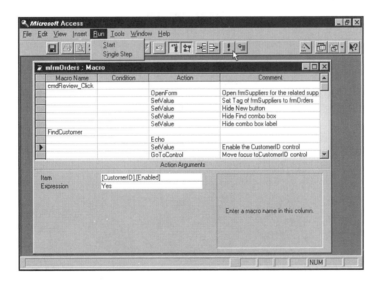

Fig. 16.15 Clicking the toolbar's Run button to run the first macro in the active macrosheet.

To run a specific macro in a macro group, choose Tools, Macro. When the Run Macro dialog appears (see fig. 16.16), type or select from the combo list the macro's full name: the macro group name, followed by a dot, followed by the macro name. Then click OK or press Enter.

> **Tip**
>
> Customize the Macro Design toolbar by adding the Run Macro button to speed the process of running a specific macro.

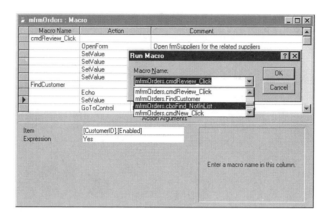

Fig. 16.16 Using the Run Macro dialog to run a macro.

If the macro doesn't run as expected, or if an Action Failed dialog appears (see fig. 16.17), you might not have the correct forms, reports, or windows open for the macro to work correctly. Some macros might require a specific form to be active or open when they run. In this case, open or activate the necessary objects and run the macro by choosing Tools, Macro, as just described.

 ▶▶ See "Troubleshooting Macro Errors," p. 692

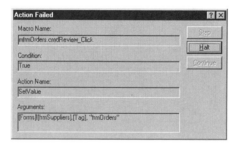

Fig. 16.17 The Action Failed dialog.

Running a Macro with Any Window Active

 To run a macro using the Run Macro dialog from any active window, choose Tools, Macro. This command is available in any view of any database object except the module window.

Tip

Customize the Form View toolbar by adding the Run Macro button.

Running a Macro from the Database Window

When the Database window is active, you can run a macro by choosing <u>T</u>ools, <u>M</u>acro and using the Run Macro dialog. Another convenient method of running the first or a single macro within a macrosheet is to click the Run button in the Database window. Follow these steps:

1. Open any database objects named as values of the macro's arguments, such as forms or reports.

2. Click the Macro tab in the Database window to display the list of macros.

3. Double-click the macro name, or select the macro name and click the Run button in the Database window.

Running Macros from Another Macro

You can run a macro from within another macro by calling the macro that you want to run with the RunMacro action. After the called macro runs, Access returns control to the next action in the calling macro. To run a macro from within another macro, enter the RunMacro action in the Action column. In the Macro Name argument, type or select the macro's full name from the combo list. You must use the full macro name, including the macro group name, even if both the calling macro and the called macro are in the same macro group. Figure 16.18 shows a macro group with both a calling and a called macro.

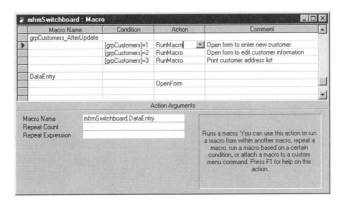

Fig. 16.18 Calling a macro from another macro.

Table 16.12 shows the arguments used with the RunMacro action.

Table 16.12 RunMacro **Arguments**	
Argument	**Description**
Macro Name	Selects the name of the macro to run from the combo list. If you are using one macro from a macro group, select the full macro name, in the form *MacroGroupName.MacroName*, from the combo list.

(continues)

Table 16.12 Continued	
Argument	**Description**
Repeat Count	Specifies the number of times that you want the macro to repeat.
Repeat Expression	Creates an expression that can be evaluated as **True** or **False**. The macro repeats until the Repeat Expression argument evaluates as **False**.

If you leave both Repeat arguments blank, the called macro runs once. The "Using Loops for Repetitive Operations" section, near the end of this chapter, describes the use of the Repeat Count and Repeat Expression actions.

Running a Macro from a Custom Toolbar Button

You can run a macro from a custom toolbar button on either a built-in toolbar or on a custom toolbar. Chapter 18, "Taking Advantage of Advanced Macro Features," shows how to create custom toolbars. To run a macro from a custom button on a built-in toolbar, display the toolbar, right-click it, and select the Customize command from the shortcut menu. The Customize Toolbars dialog appears (see fig. 16.19). Select All Macros in the Categories list box.

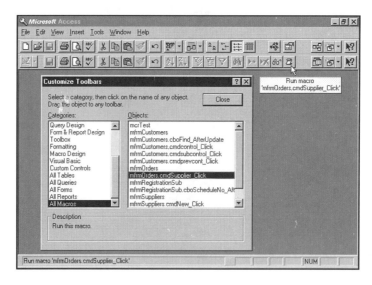

Fig. 16.19   The Customize Toolbars dialog.

Select the full name of the macro that you want to run from the Objects list box and drag the macro to the toolbar, then close the dialog. The new macro button displays the default macro icon, ToolTip, and status bar text. To run the macro, display the toolbar and click the button. When you place a custom macro button on a built-in toolbar, that button appears on the toolbar in every database you open; however, the button can run the macro in another database only if you store a copy of the macro in that database.

Note

You can customize the button's image and the ToolTip and status bar text. Right-click the toolbar and select the Customize command. With the Customize Toolbars dialog displayed, right-click the custom macro button that you placed on the toolbar and select the Choose Button Image command. You then see the Choose Button Image dialog shown in figure 16.20. Select a button and enter the new text in the Description text box. When you close the dialog, the customized button appears and the ToolTip and status bar display the new text. To edit the button's image further, right-click the button and select Edit Button Image to display the Button Editor (see fig. 16.21). When you finish editing, close the Button Editor and then close the Customize Toolbars dialog.

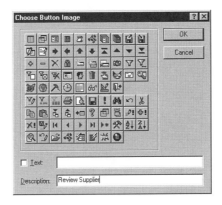

Fig. 16.20 The Choose Button Image dialog.

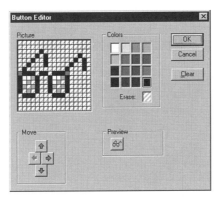

Fig. 16.21 The Button Editor.

Running a Macro from a Custom Menu Command

You can run a macro from a custom menu command on either a built-in menubar or on a custom menubar. Chapter 18, "Taking Advantage of Advanced Macro Features," shows how to create custom menu commands.

Running a Macro from a Shortcut Key

You might want to assign macros that you use frequently to a shortcut keystroke. By doing so, you can press a shortcut key such as Ctrl+N to see the next record or Ctrl+P to print. You can create a macro group named AutoKeys and use this group to store macros that assign custom commands to keystrokes. To assign a set of macro actions to a key combination, enter the key code for the key combination from the list shown in table 16.13, then enter the set of macro actions and save the macrosheet. The new key assignment is available immediately. To run the macro, press the key combination.

Figure 16.22 shows a macro group containing shortcut key codes in the Macro Name column and the macros that those codes run.

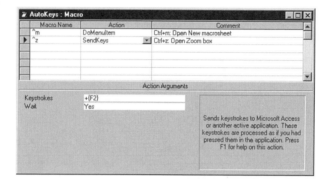

Fig. 16.22   Codes in the Macro Name column specifying which key combination runs a macro.

The list of shortcut key codes is a subset of the key codes described for the SendKeys action. Table 16.13 lists the keys and key codes to which you can assign macros.

Table 16.13   Keys and Key Codes to which You Can Assign Macros

Shortcut Key or Combination	Key Code for the Macro Name Column
Ctrl+*letter*	^*letter*
Ctrl+*number*	^*number*
Function key	{F1} and so on
Ctrl+*function key*	^{F1} and so on
Shift+*function key*	+{F1} and so on
Insert or Ins	{Insert}
Ctrl+Insert or Ctrl+Ins	^{Insert}
Shift+Insert or Shift+Ins	+{Insert}
Delete or Del	{Delete} or {Del}
Ctrl+Delete or Ctrl+Del	^{Delete} or ^{Del}
Shift+Delete or Shift+Del	+{Delete} or +{Del}

IV

> **Caution**
>
> Shortcut key combinations involving letters that are predefined in Access, such as Ctrl+C and Ctrl+X, can be assigned to your own macros. Your macro takes precedence, however, over the predefined meaning of the shortcut combination. For this reason, beware of using Ctrl+C, Ctrl+V, Ctrl+X, and Ctrl+Z.

Running a Macro at Startup

You can create a special macro that Access will run automatically when you first open the database. Create this macro in a separate macrosheet and name the macro **AutoExec**, spelled exactly this way. When you first open a database, Access looks for a macro named AutoExec and runs it immediately. You can use the AutoExec macro to open and arrange forms, import data, set defaults and change options, print a report, replace the default menubars with custom menubars, and make additional startup arrangements. After you create the AutoExec macro, Access runs it automatically the next time that you open the database. You can prevent Access from running the AutoExec macro by pressing Shift when you select the database in the Open Database dialog or in the list of recently opened databases in the File menu.

A new feature in Access 95 is a Startup dialog that enables you to set several startup properties without having to create a startup macro. Notwithstanding, the AutoExec macro provides the flexibility to set additional startup conditions and to perform operations immediately. Chapter 18, "Taking Advantage of Advanced Macro Features," shows how to use the Startup dialog and the AutoExec macro to tailor your application's opening act.

Running a Macro by Trapping an Event on a Form or Report

Of all the ways to run a macro, the most important and the most powerful is to trap an event triggered by an object. By using events to trigger macros, you minimize the need for users to know when they have to run a particular macro. For example, in a point-of-entry inventory system, when you select a product from a combo box on an order form, the AfterUpdate event of the combo box can trigger a macro that tests the current level of inventory for the product, adjusts the level to the new value, and even creates a reorder statement if inventory falls below a minimum level. By trapping the combo box's AfterUpdate event, the macro runs automatically without requiring additional action from the user.

Events are opportunities to interrupt the normal processing with your own instructions; in this sense, events are programming opportunities. Access defines events only for objects on forms and reports. You trap an event triggered by an object by entering the macro's full name in the text box of the event property in the object's property sheet. The procedure is called *attaching*, *assigning*, or *linking* the macro to the event.

Linking a Macro to an Event

To attach (assign or link) a macro to an event triggered by a control on a form, a form section, a form, a report section, or a report, follow these steps:

1. Open the form or report in Design View.

2. Select the object that recognizes the event by using one of these procedures:

Select the form or report by using one of these methods: click the gray selection square at the intersection of the rulers in the upper-left corner; if the rulers are not displayed, click the gray background outside the form or report; or choose <u>E</u>dit, Select Fo<u>r</u>m or <u>E</u>dit, Select <u>R</u>eport.

Select a form or report section by clicking the section header.

Select a form control by clicking the control. (Report controls do not trigger events.)

3. Display the property sheet by clicking the toolbar's Properties button, right-clicking the control and selecting Properties on the shortcut menu, or choosing <u>V</u>iew, <u>P</u>roperties.

4. Click the Event tab at the top of the property sheet.

5. Select the event in the property sheet that you want to run the macro, and click the event property text box.

 ▶▶ See "Writing Visual Basic for Applications Code," p. 995

6. Type or select from the event's combo list the full name of the macro that you want to trigger (see fig. 16.23). If necessary, open the Zoom box by pressing Shift+F2. The first entry in the combo list, [Event Procedure], is used for creating an Access VBA procedure triggered by the event rather than for linking a macro.

7. Save the form.

The next time that the selected object triggers the event, Access runs the macro.

You can open a new or existing macrosheet directly from an event property. To open a new macrosheet, click the Build button to display the Choose Builder dialog (see fig. 16.24). Select Macro Builder and click OK to display a new macrosheet that Access automatically links to the selected event. The next time that the selected object triggers this event, Access runs the first macro that you create in the macrosheet.

To open an existing macrosheet from an event property, select the macro group name from the combo list and click the Build button to display the macrosheet. After you create a new macro in the group, save and close the macrosheet, then link the new macro to the event by typing or selecting it from the combo list.

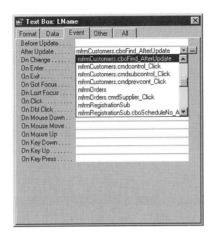

Fig. 16.23 Selecting an existing macro to link to an event.

Fig. 16.24 Selecting the Macro Builder from the Choose Builder dialog.

Note

You don't run menubar macros that replace the built-in menubars and shortcut menus from named events. You assign a menubar macro to a form or report by entering its name in the MenuBar or Shortcut MenuBar property of the form or report. The property sheet's Other category lists these properties. Chapter 18, "Taking Advantage of Advanced Macro Features," shows how to create custom menubars and shortcut menus.

Programming in Access using either macros or Access VBA is a matter of writing programs to respond to events. When you take a single action, such as tabbing from one control into another control or tabbing from one record to another record, one or more objects trigger several sequential events. To program effectively, you must know which events are available; tables 16.2 and 16.3 organize the events by cause and by object, respectively. Additionally, you must master the complex subtleties of event timing if you want macros to run at the correct moment and in the correct order.

Getting Online Help for Events

Use online help to find the most complete information on events. Follow these steps:

1. Choose <u>H</u>elp, Microsoft Access <u>H</u>elp Topics, and click the Contents tab at the top of the Help Topics window.

2. To view the event reference material, double-click "Microsoft Access Programming and Language Reference," "Events," and "Event Properties." Use the hot spots to navigate through the Help system to find information on events.

3. To view help and instructions on how to use events, return to the Help Topics window by clicking the Help Topics button at the top of any Help screen, click the book "Responding to Events" to view the help topics (see fig. 16.25). Double-click a topic icon or select a topic and choose Display to open the help window or dialog.

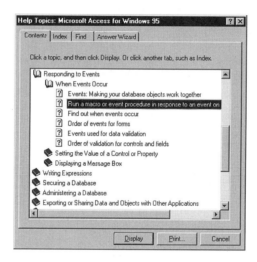

Fig. 16.25 Using the Help system to learn about events.

If you already know the event for which you want information, click the Index tab in the Help Topics window. In the text box at the top of the window, type the event's name. As you type, the list box below the text box scrolls to select the first list entry that matches the characters that you type. When the list box highlights the event, choose the Display button to display the Topics Found dialog which provides a list of subtopics (see fig. 16.26). Select one of the subtopics and choose Display to open the event's help window. Click a dotted underlined word for definition of the word (see fig. 16.27). Click any underlined word or phrase to jump to related help topics. Return to the help window for the event by clicking the Back button or pressing Alt+B.

Understanding the Update Process

One of the fundamental database operations is to enter and edit data, so it is important to understand how Access tracks data changes. When you enter or change data in the database, Access uses a two-buffer system to keep track of the changes. As you begin typing a character into a control on a record, Access places into a temporary *record buffer* a copy of the data in all the controls, and places into a temporary *control buffer* a copy of the data in the control that has the focus.

Fig. 16.26 Using the Help system to search for an event.

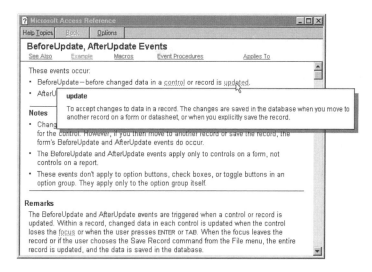

Fig. 16.27 Using online help to learn about an event.

When you move to another control by tabbing or pressing Enter, Access compares the data in the two buffers to determine whether a change was made. If a change was made, Access updates the *control* by recording the changed data from the control buffer to the record buffer. If Access doesn't detect any change, it simply doesn't perform the update operation on the control. When you attempt to save the record by tabbing to another record, pressing Shift+Enter, or choosing Records, Save Record, Access compares the data in the record buffer with the data stored in memory in the table fields. If Access detects one or more changes, it updates the *record* by recording (saving) the changed data from the record buffer to the table fields. If Access doesn't detect changes, it doesn't update the record. Figure 16.28 illustrates the two-buffer system for the update process.

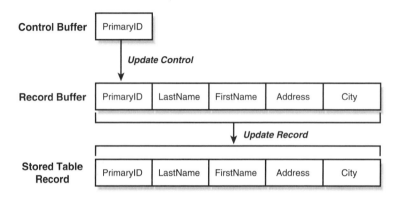

Fig. 16.28 The two-buffer update process.

The Timing of Events for Controls on Forms

When a control on a form gains or loses focus, or when you change the data and Access updates the control, that control triggers events. Table 16.3 lists the form controls and the events in each category that each control triggers. Form controls trigger 17 total events. Table 16.14 lists the nine focus and data events in the order of occurrence, and table 16.15 lists the eight mouse and keyboard events.

Table 16.14	Focus and Data Events for Form Controls	
Event	**Time at which Access Triggers the Event**	**Comments**
Enter	When you activate a control but before the control has the focus	This event occurs for the first control on a form when the form first opens; thereafter, the event occurs only when a control receives the focus from another control on the same form.
GotFocus	After the control receives the focus.	This event occurs every time that a control receives the focus. The control displays its characteristic appearance when it has the focus.

Event	Time at which Access Triggers the Event	Comments
Change	When you change a character in a text box or in the text box part of a combo box.	This event does not occur when a value in a calculated control changes or when you select a value from a combo list.
NotInList	After you enter in a combo box a value that is not on the combo list.	If the LimitToList property is set to Yes, the form triggers the Error event immediately afterward.
BeforeUpdate	When Access triggers changed data in the control buffer and just before Access updates the changed data to the record buffer.	
AfterUpdate	When Access triggers changed data in the control buffer and just after Access updates the changed data to the record buffer.	
Exit	When you leave the control but before the control loses the focus.	This event occurs for the control on a form that has the focus when the form closes; before that, the event occurs only when a control loses the focus to another control on the same form.
LostFocus	After the control loses the focus.	Access triggers the LostFocus event every time a control loses the focus.
Updated	After the data in an OLE object changes.	The order of this event depends on the application used to create the OLE object.

Table 16.15 Mouse and Keyboard Events

Event	Time at which Access Triggers the Event	Comments
Click	When you press and release the left mouse button.	For a command button, Access triggers a Click event when you choose the button.
DblClick	When you press and release the left mouse button twice within the double-click time-limit setting.	When you double-click a control, you trigger the Click event, then the DblClick event. Double-clicking a command button also triggers a second Click event after the DblClick event.
MouseDown	When you press a mouse button.	
MouseMove	When you move the mouse pointer over the object.	
MouseUp	When you release a mouse button.	
KeyDown	When you press a key or send a keystroke.	
KeyPress	When you press or send an ANSI key or ANSI key combination.	
KeyUp	When you release a key or after Access sends the keystroke.	

The Timing of Events for Forms and Form Sections

Table 16.3 lists the events in each category triggered by a form. Forms trigger 29 events.

When you open, close, and resize a form and when a form gains or loses the focus, the form triggers window and focus events. Table 16.16 shows the nine window and focus events in the order of occurrence.

Table 16.16	Window and Focus Events for Forms	
Event	**Time at which Access Triggers the Event**	**Comments**
Open	When you first open the form but before the first record displays.	
Load	After Access loads the records from memory and displays them.	
Resize	When Access first displays the form and just after you change the form's size.	
Activate	When the form receives the focus and becomes the active window.	Access triggers the Activate event only when the form is visible.
GotFocus	When the form receives the focus, but only if all controls on the form are disabled or hidden.	A form triggers the GotFocus only if all controls on the form are disabled or hidden.
Unload	When you close a form and and unload its records, but before Access removes the form from the screen.	
LostFocus	After the form loses the focus, but only if all controls on the form are disabled or hidden.	A form triggers the LostFocus event only if all controls on the form are disabled or hidden.
Deactivate	When a form loses the focus to another window in Access, except a dialog or a form whose PopUp property is set to Yes.	A form does not trigger the Deactivate event by losing the focus to another application.
Close	When you close a form and Access removes it from the screen.	

 A form triggers events when a record gains or loses the focus, when you change the data and Access updates the record, when you create a new record or delete an existing record, and when you apply or remove a filter. The form triggers eight data events and two filter events (both of which are new in Access 95) for the records. Table 16.17 shows the 10 data and filter events, and table 16.15 shows the eight mouse and keyboard events that you can trigger when interacting with a record.

Table 16.17 Data and Filter Events for Records on Forms

Event	Time at which Access Triggers the Event	Comments
Current	When you move to a record but before Access displays the record.	The Current event is followed automatically by the Enter event triggered by the first control in the record to receive the focus.
BeforeInsert	After you type the first character into a new record.	
BeforeUpdate	When Access triggers changed data in the record buffer and just before Access updates the changed data to the table fields stored in memory (saving).	
AfterUpdate	When Access triggers changed data in the record buffer and just after Access updates the changed data to the table fields stored in memory (saving).	
AfterInsert	After you save a new record in memory.	
Delete	When you take a step to delete an existing record but before Access deletes the record.	
BeforeDelConfirm	After Access removes the record from the screen and places the data in a record buffer, and just before Access displays the confirmation dialog.	
AfterDelConfirm	After Access deletes the record from memory, or after you cancel the deletion and the screen displays the record.	
Filter	When you initiate a filter with the Filter by Form or Advanced Filter/Sort command, but before Access displays the Filter or Filter by Form window.	You do not trigger the filter event by using the Filter by Selection command.
ApplyFilter	When you apply a filter by using Apply Filter/Sort or Filter by Selection but before Access displays the filtered records, when you remove a filter using Remove Filter/Sort but before Access removes the filtered records, or when you close the Filter window without applying the filter.	

Finally, a form triggers Error and Timer events. Table 16.18 lists these events.

	Table 16.18	Error **and** Timing **Events**	
Event	**Time at which Access Triggers the Event**	**Comments**	
Error	When Access detects an error while the application is running.	Access does not trigger the Error event on detecting a Visual Basic for Applications error.	
Timer	When the specified time interval passes.	You set forms' TimerInterval property to specify the interval.	

Form sections trigger the mouse events listed in table 16.15.

The Timing of Events for Reports and Report Sections

Table 16.3 lists the events in each category triggered by a report. Reports trigger a total of seven events.

 When you open or close a report to print or preview it and when a report gains or loses the focus, the report triggers window and focus events. Access 95 includes two new events, for reports, NoData and Page. Table 16.19 lists all seven events.

	Table 16.19	**Events for Reports**	
Event	**Time at which Access Triggers the Event**	**Comments**	
Open	When you first open the report but before Access displays or prints the report.		
Activate	When the report receives the focus and becomes the active window.		
Deactivate	When a report loses the focus to another Access window except a dialog or a form whose PopUp property is set to Yes.	Access does not trigger the Deactivate event when the report loses the focus to another application.	
Close	When Access removes the report from the screen.		
NoData	When you open a report and Access detects that no records are in the Recordset for the report.		
Page	When you first open a report and before Access displays each page for the first time.		
Error	When Access detects an error if the report has the focus.	An Access VBA error does not cause an Error event.	

Table 16.3, earlier in this chapter, lists the events that report sections trigger. Table 16.20 describes these three events in greater detail.

Table 16.20	Print Events for Report Sections	
Event	**Time at which Access Triggers the Event**	**Comments**
Format	After Access determines the data for a section, but before Access formats the section.	For a report detail section, the Format event occurs for each record in the section. The detail section's Format event has access to data in the current record.
Retreat	When Access returns to a previous report section during formatting.	The Retreat event occurs for each section that Access passes while retreating. For each of these sections, the Format event occurs again as Access prepares to reformat the sections.
Print	After Access formats the report section but before Access prints the section.	For a report detail section, the Print event occurs for each record in the section. If triggered by the Print event of the detail section, a macro has access to data in the current record.

Canceling Default Behavior

After an object triggers an event, Access performs default behavior. For example, when you tab out of a control with changed data into a second control, Access detects the changed data in the control buffer, the changed control triggers the BeforeUpdate event, and the following default behavior occurs in sequence:

1. Access updates the control by recording the changed data in the record buffer.

2. The changed control triggers the AfterUpdate event.

3. The changed control triggers the Exit event.

4. The changed control triggers the LostFocus event.

5. The second control triggers the Enter event.

6. The second control triggers the GotFocus event.

For certain events, Access runs the macro before performing the default behavior. For these events, you can include the CancelEvent macro action to cancel the default behavior. Table 16.21 shows the events for which you can cancel the default behavior.

Table 16.21 Events with Default Behaviors that You Can Cancel

Event	Comments
ApplyFilter	Triggers macros that display a message or take actions when the user applies or changes a filter. Such macros contain the CancelEvent action to cancel the filter.
BeforeDelConfirm	Triggers a macro that restores the deleted record or records from the temporary buffer and suppresses the display of the confirmation dialog. Although such macros contain the CancelEvent action, they nevertheless trigger the AfterDelConfirm event.
BeforeInsert	
BeforeUpdate	Triggers a macro that validates a control or record. Such macros contain the CancelEvent action to cancel the update process if the data doesn't satisfy the validation conditions.
DblClick	The CancelEvent action cancels the default behavior following the DblClick event but not the Click event that is triggered by default just before the DlbClick event.
Delete	
Error	
Exit	
Filter	Triggers macros to customize a Filter by Form window. Such macros contain the CancelEvent action to cancel the filter.
Format	
KeyPress	
MouseDown	
NoData	Triggers a macro that displays a message and takes other actions when the report has no records in its Recordset. Such macros include the CancelEvent action to cancel the printing of the report.
Open	
Print	
Unload	

Controlling the Flow of Execution with Macros

When you create a program that consists of a set of instructions, you can control the *flow of execution*—the order in which Access executes the instructions. The program can use the following three flow patterns:

- A *sequential* pattern in which Access executes the instructions one after another

- A *conditional* pattern in which at one point a decision is made and the program must take off in one of two directions

- A *looping* pattern in which Access repeats some instructions either a specified number of times or until the instructions meet a condition

In most macro-programming languages, including Access VBA, you can use all three flow patterns.

Using Sequential Macros

You enter a sequential macro in the macrosheet as a set of consecutive macro actions. Access executes the macro by executing each action in turn until there are no more actions. The macro need not end with an explicit action. Access continues moving down the macrosheet executing actions until it reaches a row with an entry in the Macro Name column or until it detects that the macrosheet has no more actions.

Making Decisions with Conditional Macros

A conditional macro provides a way for Access to make a decision based on current values in the database and to execute a set of actions if a condition is met. A *condition* is an expression that evaluates to **True** or **False** depending on current values. For example, you can use a conditional macro to test a primary key's value as soon as you enter the value. To do so, include a condition that determines whether the database has another record with the same value. If the condition is **True**, the macro can display a message and cancel the update of the control; if the condition is **False**, the entered value is valid and the macro can end.

Create conditions by using expressions and form and control references. Table 16.22 lists some examples of macro conditions.

Table 16.22   Typical Macro Conditions

Condition	Description
`[State] = "CA"`	**True** when the value of the State control is CA.
`grpOption = 2`	**True** if the value of the option group grpOption is 2.
`IsNull([Amount])`	**True** if the Amount control has no value.
`DCount("*","tblOrders") > 100`	**True** if the number of records in the table tblOrders exceeds 100.
`[Quantity] > 5`	**True** if the value in the Quantity control is greater than 5.
`Not [Quantity] > 5`	**True** if the value in the Quantity control is less than or equal to 5.

Tip

Place the **Not** operator to the left of a condition to obtain the opposite of the condition. Notice that when a condition is **True**, its opposite condition is **False**.

You can use a flow diagram to represent the flow in a conditional macro. The diamond-shaped *decision symbol* contains the condition and has two branches for the **True** and **False** alternatives. Figure 16.29 is a flow diagram for a conditional macro with two alternative sets of actions, one set of which executes only if the condition is **True** and the other which executes only if the condition is **False**. Other actions execute whether the condition is **True** or **False**.

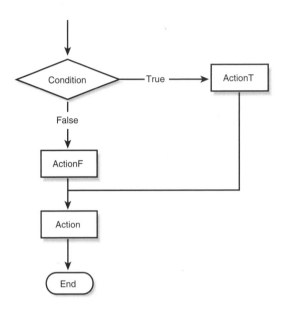

Fig. 16.29 A flow diagram for a conditional pattern with two alternatives.

Figure 16.30 is a flow diagram representing a conditional macro that executes a single set of actions only when the condition is **True**, and then executes actions whether the condition is **True** or **False**.

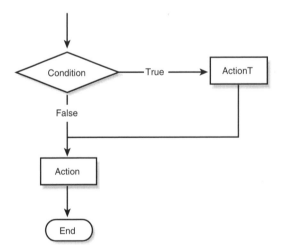

Fig. 16.30 A flow diagram for a conditional pattern with one alternative.

 If you want macro actions to run when a condition evaluates as **True**, display the Condition column in the macrosheet and enter the condition. Display the Condition column by clicking the Conditions button on the toolbar. In the adjacent Action column, enter the macro action that you want to run when the condition is **True**. If you want multiple actions to run when a condition is **True**, type in the Condition column an ellipsis (**...**) next to each action that the macro also should run. After executing the actions for the **True** alternative, Access moves to the next row and checks whether any other conditions exist. If not, Access executes the action whether the condition is **True** or **False**. If you do not want to execute this action when the condition is **True**, enter the StopMacro action as the last of the set of actions for the **True** alternative.

Figure 16.31 shows a macrosheet with conditional macros, with one alternative illustrating the case in which Access executes additional actions regardless of the condition's value. Another alternative shows the case in which an additional action runs only if the condition is **False**.

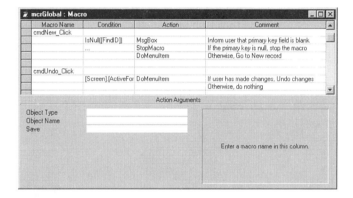

Fig. 16.31 A conditional macro with one alternative.

To create macros with actions that run when the condition evaluates as **True**, follow these steps:

1. Click the Conditions button on the Macro toolbar to display the Condition column in the macrosheet.

2. Enter the condition in the Condition column.

3. Enter in the Action column the action that you want to run when the condition is **True**.

4. If you want to run additional actions when the condition is **True**, enter them down the Action column below the action in step 3.

5. If you entered additional actions in step 4, put an ellipsis (**...**) in the Condition column next to each action. All these actions run when the condition is **True**.

6. If you want to run additional actions whether the condition is **True** or **False**, enter them below the last action in step 5. If you want to run these additional actions only when the condition is **False**, enter the StopMacro action (with an ellipsis in the Condition column) as the last action in step 5.

If you save a macrosheet with the Condition column displayed, the next time that you open the window in Design View, the Condition column is visible. If you want the Condition column for all macrosheets to be displayed, choose <u>V</u>iew, <u>O</u>ptions and then select Macro Design from the Category list. Enter **Yes** in the Show Condition Column text box.

Note

The conditional If test in Access macros differs from that of most programming languages. Access macros run actions if a test is **True** but has no **False** or **Else** portion. Access macros use an **If** condition and then action syntax. If the condition evaluates to **True**, the action runs. If the condition returns **False**, Access skips the action and jumps to the next action that doesn't have an ellipsis.

To create a conditional macro with two alternatives, enter the condition and the actions with ellipses in the subsequent Condition cells that you want to run when the condition is **True**, as was previously explained. Enter the opposite condition in the Condition column's next row and enter the actions with ellipses in the subsequent Condition cells that you want to run when the condition is **False**. Enter additional conditions that you want to run whether the condition is **True** or **False**. Terminate the set of actions for either alternative with a StopMacro action, if necessary. Figure 16.32 shows the macrosheet for a conditional macro with multiple actions that run when the condition is **True** and multiple actions that run when the condition is **False**, as well as a single action that runs in either case.

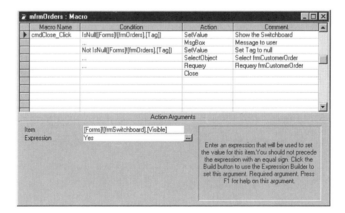

Fig. 16.32   Using a condition and its opposite for a conditional macro with two alternatives.

Using Loops for Repetitive Operations

Loop macros provide a way to repeat a set of macro actions. Using macros to repeat operations depends on the RunMacro action. Table 16.12 shows the RunMacro arguments.

Use the Macro Name argument to specify the name of the called macro and use either of the remaining arguments to repeat the macro. Use the Repeat Count argument when you know the exact number of times that you want to run the called macro. Use the Repeat Expression argument to specify a repetition condition. Access evaluates the repetition condition before running the called macro. As long as the repetition condition is **True**, the called macro runs another time; if the condition is **False**, the called macro does not run again and Access returns to the calling macro and executes the next action following the RunMacro action. If you leave both Repeat arguments blank, Access runs the called macro exactly once. When you enter a number into Repeat Count and an expression into Repeat Expression, the argument that is satisfied first ends the loop. Figure 16.33 shows a macro that loops four times.

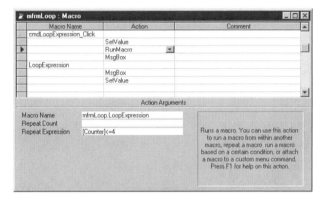

Fig. 16.33   A loop macro.

Caution

When you create a loop macro using the Repeat Expression argument, the called macro must contain actions and conditions that allow the repetition condition to become **False** eventually. Otherwise, the macro repeats in an *endless loop*. If you find yourself in an endless loop, you can usually break out of it by pressing Ctrl+Break. If this fails to end the loop, you must press Ctrl+Alt+Del to exit Access.

From Here...

Microsoft designed Access 95's macro language so that you don't need to learn Access Basic and write code to automate your Access applications. The 49 macro actions are surprisingly versatile; you can create quite complex database applications using only macros to respond to events. Even if you write Access VBA event-handling procedures, you're likely to execute many of the macro actions described in this chapter in your code.

The following chapters provide additional information on creating and using event-handling macros:

- Chapter 17, "Using Macros with Forms and Reports," provides examples of many of the most frequently used macro actions.

- Chapter 18, "Taking Advantage of Advanced Macro Features," shows you how to control the user interface, how to work with external data, and how to trouble-shoot and document macros.

- Chapter 28, "Writing Visual Basic for Applications Code," shows you how to use the DoCmd instruction to execute macro actions with Access VBA.

Chapter 17

Using Macros with Forms and Reports

In this chapter, you learn how to do the following

■ Refer to controls and properties

■ Work with data to set and display current values

■ Avoid macro errors

■ Navigate among controls, records, and forms

■ Use macro techniques for data entry

■ Automate the selection of groups of records

Being able to use macros is a valuable addition to your skills, whether you use macros occasionally as productivity tools in an interactive database or use macros to create a fully automated stand-alone database application with custom menus and toolbars, command buttons, and event-driven actions. Even if you move on to the increased power and control provided by the highest level of programming available in Access, Visual Basic for Applications, macro programming is an important transitional step.

In Chapter 16, "Understanding Access Macros and Events," you learned the fundamentals of macro programming: how to create and run macros and use the Access events as programming opportunities. In this chapter, you learn how to use macros to automate routine database operations. Reading and working through the steps of the examples in this chapter will help you to understand how macros work and prepare you to create your own macros.

Referring to Controls and Properties

For many reasons, you must know how to refer to a control, form, or report by name, and how to refer to control, form, or report properties from within a macro. You must know how to refer to objects and properties if you want to perform such tasks as the following:

■ Synchronize records in two forms by matching values of controls

■ Set a control or property to a specific value

■ Change a macro's action based on the value of a control or property

■ Check data entry values by using complex checks and responding with a message

■ Move the focus to a control on a form when the form opens or a record changes

■ Enter SQL statements in macro actions that filter or query

■ Change the RecordSource property of a form or report dynamically in a macro

Access has a basic rule for naming objects: When you name database objects, names within each group of objects must be unique, but you can use the same name for different types of database objects (except that tables and queries can't have the same name). For example, each form and each report must have a unique name, but a single form, report, macro, and module, plus a query *or* a table, can share the same name.

The names of controls within each form or report must be unique, but you can use the same name for controls on different forms and reports. Therefore, each report and form in the database can have a control with the same name. Moreover, a control on a form or report can have the same name as the form or report. Thus, you could have a control named Product on a form named Product, a control named Product on a report named Product, a field named Product in a table or query named Product, a macro named Product in a macro group named Product, and a procedure named Product in a module named Product.

A primary reason for adopting a naming convention, such as the Leszynski *Naming Conventions for Microsoft Access*, included in Appendix B, "Naming Conventions for Access Objects and Variables," is to help you to distinguish between objects by including a tag as part of the name. Access has its own way to distinguish objects. When you refer to objects in macros, you must use the syntax that Access requires. You must use different expressions to refer to an object depending on where the object is relative to the focus. The correct reference depends on whether the object is on the same form as the focus, on another form or report, or on a subform or subreport.

Referring to Forms or Reports and Their Properties

You can refer to a form or report only if it is open. Access uses the Forms and Reports collections to keep track of which forms and reports are open. The Forms collection is the set of open forms and the Reports collection is the set of open reports. Because Access lets you use the same name for a form and a report, you must distinguish between the two by specifying the collection. The syntax for the reference is the collection name followed by the *exclamation point operator* (!, more commonly called the *bang operator*) and the name of the form or report:

```
Forms![FormName]
```

```
Reports![ReportName]
```

Use the bang operator to separate the collection name from the name of an object in the collection.

A form or report has properties that define its characteristics. The syntax for referring to a property is the object name followed by the *dot operator* and the name of the property:

```
Forms![FormName].[PropertyName]
```

```
Reports![ReportName].[PropertyName]
```

Use the dot (.) operator to separate the object's name from the name of one of its properties. For example, Forms!frmProducts.RecordSource refers to the RecordSource property of the open frmProducts form.

A form's property sheet lists the form properties that you can set in Design View. Forms also have properties that you can't set in Design View and that do not appear in the property sheet, such as the `Form` property. The `Form` property refers to the collection of controls on a form. Similarly, a report's `Report` property refers to the collection of controls in a report.

Referring to Controls and Their Properties

The following is the syntax for referring to a control on a form or report:

    Forms![FormName].Form![ControlName]

    Reports![ReportName].Report![ControlName]

As before, the bang operator separates the collection name from the object name. The `Form` property is the *default property* that Access assumes for a form; therefore, you need not include the `Form` property explicitly in the reference. The following expression is the *full identifier syntax* for a form control:

    Forms![FormName]![ControlName]

Similarly, the following is the full identifier syntax for a report control:

    Reports![ReportName]![ControlName]

For example, `Forms!frmProducts!ProductName` refers to the `ProductName` control on the open `frmProducts` form.

The syntax for referring to a control's property includes the reference to the control followed by the dot operator followed by the property name:

    Forms![FormName]![ControlName].[PropertyName]

    Reports![ReportName]![ControlName].[PropertyName]

For example, `Forms!frmProducts!ProductName.Visible` refers to the `ProductName` control's `Visible` property.

A control also has a default property. The default property of a text box is the `Text` property. To refer to the value in the `ProductName` text box control in the last example, you could use any of the following equivalent references:

    Forms!frmProducts.Form!ProductName.Text

    Forms!frmProducts!ProductName.Text

    Forms!frmProducts.Form!ProductName

    Forms!frmProducts!ProductName

Notice that the last two expressions refer both to the control's text value and to the control itself.

When you refer to a control on the active form or report, you can use a shorter version of the reference and refer to the control as follows:

```
[ControlName]
```

Likewise, you can refer to the control property as follows:

```
[ControlName].[PropertyName]
```

Normally, you can use either the short or the full syntax to refer to a control on the active form or report. However, in some cases you must use the short syntax. For example, the `GoToControl` action's `ControlName` argument requires the short syntax. This chapter notes other similar exceptions. When you refer to a control on a form or report that is not the active object, you usually must use the full identifier syntax. This chapter notes the few exceptions to this rule.

Referring to Controls on a Subform or on the Main Form

The key to understanding the syntax for referring to a control on a subform is to realize that the subform is a form that is bound to a subform control on the main form. The subform control has the usual attribute properties that control its display behavior, such as size and visibility, as well as linking properties that relate the records in the subform to records in the form, including the `SourceObject`, `LinkChildFields` and `LinkMasterFields` properties. In addition, the subform control has the `Form` property. A subform control's `Form` property refers to the controls contained on the subform.

The following is the syntax for referring to the subform control:

```
Forms![FormName]![SubformControlName]
```

The syntax for referring to a control on a subform bound to a subform control is as follows:

```
Forms![FormName]![SubformControlName].Form![ControlName]
```

When the form is active, the following short syntax refers to a control on a subform of the active form:

```
[SubformControlName].Form![ControlName]
```

The `Form` property is not the subform control's default property, so you must include it explicitly in the reference. Normally, you use the subform's name as the name of the subform control. For example, if `fsubSuppliers` is the name of a form bound to a subform control also named `fsubSuppliers` on the `frmProducts` form, the following is the full syntax for referring to the the `SupplierName` control on the subform:

```
Forms!frmProducts!fsubSuppliers.Form!SupplierName
```

The short syntax is as follows:

```
fsubSuppliers.Form!SupplierName
```

When the focus is in a subform's control, you can refer to a control on the main form by using the control's `Parent` property. The `Parent` property refers to the collection of controls on the main form. In the previous example, to refer to the `ProductName` control on the main form when the focus is in the subform, use the following syntax:

    Parent!ProductName

Using the Screen Object

Access provides the `Screen` object as a way to refer to a particular form, report, or control without having to use the specific name of the object. Use the `Screen` object to refer to the active form, the active report, the active control, or the control that last had the focus by using one of the following identifiers:

    Screen.ActiveForm

    Screen.ActiveReport

    Screen.ActiveControl

    Screen.PreviousControl

For example, to refer to the active form's `Visible` property, you can use the following instead of referring to the specific form by name:

    Screen.ActiveForm.Visible

The `Screen` object is particularly useful when you are creating macros that you want to reuse in different places in your application or in another Access database. To be reusable, a macro shouldn't refer to specific objects by name.

Using the Expression Builder to Create Reference Expressions

You can use the Expression Builder for help when writing reference expressions in macros. Macros refer to objects in both action arguments and conditions. Chapter 9, "Understanding Operators and Expressions in Access," introduces the Expression Builder and shows you how the Expression Builder can help create expressions for query criteria and property settings. You start the Expression Builder by clicking the Build button that appears to the right of an action argument for which you can enter an expression, or by right-clicking a Condition cell and choosing the Build command. You also can start the Expression Builder by clicking an argument's text box or a Condition cell and then clicking the Build button on the toolbar. Figure 17.1 shows the Expression Builder.

The lower part of the window displays three lists. The list on the left contains the names of the tables, queries, forms, and reports in your database, with each category in a different folder. Additionally, the list includes folders for functions (both the built-in functions and the custom functions that you create with Access VBA), built-in constants, operators, and common expressions. The Forms folder contains a folder for all your forms and a separate folder for the open forms. Similarly, the Reports folder contains folders for all reports and all open reports. If a form that has a subform is open when you start the Expression Builder, Access indicates the relationship between the forms by showing a folder for the subform contained within the folder for the open main form. Notice in figure 17.1 that the `Orders` form is open and has a subform named `Orders Subform`.

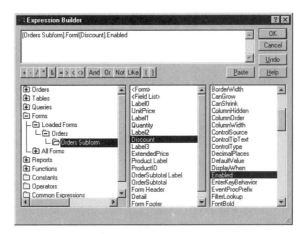

Fig. 17.1 Using the Expression Builder to create an object reference.

When you select a specific form or other database object in the Expression Builder's leftmost list, the list in the center changes to display all the objects contained in the selected object. If you selected a form, the first item in the center list is <Form> representing the form itself, the second item is <Field List> representing the field list of the underlying table or query, and the remaining items are the names of the controls and form sections. In figure 17.1, the Orders Subform has been selected in the leftmost list, so the center list displays that subform's controls.

When you select an item from the Expression Builder's center list, the rightmost list changes to display the set of properties for the selected item. Selecting <Form> displays a list of form properties, selecting <Field List> displays the field names from the record source, and selecting a control or form section displays a list of the properties of that object beginning with the object's default property. In figure 17.1, the Discount control has been selected in the center list, so the rightmost list displays this text box's properties.

When you select any pair of items from the center and rightmost lists and choose the Paste button, Access pastes your selection's full syntax into the Expression text box beginning at the insertion point. Figure 17.1 shows the reference to the Discount control's Enabled property displayed in the subform control called Orders Subform on the Orders form.

You create expressions in the Expression text box by typing, clicking the operator buttons, pasting references based on the lists, and editing as necessary to obtain a correct expression. The Expression Builder always gives the reference's full syntax, so you have to edit the reference whenever Access requires the short reference. When you finish your editing, click the OK button to copy the expression into the action argument or Condition cell. The copied expression replaces whatever expression was there when you started the Expression Builder.

> **Caution**
>
> The Expression Builder is extremely valuable as a complete list of the names of objects in your database and as an aid in preventing spelling errors. The Builder is helpful in creating references and expressions, but you should not rely on it to create the correct expression. Using the Builder can result in expressions that might appear to be correct, but which lead to errors. For example, you have to know when to use the short syntax rather than the full syntax and when to use or omit an equal sign (=). Additionally, you have to make sure that a form with a subform, or a report with a subreport, is open before you try to create a reference to a control on the subform or subreport.

Using Macros to Work with Data

This section shows you how to use macros to display the most current data, to set values of controls and properties, and to store values temporarily for later use.

Displaying Current Data

Access doesn't always display the current data in controls or records automatically. When you work interactively with a form, you can force Access to display current data in three ways.

Choose <u>R</u>ecords, Refres<u>h</u> or press F9 to show any changes to the currently displayed records in the active form or datasheet that you have made, or that others have made if you are working in a networked environment. Refres<u>h</u> doesn't show new records and doesn't remove deleted records; deleted records display the expression #Deleted in the fields. If you change a record so that it no longer meets the selection criteria of the underlying query or an applied filter, Access continues to display the record even after you use the Refres<u>h</u> command. The Refres<u>h</u> command does not rerun the query or reapply the filter for the active form or datasheet. However, Refres<u>h</u> does force the recalculation of calculated controls. If a calculated control is based on a query or table other than that on which the form is based, the Refres<u>h</u> command forces a requery of the control's source. Controls that might be based on a query or table include list boxes and combo boxes, subform controls, OLE objects, and controls containing domain aggregate functions such as Dlookup() or Dsum().

The second way to display current data is to requery the underlying records of the active form or datasheet by rerunning the query or rereading the table to reflect changes to records, retrieve newly added records, and eliminate deleted records. To requery the active form or datasheet, press Shift+F9.

> **Note**
>
> You also can use the Query Design toolbar's Run button to requery a form. Because this button is not on the default Form toolbar and the Run command is not provided as a menu command on the built-in Form View menubar, you'll have to customize the Form View toolbar by adding the Run button from the Query Design toolbar. The "Customizable Toolbars" section of Chapter 13, "Designing Custom Multitable Forms," describes how to add buttons to Access's built-in toolbars.

When you requery the active form or datasheet, Access reorders the records into the sort sequence specified in the query or the applied filter. If you haven't specified a sort order, Access reorders the records into a default sequence. After the requery, the focus moves to the first control that can receive the focus in the first record. If you change a record so that it no longer meets the criteria of the query or the applied filter, the requery removes the record from the display.

The third way to display current data is to choose Records, Remove Filter/Sort to display all the current records in the underlying table or query. The Remove Filter/Sort command removes an applied filter and then requeries the active object.

When you create macros, you can duplicate these menu commands and keystrokes to display current records with the DoMenuItem and SendKeys actions. Additionally, you can use three macro actions: RepaintObject, Requery, and ShowAllRecords.

The RepaintObject action completes any pending screen updates and recalculations of controls on the specified database object, or the active database object if none is specified, and then redraws the screen. For a form, this action does not requery the underlying table or query and does not display changes that you or others have made to the currently displayed records. You use the RepaintObject action in a macro when Access isn't updating fields as quickly as you want. For example, when you use the SetValue action to set a control's value, Access might not recalculate the value immediately; using the RepaintObject action forces immediate recalculation. The RepaintObject action is similar to the Refresh command, except that Refresh displays changes in currently displayed records and the RepaintObject action does not.

The Requery action requeries the source of the active database object or the source of a specified control on the active object. When a form contains a control that has its own underlying source, such as a combo box or a subform control, using the Requery action to requery the form does not requery the control; likewise, using the Requery action to requery a control does not requery the form. The Requery action can requery only one source, so you must include separate Requery actions for the form and the control. If you want to requery a control that is not on the active form, you use the SelectObject action to select the form and then use the Requery action to requery the control. Table 17.1 shows the macro actions to requery a combo box called cboFind on a form named frmSecond that is not the active form.

Table 17.1 Macro Actions to Requery a Control on Another Form		
Action	**Argument**	**Argument Setting**
SelectObject	Object Type	Form
	Object Name	frmSecond
	In Database Window	No
Requery	Control Name	cboFind

When two forms with the same record source are open, changes to a record in one form are immediately reflected in the second form. However, if you add or delete a record in one form, the second form does not automatically reflect that change; the second form does not acknowledge the added record, and the expression #Deleted in each of a record's fields indicates a deleted record. To display current data, apply the Requery action to the second form. When you apply the Requery action to a form, the Requery action duplicates pressing Shift+F9, but when you apply the Requery action to a control, the action is similar to pressing F9 to recalculate the control.

The ShowAllRecords action duplicates the Remove Filter/Sort command by removing an applied filter and requerying the active form.

Setting Values

Use the SetValue action to set the value of a field, a control, or a property of a form or report. Table 17.2 shows the arguments for the SetValue action.

Table 17.2 SetValue **Action Arguments**

Argument	Description
Item	The name of the field, control, or property that you want to set. If the field or control is on the active form or report, you can use the short form of the name; otherwise, use the full identifier syntax.
	For a form, you can use this action to set the value of a bound control or an unbound control that is not a calculated control. To set the value of a field in the underlying table that isn't linked to a control on the form, you use the syntax Forms![FormName]![FieldName]. When you use SetValue to set the value of a control, the control's form-level validation rule is not tested; however, if the control is bound, the corresponding field's table-level validation rule is tested.
	For a report, you can't use this action to set the value of a bound or calculated control, but you can use this action to set an unbound control that is not a calculated control. You can set the value of a field in the underlying table only if the field is bound to a report control or is referred to in a calculated control on the report.
Expression	The expression to which you want to set the object's value. Access assumes that the value entered is an expression, and an equal sign (=) is not necessary. If you do include an equal sign, Access evaluates the expression first and uses the result as the argument.

Table 17.3 shows examples of the SetValue action.

Table 17.3 Typical Examples of the SetValue **Action**

Item	Expression	Description
[Counter]	[Counter] + 1	Increments a counter on the active form.
[cmdNew].Visible	No	Hides the command button, cmdNew, on the active form.
Forms!frmSuppliers!	Yes	Unhides the cmdNew.Visible command button, cmdNew, on the inactive form frmSuppliers.
[cboFind]	Null	Displays no value in the active form's combo box control cboFind.

(continues)

Table 17.3 Continued

Item	Expression	Description
[Amount]	[fsubOrders].Form![Amount]	Sets the value of a control named Amount on a main form to the value of a control named Amount in the subform displayed in the subform control fsubOrders.
Screen.ActiveControl	Proper(Screen.ActiveControl)	Capitalizes the first letter of the value in the active control by using the Proper() custom function (in the Utility module of Nwind).
Screen.ActiveControl.Locked	Yes	Locks the active control.
[TotalCount]	DCount("*","qryOrders"	Sets the value of the control TotalCount on the active form to the total number of records in the query qryOrders.
Forms!frmSuppliers.Tag	"frmProducts"	Sets the Tag property of the inactive form frmSuppliers to frmProducts.

> **Caution**
>
> If you precede the Expression argument with an equal sign, Access first evaluates the expression that you entered. In the last example in table 17.3, if you enter the expression ="frmProducts", Access evaluates this expression as frmProducts, then uses [frmProducts] as the Expression argument and expects to find a control named frmProducts on the active form. After failing to find a control with this name, Access generates an error and the macro action fails.

When you use a form to calculate a value, you can display the result of the calculation in a calculated control on the form. The result is based on an expression entered in the control's ControlSource property. The expression can refer to controls on the same form or on another form, or on field values from a table or query other than the form's record source. The calculated value is temporary and is recalculated automatically each time that you open the form. You can recalculate the value on demand by applying the Requery action to the control. If you want to store the result of a calculation, you can use the SetValue action to set the bound control's value to the calculation's result. In the second-to-last example in table 17.3, if TotalCount is a bound control, the calculation's result of the total number of records in the record set of the qryOrders query is stored in the field to which the control is bound. If TotalCount is unbound, Access displays the calculation's result in the control but does not store the result. You cannot use the SetValue action to alter the value of bound or calculated controls on reports nor the value of calculated controls on forms.

> **Note**
>
> When you want to use an aggregate function to calculate any of the various statistics for a set of records as a macro condition or action argument, you must use one of the domain aggregate functions and not the SQL aggregate functions. For example, use DCount() rather than Count().

In addition to using the `SetValue` action to set the value of a field or control, you can use the `SetValue` action to set the properties of a control, form, or report dynamically as part of a macro. You can create functional effects as well as helpful visual cues. Here are a few examples:

- To protect data in a control from inadvertent changes, you can set the `Enabled` property to `No` and the `Locked` property to `Yes` when you design the form. To enable the user to make changes, you can place on the form a special Edit button and create a macro with `SetValue` actions to change these properties to allow edits.

- To protect a control that should have data entered only under a certain condition, you can set the control's `Visible` property and its label to `No` when you design the form. When the precondition is met, you can use the `SetValue` action in a macro to change this property to unhide the control.

- To create visual cues to indicate whether the control can be edited or a value is required, you can change the visual appearance (including colors) of a control, its label, or both.

Storing Values Temporarily

You can use the `SetValue` action to place a value needed for a subsequent operation in a temporary storage location on the same form or on another form. For example, when you run a macro with the `Requery` action to update a form, Access reorders the records and places the focus in the first record. If you want to display the record that was current before the `Requery` action, you can use a `SetValue` action to store the value of the record's primary key in a hidden text box in the form's header or footer before running the `Requery` action. Include the `FindRecord` action to find and display the record whose primary key matches the value that you stored. As another example, when you use the `RunMacro` action to run another macro repeatedly, you can keep track of the number of times that the called macro runs by storing the value of a counter in a hidden text box on the form and using the `SetValue` action in the called macro to increment the counter.

When several forms need to use values on several other forms, you need not open all the forms so that they can all share the values. Instead, you can use the `SetValue` action to store the values on a single form that you create to hold all *global variables*. When you want the values to be available the next time that you open the database, you can use a table with a single record to store the values in the global variables form.

Avoiding Macro Errors

When unable to execute a macro action, Access displays an error message followed by an Action Failed dialog (see fig. 17.2). The Action Failed dialog displays the name of the macro and the action that caused the error. If the action is preceded by a condition, the dialog indicates the condition's value. After you click the Halt button, you must trouble-shoot the error to correct whatever caused it.

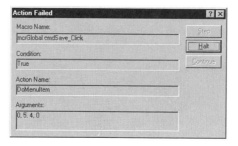

Fig. 17.2 The Action Failed dialog that indicates an error in executing a macro.

 ▶▶ See "Troubleshooting Macro Errors," p. 692

Whenever an error occurs during execution, it causes the Error event for the active form or report. Access identifies which error has occurred and places a corresponding integer value, called an *error code,* in a special *error function,* Err(). Access recognizes more than 6,000 error codes. Table 17.4 lists a few of the more common error codes and the corresponding default error messages.

Table 17.4 Common Error Codes and Error Messages

Error Code	Default Error Message
3058	Index or primary key can't have a null value.
3022	Duplicate value in index, primary key, or relationship. Changes were unsuccessful.
2237	The text you enter must match an entry in the list.
2105	Can't go to specified record.
2107	The value you entered is prohibited by the validation rule set for this field.
2169	The record being edited can't be saved. If you close the form, the changes you've made to the record will be lost. Close anyway?

Lack of Error Handling

You can use the Error event to trigger a macro, but the capability to deal with errors using macros alone is limited. If you use macros alone, you have no way to determine the error code and no way to suppress the default error message. After the error occurs, the best that you can do is have the macro test conditions to determine which error might have caused the Error event and display a custom error message in addition to the default error message. If the error that occurred causes the macro action to fail, you can't prevent Access from terminating the macro and displaying the Action Failed dialog.

The inability to handle errors is the most serious limitation of macro programming and is the primary reason that you may need to learn some Access VBA. With Access VBA, you can determine the specific error code, suppress the default error message, and write instructions on how to handle the problem. In Chapter 28, "Writing Visual Basic for Applications Code," see the section "Handling Run-Time Errors" to learn how to use Access VBA to deal with errors.

Avoiding Errors by Anticipating Preconditions

Using macros alone, the best solution is to anticipate the conditions that would make it impossible for Access to execute a macro action and then design the macro to avoid these conditions. Conditions that must be satisfied before an action can be executed successfully are called *preconditions*.

You can avoid most macro errors by entering an expression in the Conditions column to test for a precondition. If the precondition is satisfied, Access executes the action. If the precondition is not satisfied, Access executes alternative actions, such as displaying a custom message and terminating the macro with the StopMacro action before attempting the impossible action. Table 17.5 lists typical macro actions, preconditions for successful execution, and expressions to test for the precondition.

Table 17.5   Examples of Tests for Preconditions

Macro Action	Precondition	Expression to Test the Precondition
Close a specified form	The form must be open.	IsLoaded("*FormName*") The IsLoaded() custom function returns **True** if the form is open and **False** otherwise. The IsLoaded() function is available in the Utility Functions module of the Northwind.mdb database.
GoToRecord to move to the next record	There must be another record.	IsNull(*PrimaryKeyField*) When the underlying table or query has a primary-key field, the IsNull() function is **True** if the current record is the blank record at the end of the Recordset, in which case there is no next record. If the condition is **False**, there is a next record.
Undo using the DoMenuItem	The record must have been modified since the last time that it was saved.	Forms![FormName].Dirty When the form has been modified since the last save, the Dirty property is **True** and the Undo command is available. Otherwise, Undo is not available.

The examples listed in table 17.5 demonstrate situations in which the precondition depends on values that change as you work with the database. In such cases, testing for preconditions is the best way to avoid failure of the actions. Sometimes the precondition depends on a value that doesn't normally change when you work with the database. For example, a form might have controls that are locked and disabled to prevent the user from changing data. The Locked and Enabled properties don't change unless you reset them explicitly, so you need not test for their values. A disabled control cannot receive the focus, so any attempt to move to this control by using the GoToControl action fails. In such cases, you can avoid failure of the macro action by setting values to ensure that the precondition is satisfied. In this example, use the SetValue action to enable the control before using the GoToControl action to move the focus to it.

Navigating with Macros

When you work interactively with a database, you use the mouse, keystrokes, and menu commands to navigate between controls, records, forms, and reports. You can make your forms easier to use by creating macros to make navigation automatic.

For example, if certain controls need data only if a precondition is met, you can use a macro to tab past these controls when the precondition is not met. Or, if the current record is the last record in the Recordset, you can use a macro to loop back to the first record. As another example, if you want to view a report based on the data in the active form, you can use a macro to open the report in Print Preview and automatically locate the report record corresponding to the record displayed in the form.

The operation of relating the underlying records of the report and the form is called *synchronizing*. You can use macros to synchronize any two objects with sources that are tables or queries, including forms, reports, combo boxes, and list boxes.

> **Note**
>
> The examples in the rest of this chapter use specific control and form names for clarity. Use your own names when you adapt these macros for your database.

Selecting a Control on a Form or a Subform

Use the GoToControl action to move the focus to a specified control on the active form or to a specified field on an active table or query. The single argument of the action, Control Name, is the name of the control or field. You must use the short syntax for the control or field; using the full identifier causes an error message to display (see fig. 17.3) and the GoToControl action to fail.

Fig. 17.3   The error message displayed when you use the full identifer.

If you want to move the focus to a specified control on a subform of the active form, you must remember that the subform displays within a subform control. Use the GoToControl action twice: first to move to the subform control, and second to move to the specified control. The argument for each action is simply the control's name (see table 17.6).

Table 17.6   Macro Actions to Move the Focus to a Subform Control

Macro Action	Argument Value	Description
GoToControl	[SubformControlName]	Moves the focus to the subform control.
GoToControl	[ControlName]	Moves the focus to the specified control on the first record displayed in the subform.

To move the focus to a specified control on another open form, first use the SelectObject action to move the focus to the form, then use the GoToControl action to move the focus to the control. Table 17.7 lists the macro actions to move the focus to a control on another open form named frmSecond, and table 17.8 lists the actions to move the focus to a control on a subform of another open form named frmSecond.

Table 17.7   Macro Actions to Move to a Control on Another Open Form

Macro Action	Argument	Argument Value	Description
SelectObject frmSecond	Object Type Object Name In Database Window	Form frmSecond No	Moves the focus to the open form named.
GoToControl	Control Name	[*ControlName*]	Moves the focus to the specified control on the form frmSecond.

Table 17.8   Macro Actions to Move to a Control on a Subform of Another Open Form

Macro Action	Argument	Argument Value	Description
SelectObject	Object Type Object Name In Database Window	Form frmSecond No	Moves the focus to the open form named frmSecond.
GoToControl	Control Name	[*SubformControlName*]	Moves the focus to the subform control on the form frmSecond.
GoToControl	Control Name	[*ControlName*]	Moves the focus to the specified control on the first record displayed in the subform of the form frmSecond.

When you work interactively, you navigate between fields or controls by pressing Tab to move the focus to the next control, or Shift+Tab to move the focus to the previous control in the tab order. Use the SendKeys action to duplicate these keystrokes in a macro. Table 17.9 shows examples of SendKeys arguments to navigate among the controls within a record. Set the Wait argument to Yes to have the macro pause until the keystrokes are processed and the control is selected.

Table 17.9 Examples of SendKeys Action Arguments for Navigation within a Record

Keystroke Argument	Description
{tab}	Moves the focus to the next control in the tab order.
Shift+{tab}	Moves the focus to the previous control in the tab order.
{home}	Moves the focus to the first control in the tab order.
{end}	Moves the focus to the last control in the tab order.

Using Logical Navigation to Go to a Record

When you work interactively, you can use the default navigation buttons located in the lower-left corner of forms and datasheets for simple navigation between records. You can move to the first, last, previous, or next record in the Recordset by pressing the appropriate button. You can use keystrokes for simple navigation as well. Use the SendKeys action to duplicate these keystrokes in a macro.

> **Note**
>
> The examples in this chapter are based on using single fields as the primary keys for the tables. You can modify some of the techniques if the primary key is based on more than one field.

Table 17.10 shows examples of SendKeys arguments for simple navigation between records. Set the Wait argument to Yes to have the macro pause until the keystrokes are processed and the record is selected.

Table 17.10 Examples of SendKeys Action Arguments for Simple Navigation between Records

Keystrokes Argument	Description
^{pgdn}	Moves the focus to the next record.
^{pgup}	Moves the focus to the previous record.
^{home}	Moves the focus to the first control of the first record.
^{end}	Moves the focus to the last control of the last record.

Another way to move to the next record is by tabbing out of the previous record. When the focus is in the last control in a form's tab order, the next time that you press Tab the default behavior is to move the focus to the first control in the tab order for the form with the next record made the current record.

> **Note**
>
> The Cycle form property, which is new in Access 95, enables you to control whether you can tab out of a record. To prevent tabbing out of a record, set the Cycle property to Current Record; to prevent tabbing out of a page, set the Cycle property to Current Page. The default setting is All Records.

Another way to navigate among records is *logical navigation,* in which you use the information in records rather than the records' physical location in a `Recordset`. For example, when you want to work with a particular record, you don't use the default navigation buttons to browse through the records hoping to find the one for which you are looking; instead, you choose Edit, Find to display a Find dialog in which you can enter specific information to navigate directly to the first record that matches the search criteria.

Finding a Specific Record

When you search for a particular record interactively, you click into the control containing the values on which you want to search, and then choose Edit, Find or click the toolbar's Find button. When the Find dialog displays, enter in the Find What text box the value that you want to find, set the other options, and choose the Find First button.

You can automate the process of finding a record by placing a combo box displaying the available values in the form's header or footer section and duplicating the interactive find operation with a macro. When the user picks a search value in the combo list, a macro triggered by the combo box's `AfterUpdate` event uses the `GoToControl` action to move the focus to the control that contains the value on which to search, followed by the `FindRecord` action with the `Find What` argument set to the selected combo box value. As a result of these two macro actions, Access displays the first record matching the combo box value and moves the focus to the searched control. Because the user left the focus in the combo box and expects the focus to be in the combo box after Access displays the found record, you need to use another `GoToControl` action to move the focus back to the combo box. Table 17.11 lists the actions and arguments of the macro (`cboFind_AfterUpdate`) that is linked to the `cboFind` combo box and searches in the Find control.

Table 17.11   `cboFind_AfterUpdate`—**The Macro That Finds Records**

Action	Argument	Argument Value
GoToControl	Control Name	Find
FindRecord	Find What	=cboFind
GoToControl	Control Name	cboFind

Table 17.11 does not list the remaining arguments for the `FindRecord` action because you normally use the default values. Notice that you must precede the `Find What` argument with an equal sign (=).

Caution

If you omit the equal sign in the `Find What` argument's value in the `FindRecord` action, the macro runs, but doesn't find the record. If the argument value doesn't include the equal sign, Access treats the value as if it were the asterisk wild card and thus returns all the records.

> **Note**
>
> When a macro contains several actions, Access updates the screen after executing each action. The default screen-updating slows the macro's execution while Access takes time to redraw the screen. The successive screen updates result in flickering of the screen. You can avoid the flickering and improve your macro's performance by including the Echo action at the beginning of the macro. Set the Echo On argument to No to suppress screen updates while the macro runs. When the macro finishes running, Access repaints the screen with the final results of the macro and resets the Echo On argument to Yes. Use the Status Bar Text argument to display a message in the status bar while the echo is turned off. The Echo action doesn't suppress error messages, modal dialogs, or popup forms.
>
> You can use the SetWarnings action to suppress all messages and dialogs except error messages and dialogs that require the user to choose an option or enter information. Set the Warnings On argument to No. Use this action if you want to suppress the confirmation dialog that Access displays whenever you attempt to delete records, or the informational dialog that Access displays whenever you append records or use an action query to create a new table. When the macro finishes, Access resets Warnings On to Yes.
>
> If the macro takes more than a couple of seconds to run, you can provide a visual cue that the macro is running by using the Hourglass action to replace the mouse pointer with the hourglass symbol. Set the Hourglass On argument to Yes to display the hourglass symbol. When the macro finishes running, Access resets Hourglass On to No.

Returning to the Previous Record

You can use the technique described in the last section for logical navigation to specific records. Often you want to undo the search and return to the record previously displayed. To undo a search, you must keep track of which record was displayed previously. In the simplest case, in which the records have a single field as the primary key, you can place an unbound, hidden text box, PreviousFind, in the form header to hold the primary-key value of the current record. Add a SetValue action to the beginning of the cboFind_AfterUpdate macro described in the last section to update the value of PreviousFind. Place a command button called cmdPrevious on the form to run a new macro, cmdPrevious_Click, that uses the value stored in PreviousFind to search for the previous record (see fig. 17.4). Table 17.12 defines the two macros.

Table 17.12 Macros to Find a Record and Return to the Previous Record

Macro Name	Action	Argument	Argument Value
cboFind_AfterUpdate	SetValue	Item	PreviousFind
		Expression	Find
	GoToControl	Control Name	Find
	FindRecord	Find What	=cboFind
	GoToControl	Control Name	cboFind
cmdPrevious_Click	GoToControl	Control Name	Find
	FindRecord	Find What	=PreviousFind
	GoToControl	Control Name	cboFind
	SetValue	Item	cboFind
		Expression	PreviousFind

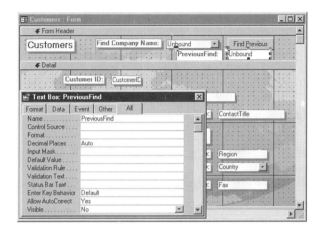

Fig. 17.4 Using a hidden control to hold the previous record's primary key.

The last action sets the value displayed in the combo box to the value stored in PreviousFind to synchronize the combo box value with the record displayed in the form.

One more macro is necessary. When the form first opens, no value is stored in the PreviousFind text box. If you click the cmdPrevious button before selecting a record, the FindRecord macro action fails. Use a macro to initialize the PreviousFind control to the value displayed in the Find control when the form first opens and displays the first record. The form triggers the Load event at this instant, so the macro is called Form_OnLoad. Table 17.13 shows the new macro.

Table 17.13 Form_OnLoad —A Macro to Initialize the PreviousFind Control

Action	Argument	Argument Value
SetValue	Item	PreviousFind
	Expression	Find

Caution

When you use this technique for returning to the record displayed previously, you must remove the default navigation buttons from the form by setting the form's Navigation Buttons property to No. Using the default navigation buttons does not update the PreviousFind control with the currently displayed record's primary key, so clicking the cmdPrevious button uses the combo box value to return to the record previously selected.

Opening a Form

Use the OpenForm macro action to open a form. Table 16.4 in the last chapter lists the arguments for the action. In the simplest case, you open a form by clicking a command button on another form. You specify only the name of the form that you are opening as the Form Name argument and accept the default values for the remaining arguments.

Sometimes you want the opened form to keep track of which form opened it. One way to keep track of this information is to use the SetValue action to set the opened form's Tag property to the opener's name. Use the MoveSize action to move to a new location by specifying the position of the form's upper-left corner within the Access window and to resize the form by specifying new width and height values. Table 17.14 lists the macro actions to open a form named frmSecond, set the Tag property to the opener's name (the form frmFirst), and move the form. The remaining arguments in the OpenForm action have the default values.

Table 17.14 Macro Actions to Open and Move a Form and Set the Tag Property

Action	Argument	Argument Value
OpenForm	Form Name	frmSecond
SetValue	Item	Forms!frmSecond.Tag
	Expression	"frmFirst"
MoveSize	Right	2
	Down	1.5

Synchronizing Two Forms

Often you want to display related information in two different forms. For example, when reviewing an order with the frmFirst form, you want to review the customer's payment history by using the frmSecond form. You can automate the process of finding the related record by placing a command button, cmdReview, on the original form and creating a macro, cmdReview_Click, with an OpenForm action that uses the Where Condition argument to specify which record to display on the opened form. To open a form and display only the records specified by the value of a control on another form, use the following syntax:

```
[FieldName]=Forms![FormName]![ControlName]
```

FieldName is the name of the matching field in the table or query that is the record source of the form that you want to open, and ControlName is the name of the control on the open form that contains the matching value. If FindSecond is the matching field for the record source of the frmSecond form, and FindFirst is the matching control on the frmFirst form, the Where Condition is as follows:

```
FindSecond = Forms!frmFirst!FindFirst
```

> **Caution**
>
> You must use the short syntax on the left side of this expression to identify the field for the form that you want to open.

Access evaluates the Where Condition only once when you run the OpenForm action. When you move to a new record on the original form, Access does not automatically update the opened form. You can force Access to update the opened form, however, by creating another macro with an OpenForm action and running the macro each time that you move to a different record on the original form.

A form triggers the `Current` event when you move to a different record, so the second macro is called `frmOnCurrent`. Clicking the `cmdReview` button is the only method that you want to provide to open the second form, so you don't want to run the `OpenForm` action if the second form is closed. (You are using the `OpenForm` action to update an open form, not to open the form.) When a form is already open, running the `OpenForm` action forces Access to evaluate the arguments again. If the second form is closed, the macro terminates.

Use the `IsLoaded()` custom function, available in the Utility Functions module of Nwind.mdb, to determine whether a form is open. Enter the name of the form enclosed in quotation marks as the function's argument. The `IsLoaded("`*FormName*`")` function returns a **True** value if the specified form is open and displays its records, and returns a **False** value otherwise.

> **Note**
>
> To use custom functions created in another database, you can import into your database the module that contains the functions.

Table 17.15 defines the two macros to open a second form and keep it synchronized with the first form.

Table 17.15   Macros to Synchronize One Form with Another Form

Macro Name	Condition	Action	Argument	Argument Value
cmdPreview_Click		OpenForm	Form Name Where Condition	frmSecond Forms!frmFirst! FindFirst
frmOnCurrent	IsLoaded ("frmSecond")	OpenForm	Form Name Where Condition	frmSecond =Forms!frmFirst! FindFirst

Closing Forms

In the simplest case, you can place a command button, `cmdClose`, in the form's header or footer and create a macro with the `Close` action. You leave the arguments blank to close the active form.

When a second form is synchronized to the form, you can modify the macro to close the second form if it is open, and take no further action if the second form is not open. You must test to determine whether the second form is open before issuing the action to close it, because telling Access to close an object that isn't open causes the `Close` action to fail. Table 17.16 shows the macro to close the active form and a synchronized form.

Table 17.16 `cmdClose`—**A Macro to Close Synchronized Forms**

Condition	Action	Argument	Argument Value
IsLoaded("frmSecond")	Close	Object Type Object Name	Form frmSecond
	Close		

Printing a Report Based on a Single Record

You can automate printing a report based on the information displayed in a form's current record by placing on the form a command button, `cmdPrint`, and using the `OpenReport` action. Table 17.17 lists the arguments for the `OpenReport` action.

Table 17.17 Action Arguments

Argument	Description
Report Name	The name of the report that you want to open.
View	The view that you want to use. The options are Design, PrintPreview, and Print.
Filter Name	The name of an existing query or filter saved as a query used to select the records in the report.
Where Condition	The expression that selects records to display or print. It can be an SQL WHERE clause (without the word *WHERE*).

Use the `Where Condition` argument to synchronize the report to the form. The syntax is identical to that for synchronizing one form to another:

```
[FieldName]=Forms![FormName]![ControlName]
```

FieldName is the name of the matching field in the table or query that is the record source of the report that you want to print, and *ControlName* is the name of the control on the open form that contains the matching value. If `FindSecond` is the matching field for the record source of the `rptSecond` report, and `FindFirst` is the matching control on the `frmFirst` form, the `Where Condition` argument is as follows:

```
FindSecond = Forms!frmFirst!FindFirst
```

Table 17.18 defines the macro to print a synchronized report.

Table 17.18 `cmdPrint_click`—A Macro to Print a Report Synchronized to a Form

Action	Argument	Argument Value
OpenReport	Report Name View Where Condition	rptFirst Print FindSecond = Forms!frmFirst!FindFirst

Macro Techniques for Data Entry

This section shows you how to automate all the basic data-entry operations. To create an error-free macro, you usually must anticipate conditions that might lead to actions failing, and design the macro to avoid the problem.

Validating Data Entry

◀◀ See "Understanding the Update Process," p. 612

Access provides built-in opportunities to validate data by setting properties in Table Design and Form Design views:

- For a field, table-level validation occurs when Access tests the field's Validation Rule property when you try to tab out of a field. If the field's Validation Rule is satisfied, Access updates the field to the record buffer. Otherwise, Access does not update the field, displays a default message, and prevents you from tabbing out of the field until you undo the changes or enter valid data.

- For a record, table-level validation occurs when Access tests the record's Validation Rule property when you try to save the record. Access also tests the referential integrity rules when you try to save the record. If the record Validation Rule is satisfied, Access updates the record to the table. Otherwise, Access does not update the record, displays a default message, and prevents you from saving until you undo the changes or enter valid data.

- For a control, form-level validation occurs when Access tests the control's ValidationRule property when you try to tab out of the control. If the control's Validation Rule is satisfied, Access updates the control to the record buffer. Otherwise, Access does not update the control, displays a default message, and prevents you from tabbing out of the control until you undo the changes or enter valid data.

The expressions that you can use for three Validation Rule properties have restrictions, as explained in Chapter 5, "Entering, Editing, and Validating Data in Tables." You can display custom validation messages for field, record, and control validation by entering a message in the corresponding Validation Text property.

You can use macros to perform complex validation that is difficult or impossible with the built-in validation properties. Use macros when you want to do any of the following:

- Display different error messages depending on the value entered

- Use the same validation rules for several controls or forms

- Use more than one rule to validate a record

- Refer to values in different tables, non-Access tables, and unbound controls on forms

- Change the timing of the validation

Normally, to validate a control, you use the BeforeUpdate event to run a validation macro that the control triggers; to validate a record, you use the BeforeUpdate event that the form triggers. When you use the SetValue action to set a control's value, Access ignores the control's form-level ValidationRule, but does test the field's table-level ValidationRule.

The next section provides an example of using a macro to change the timing of the validation of the primary key.

Validating Uniqueness of the Primary Key

By default, Access tests for the uniqueness of the primary-key values only when you try to save the record, not when you finish entering the primary key. If the primary-key values are not unique, Access displays the default error message: "Duplicate value in index, primary key, or relationship. Changes were unsuccessful."

You must press Esc to undo the record, or change the primary-key values. You can use a macro to change the timing so that Access tests the uniqueness as soon as the user enters the primary-key values. If the value entered is not unique, the macro can replace the default error message with a custom message. In the simplest case of a single-field primary key, you trigger the macro with the BeforeUpdate event triggered by the primary-key control, PrimaryID. The validation test consists of determining the number of records in the underlying table with the same value in the primary-key field as entered in the primary-key control. If the number is zero, no records in the table have the same primary key, the value in the control is unique, and the macro terminates. But if the number is 1, some records in the table share the same primary key, the macro displays a custom message and cancels the updating of the control buffer.

Use the domain aggregate function Dcount() to count the number of records in the table. The syntax is as follows:

```
DCount("*","TableName","FieldName=Forms!FormName!ControlName")
```

FieldName is the name of the matching field in the table, and *ControlName* is the name of the control on the open form that contains the matching value. The domain aggregate functions require quotation marks enclosing each argument. If the *FieldName* is PrimaryID, the table is tblFirst, the *ControlName* is PrimaryID, and the data-entry form is frmFirst, the validation condition is as follows:

```
DCount("*","tblFirst","PrimaryID=Forms!frmFirst!PrimaryID")>0
```

If the condition returns **True**, the macro displays a message and cancels the update; otherwise, the macro terminates.

Table 17.19 shows the macro linked to the primary-key control.

| Table 17.19 | PrimaryID_BeforeUpdate—A Macro to Validate the Uniqueness of the Primary Key | | |

Condition	Action	Argument	Argument Setting
DCount("*","tblFirst", "PrimaryID=Forms! !frmFirst!!PrimaryID")> 0	MsgBox	Message	There is another record with the same ID. Change the ID value or press ESC to undo the record.
		Beep	Yes
		Type	Information
		Title	ID Validation
...	CancelEvent		

Tip

Instead of using the `MsgBox` action to display a message, improve the macro by displaying the stored record with the same primary key.

Adding a Record

When working interactively with a form, you add a new record by choosing <u>E</u>dit, <u>G</u>o To, Ne<u>w</u> or by clicking the New button on the toolbar or grouped with the default navigation buttons in the form's lower-left corner. The grouping of the New button with the other navigation buttons is new in Access 95.

You can automate the process of adding a new record by creating a macro to duplicate the menu command. Run the macro from a custom command `cmdNew` button placed in a group with the other custom buttons that you create to automate data-entry operations. The <u>E</u>dit, <u>G</u>o To, Ne<u>w</u> command is not available when the currently displayed record is the blank record at the end of the `Recordset`, so the macro fails unless it tests for this precondition. In the simplest case, where the form is used to enter data into a table with a single-field primary key, you can test the value in the `PrimaryID` field, by using the following expression:

```
IsNull(PrimaryID)
```

The `IsNull()` function returns **True** if the `PrimaryID` field contains no data; this is the case when the current record is the blank record or when you are adding data to the new record but haven't yet entered data into the primary-key field. In either case, the macro terminates—in the first case, because the current record is the new record and the <u>E</u>dit, <u>G</u>o To, Ne<u>w</u> command isn't available, and in the second case because a blank primary-key field in an edited record triggers the default error message "Index or primary key can't contain a null value." Table 17.20 shows the macro to add a new record.

Table 17.20 cmdNew_Click—A Macro to Add a New Record			
Condition	**Action**	**Argument**	**Argument Value**
IsNull(PrimaryID)	StopMacro	Menu Bar	Form
	DoMenuItem	Menu Name	Edit
		Command	Go To
		Subcommand	New

Undoing Changes

◄◄ See "Duplicating a Menu Command with a Macro Action," p. 595

When working interactively with a form, you use one of the Edit, Undo commands to reverse changes to a record. You can automate the reversal of changes to a record by creating a macro to duplicate the menu command. Run the macro from a custom cmdUndo button that you place in a group with the other custom data-entry buttons. The Undo commands are available only when you have made a change to the record since the last time that you saved the record, so the macro fails unless it includes a test for this precondition. You can use the Dirty property for the test. The Dirty form property (which isn't listed in the form's property sheet because you cannot set this property) takes the value Yes if the current record changed since you last saved it, and takes the value No otherwise. Table 17.21 shows a macro to reverse changes to the current record for the frmFirst form.

Table 17.21 cmdUndo_Click—A Macro to Undo Changes to the Current Record			
Condition	**Action**	**Argument**	**Argument Value**
Forms!frmFirst.Dirty	DoMenuItem	Menu Bar	Form
		Menu Name	Edit
		Command	UndoCurrentRecord

Saving a Record

When you work interactively with a form, you save a record by choosing Records, Save Record, pressing Shift+Enter, or moving the focus to the next record. You can automate the saving process by creating a macro and running it from a custom cmdSave button placed in a group of custom data-entry buttons.

The Records, Save Record command is always available, so you need not test the command's availability as a precondition. However, under some conditions, the DoMenuItem action to save a record fails. Because issuing a command to save a record causes Access to test the validation rules, the action fails unless the new or changed data satisfies the validation rules. In particular, if you use the form for data entry into a table with a single-field primary key, the macro action fails if you have changed the record since the last time that you saved it, and the primary-key field is Null when you run the macro. (If you haven't modified the record and the primary-key field is Null, the current record must be the blank record at the end of the Recordset. In this case, the macro action doesn't fail, because Access doesn't test the validation rules for the blank record.)

The macro (see table 17.22) first tests whether the record was modified since you last saved it. The test uses the `Dirty` property introduced in the last section. If the record wasn't modified, the macro terminates. If the record was modified, the macro tests the value in the `PrimaryID` field. If the primary-key field is `Null`, the macro displays a message and terminates; otherwise, the macro saves the record.

Table 17.22   `cmdSave_Click`—A Macro to Save the Current Record

Condition	Action	Argument	Argument Value
Not Forms!frmFirst.Dirty IsNull(PrimaryID)	StopMacro MsgBox	Message	You must enter a unique value.
...	StopMacro DoMenuItem	Menu Bar Menu Name Command	Form Records SaveRecord

Caution

The macro described in table 17.22 tests only the primary-key field's "nullness" and could still fail if the new or changed data fails any of the other validation rules that the attempt to save the record might trigger. For example, the macro fails if the primary-key value entered is not unique. By default, Access tests for uniqueness of the primary-key value when you attempt to save the record. You can test for uniqueness of the primary-key value as soon as the technique explained in the section "Validating Uniqueness of a Primary Key" changes the value.

To create a bulletproof macro, you must anticipate all errors by reviewing the validation rules that you set and including additional tests of preconditions in the macro.

The macro listed in table 17.22 automates the save operation with a custom command button. If you let the user trigger the save operation in any other way, such as tabbing to a new record, you can avoid the default error message that Access displays when the user tries to save a record with a null primary-key value. To avoid this error message, create a second macro (see table 17.23) to run when Access tries to update the changed record to the table—that is, when the form triggers the `BeforeUpdate` event. The macro tests the primary-key field's value, displays a message, and cancels the update if the value is null; otherwise, the macro takes no action.

Table 17.23   `Form_BeforeUpdate`—A Macro to Cancel the Updating of a Record

Condition	Action	Argument	Argument Value
IsNull(PrimaryID) ...	MsgBox CancelEvent	Message	You must enter a unique ID value.

As the preceding Caution explains, you might have to modify this macro to include additional tests of preconditions.

Date Stamping a Record

When you edit data using a form, you can *date stamp* the changes by adding to the table a field, `DateModified`, and using a macro to set the field's value to the current date. The macro traps the `BeforeUpdate` event that the form triggers. Table 17.24 defines the macro.

Table 17.24 `Form_BeforeUpdate`—A Macro to Date Stamp Changes to a Record		
Action	**Argument**	**Argument Value**
SetValue	Item	DateModified
	Expression	Date()

Deleting a Record

 When you work interactively with a form, you delete a record by choosing <u>E</u>dit, Delete Record, a command which is new in Access 95. You might occasionally want to restrict users from deleting records when using a particular form. Access 95 provides a new form property, `AllowDeletes`, to control the availability of the deletion operation. By setting `AllowDeletes` to `No`, you disable the <u>E</u>dit, Delete <u>R</u>ecord command and make it unavailable from the form.

> **Note**
>
> To delete a record in Access 2.0, you first select the record by choosing <u>E</u>dit, Se<u>l</u>ect Record and then delete the record by choosing <u>E</u>dit, D<u>e</u>lete.

 ◄◄ See "Enforcing Referential Integrity," p. 147

When you want to enable users to delete records from within a form, you can create a macro to issue the menu command with the `DoMenuItem` action (see table 17.25).

Table 17.25 `cmdDelete_Click`—A Macro to Delete a Record without Related Records			
Condition	**Action**	**Argument**	**Argument Setting**
DCount("*"," tblRelated"," PrimaryID=Forms! frmFirst! PrimaryID")=0	SetWarnings DoMenuItem	Warnings On Menu Bar Menu Name Command	No Form Edit Delete Record
...	StopMacro MsgBox	Message	You can't delete this record since records in another table, tblRelated, depend on it.

Run the macro with a custom `cmdDelete` button placed in the group of custom data-entry buttons. Depending on the referential integrity rules that you have set for the database, the macro action will fail in some situations. For example, suppose that you want to delete a record from a table that is the one table in a one-to-many relationship for which you have turned on referential integrity. If the many table has related records, the response depends on whether you selected the Cascade Delete Related Records option for the relationship in the Relationships dialog. If you did not select this option and the many table includes related records, Access doesn't let you delete the parent record, the macro action fails, and Access displays the default error message: Can't delete or change record. Since related records exist in table "[tablename]" referential integrity rules would be violated.

You can save the macro action from failing by testing whether related records exist. Use the domain aggregate function `Dcount()` to count the number of records in the related table, `tblRelated`. The syntax is as follows:

    DCount("*","tblRelated","FieldName=Forms!FormName!ControlName")

FieldName is the name of the matching field in the related table, and *ControlName* is the name of the control on the open form that contains the matching value. If *FieldName* is `PrimaryID`, the related table is `tblRelated`, the *ControlName* is `PrimaryID`, and the data-entry form is `frmFirst`, the test condition is as follows:

    DCount("*","tblRelated","PrimaryID=Forms!frmFirst!PrimaryID")=0

If the condition is **True**, `tblRelated` has no related records, so the macro deletes the record after turning off the default warning. Otherwise, the macro displays a message and terminates.

The macro defined in table 17.25 automates the delete operation with a custom command button. If you enable the user to trigger the delete operation in any other way, such as selecting the record and pressing Delete, you can avoid having Access display its default error message when the user tries to delete a record when `tblRelated` includes related records. To do so, you create a second macro (see table 17.26) to run before Access tries to delete record—that is, when form triggers the `Delete` event. The macro determines whether related records are in `tblRelated`. If such records exist, the macro displays a message and cancels the deletion; otherwise, the macro takes no action.

Table 17.26 `Form_OnDelete`—**A Macro to Cancel the Deletion of a Record When Related Records Exist**

Condition	Action	Argument	Argument Value
Dcount("*"," tblRelated"," PrimaryID= Forms!frmFirst! PrimaryID")=0	StopMacro		
	MsgBox CancelEvent	Message	You can't delete this record since records in another table, tblRelated, depend on it.

Cascading a Delete

If you selected the Cascade Delete Related Records option, Access displays the message shown in figure 17.5.

Fig. 17.5 The confirmation dialog to delete related records.

The message indicates that if you choose to delete the displayed record, Access will delete additional related records in related tables also. You can replace the default dialog with a custom dialog that displays the names of the related tables and the number of records in each table that are at risk for deletion and that asks whether you want to continue with the deletion. The MsgBox macro action displays a message and a single OK button, and thus doesn't enable the user to make a choice. However, the MsgBox() function does display a choice of buttons and returns a value indicating which button the user selected. Use the following simplified syntax:

```
MsgBox(Message, Buttontype, Title)
```

The first and third arguments are string expressions that display the dialog's message and title bar, respectively. *Buttontype* is a numeric expression that you can use to specify the number of buttons, the type of icon displayed in the dialog, which button is the default, and the mode of the dialog window. To display Yes and No buttons with Yes as the default, to display the warning message icon, and to require that the user respond before continuing work in the database, the button argument is 20. If the user selects Yes, the function returns 6, and if the user selects No, the function returns 7. Search in the online Help for the MsgBox() function to find more information about the *Buttontype* argument, the return values, and additional arguments.

In the simplest case of a single related table named tblRelated, you can include the number of related records in the message by concatenating the domain aggregate function Dcount() with the text portions of the message, as follows:

```
"There are " &
DCount("*","tblRelated","PrimaryID=Forms!frmFirst!PrimaryID") &
"records in the related table named tblRelated that will also be
deleted. Do you wish to continue?"
```

When you use the MsgBox() function in a macro's Condition column, Access displays the dialog and suspends the macro until you select one of the buttons. When you select a button, the function returns the corresponding value, enabling Access to evaluate the condition. The condition returns **True** when you select the Yes button and **False** when you select the No button:

```
MsgBox("There are " &
DCount("*","tblRelated","PrimaryID=Forms!frmFirst!PrimaryID") &
"records in the related table named tblRelated that will also
be deleted. Do you wish to continue?",20)=6
```

If you select Yes, the macro deletes the record and the related records after turning off the default warning; otherwise, the macro terminates. Table 17.27 shows the macro.

Table 17.27 cmdDelete_Click—**A Macro to Cascade the Deletion of a Record and Related Records**

Condition	Action	Argument	Argument Value
DCount("*"," tblRelated"," PrimaryID= Forms!frmFirst! PrimaryID")=0	SetWarnings	Warning On	No
	DoMenuItem	Menu Bar	Form
		Menu Name	Edit
		Command	Delete Record
...	StopMacro		
MsgBox("There are " & DCount("*"," tblRelated"," PrimaryID=Forms!frmFirst! PrimaryID") & "records in therelated tablenamed tblRelated that will also be deleted. Do you wish to continue? ",20)=6	DoMenuItem	Menu Bar	Form
		Menu Name	Edit
		Command	Delete Record
...	StopMacro		

If you enable the user to trigger the delete operation in any other way, such as selecting a record and pressing Delete, you can replace the default message that Access displays when the user tries to delete a record with related records in tblRelated. Create a second macro (see table 17.28) to run when Access tries to delete a record—that is, when form triggers the Delete event. The macro determines whether tblRelated has related records, displays a message with the number of records in the related table, and prompts you for a decision. If you select the Yes button, the macro terminates; if you select the No button, the macro cancels the deletion.

Table 17.28 `Form_OnDelete`—**A Macro to Enable the User to Cancel the Deletion of a Record When Related Records Exist**

Condition	Action	Argument	Argument Value
`DCount("*","tblRelated", "PrimaryID=Forms!frmFirst! PrimaryID")=0`	SetWarnings StopMacro	Warnings On	No
`MsgBox("There are" & DCount("*","tblRelated", "PrimaryID=Forms!frmFirst! PrimaryID") & "records in the related table named tblRelated that will also be deleted. Do you wish to continue?",20)=6`	StopMacro		
	CancelEvent		

Macro Techniques for Selecting a Group of Records

 ◀◀ See "Filtering Table Data," p. 185

When you work interactively with a form and want to select a group of records that satisfy a single criterion or a set of criteria, you create a filter to test records against the criteria and apply the filter to select and display the records that meet the criteria. You can create the filter in the Filter window. To open the Filter window when working in Form View or any of the datasheet views, choose Records, Filter, Advanced Filter/Sort. After designing the filter, choose Records, Apply Filter/Sort to run the filter immediately. Choose, Records, Remove Filter/Sort to remove the filter and return the records to the original view. You can store a filter as a query and use the query as the filter for the form at any time.

 Access 95 introduces two new ways to create simple filters and find a group of records easily. Chapter 12, "Creating and Using Forms," discusses these interactive methods. Of the two methods, only Filter by Form enables you to save the filter as a query.

When you are working interactively with a form, follow these steps to apply and remove a filter saved as a query:

1. Choose Records, Filter, Advanced Filter/Sort to open the Filter window.

2. Choose File, Load from Query. The Applicable Filter dialog appears (see fig. 17.6), displaying a list of queries that you can apply to the form as filters.

3. Select the query that you want to apply and click OK. The Filter window displays the selected filter.

Fig. 17.6 The Applicable Filter dialog.

4. Choose Filte<u>r</u>, Appl<u>y</u> Filter/Sort or click the toolbar's Apply Filter button to display the filtered records.

5. Choose <u>R</u>ecords, <u>R</u>emove Filter/Sort or click the toolbar's Remove Filter button to remove the filter and display all the records.

You can automate the selection of records in several ways. This section describes a technique to automate the process of applying a filter to select records. The simplest case discussed in this section, for example, uses a single criteria to select records. You want to select all customers from a particular state, all orders placed after a specified date, or all products obtained from a specific supplier. In the next section, you modify the technique for multiple criteria.

You can automate the selection process by placing in the form's header or footer a combo box that displays the available selection values and creating a macro to duplicate the effect of the preceding interactive steps. The technique's concept is similar to that for finding a single record, as discussed earlier in this chapter. The details, however, are more complicated and warrant a specific example. To create a new form with a filter that you can automate by a macro, follow these steps:

1. Open Northwind.mdb and use the Auto-Form Tabular Form Wizard to create a new tabular form named `frmProducts` based on the table Products. Increase the Header section's height to one inch and move the column headings to the bottom of the header. Figure 17.7 shows the new form. Notice that the `SupplierID` and `CategoryID` controls are combo boxes. The Products table uses the Lookup Wizard, which is new in Access 95, to create these two fields as Lookup fields that automatically look up supplier and category names in the Supplier and Category tables.

2. To use Filter by Form to create a filter for selecting a supplier, choose <u>R</u>ecords, <u>Fil</u>ter, <u>F</u>ilter by Form. Select any supplier name from the Supplier combo list (see fig. 17.8). To see the filter at work, choose Filte<u>r</u>, Appl<u>y</u> Filter/Sort. After reviewing the selection, choose <u>R</u>ecords, <u>R</u>emove Filter/Sort to remove the filter and display all the records. To automate the process, you must save the filter as a filter query. Choose <u>R</u>ecords, <u>F</u>ilter, <u>F</u>ilter by Form to display the filter again. Choose <u>F</u>ile, Save <u>A</u>s Query and save the filter as the query `qfltProducts`. Close the Filter by Form window.

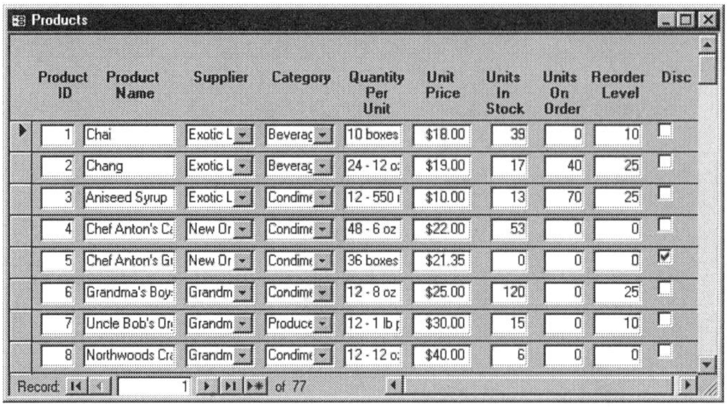

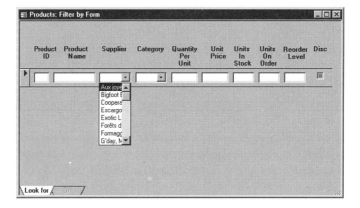

Fig. 17.7 The frmProducts form.

Fig. 17.8 Using Filter by Form to select a supplier.

3. Create the selection combo box to display the name of the selected supplier while storing the corresponding Supplier ID number. To create the selection combo box, drag the SupplierID Lookup field from the field list to the form's header. Modify the combo box by changing the name to cboSelectSupplier and deleting the default entry in the ControlSource property. Make sure that the ControlSource is blank; the selection combo box holds only the selected value and is not bound to the table. Change the label's caption to *Select Supplier*.

The next five steps automate the process by modifying the filter query so that the query obtains the criteria from the value that you select in the combo box and by creating a macro to apply the filter. The macro traps the AfterUpdate event triggered by the combo box. Here are the steps:

1. Open the qfltProducts query in Design View and delete the Lookup_Supplier field list. Delete the CompanyName field from the grid, drag the SupplierID field from the Products field list, and enter the following expression in the criteria cell:

```
Forms!frmProducts!cboSelectSupplier
```

Figure 17.9 shows the Query Design grid.

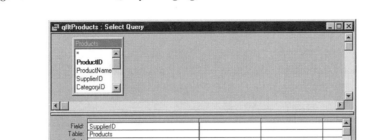

Fig. 17.9 Linking the filter query to the form in the Query Design grid.

2. Save the query.

3. Create a new macrosheet named mfrmProducts and a new macro named cboSelectSupplier_AfterUpdate that applies the filter with the ApplyFilter action. Type **qfltProducts** as the value of the Filter Name argument. Save the macro.

4. Open the AfterUpdate property of the combo box and select the macro mfrmProducts. cboSelectSupplier_AfterUpdate.

5. Save the form.

The final two steps test the selection process and remove the filter:

1. Select a supplier from the Supplier combo box and view the selection.

2. Choose Records, Remove Filter/Sort to remove the filter. Notice that the combo box continues to display the name of the supplier selected last.

You can automate the filter's removal by placing a cmdAll button in the header and creating a cmdAll_Click macro to remove the filter. The macro, shown in table 17.29, also refines the process by setting the combo box's value to Null so that the combo box provides the appropriate visual cue (blank) when displaying all records. Figure 17.10 shows the frmProducts form with the automated selection capability.

Table 17.29   cmdAll_Click—A Macro to Remove the Filter

Action	Argument	Argument Value
ShowAllRecords		
SetValue	Item	cboSelectSupplier
	Expression	Null

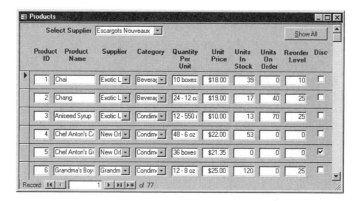

Fig. 17.10   The automated selection of a supplier.

Using Multiple Selection Criteria

You can modify the technique described in the last section if you want to use more than one criteria to select records. For example, you can select customers from a particular state that have ordered in the last six months, or employees in a particular health plan who earn less than a specified annual salary. Modify the example of the last section to select products by category as well as by supplier, as follows:

1. Create the selection combo box to display the name of the selected Category while storing the corresponding Category ID number. To create the selection combo box, drag the CategoryID Lookup field from the field list to the form's header. Modify the combo box by changing its name to cboSelectCategory and deleting the default entry in the ControlSource property. Make sure that ControlSource is blank; the selection combo box holds only the selected value and is not bound to the table. Change the label's caption to *Select Category*.

2. Open the filter query qfltProducts in Design View. Then drag CategoryID to the Query Design grid. The Criteria cell (see fig. 17.11) displays the following expression:

       Forms!frmProducts!cboSelectCategory

   Save the query.

3. Add a new macro called cboSelectCategory_AfterUpdate to the mfrmProducts macrosheet that applies the filter when you select a category. Select the ApplyFilter action and type **qfltProducts** as the value of the Filter Name argument.

4. Select the cboSelectCategory combo box's AfterUpdate property and then select the mfrmProducts.cboSelectCategory_AfterUpdate macro.

5. Save the form.

6. Modify the macro cmdAll_Click by adding a row to set the value of the combo box cboSelectCategory to Null.

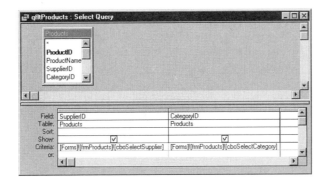

Fig. 17.11 The filter query for multiple selection.

7. Save the macro.

8. Select Bigfoot Breweries from the first combo box. Notice that no records are displayed. Then select Beverages from the second combo box. Observe that records satisfying both criteria are displayed (see fig. 17.12).

9. Click the command button to remove the filter.

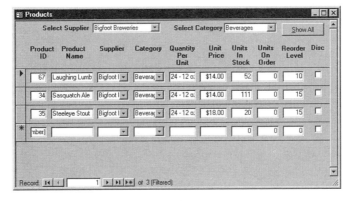

Fig. 17.12 Automating the selection using two criteria.

When the value of either combo box is Null, no records are displayed. The selection method does not function as intended. When you select a value from a combo box and the other combo box is blank, the selection should include all records satisfying the first combo box's criteria. The next step modifies the criteria in the filter query so that if a combo box is Null, the query returns records for all the combo box's values.

1. Open the filter query in Design View. Change the criteria for SupplierID to the following expression:

```
Like IIf(IsNull(Forms!frmProducts!cboSelectSupplier),"*",
   Forms!frmProducts!cboSelectSupplier)
```

2. Change the criteria for `CategoryID` to the following expression:

```
Like IIf(IsNull(Forms!frmProducts!cboSelectCategory),"*",
    Forms!frmProducts!cboSelectCategory)
```

3. Save and close the filter query.

If the value of a combo box is `Null`, the criteria becomes `Like "*"`, which includes records with any value because the wild card * replaces any characters. If a combo box value is not `Null`, the criteria is the value currently displayed in the combo box. Test the modified technique by clicking the `cmdAll` button to remove the filter and selecting a value from either combo box.

As an alternative to applying the filter query with the `ApplyFilter` action, you can use the `SetValue` action to change the value of the `RecordSource` property of the form to the name of the query. Table 17.30 shows the macros that select records by changing the record source.

Table 17.30 Macros to Select Records by Changing the Record Source

Macro Name	Action	Argument	Argument Value
cboSelectCategory_AfterUpdate	SetValue	Item Expression	Forms!frmProducts.RecordSource "qfltProducts"
cboSelectCategory_AfterUpdate	SetValue	Item Expression	Forms!frmProducts.RecordSource "qfltProducts"

Printing a Report for a Selected Group of Records

If you have selected a group of records by applying a filter query to a form's underlying table or query as described in the last section, you can automate printing a report based on the same group of records by placing a command button named `cmdPrint` on the form and using the `OpenReport` action. Synchronize the report to the form by using the Filter Name argument to apply the same filter query to the report.

Following the example of the last section, with the `frmProducts` form and the `qfltProducts` filter query, use the Auto-Report Tabular Report Wizard to create a new tabular report, called `rptProducts`, based on the Products table. Table 17.31 shows the macro to print a synchronized report.

Table 17.31 cmdPrint_Click—A Macro to Print a Report for a Selected Group of Records Synchronized to a Form

Action	Argument	Argument Value
OpenReport	Report Name View Filter Name	rptProducts PrintPreview qfltProducts

Figure 17.13 shows a portion of the synchronized report. (Notice that the Report Wizard doesn't utilize the supplier and category fields' Lookup features and displays the SupplierID and CategoryID numbers.)

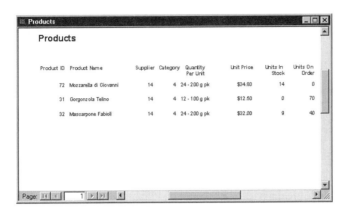

Fig. 17.13 The synchronized report.

Using a Custom Dialog to Collect Selection Criteria

The previous sections show you how to select a group of records by placing one or more combo boxes to collect selection criteria in the header or footer of the form that displays the records. If you don't need to see the data displayed in the form, you can create a separate form as a custom dialog with the sole purpose of collecting selection criteria. You can create custom dialogs that collect selection criteria while printing routine reports, without first having to display a synchronized form. This section demonstrates the technique by creating a custom dialog to select suppliers and categories for the rptProducts report created in the last section.

The first two steps in the process create the custom dialog as a form called fdlgSelect and set form properties to give the form the standard behavior of a dialog:

1. Create a new blank form (unbound) with the following controls:

Command buttons named cmdPreview, cmdPrint, and cmdCancel.

An unbound list box or combo box for each selection field for which you want to provide choices, and an unbound text box for each selection field for which you want to enable the user to type input. Either use the List Box Wizard or the Combo Box Wizard, or build these controls manually.

One or more label controls to provide instructions on how to use the dialog.

Figure 17.14 shows the Design View for the fdlgSelect form and the properties for the lstSelectSupplier list box. The properties for the lstSelectCategory list box are similar.

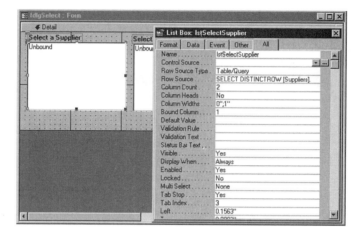

Fig. 17.14   The list box properties for `lstSelectSuppliers`.

2. Set the form properties to control the form's behavior as shown in table 17.32. Figure 17.15 shows the `fdlgSelect` form.

Table 17.32   A Dialog's Form Properties

Property	Setting	Reason
DefaultView	Single Form	The dialog is a single form.
ScrollBars	Neither	Not necessary.
RecordSelectors	No	Not necessary.
NavigationButtons	No	Not necessary.
AutoCenter	Yes	Displays the form in the center of the screen.
PopUp	Yes	To keep the form on top and, when the modal property is Yes, to disable the menus and toolbars.
Modal	Yes	To disable other windows until the modal form is closed.
BorderStyle	Dialog	To give the form a thick border.
MinMaxButtons	No	Not necessary.
ShortCutMenu	No	Not necessary.

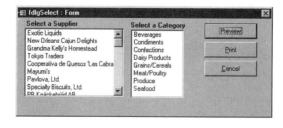

Fig. 17.15   The selection dialog `fdlgSelect`.

The next three steps create the filter query to filter the record source of the report or form, link the filter query to the custom dialog, and automate the dialog by creating macros and assigning each macro to the OnClick event of the corresponding command button:

1. Create a query based on the record source of the report or form. Set the OutputAllFields property to Yes. Drag each selection field to the design grid.

2. Link the query to the dialog by entering references to the controls on the dialog into the criteria cell for each of the corresponding selection fields. In the current example, you can use two list boxes to make selections by using the the following expressions:

```
Like IIF(IsNull(Forms!fdlgSelect!lstSelectSupplier),"*",
     Forms!fdlgSelect!lstSelectSupplier)

Like IIF(IsNull(Forms!fdlgSelect!lstSelectCategory),"*",
     Forms!fdlgSelect!lstSelectCategory)
```

3. Save the query as the filter query qfltSelect (see fig. 17.16).

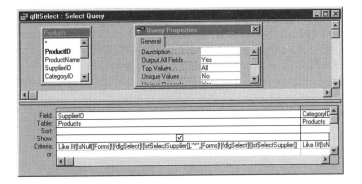

Fig. 17.16 Linking the filter query and the dialog.

4. Create a new macro group, mfdlgSelection, and macros for each of the command buttons.

   The macro cmdPreview_Click first hides the dialog, then opens the report in print preview mode by using the query filter to select the records. You hide the dialog instead of closing it so that the selected values remain available to create the filter when the report opens. When you close the report, the dialog is still hidden. To unhide the dialog when the report triggers the Close event, create a new macro group named mrptProducts by using a macro named Report_Close that unhides the dialog form.

   The cmdPrint_Click macro opens the report in print mode by using the query filter to select the records.

   The cmdCancel_Click macro closes the dialog.

Table 17.33 shows the macro `mrptProducts.Report_OnClose`, and table 17.34 shows the macro group for the `fdlgSelect` form.

Table 17.33 Report_OnClose—A Macro to Unhide the Dialog When the Report Closes

Action	Argument	Argument Value
SetValue	Item Expression	Forms!fdlgSelect.Visible Yes

Table 17.34 The Macro Group for the Dialog

Macro Name	Action	Argument	Argument Value
cmdPreview_Click	SetValue	Item Expression	Forms!fdlgSelect.Visible No
	OpenReport	Report Name View Filter	rptProducts PrintPreview qfltSelect
cmdPrint_Click	OpenReport	Report Name View Filter	rptProducts Print qfltSelect
cmdCancel_Click	Close		

Assign the macro in table 17.33 to the report's `OnClose` event, and assign the macros in table 17.34 to the corresponding command button's `OnClick` event on `fdlgSelect`.

You can modify the dialog form to include text boxes for beginning and ending dates and additional controls to collect user input and to change the filter query to accommodate the additional selection criteria.

From Here...

This chapter introduced a variety of ways to automate database operations through macro programming. With a little practice, you can easily customize the macros shown in this chapter to include additional capabilities. Macro programming is powerful enough to handle the automation of most database tasks. When you want to include capabilities that macro programming cannot provide, such as bulletproof error handling or direct communication with Windows 95, you can use Access VBA code. You can use Access VBA code to replace or supplement macros to handle events.

The following chapters provide additional information on using advanced macro features and an introduction to Access VBA:

- Chapter 18, "Taking Advantage of Advanced Macro Features," shows you how to control the user interface, how to work with external data, and how to troubleshoot and document macros.

- Chapter 28, "Writing Visual Basic for Applications Code," describes how to use Access 95's new programming language to write code to handle events for forms and reports.

■ Chapter 29, "Understanding the Data Access Object Class," shows how to work directly with the objects of Access and begin to use the full power of the VBA programming language.

Chapter 18

Taking Advantage of Advanced Macro Features

Using Macros to Control the User Interface

The *user interface* refers to all the ways that a human interacts with the computer. The user interface includes what you see on-screen, and how you use a mouse and the keyboard to give information to the computer. When you work with a commercial application such as Microsoft Access, you work with the user interface created by a team of interface-design professionals who tried to make the interface helpful, informative and, above all, easy to use.

The Microsoft Access interface is designed to allow you to communicate the information and instructions required to produce the result—the document, spreadsheet, illustration, or database—with minimum training. The screen, menu commands, toolbars, keystroke shortcuts, message dialogs, mouse movements, and mouse clicks are designed to minimize the time you must spend learning how to use the application, *before* you actually use it to do your work.

In Access the interface elements are designed to help you create a database and to use the database interactively. In an interactive database, you issue individual instructions by using the built-in interface elements: the built-in menubars, menu commands, shortcut menus, keystroke shortcuts, and mouse clicks. Chapter 17, "Using Macros with Forms and Reports," introduced ways to automate database operations with macro programming. You learned how to add to the user interface by providing command buttons and custom keystroke shortcuts that you use to issue instructions to the computer by clicking the mouse or pressing a keystroke combination. Other more subtle interface additions discussed in Chapter 17 include using events that the user causes indirectly to trigger macros, such as the update events that occur when you change data and move to the next control or record.

In this chapter, you learn the following advanced macro techniques

- To control the way your application starts up

- How to create and use custom menubars and shortcut menus

- How to use custom toolbars

- How to import and manipulate data

- How to troubleshoot problems with macros

- How to document macros

This section focuses on how to *control the user interface* by removing or hiding various built-in interface elements and replacing them with custom versions. The goal in controlling the user interface is to simplify the interface by providing only the elements necessary to use your database, but not to change its essential design. Your goals are the same as the goals of the professional interface designer—that the custom interface is helpful, informative and, above all, easy to use. Two additional goals of the custom interface are to protect the data from inadvertent changes that could invalidate it and to protect the design of the database from inadvertent changes that could cause the database to break.

What Is a Custom Database Application?

A *custom database application* is a database created in a commercial application—such as Microsoft Access—using the tools that the commercial application provides to automate tasks and replace the built-in interface elements with custom versions. In a custom application the user may not even be aware which commercial application was used. A well-designed custom application is easy to learn and use because it presents, in clear, obvious, and intuitive ways only the instructions and commands needed to perform the specific tasks the database was designed to carry out. Clearly labeled buttons, instruction labels, informative messages and dialogs, and simple menus (with commands arranged as the user expects) all help make the custom application easy to use.

The custom database application eliminates unnecessary, undesirable, or confusing interface elements—including all access to design views—and replaces them with custom versions, such as replacing the Database Explorer with a custom main-menu form to greet the user when the database first opens. The following sections show how to create custom interface elements.

Creating the Main Menu Form

The *main menu form* displays a list of the basic tasks that the custom application is designed to carry out and provides a way for the user to select a task and open the form or set of forms needed for the task. The main menu form also is known as the *switchboard* because it provides navigation to a database task and is the form to which the user returns when the task is finished. Custom applications use several design styles: some use a separate form as the switchboard, others incorporate the navigation function of the switchboard into a custom toolbar, and other designs include the navigation function in the header or footer section of each of the basic task forms.

The sample applications that come with Access are examples of three styles. The Northwind Traders application, Northwind.mdb, uses a separate switchboard form, with command buttons for navigating to the main tasks (see fig. 18.1); the Northwind Order Entry application, Orders.mdb, uses custom navigation buttons in the toolbar (see fig. 18.2); and the Solutions application, Solution.mdb, uses synchronized list boxes to display lists of the numerous examples in the application (see fig. 18.3).

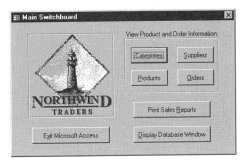

Fig. 18.1 The switchboard for Northwind Traders (Northwind.mdb).

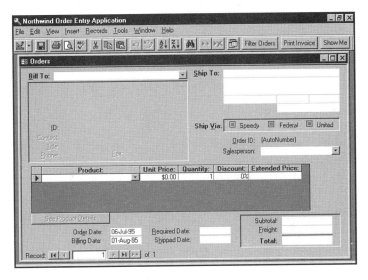

Fig. 18.2 The custom toolbar navigation buttons for Northwind Order Entry (Orders.mdb).

The navigation style you choose depends on the tasks in your database. A database application with a single main task may use the task's form as the main menu form and provide navigation to other tasks by using command buttons placed on the form or on a toolbar. The Northwind Order Entry application (Orders.mdb) uses this approach. An application with several main tasks may use a separate main menu form, as in Northwind.mdb and Solution.mdb. No matter which navigation style you choose, you need to provide the following two capabilities:

- Navigation between the main task forms by using command buttons, options groups, list boxes, or combo boxes

- Closing the database and, perhaps, quitting Access

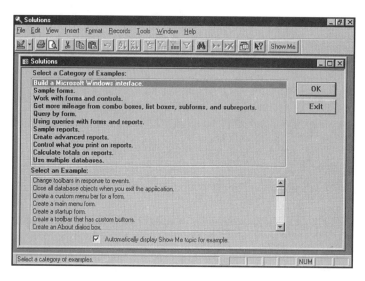

Fig. 18.3   The main menu for the Solutions application (Solution.mdb).

Starting Up Your Application

You can arrange to have the main menu form, or any other form that you choose, displayed when you first open the database by setting the new Access 95 startup options. Choose Tools, Startup to display the Startup dialog (see fig. 18.4). You use the Startup dialog to set options for the current database.

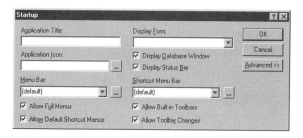

Fig. 18.4   The Startup dialog.

Click the down arrow of the Display Form combo list to display the forms in the database and select the form you want displayed when the database opens. Below the Display Form combo box are check boxes to display or hide the Database Explorer window and the status bar. In a custom application, you hide the Database window to prevent the user from seeing and having access to the tables, queries, macros, and modules in the application but you display the status bar to provide custom on-screen help.

You can change the title and the image displayed in the title bar. Enter the new title in the Application Title text box. Enter the full path name of a bitmap (.bmp) or icon (.ico) file that contains the image you want to display. Figure 18.5 shows the entries to display the cars.bmp image for a Car Inventory application. The Application Title and

Application Icon settings take effect as soon as you make the changes and click OK. All other settings you make in the Startup dialog don't take effect until the next time you open the application.

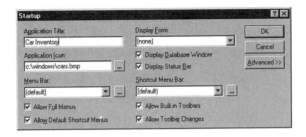

Fig. 18.5 Setting a custom application title and image.

The Menubar and Toolbar settings of the Startup dialog are discussed in following sections of this chapter.

Using an AutoExec Macro

◄◄ See "Running a Macro at Startup," p. 609

You can set additional startup conditions by creating an AutoExec macro. When you open a database, Access first sets the options that you selected in the Startup dialog, and then runs the AutoExec macro, if there is one. Although the Startup dialog has eliminated some of the need for an AutoExec macro, many custom applications include an AutoExec macro to accomplish special tasks, such as importing and modifying data from an on-line database service when the database opens.

You can use the AutoExec macro to improve the perceived performance of your application by opening and hiding the main task forms. Although there is an initial delay while Access opens the forms and retrieves the data for the tables and queries that provide the records for the forms, the subsequent performance of the application improves. Most users don't mind an initial setup delay if the subsequent responses are quicker. The time needed to unhide a form, and possibly requery it, usually is much shorter than the time to open a form and load its records.

Bypassing Startup Options

You can bypass the settings you made in the Startup dialog and the running of the AutoExec macro by holding down Shift when you open the database.

A feature new in Access 95 is the capability to prevent bypassing the startup options. You disable the bypass by using an advanced option in the Startup dialog. Choose Tools, Startup to display the Startup dialog, and then press the Advanced button (see fig. 18.6). Clearing the Use Access Special Keys check box disables the bypass of startup conditions. Clearing the Use Access Special Keys check box also disables other key sequences, such as pressing F11 to bring the Database window to the front and Ctrl+F11 to toggle between a custom menu and a built-in menu.

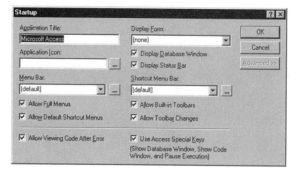

Fig. 18.6 Displaying the advanced options in the Startup dialog.

> **Troubleshooting**
>
> Be careful when you change the Advanced options in the Startup dialog. Changes you make with these options may be irreversible. When you clear both the Allow Full Menus and Use Access Special Keys check boxes, for example, the next time you open the database a reduced set of built-in menus without the Tools, Startup command is displayed. You cannot return to the full built-in menus to change the startup settings, and you will be unable to bypass the startup settings.

Creating Custom Keystroke Shortcuts

You have two ways to create custom keystroke shortcuts—assigning key combinations with an AutoKeys macro and defining access keys.

◄◄ See "Sending Keystrokes With a Macro Action," p. 597

You can assign macros to key combinations by using the AutoKeys macro. When you press a key combination, Access looks first for the AutoKeys macro, and then runs the macro assigned to the combination, if there is one. If you want a particular key combination to be effective only under certain conditions, you can include an expression to test for the preconditions in the Condition column of the AutoKeys macro. The custom keystroke combinations you assign with the AutoKeys macro are available throughout your application.

If you make custom key assignments, you need to communicate the assignments to the user by displaying an instruction label in the header or footer of the task forms, by placing a button on the form or on a toolbar that displays a list of custom key assignments for your application, or by including custom on-line help.

> **Caution**
>
> The macro actions you assign in the AutoKeys macro take precedence over the default Access key assignments. You can assign a macro, for example, to run when you press the default combination for copy, Ctrl+C. However, you should avoid reassigning the default key combinations. Your application is easier to learn and use if it is consistent with the standard Windows defaults, including location of menu commands and keystroke shortcuts.

Another way to provide keyboard stortcuts is to include *access keys* when you design forms and when you create command buttons and custom menus. You can provide a keyboard shortcut as an alternative to clicking a command button. Assign the keystroke combination Alt+*letter*, where *letter* can be any letter in the button's Caption property, by typing the ampersand (&) immediately before the letter in the Caption property. The ampersand-letter combination changes to an underlined letter in Form view. Using an underline to denote an access key that provides a keyboard shortcut (Alt+*underlined letter*) is a standard Windows interface-design convention, which needs no additional instruction.

You also can use access keys for labels associated with controls that can receive the focus. By typing the ampersand (&) immediately before a letter in the label's Caption property, you assign the Alt+letter key combination. Label controls cannot receive the focus. When Access detects that you pressed an Alt+letter combination for a label, Access moves the focus to the next control that can have the focus. When the label is "attached" to a control that can have the focus, Access moves to this control. Figure 18.7 shows a form that uses access keys for both labels and command buttons.

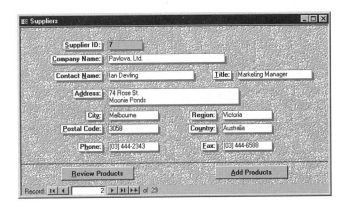

Fig. 18.7   Using access keys for labels and buttons.

Custom Menubars and Shortcut Menus

Access provides a separate built-in menubar, also known as an *Access menubar*, for each view of the database objects. Each menubar includes the menus and menu commands appropriate to the view. Each menu can have one or more commands that have submenus. A command that has a submenu displays a right-pointing arrow symbol. Figure 18.8 shows the details of the built-in menu system. Access also provides built-in shortcut menus (also called *popup* or *context* menus) for each view you display by clicking the right mouse button (see fig. 18.9). In Form view, a separate built-in shortcut menu is available for controls, in addition to the shortcut menu for the form.

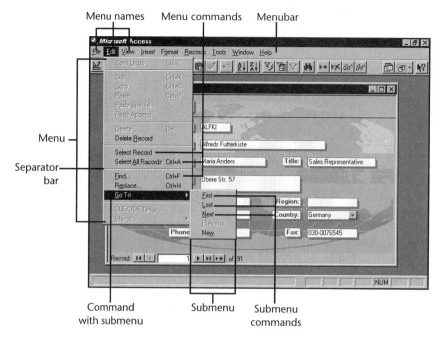

Fig. 18.8 A typical Access built-in menu with a submenu.

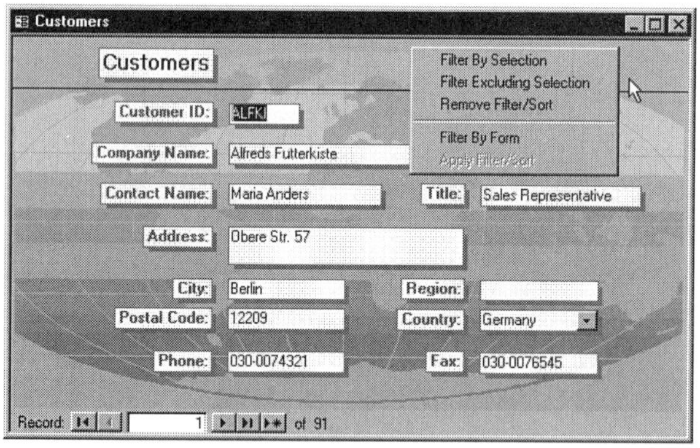

Fig. 18.9 The standard shortcut menu for an Access form.

You can change the display of the menubar in two ways—you can display a special reduced set of built-in menus or you can create custom menubars.

The capability to display a special reduced set of built-in menus is a new feature in Access 95. The reduced set doesn't include commands that enable changing the design of the database and eliminates several other commands that are not essential to working with a particular database. You can use the reduced set when you are creating applications for others to use. You choose the reduced set by clearing the Allow Full Menus check box in the Startup dialog (refer to fig. 18.4). Figure 18.10 shows the reduced built-in menus for Form view.

> **Tip**
>
> After you attach a custom menubar to a form or report, you can switch between the custom menubar and the built-in menubar by pressing Ctrl+F11. If, however, you cleared the Use Access Special Keys check box in the Startup dialog, you will not be able to toggle between the custom and built-in menubars.

You can create custom menubars that include both built-in menu commands and custom commands. You can create individual custom menubars and attach them to specific forms or reports. You can create a global custom menubar that Access displays in all windows of your applications, except for the forms and reports that have individual custom menubars. When you use custom menus, it's important to realize that the built-in menus are merely hidden and still are available, just not active. The DoMenuItem action always refers to the built-in menubars, not to a custom menubar or custom menu command.

New in Access 95 is the capability to create custom shortcut menus. You can create individual custom shortcut menus and attach them to specific forms or reports. You can create a global shortcut menu that Access displays whenever you haven't assigned an individual shortcut menu. Also new in Access 95 is the capability to attach custom shortcut menus to individual controls on forms.

Creating a Custom Menubar

You create custom menubars by using macros. Even if you use Access VBA to automate your database, you must use macros to create custom menubars and shortcut menus. A custom menubar requires the following two kinds of macros:

- A macro for the menubar itself
- A macro group for each of the menus and submenus

The menubar macro specifies which menu names are displayed on the menubar. The menubar macro is stored in its own macrosheet and contains an AddMenu action for each of the menu names. Figure 18.10 shows the menubar macro, named mmnuCustom_Data Entry, for a custom menubar with three menu names. In this example, the File menu contains commands from the built-in File menu, the Edit menu contains commands from the built-in Edit menu, including the Go To command, which has the submenu displayed in figure 18.8, and the Data Entry menu contains custom commands that open the Suppliers and Orders forms.

> **Tip**
>
> To create an access key for a menu, type an ampersand immediately to the left of the letter you want to be the access key when you enter the name of the menu in the MenuName argument of the AddMenu action.

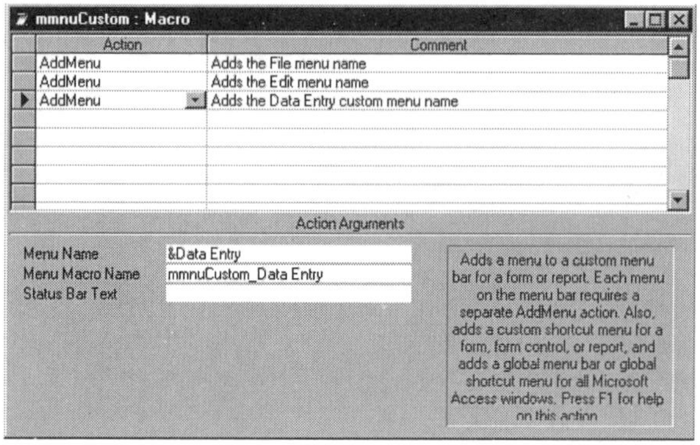

Fig. 18.10 The design of a menubar macro for File, Edit, and Data Entry menus.

Each menu has a macro group that contains a macro for each of the items listed in the menu. The Access convention is to name the macro group, using the menubar name followed by an underscore and the menu name:

    mmnuMenuBarName_MenuName

The menubar in figure 18.10 has the following three macro groups:

    mmnuCustom_File
    mmnuCustom_Edit
    mmnuCustom_Data Entry

Each submenu has a macro group that contains macros for each of the items listed in the submenu. The Access convention is to name a macro group for a submenu associated with a menu command, using the menubar name followed by an underscore, and the menu name followed by an underscore, and the following menu command:

    mmnuMenuBarName_MenuName_MenuCommand

In this example, the macro group for the Go To submenu is named

    mmnuCustom_Edit_GoTo

The macro group for a menu or submenu contains a macro for each of the items on the menu or submenu. In this example, the Edit menu contains only some of the commands from the built-in Edit menu. Figure 18.11 shows the macro group for the Edit menu.

Tip

To create an access key for a menu command, type an ampersand immediately to the left of the letter that you want as the access key when you enter the name of the menu command in the Macro Name column.

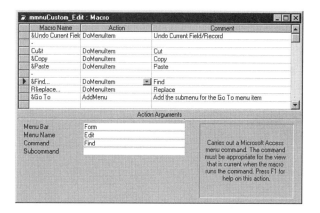

Fig. 18.11 A macro group for the Edit menu name.

Each macro in the macro group corresponds to a menu command. The name of the macro is displayed as a command in the menu. A hyphen in the Macro Name column with a blank Action cell is displayed as a line, known as a *separator bar*, between two menu commands in the menu. Notice that each item listed in the menu—except the separator bars and the Go To menu command—has a macro with a single DoMenuItem action that calls the corresponding built-in menu command. The &Find... macro, for example, runs the built-in Find... command. The Go To menu command has an associated submenu, so the macro for this command has an AddMenu action that adds the submenu to the Go To menu command. Figure 18.12 depicts the &Go To macro arguments and the macro group for the submenu, named mmnuCustom_Edit_GoTo. Each submenu command has a macro with a single DoMenuItem action that calls the corresponding built-in menu command.

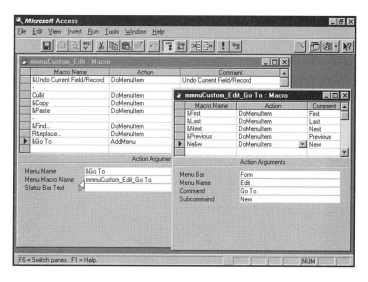

Fig. 18.12 Macros for the Go To submenu.

When a custom menu contains a menu command that calls a built-in menu command, the macro for the command contains the single DoMenuItem action to run the built-in menu command. When a custom menu contains a menu command for a custom command, however, the macro for the menu command contains the macro actions required for the command. Figure 18.13 shows the macro group for the Data Entry menu.

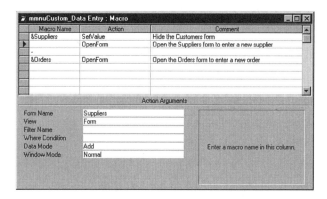

Fig. 18.13 A Macro group for custom menu commands.

> **Note**
>
> If you use the Menu Builder to create or edit custom menubars with custom menu commands, the Menu Builder requires the macro for a custom menu command to consist of a single DoMenuItem, RunMacro, or RunCode action. If you want the command to run a macro that contains several actions, or a single action other than one of the three listed, and you plan to edit the macro with the Menu Builder, create the macro for the command in a separate macrosheet. Then run the macro in the macro group for the menu command, using the RunMacro action.

Using a Custom Menubar

You can display a custom menubar when a specific form or report is active by assigning the custom menubar macro to the Menubar property of the form or report. Figure 18.14 shows the Customers form, with the custom menubar macro mmnuCustom attached. (Notice that the built-in toolbar is hidden in the figure.)

You can display a custom menubar as a global menubar that Access displays whenever the active window doesn't have an individual custom menubar. Use the Startup dialog to assign the global menubar. Click the Menubar down arrow and select the custom menubar macro from the macros displayed in the combo list (see fig. 18.15).

Creating and Using a Custom Shortcut Menu

You create a custom shortcut menu by creating a shortcut menu macro with a single menu and a macro group that contains a macro for each shortcut menu command. Figure 18.16 shows a menu macro and a macro group for a shortcut menu. Because a shortcut menu doesn't have a title bar, the menu name you enter in the MenuName argument of the AddMenu action isn't displayed.

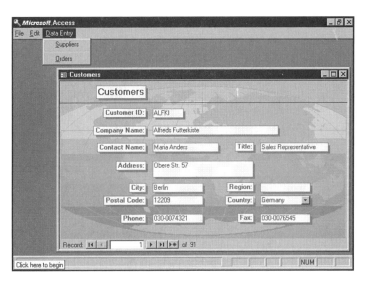

Fig. 18.14 The Customers form with a custom menubar.

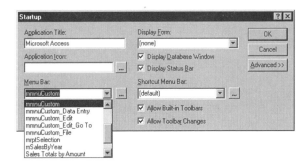

Fig. 18.15 Assigning a global custom menubar.

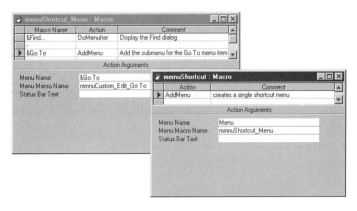

Fig. 18.16 A shortcut menubar macro and macro group.

Assign a custom shortcut menu to a form or report or a control on a form by entering the name of the shortcut menu macro in the ShortcutMenuBar property. Use the Startup dialog to assign a custom global shortcut menu that Access will display for the forms, reports, and controls on forms that don't have custom shortcut menus.

You also can use a custom menubar as a shortcut menu. When you assign a custom menubar macro to the ShortcutMenuBar property of a form, a report, or a control on a form, Access displays the first menu in the menubar. The name of the first menu doesn't appear because a shortcut menu doesn't have a title bar.

Using the Menu Builder

You can use the Menu Builder to create custom menus and custom shortcut menus. You specify the design of a custom menubar by using the Menu Builder dialogs, and then the Menu Builder creates the macros for a custom menubar or custom shortcut menu according to your specifications.

Start the Menu Builder by choosing Tools, Add-ins, Menu Builder. The first Menu Builder dialog displays a list of all macros in the database. To create a new menubar, click the New button. The second Menu Builder dialog displays a list of the built-in menubars (see fig. 18.17). You can either start from scratch by selecting <Empty Menubar> or select one of the built-in menubars to use as a template. Click OK after making a choice to display the New Menubar dialog (see fig. 18.18).

Fig. 18.17 Selecting a new menubar template.

The list box in the lower half of the dialog displays a list of the names that appear in the menubar, menus, and submenus. The symbols preceding each name indicate its role. The symbols indicate the function of each item in the list as shown in table 18.1.

Table 18.1 The Menu Builder Symbols	
Menu Builder Symbol	**Description**
&	The ampersand is placed immediately to the left of a letter to define the access key.
- - -	Indicates a menu command.
- - -_	Indicates a line dividing two menu commands.
- - - - - -	Indicates a submenu command.
- - - - - -_	Indicates a line dividing two submenu commands.

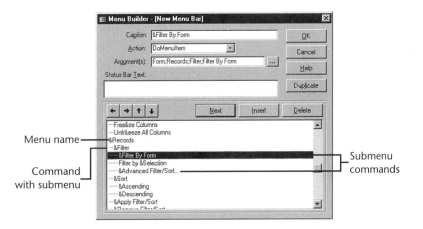

Fig. 18.18 Designing a custom menubar with the Menu Builder.

Use the up and down arrows to move through the list. The level of indentation of an item defines its role in the menubar. Items not indented are menu names. Items at the first level of indentation are menu commands. Items at the second level of indentation are submenu commands. The list in figure 18.18 displays two levels of indentation, but additional levels are possible. Use the left and right arrows to change the level of indentation to define the role of an item. Use the Insert and Delete buttons to insert a new item or delete the selected item. If a command is directly followed by one or more items indented to the next level, that command has a submenu and the indented items are the submenu items.

When an item is selected, the Caption text box in the upper part of the dialog shows the name displayed as a menu name, menu command, or submenu command. Using the Action and Argument edit boxes depends on the item selected, as explained in the following list:

- If the selected item is a menu name (not indented), the Action and Argument edit boxes are disabled (gray color) and by default, Access uses an AddMenu action to create the menu for the menu name.

- If the selected item is a menu command that has indented items immediately below it, the Action and Argument edit boxes are disabled, and Access displays a right-pointing arrow for the menu command and uses an AddMenu action to create the submenu.

- If the selected item is indented at least one level and doesn't have indented items immediately below it, the Action edit box is available. You may select the DoMenuItem, RunMacro, or RunCode action. Select the DoMenuItem action if you want the command to run a built-in menu command. If you choose the DoMenuItem action, click the Build button to set the arguments. If you choose RunMacro or RunCode, enter the name of the macro or the Access VBA function you want the menu command to run.

After you finish designing the custom menubar, click OK. Enter a name for the menubar and click OK. The Menu Builder creates the menubar macro by using the name you entered and creates a macro group for each menu and submenu.

Using the Menu Builder often is the easiest way to create a custom menubar or custom shortcut menu. You can use the Menu Builder to create a custom menubar, and then edit the macros manually. Alternatively, you can create the macros manually and use the Menu Builder to edit them if you follow the Menu Builder's conventions:

- You must use the menu naming conventions described in the last section.

- Each row in the menubar macro must contain an AddMenu action.

- The macros in a macro group must have a single macro action selected from the DoMenuItem, RunMacro, or RunCode actions.

- There can be no blank rows and no rows that contain only comments.

- There can be no conditions.

Only the last restriction represents a significant limitation in the capability of the Menu Builder. A custom menubar that you create manually can include conditions in the menubar macro, but not in a macro group for a menu or a submenu. You can use a condition, for example, to show or hide a menu on the custom menubar only if you create the menubar manually.

Using Custom Toolbars

You can make the database application easier to learn and use by providing toolbars. You can use toolbars in the following ways:

- Toolbars that display button equivalents to the menu commands in your application provide alternate visual access to the commands.

- You can create a custom toolbar to use as the switchboard for your application by providing custom buttons to navigate to the main tasks of the application.

- A form or report can have an individual custom toolbar displayed only when the form or report is active.

Toolbar design is versatile. Built-in toolbars can have both built-in and custom buttons and custom toolbars also can have both built-in and custom buttons. You can display built-in toolbars, a global toolbar, and an individual toolbar for a form or report all at the same time.

Chapter 13, "Designing Custom Multitable Forms," shows how to customize built-in toolbars by adding additional built-in toolbar buttons and how to create a custom toolbar that contains built-in toolbar buttons. Chapter 16, "Understanding Access Macros and Events," shows how to add a custom toolbar button to run a macro. You also can add a custom toolbar button to open a table, query, form, or report by using the method described in Chapter 16. To create a custom toolbar button, for example, to open a form and add it to a built-in or custom toolbar, follow these steps:

1. Choose <u>V</u>iew, <u>T</u>oolbars to display the Toolbars dialog. Make sure the built-in or custom toolbar with which you want to work is displayed.

2. Click the Customize button to open the Customize Toolbars dialog.

3. Select All Forms in the Categories list box.

4. Select the form you want to open and drag the form name to the toolbar. Access places a button on the toolbar with the form icon and with the default ToolTip and Status Bar text Open form "form name" (see fig. 18.19).

5. If desired, customize the button image and the ToolTip and Status Bar text by using the method described in Chapter 16.

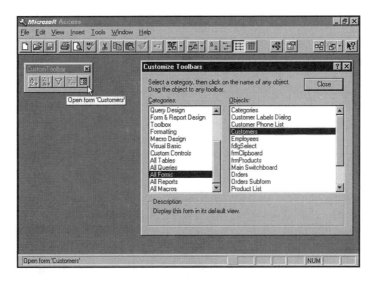

Fig. 18.19   Creating a custom button to open a form.

To display a custom toolbar at all times, choose <u>V</u>iew, <u>T</u>oolbars and select the custom toolbar. You can control the display of both built-in and custom toolbars with the Toolbars dialog. A toolbar that you select in the Toolbars dialog appears when any window is active. You can hide the toolbar for the current view by clearing its check box. To hide the Form view toolbar, for example, open any form in Form view, then open the Toolbars dialog and clear the Form view check box. You can hide all of the built-in toolbars by clearing the Allow Built-in Toolbars check box in the Startup dialog (refer to fig. 18.4).

You use a pair of macros or Access VBA event procedures to attach a toolbar to an individual form or report. For example, create a macro by using the ShowToolbar action to show a custom toolbar when the form becomes active and recognizes the Activate event. Create a second macro that uses the ShowToolbar action to hide the toolbar when the form becomes inactive and recognizes the Deactivate event. Table 18.2 shows the pair of macros to show and hide the toolbar named CustomToolbar.

Table 18.2 A Pair of Macros to Show and Hide a Custom Toolbar			
Macro Name	**Action**	**Argument**	**Argument Setting**
Form_OnActivate	ShowToolbar	Toolbar Name Show	CustomToolbar Yes
Form_OnDeactivate	ShowToolbar	Toolbar Name Show	CustomToolbar No

Using Macros to Work with External Data

Often the data needed in your database exists in a file that was created with Access or with another computer database management program, with a spreadsheet program such as Microsoft Excel, or a word-processing program such as Microsoft Word. Usually, the data isn't in the exact format or doesn't have the exact structure that you need. The imported table, for example, may contain names in a format such as "Jones, Mary" while your database uses separate fields for first names and last names. As another example, the imported table may contain data such as customer order information that your database stores in two separate tables—a customers table and an orders table. You may be able to use the program that generated the data to manipulate the data into a more useful format, or you can bring the raw data into Access and do the necessary manipulation there. In the latter case, there are three steps for bringing external data into your database:

1. Importing the data from an external file into an Access table.

2. Manipulating the imported data into the format and structure required by your database.

3. Adding, or appending, the modified data to one or more tables in your database.

Chapter 7, "Linking, Importing, and Exporting Tables," shows how to import external data into your database. When the imported data must be modified, you usually can use action queries. Use action queries to modify the data in the fields of the imported table, to split a field into two or more fields, and to append the modified data to one or more tables. Chapter 11, "Using Action Queries," shows how to use update queries to modify data and append queries to add records to a table.

Using Macros to Import and Modify Data in a Text File

If bringing data into your database is a routine occurrence, you can automate the process by using macros. You need to work interactively through the entire process of importing, manipulating data, and appending records. Automating the process is a matter of creating macros to duplicate the steps.

An example that illustrates the automation of the process is the Satellite Wild Feeds application. The scenario: a file containing the days and times of unscheduled satellite television programming (called *wildfeeds*) are downloaded on a weekly basis into a fixed-width text file named Wildfeed.txt. Figure 18.20 shows the first few dozen text entries for a specific download of Wildfeed.txt.

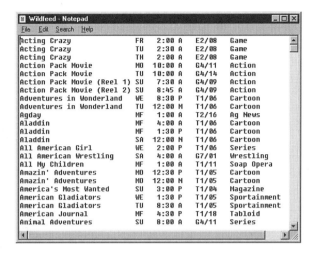

Fig. 18.20 The Wildfeed text file lists the program name, day of week, time (EST), satellite/transponder, and program class in fixed-width format.

Note

You can download a current version of Wildfeed.txt from the Full-Size Satellite library of the Consumer Electronics Video forum (GO CEVIDEO) on CompuServe. Wildfeed.txt includes information on how to subscribe to Gary Bourgois's satellite wildfeeds via an Internet listserver.

Notice there are no column headings. Table 18.3 shows the description of the data, and also the names of the fields in the tblWildFeed table in Wildfeed.mdb that stores the downloaded data after it is imported into the database.

Table 18.3   The WildFeeds Information

Column #	Description	Field names
1	Name of the program	Program_Name
2	Contains either first two letters of the name of the week or MF to stand for every weekday	Days
3	Time (in text format) the program is shown, based on Eastern Satellite Time	EST
4	Single letter code A=AM, P=PM,M=Midnight (00:00) and N=Noon (12:00)	AM_PM
5	Standard 2-character Sat Code/Transponder satellite code followed by a slash and the 2-character transponder number	
6	Type of the program	Program_Type

The following steps show the interactive process:

1. *Importing the data* from the text file into an Access table. You import the down-loaded data into the table tblWildFeed. Because the table stores only the data for the current week, you must empty the table by selecting all of its records and delet-ing them before importing the new data. When you import a file and specify that you are importing a text file, the Text Import Wizard guides you through the pro-cess. In this example, you can use the Wizard to create an import specification that splits the fifth column into a column with the satellite code (stored in the Sat-Code field) and a second column with the transponder number (stored in the Transpon-der field). The specification created for the application is named WildFeed.

2. *Manipulating the imported data* into the form needed by your database. It's necessary to modify the time of broadcast. Two kinds of modifications are required. The downloaded time information is in the text format. The first modification uses the UPDATE query named qryConvertTime to convert the text to time/date format and store the result in another field, called EST_Time, in the tblWildFeed table. The second modification uses two UPDATE queries, qryFixTimePM and qryFixMidnight, to convert the time to the twenty-four-hour clock. The qryFixTimePM query adds 12 to the PM times from 1:00 to 11:59, and the qryFixMidnight query replaces midnight with 00:00.

3. *Adding, or appending, the modified data* to one or more tables in your database. In this example you import the data directly into the tblWildFeed data table and ma-nipulate the data in the table using the update queries in the previous step. There-fore, it is not necessary to append the modified data to another table.

The frmWildFeed form displays the manipulated data and four command buttons that you use to work with the data (see fig. 18.21). The command button labeled Download Data is used to trigger the macro, mfrmWildFeed.cmdDownload_Click, that automates the importing and manipulation of the data.

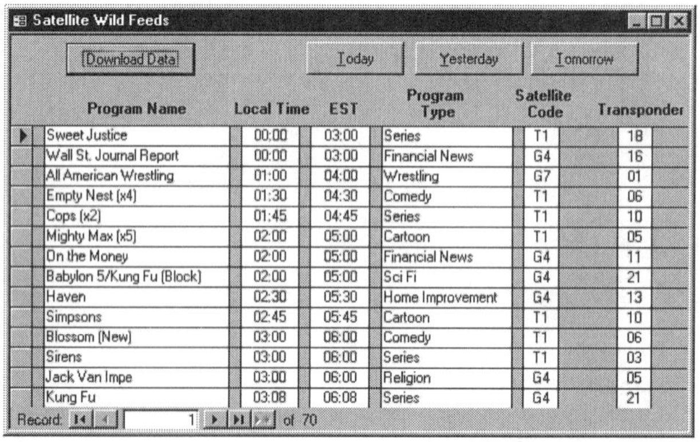

Fig. 18.21 Using the Satellite Wild Feeds form to download and select the data.

Each of the three daily command buttons—labeled Today, Yesterday, and Tomorrow—runs a query to select only the records for the appropriate day. The queries respectively are named `qryTodaysWildFeeds`, `qryYesterdaysWildFeeds`, and `qryTomorrowsWildFeeds`. These queries work by reading the current date on the computer's system clock and determining the day of the week, and then selecting records with the same day of the week from the modified downloaded records. Clicking one of the three buttons runs a macro to set the record source of the frmWildFeed form to the corresponding query. Changing the record source of the active form to a query also runs the query. Table 18.4 shows the macro that imports and manipulates the data and table 18.5 shows the macros for the daily command buttons.

Table 18.4   The cmdDownload_Click Macro to Automate the Importing and Modification of Downloaded Data

Action	Argument	Argument Setting	Comment
SetWarnings	Warnings On	No	Turn off system message boxes
Echo	Echo On Status Bar Text	No Recreating Wild Feeds table	Turn off screen updates
Open Table	Table Name	tblWildFeed	Open the tblWildFeed table
DoMenuItem	Menu Bar Menu name Command	Form Edit Select All Records	Select all tblWildFeed records
DoMenuItem	Menu Bar Menu name Command	Form Edit Delete	Delete the selected records
Close	Object Type Object name	Table tblWildFeed	Close the tblWildFeed table
TransferText	Transfer Type Specification Name Table Name File Name Has Field Names	Import Fixed Width WildFeed tblWildFeed wildfeed.txt No	Import the fixed width text file named Wildfeed.txt using the specification named WildFeed... into the table named tblWildFeed
OpenQuery	Query Name	qryConvertTime	Add entries with time/date format to the time/date field
OpenQuery	Query Name	qryFixTimePM	Add 12 hours to PM entries except 12:xx

(continues)

Table 18.4	Continued		
Action	**Argument**	**Argument Setting**	**Comment**
OpenQuery	Query Name	qryFixMidnight	Subtract 12 hours from midnight entries (12:00 to 00:00)
Requery			Requery the frmWildFeed form to display the new data

Table 18.5	The Macros to Change the Record Source of the Form	
Macro Name	**Action**	**Argument Argument Setting**
cmdToday_Click	SetValue	Item Forms!frmWildFeed.RecordSource Expression "qryTodaysWildFeeds"
cmdYesterday_Click	SetValue	Item Forms!frmWildFeed.RecordSource Expression "qryYesterdaysWildFeeds"
cmdTomorrow_Click	SetValue	Item Forms!frmWildFeed.RecordSource Expression "qryTomorrowsWildFeeds"

Finally, the Satellite Wild Feeds application uses the Startup dialog to display the frmWildFeed form when the database first opens. The Database Explorer window is not hidden so that you can explore the application on your own.

Troubleshooting Macro Errors

Like other forms of programming, building macros is a continuous process of testing and refining. Building a macro usually begins with creating a simple macro, checking to ensure that it works, and then adding more actions to it. You repeat this process until the macro is complete. The process continues from simple to complex functionality. At each stage, the macro operation is checked so that problems can be resolved while they are small. This section describes some troubleshooting aids available in Access and gives you tips about how to resolve problems.

There are three kinds of macro errors:

> **Tip**
>
> Using the Expression Builder when you create macro conditions and action arguments can help to avoid misspelling object names.

Syntax errors occur when you are creating a macro in the macrosheet and you violate one of the Access syntax rules. When you misspell a macro action or omit a parenthesis in an argument, for example, Access recognizes the error immediately and displays a default error message. Access finds most syntax errors automatically. Note that Access doesn't recognize misspellings of any of the objects you have named yourself as syntax errors.

Run-time errors occur when some condition makes it impossible for Access to run a macro action. If for example, you misspell the name of an object in an action argument, Access won't find an object with the misspelled name and can't execute the action. As another example, if you include the `Close` action to close a form that isn't open, Access won't be able to run the action.

Logic errors occur when the macro runs but doesn't give the result you intended. Logic errors occur for a variety of reasons, such as the following:

- Using the wrong operator, for example, using > when the operator should be <

- Referring to the wrong field or control

- Using the wrong macro action, or the wrong sequence of actions

- Trapping the wrong event

Handling a Failed Macro

When a macro reaches an error that causes it to halt operation, Access displays a default error message, and then displays an Action Failed dialog (refer to fig. 16.17 in Chapter 16, "Understanding Access Macros and Events"). The Action Failed dialog shows the name of the macro that failed, the action on which it failed, and the arguments for the action. Note the macro name and action that caused the problem. Note also which form or report is displayed and what action was occurring on-screen; you may find a clue to why the action failed. Click the Halt button.

Switch to the macrosheet of the macro that failed. Examine the action that failed. Some areas to check are whether the action matched the displayed view and object at the time of failure, whether the logic is correct for the procedure the macro was attempting, and whether the data in the arguments is correct.

Single-Stepping through Macro Execution

When a macro fails either with the Action Failed dialog or with a logic error, the cause of the problem may not be readily apparent. Operating the macro one step at a time often helps. This process enables you to see clearly what is happening on-screen, which view is present, and what characters are sent with the `SendKeys` action. To run a macro by using the single-step method, follow this procedure:

1. Open the macrosheet.

2. Choose <u>R</u>un, <u>S</u>ingle Step, or click the Single Step button on the Macro toolbar.

3. Arrange the screen and database system, as it appears when the macro runs.

4. Run the macro with the required window active. Depending on the macro, you may need to run the macro either with a specific form or report active or from the macrosheet. Chapter 17, "Using Macros with Forms and Reports," shows the ways you can run a macro in conjunction with forms and reports.

In single-step mode, the macro displays a Macro Single Step dialog before each action. After a single-step mode is turned on, it stays on until you turn it off. Figure 18.22 shows a Macro Single Step dialog. This dialog is similar to the Action Failed dialog, but the Step and Continue buttons are available.

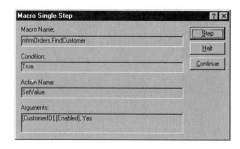

Fig. 18.22   The Macro Single Step dialog lets you step through your macro a line at a time.

Choosing the Step button runs the action displayed in the dialog, and then stops at the next action and displays this action in the dialog. If an expression is in the Condition column for the action, the Macro Single Step dialog displays whether the condition is True or False. If one of the arguments involves an expression, the dialog displays the result of the expression.

When the macro reaches a point at which you want it to continue without stepping through each action, choose the Continue button. The macro then runs at normal speed, without stopping before each action.

Troubleshooting Common Macro Problems

The troubleshooting tips in this section may help you more quickly correct problems with your macros.

Make Sure the Correct Object Is Active. When a macro runs, and then halts with the warning that a database object or control isn't available, the macro probably hasn't activated the correct database object or the object name may be misspelled or missing from the database.

◄◄ See "Avoiding Errors by Anticipating Preconditions," p. 639

This error commonly happens when the macro needs to run with a specific form active. The macro, for example, looks for a control that doesn't exist on the active object. To prevent this situation, get in the habit of testing to see if a form is open using the IsLoaded() custom function. Alternatively, you can use an Open... action or a

`SelectObject` action to open or activate the proper form, query, table, or report before the macro runs. Check the spelling of all control and database object names.

Display All Actions During a Single-Step Operation. Change the argument of all `Echo` actions so that you can see screen changes while running with Single Step.

Using the `Echo` action with the `Echo On` argument of `No` hides screen changes. This action prevents you from seeing what happens during a single-step operation. Change the `No` argument to `Yes` to see what the macro is doing. After you find and resolve the problem, change the value of the `Echo On` argument from `Yes` to `No`.

> **Tip**
>
> For another technique of tricking an `Echo` action into not running, type **False** in the Condition column next to the `Echo` action that you don't want to run.

Alert Yourself to Critical Points in Operation. Insert message boxes at critical points in a macro to announce what the macro is doing at these points.

A message box, created with the `MsgBox` action, can display which portion of the macro is ready to run or what should happen on-screen. This capability enables you to run the macro at normal operating speed and receive notices about which operations are taking place.

The message can display either a simple "Got to here" message or the value of a control. To display the value of an object in a message, use an equal sign in the Message argument, followed by a concatenation of text strings and control or object names. The following lines show examples of Message arguments to display the value in a control and a property of a form:

```
="The value in the Amount control is " & [Amount]

="The record source of the active form is " & Forms!frmFormName.RecordSource
```

Insert Breaks to Check Intermediary Results. Insert a `StopMacro` action so that you can run a macro at normal speed and stop at a specific point.

If a long macro takes a while to run, you may not want to single-step through its actions to the point where you suspect a problem. Rather, insert a `StopMacro` action after the action you suspect is causing the problem. You then can run the macro at normal speed. When it stops, check results to see whether the macro worked correctly to this point. Move the `StopMacro` action forward or backward in the macro to pinpoint the area that causes a problem. As an alternative to the `StopMacro` action, you can enter a dummy name, such as **Break**, in the Macro Name column to stop the macro.

You can use a condition in the Condition column to stop the macro for a specific condition. A condition can check the value of a control, for example, and stop the macro if the value is incorrect. Additionally, you can prevent a specific action from executing by entering False in the Condition column.

Use Segments of Reusable Macros. Learn to write reusable macros or to write large macros as collections of smaller macros. Run the reusable or small segments with the RunMacro action.

Troubleshooting a small macro is easier than troubleshooting a large one. If you build small subroutine macros that work correctly, you can join them into a larger macro by running them in the order you want with the RunMacro action. Use comments at the beginning of subroutine macros to document which larger macros or events call the subroutine. This practice helps if you have to change the subroutine. The comments help you determine how changes to the macro may affect other parts of the database.

Monitor How the Macro Is Related to other Macros and Objects. Take care in changing macros that may be used in numerous locations.

After changing a macro that seems to work correctly, other parts of your database may not work correctly. The macro you changed may have been used by other parts of the database application. Changing the macro to meet the requirements for one part of the program may change it so that it doesn't work correctly in another part of the program.

Watch that SendKeys Sends Characters to the Correct Location. If you see menus pull down by themselves, or if data is entered as though it is being typed by a ghost, you have an errant SendKeys action.

SendKeys sends keystrokes to Access just as though you are typing the keys. If the Wait argument is set incorrectly or if there is no dialog that opens to receive the sent keys, the keystrokes may be sent directly to the menubar or into a form, just as though you had typed them.

Be Careful about the Full Macro Name. If only one macro from a macro group runs, check the macro name.

If you specify only the name of a macrosheet, only the first macro in the macro group runs. To run a specific macro in a group, you must specify the macro group name, a period, and the name of the specific macro in the group. The syntax for performing this technique is shown in the following line:

    MacroGroupName.MacroName

When you copy a macro action to another macro or when you copy a macro group to a new database, the action arguments don't change. In its new environment, arguments such as form, query, or control names may be different. Check the arguments. Although the actions may be in the correct order, the arguments may be wrong.

Limiting the Use of Macros in Run-Time Applications

Minimize the number of macros you employ in applications that run with applications you plan to create with the run-time version of Access, which is part of the Microsoft Access Developer's Toolkit described in Chapter 31, "Using the Access Developer's Toolkit." If an error occurs during the execution of a macro under run-time Access, the Action Failed dialog doesn't appear. Rather, your application unceremoniously quits without warning. It takes a major testing effort to ensure that all your macros are *bullet-proof*, especially in complex macro-driven applications.

An application ideally designed for use with run-time Access should include only menubar macros with the necessary `AddMenu` actions to create the custom menubars and menu choice macros that your application needs. You cannot execute the `AddMenu` action with a `DoCmd AddMenu` instruction in Access VBA.

All macro actions or their equivalents—except for `RunCode`, `StopMacro`, `StopAllMacros`, and `AddMenu`—are available in Access VBA. You should convert all other macros in your application to their equivalent in Access VBA code. Re-create each macro as an Access VBA function, and then substitute `=FunctionName( )` for the `MacroGroup.MacroName` entry in the text box for the event to which the macro is attached. Substituting Access VBA for macros also aids in documenting your application—you can print your Access VBA code. The macro documentation created by the Database Documentor is not as convenient as code; furthermore, you cannot use the Documentor to edit macros.

Each Access VBA function you substitute for macros must include full error trapping with **On Error GoTo** *LabelName* statements and corresponding labels. In Chapter 27, the "Handling Run-Time Errors" section shows how to write error-handling routines. Untrapped errors in Access Basic functions and procedures also cause abrupt exits from applications that run under run-time Access.

> **Note**
>
> New in Access 95 is the capability to convert macros to Access VBA event procedures or modules that carry out the same tasks, using VBA code. To convert all the macros assigned to events recognized by a form and by the controls on the form, choose <u>T</u>ools, <u>M</u>acros, <u>C</u>onvert Form's Macros to Visual Basic while the form is in Design view. You can choose to include macro comments and to have Access create code for simple error handling. In the conversion process, Access creates the equivalent event procedure for each macro and assigns it automatically to the same event that triggered the macro. To convert macros that are not assigned to a specific form or report, select the macro in the Database Explorer, choose <u>F</u>ile, <u>S</u>ave As. Click Save As Visual Basic Module to convert the macro to an Access VBA module.

Documenting Macros

You can create a report to document your macros. Choose <u>T</u>ools, <u>A</u>nalyze, <u>D</u>ocumentor to display a dialog for choosing the database objects you want to document (see fig. 18.23). Select Macros in the combo list, and then select the macrosheets for the report. You can select all objects in a category by clicking the Select All button.

After you finish selecting objects, click the OK button. Access prepares a report that documents the selected objects. Figure 18.24 shows a part of the report to document the ValidateID macro in Northwind.mdb. You can print the report, but you can't modify the report or save it as an Access report.

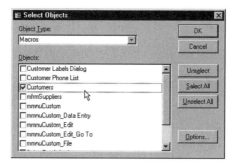

Fig. 18.23 Using Select Objects to choose objects to document.

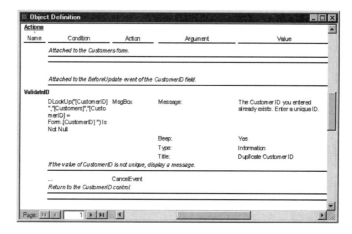

Fig. 18.24 Using the Documentor to document a macro.

From Here...

This chapter showed several of the more advanced macro features available in Access. You learned how to control the way a database starts up and how to control the user interface with custom menus and toolbars. You learned how to use macros to automate the process of importing and manipulating data from an another file. Finally, you learned how to troubleshoot a macro that isn't working as intended and how to document macros with the Documentor.

With the knowledge gained in the three chapters of Part IV, you can create a fully automated database application by using macros. To learn more about exchanging data with other applications or about using Access VBA to add error handling or the other features available only by using Access VBA, you can turn to the following chapters:

- Chapter 21, "Using Access with Microsoft Excel," describes how to embed or link Excel spreadsheets in tables, forms, and reports.

■ Chapter 22, "Using Access with Microsoft Word and Mail Merge," shows how to use Access data to provide information automatically to Work documents.

■ Chapter 28, "Writing Visual Basic for Applications Code," describes how to use Access 95's new programming language.

IV

Access with Macros

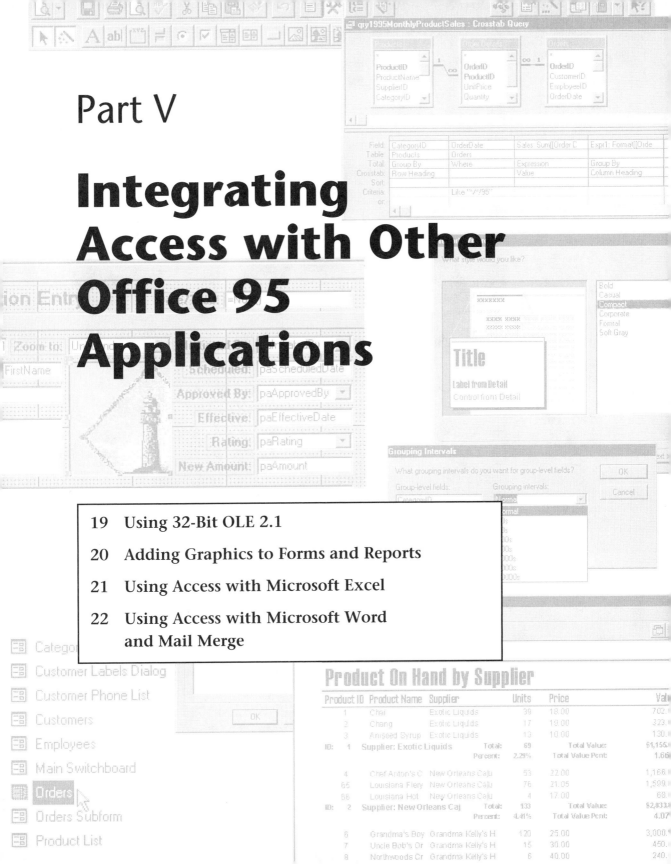

Part V

Integrating Access with Other Office 95 Applications

Using 32-Bit OLE 2.1

Windows 95 and Windows NT 3.51 introduce 32-bit *Object Linking and Embedding* (OLE, pronounced as the Spanish ¡olé!) 2.1 to the PC. The new 7.0 versions of members of the Microsoft Office 95 suite, Access 95 (in the Professional Edition only), Excel 95, Word 95, and PowerPoint 95 provide a variety of new capabilities with OLE 2.1. OLE is a method of transferring information in the form of *objects* between different Windows applications. This method is similar in concept to, although more sophisticated than, copying text or graphics to the Clipboard and pasting the copied text or graphic to other applications.

OLE 2.+ is based on Microsoft's *Component Object Model* (COM), which is likely to become the *de facto* industry standard for object-oriented application programming in the Windows environment. This chapter introduces you to the principles of OLE and how your Access 95 applications can take advantage of the features offered by 32-bit OLE 2.1.

Understanding the Importance of OLE

Understanding OLE principles is important because OLE is the sole method by which you can add graphic images to your Access forms and reports and add or edit data in OLE Object fields of Access. Using OLE as the method of applying and storing non-text information holds the following advantages over built-in graphics processing offered by some RDBMSs:

- You can use any image-processing application that functions as an OLE server to create and edit bitmapped graphics: from the simple Windows 95 Paint application to photographic-quality editors, such as Adobe Photoshop and Corel PhotoPAINT.

- You can embed or link vector-based images from template-based OLE servers, such as Visio 4.0, or from professional illustration packages, such as CorelDRAW! 6.0— both 32-bit OLE 2.1 servers designed for Windows 95. Access 95 also supports 16-bit OLE 2.0 servers. Microsoft Chart 5.0, called MSGraph5 in this book, is included with Access 95; MSGraph5 is the same 16-bit OLE 2.0 server applet included with Access 2.0.

- The added overhead associated with bitmap editors incorporated in the application is eliminated. Self-contained bitmap editors and drawing functions are seldom as capable as stand-alone, shrink-wrapped OLE server applications.

- You don't need to install a collection of import and export filters for different kinds of files. OLE server applications provide file import from, and export to, a variety of file types.

- You can export objects stored in OLE Object fields in Access tables or stored within bound or unbound object frames to other applications via the Clipboard. Bound object frames display the presentation of OLE objects stored in OLE Object fields of Access tables. Unbound object frames display the presentation of static OLE objects, such as company logos used to embellish forms and reports.

- You can store a variety of OLE objects in one OLE Object field. You can link or embed in one OLE Object field waveform audio (.WAV), MIDI music (.MID), animation (.FLI and .MMM), and audio/video interleaved (.AVI) files. You need a large-capacity fixed disk to embed .AVI and long-duration .WAV files, however.

- You can choose between embedding the data within a table, form, or report and linking the OLE object to a file that contains the data. The behavior of an OLE 2.1 object differs, depending on whether you link or embed an object.

The most common kinds of OLE objects used in Access applications are 16-color and 256-color embedded bitmap graphic images. Figure 19.1 shows a portion of a page from the Northwind Traders Catalog report that includes an embedded bitmap image. The image is a Windows 95 Paint bitmap embedded by OLE in the Picture field of the Categories table.

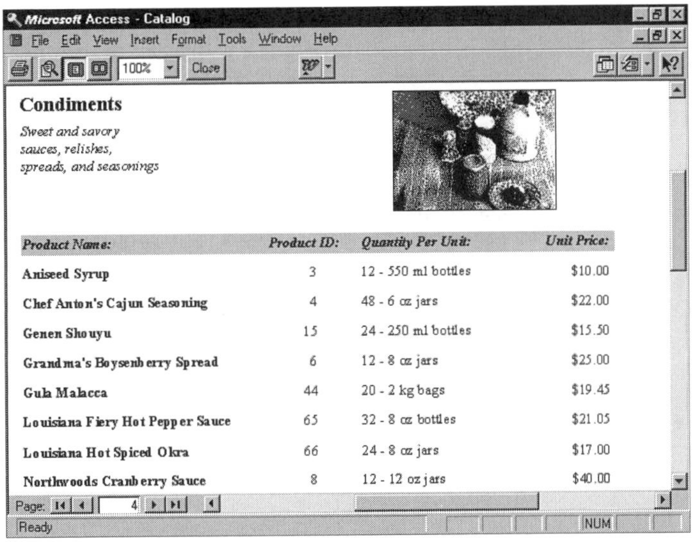

Fig. 19.1 A part of one page of the Northwind Traders Catalog report in print preview mode.

Defining OLE

OLE is a member of a class of computer operations known as *interprocess communication* (IPC). IPC operations enable different applications to send data to, and receive data from, other applications by an agreed-on procedure. The Clipboard is the primary IPC path for Windows; most present-day communication of data between running applications (other than by reading or writing to disk files) involves using the Windows Clipboard.

Windows defines a set of standard data types that you can copy to, or paste from, the Clipboard. OLE uses these standard Windows data types: bitmapped and vector-based graphic images, plain and formatted text, digital audio sound, and so on. You may have used (or tried to use) dynamic data exchange (DDE) as an IPC method to transfer data between Windows applications. OLE is a major improvement over DDE because OLE is easier to implement than DDE. OLE 2.1+ is expected to replace DDE ultimately.

OLE operations differ from conventional Windows copy-and-paste operations—performed with Ctrl+C and Ctrl+V or by way of DDE—because OLE includes a substantial amount of information about the source of the data, along with the actual data. An OLE object copied to the Clipboard by Excel 95, for example, includes the following information:

- The name of the application from which the data originated (in this case, Excel).

- The type of data, such as worksheet, macro sheet, or chart (Excel worksheet).

- The full path to the file, beginning with the drive letter and the file name, if the data is derived from a file or was saved to a file.

- A name assigned to the sheet or chart that contains the data, if the data isn't derived from or saved to a file. The name usually is a long combination of numbers and letters.

- The name or coordinates of the range of the data, if only a portion of an object is included.

- The presentation of the object in Windows Metafile Format (.WMF). If the object is not an image, the icon of the application that created the object is the object's presentation.

 - For file-based OLE 2.1 objects, a set of property values obtained from entries in the property pages of the Properties sheet for the file (see fig. 19.2).

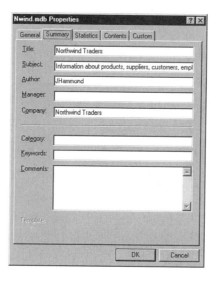

Fig. 19.2   The Summary page of the Properties sheet for Northwind.mdb.

Note

All file-based OLE 2.1-compliant server applications that qualify for the "Designed for Windows 95" logo have a File, Properties menu command that opens a standard Properties page for the file. You can edit the property values of the Summary and Custom pages; values in the General, Statistics, and Contents pages are read-only. Only documents created by OLE 2.1 servers appear as choices of the Start, Documents menu.

When you paste data copied to the Clipboard from an Excel worksheet and then double-click the cell's surface, Excel pops up to enable you to edit the data and disappears when you finish. With OLE, you paste complete objects, rather than just data, into an element of the application.

Classifying OLE 2.1-Compliant Applications

32-bit OLE 2.1-compliant applications fall into the following six categories:

- *Container applications.* These applications, such as Access 95, are stand-alone products that are capable of linking or embedding objects created by other 16-bit and 32-bit OLE 2+-compliant applications. Container applications, however, cannot create OLE objects for linking to, or embedding in, other OLE 2.0 applications. OLE container applications also are called *OLE client applications.*

- *Server-only applications.* These stand-alone applications create OLE objects for embedding in, and linking to, other applications, but you cannot embed an OLE object in, or link an OLE object to, them.

- *Mini-server applications.* Mini-servers (also called OLE applets) are similar to server-only applications, but mini-servers are not stand-alone products. You can execute an OLE mini-server only from within an OLE container application. MSGraph5 is an OLE 2.0 mini-server.

- *Full-server applications.* OLE full-servers are stand-alone applications that are capable of creating OLE objects for use by other applications and can embed or link objects created by other OLE servers. Excel 95, Word 95, and Project 4.1 are OLE 2.1 full-servers.

- *OLE Automation-compliant applications.* OLE Automation (OA) lets an OLE 2+ container application manipulate an embedded or linked object by sending programming instructions to the OLE 2+ server that created it. OA server applications are said to create *programmable objects.* Access 95 is an OA server, but not a conventional OLE 2.0 server, because you cannot embed Access 95 objects in 32-bit container applications. Excel 95 and Project 4.1 are both OA-compliant container and server applications. Word 95 has limited, but useful, OA server capabilities. OLE Automation client applications, such as Access 95, use their programming language to send instructions to programmable objects. Using OLE Automation is the subject of Chapter 30, "Exchanging Data with OLE Automation and DDE."

▶▶See "Adding OLE Custom Controls to Your Application," p. 1088

- *OLE Controls.* One of the advantages of Visual Basic as a Windows programming environment has been its extensibility through custom controls (called VBXs, Visual Basic eXtensions). Microsoft and third-party software publishers supply a variety of specialized custom control objects for Visual Basic 3.0, including mini-spreadsheets, image editors, and report writers. Access 2.0 was the first product to offer extensibility through OLE Controls (OCXs, OLE Control eXtensions). Access 95 and Visual Basic 4.0 support 32-bit OLE Controls, and the 16-bit version of Visual Basic accommodates both 16-bit OCXs and VBXs. You can expect a wide variety of 32-bit OLE Controls to become available to extend the usefulness of Access 95 forms.

> **Note**
>
> Server-only, mini-server, and full-server OLE applications collectively are called *local servers*, be-cause these OLE servers must reside on the same PC as the OLE client application. The Professional Edition of Visual Basic 4.0 lets you create *Remote Automation Objects* (RAOs), a special type of OLE server that can reside on a network server and communicate with OLE client applications on net-worked workstations. You also can create with Visual Basic 4.0 *in-process* OLE servers. These special types of OLE servers are discussed briefly in Chapter 30, "Exchanging Data with OLE Automation and DDE."

Introducing Object Building Blocks

When the term *object* is used in conjunction with a computer application or program-ming language, the term doesn't refer to a tangible object, such as a rock, a saxophone, or a book. Objects in computer programming and applications are intangible representa-tions (called *abstractions*) of real-world objects.

A computer object combines properties, such as the properties you assign to an Access control object in a form or report, and methods that define the behavior of the object. Text box properties—such as text the box contains, the size, typeface, and font the text uses, and the colors and borders employed—vary widely. The ways text box controls behave when you type new text or edit existing text are the methods associated with text box objects of forms and reports. All text boxes in Windows applications use similar, but not identical, methods.

Properties and Methods Encapsulated in Objects

A musical instrument, such as a saxophone, can serve as an example of a tangible object that has an intangible representation: sound. Some properties of a saxophone are size (soprano, alto, tenor, bass, and baritone), kind of fingering, materials of construction, and the name of the instrument's manufacturer.

The methods applicable to saxophones are the techniques used to play these instru-ments: blowing into the mouthpiece, biting the reed, and fingering the keys that deter-mine the note that you play.

If you create a programming object that simulates all the properties and all the methods of a particular kind of saxophone, and have the proper audio hardware for a computer, you can create an object that imitates the sound of Charlie Parker's, Art Pepper's, or Stan Getz's style. Stanford University's new WaveGuide acoustic synthesis computer programs create objects capable of this kind of imitation. The properties of a particular saxophone and the methods of the artist playing it are said to be encapsulated in a particular kind of saxophone object. The object acts as a container for the properties and methods that constitute the object.

One more item is found in the container of an OLE object: *presentation*. Presentation is how the user perceives the object—how the object looks or sounds. The presentation of a WaveGuide saxophone is a musical sound. If the saxophone object is used in a Windows 95 application, the sound probably is reproduced through digital audio techniques by an audio adapter card. The presentation of a large graphic image may be a miniature copy, called a *thumbnail*.

At first glance, presentation may appear to be a property. Presentation isn't a property in the true sense, however, because the presentation of an object is dependent on factors outside the object, such as the kind of hardware available, the computer operating system used, and the application in which the object is employed. The presentation of a 256-color bitmap on a 16-color VGA display, for example, is quite different from its presentation on a 256-color display driver.

Object-Enabled Applications

Applications and the programming languages—which also are applications—that programmers used to create these applications are object-enabled if the applications can encapsulate properties and methods within an object container. Before object-enabled programming was developed, programmers considered properties and methods as two separate entities. Programmers wrote code that defined the methods of an application. Separate data files contained the properties that the programmer's application manipulated. A classic example of this separation is Xbase; a set of .DBF files contains properties (data), and a separate collection of .PRG files contains the methods (programs) applicable to the set of .DBF files.

In contrast to the conventional programming technique, Access takes an object-enabled approach to database management. Access combines the data (tables) and the methods (queries, forms, reports, macros, and Access VBA code) in a single, often massive .mdb container, known as the Database object. Form and Report objects act as containers for Control objects. QueryDef objects consist of Structured Query Language (SQL) methods applied to Table or other QueryDef objects. Although lacking some characteristics of a truly object-oriented programming language (OOPL), Access VBA comes close enough to the mark that you can consider Access VBA to be an object-enabled application programming language.

The Advantages of Objects

Combining properties and methods into an object and then adding a standard presentation provides the following advantages to users of—and the programmers who create—applications:

- Objects combine data (properties) and the program code that deals with the data (methods) into one object that you can treat as a black box. You need not understand the internal elements of the box to use a box in an application. This characteristic of objects aids in the programming of large-scale applications in which many programmers participate. You can modify an object without affecting how the object is used by other programmers.

- Objects can be reused when needed. You can create and use a library of objects in many programs or applications. If you create a library of vector-based images created by CorelDRAW! in an Access table, for example, you can edit these images from within Access and then save a copy of the edited drawing in a separate file.

- Objects can be used with any Windows application that supports OLE 2+. You can use the same graphic or sound object with Access, Excel, or Word. If you copy an embedded drawing in an Excel spreadsheet to the Clipboard, you can paste the drawing as an unbound object in an Access form or report, or into a data cell of an OLE Object field in a table.

- Objects are easy to create with OLE. If you copy all or a portion of the data you create in an OLE-compliant application, you create a temporary OLE object in the Clipboard.

Object Classes, Types, Hierarchies, and Inheritance

Programming objects, like real-world objects, are organized in hierarchies of classes and subclasses and in types that have no subclasses. The hierarchy of classes of musical instrument synthesis objects is shown in figure 19.3 (the subclasses are shown for woodwinds only). At the top of the hierarchical structure, you see the master class, Simulated Musical Instruments, for example, that defines the presentation of all the subclasses as digital audio sound.

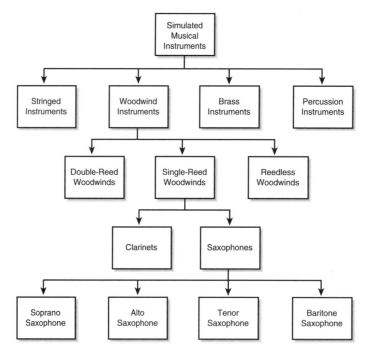

Fig. 19.3 A hierarchy diagram of objects that represents the sound of simulated musical instruments.

Musical instruments are classified by the method used to create their sounds. Saxophones are members of the general woodwind class, which you can further subclass as single-reed woodwinds (refer to fig. 19.3). Single-reed woodwinds include clarinets and saxophones and share many playing methods. Saxophones can be subclassed further by size and the musical key in which these instruments play. At the bottom of the hierarchy are types that have no further subclasses.

A B-flat (tenor) saxophone has a unique set of property values (data), but the kinds of properties are common to all saxophones. Similarly, the tenor saxophone's playing methods are common to all saxophones. The tenor saxophone type inherits both the methods and the list of properties from the saxophone subclass, which in turn inherits properties from the single-reed woodwind class. Parent classes are a level above child classes in the genealogy of classes, and siblings are members of the same class or type. Access uses the term *Master* to indicate a parent class object and *Child* to indicate a descendent of the parent class, as in the Link Master Fields and Link Child Fields properties of subform and subreport controls.

▶▶ See "Understanding Objects and Object Collections," p. 1045

Figure 19.4 illustrates the hierarchy of the objects within Access that are described up to this point in the book. `Table`, `Form`, and `Report` objects have distinctive properties and methods. `Form` and `Report` objects share the same group of `Control` objects, but some `Control` objects have different behavior when contained in `Form` or `Report` objects.

Queries (called `QueryDef` objects) aren't true objects; `QueryDef` objects comprise a set of methods applied to `Table` objects. `Control` objects can be classified further into bound and unbound `Control` objects. Only object frames can incorporate OLE objects, and only a bound object frame can display or provide access to editing capability for OLE data in tables or queries without resorting to Access VBA code.

The `Control` objects in Access inherit some methods from the object that contains the control objects. Subform and subreport controls inherit all related methods and many properties from `Form` and `Report` objects, respectively. OLE child objects inherit a large number of their properties and methods from the parent OLE class that defines how OLE objects behave (or should behave). Each OLE child, however, has a complement of properties and methods that apply only to that child. OLE object subclasses at the bottom of figure 19.4 aren't types because each subclass may have different OLE object types. The Bitmapped Graphic Class, for example, may include Paintbrush Picture, CorelPhotoPAINT Picture, and PicturePublisher Picture OLE object types.

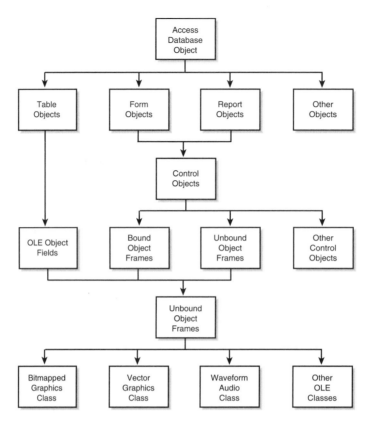

Fig. 19.4 A simplified hierarchy of database objects in Access.

Containing Objects in Other Objects

OLE is designed to allow a single *container document* to be built with contributions, known as *source documents,* from foreign applications. (Container documents were *destination documents* in OLE 1.0 terminology.) The container document may be created by most applications that are OLE compliant; Access forms and reports, proposals created in Word for Windows, Excel worksheets, and PowerPoint presentation visuals are common container documents.

When more than one application contributes to the content of a document, the document is referred to as *compound*. The application that creates the compound document is the OLE container application (formerly OLE client), and the foreign applications that contribute source documents to the compound document are OLE servers. Access 95 is an OLE 2.1 client and creates the compound container documents; Access forms, reports, and tables that incorporate OLE objects are compound documents.

Each source document created with OLE servers and contributed to a container document is an individual, identifiable object that possesses properties, behavior, and has its own presentation. You can choose to *embed* the source document within an Access container document that acts as a container for one or more source document objects. Embedding includes the object's data in the source document. You also can link the source document; in this case, the data resides in a separate file. The difference between embedding and linking objects is the subject of the next section.

> **Note**
>
> OLE 1.0 let you *activate* an embedded or linked object within the container document, but you could not activate any objects contained within the first embedded or linked object. (To activate an OLE object means to open the object for editing in the source application.) OLE 2+ eliminates this restriction. Thus, if you embed a Word 95 document containing an embedded Excel 95 worksheet in the OLE object field of an Access table, you can activate the Word document in Word 95 and then activate the worksheet object in Excel 95. There is no limit on how deeply you can nest embedded or linked OLE 2+ objects.

Whether you embed or link the source document, the code to perform the server's methods isn't incorporated in the compound document. Consider the size of an Access table that contains several copies of Excel.exe. Instead, the server's methods are incorporated by a reference to the application's name, known as the OLE type, in the source document. You need a local copy of the server application that created the source document to edit an embedded source document or to display most linked source documents. Information about OLE server applications is incorporated in your Windows 95 or Windows NT Registry, which takes the place of Windows 3.1's registration database file, REG.DAT. The importance of the Registry to OLE 2+ is explained in "The Windows 95 Registry" section at the end of this chapter.

Understanding Differences between OLE and DDE

If you previously used dynamic data exchange (DDE) between Windows applications, OLE gives you the opportunity to add a new dimension to DDE operations. The differences between OLE and DDE techniques to transfer data are illustrated by figure 19.5. DDE transfers data (properties) from the server to Access text boxes, labels, or other controls that can accommodate text and numbers; OLE transfers data and methods from the server only to unbound or bound object frames.

 See "Using DDE Links with Excel," p. 799

Access includes a function, DDE(), that you can use to create a DDE link to data in any Windows application with DDE server capability. To fully explore the capabilities of DDE with Access, you need to write an Access VBA function or procedure that includes a series of DDE functions, beginning with DDEInitiate(). You then execute the Access VBA subprocedure from the OnClick event of a command button or the function from a RunCode action in an Access macro.

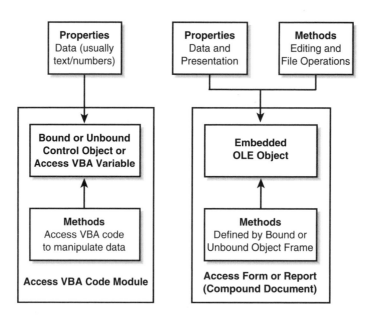

Fig. 19.5 A diagram showing the differences between DDE and OLE data transfer in Access.

Writing code to make full use of DDE with Access (one of the subjects of Chapter 29, "Understanding the Data Access Object Class") or any other Windows application, is and always was a difficult process. In specific cases discussed in the following chapter, Access creates a DDE link to an element in the source application and embeds the data transferred through the link in an OLE Object field.

Using the basic features of OLE requires no programming. Simple OLE operations in Access use the Paste Special or Insert Object choices of the Edit menu. You can copy OLE objects in Access to the Clipboard from the Edit menu so that other OLE client applications can use the objects. There are relatively few Access VBA reserved words that apply exclusively to OLE objects; Microsoft deliberately designed OLE for use by non-programmers.

You must edit a linked or embedded OLE 1.0 object manually. There is no equivalent in OLE 1.0 of the Access VBA DDEExecute instruction that lets you manipulate the data in an OLE 1.0 document with macros or Access VBA code. DDEExecute sends instructions to the DDE Server application that can modify the content of an Excel worksheet cell or of a paragraph in a Word document. The syntax of the instructions you send with DDEExecute are specific to each DDE client application.

OLE 2.+ substitutes a new programming methodology, OLE Automation, for the DDEExecute instruction. The advantage of OLE Automation is that you can alter the values of the properties of the object and apply methods to the object using conventional Access VBA syntax. OLE Automation is the foundation upon which OLE Controls are built. OLE Automation and OLE Custom Controls are discussed briefly in the "Taking Advantage of OLE Automation" section later in this chapter.

Embedding versus Linking Source Documents

When you embed a source document, Windows creates a copy of the source document data and embeds the copy permanently in the container document. The source document retains no connection to the embedded data. Subsequent editing or deletion of the file or data from which the source document was created has no effect on the embedded copy in the table or displayed on the forms and reports.

Embedding is the only option if you do not or cannot save the source document as a file. The Microsoft Graph 5.0 and Visio Express OLE 2.0 mini-servers allow you only to embed a file. These applets have no Save or Save As choices in their File menus. When you choose Exit from an applet File menu, a dialog appears asking whether you want to update the destination document with the edited source document.

Windows 95 Paint application is the OLE 2.1 source application for all graphics displayed in bound or unbound objects of the Northwind Traders sample database. Paint enables you to import and save images in monochrome, 16-bit, or 24-bit .bmp files, so you can use Paintbrush to embed or link all bitmapped graphics you possess or create in either of these file formats. (Paint can open but not save PC Paintbrush .pcx files.)

Open the Categories form and then double-click the picture. Paint appears so that you can edit the image, as shown in figure 19.6. All bitmaps in the Northwind Traders sample database are Bitmap Image objects embedded in OLE Object fields of tables and in unbound object frames on forms and reports. Notice in figure 19.6 that the menubar changes when you activate the embedded image for editing. Activating Paint grafts the Image and Options choices of Paint's menu to Access's menubar.

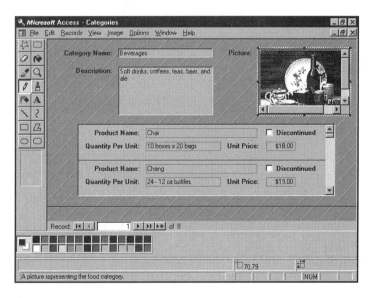

Fig. 19.6 Windows 95's Paint application editing an embedded bitmap that is displayed in a bound object frame.

If you link an object, you create a reference to the data of the source document, the name of a file. When you or others change the data in a file linked to the object, the data in the source document permanently changes. The next time you display the data, if you set the value of the Update Options property of the bound object frame to Automatic, the presentation of the object incorporates all changes made to the data in the file. The capability of automatically updating everyone's linked objects at once is useful in a networked Access application that displays data that periodically is updated by others who share these files on the network.

Caution

If you want to try the following process for linking a range of an Excel worksheet to a record of Northwind.mdb's Categories table, make a copy of Northwind.mdb and open the copy in Access. You can't undo an embedding or linking update to an Access table.

To link rather than embed an object created by an OLE server, perform the following steps:

1. Open the OLE server—Excel 95 in this example.

2. Load the file that contains the data you want to link.

3. Select the range of data (or the part of an image) to copy to the Clipboard. Most OLE 2+ server applications let you select all or a part of the open document.

4. Press Ctrl+C to copy the data to the Clipboard.

5. Activate the container, in this case an Access 95 form, and select a bound or un-bound object frame.

6. Choose Edit, Paste Special in the container application. If the application supports OLE 2+, the Paste Special dialog shown in figure 19.7 appears.

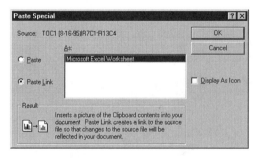

Fig. 19.7   The standard OLE 2+ Paste Special dialog.

7. Click the Paste Link option button, and then click OK to paste the image into the container document. In this example, the container is the Picture field of the first record of the Categories table.

> **Note**
>
> Before creating an OLE link in the destination application, you must open the source application and load the file because opening a file in most OLE servers breaks the existing OLE connection.

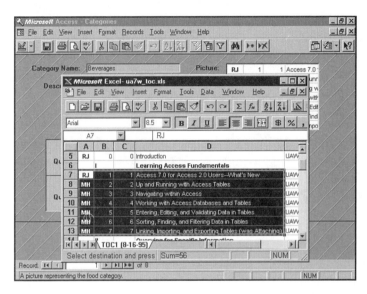

Fig. 19.8 Excel 95 editing a worksheet file with a range of cells linked to a bound object frame.

When you double-click to edit a linked object, the application opens its window and the title bar of the server's window displays the name of the file that created the image, as shown in figure 19.8. This method is one way that you quickly can determine whether an OLE object is linked, rather than embedded in most OLE client applications (including Access).

Another advantage of linking some objects whose data resides in files is that you don't waste disk space with duplicate copies of the files in the database. Access creates a copy of the source document's presentation in the table, so you don't save disk space when you link graphic images, spreadsheets, or other source documents whose presentation consists of the data. The presentation of animation, waveform audio, and digital video files is either an icon or the first image of a sequence, so the presentation is small in size. Here, the disk space saved by linking, rather than embedding, is substantial.

> **Note**
>
> Linking a bitmapped image doesn't save disk space; the presentation stored in .bmp format is the same size in bytes as the original image. (The size of the presentation is likely to be much larger if your image file was stored in a compressed format, such as .pcx, .gif, or .jpg.) If your OLE image server application lets you substitute a *thumbnail* image, the saving in file space often is substantial. A thumbnail image is a smaller version of the original image, often with less color depth (8-bit instead of 24-bit color data, for instance).

The disadvantage of linking is that the linked files must be available to all users of the application. The files must reside in the same directory for their lifetime unless you edit the linkage to reflect a new location. A fully specified path, including the drive designator or UNC server address, is included with the file name in the linking information. If your application can't open the linked file, the presentation of the source document appears in the form or report, but when you double-click the bound object frame to edit the linked object, you see an error message that the linked file is not found.

> **Note**
>
> OLE 2+ provides a limited capability to update the links to files that have moved, but it is not a wise practice to depend on the present version, OLE 2.1, to maintain links to relocated files. If the object is contained in an unbound object frame, you can change the value of the SourceDoc property to point to the file in its new location. If the object is contained in a bound object frame, you need to open the file, copy its data to the Clipboard, and then re-create the link by using Paste Special to create a new link to the file.

Activating OLE 2+ Objects in Place

One of the advantages of embedding, rather than linking, objects is that you can activate OLE 2+ objects in place. In-place activation (also called *in-situ editing* or *in-place editing*) causes the source application for the embedded object to "take over" the container application.

You activate an OLE object for editing by double-clicking the surface of the object frame that displays a simplified presentation of the worksheet. Figure 19.6 illustrates in-place activation of a Paintbrush Picture object. Figure 19.9 shows an Excel worksheet embedded in an unbound object frame of a form. The worksheet has been activated in place for editing. When an object is activated in place for editing, the object is surrounded by a frame consisting of alternating blue and white diagonal hash marks. Eight sizing handles (black squares at each corner and at the midpoints of the frame) let you adjust the size of the editing frame.

When you activate an embedded OLE 2+ object, the menubars of the application with which you created the object replace Access's menus that have the same name. This process is called *grafting* a menu. If the source application has additional menus, they are added to Access's menubar.

In figure 19.9, the Edit, View, Format, and Help menus are replaced by Excel's menus of the same name. Excel adds its own Insert, Tools, and Data menus to the menubar. Excel's anchored toolbars can become floating toolbars that you can reposition or hide. Column and row headers, sheet tabs, and scroll bars (called *adornments*) become visible when you activate an Excel worksheet. You have full control over the embedded Excel worksheet and can perform almost any operation on the worksheet that is possible if you had opened a file containing the worksheet in Excel 95.

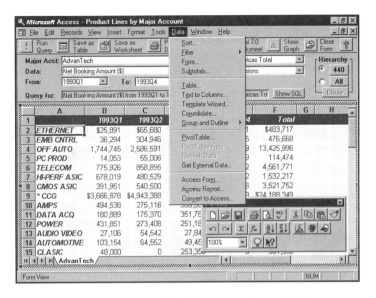

Fig. 19.9 An Excel 95 worksheet activated for editing in an Access 2.0 form.

Note

In-place activation is available only for embedded, not linked, OLE 2+ objects. When you double-click the presentation of a linked OLE 2+ object, the source application's window appears. In this respect, linked OLE 2+ objects behave identically to linked or embedded OLE 1.0 objects.

Taking Advantage of OLE Automation

▶▶ See "Manipulating an Excel 95 Workbook Object," p. 1072

OLE 2+ server and mini-server applications that support OLE Automation *expose programmable objects*. As an example, Excel 95 is an OLE Automation server application that creates programmable Excel objects. Thus, when you activate an Excel worksheet object embedded in, or linked to, an Access 95 object frame, you can gain access to the worksheet through the Object property of the object frame control. The Object property is available only with Access VBA code; the Object property does not appear in the Properties window for object frames. The Object property provides access to all the objects, and the properties and methods of the objects, that are exposed by the application that created the embedded or linked object. The Excel worksheet shown in figure 19.9 was created by Access VBA code from data contained in an Access Recordset object.

Using OLE Automation requires that you learn to program in Access VBA and that you understand the hierarchy of the collections of objects that you intend to program. Collections of objects are groups of objects of the same class that are contained within another object. As an example, the collection of Excel Worksheet objects are contained in Workbook objects. Collections of OA objects follow the same general structure as Access 95's data access objects (DAOs) described in Chapter 29, "Understanding the Data Access Object Class." Excel 95, for example, has more than 100 different types of objects and several hundred properties and methods that apply to its objects.

Access 95's DBEngine object is the top of Access DAO pyramid; the OA Application object of Excel 95 (and most other OA servers) is the equivalent of the DBEngine object. All other Excel objects are subclasses of the Application object. Access 95 exposes its Application object to OA client applications, qualifying it for OLE Automation Server status.

OLE Automation lets you construct applications using the building block approach; if you need a worksheet in your Access application, insert an Excel Worksheet object in an unbound object frame. You then set the values of properties of, and apply methods to, the Worksheet object with Access VBA code. If you want word processing features, insert a Word 95 Document object into an unbound object frame. You add command buttons or other controls to the form to execute the procedures or functions that contain the required OLE Automation commands.

OLE Custom Controls are a special class of OLE 2+ mini-servers that use OA to provide access to their properties, methods, and events. (Conventional OA objects don't expose their own events when activated.) When you embed an OLE Control in an unbound object frame, the Control object's events are not added to the Property window's list of events for unbound object frames. However, you can write Access VBA event-handling code for the events exposed by the OLE Control as procedures in code contained in forms.

The preceding brief discussion of OLE Automation may appear out of context at this point in the book because writing Access Basic code is the subject of Part VII, "Programming with Visual Basic for Applications." However, future Windows operating systems and applications will make extensive use of OA, and a general description of OLE 2.1 without including OA would be incomplete, at best.

As mentioned at the beginning of this section, taking advantage of OA and OLE Custom Controls requires that you write Access VBA code. Mastering OA programming requires a very retentive memory and much experimentation. If you need interprocess communication in your Access 95 applications, use OLE 2.1 and OA—not DDE—whenever you can. Your investment astride the OLE 2.1 learning curve will return substantial dividends as more and better OA applications and, especially, 32-bit OLE Controls become available.

The Windows 95 Registry

In Windows 95 and Windows NT, the Registry takes the place of Windows 3.1+'s REG.DAT, plus WIN.INI, SYSTEM.INI, and application-specific .INI files. (If you install Windows 95 over Windows 3.1+, setup migrates all REG.DAT and many WIN.INI and SYSTEM.INI entries to the Registry.)

The Registry consists of two hidden system files: System.dat and User.dat. Either or both of the Registry files can be on your local fixed disk drive or stored on a network server. System.dat contains information on your PC, including the hardware and software installed. User.dat contains your user profile information. If your User.dat file is stored on a server, you can move to another networked computer, log on with your user name and password, and have your desktop configuration appear at the computer you're using.

System policy information, contained in .pol files, overrides entries in System.dat and User.dat. System policy files, such as Config.pol, are primarily of interest to PC administrators for maintaining control over the extent to which users can modify their Windows 95 installation.

The registration process for early OLE 1.0 servers was relatively simple. Only a few entries in REG.DAT were required, primarily to create an association between individual file extensions and the OLE server for the type of file. The registration process for OLE 2+ servers is not so simple; much more information is required to register OLE 2+ servers, and even more entries are added for applications that support OLE Automation.

OLE Controls also register themselves in the Registry. Although the setup program registers each OLE server automatically, you must understand the use of the Registry and the Registry Editor application in case you encounter a problem when you attempt to insert an OLE 2+ object in an Access 95 object frame. The following two sections are devoted to the Registry and concentrate on the OLE 2.1 aspects of server registration.

The Registry Editor

The Registry editor, RegEdit.exe, is included with Windows 95 so that users can display and edit the Registry, formerly the registration database of Windows 3.1+. The Registry editor has a help file that explains how to use RegEdit, and the *Windows 95 Resource Kit* includes an explanation of the contents of the Registry and also describes how to use RegEdit. None of this information provides even a hint about the new Registry data structures required by OLE 2.1. If you plan to use the OLE Object field data type, use MSGraph5 to create graphs, or add sophisticated graphic images to your forms and reports, you need to know more about the Registry and RegEdit than appears in the Windows 95 and Access 95 documentation.

RegEdit.exe isn't installed by default by the Windows 95 setup application, so choose Start, Run and type **regedit.exe** in the Command Line text box, and click OK to launch RegEdit. RegEdit's opening window appears, as shown in figure 19.10.

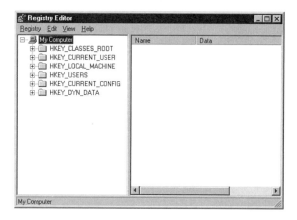

Fig. 19.10 RegEdit's opening window for editing the Registry files.

Information contained in the Registry is stored in the six subtrees, each beginning with HKEY, as shown in figure 19.10. The type of information stored in each subtree is as follows:

- *HKEY_CLASSES_ROOT* contains association mappings between applications and file types identified by the file extension, information to support drag-and-drop operations, and data on the user interface. This subtree contains information similar to that stored in the REG.DAT file of Windows 3.1+ and Windows NT 3.1+.

- *HKEY_CURRENT_USER* stores a pointer to the hive (sub-subtree) of the HKEY_USERS subtree for the user currently logged on to Windows 95.

- *HKEY_LOCAL_MACHINE* contains information on the hardware and software installed on your PC. This subtree is employed by all users who log on to your PC.

- *HKEY_USERS* stores information on all users of your PC if Windows 95 security is implemented. If only you use your PC, HKEY_USERS stores the data for HKEY_CURRENT_USER.

- *HKEY_CURRENT_CONFIGURATION* stores a pointer to a hive in HKEY_LOCAL_MACHINE that contains details about the current hardware setup of your PC.

- *HKEY_DYN_DATA* contains dynamic status information for Plug-and-Play devices, such as PC Cards (PCMCIA devices) that you "hot swap" while your PC is powered.

The primary subtrees used by OLE 2+ are HKEY_CLASSES_ROOT and the SOFTWARE hive of HKEY_LOCAL MACHINE. To display hives below subtrees, double-click the folder symbol for the subtree, then double-click folders with a + symbol to expand the hierarchical list. HKEY_CLASSES_ROOT identifies a file extension with a particular class of object, such as .doc files with the Word.Document.6 object class, called the programmatic ID or ProgID (see fig. 19.11). Word 6.0 and Word 95 share the Word.Document.6 object class because the .doc files created by both applications are identical.

When you double-click a .doc file in My Computer or the Explorer, the association launches the application's executable file specified by the ...\shell\open value that appears in the Data column of RegEdit's right pane. If you don't have Word 6.0 or Word 95 on your computer, Windows 95 launches WordPad to create a Wordpad.Document.1 object from .doc files. Similar entries associate .mdb files with the Access.Application.7 object class.

Note

You can see a list of registered file types by launching the Explorer, choosing View, Options, and clicking the File Types tab. You can change the association between a file extension and an application by clicking the Edit button of the File Types tab. Editing associations in the File Types page is similar to the process used with the Modify File Type editing feature of Windows 3.1+'s REGEDIT.EXE. The most common change to file associations is changing the editing application for bitmapped graphics files.

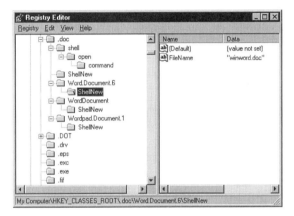

Fig. 19.11   Entries in RegEdit's HKEY_CLASSES_ROOT subtree that associate .doc files with applications.

Following the list of file extension associations in HKEY_CLASSES_ROOT is an alphabetized list of ProgIDs for registered objects. Figure 19.12 shows the HKEY_CLASSES_ROOT\Word.Document.6\shell\New\open entry that launches Word 6.0 or Word 95 with the /n parameter to specify a new (empty) document. If you move a registered application from one folder to another, you must change *every* Registry entry for the application that contains the pointer to its executable file.

Windows 95's RegEdit includes a flexible Find feature, missing in Windows 3.1+'s RegEdit, that allows searching for entries' keys, values, and/or data (see fig. 19.12). Figure 19.13 shows the Edit String dialog that appears when you double-click the "ab" icon that indicates the entry is a string of characters. Unfortunately, RegEdit doesn't include a find and replace feature, so you must make multiple Registry entries manually.

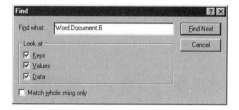

Fig. 19.12 Searching for the Registry entries that contain the `Word.Document.6` programmatic ID.

Fig. 19.13 The Edit String dialog for changing a Registry value.

    ▶▶ See "The Registry Entries for OLE Automation Servers," p. 1078

 Applications that support OLE 2+ add a variety of other entries to the Registry; an explanation of the purpose of each of these entries is beyond the scope of this chapter. What is important, however, is your ability to recover from problems that result from improper entries for OLE 2+ servers in the Registry.

Troubleshooting

When I try to insert an object into an unbound object frame, I get a message that Windows can't find the OLE server or one of its components.

The Registry contains an entry that points to the wrong location of the OLE server, the server executable has been erased (or is corrupted), or one of its .DLLs or other supporting components is missing. Although it's possible to manually change the Registry entries for relocated OLE servers, reinstalling the server from its distribution diskettes or CD-ROM is a far more foolproof process. You're likely to have a better chance of satisfactorily correcting the Registry entries for the server if you launch the Add/Remove Programs feature of Control Panel, remove the server, then reinstall it. Many older OLE server applications, however, don't display entries in the Install/Uninstall page of the Add/Remove Programs dialog.

How Access and Other OLE Applications Use the Registry

The primary Registry entries for each OLE server appear in the Object Type list box of the Insert Object dialog that appears when you choose Insert, Object in Form Design View. Figure 19.14 shows the Insert Object dialog that is standard for all OLE 2-compliant applications with the Microsoft Graph 5.0 entry (`MSGraph.Chart.5 ProgID`) selected.

If you have installed prior versions of current OLE 2.0 servers, such as Excel 5.0 and Word 6.0, entries may appear for these servers even if you have deleted the applications from your fixed disk. If you use the Uninstall option of the Maintenance Setup applications to remove applications, the Registry entries for these applications are deleted. Unfortunately, many older OLE 2.0 servers don't provide an uninstaller. All applications that display the "Designed for Windows 95" logo must include an uninstall feature that clears registry entries during the application removal process.

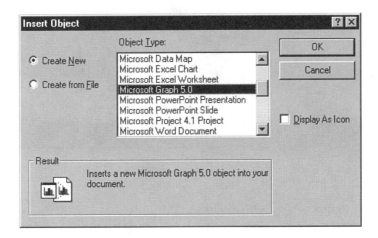

Fig. 19.14 The OLE 2+ Insert Object dialog that enables you to select an available object type based on the Registry entries.

Each Object Type in the Object Type list box is a specific type of the OLE object. The entries in the list box are derived from the Registry's value of each registered OLE server. The Microsoft Graph 5.0 type, for example, is entered from the `MSGraph.Chart.5 = Microsoft Graph 5.0` in `\HKEY_CLASSES_ROOT`. If you double-click the Microsoft Graph 5.0 entry (or select the entry and click OK), Access creates an unbound object frame and Graph5.exe opens with the example graph shown in figure 19.15.

You can enter data in the datasheet at the upper left of Microsoft Graph's window to alter the height of the bars of the chart or you can import an Excel .xlc chart file, but that's about all you can do without having a working knowledge of how graphs obtain data from Access 95. Creating graphs from Access data is one of the subjects of Chapter 20, "Adding Graphics to Forms and Reports."

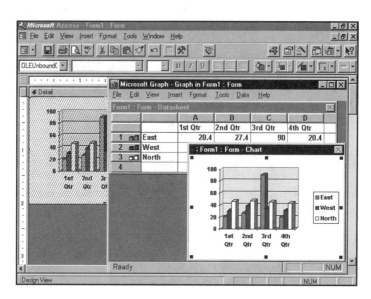

Fig. 19.15   An example graph created by inserting a new `MSGraph.5.Chart` object in Form Design View.

Replacing the Registry Files with Backups

When you start Windows 95, a backup copy of System.dat and User.dat (System.da0 and User.da0, respectively) is created automatically. If either of these files becomes corrupted, you may not be able to start Windows. If the `HKEY_CLASSES_ROOT` or `HKEY_LOCAL_MACHINE\SOFTWARE` entries for an OLE server in System.dat are incorrect or missing, the server won't appear in the Object Type list of the Insert Object dialog or you receive an error message when attempting to insert an object. Corruption of System.dat isn't a common occurrence, but it occasionally happens during installation of a new application. You can replace the corrupted System.dat file with the backup System.da0 version by following these steps:

1. If your corrupted System.dat file prevents Windows 95 from starting, launch Windows 95 and immediately press the F8 key for a fail-safe boot, then choose Safe Mode Command Prompt Only. Skip the next two steps.

2. If you can run Windows 95, open the Explorer and choose View, Options. In the View page of the Options dialog, click the Show All Files option then click OK to close the dialog.

3. Locate System.dat and System.da0 with the Explorer. The location of these two files depends on how you installed Windows 95, but they are located most commonly in your \Windows folder.

4. In MS-DOS, change to the directory containing System.dat. System.dat and System.da0 are hidden, read-only system files, so entries for these files do not appear when you execute a `dir` command.

5. At the command prompt, type the following three instructions:

    attrib -h -r -s system.dat

    attrib -h -r -s system.da0

    copy system.da0 system.dat

6. Reboot your computer. (It is not necessary to reset the attributes of System.dat.)

To replace User.dat with User.da0, follow the preceding steps and substitute **user** for **system** in step 5.

From Here...

In this chapter, you learned the principles of creating OLE 2.0 objects and the concepts behind OLE Automation and OLE Controls. A basic understanding of how OLE and the Registry work is quite useful when you see an Access or Windows 95 message box informing you that the Registry files are corrupted. Although this chapter is directed to using OLE 2.1 server applications with Access 95, these principles are the same with all OLE 2-compliant applications running under Windows 95.

For information related to the topics discussed in this chapter, refer to the following chapters:

- Chapter 20, "Adding Graphics to Forms and Reports," shows you how to use Windows Paint and other OLE 2+ servers to add bitmapped and vector images to your forms and reports, as well as to embed image data in, or link image files to, records of the OLE Object data type in Access tables.

- Chapter 21, "Using Access with Microsoft Excel," describes how to embed or link Excel Workbook objects in forms, reports, and tables.

- Chapter 22, "Using Access with Microsoft Word and Mail Merge," discusses adding OLE 2+ word-processing prowess to your Access 95 applications.

- Chapter 30, "Exchanging Data with OLE Automation and DDE," provides examples of manipulating Excel 95 and Word 95 objects with Access VBA and OLE Automation code.

Chapter 20

Adding Graphics to Forms and Reports

One of the principal incentives for using a Windows desktop database manager is the ability to display graphic images contained in (or linked to) database tables. Early Windows RDBMSs could display images stored in individual bitmapped graphic files with common formats such as .BMP, .PCX, and .TIF, but could not store the bitmap data within the database file.

A few publishers enhanced some of these early desktop database products with BLOB (binary large object) field data types. A BLOB field is of variable length and can hold any type of data, regardless of its format. Other Windows desktop RDBMSs use auxiliary files (similar to dBASE's .DBT memo files) to store graphic images and other types of non-text data. When an auxiliary file is used, a field in a database table provides a reference (called a *pointer*) to the location of the data in the auxiliary file.

Many Windows graphic images are stored as combinations of lines, shapes, and patterns, rather than as copies of the pixel pattern of an image on your video display unit. Images of this type are called *vector-based graphics*. Windows illustration applications (such as Corel Systems' CorelDRAW! 6.0 and Visio Corporation's Visio 4.0) create vector-based graphics. Microsoft Graph 5.0 (MSGraph5) uses vector-based graphics to create graphs from data in Access tables. Although each of these products has a proprietary file format, the illustration applications communicate with other applications through the Clipboard in standard Windows Metafile Format (WMF).

This chapter describes how to use both bitmapped and vector-based graphics in conjunction with Access forms and reports. It also describes how you use MSGraph5 to create graphs and charts from Access 95 data.

Adding a Bound Object Control to a Form or Report

Graphic images and other OLE objects stored in OLE Object fields of Access tables use a bound object frame control to display their presentation. The

In this chapter, you learn to

■ Add graphic images stored in tables to forms

■ Manipulate bitmapped images in bound controls

■ Use Access 95's new image control

■ Use the Chart Wizard to create graphs and charts from Access data

■ Link to a form a graph based on your own crosstab query

V

Integrating Access

bound object frame control is an OLE container within which a bitmapped or vector-based image can be displayed. Other OLE objects that rely on data stored in OLE Object fields, such as Sound Recorder and Media Player objects, plus data-bound OLE Controls, also use the bound object frame.

In the case of still graphic images, the presentation within the bound object frame is a copy of the object's data property. Animated images and video objects usually display the first image in the animation sequence or video clip. Sound objects substitute the icon of the OLE server with which their file type is associated in the Registry. Double-clicking the bound object frame launches the OLE server that was used to add the object to a data cell in an OLE Object field of your table.

In Chapter 13, "Designing Custom Multitable Forms," you were introduced to adding a bound object frame to an Access form. Here, you learn the details of displaying and editing a photograph in the Personnel Action Entry form you have built in the preceding chapters. You also learn how to scale the photograph within the bound object frame, so that you get exactly the look you want.

Including Photos in the Personnel Actions Query

 ◄◄ See "Creating the Query on Which to Base the Main Form," p. 451

The majority of Access applications use the OLE Object field data type to store only graphic images. The Northwind Traders Employees table includes a photograph for each employee as one such graphic image. You use the OLE Object field data type to add the photograph to your Personnel Actions form. The bound object frame is linked to the Photo field of the qryPersonnelActions query (see fig. 20.1).

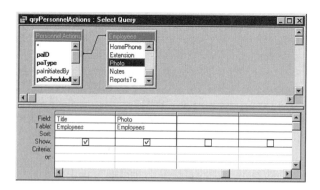

Fig. 20.1 The Photo field of the qryPersonnelActions query in Design View.

Run the qryPersonnelActions query so you can view one of the photographs in the Windows 95 Paint window; follow these steps:

1. From the Database window, open the qryPersonnelActions query.

2. Drag the Horizontal Scroll Bar button to the right to display the Photo field in the resulting table.

3. Double-click one of the Bitmap Image data cells to display the image in Windows 95 Paint. The chosen image appears in the Paint window (see fig. 20.2).

Fig. 20.2   Testing the Picture field of the qryPersonnelActions query.

4. Choose Exit & Return to qryPersonnelActions:Select Query from Paintbrush's File menu to close the editing window.

5. Choose Close from Access's File menu and save your changes to the query.

◄◄ See "The Registry Editor," p. 721

Troubleshooting

An "insufficient memory" or "application not properly registered" message appears after double-clicking a data cell in the OLE Object field.

Either of the two messages can occur under low memory conditions. First, try closing all other running applications and then double-clicking the data cell again. If you continue to receive registration error messages, exit and restart Windows. If this doesn't solve the problem, open the Registry Editor (RegEdit), choose Edit, Find, and search for the Bitmap Image value. Expand the `CLSID` entry for Bitmap Image and select the `LocalServer32` item. Verify that the value for `LocalServer32` is `C:\PROGRA~1\ACCESS~1\MSPAINT.EXE` (or the location of Mspaint.exe on your PC). If you need to change the entry, double-click the "ab" icon in the right pane to open the Edit String dialog and correct the entry as necessary.

The behavior of Paintbrush is similar to that of other OLE 2+ local server applications used to add or edit the values (contents) of data cells in OLE Object fields.

Displaying the Employee's Picture in the Personnel Actions Form

You can edit OLE objects in Access tables and queries only through the window of the OLE server you used (Paintbrush, in this example) to add the objects to the table. The presentation of OLE objects is, however, stored in the OLE field, and is displayed automatically in a bound or unbound object frame. You double-click within the object frame to edit the object.

To add a bound object frame to the Personnel Action Entry form so you can display the Photo field of your qryPersonnelActions query, follow these steps:

1. Click the Form tab of the Database window, and select the frmPersonnelActions form. If the frmPersonnelActions form is open, close it and then reopen it; the reason for this action is explained in the note at the end of this section.

2. Click the Design button of the Database window to open the form in design mode.

3. Position the mouse pointer near the upper-left corner of the Rating group frame.

4. Hold down the left mouse button and drag the mouse pointer to the lower right of the frame so that the entire frame is enclosed within the white-bordered rectangle.

5. Release the mouse pointer. The frame and all the objects within it are selected.

6. To make room for the image, press the Delete key to remove the frame and its contents from your form.

7. Click the Field List button, and select Photo from the Field List window.

8. Select the Photo field and drag the Field symbol to the approximate position of the upper-left corner of the deleted Rating object frame. Access creates a bound object frame rather than a text box when you create a control directly from a field of the OLE Object type in the Field List dialog.

9. Select the Photo label, and press the Delete key. A caption is not required for the employee photograph.

10. Position and size the new bound object frame, as shown in figure 20.3.

11. Click the Form View button to display your form with the photograph. The form appears as in figure 20.4. Note that only a portion of the photograph appears within the frame. You still need to scale the image, which is the subject of the next section.

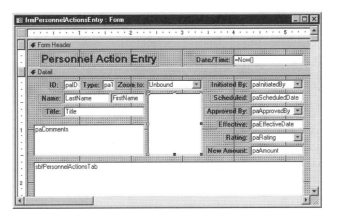

Fig. 20.3   Adding a bound object frame to frmPersonnelActions.

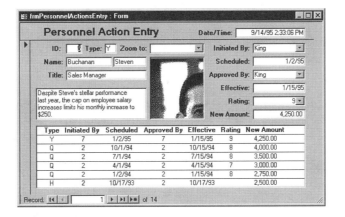

Fig. 20.4   Viewing the Personnel Action Entry form with the added Photo bound object frame.

Troubleshooting

The employee's photo does not appear in Form View.

If you add the Photo field to your query and follow the procedure for adding a bound object frame while the Personnel Action Entry form is open, your frame is likely to be empty when you display the form in run mode. In this case, the Photo field is added to the Datasheet View of your form, but the field's cells have **Null** values. Pressing Shift+F9 (Requery) does not replace the **Null** values with Bitmap Images. If this problem occurs, you must close the form and then reopen it from the Database window. Access runs the modified query when you open the form, and the pictures appear.

An alternative method for creating a bound object frame is to click the bound object frame tool of the toolbox, click the Photo field, and drag the Field symbol to the form. The extra step involved in this process serves no purpose because Access chooses a bound object frame for you when you choose a field in the Field list that is of the OLE Object data type.

When you use either the bound object frame tool or the toolbox, the value of the Enabled property is set to Yes and the Locked property is set to No. (Access 2.0 set the Enabled property to No and the Locked property to Yes when using the toolbox to create a bound object frame.) The effect of these two properties is as follows:

- When an object frame is disabled (Enabled property set to No), you can't double-click the object to launch the OLE server that created the object's content. The setting of the Locked property has no effect in this case.

- When an object is enabled and locked (Locked property set to Yes), you can launch the OLE server, but any edits you make to the content of the object are discarded when you close the server application.

> **Note**
>
> In Form View with the default values of the Enabled and Locked properties, Yes and No, respectively, double-click the Photo object frame to launch Windows 95 Paint, which assumes the role of the active application through in-place activation. Paint is an OLE 2.1 server, so Paint grafts its menu choices to the Access menubar, a process also called menu negotiation. Paint's View, Image, and Options menu choices replace several of Access's menu choices (see fig. 20.5). You can edit the bitmap in Paint, then save the changes to the OLE data in the Employees table when you close Paint. You click the form outside the Photo image to close (deactivate) Paint.

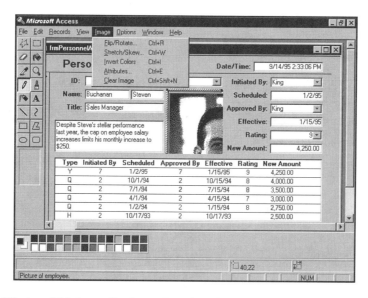

Fig. 20.5 Windows 95 Paint application activated in place to edit a Bitmap Image object.

Scaling Graphic Objects

Access provides three methods for scaling graphic objects within the confines of a bound object frame. You select one of these methods by choosing the value of the Size Mode property in the Bound Object Frame Properties window displayed in figure 20.6.

Fig. 20.6   Allowable values of the Size Mode property of object frames.

The three options offered for the value of the Size Mode property display the image in the following ways:

■ *Clip*, the default, displays the image in its original aspect ratio. The *aspect ratio* is the ratio of the width to the height of an image, measured in pixels or inches. A *pixel* is the smallest element of a bitmap that your computer can display, a single dot. The aspect ratio of the standard VGA display, for example, is 640×480 pixels, which is 1.33:1. If the entire image does not fit within the frame, the bottom or right of the image is cropped. *Cropping* an image is a graphic arts term that means cutting off the portions of an image outside of a window of a specified size, as shown in the left-hand picture of figure 20.7.

Clip   Stretch   Zoom

Fig. 20.7   Comparing the Clip, Stretch, and Zoom values of the Size Mode property.

■ *Stretch* independently enlarges or shrinks the horizontal and vertical dimensions of the image to fill the frame. If the aspect ratio of the frame is not identical to that of the image, the image is distorted, as illustrated by the center image of figure 20.7.

■ *Zoom* enlarges or shrinks the horizontal or vertical dimension of the image so the image fits within the frame, and the original aspect ratio is maintained. If your frame has an aspect ratio different from that of the image, a portion of the frame is empty, as shown in the right-hand image of figure 20.7.

The bound object frames in figure 20.7 are expanded horizontally to accent the effects of the Stretch and Zoom property values.

Access does not include the capability to specify a particular area of the image to be clipped, so zooming to maintain the original aspect ratio is the best choice in this case. When you scale or zoom a bitmapped image, the apparent contrast is likely to increase, as shown in the center and right-hand images of figure 20.7. This increase results from deleting a sufficient number of pixels in the image to make it fit the frame, which increases the graininess. The increase in graininess and contrast is less evident in 256-color (8 bits per pixel) bitmaps; the photos of employees are 16-color (4 bits per pixel) bitmaps.

To apply the Zoom property to your bound object frame in design mode, follow these steps:

1. Select the Photo bound object frame.

2. Click the Properties button on the toolbar to open the bound object frame Properties window. Click the Format tab.

3. Click the Size Mode text box, and open its list box.

4. Select Zoom.

To display the form so that you can view the photograph with its new property, follow these steps:

1. Click the Form View button of the toolbar to display your form, which now appears, as shown in figure 20.8.

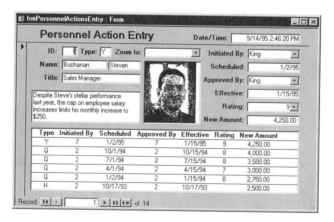

Fig. 20.8   The bound object frame with Zoom Size Mode applied.

2. If your frame includes an empty area, as illustrated in figure 20.8, return to design mode, adjust the size of the frame, and rerun the form to verify that the frame has the correct dimensions.

3. Choose File, Close, and save your changes to the Personnel Action Entry form.

The technique described in this section allows you to add a bound object frame containing a vector image created with a drawing application, a sound clip from a .WAV or .MID file, or any other OLE object type that you can select from the Insert Object dialog.

To add a bound object frame to the Detail section of a report, you also use the same method outlined here. The quality of the printed image depends on the type of image, and the laser or inkjet printer you use. Vector-based images (such as drawings created in CorelDRAW! 6.0 or Visio 4.0) result in more attractive printed reports than do bitmapped images, especially when the bitmap is scaled. The contrast problem discussed previously may be aggravated when color images are printed in black and white.

Examining Bitmap Image File Formats

Graphics files are identified by generally accepted file extensions; these serve to define most (or all) of the format's basic characteristics. The following file extensions identify bitmap image files that have achieved the status of "industry standards" for the PC. Most commercial bitmap image editing applications support these formats, though some do not import .GIF files. The "standard" extensions follow:

- *.BMP* is for Windows bitmap files in 1-, 2-, 4-, 8-, and 24-bit color depths. .BMP files contain a bitmap information *header* defining the size of the image, the number of color planes, the type of compression used (if any), and information on the palette used. A header is a block of data in the file that precedes the image data.

- *.DIB* is for device-independent bitmap files. The .DIB file format is a variant of the .BMP format; to define the RGB values of the colors used, it includes a color table in the header.

- *.PCX* is for files that are compatible with ZSoft Paint applications. The .PCX file format is the common denominator for most bitmap file format conversions; almost every graphics application created in the past five years can handle .PCX files, but Windows 95 Paint cannot save files in .PCX format. (Paint refers to .PCX files as PC Paintbrush format.) .PCX files are compressed by a method called *run-length encoding* (RLE), which can decrease the size of bitmap files by a factor of 3 or more, depending on their contents.

- *.TIF* (an abbreviated form of TIFF) is for tagged image format files. The TIFF format was originally developed by Aldus Corporation, and now is managed by Microsoft Corporation. Originally, TIFF files were used primarily for storing scanned images, but now they are used by a substantial number of applications (including those for Windows) as the preferred bitmap format.

  A special version of TIFF that uses file compression is used for fax transmission. TIFF files for conventional bitmaps are found in both uncompressed and compressed formats. A tag in the header of the file defines information similar to that found in the information header of .BMP files.

- *.JPG* is for files created by applications that offer compression and decompression options for *JPEG* graphics. JPEG is an acronym for the Joint Photographic Experts Group, which has developed a standard methodology to compress and decompress still color images. Special JPEG adapter cards are available to speed the compression and decompression processes.

JPEG compression often is used for video images, especially for digital video editing, but MPEG (Moving Pictures Experts Group) compression is expected to predominate in the video field; it provides better compression ratios for video images than does the JPEG method. MPEG compression is used by the Hughes DBS (Direct Broadcast System) satellites that beam DirecTV and USSB programming to 18-inch microwave dishes connected to RCA or Sony set-top boxes. MPEG compression requires special PC adapter cards to display live-motion video images at the standard 30 frames-per-second rate, but Pentium PCs can use software decoding at a somewhat lower frame rate.

■ *.PCD* (an abbreviation for Photo CD, a Kodak trademark) is for photographic images that are digitized and stored on CD-ROMs by photofinishers. Photo CD files use a special compression system devised by the Eastman Kodak Company; you need Kodak's Photo CD Access application for Windows or an image editor, such as Adobe Photoshop or Corel PhotoPAINT, to display the images and save them to .PCD files.

■ *.GIF* is for the graphics interchange file format used to archive bitmapped images on CompuServe and other online services. Shareware and freeware .GIF file conversion applications for all popular types of personal computers are available for downloading from CompuServe's Graphic Support forum (GO GRAPHSUP). .GIF is the standard bitmap format for background images of the Internet's World Wide Web pages, but the trend is to the use of JPEG compression.

■ *.TGA* is for files in the TARGA file format developed by Truevision for its TARGA product line of graphics adapter cards. TARGA cards were the first to offer relatively high-resolution, wide-spectrum color images with PCs by employing a separate video monitor.

If you don't have a Windows image-editing application with OLE file server capability, you need to convert bitmap files in .TIF, .GIF, .PCD, or .TGA format to .BMP or .PCX format. You can use Microsoft Word's bitmap file-conversion capability to insert a .TIF file in a new document and then copy the image to the Clipboard as a picture. You cannot edit the Word picture that you paste into an Access table with Paste Special, however, because the image is not an OLE object; it is a bitmap picture created from a DDE link to Word.

Note

If you have an application that supports the .PCX format, store individual bitmap images in .PCX and not .BMP files for use with Windows Paintbrush. Using .PCX files saves disk space compared with the .BMP format because .PCX uses RLE file compression. Line-art files (black on a white background) compress the most; 24-bit full-color photographic images compress the least. The JPEG (Joint Photographic Experts Group) compression offered by most current Windows image editing applications provides greater compression than .PCX for color images, especially images with more than 256 colors (16-bit or 24-bit color).

If your use of images is intended primarily for printing (as in desktop publishing) and you do not have a color printer, use shades of gray for vector-based images. The 256-grayscale palette is preferred for printing bitmapped images; change color images to grayscale if your image-editing application supports this conversion.

Adding an Unbound Object Frame to a Form or Report

◀◀ See "Adding a Linked Subreport to a Bound Report," p. 557

Instead of using OLE Object fields, images in unbound object frames store their properties as data in the area of your .MDB file devoted to forms or reports. Like the methods you use with bound object frames, the methods that create (or edit) unbound objects are contributed temporarily by the OLE server. After you embed or link the unbound object, the Access application supplies the methods used to display the images.

The use of unbound object frames differs from that of bound object frames in the following ways:

- You set the Enabled property of most unbound object frames to No so that the OLE server that supplied those unbound objects does not appear if you double-click the object in run mode. The Enabled property does not affect your ability to edit the object in design mode. A bound object's Enabled property is usually set to Yes (the default value when the bound object frame is created).

- Unbound object frames have properties (such as Row Source, Link Child Fields, Link Master Fields, and Column Count) that are not applicable to bound object frames. Graphs and other unbound objects use these properties to obtain or present data in an unbound object field.

- You can create a master-child linkage between the content of an unbound object frame and the value of a field in the underlying table or query (or the value entered in a text box on your form).

- Multimedia objects, such as sound, video, or animated graphics, often are contained in unbound object frames.

The following sections provide examples that utilize the important additional properties available when you use unbound object frames.

Creating a New Logo for Your Personnel Actions Form

Logotypes and symbols that identify an organization are among the most common graphic objects on forms and in reports. The bitmap example in this section uses the image of a lighthouse from the Northwind Traders database, but you can substitute your organization's logo if you have a bitmap file or a scanner to create an image of suitable dimensions. Creating a logo from a bitmap file is the subject of the "Using Access 95's New Image Control" section of this chapter.

To add an image to a new form the easiest way, copy to the Clipboard an existing unbound object frame of a form or report that contains the image. Then duplicate the image by pasting it into another form. This process is similar to the process for copying OLE objects that are to be used by other applications. You can edit the image as necessary with Windows Paint or another OLE-compliant image editor.

Northwind Traders' Forms Switchboard form contains an image that almost fits the space that now contains the employee photograph on your Personnel Action Entry form. However, the bitmap is contained in an image control, so the process is a bit more complicated than simply copying an unbound object frame from one form to another. Follow these steps to copy the Northwind Traders logo from the Forms Switchboard to your Personnel Action Entry form:

1. Click the Form tab of the Database window. Choose Forms Switchboard from the list, and then click the Design button.

2. Select the Northwind logo by clicking the lighthouse in the logo. The logo is an image control, which is new to Access 95. Image controls are the subject of the "Using Access 95's New Image Control" section, which follows shortly.

3. Press Ctrl+C or choose Edit, Copy to copy the logo's bitmap to the Clipboard. Close the Forms Switchboard form.

4. If the Personnel Action Entry form is not open, select the frmPersonnelActions form in the Database window, and click the Design button.

5. Select the Photo bound object frame that you added in the preceding sections, delete it to make room for the new logo, and then click the Detail header bar to select the detail section of the form.

6. Choose Insert, Object to display the Insert Object dialog. Select Bitmap Image from the Object Type list, making sure that the Create New option button is selected (see fig. 20.9).

7. Click OK to open Paint with an empty image, then press Ctrl+V or choose Edit, Paste to paste the image into Paint's window (see fig. 20.10). Click outside the image to expose the bitmap sizing handles.

8. Click and drag the middle bottom sizing handle to eliminate the white (empty) region below the image. Repeat the process with the middle right sizing handle to eliminate the empty region to the right of the image (see fig. 20.11).

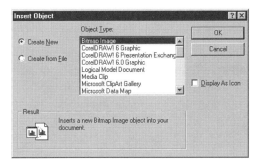

Fig. 20.9 The Insert Object dialog settings for opening an instance of Paint.

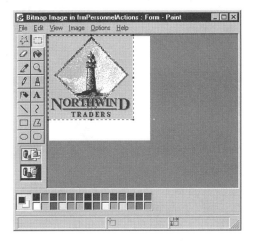

Fig. 20.10 Copying the bitmap from the Northwind logo into the open instance of Paint.

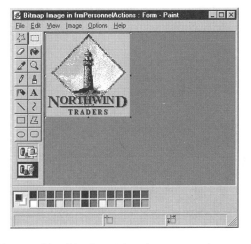

Fig. 20.11 The logo bitmap with white (empty) regions removed.

9. Choose <u>F</u>ile, Save Copy <u>A</u>s and save a copy of the bitmap as **Nwind.bmp** in your working directory (usually C:\Msoffice\Access\Samples). You use this bitmap file later with the image control.

10. Choose <u>F</u>ile, E<u>x</u>it and Return to frmPersonnelActions:Form to close Paint and place the unbound object frame in your form. The default position of the frame is at the upper left of the selected section of your form (see fig. 20.12).

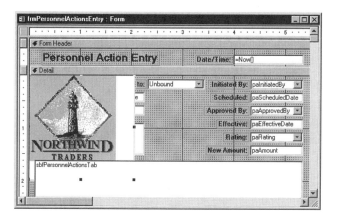

Fig. 20.12   The unbound object frame for the logo added to the Detail section of the Personnel Action Entry form.

Access applies the Size Mode property to the presentation of the image; Size Mode does not modify the image itself. The copied image extends into the area occupied by the subform; this problem is corrected when you manipulate the image in the next section.

Sizing and Setting the Properties of the Unbound Object Frame

Sizing and setting the properties of unbound object frames is similar to the process for bound object frames. To finish addition of the logo to your form, follow these steps:

1. Click and drag the unbound frame to the position previously occupied by the bound object frame.

2. Use the bottom middle and right middle sizing handles to adjust the size of the frame to fit the available space (see fig. 20.13).

 3. Open the Properties window and set the Size Mode property to Zoom to scale the bitmap to the available space, while retaining the original aspect ratio.

4. You don't need a border around the logo, so set the Special Effect property to Flat, the Border Style property to Transparent, and the Back Color property to light gray (12632256), as shown in figure 20.14.

 5. Click the Form View button to display the logo added to the Personnel Actions Entry form (see fig. 20.15).

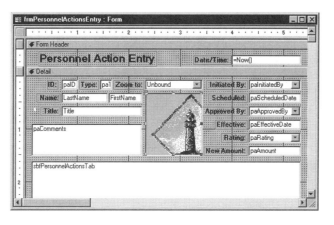

Fig. 20.13   Sizing the clipped bitmap image in the unbound object frame to the available space.

Fig. 20.14   Setting the properties for the Northwind Traders logo.

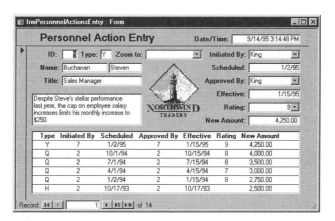

Fig. 20.15   The Northwind Traders logo in Form View.

Using Access 95's New Image Control

 Prior versions of Access required use of object frames to contain bitmapped images. Access 95 adds the image control, similar to the image control of Visual Basic 4.0, to display bitmap (.bmp), device-independent bitmap (.dib), and Windows Metafile Format (.wmf) or enhanced metafile (.emf) vector images in forms and reports. To substitute the image control for the unbound object frame of your Personnel Action Entry form, follow these steps:

1. Open frmPersonnelActions in Design View and select the logo. Press Delete to delete the unbound object frame from the form.

2. Click the Image button of the toolbox and draw the image control to the same dimensions as the deleted unbound object frame. The Insert Picture dialog appears.

3. Maneuver to the directory in which you stored the Nwind.bmp file created with Paint earlier in the chapter (see fig. 20.16). If you have an image you like better, you can substitute its .bmp file in this example.

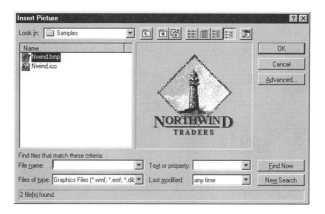

Fig. 20.16   Selecting the Nwind.bmp file created earlier in the chapter for the image control.

4. Double-click Nwind.bmp or select Nwind.bmp and click OK. Your image control appears, as shown in figure 20.17. Unlike object frames, image controls, by default, center clipped images in their frame. Image frames have a Picture Alignment property that lets you choose how the image is aligned.

5. Image controls have default Special Effect, Border Style, and Back Color properties that are suitable for adding logos to forms. Thus you need only change the Size Mode property of the image control to Zoom. Figure 20.18 shows the result of the preceding steps in Form View.

Fig. 20.17   The clipped Northwind logo in an image frame.

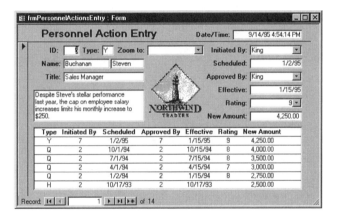

Fig. 20.18   The Northwind logo zoomed in an image frame.

If you don't need to edit a static image from within your Access application, image controls are preferred over unbound object frames for display images of the file types supported by the image control. Image controls respond faster and use fewer Windows resources than unbound object frames.

Image controls also have a variety of additional properties that you can use to customize the presentation of the image. One of the most useful of these new properties is the Palette property that you can set to a Windows palette file (.pal) or a variety of other image file types, to provide a custom set of 240 colors that enhance the appearance of 256-color bitmaps. Like its predecessors, Access 95 is limited to displaying 256-color bitmaps. Third-party 32-bit OLE Controls designed for image presentation and editing let you use high-color (16-bit color depth) and full-color (24-bit color depth) bitmaps.

Creating Graphs and Charts with Microsoft Graph 5.0

Microsoft Graph 5.0 (called by its OLE 2.0 programmatic ID, *MSGraph5*, in this book) is a 16-bit OLE 2.0 mini-server application that is almost indistinguishable from the graphing application native to Excel 5.0. Access 2.0 was the first Microsoft application to include MSGraph5 as one of a suite of OLE 2.0 mini-servers; ultimately 32-bit versions of these mini-servers will provide graphing (and other commonly required capabilities) to all Microsoft productivity applications. The sections that follow describe how to use the Graph Wizard to add MSGraph5 graphs and charts to Access 95 forms and reports.

Creating the Query on Which to Base the Graph

Most graphs required by management are the time-series type; these track the history of financial performance data, such as orders received, product sales, gross margin, and the like. In smaller firms, this data comes from tables that store entries from the original documents (such as sales orders and invoices) that underlie the summary information.

This type of data often is called a *line-item* source. Because a multi-billion-dollar firm can accumulate several million line-item records in a single year, larger firms usually store summaries of the line-item source data in tables; this technique improves the performance of queries. Summary data is referred to as *rolled-up* data, or simply *rollups*. Rollups of data on mainframe computers often are stored in client/server RDBMSs running under UNIX on minicomputers or under Windows NT on Intel-architecture or RISC PCs. Although rolling up data from relational tables violates one of the guiding principles of relational theory—don't duplicate data in tables and don't store derived data in tables—databases of rolled-up data are very common in mainframe environments.

> **Note**
>
> The Chart Wizard of Access 95 differs substantially from the Graph Wizard of Access 2.0 and its predecessors. The Chart Wizard creates a crosstab query for you; the Graph Wizard required you to create your own crosstab query. This section describes how to use the Chart Wizard in the manner Microsoft intended—from a table or a SELECT query. The "Creating a Graph from a Crosstab Query" section, later in the chapter, shows you how to change the Row Source property of a graph object to use an existing crosstab query as the source of the data.

Northwind Traders is a relatively small firm, so it is not necessary to roll up line-item data to obtain acceptable query performance on an Intel 80486-based or faster computer. To create a query designed specifically for the Chart Wizard, follow these steps:

1. In the Database window, open a new query and add the Categories, Products, Order Details, and Orders table to the query. Joins are created for you between the primary-key and foreign-key fields of each table.

2. Drag the CategoryName field of the Categories table to the first column.

3. Drag the UnitPrice field of the Order Details table to the second column. Edit the Field row of the column to read **Amount: [Order Details].[UnitPrice]* [Order Details].[Quantity]**.

4. Drag the ShippedDate field of the Orders table to the third column. Add an ascending sort on this column.

5. Add the criterion **Like "*/*/94"** to the ShippedDate column so as to only include 1994 orders. The year 1994 is used instead of 1995 in this example because data is available for all 12 months of 1994. Your query design appears, as shown in figure 20.19.

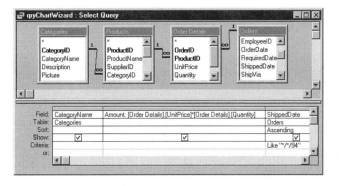

Fig. 20.19   A query design for creating a graph with Access 95's Chart Wizard.

6. Click the Run button to test your query (see fig. 20.20.) Close the query and save it with the name **qryChartWizard**.

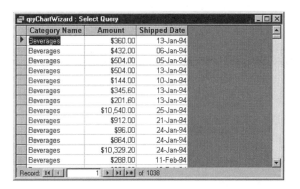

Fig. 20.20   The query result set of the query of figure 20.19.

Using the Chart Wizard to Create an Unlinked Graph

Although it's possible to create a graph or chart using the Insert Object method and selecting the Microsoft Graph 5.0 object type, the Graph Wizard makes this process much simpler. You can use the Graph Wizard to create two different classes of graphs and charts:

■ *Unlinked.* Unlinked (also called *non-linked*) line graphs display a line for each of the rows of your query. You can also create unlinked stacked column charts and multiple-area charts.

■ *Linked.* A linked graph or chart is bound to the current record of the form on which it is located and displays only a single set of values from one row of your table or query at a time.

This section shows you how to create an unlinked line graph based on a query. The next section describes how to use MSGraph5 to display alternative presentations of your data in the form of bar and area charts. In the last section of this chapter, you create a graph linked to a specific record of a query result set.

To create an unlinked graph that displays the data from the qryChartWizard query, follow these steps:

1. Open a new form, select Chart Wizard in the list box, and select qryChartWizard in the drop-down list (see fig. 20.21). Click OK to launch the first dialog of the Chart Wizard.

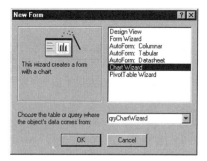

Fig. 20.21   Selecting the Chart Wizard and the query on which to base the graph.

2. Click the >> button to add all three fields to your graph (see fig. 20.22). Click the Next > button to display the Chart Wizard's second dialog.

3. Click the Line Chart button (the third from the left of the middle row of the buttons that display the available graph styles), as shown in figure 20.23. Click the Next > button to display the third Chart Wizard dialog.

4. The Chart Wizard attempts to design a crosstab query based on the data types of the query result set. In this case, the Chart Wizard makes a mistake by assuming you want months in the legend box and product categories along the graph's horizontal x-axis (see fig. 20.24).

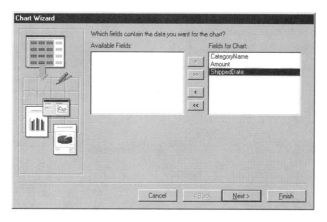

Fig. 20.22   Selecting the fields to include in the graph.

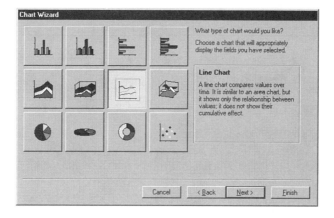

Fig. 20.23   Selecting the type of graph or chart.

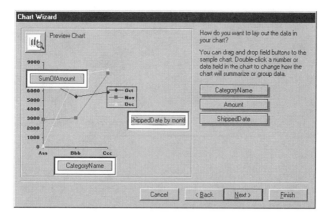

Fig. 20.24   The Chart Wizard's first try at guessing the type of crosstab query to create.

V

Integrating Access

5. You want the categories in the legend and the months of 1994 across the x-axis. Drag the CategoryName button from the right side of the dialog to the drop box under the legend and the ShippedDate button to the drop box under the x-axis. The button title, partly obscured, is ShippedDate by month (see fig. 20.25). You can double-click the ShippedDate by month button and select from a variety of GROUP BY date criteria, ranging from Year to Minute. Click the Next > button to go to the fourth and final Chart Wizard Dialog.

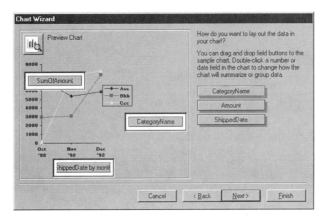

Fig. 20.25   Correcting the Chart Wizard's crosstab query guesswork.

6. Type **1994 Monthly Sales by Category** in the text box to add a title to your graph, and click the Yes, Display a Legend option button, if necessary, to display the Category Name legend (see fig. 20.26). Accept the remainder of the defaults.

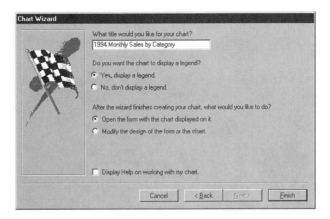

Fig. 20.26   Adding a title and legend to your graph.

7. Click the Finish button to display your graph in Form View. In the miniature version illustrated by figure 20.27, some month labels are missing and the legend crowds the graph and label. You fix these problems in the next section.

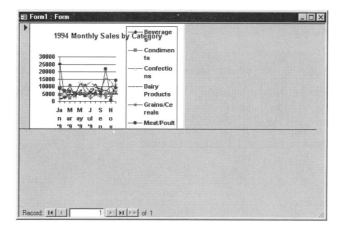

Fig. 20.27   The final unbound graph in Form View.

8. Click the Design View button of the toolbar and increase the size of your graph to at least 5.5 inches wide by 2.5 inches high (see fig. 20.28). The graph that appears in Design View at this point is an example graph included with MSGraph5.

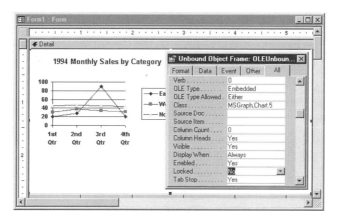

Fig. 20.28   The expanded object frame in Form Design View.

9. Set the Enabled property of the unbound object frame to Yes and the Locked Property to No.

10. The chart is in an unbound object frame, so you don't need form adornments for record manipulation. Select the form and set the Scroll Bars property of the form to Neither, Record Selectors to No, and Navigation Buttons to No.

11. Use the sizing handles of the unbound object frame to create a 1/8-inch form border around the frame. Leaving a small form area around the object makes the activation process more evident.

12. Save your form with a descriptive name, such as **frmChartWizard**. Return to Form View in preparation for changing the size and type of your graph.

> ### Tip
>
> When you complete your design, set the value of the Enabled property to No so that users of your application can't activate the graph and alter its design.

Modifying the Design Features of Your Graph

▶▶ See "Understanding OLE Automation," p. 1066

MSGraph5 is an OLE 2.0 mini-server; you can activate MSGraph5 in place, and modify the design of your graph. MSGraph5 also supports OLE Automation, so you can use Access VBA code to automate design changes. This section shows you how to use MSGraph5 to edit the design of the graph manually and how to change the line graph to an area or column chart.

To activate your graph and change its design with MSGraph5, follow these steps:

1. Double-click the graph to activate MSGraph5 in place. A diagonally hashed border surrounds the graph; MSGraph5's menus replace and supplement those of Access 95. (The activation border is missing from the left and top of the object frame if you didn't reduce the size of the object frame in step 11 of the preceding section.)

2. Drag the middle right sizing handle to the right border of your enlarged unbound object frame. Drag the middle bottom sizing handle to the bottom border of the object frame.

3. Choose View, Datasheet menu to inspect the data series that Access has transmitted to MSGraph5 (see fig. 20.29).

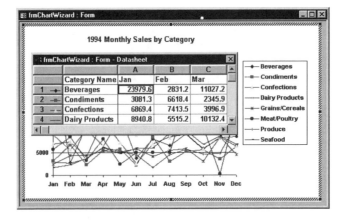

Fig. 20.29 The expanded version of the chart displaying part of the datasheet for the graph.

4. You can change the type family and font size of your chart's labels and legend. Select the graph title, and then choose F<u>o</u>rmat, <u>F</u>ont to open the Format Chart Title dialog. Set the size of the chart title to 12 points (see fig. 20.30), and then click OK to close the dialog. Select the legend, then open the Format Legend dialog and set the size of the legend font to 7 points.

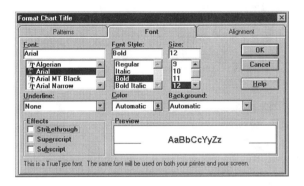

Fig. 20.30   Changing the font size of the graph's title.

5. The y-axis labels should be formatted as currency, so click one of the y-axis labels to select the y-axis. Then choose F<u>o</u>rmat, <u>S</u>elected Axis to display the Format Axis dialog.

6. Click the Number tab, select Currency formats in the Category list, and select an entry without cents (see fig. 20.31). Click OK to close the dialog and apply the new format. Your line graph appears, as shown in figure 20.32.

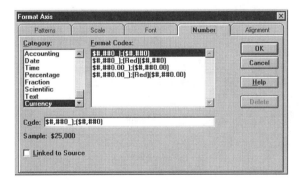

Fig. 20.31   Formatting the numeric values of the y-axis.

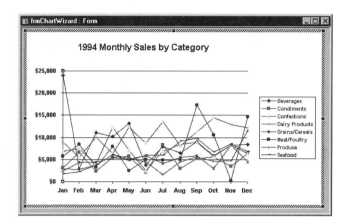

Fig. 20.32   The line graph with reformatted y-axis labels and a larger graph title.

You may want to change the line graph to some other type of chart (such as area or stacked column) for a specific purpose. Area charts, for example, are especially effective as a way to display the contribution of individual product categories to total sales. To change the line graph to another type of chart, follow these steps:

1. Choose Format, Chart Type to open the Chart Type dialog.

2. Select the Area chart picture in the Chart Type dialog (see fig. 20.33). Click OK to change your line graph into an area chart, as shown in figure 20.34. The contribution of each category appears as an individually colored area, and the uppermost line segment represents total sales.

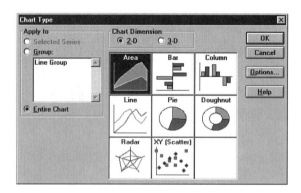

Fig. 20.33   Changing the line graph to an area chart.

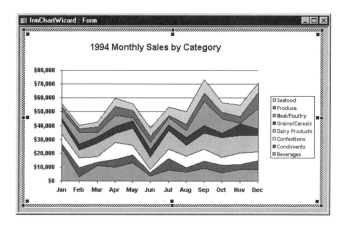

Fig. 20.34   The area chart in Form View.

3. To convert the area chart into a stacked column chart, choose F<u>o</u>rmat, <u>C</u>hart Type, select the Column picture, and then click the Options button to display the Format Column Group dialog.

4. Click the Stacked Column picture to create the column equivalent of the area chart (see fig. 20.35). (The multiple-column chart subtype is the default column chart subtype. A multiple-column chart is not suitable when you have a large number of values on the x-axis.)

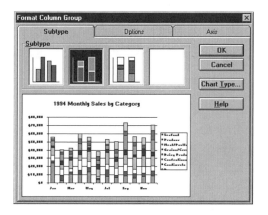

Fig. 20.35   Selecting a stacked column subtype.

5. Click OK to close the Format Column Group dialog. Your stacked column chart appears, as shown in figure 20.36.

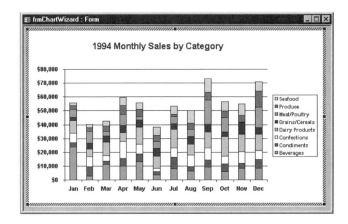

Fig. 20.36 The stacked column chart in Form View.

6. Another subtype of the area chart and the stacked column chart is the *percentage distribution* chart. To create the distribution of the sales graph shown in figure 20.37, repeat steps 3 through 5, but select the Percent Column picture with equal column heights in the Format Column Group dialog.

7. Because you set the format of the y-axis previously to eliminate the decimals, you need to change the format of the y-axis to Percent manually. Select the y-axis, choose Format, Selected Axis, select Percentage in the Categories list, select the format without decimals, then click OK to apply the format. Your chart appears as shown in figure 20.37.

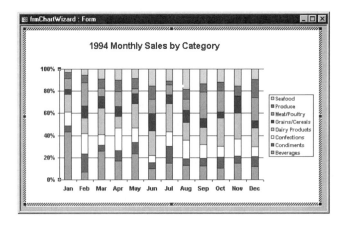

Fig. 20.37 The percentage distribution column chart.

8. Change the Chart Type to a line graph in preparation for the linked graph example of the next section. Click inside the form border but outside the object frame to deactivate the graph, and save your form. Of the four types of charts demonstrated, most users find the area chart best for displaying time series data for multiple values that have meaningful total values.

> **Note**
>
> The process of adding an unbound graph to an Access report is identical to that for forms. Unless you have a color printer, you need to select a line graph subtype that identifies data points with a different symbol for each category. For area and stacked column charts, select a series of hatched patterns to differentiate the product categories.

Creating graphs with MSGraph5 is not a speedy process. Each time you change from Design View to Form View, Access runs the query, launches MSGraph5 in the background, and passes the query data to MSGraph5. This process, using the qryChartWizard query, takes about 13 to 15 seconds on a 80486DX4/100 computer with a PCI bus video accelerator and a fast fixed-disk drive. The 32-bit graph OLE Control of Visual Basic 4.0 is much faster in operation than MSGraph5, but you must master programming OLE Automation code in Access VBA to use Graph32.ocx.

Another problem with MSGraph5 is that you cannot easily transfer data to MSGraph5's datasheet with Access VBA code. (MSGraph5 does not expose its `DataSeries` object for manipulation by OLE Automation.) You can expect third-party suppliers to provide faster-operating graphing applications, in the form of OLE 2.0 mini-servers and OLE Custom Controls. You need to write Access Basic code, however, to send the data series to these applications.

Creating a Graph from a Crosstab Query

Access 95's Chart Wizard is quite parochial: it insists on creating a crosstab query for you. Once you've created a chart with the Chart Wizard, however, you can change the Row Source property value to specify a previously created crosstab query of your own design. Thus, you can take one of the queries you created in Chapter 10, qry1994QuarterlyCategorySales, and modify this query to create the qry1994MonthlyCategorySalesGraph query that provides the same result as the crosstab query created by the wizard. You need to specify a table or query as the Record Source for the chart to create the linked chart described in the next section.

◀◀ See "Creating a Monthly Product Sales Crosstab Query," p. 357
◀◀ See "Decreasing the Level of Detail in Crosstab Queries," p. 360

> **Note**
>
> You must create the qry1994MonthlyCategorySalesGraph query and use the query as the Row Source of the unbound object frame to complete the linked graph example in the following section. The linked graph example does not work with the crosstab query created by the Chart Wizard in the preceding steps.

To create the qry1994MonthlyCategorySalesGraph query, follow these steps:

1. Open the qry1994QuarterlyCategorySales query in design mode.

2. Click the Show Table button of the toolbar and add the Categories table to the query. A join is created between the CategoryID fields of the Categories and Products tables.

3. Delete the CategoryID column that provided the Row Heading.

4. Drag the CategoryName field from the Categories table to the first column of the query, and select RowHeading in the Crosstab row.

5. Alias the CategoryName field by typing Categories: at the beginning of the field text box.

6. Change the Expr1 statement in the Fields row to Expr1:Format([OrderDate], "mmm") to use three-letter month abbreviations. Your query appears, as shown in figure 20.38.

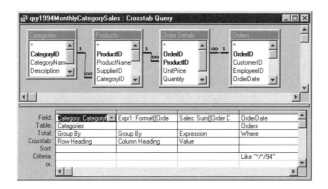

Fig. 20.38   The design of a query that displays monthly sales by product category.

7. Double-click an empty region of the upper pane to open the Query Properties dialog's General page. Delete the current entry in the Column Headings text box of the General page. Enter the 12 month abbreviations, **Jan** through **Dec**, separating the month abbreviations with commas. Access adds the double quotation marks for you, as shown in figure 20.39.

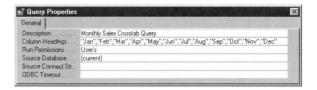

Fig. 20.39   Adding fixed column headings for 12 months.

8. Choose <u>F</u>ile, Save <u>A</u>s, and save your query as
qry1994MonthlyCategorySalesGraph.

9. Click the Run button of the toolbar to check your query result set (see fig. 20.40).

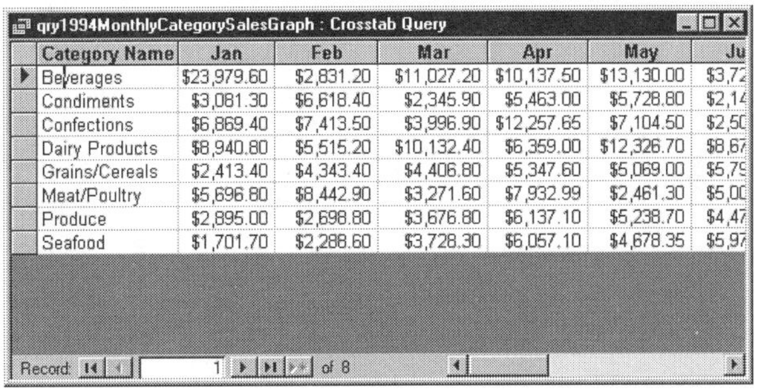

Category Name	Jan	Feb	Mar	Apr	May	Ju
Beverages	$23,979.60	$2,831.20	$11,027.20	$10,137.50	$13,130.00	$3,72
Condiments	$3,081.30	$6,618.40	$2,345.90	$5,463.00	$5,728.80	$2,14
Confections	$6,869.40	$7,413.50	$3,996.90	$12,257.65	$7,104.50	$2,50
Dairy Products	$8,940.80	$5,515.20	$10,132.40	$6,359.00	$12,326.70	$8,67
Grains/Cereals	$2,413.40	$4,343.40	$4,406.80	$5,347.60	$5,069.00	$5,79
Meat/Poultry	$5,696.80	$8,442.90	$3,271.60	$7,932.99	$2,461.30	$5,00
Produce	$2,895.00	$2,698.80	$3,676.80	$6,137.10	$5,238.70	$4,47
Seafood	$1,701.70	$2,288.60	$3,728.30	$6,057.10	$4,678.35	$5,97

Record: |◄| ◄ | 1 | ► | ►| | ►* | of 8

Fig. 20.40   Part of the result set of the qry1994MonthlyCategorySalesGraph query.

10. Open frmChartWizard in Design View, if necessary, select the unbound object frame, and open the Properties window.

11. Click the Data tab, open the Row Source list box, and select qry1994MonthlyCategorySalesGraph as the value of the Row Source property.

12. Change to Form View and verify that your line graph appears the same as that created by the Chart Wizard.

Linking the Graph to a Single Record of a Table or Query

You create a linked graph or chart by setting the values of the MSGraph5 object's Link Child Fields and Link Master Fields properties. The link is similar to that between a form and a subform. A linked graph displays the data series from the current row of the table or query that serves as the Record Source of the form. As you move the record pointer, the graph is redrawn to reflect the data values in the selected row.

To change the frmChartWizard form to accommodate a linked graph, follow these steps:

1. Open frmChartWizard in Design View; then click the Properties button of the toolbar to open the Properties window for the form.

2. Click the Data tab, open the Record Source list box, and select qry1994MonthlyCategorySalesGraph as the value of the Record Source property of the form, which binds the form to the query.

3. Your form needs record-navigation buttons for a linked query, so click the Format tab and set the value of the Navigation Buttons property to Yes.

4. Select the unbound object frame, and then click the Data tab. Type **Category** as the value of the Link Child Fields and Link Master Fields properties (see fig. 20.41).

Using this technique, you create the link between the current record of the form and the row of the query that serves as the Row Source property of the graph (through the Category field).

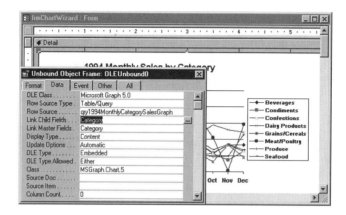

Fig. 20.41 Linking the graph's Row Source property to the current record of the form.

5. To test your linked graph, click the Form View button of the toolbar. If (in the preceding section) you saved the line graph version of the form, your graph appears, as shown in figure 20.42.

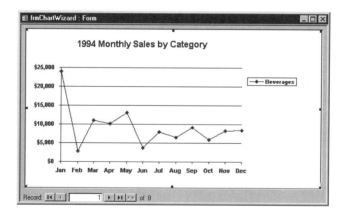

Fig. 20.42 The linked version of the 1994 Monthly Sales by Category graph.

6. The single line appears a bit anemic for a graph of this size, so double-click the graph to activate it in place. Double-click anywhere on the line to display the Format Data Series dialog. Open the Weight drop-down list, and choose the thickest line it offers. To change the data-point marker, open the Style drop-down list and select the square shape. Use the drop-down lists to set the Foreground and Background colors of the marker to a contrasting hue, such as red (see fig. 20.43). Click OK to close the dialog and implement your design changes.

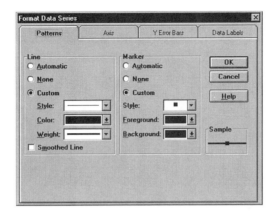

Fig. 20.43 Increasing the thickness of, and changing the markers for, the data series line.

7. Double-click the legend box to open the Format Legend dialog. Click the None option button in the Border frame to remove the border from the legend (see fig. 20.44). Click the Font tab, set the Bold attribute on, and change the font size to 11 points. Click OK to close the dialog and apply your modification to the legend.

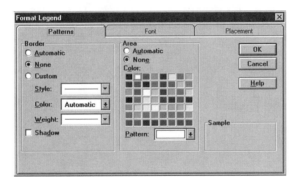

Fig. 20.44 Removing the border from the legend.

8. To use your enhanced legend as a subtitle for the chart, click and drag the legend to a location under the chart title, as shown in figure 20.45. Click the record selection buttons to display a graph of the sales for each of the eight categories.

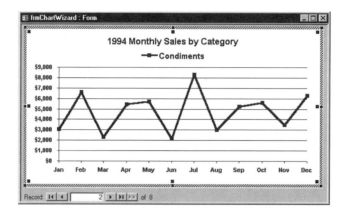

Fig. 20.45 The Form View of the graph with added design features.

9. You can smooth the data series line by activating the graph and double-clicking the line. Mark the Smoothed Line check box in the Line frame, and then click OK. Your graph now appears as shown in figure 20.46.

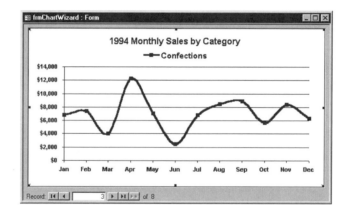

Fig. 20.46 Smoothing applied to the data series line using best-fit curves.

10. MSGraph5 offers a variety of three-dimensional chart formats. Figure 20.47 illustrates a 3-D column chart. You can change the perspective of the graph by activating the chart and clicking either of the two axes to select labels. Click one of the selection squares of the axes, and drag the square to change the perspective.

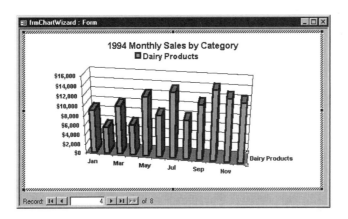

Fig. 20.47 The line graph converted to a 3-D column chart.

11. Deactivate the graph by clicking the form outside the bound object frame and choose File, Save As, and save your bound form with a new name, such as frmLinkedChart.

From Here...

This chapter introduced you to using bound and unbound object frames to contain bitmapped and vector-based images. The graphs and charts you created with MSGraph5 are dynamic vector images. Once you comprehend the operating principles of MSGraph5, you can create a variety of attractive charts and graphs based on information derived from your database application.

The following chapters expand on the subjects covered in this chapter:

- Chapter 13, "Designing Custom Multitable Forms," describes the process of linking form (master) and control (child) objects in greater detail.

- Chapter 19, "Using 32-Bit OLE 2.1," provides you with a general overview of in-place activation of OLE 2+ servers.

- Chapter 21, "Using Access with Microsoft Excel," and Chapter 22, "Using Access with Microsoft Word and Mail Merge," describe how your Access 95 applications can interact with these two popular members of the Microsoft Office 95 software suite.

- Chapter 30, "Exchanging Data with OLE Automation and DDE," describes the basic principles of using Access VBA to manipulate objects exposed by OLE Automation servers, such as MSGraph5.

V

Integrating Access

Chapter 21

Using Access with Microsoft Excel

Spreadsheet and word processing applications dominate the Windows productivity application software market. According to industry reports, more than 70 percent of all Windows installations in the business environment include a spreadsheet application. Microsoft Office 95, which includes 32-bit Excel 95 and Word 95, is likely to take over the dominant position of 16-bit Microsoft Office 4+ as Windows 95 gains popularity. Spreadsheets include the capability to emulate some of the features of database managers, such as sorting ranges of cells defined as a worksheet "database."

One of the principal uses of Access 95 is the conversion of data in large worksheets to tables in a relational database structure. Some of the primary justifications for converting from the familiar worksheet model to an Access 95 database include the following:

- Access queries provide much greater flexibility in selecting and sorting data than is offered by the limited sort and selection criteria of spreadsheet applications.

- You can create Access forms to simulate common business forms, which is difficult or impossible to do with present-day Windows spreadsheet applications. Excel 95 dialog sheets, for example, offer the choice of only a few simple control objects. Data-entry validation is much easier in Access than in worksheets.

    Access offers many more options for printing formatted reports from your data than are available with worksheets.

- Access VBA enables you to write programs in a full-featured language and does not restrict you to using a set of predetermined worksheet functions. (Spreadsheet applications that use VBA or other BASIC-like macro languages, however, don't suffer from this restriction.)

- Properly designed Access relational databases minimize the duplication of information, speed data entry, and reduce disk file storage requirements for large aggregations of data.

In this chapter, you learn to

- Import data from an Excel worksheet to a table

- Restructure the data using temporary tables

- Return the restructured data to an Excel worksheet

- Use Excel 95 as an OLE 2.1 server

- Use Access's DDE( ) and DDESend( ) function with Excel

V

Integrating Access

In many situations, however, changing a worksheet to a database is impractical. You may need to be able to view, import, or edit data contained in a worksheet within an Access application. In this case, linking the spreadsheet as an OLE object is the best method. You also can attach worksheet files in Excel 5+ formats to Access 95 tables with the Excel ODBC driver that is supplied with Microsoft Office.

The limited utility of attached worksheet files is demonstrated in the first sections of this chapter by the conversion process necessary to restructure the data to relational form. The second major topic of this chapter, "Using Excel as an OLE Server," describes how to link or embed worksheet data as OLE objects in bound or unbound object frames.

 ▶▶ See "Using Access VBA for DDE," p. 1104

This chapter also includes a brief example of the use of Access's DDE( ) function to paste the values of individual cells of a Microsoft Excel worksheet into unbound text boxes on an Access form. This technique is useful when you want to obtain the value of a specified data cell or range of cells to display or update values in Access tables. You can use the DDE( ) function with any Windows spreadsheet application that has DDE server capability. To fully exploit the DDE capabilities of Access, you need to write Access VBA functions that you execute with macros or include VBA event-handling subprocedures in code behind forms.

> **Note**
>
> Microsoft Excel 95 is used in the following examples, but you can use any Windows spreadsheet application that has OLE server capability. The first series of examples—which shows you how to reorganize spreadsheet data into Access tables—doesn't require a spreadsheet application; you only need a suitable file in Excel .xls or Lotus .wk? format to import.

Importing and Reorganizing Worksheet Data

Worksheets created by Excel and other spreadsheet applications often contain data suitable for processing with relational database techniques. The worksheet usually is organized for viewing the data quickly; however, this organization seldom is appropriate for manipulation of the data by a RDBMS.

STK_21_1 (described in the next section) is an example of a worksheet formatted for viewing data. Four rows of 22 columns each contain the equivalent of a database record—all available data for a single stock. This type of structure, where a group of individual rows constitute a database record, is common in worksheet design. This structure differs from the design of a proper worksheet database in which all the data for a single entity (in this case a stock) is contained in a single row. The examples that follow in this section illustrate how to import a spreadsheet of multiple-row-per-record type and convert the data it contains to related Access tables. Make-table and update queries assist in the reorganization of the data into relational form.

Note

The example presented in the following sections is based on a specific worksheet format that contains New York Stock Exchange trading data for common stocks. The format of the data in the worksheet is similar to that used by online sources of financial information, many of whose sources organize their transmitted data for automatic or manual importing into worksheets. You're likely to find other time-series statistical data to have been created as worksheets. The following sections are specific to a single data format, but the process of converting almost all column-row time series data to database format is similar to that presented in this chapter.

Obtaining and Converting the Example Worksheet

The file used to create many of the examples in this chapter contains the high and low prices and the trading volume of more than 300 individual stocks for a 21-day period beginning on April 10, 1992. This file was created as a Lotus 1-2-3 worksheet file (STK_21.WK1) by Ideas Unlimited and is available for downloading as STOCK.ZIP (146K in size) from the Excel for the PC Library 3 of the Microsoft Excel forum on CompuServe (GO MSEXCEL).

If you download the worksheet file to use in the following examples, you can import it directly into Access as a Lotus 1-2-3 .WK1 file. The following example uses Excel 95. If you have an earlier version of Excel or are using Lotus 1-2-3, the process is similar. Convert the file to worksheets of three different sizes by using the following steps:

1. Expand the file to STK_21.WK1 with PKUNZIP.EXE or an alternative unarchiving utility. (Type **PKUNZIP STOCK** at the DOS prompt.) If you don't have PKUNZIP.EXE, WinZip, or another ZIP-compatible utility, download PK204G.EXE from the IBM New User Library 2, Library Tools (GO IBMNEW).

   After downloading PK204G.EXE, execute the file (type **PK204G** at the DOS prompt) to obtain PKUNZIP.EXE and several other accompanying files, including user documentation.

2. Launch Excel, choose File, Open, and open STK_21.WK1 as a Lotus 1-2-3 file (.WK*) in any version of Excel. The worksheet appears in Excel 95, as shown in figure 21.1, when you click the Maximize button.

3. Choose File, Save As, and select Microsoft Excel Workbook (*.wks) in the Save As Type drop-down list to save the file as an Excel 95 workbook, STK_21.xls, in your current Access folder, C:\Msoffice\Access\Samples for the examples of this book.

4. Make A1 the selected cell of the STK_21 worksheet, and press Shift+Ctrl+End to select the entire worksheet. Choose Edit, Copy or press Ctrl+C to copy its content to the Clipboard.

5. Choose Insert, Worksheet to open a new worksheet, Sheet 1. With A1 as the selected cell, choose Edit, Paste or press Ctrl+V to copy the Clipboard contents to the new worksheet.

6. Select the STK_21 worksheet, and choose Edit, Delete Sheet.

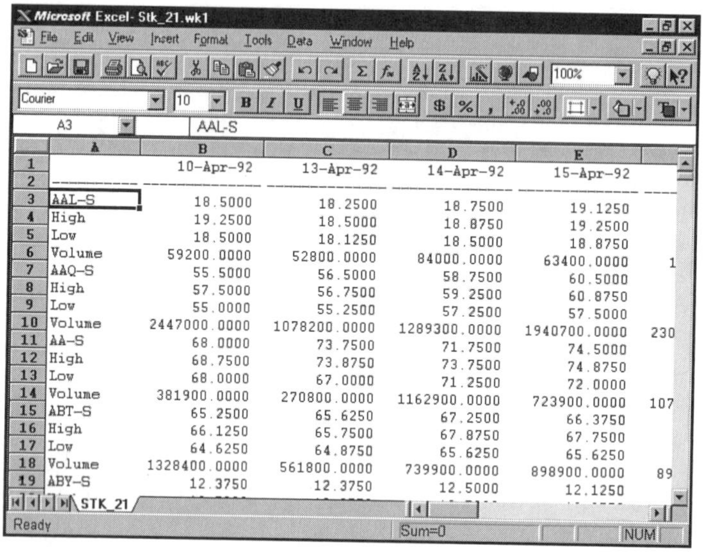

Fig. 21.1   The STK_21.WK1 worksheet opened in Excel 95.

7. Double-click the Sheet1 tab to display the Rename Sheet dialog and name the worksheet **STK_21_1**.

8. Press Shift+Ctrl+End to select the entire worksheet, if it is not fully selected, and choose Format, Cells to open the Format Cells dialog and click the Number tab. Select Number in the Category list and set the Decimal Places value to 3 with the spin button, and click OK. (Three decimal digits are adequate to display fractional prices.) The dates in row 1 change to numeric format.

9. With the entire worksheet selected, choose Format, Column, AutoFit Selection to optimize the display of the data.

10. The first row of the worksheet is used to provide field names for the table. Enter **Day** in cell A1, and replace the dates (now in Excel numeric format) in the first row of the worksheet with the numbers **1** through **21**. Follow the procedure of step 8, and select row 1 by clicking the row number button and format this row with no decimal digits (format **0**).

11. Select row 2, and choose Edit, Delete to remove the row of hyphens. The worksheet appears as shown in figure 21.2.

Now you need to make some smaller versions of the worksheet to use in the examples that follow. To create STK_21_2 (201 rows and 50 stocks) and STK_21_3 (17 rows and 4 stocks) worksheets, follow these steps:

1. Use the mouse, or the Shift key with the arrow keys to select the first 201 rows of STK_21. Choose Edit, Copy or press Ctrl+C to copy the selection to the Clipboard.

2. Insert a new worksheet. Choose Edit, Paste or press Ctrl+V to paste the 201 rows to the new worksheet. Rename the worksheet **STK_21_2**.

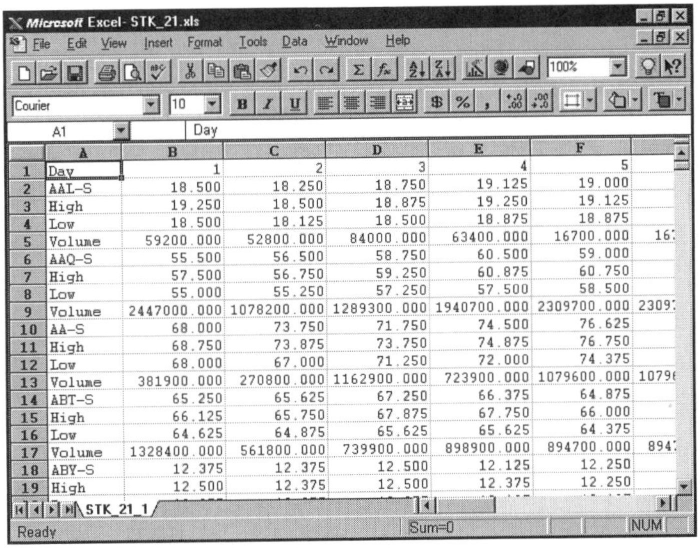

	A	B	C	D	E	F	
1	Day	1	2	3	4	5	
2	AAL-S	18.500	18.250	18.750	19.125	19.000	
3	High	19.250	18.500	18.875	19.250	19.125	
4	Low	18.500	18.125	18.500	18.875	18.875	
5	Volume	59200.000	52800.000	84000.000	63400.000	16700.000	16:
6	AAQ-S	55.500	56.500	58.750	60.500	59.000	
7	High	57.500	56.750	59.250	60.875	60.750	
8	Low	55.000	55.250	57.250	57.500	58.500	
9	Volume	2447000.000	1078200.000	1289300.000	1940700.000	2309700.000	2309:
10	AA-S	68.000	73.750	71.750	74.500	76.625	
11	High	68.750	73.875	73.750	74.875	76.750	
12	Low	68.000	67.000	71.250	72.000	74.375	
13	Volume	381900.000	270800.000	1162900.000	723900.000	1079600.000	1079(
14	ABT-S	65.250	65.625	67.250	66.375	64.875	
15	High	66.125	65.750	67.875	67.750	66.000	
16	Low	64.625	64.875	65.625	65.625	64.375	
17	Volume	1328400.000	561800.000	739900.000	898900.000	894700.000	894:
18	ABY-S	12.375	12.375	12.500	12.125	12.250	
19	High	12.500	12.375	12.500	12.375	12.250	

Fig. 21.2   The modified STK_21_1 worksheet in Excel 5.0.

3. With the entire worksheet selected, choose F<u>o</u>rmat, <u>C</u>olumn, <u>A</u>utoFit Selection.

4. Copy the first 17 rows of STK_21_2 to the Clipboard; then insert a new worksheet and paste the cells. Set AutoFit Selection for this worksheet, and rename the worksheet **STK_21_3**.

5. Exit Excel 95, and save your changes to the STK_21.xls workbook file. Don't save the large Clipboard selection.

If you are using another spreadsheet application, the procedure is likely to be quite similar. The two smaller worksheets, STK_21_2 and STK_21_3, demonstrate the effect of worksheet size on Access's performance in sections related to OLE later in this chapter. (You don't need to create the smaller files if you don't have a spreadsheet application that can act as an OLE server.)

The organization of these worksheets is especially well suited to the first example in the next section, which shows you how to reorganize a worksheet to create a properly designed table. Alternatively, you can use for the examples any Excel or .wk? file you have that contains multiple series of numbers.

Importing the Example Worksheet

◀◀ See "Creating a New Database," p. 112

◀◀ See "Creating a Table by Importing an Excel Worksheet," p. 221

The first step in the importing process is to create a new database in which to import the worksheet data. Follow these steps:

1. Launch Access if it is not open, select Blank Database in the opening dialog, and click OK. Alternatively, select the Database window if Access is open and choose File, New Database, and double-click the Blank Database icon. The New Database dialog appears.

2. In the New Database dialog, enter **Stocks.mdb** as the name of your new database; then click Create.

3. Choose File, Get External Data, Import. The Import dialog opens (see fig. 21.3).

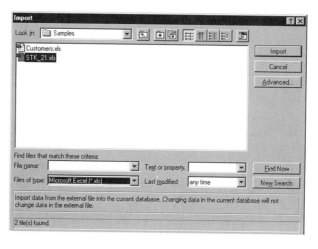

Fig. 21.3 Access 2.0's Import dialog.

4. Select Microsoft Excel (.xls) from the Files of Type drop-down list. (Support for importing all Excel file versions with a single file type selection is new with Access 95.)

5. Select STK_21.xls in the list and click the Import button to display the first dialog of the Import Spreadsheet Wizard dialog (see fig. 21.4).

6. Select STK_21_1 from the worksheet name list. (Select one of the smaller sheets if you want to save disk space.) Click Next > to display the second wizard dialog.

7. Mark the Include Field Names on First Row check box (see fig. 21.5). Click Next > to display the third wizard dialog (field options).

8. You don't need to specify field data types in this case, so click Next > to display the fourth wizard dialog (primary key options). You don't need a primary key at this point, so click the No Primary Key option button and click Finish.

9. When the wizard's message box announces that the import process has completed, click OK.

10. With the STK_21_1 table, click the Open button to display the table in Table View.

11. Select all 22 fields by clicking the Day column header button, holding down the mouse button, and dragging the mouse to the right. Choose F<u>o</u>rmat, <u>C</u>olumn Width to display the Column Width dialog (see fig. 21.6).

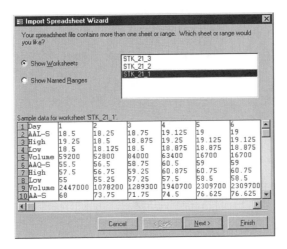

Fig. 21.4   Access 95's Import Spreadsheet Wizard's first dialog for importing worksheet files.

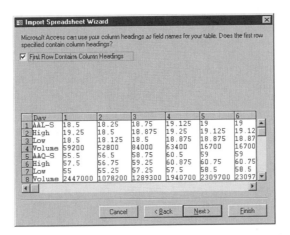

Fig. 21.5   The Import Spreadsheet Wizard's second dialog.

12. Click the Best Fit button to reduce the column widths to suit the entries in the table.

Access has interpreted the field type of the Excel 95 numeric data as double-precision, which is not required for any of the values in the table. Single-precision numbers can accommodate all of the numeric values in the table. Using single-precision, rather than double-precision, values saves about 33 percent disk space.

Fig. 21.6 Setting the column widths of the STK_21_1 table.

To change the Field Size property of the numeric fields of the STK_21_1 table, follow these steps:

1. Click the Design View button.

2. Select the first Number field—the field named 1. Change the Field Size value from Double to Single.

3. Repeat step 2 for the remaining 20 Number fields.

4. Click the Datasheet button to return to Table View. Click Yes when asked whether you want to save your changes and when notified that some data may be lost. Access converts the field sizes in the STK_21_1 table from Number to Single at this point, and no data is lost. Your table appears, as shown in figure 21.7.

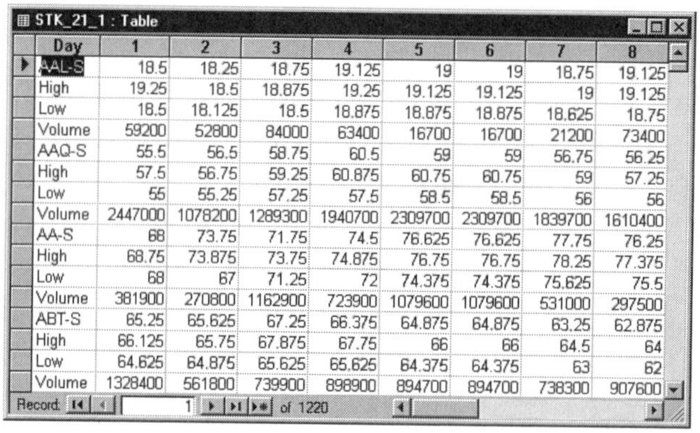

Day	1	2	3	4	5	6	7	8
AAL-S	18.5	18.25	18.75	19.125	19	19	18.75	19.125
High	19.25	18.5	18.875	19.25	19.125	19.125	19	19.125
Low	18.5	18.125	18.5	18.875	18.875	18.875	18.625	18.75
Volume	59200	52800	84000	63400	16700	16700	21200	73400
AAQ-S	55.5	56.5	58.75	60.5	59	59	56.75	56.25
High	57.5	56.75	59.25	60.875	60.75	60.75	59	57.25
Low	55	55.25	57.25	57.5	58.5	58.5	56	56
Volume	2447000	1078200	1289300	1940700	2309700	2309700	1839700	1610400
AA-S	68	73.75	71.75	74.5	76.625	76.625	77.75	76.25
High	68.75	73.875	73.75	74.875	76.75	76.75	78.25	77.375
Low	68	67	71.25	72	74.375	74.375	75.625	75.5
Volume	381900	270800	1162900	723900	1079600	1079600	531000	297500
ABT-S	65.25	65.625	67.25	66.375	64.875	64.875	63.25	62.875
High	66.125	65.75	67.875	67.75	66	66	64.5	64
Low	64.625	64.875	65.625	65.625	64.375	64.375	63	62
Volume	1328400	561800	739900	898900	894700	894700	738300	907600

Record: 1 of 1220

Fig. 21.7 The revised version of the STK_21_1 table.

Developing a Conversion Strategy

▶▶ See "Normalizing Data to the Relational Model," p. 841

The second step in the conversion process is to define the tables to be created. Very few worksheets can be converted to a single table that meets relational database standards. Designing the tables to contain the data and establishing the relationships of these tables to each other is the most important element of the conversion process. Following are the two objectives of your design strategy:

■ *A design optimized for data display, entry, and editing.* This objective is primary if you plan to use Access for data entry. In the stock prices example, data entry and editing aren't a consideration because the data is supplied in worksheet format by Ideas Unlimited and other purveyors of stock price data.

■ *A design that enables you to extract the imported data with the fewest steps.* If you obtain periodic updates to your stock price data in worksheet format, for example, ease of importing the data is the principal consideration.

The initial design usually is a compromise between these two objectives. The stock price example does not involve a compromise because data entry and editing are unnecessary.

When planning the initial design of the tables to contain the stock price and volume data, use this strategy:

▶▶ See "Fifth Normal Form and Combined Entities," p. 846

■ *The data for each element of the group—Close, High, Low, and Volume—is incorporated in an individual table.* A table with the 84 fields required to hold all the data for a stock is unwieldy at best. Reconstructing a worksheet from a table with such a design results in a cumbersome worksheet. One of the principles of relational database design is that you should be able to reconstruct your original database from the relational data.

■ *The key field of each table, Symbol, is the ticker symbol of the stock.* (Ticker symbol is the abbreviation for the name of the stock assigned by the New York Stock Exchange.) This key field enables the tables to be linked in a one-to-one relationship based on the unique values of the ticker symbols. One-to-one relationships are uncommon in relational databases, but in this example, a one-to-one relationship is quite useful.

■ *Queries organize the data in the tables as required for Access forms and reports.* Because each field in the query is prefaced by the table name, the names of the tables should be short to save keystrokes.

■ *When multiple tables are combined in a query, the records in each table must be identified by type.* The second field, Type, is a single-letter abbreviation of the type of data: C(lose), H(igh), L(ow), and V(olume).

Now you need to develop the tactics to create the required tables in accordance with your strategy. The conversion plan involves these elements:

■ The records to be included in the individual tables are extracted from the STK_21_1 table by make-table queries with criteria based on the values in the Day field.

■ The Symbol field from the Close table must be added to the High, Low, and Volume tables.

■ In the query used to create the final table, adding the Symbol field to a table requires a unique key to link the Close table and the tables that don't have symbol values. An AutoNumber field added to the Close, High, Low, and Volume tables can serve as a temporary key field.

■ Creating the new tables is a two-step process. First, the data is extracted to a temporary set of tables (Hi, Lo, and Vol). The second step combines these three tables with the Symbol field of another temporary table, Close, to create the final High, Low, and Volume tables. You need temporary tables in this case because make-table queries should never alter tables on which they are based.

■ Because the Close table lacks a type identifier field, a Type field must be added to this table. The remaining tables have a type identifier word that can be replaced by the corresponding code letter.

Now that you have a conversion strategy and have decided the tactics to carry it out, you are ready to test the merits of both, as described in the next section.

Extracting Data

  ◀◀ See "Creating Action Queries to Append Records to a Table," p. 374

Make-table queries are designed specifically for creating new tables from data in existing tables that meets a specified set of criteria. For STK_21_1, you use make-table queries to create one final table (Close) and three temporary tables (Hi, Low, and Vol). To create these four tables with make-table queries, follow these steps:

1. With the STK_21_1 table open, click the arrow of the New Object button of the toolbar and select New Query from the list to create a new query based on STK_21_1.

2. With New Query selected in the New Query dialog's list, click OK to create Query1.

3. Click the Day field, and drag the field symbol to the first column of the query.

4. Click the asterisk (*, all fields), and drag the field symbol to the second column of the query.

5. Click the Show check box in the Day field to clear the box. (Day is included in the fields in the second column of the query. You cannot include two fields of the same name in a make-table query.)

6. In the Criteria row of the Day field, enter **High** to include only records for the high price of the stock in the temporary Hi table. Your query appears, as shown in figure 21.8.

7. Choose Query, Ma<u>k</u>e Table to display the Make Table dialog.

8. Enter **Hi** in the Table Name text box and then click OK (see fig. 21.9). The default values for the remaining elements in the Make Table dialog are satisfactory.

9. Click the Run button of the toolbar to create the temporary Hi table. Access displays a message box that indicates the number of records to be added to the new table (see fig. 21.10). Click Yes.

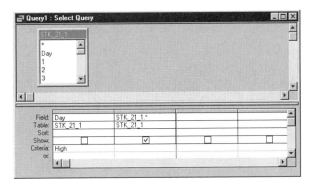

Fig. 21.8 Creating the temporary Hi table with a make-table query.

Fig. 21.9 Entering the temporary table name in the Make Table dialog.

Fig. 21.10 The message box that confirms the number of rows added to the new table.

10. Open the Database window, click the Tables tab, and double-click the Hi entry in the list to view the table (see fig. 21.11).

11. Change the Criteria value of your make-table query to **Low** and repeat steps 6 through 10, substituting **Lo** for the table name in steps 6 and 10.

12. Change the Criteria value to **Volume** and repeat steps 6 through 10, using **Vol** for the table name.

13. The closing prices are in the row with the ticker symbol. Each of the symbols has a hyphen followed by a character that identifies the type of security; -S represents a common stock. Change the Criteria value to **Like** "*-*" to select these rows and repeat steps 6 through 10, using **Close** for the table name. The expression *-* selects all records containing a hyphen. You don't need to create a temporary table in this case because the Close table includes the ticker symbols, as illustrated by figure 21.12.

Day	1	2	3	4	5	6	7	8	9	10
High	19.25	18.5	18.875	19.25	19.125	19.125	19	19.125	19.125	19.1
High	57.5	56.75	59.25	60.875	60.75	60.75	59	57.25	58	58.
High	68.75	73.875	73.75	74.875	76.75	76.75	78.25	77.375	76.375	75.6
High	66.125	65.75	67.875	67.75	66	66	64.5	64	63.375	63.8
High	12.5	12.375	12.5	12.375	12.25	12.25	12.375	23.125	12.125	12.1
High	62.625	62.75	64.375	64.75	64.75	64.75	62.375	61.75	61.625	61.3
High	25.125	25.5	26	25.875	24.5	24.5	24.125	23.5	24.375	24.
High	31.375	31.25	31.875	32	32.25	32.25	32.25	32.25	32.125	31.8
High	43.75	44.5	44.25	43.75	43.25	43.25	43.25	43.75	44.125	43.8
High	42	42	42.25	42.375	42.625	42.625	42.375	42.5	43.25	
High	40.5	40.125	41.5	42.375	42.625	42.625	42.375	41.875	41.375	39.8
High	16.625	16.625	16.75	16.875	17	17	16.875	17	17.375	17.
High	77.75	77.75	82	81.875	80	80	77.875	77.25	76.875	77
High	86	85.625	87.75	87.5	87.5	87.5	86.375	86.375	85.125	85.3
High	58.875	59.375	59.5	59.625	60.75	60.75	61.125	61.5	62.75	63.

Fig. 21.11 The temporary Hi table created by the make-table query.

Day	1	2	3	4	5	6	7	8	9
AAL-S	18.5	18.25	18.75	19.125	19	19	18.75	19.125	19
AAQ-S	55.5	56.5	58.75	60.5	59	59	56.75	56.25	57.625
AA-S	68	73.75	71.75	74.5	76.625	76.625	77.75	76.25	78
ABT-S	65.25	65.625	67.25	66.375	64.875	64.875	63.25	62.875	63.375
ABY-S	12.375	12.375	12.5	12.125	12.25	12.25	12.375	23.125	12.125
ACY-S	61.875	62.375	64.375	64.5	62.625	62.625	60.25	61.5	61
ADM-S	25	25.375	25.625	24.375	23.875	23.875	23.375	23.375	24.125
AEP-S	31.25	31.125	31.625	32	32.25	32.25	32.25	32.25	31.875
AET-S	43.5	44	43.625	43.125	43.25	43.25	43.125	43.75	43.875
AGC-S	41.875	41.375	42.125	42.375	42.625	42.625	42.25	42.5	43
AHC-S	39.375	40	41.375	42.375	42.375	42.375	41.875	41.5	40
AHM-S	16.375	16.625	16.625	16.625	16.75	16.75	16.75	16.875	17.125
AHP-S	76.875	77.75	81.625	80	78.25	78.25	76.125	77.125	76.125
AIG-S	85.375	85.5	86.75	87.25	86.75	86.75	86	85.25	84.875
AIT-S	58.75	58.875	59.375	59.625	60.75	60.75	61.125	61.125	62.625
ALD-S	53.75	53.75	54.625	55.5	57	57	56.5	56.75	56.25

Record: 14 ◀ [1] ▶ ▶I ▶* of 305

Fig. 21.12 The Close table with the ticker symbol of the stocks.

Modifying the Table Structure

> **Tip**
>
> AutoNumber fields are the fastest way of adding a primary-key field to a table that does not contain unique values on which to base a primary key.

Each table you created in the preceding section requires additional fields so that you can design an append query to create a properly-structured table. An AutoNumber field is used as a temporary key field for each of the four tables. The Close table needs a Type field added, and the Day field of each temporary table needs the name changed to Type. Follow these steps to make the changes:

1. Click the Tables tab in the Database window, select the Hi table, and click the Design button.

2. Change the name of the first field from Day to **Type** and set the Field Size property to **1**, as shown in figure 21.13. This action truncates the Type field value, High, to the required single-letter code H.

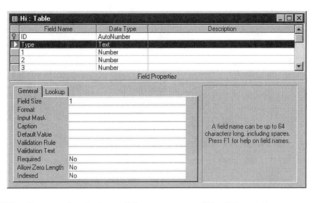

Fig. 21.13 Modifications to the design of the temporary Hi table.

3. Click the field selector button of the Type field, and press Insert to add a field at the beginning of the table. Type **ID** in the Field Name column, and select AutoNumber in the Data Type column. Click the Primary Key button of the toolbar to make the ID field the primary-key field.

4. Click the Table View button on the toolbar. Save the changes to the table. A message box advises you that some data may be lost due to truncating the length of the Type field (see fig. 21.14). Click Yes to approve the change. The table appears, as shown in figure 21.15.

Fig. 21.14 The warning that some data may be lost due to truncating the Type field.

5. Repeat steps 1 through 4 for the Lo and Vol tables.

6. Open the Close table in design mode. Change the Day field name to **Symbol**, and change its Field Size property to **10** to accommodate longer ticker symbols.

7. Click the Selection button for the Symbol field, and press Insert to add an **ID** AutoNumber field. Click the Primary Key button of the toolbar to create the primary-key index.

8. Select the first of the Number fields, and then press Insert to add a new field. Enter **Type** as the Field Name of the new field (added fields default to the Text data type) and set its Field Size property to **1**. Figure 21.16 shows the design of the Close table.

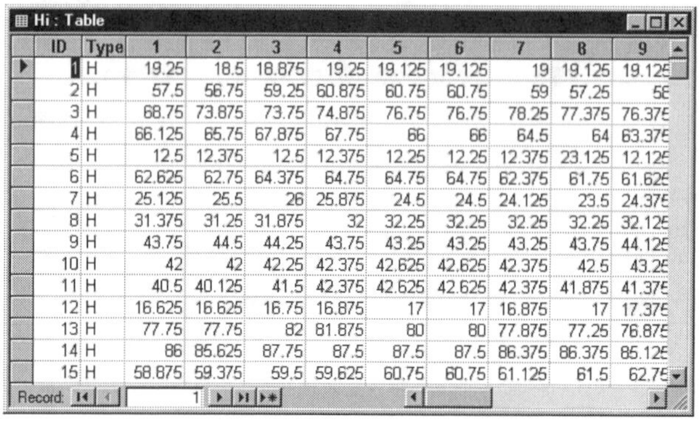

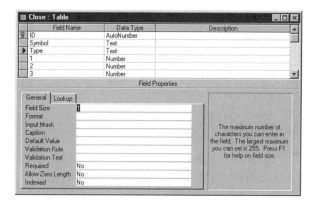

Fig. 21.15 The temporary Hi table with the ID key field added.

Fig. 21.16 Modifications made to the design of the Close table.

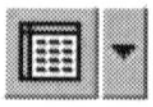

9. Click the Table View button of the toolbar, save your changes, and accept the truncated field. Figure 21.17 shows the resulting Close table.

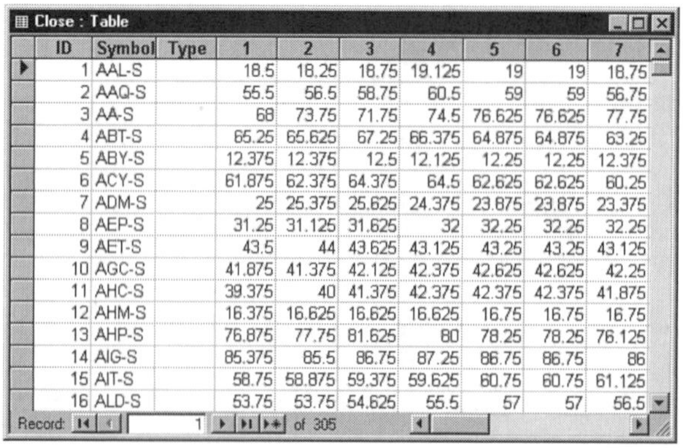

Fig. 21.17 The Close table with the ID and Type fields added.

The extraction of data from STK_21_1 to the required tables is a relatively simple process because the labels used to identify the data are consistent throughout the worksheet. You may need to write a worksheet macro that creates consistent labels for rows to be included in a specific table if the labels don't exist or aren't consistent in the original version of the worksheet.

Adding the Type Value to the Close Table

◄◄ See "Updating Values of Multiple Records in a Table," p. 379

When you need to replace data in a field containing text values, the Replace command on the Edit menu is usually a faster process than creating an UPDATE query. Because the Replace What text box in the Replace in Field dialog doesn't accept a **Null** value, however, you cannot use the Replace command on the Edit menu to add the C code (for "Close") to the Type field of the Close table. Instead, you must use an update query to change the Type field value. Follow these steps:

1. Make the Close table active. Click the arrow of the New Object button of the toolbar, and choose New Query from the menu list.

2. With the New Query item in the list selected, click the OK button of the New Query dialog to create a new query with the Close table added.

3. Choose Query, Update to change the query type from select to update.

4. Select the Type field and drag the field symbol to the first column of the query.

5. Type **C** in the Update To row. This action changes the Type field value in all records from the default **Null** to C. Figure 21.18 shows the update query design at this point.

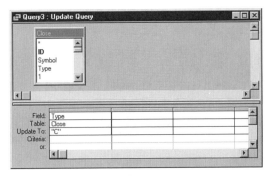

Fig. 21.18 The update query used to add C to the Type field of each record in the Close table.

6. Click the Run button on the toolbar to update the Type field of the Close table. When the message box shown in figure 21.19 appears, click Yes.

V

Integrating Access

Fig. 21.19 The message box that indicates the number of records to be updated.

Creating the Final Tables

> **Tip**
>
> If you are creating an application that uses macros to automate the conversion process, save each query with a unique name so that the query can be run by a macro.

Now you need to combine the Symbol field of the Close table with the data in the Hi, Lo, and Vol tables to create the final High, Low, and Volume tables. In this example, you use the same query each time, changing the temporary table name to create the three final tables.

To create your final High, Low, and Volume tables with make-table queries, follow these steps:

1. With the Close table active, click the arrow of the New Object button of the toolbar and select New Query, then click the OK button of the New Query dialog to create a new query based on the Close table.

2. Choose Query, Make Table to open the Make Table dialog. Enter **High** in the Table Name text box as the name of the final table to create, and click OK.

3. Select the Symbol field of the Close table, and drag it to the first column of the make-table query.

4. Click the Show Table button of the toolbar or choose Query, Show Table to open the Table/Query list. Select Hi from the Table/Query list and click OK. Then choose the Close button. Access automatically creates the join between the ID fields of the Close and Hi tables for you.

> **Caution**
>
> *This is a very important step.* If Access fails to establish this relationship and you don't add the relationship, you create a *Cartesian product* instead of the result you want. The Cartesian product is all possible combinations of all the field values contained in the two tables. In this case, the Cartesian product contains about 95,000 (305 * 305) rows.

5. Click the asterisk (*, all fields) of the Hi table, and drag the field symbol to the second column of the query. The make-table query appears, as shown in figure 21.20.

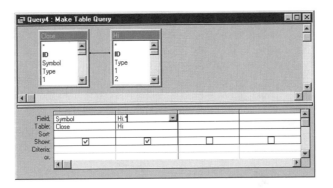

Fig. 21.20 The make-table query that creates the final Hi table.

6. Click the Run button of the toolbar to create the final Hi table. Click OK from the message box that appears.

7. Select the Hi table field list, and press Delete to remove the field list from the query. Repeat steps 4 through 6 for the Lo table, substituting **Low** as the name for the new final table in the Make Table dialog.

8. Repeat step 7 for the Vol table, entering **Volume** as the name of the final table in the Make Table dialog.

9. Close the query, and don't save the changes.

You must remove the temporary key field, ID, from the Close table so that you can make Symbol the key field. Follow these steps:

1. Open the Database window, click the Tables tab, and select the Close table. Click the Design button.

2. Click the field select button of the ID field; then press Delete. When Access displays message boxes asking you to confirm deletion of the field and deletion of the key field, click OK.

3. Select the Symbol field; then click the Primary Key button of the toolbar to make the Symbol field the primary-key field. Figure 21.21 shows the Design View of the Close table.

4. Click the Table View button on the toolbar to display the contents of the table. Click OK when asked to confirm your changes.

5. Select all columns of the table by dragging the mouse pointer over the column's field name buttons.

6. Choose Format, Column Width to open the Column Width dialog (see fig. 21.22). Click Best Fit to close the dialog.

Figure 21.23 shows the resulting Close table.

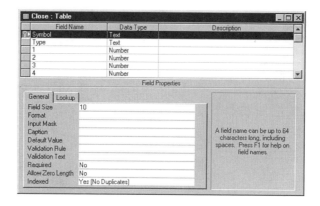

Fig. 21.21 The Close table with Symbol as the primary-key field.

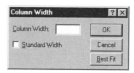

Fig. 21.22 Setting the column widths of the Close table.

Symbol	Type	1	2	3	4	5	6	7	8
AA-S	C	68	73.75	71.75	74.5	76.625	76.625	77.75	76.25
AAL-S	C	18.5	18.25	18.75	19.125	19	19	18.75	19.125
AAQ-S	C	55.5	56.5	58.75	60.5	59	59	56.75	56.25
ABT-S	C	65.25	65.625	67.25	66.375	64.875	64.875	63.25	62.875
ABY-S	C	12.375	12.375	12.5	12.125	12.25	12.25	12.375	23.125
ACY-S	C	61.875	62.375	64.375	64.5	62.625	62.625	60.25	61.5
ADM-S	C	25	25.375	25.625	24.375	23.875	23.875	23.375	23.375
AEP-S	C	31.25	31.125	31.625	32	32.25	32.25	32.25	32.25
AET-S	C	43.5	44	43.625	43.125	43.25	43.25	43.125	43.75
AGC-S	C	41.875	41.375	42.125	42.375	42.625	42.625	42.25	42.5
AHC-S	C	39.375	40	41.375	42.375	42.375	42.375	41.875	41.5
AHM-S	C	16.375	16.625	16.625	16.625	16.75	16.75	16.75	16.875
AHP-S	C	76.875	77.75	81.625	80	78.25	78.25	76.125	77.125
AIG-S	C	85.375	85.5	86.75	87.25	86.75	86.75	86	85.25
AIT-S	C	58.75	58.875	59.375	59.625	60.75	60.75	61.125	61.125
AL-S	C	19.625	20.625	20.125	20.25	20.875	20.875	21.125	20.875

Record: 1 of 305

Fig. 21.23 The final version of the Close table.

7. Choose File, Save Layout to save the column width change.

At this point, you can delete the Hi, Lo, and Vol tables. Deleting temporary tables conserves disk space, but only after you compact the database.

Verifying the Tables by Re-Creating the Worksheet

◀◀ See "Copying and Pasting Tables," p. 155

An important step when creating tables from external data sources is to verify that the tables contain the correct information. In most cases, the best method of testing is to use the tables to re-create the data in its original format—or as close to the original format as possible. This strategy enables you to make a direct comparison of the source data and the data contained in the tables.

To create a replica of the original STK_21_1 worksheet, follow these steps:

1. Make the Database window active, click the Tables tab, and select the Close table.

2. Press Ctrl+C to copy the table to the Clipboard; then press Ctrl+V to create a copy of the table. The Paste Table As dialog appears.

3. Type **tblStockPrices** as the name of the new table in the Paste Table As dialog (see fig. 21.24). Make sure that the default Structure and Data options button is selected, and then click OK. Access creates a new tblStockPrices table.

Fig. 21.24   Entering the table name in the Paste Table As dialog.

4. Select the tblStockPrices table in the Tables list of the Database window, and then click the Design button.

5. Click the Indexes button of the toolbar to display the Indexes dialog.

6. Select both the Symbol and Type fields by holding down the Shift key and clicking the two field selection buttons. Then click the Primary Key button of the toolbar.

7. Select the Symbol field and click the Indexed text box in the Field Properties section of the Design window. Choose Yes (Duplicates OK) from the Indexed drop-down list. If you choose No (No Duplicates), you cannot append records. Indexing the Symbol field can speed up queries based on a specific symbol or set of symbols. Figure 21.25 shows the design for the Stock Data table.

8. Click the Table View button of the toolbar, and click OK when asked whether you want to save your changes. Review the data in the table, and then close the tblStockPrices window.

In preparation to append the data in the other tables to the tblStockPrices table, you need to remove the primary key (ID) field. In prior versions of Access, you could append data from tables without an identical set of fields. Access 95 issues an "INSERT INTO statement contains unknown field name '*FieldName*'" message if the field names don't match in the source and destination tables. Open the High, Low, and Volume tables in Design View and delete the ID field of each of these three tables.

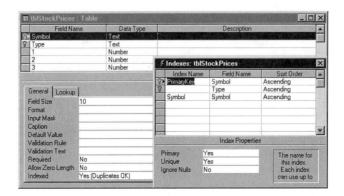

Fig. 21.25 Modifying the key field and indexing properties of the tblStockPrices table.

> **Note**
>
> An alternative to deleting the ID fields is to add all fields, except the ID field, of the High, Low, and Volume fields to the queries you create in the following series of steps.

To add the data in the High, Low, and Volume tables to the Stock Data table, follow these steps:

1. Select the High table in the Database window; then click the New Object button of the toolbar and select New Query from the menu list to display the New Query dialog.

2. With New Query selected, click OK to open a new query based on the High table.

3. Choose Query, Append to display the Append Query dialog. Open the Table Names drop-down list and select tblStockPrices (see fig. 21.26). The tblStockPrices table is the table to which you want to append the records. Click OK.

Fig. 21.26 The Append Query dialog.

4. Select the asterisk field of the High table field list and drag the field list symbol to the first column of the query. Figure 21.27 shows the append query design.

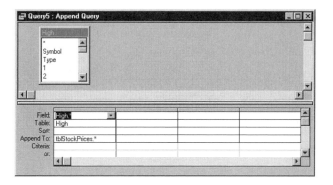

Fig. 21.27 The append query design to add records to tblStockPrices from the High table.

5. Click the Run button on the toolbar to append the High records to Stock Data. The message box shown in figure 21.28 indicates the number of records to be appended. Click Yes.

Fig. 21.28 The message box confirming the append operation.

6. Delete the High table's field list from the query, and then click the Show Table button of the toolbar. Repeat steps 4 and 5 to append the Low and Volume table data to tblStockPrices.

7. After you have appended the data from the High, Low, and Volume tables to tblStockPrices, open the tblStockPrices table from the Database window. The table appears, as shown in figure 21.29. The data for Close, High, Low, and trading Volume appears in the same sequence as in the worksheet because the table is indexed on the combination of the Symbol and the Type fields, the primary key. Access creates a no-duplicates index on the key field(s).

8. Drag the tblStockPrices table to the lower right of your display. Open the STK_21_1 table; then click the exposed surface of the tblStockPrices window to compare it with the original version (see fig. 21.30).

9. Indexing tblStockPrices has changed the order of some of the entries. Confirm that the data for a few stocks in both tables are the same.

You can add stock price data for later dates by consecutively numbering the fields in successive Excel tables. As an example, the next 21 days of prices and trading volumes would use field names 22 through 42 for the numeric values. You could name the tables you create Close2, High2, Low2, and Volume2, and then add these tables to your queries to extend the range of dates to be included. Alternatively, you could create tables that have the high, low, close, and volume data for a given stock on a specific date. Making this type of transformation, however, requires that you write Access VBA code to restructure the tables.

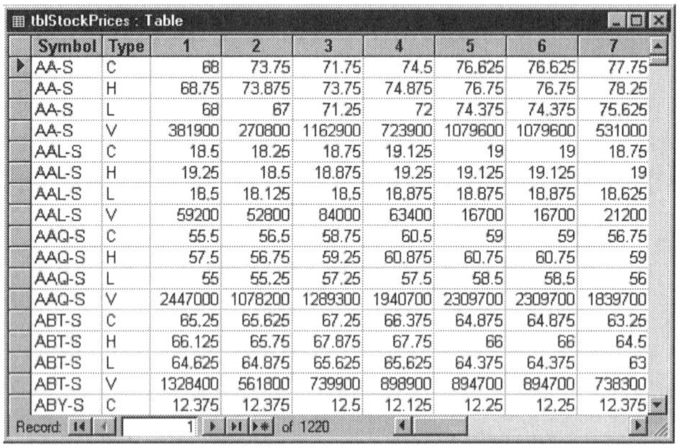

tblStockPrices : Table

Symbol	Type	1	2	3	4	5	6	7
AA-S	C	68	73.75	71.75	74.5	76.625	76.625	77.75
AA-S	H	68.75	73.875	73.75	74.875	76.75	76.75	78.25
AA-S	L	68	67	71.25	72	74.375	74.375	75.625
AA-S	V	381900	270800	1162900	723900	1079600	1079600	531000
AAL-S	C	18.5	18.25	18.75	19.125	19	19	18.75
AAL-S	H	19.25	18.5	18.875	19.25	19.125	19.125	19
AAL-S	L	18.5	18.125	18.5	18.875	18.875	18.875	18.625
AAL-S	V	59200	52800	84000	63400	16700	16700	21200
AAQ-S	C	55.5	56.5	58.75	60.5	59	59	56.75
AAQ-S	H	57.5	56.75	59.25	60.875	60.75	60.75	59
AAQ-S	L	55	55.25	57.25	57.5	58.5	58.5	56
AAQ-S	V	2447000	1078200	1289300	1940700	2309700	2309700	1839700
ABT-S	C	65.25	65.625	67.25	66.375	64.875	64.875	63.25
ABT-S	H	66.125	65.75	67.875	67.75	66	66	64.5
ABT-S	L	64.625	64.875	65.625	65.625	64.375	64.375	63
ABT-S	V	1328400	561800	739900	898900	894700	894700	738300
ABY-S	C	12.375	12.375	12.5	12.125	12.25	12.25	12.375

Record: 1 of 1220

Fig. 21.29 The final version of the tblStockPrices table with all records appended.

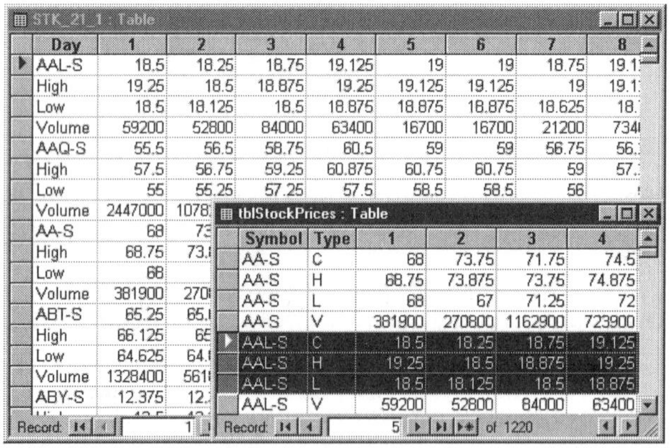

STK_21_1 : Table

Day	1	2	3	4	5	6	7	8
AAL-S	18.5	18.25	18.75	19.125	19	19	18.75	19.1
High	19.25	18.5	18.875	19.25	19.125	19.125	19	19.1
Low	18.5	18.125	18.5	18.875	18.875	18.875	18.625	18.
Volume	59200	52800	84000	63400	16700	16700	21200	734
AAQ-S	55.5	56.5	58.75	60.5	59	59	56.75	56.
High	57.5	56.75	59.25	60.875	60.75	60.75	59	57.
Low	55	55.25	57.25	57.5	58.5	58.5	56	
Volume	2447000	1078						
AA-S	68	73						
High	68.75	73.						
Low	68							
Volume	381900	270						
ABT-S	65.25	65.						
High	66.125	65						
Low	64.625	64.						
Volume	1328400	561						
ABY-S	12.375	12.						

Record: 1

tblStockPrices : Table

Symbol	Type	1	2	3	4
AA-S	C	68	73.75	71.75	74.5
AA-S	H	68.75	73.875	73.75	74.875
AA-S	L	68	67	71.25	72
AA-S	V	381900	270800	1162900	723900
AAL-S	C	18.5	18.25	18.75	19.125
AAL-S	H	19.25	18.5	18.875	19.25
AAL-S	L	18.5	18.125	18.5	18.875
AAL-S	V	59200	52800	84000	63400

Record: 5 of 1220

Fig. 21.30 Comparing the tblStockPrices table with the original version.

> **Note**
>
> The structure of the tblStockPrices table does not conform to the rules of relational databases, although its structure is an improvement over the original Excel worksheet. Using individual fields for dates constitutes *repeating groups,* a violation of first normal form for relational tables. A fully normalized table would consist of a single record for the high, low, close, and volume data for a single stock on a single date. The composite primary key of such a table would be the stock ticker symbol and the date. Creating a fully-normalized table from STK_21.xls requires the use of a complex DDE operation or the use of OLE Automation. Both of these operations require a substantial amount of Access VBA code.

Using the Tables You Created

◄◄ See "Establishing Relationships between Tables," p. 142
◄◄ See "Enforcing Referential Integrity," p. 147

In this section, queries combine the data in the tables to create forms and reports that display the data in tabular or graph form. The relationships between the tables should be established automatically for the queries you create. In addition, you need to maintain referential integrity; that is, you shouldn't be able to delete a closing price for a stock for which you have high, low, and volume data. This obligation requires that you include relationships as properties of the tables.

To establish the relationships between the tables, follow these steps:

1. Open the High table in Design View, select the ID field, and click the Primary Key button of the toolbar to make the ID field the primary key field. Repeat the process for the Low and Volume tables.

    Access 95 requires a primary key to determine whether the relationship between tables is one-to-one or one-to-many. (Access 2.0 lets you specify the type of relationship.)

2. Make the Database window active, and then click the Relationships button of the toolbar or choose <u>T</u>ools, <u>R</u>elationships. The empty Relationships window opens with the Show Table dialog active.

3. Select the High table in the Tables list box, and click the Add button.

4. Repeat step 2 for the Low, Close, and Volume tables, and then click the Close button. Your Relationships window appears, as shown in figure 21.31.

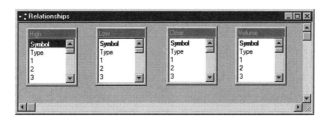

Fig. 21.31   The Relationships window with the four tables added.

5. Drag the Symbol field from the High table field list to the Symbol field of the Low table field list to create a join. Access opens the Relationships dialog.

6. Mark the Enforce Referential Integrity check box to enable cascading updates and deletions. Access automatically determines the relationship between each table as one-to-one by testing the joined fields.

7. Mark the Cascade Update Related Fields check box. This lets you change the Symbol value for a stock if its NYSE ticker symbol should change, an unlikely (but

conceivable) event. If you change one Symbol value, the Symbol values for all of the related tables change in unison.

8. Mark the Cascade Delete Related Records check box. This lets you remove all of the records for a stock that is delisted from the NYSE, a more likely event. Your Relationships dialog appears, as shown in figure 21.32.

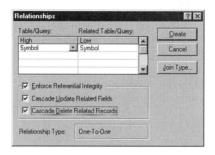

Fig. 21.32 Setting referential integrity enforcement rules in the Relationships dialog.

9. Click the Create button to create the join and close the Relationships dialog.

10. Repeat steps 4 through 8 for the join between the Low and Close tables and the join between the Close and Volume tables. The Relationships window appears, as shown in figure 21.33.

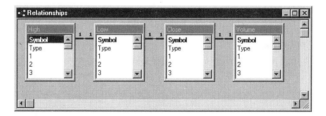

Fig. 21.33 The Relationships window with one-to-one relationships between each table.

11. Double-click the Document Control-menu box to close the Relationships window and save your changes.

Note

Always establish default relationships between the tables of your database so that these relationships are added automatically to the queries you create. If you don't establish default relationships and then Access doesn't create or you forget to add relationships to your query, you may obtain the Cartesian product (described earlier in this section) instead of the result you want. The Cartesian product of large tables can be large and take several minutes to create. Pressing Ctrl+Break may not halt the process, and Windows may exhaust its resources in creating the Cartesian product, creating an out-of-memory error.

To create a test query that includes all the data in your tables, follow these steps:

1. Select the High table in the Database window, and then click the arrow of the New Object button of the toolbar and select New Query from the button menu to display the New Query dialog.

2. With New Query selected in the list, click OK to create a query with the High table added.

3. Click the Show Table button of the toolbar to add the Low, Close, and Volume tables. The joins between the tables are established automatically (by the relationships you established in the preceding series of steps) as you add each table, as shown by the lines connecting the Symbols fields in figure 21.34. Click the Close button.

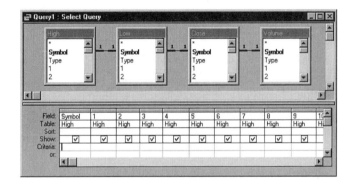

Fig. 21.34 Part of the query design for the 21-day stock prices query.

4. Double-click the header of the High table's field list to select all of the fields, and drag the multiple field column to the first column of the query.

5. Select and delete the Type column. Then use the horizontal scroll bar slider to display the first empty column after the 22 columns devoted to the High fields.

6. Repeat steps 4 and 5 for the Low, Close, and Volume tables, but also delete the Symbol field for these three tables.

7. Click the Run button of the toolbar to display the query. You can drag the columns of the query to reorder the columns in a logical sequence, as shown in figure 21.35.

8. Click the SQL button of the toolbar to display the SQL statement for the query (see fig. 21.36). The SQL statement reflects reordering of the first two sets of data (days 1 and 2) only.

V

Integrating Access

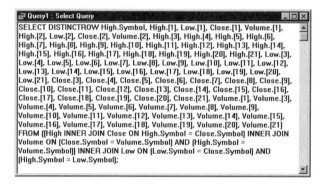

Fig. 21.35   The query result set with the columns reordered.

```
Query1 : Select Query
SELECT DISTINCTROW High.Symbol, High.[1], Low.[1], Close.[1], Volume.[1],
High.[2], Low.[2], Close.[2], Volume.[2], High.[3], High.[4], High.[5], High.[6],
High.[7], High.[8], High.[9], High.[10], High.[11], High.[12], High.[13], High.[14],
High.[15], High.[16], High.[17], High.[18], High.[19], High.[20], High.[21], Low.[3],
Low.[4], Low.[5], Low.[6], Low.[7], Low.[8], Low.[9], Low.[10], Low.[11], Low.[12],
Low.[13], Low.[14], Low.[15], Low.[16], Low.[17], Low.[18], Low.[19], Low.[20],
Low.[21], Close.[3], Close.[4], Close.[5], Close.[6], Close.[7], Close.[8], Close.[9],
Close.[10], Close.[11], Close.[12], Close.[13], Close.[14], Close.[15], Close.[16],
Close.[17], Close.[18], Close.[19], Close.[20], Close.[21], Volume.[1], Volume.[3],
Volume.[4], Volume.[5], Volume.[6], Volume.[7], Volume.[8], Volume.[9],
Volume.[10], Volume.[11], Volume.[12], Volume.[13], Volume.[14], Volume.[15],
Volume.[16], Volume.[17], Volume.[18], Volume.[19], Volume.[20], Volume.[21]
FROM ((High INNER JOIN Close ON High.Symbol = Close.Symbol) INNER JOIN
Volume ON [Close.Symbol = Volume.Symbol] AND [High.Symbol =
Volume.Symbol]) INNER JOIN Low ON [Low.Symbol = Close.Symbol] AND
[High.Symbol = Low.Symbol];
```

Fig. 21.36   The SQL statement for the queries of figures 21.34 and 21.35 with two days of data reordered.

Note

The square brackets surrounding the numbered field names in the SQL statement shown in figure 21.36 are required to prevent the numbers from being interpreted by Jet as numeric values. En-closing the field names in square brackets assures that the field names are treated as literals.

You can use queries of the preceding type to display or edit any data in the four tables by using a form or to print part or all of the stock data with an Access report. You might design other queries that display only stocks that meet a specific criterion, such as mini-mum trading volume or a range of stock closing prices. The ability to rearrange data in almost any desired row and column sequence quickly, using simple queries, demon-strates that Access query datasheets are at least as flexible as worksheets.

Exporting Stock Data as a Worksheet

When you are collecting data on the same set of common stocks, you can simplify the conversion process by modifying the design of the Excel worksheet to correspond to the design of the tables. You can avoid making a large number of changes to the worksheet in Excel by exporting the Access tblStockPrices table back to Excel in Excel 5.0 format.

To export the Stock Data table to an .XLS workbook file, follow these steps:

1. Activate the Database window, and select the tblStockPrices table.

2. Click the arrow of the Office Links button of the toolbar and choose Analyze It with Excel to export the table data and launch Excel with the tblStockPrices.xls worksheet active (see fig. 31.37).

	A	B	C	D	E	F	G	H	I	
1	Symbol	Type	1	2	3	4	5	6	7	
2	AA-S	C	68	73.75	71.75	74.5	76.625	76.625	77.75	
3	AA-S	H	68.75	73.875	73.75	74.875	76.75	76.75	78.25	
4	AA-S	L	68	67	71.25	72	74.375	74.375	75.625	
5	AA-S	V	381900	270800	1162900	723900	1079600	1079600	531000	
6	AAL-S	C	18.5	18.25	18.75	19.125	19	19	18.75	
7	AAL-S	H	19.25	18.5	18.875	19.25	19.125	19.125	19	
8	AAL-S	L	18.5	18.125	18.5	18.875	18.875	18.875	18.625	
9	AAL-S	V	59200	52800	84000	63400	16700	16700	21200	
10	AAQ-S	C	55.5	56.5	58.75	60.5	59	59	56.75	
11	AAQ-S	H	57.5	56.75	59.25	60.875	60.75	60.75	59	
12	AAQ-S	L	55	55.25	57.25	57.5	58.5	58.5	56	
13	AAQ-S	V	2447000	1078200	1289300	1940700	2309700	2309700	1839700	1
14	ABT-S	C	65.25	65.625	67.25	66.375	64.875	64.875	63.25	
15	ABT-S	H	66.125	65.75	67.875	67.75	66	66	64.5	
16	ABT-S	L	64.625	64.875	65.625	65.625	64.375	64.375	63	
17	ABT-S	V	1328400	561800	739900	898900	894700	894700	738300	
18	ABY-S	C	12.375	12.375	12.5	12.125	12.25	12.25	12.375	

Fig. 21.37   The stock price data appears in the order of the table's primary-key fields.

3. Choose File, Save to save the sorted worksheet and close Excel.

You can use the new worksheet as a template for entry or import of stock price and trading volume data for other ranges of dates. Using the new format eliminates the necessity of creating temporary tables during the conversion process.

Using Excel as an OLE Server

This section describes methods of creating links between data cells in OLE Object fields and worksheets created with Excel 95. You can duplicate some examples with Excel 3.0 and 4.0, but Version 5 and later versions—with their OLE 2+ compatibility—have several added features that simplify the process. The step-by-step examples in this section are based on the assumption that you are familiar with the use of Excel 5+.

You can embed or link an Excel worksheet or graph as a bound or unbound OLE object. You can copy data from the OLE worksheet object to the Clipboard and then paste the data into a bound or unbound text box. The following sections provide examples of these techniques.

Embedding an Excel Worksheet in a Form

You can embed an entire Excel worksheet in an unbound object frame using the simple process that follows. In this case, the presentation of an Excel worksheet (or what you can display of the worksheet in a bound object frame) is the entire content of the worksheet. Large embedded worksheets occupy considerable disk space and may require a substantial period of time to display their presentation; you may want to use a small worksheet (5K or less file size, such as a workbook file created from the STK_21_3 worksheet) if you are short on disk space.

To embed an Excel worksheet in an unbound object frame of a new form, follow these steps:

1. Open the Stocks.mdb database, if necessary, and create a new blank form. Initially, size the form to about 3.33 inches high by 6 inches wide.

2. Click the Toolbox button of the toolbar and select the unbound object frame tool. Create a frame with the left corner at about .5 inches from the form's left edge and about 0.3 inch from the top. (The dimensions of these margins are important; see the troubleshooting note at the end of this section.) The Insert Object dialog appears.

3. Click the Create from File option button, then click the Browse... button to open the Browse Dialog and locate the folder containing the tblStockPrices.xls file. Select tblStockPrices.xls (or the name of any other Excel 5+ workbook file you want to embed) in the file list, and then click OK (see fig. 21.38).

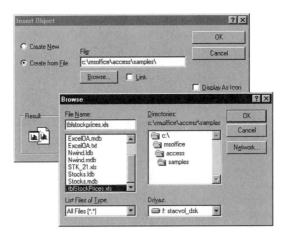

Fig. 21.38 Inserting an unbound object from an Excel 95 file.

Troubleshooting

A message box appears, indicating that the Excel worksheet is corrupted, that Excel is not properly registered, or that there is not enough memory to open Excel.

Close other open applications and try again. If the procedure continues to display error messages, exit Windows and start over. (An application has failed to release its global memory blocks on closing.) If you continue to receive error messages that refer to the Registry, you need to verify that the Registry entries for Excel are correct. See Chapter 19, "Using 32-Bit OLE 2.1," for detailed instructions on the Registry entries required for local servers.

4. Select the unbound object frame and drag the right border to about 5.8 inches. Drag the bottom border to about 3.1 inches.

5. Click the Properties button of the toolbar. Click the Data tab and set the value of the Enabled property to Yes and Locked property to No. If you don't enable and unlock the object frame, you can't activate the object (see fig. 21.39).

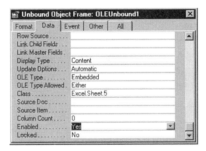

Fig. 21.39 Setting the Enabled property of the object to allow in-place activation.

6. Click the Form View button of the toolbar to display the presentation of your worksheet (see fig. 21.40). If only part of a column displays, return to Design View and adjust the width of your object frame so that a full column is displayed with a 0.25-inch border at the right. You also may need to adjust the height of the form to provide a 0.25-inch border at the bottom. (The borders inside the object frame are necessary; see the troubleshooting note below.)

7. Double-click the object frame to activate the worksheet in place. If you have set the left and top positions of your object frame and provided the proper internal borders, your activated worksheet appears, as shown in figure 21.41. Excel 95's Edit and View menus replace Access's Edit and View menus, and Excel's Insert, Format, Tools, and Data menus are added to Access's menu. The toolbars that normally appear when you open Excel are added to Access 95's toolbars. Activated mode is indicated by a hashed border around the object frame.

V

Integrating Access

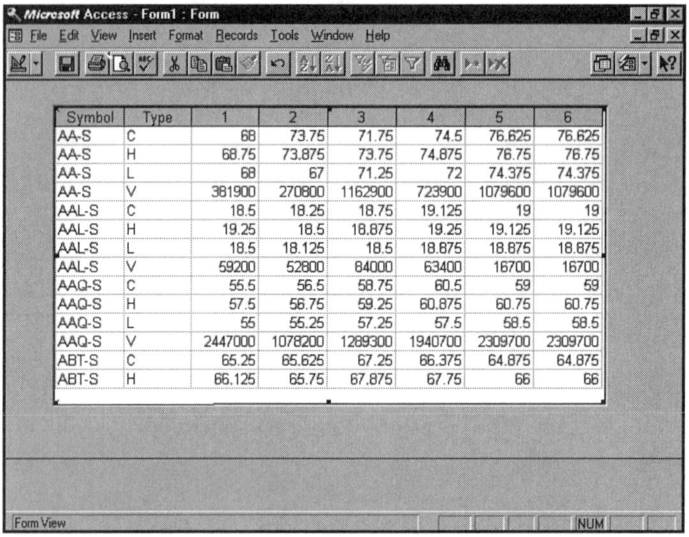

Fig. 21.40 The presentation of a worksheet in an unbound object frame.

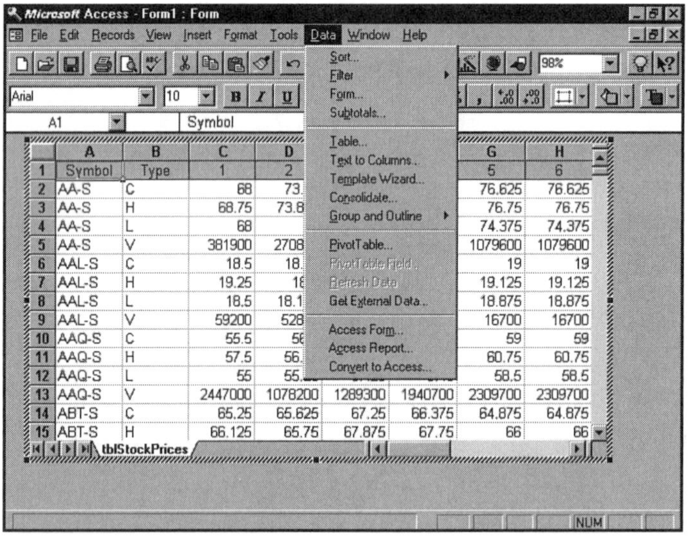

Fig. 21.41 The worksheet activated in place.

You can perform any operation that is possible in Excel 95 when the object is activated except operations that require use of Excel's File menu, such as saving the workbook to a file or printing the worksheet.

8. Click outside the bound object frame to deactivate the object, and return to presentation mode so that Access's menubar is active.

9. Choose Edit, Worksheet Object, Open to open Excel 5.0's window with the embedded data as the source of Excel's current workbook (see fig. 21.42). When you open Excel, you can print the worksheet or save the embedded workbook to a file.

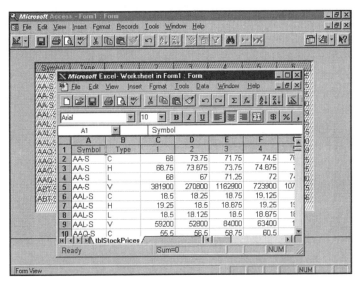

Fig. 21.42   Opening Excel 95 in its own window (from presentation mode).

10. Choose File, Exit to close the instance of Excel and return to presentation mode.

11. Close your form and save the changes.

Troubleshooting

Excel's column selection buttons, row selection buttons, worksheet tabs, horizontal scroll bar, or the vertical scroll bar don't appear when the object is activated.

Two sets of critical factors determine the visibility of *adornments*, as the preceding objects are called, when you activate an object in place. The top position of the object frame must provide room for the column selector buttons in the form area (0.25 inch), and the left position of the frame must provide space for the row selector buttons (0.5 inch). The visibility of the horizontal and vertical scroll bars is determined by the internal margin of the object, the space between the edge of the worksheet presentation, and the bottom and right edge of the object frame (0.25 inch each).

If, after setting these values, all of the adornments shown in figure 21.43 do not appear, position the mouse pointer on the upper-left corner of the activation border and drag the corner diagonally downward to reduce the size of the activation frame. You may need to make repeated adjustments to the size of the object frame and the activation frame to ensure that all adornments appear.

Extracting Values from an OLE Object

You can copy individual numeric or text values from a linked or embedded Excel OLE object and place the values in a text box. To add the close, high, and low values of the

AAL-S stock to a multiline text box added to the form you created in the preceding section, follow these steps:

1. Reduce the size of your unbound object frame containing the Excel worksheet object, and move the frame down to make room for a multiline text box at the top of the form.

2. Add a text box to the form, and set the value of the Scrollbars property to Vertical.

3. Double-click the unbound object frame to activate the workbook object.

4. Select the cell or range of cells you want to import to a text control object. In this case, select A2:I5 to return eight days of price data for the AA-S stock.

5. Choose Edit, Copy, or press Ctrl+C to copy the A2:I5 range to the Clipboard.

6. Select the text box, deactivating the object frame, and then choose Edit, Paste Special to display the Paste Special dialog. When you copy data items from an embedded object, you only have the option of pasting them as text (see fig. 21.43). Click OK.

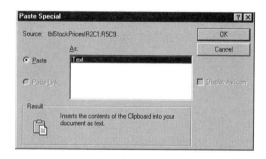

Fig. 21.43   Pasting a selection from an embedded Excel worksheet.

7. The pasted data items appear, as shown in figure 21.44. The vertical bars between the values in the text box represent the tab characters that Excel uses to separate data columns in a row.

If you create one or more bound text boxes with a numeric data type, you can paste a number from a selected single cell to each text box and then use the values to update the fields of the table to which the text box is bound. A more efficient method, however, is to use OLE Automation or Access VBA DDE... instructions to update values in tables with data from another application. (Using a simplified version of DDE is described later in this chapter.)

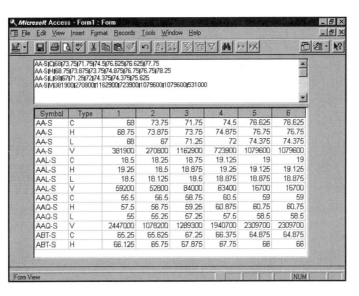

Fig. 21.44 A selection from an embedded Excel worksheet pasted into an unbound text box.

Linking to a Range of Cells of an Excel Worksheet

▶▶ See "Manipulating an Excel 95 Workbook Object," p. 1072

▶▶ See "Using Access VBA for DDE," p. 1104

Embedding Excel objects is useful if you want to use OLE Automation to transfer data from a Recordset object to embedded worksheet cells. In most cases, however, creating an OLE link to all or a range of cells in a worksheet is a more common practice. Linking enables you to display or edit the most recent version of the worksheet's data from its source file. Any changes you make in Access are reflected when you close Excel if you save the changes.

The conventional process of linking a file in Excel is similar to that for using OLE 1.0 to link graphics files; in-place activation is not available with linked objects. To create a link with a range of cells in an Excel file, perform the following steps:

1. Open a new, blank Access form.

2. Launch Excel independently of Access.

3. Choose File, Open, and in Excel's Open dialog, select the file you want to link. This example uses tblStockPrices.xls.

4. Select the cells of the worksheet to be included in your Access table; then copy the selected cells to the Clipboard with Ctrl+C. Cell range A1:E17 of the tblStockPrices.xls worksheet is used in this example.

5. In Access, choose Edit, Paste Special to display the Paste Special dialog. Click the Paste Link option button. Your only choices for a linked object are the object or the text contained in the selected data items. The data source, tblStockPrices! R1C1:R17C5, appears in the Source label (see fig. 21.45).

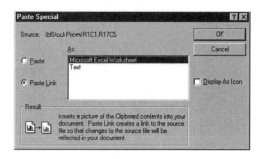

Fig. 21.45   The Paste Link dialog for a linked range of cells in an Excel worksheet.

6. Click OK to create the unbound object frame containing the presentation of the selected cells. You don't need to provide for margins in the design because in-place activation is not available with linked objects.

7. Open the Properties window and set the value of the Enabled property of the object frame to Yes and the Locked property of the frame to No.

8. Click the Form View button of the toolbar. The presentation of your linked object appears, as shown in figure 21.46.

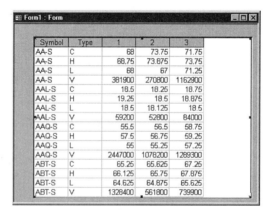

Fig. 21.46   The presentation of a linked range of worksheet cells.

9. Double-click the presentation of the worksheet to launch Excel in its own window with the linked cells selected (see fig. 21.47). As noted earlier in this section, in-place activation does not apply to linked objects.

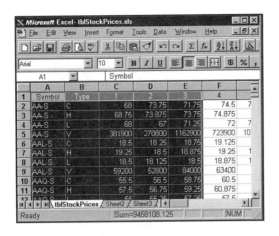

Fig. 21.47 The instance of Excel launched by double-clicking the linked cells' presentation.

10. In Excel, choose File, Exit to return the focus to Access. If you have made changes to the data, you can elect to save the changes at this point.

Using DDE Links with Excel

If you need to extract individual numeric or text values from a worksheet to update values in your database, *dynamic data exchange* (DDE) is a better method than using linked or embedded OLE objects. DDE enables you to transfer data from a specific cell within a worksheet to a bound or unbound text box on a form or report without writing OLE Automation code in Access VBA. Figure 21.48 shows the design of a form that displays the data from the tblStockPrices.xls worksheet, using Access's DDE( ) function.

The syntax of the DDE( ) function follows:

```
=DDE(AppName, TopicName, ItemName)
```

AppName, *TopicName*, and *ItemName* are enclosed within quotation marks when you use *string literals* (the actual names). The following list describes these arguments:

- *AppName* is the Windows task name of the DDE server application assigned by its publisher. *AppName* consists of a single word (no spaces allowed) and is often a contraction of the full name of the product, such as *WinWord* for Microsoft Word. You usually can find the DDE *AppName* for an application in documentation for that application.

- *TopicName* is, in the majority of cases, the full path and file name of the file that contains the data to be sent to Access.

- *ItemName* is the name of the location of the data to be sent within *TopicName*. For a worksheet, *ItemName* can be a range of cells in Excel's row-column format (R1C1) or the name of a range of cells. In Word, *ItemName* is usually a bookmark name.

If the worksheet file is located in the C:\Msoffice\Access\Samples folder, for example, and you want to extract the data from cells A2:F5, the function is as follows:

```
=DDE("Excel","c:\msoffice\access\samples\tblStockPrices.xls ",
"R2C1:R5C6")
```

Cell A2 corresponds to column 1 of row 2, and cell F5 is located in column 6 of row 5. You can substitute a named range from the worksheet for the R#C# coordinates as the DDE topic.

Figure 21.48 illustrates the design of a simple form that uses the DDE( ) function to retrieve the stock ticker symbol, plus high, low, close, and volume data, for the stock specified by the coordinates of the cells in the tblStockPrices.xls workbook with the worksheet open in Excel. (Opening Excel with the desired topic saves much typing in the text boxes.)

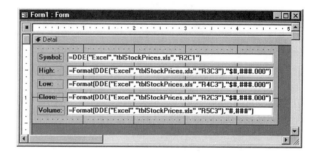

Fig. 21.48   The design of a simple form using the DDE( ) function to return cell values.

The elements of the design of the form of figure 21.48 are:

- The value of the Control Source property of each text box is `=DDE("Excel", "tblStockPrices", "RrCc")`, where r and c are the row and column coordinates of the required cell.

- The stock prices are formatted with the `$#,###.000` mask, and the volume is formatted with `#,###` to eliminate the trailing zeros.

- When you display the form in Form View and Excel is not running with the specified topic, the message box of figure 21.49 appears. Click Yes to launch Excel, minimized to an icon. (If Excel is running with another topic, a second instance of Excel is launched.) If Excel is not running with the specified topic, you must prefix the file name with the full path.

Fig. 21.49   The message box that appears if Excel is not running with the specified topic.

- Excel returns the requested values to the text boxes (see fig. 21.50).

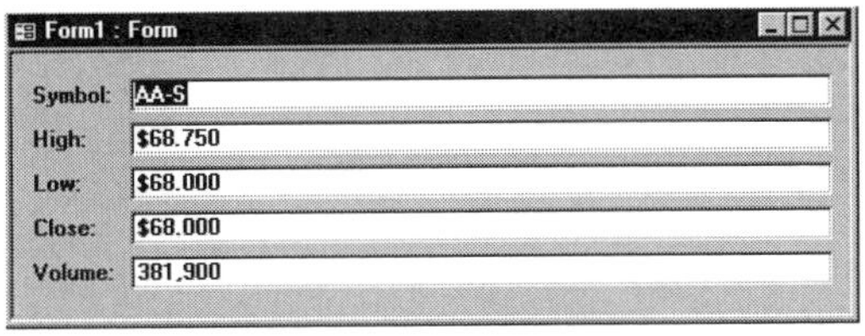

Fig. 21.50   Data returned by Excel via DDE to an Access form.

Using the DDE( ) function is cumbersome because of the amount of typing necessary to supply the argument values. You can use copy and paste methods to add additional cells. After pasting an additional set of cells, you change the column number in each DDE( ) expression.

You can use the Access DDE( ) function to obtain and display specific data items from worksheets more quickly and easily than by copying them from an OLE server that supplies worksheet objects in bound or unbound object frames. You only need to open Excel or another DDE-compliant spreadsheet application once; the server runs minimized to an icon. After loading the spreadsheet application, data transfer to the form or report is rapid, and DDE consumes much less memory than OLE during the process.

You cannot edit data in a text box supplied by the =DDE( ) expression. To use the full capabilities of DDE, you need to create an Access VBA function and then call the function from a command button or with an Access macro.

Access provides a second DDE function, DDESend( ), that enables you to transfer data, usually from a text box, from an Access form to an Excel worksheet or any other document in a Windows application that supports DDE. The syntax of the DDESend( ) function is as follows:

    =DDESend(*AppName*, *TopicName*, *ItemName*, *Data*)

AppName, *TopicName*, and *ItemName* are the same as the arguments for the DDE( ) function. *Data* is a string that can be a literal value enclosed within quotation marks, a function that returns a string, or the value of a text box control. For example, if you want to change "Day" in cell A1 of the STK_21.XLS worksheet in your C:\ACCESS directory to "Date," you add a text box control to your form and type **=DDESend("Excel", "tblStockPrices.xls", "R1C1", "Date")** as the value of the Control Source property of the text box.

You can send the value of another text box on your form by substituting the control Name of the other text box for the literal string in the preceding example. If you have a text box with the name txtClose_1, whose data you want to send to cell B2, the syntax of the DDESend( ) statement for value of the Control Source property of the DDESend( ) text box is:

    =DDESend("Excel", "tblStockPrices.xls", "R2C2", [txtClose_1])

The value of the Control Source property of a DDESend( ) text box must be that of another text box because text boxes with =DDESend() expressions as their Control Source property are read-only in run mode. The text box that contains the DDESend( ) function appears blank in Form View; thus, you set the Visible property of =DDESend() text boxes to No. You can specify the DDESend( ) function as the Control Source property of an Option Group, Check Box, or Combo Box control, but these controls are also read-only and are disabled (dimmed) in run mode.

Both the DDE( ) and DDESend( ) functions execute immediately upon the opening of the form in which they are used. If your Access application includes multiple *TopicNames*, an instance (copy) of the application specified by *AppName* is opened for each *TopicName* you add to your forms. Thus, you can rapidly deplete the resources available to Access with multiple copies of Excel (or other DDE servers), resulting in out-of-memory messages from Access. You must close each instance of the DDE server application manually by choosing the instance in Task Manager's list and clicking End Task or by clicking the DDE server's icon and choosing Close from the Application Control menu.

Using the Access VBA DDE... statements, explained in Chapter 30, "Exchanging Data with OLE Automation and DDE," is the preferred method of implementing the equivalent of the DDE( ) and DDESend( ) functions. In most cases, however, using OLE Automation to perform functions equivalent to DDE operations is the preferred method.

From Here...

This chapter provided typical examples of the ability of Access to interact with data in worksheets. Importing and reorganizing data formerly contained in worksheets is one of the most common tasks you encounter if you are using Access for business applications. If conversion isn't practical or desirable, you can use OLE to display and edit worksheet data in Access. If you only need to display values of a few specific data cells in a worksheet, DDE is the quickest and easiest approach.

The following chapters provide further information on the subject discussed in this chapter:

- Chapter 7, "Linking, Importing, and Exporting Tables," provides additional information on importing and exporting data to and from Excel workbook files.

- Chapter 19, "Using 32-Bit OLE 2.1," provides an overview of OLE and the new capabilities of Windows 95's new OLE 2.1 features.

- Chapter 22, "Using Access with Microsoft Word and Mail Merge," shows you how the Access Mail Merge Wizard uses DDE to create merge data sources for Microsoft Word 95.

- Chapter 30, "Exchanging Data with OLE Automation and DDE," describes how to use Access VBA to perform operations that are more flexible than those afforded by the DDE( ) and DDESend( ) functions.

Chapter 22

Using Access with Microsoft Word and Mail Merge

Members of the Microsoft Office 95 software suite are specifically designed to make constructing cooperative applications easy. *Cooperative applications* use two or more Windows productivity applications to perform a specified task. One of the principal uses for database applications is creating mailing lists for use in conjunction with form letters. Thus, Access 95, a member of the Professional Edition of Microsoft Office 95, includes a Mail Merge Wizard that not only automates the process of creating Word 95 merge data files, but also aids you in creating new form letters.

You also can use the reverse process and create form letters using Word 95's new mail merge process. Creating form letters from Word 95 accommodates users who do not have retail Access 95 on their computers. Word 95 uses 32-bit Microsoft Query (Msqry32.exe) and the new 32-bit Open Database Connectivity (ODBC) application programming interface (API) version 2.5 to connect to Access 95 and earlier .mdb files and to a variety of other desktop database types.

As with Excel worksheets, you can embed or link Word documents in bound or unbound object frames and add a complete word processing system to your Access application. If you embed the Word document in the object frame, you can take advantage of OLE 2.1's in-place activation to make the operating environment of Access almost identical to that of Word. Word's menu supplements the Access menu, and Word's toolbars appear as docked or floating toolbars on your display. Word's document editing window, in Page View, appears within the confines of your object frame.

Using the Access Mail Merge Wizard

Access 95's Mail Merge Wizard can help you create a new main merge document or employ an existing main merge document from which to create form letters. The Mail Merge Wizard uses a table or a query as the data source for the merge data file. The sections that follow describe the following two methods of creating a form letter:

In this chapter, you learn to

- Use Access's Mail Merge Wizard to create Word 95 form letters

- Use Access databases as the data source for the Word 95 mail merge process

- Embed and link Word 95 documents in Access tables and forms using OLE 2.1

- Create a simple form to display and edit embedded or linked documents

V

Integrating Access

- Using the Mail Merge Wizard to create a new main merge document whose merge data source is an Access table

- Using an existing main merge document with a merge data source from an Access select query

Creating and Previewing a New Form Letter

When you first try a new wizard, it's customary to create a new object rather than use the wizard to modify an existing object, such as a main merge document. The following steps use the Mail Merge Wizard to create a new main merge document from records in the Customers table of Northwind.mdb.

Note

Using the Mail Merge Wizard consumes an extraordinary amount of Windows resources because Word and two instances of Access run simultaneously. If you have less than 16M of RAM, close all running applications except Word and Access before starting the following process.

---

1. Open Northwind.mdb, if necessary, and select the Customers table in the Database window.

2. Click the arrow of the Office Links button of the toolbar, and select Merge-It from the drop-down menu to launch the Microsoft Mail Merge Wizard. The Wizard's first and only dialog appears, as shown in figure 22.1.

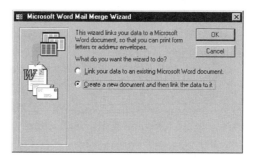

Fig. 22.1   The dialog of the Microsoft Word Mail Merge Wizard.

3. Click Create a New Document and then link the data to it option button to create a new main merge document using fields from the Customers table.

4. Click OK to launch Word 95 if it is not running, and open a new mail merge main document. The Mail Merge Wizard uses DDE to communicate with Word and opens a new instance of Access 95.

5. Click the Insert Merge Field button to verify the fields from the Customers table in the drop-down list, as shown in figure 22.2.

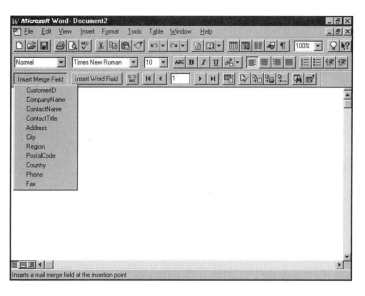

Fig. 22.2   Displaying the available merge fields in Word 95's mail merge window.

6. With the caret at the top of the document, choose <u>I</u>nsert, Date and <u>T</u>ime to add a date field to the main document.

7. Add a blank line, click the Insert Merge Field button to display the drop-down list, and insert the fields from the Customers table to create the address section of the main document (see fig. 22.3). If you click the button of the task bar for the second instance of Access launched by Word, its window appears, as shown in figure 22.3.

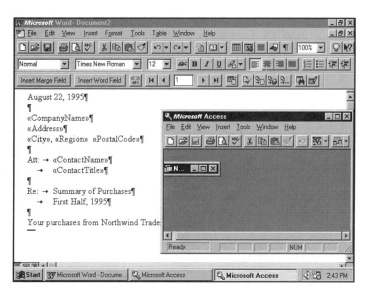

Fig. 22.3   Adding the merge fields to the main merge document.

> **Note**
>
> Spaces and other punctuation in merge data field names are not permitted by Word. The Mail Merge Wizard substitutes underscores (_) for spaces and other illegal characters in Access field names, when present.

8. Click the View Merged Data button of the Mail Merge toolbar to preview the appearance of your form letter.

> **Tip**
>
> Click the Find Record button of the toolbar, type USA in the Find What text box, and select Country from the In Field drop-down list. Click OK to find the first U.S. record.

9. The form letters go only to customers in the United States, so repeatedly click the next record button of the mail merge toolbar to find the first U.S. record. Alternatively, type **32** in the text box of the toolbar. The preview of the form letter for Great Lakes Food Market appears, as shown in figure 22.4.

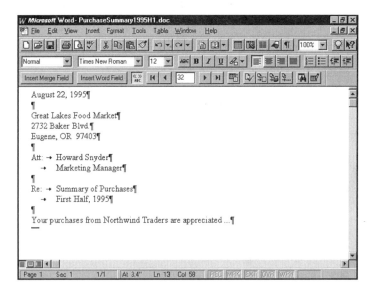

Fig. 22.4 Displaying a preview of a form letter to a U.S. customer.

10. You want to send letters to U.S. customers, so you need to create a query that returns only records whose Country column has the value "USA." Close Word, and save your main merge document with an appropriate file name, such as **PurchaseSummary1995H1.doc**. This file is used in the next section, as well as later in the chapter when you open the Access data source from Word.

> **Note**
>
> The Mail Merge Wizard uses dynamic data exchange (DDE) to communicate with Word, so you cannot use Word 95's query features to select and sort the merge data. If you attempt to do so, you break the DDE link between Word and Access. Thus, you need to base your final mail merge document on an Access query if you want to select or sort your records.

Using an Existing Main Merge Document with a New Data Source

Once you've created a standard main merge document, the most common practice is to use differing data sources to create form letters by category of addressee. Take the following steps to use the main mail merge document you created in the preceding section, PurchaseSummary1995H1.doc, with a new data source based on a simple Access query:

1. Open a new query, and add the Customers table.

2. Add the CompanyName, ContactName, ContactTitle, Address, City, Region, PostalCode, and Country fields to the query.

3. Enter **USA** as the criterion for the Country field, and clear the Show check box to prevent Country from appearing in the query. Add an ascending sort to the PostalCode field. Your query design appears, as shown in figure 22.5.

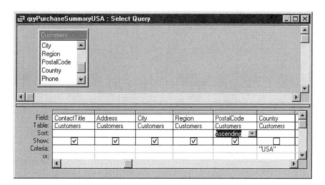

Fig. 22.5   The query design for the U.S. customers mailing list.

4. Click the Run button of the toolbar to verify the query result set (see fig. 22.6). Choose <u>F</u>ile, <u>S</u>ave or Save <u>A</u>s, and save the query with an appropriate name, such as **qryPurchaseSummaryUSA**.

qryPurchaseSummaryUSA : Select Query

Company Name	Contact Name	Contact Title	
The Cracker Box	Liu Wong	Marketing Assistant	55 Grizzly
Split Rail Beer & Ale	Art Braunschweiger	Sales Manager	P.O. Box 5
Save-a-lot Markets	Jose Pavarotti	Sales Representative	187 Suffolk
Rattlesnake Canyon Grocery	Paula Wilson	Assistant Sales Repres	2817 Milto
Let's Stop N Shop	Jaime Yorres	Owner	87 Polk St
The Big Cheese	Liz Nixon	Marketing Manager	89 Jefferso
Lonesome Pine Restaurant	Fran Wilson	Sales Manager	89 Chiaros
Great Lakes Food Market	Howard Snyder	Marketing Manager	2732 Bake
Hungry Coyote Import Store	Yoshi Latimer	Sales Representative	City Cente
Trail's Head Gourmet Provisioners	Helvetius Nagy	Sales Associate	722 DaVin
White Clover Markets	Karl Jablonski	Owner	305 - 14th
Lazy K Kountry Store	John Steel	Marketing Manager	12 Orches
Old World Delicatessen	Rene Phillips	Sales Representative	2743 Berin

Record: 1 of 13

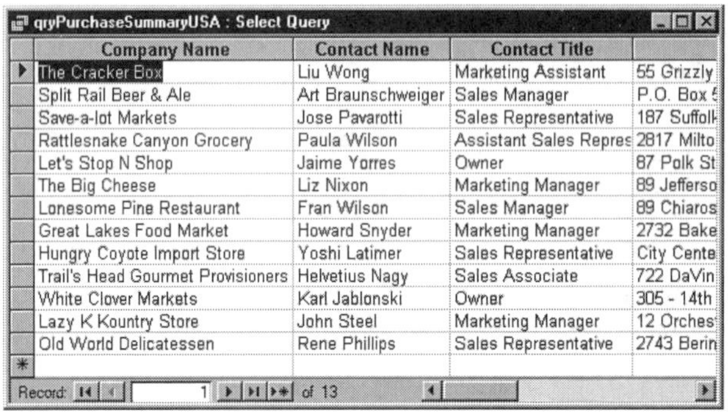

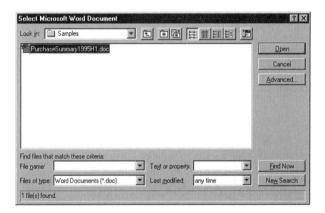

Fig. 22.6 The query result set for U.S.-based customers.

5. With the query open, choose Tools, OfficeLinks, Merge It to launch the Mail Merge Wizard. With the Link Your Data to an Existing Microsoft Word Document option button marked (the default), click OK to display the Select Microsoft Word Document dialog (see fig. 22.7).

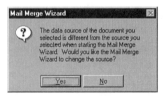

Fig. 22.7 Selecting the main merge document.

6. Select your main merge document in the file list and click OK. A message box, shown in figure 22.8, appears when you change the data source for a merge document. Click Yes to to change to the new data source.

Fig. 22.8 The message box that appears when you change the merge data source.

7. Confirm that your query is the new merge data source by clicking the Insert Merge Field button and checking the field list. (The Country field shouldn't appear.)

Alternatively, you can click the Edit Data Source button of Word's mail merge toolbar to display the query in Access, as shown in figure 22.9. (Click the Minimize button of Access's Query window, then click the Word document to return the focus to Word.)

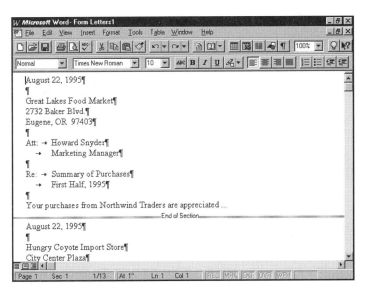

Fig. 22.9 Displaying the query result set from Word.

8. You can merge the main document and the data source directly to the printer or create a series of form letters in a new document. The latter choice lets you inspect the letters before you print them. Click the Merge To New Document button to create the new form letter. The top of the first form letter—in ZIP code sequence—appears, as shown in figure 22.10.

Fig. 22.10 The final version of the form letter addressed to U.S. customers.

If you close Word at this point, make sure you save your changes to
PurchaseSummary1995H1.doc. This file is used as the main merge document
in the sections that follow.

Using Word 95's Mail Merge Feature with Access Databases

 ▶▶ See "Understanding ODBC Drivers," p. 953

In many cases, Access 95 isn't available to users of Word who need to create form letters
from data contained in Access .mdb files. Office 95 includes a copy of Microsoft Query
and the necessary 32-bit ODBC drivers to connect to Access .mdb files (all versions) and
Microsoft SQL Server databases, plus dBASE, FoxPro, and Paradox 3+ table files. (ODBC
drivers for Excel worksheets and text files also are included.) Microsoft Query is modeled
on Access's query design window, but Microsoft Query displays the query result set automatically in a separate pane below the design pane as you construct the query. Office 95
applications launch and control Microsoft Query with DDE.

> **Note**
>
> You need Microsoft Office 95 installed on your PC to create the examples in this section. Access 95
> and Jet 3.0 require the 32-bit ODBC 2.5 drivers. Office 95 includes the 32-bit ODBC driver for
> Access 95 databases. The prior, 16-bit, Access drivers do not support 32-bit Access 95 .mdb files.

Word 95 includes the Mail Merge Helper, which is similar in concept to an Access wizard. The following three sections use the Mail Merge Helper to create a new Microsoft
Query (MSQuery) data source and to use an existing MSQuery data source.

Setting Up the ODBC Data Source

 When you install Office 95, the Setup program creates an ODBC data source named MS
Access 95 Database (Microsoft Access Driver (*.mdb)). Follow these steps to set up the
data source to use the Northwind.mdb database:

 1. Launch Control Panel and double-click the 32-bit ODBC Administrator icon to
   open the Data Sources dialog.

2. Select the MS Access 95 Database item in the User Data Sources (Driver) list and
   click the Setup button to display the ODBC Microsoft Access 95 Setup dialog.

3. Click the Select button in the Database frame to open the Select Database dialog.
   Maneuver to the folder containing Northwind.mdb (usually
   C:\Msoffice\Access\Samples), and select Northwind.mdb in the Database Name
   list (see fig. 22.11). Click OK to close the dialog.

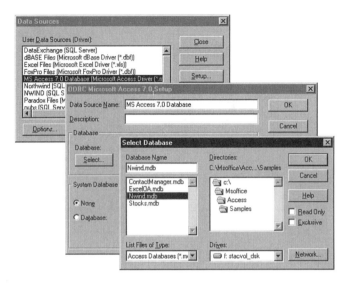

Fig. 22.11   Specifying the name and location of the Access database for the ODBC data source.

4. If you have secured Access or Northwind.mdb, click the Database option button in the System Database frame, then click the System Database button to open the System Database dialog. Select the System Database you're using, then click OK to close the dialog. Click the Advanced button to open the Advanced dialog and enter your login name and password in the text boxes, then click OK to close the Advanced dialog.

5. Click OK to close the ODBC Microsoft Access 95 Setup dialog, then click OK again to close the Data sources dialog.

Creating a New Mail Merge Data Source with Microsoft Query and an ODBC Data Source

To use Microsoft Query to create a merge data source from a Microsoft Access 1.1 database, follow these steps:

1. Launch Word 95, if necessary, and open the PurchaseSummary1995H1.doc main merge document you created earlier in this chapter.

▶▶ See "Using Access as a DDE Server," p. 1108

2. Click the Mail Merge Helper button of the mail merge toolbar to open the Mail Merge Helper dialog (see fig. 22.12). The entry in the Data label of the Data Source section is Northwind.mdb!Query qryPurchaseSummaryUSA. This is the syntax for specifying the topic of a DDE conversation when you use Access as a DDE server.

V

Integrating Access

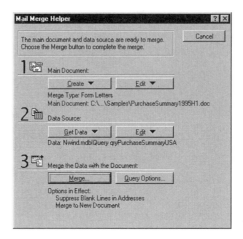

Fig. 22.12 The Mail Merge Helper dialog with an Access DDE merge data source specified.

3. Click the Get Data button, and select Create Data Source from the drop-down list to open the Create Data Source dialog. Word includes a set of default field names you can use to create merge data files (see fig. 22.13).

Fig. 22.13 Word 95's Create Data Source dialog.

4. This example uses MSQuery to create the data source, so click the MS Query button to launch MSQuery. MSQuery opens with the Select Data Source dialog active (see fig. 22.14).

Fig. 22.14 Microsoft Query launched with the Select Data Source dialog open.

5. Select the MS Access 95 Database item in the Available Data Sources list and click the Use button to open the Add Tables dialog.

6. In the Add Tables dialog, select the Customers item of the Table list (see fig. 22.15). Click Add to add the Customers table to MSQuery's graphical QBE panel, then click the Close button. MSQuery is quite similar in use to the Query Design window of Access.

Fig. 22.15   Selecting the Customers table in the Add Tables dialog.

7. Click and drag the following fields to the columns of the Query Result panel: CompanyName, ContactName, ContactTitle, Address, City, Region, PostalCode, and Country. (The sequence in which the columns appear is not significant.)

8. Click the header bar of the PostalCode column to select the column, and then click the Sort Ascending button of MSQuery's toolbar to sort the query in ZIP code sequence.

9. Place the caret in the Criteria Field text box, and open the drop-down list of fields. Select County, and type **USA** in the Value text box. (MSQuery adds the single quote marks for you; MSQuery uses single quotes in place of Access 95's default double quote marks to identify literal string values.) Your query design appears, as shown in figure 22.16.

10. Choose File, Save Query to open the Save Query dialog. Assign your query a name, such as **PurchaseSummary.qry**, and click OK. By default, queries are saved in your \Msoffice\Winword folder. You use the saved query in the section that follows.

V

Integrating Access

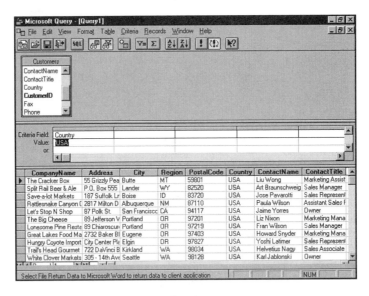

Fig. 22.16 The query design for the U.S. mailing list.

 11. Choose File, Return Data to Microsoft Word to close MSQuery and return to the Mail Merge Helper. The entry in the Data label of the Data Source section is now C:\Msoffice\Access\Samples\Northwind.mdb (see fig. 22.17). Click the Merge button of Mail Merge Helper to open the Merge dialog.

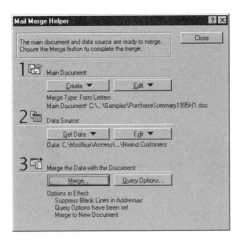

Fig. 22.17 The Mail Merge Helper dialog with an Access 1.1 file specified as the merge data source.

12. Accept the default New Document selection in the Merge To drop-down list. Click the Check Errors button of the Merge dialog to display the Checking and Reporting Errors dialog. Click the Complete the Merge, Pausing to Report Each Error As It Occurs option button (see fig. 22.18).

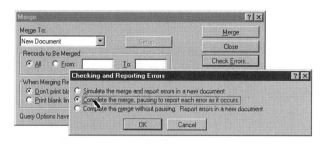

Fig. 22.18 The Merge dialog and the Checking and Reporting Errors dialog.

13. Click OK to close the Checking and Reporting Errors dialog, and click Merge to perform the merge.

14. Click the Merge To Document button to review the final form letter. The final form letter is designated Form Letters2 to distinguish it from the preview version, Form Letters1.

Creating Form Letters from an Existing Query

Once you've created and saved a query with MSQuery, you can use the saved query to create another set of form letters. MSQuery's saved queries are similar to Access queries saved as QueryDef objects in .mdb files. To use an existing .qry file as the data source for a merge document, follow these steps:

1. In Word 95, click the Mail Merge Helper button to display the dialog.

2. Click the Get Data button, and select Open Data Source from the drop-down list to display the Open Data Source dialog.

3. Choose the MS Query Files (*.qry) item in the Files of Type drop-down list.

4. Select the PurchaseSummary.qry file you saved in the preceding section, and click Open (see fig. 22.19). The message box shown in figure 22.20 appears.

Fig. 22.19 Choosing an existing MSQuery .qry file in the Open Data Source dialog.

V

Integrating Access

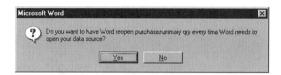

Fig. 22.20   Making the .qry file the permanent source of data for the main merge document.

5. To make the PurchaseSummary.qry the permanent source of data for the PurchaseSummary1995H1.doc main merge document, click the Yes button of the message box to return to the Mail Merge Helper dialog (see fig. 22.21). *The path to, and the name of, your query file* appears in the Data label of the Data Source section.

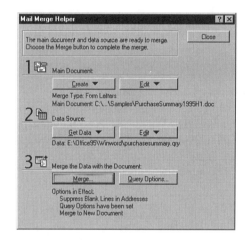

Fig. 22.21   The Mail Merge Helper dialog with the .qry file specified as the data source.

Embedding or Linking Word Documents in Access Tables

Many word processing documents are a collection of individual paragraphs, each of which may change depending on the purpose of the document. If the document is a contract, many of the paragraphs are likely to be *boilerplate:* standard paragraphs that are added based on the jurisdiction and purpose of the contract and the relationship be-tween the parties. Similarly, books are collections of chapters; when an author is writing a book, each chapter may go through several editing stages. Keeping track of boilerplate files and maintaining collections of book chapter files in various editing stages can be a daunting project. Even if you establish a workable DOS file-naming convention, you can easily lose track of the relationship between the file name and the content of the file.

Applications that track documents and maintain revision records for documents fall into the category of *document management systems*. Document management systems differ from image management systems; the latter handle static bitmapped images (usually created by scanners), rather than dynamic document content (editable data). With its

OLE 2.1 capability, Access 95 is a logical candidate for the creation of document management applications.

You can create a simple document management system by designing a table with one or more fields of the OLE Object data type to contain embedded documents or links to individual document files. You need a minimum of two other fields: one to identify the source file name of the document and the other to provide a document description. Additional fields can be added to indicate document ownership, track document status, hold key terms, and control who can modify the document. Figure 22.22 shows the design of a simple table devised to store the manuscript of this edition in the form of individual chapters in an OLE Object field.

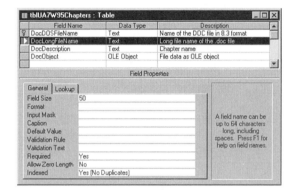

Fig. 22.22   The design of the table for a simple document management system.

After you define the fields for your document table, you need to determine whether you want to embed the document's data in the table or link the documents to their source files. Make your choice based on the following criteria:

- Embedding the document lets you use in-place activation to review the document within Access. In-place activation is a less-intrusive process.

- Activating a linked document launches Word 95 in its own window.

- Embedding the document provides an independent copy of the document that can serve as an archive. You can set the value of the Locked property of the object to Yes to allow the object to be activated, but not altered.

- Linking the document allows you to view changes to the document as they occur.

- Linking requires that the document remain in the same location. In most cases, moving the document to another drive or directory breaks the link.

- You cannot save an embedded Word 95 or Excel 95 document to a file or print the embedded document using File menu choices in the in-place activated mode. The file menus of these applications do not replace the File menu of Access 95 when the embedded objects are activated. However, you can open Word's window to make the Word File menu accessible.

> **Note**
>
> You can use OLE Automation instructions in Access Basic modules to save an embedded Word 95 document to a file or print the document. The Object property of the object frame lets you manipulate embedded or linked objects with Access Basic code. Chapter 30, "Exchanging Data with OLE Automation and DDE," describes how to apply OLE Automation methods to Word documents.

Embedding or Linking a Word 95 Document in a Table

To embed or link a Word 95 document in an OLE Object field of a table with a design similar to that shown in figure 22.22, follow these steps:

1. Place the caret in the OLE Object field, and choose Insert, Object to display the Insert Object dialog (see fig. 22.23).

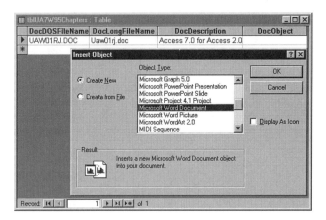

Fig. 22.23 The Insert Object dialog.

2. You can create an empty Word document by accepting the default, Create New. To link or embed an existing document, click the Create from File option and then click OK. (You don't need to select Microsoft Word Document when you insert an object from a file.) The Object Type list changes to the File text box.

3. You can type the path and file name in the File text box or click the Browse button to display the Browse dialog (see fig. 22.24). Select the file you want to use in the File Name list, and then click OK to close the Browse dialog and return to the Insert Object dialog.

4. The file you selected in the preceding step appears in the File text box. At this point, you can choose between linking and embedding the file. The example that follows uses embedded objects to demonstrate in-place activation (see fig. 22.25). If you want to link the file, mark the Link text box. Click OK.

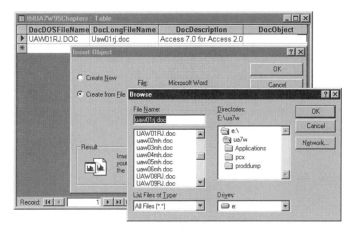

Fig. 22.24 Selecting a source document file in the Browse dialog.

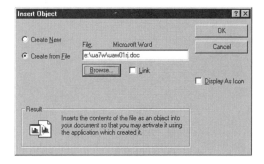

Fig. 22.25 Embedding a Word 95 document object from a file.

5. Position the record selector of the table to a different record to save the embedded object or link to the object's file in your table, together with its OLE presentation.

Repeat the above steps for each document you want to add to the table. You can activate the document object in Word 95's window by double-clicking the OLE Object cell. Viewing the documents you insert in the file lets you verify that their contents correspond to their description.

Troubleshooting

The Microsoft Word 95 Document entry does not appear in the Insert Object dialog's Object Type list, or attempting to insert a Word 95 document results in a message box stating that the registration database entry is invalid or corrupted.

The Registry entries for Word 95 are missing or invalid. If the Word 95 entry is missing, it is likely that Word's Setup program did not complete its operation. (The last step of Setup adds entries to

(continues)

(continued)

the Registry). If the "corrupted" message appears, it is likely that you moved the Word files from the original directory in which Setup installed the files into a different directory. In either case, you need to use the Registry Editor (RegEdit.exe) to correct the problem. See the instructions for using the Registry editor in Chapter 19, "Using 32-Bit OLE 2.1."

Creating a Form to Display the Document

If your table contains only a few fields, you can use the AutoForm feature to create a simple form to display and edit your linked or embedded object. To create the document display form, follow these steps:

1. With the table that contains your Word objects open with the focus in Datasheet View, click the arrow of the New Object button of the toolbar and select AutoForm from the drop-down menu. The Form Wizard automatically creates a standard form.

2. Click the Design View button of the toolbar, and then relocate and resize the controls as necessary. Your bound object frame should occupy most of the display area. To view the entire document in its original format, set the Height property of the object frame to 11 inches and the Width property to 8.5 inches.

3. Return to Form View to display the presentation of the document. Figure 22.26 shows the presentation of the initial version of the manuscript for the first chapter of this edition. The size of the bound object frame of figure 22.26 is about 9 by 11.5 inches.

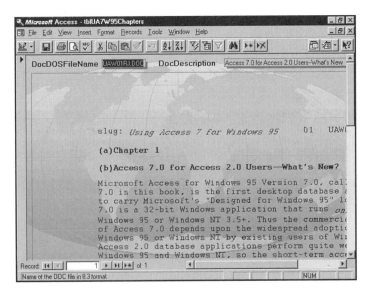

Fig. 22.26   The presentation of a Word 95 document in a bound object frame.

4. Double-click the surface of the object frame to activate the object. Activating the object launches Word 95 if it is not running. If you embedded the document, activation adds Word's toolbars to the display as docked toolbars. Word's menu choices take over Access's Edit and View menus, and Word adds its Insert, Format, Tools, and Table menus to the menubar (see fig. 22.27).

You can move through the document with the Page Up and Page Down keys. All the editing features of Word 95 are available when the document object is activated, but you cannot use Word's Zoom feature to change the presentation. You must use the scroll bar of the Access form to view parts of the page that are not visible on your display. (Using 800- by 600-pixel or higher resolution solves the partial display problem).

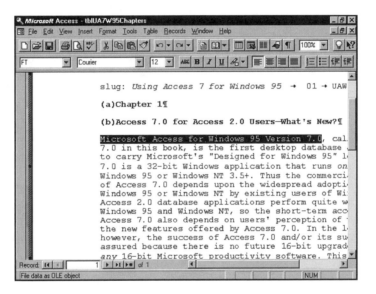

Fig. 22.27 A Word 95 document activated in a bound object frame.

5. Click the surface of the form, outside of the area of the bound object frame, to deactivate the object and return to presentation view of the document.

6. To save the document to a file, alter the page layout, or print an embedded document, choose Edit, Document Object, and select Open. Word's window takes over your display, and you can access the File menu of Word to save changes, as shown in figure 22.28.

7. Choose File, Close and Return to *FormName* to close Word's window and return to Access.

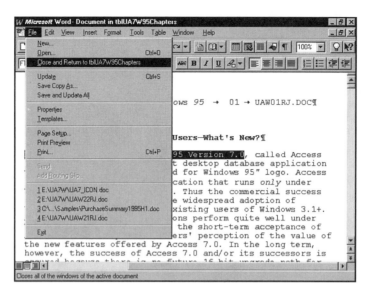

Fig. 22.28 Opening the embedded document in Word 95's window.

> **Note**
>
> The only view of a Word document available when the object is embedded is Page Layout View. You can change the layout of the embedded document by opening the document in Word (see the preceding step 8), choosing File, Page Setup, and then making the required adjustments.

You also can insert additional document objects directly into the form. To embed or link an object in Form View, position the record pointer on the blank (tentative append) record. An empty presentation appears in the bound object frame. Choose Insert, Object, and follow steps 2 through 5 of the preceding section to embed or link additional document objects.

From Here...

This chapter concentrated on the methodology for creating form letters based on data in Access tables because creating form letters is one of the most common applications for database management systems. You learned how to use Access 95's Mail Merge Wizard and the Mail Merge Helper of Word 95 to create merge data sources from database tables. The chapter concluded with a description of how to create a simple Access document management system that takes advantage of in-place activation to display and edit Word 95 documents.

For information on topics related to those in this chapter, refer to the following chapters:

- Chapter 4, "Working with Access Databases and Tables," shows you how to design tables for a variety of database applications.

- Chapter 8, "Using Query by Example," introduces you to the design of simple queries similar to those used for creating most merge data sources.

- Chapter 12, "Creating and Using Forms," describes the use of other Access Form Wizards to create more complex forms.

- Chapter 30, "Exchanging Data with OLE Automation and DDE," shows you how to manipulate Word 95 documents using the Word.Basic object and Access VBA OLE Automation code.

V

Integrating Access

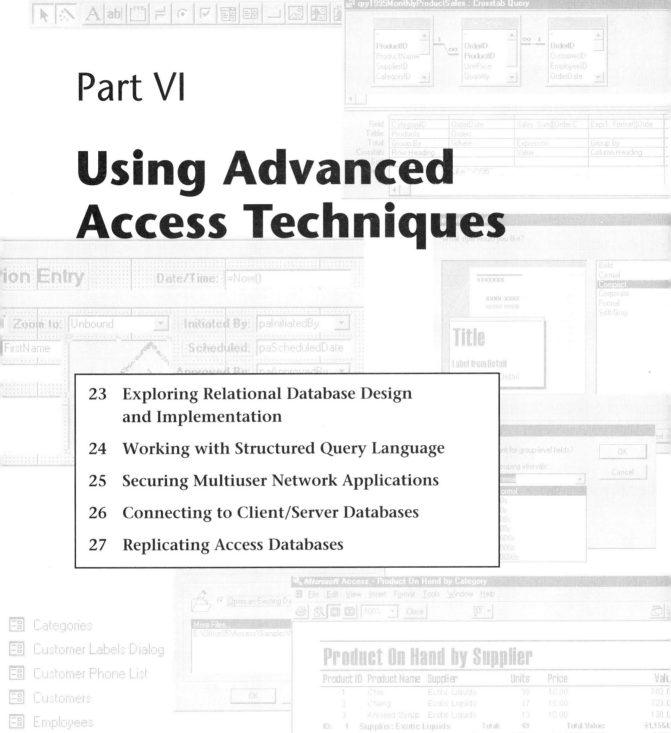

Part VI

Using Advanced Access Techniques

Chapter 23

Exploring Relational Database Design and Implementation

You were introduced to a few of the elements of relational database design when you created the Personnel Actions table and joined it with the Employees table of the Northwind Traders database in Chapter 10, "Creating Multitable and Crosstab Queries." Chapter 21, "Using Access with Microsoft Excel," gave you a bit more insight into how to create a relational database from information contained in a worksheet. When you're presented with the challenge of designing a database from ground zero, however—especially a complex or potentially complex database—you need to understand the theory of relational database design and its terminology.

This chapter takes a step back and starts with the definition of data objects and how you identify them. Because Access is an object-enabled database development tool, the concepts of database design presented in this chapter have an object-oriented bent. The reason for this approach is twofold:

- Access's relational tables incorporate many of the features of client/server databases. Properties, such as validation rules and indexes, and methods that include preventing duplicate primary key entries, are combined in the table object. Details of relationships between tables, and methods of enforcing referential integrity, are stored in the database object.

- Access VBA treats the database itself and each of Access's database elements—tables, queries, forms, and reports—as programming objects.

After you've identified the data objects that are to be included in the tables of your database, you need to design the tables to contain the data objects. You use a process called *data normalization* to create tables that conform to the relational database model. Normalization is the process of eliminating duplicate information in tables by extracting the duplicate data to new tables that contain records with unique data values. You then join the tables you create by fields with common data values to create a relational database structure. Normalizing data is the subject of the "Normalizing Data to the Relational Model" section, later in this chapter.

In this chapter, you learn to

- Design a relational database system

- Create tables that comply with the rules of relational database design

- Document your Access database application with a data dictionary

- Understand how Access uses indexes to speed queries

- Prevent deletion of records in tables on which other tables depend

VI

Advanced Techniques

The role of indexes in maintaining unique values in primary-key fields and organizing data tables was described briefly in preceding chapters. This chapter provides an explanation of how indexes are constructed and maintained by Access. Properly designed indexes improve the performance of your applications without consuming excessive amounts of disk space or slowing the appending of new records to a crawl.

This chapter also deals with the rules that establish and maintain referential integrity, one of the most important considerations in designing a database. Referential integrity enforces uniqueness in primary keys and prevents the occurrence of orphaned records, such as records of invoices whose customer data records have been deleted.

Understanding Database Systems

Prior to this chapter, you've used the Northwind Traders demonstration database, created a few simple databases, and perhaps imported your own data in another database format into an Access table. No formal theories were presented to aid or hinder your understanding of the underlying design of the database examples. Now that you've gained some experience using Access, the more theoretical concepts of database design should be easier to understand.

This section takes a systems approach to database design, starting with a generalized set of objectives, outlining the steps necessary to accomplish the objectives, and then explaining the theory and practice behind each step.

The Objectives of Database Design

The strategy of database design is to accomplish the following objectives:

- Fulfilling your own needs or the needs of the organization for information in a timely, consistent, and economical manner.

- Eliminating or minimizing the duplication of database content across the organization. In a large organization, eliminating duplication may require a *distributed database*. Distributed databases use multiple servers to store individual databases. The individual databases are *linked* to one another (to use Access terminology) through a local-area network (LAN) or wide-area network (WAN) so that they appear as a single database to the user.

- Providing rapid access to the specific elements of information in the database required by each user category. Operating speed is a function of the relational database management system (RDBMS) itself, the design of the applications you create, the capabilities of the server and client computers, and network characteristics.

- Accommodating expansion of databases to adapt to the needs of a growing organization, such as the addition of new products and processes, complying with governmental reporting requirements, and incorporating new transaction-processing and decision-support applications.

- Maintaining the integrity of the database so that it contains only validated, auditable information. Some client/server databases, such as Microsoft SQL Server, provide built-in *triggers* to maintain database integrity. Triggers are a set of rules that are included in the database. If you violate a rule, the trigger sends an error message instead of performing the transaction. The Enforce Referential Integrity check box in Access's Relationships dialog creates the equivalent of a trigger.

■ Preventing access to the database by unauthorized persons. Access provides a security system that requires users to enter a password to use a particular database.

■ Permitting access only to those elements of the database information that individual users or categories of users need in the course of their work. You can permit or deny users the right to view the data in specific tables of the database.

■ Allowing only authorized persons to add or edit information in the database. Permissions in Access are multilevel; you can selectively allow users to edit tables or alter their structure, as well as edit or create their own applications.

■ Easing the creation of data entry, editing, display, and reporting applications that efficiently serve the needs of the users of the database. The design of the RDBMS's front-end features determines the ease with which new applications are created or existing ones can be modified. You have seen in the preceding chapters that Access is especially adept as a front-end application generator.

The first two objectives are independent of the database manager you choose. The RDBMS influences or determines the other objectives. Operating speed, data validation, data security, and application creation are limited by the capabilities built into the RDBMS and the computer environment under which it operates. If your database is shared on a network, you need to consider the security features of the network operating system and the client/server database system (if one is used) in the security strategy.

Note

Database replication presents an exception to the objective of minimizing data duplication. Replication of entire databases or specific tables of databases often is used to improve performance of queries against remote databases accessed over a WAN. A local copy of the remote database is maintained on a LAN server. Updates to the tables of the remote database periodically are propagated over the WAN to the local replicate databases. If users don't need current information, replication is scheduled in the middle of the night when WAN traffic is minimal. Access 95 incorporates a small-scale replication system designed primarily to accommodate mobile computer users who maintain a copy of a database on their laptop PCs. Chapter 27, "Replicating Access Databases," describes Access 95's new replication feature that takes advantage of Windows 95's Briefcase feature.

The Process of Database Design

The process of designing a relational database system consists of 10 basic steps:

1. Identifying the objects (data sources) that the database system is to represent

2. Discovering associations between the objects (when you have more than one object)

3. Determining the significant properties and behaviors of the objects

4. Ascertaining how the properties of the objects relate to one another

5. Creating a preliminary data dictionary to define the tables that comprise the database

6. Designating the relationships between database tables based on the associations between data objects contained in the tables, and incorporating this information in the data dictionary

7. Establishing the types of updates and transactions that create and modify the data in the tables, including any necessary data integrity requirements

8. Determining how to use indexes to speed up query operations without excessively slowing down the addition of data to tables or consuming excessive amounts of disk space

9. Deciding who can access and who can modify data in each table (data security), and altering the structure of the tables if necessary to assure data security

10. Documenting the design of the database as a whole; completing data dictionaries for the database as a whole and each table it contains; and writing procedures for database maintenance, including file backup and restoration

Each step in the design process depends on preceding steps. The sections in this chapter follow steps 1 through 8 in sequence. Database security is the subject of Chapter 25, "Securing Multiuser Network Applications." A full discussion of database documentation is beyond the scope of this book, but this chapter explains how to use Access 95's improved Documentor feature to create a data dictionary.

The Object-Oriented Approach to Database Design

Databases contain information about objects that exist in the real world. These objects may be people, books in a library, paper invoices or sales orders, maps, money in bank accounts, or printed circuit boards. Such objects are *tangible*. Whatever the object, it must have a physical representation, even if only an image on a computer display that never finds its way to the printer, as in the mythical "paperless office." References to objects in this book, if not preceded by a word describing the type of object—such as "table object" or "OLE object"—indicate real-world, tangible objects.

Tangible objects possess *properties* and *behavior*, just as the OLE objects discussed in Chapter 19, "Using 32-Bit OLE 2.1," have properties and methods. At first, this combination might appear to be applicable only to databases of persons, not books or bank balances; however, all database objects other than those in archival databases have both properties and behavior. (Archival databases are used to store information that never changes—new data is simply added to such databases. An example of an archival database is one containing the text of previously published newspapers.)

Considering Static and Dynamic Properties of Objects. An object's properties determine the content of a database or table that contains object representations of the same type. Books are assigned subject codes, derived from the Dewey decimal system. Modern books have an identifying ISBN code, and most now have a Library of Congress catalog number. These numbers are properties of a book, as are the title, author, number of pages, and binding type. Such properties are *static*: they are the same whether the book is in the stacks of a library or checked out by a cardholder. Customer information for a bank account, such as account number, name, and address, also is considered static, even though customers occasionally change addresses. Book circulation status and bank account balances are *dynamic* properties: they change from day to day, or hour to hour.

Describing Data Entities and Their Attributes. A single object, including all its static properties, is called a *data entity*. Each individual data entity must be unique so that you can distinguish it from others. A bank's checking account customer is a data entity, for example, but money in the customer's account is not, because the money cannot (and doesn't need to be) uniquely identified. Because a customer may have more than one account, a Social Security number or federal employer identification number doesn't suffice as a unique identifier; an account number must be assigned to ensure the uniqueness of each customer data entity.

Deposit slips and checks are objects that are represented in the database as other data entities that *relate* to the customer entity. Check numbers aren't unique enough to distinguish them as entities; many different customers might use a check numbered 1553. Combining the customer number and the check number doesn't suffice as a unique identifier because different banking firms might use the same customer number to identify different people. A bank identification number, customer number, and check number together can uniquely identify a debit entity. Each check contains this information printed in magnetic ink. The amount property of each debit (check) or credit (deposit) entity is used to adjust the balance in the customer's account by simple subtraction and addition, a process called a *transaction*.

You don't want to wait while an ATM (originally Automated Transaction Machine, now commonly called an Automatic Teller Machine) calculates your balance by processing every transaction since you opened your account. Therefore, a *derived* static property, the last statement balance, can be included in the customer data entity and updated once per month. Only last-statement-to-date transactions need to be processed to determine the current balance—a dynamic, *calculated* property. In figure 23.1, lines connect static properties of bank account objects to the data entities derived from them. Properties of objects included in data entities, such as account number and customer name, are called *attributes*.

Accounting for the Behavior of Objects with Methods. The behaviors of related database objects determine the characteristics of transactions in which their data entities participate. Books in a library may be acquired, checked out, returned, and lost. Bank account behavior is very easy to describe: A customer opens the account, deposit transactions and interest accumulations (credits) increase the account balance, and checks, cash withdrawn from an ATM, and bank charges incurred (debits) reduce the balance. Crediting or debiting a bank account is an example of a transaction. Transactions occur in response to *events*, such as making a deposit or withdrawal at an ATM. Access implements transactions by using *methods* in response to events initiated by the user, such as opening a form or clicking a command button.

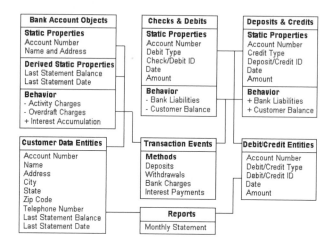

Fig. 23.1   Relationships between objects, entities, events, and methods in a banking database.

In conventional relational databases, you can represent tangible objects and object properties as data entities, but not an object's real-world behavior. The OLE Object field data type, described in Chapter 13, "Designing Custom Multitable Forms," is an exception to this rule. The behavior of an OLE data object is determined by the methods available in the OLE server used to create the object or add the object to the OLE Object field. With conventional data entities, you emulate the behavior of tangible objects by using the methods that you incorporate into your applications.

Programs that you write using the RDBMS's native language implement database methods. In the case of Access, macros consisting of one or more *actions*, or Access VBA functions and procedures, implement the methods. A macro action is a prepackaged set of methods designed for a specific purpose. If one of the standard actions doesn't fit your requirements, you can use the RunCode() macro action to use Access VBA functions that include the methods you need. Alternatively, you can execute an Access function or invoke an event-handling procedure directly from the event property. As you learned in Part IV, "Powering Access with Macros," the events that you can use to initiate macro action methods are listed in the Properties windows of forms, reports, and control objects.

Access is unique among today's PC database managers because, by default, Access saves *application objects* (the queries, forms, reports, macros, and VBA code that you create for the database) within the database file itself, not in separate .SC, .PRG, or .EXE files as do other PC RDBMSs. Access *data objects* (tables) have self-contained properties and methods; other PC RDBMSs require separate programs to validate data, display status text, and create indexes. Therefore, Access database files, and the tables they contain, conform to the object "paradigm"—a synonym for the word "model" that has become an object-oriented cliché.

> **Note**
>
> As mentioned elsewhere in this book, it has become a generally accepted database design practice (GADDP) to use separate .MDB files to contain application objects and data objects. Keeping your tables in a *Tables*.mdb file and linking the tables to your *AppObjs*.mdb file lets you update the application objects without affecting the existing data in the table objects. A separate *Tables*.mdb file in Access 2.0 format is necessary if you must continue to support users running 16-bit Windows 3.1+. (You must also maintain a duplicate of your *AppObjs*.mdb file in Access 2.0 format.) Issues relating to 16-bit and 32-bit Access application versioning are covered in Chapter 33, "Migrating Access 2.0 Applications to Access 95."

Combining Different Entities in a Single Table. You can include representations of different types of objects in a single table as long as you can represent their properties and behavior in the same manner, and yet distinguish the different object types. For example, checks and debits are shown as a single data-object type in preceding figure 23.1, although one originates from a paper check and the other from an Electronic Funds Transfer debit. A Debit Type field can indicate the different sources. You can combine cash deposits and transfers from a savings account into a single data-entity type in a Credits table. You might want to combine both debits and credits in a single table, which you can do by using different codes for Debit Types and Credit Types.

To identify a debit or credit uniquely, you need to include fields for bank ID, customer number, debit/credit type, and transaction number. Although a check number can serve as the transaction number, the system must assign transaction numbers to other types of transactions, such as those conducted at ATMs. Access 95 can use an AutoNumber field, called a Counter field in earlier versions of Access, to add a unique transaction number (either incremented or random) to each data entity, including checks. The check number becomes a separate attribute.

Database Terminology

The terms used to describe formally a database and the elements that comprise it derive from four different sources. The data-description language, of which *entity* and *attribute* are members, derives from the terminology of statistics. Another set of terms, which describe the same set of elements, is based on computer terminology and relates to how the elements are stored within disk files. Query by Example introduced new terms—for example, row, column, and cell—to the language of databases, and Structured Query Language adopted these terms. Table 23.1 compares words that are used for data description, in QBE and SQL, and for describing data-storage methodologies employed by Access, xBase, and Paradox. The Access VBA language takes an object-oriented approach to programming, so table 23.1 also includes terms applicable to object-oriented programming (OOP).

Table 23.1   A Comparison of Data-Description and Data-Storage Terminology

Data Description	QBE and SQL	Object-Oriented	Access Storage	xBase/ Paradox
Heterogeneous Universe	Database	Base Object Class	File	Directory
Universe (homogeneous)	Table	Object Class	Table (Sub-File)	Data File
Entity (object, instance)	Row	Data Object	Record	Record
Attribute	Cell	Object Property	Field	Field
Attribute Data Type	Datatype	Data Type	Field Data Type	Field Type
Attribute Domain	Validation Rule	Enumeration	Validation Rule	Valid Statement
Attribute Value	Cell Value	Property Value	Field Value	Field Value
Identifier	Primary Key	Property Value	Key, Index	Index File

The real-world object is the basic source of information that is represented in a database as an entity. In explaining the terms included in table 23.1, therefore, the following definition list begins with an entity, breaks it down into its component parts, and then establishes its position in the hierarchy of databases and tables.

- *Entity.* A unique representation of a single real-world object, created using the values of its attributes in computer-readable form. To ensure uniqueness, one or more of an entity's attributes must have values unlike the corresponding values of any other entity of the same class. An entity corresponds to a *row* in QBE and SQL, or a *record* in data-storage terminology. Entities are also called *data entities, data objects, data instances,* or *instances.*

- *Attribute.* A significant property of a real-world object. Every attribute carries a value that assists in identifying the entity of which it is a part, and in distinguishing the entity from other members of the same entity class. Attributes are contained in *fields* (data-storage terminology) or *columns* (QBE and SQL). An attribute also is called a *cell* or *data cell*, terms that describe the intersection of a row and a column (or a field and a record).

- *Attribute data type.* Basic attribute data types consist of all numeric (integer, floating-point, and so forth) and string (text or alphanumeric) data types without embedded spaces or separating punctuation. The string data type can contain letters, numbers, and special characters (such as those used in languages other than English). An attribute with a basic attribute data type is indivisible and is called an *atomic* type. Text data types with spaces or other separating punctuation characters are called *composite attribute data types.* You can divide most composite types into basic data types by *parsing.* Parsing means to separate a composite attribute into basic attributes. For example, you can parse "Smith, Dr. John D., Jr." to Last Name (Smith), Title (Dr), First Name (John), Middle Initial, and Suffix (Jr) basic attribute types. Special field types, such as Memo and OLE, are composite attribute data types that cannot be parsed to basic data types by conventional methods. You cannot, therefore, create Access indexes that include Memo or OLE attribute data types; only attributes with basic attribute data types can be indexed.

- *Attribute domain.* The allowable range of values for an attribute of a given attribute data type. The attribute data type determines the domain unless the domain is limited by a process external to the data in the table. As an example of attribute domain limitation, the domain of an employee age attribute that has an integer data type might be limited by a data validation method to any integer greater than 13 and less than 90. In object-oriented terms, the domain consists of an *enumeration* of acceptable values. A days-of-the-week enumeration (the domain of days) consists of a list of its members: Monday, Tuesday, and so on. Access validation rules, stored in tables, maintain *domain integrity*, limiting data entry to limits set by the data validation expression.

- *Attribute value.* The smallest indivisible unit of data in an entity. Attribute values are limited to those within the attribute domain. *Cell value* and *data value* are synonyms for attribute value.

- *Identifier.* An attribute or combination of attributes required to uniquely identify a specific entity (and no others). Identifiers are called *primary-key fields* in Access and are used to create the primary index of the entities. When an entity's attribute values are duplicated in other entities' corresponding attributes, you need to combine various attributes to ensure a unique identifier for the entity. When more than one attribute is used as an identifier, the key fields are called a *composite* or *compound* primary key.

- *Homogeneous universe.* The collection (set) of all data entities of a single data entity type. The data entities must have an identical set of attributes, attribute data types, and attribute domains. This set corresponds to an Access or Paradox *table*, or a *data file* in xBase. The set also is called an *entity class* or *entity type*, and its members are sometimes called *entity instances*, or just *instances*.

- *Heterogeneous universe.* The collection (set) of related entity classes comprising related homogeneous universes—the *database*. A database is stored as a single file in Access and most client/server databases. Paradox and xBase store databases as collections of related files, usually in a single directory. A dBASE catalog is a file that includes records to identify the individual files that comprise the entire database. Access databases include a special table that catalogs the objects that the databases contain. You can reveal the content of the catalog by using the techniques described in the "Access's Integrated Data Dictionary System" section near the end of this chapter.

Much of the formal terminology used to describe data objects in relational databases is quite technical and rather abstract. You need to understand the meaning of these terms, however, when you create the data models that form the basis of the design of your database.

Types of Tables and Keys in Relational Databases

Specific to relational databases are certain types of tables and keys that enable relationships between tables. Understanding these tables and keys is essential to comprehending relational databases and the rules of data normalization, which are discussed in the "Normalizing Data to the Relational Model" section. The following list defines the various relational keys and tables:

- *Base table.* In a relational database, a base table is the table that incorporates one or more columns of an object's properties and contains the primary key that uniquely identifies that object as a data entity. A base table must have a primary key. Base tables are often called *primary tables* because of the requirement for a primary key.

- *Relation table.* A table that is used to provide linkages between other tables and isn't a base table (because it doesn't incorporate properties of an object or because it doesn't have a primary key field) is called a *relation table.* Key fields in relation tables each must be foreign keys, related to a primary key in a base table.

  Technically, a true relation table is comprised wholly of foreign keys and contains no independent data entities. The Order Details table of the Northwind Traders database is an example of a relation table that contains data values that aren't foreign keys (the UnitPrice and Quantity fields, for example). Its OrderID field is related to the field of the same name in the Orders table. Likewise, the ProductID field is related to the ProductID field of the Products table. Although the Order Details table has a composite key, it isn't a true primary key; its purpose is to prevent duplication of a product entry in a specific order.

- *Primary key.* A primary key consists of a set of values that uniquely specifies a row of a base table, which in Access is the primary table. For any primary-key value, one and only one row in the table matches this value. You can base the primary key on a single field if each data cell's value is unique at all times.

- *Candidate keys.* Any column or group of columns that meets the requirements for a primary key is a candidate to become the primary key for the table. Name and Social Security number are candidate keys to identify a person in the United States; however, Social Security number is the more appropriate choice because two people can have the same name but not the same valid Social Security number.

- *Composite keys.* If you need data from more than one column of the table to meet the uniqueness requirement of a primary key, the key is said to be a composite or *concatenated key.*

- *Foreign keys.* A foreign key is a column whose values correspond to those contained in a primary key, or the far-left portion of a composite key, in another related table. A foreign key can consist of one column or a group of columns (a *composite foreign key*). If the length of a foreign key is less than the corresponding primary key, the key is called a *partial* or *truncated foreign key.*

Examples of the preceding keys and tables occur in the discussions of normal forms in the "Normalizing Data to the Relational Model" section, later in this chapter. First, the following sections examine the process of data modeling.

Data Modeling

The first step in designing a database is to determine which objects to represent within the database and which of the objects' properties to include. This process is called *data modeling.* The purpose of a data model is to create a logical representation of the data structure that is used to create a database. Data modeling can encompass an entire organization, a division or department, or a single type of object. Models that deal with objects, rather than the tables that you later create from the objects, are called *conceptual data models*.

Figure 23.2 illustrates two different approaches (conceptual data models) to database design: the bottom-up approach to create an application database, and the top-down method to develop subject databases. These two approaches, discussed in the following sections, result in databases with quite different structures.

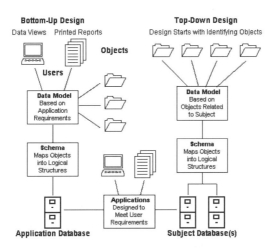

Fig. 23.2   A comparison of bottom-up and top-down database designs.

Application Databases. You can base data models on specific needs for data presented in a particular manner. For such a needs-based model, you can use the *bottom-up* approach and start with a view of the data on a display, a printed report, or both, as shown in the lefthand example of figure 23.2. This approach results in an *application database*. If you are creating a simple database for your own use, or dealing with a single type of data object, the *bottom-up* approach might suffice because the presentation requirements and the properties of the objects involved are usually well defined. The problem with the bottom-up approach is that it often leads to multiple individual databases that may duplicate each other's information. Several persons or groups within an organization might have a requirement for an application database that includes, for example, a customers table. When a new customer is added—or data for an existing customer is changed—in one application database, you need to update each of the other application databases. The updating process is time-consuming and subject to error.

Conceptual data models, such as those shown in figure 23.2, are independent of the database manager you use and the type of database files it accesses. Therefore, the same data model accommodates databases in Access's native format, as well as others with which Access is compatible. Data models aren't connected with any programming language or tools used to create applications. The applications box in figure 23.2 isn't a component of conventional data models, but is added to show where application design fits into the overall picture.

Subject Databases. A better approach is to base the design of the database on groups of objects that are related by subject matter. For a manufacturing firm, tables are usually grouped into databases devoted to a single department or function. The following lists some database examples:

- *Sales* database consisting of customer, sales order, sales quota, product discount, and invoice tables

- *Production* database including product, price, parts, vendor, and cost accounting tables

- *Personnel* database with employee, payroll, and benefits tables (large firms may include tables relating to health care providers and employment applicants)

- *Accounting* database incorporating general ledger and various journal tables

Databases that consist of tables relating to a single class of subjects or functions are called *subject databases*. Even if you are creating the first database application for a small organization, starting with an overall plan for the organization's total information requirements in subject databases pays long-term dividends. If you decide or are assigned to create an invoicing application, for instance, you can establish sales, production, and personnel databases from the beginning, rather than have to split up a single invoice database at a later time and rewrite all your applications to access tables within multiple databases.

Subject databases require *top-down* design, depicted in the righthand diagram of figure 23.2. In this case, the properties of the data objects, not the applications used with them, determine the design. Designing subject databases involves creating a diagram of the relevant objects and the associations between them, and then creating models for each database involved. You distribute the model diagrams to users, and then interview the users to determine their information needs based on the content of the model databases.

Diagrammatic Data Models. Large, complex data models resemble the work-flow and paper-flow diagrams commonly used in analyzing organizations' administrative procedures. If you have such diagrams or descriptions, they make the data-modeling process much easier. Generating an organization-wide data model may involve a substantial amount of research to determine the needs of the organization as a whole and of individuals using specialized applications. In many cases, users and potential users aren't able to define what information they need or how they want to see it presented.

Many methods exist of creating diagrams to represent data models. One of the more useful methods is the Entity-Relationship (E-R) diagram, developed by Peter Chen in 1976 and expanded on by David R. McClanahan in a series of articles entitled "Database Foundations: Conceptual Designs" in *DBMS* magazine (see fig. 23.3). You can use E-R diagrams to represent relationships between objects and to depict their behavior.

Fig. 23.3   An Entity-Relationship diagram of two data entities from figure 23.1.

Data entities are enclosed within rectangles, data attributes within ovals, and relationships between entities within diamonds. Relationships between database objects, at the conceptual stage, can be defined by their behavior; therefore, E-R diagrams include at least one verb whose object, unless otherwise indicated, is to the right of the diamond relationship symbol. You add symbols to the diagram as the model's detail increases. One of the advantages of the E-R diagram is that you can use it to represent the conceptual design of very large systems with multiple databases in a relatively small amount of space.

Database Schema. A graphic description of the layout of tables in the form of bars that contain their field names and show a simplified version of relationships between them can be employed to aid users to grasp the concept of the database. A diagram that shows the logical representation of data is called a *schema*. A schema, such as the one shown in figure 23.4 for an ocean shipping line, is independent of the RDBMS used to implement the database.

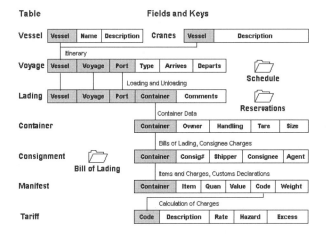

Fig. 23.4   The schema for the operations database of a shipping line.

In figure 23.4, the primary keys are shaded, and the relationships between the table keys are indicated by lines that connect the keys. Foreign keys are unshaded, except when they correspond to a component of a composite primary key. The descriptions shown between the bars are optional; they are useful in describing the relationships to users. You can expand a schema of this type to include the source documents involved, the reports to be generated, and the applications that pertain to all (or a portion) of the tables.

External Determinants of Database Design. Finding the data objects that provide the information to meet all of an organization's requirements may require extensive detective work. Many objects might not be available within the organization itself. For instance, if you're developing a database application that involves geographic positioning (called *geocoding*), you might need map tables such as the U.S. Census Bureau's TIGER/ Line files, or tables derived from them by others. Images to be incorporated as OLE objects might not be available in file formats that are compatible with your OLE server applications; they would require file-type conversion. If the accounting department is using packaged accounting software, you must incorporate representations of the structure of its database into your model. In this case, you also must plan how to exchange information with the accounting data, but you need not include the access methodology in your conceptual data model.

Using Data Modeling Tools to Create Access Databases

Data modeling tools are available from several publishers for designing and then automatically creating the structure of client/server relational databases, such as SQL Server, ORACLE, and SQLBase. Data modeling tools that run under Windows let you use graphic techniques, such as E-R diagrams, to design the structure of the tables and establish relationships between the tables. Database CASE tools save much time and prevent many errors when you implement a large and complex relational database.

Note

Data modeling tools often are called CASE (Computer-Aided Software Engineering) tools. CASE tools designed for enterprise-wide software design usually include data modeling as one of their features. Today's high-end CASE tools, some of which carry license fees of $100,000 or more, offer many additional capabilities. This edition positions data modeling tools as a subset of CASE tools.

Most data modeling tools contain a *repository* that stores information about table design, primary and foreign key fields, constraints (validation rules) for fields, and types of relationships between the tables. The repository is a database maintained by the data modeling application itself. You can print database schema and generate data dictionaries from records in the repository. When your database design appears satisfactory, the data modeling tool translates the data in the repository to an SQL Data Definition Language (DDL) statement. You send the DDL statement to the client/server RDBMS on the server. This RDBMS can be used to create the entire database, or just to add tables to the database. SQL's DDL commands are one of the subjects of the next chapter.

At the time of this edition's printing, InfoModeler, published by Asymetrix of Bellevue, Washington, was the most popular data modeling tool for Access databases. InfoModeler uses a new approach to designing databases called *Object Role Modeling* (ORM) developed by Professor Terry Halpin of the University of Queensland, Australia. ORM lets you express the design of a database in simple, English terms through a structured language called *Formal Object Role Modeling Language* (FORML). InfoModeler translates FORML statements into a graphic schema, related to but more flexible than E-R diagrams. Figure 23.5 shows a portion of the ORM database diagram for a tutorial application of Info-Modeler 2.0 derived from the pubs sample database included with Microsoft SQL Server 4+.

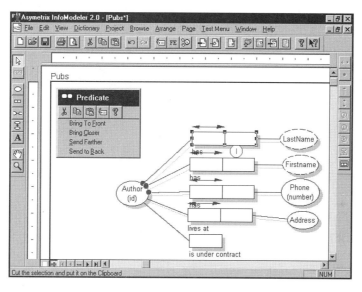

Fig. 23.5   An Object Role Modeling diagram for an Access database.

InfoModeler lets you print the ORM graphic schema and creates a data dictionary for the database. This reduces the time required to describe the structure of the database to others, as well as much of the drudgery of creating a comprehensive data dictionary. 32-bit InfoModeler 2.0 for Windows 95 and Windows NT 3.5+, which was in the final beta testing stage when this edition was printed, offers a number of other useful features, such as reverse-engineering your Access database (creating an ORM schema from an .MDB file or client/server database), database structure version tracking, and automatic restructuring of databases and tables.

Normalizing Data to the Relational Model

Up to this point, most of the subject matter in this chapter has been applicable to any type of database—hierarchical, relational, or even the new class of object database systems. However, because Access is a relational database management system (RDBMS), the balance of the chapter is devoted to relational databases. Because Access fully implements the relational model in its native database structure and you can link tables from other RDBMSs—including client/server tables—to Access databases, the discussion that follows is general in nature and applies to any database system with which Access is compatible, or for which you have the appropriate 32-bit Open Database Connectivity (ODBC) driver. (Access 95 requires the use of 32-bit ODBC drivers.)

The theory of relational database design is founded in a branch of mathematics called *set theory*, with a great deal of combinatorial analysis and some statistical methodology added. The set of rules and symbols by which relational databases are defined is called *relational algebra*. This chapter doesn't delve into the symbolic representation of relational algebra, nor does it require you to comprehend advanced mathematics. The chapter does, however, introduce you to many of the terms used in relational algebra for the sake of consistency with advanced texts that you may want to consult on the subject of database design.

Normalization Rules

Normalization is a formalized procedure by which data attributes are grouped into tables, and tables are grouped into databases. The purposes of normalization include the following:

- Eliminating duplicate information in tables

- Accommodating future changes in the structure of tables

- Minimizing the impact of database structural change on user applications that access the data

Normalization is done in steps; the first three and most common steps were described by Dr. E. F. Codd in his 1972 paper, "Further Normalization of the Data Base Relational Model." These steps are depicted in figure 23.6. The following sections describe each of the five steps that comprise the normalizing process.

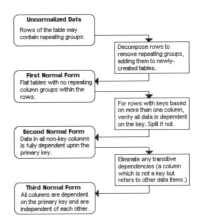

Fig. 23.6 A graphic representation of relational database normalization to the third normal form.

First Normal Form. First normal form requires that tables be flat and contain no repeating groups. A flat table has only two dimensions—length (number of records or rows) and width (number of fields or columns)—and cannot contain data cells with more than one value. For a single cell to contain more than one data value, the representation of the cell's contents requires a third dimension, depth, to display the multiple data values. Flat tables and the flat-file databases referred to in prior chapters are similar in that both have two dimensions. Flat-file databases, however, consist of only one table and have no restrictions on the content of the data cells within the table.

> **Note**
>
> Access 95's new TableAnalyzer Wizard does a good job of detecting duplicate information in tables created from flat files, but the files must be in first normal form (no repeating groups) for the analysis to succeed. The "Using Access 95's New TableAnalyzer Wizard" section, later in this chapter, describes how to use the TableAnalyzer Wizard to check for duplicate data, and to create a set of related tables to minimize or eliminate the duplication.

An example of unnormalized data for a shipping line appears in figure 23.7. This presentation often is seen in the schedules published by transportation firms where the stops are displayed across the page. This example is representative of a schedule created by importing the worksheet file that was used to create the printed version of the schedule. In the various examples of tables that follow, missing borders are the equivalent of an ellipsis; that is, a missing right border indicates that additional columns (fields) exist beyond the far right column, and a missing bottom border means that more rows (records) follow. (Those readers who are mariners will recognize the example as a mythical schedule for vessels of the former Pacific Far East Lines.)

Vessel	Name	Voyage	Embarks	From	Arrives	Port	Departs	Arrives	Port	Departs
528	Japan Bear	9203W	5/31/92	SFO	6/6/92	HNL	6/8/92	7/15/92	OSA	7/18/92
603	Korea Bear	9203W	6/05/92	OAK	6/19/92	OSA	6/21/92	6/25/92	INC	6/28/92
531	China Bear	9204W	6/20/92	LAX	7/10/92	PAP	7/11/92	8/28/92	SYD	9/2/92
528	Japan Bear	9204W	8/20/92	SFO	8/27/92	HNL	8/29/92	9/30/92	OSA	10/2/92

Fig. 23.7 A partial schedule of voyages for a shipping line.

Because the vessels stop at a number of ports, the Arrives, Port, and Departs columns are duplicated for each stop in the voyage. This type of data structure is allowed in COBOL, where the repeating group (Arrives, Port, and Departs) OCCURS any number of TIMES, but not in relational databases. The data in the preceding schedule isn't in first normal form because it contains repeating groups. The table must be *decomposed* (divided) into two tables, therefore, with the repeating groups (shown in shaded type in figure 23.7) removed from the Schedule table and placed in two new tables, Ports and Vessel Voyages, as shown in figure 23.8.

Now you need to provide for a link between the Ports and Vessel Voyages tables to retain the relationship between the data. Because this shipping line numbers voyages for each vessel with the year and which voyage this is for the year, as well as the general direction of travel (9204W is the fourth voyage of 1992, westbound), both Vessel and Voyage need to be used to relate the two tables. Neither Vessel nor Voyage is sufficient in itself because a vessel has multiple voyages during the year and the voyage numbers used here recur for other vessels. Because you must create a new Ports table to meet the requirements of the first normal form, you have the chance to order the columns in the order of their significance. Columns used to establish relationships are usually listed first, in the sequence in which they appear in the composite primary key, when more than one column is included in the key (see fig. 23.9).

Vessel	Name	Voyage	Embarks	From		Arrives	Port	Departs
528	Japan Bear	9203W	5/31/92	SFO		6/6/92	HNL	6/8/92
603	Korea Bear	9203W	6/5/92	OAK		6/19/92	OSA	6/21/92
531	China Bear	9204W	6/20/92	LAX		7/10/92	PAP	7/11/92
528	Japan Bear	9204W	8/20/92	SFO		8/27/92	HNL	8/29/92
						7/15/92	OSA	7/18/92
						6/25/92	INC	6/28/92
						8/28/92	SYD	9/2/92
						9/30/92	OSA	10/2/92

Fig. 23.8 The Ports and Vessel Voyages tables created from the Schedule table.

Vessel	Voyage	Port	Arrives	Departs
528	9203W	HNL	6/6/92	6/8/92
603	9203W	OSA	6/19/92	6/21/92
531	9204W	PAP	7/10/92	7/11/92
528	9204W	HNL	8/27/92	8/29/92
528	9203W	OSA	7/15/92	7/18/92
603	9203W	INC	6/25/92	6/28/92
531	9204W	SYD	8/28/92	9/2/92
528	9204W	OSA	9/30/92	10/2/92

Fig. 23.9 Linking fields are added to the Ports relation table.

Next, you establish the key fields for the Ports table that uniquely identify a record in the table. You need a primary key for the Ports table because other tables may be dependent on this table. Clearly, Vessel and Voyage must be included because these columns constitute the relationship to the Vessel Voyages table. You need to add the Port field to create a unique key (Vessel + Voyage can have duplicate values). Vessel + Voyage + Port creates a unique composite primary key because the combination takes into account stopping at a port twice—when returning eastbound, the voyage carries an "E" suffix.

> **Note**
>
> A spreadsheet application, such as Microsoft Excel 95, can speed up the process of normalizing existing data, especially when the data contains repeating groups. Import the data into a worksheet; then cut-and-paste the data in the repeating groups into a new worksheet. When the data for both of the tables is normalized, save the worksheets and then import the files to Access tables. This process is usually faster than creating make-table queries to generate normalized tables.

Second Normal Form. Second normal form requires that data in all non-key columns be fully dependent on the primary key and on each element (column) of the primary key when it is a composite primary key. *Fully dependent* means that the data value in each non-key column of a record is determined uniquely by the value of the primary key. If a composite primary key is required to establish the uniqueness of a record, the same rule applies to each value of the fields that comprise the composite key of the record.

Your table must be in first normal form before examining it for conformity to second normal form. Second normal form removes much of the data redundancy that is likely to occur in a first normal table.

Returning to the Vessel Voyages table, you can see that it requires a composite key, Vessel + Voyage, to create a unique key because the vessel number and vessel name recur. When you create such a key, however, you observe that Vessel and Name aren't dependent on the entire primary key because neither is determined by Voyage. You also find that the vessel name occurs for each of a vessel's voyages; for example, the *Japan Bear* appears twice. This lack of dependency violates the rules of the second normal form and requires Vessel Voyages to be split into two tables, Vessels and Voyages. One row is required in the Vessels table for each ship and one row in the Voyages table for each voyage made by each ship (eastbound and westbound directions are considered separate voyages for database purposes). As was the case for Ports, a unique key is required to relate voyages to the vessel, so the vessel number column is added to the Voyages table, as shown in figure 23.10.

Vessel	Vessel Name
528	Japan Bear
603	Korea Bear
531	China Bear

Vessel	Voyage	Embarks	From
528	9203W	5/31/92	SFO
603	9203W	6/5/92	OAK
531	9204W	6/20/92	LAX
528	9204W	8/20/92	SFO

Fig. 23.10 The Vessels and Voyages tables created from the Vessel Voyages table.

Third Normal Form. Third normal form requires that all non-key columns of a table be dependent on the table's primary key and independent of one another. Tables must conform to both first and second normal forms to qualify for third normal status.

Your Vessels and Voyages tables are now in third normal form because there are no repeating groups of columns, and the data in non-key columns is dependent on the primary key field. The non-key columns of Ports, Arrives, and Departs are dependent on the composite key (Vessel + Voyage + Port) and independent of one another. Ports, therefore, meets the requirements of first, second, and third normal forms. The departure date is independent of the arrival date because the difference between the two dates is based on the vessel's lading into and out of the port, the availability of berths and container cranes, and the weather.

To demonstrate normalization to the third normal form, suppose that you want to identify the officers of the vessel—master, chief engineer, and so on—in the database. Your first impulse might be to add their employee numbers, the primary key of an Employee table, to the Vessels table (see fig. 23.11).

This table violates the third normal rule because none of the officers assigned to a vessel is dependent on the vessel itself. This type of dependency is called *transitive*. The master's, chief's, and first mate's maritime licenses allow them to act in their respective capacities on any vessel for which the license is valid. Any officer may be assigned to other vessels as the need arises, or remain on board for only a portion of the voyage.

VI

Advanced Techniques

Vessel	Vessel Name	Master	Chief	1st Mate
528	Japan Bear	01023	01155	01367
603	Korea Bear	00955	01203	00823
531	China Bear	00721	00912	01251

Fig. 23.11 A table with a transitive dependency between vessels and crew members.

One method of removing the transitive dependency might be to add the employee numbers column to the Voyages table. This method doesn't provide a satisfactory solution, however, because the vessel may arrive at a port with one group of crew members and depart with another group. In addition, you need to specify the crew members who remain with the vessel while it is in port. A relation table, such as that shown for the *Japan Bear* in figure 23.12, solves the problem. Duplicate values in the Port (departure port) and To (destination port) fields designate records for crew members responsible for the vessel while in port. The Crew table of figure 23.12 qualifies as a relation table because all its fields correspond to primary keys or parts of primary keys in the base tables—Vessels, Voyages, Ports, and Employees.

Vessel	Voyage	Port	To	Master	Chief	1st Mate
528	9203W	SFO	HNL	01023	01156	01367
528	9203W	HNL	HNL	01023	01156	01367
528	9203W	HNL	OSA	01023	01156	01367
528	9203W	OSA	OSA	01023	01156	01367
528	9203W	OSA	INC	01023	01156	01367

Fig. 23.12 Removing transitive dependency with a relation table.

All your tables are now flat, contain no duplicate information other than that in the columns used for keys, and conform to the first through third normal forms.

Fourth Normal Form. Many database designers disregard the fourth and fifth normal forms; those designers consider these forms too esoteric, or applicable only in specialized cases. Disregarding fourth normal form often results in poorly designed databases, but not necessarily malfunctioning ones.

Fourth normal form requires that independent data entities not be stored in the same table when many-to-many relationships exist between these entities. The table of figure 23.12 violates fourth normal form because many-to-many relationships exist between the Vessel and the fields that identify crew members. The fourth normal form is discussed in the "Many-to-Many Relationships and Fourth Normal Form" section, later in this chapter, because it is the only normalization rule that is dependent on a specific type of relationship.

Fifth Normal Form and Combined Entities. Fifth normal form requires that you be able to reconstruct exactly the original table from those tables into which it was decomposed. Re-creating the Excel spreadsheet from the tables in the example in Chapter 21, "Using Access with Microsoft Excel," demonstrates compliance with fifth normal form. Fifth normal form requires that the tables comply with the rules for third normal form and, when many-to-many relationships are present, with the rule for fourth normal form.

The Voyages table appears quite similar to that of Ports. The From column is equivalent to Port, and Embarks is the same as Departure. Therefore, you can move the data in the Voyages table to the Ports table and delete the Voyages table. Figure 23.13 shows the new Ports table. The rows from the Voyages table don't have values in the Arrives column because they represent points of departure.

Vessel	Voyage	Port	Arrives	Departs
528	9203W	HNL	6/6/92	6/8/92
603	9203W	OSA	6/19/92	6/21/92
531	9204W	PAP	7/10/92	7/11/92
528	9204W	HNL	8/27/92	8/29/92
528	9203W	OSA	7/15/92	7/18/92
603	9203W	INC	6/25/92	6/28/92
531	9204W	SYD	8/28/92	9/2/92
528	9204W	OSA	9/30/92	10/2/92
528	9203W	SFO		5/31/92
603	9203W	OAK		6/5/92
531	9204W	LAX		6/20/92
528	9204W	SFO		8/20/92

Fig. 23.13 Records from the Voyages table appended to the Ports table.

However, you cannot explicitly reconstruct the original table from the combined Voyages and Ports tables in all cases, because you cannot distinguish an embarkation row from the other rows by a value in the table. A null value in the Arrives field is a candidate to distinguish an embarkation, but most PC RDBMSs don't support null values. You eliminate any ambiguity that using a null value might cause—and bring the table into fifth normal form—by adding a single-character field, Type, with single-letter codes to define the type of call. In figure 23.14, the codes E and S represent Embarkation and Scheduled call, respectively. Other codes might include M for Maintenance stop and R for Return voyage.

Vessel	Voyage	Port	Type	Arrives	Departs
528	9203W	HNL	S	6/6/92	6/8/92
603	9203W	OSA	S	6/19/92	6/21/92
531	9204W	PAP	S	7/10/92	7/11/92
528	9204W	HNL	S	8/27/92	8/29/92
528	9203W	OSA	S	7/15/92	7/18/92
603	9203W	INC	S	6/25/92	6/28/92
531	9204W	SYD	S	8/28/92	9/2/92
528	9204W	OSA	S	9/30/92	10/2/92
528	9203W	SFO	E		5/31/92
603	9203W	OAK	E		6/5/92
531	9204W	LAX	E		6/20/92
528	9204W	SFO	E		8/20/92

Fig. 23.14 The Type field has been added to comply with fifth normal form.

Figure 23.15 demonstrates that you can reconstruct the content of the original Schedule table from the Vessels and Ports tables. Query1 creates the first five columns of the Schedule table by adding the criterion E for the Type field, which isn't shown. You can re-create the remaining columns of the Schedule table from Query2, which uses the criterion S for the Type field.

Types of Relationships

The subject of relationships between entities usually precedes discussions of normalization. Relationships come second in this book, however, because you can only create valid relationships between tables that have been structured in accordance with at least the first three normalization rules described in the preceding sections. This section describes the four basic types of relationships between tables, and employs E-R diagrams to depict the relationships graphically.

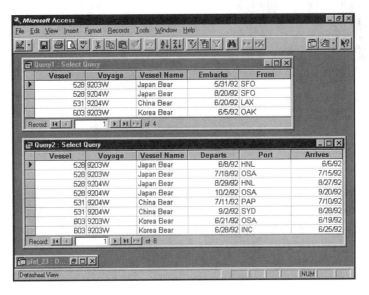

Fig. 23.15   The datasheets of the two queries required to reconstruct the Schedule table.

One-to-One Relationships. The simplest relationship between tables is a one-to-one relationship. In such a relationship, the tables have exact one-to-one row correspondence; no row in one table has more than one corresponding row in the other table. You can combine one-to-one-related tables into a single table consisting of all the tables' columns.

One-to-one relationships are often used to divide very wide base tables into narrower ones. You might want to divide a wide table to reduce the time needed to view fields containing specific sets of data, such as the stock prices table in the example of Chapter 15, "Preparing Advanced Reports." Often you need to control access to the parts of tables that contain sensitive or confidential data. An example is an employee file; everyone might have read-only access to the employees' names, but only members of the personnel department are authorized to view salary and other payroll information (see fig. 23.16).

Employee	Position	Last	First	MI
00668	Master	Johansson	Lars	F.
00721	Master	Karlsson	Bo	B.
00885	Chief	MacGregor	Paul	C.
00912	Chief	McDermott	John	R.
00955	Master	Olafson	Karl	T.
01023	Master	Kekkonen	Eino	K.
01156	Chief	McDougal	William	U.
01203	Chief	Kashihara	Matsuo	

Employee	Salary
00668	6500.00
00721	6250.00
00885	5100.00
00912	5000.00
00955	6100.00
01023	6050.00
01156	4900.00
01203	4850.00

Fig. 23.16   Two tables with a one-to-one relationship.

If you are sharing tables on a network, dividing large tables can improve response time when many users are updating the tables' data. Chapter 25, "Securing Multiuser Network Applications," explains the reason for the speed improvement.

Figure 23.17 shows the E-R diagram for the Employees and Salaries tables. The 1s added to each side of the relationship diamond indicate a one-to-one relationship. The participation of entities in relationships can be mandatory or optional. Optional relationships are symbolized by a circle drawn on the line connecting the optional entity with the relationship diamond. In the figure, the Paid-Salaries relationship is optional because some employees can be paid on an hourly basis and linked to a Wages table. Tables with mandatory one-to-one relationships are base tables. A table with an optional one-to-one relationship to a base table is a related table. Multiple tables with one-to-one relationships where the corresponding records in the other tables are optional can reduce the database's disk space requirement.

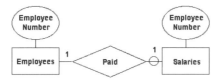

Fig. 23.17 An E-R diagram for an optional one-to-one relationship.

Another example of a one-to-one relationship is that between an xBase memo field and a corresponding entry in a memo (DBT) file. Access treats free-text as the content of a data cell in the table, so no relationship is involved.

One-to-Many Relationships. One-to-many relationships link a single row in one table with two or more rows in another table, through a relationship between the primary key of the base table and the corresponding foreign key in the related table. Although the foreign key in the table containing the many relationships may be a component of a composite primary key in its own table, it is a foreign key for the purposes of the relationship. One-to-many relationships are the most common type of relationships.

The one-to-many relationship shown in figure 23.18 links all records in the Ports table to one record in the Vessels table. The one-to-many relationship enables you to display all records in the Ports table for scheduled ports of call of the *Japan Bear*.

Vessel	Vessel Name		Vessel	Voyage	Port	Type	Arrives	Departs
528	Japan Bear		528	9203W	HNL	S	6/6/92	6/8/92
			528	9204W	HNL	S	8/27/92	8/29/92
			528	9203W	OSA	S	7/15/92	7/18/92
			528	9204W	OSA	S	9/30/92	10/2/92
			528	9203W	SFO	E		5/31/92
			528	9204W	SFO	E		8/20/92

Fig. 23.18 A one-to-many relationship between the Vessels and Ports tables.

The E-R diagram of figure 23.19 expresses this relationship, where the degree of the Vessel entity relationships between the two tables is indicated by the "1" and "m" adjacent to their entities.

Fig. 23.19 The E-R diagram for the one-to-many relationship of figure 23.17.

Many-to-One Relationships. Many-to-one relationships are the converse of the one-to-many type. The many-to-one relationship enables you to display the vessel name for any record in the Ports table. If the roles of the participating entities are simply reversed to create the many-to-one relationship, the relationship is said to be *reflexive*; that is, the many-to-one relationship is the reflection of its one-to-many counterpart (see fig. 23.20). All many-to-one relationships in Access are reflexive; you can specify only a one-to-one or one-to-many relationship between the primary table and the related table, using the two option buttons in Access's Relationship dialog.

Vessel	Voyage	Port	Type	Arrives	Departs		Vessel	Vessel Name
528	9203W	HNL	S	6/6/92	6/8/92		528	Japan Bear
528	9204W	HNL	S	8/27/92	8/29/92			
528	9203W	OSA	S	7/15/92	7/18/92			
528	9204W	OSA	S	9/30/92	10/2/92			
528	9203W	SFO	E		5/31/92			
528	9204W	SFO	E		8/20/92			

Fig. 23.20 The Ports and Vessels tables in a reflexive many-to-one relationship.

If you select a record on the many side of the relationship, you can display the record corresponding to its foreign key on the one side. E-R diagrams for reflexive relationships are often drawn like the diagram in figure 23.21. Reflexive relationships are indicated by the appropriate form of the verb placed outside the diamond that defines the relationship.

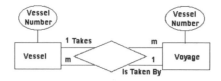

Fig. 23.21 The E-R diagram for a reflexive many-to-one relationship.

Many-to-Many Relationships and Fourth Normal Form. Many-to-many relationships cannot be expressed as simple relationships between two participating entities. You create many-to-many relationships by making a table that has many-to-one relationships with two base tables.

The Crews relation table created in the "Third Normal Form" section to assign crew members to legs of the voyage is shown again in figure 23.22. The Crews table creates a many-to-many relationship between the Vessels table, based on the Vessel entity, and the Employees table, based on the employee number entities in the Master, Chief, and 1stMate fields.

Vessel	Voyage	Port	To	Master	Chief	1st Mate
528	9203W	SFO	HNL	01023	01156	01367
528	9203W	HNL	HNL	01023	01156	01367
528	9203W	HNL	OSA	01023	01156	01367
528	9203W	OSA	OSA	01023	01156	01367
528	9203W	OSA	INC	01023	01156	01367

Fig. 23.22 The first version of the Crews relation table.

The table in figure 23.22 has a many-to-one relationship with the Vessels table and a many-to-one relationship with the Employees table. This version of the Crews table creates a many-to-many relationship between the Vessels and Employees tables. The employees who crew the vessel are independent of one another; any qualified employee can, in theory, be assigned to fill a crew position on any leg of a voyage. The table in figure 23.22 violates the fourth normal form, therefore, because it contains independent entities.

Figure 23.23 shows the restructured Crews relation table needed to assign employees to legs of voyages. The table has one record for each employee for each leg of the voyage.

Employee	Vessel	Voyage	Port	To
01023	528	9203W	SFO	HNL
01156	528	9203W	SFO	HNL
01367	528	9203W	SFO	HNL
01023	528	9203W	HNL	HNL
01156	528	9203W	HNL	HNL
01367	528	9203W	HNL	HNL
01023	528	9203W	HNL	OSA
01156	528	9203W	HNL	OSA
01367	528	9203W	HNL	OSA
01023	528	9203W	OSA	OSA
01156	528	9203W	OSA	OSA
01367	528	9203W	OSA	OSA
01023	528	9203W	OSA	INC
01156	528	9203W	OSA	INC
01367	528	9203W	OSA	INC

Fig. 23.23 The Crews table restructured to fourth normal form.

You can add new entities to this table, provided that the entities are wholly dependent on all the foreign key fields. An example of a dependent entity is payroll data that might include data attributes such as regular hours worked, overtime hours, and chargeable expenses incurred by each employee on each leg of a voyage. Such entities are called *weak* or *associative* entities because they rely on other base tables for their relevance. The Crews table is no longer considered strictly a relation table when you add associative entities because it no longer consists wholly of fields that constitute foreign keys.

The E-R diagram for the many-to-many relation table relating employees and the legs of a voyage to which the employees are assigned is shown in figure 23.24. The encircled Date connected to the Assigned Crew relationship expresses *cardinality:* one employee can be assigned to only one voyage on a given date. The cardinality of the relationship, therefore, is based on the departure and arrival dates for the leg. Automatically enforcing the condition that employees not be in more than one place at one time can be accomplished by creating a no-duplicates index consisting of all the Crews table's fields. Associative entities are shown in E-R diagrams as a relationship diamond within an entity rectangle. If you add payroll data to the Crews table, an associative entity is created. Assignment of an employee to a voyage is optional, as indicated by the circled lines; employees may have shore leave, be indisposed, or be assigned to shoreside duties.

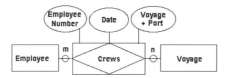

Fig. 23.24 An E-R diagram for a many-to-many relationship with an associative entity.

Using graphic schema and E-R diagrams when you design an Access database helps ensure that the database meets your initial objectives. Schema also are useful in explaining the structure of your database to its users. E-R diagrams can uncover design errors, such as the failure to normalize tables at least to fourth normal form. Few experiences are more frustrating than having to restructure a large table because you realize its design wasn't fully normalized. Forethought, planning, and diagramming are the watchwords of success in database design.

Using Access 95's New TableAnalyzer Wizard

◀◀ See "Lookup Fields in Access Tables and the Lookup Wizard," p. 42

Access 95's TableAnalyzer Wizard detects cells containing repeated data in table columns, and proposes to create two new related tables to eliminate the repetition. This wizard uses Access 95's new Lookup Wizard, described in Chapter 4, "Working with Access Databases and Tables," to create the relationship between the two new tables. After the wizard creates the new related tables, your original table is renamed to *TableName*_OLD, and the wizard creates a one-to-many INNER JOIN query named *TableName* to return a result set that duplicates the Datasheet View of the original table. Thus you need not change the references to *TableName* in your Access application objects.

The tlkp*Lookup* table must have a valid primary key field to provide unambiguous association of a single record in the tlkp*Lookup* table with a foreign key field in the tbl*NewName* table. One of the problems associated with repetitive data is data entry errors, such as occasional misspelling of a company name or an address element. The TableAnalyzer Wizard detects and displays instances of minor mismatch in repeated cell values, such as a missing apostrophe, for correction. If such errors are not corrected, the tlkp*Lookup* table includes spurious almost-duplicate entries that violate the rules of table normalization.

To demonstrate use of the TableAnalyzer Wizard to eliminate duplicate shipping address information in the Orders table of Northwind.mdb, follow these steps:

1. Open Northwind.mdb, if necessary, and launch the TableAnalyzer Wizard by choosing Tools, Analyze, Table.

2. Skip the two introductory dialogs by clicking the Next button twice; you'll reach the table selection dialog shown in figure 23.25.

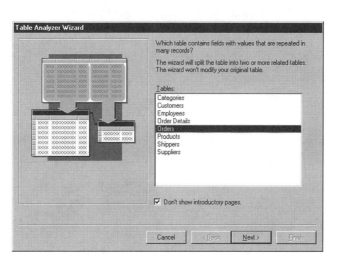

Fig. 23.25   You select the table to analyze in the third TableAnalyzer Wizard dialog.

3. Select the table with the duplicated data in the Tables list box (for this example, you need the Orders table). Next, mark the Don't show introductory pages check box to skip the two introductory dialogs whenever you use the TableAnalyzer Wizard again. Click the Next button to display the next dialog.

4. Accept the default option—Yes, let the wizard decide—and click Next to start the analysis process. A progress bar monitors the status of the analysis (see fig. 23.26.)

5. After the analysis completes, the wizard creates two tables with default names Table1 (the original table with duplicate data removed) and Table2 (the lookup table). The wizard establishes a relationship between the two tables based on the proposed primary key field of Table2 and the corresponding foreign key field of Table1.

6. Select Table1 and click the table rename button (the leftmost button in the group of three buttons at the top of the dialog) to display the Table Name input box. Give the table a new name—in this case, **Sales Orders**—and click OK to close the input box. Repeat this process for Table2, assigning the name **Ship Addresses** (see fig. 23.27). Click Next to continue.

VI

Advanced Techniques

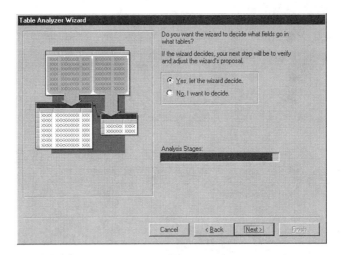

Fig. 23.26   Analyzing the Orders table by letting the wizard decide which table fields contain duplicate data.

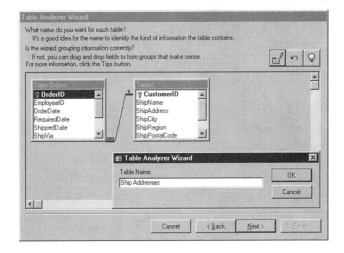

Fig. 23.27   Renaming the two tables which were created from the Orders table by the TableAnalyzer Wizard.

[Next >]   **7.** Verify that the new Lookup field, Lookup to Ship Addresses, of the Sales Orders table has a many-to-one relationship with the key field of the lookup table, in this case the CustomerID field of the Ship Addresses table (see fig. 23.28). If the wizard can't identify a candidate primary key, the wizard suggests using a field of the AutoNumber data type to create a primary key. Click Next to continue.

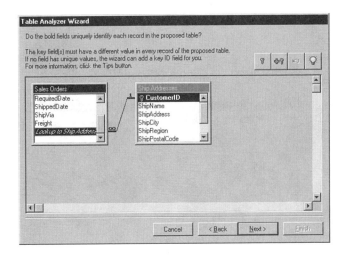

Fig. 23.28 Verifying that the CustomerID field of the Ship Addresses table is the appropriate primary key.

8. If the wizard detects a misspelling of an entry in the lookup table, the dialog shown in figure 23.29 appears. The wizard bases the marked check box in the Correct Record column on the frequency of exact duplication of records ("Alfred's Futterkiste" appears several times and "Alfreds Futterkiste" only once in the ShipName column). Verify which record is correct, and click the Correct Record check box for the incorrect record(s). The Wizard automatically corrects the misspelled entries. Click Next to continue.

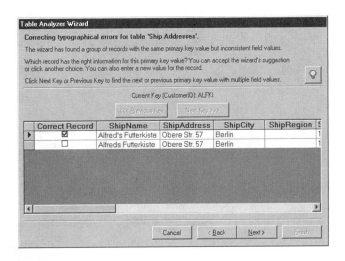

Fig. 23.29 Correcting a misspelled entry in the ShipName field.

9. The wizard proposes to create a query, in this case named Orders, that substitutes for the original Orders table. Deselect the Show Me Help... check box to prevent the two Lookup Wizard Help screens from appearing when you complete the operation (see fig. 23.30).

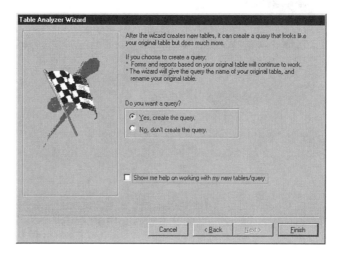

Fig. 23.30 Creating an Orders query as a substitute for the original Orders table.

 10. Click Finish to create the Orders query and display the temporary Orders query datasheet as shown in figure 23.31. Click OK in the message box to create the final Orders query.

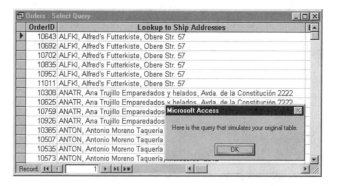

Fig. 23.31 The temporary Orders query displaying the Lookup to Ship Addresses column.

11. Verify that the Datasheet View of the final Orders query result set, which does not include the Lookup to Ship Addresses column, duplicates the original orders table. Figure 23.32 shows the Orders query in Query Design view.

12. The wizard has renamed the original Orders table to Orders_OLD. To return Northwind.mdb to its original state, open the Database window and delete the Orders query plus the Sales Orders and Ship Addresses tables, then rename the Orders_OLD table to **Orders**.

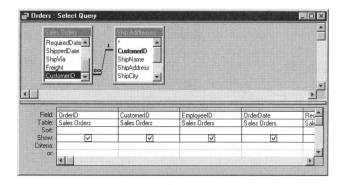

Fig. 23.32 The final Orders query in Query Design view.

> **Caution**
>
> Extracting the duplicate shipping address information from the Orders table to a new Ship Addresses table is useful to demonstrate use of the TableAnalyzer Wizard, but is not practical in the real world where individual customers may have several shipping addresses. To make the Shipping Addresses table useful, you must add a field, such as ShipToID, to identify multiple shipping addresses for a single customer. Assign a value of 0 for the ShipToID field for the default shipping information created by the wizard. Additional shipping addresses for a particular CustomerID are numbered 1, 2, 3, … You need to redesign forms that specify shipping addresses to allow adding new Shipping Addresses records for customers. You must change the primary key to a composite primary key consisting of CustomerID + ShipToID, and use Access VBA code to create successive ShipToID values automatically for a particular CustomerID.

If you use object type identifiers based on the Leszynski naming conventions, however, as described in Appendix B, you must follow these steps to assign appropriate names to the new objects:

1. Name the new table with the repeated data removed tbl*NewName*.

2. Name the new lookup table tlkp*Lookup*.

3. Name the associated query qlkp*Lookup*.

4. Change the references in your application objects from tbl*TableName* to qlkp*Lookup*.

Working with Data Dictionaries

After you've determined the individual data entities that comprise the tables of your database, and have established the relationships between them, the next step is to prepare a preliminary written description of the database, called a *data dictionary*. Data dictionaries are indispensable to database systems; an undocumented database system is almost impossible to administer and maintain properly. Errors and omissions in database design often are uncovered when you prepare the preliminary data dictionary.

When you have completed and tested your database design, you prepare the final detailed version of the data dictionary. As you add new forms and reports to applications, or modify existing forms and reports, you update the data dictionary to keep it current. Even if you're making a database for your personal use, a simplified version of a data dictionary pays many dividends on your time investment.

Conventional Data Dictionaries

Data dictionaries contain a text description of the database as a whole, each table it contains, the fields that comprise the table, primary and foreign keys, and values that may be assigned to fields when they contain coded or enumerated information. The purpose and description of each application that uses the database is included. Data dictionaries shouldn't be dependent on the particular RDBMS used to create and manipulate the database. Because data dictionaries are hierarchical in nature, they lend themselves to the use of traditional outline formats that are implemented in Windows word processing applications. The following illustrates the structure of a conventional data dictionary using legal-style outline headings:

1. DATABASE - Proper name and file name

   A text description of the purpose and general content of the database and who may use it. A list of applications that operate on the database is useful, along with references to any other databases that use the information that the database contains. If any graphic schema of the database have been prepared, they appear in this section.

   1.1. DATA AREA - Name of the group of which tables are a member

   When tables are classified by group, such as the Payroll group within the Human Resources database, include a description of the group.

   1.1.1. TABLE - Individual tables that comprise the data area

      1.1.1.1. PERMISSIONS - User domains with access to the table

      1.1.1.2. RECORD - General definition of the data entities

         1.1.1.2.1. PRIMARY KEY - Field(s) in the primary key

            1.1.1.2.1.1. INDEX - Primary key index specification

         1.1.1.2.2. FOREIGN KEY(S) - Other key fields

            1.1.1.2.2.1 INDEX - Indexes on foreign keys

         1.1.1.2.3. FIELDS - Non-key fields

            1.1.1.2.3.1 ENUMERATIONS - Valid codes for fields

Text follows each heading and describes the purpose of the database element to which the heading refers. Subsequent headings include descriptions of the applications that use the database tables, with subheadings for queries, forms, and reports. Captured images of displays and copies of reports add to the usefulness of the data dictionary. Printouts of programming code usually are contained in appendixes. Complete data dictionaries are essential for database maintenance. An alternative format consists of content descriptions of each table in tabular form.

Access's Integrated Data Dictionary System

Access 95's Database Documentor add-in, introduced in Access 2.0, replaces the Database Analyzer library included with Access 1.x. The Documentor creates a report that details the objects, and the values of the properties of the objects, in the current database. Thus Documentor is a substantial improvement over Analyzer, which only created tables that contained lists of objects and their properties; you had to design your own reports based on the *@ObjectName* tables created by Analyzer, or export the table data to Excel or Word tables to create the dictionary.

> **Note**
>
> The Access 2.0 version of Documentor printed reports, but couldn't export its data to tables or files. Access 95's Publish It with MS Word feature of the Office Links toolbar button allows you to save the report as an .RTF file (doc_rptObjects.rtf) for import into Microsoft Word or any other word processor, such as WordPad, that handles rich-text files. Alternatively, you can export the report in BIFF format to an Excel doc_rptObjects.xls file by choosing the Analyze It with MS Excel option.

In many cases, Documentor tells you more than you want to know about your database; the full report for all the objects in Northwind.mdb, for example, requires about 392 printed pages. Most often, you only want to document your tables and, perhaps, your queries to create a complete data dictionary. The following steps show you how to create a data dictionary with Database Documentor:

1. Open the database you want to document, and then choose Tools, Analyze, Documentor. Documentor's Select Objects opening dialog appears, as shown in figure 23.33 for Northwind.mdb.

2. Select the type of object you want to document from the Object Type drop-down list. The All Object Types item adds every object in the database to the Objects list when you click Select All.

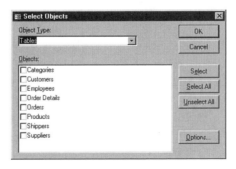

Fig. 23.33 Database Documentor's opening window.

3. Click Options to display the Print Table Definition dialog. The most detailed set of information for tables and indexes is the default. If your Access database is not secure, you can click the Permissions by User and Group check box to eliminate reporting permissions data (see fig. 23.34). Click OK to return to the opening dialog.

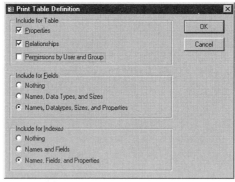

Fig. 23.34 Setting options for documenting tables.

4. Select the table(s) you want to document in the Objects list, and then click Select. This marks the table's check box, as shown in figure 23.35. (Double-clicking the list item has the same effect.) Alternatively, if you want to document all the tables of your database, click Select All. For this example, only the Orders and Order Details tables are documented.

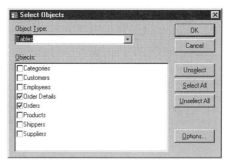

Fig. 23.35 Two tables selected for documenting.

5. Select Queries from the Object Type drop-down list to display the QueryDef objects in your database. Click the Options button to display the Print Query Definition dialog. Select the Permissions by User and Group check box to eliminate security data from the report, and select the other options shown in figure 23.36 to minimize duplication of table field data. Click OK to continue.

6. Double-click the Order Information query entry to add this query to the documentation, and then click OK to create the report.

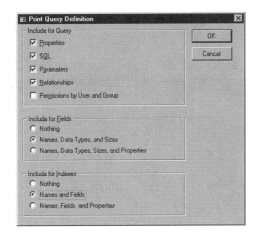

Fig. 23.36 Selecting the options for printing query definitions.

7. After a short period, the Object Definition print preview window appears (see fig. 23.37). Note that the report for three objects is one page in length. Click the last page button to view the documentation for the Order Information query.

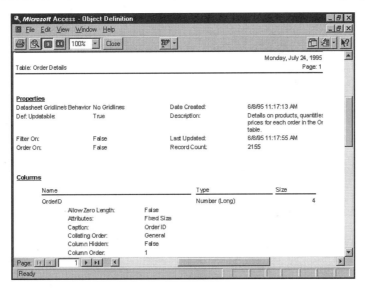

Fig. 23.37 The first page of Database Documentor's report.

8. Click the Print button on the toolbar to print the report, or click the Office Links button to create a doc_rptObjects.rtf or doc_rptObjects.xls file. Figure 23.38 shows part of a doc_rptObjects.xls file pertaining to the Orders table.

9. Click the Close button on the toolbar, or double-click the Document Control-menu box to close the print preview window.

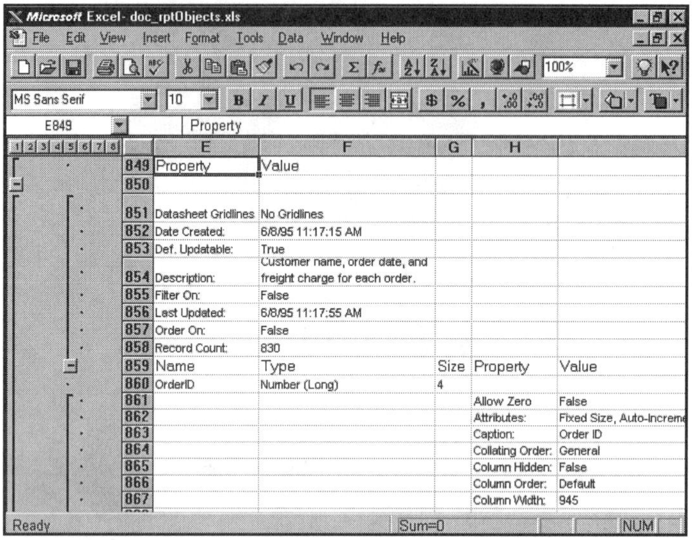

Fig. 23.38 Part of the doc_rptObjects.xls is displayed here in Microsoft Excel 95.

Documenting other objects in your database follows the same method outlined in the preceding steps. You can print data for the database itself (<Current Database> in the Object Type list) or for selected forms, reports, macros, and modules.

Using Access Indexes

Database managers use indexes to relate the values of key fields to the location of the data entity on the disk. The basic purpose of an index is to speed up access to specific rows or groups of rows within a database table. You also use indexes to enforce unique-ness of primary keys, and to establish upper and lower limits for queries. Using an index eliminates the necessity of re-sorting the table each time you need to create a sequenced list based on a foreign key.

Different PC database managers create and use indexes in a variety of ways. Paradox uses a mandatory primary index (.PX) to speed up queries and to ensure nonduplicate keys. Secondary indexes on nonprimary-key fields are permitted by Paradox (.X## and .Y##), created either by the QuerySpeedUp menu choice or the PAL INDEX instruction. dBASE and some of its xBase dialects enable any number of indexes to be created in the form of individual .NDX files, for a single file or table. The number of xBase indexes that you can have open at once, so as to keep them current, is determined by the xBase RDBMS you choose. You select the index you want to use with the SET ORDER TO *IndexFileName* in-struction. Several xBase languages have their own index structures, such as Clipper's .NTX and FoxPro's .IDX. dBASE IV and FoxPro go one step beyond, with their multiple index structures (.MDX and .CDX) that combine several indexes in a single file. You specify a TAG name to identify which index is to be used to find the records you want.

Indexed Sequential Access Method (ISAM)

Indexed Sequential Access Method (ISAM) describes a file structure in which the records are logically located (sorted) in the sequence of the values of their primary key, with an index used to provide random access to individual records. The term *logically* is applied to record location because the records' physical location on the disk may not be sequential; their physical location is determined by the disk's file allocation table (FAT) and the degree of file fragmentation on the drive. ISAM is often used to describe any database structure that uses indexes for searching. This book adheres to the original definition, in which the records must be in the order of their primary key.

Classic mainframe ISAM databases have file structures that use *overflow sectors*, space reserved on the disk to handle insertion of new records. The database administrator periodically sorts the file to insert the data from the overflow sectors into the body of the table structure at appropriate locations. The periodic sorting clears the overflow sectors for future additions. The process is called *file maintenance*. Improved insertion techniques have been applied to databases created by PC and client/server RDBMSs. These methods are described in the sections that follow.

DOS RDBMSs duplicate ISAM structures by using an insertion technique. For instance, many xBase dialects enable you to INSERT a record in the middle of a file (the ISAM method), rather than APPEND a BLANK to the end of a file (the *heap* technique). When you INSERT a record near the top of a large, indexed xBase file, you can catch up on your sleep while the RDBMS moves all the following records to make room for the new one, adjusting all the index entries to refer to new locations. Figure 23.39 shows the difference between a record INSERT and APPEND. Paradox's native mode is ISAM, which explains why some of its operations, such as canceling an edit on a large table, take so long to complete.

Fig. 23.39   Inserting versus appending new records in an xBase file.

Certain types of files created by DOS RDBMSs inherently fit the ISAM mold—sales order and invoice records with a numeric key incremented by one for each addition are the best examples; Access's AutoNumber field data type performs the numbering function automatically. Other types of tables, such as lists of customers, are often sorted alphabetically. You have to INSERT each record in the proper location or re-sort the file each time you add a new customer to maintain a true ISAM structure. The faster method with xBase is to APPEND BLANKS and REPLACE the blanks WITH data; this procedure adds the new records in a heap at the bottom of the file. Periodically, DOS adds another cluster to the file to accommodate the newly added data. Some xBase dialects, such as Clipper, don't include the INSERT command.

The header of an xBase .DBF file, such as the one in figure 23.39, includes the name of each field, its field data type, its length in bytes, and some additional data. All data records in the file are the same length, representing the sum of the field lengths, plus one byte to indicate whether the record is marked for deletion. xBase files are called the *fixed-length record* type. Values that don't fill the length of a field are padded with spaces; character fields are padded with spaces to the right of the text, and numbers are right-justified by padding to the left. xBase files often incorporate much more padding than data.

The record numbers shown in figure 23.39 aren't present in the data, but are deduced by calculating the offset (the intervening number of bytes) of the record from the beginning of the file. If the header is 300 bytes long, record 1 begins at offset 300, corresponding to the 301st byte (the offset of the first byte is 0). Assuming the fields total 80 bytes in width, record 2 begins at offset 380, 3 at offset 460, and so forth. The location of a data item's value is determined by calculating the offset of the desired record, then adding the offset to the beginning of the column (field) containing the data.

Access Data Pages and Variable Length Records

Access, like Microsoft SQL Server and many other SQL databases, divides the data stored in its table structures into 2K *data pages*, corresponding to the size of a conventional DOS fixed-disk file cluster. A header, similar to the one in figure 23.40, is added to each page to create the foundation for a *linked list* of data pages. The header contains a reference, called a *pointer*, to the page that precedes it, and another pointer to the page that follows. Linked lists use pointers to link the data pages to one another in order to organize the data table. If no indexes are in use, new data is added to the last page of the table until the page is full, and then another page is added at the end. The process is much like the heap method used by xBase, or the manner in which DOS creates entries that link fixed-disk data clusters in its file allocation table (FAT).

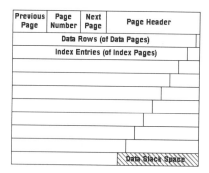

Fig. 23.40 The structure of a data page in an Access table.

Data pages contain only integral numbers of rows. The space that remains after the last row that fits in the page is called *slack*. You may be familiar with the concept of slack from the characteristic of current DOS versions that allocate fixed-disk file space in 2K clusters. A small batch file, for example, may be displayed as having a file size of 120 bytes, but the file actually occupies 2,048 bytes of disk space; the unused space is slack.

Access uses variable-length records for its data rows instead of the fixed-length record structure of xBase. Variable-length records don't require padding for data that is shorter than the designated field size.

Data rows longer than 2K are contained in multiple pages. Avoid long rows if possible, as they can reduce storage efficiency by increasing the percentage of slack space in data pages. Access files with relatively short rows store data, especially character-based data, more efficiently than xBase or Paradox. Special fields containing text and images are stored in separate data structures linked to the data item in the data page. The storage concept is similar to that for xBase memo files, but the implementation differs in Access.

The advantage of data pages with their own headers, over the single-header, record-based xBase structure shown earlier in figure 23.39, is that you can keep a table's data pages in ISAM order by altering only the pointers in the page header, and not the structure of the file itself. This process, which uses a *nonclustered index* (discussed later in this chapter, in the "Nonclustered and Clustered Indexes" section), is much faster than the INSERT method for xBase files and usually matches the speed of the APPEND technique.

Balanced Binary Trees, Roots, and Leaves

Most database managers use an indexing method called a *binary tree* or *B-tree*. In describing an index structure, the tree is inverted, with its root and trunk at the top, progressing downward to branches and leaves, the direction taken by the searching process. A binary tree is defined as a tree in which the trunk divides into two branches, with each branch dividing into two sub-branches, and then further twofold divisions occurring until you reach the leaves, which are indivisible. The points of the two-way divisions are called *nodes*. B-trees for computer-based searching were first proposed by John Mauchly, one of the pioneers of electronic computers, in 1946.

When you make many insertions and deletions in a database, conventional B-tree structures can become very lopsided, with many sub-branches and leaves stemming from one branch, and few from another. The reason for this is explained by mathematical theory that is beyond the scope of this book. Lopsided B-trees slow the searching process for records that are in an especially active area of the database. This situation causes undesirable effects in, for example, an airline reservation system where passenger reservations are being added to or deleted from a flight at a rapid rate immediately prior to its scheduled departure.

To solve the lopsided B-tree problem, two Russian mathematicians, G. M. Adelson-Velski and E. M. Landis, proposed a balanced B-tree structure in 1963. In a balanced B-tree structure, the length of the search path to any leaf is never more than 45-percent longer than the optimum. Each time a new row is added to the index, a new node is inserted and the tree is rebalanced if necessary. A small balanced B-tree structure appears in figure 23.41. Its nodes are labeled + (plus) or – (minus), called the *balance factor*, according to whether the right subtree height minus the left subtree height is +1 or –1. If the subtrees are the same height, the node is empty. Balance factors are used to determine where a new node is added to maintain the tree in balance.

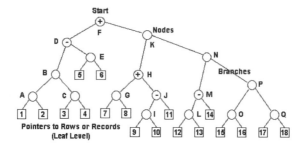

Fig. 23.41   A diagram of a simple balanced B-tree index.

Access and most other modern RDBMSs use the balanced B-tree structure to create indexes. Balanced B-trees improve search speed, at the expense of increasing the time necessary to add new records, especially when the table is indexed on several keys. In a multitasking or client/server environment, however, the server conducts the addition process independently. The user can then perform other client operations, such as entering the key to search for another record, while the server's insertion and index rebalancing operations are going on.

Nonclustered and Clustered Indexes

Most RDBMSs, including Access, use *nonclustered indexes* to locate records with specific key values. Nonclustered means that the RDBMS adds data by the heap or APPEND method, and the rows of the table aren't in the sequence of their primary key—that is, the table isn't structured as an ISAM table. Figure 23.42 shows the structure, compressed and truncated, of a nonclustered Access index. xBase indexes have a similar structure, substituting records for data pages.

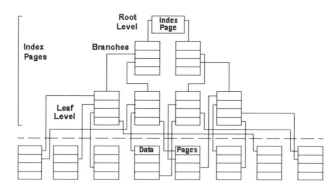

Fig. 23.42   A diagram of a conventional nonclustered index.

Notice the more-or-less random association of the data pages to the location of the pointers at the leaf level of the index. This lack of order is typical for indexes on foreign keys in all types of databases, and for indexes on primary keys in non-ISAM files. If organized into an ISAM structure with the index created on the primary key, the file would have the more organized appearance of the diagram in figure 23.43.

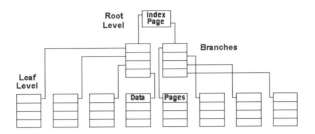

Fig. 23.43   A diagram of a clustered index.

Many client/server databases, such as Microsoft SQL Server and Sybase SQL Server, can use a clustered index to create ISAM order out of heap-induced chaos. When you use a clustered index, its table converts from heap-based row-insertion structure to the balanced B-tree structure you saw in figure 23.41. In this case, the leaf level of the index consists of the data pages themselves. This organization is accomplished by rewriting the pointers in each data page's header in the order of the key on which the clustered index is based. Because the header can have only one set of pointers, fore and aft, you can have only one clustered index per table. In almost all cases, you create the clustered index from the primary key.

To retain the balanced B-tree organization of data pages, an RDBMS needs a balancing technique for insertions. Instead of using overflow sectors, the RDBMS adds a new page, readjusts the header pointers to include the new page in the linked list, and then moves the last half of the rows in the original page to the new page. The RDBMS then updates the index to reflect the changes. This process speeds up data access, but slows updating; therefore, the process is practical only for an RDBMS running on a high-speed server computer under an advanced operating system, such as Windows NT or OS/2, and having large amounts of RAM.

Query Speed versus Update Performance

Access, like Paradox, automatically creates an index on the primary key field. Adding other indexes to Access tables, which is similar to using Paradox's QuerySpeedUp menu command, is a two-edged sword. You can speed up the performance of queries because the index assists the sort sequence; you don't need to sort the query's Recordset object on a primary key index, and sorts in the order of other indexes you specify are speeded. On the other hand, when you append a new record, Access must take the time to update all the table's indexes. When you edit a field of a record that is included in one or more indexes, Access has to update each of the indexes affected by the edit.

Beginning with version 2.0, Access incorporates FoxPro's Rushmore technology that optimizes query operations on indexed tables with large numbers of records. Many decision-support queries can be speeded by a factor of 10 to 25 or more by adding the appropriate indexes, in addition to the index on the primary key field that is created for you. You can improve the performance of Access applications, especially when tables with large numbers of records or queries that join several tables are involved, by observing these guidelines:

■ Minimize the number of indexes used with transaction-based tables, especially in networked multiuser applications that share tables. Access locks pages so that they aren't editable by other users while you are editing records, and during the time it takes Access to update the indexes when you are finished.

■ Minimize the number of indexes in tables that are used regularly with append and delete queries. The time required to update indexes is especially evident when making changes to the data in bulk.

■ Add indexes judiciously to tables that have large numbers of records and are used primarily in decision-support applications.

■ Add indexes to foreign key fields of tables that participate in joins with primary tables. However, when specifying a selection criterion on the key field, always use the key field of the primary table rather than the foreign key field of the related table.

■ Add indexes to fields on which you set criteria. If transaction-processing performance is more important than the speed of decision-support applications, add indexes only to those fields that occur most often in the criteria of your select queries.

Indexing becomes more important as the number of records in your tables increases. You might need to experiment to determine whether an index is effective in significantly increasing the speed of a query. If you find the index is warranted by improved query performance, check the speed of transaction processes with the new index before committing to its use.

Note

If you are using a shared database on a peer-to-peer network, such as Windows for Workgroups, and the database is located on your computer, use another workgroup member's computer to test the effectiveness of indexes. Network characteristics may affect the performance of indexes significantly. Try to make the test during periods of maximum network traffic, not during off hours when no one is contributing to network congestion.

Enforcing Database Integrity

The integrity of a database is comprised of two elements: entity integrity and referential integrity. *Entity integrity* requires that all primary keys must be unique within a table, and *referential integrity* dictates that all foreign keys must have corresponding values within a base table's primary key. Although the normalization process creates entity and referential integrity, either the RDBMS itself or your application must maintain that integrity during the data-entry process. Failure to maintain database integrity can result in erroneous data values and ultimately in widespread corruption of the entire database.

Ensuring Entity Integrity and Auditability

Database managers differ widely in their capabilities to maintain entity integrity through unique primary key values. Paradox, for instance, enforces unique primary keys within the RDBMS by flagging as a *key violation* any attempt to insert a row with an identical primary key, and placing the offending record in the KeyViol table. Access uses a similar technique when you specify a no-duplicates index; if you paste or append records that have duplicate primary keys, Access appends those records to a Paste Errors or Append Errors table.

In xBase, you can add as many records with duplicate index keys as you want. If you use SET UNIQUE ON, a SEEK finds only the first record with the same key; however, any duplicate keys remain in the file and, for example, appear in an indexed LIST operation. Indexed DELETEs affect only the first undeleted record found for the SEEK parameter; you must perform a DELETE for each duplicate. You need to write xBase code, therefore, to test for data duplicates before you APPEND the record that adds the data to the file.

Enforcing entity integrity within the table itself, the process used by Access and Paradox, is more reliable than using application programming code to prevent duplication of primary key values. Access provides two methods of ensuring entity integrity that are independent of the applications employing the tables:

- A key field that uses the AutoNumber data type that creates unique values based on an automatically incremented or random long integer. Incremental AutoNumber fields are the most common method for creating primary key fields. You cannot create a duplicate primary key in this case because you cannot edit the values in fields of the AutoNumber data type.

- An index on the primary key field with the No Duplicates property. If you attempt to enter a duplicate value in the key field, Access displays an error message.

Either of these methods ensures unique key fields, but an AutoNumber field is helpful so that documents such as sales orders, invoices, and checks are sequentially numbered. Sequential numbering is necessary for internal control and auditing purposes. Auto-Number (incremental) fields normally begin with 1 as the first record in a table, but rarely does a real-world cash disbursement or invoice table need 1 as its starting number. You cannot create a table with a Long Integer Number field, enter the beginning number, and then change the field data type to AutoNumber. Access issues a warning message if you attempt this procedure. You can use an append query, however, to establish a specific beginning AutoNumber value.

> **Note**
>
> Access increments the value of the AutoNumber field even if Access prevents you from adding a record to a table with a counter field. Such a situation can occur if domain or referential integrity rules are violated when addition of a record is attempted. For this reason, an Access counter field might not be satisfactory for applications where sequential documents must be accounted for.

To create a starting AutoNumber field value of 123456 in the Invoice field of the tblInvoices table's first record, perform the following steps:

1. Open the Database window, select the Orders table, and press Ctrl+C to copy the table to the Clipboard.

2. Press Ctrl+V, and enter **tblInvoices** as the name of the table to create. Then click the Structure Only option button to create the new tblInvoices table with no records.

3. Open the tblInvoices table in Design mode, click the select button of the Order ID field, and change the field data type from AutoNumber to Number (Long Integer).

4. Click the Datasheet View button on the toolbar, and click OK to save your changes. (Access 95 does not allow two or more operations on AutoNumber fields in a single design session.)

5. Reopen the table in Design mode, select the OrderID field, and press Insert to add a new field.

6. Enter **InvoiceID** as the Field Name, and choose AutoNumber (Increment) as the Data Type.

7. Click the Indexes button on the toolbar. Delete the Primary Key index on OrderID, which enables you to append a record that doesn't have a value for the key field (**Null** values aren't allowed in key fields). The tblInvoices table design appears as shown in figure 23.44. Close the Indexes window.

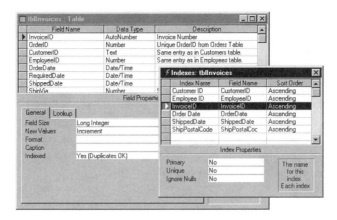

Fig. 23.44 A table designed for adding an AutoNumber field with an arbitrary starting number.

You also need to set the value of the Required property of the CustomerID field to No and the Allow Zero Length property to Yes. Otherwise, the append query that follows will not execute.

8. Close the tblInvoices table and save your changes. Don't create a primary key field at this point.

9. Create a new temporary table named tblFirstInvoice with one field, named InvoiceID.

10. Set the InvoiceID field's Data Type property to Number and the Field Size property to Long Integer.

11. Change to Datasheet View and enter a value in InvoiceID that is 1 less than the starting number you want (for this example, type **123455**).

12. Close the tblFirstInvoice table, save your changes, and don't create a primary key field.

13. Create a new query and add the tblFirstInvoice table. Click and drag the InvoiceID field symbol to the first column of the Query Design grid.

14. Choose Query, Append and enter **tblInvoices** as the table to which to append the record. Click OK. Invoice automatically appears as the Append To field. Click the Run Query button on the toolbar to add the single record in tblFirstInvoice to the tblInvoices table.

15. Close Query1 without saving your changes.

The next record you append to tblInvoices is assigned the value 123456 in the InvoiceID (AutoNumber) field. To verify that this technique works properly for appended records, perform the following steps:

1. Create a new query, and add the Orders table. Click and drag the * symbol to the first column of the Query Design grid.

2. Choose Query, Append and enter tblInvoiceData as the table to which to append the records from the Orders table. Click the Run Query button on the toolbar to add the records from the Orders table.

3. Close Query1 and don't save the changes.

4. Open the tblInvoices table.

Access has added numbers beginning with 123456 to the new Invoice field, corresponding to Order ID values of 10000 and higher, as shown in figure 23.45.

If you were adding an AutoNumber field to real-world data, you would delete the first blank record and then make the InvoiceID field the primary key field. Access creates a no-duplicates index when you assign an AutoNumber field as a primary key field.

VI

Advanced Techniques

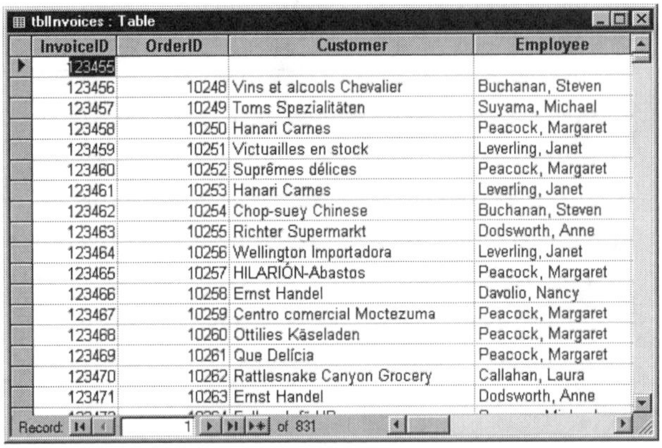
tblInvoices : Table

InvoiceID	OrderID	Customer	Employee
123455			
123456	10248	Vins et alcools Chevalier	Buchanan, Steven
123457	10249	Toms Spezialitäten	Suyama, Michael
123458	10250	Hanari Carnes	Peacock, Margaret
123459	10251	Victuailles en stock	Leverling, Janet
123460	10252	Suprêmes délices	Peacock, Margaret
123461	10253	Hanari Carnes	Leverling, Janet
123462	10254	Chop-suey Chinese	Buchanan, Steven
123463	10255	Richter Supermarkt	Dodsworth, Anne
123464	10256	Wellington Importadora	Leverling, Janet
123465	10257	HILARIÓN-Abastos	Peacock, Margaret
123466	10258	Ernst Handel	Davolio, Nancy
123467	10259	Centro comercial Moctezuma	Peacock, Margaret
123468	10260	Ottilies Käseladen	Peacock, Margaret
123469	10261	Que Delícia	Peacock, Margaret
123470	10262	Rattlesnake Canyon Grocery	Callahan, Laura
123471	10263	Ernst Handel	Dodsworth, Anne

Record: 1 of 831

Fig. 23.45 The Invoice Data table with AutoNumber values starting with 123456.

Troubleshooting

When I try to execute the append query that provides the starting value minus 1 to my table structure, I get an error message.

You have constraints on the fields of your destination table that do not allow **Null** values or empty strings in fields. Open your destination table in Design mode, and make sure that the Required property of each field is set to No and that the Allow Zero Length property of each field of the Text data type is set to Yes. Also make sure that your destination table does not have a primary key field specified.

Maintaining Referential Integrity

Prior chapters have discussed the use of Access's database-level referential integrity enforcement capabilities, which were introduced in Access 2.0. Maintaining referential integrity requires strict adherence to a single rule: *Each foreign key field in a related table must correspond to a primary key field in a base or primary table.* This rule requires that the following types of transactions be prevented:

- Adding a record on the many side of a one-to-many relationship without the existence of a corresponding record on the one side of the relationship
- Deleting a record on the one side of a one-to-many relationship without first deleting all corresponding records on the many side of the relationship
- Deleting or adding a record to a table in a one-to-one relationship with another table without deleting or adding a corresponding record in the related table
- Changing the value of a primary key field of a base table on which records in a relation table depend
- Changing the value of a foreign key field in a relation table to a value that doesn't exist in the primary key field of a base table

A record in a relation table that has a foreign key with a value that doesn't correspond to the value of a primary key in a relation table is called an *orphan record*.

Whenever possible, use Access's built-in join features to maintain referential integrity at the database level, and don't rely on applications to test for referential integrity violations when adding records to relation tables or deleting records from base tables. Access gives you the opportunity to enforce referential integrity automatically between tables in a database by marking the Enforce Referential Integrity check box in the Relationships dialog. As noted in Chapter 11, "Using Action Queries," you can specify cascade updates and cascade deletes when you use Access's referential integrity enforcement capabilities. Access also enforces referential integrity in linked Access tables.

Paradox versions 3.0 and later automatically enforce referential integrity between master and detail table records. Paradox handles changes to the values of primary key (link) fields with dependent records in relation (detail) tables in a different manner than Access. When you change a value in a Paradox link field, the corresponding fields of linked records in detail tables change automatically. This process is identical to Access's cascade update feature.

Most xBase RDBMSs don't have the capability to enforce referential integrity automatically. You need to write xBase code that tests for the required records with SEEK commands on indexed files.

From Here...

This chapter covered the fundamental principles of relational database design, and showed you how to restructure tables so that they conform to these principles. Methods of documenting your database design, both in the preliminary and final stages, with text and graphical descriptions of data structures and relationships were emphasized. Many entire books have been written on each of these subjects. Indexing techniques were covered in detail because of the differences between Access's approach to indexes and the approach taken by xBase and other desktop databases. Indexes play a critical role in maintaining entity integrity by preventing duplication of values in key fields. Access's automatic enforcement of relational integrity at the database level, combined with cascade updates and deletes, provides protection against orphan records in your relation tables.

- Chapter 24, "Working with Structured Query Language," describes how to write queries in SQL, instead of using Access's graphical QBE design window.

- Chapter 25, "Securing Multiuser Network Applications," shows you how to share databases between workgroup members and how to secure your Access applications and data.

VI

Advanced Techniques

■ Chapter 26, "Connecting to Client/Server Databases," covers the use of Access for creating front-end applications for database server back-ends, such as Microsoft SQL Server, Sybase SQL Server, Oracle, Informix, and other popular client/server RDBMSs.

■ Chapter 27, "Replicating Access Databases," describes how to use Access 95 and Windows 95's Briefcase feature to automatically maintain the currency of multiple copies of your Access databases.

Chapter 24

Working with Structured Query Language

This chapter describes Structured Query Language (SQL), the structure and syntax of the language, and how Access translates queries you design with Access's graphical query-by-example technique into SQL statements. An SQL background helps you understand the query process and design more efficient queries. A knowledge of SQL syntax is necessary to use the new subquery and UNION query capabilities introduced by Access 2.0 and for many of the applications you write in Access VBA. Examples of SQL have been presented in other chapters in this book. These examples, usually figures that illustrate an SQL statement created by Access, demonstrate what occurs behind the scenes when you create a query or a graph.

> **Note**
>
> There are no significant differences between the Access 2.0 and Access 95 versions of Access SQL. The primary additions to Access SQL occurred during the upgrade from Access 1.1 to Access 2.0.

Access is a useful learning tool for gaining fluency in SQL. This chapter shows you how to create Access query-by-example (QBE) queries from SQL statements entered in the SQL dialog. If you use SQL with another RDBMS, such as dBASE IV or Microsoft SQL Server, this chapter can help you make the transition from ANSI SQL or Transact-SQL, the extended version of SQL used by Microsoft SQL Server and Sybase System 10+, to Access's implementation of SQL. An knowledge of SQL also is necessary for Visual Basic programmers because Visual Basic doesn't include a graphical QBE feature.

Many users of Access decision-support applications want to be able to define their own queries. When you open an Access 95 database with the runtime version of Access, the query design window is hidden. Thus, you need to design forms that include control objects that users can manipulate to construct an Access SQL statement to return the query result set they need. You write Access VBA code to translate users' choices on the form into an Access

In this chapter, you learn

■ The categories of SQL reserved words

■ The syntax of SQL statements

■ To write SELECT statements

■ To join tables with an SQL statement

■ To write SQL action queries

VI

Advanced Techniques

SQL statement; then create a `QueryDef` object (a persistent query definition whose name appears in the Database window) in the current database.

> **Note**
>
> This book uses the term *Access VBA* to mean the Access "flavor" of VBA that includes preestablished references to Microsoft Access 95 object collections, such as `Forms` and `Reports`, and Jet 2.5/3.0 Data Access Objects (DAOs), as well as Visual Basic for Applications itself. The "flavor" of other VBA-enabled applications, such as Excel VBA or Project VBA, is determined by the application's object collections that are referenced by default.

What Is Structured Query Language?

Structured Query Language, abbreviated SQL (usually pronounced "sequel" or "seekel," but more properly "ess-cue-ell"), is the common language of client/server database management. The principal advantage of SQL is that it's standardized—you can use a common set of SQL statements with all SQL-compliant database management systems. The first U.S. SQL standard was established in 1986 as ANSI X3.135-1986. The current version is ANSI X3.135-1992, usually known as SQL-92.

> **Note**
>
> ANSI, an acronym for the American National Standards Institute, is an organization devoted to establishing and maintaining scientific and engineering standards. ANSI-standard SQL was first adopted as a worldwide standard in 1987 by the International Standards Organization (ISO), a branch of the United Nations.

SQL is an application language for relational databases, not a system or programming language. SQL is a set-oriented language; thus, ANSI SQL includes neither a provision for program flow control (branching and looping) nor keywords to create data entry forms and print reports. Programming functions usually are implemented in a system language such as xBase, PAL, C, or COBOL. Some implementations of SQL, such as Transact-SQL used by Microsoft and Sybase SQL Server, add flow control statements (`IF...ELSE` and `WHILE`) to the language. Publishers of ANSI SQL-compliant RDBMSs are free to extend the language if the basic ANSI commands are supported. The ANSI/ISO implementation of SQL is independent of any system language with which it might be used.

ANSI SQL includes a set of standard commands (keyword verbs) that are broadly grouped into six categories: data definition, data query, data manipulation, cursor control, transaction processing, and administration or control. Provisions for SQL keywords that maintain data integrity were added in a 1989 revision of the original standard as ANSI X3.135-1989, *Database Language—SQL with Integrity Enhancement*. Access 95's implementation of SQL includes the data integrity keywords.

SQL has three different methods of implementation: Direct Invocation, Module Language, and Embedded SQL. Direct Invocation sends a series of SQL statements to the RDBMS. The DBM responds to the query by creating a table that contains the result and displays the table. Entering SQL commands at the dBASE IV SQL prompt is an example of Direct Invocation. Embedded SQL is the most common implementation; the SQL statements are generated by the application or included as strings of text in a command of an application language. Access queries, whether created by graphical QBE, by an SQL property in Access VBA, or by the Row Source property of a graph, use Embedded SQL.

Looking at the Development of SQL

SQL was created because, early in the 1970s, IBM wanted a method with which nonprogrammers could extract and display the information they wanted from a database. Languages that nonprogrammers can use are called *fourth generation*, or 4GL, and sometimes are referred to as *structured English*. The first commercial result of this effort was *query by example* (QBE), developed at IBM's laboratories in Yorktown Heights, New York. QBE was used, beginning in the late 1970s, on terminals connected to IBM System 370 mainframes. A user could obtain a result with less than an 80-character line of QBE code that required 100 or more lines to implement in COBOL or the other 3GL languages of the day. Access, dBASE IV and 5, and Paradox use QBE to display selected data from tables.

At the other end of the country, programmers at IBM's San Jose, California facility were developing System R, the progenitor of SQL/DS and IBM's DB2 relational database. In the mid-1970s, IBM scientist Dr. E.F. Codd proposed SQL (then known as SEQUEL for *S*tructured *E*nglish *Q*uery *L*anguage) as a means of accessing information from the relational database model he had developed in 1970. Relational databases based on the Codd model that use the SQL language to retrieve and update data within them have become, like QBE, computer-industry standards.

SQL has achieved the status of being the exclusive language of client/server databases. A database server (the back end) application holds the data. Client applications (front ends) add to or edit the data. The client application generates SQL statements. If you deal regularly with databases of any type, the odds are great that you ultimately will need to learn SQL. You need to learn Access SQL *now* if you plan to create applications with user-defined queries that are usable with the runtime version of Access.

Comparing ANSI and Access SQL

Access SQL is designed for creating queries, not for creating or modifying tables. Access SQL, therefore, doesn't include many of the approximately 100 keywords incorporated in the ANSI standard for SQL. Few, if any, commercial SQL-compliant RDBMSs for the PC implement much more than half of the standard SQL keywords. The majority of the common SQL keywords missing from Access's implementation are provided by the expressions you create with operators, built-in Access functions, or user-defined functions you write in Access VBA. The effect of many unsupported ANSI SQL keywords related to tables is achieved by making selections from Access's Database window or from menus.

When you learn a new language, it's helpful to categorize the vocabulary of the language by usage and then into the familiar parts of speech. SQL commands, therefore, first are divided into six usage categories:

- *Data Query Language* (DQL) commands, sometimes referred to as *data retrieval* commands, obtain data from tables and determine how the results of the retrieval are presented. The SELECT command is the principal instruction in this category. DQL commands often are considered members of the Data Manipulation Language category.

- *Data Manipulation Language* (DML) commands provide INSERT and DELETE commands, which add or delete entire rows, and the UPDATE command, which can change the values of data in specified columns within rows.

- *Transaction Processing Language* (TPL) commands include BEGIN TRANSACTION, COMMIT [WORK], and ROLLBACK [WORK], which group multiple DML operations. If one DML operation of a transaction fails, the preceding DML operations are canceled (rolled back).

- *Data Definition Language* (DDL) commands include CREATE TABLE and CREATE VIEW instructions that define the structure of tables and views. DDL commands are used also to modify tables and to create and delete indexes. The keywords that implement data integrity are used in conjunction with DDL statements.

- *Cursor Control Language* (CCL) commands can select a single row of a query result set for processing. Cursor control constructs, such as UPDATE WHERE CURRENT, are implemented by the Jet database engine, so these commands are not discussed in this chapter.

- *Data Control Language* (DCL) commands, such as GRANT and REVOKE, perform administrative functions that grant and revoke privileges to use the database, a set of tables within the database, or specific SQL commands. Access SQL does not include DCL; instead, you use Access's security objects for implementing security.

Keywords that comprise the vocabulary of SQL are identified further in the following categories:

- *Commands,* such as SELECT, are verbs that cause an action to be performed.

- *Qualifiers,* such as WHERE, limit the range of values of the entities that comprise the query.

- *Clauses,* such as ORDER BY, modify the action of an instruction.

- *Operators,* such as =, <, or >, compare values and are used to create joins when JOIN syntax is not used.

- *Group aggregate functions,* such as MIN(), return a single result for a set of values.

- *Other* keywords modify the action of a clause or manipulate cursors that are used to select specific rows of queries.

> **Note**
>
> SQL keywords usually are capitalized, but the keywords aren't case-sensitive. The uppercase convention is used in this book, and SQL keywords are set in the monospace type. You use *parameters*, such as *column_list*, to define or modify the action specified by keywords. Names of replaceable parameters are printed in lowercase italicized monospace type.

SQL Reserved Words in Access

Access doesn't support all the ANSI SQL keywords with identical reserved words in the Access SQL language. In this chapter, *keywords* are defined as the commands and functions that comprise the ANSI SQL language. Access SQL commands and functions, however, are referred to here as *reserved words* to distinguish them from ANSI SQL.

The tables in the following section are intended to acquaint readers who are familiar with ANSI or similar implementations of SQL in other DBMs or database front-end applications with the Access implementation of SQL. If you haven't used SQL, the tables demonstrate that SQL is a relatively sparse language, which has far fewer keywords than programming languages like Access VBA, and that Access SQL is even more sparse. Access SQL has few reserved words to learn. You learned in Chapter 9, "Understanding Operators and Expressions in Access," to use the Access operators and functions in expressions that Access substitutes for ANSI SQL keywords.

Access SQL Reserved Words Corresponding to ANSI SQL Keywords

Access supports the ANSI SQL keywords listed in table 24.1 as identical reserved words in Access SQL. Don't use these Access SQL reserved words as the names of tables, fields, or variables. The reserved words in table 24.1 appear in all capital letters in the Access SQL statements Access creates for you when you design a query or when you add a graph to a form or report. Reserved words in table 24.1 marked with an asterisk are newly available with Access 95.

Table 24.1   ANSI SQL-92 Keywords Corresponding to Access SQL Reserved Words

ADD*	CONSTRAINT*	HAVING	MAX	REFERENCES*
ALL	COUNT	IN	MIN	RIGHT
ALTER*	CREATE*	INDEX*	NOT	SELECT
ANY*	DELETE	INNER	NULL	SET
AS	DESC	INSERT	ON	SOME*
ALIAS	DISALLOW*	INTO	OR	UNION*
ASC	DISTINCT	IS	ORDER	UNIQUE*
AVG	DROP*	JOIN	OUTER	UPDATE
BETWEEN	EXISTS*	KEY*	PARAMETERS	VALUE*
BY	FOREIGN*	LEFT	PRIMARY*	VALUES*
COLUMN*	FROM	LIKE	PROCEDURE	WHERE

The keywords that relate to data types, CHAR[ACTER], FLOAT, INT[EGER], and REAL, aren't included in table 24.1 because Access SQL uses a different reserved word to specify these SQL data types (refer to table 24.3 later in this chapter). The comparison operators (=, <, <=, >, and =>) are common to both ANSI SQL and Access SQL. Access substitutes the <> operator for ANSI SQL's not-equal (!=) operator.

As in ANSI SQL, the IN reserved word in Access SQL can be used as an operator to specify a list of values to match in a WHERE clause or a list created by a subquery. (Beginning with Access 2.0, Access SQL supports subqueries.) You also can use IN to identify a table in another database; this use is discussed near the end of this chapter, in the "Adding IN to Use Tables in Another Database" section.

Access Functions and Operators Used in Place of ANSI SQL Keywords

Table 24.2 shows reserved words in Access that correspond to ANSI SQL keywords but are operators or functions used in Access expressions. Access doesn't use ANSI SQL syntax for its aggregate functions; you cannot use the SUM(DISTINCT *field_name*) syntax of ANSI SQL, for instance. Access, therefore, distinguishes between its use of the Sum() aggregate function and the SQL implementation, SUM(). Expressions that use operators such as And and Or are enclosed in parentheses in Access SQL statements; Access uses uppercase AND and OR (refer to table 24.1) when criteria are added to more than one column.

Table 24.2 Access Reserved Words that Substitute for ANSI SQL Keywords			
Access	**ANSI SQL**	**Access**	**ANSI SQL**
And	AND	Max()	MAX()
Avg()	AVG()	Min()	MIN()
Between	BETWEEN	Not	NOT
Count()	COUNT()	Null	NULL
Is	IS	Or	OR
Like	LIKE	Sum()	SUM()

The Access IsNull() function that returns True (–1) or False (0), depending on whether IsNull()'s argument has a Null value, has no equivalent in ANSI SQL and isn't a substitute for Is Null or Is Not Null qualifiers in WHERE clauses. Access SQL does not support distinct aggregate function references, such as AVG(DISTINCT *field_name*); the default DISTINCTROW qualifier added to the SELECT statement by Access serves this purpose.

Access SQL Reserved Words, Operators, and Functions Not in ANSI SQL

Access SQL contains a number of reserved words that aren't ANSI SQL keywords (see table 24.3). Most of these reserved words define Access data types; some reserved words have equivalents in ANSI SQL, and others don't. You use Access DDL reserved words to modify the properties of tables. Access VBA's SQL property DISTINCTROW is described in the following section. PIVOT and TRANSFORM are used in creating crosstab queries that are unique to Access.

Table 24.3 Access SQL Reserved Words Not in ANSI SQL

Access SQL	ANSI SQL	Category	Purpose
BINARY	No equivalent	DDL	Not an official Access field data type
BOOLEAN	No equivalent	DDL	Access Yes/No field data type
BYTE	No equivalent	DDL	Byte field data type, 1 byte integer
CURRENCY	No equivalent	DDL	Access Currency field data type
DATETIME	No equivalent	DDL	Access Date/Time field data type
DISTINCTROW	No equivalent	DQL	Updatable Access Recordset objects
DOUBLE	REAL	DDL	High-precision decimal numbers
LONG	INT[EGER]	DDL	Long Integer field data type
LONGBINARY	No equivalent	DDL	OLE Object field data type
LONGTEXT	VARCHAR	DDL	Memo field data type
OWNERACCESS	No equivalent	DQL	Run with owner's privileges parameters
PIVOT	No equivalent	DQL	Used in crosstab queries
SHORT	SMALLINT	DDL	Integer field data type, 2 bytes
SINGLE	No equivalent	DDL	Single-precision real number
TEXT	CHAR[ACTER]	DDL	Text field data type
TRANSFORM	No equivalent	DQL	Creates crosstab query
? (LIKE wild card)	_ (wild card)	DQL	Single character with LIKE
* (LIKE wild card)	% (wild card)	DQL	Zero or more characters
# (LIKE wild card)	No equivalent	DQL	Single digit, 0–9
# (date specifier)	No equivalent	DQL	Encloses date/time values
<> (not equal)	!=	DQL	Access uses ! as a separator

Access provides four statistical aggregate functions that aren't incorporated in ANSI SQL. These functions are listed in table 24.4.

Table 24.4 Aggregate SQL Functions Added in Access SQL

Access Function	Category	Purpose
StdDev()	DQL	Standard deviation of a population sample
StdDevP()	DQL	Standard deviation of a population
Var()	DQL	Statistical variation of a population sample
VarP()	DQL	Statistical variation of a population

Access's DISTINCTROW and SQL's DISTINCT Keywords

The DISTINCTROW reserved word that follows the SQL SELECT keywords causes Access to eliminate duplicated rows from the query's result. The effect of DISTINCTROW is especially dramatic in queries used to display records in tables that have indirect relationships. To create an example of a query that you can use to demonstrate the effect of Access DISTINCTROW SQL reserved word, follow these steps:

1. Open a new query in Northwind.mdb by clicking the Query tab in the Database window and then clicking the New button. Select New Query in the list box of the New Query window, and then click OK to bypass the Query Wizards.

2. Add the Customers, Orders, OrderDetails, Products, and Categories tables to the query, in sequence. Access automatically creates the required joins.

3. Drag the CompanyName field from the Customers field list to the Field row of the first column of the query design grid. Select the Sort cell, open the drop-down list with F4, and choose Ascending Sort Order.

4. Drag the CategoryName field from the Categories field list to the Field row of the second column of the grid. Add an ascending sort to this field.

5. Choose View, SQL. The SQL statement that creates the query is shown in the SQL window in figure 24.1.

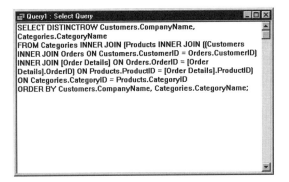

Fig. 24.1 The SQL statement that creates the query to determine customers purchasing categories of products.

6. Click the Run button on the toolbar to execute the query. The number of rows (records) returned by the query, 598 at the time of this writing, appears to the right of the navigation buttons at the bottom of the Query Datasheet window.

To demonstrate the effect of removing the DISTINCTROW reserved word from the SQL statement and to verify, in this case, that the effect of ANSI SQL's DISTINCT keyword and Access SQL's DISTINCTROW reserved word is the same, follow these steps:

1. Choose View, SQL to edit the SQL statement.

2. Delete the DISTINCTROW keyword from the SQL statement.

3. Click the Run button. The new query result set has 2,155 rows with many duplicated rows.

4. Choose <u>V</u>iew, <u>S</u>QL to edit the SQL statement again. Add DISTINCT after the keyword SELECT.

5. Click the Run button again. You get the same result of 598 records that you obtain when you use the DISTINCTROW keyword.

6. Close, but do not save, the query.

Note

As an alternative to choosing <u>V</u>iew, <u>S</u>QL from the Query menu, you can click the arrow adjacent to the Query Type button of the toolbar, and then select SQL from the drop-down Query Type menu. The number of mouse clicks is the same in either case. Another alternative is to left-click the Query Design toolbar, and then choose Customize from the popup menu to open the Customize dialog. Select Query Design from the Categories list box, and then drag the SQL button to an empty spot on the toolbar. You click the new SQL button to open the SQL window. A third option is to right-click the mouse button on a blank area of the upper pane of the Query Design window and choose View SQL from the popup menu.

DISTINCTROW is a special Access SQL reserved word and is unavailable in standard (ANSI) SQL; DISTINCTROW is related to, but not the same as, the DISTINCT keyword in ANSI SQL. Both words eliminate duplicate rows of data in query result tables, but they differ in execution. DISTINCT in ANSI SQL eliminates duplicate rows based only on the values of the data contained in the rows of the query, from left to right. You cannot update values from multiple-table queries that include the keyword DISTINCT.

DISTINCTROW, available only in Access, eliminates duplicate rows based on the content of the underlying table, regardless of whether additional field(s) that distinguish records in the table are included. DISTINCTROW allows values in special kinds of multiple-table Recordset objects to be updated.

To distinguish between these two keywords, assume that you have a table with a Last_Name field and a First_Name field and only 10 records, each with the Last_Name value, *Smith*. Each record has a different First_Name value. You create a query that in-cludes the Last_Name field but not the First_Name field. DISTINCTROW returns all 10 Smith records because the First_Name values differ in the table. DISTINCT returns one record because the First_Name field that distinguishes the records in the table is absent in the query result table.

All SQL statements created by Access include the default reserved word DISTINCTROW, unless you purposely replace it with the DISTINCT keyword by using the Query Properties dialog's Unique Values Only option. The only way of eliminating DISTINCTROW from que-ries is to delete it by editing the SQL statement. You probably will never need to delete DISTINCTROW.

Creating Tables with Access DDL
You can create new tables in your current database with Access 95's Data Definition Language reserved words. Using SQL to create new tables is of primary interest to

developers of Access applications because it is much easier to create new tables with the Access user interface. For the sake of completeness, however, a brief description of Access 95 SQL DDL statements follows:

- CREATE TABLE *table_name* (*field_name data_type* [*field_size*][, *field_name data_type...*]) creates a new table with the fields specified by a comma-separated list. Properties of fields are space-delimited, so you need to enclose entries for *field names* with spaces in square brackets ([]). The *data_type* can be any valid Access SQL field data type, such as TEXT or INTEGER. The *field_size* entry is optional for TEXT fields only. (The default value is 50 characters.)

- CONSTRAINT *index_name* {PRIMARYKEY¦UNIQUE¦REFERENCES *foreign_table* [(*foreign_field*)]} creates an index on the field name that precedes the expression. You can specify the index as the PRIMARYKEY or as an UNIQUE index. You also can establish a relationship between the field and the field of a foreign table with the REFERENCES *foreign_table* [*foreign_field*] entry. (The [*foreign_field*] item is required if the *foreign_field* is not a primary-key field.)

- ALTER TABLE allows you to add new fields (ADD COLUMN *field_name...*) or delete existing fields (DROP COLUMN *field_name...*).

- DROP INDEX *index_name* ON *table_name* deletes the index from a table specified by *table_name*.

- DROP TABLE *table_name* deletes a table from the database.

Common ANSI SQL Keywords and Features Not Supported by Access SQL Reserved Words

The majority of the ANSI SQL keywords that aren't supported by Access 95 are elements of SQL's Data Control Language. Transactions, which are implemented automatically for most operations by the Jet 3.0 database engine, can be explicitly declared only in Access VBA code. The record position buttons of Access queries and forms substitute for most cursor-control (CCL) statements in ANSI SQL that choose a particular row in a query. Table 24.5 lists these substitutes.

Table 24.5 Common ANSI SQL Reserved Words Not Supported in Access SQL

Reserved Word	Category	Substitute
AUTHORIZATION	DCL	Privileges dialog
BEGIN	TPL	Access VBA BeginTrans method
CHECK	DQL	Table Validation Rule property
CLOSE	CCL	Document Control menu of query
COMMIT	TPL	Access VBA CommitTrans method
CREATE VIEW	DDL	Query design mode and filters
CURRENT	CCL	Query run mode, record position buttons
CURSOR	CCL	Query run mode
DECLARE	CCL	Query run mode (cursors are automatic)

Reserved Word	Category	Substitute
DROP VIEW	DDL	Query design mode
FETCH	DQL	Text boxes on a form or report
GRANT	DCL	Privileges dialog
PRIVILEGES	DCL	Privileges dialog
REVOKE	DCL	Privileges dialog
ROLLBACK	TPL	Access VBA RollbackTrans method
TRANSACTION	TPL	Access VBA transaction methods
VALUES	DML	Data values entered in tables or forms
WORK	TPL	Access VBA BeginTrans method
: (variable)	DQL	Access VBA Dim statement prefix
!= (not equal)	DQL	Access <> not-equal operator

The Jet 3.0 database engine uses transaction processing for all Access DML commands executed by action queries. You implement transaction processing (SQL's COMMIT and ROLLBACK [WORK]) on Recordset objects you create with code by writing Access VBA functions or procedures that contain the BeginTrans, CommitTrans, and Rollback reserved words. Many other less commonly used SQL keywords, such as COBOL and PASCAL, don't have Access SQL reserved word equivalents.

Writing Select Queries in SQL

When you create a select query in query design mode, Access translates the QBE query design into an Access SQL statement. You can view the Access SQL equivalent of your design by clicking the SQL button of the toolbar. Displaying and analyzing the SQL statements that correspond to queries you design or queries in the Northwind Traders sample database is useful when you are learning SQL.

The heart of SQL is the SELECT statement used to create a select query. Every select query begins with the SELECT statement. The following lines of syntax are used for a SQL SELECT statement that returns a query table (called a result set, usually a Recordset object of the Dynaset type) of all or selected columns (fields) from all or qualifying rows (records) of a source table:

```
SELECT [ALL¦DISTINCT¦DISTINCTROW] select_list
    FROM table_names
    [WHERE search_criteria]
    [ORDER BY column_criteria [ASC¦DESC]]
```

The following list shows the purpose of the elements in this basic select query statement:

- SELECT is the basic command that specifies a query. The *select_list* parameter determines the fields (columns) that are included in the result table of the query. When you design an Access QBE query, the *select_list* parameter is determined by the fields you add to the Fields row in the Query grid. Only those fields with the Show check box marked are included in *select_list*. Multiple field names are separated by commas.

The optional ALL, DISTINCT, and DISTINCTROW qualifiers determine how rows are handled. ALL specifies that all rows are to be included, subject to subsequent limitation. DISTINCT eliminates rows with duplicate data. As discussed earlier in the chapter, DISTINCTROW is an Access SQL keyword, similar to DISTINCT, that eliminates duplicate rows but also enables you to modify the query result set.

■ FROM *table_name* specifies the name or names of the table or tables that form the basis for the query. The *table_names* parameter is created in Access QBE by the entries you make in the Add Table dialog. If fields from more than one table are included in the select_list, each table has to be specified in the table_names parameter. Commas are used to separate the names of multiple tables.

■ WHERE *search_criteria* determines which records from the select list are displayed. The search_criteria parameter is an expression with a text (string) operator, such as LIKE, for text fields or a numeric operator, such as >=, for fields with numeric values. The WHERE clause is optional; if you don't add a WHERE clause, all the rows that meet the SELECT criteria are returned.

■ ORDER BY *column_criteria* specifies the sorting order of a Recordset object of the Dynaset or Snapshot type created by the query. A Recordset object of the Snapshot type is a query result set that is not updatable. Like the WHERE clause, ORDER BY is optional. You can specify an ascending or descending sort by the optional ASC or DESC keywords. If you don't specify a sort direction, ascending is the default.

The following lines show an example of a simple SQL query statement:

```
SELECT [Company Name],[Customer ID],[Postal Code]
   FROM Customers
   WHERE [Postal Code] LIKE "9*"
   ORDER BY [Company Name];
```

You must terminate an Access SQL statement by adding a semicolon immediately after the last character on the last line.

Note

Examples of SQL statements in this book are formatted to make the examples more readable. Access doesn't format the SQL statements. When you enter or edit SQL statements in the Access SQL window, formatting these statements so that commands appear on individual lines makes the SQL statements more intelligible. Use Ctrl+Enter to insert newline pairs (the return and new line characters) before SQL keywords. Access ignores spaces and newline pairs when it processes the SQL statement.

The preceding query results in an Access Recordset object of three columns and as many rows as the number of records in the Customers table for companies located in ZIP codes with values that begin with the character 9, sorted alphabetically by the company name. You don't have to specify the table name with the field name in the *select_list* because only one table is used in this query. When Access creates an SQL statement, the table name always precedes the field name. Usually, Access processes queries you write in either ANSI SQL or Access SQL syntax. This example differs from ANSI SQL only in the substitution of the Access SQL * (asterisk) for ANSI SQL's % wild card.

Programming Statements in xBase Equivalent to SQL

If you are accustomed to using the dot prompt with xBase dialects that include interactive capability or writing xBase programs, you can use much of your xBase experience in learning SQL. In xBase, you achieve a result identical to the preceding simple SQL query by the following set of statements, assuming that the CustName index exists:

```
USE Customers INDEX CustName
LIST FIELDS Company, CompanyID, PostalCode
FOR SUBSTR(PostalCode,1,1) = "9"
```

The CustName index is needed to provide the equivalent of the ORDER BY clause so that the list appears in customer name sequence. If the Customer table was sorted previously by customer name (which is unlikely), you would not need the index. The dot-prompt commands in xBase are closely related to SQL statements invoked directly. Many of the keywords differ between the two languages, but you can achieve similar results with either language. The advantage of SQL over xBase dialects is that SQL syntax is simpler and usually requires fewer keywords to obtain the same result.

Using SQL Punctuation and Symbols

In addition to the comparison operators used for expressions, SQL uses commas, periods, semicolons, and colons as punctuation. The following list of symbols and punctuation is used in ANSI SQL and the Access SQL dialect; differences between the two forms of SQL are noted where appropriate:

- Commas are used to separate members of lists of parameters, such as multiple field names, as in Name, Address, City, ZIP.

- Square brackets surrounding field names are required only when the field name includes spaces or other symbols, including punctuation, not allowed by SQL, as in [Company Name].

- If fields of more than one table are involved in the query, a period is used to separate the table name from the field name, as in Customers.[Company Name].

- ANSI SQL uses the single quote symbol (') to enclose literal string values. You can use the double quote (") or the single quote symbol to enclose literal values in Access SQL statements. Using the single quote makes writing SQL statements in Access VBA easier.

- ANSI SQL uses % and _ (underscore) symbols as the wild cards for the LIKE statement, rather than the * (asterisk) and ? used by Access SQL to specify zero or more characters and a single character, respectively. The Access wild cards correspond to the wild cards used in specifying DOS group file names.

- Access provides the # wild card for the LIKE statement to represent any single digit. Access also uses the # symbol to enclose date/time values in expressions. This symbol isn't available in ANSI SQL.

■ The end of an Access SQL statement is indicated by a mandatory semicolon.

■ In Access, you cannot use colons as prefixes to indicate user-declared variables you create in ANSI SQL. You cannot create variables with Access SQL; user-declared variables in Access are limited to the Access VBA functions and procedures you write. You can, however, pass variable values as parameters to stored procedures of client/server RDBMSs. Using stored procedures requires employing Access's SQL pass-through option, which is beyond the scope of this book.

■ ANSI SQL uses the ! (bang symbol or exclamation mark) as a *not in* operator for character lists used with LIKE. ANSI SQL uses != for not equal; Access SQL uses <>.

As the preceding list demonstrates, relatively minor differences exist in the availability and use of punctuation and symbols between ANSI and Access SQL.

Note

Indentation often is used in writing multiple-line SQL statements. Indented lines indicate continuation of a preceding line or a clause that is dependent on a keyword in a preceding line.

Using SQL Statements to Create Access Queries

You can enter SQL statements in query design mode to create simple Access queries that are reflected in changes to the design of the Query grid. This method is another useful way to learn the syntax of SQL. If your entries contain errors in spelling or punctuation, Access displays a message box that describes the error and its approximate location in the statement. When you choose OK in the SQL dialog, Access translates your SQL statement into a QBE query design.

To create an Access QBE select query with the SQL statement, follow these steps:

1. Open the Northwind Traders database, if necessary, and then open a new query.

2. Close the Show Table dialog without adding a table name.

3. Choose <u>V</u>iew, <u>S</u>QL to open the SQL window.

4. Delete any text, such as SELECT DISTINCTROW;, that may appear in the SQL window.

5. Enter the following SQL statement in the SQL window. Use Ctrl+Enter to create new lines. Your SQL statement appears as shown in figure 24.2.

```
SELECT CompanyName, CustomerID, PostalCode
    FROM Customers
    WHERE PostalCode LIKE "9*"
    ORDER BY CompanyName;
```

Fig. 24.2   An SQL statement for a simple select query.

6. Choose <u>V</u>iew, Query <u>D</u>esign. Access creates the equivalent of your SQL statement in graphical QBE (see fig. 24.3).

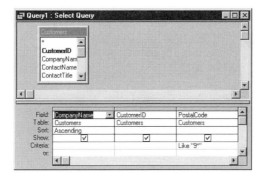

Fig. 24.3   The QBE design created by Access from the query in figure 24.2.

7. Click the Run Query button on the toolbar. The result of your query in Datasheet View appears as shown in figure 24.4.

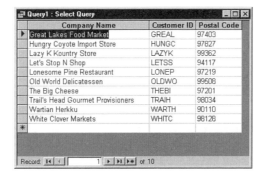

Fig. 24.4   The query in figure 24.3 in Datasheet View.

To change the order by which the query result is sorted, follow these steps:

1. Choose <u>V</u>iew, <u>S</u>QL to open the SQL window.

2. Change ORDER BY [CompanyName] to ORDER BY [PostalCode], and choose View, Query Design to open the Query Design window.

   The Query grid in design mode displays Ascending in the PostalCode column rather than in the CompanyName column, indicating that the query result set is sorted by ZIP code.

3. Click the Run button of the toolbar to display the result set sorted in ZIP code sequence (see fig. 24.5).

4. Close, but do not save, the query.

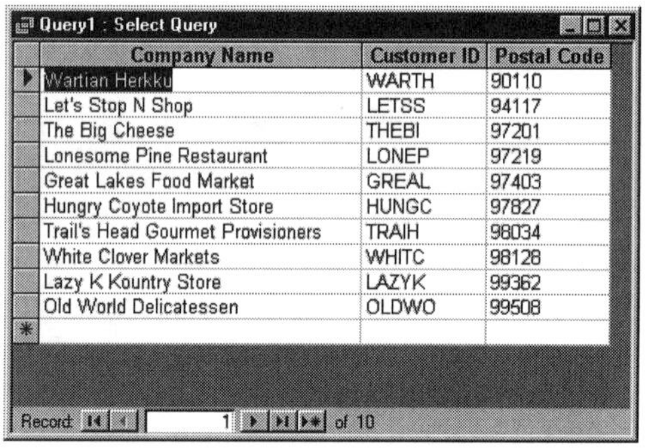

Company Name	Customer ID	Postal Code
Wartian Herkku	WARTH	90110
Let's Stop N Shop	LETSS	94117
The Big Cheese	THEBI	97201
Lonesome Pine Restaurant	LONEP	97219
Great Lakes Food Market	GREAL	97403
Hungry Coyote Import Store	HUNGC	97827
Trail's Head Gourmet Provisioners	TRAIH	98034
White Clover Markets	WHITC	98128
Lazy K Kountry Store	LAZYK	99362
Old World Delicatessen	OLDWO	99508

Record: ◄◄ ◄ 1 ► ►► ►* of 10

Fig. 24.5 The query of figure 24.4 in ZIP code order.

Using the SQL Aggregate Functions

If you want to use the aggregate functions to determine totals, averages, or statistical data for groups of records with a common attribute value, you add a GROUP BY clause to your SQL statement. You can further limit the result of the GROUP BY clause with the optional HAVING qualifier:

```
SELECT [ALL|DISTINCT|DISTINCTROW]
     aggregate_function(field_name) AS alias
     [, select_list]
   FROM table_names
   [WHERE search_criteria]
   GROUP BY group_criteria
     [HAVING aggregate_criteria]
     [ORDER BY column_criteria]
```

The *select_list* includes the *aggregate_function* with a *field_name* as its argument. The field used as the argument of an aggregate function must have a numeric data type. The additional SQL keywords and parameters required to create a GROUP BY query are described in the following list:

- AS *alias* assigns a caption to the column. The caption is created in an Access QBE query by the *alias:aggregate_function(field name)* entry in the Field row of the Query grid.

- GROUP BY *group_criteria* establishes the column on which the grouping is based. In this column, GROUP BY appears in the Totals row of the Query grid.

■ HAVING *aggregate_criteria* is one or more criteria applied to the column that contains the *aggregate_function*. The *aggregate_criteria* of HAVING is applied after the grouping is completed. WHERE *search_criteria* operates before the grouping occurs; at this point, no aggregate values exist to test against *aggregate_criteria*. Access substitutes HAVING for WHERE when you add criteria to a column with the *aggregate_function*.

Note

Not all client/server RDBMSs us the ANSI SQL AS *alias* construct. Microsoft SQL Server, Sybase System 10+, and IBM DB2, as examples, substitute a space for the AS keyword, as in SELECT *field_name alias*.... The ODBC driver for these databases uses *escape syntax* to change from Access/ANSI use of AS to the space separator. If you use Access's SQL pass-through feature with Access VBA, you must use the space separator, not the AS keyword.

The following GROUP BY query is written in ANSI SQL, except for the # symbols that enclose date and time values:

```
SELECT ShipRegion, SUM(Freight) AS [Total Freight]
    FROM Orders
    WHERE ShipCountry="USA"
        AND OrderDate BETWEEN #07/1/93# AND #12/31/94#
    GROUP BY ShipRegion
        HAVING SUM(Freight) >50
    ORDER BY SUM(Freight) DESC;
```

The query returns a result set that consists of two columns: Ship Region (states) and the totals of Freight for each Ship Region in the United States, for the years 1991 through 1994. The result set is sorted in descending order.

To create an SQL GROUP BY query in Access, follow these steps:

1. Open a new query, choose <u>V</u>iew, <u>S</u>QL, and enter the preceding GROUP BY example code in the SQL dialog (see fig. 24.6).

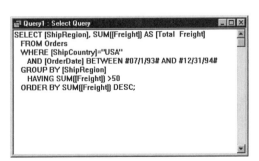

Fig. 24.6   An SQL statement that uses the *SUM()* aggregate function.

2. Choose <u>V</u>iew, Query <u>D</u>esign. Your QBE GROUP BY query design appears as shown in figure 24.7.

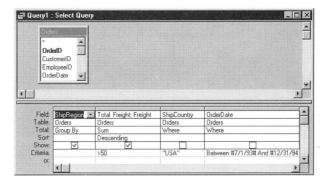

Fig. 24.7 Access's QBE design for the query in figure 24.6.

3. Click the Run Query button on the toolbar. The states with orders having freight charges equal to $50 or more during the period 7/1/93 through 12/31/94 are shown ranked by total freight costs and are displayed in Datasheet View (see fig. 24.8).

4. Close, but do not save, your query.

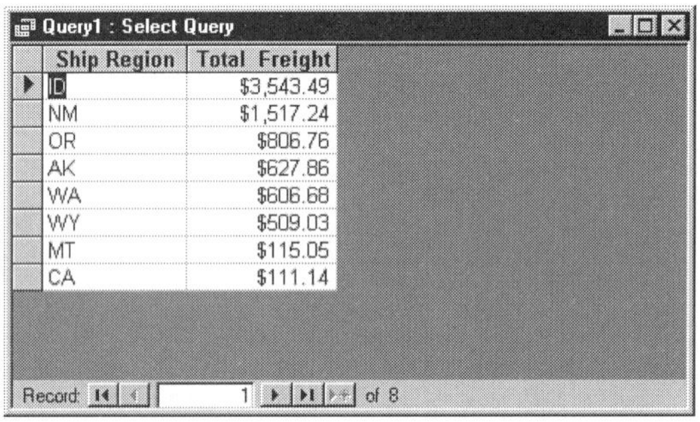

Fig. 24.8 The aggregate query design in figure 24.7 in Datasheet View.

Creating Joins with SQL

Joining two or more tables with Access QBE uses the JOIN_ON structure that specifies the table to be joined and the relationship between the fields on which the JOIN is based:

```
SELECT [ALL¦DISTINCT¦DISTINCTROW]select_list
   FROM table_names
   {INNER¦LEFT¦RIGHT} table_name JOIN join_table ON
      join_criteria
   [{INNER¦LEFT¦RIGHT} table name JOIN join_table ON
    join_criteria]
   [WHERE search_criteria]
   [ORDER BY column_criteria]
```

The elements of the JOIN statement are shown in the following list:

- *table_name* JOIN *join_table* specifies the name of the table that is joined with other tables listed in *table_names*. Each of the tables participating in a join must be included in the *table_names* list and before and after JOIN. When you specify a self-join by including two copies of the field list for a single table, the second table is distinguished from the first by adding an underscore and a digit to the table name.

  One of the three types of joins, INNER, LEFT, or RIGHT, must precede the JOIN statement. INNER specifies an equi-join; LEFT specifies a left outer join, and RIGHT specifies a right outer join. The type of join is determined in Access QBE by double-clicking the line connecting the joined fields in the table and clicking option button 1, 2, or 3 in the Join Properties dialog.

- ON *join_criteria* specifies the two fields to be joined and the relationship between the joined fields. One field is in *join_table* and the other is in a table in *table_names*. The join_criteria expression contains an equal sign (=) comparison operator and returns a True or False value. If the value of the expression is True, the record in the joined table is included in the query.

The number of JOIN statements you can add to a query usually is the total number of tables participating in the query minus one. You can create more than one JOIN between a pair of tables, but the result is often difficult to predict.

The Access SQL statement for the equi-join between the Personnel Actions and Employees tables based on ID values in each table is shown in figure 24.9, and Employees is repeated in the FROM clause. The copy of Employees is associated with the JOIN statement and is required in Access SQL joins. The JOIN reserved word in Access SQL creates the lines that connect the joined fields in Query Design View.

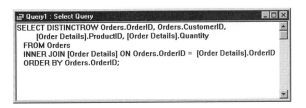

Fig. 24.9 The Access SQL implementation of an equi-join.

You create equi-joins in ANSI SQL with the WHERE clause, using the same expression to join the fields as that of the ON clause in the JOIN command. The WHERE clause is more flexible than the JOIN...ON structure because you can use other operators such as BETWEEN...AND, LIKE, >, and <. These operators result in error messages when they are substituted for the equal sign (=) in the ON clause of the JOIN statement. You don't have to repeat the Employees field in this case. The ANSI SQL statement in Figure 24.10, and in the following text, gives the same result as the Access SQL statement in figure 24.9:

```
SELECT DISTINCTROW Orders.OrderID, Orders.CustomerID,
    [Order Details].ProductID, [Order Details].Quantity
FROM Orders
INNER JOIN OrderDetails ON Orders.Order ID =
    [Order Details].OrderID
ORDER BY Orders.OrderID;
```

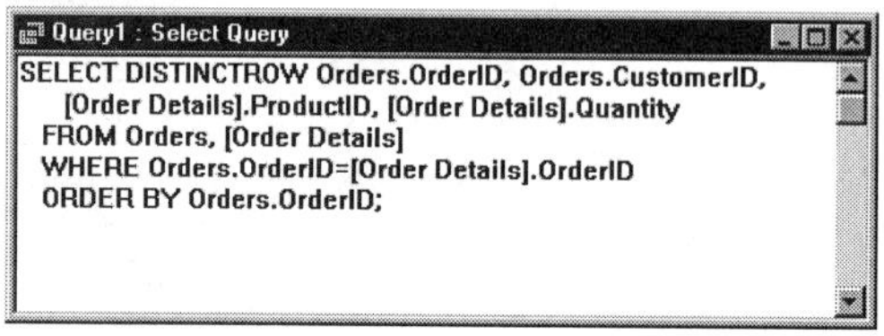

Fig. 24.10 The equi-join in figure 24.9 created by a WHERE clause.

You create multiple joins with WHERE clauses by separating each JOIN expression with an AND operator. When you use the WHERE clause to create joins in Access, the join lines don't appear between the fields in query design mode.

Using UNION Queries

UNION queries let you combine the result set of two or more SELECT queries into a single result set. Northwind.mdb includes an example of a UNION query, which has the special symbol of two overlapping circles, in the Database window. You can create UNION queries only with SQL statements; if you add the UNION keyword to a query, the query design mode button on the toolbar and the Query Design choice on the View menu are disabled. The general syntax of UNION queries is as follows:

```
SELECT select_statement
  UNION SELECT select_statement
  [GROUP BY group_criteria]
      [HAVING aggregate criteria]
  [UNION SELECT select_statement
  [GROUP BY group_criteria]
      [HAVING aggregate criteria]]
  [UNION. . .]
  [SORT BY sort_criteria]
```

The restrictions on statements that create UNION queries are the following:

- The number of fields in the *field_list* of each SELECT and UNION SELECT query must be the same. You receive an error message if the number of fields is not the same.

- The sequence of the field names in each *field_list* must correspond to similar entities. You don't receive an error message for dissimilar entities, but the result set is likely to be unfathomable. The field data types in a single column need not correspond; however, if the column of the result set contains both numeric and Text data types, the data type of the column is set to Text.

- Only one SORT BY clause is allowed, and it must follow the last UNION SELECT statement. You can add GROUP BY and HAVING clauses to each SELECT and UNION SELECT statement, if needed.

Figure 24.11 shows the SQL statement to create a UNION query derived from the Union Query included in Northwind.mdb. The syntax of the SQL statement illustrates the ability of UNION queries to include values from two different field data types, Text (Customer ID) and Long Integer (Supplier ID), in the single, aliased ID column. The query result set appears in figure 24.12 with the single record included from the Suppliers table selected.

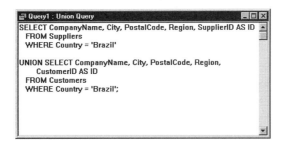

Fig. 24.11 Creating a multiple-column UNION query.

	CompanyName	City	PostalCode	Region	ID
	Comércio Mineiro	São Paulo	05432-043	SP	COMMI
	Familia Arquibaldo	São Paulo	05442-030	SP	FAMIA
	Gourmet Lanchonetes	Campinas	04876-786	SP	GOURL
	Hanari Carnes	Rio de Janeiro	05454-876	RJ	HANAR
	Que Delícia	Rio de Janeiro	02389-673	RJ	QUEDE
	Queen Cozinha	São Paulo	05487-020	SP	QUEEN
▶	Refrescos Americanas L	São Paulo	5442		10
	Ricardo Adocicados	Rio de Janeiro	02389-890	RJ	RICAR
	Tradição Hipermercados	São Paulo	05634-030	SP	TRADH
	Wellington Importadora	Resende	08737-363	SP	WELLI

Record: ⏮ ◀ | 7 | ▶ ⏭ ▶* of 10

Fig. 24.12 The result of the UNION query of figure 24.11.

Implementing Subqueries

Versions of Access prior to 2.0 used nested queries to emulate the subquery capability of ANSI SQL. (A *nested query* is a query executed against the result set of another query.) Access 7.0 lets you write a SELECT query that uses another SELECT query to supply the criteria for the WHERE clause. Depending on the complexity of your query, using a subquery instead of nested queries often improves performance. The general syntax of subqueries is as follows:

```
SELECT field_list
   FROM table_list
   WHERE [table_name.]field_name
      IN SELECT select_statement
   [GROUP BY group_criteria]
      [HAVING aggregate_criteria]
   [ORDER BY sort_criteria];
```

Figure 24.13 shows the SQL statement for the example subquery included in Northwind.mdb with formatting added for clarity. This query returns names and addresses of customers who placed orders between April 1, 1994 and June 30, 1994. The

SELECT subquery that begins after the IN predicate returns the CustomerID values from the Orders table against which the CustomerID values of the Customers table are compared.

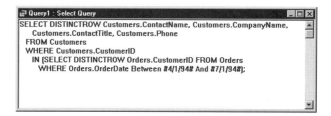

Fig. 24.13 The SQL statement for a subquery.

Unlike UNION queries, you can create a subquery in query design mode. You type **IN**, followed by the SELECT statement as the criterion of the appropriate column. Figure 24.14 shows the query design with part of the IN SELECT statement in the Criteria row of the Customer ID column. Figure 24.15 shows the result set returned by the SQL statement of figure 24.13.

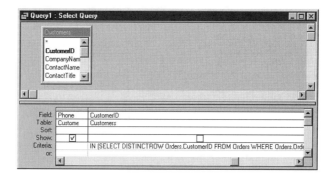

Fig. 24.14 Entering the SQL statement for a subquery in the Criteria row.

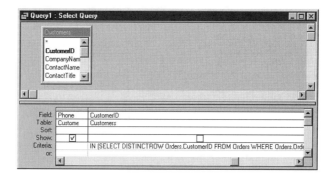

Fig. 24.15 The query result set from the subquery of figures 24.13 and 24.14.

Specifying Action Query Syntax

Data Manipulation Language (DML) commands are implemented by Access's action queries: append, delete, make-table, and update. Access SQL reserved words that create crosstab queries, TRANSFORM and PIVOT, are included in this section because crosstab queries are related to DML queries. This sections shows the syntax for each type of Access action query.

Append queries use the following syntax:

```
INSERT INTO dest_table
   SELECT [ALL¦DISTINCT¦DISTINCTROW] select_list
      FROM source_table
   [WHERE append_criteria]
```

If you omit the WHERE clause, all the records of *source_table* are appended to *dest_table*.

Delete queries take the following form:

```
DELETE FROM table_name
   [WHERE delete_criteria]
```

If you omit the optional WHERE clause in a delete query, you delete all data in *table_name*.

Make-table queries use the following syntax:

```
SELECT [ALL¦DISTINCT¦DISTINCTROW] select_list
   INTO new_table
   FROM source_table
   [WHERE append_criteria]
```

To copy the original table, substitute an asterisk (*) for *select_list* and omit the optional WHERE clause.

Update queries use the SET command to assign values to individual columns:

```
UPDATE table_name
   SET column_name = value [, column_name = value]
   [WHERE update_criteria]
```

Separate multiple column_name entries and corresponding values by commas if you want to update the data in more than one field. Access 7.0 SQL supports the ANSI SQL VALUES keyword for adding records to tables the hard way (specifying the VALUE of each column of each record).

Crosstab queries use the Access SQL keywords TRANSFORM and PIVOT to create various types of summary queries using the SQL aggregate functions. The following syntax applies to time-series crosstab queries:

```
TRANSFORM aggregate_function(field_name) [AS alias]
   SELECT [ALL¦DISTINCT¦DISTINCTROW] select_list
      FROM table_name
   PIVOT Format(field_name),"format_type")
   [IN (column_list)]
```

VI

Advanced Techniques

TRANSFORM defines a crosstab query, and PIVOT specifies the GROUP BY characteristics plus the fixed column names specified by the optional IN predicate. Crosstab queries, like queries with multiple or nested JOINs, are better left to Access QBE to create the query. You can edit the query as necessary after Access has written the initial SQL statement.

Troubleshooting

When I try to execute a query from my SQL statement, an Enter Parameter dialog appears.

You misspelled one of the table names in your *table_list*, one of the field names in your *field_list*, or both. If the Jet engine's query parser can't match a table name or a field name with those specified in the FROM clause, Jet assumes that the entry is a parameter and requests its value. Check the spelling of the database objects in your SQL statement. (If you misspell an SQL keyword, you usually receive a syntax error message box.)

Adding IN to Use Tables in Another Database

Access enables you to open only one database at a time, unless you write code to open another table with an Access VBA function or procedure. However, you can use Access SQL's IN clause with a make-table, append, update, or delete query to create or modify tables in another database. Access provides the capability to make a table or append records to a table in another Access database through graphical QBE only. You click the Another Database option in the Query Properties dialog for the make-table or append query and type the file name of the other database.

You have to write an SQL query or edit a query created by Access to update data or delete records in tables contained in another database of any type, or to perform any operation on a dBASE, Paradox, or Btrieve file that isn't attached to your database. The SQL query uses the IN clause to specify the external database or table file. The advantage of using the IN clause is simplicity—you don't have to attach the table before using it. The disadvantage of using the IN clause is that indexes associated with dBASE and Paradox tables aren't updated when the content of the table is modified.

Working with Another Access Database

You can create a table in another Access database, delete all the records, and then append the records back to the table from which the records were deleted, using the IN clause to specify the name of the other database that contains the table. To try using the IN clause, open a new query or an existing query and follow these steps:

1. Choose <u>V</u>iew, <u>S</u>QL to open the SQL window.

2. Delete any existing text if you have a query open, and type the following line in the SQL window (see fig. 24.16).

   SELECT * INTO Customers IN "OLE Objects.mdb" FROM Customers;

SELECT...INTO creates a make-table query. If you haven't created OLE_Objects.mdb, choose New Database from the File menu and create a new blank database named OLE_Objects.mdb or whatever you like in your \Access\Samples folder. If the new database is in a different location, you need to add the path to the IN string. Re-open Northwind.mdb.

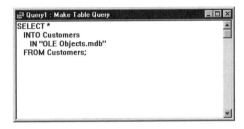

Fig. 24.16 A query that creates a table in another database.

3. Click the Run Query button of the toolbar to make the new Customers table in your OLE Objects database. Click OK when the message box advises you of the number of records that are copied to the new Customers table created in OLE Objects. You can open OLE Objects.mdb to verify the existence of the new table.

4. Choose <u>V</u>iew, <u>S</u>QL again, delete the existing text, and type the following line (see fig. 24.17):

DELETE * FROM Customers IN "OLE Objects.mdb"

DELETE...FROM creates a delete query.

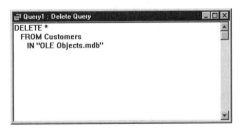

Fig. 24.17 Deleting all records from a table in another database.

5. Click the Run Query button on the toolbar to delete the records in the OLE_Objects Customers table. Click OK to confirm the deletion of the records.

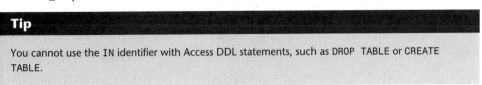

Tip

You cannot use the IN identifier with Access DDL statements, such as DROP TABLE or CREATE TABLE.

To append the records you deleted back into the Customers table of the OLE Objects database, follow these steps:

1. Choose <u>F</u>ile, <u>O</u>pen Database and select your OLE Objects database, which contains the Customers table with no records.

2. Click the Query tab of the Database window, and then click the New button. Close the Show Table dialog without adding a table.

3. Choose <u>V</u>iew, <u>S</u>QL and type the following line in the SQL Text box (see fig. 24.18):

   INSERT INTO Customers SELECT * FROM Customers IN "Northwind.mdb"

   `INSERT INTO` creates an append query. If your OLE Objects database is located elsewhere, add the path to Northwind.mdb to the preceding statement.

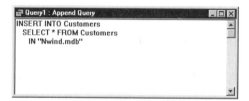

Fig. 24.18 A query to append records to a table in another database.

4. Click the Run Query button on the toolbar to add the records from Northwind's Customers table. Confirm the append by clicking OK in the message box.

Although you accomplish the same objectives by attaching a table from another database or copying tables to the Clipboard and pasting the table into another database, using an SQL query for this purpose is a more straightforward process.

Using the `IN` Clause with Other Types of Databases

You can create or modify dBASE, Paradox, and Btrieve tables by specifying in an `IN` statement the path to the file and the file type using the following special Access SQL syntax reserved for foreign database file types:

```
IN "[drive:\]path" "database_type"
```

The *path* to the file is required, even if the database is located in your \Access folder; you receive an error if you omit the *path* entry. You can use an empty string, `""`, to identify the current folder.

The *database_type* expression must be enclosed in quotation marks. It consists of one of the seven foreign file types supported by ISAM DLLs supplied with Access 95, followed by a semicolon: `dBASE III;`, `dBASE IV;`, `dBASE 5;`, `FoxPro;` (.dbf), `FoxPro 3.0;` (.dbc), `Paradox;` (db), or `Btrieve;`. The semicolon after the file type name is required, but the database file type names are not case-sensitive—*dbase iii;* is acceptable to Access.

You can create a dBASE IV table from a query by using the syntax shown in figure 24.19.

You can append records to a dBASE IV file with the syntax shown in figure 24.20. In deleting and updating records in foreign tables, use the syntax shown in the "Specifying

Action Query Syntax" section, with the IN clause added. When you append records to or delete records from a foreign database type that does not support transaction processing, you receive the warning message shown in figure 24.21.

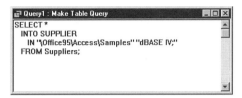

Fig. 24.19   Creating a dBASE IV table from an SQL query.

Fig. 24.20   Appending records to a dBASE IV table with an SQL query.

Fig. 24.21   The warning message that appears when appending records to an attached table of a foreign database type that does not support transactions.

Using SQL Statements in Forms, Reports, and Macros

If you create a large number of forms and reports based on queries or that use queries, or if you use macros to run select and action queries, the query list in your Database window can become cluttered. You can use SQL queries you write or copy from the SQL dialog in place of the names of query objects and then delete the query from your database. You can use SQL statements for the following purposes:

■ *Record Source property of forms and reports.* Substitute the SQL query text for the name of the query in the Record Source text box.

■ *Row Source property in lists and drop-down combo lists on a form.* Using an SQL statement rather than a query object gives you greater control over the sequence of the columns in your list.

■ *Argument of the* RunSQL() *macro action.* Only SQL statements that create action queries can be used with the RunSQL() macro action.

■ *Parameter of the SQL property of an Access VBA function that creates a select query or modifies an existing query.* You use the RunCode() macro action to create the query with an Access VBA function and then display the query with the OpenQuery() macro action. Using this technique creates the equivalent of the RunSQL() macro action for select queries.

You can create and test your Access SQL statement in Query Design mode and then copy the statement to the Clipboard. Paste the text into the text box for the property or into your Access VBA module. Then close the test query design without saving it.

From Here...

This chapter described the basic details of the use of Structured Query Language in Access. Important differences between the ANSI and Access implementations of SQL were outlined for readers who have used SQL in other database management applications. The syntax of the SQL example statements in this chapter adhere to ANSI standard syntax as much as possible. Using WHERE clauses rather than JOIN statements can save substantial amounts of typing when you write your own SQL statements. Writing your own SQL statements frees you from having to use some of the rigid conventions of the QBE methods implemented by Access.

■ Chapter 9, "Understanding Operators and Expressions in Access," describes how to use all of the operators discussed in this chapter.

■ Chapter 10, "Creating Multitable and Crosstab Queries," shows you how to use Access's graphical QBE window to create the Access SQL statements that underlie all Access queries.

■ Chapter 25, "Securing Multiuser Network Applications," introduces the use of Access in a network environment. Both client/server and peer-to-peer network applications are described.

Chapter 25

Securing Multiuser Network Applications

Personal computer networking continues to be one of the fastest-growing areas in the PC marketplace. Many large organizations are downsizing database applications to personal computer networks. *Downsizing* means moving a database system that runs on a costly, large-scale computer, such as a mainframe, to smaller, lower-priced computers, usually server PCs running network operating systems such as Windows NT 3.5+ Server or Novell NetWare. These networks use a dedicated server PC; PCs connected by the network to the server are called *clients* or *workstations*. Small- to moderate-size organizations have discovered that installing a simple PC network can increase productivity and reduce the required investment in computing hardware. An organization need purchase only a single laser printer if all users can share it on a network. The cost of purchasing large fixed disk drives is reduced when users share large files rather than keep multiple independent copies on local disk drives. Even families with more than one home PC are installing low-cost networks in order to share peripherals and files among family members.

Reducing capital expenditures and operating costs are the principal incentives for installing PC networks. In many cases, savings in the amount spent on peripheral equipment is the sole consideration in the decision to use a network. When you use a database application, however, productivity plays the most important role in the network decision-making process. The capability to share up-to-date information contained in a database file among many users is a strong incentive to install a PC network because it increases productivity. Increasing productivity with a networked database system can, in turn, reduce operating costs by many times the savings offered by the reduction of the investment when you share computer peripheral equipment.

Access will be the first networked Windows application many readers of this book have ever used. Windows 95's simple installation of low-cost and easy-to-administer PC networks should appeal to first-time network users. If you don't have a network now and you plan to create Access applications for other users to share, Windows 95's built-in network operating system is a

In this chapter, you learn to:

- Share Access databases in a workgroup environment

- Use Access 95's new Database Splitter add-in

- Use the Workgroup Administrator to change workgroups

- Secure your Access application

- Grant permissions to others to use your application

- Encrypt your databases for greater security

- Share database files with peer-to-peer and Windows NT 3.51 Server networking

VI

Advanced Techniques

logical choice as a *peer-to-peer* "starter" network. A *peer-to-peer* network is a network in which any PC connected to the network is capable of sharing files in all or designated folders with any other PC connected to the network. PCs connected by peer-to-peer networks often are called members of a workgroup. Access applications that share .MDB files are termed *multiuser* applications.

Microsoft Corporation designed Access specifically for multiuser operation in a networked, workgroup environment. For example, Microsoft added a security system to Access. If your network is already set up, you can choose to install Access on the network or install only the .mdb files you intend to share. If you don't have a network when you begin using Access, the process is simple to change your database files from single-user to shared status when you install a network. This chapter explains how to set up and use Access in a variety of network environments, share database files, establish database security, and administer a multiuser database system.

> **Caution**
>
> Access 95 has a new .mdb file structure and uses entries in the Windows 95 or Windows NT registry, not MSACC??0.INI, to hold the locations and names of workgroup system files. If you are upgrading to Access 95 from a prior version and share existing .MDB and workgroup system (.MDA) files, do not convert the .MDB or .MDA files to Access 95 format unless all members of the workgroup have installed Access 95. Access 2.0 and earlier versions cannot open Access 95 .mdb or .mdw files. Access 95, however can link files created by earlier versions.

Installing Access in a Networked Environment

> **Tip**
>
> Use the Custom installation option if you want to create shared Access .mdb files or connect to client/server databases with Open Database Connectivity (ODBC). The Typical option does not install the Workgroup Administrator or ODBC files.

If you are using a network operating system with application server capabilities, such as Novell NetWare 3.x/4.x or Windows NT 3.5+ Server, you can use either of the following methods to install Access in a network environment:

- Install Access on the network server. All workstations run the server's copy of Access 95 and don't require a copy of Access on their local disk drives. This approach saves disk space on the workstations but usually results in much slower operation of Access. If workstations also run Windows 95 from the server, operation can slow down even more. The degree to which the operating speed will be affected depends on your network's performance and the number of users accessing the network simultaneously.

■ Install a copy of Windows 95 and Access 95 on each workstation. In this case, users share only Access .mdb files. Access requires between about 20M and 50M of disk space, depending on the features you include in the workstation installation and whether you previously have installed OLE 2+ server applications such as Microsoft Word 95 and/or Excel 95. Use this installation method for computers connected in a peer-to-peer network.

Tip

If many users need to install or upgrade to Access 95, it usually is faster to use the administrator's installation on a network server and then install Access 95 on the workstations from the administrator's installation, rather than from the distribution diskettes. (See Acreadme.txt and other .txt files on the CD-ROM or Setup diskette 1.)

You need an individual copy of the Access software for each workstation that uses Access or a license for each workstation that runs an Access application with the retail version of Access 95. For additional details, refer to the license information that Microsoft supplies with Access.

The Microsoft Access Developer's Toolkit (ADT) lets you distribute a runtime version of Access. Runtime Access 95 enables users to run applications you create but not to create or modify applications. Runtime Access enables multiple workstations to run Access applications without an individual license for each workstation. Unlike prior versions of Access, which used a separate runtime executable file (MSARN??0.EXE), Access 95 runtime uses the retail executable (Msaccess.exe) with a setting in the user's Registry that turns off the user's ability to use Msaccess.exe in design mode. You can install runtime Access on the server or local workstations; installation of runtime Access on each workstation is recommended because you gain operating speed. A runtime Access installation consumes less disk space than the retail version of Access because runtime Access does not include (and cannot be used with) the Access help file and the Access wizards and builders.

Note

Do not attempt to share the retail or runtime version of Access on a peer-to-peer network. Peer-to-peer networks are designed for sharing printers and data files, not the executable (.exe) and help (.hlp) files of large applications such as Access. The computer and network resources required to run Access from a peer server slow applications running on the server to a crawl and greatly increase network traffic.

VI

Advanced Techniques

Sharing Your Access Database Files with Other Users

▶▶ See "Examining the Content of the Access Developer's Toolkit," p. 1117

While you're learning to use Access and designing your first Access applications, you use Access in single-user mode and maintain exclusive use of the database files you create. If your application is designed for use in a networked environment, however, you need to set up a workgroup for the users who will share the database you created. The sections that follow describe how to create a directory for sharing files, modify Access applications for a multiuser environment, and set up a workgroup to provide security for shared .mdb files.

Creating a Directory and System File for File Sharing

> **Tip**
>
> If you intend to share your Access applications, make a backup copy of System.mdw, preferably on disk. Use the backup copy to make a new System.mda file in case your original System.mda file becomes corrupted.

Sharing a database application requires that each user of the database share a common system file, derived from Access' System.mdw workgroup file, that contains information on the members of the workgroup, such as their logon names, passwords, and the groups of which they are members. Permissions for individual users to open and to modify objects are stored in the .mdb file. Permissions are discussed in a later section, "Maintaining Database Security."

 When you develop an application intended for shared use, it's a common practice to create a new local folder to hold the application's .mdb file(s). You then use the Workgroup Administrator application (Wrkgadm.exe) to create a new system file specifically for the application and develop the application in its own directory. Access 95's new default extension for workgroup system files is *.mdw*. When the application is completed, you can copy the .mdb and .mdw files in this directory to the workgroup directory of the network or peer-to-peer server that is used to share them.

 The location and name of the system file that Access 95 uses when it is launched is specified by the SystemDB entry of the HKEY_LOCAL_MACHINE\SOFTWARE\Microsoft\ Access\7.0\Jet\3.0\Engines\Jet section of the Registry. If you installed Access in the default folder, \MSOffice\Access, the default Registry entry (key) for SystemDB is "\msoffice\Access\System.mdw," as shown in figure 25.1. Unless you're familiar with editing Windows 95's or Windows NT's Registry with the Registry Editor application (RegEdit.exe), don't edit Registry entries manually. An incorrect entry can cause Access or Windows to behave unexpectedly.

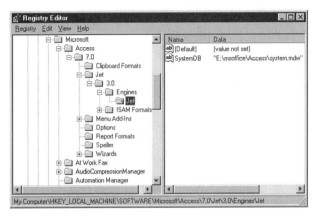

Fig. 25.1 The Registry Editor displaying the Registry value for the SystemDB key that specifies the name and location of your system file.

To establish a directory and a workgroup system file for the development of an example shared database application, complete the following steps:

1. Launch Explorer and add a new folder, called \Shared in this example, to the root folder of a local drive on your PC.

2. Open the \Shared folder and create a new subfolder, \Shared\Nwind.

3. Create a copy of Northwind.mdb in \Shared\Nwind, and then close Explorer.

4. Launch Workgroup Administrator (Wrkgadm.exe). The location of Workgroup Administrator in your Start menu hierarchy depends on how you installed Access. Wrkgadm.exe is located by default in your \Msoffice\Access folder. Create a Desktop shortcut to Wrkgadm.exe if Workgroup Administrator does not appear in your Start, Programs, or Office menu. The opening dialog of Workgroup Administrator displays the name and location of the default system file, System.mdw (see fig. 25.2).

Fig. 25.2 Workgroup Administrator's opening dialog.

5. Click the Create button to open the Workgroup Owner dialog in which you specify the Name, Organization, and optional Workgroup ID for the new workgroup system file (see fig. 25.3). The Name and Organization entries default to entries you made when installing Office 95 or Access 95. Write down the Name, Organization,

and Workgroup ID entries, which are case-sensitive, and keep them in a safe place. If you need to re-create the workgroup system file in the future, your entries must exactly match the original entries.

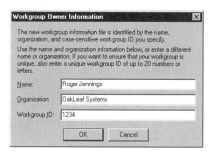

Fig. 25.3 Specifying the Name, Organization, and optional Workgroup ID for a new workgroup system file.

6. Click the OK button to display the Workgroup System Database dialog. Type the path and name of your workgroup folder, **E:\SHARED\NWIND\SYSTEM.MDW** in this case, in the Database text box (see fig. 25.4).

Fig. 25.4 You type the location and name of the share workgroup file in the Workgroup Information File dialog.

7. Click the OK button to display the Confirm Workgroup Information dialog (see fig. 25.5). If the workgroup information is correct, click the OK button. A message appears to confirm that the new workgroup system file has been created (see fig. 25.6). Click OK to close the message box and return to the initial Workgroup Administrator dialog (see fig. 25.7).

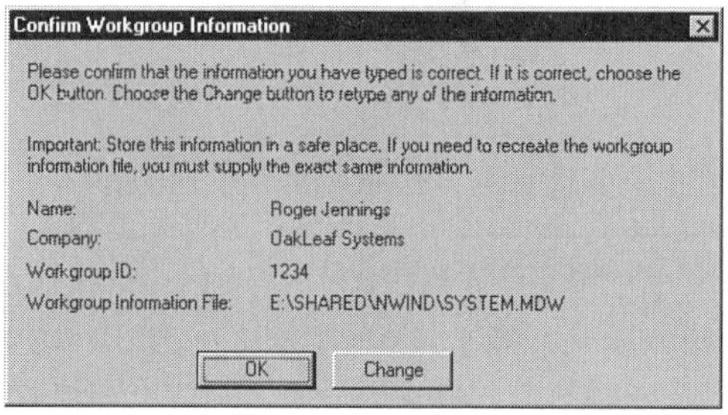

Fig. 25.5 Confirming the owner information for the new workgroup system file.

Fig. 25.6 Access confirms that the new System.mdw workgroup system file is created.

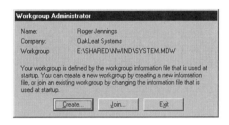

Fig. 25.7 The Workgroup Administrator dialog displays the name and location of the new workgroup system file.

8. Click Exit to close Workgroup Administrator. Access doesn't use the new workgroup system file until you close and relaunch Access.

9. Launch Explorer to verify that the copy of Northwind.mdb and System.mdw appear in \Shared\Nwind, as shown in figure 25.8.

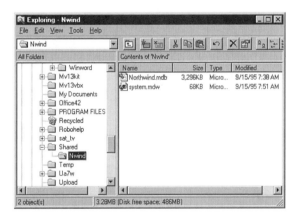

Fig. 25.8 Windows Explorer displaying the files in the \Shared\Nwind folder.

10. Close Access, if it is open. Launch Access and open the \Shared\Nwind\ Northwind.mdb database file with the System.mdw system file active.

The dedicated System.mdw file contains information pertaining only to the database applications that you open when System.mdw is your active system file. You can develop an application using Access' default operating options and System.mda and then change the options and create a new workgroup system file to provide for file sharing when you complete the application.

You can change with the Workgroup Administrator the system database file that Access uses when launched. The procedure is described in the section, "Choosing Workgroups with the Workgroup Administrator," later in this chapter.

> **Note**
>
> Minimize the number of database objects you create when you develop applications to be shared. You must specifically grant or revoke permissions to groups or individual users for each object you create. Use SQL statements to replace query objects when possible (see Chapter 24, "Working with Structured Query Language"). Combine related Access macros so that you have as few individual macro objects as possible (see Part IV, "Powering Access with Macros"). Criteria for combining macros are the subject of a tip in the "Granting and Revoking Permissions for Database Objects" section, later in this chapter. Minimizing the number of objects also reduces the number of entries you need to make when you establish database security restrictions (permissions) for your application.

Preparing to Share Your Database Files

 To set up Access to share database files, you must make several changes to the settings in the Advanced page of the Options properties sheet. You open the Advanced page by choosing <u>T</u>ools, <u>O</u>ptions and then clicking the Advanced tab (see fig. 25.9). The changes you make to Access options (called *preferences*) are stored for your account (*Admin*, the default) in the system database and apply to all databases you open thereafter using that system database.

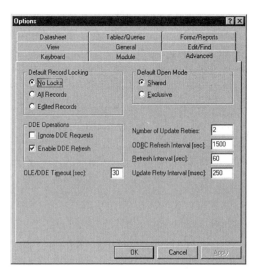

Fig. 25.9   The Advanced page of the Options property sheet.

Following is a list of the Advanced options that affect multiuser applications:

■ The Default Open Mode is set to Shared by default. Changing this setting to Exclusive so that only one user can open files improves performance. If you've changed the file open mode to Exclusive, you must return to the default Shared mode so that more than one user can open the file.

- Default Record Locking has three options designed to prevent more than one user from making simultaneous changes to the same record. No Locks, the default, only causes a lock when the edit occurs. All Records locks the entire table when a user opens it for editing. Edited Records locks only the record(s) during the editing process.

- Access attempts to update a locked record for the value in the Number of Update Retries text box at a rate determined by the value in the Update Retry Interval text box, before issuing a message box that the record is locked and cannot be updated.

- Refresh Interval determines how often the data displayed in a datasheet or form is rewritten automatically to reflect changes made by other members of the workgroup. ODBC Refresh Interval applies only to tables attached using the ODBC driver for tables linked from a foreign database, usually a client/server database.

Access 95's default values are suitable for most multiuser applications. Unless you have a specific reason for making changes, accept the default values.

Note

Record locking is a misnomer in Access. An Edited Record lock is applied to a 2K page that may contain many records if the fields of the records have small Size property values. Using No Locks, the default, speeds operation of Access in a multiuser environment because the time required to lock and unlock table pages is saved. No Locks is called *optimistic locking*; optimistic locking assumes that the probability is low that two or more users might attempt to alter the same record simultaneously. If you attempt to update a record in a table with No Locks that is being updated simultaneously by another user, Access displays a message box that lets you choose to accept or overwrite the other user's changes. The conservative approach is to use Edited Record locking, but doing so may impair performance when many users simultaneously update data in a single table.

Splitting Databases for File Sharing

◀◀ See "The Database Splitter Add-In," p. 31

Most Access developers agree that Access applications should be divided into two .mdb files, one containing only Access tables (also called *data objects*) and the other containing all other objects (called *application objects*). Splitting Access applications lets you link (attach) tables from the shared .mdb to your application objects in a local .mdb file. Keeping the application objects on the user's computer minimizes network traffic and improves performance, especially on peer-to-peer networks. The major benefit of splitting Access applications, however, is the ability to easily update a user's application .mdb file without affecting current data stored in Access tables.

Microsoft recognized that most production database applications created with Access use the split design, so Access 95 now has an add-in to automate the process. Chapter 1,

VI

Advanced Techniques

"Access 95 for Access 2 Users—What's New," includes a brief description of the Database Splitter add-in. Follow these steps to separate the tables from the application objects of the Northwind.mdb file using the Database Splitter add-in:

1. Open the copy of Northwind.mdb in your \Shared\Nwind folder with \Shared\Nwind\System.mdw as your system database, if necessary. (Do *not* use your original copy of Northwind.mdb in \Msoffice\Access\Samples for this example.)

2. With the Database window active, choose Tools, Add-Ins, Database Splitter to open the Database Splitter add-in's dialog, as shown in figure 25.10.

Fig. 25.10   The Database Splitter add-in's opening dialog.

3. Verify that you have the copy of Northwind.mdb open, and then click the Split button to display the Database Splitter's Save As dialog. The default file name is Northwind_be.mdb; "be" is an abbreviation for "back-end."

4. Move to the \Shared\Nwind folder and type NwindData.mdb as the name of your back-end database file containing tables to link to application objects in Northwind.mdb (see fig. 25.11).

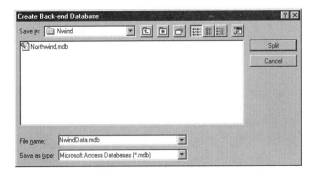

Fig. 25.11   Selecting the directory and naming the the back-end database file to contain the table objects.

5. Click the Split button to create the back-end database. After a minute or so (depending on your computer's speed) of disk activity, you receive the message shown in figure 25.12.

Fig. 25.12 The message that informs you the tables are split from your source .mdb file and links to the tables are created.

6. Click OK to close the Database Splitter add-in. The tables page of your Database window appears as shown in figure 25.13. Arrows to the left of the table icons indicate linked files.

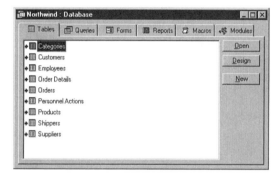

Fig. 25.13 Newly created links to the tables moved to the back-end database.

7. To verify that the links to the tables are correct, choose <u>T</u>ools, Add-Ins, <u>L</u>inked Table Manager to display the Linked Table Manager's dialog, as shown in figure 25.14.

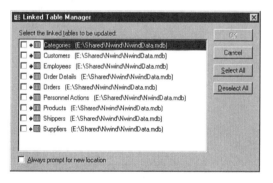

Fig. 25.14 The Linked Table Manager add-in confirms the location and name of the back-end .mdb file containing the linked tables.

Choosing Workgroups with the Workgroup Administrator

If you have several workgroups that have overlapping user membership, you might want to place all of the workgroup system databases in a single directory, such as \Shared, to make it easy for users to choose a particular workgroup. (The workgroup system database does not have to be in the same directory as the shared .mdb file(s).) To use the Workgroup Administrator to change workgroups, follow these steps:

1. Launch Workgroup Administrator. Your current workgroup is identified by the .mdw file that appears in Workgroup Administrator's opening dialog.

2. Click the Join button to open the Workgroup Information File dialog. Your current workgroup system file appears in the Database text box (see fig. 25.15).

Fig. 25.15 Your current workgroup displayed in the Workgroup Information File dialog.

3. Enter the well-formed path and name of the workgroup database file for the workgroup you want to join in the Database text box, or click the Browse button to display the Select Workgroup Information File dialog shown in figure 25.16. In this case, choose the System.mdw in your \MSOffice\Access folder to return to the normal Access configuration.

Fig. 25.16 Selecting the workgroup database file for the new workgroup.

4. Select the drive and directory in which the System.mdw file for the new workgroup is located, and click Open to close the Select Workgroup Information File dialog. Your selection appears in the Select Workgroup Information File dialog shown in figure 25.17.

5. Click OK to confirm your new workgroup selection; click OK when the message box confirms that you have joined the workgroup, and then click the Exit button of the Microsoft Workgroup Administrator's dialog (see fig. 25.18) to complete the process.

Fig. 25.17 Confirming the workgroup system file for the new workgroup.

Fig. 25.18 The Workgroup Administrator dialog after changing to a new workgroup.

Using Command Line Options to Open a Shared Database

Access provides a number of options that you can employ to customize how Access starts for each user. All users in a workgroup may share a common database, but you may want individual users to start Access with a different form. You can open a workgroup database automatically, execute a macro that opens a specific form, and supply a user name or password when you start Access by entering options on the command line that you use to start Access for each workgroup member, as in the following example:

```
d:\msa_path\msaccess.exe [n:\mdb_path\mdb_name.mdb]
  [/User user_name ][/Pwd pass_word ][/X macro_name]
[/Ro ][/Excl ] [/Profile profile.ini] [/Repair] [/Nostartup]
[/Compact [target.mdb]] [/Convert target.mdb] [/Runtime]
[/Cmd cmd_value]
```

Spaces separate each of the optional command line parameters. Table 25.1 describes the elements of the Access startup command line options.

Table 25.1 Command Line Options for Launching Access	
Command Line Element	**Function**
d:\msa_path\msaccess.exe	Command to launch Access
n:\mdb_path\mdb_name.mdb	Path and name of startup database file
/User user_name	Start with user_name as user name
/Pwd pass_word	Start with pass_word as password
/X macro_name	Run macro_name on startup
/Ro	Open mdb_name for read-only use

(continues)

Table 25.1   Continued

Command Line Element	Function
/Excl	Open *mdb_name* for exclusive use
/Profile *profile*.ini	Open \Windows*profile*.ini instead of using Registry entries
/Repair	Repair the database, and then close Access
/NoStartup	Don't display the Access startup dialog
/Compact *target*.mdb	Compact into *target*.mdb or into the startup database if you omit *target*.mdb
/Convert *target*.mdb	Converts a prior version .MDB file to an Access 95 .mdb file with the name specified by *target*.mdb
/Runtime	Starts Msaccess.exe in runtime mode
/Cmd *cmd_value*	Specifies a value to be returned by the Access Basic Command function

Tip

Opening the local application .mdb with the /Excl parameter speeds operation of the application. The /Excl option applies to the local database, not the attached tables of the shared data .mdb file. Do not use the /Excl option if you want other users to be able to share the database. When you omit the /Excl option, shared or exclusive use of databases is determined by the Default Open Mode for Databases choice of the Multiuser Options, discussed in a previous section, "Preparing to Share Your Database Files."

Note

Do not use the /Ro option if you want some members of the workgroup to be able to modify the tables or other objects of the database. If you specify the /Ro option for one workstation, all workstations in the workgroup are restricted to read-only use of the database. Use the permissions features of Access, described in the "Maintaining Database Security" section of this chapter, to designate the users who can update the data in tables and those who cannot.

The sequence in which you enter the command line options doesn't affect the options' operation; however, a convention is that the name of the file to open always immediately follows the command that launches the application.

The /Profile parameter replaces the /ini option of the runtime version of Access 2.0, but requires a substantial amount of editing of your Registry to use. You can use the argument of the /Profile parameter to point to a private profile (.ini) file, such as Northwind.ini, in your \Windows folder. (You can locate the .ini file in another folder by prefixing the well-formed path to the .ini file.) This feature is useful because you can create a shortcut for users that specifies a particular workgroup system file in the [Options] section of the .ini file. To create and use a profile with the /ini option, follow these steps:

1. Launch Notepad and type **[Options]** as the first line.

2. Type **SystemDB=** and the well-formed path and name of your workgroup system database as the second line.

3. Choose File, Save and save your text file in your \Windows directory as *Profile*.ini (see fig. 25.19), and then close Notepad.

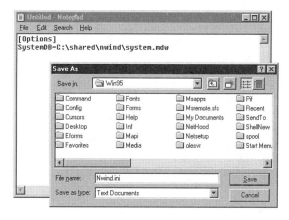

Fig. 25.19   Specifying a workgroup database file in a profile (.ini) file.

4. Create a desktop shortcut to Msaccess.exe, and then left-click the shortcut and choose Rename from the popup menu. Give the shortcut an appropriate name, in this case **NorthWind**.

5. Right-click the shortcut again and choose Properties from the popup menu. Click the Shortcut tab to display the Shortcut properties page.

6. After ...\MSACCESS.EXE, add the path and name of your .mdb file, **/ini** and the name of your .ini file, and then add **/Nostartup**. For this example, the full command line for the shortcut is **C:\MSOffice\Access\MSACCESS.EXE c:\shared\nwind\Northwind.mdb /ini Nwind.ini /Nostartup** (see fig. 25.20).

7. If you want to change the icon for your shortcut, click the Change Icon button to display a collection of icons in Shell32.dll from which to choose (see fig. 25.21). Select the icon you want, then click OK to close the Change Icon dialog.

When you double-click the new shortcut, Access launches, uses the workgroup system database specified by the /Profile command line parameter, and automatically opens the file specified on the command line parameter. When you distribute your Access application .mdb to other users, include a copy of the shortcut and the .ini file.

VI

Advanced Techniques

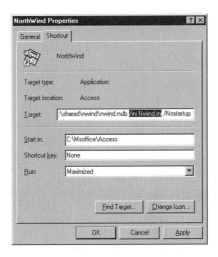

Fig. 25.20   Entering command line parameters for an Access shortcut.

Fig. 25.21   Changing the icon for an Access shortcut.

Note

Adding a user's password as an option to the startup command line violates one of the basic rules of database security: do not disclose your password to any other person. The preceding example that uses a password as a command line option does so only for the purpose of completely defining the options available. You should not use the /Pwd command line option under any circumstances.

Maintaining Database Security

Database security prevents unauthorized persons from accidentally or intentionally viewing, modifying, deleting, or destroying information contained in a database. Database security is of primary concern in a multiuser environment, although you may want to use Access' security features to prevent others from viewing or modifying databases stored on your single-user computer. This section describes the multilayered security features of networked Access databases and how you use these features to ensure a secure database system.

Specifying the Principles of Database Security on a LAN

Ten basic principles of database security exist for databases installed on a LAN. Five of these principles are associated with the network operating system:

- Each user of a network must be positively identified before the user can gain access to the network. Identification requires a unique user name and secret password for each user. Users must not share their passwords with one another, and all passwords used should be changed every 60 to 90 days.

- Each identified user of the network must be authorized to have access to specific elements of the network, such as server directories, printers, and other shared resources. Each user has a network account that incorporates the user's identification data and authorizations. The network file that contains this information is always encrypted and is accessible only by the network administrator(s).

- Actions of network users should be monitored to determine whether users are attempting to access elements of the network for which they don't have authorization. Users that repeatedly attempt to breach network security should be locked out of the network until appropriate administrative action can be taken.

- The network should be tamper-proof. Tamper-proofing includes installing security systems immune to *hacking* by ingenious programmers and testing routinely for the presence of viruses.

- Data stored on network servers must be protected against hardware failure and catastrophic destruction (fires, earthquakes, hurricanes, and so on) by adequate and timely backup. Backup systems enable you to reconstruct the data to its state at the time the last backup occurred.

The measures required to establish the first five principles are the responsibility of the network administrator for a server-based system. In a peer-to-peer network, network security measures are the responsibility of each person that shares his or her resources with others. The remaining five principles of database security are determined by the security capabilities of the database management system and the applications you create with it:

- The contents of tables in a database should be encrypted to prevent viewing the data with a file-reading or other *snooping* utility.

- Users must be further identified before they are allowed to open a database file. A secret password, different from a user's network access password, should be used. The database file that contains user identification and password data (database user accounts) must be encrypted. The encryption technique used should be sophisticated enough to prevent hackers from deciphering it. Only the database administrator(s) have access to this file.

- Users must be assigned specific permission to use the database and the tables it contains. If users are to be restricted from viewing specific columns of a table, access to the table should be in the form of a query that includes only the fields that the user is authorized to view. The database management system must provide for revoking specific permissions as the need arises.

■ The data in tables should be auditable. Lack of auditability is an incentive to computer-based embezzling. Updates made by users to tables that contain financial data should be maintained in a log, preferably in another database, that identifies the user who made the entry and the date and time the update was made. Logs are useful in reconstructing database entries that occurred between the time the database was last backed up and the time data was restored from the backup copy.

■ Operations that update records in more than one table should be accomplished by transaction techniques that can be reversed (rolled back) if updates to all the tables involved cannot be completed immediately.

Most network operating systems in use on PCs provide for the first five database security principles, but enforcement of password secrecy, monitoring of user transgressions, and virus surveillance often are ignored, especially in peer-to-peer networks. Access provides all five of the database security principles, but you must take specific actions to invoke and maintain these principles.

> **Note**
>
> One of the most frequent breaches of database security occurs when a temporary worker is hired to stand in for a user who is ill or on vacation. Instead of establishing a new network account, including a user name, password, and new user (or guest) account for the database, the employee's user names and passwords are divulged to the temporary worker for the sake of expediency. A temporary worker should be assigned his or her own identification for the network and database; the temporary worker's authorizations should be removed when the regular employee returns to the job.

Password-Protecting a Single Database

 Access 95 adds password protection for individual database files. Setting a database password is the easiest way to partially secure a database while allowing others who don't know the password to use the copy of Access on your PC. To activate the database password for a specific .mdb file, complete the following steps:

1. You cannot set a database password in shared access mode, so close the open database, and then choose File, Open Database to display the Open dialog. Select your .mdb file, mark the Exclusive check box, and click Open to open the database in exclusive access mode.

2. Choose Tools, Security, Set Database Password to display the Set Database Password dialog shown in figure 25.22.

3. Type a password in the Password text box. Your entry is shown as a series of asterisks to prevent disclosing your password to others as you enter it. Passwords are case-sensitive, so *Uxmal* is a different password from *uxmal*.

Fig. 25.22 The Set Database Password dialog used to establish a password required to open a specific database.

4. Type the password in the Verify text box to test your entry. The verification test is not case-sensitive. Click OK.

5. Close the database, and then re-open it. The Password Required dialog shown in figure 25.23 appears.

Fig. 25.23 The dialog that appears when you try to open a password-protected database.

6. Enter the password exactly as you typed it in step 3. Press Enter or click OK. If you enter the password correctly, Access continues the startup procedure. If you type an incorrect password, Access displays an error message and won't open the database.

To remove a password protection from a database, open the database for exclusive access, and then choose Tools, Security, Unset Database Password. Type the password in the Password text box of the Unset Database Password dialog, and then click OK.

Managing Groups and Users

Most client/server databases establish the following three groups of database users:

- *Administrators* (Admins) have the authority to view and update existing tables and add or delete tables and other database objects from the database. Members of the Admins group usually have permission to modify the applications contained in databases.

- *Regular members of workgroups* (Users) are assigned permission to open the database and are granted permission to view and modify databases on a selective basis. Users ordinarily aren't granted permission to modify Access applications.

- *Occasional users of databases* (Guests) are granted limited rights to use a database and the objects it contains but aren't assigned a user account. Guest privileges often are assigned to persons being trained in the use of a database application. Access 95 does not define a Guests group.

When you install Access, you automatically are made a member of the Admins group with the name Admin and have all permissions granted. You have an empty password and Personal ID Number (PIN), which means that you don't need to enter a password to

VI

Advanced Techniques

log on to the database(s) associated with the System.mda database installed in the ...\Access folder. When you are learning Access, you have little reason to establish database security. After you begin to create a useful database application, you should implement basic security provisions on your own computer.

Establishing Your Own Admins Name, Password, and PIN. Access has two levels of security: *application* level and *file* level. The application-level security system requires each user of Access to enter a user name and a password to start Access. Establishing single-user application-level security and preparing for multiuser security requires that you perform the following tasks:

- Activate the logon procedure for Access. This action requires that you add a password for the Admin user. To remain Admin, you need not complete the remaining steps, but the only security is your password.

- Create a new account for yourself as a member of the Admins group.

- Log on to Access using your new Admins user account.

- Delete the default Admin user account from the Admins group. The Admins group should include entries for active database administrators only. You cannot delete the Admin user from the Users group.

Before you begin the following procedure, make a disk backup copy of the System.mda file in use and any database files that you created or modified while using this System.mda. If you forget the user name or password you assigned to yourself after deleting the Admin user, you cannot log on to Access. In this case, you must restore the original version of the System.mda file. Then you may not be able to open the database files with which the original version of the System.mda file is associated unless you restore the backed-up versions. It is recommended that you modify the System.mdw file you created in the \Shared\Nwind folder as your system database for all of the examples that follow in this chapter.

> **Caution**
>
> Do not use the Northwind.mdb database in your ...\Access\Samples folder for the examples that follow. You should preserve Northwind.mdb and the System.mdw file of your \MSOffice\ Access folder in the original state. Use the Nwind.mdb file created earlier in this chapter with the Database Splitter and use the System.mdw workgroup file located in the \Shared\Nwind directory.

To activate the logon procedure for Access, complete the following steps:

1. A temporary password to the Admin user is necessary to activate Access's logon procedure. Choose Tools, Security, User and Group Accounts to open the User and Group Accounts dialog (see fig. 25.24). You are logged on as Admin, a member of the Admins and Users group, by default.

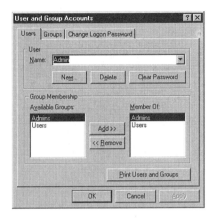

Fig. 25.24   The default opening page, Users, of the User and Group Accounts dialog.

   2. Click the Change Logon Password tab to display the Change Logon Password dialog page in figure 25.25.

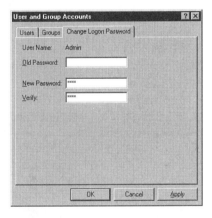

Fig. 25.25   The Change Logon Password page used to establish your new Admin password.

> **Note**
>
> If you don't change the Admin user's password, you automatically are logged on as Admin with a blank password each time you start Access.

   3. Press the Tab key to bypass the Old Password text box (this enters the equivalent of an empty password), and enter a temporary password, such as **Temp**, in the New Password text box. Your entry is shown as a series of asterisks to prevent disclosing your password to others as you enter it. Passwords are case-sensitive, so *Temp* is a different password from *temp*.

   4. Type the password in the Verify text box to test your entry. The verification test is not case-sensitive. Click OK to close the dialog.

5. Exit Access and launch it again. The Logon dialog shown in figure 25.26 appears.

Fig. 25.26 The Logon dialog that appears when you start Access with a user name and password.

6. Type **admin** in the Name text box, press Tab, and enter the password exactly as you typed it in step 3.

7. Clear the Save This Password In Your Password List check box. Press Enter or click OK. If you enter the password correctly, Access continues the startup procedure.

To add your new user account in the Admins group, perform the following steps:

1. Choose Tools, Security, User and Group Accounts to display the User and Group Accounts dialog shown in figure 25.24. All members of the Admins group automatically are included (and must be included) in the Users group. Both Admins and Users appear in the Member Of list.

2. Click the New button to add your new account. The New User/Group dialog appears (see fig. 25.27).

3. Type the name you want to use to identify yourself to Access in the Name text box and enter a four-digit PIN (personal identification number) in the Personal ID text box. The PIN, with the Name entry, uniquely identifies your account. This precaution is necessary because two people may use the same logon name; the Name and PIN values are combined to create a no-duplicates index on the Users table in your current system database file. Click OK to close the New User/Group dialog and return to the User and Group Accounts page.

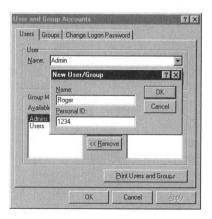

Fig. 25.27 The New User/Group dialog.

4. *This is a critical step.* Select Admins in the Available Groups dialog and click the Add button to add the Admins group to your new user name (see fig. 25.28). If you fail to do this, you cannot delete the Admin user. (Access requires that there be at least one member of the Admins group in each system database file.)

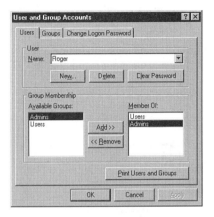

Fig. 25.28   Adding the Admins group to your new user account.

> **Tip**
>
> When you log on with your new user name, you can't see the names of the last four data-bases you opened as Admin when you choose File, Open. Prior database selections are specific to each user.

5. You don't enter a password for the new user at this time because you still are logged on to Access as Admin. Click the OK button to close the Users dialog and then exit Access.

6. Launch Access, type your new user name in the Logon dialog, clear the Save This Password in Your Password List checkbox, and press Enter or click OK. Do not enter a password because you have an empty password at this point. User names aren't case-sensitive; Access considers *NewAdmin* and *newadmin* to be the same user.

7. Choose Tools, Security, User and Group Accounts, select your new user name from the Name drop-down list, and click the Change Logon Password Tab. Press Tab to bypass the Old Password text box and type the password you plan to use until it is time to change your password (to maintain system security). Passwords can be up to 14 characters long and can contain any character, except ASCII character 0, the Null character. Verify your password, and then press Enter or click OK to close the Password dialog.

8. Close and reopen Access and log on with your new user name and password. This step verifies that your new Admins user name and password are valid. This time, you can allow the password to be saved in your password list.

VI

Advanced Techniques

9. Choose <u>T</u>ools, Securi<u>t</u>y, User and Group <u>A</u>ccounts. Open the Users list of the User and Group Accounts page and select your new user name from the list. Verify that you are a member of the Admins and Users group.

10. Open the Users list again and select the Admin user. Select Admins in the Member Of list; then click Remove. Admin remains a member of the Users group, as shown in figure 25.29. Click OK to close the dialog.

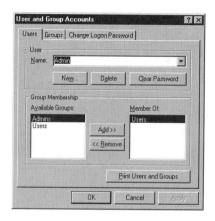

Fig. 25.29 Removing the Admin user from the Admins group.

You use the same procedure to add other users as members of the default Admins, Users, or Guests group or of new workgroups you create. You have not fully secured the open database because the Admin user still has full permissions for the objects in the database. Revoking the Admin user's permissions is discussed in the "Changing the Ownership of Database Objects" section later in the chapter.

> **Note**
>
> Write down and save your PIN and the PIN of every user you add to the workgroup for future reference. User names and PINs aren't secure elements, so you can safely keep a list without compromising system security. This list should be accessible only to database administrators. You need a user's PIN so that the user can be recognized as a member of another workgroup when the need arises. (See the "Granting Permissions for a Database in Another Workgroup" section near the end of this chapter.)

Establishing Members of Access Groups. Groups within Access's security system are not the same as workgroups. As discussed previously, a workgroup shares the same system database file that is located in a designated directory. The entries you made in the preceding steps were saved in the workgroup or system database file that was active when you launched Access. This section describes how to add new users to a group, a process similar to the one you used to add your new Admins account.

To add a new user to a group, you must be logged on to Access as a member of the Admins group and complete the following steps:

1. Choose Tools, Security, User and Group Accounts to open the User and Group Accounts dialog.

2. With the Users page active, click New. The New User/Group dialog appears. Type the new user's name and PIN. Click OK to create the account and close the dialog. The Users dialog reappears. Make a note of the PIN you used to add the new user. You need to know the user's PIN so that you can duplicate an entry for the new user in other workgroups.

3. The default group for all new users is Users. To add the user to the Admins group, select Admins in the Available Groups list and click the Add button to add Admins to the Member Of list (refer to fig. 25.24). All users must be members of the Users group, except for members of the Guests group. To change the group membership of a current user to the Guests group, delete the user's account and then add the user with only Guests appearing in the Member Of list. Use the Remove button to delete the User group assignment. Click OK to return to Access's main window when your selections are complete.

4. Request the new user to log on to Access with the user name and change his or her password from the default empty value to a legitimate password.

   You can improve the level of security by typing the new user's password yourself, so that users cannot bypass the password step by leaving their passwords blank. To enter a password for a new user, close Access, log on as the new user, and enter the user's chosen password in the Change Logon Password page.

Before you add a significant number of users, decide whether you need additional groups and determine the permissions that should be assigned to each group other than Admins. These aspects of database security are discussed in the following sections.

> **Note**
>
> When requesting new users to enter their first password, emphasize the advantage of the use of longer passwords that combine upper- and lowercase characters and numbers because they improve system security. Users should not use their initials, names of spouses or children, birth dates, or nicknames; these are the entries that unauthorized users try first to gain access to the system.

Adding a New Group. In most cases, Admins and Users are the only groups necessary for each workgroup you create. Members of a group usually share the same permissions to use database objects (which is the subject of the next section). Adding a new Access group is not necessary, therefore, unless you have a category of users who are to have a different set of permissions than members of the Users or Guests groups. Such a category may distinguish Users (who may be limited to viewing data) from members of Data Entry who have permission to update the data in tables.

To add a new group, perform the following steps:

1. Choose <u>T</u>ools, Security, User and Group <u>A</u>ccounts. Then click the Groups tab. The Groups page shown in figure 25.30 appears.

Fig. 25.30   The Groups page for adding a new user group to a database.

2. Click the New button to open the New User/Group dialog.

3. Type the name of the group in the Name dialog and a four-digit Personal ID Number, as shown in figure 25.31. Group names can be up to 20 characters long and can contain spaces, but punctuation symbols aren't allowed. You don't need to make a note of the PIN in the case of groups because the PIN is used only for indexing purposes.

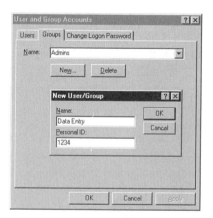

Fig. 25.31   Adding a new Data Entry group to the workgroup.

4. Press Enter or click OK. The Groups dialog reappears.

5. Click OK from the Groups dialog. You can delete the newly added group by clicking the Delete button now.

After you add a new group, you need to assign the default permissions that apply to all members of the group by the procedure outlined in the "Granting and Revoking Permissions for Database Objects" section that follows.

Deleting Users and Groups. Members of the Admins group have the authority to delete users from any group and to delete any group except Admins, Users, and Guests. To delete a user or group, choose Tools, Security, User and Group Accounts, select the user or group to delete from the list box, and click Delete. You are asked to confirm the deletion. Admins, Users, and Guests groups must each contain one user account; you cannot delete all users for any of these groups.

Clearing Forgotten Passwords. If a user forgets his or her password and you are logged in to Access as a member of the Admins group, you can delete the user's password, so that you or the user can enter a new password.

To clear a user's password, complete the following steps:

1. Choose Tools, Security, User and Group Accounts. Make sure the Users tab is active.

2. Open the Name list and select the user whose password you want to clear.

3. Click the Clear Password button (refer to preceding fig. 25.29).

4. Make sure that the user whose password you cleared enters a new password, or log on to Access as the new user and enter a new password for the user.

As mentioned previously, entering the user's password as the database administrator is the only means of ensuring that the database security is enforced. There is no other means of ensuring that users assign themselves passwords. (Of course, perverse users can change their passwords to empty strings if they choose to do so.)

Understanding Database Object Ownership

The user who creates an object becomes the *owner* of the object. (Access calls the owner of an object the object's *creator*.) Object owners have special status within the Access security system. The following two sections briefly describe owners' permissions and how to change the ownership of database objects. A more detailed description of object ownership is contained in the file SECURE.ZIP, written for Access 2.0, that you can download from the MSACCESS Forum of CompuServe.

Owner Permissions for Objects

The owner of an object has full (Administer) permissions for the object. No other user, including members of the Admins group, can alter the object owner's permissions for the object. For example, the Admin user is the owner of all the database objects in Northwind.mdb. Thus, anyone who uses the Admin user account has full permissions for all objects in Northwind.mdb.

When a user other than the object's creator adds a new object to the database or to one of the existing objects in the database, this user becomes the owner of the object. For

VI

Advanced Techniques

example, if user Margaret adds a control object to a form created by Larry, Margaret is the owner of the control object, not Larry. Mixed ownership of objects can lead to bizarre situations, such as the inability of the owner of a query to execute the query because the owner of the underlying tables has changed. (You can overcome this problem, however, by adding the WITH OWNERACCESS OPTION to the SQL statement for the query.)

When you create new database objects using the default Admin user ID, anyone else who has a retail copy of Access 95 and uses the default Admin user ID also has full permissions for these objects. Thus, when you begin development of an application that you intend to share with others or that you want to prevent others from using or modifying, create a new account in the Admins group as described earlier in the chapter. Use your new Admins account when you create new applications.

Changing the Ownership of Database Objects

Following are the three methods of changing the ownership of existing Access database objects:

- Create a new database file, and then choose File, Get External Data, Import. Open the .mdb file containing the objects, and import all of the objects into the new .mdb file. The user who creates the new .mdb file becomes the owner of the imported objects.

- Use the Change Owner page of the User and Group Permissions dialog.

- Use the Security Wizard to create a new secure database file, import the objects, and then encrypt the new database.

The following two sections describe the second and third methods for changing database object ownership.

 Using Access 95's New Change Owner Feature. To use the new Change Owner feature of Access 95, you must be a member of the Admins group for the database, and must follow these steps:

1. Open the database containing the objects whose ownership you want to change.

2. Choose Tools, Security, User and Group Permissions to open the User and Group Permissions dialog, and then click the Change Owner tab.

3. Choose the class of object you want to change in the Object Type drop-down list.

4. If you want to change the ownership of all of the objects of the selected class, select the first item in the Object list, move to the bottom of the list, press the Shift key, and click the last item of the list.

5. Select the new owner's name from the New Owner drop-down list.

6. Click the Change Owner button to change the ownership of the selected items, from Admin to Roger in this example (see fig. 25.32).

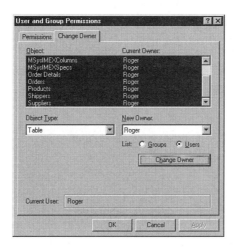

Fig. 25.32 Changing the ownership of all Table objects from Admin to a new owner.

7. Repeat steps 3 through 6 for each class of objects whose ownership you want to change.

The preceding process is the fastest way to remove permissions of the Admin user accrued from ownership of the original objects.

Using the New Security Wizard. You can change the ownership of all the objects in a database for which you have Administer permissions by importing all the database objects into a new database you create with a user ID other than Admin. Access 2.0 made it easy to import all the database objects from one .MDB file into another .MDB file with its Import Database add-in. Access 95's new Security Wizard goes the Import Database add-in one better by letting you choose the database objects to secure and encrypting the new secure copy of the database in a single (long) step. The Security Wizard automatically imports every object in the source database into the new encrypted destination database.

> **Caution**
>
> Do not use the Security Wizard with the Northwind.mdb database in your ...\Access\Samples directory. Use the NwindData.mdb file created earlier in this chapter with the Database Splitter, and use the System.mdw file in your \Shared\Nwind directory. The Security Wizard takes a long time to perform its operations, so using the smaller NwindData.mdb file is recommended.

To test the Security Wizard, follow these steps:

1. If you aren't logged on to Access, launch Access and log on with your new user ID that includes Admins group membership and open the database to secure.

2. Choose Tools, Security, User-Level Security Wizard to display the Security Wizard's opening dialog.

3. Clear the checkbox that corresponds to the class of database objects that you don't want to make secure. If you want to secure all database objects, accept the Wizard's default (see fig. 25.33).

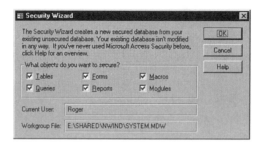

Fig. 25.33 Setting the types of objects to secure in the new database.

4. Click the OK button to open the Destination Database dialog. Select the folder in which to store the new secure database file and give the file a new name. The default is Secure *database*.mdb (see fig. 25.34).

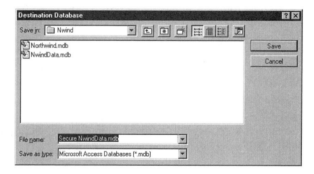

Fig. 25.34 Specifying the path and file name for the new secure database file.

5. Click the Save button to put the Security Wizard to work. After a few minutes, the message shown in figure 25.35 appears, indicating successful creation of the new secure database. Click OK to close the dialog.

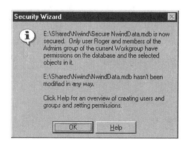

Fig. 25.35 The message indicating successful completion of the Security Wizard's task.

The owner of all the objects in the new database is the user ID you used when you opened the source database.

> **Note**
>
> This chapter uses the term *user ID* to identify users of Access. Internally, Access uses a *system ID* (SID) to identify users. The SID is a value that Access computes from the user ID, password, and PIN. The SID is stored in the MSysUsers table of System.mda as an encrypted binary value in a field of the Binary (varbinary) data type.

Granting and Revoking Permissions for Database Objects

The second layer of Access security is at the database level. Access lets the database administrator grant or revoke *permissions* to use specific database objects to all members of a group or to specific members of a group. Permissions grant authority for users to view or alter specific database objects. The permissions granted to the group are inherited by each member as he or she is added to the group. Thus it is important that you establish the group permissions you want *before* adding users to a group. Users who are members of more than one group, such as Admins and Users, inherit database object permissions from each group. You can grant additional permissions to individual members of a group, but you cannot revoke permissions that individual members inherit from the group. Permissions are stored within the database file as properties of individual database objects. Only members of the Admins group or users who have Administer permission can grant or revoke permissions for database objects.

> **Caution**
>
> If you use the split-database design, you do not need to add groups and users to the data .mdb. Permissions for use of the linked data .mdb file are managed by the permissions for links to the tables in your application .mdb file. However, it is important that you change the ownership of Table objects in the data .mdb file from the Admin account to your secure account in Admins. If you do not change ownership, any user of retail Access who uses the default Admin account can open the data .mdb file and make changes at will to the file.

Table 25.2 lists the permissions offered by Access for database objects, ranked in descending level of authority. Full Permissions allow the user to use all the features of Access, including design functions. The description of the specific action allowed by a permission is listed in the Explicit Permissions column. Permissions at an authority level below Full Permissions require other permissions to operate; these required permissions are called *implicit permissions*.

Table 25.2   Permissions to Use Access Database Objects

Permission	Database Objects	Explicit Permissions	Implicit Permissions
Open/Run	Forms, reports, macros	Use or run objects	Read Data
Read Design	All	View objects	Execute for macros only
Modify Design	All	Alter, replace, or delete objects	Update Data and Execute
Administer	All database objects	All permissions	Not applicable
Read Data	Tables, queries, forms	View data in objects	Read Design
Update Data	Tables, queries, forms	Edit table data	Read Data
Insert Data	Tables, queries, forms	Append data in tables	Read Data
Delete Data	Tables, queries, forms	Delete data in tables	Read Data

If, for example, you allow a user to modify design, this user also must be able to modify data and execute objects. Therefore, Update Data and Open/Run permissions are implied by the Modify Design permission. This user, and any other users allowed to modify data, must be able to read data. All users having permission to read data must be able to read designs. When you establish permissions for a database object, Access adds the implicit permissions automatically.

The Admins and Users groups have full permissions for any new database objects you create. If you intend to share the database with other users, you probably don't want all members of the Users group to have permission to update database tables. A more conservative set of permissions for the two groups follows:

- The Admins group has full permissions for all objects. Admins privileges should be assigned to as few individuals as possible. Make sure you have enough backup database administrators with Admins privileges to cover for the absence of the primary administrator. Members of the Admins group also must be members of the Users group.

- The Users group has Open/Run and Read Data permissions. Update, Insert, and Delete Data permissions are granted for specific forms and reports. Users ordinarily aren't granted Modify Design permission in databases.

You can add new groups with specific group permissions, such as Data Entry or Developers, to make assigning individual user permissions for database objects simpler.

> **Note**
>
> You can use the Run with Owner's Permissions checkbox or add the WITH OWNERACCESS OPTION to SQL statements to enable users without the required permissions to execute a query.

Altering Group Permissions

After you design your hierarchy of permissions and add any new user groups you need, you are ready to assign group permissions for each of the objects in your database. Only members of the Admins group can alter permissions for Groups or Users. The Permissions check boxes that are enabled depend on the type of object you choose. Open/Run, for example, is enabled only for database, form, report, and macro objects.

> **Note**
>
> When you first select the Admins group, none of the Admins group's permission check boxes are marked. Members of the Admins group inherit full object permissions from membership in the Users group. (By default, Users have full permissions for all objects.) If you revoke object permissions for the Users group, you add Administer permissions for the Admins group.

To change the permissions for a group, complete the following steps:

1. Open the database for which group permissions are to be granted or revoked with the appropriate workgroup system database active.

2. Choose Tools, Security, User and Group Permissions. The User and Group Permissions dialog appears.

3. Click the Groups option button to display the permissions for groups of users; then select Users in the User/Group Name list.

4. Open the Object Type drop-down list and select the type of database object whose permissions you want to change.

5. Select the specific object to which the new permissions will apply in the Object Name list. To select all objects, click the first item in the list, press the Shift key, and then click the last item in the list. Do not include <New *ObjectType*> in your multiple selection.

6. In the User/Group Names list, select the Group whose permissions you want to revise, Users for this example. Figure 25.36 shows the full permissions for Table objects that Access assigns by default to the Users group.

7. Permissions currently granted to the group are shown by a check mark in the Permissions check boxes. Click the Modify Design, Update Data, Insert Data, and Delete Data check boxes to allow the users groups only to display forms and read table data. If you have made multiple selections, you may need to click the check

box twice to make a selection effective. When you remove a permission, Access automatically removes the Administer permission. Your Permissions dialog appears as shown in figure 25.37.

Fig. 25.36 The default permissions for the Users group.

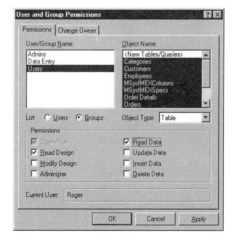

Fig. 25.37 Revising permissions for all Table objects for the Users group.

8. Click the Apply button to make the new permissions effective for the selected database object(s).

9. With the object(s) selected in step 5, select the Admins group, mark the Administer check box, and click the Apply button. This step assures that the Admin users continue to have full permissions for the objects (see fig. 25.38).

Fig. 25.38 Granting Administer permissions for all Table objects to the Admins group.

10. Repeat steps 4 through 9 for each database object and object type whose User group permissions you want to change.

> **Note**
>
> When you create macro objects that contain several individual named macros (to minimize the number of objects in the database), make sure that each macro object contains named macros that correspond to a specific category of permissions. Named macros, for example, that invoke action queries to modify tables or add new records should be grouped in one macro object, and named macros that only display the contents of database objects should be located in a different macro object. When you assign permissions to execute macro objects, you need to assign Modify Data permission to those users who can execute macro objects that run action queries.

Granting Additional Permissions to Specific Users

The process of granting additional permissions to a specific user is similar to the process used to alter group permissions. Permissions inherited by the user from the group to which the user is assigned are not shown in the Permissions dialog. To grant additional permissions to a specific user, complete the following steps:

1. Choose Tools, Security, User and Group Permissions. The Users option is the default for the User and Group Permissions dialog.

2. Select the user to whom additional permissions are to be granted in the User/Group Name list (see fig. 25.39).

TestUser is a member of the Users group whose account was added after the changes to User group permissions were made in the preceding section. As mentioned in the introduction to this section, the Read Design and Read Data permissions that were inherited by TestUser from the modified permissions of the Users group aren't shown in the Permissions check boxes.

Fig. 25.39   The Permissions dialog for a new user with inherited permissions.

   3. To assign permissions to a specific user so that the user can update data for an object, select the object using the Object Type and Object Name lists, and then click the Update Data, Insert Data, and Delete Data check boxes. Access automatically marks the implicit permissions, Read Design and Read Data, associated with the explicit permission, Update Data (see fig. 25.40). Click the Apply button after selecting each object whose permissions you want to change.

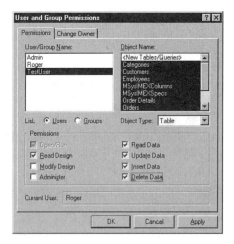

Fig. 25.40   The Permissions dialog for a new user with the new data permissions added.

   Implicit permissions for individual users are displayed in the Permissions check boxes regardless of whether the implicit permissions also were inherited from group membership.

   4. Repeat step 3 for each user who requires permissions for an object that aren't inherited from the user's group permissions. Click the OK button when you complete the permission changes for all users who require such changes.

> **Note**
>
> You can use the /Ro command line option, described in the preceding section, "Using Command Line Options to Open a Shared Database," to revoke Update Data, Insert Data, and Delete Data permissions for the database on specific workstations. This method isn't secure because the user can edit the command line option, remove the /Ro entry, and log on again with read-write privileges. If you use this method, Access displays a message box indicating that the database is being opened in read-only mode and that the user cannot modify data.

Granting Permissions for a Database in Another Workgroup

If your application requires that you attach a table in a secure database used by a different workgroup, the user needs to be a member of a group in the other workgroup and needs to be assigned appropriate permissions for the attached table. At this point, you need the list of PINs for users, mentioned in the "Establishing Your Own Admins Name, Password, and PIN" section earlier in this chapter.

To grant permission for a user to modify data in a table attached from another workgroup's database, perform the following steps:

1. Close Access; you need to relaunch Access when you select another workgroup.

2. Launch the Workgroup Administrator application and specify the path to the workgroup database file of the workgroup that uses the database that contains the table to be attached.

3. Launch Access and open the database that contains the table to be attached.

4. Add an account for the user to the Users group with exactly the same user name and PIN as was used to add the user account to his or her workgroup.

5. If you don't want this user to join the other workgroup, enter a password and don't disclose the password to the user.

6. Open the Permissions dialog, select the table object to be attached, and assign the appropriate data permission for the table to the user.

You need to use the same PIN for the user in both workgroups because the account for the user is created from the user name and PIN, and the accounts must be identical in both databases. You also must use the same PIN number to reinstate the user's account if the workgroup system file becomes corrupted; you don't have a current backup, and Access cannot repair it.

Sharing Databases on the Network

Once you've set up your user groups and modified the database object permissions for the groups as necessary, you can safely share the workgroup system database and your data .mdb file, and then distribute copies of your application .mdb file to the users. Before sharing the files, make sure to create a backup copy of each of the shared files and store the copies in a safe location. The following sections describe how to share files.

VI

Advanced Techniques

Sharing Database Files on a Windows 95 Network

With a peer-to-peer Windows 95 network, you need only set up a network share of the folder in which you developed the application, \Shared\Nwind for the example of this chapter. To share a folder on your computer, follow these steps:

1. Launch Explorer and select the folder to be shared, \Shared\Nwind for this example.

2. Choose File, Properties and click the tab of the Sharing properties page.

3. Click the Shared As option button. The name of the folder appears as the default sharename, NWIND in this example. Share names are limited to 12 characters and must not contain names, puctuation, or other special characters.

4. To update data, users must have read-write access to the shared folder (often simply called a *share*). Click the Full option button in the Access Type frame.

5. For additional security, you can require users of your application to enter a password to gain access to the share. Type the password in the Full Access Password text box, as shown in figure 25.41, and then click the OK button to create the share.

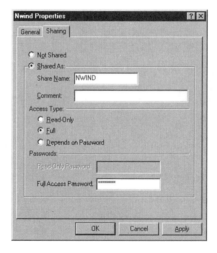

Fig. 25.41   Creating a shared subfolder for a peer-to-peer Windows 95 network server.

6. Enter the password in the Full Access Password dialog, and click the OK button to confirm the password.

In the example presented in this chapter, both Northwind.mdb (the application database) and NWData.mdb (the data .mdb file) are shared for read-write access, allowing users to launch Northwind.mdb from the server if they choose. Users should copy Northwind.mdb from the server share to their local computer and run the local copy to minimize network traffic.

Sharing Database Files from a Network Server

The specific method of creating a server share on a dedicated network server depends on the network operating system (NOS) in use. Ordinarily, the network administrator will create the server share for you, and you need only move the files to be shared from your local folder to the shared server directory. If your NOS supports permissions for individual files, request read-write access to your workgroup database and data .mdb files. If you want users to be able to run the application .mdb from the server, grant read-write access; otherwise, grant copy-only access so users can copy the application .mdb file to their local computer. Make sure, however, that you (the share owner) have *full network permissions* for all of the shared files. Do not grant users any other permissions for the shared files.

Accessing the Shared Files

Users access the server share by mapping the server share to a drive letter or by using Uniform Naming Convention (UNC). Using UNC eliminates the problem with users assigning different logical drive letters to server shares when mapping the share to their computer. Unlike Access 2.0, Access 95 supports UNC, as well as long file names (LFNs).

The network share you create, whether from your computer or from a network server, appears in the Network Neighborhood window for the selected server. In this example, Oakleaf0 is a Windows NT 3.51 Server and Oakleaf1 is the workstation used to write this edition. The \Shared\Nwind directory of Oakleaf0 is shared as "NWIND," but appears as "nwind" in the list of shares available from Oakleaf0 (see fig. 25.42). Double-clicking the nwind share displays icons for the shared files. (Use of the term *directory*, rather than *folder*, is more common when referring to file servers.)

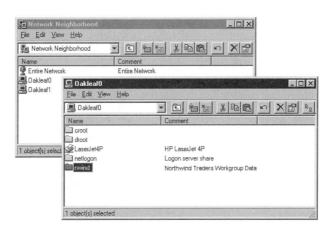

Fig. 25.42   The \Shared\Nwind directory shared as NWIND on the Oakleaf0 server appears in Network Neighborhood as nwind.

Attaching the Shared Workgroup System File. Users of your application ordinarily use Workgroup Administrator to join the workgroup using the shared workgroup database file. You copy the shared data .mdb file and the System.mdw file to the server's

shared directory. To access files using UNC, you type ***ServerName\ShareName**
***FileName.ext**. If you're sharing files from your computer, *ServerName* is the name you
assigned to your computer when you installed Windows 95. Figure 25.43 shows how to
specify a workgroup database file using UNC. (Do not use a logical drive letter mapped
from a share to specify the location of System.mdw. Users are likely to map shares to
different logical drive letters.)

Fig. 25.43 Specifying the workgroup to join using the Uniform Naming Convention (UNC).

Troubleshooting

*After changing the location of the workgroup database file, Access opens with a
"'d:\path\filename.mdw' isn't a valid path" message, and then Access closes.*

Either the drive letter, path, or file name entry isn't valid, or you cannot connect to the server share
specified by the UNC name, or, if mapped to a drive letter n:[\path]. Use Explorer or Network
Neighborhood to verify that your entry is correct and that your network connection to the server is
working. Choose Explorer's View, Refresh command to verify that the server connection currently
is valid.

Refreshing the Links to the Shared Data File. Prior to distributing your application
.mdb file, you must change the links to point to the shared data .mdb file. This step is
especially important if you have revoked the design mode permissions for the Users
group because the revocation prevents members of the Users group from refreshing the
links. To refresh the links to point to the shared data .mdb file, follow these steps:

1. As a member of the Admins group, open the application .mdb file and choose
   Tools, Add-Ins, Linked Table Manager.

   If you share the files from your computer with the Windows 95 network, you must
   perform this step on another networked computer because your share does not
   appear in Network Neighborhood and you do not have access to files on your computer through UNC file names. In this case, open the shared application .mdb to
   refresh the links.

2. Click the Select All button, and then mark the Always Prompt for New Location
   checkbox. (If you don't mark this checkbox and the existing links are valid, you
   won't be able to refresh the links.) The Linked Table Manager's dialog appears as
   shown in figure 25.44, assuming you performed the database splitting and Security
   Wizard exercises earlier in this chapter.

3. Click the OK button to open the Select New Location of Categories dialog.

Fig. 25.44 Preparing to move table links to a shared data .mdb file with the Linked Table Manager.

4. Open the Look In list and select Network Neighborhood, and then select the server and share to display the files in the share (see fig. 25.45). Select the data .mdb file and click the Open button.

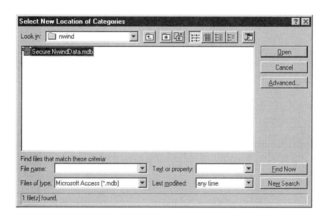

Fig. 25.45 Selecting the shared data .mdb file in the \Network Neighborhood*ServerName**ShareName* folder.

5. The Linked File Manager automatically refreshes links for all of the linked tables it finds in the selected data .mdb file. On completion of the refresh process, a message confirms that all linkages were refreshed and the Linked File Manager's dialog appears as shown in figure 25.46. Click the OK button to close both the message box and the dialog.

VI

Advanced Techniques

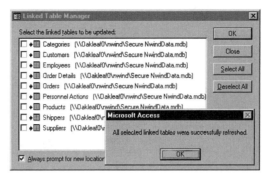

Fig. 25.46   The Linked File Manager confirms the links to the data .mdb on the file server.

Once you refresh the links with the UNC location of the shared data .mdb file, you can distribute the application .mdb file to users.

Administering Databases and Applications

Administering a multiuser database involves a number of duties besides adding and maintaining user accounts. The most important function of the database administrator is to ensure that periodic valid backup copies are made of database and system files. The database administrator's other responsibilities consist of routine database maintenance, periodic compacting of database files, and repairing databases.

Backing Up and Restoring Databases

The following maxims relate to maintaining backup copies of database files:

■ The time interval between successive backups of databases is equal to the amount of data you are willing and able to reenter in the event of a fixed disk failure. Except in unusual circumstances, such as little or no update activity, daily backup is the rule.

■ Rotate backup copies. Make successive backups on different tapes or disk sets. One of the tapes or disks may have defects that could prevent you from restoring the backup. The backup device, such as a tape drive, can fail without warning you that the recorded data isn't valid.

■ Test backup copies of databases periodically. You should test one different copy in the backup rotation sequence for restorability. If you rotate five daily backup tapes, for example, you should randomly choose one of the tapes, restore the database file from the tape, and open it with Access to ensure its validity every fifth day. Access tests each database object for integrity when you open the database file.

■ Maintain off-site backups that you can use to restore data in case of a disaster, such as a fire or flood. The copy of the backup tape or disk that you test for restorability is a good candidate for an off-site backup copy.

You can back up database files on a network server by copying them to a workstation that has a fixed disk, but this technique doesn't provide backup security. The user of the workstation can erase or damage the backup copy if you don't create the off-site copy required for security against disasters.

Backing up data on network and peer-to-peer servers usually is accomplished with a tape drive device. These devices usually include an application that backs up all data on a network server or selected files on peer-to-peer servers at intervals and times you select. The simpler the backup operation, the more likely you are to have current backups. Regardless of how automated the backup procedure is, however, you need to manually restore the test copy.

Compacting and Repairing Database Files

Compacting and repairing database files was discussed in Chapter 3, "Navigating within Access." You should compact database files in which applications add and delete data to recover the disk space occupied by the deleted data. The procedure for compacting a database is similar to that described for encrypting and decrypting databases, the subject of the next section, except that you choose Tools, Database Utilities, Compact Database rather than Tools, Security, Encrypt/Decrypt Database.

> **Note**
>
> You can improve the operating speed of Access if you periodically defragment database files. Windows 95's Disk Defragmenter utility tells you whether a disk drive has sufficient fragmentation to justify running the utility.

If you receive a message that a database is corrupted or if the database behaves in an irregular manner, one or more of the objects it contains may be corrupt as the result of a hardware error. Databases can become corrupt as the result of a power failure when the computer is writing to the database file. The Repair Database choice of Access's File menu attempts to repair the damage. If Access cannot repair the corruption, you must restore the latest backup copy. Test the backup copy with the existing System.mda or *Workgroup*.mdw file; in some cases, you may need to restore the prior .mda or .mdw file that contains the user account data for the database.

Encrypting and Decrypting Database Files

File-level security isn't complete until you encrypt the database. Encrypting the database prevents others from reading its contents with a text editing or disk utility application, such as is included with Symantec's Norton Utilities. Encryption of databases causes Access' operations on tables to slow perceptibly because of the time required to decrypt the data. Only members of the Admins group can encrypt or decrypt a database.

> **Note**
>
> If you are using a fixed disk data-compression utility, you will find that encrypting your database files reduces the percentage of compression to zero or a very small number. Encrypting files eliminates the groups of repeating characters that form the basis of most data-compression algorithms.

To encrypt or decrypt an Access database file, complete the following steps:

1. Make sure that the disk drive of the computer on which the database is stored has sufficient free space to create a copy of the database you intend to encrypt or decrypt. Access makes a new copy of the file during the process.

2. All other workstations, including your own, need to close the database file to be encrypted. You cannot encrypt or decrypt a database file that is in use on any workstation.

3. Choose Tools, Security, Encrypt/Decrypt Database. The Encrypt/Decrypt Database dialog appears.

4. Select the name of the database file to be encrypted and click OK.

5. If the file already is encrypted, it is decrypted, and vice-versa. The title bar of the dialog that opens indicates whether the file will be encrypted or decrypted in this operation. If you are interested only in whether the file has been encrypted, you can click Cancel now.

6. Type the name of the encrypted or decrypted file to create in the Encrypt *FileName* As dialog, and click OK. Normally, you type the same name as the original file; Access does not replace the original copy of the file if the process does not succeed.

Databases are compacted by Access when they are encrypted or decrypted.

> **Note**
>
> You do not need to encrypt files while you're developing applications using files that aren't shared with others unless the files contain sensitive information. After the files are made shareable, a good security practice is to encrypt them, even if they don't contain confidential data.

From Here...

Although this chapter was devoted primarily to using Access in a multiuser environment, many elements of database security discussed here apply to single-user applications. Even if you don't have a network now, if you use Access in an organization of more than ten employees, multiuser applications will likely be a part of your future. The following chapters contain related information:

- Chapter 3, "Navigating within Access," explains the processes of encrypting, converting, and compacting Access databases.

- Chapter 7, "Linking, Importing, and Exporting Tables," describes how you attach tables contained in shared Access databases to local application .mdbs.

- Chapter 26, "Connecting to Client/Server Databases," discusses the special techniques you use to attach tables of client/server RDBMSs using the new 32-bit ODBC drivers and the ODBC Administrator application.

VI

Advanced Techniques

Chapter 26

Connecting to Client/ Server Databases

One of the computer buzz words of the mid-1990s, *downsizing*, was mentioned in the context of local area networks (LANs) in the preceding chapter. Downsizing has another element: moving database management systems from mainframe computers to client/server RDBMSs running on PCs and RISC (reduced instruction set computing) workstation-servers. Another newly minted term, *rightsizing*, means choosing the best combination of computer platforms to ensure maximum availability of corporate data to those who need it. Rightsizing often involves retaining mainframe computers as giant database servers, but moving the applications that access and manipulate the data from the mainframe to PCs. The final member of the ...sizing trio is *upsizing*. Upsizing means moving tables from a desktop database, such as Access, dBASE, or Paradox, to a client/server RDBMS. You can continue to use the application components of your desktop database if the desktop database can link to the tables of the client/server RDBMS.

Regardless of the linguistic legitimacy of terms such as rightsizing, these words have become ingrained in today's computerese. Each of these expressions relates to the *scalability* of applications; scalable applications can run on a variety of platforms, communicate by industry-standard LAN protocols, and access data stored in a variety of different types of databases. 32-bit Access 95 presently runs under Windows 95 or Windows NT 3.5+, so Access itself is moderately scalable. Access 95 is a threaded application and Jet 3.0 is multithreaded; thus Access can take advantage of the symmetrical multiprocessing (SMP) capabilities of Windows NT running on workstations with multiple processors. Windows NT runs on Intel-based PCs and RISC systems, such as DEC Alpha servers and IBM PowerPC platforms, but you need a version of Access 95 that's compiled for the specific RISC processor in use. It remains to be seen if Microsoft intends to release versions of Access 95 for use with Windows NT running on RISC servers.

The 32-bit version of Microsoft Windows network operating system (NOS) included with Windows 95, Windows NT 3.51+, and Novell NetWare 3.1+/4.1+ offers common NOS protocols (NetBEUI and IPX/SPX), but also

In this chapter, you learn how to do the following

■ Understand the Open Database Connectivity API

■ Install the 32-bit Microsoft ODBC 2.5 driver for SQL Server

■ Add and remove ODBC data sources

■ Attach client/server tables to Access databases

■ Use Access's SQL pass-through queries

■ Export Access 95 tables to SQL Server

offers TCP/IP (Transport Control Protocol/Internet Protocol). TCP/IP rapidly is becoming the worldwide standard for heterogeneous networks—networks that connect servers and workstations using different hardware and operating systems. The scalability of Access applications therefore can be enhanced by a NOS that connects a multiuser Access application to the shared database files. For example, it is a relatively simple process to use TCP/IP to share database files located on a Network File System (NFS) server running under UNIX.

The third element of scalability, the capability to access data that resides in a variety of SQL-compliant databases, is provided by Microsoft's Open Database Connectivity (ODBC) products. Access 95 includes the 32-bit ODBC Administrator application and a 32-bit ODBC version 2.5 driver for Microsoft SQL Server. When this edition of *Special Edition Using Access* was written, there were about 100 suppliers of ODBC drivers, and the number of individual drivers numbered in the hundreds. ODBC provides Access with the capability to connect to virtually any popular mainframe-, minicomputer-, RISC-, and PC-resident SQL-compliant database through Microsoft and third-party 32-bit ODBC drivers. This chapter describes how ODBC works, and how you can connect to client/server databases with ODBC drivers.

> **Note**
>
> Access 95 requires 32-bit ODBC 2.5 drivers to connect to client/server RDBMSs. Existing 16-bit ODBC 2.0 drivers used with Access 2.0 and its predecessors do not work with Access 95. If you are upgrading from Access 2.0 (or an earlier version) and are using 16-bit ODBC drivers for RDBMSs other than Microsoft SQL Server, you need to obtain 32-bit versions of those ODBC drivers from the RDBMS publisher or a third party.

Defining the Client/Server Environment

Client/server databases are designed specifically for use on *application server*-based networks. An application server uses a network operating system, such as Windows NT Server, optimized specifically for running applications rather than for sharing files or peripheral devices. Client/server databases have many advantages over conventional database systems, including increased database security, incorporation of all components of the database (and sometimes all databases) in a single file, and faster access to data. The clients of a client/server database are workstations, often called *front-ends*, connected to the server, called the *back-end*. In these respects, the "split" Access databases, described in the preceding chapter, and client/server databases are similar. The principal difference between Access and a typical client/server database manager, such as Microsoft SQL Server, is that the client/server RDBMS itself performs many operations on the server that traditionally are done by database applications running on the client workstation.

Client/server database managers accept SQL statements from client applications. The client/server RDBMS interprets the SQL statement and executes the actions specified in the statement. If you send a SELECT query SQL statement to the server, the server returns only the result set to the client; processing of the query occurs on the server computer.

This action speeds query generation two ways: The amount of information traveling over the network is reduced, and server computers often have much more powerful and faster microprocessors than do the workstation clients.

To understand many of the examples in this chapter, you need to know how the computers that created the examples are set up. The following list describes the computers and the network used to create this chapter's examples of employing ODBC for connecting to client/server databases:

- The server (\\OAKLEAF0) is an 80486DX2-66 ISA clone with local bus video, 32M of RAM, and a 1.2G Maxtor SCSI-2 fixed disk drive (8 ms average access time). An Ultrastor 34F SCSI fixed disk controller on the local bus uses Corel SCSI to provide ASPI services when running under DOS 5.0. Dual-boot Windows 95/Windows NT 3.51 Server is installed on the 600M C drive (a FAT partition). The remaining 600M of the fixed drive is a D partition using NTFS (Windows NT's New Technology File System). The E drive is a Texel DM-3024 double-speed SCSI CD-ROM drive.

- Microsoft SQL Server 4.2 for Windows NT (Enterprise Edition, SQLSNT for short) and a late beta version of SQL Server 6.0 run as *processes* under Windows NT Server 3.51 (NTS) on the \\OAKLEAF0 server. (A Windows NT process is an application that starts automatically when you boot Windows NT, before the user logs on.) This combination, a subset of Microsoft BackOffice, was selected because it represents the highest price-performance value of any full-fledged client/server RDBMS/NOS available at the time this edition was written. SQLSNT is a multithreaded, symmetrical multiprocessing (SMP) server that achieves very high data throughput with 250 or more simultaneous users. The 16-bit versions of SQLSNT 4.2's SQL Administrator, SQL Object Manager, SQL Client Configuration Utility, and ISQL/w, the Windows version of the ISQL command line utility, are installed on each client.

- The client used to write this edition (\\OAKLEAF1) is an 80486DX4-100 PCI-bus clone with 16M of RAM, a 300M IDE fixed disk with a conventional FAT drive C partition, and a legacy drive F partition compressed with Stac Electronics' Stacker 3.0; a 300M IDE drive D devoted primarily to Windows 95; and a 1G IDE drive E for storing 32-bit applications and their document files. A Texel DM-3024 connected to the SCSI-2 port of a Sound Blaster 16 SCSI card is drive H (Stacker 3.0 occupies the drive G partition). Thus, *server shares* (logical drives attached from the server) begin as drive I. Figure 26.1 shows My Computer (renamed Oakleaf1 Workstation) displaying the drive assignments of \\OAKLEAF1. Drives I (croot) and J (droot) are mapped to the root directory of \\OAKLEAF0's C and D partitions, respectively. \\OAKLEAF1 runs Windows NT 3.51 Workstation, Windows 95, and DOS/Windows for Workgroups 3.11 in a triple-boot configuration.

- Another client (\\OAKLEAF2) is an 80386DX-33 ISA clone with a 300M disk running Windows 95. \\OAKLEAF2 is used primarily for composing and sequencing music. It is equipped with a variety of legacy (pre-Plug and Play) sound cards and MIDI synthesizer modules. The 80386 client is used for testing the performance of

Access applications on yesterday's average client workstation. 16-bit MIDI sequencing applications run fine under Windows 95 on \\OAKLEAF2, but running Access 95 applications on 80386DX-33 PCs with 8M of RAM is *not* recommended.

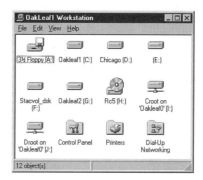

Fig. 26.1 The diskette, fixed disk, and CD-ROM drive assignments of the \\OAKLEAF1 workstation.

- A third client (\\OAKLEAF3) is a 90MHz Pentium PC with a PCI bus, 32M of RAM, and several 1G and larger fast SCSI-2 fixed disk drives. \\OAKLEAF3, which runs Windows 95 and Windows NT 3.51 Workstation, is used primarily for digital video capture and non-linear digital video editing.

- The server and the clients are equipped with Intel EtherExpress 16 network interface cards (NICs) connected via thin Ethernet coaxial cabling. Both NetBEUI (NetBIOS Extended User Interface, the native protocol for Windows for Workgroups and Windows NT networks) and TCP/IP network protocols are used. Remote Access Services (RAS), which allow dial-up (modem) connection to the Windows NT 3.51 Server, also are implemented.

If the preceding description appears to be written in Greek, don't despair; knowing the computer setup is only necessary to explain the entries in the text boxes of the dialogs illustrated in this chapter. Network systems of the complexity of the above configuration are common where a variety of operating systems, sometimes in both retail and beta versions, are used.

Defining Open Database Connectivity

Access uses the Microsoft Open Data Base Connectivity (ODBC) application programming interface (API) to provide access to any database system for which ODBC drivers are available. An API is a standardized method by which an application communicates with elements of the computer's operating system or environment. For example, applications use the Windows API in GDI32.EXE, a mostly 32-bit Windows 95 dynamic link library (DLL), to perform all display operations. The ODBC API enables a standard set of SQL statements in any application to be translated to commands recognized by the server database. The role of ODBC drivers is explained in the following section.

The ODBC API is the first element of Microsoft's Windows Open Services Architecture (WOSA) that is intended to be used to create a variety of classes of commercial Windows applications. (Version 2.5 is the third iteration of the ODBC API; 32-bit ODBC 3.0 is expected to be available in late 1996.) MAPI (Messaging API) and TAPI (Telephony API) also are members of WOSA, which includes industry-specific APIs such as WOSA/XRT for handling real-time stock market data. Today, WOSA includes a group of APIs that enable Windows applications to manipulate data residing in virtually any format on any type of computer located anywhere in the world. Enterprise-wide data sharing through local and wide area networks (LANs and WANs) employs large mainframe computers as centralized database servers that feed data to or through client/server RDBMSs. It is a recent trend in enterprise-scale computing to have PC clients connect to client/server RDBMSs, rather than to mainframe computers.

One of today's trends in enterprise-wide computing is the use of *distributed database systems*. Distributed database systems enable elements of a large database to be stored on servers in different locations that act as if they were a single large server. As advanced Windows operating systems—such as the next version of Windows NT (presently called Cairo)—are developed, and as additional members of WOSA become a commercial reality, PCs using Intel 80x86 architecture and RISC processors will capture a larger share of the server market. Access is designed to play an important role in enterprise-wide, distributed database systems: creating the applications that users need to view and update the myriad databases to which they can connect.

Understanding ODBC Drivers

The ODBC API consists of a driver manager and one or more ODBC drivers, as illustrated by the shaded boxes in figure 26.2. Windows uses drivers to adapt its standard API to specific combinations of hardware such as displays, keyboards, and printers. Likewise, the ODBC API uses drivers to translate instructions passed from the application through the driver manager to instructions compatible with various RDBMSs. When the ODBC driver manager receives instructions from Access intended for a data source, such as an SQL Server database, the driver manager opens the appropriate ODBC driver for the database. The relationship of the ODBC driver manager and ODBC drivers parallels the relationship of Access 95's built-in 32-bit Jet 3.0 database engine and the 32-bit ISAM drivers used to connect to Access, dBASE, FoxPro, and Paradox files.

ODBC drivers are classified as one of the following two types:

- *Single-tier drivers* translate SQL statements into low-level instructions that operate directly on files. Single-tier drivers are required for RDBMSs that don't process SQL statements directly. The widely used PC RDBMSs fall into this category. The 32-bit ISAM drivers included with Access for connecting to dBASE, FoxPro, and Paradox databases are single-tier drivers (but they aren't ODBC drivers). The Access, dBASE, FoxPro, Paradox, Excel, and Text Desktop Database drivers included with Microsoft Office 95 are 32-bit ODBC drivers.

■ *Multiple-tier drivers* process ODBC actions, but pass SQL statements directly to the data source using SQL syntax acceptable to the back-end RDBMS. All popular client/server RDBMSs that can run on PCs—and most mini- and mainframe RDBMSs—process SQL statements directly. The ODBC drivers shown in the list that follows are multiple-tier drivers because the client/server RDBMSs with which the drivers are used process SQL statements directly.

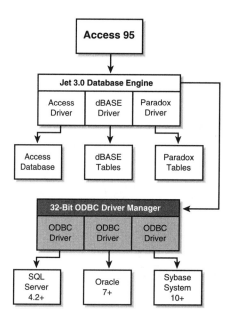

Fig. 26.2 A comparison of the ODBC and Jet driver systems used with Access.

One 32-bit ODBC driver is required for each type of client/server database whose tables you want to attach to an Access 95 database, but a single driver can be used to connect to several databases of the same type. Each connection to a database is called an *instance* of a driver. In addition to the ODBC driver, you may need additional files (usually license and/or communication files supplied by the RDBMS publisher) to connect to the back-end RDBMS. As an example, Microsoft supplies the required named pipes DLLs, 16-bit Dbnmp3.dll and 32-bit Dbnmpntw.dll, to connect to Microsoft SQL Server. *Named pipes* is the protocol through which you make connections to SQL Server. To connect to an Oracle database, you need a local copy of SQLNet.dll.

The ODBC API is based on a standard called the X/Open SQL Call Level Interface (CLI) developed by the SQL Access Group, an organization comprised of hardware manufacturers, software suppliers, and users of SQL databases. Microsoft published the standards for creating ODBC drivers, so any RDBMS supplier can make its database product compatible with Access by writing the appropriate driver. Microsoft provides with Access a single 32-bit ODBC driver that is compatible with the following client/server databases:

- Microsoft SQL Server databases running under Windows NT Server or the Microsoft version of OS/2.

- Sybase SQL Server databases up to (but not including) Sybase System 10, running on UNIX servers and as NetWare-Loadable Modules (NLMs) on Novell servers. (You can use the SQL Server driver with Sybase System 10, but you cannot avail yourself of many of the new System 10 features with this driver.)

Most publishers of major client/server database management systems provide ODBC drivers for their database products. Prior versions of Access included a driver for Oracle databases through version 6.0; this driver is not included with Access 95. (Microsoft is expected to provide a 32-bit Oracle7+ driver after the initial release of retail Access 95.) Oracle Corporation (Redwood Shores, CA) now provides and supports ODBC drivers for its Oracle Server RDBMSs. Intersolv (which purchased Q+E Software, formerly Pioneer Software, in 1994), supplies a variety of third-party ODBC drivers for client/server and other databases and files. If the client/server RDBMS you are using is not included in the preceding list, check with the supplier to determine whether a 32-bit ODBC-compliant driver is available for the RDBMS, and whether the driver is compatible with Access 95.

Installing the Access ODBC Driver for SQL Server

Installing the 32-bit Access ODBC driver for Microsoft SQL Server 4.2 and later is a three-stage process. Following are the basic steps in the process:

- Grant permissions to the users of workstations that access tables or views of tables in SQL Server databases. (Table views are not updatable in SQL Server 4.2.)

- Install the ODBC Administrator application and SQL Server ODBC driver on each workstation that needs to attach SQL Server tables to Access databases. (If you use the Custom installation and specify that the SQL Server ODBC driver be installed, you can skip this step.)

- Establish connections to specific SQL Server databases with the Access ODBC Administrator application.

The last two steps are described in sections that follow. SQL Server's documentation covers granting permissions to users of SQL Server databases. Granting permissions usually is performed by the database administrator or the database owner. The examples in this chapter use SQL Server's default system administrator (sa) login with no password, which is common for test installations of SQL Server.

VI

Advanced Techniques

Installing the ODBC Administrator and SQL Server Driver

> **Tip**
>
> You don't need to install the ODBC Administrator if you previously installed Microsoft Excel 95 or Word 95 with the database options, and installed the SQL Server driver. Open Control Panel and check to see whether the 32-bit ODBC icon is present. If it is, double-click the 32-bit ODBC icon to open the ODBC Administrator feature, then click the Drivers button. If the SQL Server driver appears in the list, close the dialogs and proceed to the next section.

 Each workstation that needs to attach SQL Server tables to Access databases must be connected to the SQL Server through the NOS: Microsoft Windows Network, TCP/IP, Microsoft LAN Manager, IBM LAN Server, Banyan VINES, or Novell NetWare. In most cases, you set up your network adapter card and established the network protocol(s) in use when you installed Windows 95. You can modify your network configuration with Control Panel's Network option.

> **Note**
>
> If you have installed Microsoft Access 2.0, Word 6.0, or Excel 5.0 under Windows 95, and elected to install the ODBC driver for Access or the Desktop Database Drivers for Word or Excel, you see an ODBC icon in Control Panel. This is the icon for the 16-bit ODBC Administrator and drivers, which *do not* work with Access 95. You need to install the 32-bit ODBC Administrator and drivers for use with Access 95, Word 95, or Excel 95.

To install Access 95's ODBC Administrator application and the SQL Server ODBC driver on a workstation on which Access 95 is installed, but where ODBC was not specified during installation or you did not install the SQL Server driver, perform the following steps:

1. Close all open Windows applications and launch the Add/Remove Programs feature of Control Panel. When you install Access 95, the Setup program creates an entry in the list of installed programs that conform to the Windows 95 logo requirements (see fig. 26.3).

2. Insert disk 1 of the Access distribution disk set into drive A or drive B, or insert the Microsoft Office Professional CD-ROM into the CD-ROM drive.

3. Select the Microsoft Access 95 item in the list, and click the Add/Remove button to launch the Access installation maintenance program. The first dialog appears as shown in figure 26.4.

4. Click the Add/Remove button to display the installation options dialog shown in figure 26.5. The entry in the dialog varies, depending on how you originally installed Access.

5. With the entry in the list box selected, click the Change Option button to display the second installation options dialog (see fig. 26.6).

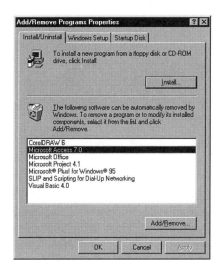

Fig. 26.3   The Add/Remove Programs feature of Control Panel lists previously installed 32-bit applications.

Fig. 26.4   The first dialog of the Access 95 installation maintenance program.

6. The ODBC Drivers check box is cleared if you did not install the ODBC files. ODBC Drivers installs both the ODBC Administrator application, if it is not already installed, and the SQL Server ODBC driver. Mark the ODBC Drivers check box, then click OK to continue.

7. When installation is complete, click the OK button of the Add/Remove Programs Properties sheet to close it.

The Access 95 Setup process automatically installs the SQL Administrator application, Odbcad32.exe and Odbccp32.dll, as a component of the Windows Control Panel. Figure 26.7 shows the appearance of Control Panel's application group after installing the ODBC Administrator. Setup also installs the SQL Server ODBC driver and creates the required entries for SQLsrv32.dll in the Registry in the HKEY_LOCAL_MACHINE\ SOFTWARE\ODBC hive (see fig. 26.8). (Previous versions of ODBC stored installation

and driver data in ODBCINST.INI and ODBC.INI files in your \WINDOWS directory.)
The next section describes how to add an SQL Server data source.

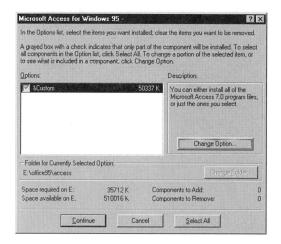

Fig. 26.5   The installation options dialog.

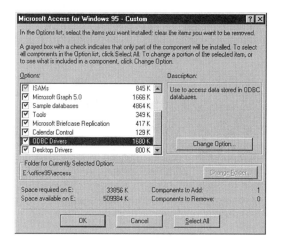

Fig. 26.6   Specifying installation of the ODBC Administrator and ODBC driver for SQL Server.

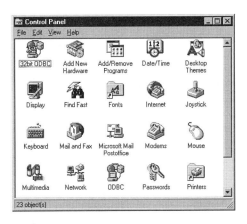

Fig. 26.7   Control Panel with the ODBC Administrator application installed.

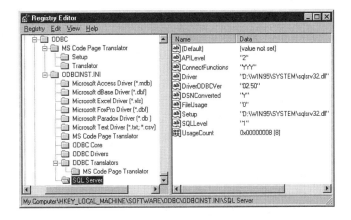

Fig. 26.8   The Registry Editor (RegEdit.exe) displaying the Registry entries for the SQL Server driver.

Adding and Removing SQL Server Data Sources

You use Control Panel's ODBC Administrator application to add or remove SQL Server data sources. An ODBC *data source* is a definition of a database (usually a client/server database), including the server on which the RDBMS is located, the ODBC driver required to connect to the database, and, optionally, the name of the data source. You need at least one SQL Server data source to enable Access to attach, export, or import SQL Server tables. To add an SQL Server data source, follow these steps:

1. Double-click the 32-bit ODBC icon in Control Panel to launch the ODBC Administrator. ODBC Administrator's Data Sources dialog appears (see fig. 26.9).

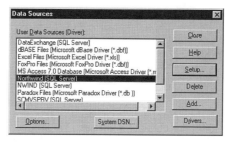

Fig. 26.9 The Data Sources dialog of the ODBC Administrator.

Figure 26.9 shows a multitude of ODBC data sources. If you have not previously installed ODBC data sources, the User Data Sources (Driver) list is empty. Microsoft Office 95 installs the ODBC drivers for dBASE, Excel, FoxPro, Access 95, Paradox, and Text files. If you are installing the SQL Server data source on another user's workstation, there may be a variety of ODBC data sources installed for use with other Microsoft applications.

2. Click the Add button to add a new ODBC data source with the Add Data Source dialog. If there is more than one ODBC driver in the Installed ODBC Drivers list, select the SQL Server item, as shown in figure 26.10.

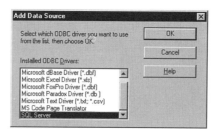

Fig. 26.10 You can choose the SQL Server ODBC driver in the Add Data Source dialog.

> **Note**
>
> Figure 26.10 is representative of the appearance of the Add Data Source dialog after installing Microsoft Office 95 or any Microsoft application that includes the Microsoft Query DDE server applet.

3. Click OK to display the ODBC SQL Server Setup dialog. Enter a short descriptive name of the SQL Server database in the Data Source Name text box. Unless you have a particular database that contains the tables you want to attach to Access, type **pubs** to specify the pubs sample database supplied with SQL Server. Type a description of the database, such as **SQL Server Sample Database**, in the Description text box.

4. Select the name of the server that holds the SQL Server database you want to use from the Server combo list. If no entries appear in the combo list, type the name of the server (without the preceding \\) in the text box. Unless you are using TCP/IP as your network protocol, or are using a special network library (netlib) for the data source, accept the (Default) entries for the Network Address and Network Library text boxes (see fig. 26.11). (The default network library for SQL Server is Dbnmpntw.dll.)

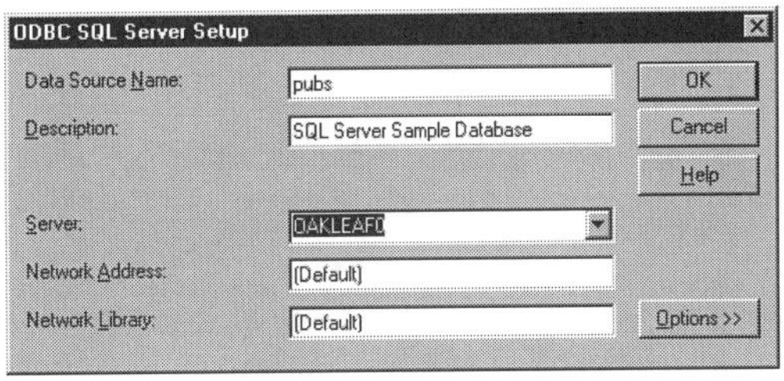

Fig. 26.11 Beginning the definition of a new ODBC data source.

5. Click the Options button to expand the dialog to specify a default database. Type **pubs** in the Database Name text box, as shown in figure 26.12.

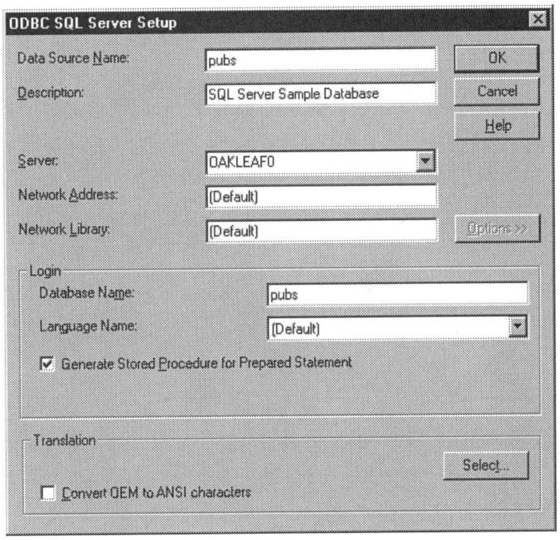

Fig. 26.12 Completing the definition of the ODBC data source.

The Generate Stored Procedure for Prepared Statement check box, when marked, creates a temporary SQL Server stored procedure (a precompiled query) from prepared statements written in Transact-SQL, the SQL dialect of SQL Server. Access 95 does not generate prepared statements. The Remote Data Object of Visual Basic 4.0, which you can implement with Access VBA, is capable of creating multiple prepared statements.

The Language Name drop-down list displays the national languages that the database supports. (The national language of the database is not necessarily the same as the Locale of Windows 95.)

VI

Advanced Techniques

The Convert OEM to ANSI characters check box changes special characters in SQL Server database tables to their Windows (ANSI) equivalents, when an ANSI equivalent is available. If you or the database administrator installed SQL Server with the default code page, you don't need to be concerned with OEM-to-ANSI conversion.

6. Click OK to add the new data source and close the Data Source dialog. Your new data source is added to the User Data Sources (Driver) list of the Data Sources dialog, as shown in figure 26.13.

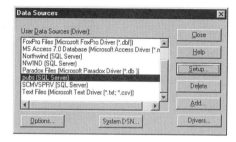

Fig. 26.13 The new pubs SQL Server data source has been installed for use with the ODBC API.

7. Click Close to close the ODBC Administrator application, and then close Control Panel.

You can add additional SQL Server data sources for a workstation by repeating steps 1 through 6 before exiting the ODBC Administrator application. The entries you make for each new data source are added to the hive of the Registry, as in

HKEY_CURRENT_USER\Software\ODBC\ODBC.INI

and as shown in figure 26.14. The ODBC data source entries are located under the HKEY_CURRENT_USER key, because other users of your PC may have different sets of ODBC data sources.

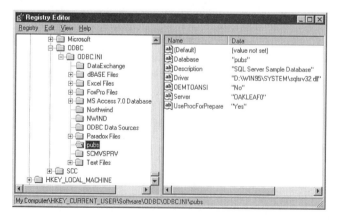

Fig. 26.14 The Registry now contains an entry for the pubs database of SQL Server 4.21a on the \\OAKLEAF0 server.

> **Note**
>
> Examples of entries in the Windows 95 Registry are provided in this chapter so that you can compare Registry entries for your computer in the event that you have problems making a connection to a client/server database. Each ODBC driver for a particular client/server RDBMS has its own set of properties, but the entries for the driver and the data source should resemble figures 26.8 and 26.14, respectively. If you have problems that you can't solve yourself while connecting to a client/server database, it's likely that the vendor's technical support person will ask for the values of your Registry entries for the ODBC driver and/or data source.

If you have problems connecting to your ODBC data source, you can turn *ODBC tracing* on by clicking the Options button of the ODBC Administrator's Data Sources dialog to display the ODBC Options dialog. Mark the Trace ODBC Calls check box to create an ODBC log in the default SQL.LOG file (see fig. 26.15). Examples of entries in SQL.LOG appear in the next section.

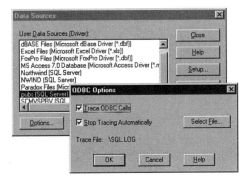

Fig. 26.15   Turning on the trace feature of the SQL Server ODBC driver.

Using Databases Connected by ODBC

After you add the SQL Server database as a data source, you can attach, import, or export tables in the SQL Server database to your Access database, depending on the permissions granted by SQL Server to each connected workstation. You use tables in the client/server database in the same manner that you use attached Access, dBASE, FoxPro, Paradox, or Btrieve tables. (See Chapter 7, "Linking, Importing, and Exporting Tables.") You don't specify indexes to be used with client/server tables because indexes are opened automatically when you open the table for which indexes have been created, just as with Access tables.

Pubs is a demonstration database, supplied with Microsoft and Sybase SQL Server, that contains tables for a fictional book distributor. Pubs' tables include information on imaginary book publishers, titles, and authors. (The name is "pubs" because using all-lowercase names for SQL Server objects is a long-standing convention.) To attach the tables in the pubs SQL Server database to a new Access database (pubs.mdb in this example), follow these steps:

1. Launch Access and create a new database named pubs.mdb. Choose File, Get External Data, Link Tables to display the Link dialog.

2. Open the Files of type drop-down list. Use the vertical scroll bar to reach the ODBC Databases() entry in the list, as shown in figure 26.16. Select this entry and click OK. The SQL Data Sources dialog appears.

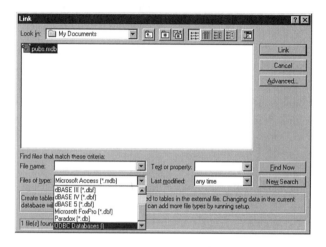

Fig. 26.16   The Link dialog with the ODBC Databases() data source added by the ODBC Administrator.

3. Double-click the data source name—in this case, pubs—in the Select Data Source list (see fig. 26.17). The SQL Server Login dialog appears.

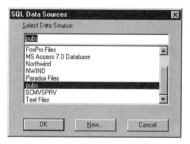

Fig. 26.17   Selecting the SQL data source.

4. Type your login identification and password in the Login ID and Password text boxes, respectively. **sa** (system administrator) is used as the login ID, and no password is used in this example (see fig. 26.18).

5. Click the Options button to display the additional login options shown in figure 26.19. Open the Database drop-down list to display other databases installed on the server whose names are accessible to users not logged in. The entries in the

Application Name and WorkStation ID text boxes are added automatically for you by Access. Select pubs from the Database drop-down list, and then click OK to log in to SQL Server.

Fig. 26.18 Logging in to the pubs SQL Server database as the system administrator with no password.

Fig. 26.19 The expanded version of the SQL Server Login dialog.

After you are connected to the pubs database with the ODBC API, the Link Tables dialog appears, as shown in figure 26.20. The names of tables are prefixed with dbo., an SQL Server abbreviation for *database owner*.

Fig. 26.20 Tables available in the pubs database of SQL Server 4.21a are available for linking to an Access database.

  6. Click the Select All button and mark the Save login ID and password locally check box. Click OK to attach all the tables to pubs.mdb.

Selecting the Save login ID and password locally check box eliminates the need to reenter your login ID and password each time you attach another table. If the database administrator adds additional security provisions to a database (by adding a special MSysConf table to the database), this check box is disabled.

7. To make the tables updatable by Access, a unique index is required on one or more fields to uniquely identify each record in the table. If the SQL Server table does not have a primary-key index, Access 95 opens the Select Unique Record Identifier dialog and offers to create a local "pseudo-index" on the table. As an example, the discounttype and stor_id fields of the dbo.discounts table create a composite primary key (see fig. 26.21). Select the field(s) for the primary key and click OK (or click Cancel to omit the pseudo-index). Do not add a pseudo-index for the dbo.royaltysched or dbo.titleview tables (dbo.titleview is an SQL VIEW and is not updatable.) Add a pseudo-index on the stor_id, ord_num, and title_id fields of the dbo.sales table.

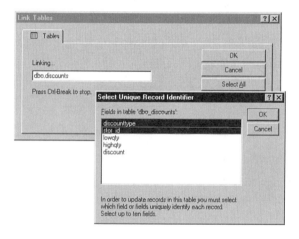

Fig. 26.21 The Select Unique Record Identifier dialog requests that you choose fields to create a local pseudo-index for the table.

8. When the linking process is complete, the linked tables appear in the Tables page of the Database window (see fig. 26.22). The globe to the left of the table name indicates that the table is attached by ODBC. An underscore substitutes for the period between dbo and the table name because periods are not allowed within Access table names. (Periods are separators between objects and properties or methods in Access 95.)

Double-click the dbo_*table_name* item you want to examine. To verify that you can update or append dbo_sales records, for which you created an Access pseudo-index, click the Last Record button to check for a tentative append record at the bottom of the table (see fig. 26.23).

Fig. 26.22   The Tables page of this Database window shows eight tables and one view attached from the pubs database.

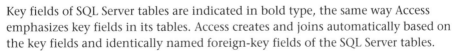

Fig. 26.23   This dbo_sales table displays the tentative append record added by specifying a local Access pseudo-index for the table.

To create a query that joins the tables, and that displays the author name, book title, and book publisher, follow these steps:

1. Create a new query and add the dbo_authors, dbo_titleauthor, dbo_titles, and dbo_publishers tables to your query. Click the Close button of the Add Tables dialog.

    Key fields of SQL Server tables are indicated in bold type, the same way Access emphasizes key fields in its tables. Access creates and joins automatically based on the key fields and identically named foreign-key fields of the SQL Server tables.

2. Click and drag the au_lname field from the dbo_authors table to the field row of the first column of the query.

3. Repeat step 2 for the title field of the dbo_titles table and the pub_name field of the dbo_publishers table. Your Query Design window looks like the one shown in figure 26.24.

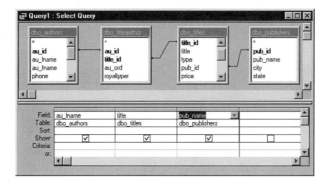

Fig. 26.24 The Query Design window for the example, based on tables attached from the pubs database.

 4. Click the Run button on the toolbar to display your query result set, as shown in figure 26.25.

au_lname	title	pub_name
White	Prolonged Data Deprivation: Four Case Studies	New Moon Books
Green	The Busy Executive's Database Guide	Algodata Infosystems
Green	You Can Combat Computer Stress!	New Moon Books
Carson	But Is It User Friendly?	Algodata Infosystems
O'Leary	Cooking with Computers: Surreptitious Balance	Algodata Infosystems
O'Leary	Sushi, Anyone?	Binnet & Hardley
Straight	Straight Talk About Computers	Algodata Infosystems
Bennet	The Busy Executive's Database Guide	Algodata Infosystems
Dull	Secrets of Silicon Valley	Algodata Infosystems
Gringlesby	Sushi, Anyone?	Binnet & Hardley
Locksley	Net Etiquette	Algodata Infosystems
Locksley	Emotional Security: A New Algorithm	New Moon Books
Blotchet-Halls	Fifty Years in Buckingham Palace Kitchens	Binnet & Hardley
Yokomoto	Sushi, Anyone?	Binnet & Hardley

Fig. 26.25 The query result set from the query design shown in figure 26.17.

5. Close and save your query for use in the next section.

To remove the linked tables from the Northwind Traders database, close your query and save it for the example in the next section. Click the Show Database window button on the toolbar, click the Tables button in the Database Window, and select the name of the linked table to delete. Press Del. A message box appears, asking you to confirm that you want to delete the link to the table (see fig. 26.26). Click No because you need to use the linked SQL Server tables in the next section.

> **Note**
>
> You can eliminate the need to add the dbo_ prefix to a table name by renaming the attachments to the table name without the dbo_ prefix. Close any open attached tables, select the table, and then choose Edit, Rename to enter the new name. Alternatively, right-click the table name, then choose Rename from the popup menu.

Fig. 26.26 This message box confirms the deletion of a link to a table.

The preceding example, using the pubs database, is typical of the procedure that you use to attach tables from any client/server database for which an ODBC driver is available.

Troubleshooting

A "Cannot connect to server" or similar error message occurs when I attempt to attach to SQL Server.

There are a variety of problems that can lead to your inability to connect to SQL Server. The most common cause is the lack of (or an outdated version of) the Dbnmpntw.dll library on your computer. Dbnmpntw.dll is the 32-bit named pipes library required to connect to SQL server. Choose Start, Find, Files or Folders and verify that Dbnmpntw.dll is installed in your \Windows\System folder. (The size of the version of Dbnmpntw.dll that was current when this edition was written is 17K. The date should correspond to the dates of other files installed by Access or other applications that install Dbnmpntw.dll.) If you have additional copies of Dbnmpntw.dll with earlier dates in folders other than \Windows\System, delete these unneeded copies.

Using Access 95's SQL Pass-Through Queries

SQL *pass-through queries* enable you to write queries in the dialect of SQL used by the server RDBMS. SQL Server, as an example, lets you write stored procedures that you can execute by name, instead of by sending individual SQL statements to the server. Executing a stored procedure query is faster than executing the query through Access's Jet database engine because of reduced network traffic and faster execution of the query by the server. (Stored procedure queries are pre-compiled by SQL Server.) You also need to use SQL pass-through if you want to take advantage of special Transact-SQL reserved words not included in Access SQL.

Access 1.x required that you use Access Basic to declare the functions of MSASP110.DLL, an SQL pass-through library supplied by Microsoft. Access 2.0 and 95 have built-in SQL pass-through capability, similar to that offered by Visual Basic 3.0 and 4.0. You can convert the query you created in the preceding section to an SQL pass-through query by following these steps:

1. Open the saved query you created in the previous section in Query Design View; then choose Query, SQL-Specific, Pass-through.

2. The SQL window opens with the SQL statement behind your query, as shown in figure 26.27. The Query Design button is disabled when you convert a conventional Access query to the SQL pass-through type.

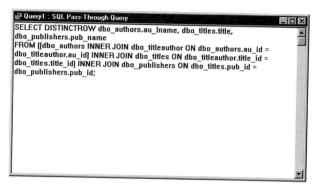

Fig. 26.27   The SQL window for an SQL pass-through query.

3. Click the Run button on the toolbar to execute your pass-through query. You receive the same query result set as that from the conventional query executed through the Jet database engine.

> **Note**
>
> Query result sets returned by SQL pass-through queries are Recordset objects of the Snapshot type, which are not updatable. Other query result sets against databases linked by ODBC are Recordset objects of the Dynaset type, but may or may not be updatable, depending on the query design and whether you set a local pseudo-index on the table.

When you save an SQL pass-through query, the ODBC symbol appears next to the name of the pass-through query in the Queries list of the Database window (see fig. 26.28). The ODBC API function call for SQL pass-through queries is SQLExecDirect(). Figure 26.29 shows the SQLExecDirect() function call created by the preceding SQL pass-through query, followed by the SQLFetch() function call, and then five SQLGetData() function calls to return the first five rows of the query result set.

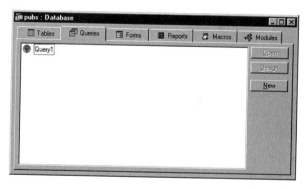

Fig. 26.28   The Queries page of the Database window with a saved SQL pass-through query.

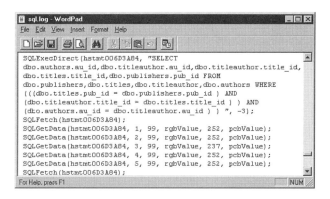

Fig. 26.29 A few of the ODBC API function calls that result from executing an SQL pass-through query.

> **Note**
>
> SQL pass-through queries bypass the query parser of the Jet database engine, but Access SQL and ANSI SQL-92 INNER JOIN statements are not accepted by version 4.x of SQL Server. (SQL Server uses WHERE clauses to create joins.) The Microsoft ODBC driver for SQL Server traps the INNER JOIN statement and converts (in ODBC terminology, it *escapes*) the Access/ANSI SQL statements to an equivalent SQL WHERE clause.

Exporting Access Tables to a Client/Server Database

Creating the definition of tables in a client/server database can be a very lengthy process, especially if you need to write SQL DDL statements at the ISQL prompt or in ISQL/Windows to create the tables. Tools for SQL Server 4.2, such as SQL Object Manager, simplify the process of creating new client/server tables. It's even easier, however, to export your existing Access tables to a database in SQL Server. When you export Access tables to SQL Server, you ensure that the SQL Server table's field data types correspond to the data types of your Access table.

To export a table from Northwind.mdb to the pubs database, follow these steps:

1. Open Northwind.mdb. In the Tables page of the Database window, select the table you want to export to the SQL data source.

2. Choose File, Save As/Export; click OK when the Save As dialog with the To an External File or Database option selected appears to display the Export dialog. Select ODBC Databases( ) in the Save as type drop-down list (see fig. 26.30). The Export dialog appears to confirm your selection (see fig. 26.31). Click OK to display the SQL Data Sources dialog.

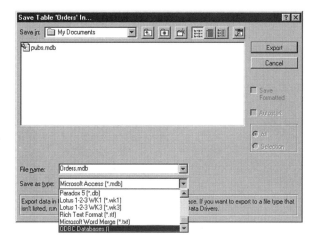

Fig. 26.30   Initiating the export of an Access table to SQL Server.

Fig. 26.31   Confirming the export of a table to SQL Server.

3. Click to select the data source for the database to which you want to export the table (see fig. 26.32). The Northwind data source was created previously for this purpose. Click OK to display the SQL Server Login dialog.

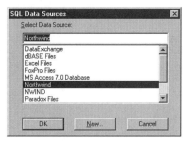

Fig. 26.32   In the SQL Data Sources dialog, you select the data source for the database to which to export the table.

4. Enter your user ID and password, then click OK to export the table to the server database. You don't need to add the dbo_ prefix for SQL Server tables.

The status bar shows the progress of exporting the table to the server. Exporting an Access table with a large number of records is not as fast as importing the content of the table to SQL Server from an ASCII text file with a bulk copy program (BCP). However, exporting the table is much quicker when the table contains less than 10,000 records. You can view the result of the export operation with SQL Object Manager or a similar application.

Figure 26.33 shows SQL Server 4.2's SQL Object Manager displaying the structure of the Orders table of Northwind.mdb exported to the pubs database. The SQL Server ODBC driver replaces spaces in the field names of tables with underscores. (Spaces are not allowed in SQL Server table or field names.)

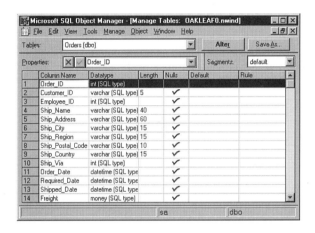

Fig. 26.33 SQL Object Manager is displaying the structure of the dbo_orders table.

> **Note**
>
> When you export an Access table to SQL Server, the indexes, validation rules, default values, and other properties of the table are not exported. You need to use SQL Object Manager or a similar tool to add indexes and other properties to the new server table. Alternatively, you can use ISQL and SQL ALTER TABLE statements to add the indexes and other properties. The Access Upsizing Wizard, which was not yet available for Access 95 when this chapter was written, is the most effective method of exporting Access tables to SQL Server, because the Upsizing Wizard creates indexes, default values, and triggers to enforce referential integrity.

From Here...

This chapter provided you with a brief introduction to the use of the ODBC Administrator application with Microsoft SQL Server for Windows NT version 4.2. The examples included in this chapter also are applicable to SQL Server 6.0 and Sybase System 10+. Adding data sources for other client/server RDBMSs for which ODBC drivers are available is similar, but the dialogs to specify the details of the data source differ.

VI

Advanced Techniques

You also can execute queries against client/server databases with Access VBA code. To learn about programming with Access VBA and related topics, refer to the following chapters:

- Chapter 28, "Writing Visual Basic for Applications Code," describes how to use Access 95's Code Behind Forms feature to write event-handling code for forms and reports.

- Chapter 29, "Understanding the Data Access Object Class," explains Access 95's hierarchy of objects created by Access and the Jet database engine.

- Chapter 30, "Exchanging Data with OLE Automation and DDE," gives examples of code for programming objects created by other OLE 2-compliant applications, as well as OLE Controls (OCXs).

Chapter 27

Replicating Access Databases

Laptop and notebook computers now comprise a substantial percentage of PCs running Windows, and the market share of portable PCs is expected to increase during the late 1990s. Microsoft designed Windows 95 specifically to accommodate the needs of mobile computing by adding features such as hot-swapping of PC Card (formerly PCMCIA) adapters and hot-docking to connect portable PCs to stationary keyboards and displays (called *docking stations*). The growing number of home PCs that also are used part-time for business purposes also fit the mobile computing pattern. A large percentage of portable and home PC users connect to office networks by modem using Windows 95's Dial-Up Networking client and Windows NT Server's Remote Access Services (RAS) or the Windows 95 Dial-Up Networking Server included with Microsoft Plus! Using RAS or Dial-Up Networking lets mobile computer users update the current versions of files on the server or their office PC.

If you don't have a RAS or Dial-Up Networking connection to a server or your office PC, Windows 95 provides a Briefcase feature to synchronize the contents of multiple copies of a file. This chapter explains the principles of Briefcase synchronization and how Access 95 synchronizes updates to table data using database replicas stored in Windows 95 Briefcases. Briefcase synchronization is new in Access 95, so the icon indicating a new Access 95 feature appears only once in this chapter.

> **Note**
>
> Windows 95's My Briefcase icon appears on the desktop only if you chose Windows 95's Portable installation option or used the Custom installation option and specified that Briefcase be included when you originally installed Windows 95. If you didn't install Briefcase and want to try this chapter's examples of Briefcase synchronization, launch Control Panel's Add/Remove Programs feature and add the Briefcase files from your Windows 95 CD-ROM or distribution disks.

Understanding the Principles of Briefcase Replication

To synchronize updates to Access 95 databases, you must create a *replica set*. An Access 95 replica set consists of one *design-master* replica, to which you can make design changes, and one or more replicas that do not support design mode. One (and only one) design-master and all other replicas comprise an Access *replica set*. The design-master replica is the .mdb file from which all Briefcase replicas are created. In most cases, the .mdb file designated the design-master replica is the original application or, more often, the original data .mdb file stored on your local fixed disk or shared from a file server. You can designate one of the Briefcase replicas as the design-master, if desired.

OLE (Object Linking and Embedding) 2.0 provides a set of functions, called OLE interfaces, that support operations such as embedding or linking objects within container documents. The chapters in Part V of this book, "Integrating Access with Other Office 95 Applications," describe the basic features of OLE 2.1 as they apply to Access 95. Windows 95's implementation of OLE 2.1 includes an additional OLE 2.1 interface, not discussed in Part V, that adds the following Briefcase functions:

- *Binding a reconciliation handler to an application.* A *reconciliation handler* is a set of methods, specific to the type of document created by the application, to reconcile accumulated changes to replicas of a particular document file made at different times by multiple users. *Binding* is a Windows programming term that means attaching a process to an application when the application needs to use the process.

 ◀◀ See "The Registry Editor," p. 721

- *Tracking the contents of the Briefcase.* Access replica sets are identified by an unique number, called a Globally Unique ID (GUID, also called an Universally Unique ID, UUID), created by Windows 95. Each member of a replica set uses the same GUID. GUIDs are automatically generated, 128-bit hexadecimal numbers that have an almost infinitesimal probability of duplication. (Access 95 provides the GUID data type for creating and manipulating GUIDs.) If you have explored the Windows 95 Registry with the Registry Editor (RegEdit.exe), you probably have seen a large number of entries with 32-character GUIDs. (The OLE Class ID, CLSID, entries in the Registry are GUIDs assigned to each OLE object class and interface by the author of the object.) Only classes of documents that are supported by an OLE 2.1 application with a reconciliation handler are candidates for Briefcase synchronization.

- *Reconciling the contents of the Briefcase.* Reconciling Briefcase documents updates the original design-master file with the content of the replica file(s) in Briefcase(s) with accumulated changes. The updating process is relatively simple for a conventional OLE document, such as a Microsoft Word 95 or Excel 95 file, that has built-in revision handling features, but it is a much more involved procedure for Access .mdb files, which may include a wide variety of different objects.

All participants in the Briefcase replication process must use Windows 95. The versions of Windows NT Workstation and Server available when this edition was written (version 3.55) do not support Briefcase replication. When Windows NT gains the Windows 95 user interface, it is likely that Windows NT users also will be able to take advantage of the Briefcase feature.

Creating and Updating a Briefcase Replica

To create a design-master and Briefcase replica of a document, you follow these basic steps:

1. Drag the database's icon from Windows 95's Explorer into Briefcase's window. (Access 95 also offers the Tools, Replication, Convert Database to Replica command to create a design-master replica. You use the menu commands to create replicas under Windows NT.)

2. Create additional Briefcases containing replicas by copying and pasting My Briefcase to the desktop, and then renaming the copy. Other database users update the Briefcase replica(s).

3. Open My Briefcase, and choose Briefcase, Update All. All replicas of the same replica set in all Briefcases on the desktop update the design-master replica.

Figure 27.1 illustrates the steps involved in Briefcase replication of Access 95 databases.

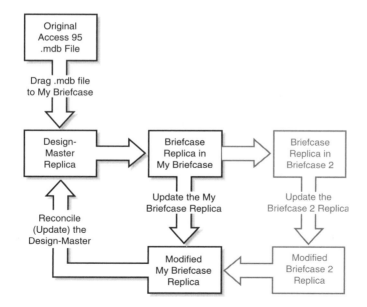

Fig. 27.1   Creating an Access replica set and updating the design-master replica with updates made to Briefcase replicas.

Once the replica is in the Briefcase of the *host* computer, mobile users can update the Briefcase replica on the host or on the *guest* (mobile) computer by the following four methods:

- *Network connection.* If you can connect your guest computer to the host computer's Briefcase, you can update the Briefcase replica directly. If the replica is opened in shared mode (the default), multiple users can update the Briefcase replica simultaneously. Unless there is a particular reason to use the Briefcase replica, networked users should connect directly to and update the design-master (original) .mdb file.

- *Direct cable connection.* You can use a serial cable (called a null-modem cable) between the serial (COM) ports of host and guest computers to make the host Briefcase accessible to the guest computer. If you have an ECP-enabled parallel port, you can use an ECP (Extended Communication Protocol) cable to connect the parallel (LPT) ports of the host and guest PCs. A parallel ECP connection is much faster than a serial connection. You can use a Universal Cable Module (UCM) cable to connect different types of PC parallel ports.

- *Dial-up modem connection.* If you've installed on the host computer the Dial-Up Networking Server component included on the Microsoft Windows 95 Plus! Pack, your guest computer can connect to the Briefcase on the host computer and update the Briefcase replica.

- *Disk.* You can move the Briefcase replica on the host computer to a disk, and then move the Briefcase replica from the disk to a Briefcase on the desktop of the guest PC. After you make changes on the guest PC, you reverse the process and move the updated files from the disk to the host PC's Briefcase. Most Briefcase users are likely to employ the disk method, so the example in this chapter uses disks for synchronizing changes to Access tables.

> **Note**
>
> To use the network, direct cable, or dial-up modem connection method, you need to have the File and Printer Sharing services for either the Microsoft or Novell networks installed. The version of the Banyan VINES network available when this edition was written does not support Briefcase replication.

Creating the Contact Management Application for Replication

Contact management is one of the most common applications for Briefcase replication. Salespersons take their laptops on sales calls and record important information relating to sales contacts. To use the Database Wizard to create a new Contact Management database, ContactManager.mdb, follow these steps:

1. Launch Access and select Database Wizard from the opening window or, if Access is open, choose <u>F</u>ile, <u>N</u>ew Database to open the New dialog (see fig. 27.2); then click the Database tab.

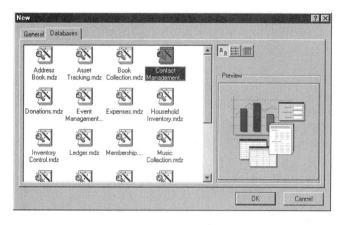

Fig. 27.2 The New dialog displaying icons for databases you can create with the Database Wizard.

2. Double-click the Contact Management icon in the Database list to create a new database based on the Contact Management template. The File New Database dialog opens.

3. Navigate to the directory for the new database and give the file a name, such as **ContactManager.mdb** (ContactManagement1.mdb is the default file name), as shown in figure 27.3. The location of the file is not important; in this example, the new database is located in C:\Msoffice\Access. Click Create to have the Database Wizard generate the new database.

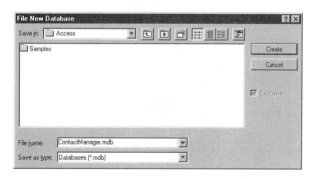

Fig. 27.3 Specifying a name and location for the new Contact Management database.

4. When the first Database Wizard screen appears, click the Next button to display the tables and fields dialog. Mark the Yes, Include Sample Data checkbox to add the sample data to the tables (see fig. 27.4). Accept the remainder of the dialog's defaults and click the Next button.

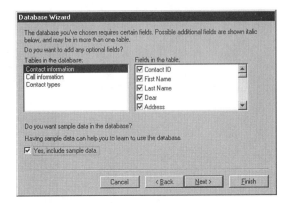

Fig. 27.4   Specifying addition of sample data to the Contact Management database.

5. In the first style selection dialog, select the style you like for forms and click the Next button. This example uses the International style.

6. In the second style selection dialog, select the report style you want and click the Finish button to accept the remainder of the Database Wizard's defaults.

After a few minutes of intense disk activity, the Database Wizard completes the task of building the ContactManager.mdb database and the Contact Management Switchboard appears (see fig. 27.5).

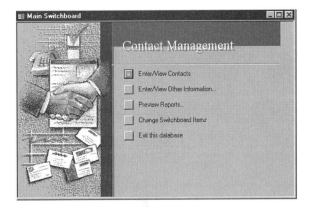

Fig. 27.5   The Switchboard form of the Contact Manager database.

Replicating only the tables of the database is more efficient than replicating the entire database, so follow these steps to split the tables of ContactManager.mdb into ContactData.mdb and create the links to the tables:

1. With ContactManager.mdb open and the Main Switchboard form closed, choose Tools, Add-Ins, Database Splitter to open the Database Splitter dialog.

2. Click the Split Database button to open the Database Splitter's save as dialog. Maneuver to the same folder that contains ContactManger.mdb, if necessary, and type **ContactData.mdb** in the File Name text box (see fig. 27.6).

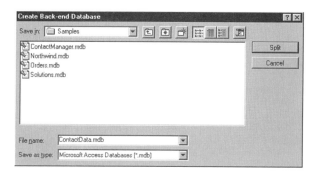

Fig. 27.6   Naming the "back-end" database to contain the Contact Management tables.

3. Click the Split button to complete the splitting and linking process. The Tables page of the Database window appears as shown in figure 27.7.

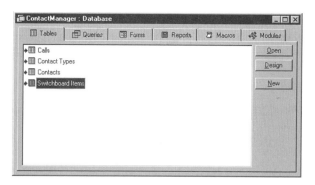

Fig. 27.7   The tables linked from ContactData.mdb to ContactManager.mdb.

4. Choose Tools, Add-Ins, Linked Table Manager to display the links from ContactManager.mdb's application objects to the tables of ContactData.mdb (see fig. 27.8). Close Linked Table Manager.

Caution

Do not password-protect Access .mdb files that you intend to use with Briefcase replication. Providing a password requires opening Access. All reconciliation operations operate behind the scenes (using the Jet 3.0 database engine directly) and do not launch Access. You receive an error message if you attempt to reconcile updates to a password-protected replica.

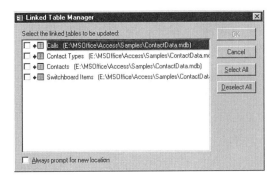

Fig. 27.8 Verifying the links between the application and data .mdb file for the Contact Management application.

Creating a Replica Set

To create a design-master and a Briefcase replica (a replica set) from ContactData.mdb, follow these steps:

1. Close Access and launch Explorer. Open the Explorer folder that contains ContactData.mdb.

2. Move Explorer's window, if necessary, to expose the My Briefcase desktop icon. Drag ContactData.mdb's icon to the desktop and drop the icon on the My Briefcase icon. (If My Briefcase is open, you can drop the icon in My Briefcase's window.) My Briefcase begins to create a replica set of ContactData.mdb.

3. After a brief period of disk activity, the message shown in figure 27.9 appears. Click Yes to continue.

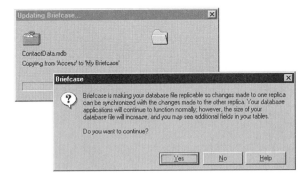

Fig. 27.9 The message requesting confirmation for creating the Access replica set.

4. A second message appears offering you the option to make a backup copy of your replicated database (see fig. 27.10). Click No to continue because you don't need a backup copy of this example database. (Ordinarily, you create a backup copy of your database at this point.)

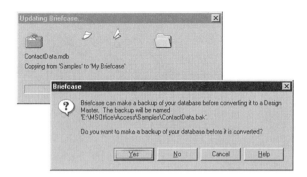

Fig. 27.10 The message offering to create a backup copy of your design-master replica database.

5. A third message appears that lets you select whether to make the Original Copy or the Briefcase Copy the design-master set (see fig. 27.11). Unless you plan to do off-site development work on your database, select the default (Original Copy) option. Ordinarily, you don't want users making changes to the design of your tables, especially if the tables are attached to an Access application. Click OK to complete the replication process.

Fig. 27.11 This dialog lets you select whether the original or the Briefcase copy is the design-master replica.

6. Launch My Briefcase, if necessary. Your replica copy appears in My Briefcase's file list, as shown in figure 27.12.

7. Right-click ContactData.mdb's icon and choose Properties from the popup menu to open the properties sheet. Click the Update Status tab to display the synchronization status. The original and replica of ContactData.mdb are Unmodified and the status is Up-to-Date because you haven't yet made changes to either replica (see fig. 25.13). Click Close to return to Briefcase.

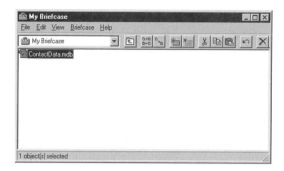

Fig. 27.12 The Briefcase copy of ContactData.mdb in My Briefcase's file list.

Fig. 27.13 The Update Status properties page of the of ContactData.mdb Briefcase replica.

8. To view the tables of the replica, double-click ContactData.mdb's Briefcase icon. Access launches with the replica copy of ContactData.mdb active. `Replicable Database` appears in the title bar of the Database window, indicating you're working with a replica of the original database.

9. Choose Tools, Options and click the View tab. Mark the Hidden Objects and System Objects checkboxes of the Show frame and click OK to close the Options sheet. Note that many new hidden tables for replication management, such as MSysReplicas and MSysTombstones, have been added to ContactData.mdb (see fig. 27.14).

10. Choose Tools, Options again, and clear the Hidden Objects and System Objects check boxes. Then click OK to close the Options sheet. Close the Briefcase copy of ContactData.mdb.

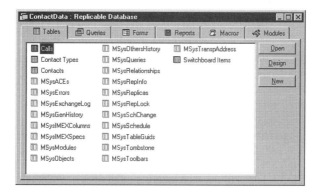

Fig. 27.14   The Tables page of the Database window displaying hidden and system tables, including hidden and system tables for replication management.

Synchronizing the Design-Master and Briefcase Replicas

Modifying data or options in either the Briefcase replica or the design-master sets the status of the file to Modified. If either of the replicas has been modified since the last reconciliation, either the Briefcase or the design-master replica is a candidate for updating. Follow these steps to verify the preceding statements:

1. Open Briefcase, if necessary. Right-click ContactData.mdb's icon, and select Properties from the popup menu. Click the Update Status tab of the Properties sheet. The status of the Briefcase copy is Modified, as shown in figure 27.15, although you didn't change any data in the preceding steps. Changing the View options in preceding steps 9 and 10 set the "Dirty" flag for the Briefcase copy, which determines if the copy's status is set to Modified.

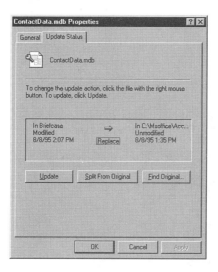

Fig. 27.15   The Update Status properties page of the modified Briefcase replica.

2. Click Update to update the design-master replica.

3. Open the original (design-master) copy of ContactData.mdb. The title bar of the Database window displays Replicable Database (Design-Master), as shown in figure 27.16.

Fig. 27.16   The Tables page of the Database window for the design-master replica of ContactData.mdb.

4. Open the Calls table of ContactData.mdb and modify an entry, such as changing the date in the Call Date field of a record.

5. Open Briefcase, if necessary, and check the Update status using the procedure of step 1. Both the Briefcase and the design-master version show Unmodified status. (The modification you made in the preceding step to the Calls table is cached by Access and has not yet been written to the design-master ContactData.mdb file.)

6. Close ContactData.mdb to write the changes to the .mdb file and repeat step 5. The original version now shows modified status and the Update button is enabled (see fig. 27.17). Click Update to propagate the change from the original (design-master replica) file to the Briefcase replica.

Fig. 27.17   Updating the Briefcase replica with changes made to the design-master replica.

Emulating Replica Set Reconciliation with Disks

As noted earlier in this chapter, most Access 95 users will use disks to replicate Briefcases and reconcile replica sets. You can emulate floppy disk Briefcase update operations on a single computer by following these steps:

1. Create a copy of your application .mdb file. For example, copy ContactManager.mdb and name the copy ContactRemote.mdb.

2. Right-click the My Briefcase icon and choose Copy from the popup menu. Right-click the desktop and choose Paste to add a copy of My Briefcase icon to the desktop. (The copy of My Briefcase is a backup.)

3. Insert a blank formatted disk in your A: drive. Open Explorer and drag the My Briefcase icon to Explorer and drop the icon on the A: drive icon. This step *moves* My Briefcase from the desktop to the A: drive.

   Moving the Briefcase is an important step in understanding the concept of a Windows Briefcase. You keep replicas of all of the office files you want to update while on the road in My Briefcase. You take My Briefcase with you when you leave; a real briefcase cannot be two places at once and neither can a briefcase's abstraction as a Windows desktop object. When you return, you *move* My Briefcase from the disk to the desktop, as described later in this procedure. If you share your Briefcase on a network, the real-world object corresponding to the Briefcase is an in-basket.

4. You now need to change the links to ContactData.mdb to the copy of ContactData.mdb in the \My Briefcase folder on the disk to emulate disk operations with your guest computer. Open ContactRemote.mdb, and then choose Tools, Add-Ins, Linked Table Manager to open the Linked Table Manager's dialog.

5. Click the Select All button and mark the Always Prompt for New Location checkbox (see fig. 27.18). Click the OK button to open the Select New Location of Calls dialog.

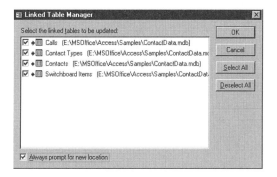

Fig. 27.18 Selecting all links for refreshing by the Linked Table Manager add-in.

6. Open the Look In drop-down list and select the A:\My Briefcase folder, which contains the replica of ContactData.mdb, as shown in figure 27.19.

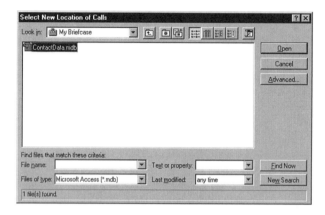

Fig. 27.19   Selecting A:\My Briefcase as the location of the ContactData.mdb file for linking.

7. Select ContactData.mdb and click the Open button to close the dialog and refresh the table links. Linked Table Manager's dialog appears as shown in figure 27.20. Click Cancel to close the dialog.

8. Open the Contacts form and change an entry, such as giving Nancy Davolio a promotion from Sales Representative to **Sales Director** (see fig. 27.21), and then close ContactManage.mdb.

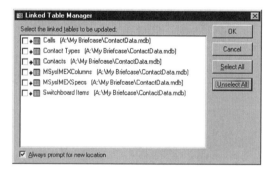

Fig. 27.20   Tables in ContactManager.mdb linked to the My Briefcase replica of ContactData.mdb on the disk.

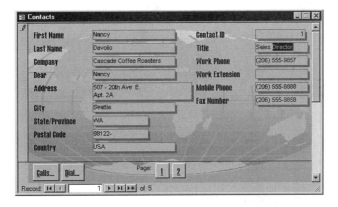

Fig. 27.21 Changing an entry in the Contacts form of the Contact Management application.

Operations using .mdb files stored on disk are very slow; you need patience to perform steps 7 and 8. In real-world applications, you move the Briefcase from the disk to the desktop of your guest PC and attach the files from My Briefcase (or whatever you've named your Briefcase) to the desktop. When returning to the office, you move the Briefcase back to the disk.

9. Open Explorer and select the A: drive, as shown in figure 27.22. Briefcase folders in Explorer are indicated by a small Briefcase icon. Drag the small My Briefcase icon in Explorer's window back to your desktop.

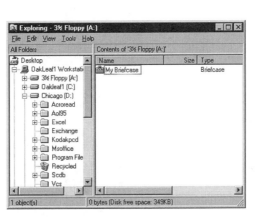

Fig. 27.22 Explorer displaying the My Briefcase folder on the disk.

10. Open My Briefcase from the desktop and choose View, Details to display the location of the design-master copy to synchronize, the status of the replica set, and other file details, as illustrated by figure 27.23.

VI

Advanced Techniques

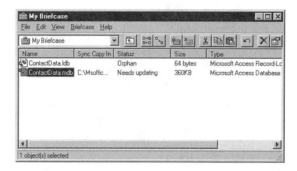

Fig. 27.23 My Briefcase's windows displaying details of the modified Briefcase replica.

Note

When you open an Access database, Access creates a lock file, *Filename*.ldb. The lock file is an *Orphan* file in the Briefcase because the lock file does not have a corresponding synchronized copy. You don't need to worry about the presence (or absence) of an Access lock file in your Briefcase.

---

11. Choose Briefcase, Update All to update the design-master .mdb. The Update My Briefcase dialog appears as shown in figure 27.24. Click Update to make the changes to the design-master copy of ContactData.mdb.

The Update All menu choice updates the design-master .mdb from *all* Briefcases on the desktop that are synchronized with the .mdb, not just the open Briefcase.

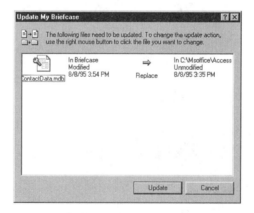

Fig. 27.24 The Update My Briefcase dialog that confirms reconciliation of the design-master replica with the updated Briefcase replica.

12. Re-open My Briefcase to check the status of your Briefcase replica, which now is Up-to-Date (see fig. 27.25).

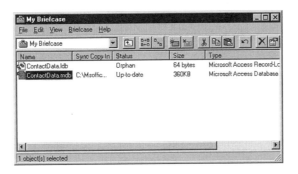

Fig. 27.25   My Briefcase's window displaying the status of an up-to-date replica set.

13. Close My Briefcase and delete the copy of My Briefcase on the desktop.

Tip

If you create multiple Briefcases to accommodate several mobile users who update Briefcase replicas using disks, try to organize the process so that you obtain the disks from all users at the same time. This allows you to use a single Update All operation to reconcile all changes for a given period simultaneously.

From Here...

Briefcase replication and reconciliation of Briefcase replica updates to Access design-master replicas is a useful method for maintaining "soon-enough" rather than real-time currency of data in Access databases. For information on subjects related to the process of Briefcase replication, see:

- Chapter 28, "Writing Visual Basic for Applications Code," describes how to use Access 95's Code Behind Forms feature to write event-handling code for forms and reports. You can write Access VBA code to automate the Briefcase replication processes described in this chapter.

- Chapter 29, "Understanding the Data Access Object Class," explains Access 95's hierarchy of objects created by Access and the Jet 3.0 database engine, including objects related specifically to Briefcase replication.

- Chapter 30, "Exchanging Data with OLE Automation and DDE," gives examples of code for programming objects created by other OLE 2.1-compliant applications, as well as OLE Custom Controls. The Briefcase replication process uses OLE Automation operations on the Jet 3.0 Data Access Object to perform many of its functions.

VI

Advanced Techniques

Part VII

Programming with Visual Basic for Applications

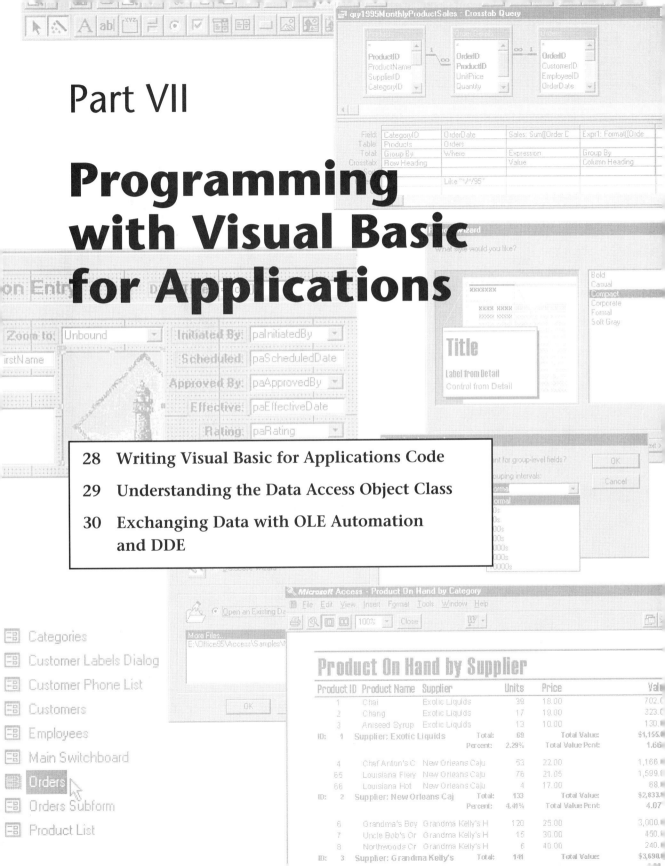

Chapter 28

Writing Visual Basic for Applications Code

Most Access applications you create do not require you to write a single line of Access VBA code. A few commercial Access applications rely primarily on macros rather than Access VBA code for automating applications. Sequences of Access actions, contained in macro objects, usually are sufficient to provide the methods needed by simple applications to respond to events, such as running queries, displaying forms, and printing reports. The built-in functions of Access enable you to perform complex calculations in queries. You may, however, want or need to use Access VBA code for any of the following reasons:

- To create user-defined functions (UDFs) that substitute for complex expressions you use repeatedly to validate data, compute values for text boxes, and perform other duties. Creating a UDF that you refer to by a short name minimizes potential typing errors and enables you to document the way your expression works.

- To write expressions that include more complex decision structures than allowed by the standard IIf() function (in an **If...Then...Else...End If** structure, for example), or to write expressions that need loops for repetitive operations.

- To perform actions not available from standard Access macros, such as transaction processing with the Access VBA equivalents of SQL COMMIT and ROLLBACK statements.

- To execute DDE operations that you cannot perform with the standard DDE() and DDESend() functions of Access, or to execute DDE operations over which you need more control than is offered by these functions. Using Access VBA's DDE capabilities is one of the subjects of Chapter 30, "Exchanging Data with OLE Automation and DDE."

- To manipulate other applications' objects with OLE Automation code. Using OLE Automation is the primary subject of Chapter 30, "Exchanging Data with OLE Automation and DDE."

In this chapter, you learn to

- Modify a sample Access VBA function

- Use the Debug Window to evaluate Access VBA functions

- Use the **Debug.Print** object to print values of Access VBA variables

- Write and test your own user-defined function

- Use the Code Builder to create an event-handling subprocedure

■ To open more than one database in an application where attaching a table or using the SQL IN statement is not sufficient for your application.

■ To provide hard-copy documentation for your application. If you include actions in Access VBA code rather than macros, you can print the Access VBA code to improve the documentation for your application. Well-documented code is likely to be easier to understand than the documentation for macros created by the Documentor add-in.

■ To create run-time applications that substitute Access VBA functions for macros so that execution errors do not cause your application to quit without warning.

This chapter describes Access VBA, introduces you to Access VBA modules and procedures, shows you how to use the Module window to enter and test Access VBA code, and helps you start writing user-defined functions. The chapter also includes examples of Access VBA programs.

Introducing Access VBA

Several years ago, Bill Gates, the founder and chairman of Microsoft Corporation, stated that all Microsoft applications that use macros would share a common macro language built on BASIC. BASIC is the acronym for Beginner's All-Purpose Symbolic Instruction Code, originally developed at Dartmouth College. Gates's choice of BASIC is not surprising when you consider that Microsoft was built on the foundation of Gates's BASIC interpreter that ran in 8K on the early predecessors of the PC. He reiterated his desire for a common macro language in an article that appeared in *One-to-One with Microsoft* in late 1991.

Before Access 1.0 was released, the results of Gates's edict were observed in only one Microsoft product, Word for Windows. If you have created Microsoft Word macros or just made minor changes to macros you have recorded, you will find that Access VBA is similar to WordBasic. With the arrival of Excel 5.0, Visual Basic, Applications Edition (more commonly known as Visual Basic for Applications or VBA), became the *lingua franca* for programming Microsoft's productivity applications.

Access 95 now joins Excel 5+, Project 4+, and Visual Basic 4.0 in implementing VBA as Microsoft's "common macro language." Microsoft says future versions of Word and PowerPoint also will use VBA, and the Blackbird developer tools for creating applications for the Microsoft Network are scheduled for the addition of VBA in 1996.

Note

Each application that uses VBA automatically adds references to its built-in application objects to the language. Thus, each application has its own "flavor" of VBA. As an example, the Access DoCmd object used to execute macro actions in code is specific to the Access "flavor" of VBA. For this reason, this book uses the term *Access VBA* to describe VBA with the standard set of Access object references added to the root language.

VBA is a real programming language, not a "macro language;" Access has its own macro "language." You create the equivalent of macros with Access VBA functions and subprocedures. To execute the Access VBA functions and subprocedures that you write, you use Access's macro language or specify the name of an Access VBA function as the value of an event.

You can execute any macro action from Access VBA by preceding the keyword with a DoCmd and a space. The names of many macro actions appear to be the same as Access VBA reserved words. Except for MsgBox and SendKeys, macro action names and Access VBA reserved words that are identical in name use a different syntax and perform different, but usually related, functions.

Access VBA Compared with Xbase, PAL, and Visual VBA

Programmers who have experience with dBASE or other DOS Xbase dialects, such as Clipper and FoxBase, will find that Access VBA uses many of the same Xbase keywords or minor variations of familiar Xbase keywords. Borland's PAL is related to Xbase, so PAL and ObjectPAL programmers will also find the translation of PAL to Access VBA keywords straightforward. There remains a large number of DOS-based RDBMS applications running on PCs; many of these applications are likely to be converted to 32-bit Access applications running under Windows 95 or Windows NT. Therefore, a comparison of Access VBA and DOS database applications continues to be warranted.

User-defined functions are almost identical in structure in Access VBA and the DOS versions of Xbase and PAL. This similarity in code structure ends, however, with user-defined functions. Writing code for Windows applications in general, and for Access in particular, requires an entirely different code structure. Applications for DOS RDBMSs use top-down programming techniques, which means that a main program calls (executes) other subprograms or procedures that perform specific actions. The user of the application makes choices from a menu that determine which subprograms or procedures are invoked. Menus that let the application remain idle are enclosed within DO WHILE...ENDDO loops while the user decides what menu command to choose next. Your code is responsible for all actions that occur while the application is running.

The situation with Windows and Access differs from that of top-down programming. Access itself is the main program, and Windows is responsible for many functions that you must code in DOS RDBMS languages. This fact is a blessing for new programmers because Windows and Access simplify the development of complex applications. However, Access's and Windows' contributions are a curse for top-down DOS programmers because Access and Windows require an entirely new approach to writing RDBMS code.

The guiding principles for DOS RDBMS developers writing Access VBA applications are the following:

- Don't even *think* about writing Access VBA code during the development stage of your first applications; use macros. Most applications do not need any code other than an occasional user-defined function. Those applications that do need code usually do not require very much of it. The exceptions are run-time Access applications for which using Access VBA code is preferred.

■ Use command buttons and associated macro actions to substitute for the traditional menu commands of DOS RDBMSs. In many applications, you create a menu that gives the user only the File, Exit command. All other user-initiated choices in the application are handled by control objects on forms.

■ Concentrate on using macro actions to respond to user- and application-initiated events, such as opening forms. Study the event-oriented properties of form and control objects and the macro actions available to respond to the event properties. Learn the full capabilities of each macro action native to Access before you write your own actions in Access VBA. Event properties combined with the appropriate macro actions usually can substitute for about 95 percent of the code you write for DOS RDBMSs.

■ After your application is up and running, consider writing Access VBA code to add the nuances that distinguish professionally written database applications. If you are a programmer, you may find that implementing macro actions in code is preferable to using macro objects to contain those actions because you can print the code to document your application.

Where You Use Access VBA Code

You probably will first use Access VBA to create functions that make complex calculations. Creating an Access VBA function to substitute for calculations with many sets of parentheses is relatively simple and a good introduction to writing Access VBA code. Writing expressions as Access VBA functions enables you to add comments to the code that make the purpose and construction of the code clear to others. Also, comments aid your memory when you decide to revise an application after using it for a few months.

Your next step is to create Access VBA event-handling subprocedures in form or report modules to replace macros. You use event-handling subprocedures to perform operations that are cumbersome to implement with, or that cannot be accomplished by, macro actions. For example, the `RunCode` macro action executes Access VBA functions, but the `RunCode` action ignores the function's return value if it has one. Access 95 gives you the choice of calling a function contained in an Access module, or executing an event-handling subprocedure contained in a form or report module. Microsoft calls Access VBA contained in forms or reports *Code Behind Forms* (CBF).

Typographic and Naming Conventions Used for Access VBA

This book uses a special set of typographic conventions for references to Access VBA keywords and object variable names in Access VBA examples:

■ Monospace type is used for all Access VBA code in the examples, as in `lngItemCounter`.

■ Bold monospace type is used for all VBA reserved words and type-declaration symbols, as in **Dim** and **%**. Standard function names in Access VBA, as described in Chapter 9, "Understanding Operators and Expressions in Access," also are set in bold type so that reserved words, standard function names, and reserved symbols stand out from variable and function names and values you assign to variables. Key words incorporated by reference by Access, such as `DoCmd`, are not set in bold.

■ Italic monospace type indicates a replaceable item, as in `Dim DataItem As String`.

■ Bold italic monospace type indicates a replaceable reserved word, such as a data type, as in `Dim DataItem As DataType`; `DataType` is replaced by a VBA reserved word corresponding to the desired VBA data type.

■ Names of variables that refer to Access objects, such as forms or reports, use a three-letter prefix derived from the object name, as in `frmFormName` and `rptReportName`. The prefixes for object variables are listed in Appendix B, "Naming Conventions for Access Objects and Variables."

■ Names of other variables are preceded by a one-letter or three-letter data type identifier, such as `varVariantVariable` and `intIntegerVariable`. Boolean variables (flags) that return only `True` or `False` values use the f prefix, as in `fIsLoaded`.

■ Optional elements are included within square brackets, as in `[OptionItem]`. Square brackets also enclose object names that contain spaces or special punctuation symbols.

■ An ellipsis (. . .) substitutes for code not shown in syntax and code examples, as in `If...Then...Else...End If`.

Modules, Functions, and Subprocedures

A *module* is a container for Access VBA code just as a form is a container for control objects. Access 95 provides the following three types of modules:

■ *Access Modules.* You create an Access module to contain your Access VBA code the same way that you create any other new database object: click the Module tab in the Database window and then click the New button. Alternatively, you can click the New Object button on the toolbar and choose New Module from the drop-down menu. Figure 28.1 shows the `IsLoaded()` function of the Utility Functions module of Northwind.mdb.

Tip

Using Access modules to contain all your Access VBA code speeds the opening of forms and reports, but slows the initial opening of your application.

■ *Form Modules.* Form modules contain code to respond to events triggered by forms or controls on forms called Code Behind Forms (CBF). You open a form module by clicking the Code button of the toolbar in Form Design View. Alternatively, choose View, Code. Either of these methods opens a module that Access automatically names Form_*FormName*, where *FormName* is the name of the selected form. (Access 2.0 named the modules Form.*FormName*.)

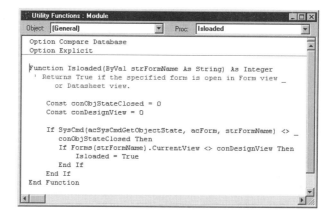

Fig. 28.1   The Access module window for the IsLoaded() function.

Another method of opening a form module is to click the ellipsis button for one of the event properties for a form or a control object on a form. Selecting Code Builder from the Choose Builder dialog displays the *Form_FormName* module with a procedure stub, **Private Sub** *ObjectName_EventName*()...**End Sub**, written for you. Access 95 adds the VBA **Private** prefix by default. Figure 28.2 shows the Access VBA code for the CustomerID_AfterUpdate procedure of Northwind.mdb's Orders form.

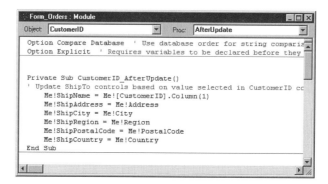

Fig. 28.2   A typical Code Behind Forms event-handling procedure.

- *Report Modules.* Report modules contain code to respond to events triggered by reports, sections of reports, or group headers and footers. (Control objects on reports do not trigger events.) You open report modules in the same way you open form modules. Report modules are named Report_*ReportName* automatically.

A module consists of a *Declarations section* and usually one or more *procedures* or *functions*. As the name suggests, the Declarations section of a module is used to declare items (usually variables and constants, the subjects of following sections) used by the procedures and functions contained in the module. You can use a module without functions or procedures to declare **Public** variables and constants that can be used by any function or procedure in any module. Similarly, you use the **Public** prefix for functions and subprocedures to allow their use by code in any module. (**Public** replaces Access 2.0's **Global** keyword, but **Global** continues to work in Access 95.)

> **Note**
>
> The Module windows of figures 28.1 and 28.2 show the Declarations section and a function or procedure separated by a horizontal line. The ability to display the Declarations sections and all procedures in a single scrollable window, called Full Module View, is a feature shared by the Module windows of all flavors of VBA. If you see only the Declarations section when you open a module, choose Tools, Options to display the Options dialog. Click the Module tab and mark the Full Module View and Procedure Separator check boxes.

Procedures are typically defined as subprograms referred to by name in another program. Referring to a procedure by name *calls* or *invokes* the procedure; the code in the procedure executes, and then the sequence of execution returns to the program that called the procedure. Another name for a procedure is *subroutine*. Procedures can call other procedures, in which case the called procedures are called *subprocedures*. Procedures are defined by beginning (**Sub**) and end (**End Sub**) reserved words, with a **Public**, **Private**, or **Static** prefix, as in the following example:

```
Private Sub ProcName
    [Start of procedure code]
    ...
    [End of procedure code]
End Sub
```

> **Note**
>
> You can refer to the procedure name to invoke the procedure, but Access VBA provides a keyword, **Call**, that explicitly invokes a procedure. Prefixing the procedure name with **Call** is a good programming practice because this keyword identifies the name that follows as the name of a procedure rather than a variable.

Functions are a class of procedures that return values to their names, as explained in Chapter 9, "Understanding Operators and Expressions in Access." C programmers would argue that procedures are a class of functions, called *void* functions, that do not return values. Regardless of how you view the difference between functions and subprocedures, keep the following points in mind:

- Access macros require that you write Access VBA functions (not subprocedures) to act in place of macro actions when using the RunCode macro action.

- The only way you can call a subprocedure in an Access VBA module is from an Access VBA function or from another procedure. You cannot directly execute a procedure in an Access module from any Access database object.

■ Unlike Access modules, form and report modules use subprocedures (not functions) to respond to events. Using form- and report-level subprocedures for event-handling code mimics Visual VBA's approach for events triggered by forms and controls on forms.

■ Function names in Access modules are global in scope with respect to Access modules unless they are declared **Private**. Thus, you cannot have duplicate **Public** function names in any Access module in your application. However, form and report modules can have a function with the same name as a **Public** function in a module because form and report function and procedure names have form- or report-level scope. A function in a form module with the same name as a function in an Access module function takes priority over the Access module version. Therefore, if you include the IsLoaded() function in a form module and you call the IsLoaded() function from a procedure in the form module, the IsLoaded() function in the form module executes.

■ To execute an Access VBA function in Access VBA code, you must use the function in an expression, such as

```
intReturnValue = nilFunctionName([Arguments])
```

even when the function returns no value.

Functions are created within a structure similar to procedures, as in the following example:

```
Private Function FuncName([Arguments])
   [Start of function code]
   ...
   [End of function code]
End Function
```

You cannot use **Call** to execute a function; you must refer to the function by name. Function calls are identified by the parentheses that follow the function name—even if the function requires no arguments.

You can add as many individual procedures and functions as you want to a module. If you write a substantial amount of Access VBA code, you should take one of the following two approaches:

■ Use form and report modules to contain the code that responds to the events on forms. Procedures common to several forms, however, should be incorporated in Access modules. As mentioned in the tip earlier in this chapter, adding substantial amounts of code to form modules slows the opening of the form.

■ Create separate Access modules for code associated with a particular class of object, such as forms. A form that requires an appreciable amount of code usually deserves its own module. When you take the Access module approach, your application opens more slowly, but forms open more rapidly. Users are likely to favor applications that respond more quickly after they are launched.

Access VBA introduces another class of procedure called *property procedures* that use the
`{Property Let|Property Get| Property Set}...End Property` structure to create custom
properties for Access objects, such as forms or controls. Property procedures are used by
VBA developers primarily for creating custom wizards. A discussion of property procedures is beyond the scope of this book.

References to VBA and Access Modules

Access 95 uses references to make objects available for use in modules. Access 95's default
references are Visual Basic for Applications, Microsoft Access 95, Microsoft DAO 3.0 Object Library, and the currently open database. To view the default references, open a
module, then choose Tools, References to open the References dialog (see fig. 28.3). Current references, except to the open database, are indicated by a mark in the adjacent
check box.

Access 95 implements VBA by establishing references to collections of objects exposed
by VBA's object library, ven2132.olb. Ven2132.olb is the English (en) version of VBA 2.1
(21), 32-bit version (32). Similarly, Access exposes its application objects through a type
library, MSACCESS.TLB, and the Jet database engine exposes data access objects (DAOs)
through an OLE .DLL, DAO3032.DLL. Each application that supports VBA has a similar,
but not identical, set of default references.

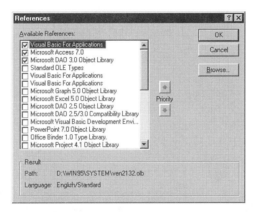

Fig. 28.3   Three of the four default object references for Access 95.

Referenced objects appear in the Libraries/Databases drop-down list of the Object
Browser. To view the Object Browser, open a module and click the Object Browser button
on the tool bar (or choose View, Object Browser). The current database is the default
object in the Libraries/Databases list. Figure 28.4 shows a few of the references to Report
objects in Northwind.mdb and the Utility Functions module in the Modules/Classes list.
Only objects that can act as VBA containers appear in the Module/Classes list.

When you select a function or subprocedure name in a module, the function or
subprocedure name and arguments, if any, appear adjacent to the help (?) button, which
is disabled for user-defined functions and the event-handling subprocedures you write.

Chapter 29, "Understanding the Data Access Object Class," describes object classes and the use of the Object Browser in detail.

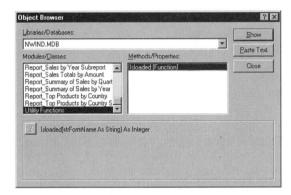

Fig. 28.4 The Object Browser displaying the calling syntax for the IsLoaded() function.

Data Types and Database Objects in Access VBA

When you create Access VBA tables, all data types that you use to assign field data types and sizes (except for OLE and Memo field data types) have data type counterparts in Access VBA. With the exception of the **Variant** and **Currency** data types, Access VBA data types are represented in most other dialects of BASIC, such as Microsoft QuickBASIC and the QBasic interpreter supplied with MS-DOS 5 and later.

Traditional BASIC dialects use a punctuation symbol called the *type-declaration character*, such as $ for the String data type, to designate the data type. The Access VBA data types, the type-declaration characters, the corresponding field data types, and the ranges of values are shown in the AB Type, Symbol, Field Type, Minimum Value, and Maximum Value columns of table 28.1, respectively. The Field Types Byte, Integer, Long Integer, Single, and Double correspond to the Field size property of the Number data type in tables, queries, forms, and reports. Access VBA adds the **Byte** and **Boolean** data types to support the 8-bit Byte and 16-bit Yes/No field data types.

Table 28.1 Access VBA and Corresponding Field Data Types

AB Type	Symbol	Field Type	Minimum Value	Maximum Value
Byte	None	Byte	0	255
Integer	%	Integer,	–2,768	32,767
Boolean	None	Yes/No	**True**	**False**
Long	&	Long Integer, Counter	–2,147,483,648	2,147,483,647
Single	!	Single	–3.402823E38 1.401298E –45	–1.401298E–5 3.402823E38

AB Type	Symbol	Field Type	Minimum Value	Maximum Value
Double	#	Double	–1.79769313486232E308 4.94065645841247E –324	4.9406564841247E–324 1.79769313486232E308
Currency	@	Currency	–922,337,203,685, 477.5808	922,337,203,685, 477.5807
String	$	Text	0 characters	65,500 characters (+/–)
Variant	None	Any	January 1, 0000 (date)	December 31, 1999 (date)
			Same as **Double** (numbers)	Same as **Double** (numbers)
			Same as **String** (text)	Same as **String** (text)

Tip

All data returned from fields of tables or queries is of the **Variant** data type by default. If you assign the field value to a conventional data type, such as **Integer**, the data type is said to be *coerced*.

You can dispense with the type-declaration character if you explicitly declare your variables with the **Dim...As** *DataType* statement, discussed later in this section. If you do not explicitly declare the variables' data type or use a symbol to define an implicit data type, Access VBA variables default to the **Variant** data type.

The # sign is also used to enclose values specified as dates, as in varNewYears = #1/1/96#. In this case, bold type is not used for the enclosing # signs because these symbols are not intended for the purpose of the # reserved symbol that indicates the **Double** data type.

Database objects—such as databases, tables, and queries—and application objects (forms and reports), all of which you used in prior chapters, also have corresponding object data types in Access VBA. Here Access VBA departs from other BASIC languages with the exception of Visual Basic. The most commonly used object data types of Access VBA and the object library that includes the objects are listed in table 28.2.

Table 28.2   The Most Common Database Object Data Types Supported by Access VBA

Object Data	Library	Corresponding Database Object Type
Database	DAO 3.0	Databases opened by the Jet database engine
Form	Access 95	Forms, including subforms
Report	Access 95	Reports, including subreports
Control	Access 95	Controls on forms and reports
QueryDef	DAO 3.0	Query definitions (SQL statement equivalents)
TableDef	DAO 3.0	Table definitions (structure, indexes, and other table properties)
Recordset	DAO 3.0	A virtual representation of a table or the result set of a query

> **Note**
>
> The Table, Dynaset, and Snapshot object data types of Access 1.x have been replaced by the all-encompassing Recordset data type of Access 2+. You distinguish the type of Recordset object (Table, Dynaset, or Snapshot) by the Recordset object's Type property. The Table, Dynaset, and Snapshot object types are supported by Access 95 for backward compatibility with Access 1.x code. However, it is a good practice to use the new Recordset data type because there is no guarantee that the obsolete Access 1.x object data types will be supported in future versions of Access. Data access object data types and object collections are discussed in Chapter 29, "Understanding the Data Access Object Class."

Variables and Naming Conventions

Variables are named placeholders for values of a specified data type that change when your Access VBA code is executed. You give variables names, as you name fields, but the names of variables cannot include spaces or any other punctuation except the underscore character (_). The other restriction is that a variable cannot use an Access VBA keyword by itself as a name; keywords are called *reserved words* for this reason. The same rules apply to giving names to functions and procedures. Variable names in Access VBA typically employ a combination of upper- and lowercase letters to make them more readable.

Implicit Variables. You can create variables by assigning a value to a variable name, as in the following example:

```
NewVar = 1234
```

A statement of this type *declares* a variable, which means to create a new variable with a name you choose. The statement in the example creates a new implicit variable, NewVar, of the **Variant** data type with a value of 1234. (Thus **NewVar** would be more appropriately named varNewVar.) When you do not specify a data type for an implicit variable by appending one of the type-declaration characters to the variable name, the **Variant** data type is assigned by default. The following statement creates a variable of the Integer data type:

```
NewVar% = 1234
```

Declaring variables of the **Integer** or **Long** (integer) type when decimal fractions are not required speeds the operation of your code. Access takes longer to compute values for **Variant**, **Double**, and **Single** variables.

Explicit Variables. It is better programming practice to declare your variables and assign those variables a data type before you give variables a value. Programming languages such as C, C++, and Turbo Pascal require you to declare variables before you use them. The most common method of declaring variables is by using the **Dim...As** *Datatype* structure where **As** specifies the data type. This method declares explicit variables. An example follows:

```
Dim intNewVar As Integer
```

If you do not add the **As Integer** keywords, intNewVar is assigned the **Variant** data type by default.

You can require that all variables must be explicitly declared prior to their use by adding the statement, **Option Explicit**, in the Declarations section of a module. The advantage of using **Option Explicit** is that Access detects misspelled variable names and displays an error message when misspellings are encountered. If you do not use **Option Explicit** and you misspell a variable name, Access creates a new implicit variable with the misspelled name. The resulting errors in your code's operation can be difficult to diagnose. Access automatically adds an Option Explicit statement to the Declarations section of each module if you set the Require Variable Declaration option on in the Module sheet of the Options dialog (see fig. 28.5).

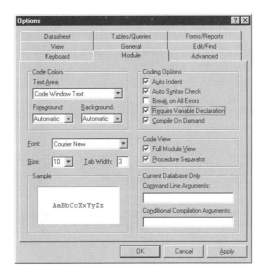

Fig. 28.5   Setting the Require Variable Declaration option in the Modules sheet of the Options dialog.

Scope and Duration of Variables. Variables have a property called *scope*, which determines when they appear and disappear in your Access VBA code. Variables appear the first time you declare them and then disappear and reappear on the basis of the scope you assign to them. When a variable appears, it is said to be *visible*, meaning that you can assign the variable a value, change its value, and use it in expressions. Otherwise, the variable is *invisible*; if you use a variable's name while it is invisible, you create a new variable with the same name instead.

The following lists the four scope levels in Access VBA:

■ *Local (procedure-level) scope.* The variable is visible only during the time when the procedure in which the variable is declared is executed. Variables that you declare, with or without using **Dim...As** *Datatype* in a procedure or function, are local in scope.

■ *Form-level and report-level scope.* The variable is visible only when the form or report in which it is declared is open. You declare form-level and report-level variables in the Declarations section of form and report modules with **Private...As *Datatype***. (**Dim...As *Datatype*** also works).

■ *Module-level scope.* The variable is visible to all procedures and functions contained in the module in which the variable was declared. (Modules open when you open the database.) You declare variables with module scope in the Declarations section of the module with the same syntax as form- and report-level variables.

■ *Global or public scope.* The variable is visible to all procedures and functions within all modules. You declare variables with global scope in the Declarations section of a module using **Public...As *Datatype***.

The scope and visibility of variables declared in two different Access modules of the same database, both having two procedures, are illustrated by the diagram in figure 28.6. In each procedure, variables declared with different scopes are used to assign values to variables declared within the procedure. Invalid assignment statements are shown crossed out in the figure. These assignment statements are invalid because the variable used to assign the value to the variable declared in the procedure is not visible in the procedure.

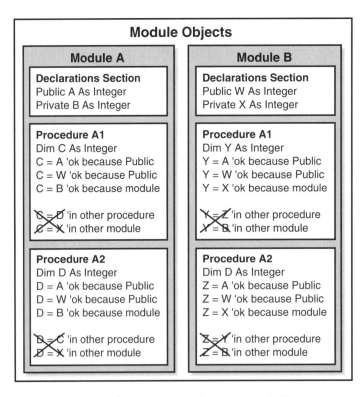

Fig. 28.6   Valid and invalid assignment statements for variables of different scopes.

Variables also have a property called *duration*, or *lifetime*. The duration of a variable is your code's execution time between the first appearance of the variable (its declaration) and its disappearance. Each time a procedure or function is called, local variables declared with the `Dim...As Datatype` statement are set to default values with 0 for numeric data types and the empty string ("") for string variables. These local variables ordinarily have a duration equal to the lifetime of the function or procedure—from the time the function or procedure is called until the `End Function` or `End Sub` statement is executed.

To preserve the values of local variables between occurrences (called *instances*) of a procedure or function, you substitute the reserved word `Static` for `Dim`. Static variables have a duration of your Access application, but their scope is determined by where you declare them. Static variables are useful when you want to count the number of occurrences of an event. You can make all variables in a function or procedure static variables by preceding `Function` or `Sub` with the `Static` keyword.

> **Note**
>
> Minimize the number of local variables that you declare `Static`. Local variables do not consume memory when they are not visible. This characteristic of local variables is especially important in the case of arrays, discussed in the "Access VBA Arrays" section that follows shortly, because arrays are often very large.

User-Defined Data Types. You can create your own data type consisting of one or more Access data types. User-defined data types are discussed in this section pertaining to variables because you need to know what a variable is before you can declare a user-defined data type. You declare a user-defined data type between the `Type...End Type` keywords, as in the following example:

```
Type DupRec
    Field1 As Long
    Field2 As String * 20
    Field3 As Single
    Field4 As Double
End Type
```

User-defined data types are particularly useful when you create a variable to hold the values of one or more records of a table that uses fields of different data types. The `String * 20` statement defines `Field2` of the user-defined data type as a *fixed-length* string of 20 characters, usually corresponding to the Size property of the Text field data type. String variables in user-defined data types are always specified with a fixed length. You must declare your user-defined data type (called a *record* or a *structure* in other programming languages) in the Declarations section of a module.

You must explicitly declare variables to be of the user-defined type with the `Dim`, `Private`, `Public`, or `Static` keywords because there is no reserved symbol to declare a user-defined data type, as in `Dim usrCurrentRec As tagDupRec`. To assign a value to a field of a variable with a user-defined data type, you specify the name of the variable and the field name, separating them with a period, as in `usrCurrentRec.lngField1 = 2048`.

Access VBA Arrays. *Arrays* are variables that consist of a collection of values, called elements of the array, of a single data type in a regularly ordered structure. Implicitly declared arrays are not allowed in Access VBA (or in Visual VBA). You declare an array with the Dim statement, adding the number of elements in parentheses to the variable name for the array, as in the following example:

```
Dim astrNewArray (20) As String
```

This statement creates an array of 21 elements, each of which is a conventional, variable-length string variable. You create 21 elements because the first element of an array is the 0 (zero) element unless you specify otherwise by adding the **To** modifier, as in the following example:

```
Dim astrNewArray (1 To 20) As String
```

The preceding statement creates an array with 20 elements.

You can create multidimensional arrays by adding more values separated by commas. The statement

```
Dim alngNewArray (9, 9, 9) As Long
```

creates a three-dimensional array of 10 elements per dimension. This array, when visible, occupies 4,000 bytes of memory ($10 \times 10 \times 10 \times 4$ bytes/long integer).

You can create a dynamic array by declaring the array using Dim without specifying the number of elements and then using the **ReDim** reserved word to determine the number of elements the array contains. You can **ReDim** an array as many times as you want; each time you do so, the values stored in the array are reinitialized to their default values, determined by the data type, unless you follow **ReDim** with the reserved word, **Preserve**. The following sample statements create a dynamic array:

```
Dim alngNewArray ( ) As Long          'In Declarations sections
ReDim Preserve alngNewArray (9, 9, 9) 'In procedure, preserves prior values
ReDim alngNewArray (9, 9, 9)          'In procedure, reinitializes all
```

Dynamic arrays are useful when you don't know how many elements an array requires when you declare it. You can **ReDim** a dynamic array to zero elements when you no longer need the values it contains; this enables you to recover the memory that the array consumes while it is visible. Arrays declared with **Dim** are limited to eight dimensions. You can use the **ReDim** statement within a procedure without preceding it with the **Dim** statement to create local-scope arrays with up to 60 dimensions.

Scope, duration rules, and keywords apply to arrays in the same way in which they apply to conventional variables. You can declare dynamic arrays with global and module-level scope by adding the **Public** or **Private** statement to the Declarations section of a module and then using the **ReDim** statement by itself in a procedure. If you declare an array with **Static**, rather than **Dim**, the array retains its values between instances of a procedure.

> **Note**
>
> Do not use the **Option Base** keywords to change the default initial element of arrays from 0 to 1. **Option Base** is included in Access VBA for compatibility with other BASIC dialects. Many arrays you create from Access VBA objects must begin with element 0. If you are concerned about the memory occupied by an unused zeroth element of an array, use the **Dim** *ArrayName* (1 **To** *N*) **As** *DataType* declaration. In most cases, you can disregard the zeroth element.

Named Database Objects as Variables in Access VBA Code. Properties of database objects you create with Access can be treated as variables and assigned values within Access VBA code. You can assign a new value to the text box that contains the address information for a customer by name, for example. Use the following statement:

```
Forms!Customers!Address = "123 Elm St."
```

The collection name Forms defines the type of object. The exclamation point (called the *bang* symbol by programmers) separates the name of the form and the name of the control object. The ! symbol is analogous to the \ path separator that you use when you are dealing with files. If the name of the form or the control object contains a space or other punctuation, you need to enclose the name within square brackets, as in the following statement:

```
Forms!Customers![Contact Name] = "Joe Hill"
```

Alternatively, you can use the **Set** keyword to create your own named variable for the control object. This procedure is convenient when you need to refer to the control object several times; it is more convenient to type txtContact than the full "path" to the control object, in this case a text box.

```
Dim txtContact As Control
Set txtContact = Forms!Customers![Contact Name]
txtContact = "Joe Hill"
```

You can assign any database object to a variable name by declaring the variable as the object type and using the **Set** statement to assign the object to the variable. You do not create a copy of the object in memory when you assign it a variable name; the variable refers to the object in memory. Referring to an object in memory is often called *pointing* to an object; many languages have a pointer data type that holds the value of the location in memory where the variable is stored. Access VBA does not support pointers. Chapter 29, "Understanding the Data Access Object Class," deals with creating variables that point to the Access 95 database objects supplied by the Jet 3.0 DAO.

Object Properties and the With...End With Structure. Access VBA introduces the With...End With structure that offers a shorthand method of setting the values of object properties, such as the dimensions and other characteristics of a form. The With...End With structure also lets you set the values of fields of a user-defined data type without repeating the variable name in each instance. To use the With...End With structure to set object property values, you must first declare and set an object variable, as in the following example:

```
Dim frmFormName As Form
Set frmFormName = Forms!FormName
With frmFormName
    .Top = 1000
    .Left = 1000
    .Width = 5000
    .Height = 4000
End With
```

When using the **With...End With** structure with user-defined data types, you don't use the **Set** statement. Names of properties or fields within the structure are preceded by periods.

Variable Naming Conventions. In the event that you need to write large amounts of Access VBA code, you probably will employ a large number of variable names and many different data types. On forms and reports, many different types of named control objects can be used, each of which you can assign to a variable name with the **Set** keyword in your Access VBA code. As your code grows in size, remembering the data types of all the variables becomes difficult.

Stan Leszynski, a Seattle database consultant, has created a set of variable-naming conventions for Access VBA. The *Leszynski Naming Conventions for Microsoft Access* employs *Hungarian notation*, which is used primarily in the C and C++ languages. Hungarian refers to the nationality of the method's inventor, Charles Simonyi, who was involved in the development of Access, and the fact that only Hungarians are likely to be able to correctly pronounce some of the abbreviations involved, such as "lpsz." Leszynski adapted Hungarian notation for use in the Access VBA environment.

Hungarian notation uses a set of codes for the data type. You prefix the variable name with the code in lowercase letters. For example, the prefix code for a text box is txt, so the variable name for the text box in the preceding example is txtContact. Strings in C code are identified by the prefix lpsz, an abbreviation for long pointer to a string, zero-terminated (with **Chr$(0)** or ASCII **Null**). Access VBA does not support the pointer data type (but it does use pointers for the location of string variables), and it does not use zero-terminated strings. Therefore, str is a more appropriate prefix for Access VBA strings.

The data type identifier of a user-defined data type is called a *created tag*. In Hungarian notation, created tags are capitalized as in the following:

```
Type REC
    lngField1 As Long
    strField2 As String
    sngField3 As Single
    dblField4 As Double
End Type
```

A variable of type REC is declared with the lowercase rec prefix, such as in the following:

```
Dim recCurRecord As REC
```

Created tags should be short, but should not duplicate one of the standard data type prefix codes.

Using standard data type prefixes makes your code easier to read and understand. Many of the code examples in this book use the new proposed naming conventions. The complete list of the Leszynski notation for Access VBA objects and variables appears in Appendix B, "Naming Conventions for Access Objects and Variables."

Symbolic Constants

Symbolic constants are named placeholders for values of a specified data type that do not change when your Access VBA code is executed. You precede the name of a symbolic constant with the keyword, **Const**, as in **Const** sngPI **As Single** = 3.1416. You declare symbolic constants in the Declarations section of a module or within a function or procedure. Precede **Const** with the **Public** keyword if you want to create a global constant visible to all modules, as in **Public Const** gsngPI = 3.1416. Public constants only can be declared in the Declarations section of an Access VBA module.

Typically, symbolic constants take names in all capital letters to distinguish them from variables. Often, underscores are used to make the names of symbolic constants more readable, as in sngVALUE_OF_PI. This naming convention no longer applies to system-defined constants in Access 95. System-defined intrinsic constants are the subject of the next section.

You do not need to specify a data type for constants because Access VBA chooses the data type that stores the data most efficiently. Access VBA can do this because it knows the value of the data when it "compiles" your code. It is a good programming practice, however, to add **As** *Datatype* when declaring constants.

> **Note**
>
> Access is an interpreted language, so the term "compile" in an Access VBA context is a misnomer. When you "compile" the Access VBA source that you write in code editing windows, Access creates a tokenized version of the code (called *pseudo-code* or *p-code*). This subject is discussed in the section "The Access VBA Compiler," later in the chapter.

Access System-Defined Constants. Access VBA includes seven system-defined constants, **True**, **False**, Yes, No, On, Off, and **Null**, that are created by the VBA and Access type libraries when launched. Of these seven, you can use **True**, **False**, and **Null**, which are declared by the VBA library, in Access VBA code. The remaining four are declared by the Access type library and are valid for use with all database objects except modules. When the system-defined constants **True**, **False**, and **Null** are used in Access VBA code examples in this book, they appear in bold monospace type.

Access Intrinsic Constants. Access VBA provides a number of pre-declared intrinsic symbolic constants primarily for use as arguments of DoCmd.*MacroAction* statements, which let you execute macro actions in Access VBA. Access 95 intrinsic constants carry the prefix ac, as in acExportMerge. You can display the list of Access intrinsic constants in the Object Browser by selecting Access - Microsoft Access 95 in the Libraries/Databases list and then selecting Constants in the Modules/Classes list.

When you select a constant in Methods/Properties list, its numeric value appears adjacent to the help (?) button (see fig. 28.7). It is a good programming practice to use constants, rather than their numeric values, when applicable. You may not use any of these intrinsic constants' names as names for constants or variables that you define.

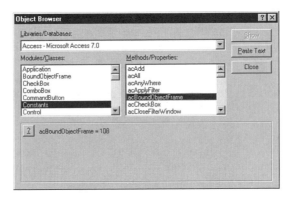

Fig. 28.7 Displaying Access 95 intrinsic constants in the Object Browser.

> **Note**
>
> In Access 2.0 and earlier, intrinsic constants were classified as action constants (prefixed with A_), database constants (prefixed with DB_), and the Variant data type constants (prefixed with V_). In Access 95, each object library contributes its own set of intrinsic constants, prefixed with db for Jet 3.0 DAO constants and with vb for VBA constants. If you convert an Access 2.0 or earlier application to Access 95, the prior constant names are valid. These prior constants appear when you select OldConstants in the Modules/Classes list.

Access VBA Named and Optional Arguments

Procedures often have one or more arguments that pass values from the calling statement to the called procedure. Traditionally, you must pass all of the values required by the procedure in your calling statement. As an example, if a procedure accepts four arguments, *Arg1...Arg4*, your calling statement must provide values for *Arg1...Arg4*, as in the following example:

```
Sub CallingProc ()
   ...
   Call CalledProc(100000, 200000, 300000, 400000)
   ...
End Sub

Sub CalledProc (Arg1 As Long, Arg2 As Long, Arg3 As Long, _
    Arg4 As Long)
   [Subprocedure code]
End Sub
```

Access 95 lets you declare the arguments of the subprocedure to be **Optional**, eliminating the need to pass every parameter to the procedure. You use *named arguments* to pass values to specific arguments, as in the following example:

```
Sub CallingProc ()
    ...
    Call CalledProc(Arg2 := 200000, Arg3 := 300000)
    ...
End Sub

Sub CalledProc (Optional Arg1, Optional Arg2, Optional Arg3, _
        Optional Arg4)
    [Subprocedure code]
End Sub
```

The := operator specifies that the preceding element is the name of an argument; named arguments need not be entered in the order the arguments appear in the called procedure. However, if you want to omit argument(s), the corresponding argument name(s) of the called procedure must be preceded by the keyword **Optional**. Optional arguments must be of the **Variant** data type, and missing arguments return **Null** values to subprocedure code. If you omit the **As *Datatype*** modifier of an argument in the called procedure, the argument assumes the default **Variant** data type.

Controlling Program Flow

Useful procedures must be able to make decisions based on the values of variables and then take specified actions based on those decisions. Blocks of code, for example, may need to be repeated until a specified condition occurs. Statements used to make decisions and repeat blocks of code are the fundamental elements that control program flow in Access VBA and all other programming languages.

All programming languages require methods of executing different algorithms based on the results of one or more comparison operations. You can control the flow of any program in any programming language with just three types of statements: conditional execution (**If...Then...End If**), repetition (**Do While...Loop** and related structures), and termination (**End...**). The additional flow control statements in Access VBA and other programming languages make writing code more straightforward.

The code examples used in the following sections do not include **Dim** statements, so Hungarian notation is not used here. Data type identification symbols are used for brevity to indicate the data types of variables.

Branching and Labels

◀◀ See "Assignment and Comparison Operators," p. 288

If you have written DOS batch files or WordPerfect macros, you are probably acquainted with branching and labels. Both the DOS batch language and the WordPerfect macro language include the GoTo Label command. DOS defines any word that begins a line with a colon as a label; WordPerfect requires the use of the keyword LABEL and then the label name.

When BASIC was first developed, the *only* method of controlling program flow was through its GOTO *LineNumber* and GOSUB *LineNumber* statements. Every line in the program required a number that could be used as a substitute for a label. GOTO *LineNumber* caused the interpreter to skip to the designated line and continue executing the program from that point. GOSUB *LineNumber* caused the program to follow that same branch, but when the BASIC interpreter that executed the code encountered a RETURN statement, program execution jumped back to the line following the GOSUB statement and continued executing at that point.

Skipping Blocks of Code with GoTo. Procedural BASIC introduced named labels that replaced the line numbers for GOTO and GOSUB statements. Access VBA's **GoTo** *Label* statement causes your code to branch to the location named *Label:* and continue from that point. Note the colon following *Label:*, which identifies the single word you assigned as a label. However, the colon is not required after the label name following the **GoTo**. In fact, if you add the colon, you get a "label not found" error message.

A label name *must* begin in the far left column (1) of your code. This often interferes with orderly indenting of your code, explained in the next section, which is just one more reason, in addition to those below, for not using **GoTo**.

Avoiding Spaghetti Code by Not Using GoTo. The sequence of statements in code that uses multiple **GoTo** statements is very difficult to follow. It is almost impossible to understand the flow of a large program written in line-numbered BASIC because of the jumps here and there in the code. Programs with multiple **GoTo** statements are derisively said to contain "spaghetti code."

The **GoTo** statement is required for only one purpose in Access VBA: handling errors with the **On Error GoTo** *Label* statement. Although Access VBA supports BASIC's ON...GOTO and ON...GOSUB statements, using those statements is not considered good programming practice. You can eliminate all **GoTo** statements in form and report modules by using Access's Error event and DAO 3.0's new Errors collection. The Error event is described in the "Handling Run-Time Errors" section later in this chapter and the Errors collection is explained in Chapter 29, "Understanding the Data Access Object Class."

Conditional Statements

A conditional statement executes the statements between its occurrence and the terminating statement if the result of the relational operator is true. Statements that consist of or require more than one statement for completion are called *structured statements*, *control structures*, or just *structures*.

The If...Then...End If Structure. The syntax of the primary conditional statement of procedural BASIC is as follows:

```
If Condition1% [= True] Then
    Statements to be executed if Condition1 is true
[Else[If Condition2%[ = True] Then]]
```

```
        Optional statements to be executed if Condition1%
        is false [and Condition2% is true]
    End If
```

The = **True** elements of the preceding conditional statement are optional and typically not included when you write actual code. **If** *Condition1%* **Then** and **If** *Condition1%* = **True Then** produce the same result.

You can add a second condition with the **ElseIf** statement that must be true to control execution of the statements that are executed if *Condition1%* is false. Note that no space is used between **Else** and **If**. An **If...End If** structure that incorporates the **ElseIf** statement is the simplified equivalent of the following:

```
If Condition1% Then
    Statements to be executed if Expression1 is true
Else
    If Condition2% Then
        Statements to be executed if Condition1% is
        false and Condition2% is true]
    End If
End If
```

Whether a statement is executed is based on the evaluation of the immediately preceding expression. Expressions that include **If...End If** or other flow control structures within other **If...End If** structures are said to be *nested*, as in the preceding example. The number, or *depth*, of **If...End If** structures that can be nested within one another is unlimited.

Note that the code between the individual keywords that make up the flow control structure is indented. Indentation makes code within structures easier to read. You usually use the Tab key to create indentation.

To evaluate whether a character is a letter and to determine its case, you can use the following code:

```
If Asc(Char$) > 63 And Asc(Char$) < 91 Then
    CharType$ = "Uppercase Letter"
ElseIf Asc(Char$) > 96 And Asc(Char$) < 123 Then
    CharType$ = "Lowercase Letter"
End If
```

Note

You have seen a single-line version of the **If...End If** statement, IIf( ), in the "Assignment and Comparison Operators" section of Chapter 9, "Understanding Operators and Expressions in Access." The single-line (also called inline) version in Access VBA, **If** *Condition%* **Then** ... does not require the terminating **End If** statement. Although acceptable for simple statements, the use of the single-line version is questionable (not necessarily poor) programming practice, so this book avoids it.

You use the **If...End If** structure more often than any other flow control.

The Select Case...End Select Construct. When you must choose among many alternatives, **If...End If** structures can become very complex and deeply nested. The **Select Case...End Select** construct was added to procedural BASIC to overcome this complexity. In addition to testing whether an expression evaluates to true or false, **Select Case** can evaluate variables to determine whether those variables fall within specified ranges. The generalized syntax is in the following example:

```
Select Case VarName
    Case Expression1[, Expressions, ...]
        (Statements executed if the value of VarName
         = Expression1 or Expressions)
    [Case Expression2 To Expression3
        (Statements executed if the value of VarName
         is in the range of Expression2 to Expression3)]
    [Case Is RelationalExpression
        (Statements executed if the value of
         VarName = RelationalExpression)]
    [Case Else
        (Statements executed if none of the
         above cases is met)]
End Select
```

Select Case evaluates *VarName*, which can be a string, a numeric variable, or an expression. It then tests each **Case** expression in sequence. **Case** expressions can take one of the following four forms:

- A single or list of values to which to compare the value of *VarName*. Successive members of the list are separated from their predecessors by commas.

- A range of values separated by the keyword **To**. The value of the first member of the range limits must be less than the value of the second. Each string is compared by the ASCII value of its first character.

- The keyword **Is**, followed by a relational operator, such as <>, <, <=, =, >=, or >, and a variable or literal value.

- The keyword **Else**. Expressions following **Case Else** are executed if no prior **Case** condition is satisfied.

The **Case** statements are tested in sequence, and the code associated with the first matching **Case** condition is executed. If no match is found and the **Case Else** statement is present, the code following the statement is executed. Program execution then continues at the line of code following the **End Select** terminating statement.

If *VarName* is a numeric type, all expressions with which it is to be compared by **Case** are forced to the same data type.

The following example is of **Select Case** using a numeric variable, Sales#:

```
Select Case Sales#
    Case 10000 To 49999.99
        Class% = 1
    Case 50000 To 100000
        Class% = 2
```

```
        Case Is < 10000
            Class% = 0
        Case Else
            Class% = 3
    End Select
```

Note that because `Sales#` is a double-precision real number, all the comparison literals also are treated as double-precision (not the default single-precision) real numbers for the purposes of comparison.

A more complex example that evaluates a single character follows:

```
    Select Case Char$
        Case "A" To "Z"
            CharType$ = "Upper Case"
        Case "a" To "z'
            CharType$ = "Lower Case"
        Case "0" To "9"
            CharType$ = "Number"
        Case "!", "?", ".", ",", ";"
            CharType$ = "Punctuation"
        Case ""
            CharType$ = "Empty String"
        Case < 32
            CharType$ = "Special Character"
        Case Else
            CharType$ = "Unknown Character"
    End Select
```

This example demonstrates that **Select Case**, when used with strings, evaluates the ASCII value of the first character of the string—either as the variable being tested or the expressions following **Case** statements. Thus, **Case < 32** is a valid test, although `Char$` is a string variable.

Repetitive Operations—Looping

In many instances, you must repeat an operation until a given condition is satisfied, whereupon the repetitions terminate. You may want to examine each character in a word, sentence, or document, or assign values to an array with many elements. Loops are used for these and many other purposes.

Using the For...Next Statement. Access VBA's **For...Next** statement enables you to repeat a block of code a specified number of times, as shown in the following example:

```
    For Counter% = StartValue% To EndValue% [Step
            Increment%]
        Statements to be executed
    [Conditional statement
        Exit For
        End of conditional statement]
    Next [Counter%]
```

The block of statements between the **For** and **Next** keywords is executed (*EndValue%* - *StartValue%* + 1) / *Increment%* times. As an example, if *StartValue%* = 5, *EndValue%* = 10, and *Increment%* = 1, execution of the statement block is repeated six times. You need not add the keyword **Step** in this case—the default increment is 1. Although **Integer** data types are shown, **Long** (integers) may be used. The use of real numbers (**Single** or **Double** data types) as values for counters and increments is possible, but uncommon.

The dividend of the above expression must always be a positive number if execution of the internal statement block is to occur. If *EndValue%* is less than *StartValue%*, *Increment%* must be negative; otherwise, the **For...Next** statement is ignored by Access VBA.

The optional **Exit For** statement is provided so that you can prematurely terminate the loop using a surrounding **If...Then...End If** conditional statement. Changing the value of the counter variable within the loop itself to terminate its operation is discouraged as a dangerous programming practice. You might make a change that would cause an infinite loop.

> **Note**
>
> If you use a numeric variable for *Increment%* in a **For...Next** loop and the value of the variable becomes **0**, the loop repeats indefinitely and locks up your computer, requiring you to reboot the application. Make sure that your code traps any condition that could result in *Increment%* becoming **0**.

The repetition of *Counter%* following the **Next** statement is optional, but is considered good programming practice—especially if you are using nested **For...Next** loops. Adding *Counter%* keeps you informed of which loop you are counting. If you try to use the same variable name for a counter of a nested **For...Next** loop, you receive an error message.

When the value of *Counter%* exceeds *EndValue%* or the **Exit For** statement is executed, execution proceeds to the line of code following **Next**.

Using For...Next Loops to Assign Values to Array Elements. One of the most common applications of the **For...Next** loop is to assign successive values to the elements of an array. If you have declared a 26-element array named Alphabet$(), the following example assigns the capital letters *A* through *Z* to its elements:

```
For Letter% = 1 To 26
    Alphabet$(Letter%) = Chr$(Letter% + 63)
Next Letter%
```

The preceding example assigns 26 of the array's 27 elements if you used **Dim** Alphabet$(26) rather than **Dim** Alphabet$(1 To 26). 63 is added to Letter% because the ASCII value of the letter *A* is 64, and the initial value of Letter% is 1.

Understanding Do While...Loop and While...Wend. A more general form of the loop structure is **Do While...Loop**, which uses the following syntax:

```
Do While Condition% [= True]
    Statements to be executed
    [Conditional statement
        Exit Do
    End of conditional statement]
Loop
```

This loop structure executes the intervening statements only if `Condition%` equals **True** (**Not False**, a value other than 0), and it continues to do so until `Condition%` becomes **False** (0) or the optional **Exit Do** statement is executed.

From the preceding syntax, the previous **For...Next** array assignment example can be duplicated by the following structure:

```
Letter% = 1
Do While Letter% <= 27
    Alphabet(Letter%) = Chr$(Letter% + 63)
    Letter% = Letter% + 1
Loop
```

Another example of a **Do** loop is the **Do Until...Loop** structure, which loops as long as the condition is not satisfied, as in the following example:

```
Do Until Condition% <> True
    Statements to be executed
    [Conditional statement
        Exit Do
    End of conditional statement]
Loop
```

The **While...Wend** loop is identical to the **Do While...Loop** structure, but you cannot use the **Exit Do** statement within it. The **While...Wend** structure is provided for compatibility with earlier versions of BASIC and should be abandoned in favor of **Do** **{While¦Until}...Loop** in Access VBA.

Making Sure Statements in a Loop Occur at Least Once. You may have observed that the statements within a **Do While...Loop** structure are never executed if `Condition%` is **Not True** when the structure is encountered in your application. You also can use a structure in which the conditional statement that causes loop termination is associated with the **Loop** statement. The syntax of this format is in the following example:

```
Do
    Statements to be executed
    [Conditional statement then
        Exit Do
    End of conditional statement]
Loop While Condition%[ = True]
```

A similar structure is available for **Do Until...Loop**:

```
Do
    Statements to be executed
    [Conditional statement
        Exit Do
    End of conditional statement]
Loop Until Condition%[ = False]
```

These structures ensure that the loop executes at least once *before* the condition is tested.

Avoiding Infinite Loops. You have already received warnings about infinite loops in the descriptions of each of the loop structures. If you create a *tight* loop (one with few statements between Do and Loop) that never terminates, executing the code causes Access VBA to appear to freeze. You cannot terminate operation, and you must use Ctrl+Alt+Delete to reboot, relaunch Access VBA, and correct the code.

These apparent infinite loops are often created intentionally with code, such as the following:

```
Temp% = True
ExitLoop% = False
Do While Temp% [= True]
   Call TestProc(ExitLoop%)
   If ExitLoop%[ = True] Then
      Exit Do
   End If
Loop
```

The preceding example repeatedly calls the procedure TestProc, whose statements are executed, until ExitLoop% is set True by code in TestProc. Structures of this type are the equivalent of DO WHILE .T. ... ENDDO structures in dBASE. You must make sure that ExitLoop% eventually becomes True, one way or another, no matter what happens when the code in TestProc is executed.

Note

To avoid locking up Access VBA with tight infinite loops, include the **DoEvents** command in loops during the testing stage, as in the following example:

```
Do While Temp%[ = True]
   Call TestProc(ExitLoop%)
   If ExitLoop% Then
      Exit Do
   End If
   DoEvents
Loop
```

DoEvents tests the Windows environment to determine whether any other event messages, such as a mouse click, are pending. If so, **DoEvents** allows the messages to be processed and then continues at the next line of code. You can then remove **DoEvents** to speed up the loop after your testing verifies that infinite looping cannot occur. The **DoEvents** statement should not be required in production 32-bit VBA code because threaded applications, such as Access 95, take advantage of preemptive multitasking in Windows 95 and Windows NT. However, not all 32-bit Windows applications are threaded, so **DoEvents** is likely to remain in use for some time.

Handling Run-Time Errors

No matter how thoroughly you test and debug your code, run-time errors appear eventually. Run-time errors are errors that occur when Access executes your code. Use the **On Error GoTo** instruction to control what happens in your application when a run-time error occurs. **On Error** is not a very sophisticated instruction, but it is your only choice for error processing in Access modules. You can branch to a label, or you can ignore the error. The general syntax of **On Error...** follows:

```
On Error GoTo LabelName
On Error Resume Next
On Error GoTo 0
```

On Error GoTo *LabelName* branches to the portion of your code with the label *LabelName*:. *LabelName* must be a label; it cannot be the name of a procedure. The code following *LabelName*, however, can (and often does) include a procedure call to an error-handling procedure, such as ErrorProc, as in:

```
On Error GoTo ErrHandler
   ...
[RepeatCode:
  (Code using ErrProc to handle errors)]
   ...
   GoTo SkipHandler
ErrHandler:
   Call ErrorProc
  [GoTo Repeat Code]
SkipHandler:
   ...
  (Additional code)
```

In this example, the **On Error GoTo** instruction causes program flow to branch to the ErrHandler label that executes the error-handling procedure ErrorProc. Ordinarily, the error handler code is located at the end of the procedure. If you have more than one error handler or if the error handler is in the middle of a group of instructions, you need to bypass it if the preceding code is error-free. Use the **GoTo** SkipHandler statement that bypasses ErrHandler: instructions. To repeat the code that generated the error after ErrorProc has done its job, add a label such as RepeatCode: at the beginning of the re-peated code, and then branch to the code in the ErrHandler: code. Alternatively, you can add the keyword **Resume** at the end of your code to resume processing at the line that created the error.

On Error Resume Next disregards the error and continues processing the succeeding in-structions.

After an **On Error GoTo** statement executes, it remains in effect for all succeeding errors until another **On Error GoTo** instruction is encountered or until error processing is explic-itly turned off with the **On Error GoTo 0** form of the statement.

If you do not trap errors with an **On Error GoTo** statement or if you have turned error trapping off with **On Error GoTo 0**, a dialog with the appropriate error message appears when a run-time error is encountered.

If you do not provide at least one error-handling routine in your Access VBA code for run-time applications, your application quits abruptly when the error occurs.

Detecting the Type of Error with the **Err** Function

The **Err** function (no arguments) returns an integer representing the code of the last error or 0 if no error occurs. This function is ordinarily used within a **Select Case** structure to determine the action to take in the error handler based on the type of error incurred. Use the `Error$()` function to return the text name of the error number specified as its argument, as in the following example:

```
ErrorName$ = Error$(Err)
Select Case Err
   Case 58 To 76
      Call FileError 'procedure for handling file errors
   Case 281 To 297
      Call DDEError 'procedure for handling DDE errors
   Case 340 To 344
      Call ArrayError 'procedure for control array errors
End Select
Err = 0
```

Some of the error codes returned by the `Err` function are listed in the Error Codes topic of the Access help file. Choose Help, Microsoft Access Help Topics to display the Help Topics dialog. Then type **Error Codes** in the text box and press Enter. Double-click Error Codes in the Topics Found dialog to display a Help window with an abbreviated list of code numbers and their descriptions. Click the underlined description text to display a window that describes each error code in detail.

You can substitute the actual error processing code for the `Call` instructions shown in the preceding example, but using individual procedures for error handling is the recommended approach. The `Err` *statement* is used to set the error code to a specific integer. This statement should be used to reset the error code to 0 after your error handler has completed its operation, as shown in the preceding example.

The `Error` statement is used to simulate an error so that you can test any error handlers you have written. You can specify any of the valid integer error codes or create a user-defined error code by selecting an integer not included in the list. A user-defined error code returns "User-defined error" to `Error$()`.

Using the `Error` Event in Form and Report Modules

Access includes an event, `Error`, triggered when an error occurs on a form or report. You can use an event-handling procedure in a form or report to process the error, or you can assign a generic error-handling function in an Access module to the `Error` event with an =ErrorHandler() entry to call the ErrorHandler() function. (You also can attach a macro to the `Error` event, but macros have limited means of dealing with run-time errors.)

When you invoke an error-handling function from the `Error` event, you need to use the `Err` function to detect the error that occurred and take corrective action, as described in the preceding section.

Exploring the Module Window

You write Access VBA functions and procedures in the Module window. To display a Module window, click the Module tab of the Database window; then, double-click the name of the module you want to display. To open a new Access VBA module, click the New button. A Module code editing window appears, as shown in figure 28.8. This figure shows part of the `Proper()` function of the Utility Functions module included in Access 2.0's NWIND.MDB example database, displayed in Access 95. You choose the function or procedure to display from the procedures drop-down list. The Module window incorporates a text editor, similar to Windows Notepad, in which you type your Access VBA code. Access VBA now color-codes keywords and comments.

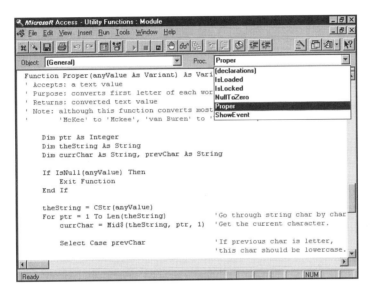

Fig. 28.8   Opening an Access VBA function in the Module window.

The Access VBA code in figure 28.8 demonstrates two principles of writing code in any language: adding comments that explain the purpose of the statements and using indentation to make your code more readable. Comments in Access VBA are preceded with an apostrophe (`'`); alternatively, use the prefix **Rem** (for "remark" in earlier versions of BASIC) to indicate that the text on the line is a comment. **Rem** must be the first statement on a line (unless preceded by a colon that separates statements), but the apostrophe prefix can be used anywhere in your code.

Comments that precede the code identify the procedure, explain its purpose, and indicate the macro or other procedure that calls the code. If the function returns a value, a description of the returned value and its data type is included.

The Toolbar of the Module Window

Table 28.3 lists the purpose of each item in the toolbar of the Module window and the menu commands and key combinations that you can substitute for toolbar components. Buttons marked with an asterisk (*) in the Items column are new with Access 95. Buttons whose design or name has changed but perform the same function in Access 95 as in Access 2.0 are not marked with an asterisk.

Table 28.3	**Elements of the Module Window's Toolbar**		
Button	**Item**	**Alternate Method**	**Purpose**
	Insert Module*	Insert, Module	Creates a new, empty module.
	Insert Procedure	Insert, Procedure	Opens the Insert Procedures dialog that lets you select Function or Sub and name the new procedure.
	Save	File, Save	Saves changes to the current procedure.
	Print*	File, Print	Prints the content of the module as text.
	Undo	Edit, Undo	Rescinds the last keyboard or mouse operation performed, if possible.
	Redo*	Edit, Redo	Rescinds the last undo operation, if possible.
	Debug Window*	View, Debug Window	Opens the Debug Window.
	Object Browser	View, Object Browser	Opens the Object Browser dialog.
	Continue	Run, Continue or press F5	Continues execution of the procedure after execution of a procedure has been halted by a break condition or after use of the Single Step or Procedure Step button.
	End*	Run, End	Terminates execution of a procedure.
	Reset	Run, Reset or press Shift+F5	Terminates execution of an Access VBA procedure and reinitializes all variables to their default values.
	Breakpoint	Run, Toggle Breakpoint or press F9	Toggles a breakpoint at the line of the code in which the caret is located. Breakpoints are used to halt execution at a specific line. If a breakpoint is set, the Breakpoint button turns it off.
	Instant Watch*	Tools, Instant Watch or Shift+F9	Adds a watch expression to the Debug Window that causes a break in execution when the expression returns**True**.
	Calls	View Calls	Displays the Calls dialog that lists all procedures called prior to reaching a breakpoint in your code.
	Step Into	Run, Step Into or press F8	Moves through an Access VBA procedure one statement (line) at a time.
	Step Over	Run, Step Over or press Shift+F8	Moves through an Access VBA procedure one subprocedure at a time.

Button	Item	Alternate Method	Purpose
	Compile Loaded Modules	Run, Compile Loaded Modules	Creates pseudo-code (p-code) from the text version of all Access modules and all form and report modules currently open.
	Indent	Edit, Indent	Indents selected code by the number of characters specified in the Module Options sheet.
	Outdent	Edit, Outdent	Reverses the indent process.
	Build*	None	Opens the Expression Builder dialog.
	Database Window	Window, 1	Opens the Database window.
	New Object	None	Clicking the arrow opens a drop-down menu to select the type of new object to create.
	Help	F1 key	Displays help for the user interface of the Module window.
N/A	Object List*	None	Displays a list of objects in form or report modules. (Only (general)appears for Access modules.)
N/A	Proc(edure)	None. List	Displays a function or procedure in a module.Select the procedure or event name from the drop-down list. Procedures are listed in alphabetical order by name.

Module Shortcut Keys

Additional shortcut keys and key combinations listed in table 28.4 can help you as you write and edit Access VBA code. Only the most commonly used shortcut keys are listed in table 28.4.

Table 28.4 Primary Key Combinations for Entering and Editing Access VBA Code	
Key Combination	**Purpose**
F3	Finds next occurrence of a search string.
Shift+F3	Finds previous occurrence of a search string.
F9	Sets or clears a breakpoint on the current line.
Ctrl+Shift+F9	Clears all breakpoints.
Tab	Indents a single line of code by four (default value) characters.

(continues)

Table 28.4 Continued	
Key Combination	**Purpose**
Tab with selected text	Indents multiple lines of selected code by four (default) characters.
Shift+Tab	Outdents a single line of code by four characters.
Shift+Tab with selected text	Outdents multiple lines of selected code by four characters.
Ctrl+Y	Deletes the line on which the caret is located.

You can change the default indentation of four characters per tab stop by choosing Tools, Options, clicking the Module tab, and entering the desired number of characters in the Tab Width text box.

Menu Commands in the Module Window

Menu commands to perform operations not included in table 28.3 are listed in table 28.5. Menu commands common to other database objects, such as File, Save, are not included in the table.

Table 28.5 Module Window Menu Commands		
Menu	**Commands**	**Purpose**
File	Save As Text	Displays the Save Text dialog to save the module's code to a text file in ASCII format.
Edit	Find	Displays the Find dialog to search for specific text strings or regular expressions entered in the Find text box.
	Replace	Replaces all or selected occurrences of the text entered in the Find text box with the text in the Replace text box.
View	Procedure Definition	If the caret is on a line that contains a procedure call, finds and displays the called procedure.
Insert	File	Opens the Insert File dialog to allow insertion of code contained in a text file.
Run	Step to Cursor	Continues execution until reaching the line above the position of the caret.
	Set Next Statement	Sets the next statement to be executed, bypassing other code.
	Show Next Statement	Displays the next statement to be executed.
	Clear All Breakpoints	Clears all breakpoints set in the module. Active only when breakpoint(s) are set. (See "Adding a Breakpoint to the IsLoaded() Function" in this chapter.)
	Compile All Modules	Compiles all modules in the database.

Menu	Commands	Purpose
Tools	Add Watch	Opens the Add Watch dialog to add a watchpoint.
	Edit Watch	Opens the Edit Watch dialog to modify or delete a watchpoint.
	Custom Controls	Opens the Custom Controls dialog to display a list of registered OLE Controls and provides for registering new OLE Controls.
	References	Opens the References dialog for adding or deleting references to objects exposed by libraries.

The Access VBA Help System

Microsoft provides an extensive, multilevel Help system to help you learn and use Access VBA. The majority of the help topics for Access VBA are supplied by a generic VBA help file that's applicable to all flavors of VBA. If you place the caret on a keyword, select a keyword and then press the F1 key, or click the Help button on the toolbar, for example, a help window for the keyword appears. If you click the "Example" hot spot under the name of the keyword and an example specific to Access VBA is available, the Topics Found dialog appears to let you choose between the generic VBA and Access VBA example (see fig. 28.9). Double-clicking the topic with the (Microsoft Access) suffix displays the example that is specific to Access VBA (see fig. 28.10).

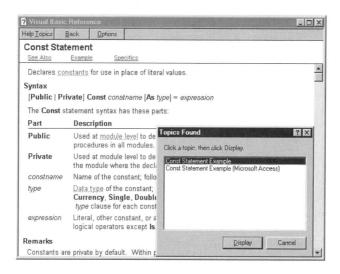

Fig. 28.9 A help window for the Const keyword with generic VBA and Access VBA examples available.

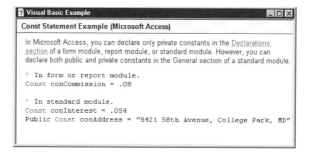

Fig. 28.10   The example that is specific to Access VBA for the Const keyword.

If you press F1 when the caret is not located on a keyword, the Help system displays a Keyword Not Found topic. Choosing Help, Microsoft Access Help Topics and then clicking the Contents Tab displays a list of "books" that comprise the entire Access 95 Help system. To obtain additional information on VBA programming, double-click the Visual Basic for Applications book; then, double-click the topic you want, such as Keywords by Task. Expanding the Keywords by Task item displays a list of chapters (represented by a "?" icon) devoted to specific programming subjects (see fig. 28.11). When you double-click the chapter icon, a keyword summary for the topic appears (see fig. 28.12). Clicking an underlined keyword hotspot displays the corresponding help topic.

Fig. 28.11   Help topics for VBA tasks beginning with the letters A through D.

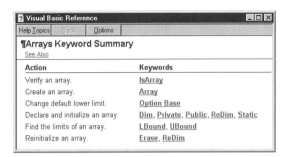

Fig. 28.12   The Keyword Summary help topic for tasks related to arrays.

The Access VBA Compiler

Programming languages, such as Pascal and C, use compilers. *Compilers* are applications that convert the code statements—*source code*—you write into instructions the computer can understand—*object code*. These languages use punctuation symbols to identify where statements begin and end; Pascal, for example, uses a semicolon to tell the compiler that a statement is complete. Separating code into individual statements and determining which words in a statement are keywords is *parsing* the code.

After you compile Pascal or C code, you link the code with *libraries* to create an *executable* file. *Libraries* are additional object code that perform standard operations, such as mathematical calculations. Access libraries, such as Utlity.mda, have a similar purpose. An executable file for a Windows application has the extension .exe; you run executable files as independent applications. Compiling and linking an application, especially a Windows application, can be a complex process. Microsoft Visual C++, Professional Edition, for example, requires more than 60M for a typical installation. (A minimum installation consumes about 10M.)

Traditional BASIC languages, such as QBasic and also the native dBASE and Paradox programming languages, employ interpreters to execute code. An *interpreter* is an application that reads each line of code, translates the code into instructions for your computer, and then tells the computer to execute these instructions. The interpreter parses code line by line, beginning with the first non-blank character on a line and ending with the newline pair, carriage return (CR, `Chr$(13)`), and line feed (LF, `Chr$(10)`). A *newline pair* is created by pressing the Enter key. Compilers for the dBASE language, such as the Borland dBASE compiler and CA-Clipper, also use the newline pair to indicate the end of a statement.

You must execute interpreted code within the application in which the code was created. You run QBasic code, for example, from QBasic, not as a stand-alone application. An interpreter's advantage is that it can test the statements you enter for proper syntax as you write them. Compiled languages don't issue error messages until you compile the source code to object code. Another advantage of interpreters is that you don't need to go through the process of compiling and linking the source code every time you make a change in the code. Unfortunately, interpreters usually execute code more slowly than the computer executes a compiled (.exe) application.

Access VBA combines the features of both a compiler and an interpreter. VBA interprets the code you write when you terminate a line with the Enter key. If possible, the VBA interpreter corrects your syntax; otherwise you receive a syntax error message, which usually is accompanied by a suggestion for correcting the mistake. Each line of code, therefore, usually contains a syntactically correct statement. (In some cases, you must run the "compiler" to interpret the source code.) Most languages, such as Xbase and Paradox, enable you to continue a statement on another line; Xbase, including Clipper, uses the semicolon for this purpose. Access VBA now offers a statement continuation character, a space followed by an underscore.

After you write the source code, the VBA interpreter converts this code into a cross between interpreted and object code known as pseudo-code, or p-code. Pseudo-code runs faster than conventional interpreted code. Access compiles to p-code the code you write or modify the first time the code is used in an application. Access discovers most errors not caught during entry as the code compiles. You can choose Run, Compile All Modules to force the VBA interpreter to compile all the code in Access modules and in form/report modules. Forcing compilation before running the code—especially if the form or macro that executes the code takes a long time to load—can save substantial time during development.

Examining the Utility Functions Module

One recommended way to learn a new programming language is to examine simple examples of code and analyze the statements used in the example.

The sections that follow show how to open a module, display a function in the Module window, add a breakpoint to the code, and then use the Debug Window to execute the function.

Adding a Breakpoint to the IsLoaded() Function

When you examine the execution of Access VBA code written by others, and when you debug your own application, breakpoints are very useful. This section explains how to add a breakpoint to the IsLoaded() function so that the Suppliers form stops executing when the Suppliers macro calls the IsLoaded() function and Access displays the code in the Module window.

To add a breakpoint to the IsLoaded() function, follow these steps:

1. Choose Window, Module: Utility Functions to make the Module window active.

2. Place the caret on the line that begins with If SysCmd(acSysCmdGetObjectState,...).

 3. Click the Breakpoint button of the toolbar, choose Run, Toggle Breakpoint, or press F9. The breakpoint you create is indicated by changing the display of the line to reverse red (see fig. 28.13).

Fig. 28.13   The IsLoaded() function with a breakpoint set.

4. Close the Utility Functions module and open the Suppliers form.

5. Close the Suppliers form to execute the Suppliers.Close macro that is attached to the On Close event of the form. When the Suppliers.Close macro calls the IsLoaded() function, execution of IsLoaded() begins with the **Const** conObjStateClosed = 0 line and halts at the line with the breakpoint. When execution encounters a breakpoint, the module containing the breakpoint opens automatically. The line with the breakpoint is enclosed in a highlighted rectangle (see fig. 28.14).

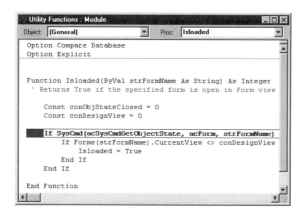

Fig. 28.14   The IsLoaded() procedure when the breakpoint is reached and the Utility Function module opens.

The element of the Forms collection tested is specified by strFormName. Access's SysCmd() function tests the Forms collection for the value of strFormName with the SysCmd(acSysCmdGetObjectState, acForm, strFormName) statement. If the specified form is open in either Form or Design View, SysCmd() returns **True**. The second test checks the value of the CurrentView property of the form to see if the form is open in Form View. If the result of the CurrentView comparison is **True**, the IsLoaded = **True** line executes and the IsLoaded() function returns **True** to the calling procedure, in this case the Suppliers.Close macro.

Using the Debug Window

In the "Using the Debug Window" section of Chapter 9, "Understanding Operators and Expressions in Access," you learned to use the Debug Window to display the results of computations and values returned by functions. The Debug Window also is useful when you want to display the value of variables when the breakpoint is encountered. To display the value of local (procedure-level) variables, execution of your code must be halted at a breakpoint beyond the point at which the variables are assigned their values.

To open the Debug Window and display the value of a variable while execution is halted at the breakpoint shown in figure 28.14, follow these steps:

1. Click the Debug Window button of the toolbar or choose <u>V</u>iew, Debug Window.

2. Type **? strFormName** and press Enter to display the value of this variable (see fig. 28.15). The ? symbol is shorthand for the reserved word **Print**.

3. Click the Step Into button of the toolbar, choose <u>R</u>un, Single Step, or press F8 to continue execution of the function a line at a time. The **End If** statement is encountered. Press F8 again and execution moves to the **End Function** line. Press F8 again and execution proceeds to the **Sub** Form_Close procedure of the Suppliers form.

4. Press F5 twice to continue execution of the code, closing the Suppliers form.

5. Choose <u>R</u>un, Clear <u>A</u>ll Breakpoints, or press Ctrl+Shift+F9 to toggle the breakpoint off.

When you write your own code, the Debug Window is *very* handy for debugging purposes.

Printing to the Debug Window with the Debug Object

When you need to view the values of several variables, you can use the **Debug** object to automate printing to the Debug Window. If you add the **Debug** object to a function that tests the names of each open form, you can create a list in the Debug Window of all the forms that are open.

To create a WhatsLoaded() function to list all open forms, follow these steps:

1. Load three or more forms by repeatedly opening the Database window, clicking the Form tab, and double-clicking a form icon. The Customers, Categories, Forms Switchboard, and Main Switchboard forms are good choices because these forms load quickly.

2. Choose Module: Utility Functions from the Window menu and type **Function WhatsLoaded() As Integer** below the End Function line of the **IsLoaded()** function. The VBA interpreter adds the **End Function** statement for you automatically.

3. Type the following code between the **Function...** and **End Function** lines:

```
Dim intCtr As Integer
   For intCtr = 0 To Forms.Count - 1
      Debug.Print Forms(intCtr).FormName
Next intCtr
```

The **For...Next** loop iterates the Forms collection. The **Debug.Print** statement prints the name of each open form in the Debug Window.

4. Click the Debug Window button to open Debug Window. Type **? WhatsLoaded()** and press Enter. The name of each form is added to the Debug Window by the **Debug.Print** statement followed by 0, the default value returned by the function (see fig. 28.15).

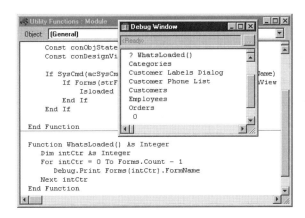

Fig. 28.15 The Debug object used to print values of variables to the Debug Window.

5. Close and don't save changes to the Utility Function module. Then close the other forms that you opened for this example.

The **Debug.Print** statement is particularly useful for displaying the values of variables that change when you execute a loop. When you have completed testing of your procedure, you delete the **Debug** statements.

Using Text Comparison Options

Tests of text data in fields of tables, query result sets, and Recordset object against **String** or **Variant** text data in modules depends upon the value of the **Option** Compare... statement, which appears in the Declarations section of the Utility Functions module. To determine how text comparisons are made in the module, you can use any of the following statements:

■ **Option** Compare Binary comparisons are case-sensitive. Lowercase letters are not equivalent to uppercase letters. To determine the sort order of characters, Access uses the character value assigned by the Windows ANSI character set.

- **Option** Compare Text comparisons are not case-sensitive. Lowercase letters are treated as the equivalent of uppercase letters. For most North American users, the sort order is the same as Option Compare Binary, ANSI. Unless you have a reason to specify a different comparison method, use **Option** Compare Text.

- **Option** Compare Database comparisons are case-sensitive and the sort order is that specified for the database.

Option Compare Binary is the default if you do not include an **Option** Compare... statement in the Declarations section of the module. However, Access adds **Option** Compare Database to the Declarations section when you create a new module, overriding the default. **Binary** and Database are keywords in Access VBA, but these words do not have the same meaning when used in the **Option** Compare... statement. For compatibility with changes in possible future releases of Access, you should not use Compare or Text as names of variables.

Writing Your Own Functions and Procedures

You do not need to be an Access VBA expert to write a user-defined function. The information you learned about operators and expressions in Chapter 9, "Understanding Operators and Expressions in Access," as well as the introduction to Access VBA statements presented in this chapter, enable you to create UDFs that supplement Access VBA's repertoire of standard functions.

After you master user-defined functions, you can try your hand at writing functions—actually, procedures in the form of functions—executed by the RunCode action of macro objects. Access VBA procedures offer flexibility in manipulating database and control objects, but require more knowledge of programming techniques than is needed to create UDFs. This section describes how you write a simple user-defined function.

User-defined functions are required when you need a conditional statement more complex than that accommodated by the IIf() function. An example is a fixed set of quantity discounts that apply to all or a group of products. You can create a table of quantity discounts; however, a user-defined function that returns the discount is easier to implement and faster to execute.

For this example, the discounts are 50 percent for 1,000 or more of an item; 40 percent for 500 to 999; 30 percent for 100 to 499; 20 percent for 50 to 99; 10 percent for 10 to 49; and no discount for purchases of fewer than 10 items. Discount structures of this type lend themselves well to **Select Case...End Select** structures.

To create the user-defined function sngDiscount() that returns a fractional percent discount based on the value of the argument, intQuantity, follow these steps:

1. Click the Modules button of the Database window, and double-click the Utility Functions module.

2. Position the cursor on the line following the last **End Function** statement and type **Function sngDiscount(intQuantity As Integer)**. After you press Enter, Access adds the **End Function** statement. This process is quicker than clicking the New Procedure button or choosing Insert, Procedure.

The sng prefix of the function name indicates that the function returns the Single data type. The **As Integer** modifier for the intQuantity argument specifies that the function treats intQuantity as an **Integer** data type. If you do not specify the data type, your function assigns the default **Variant** data type to intQuantity.

> **Tip**
>
> You don't need to enter the **Is** keyword because Access checks the syntax of each statement you write when you press Enter. If you omit the **Is** keyword, Access adds it for you.

3. Position the caret at the beginning of the blank line and press Tab. To establish the discount schedule, enter the following lines of code:

```
Select Case intQuantity
    Case Is >= 1000
        sngDiscount = .5
    Case Is >= 500
        sngDiscount = .4
    Case Is >= 100
        sngDiscount = .3
    Case Is >= 50
        sngDiscount = .2
    Case Is >= 10
        sngDiscount = .1
    Case Else
        sngDiscount = 0
End Select
```

Use the Tab key to duplicate the indentation illustrated in the preceding example. **Case** statements are executed from the first statement to the last, so quantities are entered in descending sequence. If sngQuantity = 552, the criterion is not met for **Case Is >= 1000**, so the next **Case** statement is tested. **Case Is >= 500** is satisfied, so sngDiscount receives the value .4 and execution proceeds directly to the **End Select** statement.

4. To make sure that the function is acceptable to Access VBA's compiler, click the Compile Loaded Modules button of the toolbar or choose Run, Compile Loaded Modules. Access converts the entries to a form that it can process. When you compile the code, Access indicates any errors not caught by line-by-line syntax checking.

5. You do not need to create a table or macro to test the function; the Debug Window performs this task adequately for sample code. If the Debug Window is not open, click the Debug Window button of the toolbar or choose View, Debug Window.

6. Test the `sngDiscount()` function by entering **? sngDiscount(*Quantity*)** in the Debug Window, and then press Enter. Substitute numeric values for *Quantity*, (see fig. 28.16).

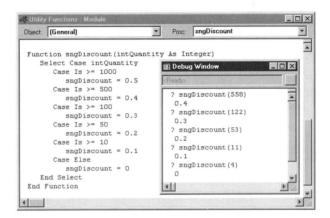

Fig. 28.16 Code for the `sngDiscount()` user-defined function.

7. To save the UDF, click the Save button of the toolbar or choose <u>F</u>ile, <u>S</u>ave.

You can employ user-defined functions in expressions to compute values for calculated fields, validate data entry, construct queries, and other purposes where an expression can be used.

Troubleshooting

An "Expected Shared or identifier" message box appears when entering a **Dim** *VariableName* **As** **DataType** *statement.*

You attempted to name a variable with a reserved word. For example, you receive the preceding error message if you attempt to create a **Dim** **Option** **As** **Integer** statement. **Option** is a VBA reserved word. Change the name of the object, preferably using the data type tag prefix, as in `intOption`.

Writing Code Behind Forms with the Code Builder

This section describes the process you use to write event-handling code in form or report modules. Simple event-handling procedures (*event-handlers*) can take the place of macros. This example replaces the Customer Labels Dialog.Cancel macro, which closes the Country Filter Dialog form with an event-handling procedure that performs the same function.

To create an event-handler to replace the Customer Labels Dialog.Cancel macro, follow these steps:

1. Close any forms or modules you have open; then, open the Customer Labels Dialog form in Design View.

2. Pull down the bottom of the Customer Labels Dialog's window to expose the Cancel button; then, click the Cancel button to select it.

3. Click the Properties button of the toolbar to open the Properties windows, and click the Event tab.

4. Place the caret in the On Click event text box (see fig. 28.17), and click the ellipsis button to display the Customer Labels Dialog macrosheet.

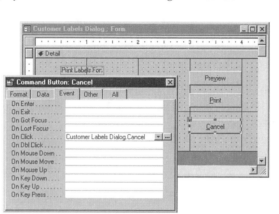

Fig. 28.17 The Customer Labels Dialog.Cancel macro assigned to the `OnClick` event of the Cancel button.

5. Place the caret in the Cancel cell of the macrosheet to display the arguments of the Close action (see fig. 28.18). Clicking the Cancel button of the Customer Labels Dialog closes the form.

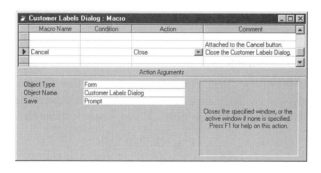

Fig. 28.18 The Cancel macro shown in the Customer Labels Dialog macrosheet.

VII

Programming with VBA

6. Close the macrosheet to return to the Customer Labels Dialog form's Design View.

7. Delete the Customer Labels Dialog.Cancel entry for the OnClick event, and then click the ellipsis button to display the Choose Builder dialog (see fig. 28.19).

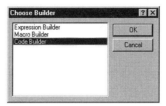

Fig. 28.19   Selecting the Code Builder with the Choose Builder dialog.

8. Select Code Builder and click OK to open the Form_Customer Labels Dialog module. Access creates a **Sub** Cancel_Click()...**End Sub** event-handler stub for you.

9. Type **DoCmd.Close acForm, "Customer Labels Dialog", acPrompt** between the **Sub...** and **End Sub** lines (see fig. 28.20). The Close method of the DoCmd object is the Access VBA equivalent of the Close macro action. The acForm and acPrompt arguments of the Close method are Access 95 intrinsic constants. (Access 95 substitutes a period for Access 2.0's space between DoCmd and the method name.)

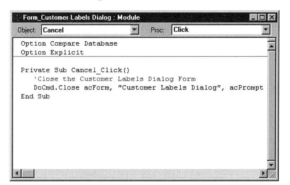

Fig. 28.20   Writing the event-handling code to close the Customer Labels Dialog.

10. To view the syntax of the Close method, place the caret between the period and Close and then press F1. The Context Help On: Close dialog appears with a list of all current object references that expose the Close method (see fig. 28.21).

11. Double-click the Access entry to open the help topic for the DoCmd.Close method (see fig. 28.22). The DoCmd object is specific to Access 95; it is not available in other versions of VBA.

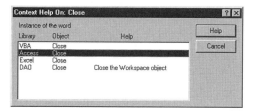

Fig. 28.21   The Context Help On: Close dialog displaying object references that expose the `Close` method.

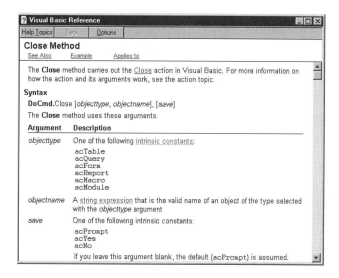

Fig. 28.22   The help topic for the `Close` method.

12. Click the Compile All Modules button to compile your added code, which performs a final syntax check of your event-handler.

13. Close the Form_Customer Labels Dialog module. The event-handling procedure you wrote ([Event Procedure]) is attached to the On Click event of the Cancel command button (see fig. 28.23).

14. Close the Customer Labels Dialog form and save your changes.

15. Open the Customer Labels Dialog and click Cancel to check operation of your code. Your event-handler for the Cancel button performs identically to the Customer Labels Dialog.Cancel macro.

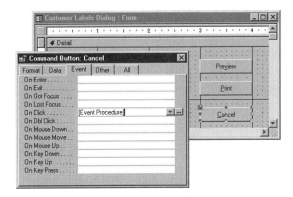

Fig. 28.23 The `Cancel_Click` event handler attached to the `OnClick` event of the Cancel button.

Note

The arguments of the `DoCmd.Close` method you entered in step 9 are not required to close the active form. The arguments are included to demonstrate the full syntax of the instruction. `DoCmd.Close` (no arguments) closes the currently active form.

Most Access developers choose to use event-handling procedures, rather than macros, to process all events triggered on forms and reports. An advantage of using macros is that all the event-handling macros can be located in a single macrosheet so that all the event processing for a form appears in a single window. This advantage is overshadowed by the lack of error trapping in macros. Event-handling procedures are well suited for events that require complex operations, such as manipulating database objects "behind the scene."

From Here...

This chapter introduced you to Access VBA code so that you can create user-defined functions and replace macros with simple event-handling procedures. This chapter described ways to use the Module window to enter and edit code, and explained the compiling process for Access VBA in the context of compilers and interpreters for other programming languages.

The use of conditional statements and different types of loops were covered. You combined the expressions you learned in Chapter 9, "Understanding Operators and Expressions in Access," with the Access VBA keywords presented here so you could write short examples of Access VBA code. The methods you use to handle run-time errors were explained briefly.

For more information about these concepts, consult the following chapters:

■ Chapter 9, "Understanding Operators and Expressions in Access," provides a thorough description of Access's operators and functions that you can employ in Access VBA code.

- Chapter 16, "Understanding Access Macros and Events," lists all the macro actions of Access 95. Each of these actions is a candidate for replacement by Access VBA event-handling code.

- Chapter 29, "Understanding the Data Access Object Class," describes the Jet 3.0 database engine's set of database objects and the collections in which they are contained.

Chapter 29

Understanding the Data Access Object Class

Access 95 offers Access VBA programmers the opportunity to change the values of almost all properties of its database objects in run mode, a feature that commenced with Access 2.0. The majority of Access 1.x object properties were read-only in run mode; you could alter the property values only in design mode. (The term *run-time* often is used in this context; however, this book uses *run mode* to avoid confusion with the term *run-time*, which is applied to applications that use the run-time-limited version of Access.) In addition, Access 95 lets you create new database objects, including `Database` and `Table` objects, with Access VBA code. Microsoft calls this ability *creating objects programmatically*. Access 1.x required that you employ the user interface to create new databases and tables. (You could use a special library, MSADDL11.DLL, to create Access 1.1 tables programmatically, albeit with difficulty.)

This chapter introduces you to the many data access objects (DAOs) of Access 95 and explains how you can manipulate the DAOs with Access VBA code. There is no "Data Access Object," *per se*; the term refers to all the collections of Access 95 objects. The structure of the hierarchy of DAOs is, to a major extent, designed to conform to the requirements and recommendations of the Object Linking and Embedding (OLE) 2.0 specification. Thus, much of this chapter uses OLE 2.0 terminology.

The principal topics in this chapter include

- The hierarchy of the data access objects of Access 2.0

- Referring to the current `Database` object

- Creating new `Recordset` objects in the Debug Window

- Creating a `QueryDef` object

- Writing a function to display a `QueryDef` result set.

Understanding Objects and Object Collections

The specification for Object Linking and Embedding (OLE) 2.0 requires that OLE 2.0-compliant applications, such as Access 2.0, organize programmable objects into a hierarchical structure of *classes* of objects. Two members of Access object classes that you have used extensively are `Forms` and `Reports`. You use these class names as identifiers, such as `Forms!FormName.PropertyName` and `Reports!ReportName!ControlName.PropertyName`, in expressions. In these expressions, `Forms` or `Reports` is the class name, and *FormName* or *ReportName* is the literal name of the member object of the class.

In OLE 2.0 jargon, groups of objects of the same class are called *object collections*. `Forms` is the collection of open `Form` objects and `Reports` is the collection of open `Report` objects. Objects that you have not opened with the `DoCmd` `OpenObjectType` statement, or its equivalent, do not appear in these collections. Collections are similar to arrays except that collections consist of references (called *pointers*) to member objects, whereas Access VBA arrays consist of elements that have assigned values. Unlike arrays, the members of collections may appear or disappear without your intervention. As an example, the members of the `Forms` collection change as you open and close the `Form` objects of your application. Access 95 adds the capability of creating user-defined collections with the **Dim** `colUserDefined` **As New** `Collection` statement. You then can add user-defined objects to the collection by invoking the `AddItem` method of `Collection` objects.

Naming Standards for Object Collections

To conform to OLE 2.0 standards for creating programmable objects, collections are named by the English-language plural of the class name of objects contained in the collection. As an example, Microsoft Graph 5 (MSGraph5) has `Axis` objects; the collection of these objects is called the `Axes` collection. Collections have relatively few properties; the most common property is `Count`. The `IsLoaded()` function, discussed in Chapter 28, "Writing Visual Basic for Applications Code," makes use of the value of the `Count` property in the **For** `i = 0` **To** `Forms.Count - 1` statement to *iterate* or *enumerate* the Forms collection. To iterate or enumerate a collection usually means to test all (or a particular set of) members of a collection for values of a specified property. The `IsLoaded()` function tests the `FormName` property of members of the `Forms` collection in the **If** `Forms(i).FormName = MyFormName` **Then** statement.

Figure 29.1 shows the hierarchy of the data access objects of Access 95. The topmost member of the hierarchy is the `DBEngine` object, representing the Jet database engine, which contains the `Workspaces` and new `Errors` collection. The `Workspaces` collection contains `Databases`, `Users`, and `Groups` collections. None of these collections were *exposed* by Access 1.x. Exposing a collection makes the members of the collection accessible to Access VBA code. As an example, the Errors collection contains one or more Error objects when an error is encountered by Jet 3.0. Notice that the Forms and Reports collections do not appear in figure 29.1. The Forms and Reports collections of Access 1.x and 2.0, like the Scripts (macros) and Modules collections added by Access 2.0, are not DAOs. The Forms and Reports collections are defined by Access, not by Jet, and have two distinct identities:

- ■ `Documents` collections, which consist of all saved forms and reports, are members of the `Containers` collection.

- ■ `Forms` and `Reports` collections, which contain only members of the `Forms` and `Reports` `Containers` collection that are currently open in your application.

In the case of `Containers` and `Documents`, Access departs from the OLE 2+ rules for naming collections. `Documents` are collections that are members of the `Containers` collection; there are no "`Container`" objects in the collection. The list in the Database window enumerates the `Name` property of members of the class of the `Documents` collection you select by clicking a tab. When you refer to `Form` and `Report` objects in expressions, you use the

Forms and Reports collections, *not* the member of the Containers collection with the same name.

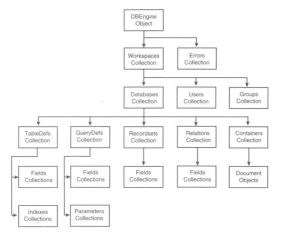

Fig. 29.1   The hierarchy of Access 2.0's data access objects.

Creating a Reference to the Data Access Object

VBA requires references to OLE objects exposed by components of OLE container applications. All flavors of VBA, including the Access, Excel, Project, and Visual Basic 4.0 versions, include references to application objects and VBA itself. When you install Access 95, references are created automatically to the following three object libraries stored in your \Windows\System folder:

- Visual Basic for Applications (Ven2132.olb, 32-bit VBA English Version 2.1), which contains references to all of the commands and constants of VBA

- Microsoft Access 95 (Msaccess.tlb), which contains references to all Access-specific objects, VBA commands (for example, DoCmd), and constants

- Microsoft DAO 3.0 Object Library (Dao3032.dll), which contains references to all of the objects exposed by the Jet 3.0 database engine

References to object libraries (.olb), object type libraries (.tlb), and OLE Dynamic Link Libraries (.dll) appear in the References dialog shown in figure 29.2. To open the References dialog, open the Utility Functions module of Northwind.mdb in Design View, and choose Tools, References. The items that appear in the Available References list depend on the OLE-compliant applications installed on your computer. You cannot remove the references to, or change the priority of, Visual Basic for Applications or Microsoft Access 95. You can, however, click the check box for the Microsoft DAO 3.0 Object library to remove references to the Jet 3.0 DAO.

If you remove the DAO reference, you cannot use data access objects in your VBA code. The references you establish with the References dialog apply only to VBA code, not to operations involving the Access user interface. You establish references to objects of other OLE Automation server applications to manipulate the Automation Objects with VBA code, the subject of Chapter 30, "Exchanging Data with OLE Automation and DDE." All OLE Automation client applications that use VBA as their application programming language have a References dialog similar to that of Access 95.

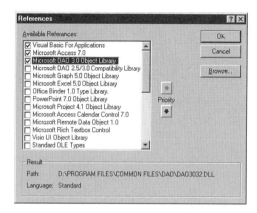

Fig. 29.2   Access 95's default VBA references displayed by the References dialog.

Note

The Available References list of the References dialog also includes a reference for the 32-bit version of the Microsoft DAO 2.5/3.0 Compatibility Library (Dao2532.tlb). You can substitute Dao2532.tlb for Dao3032.dll to preserve compatibility with Access Basic code in Access 1.x and 2.0 applications that you convert to Access 95. You cannot add references to both Dao3032.dll and Dao2532.dll; you receive an error message if you attempt to do so. To assure compatibility of your VBA code with future versions of Access, it is advisable to use the Dao3032.dll reference and change your VBA code to comply with Access 95 VBA syntax for data access objects.

Using the Object Browser

Access 95's new Object Browser displays the objects exposed by OLE Automation servers to which references have been created, plus the properties and methods of the objects. To open Access 95's Object Browser dialog, press F2 and click the Object Browser button in the toolbar, or choose View, Object Browser. To choose the class of objects to view, open the Libraries/Databases drop-down list. You can select from the object classes supplied by the three references described in the preceding section, any additional references you have added, plus objects in the current database (Northwind.mdb in this example). This chapter is devoted to data access objects, so select DAO—Microsoft DAO 3.0 Object Library.

The Object Browser is very useful for becoming acquainted with the names of objects exposed by the Jet 3.0 DAO and the properties and methods of data access objects. When you select an object or collection in the Modules/Classes list and a member function of the object or collection in the Method/Properties list, the syntax for the method or property appears next to the ? button below the lists. Figure 29.3 shows the Object Browser displaying the syntax for the `OpenDatabase()` method of the `Workspace` object. All VBA-enabled applications have a similar Object Browser.

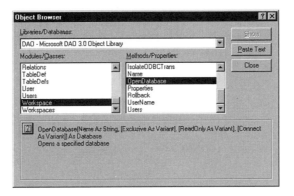

Fig. 29.3 Object Browser displaying the syntax for the `OpenDatabase()` method of the `Workspace` object.

Clicking the ? button displays the help topic for the method or property, in this case for the `OpenDatabase()` method (see fig. 29.4). Clicking the Paste Text button pastes a prototype expression for the method or property into a procedure of a module at the current caret position. If the Debug window is open with the focus, the expression is pasted to the current line of the Debug window. The expression uses named arguments and does not supply argument values. Figure 29.5 shows the prototype expression for the OpenDatabase() method pasted into the Debug window. When you use the Paste Text button, Object Browser's dialog closes before pasting the prototype expression. You cannot execute the prototype statement because the object reference prefix and the argument values are missing.

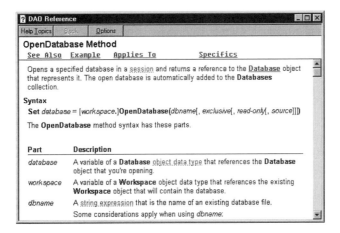

Fig. 29.4 The help topic for the `OpenDatabase()` method opened by clicking the ? button of the Object Browser.

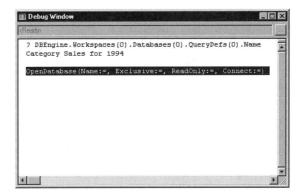

Fig. 29.5   Pasting an expression prototype for the `OpenDatabase()` method into the Debug window with the Paste Text button.

Referring to Data Access Objects in VBA

Knowing the hierarchy of data access objects is critical to their manipulation by your Access VBA code. As an example, if you want to refer to the currently open database, you specify the full "path" through the hierarchy to your object and its properties or methods with an expression similar to the following:

```
DBEngine.Workspaces(0).Databases(0).QueryDefs(0).Name
```

The zeroth member of the `Workspaces` collection is the current `Workspace` object, also called the current *session* or *instance* of the Jet database engine. The current session comes into existence when you first launch Access. Similarly, `Databases(0)` specifies the database you open after launching Access, called the *current database*. `QueryDefs(0)` specifies the first `QueryDef` object of the `QueryDefs` collection. `Name` is a property of the `QueryDef` object. The second line of the preceding figure 29.5 shows the result of executing the expression in the Debug window. You can open additional `Workspace` objects and add one or more Database objects to the newly created `Workspace` object with Access VBA code. Adding new members to collections is described in sections that follow.

Note

The currently open `Database` object, specified by `DBEngine.Workspaces(0).Databases(0)`, is the same object identified by the `CurrentDB()` function in all versions of Access. Access 2.0 introduced *Container(i)* syntax, as in

```
Set dbCurrent = DBEngine.Workspaces(0).Databases(0)
```

The preferred statement in Access 95 to refer to the database opened in Access is

```
Set dbCurrent = CurrentDB()
```

that creates an instance of the current database. Using the `CurrentDB()` function is advisable to assure compatibility with future versions of Access. (See the "Creating Object Variables" section that follows.) The CurrentDB() function (method) is a member function of the Access `Application` object, not the DAO. Thus, CurrentDB() is not applicable when using Visual Basic 4.0, Excel VBA or Project VBA.

A Database object can contain `TableDef`, `QueryDef`, `Recordset`, and `Relation` objects, as well as `Documents` collections in the `Containers` collection. A brief description of each of these objects, except the `Containers` collection, follows:

- `TableDef` objects represent the definition of saved tables. `TableDef` objects contain `Fields` and `Indexes` collections, which contain one member for each field and index of the table represented by the `TableDef` object. `TableDef` objects have several properties, such as `Name`, `RecordCount`, and `ValidationRule`, that apply to the table as a whole. The `Field` and `Index` objects have their own sets of properties.

- `QueryDef` objects represent the definition of saved queries and contain `Fields` (which might better have been named `Columns`) and `Parameters` collections. `QueryDef` objects have properties, such as `Name`, `SQL`, and `Updatable`.

- `Recordset` objects, which have been mentioned throughout this book, represent virtual tables (images) that are stored in RAM. `Recordset` objects are said to be "created over" a table or a query result set. `Recordset` objects, which mimic the behavior of the underlying object, can be of the `Table`, `Dynaset`, or `Snapshot` type. As mentioned in earlier chapters of this book, the `Table`, `Dynaset`, and `Snapshot` data types appear in Access 95 for compatibility with Access 1.x code. You should use Access 95's `Recordset` objects to assure compatibility with future versions of Access.

- `Relation`objects represent default relationships between fields of tables that, in most cases, you create in the Relationships window. `Relation` objects contain a `Fields` collection.

Note

If the size of a Recordset object exceeds the available RAM, the remainder of the object is placed in a temporary "spill file" in the \Windows\Temp folder.

Following are the three different methods of creating a reference to a member of a collection:

- The *index* method uses conventional array subscripts to specify a particular member of a collection by its position in the collection: *CollectionName(i)*, where *i* ranges from 0 to *CollectionName*.Count –1. Using the index to the object is the fastest method of referring to members of collections. The problem with the index method is that the index of a particular member object is likely to change as you open (add) and close (remove) objects in the collection.

- The *argument* method uses a literal identifier, either a quoted string or a variable holding the value of a literal identifier: *CollectionName("ObjectName")* or *CollectionName(strObjectName)*. This method is preferred when you know the name of the member object.

- The *literal* method uses the bang operator to separate the literal name of the object from the collection name: *CollectionName!ObjectName*. If the literal name contains spaces or punctuation other than the underscore, enclose the literal in square brackets, as in *CollectionName*![*Object Name*]. This method is used primarily with Form and Report objects, but is applicable to members of any collection. In this case, you can't use a variable in place of the name of the member object. The literal method is the least flexible of the three.

Properties of, and Methods Applicable to, DAOs

Most objects have a Properties collection that you can use to enumerate the properties of the object. You can read (get) the value of properties and set the value of most properties of an object in run mode. The Debug Window is a handy tool to experiment with getting and setting the values of properties as well as invoking methods. The example statements in this section use the Debug Window syntax to print the value of properties.

The ? DBEngine.Workspaces(0).Properties.Count statement returns 3, the number of properties of the Workspace object. You can obtain the name of a property with the *CollectionName*(*i*).Properties(*j*).Name statement, where *j* = 0 to *CollectionName*(*i*).Properties.Count - 1. As an example, ? DBEngine.Workspaces(0).Properties(0) returns the value of the Name property. Name is the zeroth property of almost all DAOs. ? DBEngine.Workspaces(0).Properties(0) returns #DefaultWorkspace#, ...Properties(1) returns the value of UserName, admin for unsecure databases, and ...Properties(2) returns the value of the IsolateODBCTrans property, 0 (**False**), as shown in figure 29.6.

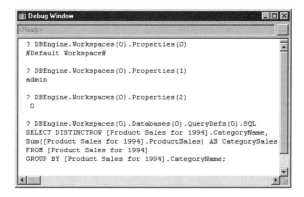

Fig. 29.6 Using the Debug Window to print the values of properties of data access objects.

> ### Note
>
> In Access 2.0, the Workspaces object had four properties. DBEngine.Workspaces(0) .Properties(2) held the Password property of the user. This property was write-only; you could set this value but not read it. The Password property has been removed from the Workspaces object of Access 95.

To read or set property values of objects lower in the hierarchy than Workspaces, you should declare an object variable and then assign the object variable the object you want to manipulate from its collection. Creating object variables is the subject of the next section.

You can apply methods to members of collections, such as Append to add a new member to a collection. The Properties collection is interesting in this respect: Access 2.0 and later allows you to append user-defined properties to the Properties collection. Some properties of objects are called Access-defined properties; you must append the Access-defined property to the collection in order for Access to assign the property a value. (This obscure methodology is of principal interest to Access developers using SQL pass-through queries, one of the subjects of Chapter 26, "Connecting to Client/Server Databases.")

> **Note**
>
> Publishing limitations preclude listing the properties and methods for each DAO. Use the Object Browser's ? button to display the online help topic for the object class (selection only in the Classes/Modules list), as shown in figure 29.7. You also can open the help topic for a specific member function (selection in both the Classes/Modules and Methods/Properties lists), as illustrated by the preceding figure 29.4. Using the Object Browser to open a help topic for a data access object is a much easier process than choosing Help, Microsoft Access Help Topics, selecting the Microsoft Data Access Objects (DAO) book, and then attempting to find what you want in the book's table of contents.

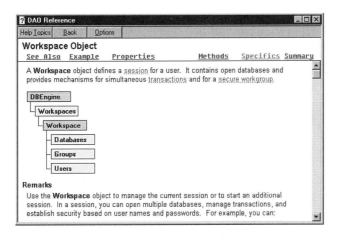

Fig. 29.7 The help topic for the Workspace object class.

Creating Object Variables

You need to declare *object variables* to represent a specified object lower than Workspace objects in the DAO hierarchy. All object variables must be declared explicitly. Object variables are declared with **Private** obj*Name* **As** *ObjectType* statements in the Declarations section of a module to create an object variable with module-level scope or in a procedure to create a local object variable. Use the **Public** reserved word to create a variable with global scope. **Private** and **Public** replace the **Dim** and **Global** reserved words of Access VBA, although you can continue to use **Dim** and **Global**. The following code creates an object variable, dbCurrent, that refers to the current database:

```
Private dbCurrent As Database
Set dbCurrent = CurrentDB()
```

The **Set** reserved word is used to assign values to variables of object data types. The value of the variable is a reference (pointer) to a block of memory in which the object is located. Thus, dbCurrent is said to *point to* the current database.

Once you've declared a Database variable, such as dbCurrent, you can use dbCurrent as a shorthand method of assigning pointers to the database objects. To refer to the TableDefs collection of the current database, which is a *subclass* of the Database object, use the following statements:

```
Private tdfCurrent As TableDef
Set tdfCurrent = dbCurrent.TableDefs("Categories")
```

As a general practice, you create a module-level variable of the Database type to point to the current database. If more than one module contains DAO manipulation code, substitute **Public** dbCurrent **As** Database for **Private** dbCurrent **As** Database. The scope of subclasses of your dbCurrent object depends on your use of the object subclasses in your code.

Using Object Variables in the Debug Window

 You cannot declare variables explicitly in the Debug Window; thus, you need to declare object variables in the Declarations section of a module and then enter **Set** statements in the Debug Window to assign object pointers to the variables. Figure 29.8 provides examples of declaring object variables at the module level and of assigning pointer values to the variables in the Debug Window. Database objects contain one TableDef object for each table listed in the Database window, and each TableDef object contains one Field object for each field of the table.

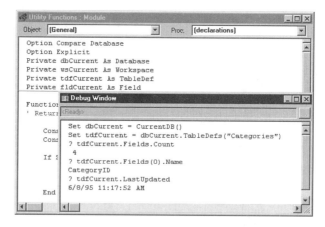

Fig. 29.8 Declaring and assigning values to object variables.

Creating New Data Access Objects

As mentioned in "Creating Object Variables," earlier in this chapter, Access 95 lets you create new DAOs with Access VBA code. The most common DAOs you create with Access VBA are Recordset and QueryDef objects. QueryDef objects, like TableDef objects, are called *persistent* objects because QueryDef and TableDef objects also are Document objects: Query and Table objects, respectively. QueryDef and TableDef objects are stored as elements of your .mdb file and appear in the Queries and Tables lists, respectively, of the Database window. Recordset objects are *impersistent* objects; Recordset objects exist in memory only from the time you open them until they are closed. You can close a Recordset object by applying the Close method; Recordset objects are closed automatically when the variable that points to them goes out of scope. When you close a Recordset object, the memory that the object consumes is released to your application.

> **Note**
>
> Using Access VBA to create new Workspace, Database, User, Group, TableDef, and Relation objects is beyond the scope of this book. You can create these objects, with the exception of the Workspace object, much easier with Access's user interface. You also can create new TableDef objects with make-table queries or by using Access SQL Data Definition Language statements.

Opening a New Recordset Object

You create a new Recordset object with the OpenRecordset() method of Database, TableDef, and QueryDef objects. The general syntax of the OpenRecordset() method has two forms:

```
Set rsdName = dbName.OpenRecordset(strSource[, intType[,
intOptions]])
Set rsoName = objName.OpenRecordset([intType[, intOptions]])
```

The first form, which is applicable only to Recordset objects created over Database objects, requires a value for the strSource argument. The value of the strSource argument can be the name of a TableDef or QueryDef object or an Access SQL statement. You also can use VBA's named arguments feature in the following statements:

```
Set rsdName = OpenRecordset(Name:=strSource[, Type:=intType[,
Options:=intOptions]])
Set rsoName = objName.OpenRecordset([Type:=intType[,
Options:=intOptions]])
```

Tables 29.1 and 29.2 list values allowed for the intType and intOptions arguments for both of the preceding syntax examples. The values shown in the table are the names of predefined (intrinsic) global constants that are defined by the Jet 3.0 DAO. In previous versions of Access, Access intrinsic global database constants names were uppercase and included underscore separators for readability, as in DB_OPEN_TABLE. Database intrinsic constants now are supplied by the Constants collection of the Jet 3.0 DAO and use the lowercase prefix db, with intermediate capitalization to improve readability (see fig. 29.9). In the case of the intOptions values listed in table 29.2, you can combine the options you want with the VBA **Or** operator, as in dbDenyWrite **Or** dbDenyRead.

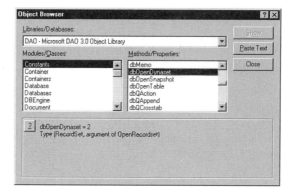

Fig. 29.9 Some of the predefined (intrinsic) constants supplied by the Jet 3.0 Data Access Object.

Table 29.1   Values for the `intType` Argument of the `OpenRecordset()` Method Using DAO 3.0 and Access 2.0 Intrinsic Constants

DAO 3.0	Access 2.0	Description of Type
dbOpenTable	DB_OPEN_TABLE	Table (default value for local `TableDef` source)
dbOpenDynaset	DB_OPEN_DYNASET	Dynaset (default value for `Database`, `QueryDef`, `Recordset`, or an attached `TableDef`)
dbOpenSnapshot	DB_OPEN_SNAPSHOT	Snapshot (not updatable)

Table 29.2   Values for the `intOptions` Argument of the `OpenRecordset()` Method Using DAO 3.0 and Access 2.0 Intrinsic Constants

DAO 3.0	Access 2.0	Purpose of Option
dbDenyWrite	DB_DENYWRITE	Prevents others from making changes to any records in the underlying table(s) while the `Recordset` is open.
dbDenyRead	DB_DENYREAD	Prevents others from reading any records in the underlying table while the `Recordset` is open. This option, which applies to `Table`-type `Recordset` objects only, should be used for administrative purposes only in a multiuser environment.
dbReadOnly	DB_READONLY	Does not allow updates to records in the table. Read-only access increases the speed of some operations.
dbAppendOnly	DB_APPENDONLY	Only allows appending new records. (Applies to Dynaset-type `Recordset` objects only.)
dbInconsistent	DB_INCONSISTENT	You can update the one-side of a one-to-many relationship. (Applies to Dynaset-type `Recordset` objects only.)
dbConsistent	DB_CONSISTENT	You cannot update the one-side of a one-to-many relationship, the default. (Applies to Dynaset-type `Recordset` objects only.)
dbForwardScroll	DB_FORWARDSCROLL	Creates a `Recordset` object of the forward-scrolling-only Snapshot type.

The following two sections show how to create two different types of Recordset objects.

A Recordset Object That Represents the Image of a Table. You can create the following two types of Recordset objects over a table, both of which create a virtual table in memory:

■ A Recordset object of the Dynaset type created from the current Database object. To open a Dynaset-type Recordset object over the Orders table, add the **Private** rstCurrent **As** Recordset variable declaration statement to the Declarations section of the module; then use the following statement to assign the pointer:

```
Set rstCurrent = dbCurrent.OpenRecordset("Orders", dbOpenDynaset)
```

A more appropriate object tag for rstCurrent is rsdOrders, representing the Dynaset Recordset object created over the Orders table.

■ A Recordset object of the Table type created from a TableDef object. To open a Table Recordset object over the Orders table, add the **Private** tdfCurrent **As** TableDef variable declaration statement to the Declarations section of the module; then use the following statements to assign the pointers:

```
Set tdfCurrent = dbCurrent.TableDefs("Orders")
Set rstCurrent = tdfCurrent.OpenRecordset(dbOpenTable).
```

Figure 29.10 illustrates the creation of both of the preceding types of Recordset objects in the Debug Window.

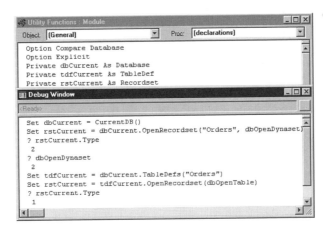

Fig. 29.10   Creating Recordset objects of the Dynaset and Table type in the Debug Window.

Moving to a Specific Record in a Recordset Object. Opening a Recordset of the Table type lets you quickly find a record in a table with the Seek method. This method is applicable only to Table-type Recordset objects whose underlying table contains an index on the field in which the value you want to find is located. To apply the Seek method, you first must specify the index name. The following example sets the record pointer to the record in the Orders table of Northwind.mdb with a value of 10833 in the OrderID field, the primary key of the table:

```
Set tdfCurrent = dbCurrent.TableDefs("Orders")
Set rstCurrent = tdfCurrent.OpenRecordset()
rstCurrent.Index = "PrimaryKey"
rstCurrent.Seek "=", 10833
If rstCurrent.NoMatch Then
    'Record not found, display message box
Else
    'Record found, add code to process the record here
En d If
```

> **Note**
>
> You can't enter conditional statements in the Debug Window, but you can test the preceding code by typing the entries up to and including the Seek line, and then executing ? rstCurrent.NoMatch to determine if the Seek method was successful in finding a matching record. The NoMatch property uses the new **Boolean** data type. If **False** is returned, the record pointer rests on the matching record.

If the field in which you are Seeking the value is not the primary key field, you specify the field's name. The NoMatch property returns **False** if the value specified by the Seek expression is found; it returns **True** if a matching record is not found. Note that the behavior of the NoMatch property is the opposite of the FOUND() function of Xbase. Figure 29.11 shows typical entries to test the Seek method in the Debug Windows. Test the Indexes collection of the TableDef object to verify that the index you specify exists. The Seek method allows the use of a variety of other operators, such as < or >=, in place of the = operator. Thus, the Seek method is more flexible than Xbase's FOUND() function.

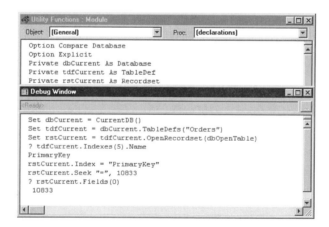

Fig. 29.11   Applying the Seek method to Recordset objects of the Table type.

> **Tip**
>
> You cannot apply the Find. . .methods to a forward-scrolling-only Recordset object of the Snapshot type. The only method applicable to such objects is MoveNext.

You use the `Find. . .`methods to locate a specific record in `Recordset` objects of the `Dynaset` and `Snapshot` type. There are four `Find. . .`methods: `FindFirst`, `FindNext`, `FindLast`, and `FindPrevious`. Not surprisingly, each method does what its name indicates. The general syntax of the `Find. . .`methods is

```
rsdName.Find{First¦Next¦Last¦Previous} strCriteria
```

The single `strCriteria` argument of the `Find. . .`methods must be a valid SQL `WHERE` clause without the `WHERE` reserved word. As with the `Seek` method, the `NoMatch` property returns **False** if a match occurs. Figure 29.12 shows examples of the use of the four `Find. . .`methods.

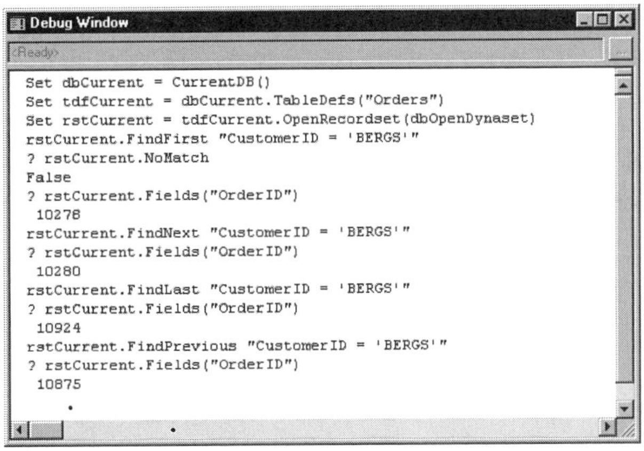

```
Debug Window
<Ready>
Set dbCurrent = CurrentDB()
Set tdfCurrent = dbCurrent.TableDefs("Orders")
Set rstCurrent = tdfCurrent.OpenRecordset(dbOpenDynaset)
rstCurrent.FindFirst "CustomerID = 'BERGS'"
? rstCurrent.NoMatch
False
? rstCurrent.Fields("OrderID")
 10278
rstCurrent.FindNext "CustomerID = 'BERGS'"
? rstCurrent.Fields("OrderID")
 10280
rstCurrent.FindLast "CustomerID = 'BERGS'"
? rstCurrent.Fields("OrderID")
 10924
rstCurrent.FindPrevious "CustomerID = 'BERGS'"
? rstCurrent.Fields("OrderID")
 10875
       .
```

Fig. 29.12 Applying the `Find` methods to `Recordset` objects of the `Dynaset` or `Snapshot` type.

A Recordset That Emulates a `QueryDef` Object. You can substitute a valid Access SQL statement for a table or query name as the value of the strSource property to create a `Recordset` object of the `Dynaset` or `Snapshot` type over selected records of one or more tables. You only can create such a `Recordset` over the `Database` object because more than one `TableDef` object may participate in the query. Such a `Recordset` is the equivalent of an "impersistent `QueryDef`" object (a `QueryDef` object that is not a Document object). Figure 29.13 shows you how to create a `Recordset` object using an SQL statement in the Debug Window. You must add a **Private** strSQL **As String** statement to the Declarations section of the module if the `Option Explicit` statement has been executed. The entire strSQL = ... statement is

```
strSQL = "SELECT * FROM Orders, [Order Details]
WHERE [Order Details].OrderID = Orders.OrderID
AND Orders.CustomerID = 'BERGS'"
```

If you only need to manipulate a `Recordset`'s records temporarily, creating the "impersistent `QueryDef`" `Recordset` is faster than creating a legitimate, persistent `QueryDef` object.

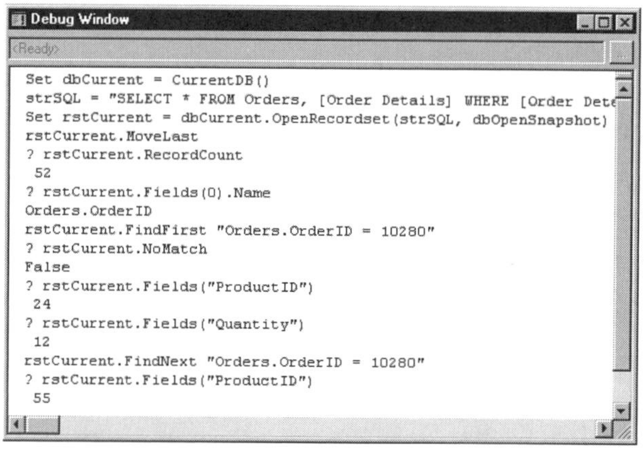

Fig. 29.13 Creating a `Recordset` object with an Access SQL statement.

Defining a New `QueryDef` Object

> **Tip**
>
> You need to apply the `MoveLast` method before testing the value of the `RecordCount` property. If you omit the `MoveLast` method, you usually receive an erroneous `RecordCount` value (1). However, you can test whether any recorders were returned by testing with an **If** rst*Name*.`RecordCount` **Then** ... **End If** structure.

You use the `CreateQueryDef()` method to create a new, persistent `QueryDef` object and add it to the `QueryDefs` collection. One of the advantages of creating a `QueryDef` is that you can use the name you give the `QueryDef` in place of a table name in an Access SQL statement. The name of the `QueryDef` must not duplicate the name of an existing `QueryDef` *or* `TableDef` object. The syntax for creating a new `QueryDef` object is

> **Set** qdf*Name* = db*Name*.`CreateQueryDef`(str*Name*, str*SQL*)

`QueryDef` objects are what their object class name implies: the definition of a query. If str*SQL*'s SQL statement represents an action query, you apply the `Execute` method to the `QueryDef` object to execute the query. You must create a `Recordset` over `QueryDef` objects that define select queries in order to read values in the query result set. Figure 29.14 illustrates how you create a new `QueryDef` object and open a `Recordset` object based on the `QueryDef`. You need to add **Private** qdfCurrent **As** `QueryDef` to the Declarations section of your code before you can execute the code shown in the Debug Window of figure 29.14. When you execute a statement that includes the `CreateQueryDef()` method, the new `QueryDef` appears in the Queries page of the Database window. You can open a `QueryDef` created by Access VBA, as shown in figure 29.15.

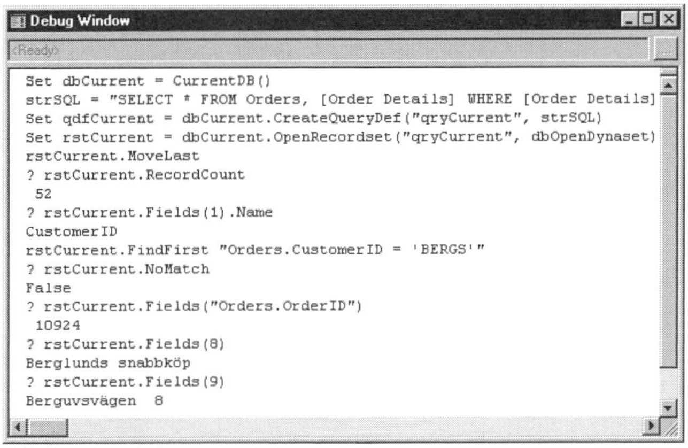

```
Debug Window                                                        _ □ ×
<Ready>
Set dbCurrent = CurrentDB()
strSQL = "SELECT * FROM Orders, [Order Details] WHERE [Order Details]
Set qdfCurrent = dbCurrent.CreateQueryDef("qryCurrent", strSQL)
Set rstCurrent = dbCurrent.OpenRecordset("qryCurrent", dbOpenDynaset)
rstCurrent.MoveLast
? rstCurrent.RecordCount
  52
? rstCurrent.Fields(1).Name
CustomerID
rstCurrent.FindFirst "Orders.CustomerID = 'BERGS'"
? rstCurrent.NoMatch
False
? rstCurrent.Fields("Orders.OrderID")
  10924
? rstCurrent.Fields(8)
Berglunds snabbköp
? rstCurrent.Fields(9)
Berguvsvägen  8
```

Fig. 29.14 Creating a new QueryDef object and opening a Recordset over the QueryDef.

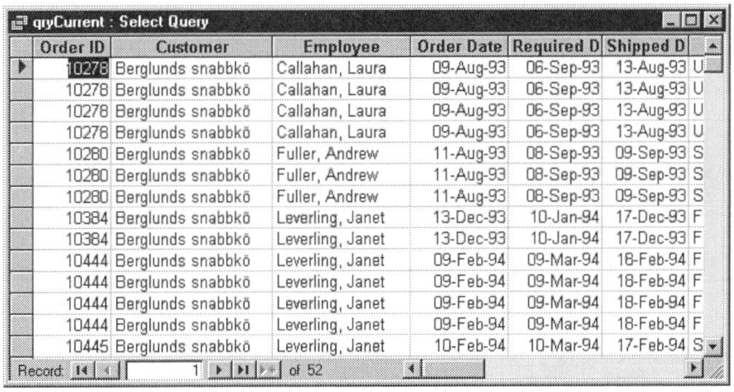

Order ID	Customer	Employee	Order Date	Required D	Shipped D	
10278	Berglunds snabbkö	Callahan, Laura	09-Aug-93	06-Sep-93	13-Aug-93	U
10278	Berglunds snabbkö	Callahan, Laura	09-Aug-93	06-Sep-93	13-Aug-93	U
10278	Berglunds snabbkö	Callahan, Laura	09-Aug-93	06-Sep-93	13-Aug-93	U
10278	Berglunds snabbkö	Callahan, Laura	09-Aug-93	06-Sep-93	13-Aug-93	U
10280	Berglunds snabbkö	Fuller, Andrew	11-Aug-93	08-Sep-93	09-Sep-93	S
10280	Berglunds snabbkö	Fuller, Andrew	11-Aug-93	08-Sep-93	09-Sep-93	S
10280	Berglunds snabbkö	Fuller, Andrew	11-Aug-93	08-Sep-93	09-Sep-93	S
10384	Berglunds snabbkö	Leverling, Janet	13-Dec-93	10-Jan-94	17-Dec-93	F
10384	Berglunds snabbkö	Leverling, Janet	13-Dec-93	10-Jan-94	17-Dec-93	F
10444	Berglunds snabbkö	Leverling, Janet	09-Feb-94	09-Mar-94	18-Feb-94	F
10444	Berglunds snabbkö	Leverling, Janet	09-Feb-94	09-Mar-94	18-Feb-94	F
10444	Berglunds snabbkö	Leverling, Janet	09-Feb-94	09-Mar-94	18-Feb-94	F
10444	Berglunds snabbkö	Leverling, Janet	09-Feb-94	09-Mar-94	18-Feb-94	F
10445	Berglunds snabbkö	Leverling, Janet	10-Feb-94	10-Mar-94	17-Feb-94	S

Record: |◄| ◄| 1 |►|►|| ►*| of 52

Fig. 29.15 Opening a new QueryDef object created with Access VBA code.

Writing a Function that Uses Database Objects

All database objects that you can create and manipulate with Access's graphical development environment also can be created and manipulated with Access VBA code. You can use Access VBA to create a new table, add records to the table, define a query to select records from the table, create a form to display the data, and then print a report. In other words, you can use Access VBA to create an application exactly the same way you use the dBASE language or PAL. The purpose of Access's graphical development environment, however, is to minimize the need for code in applications.

The nilTestQuery() function you write in the following example uses the QueryDef and Database object data types to create a query with an SQL statement and then displays that query in Datasheet View.

The `nilTestQuery()` function contains a number of Access VBA reserved words that have been explained in the preceding sections of this chapter, but an example of one reserved word (`DoCmd`) has not yet been provided. Describing every Access VBA reserved word requires a book in itself, as you can see by the length of the *Access VBA Language Reference* if you have the Access Developer's Toolkit. As you enter the keywords in this example, place the caret inside the keyword and press the F1 key to obtain a detailed explanation of the keyword and its use from Access VBA's Help system.

To create the `nilTestQuery()` function, follow these steps:

1. Close any module you have open; then make the Database window active, click the Module tab, and click the New button to create a new module.

2. You can accept the default `Option Compare Database` statement that Access adds to the Declarations section of a new module, or change the compare modifier to `Text` to make comparisons not case-sensitive. Add the `Option Explicit` statement, to force explicit declaration of variables, if you haven't specified Require Variable Declaration in the options for modules.

3. To create the new procedure, type **Function nilTestQuery( )** below the `Option Explicit` statement. Access VBA procedures called by macros must be written as functions, although these procedures do not return usable values to the macro action (thus the `nil` prefix).

4. You need to declare and assign data types to the variables that the procedure uses. Below `Function nilTestQuery()`, enter the following statements to create object variables with local (procedure-level) scope:

   ```
   Private dbNWind As Database
   Private qdfTest As QueryDef
   ```

5. You need to specify the database, in this case Northwind.mdb, that contains the table for the query. Type the following statement:

   ```
   Set dbNWind = CurrentDB()
   ```

6. You cannot have two `QueryDef` objects of the same name, so you need to delete the `QueryDef` created by multiple executions of the procedure with the `Collection.Delete` method. Enter the following statements:

   ```
   On Error Resume Next
   dbNWind.QueryDefs.Delete "qryTest"
   On Error GoTo 0
   ```

An error is generated if the `QueryDef` you attempt to delete doesn't exist; `qryTest` doesn't exist the first time you run the function, so an error occurs. The **On Error Resume Next** statement causes Access to disregard errors that occur in code below the statement. **On Error GoTo 0** resumes run-time error checking.

7. You need a variable to hold (point to) the definition of the query. Enter the following:

```
Set qdfTest = dbNWind.CreateQueryDef("qryTest")
```

8. Now you enter the SQL statement that you use to create and run the query. You can add the SQL statement as the optional second argument of the `CreateQueryDef` method instead of setting the value of its SQL property. Enter the following:

```
qdfTest.SQL = "SELECT * FROM Suppliers WHERE SupplierID < 11;"
```

9. Finally, you need to execute the query and display the `Recordset` object created over the `QueryDef` in a datasheet. The macro action, `OpenQuery`, creates a Recordset and displays the rows of the `Recordset` in Datasheet View. You use the `DoCmd` object (a reserved word in Access) to execute macro actions in Access VBA. Enter the following statement:

```
DoCmd.OpenQuery "qryTestQuery"
```

10. Your Module window appears, as shown in figure 29.16.

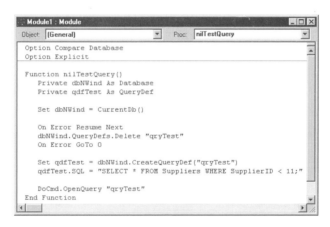

```
Module1 : Module                                                _ □ ×
Object: [General]          ▼      Proc:  nilTestQuery            ▼

Option Compare Database
Option Explicit

Function nilTestQuery()
    Private dbNWind As Database
    Private qdfTest As QueryDef

    Set dbNWind = CurrentDb()

    On Error Resume Next
    dbNWind.QueryDefs.Delete "qryTest"
    On Error GoTo 0

    Set qdfTest = dbNWind.CreateQueryDef("qryTest")
    qdfTest.SQL = "SELECT * FROM Suppliers WHERE SupplierID < 11;"

    DoCmd.OpenQuery "qryTest"
End Function
```

Fig. 29.16   Code for the `nilTestQuery()` function.

11. Click the Compile All Modules button of the toolbar or choose <u>R</u>un, Compile All <u>M</u>odules to verify the syntax of the Access VBA statements you entered.

12. Click the Save button of the toolbar, or choose File, Save, and give the new module a name, such as `modTestQuery`.

13. Open the Debug Window and delete any existing entries. Type **? nilTestQuery()** and press Enter. Your query result set appears in the datasheet (see fig. 29.17).

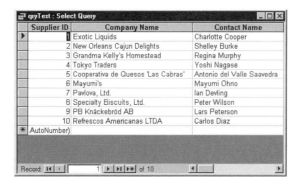

Fig. 29.17 The Datasheet View of the query result set created by the `nilTestQuery()` function.

From Here...

This chapter introduced you to the data access objects of Access 95. Exploring all of the properties and methods of every type of data access object and giving examples of their use requires a book in itself. Thus, the examples of this chapter were limited to creating and manipulating the most commonly used DAOs: `Recordset` and `QueryDef` objects.

For information related to the topics discussed in this chapter, refer to the following chapters:

- Chapter 16, "Understanding Access Macros and Events," provides a complete list of all of the macro actions you can execute with Access VBA's `DoCmd` reserved word.

- Chapter 28, "Writing Visual Basic for Applications Code," explains the structure and syntax of Access VBA.

- Chapter 30, "Exchanging Data with OLE Automation and DDE," describes how you manipulate with Access VBA code the objects you create from other applications' repertoires of objects.

Chapter 30

Exchanging Data with OLE Automation and DDE

One of the major challenges that faced Microsoft Corporation during the early development of Windows was to establish a standard method of *interprocess communication* (IPC). Interprocess communication is the ability to transfer data, including graphic images, and to execute commands between two different applications running on the same computer. Microsoft elected to use the Windows Clipboard as the intermediary in the process and named the IPC methodology *dynamic data exchange* (DDE).

Almost all commercial Windows productivity applications, such as word processors, spreadsheets, and project managers, implement DDE to transfer data. Windows 95 and Windows NT let you implement DDE conversations over a network using NetDDE. DDE's principal problems are the independence of the source of the data and its destination and the need for rather complex application programming to implement the DDE process.

The next major step in IPC technology was OLE 1.0, originally implemented by Excel 3.0, Word for Windows 2.0, and PowerPoint 2.0. Windows 3.1 included the .DLLs necessary to implement OLE 1.0, OLECLI.DLL, and OLESVR.DLL. Providing OLE 1.0 client and server capability became *de rigueur* for all mainstream Windows applications. The primary advantage of OLE 1.0 was that you could build compound documents in which a source document created by one application, the OLE server, is embedded within a destination document created by another application, the OLE client. Thus there is a much closer relationship between the source and destination documents when you use OLE.

OLE 1.0 overcame the need for most of the application programming requirements of DDE. On the other hand, OLE 1.0 did not provide programmers the ability to easily manipulate individual pieces of data, such as a specific cell value in a worksheet. Thus, OLE 1.0 was unable to replace DDE in many applications that required IPC. OLE presently lacks DDE's ability to operate over a network; today, both the OLE client and OLE server application must reside on the same computer.

In this chapter, you learn to

- Send data to an Excel 95 Worksheet and a Word 95 document

- Add OLE Controls to an Access application

- Manipulate OLE Controls

- Use Access as an OLE Automation server

- Use Access VBA DDE to retreive data from an Excel worksheet

- Employ Access as a DDE server

Microsoft's solution to the IPC limitations of OLE 1.0 is OLE 2 and OLE Automation (OA), an optional component of the OLE 2+ specification. (OLE 2.1 was the current version of the OLE 2 specification when this edition was written; both Windows 95 and Windows NT 3.51+ support OLE 2.1.) Applications that implement OA expose their objects so that these objects can be manipulated by code contained in other applications. Microsoft calls the objects exposed by an OA server *programmable objects*. Programmable objects let you assemble customized applications using the "cinder block" approach: programmable objects are the blocks and OA code acts as the mortar.

OLE 2.1 and OA still require that both the client and server application reside on a single computer. Microsoft Corporation and Digital Equipment Corporation have announced a joint development program to add network transportability and cross-platform compatibility to programmable objects using DEC's ObjectBroker technology. Visual Basic 4.0 lets you create Remote Automation Objects (RAOs) that can communicate over networks.

Microsoft's Bill Gates has stated that future versions of Windows 95 and Windows NT will include OLE 2+ as part of the operating system and also will make extensive use of programmable objects. Building applications with reusable, programmable objects minimizes the development time for (and thus the cost of) creating custom Windows applications. Common programmable objects, such as drawing, graphing, and spell-checking objects, ultimately will reduce the fixed disk space required by the mega-apps that can share these objects.

Another advantage to shared programmable objects is that upgrades for multiple applications can be implemented by releasing a single improved version of the shared object. Visual Basic 4.0 lets you create 32-bit custom programmable objects for use with Access 95 or Visual Basic 4.0 applications, plus any other applications that can act as OA clients.

This chapter has two objectives: to show you how to best take advantage of OA in your Access 95 applications and to use DDE for IPC with applications that are not OA-compliant. Although many new OA-compliant applications are appearing in the Windows software market, there are many existing applications that support only DDE. The first part of this chapter covers OA and the use of OLE Controls (OCXs) with Access 95. Examples that demonstrate Access's capabilities as a DDE client and server, which have not changed significantly since version 1.x, complete the chapter.

Understanding OLE Automation

 Access 95 is an OLE 2.1 client and server application; Access 2.0 was an OLE 2.01 client only. The Jet 3.0 database engine is a programmable OA object, so VBA-enabled applications, such as Microsoft Excel and Project, can manipulate the Jet 3.0 Data Access Object (DAO) with code similar to the Access VBA examples in Chapter 29, "Understanding the Data Access Object Class."

Referencing the Jet 3.0 engine directly, rather than using Access 95 as an OA server is much faster and uses far fewer resources. Therefore, your primary use of Access 95 is likely to be as an OA client that manipulates various types of OA servers. The sections that follow describe the types of OA servers defined by the OLE 2.1 specification and how 16-bit and 32-bit OA components interact.

Categorizing OLE Automation Servers

Understanding OLE Automation requires an explanation of the categories of OA components that you can use in building desktop database applications. OA servers are of five basic types:

- *Full servers* are programs, such as 32-bit Microsoft Excel 95 and Project 4.1, and Visio Corp.'s Visio 4.0, that are stand-alone productivity applications with OLE Automation capability added. Like Access 95, Excel 95 and Project 4.1 expose their application objects to their own flavor of VBA. Microsoft Word 6.0 exposes its menu commands, rather than objects, and uses WordBasic, not VBA, as its macro language. The next version of Word is expected to become a full server and substitute VBA for WordBasic. Full servers also are called *local servers* because the server must reside on the same PC as the OLE client application.

- *Automation servers* are full (local) servers that are not insertable objects. Access 95 is an automation server only. Access 95 does not appear in the Object Type list of the Create New page of the Insert Object dialog of Word 95 or Excel 95. If you attempt to specify an .mdb file in the Create From File page, Object Packager attempts to create a package from the .mdb file.

- *Mini-servers* are applications, such as Microsoft Graph 5.0 (MSGraph5) and Visio Express, that only can be executed from within an OLE Automation client application. Mini-servers are similar to the OLE 1.0 applets supplied with Word for Windows 2.0 and other early Microsoft OLE 1.0 applications, such as Microsoft Draw. (Visio Express is a mini-server version of Visio 3.0.)

  To qualify for mini-server status, the application must be an executable file (.exe) capable of displaying a window. Mini-servers that display a particular class of objects, such as video clips, are called *viewers*. Using the Graph Wizard to create MSGraph5 charts is one of the subjects of Chapter 20, "Adding Graphics to Forms and Reports." You also can create custom graphs and charts by programming MSGraph5 with Access VBA code.

- *OLE Controls* (OCXs) are a special type of mini-server. OLE Controls, which use the .ocx file extension, expose events in addition to properties and methods. They are the object-oriented equivalent of Visual Basic's VBX custom controls. Like VBXs, some OCXs, such as Graph32.ocx, are visible at run time. Others, like Msmapi32.ocx, are not.

  Access 2.0 was the first Microsoft application to be compatible with 16-bit OLE Controls. Access 2.0 required the Access Developer's Toolkit (ADT) to add OCXs to your Access applications; the retail version of Access 95 includes full support for 32-bit OLE Controls and includes the 32-bit version of the Microsoft Calendar control. The Access 95 ADT includes the Data Outline OLE Control and several additional

32-bit OCXs that also are included with the Professional and Enterprise Editions of Visual Basic 4.0.

■ *Process servers* are a sub-class of automation servers used to perform functions that do not involve interaction at the user interface. Process servers come in two flavors: OutOfProc(ess) and InProc(ess) servers. OutOfProc servers are executable files that run in their own process space, that is, they have their own block of allocated memory. (Full servers and mini-servers are OutOfProc servers.) InProc servers share memory with the client application. (OCXs are InProc servers.)

OutOfProc servers communicate with the client application through Lightweight Remote Procedure Calls (LRPCs), while InProc servers, also called *OLE .DLLs*, use conventional Windows function calls. Thus InProc servers respond considerably faster to client instructions than OutOfProc servers. The Microsoft DAO 3.0 Object Library (Dao3032.dll, AKA the Jet 3.0 database engine) is an InProc server.

Note

Process server is not an "official" OLE 2+ category. The term is used here to distinguish invisible programmable process server objects that run in the background from programmable objects that have a visible representation in Access 95's run or design modes, even if the visible representation is optional.

One of the primary applications for process servers is creating "three-tier" client/server database applications. A three-tier application interposes an OA process server between the client front end and the RDBMS back end. The process server manages connecting to the RDBMS and processing of queries, and may include code to enforce "business rules" that are common to all front-end applications. The middle-tier OA process server isn't visible to the user.

One of the advantages of OA is that you can manipulate programmable full-server and mini-server objects without creating a visible instance of the OA server. Unlike DDE, which requires that the server application be launched in a window or as an icon, OA automatically launches the application for you. Unless you instruct the server to activate its window, the server is invisible; the server's name usually does not appear in the Windows Task List.

Note

Although an OA full or automation server's window is not visible, OA full and automation servers can consume a substantial percentage of the available resources of your computer. This is particularly true of mega-apps, such as Excel 95 and Word 95, when used as OA servers. You can speed the opening of Excel 95 as an OA server and minimize the resources Excel consumes by not loading unneeded add-ins. If you plan to make extensive use of OA in your applications, you should have a minimum of 16M of RAM (preferably 24M or more) and make sure that you have plenty of disk space (30M or more) for Windows 95's swap file.

Interacting with 16-Bit OLE Automation Servers

Windows 95 and Windows NT 3.51+ share the same 32-bit .DLLs to support OLE 2+. You can prove this statement by opening Windows 95's Find application, entering **ole*.*** in the Named text box, and clicking the Find Now button. Right-click one of the found files, such as Oleprx32.dll, choose Properties from the popup menu, then click the Version tab of the Oleprx32.dll Properties sheet. The Comments property of the Version page displays "Microsoft OLE 2.1 for Windows NT (TM) Operating System" (see fig. 30.1).

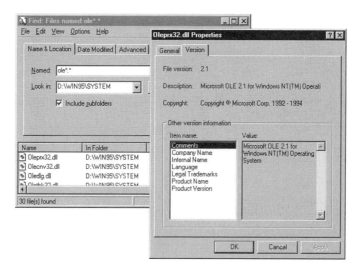

Fig. 30.1 The Version page of the Oleprx32.dll Properties sheet displaying the Comments property of Windows 95's Oleprx32.dll.

You can use most 16-bit OLE 1 and 2+ OutOfProc servers with 32-bit OLE clients. The rules for use of 16-bit and 32-bit programmable objects in both Windows 95 and Windows NT 3.51+ are as follows:

- 32-bit OLE 2+ clients can employ 16-bit OLE 1.0 and 16-bit and 32-bit OLE 2+ full servers and mini-servers. The conversion to and from 16-bit operations is accomplished by a process called *thunking* implemented by Olethk32.dll.

- 16-bit OLE clients cannot employ 32-bit OLE 2+ servers.

- 32-bit applications that support OLE Controls—Access 95 and 32-bit Visual Basic 4.0 when this edition was written—must use 32-bit OCXs. Future 32-bit versions of other OLE 2+ OA clients, such as Excel and Project, are likely to be able to act as 32-bit OLE Control containers.

- 16-bit applications that support OLE Controls—only Access 2.0 and 16-bit Visual Basic 4.0 when this edition was written—must use 16-bit OCXs. Full support for current 16-bit OCXs in Access 2.0 requires installation of several updated files.

■ InProc servers (OLE .DLLs) must have the same "bitness" as the client application. As an example, you cannot use the 16-bit Jet 2+ database engine with Access 95 nor the 32-bit Jet 3.0 database engine with Access 2.0.

> **Note**
>
> The thunking process for IPC between 32-bit OLE 2+ clients and 16-bit OLE 1.0 and 2+ servers imposes additional overhead on LRPCs and extracts an application performance toll. If you intend to make extensive use of OLE 2.0 with Access 95, an investment in 32-bit versions of OLE 2+ servers will return substantial performance dividends.

On the whole, the limitations associated with interoperability of 16-bit and 32-bit OLE Automation components are unlikely to be a problem for Access 95 users running either Windows 95 or Windows NT 3.51+. Beginning in early 1995, the vast majority of Microsoft and third-party Windows application development has been devoted to 32-bit Windows software. There is little likelihood that software publishers will make major upgrades to their existing 16-bit applications for use with Windows 3.1+ or OS/2 Warp.

Using OLE Automation Servers with Access 95

To use OLE Automation, you must first write the code to create an instance in your application of the object you plan to program. Access VBA contains the following four reserved words that you use to create an instance of a programmable object with Access VBA code:

■ The **Object** data type for the programmable object variables you declare with {**Private**¦**Dim**¦**Public**} obj*Name* **As Object** statements. The Object property of a programmable OA object, such as an OLE Control, contained in a bound or unbound object frame control points to the instance of the object. You can assign to an **Object** variable a pointer to the OA object with the general syntax

    Set obj*Name* = Forms!frm*Name*!uof*Name*.Object

■ The **CreateObject**() function assigns a pointer to a new instance of an empty programmable object, such as a blank Excel 95 worksheet. The general syntax of the **CreateObject**() function is

    Set obj*Name* = **CreateObject**("*ServerName.ObjectType*")

■ The **New** keyword declares an **Object** variable and assigns in a single command a pointer to a new instance of an empty programmable object, such as an empty Word 95 document. The general syntax for creating an instance of a programmable object with **New** is

    {**Private**¦**Dim**¦**Public**¦**Static**} obj*Name* **As New** *ServerName.ObjectType*

To use the **New** keyword to create an instance of an **Object** variable, you must add a reference to the OA server in Access 95's References dialog.

- The **GetObject**() function assigns a pointer to a new instance of a programmable object whose data is contained in an existing file, str*PathFileName*, in the following syntax example:

```
Set objName = GetObject(strPathFileName[,
    "ServerName.ObjectType"])
```

You can omit the *ServerName.ObjectType* argument if an entry in the Registry associates the file's extension with the object of the application you want to program. In the case of Excel 95, the default object type for .xls files is Excel.Workbook. If you substitute an empty string ("") for str*PathFileName*, the preceding statement assigns a pointer to an object of *ServerName.ObjectType* if such an object is open. If an object of the specified type is not open when the statement is executed, a trappable error occurs.

If the OA server application is open when you use the **CreateObject**() or **GetObject**() functions or the **New** reserved word, the type of the OA server determines whether a new instance of the server is launched or the open instance is used. If the server type is Creatable Single-Instance, as is the case for Word 95, the open instance of Word is used with an empty document (**CreateObject**()) or with a document created from the specified file (**GetObject**()).

Note

Names of programmable objects created by OA server applications appear in regular (not bold) monospace type because the names of these objects are not Access VBA object data types.

This book uses the common lowercase file extensions as the prefix to identify objects created by full servers, rather than the object tags specified by the *Leszynski Naming Conventions for Microsoft Access* (*LNC*) incorporated as Appendix A, "Naming Conventions for Access Objects and Variables." Examples are xla*App* for the Excel application, xlw*Book* for Excel 5+ workbooks, xls*Sheet* for worksheets, xlc*Chart* for Excel charts, and xlm*Module* for Excel VBA modules (although Excel 5+ does not create .xla, .xlw, .xlc, or .xlm files in Excel 5.0+ format). (*LNC* uses xlsa*App*, xlsw*Sheet*, and xlsc*Chart*; LNC does not include a tag for Excel workbooks or VBA modules.) Word 6+ Document objects are identified in this book by doc*Name*, and pseudo-objects of the Word.Basic menu command type are identified by doc*Command*. Visio 2+ drawings are identified by vsd*Name*.

These four reserved words of the preceding list also are used by VBA to program objects of other applications. To write OA code, you need to know the server name of the OA server and the names of the object types created by the server. The best way to become familiar with the object hierarchy of an OLE server is to create a reference to the server and explore the object hierarchy with Access 95's Object Browser.

Word 6+ users are not so lucky; neither Word 6.0 or Word 95 provides a .tlb or .olb type or object library file. Thus you cannot establish a reference to the Word.Basic object. You must use the Word Basic Reference help topics or purchase the Word Basic manual (see the note that follows). The two sections that follow show you how to create and manipulate Excel 95 Workbook and Worksheet objects, and the Cells collection, as well as a Word 95 Document object.

Note

A printed version of the Excel 5.0 online help file for VBA, *Microsoft Excel Visual VBA for Applications Reference* (ISBN 1-55615-624-3), and a guide to Word 6.0 Word Basic, *Microsoft Word Developer's Kit* (ISBN 1-55615-630-8), are available from Microsoft Corporation. The *Function Reference* is no longer included with the retail or Microsoft Office versions of Excel; you now must purchase the *Microsoft Excel Worksheet Function Reference* (ISBN 1-55615-637-5) from Microsoft. It's likely that updated Excel 95 and Word 95 versions will be available by the time you read this edition.

Manipulating an Excel 95 Workbook Object

The hierarchy of Excel 95 programmable objects is at least as complex as that of Access 95. Fortunately, the concepts of addressing objects in all OA-compatible applications is nearly identical. Thus, the techniques you learned in Chapter 29, "Understanding the Data Access Object Class," stand you in good stead when you encounter Excel 95's `Excel.Application` object. The following sections describe how to create a test workbook, Customers.xls, with a single worksheet, Customer, and how to transfer data to and from the worksheet using Access VBA and OLE Automation.

Creating Customers.xls. The examples that follow use the Customers.xls workbook file with data from the Customers table of Northwind.mdb. The example of OLE Automation with Excel 95 in this chapter uses the `GetObject()` function to open the Customers.xls file and manipulate the data in the worksheet. To create Customers.xls, follow these steps:

1. Select the Customers table in the Database window, and click the selection arrow of the Office Links button. Choose Analyze It with MS Excel from the drop-down menu to export the data in the table to Customers.xls and open the file in Excel 95 (see fig. 30.2).

	A	B	C	D
1	Customer ID	Company Name	Contact Name	Contact Title
2	ALFKI	Alfreds Futterkiste	Maria Anders	Sales Representative
3	ANATR	Ana Trujillo Emparedados y helados	Ana Trujillo	Owner
4	ANTON	Antonio Moreno Taquería	Antonio Moreno	Owner
5	AROUT	Around the Horn	Thomas Hardy	Sales Representative
6	BERGS	Berglunds snabbköp	Christina Berglund	Order Administrator
7	BLAUS	Blauer See Delikatessen	Hanna Moos	Sales Representative
8	BLONP	Blondel père et fils	Frédérique Citeaux	Marketing Manager
9	BOLID	Bólido Comidas preparadas	Martín Sommer	Owner
10	BONAP	Bon app'	Laurence Lebihan	Owner
11	BOTTM	Bottom-Dollar Markets	Elizabeth Lincoln	Accounting Manager
12	BSBEV	B's Beverages	Victoria Ashworth	Sales Representative
13	CACTU	Cactus Comidas para llevar	Patricio Simpson	Sales Agent
14	CENTC	Centro comercial Moctezuma	Francisco Chang	Marketing Manager
15	CHOPS	Chop-suey Chinese	Yang Wang	Owner
16	COMMI	Comércio Mineiro	Pedro Afonso	Sales Associate
17	CONSH	Consolidated Holdings	Elizabeth Brown	Sales Representative
18	DRACD	Drachenblut Delikatessen	Sven Ottlieb	Order Administrator

Fig. 30.2 The data of the Customers table exported to a Microsoft Excel 95 workbook.

2. Select cells A2 through D9 of the worksheet. Choose <u>I</u>nsert, <u>N</u>ame, and select <u>D</u>efine. Type **TestRange** in the Names in Workbook text box and click OK. This creates a named range that you use in the examples that follow.

3. Choose <u>F</u>ile, Save <u>A</u>s from Excel's File menu, and select Microsoft Excel Workbook in the Save As Type drop-down list to save the file in Excel 5.0 format.

4. Change the Save In folder to C:\Msoffice\Access, and accept the default name for the file, Customers.xls, unless you have a reason to do otherwise. Click OK to save the file and close the dialog.

5. Choose <u>T</u>ools, Add-<u>I</u>ns menu and clear all of the check boxes in the Add-Ins dialog's Add-Ins Available list. Eliminating add-ins decreases the time required to launch Excel. Click OK to close the Add-Ins dialog.

6. Close Microsoft Excel.

The Hierarchy of VBA Excel 95 Objects. The following list describes the hierarchy of the most commonly used programmable objects exposed by Excel 95:

■ Application represents an instance of Excel 95. Using the Application object, you can execute almost all of Excel's menu commands by applying methods to the Application object. The Application object has properties such as ActiveWorkbook and ActiveSheet that specify the current Workbook and Worksheet objects. You can specify Excel.Application as the value of the *ServerName.ObjectType* argument of the **CreateObject**() and **GetObject**() functions, plus the **Dim** *objName* **As New** *ServerName.ObjectType* statement.

■ Workbook is the primary object of Excel 95. Workbook objects are files that contain the other objects you create with Excel 95: Worksheet and Chart objects. Worksheet and Chart objects are contained in Worksheets and Charts collections, respectively. The Excel implementation of VBA does not distinguish between collections and objects; for example, the Excel VBA help file calls the Worksheets collection an object.

■ Worksheet objects are elements of the Workbook object that contain data. The primary interaction between Access 95 and Excel 95 takes place with Worksheet objects. You can transfer data contained in rows and columns of an Access Recordset object to cells in an Excel Worksheet object, and vice versa. If you specify Excel.Sheet as the value of the *ServerName.ObjectName* argument of the **GetObject**() function or the **Dim** *objName* **As New** *ServerName.ObjectType* statement, the first member of the Worksheets collection—the ActiveSheet property of the Workbook object—is opened by default.

■ Range objects are groups of cells specified by sets of cell coordinates. You can get or set the values of a single cell or a group of cells by specifying the Range object. If the cells are contained in a named range, you can use the range name to refer to the group of cells. (A group of cells is not the same as a collection of cells; there is no "Cells" collection in Excel 95.)

The `Cells` method specifies the coordinates of a `Range` object. There is no "Cell" object in Excel 95, but you can use the `Cells` method to read or set the value of a single cell or group of cells, specified by coordinate sets.

Excel 95 exposes a variety of other objects. The preceding four objects, however, are those that you use most often in conjunction with OA operations executed with Access VBA code.

Using Excel's Online Help File for VBA. If you don't have a copy of the *Microsoft Excel Visual VBA for Applications Reference*, you can open the Vba_xl.hlp online help file to act as a reference for the objects, methods, and properties exposed by Excel 95. To open Vba_xl.hlp while running Access and display objects and methods references, follow these steps:

1. Launch the Windows Explorer from the Start, Applications menu.

2. Select your Excel 95 folder (usually C:\Msoffice\Excel), and double-click Vba_xl.hlp in the Contents of 'Excel' list to open the Help Topics: Microsoft Excel Visual Basic dialog's Contents page (see fig. 30.3).

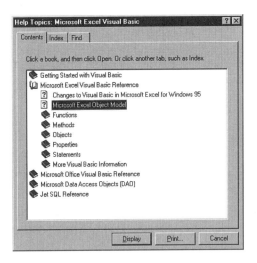

Fig. 30.3   The Contents page of the Vba_xl.hlp file.

3. Double-click the Microsoft Excel Visual Basic Reference chapter icon, then double-click the Microsoft Object Model icon to display a diagram of the hierarchy of objects exposed by Excel 95 (see fig. 30.4). Objects exposed to Excel VBA are exposed also to OA client applications.

4. Click the "Worksheet" hot spot of the diagram to display the help topic for the `Worksheet` object, and then click the Methods hot spot to display the list of

methods applicable to the Worksheet object in the Topics Found dialog (see fig. 30.5). You can obtain a similar list of properties of the object by clicking the Properties hot spot.

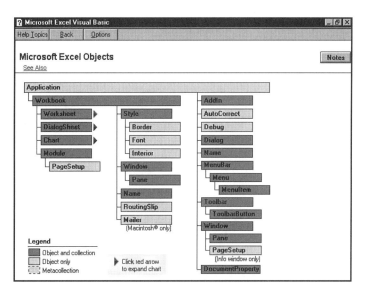

Fig. 30.4 The Microsoft Excel Object Model from the Excel VBA help file.

Fig. 30.5 Methods applicable to the Excel Worksheet object displayed in the Topics Found window.

   5. Click the "Cells" hot spot to display the help window for the Cells method (see fig. 30.6).

   6. Click the Examples hot spot to display an example of VBA code applicable to the Cells method (see fig. 30.7). Most of the Excel VBA code examples are compatible with Access VBA OLE Automation code.

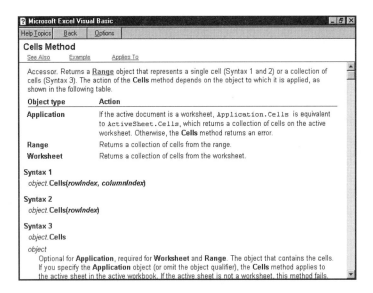

Fig. 30.6 The syntax reference for the `Cells` method.

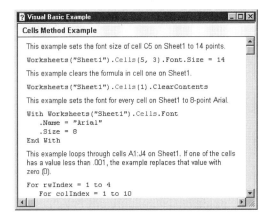

Fig. 30.7 VBA example code for the `Cells` method of the `Workbook` object.

 Creating an Excel Reference and Using Access 95's Object Browser. Creating a reference to the object or type library of OA servers offers the following advantages:

- The Access VBA compiler checks the syntax of your OA code for consistency with the properties and methods of the objects you declare. This test is not made if you don't declare a reference to the OA server object.

- You can use the Object Browser to determine the proper syntax for object properties and methods.

- You can gain quick access to the help topic for the object, property, or method selected in the Object Browser's list boxes.

- You can use the shorthand `Dim` obj*Name* `As New` *ServerName.ObjectType* statement to instantiate (create an instance of) the server object.

- You can use the intrinsic constants predefined for the object as argument values.

Excel 95 uses the 32-bit version of the Excel 5.0 type library for 16-bit Excel 5.0. To create a reference to the Excel 5.0 object library and explore Excel objects with the Access Object Browser, follow these steps:

1. Launch Access and open Northwind.mdb, if necessary. Open the Utility Functions module and choose Tools, References to display the References dialog.

2. Mark the check box for the Microsoft Excel 5.0 Object Library, Xl5en32.olb (see fig. 30.8), then click the OK button to close the References dialog and create the reference.

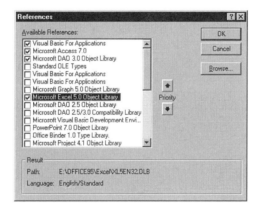

Fig. 30.8 Adding an Access VBA reference to the Excel 5.0 Object Library.

3. Open Access's Object Browser and choose Excel - Microsoft Excel 5.0 Object Library in the Libraries/Databases drop-down list (see fig. 30.9).

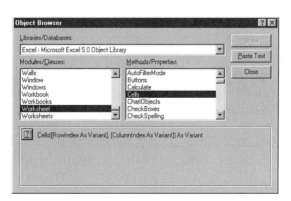

Fig. 30.9 Displaying the syntax example for the `Cells` method of the `Worksheet` object in Access 95's Object Browser.

4. Select Worksheet in the Modules/Classes list and Cells in the Methods/Properties list. The syntax example for the Cells method appears to the right of the help (?) button. Clicking the help button displays the help topic for the `Cells` method, which is identical to the topic shown in figure 30.7.

5. When you finish exploring properties and methods of the Worksheet object, click the Close button to close Object Browser.

The Registry Entries for OLE Automation Servers. You can specify any object listed in the Registry that is identified by a *ServerName.ObjectType[.Version]* entry at the HKEY_CLASSES_ROOT level of the Registry, as shown in figure 30.10. The optional *.Version* suffix, shown in the line below the entry for `Excel.Sheet`, indicates the version number of *ServerName*; if you have two versions of the same OA server, you can use the *.Version* suffix to specify one of the two. Excel 95 objects retain the .5 version suffix of Excel 5.0.

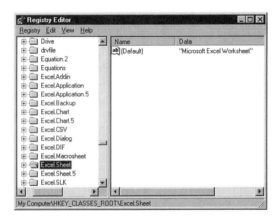

Fig. 30.10 Primary Registry entries for Excel 95 `Application`, `Worksheet`, and `Chart` objects.

In addition to the primary Registry entries for Excel 95 objects that you can open, additional data for creating or opening programmable objects appear in the \HKEY_LOCAL_MACHINE\Software\CLSID section of the Registry. CLSID is the abbreviation for ClassID, a unique 32-character (plus hyphens) identifier for each object exposed by OLE 2 servers. A part of the additional Registry entries for the `Excel.Application` and `Excel.Sheet` objects appears in figure 30.11. The majority of entries for Excel 5.0 and 95 in the Registry are identical. If you have installed Excel 5.0 and Excel 95 under Windows 95 or Windows NT, the `LocalServer` entry points to the location of Excel.exe for 16-bit Excel 5.0 and `LocalServer32` points to 32-bit Excel 95.

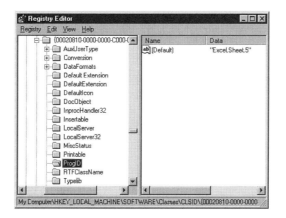

Fig. 30.11 Additional registration database entries for Excel 95 `Application` and `Worksheet` objects.

Opening and Manipulating an Existing Excel Worksheet Object

Learning to write OLE Automation code is a much quicker process if you use the Debug Window to try OA instructions before you begin writing complex OA code in modules.

> **Note**
>
> In all examples of this chapter that use the Debug Window, pressing the Enter key after typing **?** **_Expression_** is implied.

To open the Worksheet object of the Customers.xls Workbook object, follow these steps:

1. Close Excel if it is running. Open a new module in the Northwind Traders database and add the following Object variable declarations in the Declarations section:

```
Private xlaAppXL5 As Object   'Application object
Private xlwCust As Object     'Workbook object
Private xlsCust As Object     'Sheet object
```

2. Open the Debug Window and type the following statement to create an object of the `Excel.Sheet` (`Worksheet`) type. When you press Enter, Excel 95 is launched in `/automation` mode.

```
Set xlsCust = GetObject(CurDir & "\customers.xls",
"Excel.Sheet")
```

`CurDir` returns the well formed path of your current directory, \Msoffice\Access\Samples if you have opened Northwind.mdb in its default location. If you saved Customers.xls elsewhere, add the path to the file name in the preceding statement. Depending on the speed of your computer, opening Excel 95 may take an appreciable period. (When <Running> returns to <Ready> in the status bar of the Debug Window, Excel has finished loading.) Customers.xls only includes one `Worksheet` object, so the Customer worksheet is the `ActiveSheet` object.

3. Verify that you have a valid `Worksheet` object by typing **? xlsCust.Cells(1, 1)**. After a brief interval, the expected result, Customer ID, appears.

4. You can test the ability of the `Cells` method to return the values of other cells by typing **? xlsCust.Cells(R, C)**, where **R** is the row and **C** is the column of the cell coordinates (see fig. 30.12).

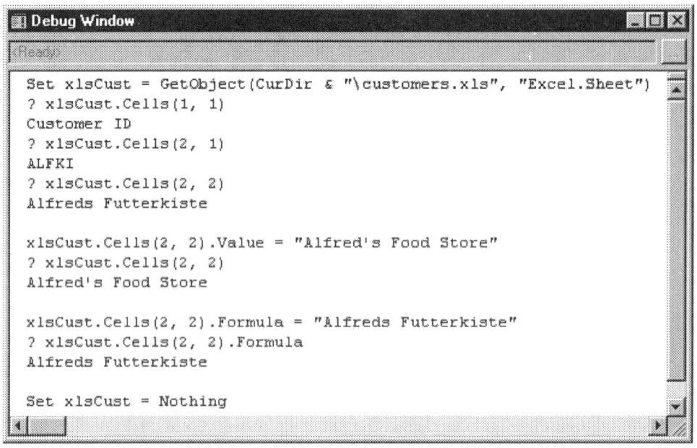

```
Set xlsCust = GetObject(CurDir & "\customers.xls", "Excel.Sheet")
? xlsCust.Cells(1, 1)
Customer ID
? xlsCust.Cells(2, 1)
ALFKI
? xlsCust.Cells(2, 2)
Alfreds Futterkiste

xlsCust.Cells(2, 2).Value = "Alfred's Food Store"
? xlsCust.Cells(2, 2)
Alfred's Food Store

xlsCust.Cells(2, 2).Formula = "Alfreds Futterkiste"
? xlsCust.Cells(2, 2).Formula
Alfreds Futterkiste

Set xlsCust = Nothing
```

Fig. 30.12   The command to read and set the values of a single cell in the Customers worksheet.

5. You can alter the content of a cell by entering an expression such as `xlsCust.Cells(2, 2).Value = "Alfred's Food Shop"`. Like many Access control objects, in which the name of an object returns its value, the `Cells` method does not require that you explicitly specify the default `Value` property. Verify that the content changed by typing **? xlsCust.Cells(2, 2)**, with and without appending **.Value** (see fig. 30.12).

6. When you are finished using an OA object, you should close the object to free the memory resources it consumes. To disassociate an object from an object variable, use a **Set** *objName* = **Nothing** statement (see fig. 30.12). Type **Set xlsCust = Nothing** to close the invisible instance of Excel. Multiple object variables can point to a single object, so the OA object is not closed until all object variables have gone out of scope or have been **Set** explicitly to **Nothing**.

You also can use the `Formula` property to set the value of a cell. The advantage of the `Formula` property is that you can also use this property to enter a formula using Excel A1 syntax, such as "=A10+B15".

Using Named Ranges of Cells. If you created the named range, TestRange, in Customers.xls, you can return the values of the cells in the range by referring to the `Range` object of the Worksheet object. Figure 30.13 shows typical expressions that operate on the `Range` object of a `Worksheet` object and the `Ranges` collection of a `Workbook` object.

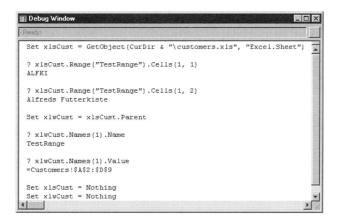

Fig. 30.13 Expressions that return the values in Range objects and the Ranges collection.

To specify a cell within a named Range object, use the following general syntax:

```
wksWorksheet.Range(strRangeName).Cells(intRow, intCol)
```

Because named ranges are global for all worksheets in an Excel workbook, the Names collection is a member of the Workbook object. Therefore, you need to refer to the Workbook object that contains the Worksheet object. The wksWorksheet.Parent property returns a pointer to the Workbook object that contains the Worksheet object, as in the following example:

```
Set xlwWorkbook = xlsWorksheet.Parent
```

You then can refer to the Ranges collection of the Workbook object with statements such as

```
strRangeName = xlwWorkbook.Names(intIndex).Name
strRangeValue = xlwWorkbook.Names(intIndex).Value
```

Unlike Access object collections, which begin with an index value of 0, the first member of a VBA collection has an index value of 1.

Explicitly Closing a Workbook and the Application Object. Just as a Workbook object is the value of the Parent property of a Worksheet object, the Application object is the Parent property of a Workbook object. The value of Excel 5.0's Application object is Microsoft Excel. Figure 30.14 illustrates expressions that work their way upward in Excel's object hierarchy, from Worksheet to Application objects. You can shortcut the process by using xlsCust.Parent.Parent to point to the Application object from a Worksheet object.

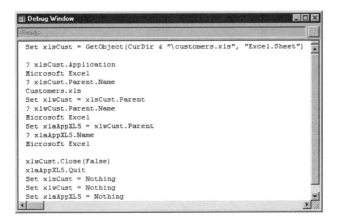

Fig. 30.14 Assigning objects higher in the hierarchy, and closing `Workbook` and `Application` objects.

 You can use the `Close` method to explicitly close an Excel Workbook object (you can't close a `Worksheet` object) and the `Quit` method to exit the application. It is a good practice to explicitly exit the OA server application to conserve scarce system resources if you have multiple references to the OA server object. (Access 2.0 required brackets around `Close` and `Quit` because of conflicts with Access Basic reserved words.) For example, the following statements close the `Workbook` object and then exit the OA server application, freeing the memory reserved by the server:

```
Set xlaAppXL5 = xlsCust.Parent.Parent
xlsCust.Parent.Close(False)
xlaAppXL5.Quit
```

The **False** argument of the Close method closes the Workbook without displaying the message box that asks if you want to save changes to the Workbook. When using the `Quit` method to exit the application, you receive that message regardless of whether you modified the worksheet. To avoid this message when reading Excel 95 worksheets, close the worksheet before applying the `Quit` method. You must create an `Application` object because you cannot execute the `xlsCust.Parent.Parent.Quit` statement after closing the `xlsCust` object. (You receive an "Object has no value" error message if you try.)

Creating a New Excel Worksheet with Access VBA Code

You can emulate the Analyze It with MS Excel feature of Access 95 with Access VBA OLE Automation code. The following function, `CreateCust()`, creates a new `Workbook` object, Cust.xls, and copies the data from the Customers table to a Worksheet named Customers. One of the primary incentives for writing your own version of the Analyze It with MS Excel feature is the ability to format the `Worksheet` object the way you want. You also can add custom column headers. (The code to add column headers is not included in the `CreateCust()` function.)

```
Function CreateCust() As Integer
    'Purpose: Create new Excel 95 worksheet from Customers table
```

```
'Declare local variables (Object variables are module-level)
Dim dbNWind As Database      'Current database
Dim rstCust As Recordset     'Table Recordset over Customers
Dim intRow As Integer        'Row counter
Dim intCol As Integer        'Column counter

'Assign DAO pointers
Set dbNWind = CurrentDB()
Set rstCust = dbNWind.OpenRecordset("Customers", dbOpenTable)

DoCmd.Hourglass True

'Create a new Excel Worksheet object
Set xlsCust = CreateObject("Excel.Sheet")

'Give the new worksheet a name
xlsCust.Name = "Customers"

'Get the Application object for the Quit method
Set xlaAppXL5 = xlsCust.Parent.Parent

intRow = 1
intCol = 1

rstCust.MoveFirst    'Go to the first record (safety)
Do Until rstCust.EOF
   'Loop through each record
   For intCol = 1 To rstCust.Fields.Count
      'Loop through each field
      If Not IsNull(rstCust.Fields(intCol - 1)) Then
         xlsCust.Cells(intRow, intCol).Value = _
            CStr(rstCust.Fields(intCol - 1))
      End If
   Next intCol
   rstCust.MoveNext
   intRow = intRow + 1
Loop

For intCol = 1 To xlsCust.Columns.Count
   'Format each column of the worksheet
   xlsCust.Columns(intCol).Font.Size = 8
   xlsCust.Columns(intCol).AutoFit
   If intCol = 8 Then
      'Align numeric and alphanumeric postal codes left
      xlsCust.Columns(intCol).HorizontalAlignment = xlLeft
   End If
Next intCol

DoCmd.Hourglass False

xlsCust.SaveAs ("Cust.xls")
xlaAppXL5.Quit
End Function
```

Figure 30.15 shows the **Private Object** variable declarations in the Declarations section
of the module, followed by the first few lines of the preceding code.

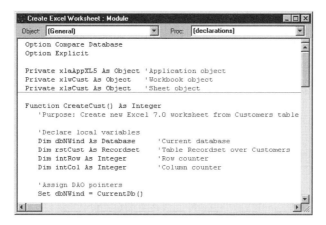

Fig. 30.15 The Declarations section and the first few lines of code for the `CreateCust()` function.

 You must coerce to **String** the data type of the **Variant** values returned by `rstCust.Fields(intCol -1)` with the **CStr()** function. If you omit the **CStr()** function, Excel 95 displays #N/A# instead of the proper value. If the `Recordset` contains field data types other than Text, use the appropriate **CType()** function to determine the data type for the column.

The `xlLeft` constant, assigned to the value of the `HorizontalAlignment` property of the eighth column is an Excel intrinsic constant defined when you create a reference to the Microsoft Excel 5.0 Object library. Selecting Constants in the Modules/Classes list of the Object Browser with the Excel library active displays the `xlConst` constants. Figure 30.16 shows the numeric value of `xlLeft`, one of the constant values that is valid for the `HorizontalAlignment` property.

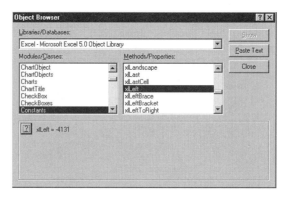

Fig. 30.16 Obtaining values of `xlConst` intrinsic constants in Access 95's Object Browser.

Run the function shown in the preceding listing by typing **? CreateCust()** in the Debug Window. Figure 30.17 shows the Cust.xls workbook with the Customer worksheet created by the `CreateCust()` function opened in Excel 95. Unless you specify a path, Excel saves Cust.xls in the folder that contains Excel.exe, usually the \Msoffice\Excel folder.

Fig. 30.17   Part of the Excel 95 worksheet created from the Customers table.

Sending Data to Microsoft Word 95 with OLE Automation

Chapter 22, "Using Access with Microsoft Word and Mail Merge," demonstrates that Access 95's Mail Merge Wizard does a very competent job of creating merge data files for use with Microsoft Word 95. The Mail Merge Wizard uses DDE, rather than OLE Automation, to communicate with Word.

Although Word 95 is not a full-fledged OA server application, Word exposes one programmable object with two names: `Word.Basic` alias `WordBasic`. You use the `Word.Basic` object type with the **CreateObject**() function; the `Word.Basic` object type corresponds to Excel's `Excel.Application` object. You use the `WordBasic` object when you want to manipulate the `Object` of a bound or unbound object frame. The `WordBasic` object is a member of the `Application` class. An object of either the `Word.Basic` or `WordBasic` type lets you use `WordBasic` document manipulation commands as methods of the object.

> **Tip**
>
> You cannot use the **GetObject**(`"docname.doc"`) function to open an existing Word 95 document from a file.

To create an independently programmable Word document object (a Word document that is not contained in an object frame of your application), you use the following generic code:

```
Dim docName As Object
Set docName = CreateObject("Word.Basic")

docName.FileOpen "d:\path\filename.doc"     'Open a file

    'Code to manipulate document goes here
docName.FileClose(1)                         'Save and close the file
Set docName = Nothing                        'Close Word
```

> **Note**
>
> Even if you do not make changes in the document file, use the FileClose(1) statement to save the file. The version of Word 95 available when this edition was written sets the "dirty" flag even when the code does not change the content of the document.

As noted in the "Opening and Manipulating an Existing Excel Worksheet Object" section earlier in this chapter, the **Set** objName = **Nothing** statement closes the instance of the server application and frees the resources the server consumes. This statement is similar to the Quit method applied to the Application object; a Word object does not support the Quit method or the FileExit WordBasic command. Figure 30.12 shows an example of using the Debug Window to test the preceding example code. The document opened by the WordBasic FileOpen command of figure 30.18 is the manuscript for this chapter with the section heading identified by the bookmark "WordHead."

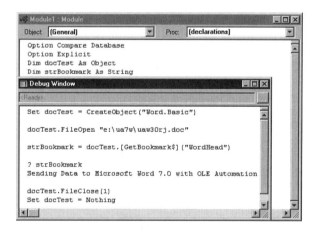

Fig. 30.18 Using the Debug Window to manipulate a Word 95 document object.

Most persons who alter word processing documents want to view the modifications before final acceptance. Thus, the majority of Access applications that use OA with Word 95 are more likely to involve Word documents contained in bound or unbound object frames. Chapter 22, "Using Access with Microsoft Word and Mail Merge," explains how to add an unbound object frame containing an embedded Word document. The following generic code lets you apply WordBasic commands to the document contained in a bound or unbound object frame:

```
Dim uofName As Control
Dim docName As Object
Set uofName = Forms!FormName!ControlName
uofName.Action = 7    'Activate the object
Set docName = uofName.Object.Application.WordBasic
    'Code to manipulate object
Set docName = Nothing
```

The uof*Name*.Action = 7 statement is required if the embedded object has not been activated when you execute the preceding code example. An embedded object in a frame must be activated before you can refer to its Object.Application.*PropertyName* property. Linked objects in object frames do not support OLE Automation. You receive a "This object does not support OLE Automation" error message when you execute the **Set** doc*Name* = uof*Name*.Object.Application.WordBasic for a linked file.

Figure 30.19 shows an example of activating an embedded Word 95 object and then reading and setting the value of bookmarked text. To execute the code shown in figure 30.19, you must first insert an unbound Word 95 object created from a file, uofWord, with a bookmark named "WordHead" in a form named frmWordDoc. When you execute the docTest.EditGoTo "WordHead" statement, Word selects the bookmark. The docTest.Insert "New Section Head" statement replaces the existing bookmarked text with "New Section Head". Figure 30.20 shows the result of executing the Insert command with revision marks turned on.

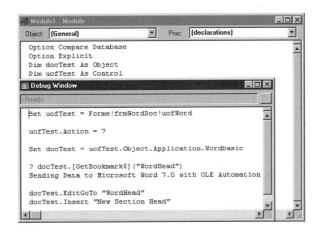

Fig. 30.19   Replacing the text of a bookmark in an embedded OLE object.

Using OLE Automation and code similar to that shown in figure 30.20, you can create a document that consists of nothing but empty bookmarks and then fill the bookmarks with text contained in Text or Memo fields of tables or from the Value property of control objects on forms. Using OLE Automation provides a much more flexible method of creating specialized documents than using Access 95's Merge It feature.

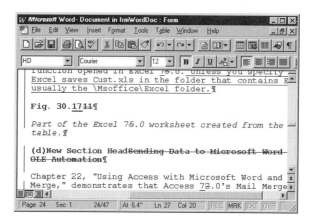

Fig. 30.20   The result of executing the code shown in figure 30.19.

Adding OLE Controls to Your Application

OLE Controls (OCXs) are a special class of programmable OA objects that expose their own events in addition to their properties and methods. You embed the OLE Control in an unbound object frame and program the Object property of the control, employing the same types of statements used with other embedded programmable objects. Some OCXs are data-bound controls, in which case you embed the OLE Control in a bound object frame.

OCXs are similar to Visual Basic custom controls (VBXs) in concept and use; the principal difference in the use of OCXs and VBXs is that OCXs are embedded within object frames while VBXs create independent controls on 16-bit Visual Basic forms. VBXs are 16-bit only; OCXs come in 16-bit and 32-bit versions. As noted in the "Categorizing OLE Automation Servers" section earlier in the chapter, Access 95 is a 32-bit application and thus requires 32-bit OCXs. (Access 2.0 required 16-bit OCXs.)

The sections that follow describe the OLE Controls supplied with retail Access 95, explain how to register an OCX when necessary, and show you how to insert and program the Microsoft Calendar OLE Control.

Using OLE Controls Included with Access 95 and Visual Basic 4.0

Access 95 includes the two following OLE Controls designed specifically for use with Access:

- *Calendar* (Msacal70.ocx) provides a programmable calendar object. When the calendar opens, its date is set to the value of **Now**. You can change the date by applying Next*Period* and Previous*Period* methods or by setting the Calendar Control's **Value** property. You access lists of the properties, methods, and events of the Calendar Control through the Calendar Control topic of Access's online help file. The Calendar control is included in the retail version of Access 95.

- *Data Outline* (OUTL2032.OCX), which is included with the Access Developer's Toolkit, provides a means of displaying data contained in tables or queries in an outline structure. The Data Outline Control, originally known as the Navigator Control, is derived from the design of the outline custom control (MSOUTLIN.VBX) of the Professional Edition of Visual VBA 3.0. When you double-click an entry in the Control, the form associated with the data item appears. Figure 30.21 shows the Data Outline Control displaying part of the Categories-Products-Suppliers table hierarchy of Northwind.mdb. The Data Outline Control appears as the left pane of the form of figure 30.21.

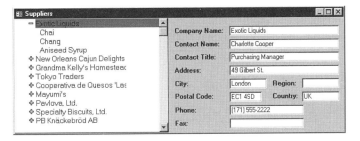

Fig. 30.21   The Data Outline (Navigator) Control displaying data from tables in Northwind.mdb.

Note

Using OLE Controls with Access 2.0 required purchasing the Access Developer's Toolkit (ADT), which included three OCXs and the necessary 16-bit support .DLLs for Access 2.0 to act as an OLE Control container. The retail version of Access 95, the Access 95 ADT, and Visual Basic 4.0 install the OCXs and required OLE Control support .dlls in your \Windows\System folder during the setup process.

The Professional and Enterprise Editions of Visual Basic 4.0 include a variety of 16-bit and 32-bit OLE Controls. You can use most of the 32-bit OCXs included with Visual Basic 4.0 in your Access 95 database applications if you have a license for Visual Basic 4.0. (You cannot use Visual Basic 4.0's data aware controls, such as DBGrid32.ocx with Access 95.) The ADT for Access 95 includes several useful 32-bit OCXs from the Professional Edition of Visual Basic 4.0. The Enterprise Edition of Visual Basic 4.0 also includes the 32-bit Remote Data Object (RDO): an OLE Automation process server that you can use in Access 95 applications to speed queries against client/server RDBMSs.

Registering OLE Controls

OLE Controls must be registered before they appear in the list of OCXs available for use with Access 95. Most commercial OCXs, including the OCXs supplied with Access 95 and Visual Basic 4.0, create the required Registry entries during the installation process. Figure 30.22 shows in RegEdit.exe the Registry entries for the Access 95 Calendar Control.

Many shareware OCXs don't come with a Setup application, so you must register the OCXs yourself. If your Windows 95 or Windows NT Registry file becomes corrupted and you cannot solve the problem by restoring the Registry backup file, you must re-register your OLE Controls. (If the Registry file becomes irreparably corrupted, you also are likely to need to reinstall all of your Windows applications and, perhaps, Windows 95.)

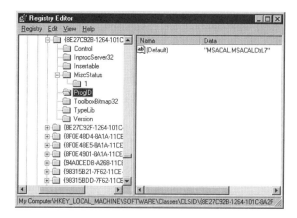

Fig. 30.22   The Registry hive for the Calendar Control displayed in RegEdit.exe.

To register a 32-bit OLE Control for Access 95 and for all other applications that use 32-bit OCXs, follow these steps:

1. Choose <u>T</u>ools, <u>C</u>ustom Controls to open the Custom Controls dialog, then click the Register button to open the Add Custom Control dialog. Although the "official" name for OCXs is *OLE Controls*, Access 95 calls them *Custom Controls*.

2. Maneuver to the \Windows\System folder, the standard location for OLE controls, and select the .ocx file you want to register or re-register (see fig. 30.23). The Mv1332.ocx file shown in figure 30.23 is a shareware 32-bit OLE control for displaying MediaView 1.3 documents. A related version (1.4) of MediaView is the viewer used to display much of the graphic content of the Microsoft Network.

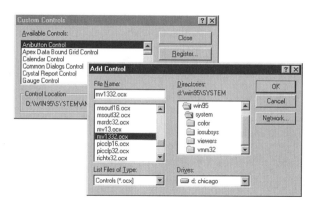

Fig. 30.23   Selecting the .ocx file to register.

3. Click the OK button to close the Add Control dialog and register the OLE Control. After registration, the name of the OLE Control appears in the Available Controls list of the Custom Controls dialog (see fig. 30.24).

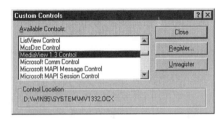

Fig. 30.24 A newly registered OLE Control displayed in Access 95's Custom Controls dialog.

If you delete a custom control from your fixed disk, it is advisable to delete the Registry entry for the control. Select the name of the control in the Available Controls list of the Custom Control dialog, then click the Unregister button to remove the Registry entry for the control.

Note

The Regsvr32.exe application provides an alternative method of registering and unregistering OLE Controls. Some OLE Controls include Regsvr32.exe for this purpose. Registering OCXs using Access 95's Custom Control dialog is a simpler and more foolproof process.

Using the Calendar Control

The Microsoft Calendar Control was one of the three original OLE Controls introduced with Access 2.0. Msacal70.exe, included with Access 95, is an improved, 32-bit version of the original Calendar Control. Msacal70.exe is a data-bound control, that is, you can bind the Control to a field of the Date/Time data type. The data-bound Calendar Control displays the date in calendar form.

The following sections describe how to add the Calendar Control to a form and how to program the Calendar Control.

Adding the Calendar Control to a Form. To add a Calendar Control in an unbound object frame of a form, follow these steps:

1. Create a new blank (unbound) form about 5 inches wide and 3 inches deep.

2. Choose Insert, Custom Controls to display the Insert Custom Controls dialog.

3. Select the Calendar Control from the Select a Custom Control list (see fig. 30.25). Click OK to add the Calendar Control to the form.

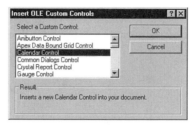

Fig. 30.25 Adding the Calendar Control with the Insert Custom Controls dialog.

4. Size the Calendar Control to about 3 by 2 inches, position the mouse pointer on the Control, and then click the right mouse button to display the floating menu for the unbound object frame.

5. Choose Calendar Control Object from the floating menu with the left mouse button to open the object's submenu (see fig. 30.26). Choose Properties to open the properties dialog for the Control.

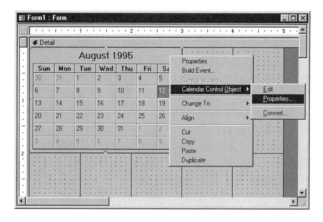

Fig. 30.26 The floating menus for an OLE Custom Control.

6. The tabbed properties dialog opens to let you set a variety of General properties for the Calendar control. Click the Font tab to open the Fonts properties page.

Note

Technically speaking, the properties dialog of an OLE Control is called a *property frame* or, more commonly, *properties sheet,* and the content of the property frame is stored in *property pages*. Entries for the property sheet and property page(s) are added to the entries for the OCX in the Registry.

---

7. With DayFont selected in the Property Name list, select Arial from the Font combo list, apply the Bold attribute, set the font size to 10 points, and click the Apply button. The size of the Calendar Control's columns limits the DayFont size to 9.75 points (see fig. 30.27).

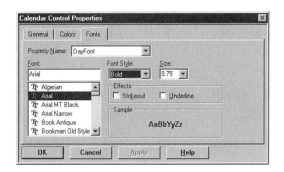

Fig. 30.27 The Fonts page of the Calendar Control Properties.

8. Repeat the font selection process of the preceding step for the `GridFont` property (9 point Arial bold) and the `TitleFont` property (12 point Arial bold).

9. Click the Colors tab to display the Colors properties page. You can change the color of the background (BackColor), DayFont, GridFont, TitleFont, and GridLines to one of the 16 standard colors or the Windows system colors (see fig. 30.28).

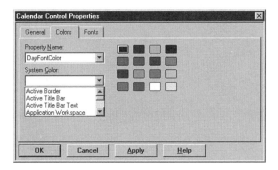

Fig. 30.28 The Colors page of the Calendar Control Properties.

10. Click OK to close the properties sheet. Double-click a blank area of the form to display the Form properties window, and then set the `ScrollBars` property to Neither and the `RecordSelectors` and `NavigationButtons` properties to No. Name the unbound object frame control that contains the Calendar Control **ocxCalendar**. Your Calendar Control appears in run mode, as shown in figure 30.29.

11. To eliminate the month and year drop-down lists, return to Design View and open the properties sheet for ocxCalendar. In the General properties page, clear the Month/Year selectors check box and select Sunken in the Grid Cell Effect list.

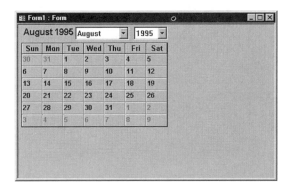

Fig. 30.29   The modified Calendar Control in run mode with month and year drop-down lists.

    12. Click OK to close the properties sheet. Change to form run mode; the modified Calendar Control appears, as shown in figure 30.30.

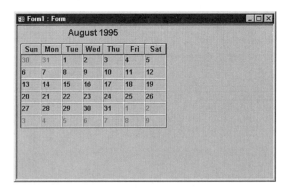

Fig. 30.30   The modified Calendar Control in run mode without the drop-down lists.

13. Save your form with a descriptive name, such as **frmCalendar**.

The procedure for adding the Data Outline control supplied with retail Access and other OCXs included with the ADT and Visual Basic 4.0 is similar to the preceding process.

Programming the Calendar Control. Each OLE Control has its own collection of properties, methods, and events. Each of the OCXs supplied with the retail version of Access and the ADT has an individual online help file to assist you in programming the control. You can open the help file by clicking the Help button of a Control's properties sheet, if present. Otherwise, choose Start, Find and enter *.hlp in the Named text box and click the Find button; the help file usually is the file name for the control with a .hlp extension (see fig. 30.31). Double-click the help file for the OLE Control to display the Help Topics dialog for the control (see fig. 30.32). Figure 30.33 shows the help topic for the PreviousMonth method for the Calendar Control. As is the case for any object contained in a bound or unbound OLE object frame, you apply methods to the Object property of the frame.

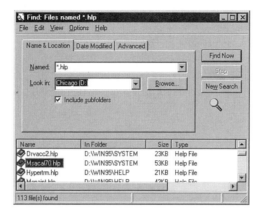

Fig. 30.31   Finding help files for OLE Controls.

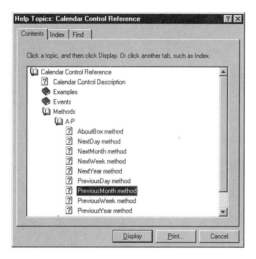

Fig. 30.32   The Help Topics dialog for the Calendar Control.

To program the Calendar Control and complete the design of the frmCalendar form, follow these steps:

1. Add six command buttons, stacked vertically to the right of the calendar. Assign **Next Week**, **Last Week**, **Next Month**, **Last Month**, **Next Year**, and **Last Year** as the value of the Caption property for the six buttons in sequence. Name the buttons **cmdNextWeek**, **cmdLastWeek**, and so forth.

2. Add an unbound text box under the calendar. Assign **lblDate** and **txtDate** as the values of the Name property of the label and text box, respectively (see fig. 30.34).

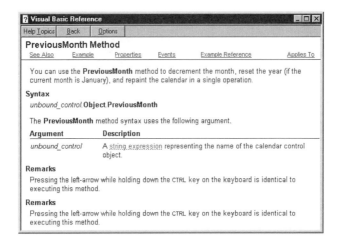

Fig. 30.33 The online help topic for the PreviousMonth method of the Calendar Control.

Fig. 30.34 The final design of the Calendar Control form.

3. Click the Calendar Control with the right mouse button and choose Build Event from the floating menu. Select Code Builder in the Choose Builder dialog to open the code editing window for ocxCalendar. Select the Updated event from the events drop-down list to create the **Private** Sub ocxCalendar_Updated()...**End Sub** stub. Note that the events exposed by the Calendar Control, such as Updated, NewMonth, and NewYear, appear in the list of events for the ocxCalendar unbound object frame.

4. Enter the following code (see fig. 30.35) for the Updated event to display the date when the form opens:

```
Private Sub ocxCalendar_Updated ()
'Purpose: Update the text boxes
    lblDate.Caption = Format(ocxCalendar.Object.Value, _
      "mm/dd/yy")
    txtDate.Value = Format(ocxCalendar.Object.Value, "dddddd")
End Sub
```

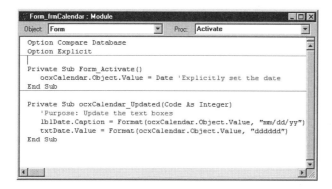

Fig. 30.35 Entering the code for the Updated event.

5. Enter the following code to set the date explicitly when opening the form:

```
Private Sub Form_Activate()
    ocxCalendar.Object.Value = Date 'Explicitly set the date
End Sub
```

6. Msacal70.ocx has methods for changing the week, month, and year (see fig. 30.33), so you can add the following code to apply the appropriate method to the Calendar Control with each Click event of each of the command buttons:

```
Sub cmd{Next¦Previous}{Week¦Month¦Year}_Click ()
    'Purpose: Use the Next or Previous period method
    to increment or decrement the period
    ocxCalendar.Object.{Next¦Previous}{Week¦Month¦Year}
End Sub
```

7. Complete the design of the form by setting the value of the MinMaxButtons property to None.

8. Click the Form View button of the toolbar to open your Calendar Control form (see fig. 30.36). Verify your event-handling procedures by testing the action of each of the six buttons.

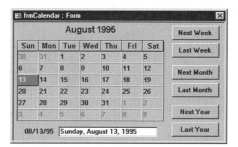

Fig. 30.36 The finished Calendar Control in Form View.

Using Access 95 as an OLE Automation Server

Access 95 exposes all of its application objects to other 32-bit automation-enabled applications through the `Access.Application.7` object. To use Access as an automation server, you create in a module a reference to the Microsoft Access 95 type library, Msaccess.tlb, which is located in the Access folder, not in \Windows\System. When this edition was written, only Microsoft Excel 95 and Project 4.1 were capable of manipulating 32-bit Access 95 application objects.

The extent to which developers will use Access 95 application objects instead of the Jet 3.0 database engine remains to be seen. Using the Jet 3.0 data access object to manipulate databases is much faster and consumes far fewer resources than launching an instance of Access to perform ordinary database-related operations.

You use the **CreateObject**() function to open a minimized instance of Access, then open a database with the OpenCurrentDatabase "*DatabasePathName*" method. Alternatively, you can use the **GetObject**("*path\filename*.mdb", "Access.Application.7") function. From this point on, you program the objects with Access VBA code in the other application. You even can invoke Access VBA's DoCmd object from the OLE Automation client with objName.DoCmd.*Action Argument(s)* statements.

As with using Access to manipulate objects of other applications described earlier in the chapter, the Debug Window is the best way to gain familiarity with the Access Application object. To experiment with Access 95's Application object in Excel 95, follow these steps:

1. Close Access if it is open, and launch Excel 95.

2. Choose Insert, Macro, Module to open an empty Module1 sheet.

3. Choose Tools, References to open Excel's References dialog. In the Available References list, mark the check box for Microsoft Access 95 (see fig. 30.37). Mark the Microsoft DAO 3.0 check box if you want to use database intrinsic constants. Click OK to close the dialog.

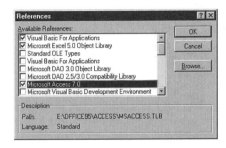

Fig. 30.37 Adding a reference to the Microsoft Access 95 type library to Excel 95.

4. Press F2 or choose <u>V</u>iew, <u>O</u>bject Browser to open Excel's Object Browser. Select Access from the Libraries/Workbooks list to display the objects exposed by the Access 95 type library (see fig. 30.38). Click Close when you've finished exploring the Access Application objects.

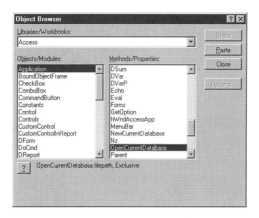

Fig. 30.38 Some of the Access Application objects displayed in Excel 95's Object Browser.

5. Add the following object variable declarations to the module:

```
Dim appAccess7 As Object
Dim dbCurrent As Database
Dim rstCurrent As Recordset
```

6. Press Ctrl+G or choose <u>V</u>iew, <u>D</u>ebug Window to open Excel's Debug Window. The object variable declarations appear in the lower pane.

7. Type **Set appAccess7 = CreateObject("Access.Application.7")** in the upper pane of the Debug Window. When you press Enter, the command eventually launches an iconic instance of Access.

8. When <Ready> appears in the status line, type **appAccess7.OpenCurrentDatabase "c:\msoffice\access\samples\northwind.mdb"**. (Alter the path if Northwind.mdb is in a different location.) Pressing Enter opens Northwind.mdb.

9. Type **Set dbCurrent = appAccess7.CurrentDB()**. After executing this statement, most of the commands to manipulate database objects are identical to those of Access VBA.

10. Type **Set rstCurrent = dbCurrent.OpenRecordset("Customers")** to open a Recordset object over the Customers table. Apply typical methods and check some property values of the Recordset object, as shown in figure 30.39.

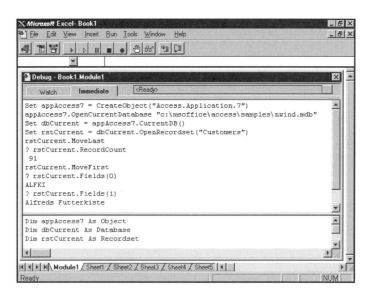

Fig. 30.39 Creating and manipulating an Access 95 Recordset object with Excel VBA.

11. When you finish experimenting with Access Application objects, type **Set appAccess7 = Nothing** to close the instance of Access.

Experimenting with Access as an OLE Automation server demonstrates that Visual Basic for Applications truly is the *lingua franca* of application programming (also called macro) languages. Although the hierarchy of the objects exposed to VBA varies with server applications, the programming language and methodology is independent of the client and server applications. Once Microsoft Word gains Word VBA, Microsoft's Bill Gates will have achieved his 1989 vision of a "common macro language" for all Microsoft productivity applications.

> **Note**
>
> One of the more interesting potential uses for Access as an OLE Automation server is the ability to create wizards with Visual Basic 4.0 or Visual C++ 4.0 that generate database applications in Access 95 and/or Visual Basic 4.0. The Access "wizard" functions, CreateForm(), CreateControl(), and CreateReportControl(), let you create application objects programmatically, just as you can create objects with Visual Basic 4.0's Development Environment objects exposed by the Vbext32.olb object library.

Exploring Dynamic Data Exchange

Chapter 21, "Using Access with Microsoft Excel," demonstrated how you can use Windows' dynamic data exchange (DDE) capabilities, the DDE() and DDESend() functions in particular, to transfer data between Excel and Access using the Clipboard as an intermediary. Using the DDE() and DDESend() functions doesn't require programming. Access VBA has its own set of DDE methods that provide more flexibility than the DDE() and DDESend() functions. Using Access VBA for DDE data transfers is faster than using the DDE() and DDESend() functions because you can make multiple requests for data after you establish a DDE communications channel.

The sections that follow describe how DDE works and how to use the DDE... statements and functions of Access VBA to exchange information with other Windows applications.

Principles of Dynamic Data Exchange

DDE is Windows' traditional method of interprocess communication; DDE allows applications that are not OLE 2.0 compliant to exchange data on a real-time basis. The process of exchanging data is called a DDE *conversation*. The application that initiates the conversation is called the DDE *client*, and the application that provides the data is called the DDE *server*. DDE clients also can supply unsolicited data to DDE servers (called *poking* data) and can send commands for servers to execute. An application can engage in several DDE conversations simultaneously, acting as a server in some and a client in others.

The basic elements of a DDE conversation consist of a request from a client to a server to initiate a conversation, exchange of information between the server and the client, and termination of the conversation. These elements, called DDE *transactions*, comprise the DDE protocol. DDE transactions take place between windows in each of the participating applications that are dedicated to the DDE conversation. These windows are usually invisible. Figure 30.40 is a diagram of a DDE conversation; optional transactions of the conversation are shown in gray type.

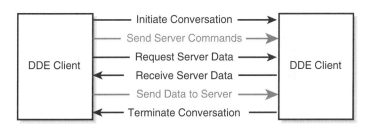

Fig. 30.40 The elements of a DDE conversation.

> **Tip**
>
> The client usually initiates the Terminate Conversation transaction, but the server can also terminate a transaction.

To execute the DDE protocol, the client and server send a series of Windows messages to the message queue maintained by the Windows operating system. Windows processes the messages and then removes each message from the message queue in first-in, first-out (FIFO) sequence.

The six elements of the conversation shown in figure 30.40 involve many Windows messages. Several messages may be passed between the client and server to implement one element of the conversation. To maintain the proper timing of messages, the client can request that the server acknowledge all request messages. This type of conversation is called an *asynchronous* DDE conversation.

In an asynchronous conversation, the client waits until it receives an acknowledgment from the server, indicating that it has processed a request message, before the client sends the server the next message. Most DDE conversations are asynchronous. *Synchronous* conversations use a time-out method; the client sends a series of messages and then awaits a response. If the expected response isn't received within the time-out period, an error message results.

Understanding Service Names, Topics, and Items

DDE uses a three-level hierarchy to identify the data that the client transmits to the server:

- *Service name* identifies the server application. Prior to Windows 3.1, *service name* was called *application name*. The service name is usually the name of the application's executable file, less the .exe extension, such as EXCEL, WINWORD, or MSACCESS. An application may have more than one service name; the application's documentation usually provides the application's DDE service name(s).

- *Topic* identifies the context of the information that is the subject of the conversation. In most cases, the topic is the name of a file, such as an Excel worksheet or a Word document. If an application doesn't use files, the topic is usually a string that is specific to the application. A third type of topic, the System topic, is described in the following section.

- *Item* is a specific piece of data contained in a topic, such as text specified by a bookmark in a word processing document.

Understanding the System Topic

Most applications that support DDE provide an additional topic called System. If the server application fully supports the System topic, you can use SysItems to obtain information about the server and its status. SysItems returns a comma-separated list of all valid items that you can use in conjunction with the System topic. In most cases, at least the following two SysItems are supported:

- *Topics* provides a list of the files that are open in the application if the application is file-based. Otherwise, it provides a list of the names of application-specific strings.

- *Formats* supplies a list of the Clipboard formats that the server application supports. Excel, for example, supports 11 different Clipboard formats for DDE data. The client application automatically selects the format that suits it best. Access requires that the format be plain text (the Clipboard's CF_TEXT format). Access cannot, for instance, process graphic images (using Clipboard's CF_BITMAP format) with DDE. You cannot alter the DDE Clipboard format in Access VBA.

Many applications don't include the information returned by SysItems in the product documentation. You must write a short DDE application to find out this information. The SysItems supported by Access as a DDE server are listed in the section "Using the System Topic," near the end of this chapter.

Choosing between DDE and OLE Automation

Access is biased toward the use of OLE 2.0 and OLE Automation for interprocess communication because OLE 2.0 is easier to implement and OA is a more reliable method of interprocess communication than DDE. OLE Automation overcomes OLE 1.0's inability to manipulate individual data items contained in an OLE object. OLE is the only practical method of transferring large blocks of data, such as graphic images, between Access and other applications. The maximum length of a DDE string in Access is about 32K, and Access, as noted previously, cannot handle graphic formats with DDE.

> **Tip**
>
> You can use the Access VBA GetChunk and AppendChunk methods to transfer data that exceeds 32K in length to and from fields of the Memo and OLE Object field data types.

If you need to communicate with applications that are not OLE 1.0 or 2.0 servers, DDE is your only option. DDE also allows communication between a 32-bit server to a 16-bit client application. Most major publishers of Windows applications have incorporated OLE 2.0 features, but many of today's OLE 2.0-compliant applications do not support OLE Automation. Qualifying for Microsoft's "Designed for Windows 95" logo requires implementing OLE 2.0 (at least for most applications), but qualification does not require exposing objects as an OLE Automation server.

If your access application must address specific data items in a container document, and the OLE 2.0 server you want to use with Access doesn't support OLE Automation, you must use DDE. Implementing OA in a mega-app, such as Excel 5.0, was a major undertaking; the fact that Microsoft's own Word 95 still does not conform to the object structure of OA is ample testimony to the complexity of the code required.

As mentioned at the beginning of this chapter, you must currently use DDE if you need to use interprocess communication between two computers on a network. The NetDDE features of Windows 95 and Windows NT let users transfer data between client and server Clipboards. Thus, you can obtain data via DDE from a remote computer. As a rule, however, NetDDE operations usually are confined to DDE links you create with the built-in DDE features of applications, rather than with the DDE... functions of Access VBA.

Choosing among DDE(), DDESend(), and Access VBA DDE

If you are faced with using Access as a DDE client, you must determine the best way of implementing DDE. When you used the DDE() and DDESend() functions in Chapter 21, "Using Access with Microsoft Excel," to obtain data from, or send data to, an Excel spreadsheet, you specified the service name, topic, and item for each transaction. When you use these two functions, Access does most of the work for you. DDE() initiates a conversation, specifies the topic, requests the particular data item, and then terminates the conversation with a single command. Similarly, DDESend() transfers a data item to a server with a single function.

If you need to transfer substantial numbers of data items between two applications, using DDE() or DDESend becomes quite cumbersome. In the majority of cases, you need a separate control object to hold the value of each data item. The alternative is to use a table with records that contain the values to identify the data item; this technique was used for the Stock Prices example in Chapter 21, "Using Access with Microsoft Excel." Creating a table to specify the addresses of a large number of data items is, at best, a tedious process. If the data items are properly organized, you can write an Access VBA procedure to append the data to a table.

Using Access VBA for DDE

Access VBA includes a set of six keywords that are used to initiate, process, and terminate DDE conversations. The four statements and two functions that comprise the DDE keywords of Access VBA are listed in table 30.1.

If you have written macros using DDE in Word's WordBasic language, you already know how to use these commands. The one difference is the lack of the string type identification character in the DDERequest() function; DDERequest() in Access VBA returns data of the **Variant** data type; DDERequest$() in WordBasic always returns a string. Pre-Excel 5.0 DDE macro functions dispense with the DDE prefix, but otherwise use similar commands. Visual Basic 3.0 and earlier substitutes Link... for DDE... and requires more statements to process a DDE conversation, but the overall approach of Visual Basic 3.0 to DDE is similar to that of other Microsoft applications.

Table 30.1	DDE Keywords of Access VBA	
Keyword	**Type**	**Purpose**
DDEExecute	Statement	Sends a command recognized by a DDE server over an open DDE channel.
DDEInitiate()	Function	Initiates a conversation with a DDE server and returns an integer that serves as the DDE channel number.
DDEPoke	Statement	Sends unsolicited data to a DDE server.
DDERequest()	Function	Requests a specific item of information from a DDE server over an open DDE channel.
DDETerminate	Statement	Closes an open DDE channel specified by number.
DDETerminateAll	Statement	Closes all open DDE channels.

Understanding the Structure and Syntax of Access VBA DDE Statements

The structure of a simple Access VBA generic DDE code that requests a data item (*ItemName*) from a topic (*TopicName*) of an application (*ServiceName*) follows:

```
lngChannel = DDEInitiate("ServiceName", "TopicName")
DDERequest(lngChannel, "ItemName")
DDETerminate lngChannel
```

The DDEInitiate() function returns a **Long** integer, lng*Channel*, that all succeeding DDE statements use to identify the communication channel for the service name and topic. (Windows 3.1+ DDE channel numbers were of the **Integer** data type.) This set of instructions assumes the application is loaded before the DDEInitiate() function is called. Unlike OLE, if the application isn't loaded, you receive an error message. You then must start the application with Access VBA's **Shell**() function.

Using the Shell() Function to Load an Application

The operation of the **Shell**() function is similar to running an application from the Run dialog opened from the Start menu. The syntax of the **Shell**() function is as follows:

```
hTask = Shell("AppFile", intStyle)
```

The handle to the Windows task, hTask, is a **Long** integer value in Windows 95 and Windows NT. In this case, *AppFile* is the full file name, including the .exe extension, of the application you want to run, Excel.exe, for example. If *AppFile* isn't in your \Windows or \Windows\System folder, or on your path, you need to add the well-formed path to the file name.

The int*Style* argument specifies the presentation of the application when it is loaded. Assigning an int*Style* of 6 is the equivalent of checking the Run Minimized check box in the Run dialog of Windows NT; Windows starts the application in iconic style without the focus. (There is no Run Minimized check box in Windows 95's Run dialog.) Unless you have a specific reason to display the server in a window, always use the iconic style without the focus when opening a DDE server.

If you call the **Shell**() function when an application is already running, you launch another instance of most applications. This consumes resources that you may need to keep Access operating. To determine whether the application is presently running, you can use the **On Error GoTo** instruction, but the most straightforward method is to test the error value with the **Err** function and then use **Shell**().

Experimenting with DDE in the Debug Window

 ◀◀ See "Exporting Data in other File Formats," p. 256

The Customers.xls workbook you created in the "Creating Customers.xls" section earlier in this chapter provides an Excel 5.0 worksheet, Customers, that you can use to experiment with Access VBA DDE... functions. If you didn't create Customers.xls, export the Customers table of Northwind.mdb to Customers.xls in a format appropriate for your present version of Microsoft Excel. The sequence of DDE... instructions shown in figure 30.41 requires that an instance of Excel be open with the CUSTOMER.XLS worksheet active.

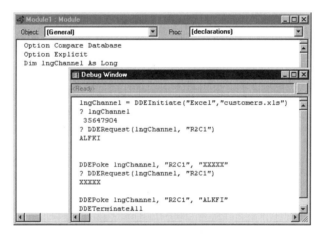

Fig. 30.41 Communicating with an open application and topic using DDE.

The first statement in figure 30.28, lngChannel = DDEInitiate("Excel", "customers.xls"), opens a DDE channel to Excel and the worksheet. A lngChannel value of 0 indicates an error; the most likely cause of the error is that Excel is not open or the topic you specified is not one of the items that is returned by the System topic. You can obtain a list of valid topics with a **? DDERequest(lngChannel, "Topics")** statement with a channel opened to the System topic. This statement returns [Customers.xls]Customers, specifying the Customers worksheet of the Customers.xls workbook, the names of other sheets and modules in the workbook, and finally System.

Unlike the prior OLE Automation example, you use Excel's RC (row, channel) nomenclature to specify the cell coordinates in DDE conversations. Thus, the ? DDERequest(lngChannel, "R2C1") statement returns the value in cell A2. You can send unrequested data to a DDE server with the DDEPoke statement. For example, the DDEPoke lngChannel, "R2C1", "XXXXX" statement replaces "ALKFI" with "XXXXX", as shown in figure 30.42. Using the `DDETerminateAll` instruction is recommended when you have completed the conversation unless you need to maintain other DDE channels in use. In the latter case, use the `DDETerminate lngChannel` statement to terminate a specific channel.

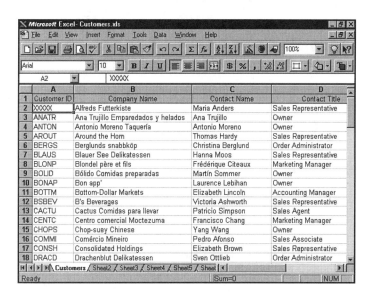

Fig. 30.42   Using the `DDEPoke` statement to change a cell value in a worksheet.

Figure 30.43 illustrates the use of the **Shell**() function to launch the DDE server application. To experiment with the **Shell**() function, close Excel and don't save the changes to your worksheet. The **Shell**() function launches the application and returns the Windows Task Manager's task handle (`hTask`) to the instance of the application. With Excel 95, the **? Shell**(`"excel.exe"`) statement without the optional `intStyle` parameter opens an iconized instance of Excel 95 with an empty workbook (Book1) and worksheet (Sheet1). (Versions of Excel earlier than 5.0 open with an empty worksheet.)

You must use a valid topic to open a DDE channel; the `System` topic is valid for almost all DDE server applications. Most DDE servers accept commands from DDE client applications via a channel to their `System` topic. You use Excel's function syntax with the `DDEExecute` statement to perform Excel's menu commands. Thus, the statement `DDEExecute lngChannel, "[OPEN(""c:\msoffice\excel\customers.xls"")]"` opens the Customers.xls workbook. You must open another DDE channel, identical to the one you use when Excel is already open, to communicate with the worksheet in the workbook.

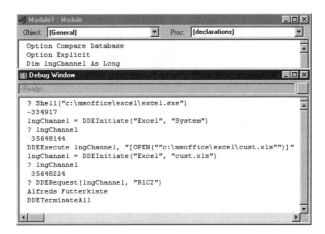

Fig. 30.43   Using the **Shell()** function and the DDEExecute statement to open a channel to a worksheet.

Note

The double quotation marks (" ") that surround the path and file name create the single quotation marks required by Excel's function syntax. Most applications require commands passed by DDE to be enclosed within square brackets.

Although the examples of this section are devoted to communicating with Microsoft Excel, the process is similar for almost all other DDE servers. You can use DDE to provide interprocess communication with Lotus 1-2-3, WordPerfect for Windows, and even fax applications, such as WinFax PRO. As mentioned earlier in this chapter, the Mail Merge feature of Access relies solely on DDE to communicate with Word.

Using Access as a DDE Server

Access can act as a DDE server to other DDE client applications. Access recognizes a set of DDE instructions issued by the client applications that is more versatile than the set offered by most DDE server applications. The flexibility of Access's DDE server instruction set was designed to compensate for the inability of earlier versions of Access to act as an OLE Automation server. In some cases, DDE is a better choice than OLE Automation for transferring columnar data to a client spreadsheet application. If, as an example, you want to transfer data from 32-bit Access 95 to a 16-bit Excel 5.0 worksheet, DDE is the best choice.

Using the System Topic

When a client application initiates a DDE channel on the System topic and specifies Topics as the data item in a DDERequest() statement, Access returns a list of the topics it currently supports. With Access running and Northwind.mdb open, type and then execute the following Word macro:

```
Sub MAIN
    Channel = DDEInitiate("MSAccess", "System")
    Topics$ = DDERequest$(Channel, "Topics")
    DDETerminate(Channel)
    Insert Topics$
End Sub
```

Access returns a tab-separated string and Word inserts this string, similar to that in the following example, at Word's current insertion point:

```
System      C:\MSOFFICE\ACCESS\SYSTEM.MDW
        C:\MSOFFICE\ACCESS\UTILITY.MDA
        C:\MSOFFICE\ACCESS\WZMAIN70.MDA
        C:\MSOFFICE\ACCESS\WZTOOL70.MDA
        C:\MSOFFICE\ACCESS\WZLIB70.MDA
        C:\MSOFFICE\ACCESS\SAMPLES\NORTHWIND.MDB
```

As mentioned in the preceding section, the System topic is supported by all Windows DDE servers. Unlike Access 1.1, which returned UTILITY, WIZARD, and NORTHWIND, Access 2.0 and Access 95 return the path, file name, and extension of all open topics.

The System topic supports the SysItems data item that returns a list of valid data items that you can use to determine additional information about Access's capabilities as a server. Run the following Word macro:

```
Sub MAIN
    Channel = DDEInitiate("MSAccess", "System")
    SysItems$ = DDERequest$(Channel, "SysItems")
    DDETerminate(Channel)
    Insert SysItems$
End Sub
```

The macro inserts the following tab-separated list of valid data items for the System topic:

```
Status      Formats     SysItems     Topics
```

If you substitute Formats for SysItems in the preceding macro, Access 95 returns the three types of Clipboard formats it supports:

```
Text    Csv    XlTable
```

```
Text    Csv    XLTable
```

Csv is an abbreviation for comma-separated values, the format in which Access returns the examples shown previously. XLTable is an Excel 5.0 format added to Access 2+.

The data items supported by the System topic are summarized in table 30.2.

Table 30.2 Data Items Supported by Access's System Topic	
Data Item	**Purpose**
Status	Returns Ready or Busy.
Formats	Returns a list of the formats Access can copy onto the Clipboard, presently CSV, Text, and XLTable.
SysItems	Returns a list of the data items, except MacroName, supported by the System topic.
Topics	Returns a list of all open databases, including libraries.
MacroName	Enables a macro in the current database to be executed with the DDEExecute statement using the System topic.

Returning Information about Other Topics

You can obtain four different sets of data by specifying the name of the open database:

- *Database object lists.* To obtain these lists, use the name of the database as the topic in the DDEInitiate() statement and use one of the following keywords as the data item in a DDERequest() statement: TableList, QueryList, FormList, ReportList, MacroList, and ModuleList.

- *Data from tables.* To obtain this data, specify the database (followed by a semicolon), the keyword TABLE, and the name of the table as the topic in the DDEInitiate() statement. Then use one of the following keywords as the data item in a DDERequest() statement: All, Data, FieldNames, FirstRow, NextRow, PrevRow, LastRow, and FieldCount.

- *Data from a query.* To obtain this data, specify the database (followed by a semicolon), the keyword QUERY, and the name of the query as the topic in the DDEInitiate() statement. Then use one of the same keywords for the TABLE topic as the data item in a DDERequest() statement.

- *Data from an SQL statement.* To obtain this data, specify the database (followed by a semicolon), the keyword SQL, and a valid SQL statement in the DDEInitiate() statement. Then use one of the same keywords for the TABLE topic as the data item in a DDERequest() statement.

The sections that follow give the syntax and an example of an Excel 4.0 macro that executes each of these DDE client processes. The information in these sections assumes some familiarity with the command macros features of Excel 4.0. Excel 5.0 is backward compatible with Excel 4.0 macros, so these macros also are operable in Excel 5.0 and 95.

You can execute macros over DDE channels initiated with the *DatabaseName* topic in the same manner as those initiated with the System topic. You specify the *MacroName* of a macro contained in the open database as the data item in a DDERequest() statement.

Listing Database Object Names with the DatabaseName Topic. You can obtain lists of all database objects in an Access database you specify with the *DatabaseName* topic. *DatabaseName* can be NORTHWIND or Northwind.mdb, for example, if Northwind.mdb is open. Otherwise, you need to include the **Shell**() function command in your macro.

After initiating the DDE conversation with the *DatabaseName* topic, you can use the data items listed in table 30.3 with the DDERequest() request function to return a Csv string listing the names of database objects in the database.

Table 30.3 Data Items Recognized with the DatabaseName Topic	
Data Item	**Purpose**
TableList	A list of tables in *DatabaseName*
QueryList	A list of queries in *DatabaseName*
MacroList	A list of macros in *DatabaseName*
ReportList	A list of reports in *DatabaseName*
FormList	A list of forms in *DatabaseName*
ModuleList	A list of modules in *DatabaseName*

For example, the following Excel 4.0 macro returns the first three entries in a list of the tables in the Northwind Traders sample database, assuming Northwind.mdb is open:

```
=INITIATE("MSAccess","NORTHWIND")
=INDEX(REQUEST(A2,"TableList"),1)    Categories
=FORMULA(A3,B3)
=INDEX(REQUEST(A2,"TableList"),2)    Customers
=FORMULA(A5,B5)
=INDEX(REQUEST(A2,"TableList"),3)    Employees
=FORMULA(A7,B7)
=TERMINATE(A2)
=RETURN()
```

Enter the macro statements of the example in a macrosheet in rows 1 through 9 of column A. Select cell A1, and then choose Run from Excel's Macros menu. Choose OK or press Enter when the Run Macro dialog appears. The values appear in cells B3, B5, and B7.

Using the *TableName* and *QueryName* Topics to Obtain Data. You can add a qualifier to *DatabaseName* to specify a table or query object contained in *DatabaseName* as the topic. The syntax is as follows:

```
DatabaseName;TABLE TableName
DatabaseName;QUERY QueryName
```

Table 30.4 lists the data items that are valid for use with both the *TableName* and *QueryName* topics, plus the *SQLStatement* topic discussed in the next section.

Table 30.4 Data Items Recognized by the TableName, QueryName, and SQLStatement Topics	
Data Item	**Purpose**
All	Returns all data in the table, preceded by a row of field names.
Data	Returns all rows of data without a row of field names.
FieldNames	Returns a list consisting of all field names.
FirstRow	Returns the data in the first row of the table or query.

(continues)

Table 30.4 Continued	
Data Item	**Purpose**
NextRow	Returns the data in the next row in the table or query. If NextRow is the first request, the data in the first row is returned. NextRow fails if the current row is the last record.
PrevRow	Returns the previous row in the table or query. If PrevRow is the first request, the data in the last row of the table or query is returned. PrevRow fails if the current row is the first record.
LastRow	Returns the data in the last row of the table or query.
FieldCount	Returns the number of fields in the table or query.
MacroName	Enables a macro in the current database to be executed with the DDEExecute() statement using the System topic.

The following Excel 4.0 macro returns the first three fields of the first row of the Categories table:

```
=INITIATE("MSAccess","NORTHWIND;TABLE Categories")
=INDEX(REQUEST(A2,"FirstRow"),1)          BEVR
=FORMULA(A3,B3)
=INDEX(REQUEST(A2,"FirstRow"),2)          Beverages
=FORMULA(A5,B5)
=INDEX(REQUEST(A2,"FirstRow"),3)          Soft drinks, _
=FORMULA(A7,B7)
=TERMINATE(A2)
=RETURN()
```

Enter and run the macro using the procedure described previously in the *DatabaseName* section.

Running a Query with the *SQLStatement* Topic. The *SQLStatement* topic returns a valid SQL statement following the SQL keyword. The syntax for the *SQLStatement* topic is as follows:

```
DatabaseName;SQL SQLStatement;
```

The SQL statement must end with a semicolon.

An Excel 4.0 macro that executes the SQL statement, SELECT * FROM Customers, and lists the names of the first three customers in the resulting Recordset object is as follows:

```
=INITIATE("MSAccess","NORTHWIND;SQL SELECT * FROM Customers;")
=INDEX(REQUEST(A2,"FirstRow"),2)    Alfreds Futterkiste
=FORMULA(A3,B3)
=INDEX(REQUEST(A2,"NextRow"),2)     Ana Trujillo Emparedados y _
                                    helados
=FORMULA(A5,B5)
=INDEX(REQUEST(A2,"NextRow"),2)     Antonio Moreno Taquería
=FORMULA(A7,B7)
=TERMINATE(A2)
=RETURN()
```

In the majority of cases, you write macros in the client application's macro language that contain loops to process multiple rows of data. Excel VBA and even WordBasic makes writing macros with loops and conditional branching easy. However, the design of macros in the languages of applications other than Access is beyond the scope of this book.

From Here...

The primary emphasis of this chapter is on Access 95's OLE Automation capabilities and OLE Custom Controls because OA and OCXs represent the future direction of interprocess communication for Windows applications, as well as for applications running under a variety of other operating systems. Many Windows applications do not support OLE 1.0 and, thus, are not likely to support OLE 2.0, either. Therefore, the chapter provided you with the basics using Access 95 as a DDE client. Finally, you must use DDE if you want to use Access 95 as the source of data for a 16-bit client application. This chapter demonstrates that Access 95 has a much richer set of DDE server capabilities than most other Windows database applications.

The following chapters provide additional information on the use of OLE 2.0 and the simplified version of DDE offered by Access's DDE() and DDESend() functions:

- Chapter 19, "Using 32-Bit OLE 2.1," gives an overview of Access 2.0's implementation of OLE 2.0 and OLE Automation.

- Chapter 20, "Adding Graphics to Forms and Reports," shows you how to use OLE 1.0- and OLE 2.0-compliant applications with Access 95 and describes how to use the Graph Wizard with Microsoft Graph 5.0 to create bound and unbound graphs and charts.

- Chapter 21, "Using Access with Microsoft Excel," and Chapter 22, "Using Access with Microsoft Word and Mail Merge," describe the use of the DDE() and DDESend() functions with these two popular productivity applications.

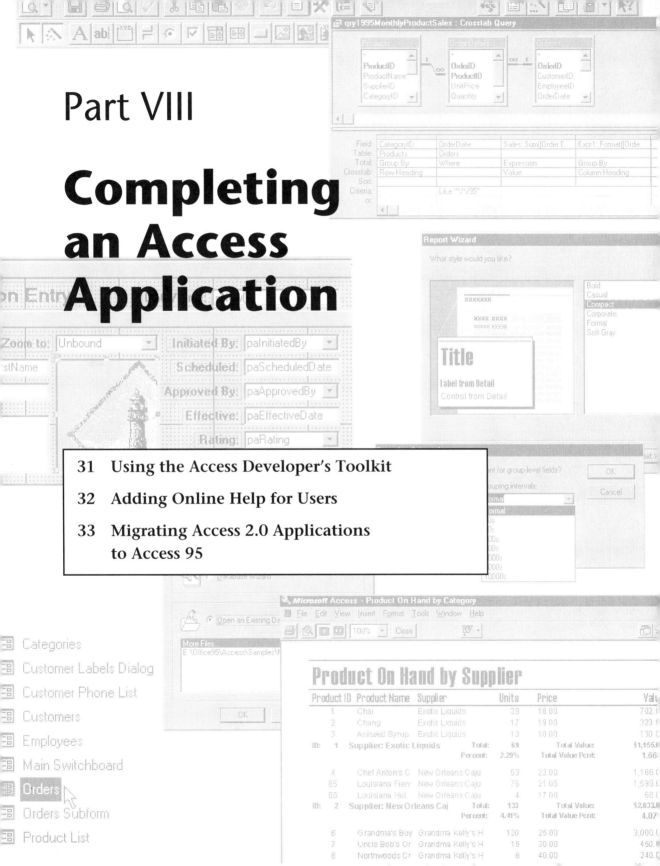

Part VIII

Completing an Access Application

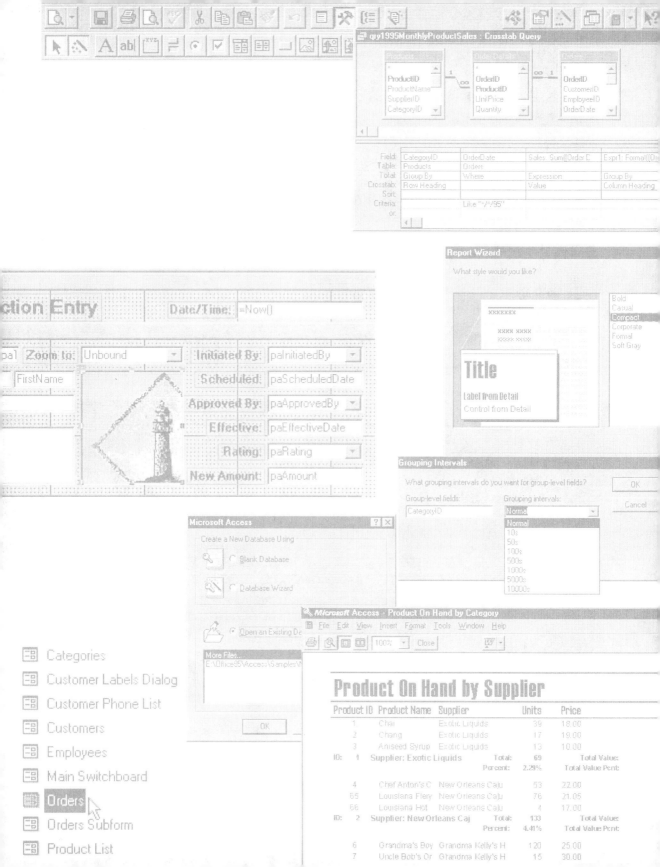

Chapter 31

Using the Access Developer's Toolkit

The Access Developer's Toolkit (ADT) for Access 95 differs greatly from the Access 2.0 ADT. Previous versions of Access used a separate runtime executable file, MSARN??0.EXE; Access 95 uses the retail version of Msaccess.exe set to runtime mode for distributing Access 95 applications. The Access 95 ADT includes a variety of new components that were not included in the Access 1.1 ADK (Access Distribution Kit) or the Access 2.0 ADT. Even if you don't intend to distribute your applications to others, you might want to acquire the Access 95 ADT because of the additional OLE Controls and printed documentation the ADT provides. This chapter describes what's in the ADT, how to use the Setup Wizard to create runtime distribution disks for your Access 95 applications, and how to use the API Viewer to add 32-bit Windows (Win32) API function prototype declarations to your Access VBA code.

Examining the Content of the Access Developer's Toolkit

The new ADT for Access 95 is directed at both the Access developer and power-user communities. The new ADT contains the following components:

- A royalty-free license to distribute Msaccess.exe for runtime use, the runtime version of Microsoft Graph 5.0 (Gr5run.exe), and the other distributable components of Access 95, such as the Jet 3.0 database engine, OLE Controls, ODBC, and ISAM drivers.

- An improved version of the Setup Wizard you use to create images of the distribution disks for your application. The Setup Wizard also writes the Setup.inf and other data files required by Setup.exe. The data files are more complex because Access 95 uses the Registry, rather than an *APPNAME*.INI file, to specify custom entries needed to run your application.

- The two-volume *Microsoft Visual Basic, Applications Edition Reference Manual* and the *Jet 3.0 Data Access Object Reference Manual*. (The content

In this chapter, you learn

- What's in the Access 95 Developer's Toolkit

- How to modify the design of your Access applications for runtime execution and distribution

- To use the Setup Wizard to create distribution diskettes

- How to add 32-bit Windows API function declarations to your Access VBA code with the API Viewer

VIII

Completing an App

of the these manuals is included in Access 95's online help files, but most Access power users are likely to want a printed version.)

◀◀ See "Adding OLE Controls to Your Application," p. 1088

■ The 32-bit Common Dialog (Comdlg32.ocx), Spinner (Spin32.ocx), and Rich Text (Richtx32.ocx) OLE Controls of Visual Basic 4.0 and the Windows 95 common controls (Image List, Status Bar, Tab Strip, and Tree View), which also are included with Visual Basic 4.0. The ADT also includes Version 1.1 of the Data Outline control (Msdboutl.ocx), together with the Data Outline Control Wizard (Wzdboutl.mda) to set the Data Outline control's properties, and an example database (Outline.mdb) that contains several forms to show you how to use the Data Outline control.

■ The Replication Manager (Replman.exe) to automate Briefcase replication operations between multiple sites. The Microsoft Access Replication Configuration Wizard aids in setting up replication scenarios.

▶▶ See "Compiling and Displaying Your Skeleton Help File," p. 1148

■ The Microsoft help compiler for Windows 95 (Hcrtf.exe), the graphic front-end for the help compiler (Hcw.exe), and the files needed to create Sample.hlp, a Windows 95 example help file.

■ A Windows API Viewer application, Apilod32.exe, which also is part of Visual Basic 4.0. The API Viewer aids in converting your 16-bit Windows API function prototype declarations to the Win32 API.

■ The *Microsoft Office Compatible Basic Toolkit for 32-Bit Products*, Ocbtk.doc, a Word document that describes the requirement for applications to gain "Microsoft Office Compatible" certification.

■ A Microsoft Developer Network (MSDN) sample CD-ROM that describes the benefits of subscribing to MSDN and provides examples of the content of recent MSDN CD-ROMs.

Except for the Data Outline OLE Control, which is a 32-bit version of the control supplied with the Access 2.0 ADT, all of the preceding components are new for Access 95.

Differences between Runtime and Retail Access

The behavior of your 32-bit Access applications differs when you execute the applications for use with the runtime, rather than the full (retail), version of Access 95. Following are the principal differences that distinguish runtime execution:

- All design-related menu choices and corresponding object views are removed. Your runtime applications should use menu macros to create the menu bars and menu items your application requires.

- Built-in toolbars aren't supported, but you can create custom toolbars for your application. (Custom toolbars are stored in the System.mdw file you distribute with your application.)

- The Database window is not visible, and macro and module windows are hidden. You specify the form to open by selecting the form in the Startup dialog opened by choosing <u>T</u>ools, Start<u>u</u>p. Most of the information contained in the *APPNAME*.INI file required by the runtime version of Access 1.x and 2.0 now is provided by entries in the Startup dialog.

- Special-purpose keys and combinations are disabled. Shift is disabled during the database opening process. Ctrl+Break is disabled so that users cannot halt Access VBA code or macro operation. (Ctrl+Break remains active during query execution so that users can halt a "run-away" query that returns very large numbers of records.)

- Pressing F1 for online help results in an error message if you don't supply a custom online help file for your application and assign the file name to the Help File property of every visible object of your application. (You also must include a valid Help Context ID value.) Supplying even a very simple help file is a better practice than allowing an error to occur when the user presses F1. (You are not allowed to distribute the Access online help file.)

- All errors that occur in the execution of macros and untrapped errors that occur while executing Access VBA code result in an instantaneous exit of Access. The user receives no warning of the impending disappearance of your application. As mentioned in the previous chapters of this book, you cannot trap macro errors. Thus, you should use Access VBA code with error trapping rather than macros for all event-handling operations. Macros should be limited to the AutoKeys macro to assign key combinations to execute functions and to add custom menu bars and menu choices to your application's user interface.

- If you use separate data and application .mdb files, you need to provide Access VBA that test to determine if the data.mdb file is on the expected drive and in the specified folder. If not, a special form and another routine is required to specify the location of the data.mdb file. The Outline.mdb database includes a module, Reattach Northwind, that provides example code to test whether the required file(s) are linked and, if not, to determine the location of the file(s) to link.

No significant change in the preceding list has occurred with Access 95. Thus, the Access 1.x or 2.0 runtime applications you convert to Access 95 are likely to behave identically. Chapter 33, "Migrating Access 2.0 Applications to Access 95," describes the changes you need to make to execute your applications with runtime Access 95. These changes also are necessary for the applications to execute with the retail version of Access 95.

> ### Tip
>
> You can emulate runtime operation by creating a desktop shortcut that includes the path and file name with the /Runtime command-line switch for Msaccess.exe in the Target text box of the Shortcut page of the *Shortcut Name* Properties sheet. As an example, type **C:\MSOffice\Access\Msaccess.exe C:\MSOffice\Access\Samples\Nwind.mdb /Runtime** in the Target text box to specify the .mdb file used in the following example. It's a good practice to specify the current directory in the Start In text box, **C:\MSOffice\Access\Samples** for this example.

Creating Distribution Disks with the Setup Wizard

Microsoft Corporation's standard Setup program changed with the introduction of the Windows 95 round of Microsoft productivity application upgrades. The Setup application for users of your Access 95 runtime applications uses the standard Microsoft Office 95 Setup program, often called *Acme Setup*. The Access 95 Setup Wizard (Wzstp70.mda, a database disguised as a library) also has been given a major facelift.

The description of using the Setup Wizard that follows assumes that you have created or appropriated an icon file for your application and have an online help and help contents files, such as Nwind.hlp and Nwind.cnt (described in the next chapter, "Adding Online Help for Users"). The following steps prepare the files necessary to create runtime disk images:

1. The example uses a split version of the Northwind.mdb file (Nwind.mdb as the application file and Nwind_be.mdb as the data file). Compact Northwind.mdb into a copy named Nwind.mdb, open Nwind.mdb, and use the Database Splitter add-in to move the tables to Nwind_be.mdb in your \MSOffice\Access\Samples folder, the default folder for this example.

   See the "Splitting Databases for File Sharing" section of Chapter 25, "Securing Multiuser Network Applications," for instructions on using the Database Splitter add-in.

2. Copy any icon (*Iconname*.ico) file on your disk to the default folder. (Use Start, Find, Files or Folders and enter ***.ico** in the Named text box, then Find Now to locate an icon file to copy.) Rename the icon file copy to **Nwind.ico**.

3. If you didn't create the Nwind.hlp file, also copy to the default folder \MSOffice\Access\ADT\Help Compiler\Sample.hlp and rename Sample.hlp to **Nwind.hlp**. Repeat this process for Sample.cnt.

4. Copy \MSOffice\Access\System.mdw to the default folder. You cannot create a distribution copy of the System.mdw file that Access automatically opens when launched.

To create images of the distribution disks for the Northwind Traders (Runtime) application on your fixed disk (or a server drive), follow these steps:

> ### Tip
>
> Make sure you have at least 20M of free disk space on the drive that you use to store the disk images before you start creating distribution disks. The following example requires about 10.7M to store the disk images and compressed files.

1. Open Nwind.mdb and choose <u>T</u>ools, Start<u>u</u>p to open the Startup dialog. Type your application's name, such as **Northwind Traders (Runtime)**, in the Application Title text box; click the Builder button and select Nwind.ico in the Icon Browser dialog; and then select Main Switchboard from the Display Form drop-down list (see fig. 31.1). Accept the remaining defaults and click OK to close the dialog.

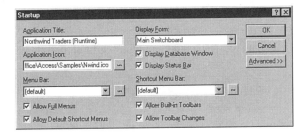

Fig. 31.1 Setting the startup parameters for Nwind.mdb.

2. Open the Wzstp70.mda database in your \MSOffice\Access\ADT\Setup Wizard folder. (If Access isn't running, you can launch the Wizard from Start, Programs, Microsoft ADT, Setup Wizard.) The Setup Wizard displays the opening dialog shown in figure 31.2. Accept the default Create a New Set of Setup Options choice and click Next > to display the second Wizard dialog.

3. Click the Add button to open the Select Files dialog. Select All Files(*.*) from the Files of Type drop-down list. (If you don't select All Files, the Nwind.cnt file might not appear in the list.) Press the Ctrl key and select Nwind.cnt, Nwind.hlp, Nwind.ico, Nwind.mdb, Nwind_be.db, and System.mdw (see fig. 31.3). Click Add to add the files to List of Files list box of the Setup Wizard's dialog. (For a multiuser application, you install Nwind_be.mdb and System.mdw on the file server and do not include either of these two files in the List of Files.)

4. Select Nwind.mdb in the List of Files list box and mark the Set As Application's Mail File check box (see fig. 31.4). Accept the default $(AppPath) for the Destination Folder, Older for Overwrite Existing File, and accept Application as the Component Name for the files.

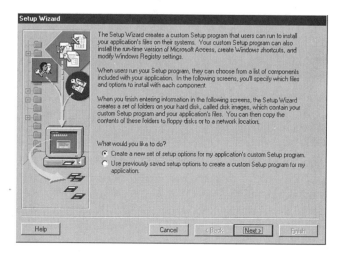

Fig. 31.2 The opening dialog of the Setup Wizard.

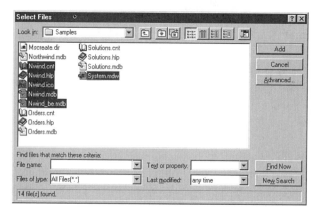

Fig. 31.3 Selecting the required application files in the MSOffice\Access\Samples folder.

5. Select System.mdw and mark the Set as Workgroup File check box, as shown in figure 31.5. If you include the workgroup file, this is an important step because marking the Set As Workgroup File checkbox causes setup to make the appropriate Registry entries for System.mdw.

For multiuser applications, you must include the Workgroup Administrator application so that the user can specify the location of the workgroup file before launching your application.

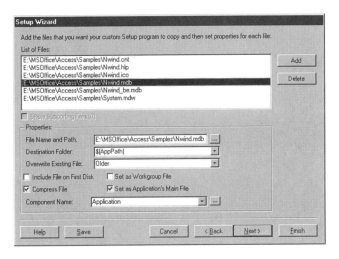

Fig. 31.4 Adding the application files to the List of Files list box and setting the application's main file.

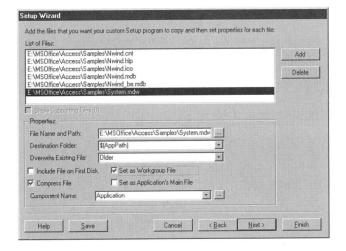

Fig. 31.5 Adding System.mdw from the \MSOffice\Access\Samples folder as the workgroup file.

6. With System.mdw selected, click the Builder button (to the right of the Component Name drop-down list) to open the Components Builder dialog, then click the Add button. Type **Workgroup File** in the Name text box and click the Close button to add Workgroup File to the Components list. Optionally, you can add other component names, such as Database, and Help Files, before you close the Components Builder (see fig. 31.6). You can change the order of the components with the blue up and down arrows to the left of the List of Components.

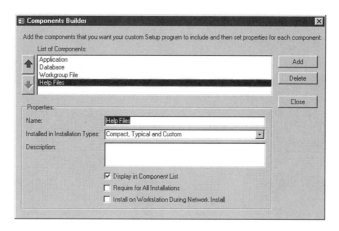

Fig. 31.6   Adding new component categories to the List of Components.

7. With System.mdw selected, open the Component Name drop-down list and select Workgroup File (see fig. 31.7). If you added additional components in the preceding step, select each file and assign the appropriate component name. Click Next > to continue.

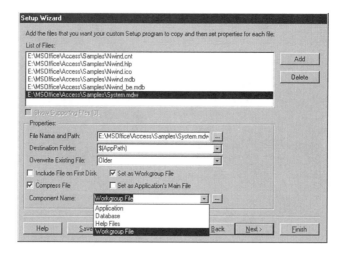

Fig. 31.7   Assigning a component name to the workgroup file.

8. The Wizard lets you create shortcuts to run, compact, and repair your application. To provide a shortcut to launch Nwind.mdb, type **Northwind Runtime** in the Description text box, accept the remaining defaults, and click the Add button. Repeat this process for Compact Northwind (select the Compact option button) and Repair Northwind (select the Repair option button). When you select Compact, a message appears asking if you want to include the Access Runtime Executable file; click Yes to include Msaccess.exe with your files. You also can add a shortcut for your help file by selecting Nwind.hlp in the File to Open drop-down list (see fig. 31.8). Click the Next > button to continue.

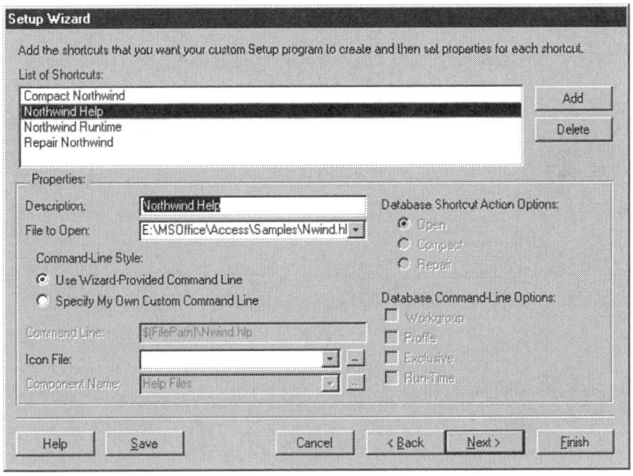

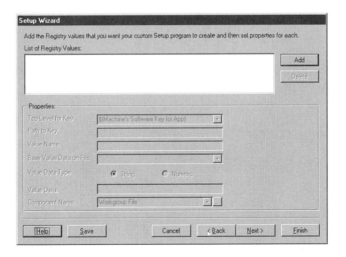

Fig. 31.8 Creating shortcuts for opening, compacting, and repairing the .mdb file and opening the help file.

9. The Setup Wizard automatically creates all of the Registry keys and values needed to run your application. You can add custom Registry keys, if needed, in the Wizard's dialog shown in figure 31.9. For this example, click Next > to continue.

Fig. 31.9 You can add custom Registry keys, if needed by your application.

10. Click the entries in the list box to select additional components to include on your distribution diskettes or in your network setup directory. An X indicates selected components (see fig. 31.10). If you answered Yes to the message described in step 8, the Wizard selects Microsoft Access Runtime for you; if not, make sure to select this component. Also make sure to select Microsoft Graph 5 Runtime, if your application includes graphs or charts. Click Next > to continue. (You must include the

Workgroup Administrator application with multiuser applications so that users can connect to the workgroup file on the workgroup server.)

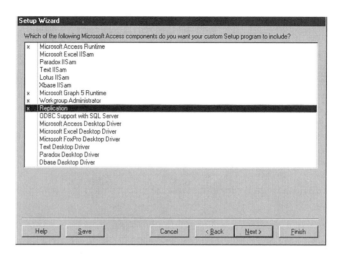

Fig. 31.10 Adding required components to the distribution files.

11. If you selected Replication in the preceding list of additional components, the dialog shown in figure 31.11 appears. You can choose to place replicated files in the user's application folder, $(AppPath) or in a Replicas subfolder, $(AppPath)\Replicas. Enter the UNC location of the folder (called the *dropbox* folder) in which updated versions of replica sets are stored for periodic pickup by your application. You can include Replication Manager with your installation files, if desired. (If your application is a conventional networked multiuser application, you usually don't need replication.) Click Next > to continue.

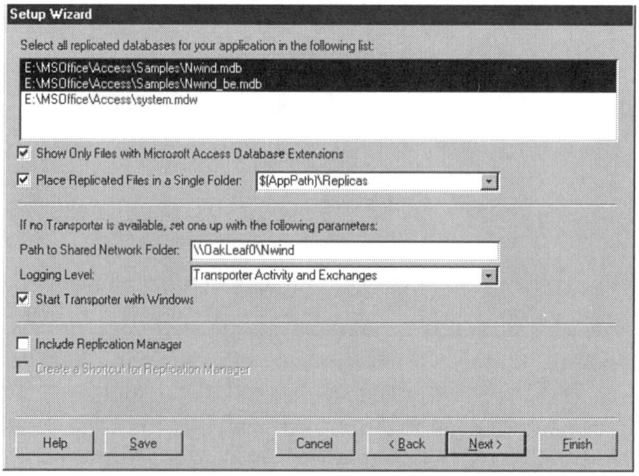

Fig. 31.11 Setting up replication operations, including the location of the dropbox folder.

12. Verify that the components required for your application are installed in all three installation types, Compact, Typical, and Custom (see fig. 31.12). Mark the Require for All Installations check box for needed files. (Require for All Installations prevents users from failing to install required files when choosing Custom setup.) If you supply Replication Manager, you can select Custom from the Installed in Installation Types drop-down list so that Replication Manager only is installed when needed. Click Next > to continue.

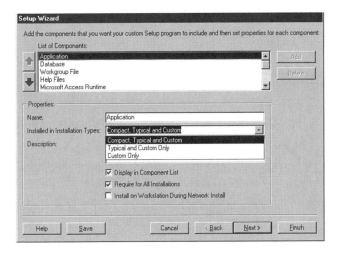

Fig. 31.12 Setting the property values of installation components.

13. Type the name and version number of your application, your firm name, and the drive and name of the folder that corresponds to $(AppPath). Provision is made for a conventional DOS folder name, if your application is installed on a PC that doesn't support long file names, such as versions of Windows NT earlier than 3.51 (see fig. 31.13). Click Next > to continue.

14. If you need to run an executable file when the setup operation completes, select the .exe file in the Run the Following File... drop-down list. The executable file and any supporting .dll files must have been included in the file list created in preceding step 3, unless the file is known to be on the user's computer. You can include a Readme.wri file and type **Wordpad.exe $(AppPath)\Readme.wri** in the Enter or Edit the Command Line... text box to display the file on completion of setup (see fig. 31.14). For a Readme file, make sure to mark the Allow Setup to Complete... check box so Setup announces that it has completed successfully before your Readme file appears. Click Next > to continue.

VIII

Completing an App

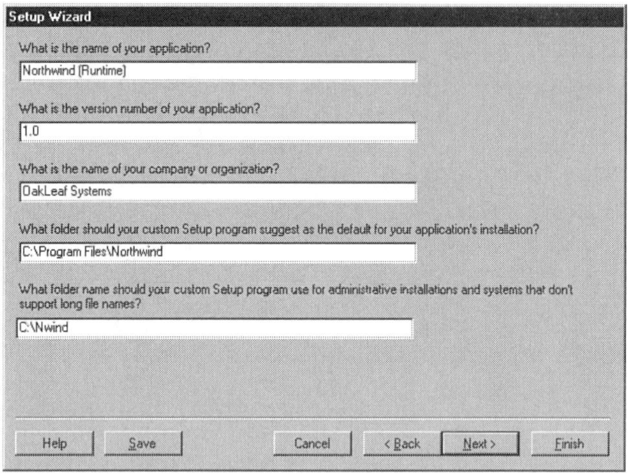

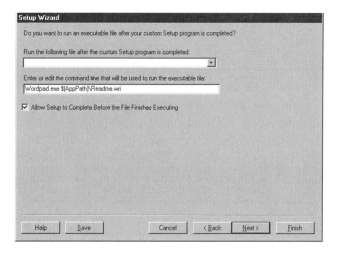

Fig. 31.13 Setting the property values for your application.

Fig. 31.14 Specifying an executable file to run on completion of the setup operation.

15. Enter the path and folder name of the directory in which to store the disk images, each of which is stored in a ...\DISK1...\DISK*n* folder (see fig. 31.15). Alternatively, you can elect to create a single network setup folder in a server share. Compressed network setup files save space on the server, but installation takes slightly longer. Storing a local copy of compressed files makes recreating your diskette images or server files quicker. Click Finish to create your diskette or server file images.

16. The Wizard asks if you want to save your setup data as a template. Click Yes to open the Save Template dialog (see fig. 31.16). Give your template an appropriate name, such as Northwind.mdt, and click the Save button to close the dialog.

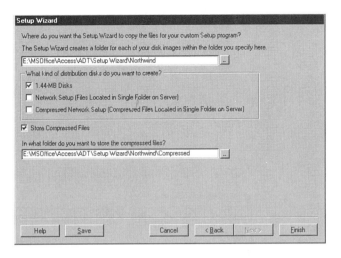

Fig. 31.15 Specifying the location of network or diskette image distribution files and optional compressed files.

Fig. 31.16 Assigning a name to and saving a template for your setup data.

17. The Wizard starts creating the compressed files and disk images and provides a status dialog as shown in figure 31.17. This is a good time to have a cup of coffee (or lunch), because the process may take 5 to 30 minutes, depending on the size of your application files, the component options you select, and the speed of your PC and disk drive. When the process completes, you receive the message shown in figure 31.18.

The setup files that the Wizard creates for your application result in an installation process that is very similar to that for Access 95 and other members of the Office 95 suite. You can quickly check your setup application by displaying the first few windows; figure 31.19 shows the opening Setup window for the example created in the preceding steps. To fully validate your setup application, however, you need to run Setup.exe from the diskettes or network file server on a workstation without either the retail or runtime version of Access 95 installed.

Fig. 31.17   The Setup Wizard keeps you informed of the progress of setup file generation.

Fig. 31.18   Success at last; the Wizard notifies you of the completion of the process.

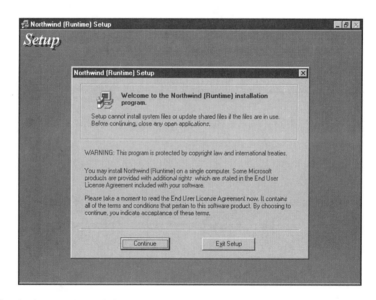

Fig. 31.19   The first window of the example Northwind (Runtime) setup program.

Using the 32-Bit Windows API Viewer

The Windows API Viewer, which also is included with Visual Basic 4.0, is intended as an aid to converting your existing 16-bit Windows 3.1+ (Win16) API calls to Win32 format. To add Win32 function prototype declarations to your Access VBA code, follow these steps:

1. Launch the API Viewer, Apilod32.exe, from your \MSOffice\Access\ADT\Win API Viewer folder.

2. Choose File, Load Database File to open the Select a Jet Database dialog and select Win32api.mdb (see fig. 31.20). Click the Open button to load the database file and close the dialog.

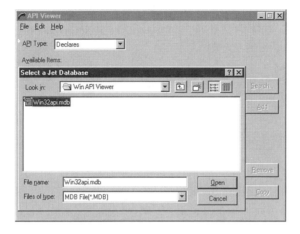

Fig. 31.20   Loading the Win32api.mdb file into the API Viewer.

3. With Declares selected in the API Type drop-down list, click the Available Items list box to give it the focus. Type the initial letter(s) of the Windows API function you want to add to your code. The corresponding API function entries appear.

4. Select the API function you want to include in the Declarations section of your Access VBA code and click the Add button to add the entry to the Selected Items list box. Repeat this process for as many API functions as you need.

5. Click the Copy button to copy the function prototype declarations to the Clipboard (see fig. 31.21).

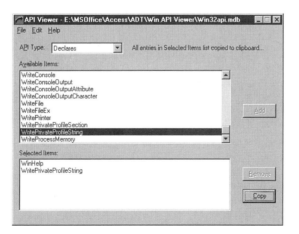

Fig. 31.21   Selecting the function prototype declarations to add to your Access VBA code.

VIII

Completing an App

6. Launch Access, if necessary, and open an existing or a new module.

7. Position the cursor at the line below the **Option** Explicit line in the Declarations section of the module and press Ctrl+V to paste the copied declarations.

8. Reformat the function prototype declarations using the line continuation pair (space plus underscore), as shown in figure 31.22. Reformatting the declarations makes your code easier to read.

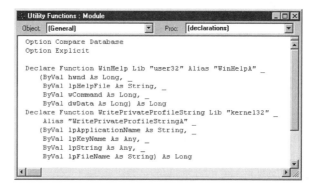

Fig. 31.22 The function prototype declarations pasted into a module and reformatted for readability.

▶▶ See "Declaring Windows Functions in Access VBA," p. 1164

You also can use the API Viewer to add Win32 structures (user-defined data types) and constant declarations to your Access VBA code. The API Viewer is capable of using either specially-formatted .txt or .mdb files and can convert .txt files into .mdb files for faster access to a specific function.

From Here...

The Access Developer's Toolkit is a necessity if you plan to develop Access 95 applications for others to use. In addition to the runtime license for Access 95, the ADT's help compiler, OLE Controls, and other features justify purchase of the ADT by serious Access developers. Refer to the following chapters to learn more about the subjects discussed in this chapter:

■ Chapter 25, "Securing Multiuser Network Applications," describes how to set up your applications for sharing on a peer-to-peer or network server.

■ Chapter 32, "Adding Online Help for Users," describes how to add function prototype declarations and call the WinHelp() function with Access VBA.

Chapter 32

Adding Online Help for Users

Online help is an indispensable element of the Access applications you create for others to use, especially if the applications are complex. Users of Windows applications are reported to take advantage of online help more frequently than those using the same applications under DOS. One reason is undoubtedly the easy-to-use Windows 95 WinHelp engine as well as its navigation and search features. Another reason is that software publishers are reducing the size of (or eliminating) printed manuals, relying on the Help system to guide new users through the intricacies of their products.

This chapter explains how to create Windows help files to provide context-sensitive help for your applications. To create help files, you need a word processing application that creates *Rich Text Format* (.rtf) files, such as Word 2.0+. (.RTF is a method of including formatting instructions with text in a readable ASCII file; .RTF is described in "Taking a Brief Look at the Rich Text Format" later in this chapter.) You also need Hcrtf.exe, the Microsoft help compiler that converts the .rtf files to a form readable by the Windows 95 help engine, Winhlp32.exe, called WinHelp in this book. Hcw.exe, the Help Compiler Workshop, acts as the user interface for Hcrtf.exe.

Neither Hcrtf.exe or Hcw.exe are included with the retail version of Access 95, but are provided with the Access 95 Developer's Toolkit (ADT), the Professional Edition of Visual Basic 4.0, and on the Microsoft Developer Network (MSDN) Level II CD-ROMs. Recent versions of most language compilers designed for creating Windows applications, such as Microsoft Visual C++, Symantec C++, and Borland C++, also include the Windows 95 help compiler files.

In this chapter, you learn to

- Use a commercial help authoring tool to create Windows 95 and Windows NT help files

- Add new Windows 95 features to your existing help files

- Compile your help file with the new Microsoft help compiler for Windows 95

- Add bitmapped images and graphic hotspots to help files

- Add Context ID values for context-sensitive online help for your Access applications

VIII

Completing an App

> **Note**
>
> Microsoft Word 6.0 is used in the examples of this chapter because many of the help-authoring tools that were available when this edition was written were not compatible with Word 95. Updated versions of all help-authoring tools designed to take advantage of the features of Word 95, such as Sky Software's RoboHELP 95, are likely to be available by the time you read this.

> **Note**
>
> The information in this chapter is intended to be a supplement to—not a substitute for—the help file for the Windows Help Workshop and books devoted specifically to creating Windows 95 help files. As an example, the WinHelp Reference book of the Windows Help Workshop help file deals with advanced topics, such as help macros, which are not covered in this chapter.

Checking Out the New Features of Windows 95 Help

The Windows 95 WinHelp system (WinHelp95) represents a significant departure from prior versions of WinHelp. WinHelp95 is fully compatible with Windows 3.1+ help files, but WinHelp95 doesn't extend its new features to Windows 3.1+ .HLP files. Following are the major differences between the Windows 3.1+ and Windows 95 Help system:

- Standard Help menu choices differ. Most Windows 95 applications offer a single choice, usually *ProductName* Help Topics, which replaces the <u>C</u>ontents, <u>S</u>earch, <u>I</u>ndex, <u>C</u>ue Cards, and other <u>H</u>elp menu choices associated with Windows 3.1+ applications. (The Answer Wizard choice is a proprietary feature of Office 95 and other Microsoft applications; Answer Wizards are not covered in this chapter.)

- Help features previously selected from <u>H</u>elp menu choices are accessed by Contents, Index, and Find tabs in the opening Help Topics dialog.

- The Help Topics dialog has a fixed size, is non-modal or application-modal, and resembles a properties sheet. The Contents window of Windows 3.1+ help files is non-modal and resizable. Figures 32.1 and 32.2 compare the appearance of the Contents windows for Access 2.0 and Access 95 help, respectively.

- Help topics in the Contents page are arranged in a hierarchical collection of *books*. When you double-click a closed book icon, it changes to an open book and help topic icons (?) and/or additional closed book icons appear, depending on the depth of the hierarchy (see fig. 32.2). The topic hierarchy is established by a .cnt (help contents) file that contains pointers to the location of topics in the .hlp file. When you first open a WinHelp95 .hlp file, a .gid (contents database) file is created automatically.

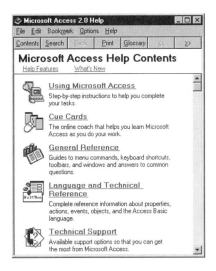

Fig. 32.1   WinHelp95 displays the Contents window of the Access 2.0 help file with the same menu choices and buttons as Windows 3.1+ WinHelp.

Fig. 32.2   WinHelp95 displays the Contents page of the Access 95 help file in a non-modal dialog that appears similar to a properties sheet.

- WinHelp95 provides second-level index entries (see fig. 32.3). Windows 3.1+ help provided only a single-level index.

- The Find page of the Help Topics dialog provides an indexed, full-text search of the .hlp file's contents. The first time you open the Find page for a WinHelp95 .hlp file, you receive a "Preparing help file for first use" message. This message indicates that WinHelp32 is creating an .fts (full-text search) file that contains pointers to the location of indexed words in the .hlp file.

VIII

Completing an App

Fig. 32.3   Second-level indexes are new to WinHelp95.

- The Help Topics dialog does not include a menu. Most of the features you access through Windows 3.1 help menu choices appear as a drop-down menu of the Options button when you display a help topic. You cannot open another help file from the Help Topics dialog; use the Windows Explorer to open other help files. (If the help file contains a main window, the menu appears when the main window is displayed. Most help topics appear in secondary windows.)

- A built-in jump button (called a *Chiclet*) substitutes for a hotspot. In Access 95, the jump button often is preceded by "How?"

- A built-in Related Topics or See Also button opens a dialog from which you can select an item in a list of related help topics.

- A built-in shortcut button lets you create a shortcut to a related application. The application opens when you click the shortcut button.

- You can easily add multimedia elements, such as video (.avi), sound (.wav), and MIDI music (.mid), to your help files.

If you've created Windows 3.1 help files, you can change the .rtf files to WinHelp95 format and automatically add new WinHelp95 features with commercial help porting tools, such as Blue Sky Software Corporation's Moving to WinHelp '95 product. Moving to WinHelp '95 is described in the "Porting Your Windows 3.1 Help Files to WinHelp95" section later in this chapter.

Understanding How the WinHelp95 Engine Works

The WinHelp95 engine is used by all applications to display the contents of help files. Winhlp32.exe contains a function, WinHelp(), whose arguments determine the name of the help file to use and the topic to display. WinHelp files are a special type of file, with the extension .hlp, designed for use with the WinHelp95 engine.

WinHelp files are created from .rtf files that use special codes, embedded as footnote markers, to create indexes to topics. These indexes then are used by `WinHelp()` to locate the topics in the file, find keyword search entries, enable the user to browse topics in sequence, and create a history of the help screens viewed by the user. Special formatting within the body of the .rtf file creates hotspots that, when clicked, cause a jump to the specified topic.

The techniques for creating help files that use WinHelp features are explained in this chapter. However, first you need to understand the features of the WinHelp95 engine and how links between help topics are created. These subjects are included in the two sections that follow.

Using the Features of the WinHelp Engine

Creating help files for Windows applications is a more complex process than writing application documentation. You need to create an .rtf file with special topic, browsing, and keyword entries; create a *project file* (.hpj, sometimes called a *make file*); edit the project file, if necessary; and then compile your .rtf files to *AppName*.hlp with the Windows 95 help compiler.

WinHelp95 enables you to illustrate your help files with bitmaps and Windows metafiles, add video, music, or sound to the help windows, and format your text in any TrueType typeface and font available on the user's computer. This chapter shows you how to create WinHelp files that use the following methods to display Help windows explaining specific topics:

- *Context strings* enable you to use *hotspots* to display a window identified by the context string. Hotspots add hypertext-like capabilities to your application's Help system. (Hypertext is explained in the next section, "Understanding Hypertext Links in Help Files.") Context strings are names that identify a particular help window. When the user clicks a green hotspot with which a context string is associated, a new help window identified by the context string appears. You can choose between conventional non-modal windows for help text and graphics and modal popup windows that usually provide definitions of terms.

- *Keywords* assigned to a topic enable the user to use the Index page to search the WinHelp file for other topics that include the same word in a keyword list of the Topics Found dialog. A list box of all topics identified with the chosen keyword enables the user, rather than the WinHelp file, to make the navigation decisions.

- *Content entries* in the separate *AppName*.cnt file establish the items in the Contents page and determine their level in the hierarchy.

- *Browse-sequence numbers* establish the sequence in which windows for topics appear when the user clicks the << and >> buttons of the Help window. Browse buttons are not a standard WinHelp95 feature; you use the BrowseButton macro to add browse buttons to your help windows.

■ *Context-sensitive help* uses context ID numbers coupled to the context strings associated with individual topics. You can specify the WinHelp file to be used for a form or report by assigning the file name to the Help File property of a form or report or a control object on a form or report. Then you assign the context ID value to the Help Context ID property of a control object. You select the control to give it the focus, press the F1 key, and the Help window with the designated topic appears. Alternatively, you use the What's This? button to open the help topic for the object.

Context strings, keywords, content entries, browse-sequence numbers, and context ID numbers are placed in footnotes in the help text files. The help compiler uses the footnote text to create the indexes needed to make the WinHelp file operable.

Understanding Hypertext Links in Help Files

Hypertext was invented to make related items in complex documents easily accessible. A table of contents presents the topics of a book in an orderly, linear form, telling you where to find topics from the front to the back of the book. Hypertext works differently. Hypertext links are nonlinear and are similar to the non-clustered indexes for database tables described in Chapter 23, "Exploring Relational Database Design and Implementation."

Hypertext links, also called *jumps*, save you the trouble of looking up a topic in the index and turning to the appropriate pages. The green hotspots of the Access help windows are hypertext links to other related topics. These related topics have hotspots that link to even more related topics. Glossary-type hotspots provide jumps to definitions of unfamiliar terms in a popup window.

Planning Help Files for Your Applications

Creating a help file is much like writing a book. You determine your intended audience, develop a master outline of the parts of the Help system, and then fill in the lower outline levels of each part with the topic titles covering each aspect of your application. This process creates the hierarchy of your help file. Finally, you add the text for each topic, written to accommodate the user's level of familiarity with computers in general, the operating system in use, and similar applications.

With the advent of the CD-ROM, you can expect help files to grow to encyclopedic length. Microsoft's Multimedia Works and Lotus's SmartHelp for Lotus 1-2-3 for Windows were early examples of this trend—the help files are contained in CD-ROM tracks and consist of 500M to 600M of text and images. Help files and multimedia computer-based training (CBT) files have much in common.

Note

Stand-alone Microsoft multimedia applications (Multimedia Viewer 2.0), multimedia display tools (Media View 1.3+), and publishing tools for The Microsoft Network (code-named Blackbird when

---

this edition was written) use .rtf source files with embedded formatting commands similar to those used to create help files. Learning to create WinHelp files is very valuable if you intend to author files for Viewer 2.0 or other Microsoft interactive media tools.

The help file and your application's operating manual usually cover much of the same material. A good help file can reduce by more than half the time needed to prepare printed documentation. You can use standardized help files for various, related applications because WinHelp can find topics in any file that you include in your final help file list.

Build your help file as you develop the Access application. One of the advantages of this approach is that you can evaluate the application's ease of use. If you can explain a step clearly in a paragraph or two of a help file, the user probably will understand what you intend; otherwise, consider altering the application to clarify the actions required of the user.

Simultaneous creation of help files also aids in eliminating the omission of important topics. The topic that you forget to include in your WinHelp file is always the one that users don't understand. Another benefit is the help file's capability to document your application as you proceed with its development. When you return to writing code after your vacation, use the help file to refresh your recollection of what the application was intended to accomplish and to remind you of where you were when you left.

Aiming at the User's Level of Expertise

You should direct the structure and contents of your help file to the experience level of your audience: not only with computers in general and Windows in particular, but also with applications that are similar to the one you are creating. If you are developing a database front end for your firm, for example, your users may be experienced data-entry persons or management colleagues who are familiar with the terminology of your industry and the content of your databases. But what happens when a temporary replaces your vacationing data-entry person, and you are in Teaneck training sales representatives?

Users can be classified within five basic groups with increasing levels of competence:

1. *Computing novice.* A person who has never used a personal computer or who is making the transition from the use of a mainframe terminal to a self-contained or networked PC. Special applications often are written for trainees or employees in transition from one job classification to another.

2. *Windows novice.* An individual who is familiar with DOS or uses an Apple Macintosh, but is new to the Windows GUI. Your help file should include details on the effective use of the mouse and keyboard shortcuts. A glossary of Windows terminology is a definite requirement, and diagrams for menu choices are helpful. Simple diagrams created with Visio 4.0 usually suffice, but you can use CorelDRAW! 6.0 or other illustration packages to give your help files "glitz."

VIII

Completing an App

3. *Application novice.* One who is experienced with Windows but not with the type of application you are creating. An example is a word processing operator assigned to use your database front end. You may not need to include information on how to use the keyboard and mouse for these users.

4. *Application-familiar user.* A person who is familiar with Windows and the type of application you are developing. Such a person may be a data entry operator who regularly uses the database features of a Windows spreadsheet application, or an executive who has used applications developed with a client/server front end for Windows. The help file need only explain those elements of the application that are not intuitive or that differ from commercial implementations of similar applications. You may be able to dispense with printed documentation for application-familiar users.

5. *Power user.* A person who does not read the documentation or use your help file. Power users believe no application has ever left the beta stage. They find warts (anomalies) and bugs in version 7.6 of your application.

The first four classifications require distinctly different contents in their help files. One way of accomplishing this differentiation is to create a different help file for each user level and supply the appropriate file or include a dialog to select the appropriate help file at startup. An alternative is to create a single help file and change the topic name of the entry point in the file for each subject at different skill levels. You can create a browse sequence to enable the user to obtain information about the subject at a higher or lower level of detail.

Examining the Standard Structure of Help Topics

Most help files are arranged in a structure corresponding to the basic subject matter covered by the application and include assistance to users in the translation of menu commands. The structure of a typical help file for a full-scale Access application appears in figure 32.4. Solid lines show the topic selection paths in a linear, hierarchical structure suitable for display in the Contents page. Topic windows comprise the lowest level of the hierarchy. Gray lines show nonlinear, hypertext links.

In this example, the Commands book and Procedures book are first-level books that lead to second-level books that provide quick access to a specific topic. Individual topics in different categories, however, may be related, so they are joined by gray lines in figure 32.4. The dashed lines do not follow the usual top-to-bottom sequence in a category of related topics. You can provide hotspots or use Chiclet buttons to create cross-category jumps or use common keywords that give the user quick access to a related topic in another category.

If you plan to create a number of related applications, you may want to create individual help files for each category or for a particular category that is the same for all the applications. As an example, if you are writing a number of database front ends for your firm, the glossary portion of the help file may be the same for all applications. You therefore can create the glossary as a separate .rtf file and then compile it with other .rtf files written specifically for the particular applications. The project file for the help compiler can include as many .rtf help files as you want to include in the compiled WinHelp .hlp file.

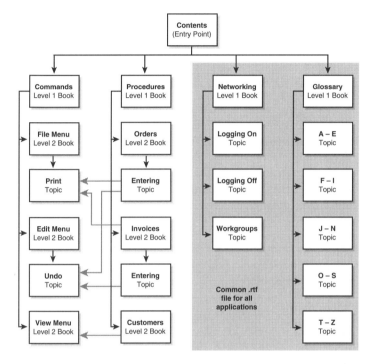

Fig. 32.4 A sample help file structure for an order entry and billing application.

Creating the Text for Help Files

As mentioned at the beginning of this chapter, you must create Windows help files in a word processing application that exports .rtf files and is capable of creating hidden text. Alternatively, you can manually add the required .RTF control words and symbols to unformatted text with a conventional text editor such as Windows WordPad, but this process is extremely laborious. Microsoft Word 2.0, 6.0 and 7.0, Lotus Word Pro, and WordPerfect for Windows provide .rtf file export capability.

The following paragraphs take a look at the Rich Text Format needed for help files and familiarize you with many of the common codes used in a help file. Then you learn how to create help files by using a commercial help authoring system.

Taking a Brief Look at the Rich Text Format

Rich Text Format is a Microsoft Corporation standard for interprocess communication (IPC) transfer of formatted text and graphics. RTF is a valid Windows Clipboard format for many applications. You can use .rtf files for IPC transfers between Windows applications and DOS, OS/2, or Apple Macintosh applications created by Microsoft and many other software publishers.

An .rtf file consists of control words, symbols, and groups combined with unformatted text in ANSI (Windows), PC-8 (used by Hewlett-Packard laser printers), Macintosh, or IBM PC character sets. An .rtf file of the first two sentences of the preceding paragraph (less most of the header section added by Word for Windows) appears as

```
\paperw12240\paperh31680\margl1800\margr1800\margt1440
\margb1440\gutter0\deftab360\widowctrl\ftnbj{\*\templa
te F:\\WINWORD2\\QUE_BOOK.DOT}\sectd \linex0\endnhere
\pard\plain \qj\fi504\sa120\keep \f4\fs21\lang1033
Rich Text Format is a Microsoft Corporation standard
for interprocess communication (IPC) transfer of formatted
text and graphics. RTF is a valid Windows Clipboard format
for many applications.\par
```

A backslash character precedes RTF control words and symbols, which are used to indicate text formatting. Double backslashes are used to include a backslash in the text. Documentation for the full command set of Microsoft RTF is difficult to obtain, and new commands frequently are added to RTF in order to accommodate multimedia publishing requirements. Fortunately, you do not need a full understanding of RTF syntax to write Windows help files.

Examining the Basic Elements of Help Files

Windows help files consist of a combination of formatted text, double-underlined hotspots that specify hypertext jumps, single-underlined hotspots for popup windows, footnote symbols and text, and hidden text. Footnote symbols serve as codes to tell Hcrtf.exe how to use the information included in the footnotes and hidden text. Context strings (hidden text used to identify hotspots), footnote symbols, and footnote text do not appear in the help window viewed by the user. Table 32.1 lists the most common footnote codes.

Table 32.1 Common Footnote Codes Used in RTF Help Documents

Help Element	Footnote Code	Description
Context string	#	Identifies each topic in a help file. Context strings are optional and are used by WinHelp to find a specific topic when the user initiates a jump to it.
Topic title	$	Displays topics in the dialogs for the Search and History buttons, as well as those topics marked by using the Bookmark choice of the drop-down Option button menu.
Keyword	K	Provides entries for lists that appear in the Index page, enabling the user to jump to any topic that contains the keyword. (Also called Klinks.)
Associative keyword	A	Keywords that don't appear in Index page but enable jumps to a specified topic. (New for Windows 95 help; also called Alinks.)
Browse sequence	+	Displays groups of topics in a predetermined sequence. These topics are accessed in sequence by the optional << and >> buttons. If you don't use browse buttons, you don't need browse sequence entries.

Each of the commonly used RTF codes for WinHelp files is described in table 32.2. Lowercase codes shown in bold type are RTF formatting instructions (\v stands for hidden text, for example).

Table 32.2 Common RTF Codes Used in Help Documents		
Help Element	**RTF Code**	**Description**
Jump	**uldb** *JumpText* **v** *TopicName*	Links related topics in a manner similar to hypertext. When the user clicks a coded word or bitmap, *JumpText*, WinHelp moves to *TopicName*. You identify a jump by double-underlining the text.
Popup window	**ul** *JumpText* **v** *TopicName*	Displays the text topic identified by *TopicName* in a modal dialog when the user clicks a single-under lined hotspot, *JumpText*, in the help file.
16-color bitmap reference	bmc *Picture.ext*	Inserts a 16-color bitmap (.bmp or .dib) or metafile (.wmf) image, *Picture.ext*, into a help file. Images are positioned as if they were characters or may be formatted with optional parameters. You also may copy a bitmap to the Clipboard with CopyBmp if the bitmap is identified as a hot spot. (If you are using Microsoft Word, you can simply use Insert, Picture to insert the bitmap in the text.)
Nonscrolling region	\keepn	Keeps a region containing text immediately below the menubar from scrolling with the balance of the text when the scroll bar is used.
Nonwrapping text	\keep	(Keep with next formatting.) Prevents an area of the screen from wrapping if the user reduces the width of the help window. This option is frequently used with tabular information.
Embedded window	ew...	Enables the display of bitmaps or animation sequences and can play sound files. (The ew... instruction is replaced by WinHelp95's {mci Filename.ext} instruction for playing .avi, .wav, and .mid files).

Depending on the Windows word processing program (and its version) that you use, the program usually inserts most or all of the preceding codes when you save a file in .rtf format. You can use many other codes in addition to those shown in tables 32.1 and 32.2 when authoring WinHelp files, but the use of special-purpose codes is beyond the scope of this book. The documentation accompanying the help compiler or commercial help authoring packages explains the use of special-purpose codes not listed here.

Using Commercial Help Authoring Systems to Create Help Files

You can speed up the process of creating help files by using a commercial help authoring system. One example is RoboHELP 3.0, which is offered by Blue Sky Software Corporation of La Jolla, California. Specifically designed for use with Word for Windows 6.0, RoboHELP uses a sophisticated template, ROBOHELP.DOT, and includes the additional files required to automate the process of creating help files. In the following sections, you learn how to use these templates to help you create your help files.

VIII

Completing an App

Using RoboHELP 3.0 to Create a Help Document

The main advantage of using a commercial help authoring system is that you can create WinHelp files quickly. RoboHELP also does most of the housekeeping for you, such as adding footnotes and assigning help context strings, which can save more than 50 percent of the time needed to create a help file. When you finish your help file, you can compile the file for use with Windows 3.1+. You also can use RoboHELP's Moving to WinHelp '95 porting tool to create the associated content (.cnt) file and compile the help file for use with the WinHelp95 help engine.

To create an example help file after installing RoboHELP 3.0 under Windows 95, follow these steps:

1. Choose Start, Programs, RoboHELP, and double-click Here to Begin to open RoboHELP's opening dialog. Click the New Project button to launch Word 6.0 with the RoboHELP enhancements active. RoboHELP's Create New Help Project dialog appears.

2. Enter the title of your help file and the name of your help project file (*APPNAME*.HPJ) in the Title and File Name text boxes, respectively. Select the drive and folder to contain your help files, in this case, \Msoffice\Access\Samples. Select Access from the Development Environment drop-down list, and accept Windows 3.1 as the Help Version and HCP.EXE, the Windows 3.1+ protected-mode help compiler, as the Compiler. The Browse Buttons is marked by default. Mark the Glossary Topic check box to automatically create a Glossary topic (see fig. 32.5).

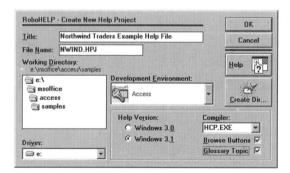

Fig. 32.5   RoboHELP 3.0's Create New Help Project dialog lets you name the help file, select your operating environment, and select other options.

3. Click OK to close the Create New Help Project dialog. RoboHELP creates NWIND.DOC and NWIND.HPJ for you. RoboHELP automatically inserts the Contents topic for Windows 3.1 help when you start a new help file and, if you specify a Glossary topic, creates the Glossary topic for you (see fig. 32.6).

   By default, RoboHELP adds a floating toolbar to Word. You can change the floating toolbar to a custom Word toolbar, shown docked at the bottom of figure 32.6, by choosing View, Toolbars, then marking the RoboHELP item in the list of the Toolbars dialog.

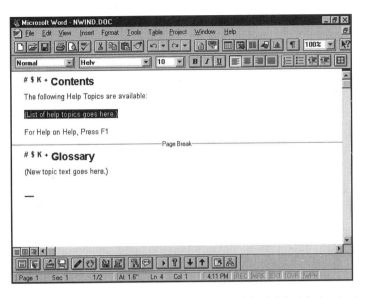

Fig. 32.6   When you create a new project, RoboHELP opens Word 6.0 with the Contents and Glossary topics.

4. Place the caret on the Page Break line and click RoboHELP's Create Topic button or press Ctrl+T to add a topic. RoboHELP displays an Insert New Help Topic dialog.

5. Enter the topic title, such as **Menu Commands**, in the Help Topic Title text box. RoboHELP automatically adds the same title to the Search Key Word(s) text box. You can add more search words if you prefer; separate each word from the preceding word with a semicolon (see fig. 32.7). Search words appear in the list of the Index page of the Help Topics dialog.

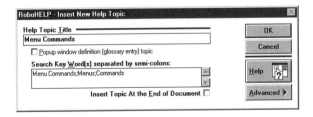

Fig. 32.7   RoboHELP's dialog for adding a new help topic.

6. Click OK to add the new topic to your help document. RoboHELP simultaneously adds the footnotes for the context string (#), topic title ($), keywords (K), and browse sequence (NWIND:0). Figure 32.8 shows the default body text and footnote entries for the added Menu Commands topic.

VIII

Completing an App

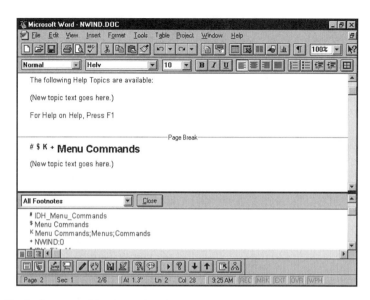

Fig. 32.8   The body text and footnotes for the new Menu Commands topic.

It is a good practice to add the IDH prefix to the context string because the Windows 95 help compiler automatically tests topics with this prefix for context ID mapping, a subject covered in the "Adding Context-Sensitive Help to Your Access Application" section, later in the chapter. Choose Tools, RoboHELP Options to open the RoboHELP Options dialog, mark the Prefix Context Strings check box, and type **IDH_** in the text box.

7. Add additional topics that constitute the first and second levels of help books plus the help topic pages.

> **Note**
>
> As a rule, you don't add the text for help topics until you create at least the basic structure of your help document and test its navigation features. RoboHELP and other commercial help authoring tools, such as the Doc-To-Help application by Wextech, Inc., can import and automatically convert the manuscript for product documentation to help files.

Adding Hotspot Jumps to the Help Document

Adding help topics is similar to creating the outline for a book, but there is no inherent hierarchy when you add topics to a help document. Windows 3.1 help uses hotspot jumps to create a hierarchy; WinHelp95 relies on the .cnt file to establish the topic hierarchy. This section describes how to create hotspot jumps to establish the topic hierarchy for Windows 3.1 help files, which is important if you are creating Access 95 applications for use with Windows NT 3.1+ because Windows NT 3.1+ uses a help engine based on that of Windows 3.1+. Follow these steps to create the hotspot jumps to establish the help file hierarchy:

1. Position the caret on the line in the Contents page where you want to create the hotspot for the new topic (Menu Commands, in this example). Click the Create Jump Hotspot button on the RoboHELP toolbar to create a hypertext link between the hotspot and the topic. The Create Hypertext Jump to Help Topic dialog appears.

2. Select the context string (IDH_Menu_Commands, in this example) from the Choose Help Topic list box. The help topic title automatically appears in the Hotspot Text text box. Your Create Hypertext Jump to Help Topic dialog is shown in figure 32.9.

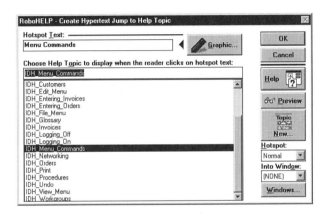

Fig. 32.9   The Create Hypertext Jump to Help Topic dialog.

3. Click the OK button to add the jump hotspot. The double-underlined green text appears as single-underlined green text in the help window. The context string for the jump is formatted as hidden text. You add explanatory text after the context string.

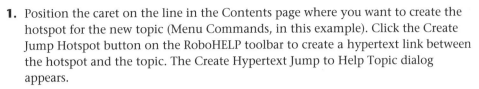

4. Repeat step 2 for the IDH_Procedures and IDH_Networking topics. You don't need to add IDH_Glossary because you specified a Glossary topic and its associated help button when you started the help project. Your three hotspot jumps for the Contents pages appear, as shown in figure 32.10. (Explanatory text has been added to the hotspot text.).

5. Add the hotspot jumps to help topics at the second and third levels of the hierarchy.

6. When you have created the basic structure of your Help system, click the Save as Rich Text button on the RoboHELP toolbar to save Nwind.doc as Nwind.rtf. RoboHELP checks the syntax of your entries before creating the .rtf file.

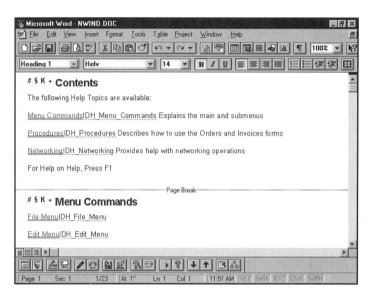

Fig. 32.10   The three hotspot jumps for the first level and two of the jumps for the second level of the help topic hierarchy.

Compiling and Displaying Your Skeleton Help File

RoboHELP has created Nwind.rtf, the file that serves as the source code for your Nwind.hlp file. To use the Windows 3.1 help compiler, HCP.EXE, to compile Nwind.rtf to Nwind.hlp and display the help file, follow these steps:

1. Click the Make Help Project button on the RoboHELP toolbar to open the Make Project dialog (see fig. 32.11).

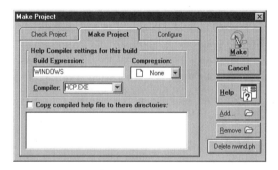

Fig. 32.11   RoboHELP's Make Project dialog.

2. Click the Make button to compile your Nwind.rtf file. The Make Help Project into Help File dialog appears, and messages from HCP.EXE are added to the list box as compilation proceeds (see fig. 32.12).

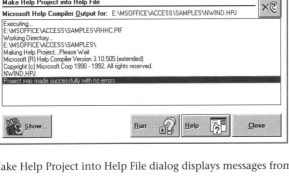

Fig. 32.12 The Make Help Project into Help File dialog displays messages from the help compiler.

3. Click the Run button. Your new Windows 3.1+ WinHelp file appears. Figure 32.13 shows the help window created from the sample structure given in figure 32.4.

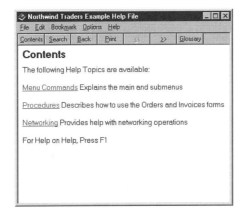

Fig. 32.13 A help window created with the aid of RoboHELP.

From the Contents topic, you can click the green Menu Commands hotspot to display the topic. To verify the help file navigation features, click another topic, such as File Menu, that you entered at lower levels in the hierarchy. The keyword entries you created as *K* footnotes appear on the Index page when you click the Search button. Figure 32.14 shows the result of double-clicking the Commands index entry with "Commands" added as a keyword to all of the topics in the Menu Commands hierarchy.

When you click the Find tab, the Find Setup Wizard offers you options for creating the full-text search (Nwind.fts) file for your help file. After the Find Setup Wizard completes the indexing task, your Find page appears, as shown in figure 32.15.

Index

Find

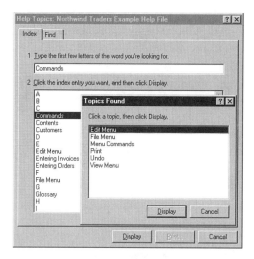

Fig. 32.14 The Topics Found dialog appears when more than one topic is indexed with the selected keyword.

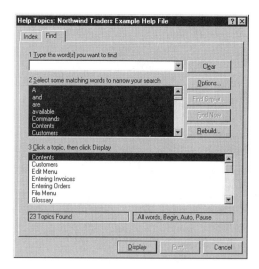

Fig. 32.15 The Find page of the Help Topics dialog adds full-text search capability to your help file.

Porting Your Windows 3.1 Help Files to WinHelp95

Blue Sky Software's Moving to WinHelp '95 application is a stand-alone porting tool to convert Windows 3.1+ help files to Windows 95. Moving to WinHelp '95 is included in Blue Sky's WinHelp Office product or you can purchase it as a separate product. You can use Moving to WinHelp '95 with help documents and project files created by other help authoring tools, such as Doc-To-Help. You must have the WinHelp95 help compiler (Hcrtf.exe and Hcw.exe) to use early releases of Moving to WinHelp '95.

> **Caution**
>
> When you run the porting tool to compile your help file in WinHelp32 format, your existing project (Nwind.hpj) and help (Nwind.hlp) files are overwritten. If you intend to maintain two versions of your help file, rename your existing Windows 3.1+ project and help files to prevent overwriting after the porting process. Using Moving to WinHelp '95 does not alter your help document files (Nwind.doc and Nwind.rtf).

You substitute books for topics that contain only jumps to other topics and add lowest-level topics as pages of books. To add a content (.cnt) file and convert your Nwind.rtf file to WinHelp95 format with Moving to WinHelp '95, follow these steps:

1. Close Word 6.0 and save the changes to your Nwind.doc file.

2. Launch Moving to WinHelp '95, choose <u>F</u>ile, <u>O</u>pen, and open your .prj file (in this case, Nwind.hpj). A list of context strings included in Nwind.rtf appears in the Topics list box.

3. Click the Add Book button to open the New Book dialog. Type the name of a level 1 topic, Menu Commands in this case, in the Book Name text box (see fig. 32.16). Alternatively, mark the Show by Title check box and select the topic name in the Topics list; then, click the Add Book button to add the topic title automatically. Click OK to add the new book and close the dialog.

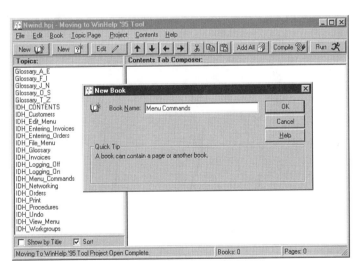

Fig. 32.16 Adding a new book to the contents file.

4. Repeat step 2 for each of the level 1 and 2 help topics that contain only jumps to other topics. Select the book in the Contents Tab Composer window and use the arrow buttons to establish the topic sequence and to make "subbooks" from level 2 books. You also can use drag-and-drop methods to create the proper hierarchy.

5. Select a book that contains lowest-level topics, then select the topic name in the Topics list.

6. Click the Add Page button to open the New Topic Page dialog. The selected topic name appears in the Topic Page Name text box (see fig. 32.17).

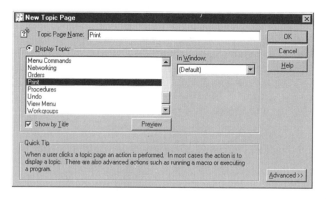

Fig. 32.17   Adding an existing topic page to the contents file.

7. Repeat step 5 for each of the lowest-level topic pages. When you're finished, the Moving to WinHelp '95 Tool window appears, as shown in figure 32.18.

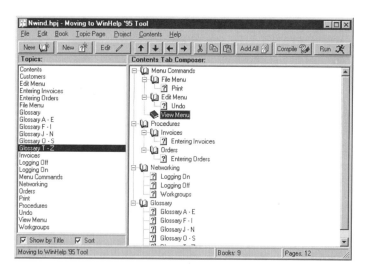

Fig. 32.18   The Moving to WinHelp '95 Tool window after entering books and pages.

8. Click the Compile Help System button to compile Nwind.rtf and create the Nwind.cnt file. The Help Workshop window appears briefly during the process.

9. When the compilation completes, click the Run Help System button to display your WinHelp95 Help Topics Contents page (see fig. 32.19).

Fig. 32.19 The Help Topics Contents page of the WinHelp95 file created with Moving to WinHelp '95.

Creating WinHelp95 help files with version 3.0 of RoboHELP and Moving to WinHelp '95 is a two-step process. Future versions of RoboHELP are likely to provide a one-step process for creating Windows 95 help files. Many developers require Windows 3.1+/ Windows NT and Windows 95 help files, so the two-step process is not detrimental.

Adding Illustrations to Your Help Files

◄◄ See "Creating a New Logo for Your Personnel Actions Form," p. 739

RoboHELP 3.0 includes graphics features that let you add bitmap or vector graphics to your help topics. To add the Nwind.bmp bitmap file that you created from the Switchboard form of Northwind.mdb in Chapter 20, "Adding Graphics to Forms and Reports," follow these steps:

1. Launch RoboHELP 3.0 and open your Nwind.hpj project.

2. In one of the lowest-level topics, such as Print, delete the "(New topic text goes here.)" text.

3. Click the Graphic button to open the Insert Graphics Object dialog. The Graphics combo list displays all graphics files in your default folder (see fig. 32.20).

4. If the graphics file you want isn't in the default folder for Nwind.hpj, click the Files button and locate the graphics file to insert: Nwind.bmp in this case.

5. Clicking the Left, Character, or Right button inserts the graphic file at the left margin, insertion point, or right margin, respectively. Click the Right button to insert the reference to the bitmap file and close the dialog.

6. RoboHELP inserts a {bmr NWIND.BMP} macro instruction into the help document.

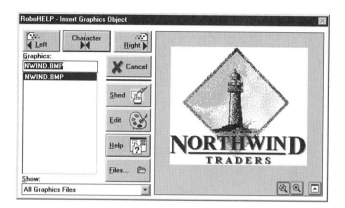

Fig. 32.20 RoboHELP's Insert Graphics Object dialog lists all graphics files in your default help project folder.

7. Click the Save as Rich Text and then Make Help Project buttons to compile your project as a Windows 3.1+ help file. You can safely ignore warnings received from the help compiler as a result of changes made to your Nwind.hpj file by porting with Moving to WinHelp '95.

8. Click the Run button to display your help file. Porting your help file to WinHelp95 created Nwind.cnt, so the Contents page appears in the Windows 3.1+ version of your help file. Click the topic page into which you inserted the bitmap image. Your help topic window appears, as shown in figure 32.21.

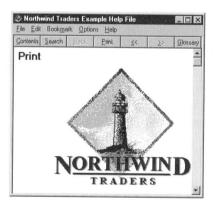

Fig. 32.21 A bitmapped graphic inserted by RoboHELP into a help topic with the {bmr *filename*.bmp} macro.

Using Hypergraphics Hotspots and Displaying Popup Windows

You can add hotspots to bitmap (.bmp) images that create jumps to particular topics. Bitmap files with hotspots are called *hypergraphic* files and use the .shg extension. Popup windows are useful for displaying glossary entries. Text jumps to popup windows appear in green with a dotted underscore. This section describes how to use RoboHELP 3.0 to change the bitmap you added in the prior topic to a hypergraphic. The hotspot of the hypergraphic opens a popup window.

To add the popup window topic and create a hypergraphic that jumps to the popup window, follow these steps:

1. Click the Create Topic button on the RoboHELP toolbar to display the Insert New Help Topic dialog.

2. Mark the Popup Window Definition and Insert Topic At the End of Document check boxes. Type **About Northwind Traders** in the Help Topic Title text box (see fig. 32.22). Click the OK button to create the new popup window.

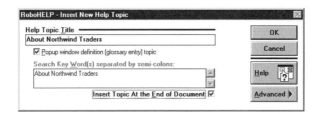

Fig. 32.22 Adding a popup help window topic to the end of your help document.

3. After RoboHELP creates the popup window topic, replace the (New topic text goes here.) entry with your own description of Northwind Traders.

4. Move to the topic with the bitmap macro and position the caret on the line of your help document with the {bmr Nwind.bmp} entry, and click the Graphics button to display the bitmap in the Insert Graphic Object dialog.

5. Click the Shed button to display the hypergraphics Hotspot Editor (Shed) with Nwind.bmp file loaded. If Nwind.bmp isn't loaded, choose File, Open and load the bitmap.

6. Position the mouse pointer at the upper-left corner of the hotspot area of the graphic. Hold the left mouse button down and drag a rectangle to define the hotspot area, then release the mouse button (see fig. 32.23).

7. Choose Edit, Attributes from Shed's menu to open the Enhanced Hotspot Attributes dialog. Select Popup from the Type drop-down list, then click the Choose button to display the list of context strings in your help document.

8. Select the context string for your popup window, IDH_About_Northwind_Traders in this case (see fig. 32.24). Click the OK button to assign the context string to the graphic hotspot.

9. Choose File, Save As in Shed and save your hypergraphic as **Nwind.shg** in the current folder. Click OK to close the Enhanced Hotspot Attributes dialog and close Shed.

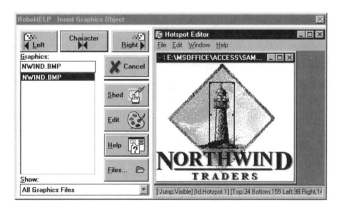

Fig. 32.23 The Hotspot Editor (Shed) lets you define one or more hotspots in a graphic.

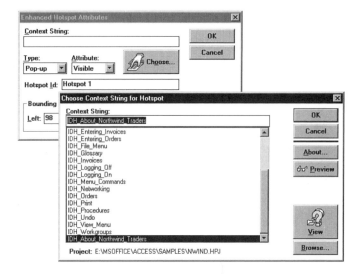

Fig. 32.24 Selecting the context string for the popup window to appear when you click the graphic hotspot.

10. Click Cancel to close the Insert Graphics Object dialog because you already have a macro for the graphic.

11. Change the bitmap macro to specify NWIND.SHG as the bitmap source. Save your Nwind.doc help document, then click the Save As Rich Text button to save the modified Nwind.rtf file.

12. Click the Make Help File button to create the Windows 3.1+ version of Nwind.hlp, then click the Run button to open the help file.

13. When you open the help topic that contains the bitmap, a dashed line surrounds the hotspot you added. Click within the hotspot to open the popup window (see fig. 32.25).

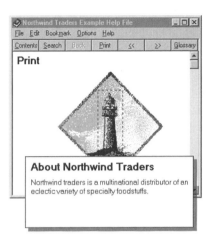

Fig. 32.25 The hotspot and popup window in a Windows 3.1+ help file.

The appearance and behavior of popup windows in WinHelp95 help files is identical to that of the Windows 3.1+ version. You can verify this statement by recompiling the help file with Moving to WinHelp '95.

Adding Context-Sensitive Help to Your Access Application

Applications, such as Access 95 and Visual Basic 4.0, that enable you to add context-sensitive help with Help File and Context ID properties of forms and controls require that you add a [MAP] section to your project file. This procedure enables you to assign a context ID number to each of the help windows that you want to associate with an object in the application you create.

The sections that follow describe how to add entries to the [MAP] section of a help project file and how to assign values to the Help File and Context ID properties of Access forms, reports, and control objects. These sections demonstrate the use of the Microsoft Help Workshop to create WinHelp95 help files from existing .rtf and .hpj files. As mentioned earlier in the chapter, the Help Workshop is included with Blue Sky Software's Moving to WinHelp '95 and the Access Developer's Toolkit (ADT).

Adding a [MAP] Section for Context ID Numbers

Help context IDs are entries in the [MAP] section of your help project file that contain integers associated with context strings. The numbers that correspond to context strings can be arbitrary, but following a regular pattern is a good practice. As an example, the .rtf file used as a demonstration in the preceding sections has a Contents topic (book) and four categories of first-level help topics (books), as shown in table 32.3. You assign the Contents topic a low value, such as 1 or 10. You give first-level help categories numbers such as 100 or 1000 so that you can assign numbers such as 110 to topics belonging to the 100 category. Using even hundreds to identify categories enables you to establish a four-level hierarchy: contents (index), category, subcategory, and topic.

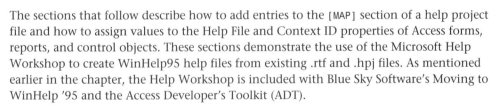

Four levels is usually sufficient for even the most complex application. Adding a help context ID number to the Contents topic lets you set the Contents window as the context when there is no help window applicable to the object you select in Access.

> **Note**
>
> If you're creating a help file for use under Windows 95 only, you usually don't need to assign help context ID numbers to context strings that correspond to first-level books. To make your help file compatible with Windows 3.1+ and NT, however, it is a good practice to assign help context ID values to all topics in your help document.

Using a help file-tracking database can assist in preventing duplication of context ID numbers if you assign the Context ID field as the primary key or create a No Duplicates index on the Context ID field.

Table 32.3 Sample Context ID Numbers Assigned to Context Strings

Category Context String	Context ID	Topic Context String	Context ID
IDH_Contents	10		
IDH_Menu_Commands	100		
IDH_File	110	IDH_New	111
		IDH_Open	113
		IDH_Close	115
		IDH_Print	117
		IDH_Exit	119
IDH_Edit	120	IDH_Undo	121
IDH_Procedures	200	IDH_Orders	211_219
		IDH_Invoices	221_229
		IDH_Customers	231_239
IDH_Network	300	IDH_Logon	311
		IDH_Logoff	321
		IDH_Workgroups	331

After you determine the context ID values for each of your help windows, you add the [MAP] section to your help project file, if necessary, and then add the context ID strings, an equal sign (you also can use a space or tab character as a separator), and the corresponding context ID value, as in the following example:

```
[MAP]
IDH_Contents=10
IDH_Menu_Commands=100
IDH_Procedures=200
IDH_Network=300
```

You can add the lines to complete the context ID assignment for help topic windows under the category entries or in groups that follow the category assignments; the entries do not need to be in numerical sequence. Although you can use Notepad (WordPad in Windows 95) or any other text editor to add the help context ID entries, the recommended method is to use the Help Workshop to add entries to project files.

Follow these steps to add the help context ID values to your Nwind.hpj help project file:

1. Launch Hcw.exe, choose File, Open, and open your Nwind.hpj file in the Microsoft Help Workshop. Figure 32.26 shows the Nwind.hpj file created by RoboHELP 3.0 in the preceding examples. Lines of text preceded by a semicolon (;) are comments and are disregarded by the help compiler.

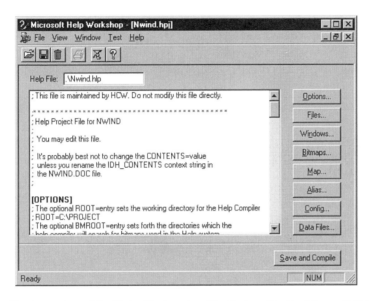

Fig. 32.26   The beginning of the Nwind.hpj project file displayed in the Microsoft Help Workshop window.

2. Click the Map button to open the Map dialog, and delete the IDHxxx entry in the Instead of IDH, Check These Prefixes text box.

3. Click the Add button to open the Add Map Entry dialog. Enter the context string in the Topic ID text box and the context ID value in the Mapped Numeric Value text box (see fig. 32.27). Click OK to close the dialog and add the entry to the list box of the Map dialog.

4. Repeat step 3 for each of the topics that require a context ID value. The About Northwind Traders and Glossary topics don't need a context ID. Help Workshop adds your context ID entries in alphabetical order.

5. When you've added all of the context IDs, click OK to close the Map dialog. Your [Map] section entries are shown in figure 32.28. (RoboHELP's comments have been deleted in figure 32.28).

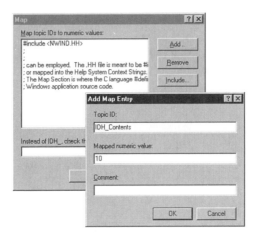

Fig. 32.27   You enter the context string and the context ID for context-sensitive topics in the Add Map Entry dialog.

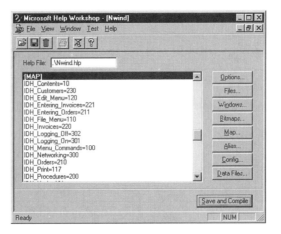

Fig. 32.28   The completed [Map] section of the Nwind.hpj project file.

6. Click the Save and Compile button to save your Nwind.hpj file and compile the Nwind.rtf file. If you typed all of the context strings correctly, a message such as that shown in figure 32.29 appears. Errors are reported so that you can easily find incorrect entries in the map section and edit the entries with the Map dialog's Edit Map Entry dialog.

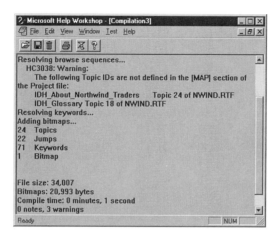

Fig. 32.29   This typical help compiler message appears when your context string entries are correct.

Linking Help Topics to Your Access Application

You can create links to context-sensitive help for your Access applications, similar to that used by Access's own Help system, by using one of two methods:

■ You can use the Help File property of a form or report to designate the WinHelp95 file that is to be used. You then assign the context ID number as the value of the Context ID property of a form, report, or control to display a specific help window when the user selects the control and presses F1 for help or clicks the What's This and selects the object.

■ You can use the WinHelp() function of the WinHelp95 engine in Access VBA procedures and functions. The Access VBA code you use to declare and then use WinHelp() is typical of the method for using any of the Win32 API functions and third-party Dynamic Link Libraries (.DLLs).

The following sections give you more details about these two procedures.

Assigning Help Files and Context IDs to Access Objects

You can specify a help file and a help context ID value to be used for a form or report plus each control object on the form. (Online help seldom is appropriate for controls of reports.) The capability to assign a specific help file to a form or report enables you to write smaller help files that load faster.

To assign a help file and a context ID number to a form and a control on a form, follow these steps:

1. Open Northwind.mdb's Orders form for this example, and click the Design View button.

2. Click the Properties icon of the toolbar to display the properties window. Choose Edit, Select Form to select the form as a whole, if necessary, rather than one of its sections.

3. Click the Other tab of the properties window. In the Help File text box of the Other properties window, type the name of your WinHelp file. For this example, type **Nwind.hlp**. If you have the Access 95 ADT, you can substitute the Sample.hlp file in \Msoffice\Access\ADT\Help Compiler. If you don't copy Sample.hlp to your \Msoffice\Access\Samples folder, make sure you include the full path to the file in the Help File text box.

4. In the Help Context Id text box, type the value of the context ID of the help topic that applies to the form as a whole. In the Nwind.hlp example, the value 211 is used for Entering Orders topic, so type **211** in the Help Context Id text box. Your properties window is shown in figure 32.30.

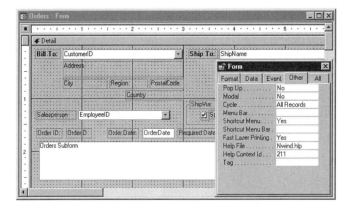

Fig. 32.30   The properties window when assigning a help file and context ID value for a form or report.

5. Select the CustomerID bound Combo Box and enter the context ID value for the help topic that applies to the control object in the Help Context Id text box, as shown in figure 32.31. The value assigned to the Customers topic is 230 in the Nwind.hpj file, so enter **230** in the Help Context Id text box. Properties dialogs for control objects do not have a Help File text box because the value of the Help File property applies to the form or report and all the control objects it contains.

6. Click the Form View button on the toolbar. The CustomerID Combo Box is selected when the Orders form loads. Press the F1 key, and the Customers topic appears in the Northwind Traders help window, as shown in figure 32.32.

7. Click the What's This button, drag the cursor to a blank area of the form, and click the mouse. The Entering Orders topic appears (see fig. 32.33).

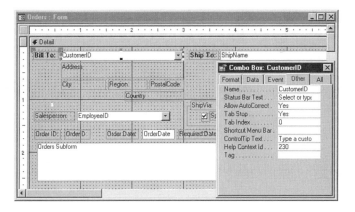

Fig. 32.31 The Combo Box properties window when you're assigning context ID value to a control object.

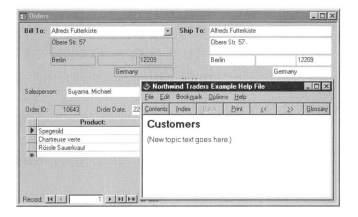

Fig. 32.32 The help topic selected by the context ID value of the CustomerID Combo Box.

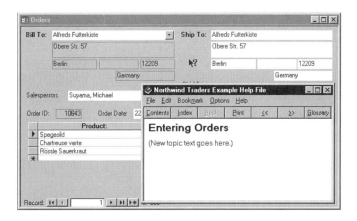

Fig. 32.33 The help topic selected by the context ID value of the form.

You can create help topics for each of the form's fields by assigning different Context ID property values to each text box or other control object on the form. Alternatively, you can assign to control objects a context ID value equal to that of the form so that all control objects on the form display the help topic assigned to the form. If you set the context ID value of the form to 0, Access displays its own help window when you press the F1 key. With the exception of control objects, the procedure described in the preceding steps also applies to reports.

Adding Calls to `WinHelp()` in Access VBA Code

Assigning help files to forms and reports and Help Context ID values to forms, reports, and control objects provides all the WinHelp capabilities you need for most applications. If you use Access VBA procedures that change how control objects behave, however, you may need to set the `HelpContextID` property value in your Access VBA procedures.

To control the action of the WinHelp32 engine with Access VBA code, you call the `WinHelp()` function when you need to change a help file name or context ID value. The syntax of the `WinHelp()` function is as follows:

```
lngHelpOK = WinHelp(hWnd, strHelpFile, lngCommand, lngData)
```

In the preceding syntax, lngHelpOK is a **Long** variable used to receive the return value of the `WinHelp()` function. The arguments of the `WinHelp()` function are explained in the following sections.

Declaring Windows Functions in Access VBA

◄◄ See "Data Types and Database Objects in Access VBA," p. 1004
▶▶ See "Naming Conventions for Access Objects and Variables," p. 1219

You call Windows functions in the same manner that you call Access VBA functions within Access VBA procedures. You need to inform Access VBA of your intention to use an external function, however, before using that function in your code. For this task, which is called *declaring a function prototype*, you use the **Declare** keyword. The syntax of the declaration statement for `WinHelp()`, copied from the WinHelp declaration entry in the API Viewer included with the ADT, follows:

```
Declare Function WinHelp Lib "user32" Alias "WinHelpA" _
    (ByVal hWnd As Long, _
     ByVal lpHelpFile As String, _
     ByVal wCommand As Long, _
     ByVal dwData As Long) As Long _
```

> **Note**
>
> The prefixes lp (long pointer, in this case to a **String**), w (word, **Integer**), and dw (**Long** integer) are prefixes commonly used in C programming. There is a conflict between the w prefix of wCommand and its data type, **Long**. wCommand is an **Integer** in the Win16 API.

The following list explains the statement's components:

- **Lib**. The name of the library that contains the function. WinHelp() is included in User32.exe.

- **Alias**. Win32 API functions that have string arguments come in two flavors: ANSI (suffix *A*) and Unicode (suffix *W* for wide). VBA uses the ANSI version of the function, which is aliased to WinHelp for backward compatibility with Win16 function calls.

- **ByVal**. A keyword that tells Access to transfer the data in the argument to the Windows function with a data type that is compatible with the C language in which Windows is written.

- hWnd. A Windows handle (code number, Long in Win32) to the window that is active when the function is called with the F1 key or by the What's This button.

- str*HelpFile*. The name of the help file, including the .hlp extension, assuming the help file is in the current folder, \Windows, or \Windows\System.

- lng*Command*. Table 32.4 lists and describes the common lng*Command* constant values for you.

- lng*Data*. An argument whose data type depends on the value of the lng*Command* argument you choose, so the lng*Data* argument is declared an **As Any** data type.

Table 32.4 WinHelp() lng*Command* **Constant Values and Their Actions**

lng*Command* Constant	Value	Description
HELP_CONTEXT	1	Causes a specific help topic, identified by a **Long** integer and specified as the lng*Data* argument, to be displayed.
HELP_QUIT	2	Notifies WinHelp() that the specified help file is no longer in use and can be closed. The lng*Data* argument is ignored.
HELP_INDEX	3	Displays the index of the specified help file, as designated by the author. The lng*Data* argument is ignored.
HELP_HELPONHELP	4	Displays help for using the WinHelp application itself. The lng*Data* argument is ignored.
HELP_SETINDEX	5	Sets the context number specified by the lng*Data* argument, a long integer, as the current index for the specified help file.
HELP_KEY	257	Displays the first corresponding topic found in a search for the keyword specified by the dw*Data* argument, in this case, As String (as a string variable).
HELP_MULTIKEY	513	Displays help for a keyword found in an alternate keyword table. The lng*Data* argument is a data structure containing the size of the string, the letter of the alternate table, and the keyword string.

Table 32.4 describes how the data type of the lng*Data* argument changes with the value of lng*Command*. The lng*Data* argument may be a **Long** integer, a **String**, or a user-defined data type. Therefore, lng*Data* is declared **As Any**. When you want lng*Data* to be ignored by WinHelp(), you should set lng*Data* to &H0 (**Null**, rather than decimal 0) in your application.

So you can take advantage of all the features that WinHelp() offers, the additions to the Declarations section of your module—called WinHelp Declarations in this example—follow:

```
Declare Function WinHelp Lib "user32" Alias "WinHelpA" _
  (ByVal hwnd As Long, _
    ByVal lpHelpFile As String, _
    ByVal wCommand As Long, _
    ByVal dwData As Long) As Long

'Declare Public constants for wCommand (lngCommand)
Public Const HELP_CONTEXT = &H1       'Display a specified topic
Public Const HELP_QUIT = &H2          'Terminate WinHelp for application
Public Const HELP_INDEX = &H3         'Display the help index
Public Const HELP_HELPONHELP = &H4    'Display help on using WinHelp
Public Const HELP_SETINDEX = &H5      'Set the current help index
Public Const HELP_KEY = &H101         'Display a topic for keyword
Public Const HELP_MULTIKEY = &H201    'Use alternate keyword table
Public Const KEY_F1 = &H70            'Key code for help key

'Declare the multikey help user-defined variable type (structure)
Type MKH 'Multikey Help
    intSize        As Integer       'Size of record
    strKeylist     As String * 1    'Code letter for keylist
    strKeyphrase   As String * 100  'String length is arbitrary
End Type

'Declare Public help variables
Public strHelpFile  As String  'Name of help file
Public lngCommand   As Long    'Help command constant
Public lngHelpCtx   As Long    'Help context value when numeric
Public strHelpKey   As String  'Help keyword for search when string
Public lngHelpOK    As Integer 'Return value from WinHelp()
```

You do not need to add the constants to the Declarations section of your module if you want to substitute the integer values shown in table 32.4 as the lng*Command* argument when you use the WinHelp() function. You must, however, declare the MKH (multikey help) structure in your global module, declare a record variable, and assign values to its fields in your code if you plan to use more than one help key in your application. A good practice is to make the name of your help file a **Public** variable.

Using the WinHelp API Function in Your Access VBA Code

Assign the name of your help file to `strHelpFile` and default values to `lngCommand` and `lngHelpCtx` in the Declarations section of the first form opened by your application. These variables are made **Public** so that they retain the last value set to all modules contained in your Access database. You set `lngHelpCtx` to the value of the context ID of the topic you want to display when the user requests help at a particular point in your code. For example:

```
Private Sub Form_Load()
    'Assign initial values to hHelp variables
    strHelpFile = "Nwind.hlp"
    lngCommand = HELP_CONTEXT
    lngHelpCtx = 211
End Sub
```

To display help from a Help button, add the button and add the following code for the `Click` event:

```
Private Sub cmdHelp_Click()
    lngHelpOK = WinHelp(Me.hWnd, strHelpFile, lngCommand, _
        lngHelpCtx)
End Sub
```

The **Me.**hWnd argument passes the window handle of the form on which the button is placed. Compile your code by clicking the Compile All Modules button, choose File, Save All Modules, then close the form and reopen it in Form View. When you click the Help button, `WinHelp()` displays the appropriate topic (see fig. 32.34).

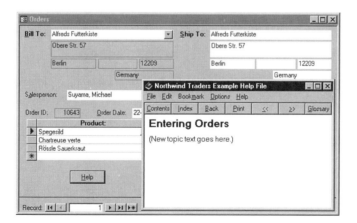

Fig. 32.34 The help topic opened by clicking the Help button added to the orders form.

If `lngCommand` is set to the value of `HELP_KEY` for a keyword search, the syntax of the call to `WinHelp()` is as follows:

```
lngCommand = HELP_KEY
strHelpKey = "Invoice"
intHelpOK = WinHelp(hWnd, strHelpFile, lngCommand,
strHelpKey)
```

From Here...

This chapter showed you the basic steps for creating custom help files for your Access applications. You learned how to create the help file document with a commercial help file authoring application for Word 6.0. The chapter explained how to create help project files and use them with Hcrtf.exe, the Microsoft help compiler, to compile documents in Rich Text Format to WinHelp files. You also learned the methods for assigning custom help files to forms and reports and setting the help context ID values for control objects to display specific topics. A description of how you use the `WinHelp()` function of Windows with your Access VBA code concluded the chapter.

For information on manipulating graphic images, naming of Access VBA variables, and upgrading your Access 1.x and 2.0 applications to Access 95, refer to these chapters:

- Chapter 20, "Adding Graphics to Forms and Reports," includes examples of how you edit bitmap images with the Windows 95 Paint applet.

- Chapter 33, "Migrating Access 2.0 Applications to Access 95," describes the process of converting Access 1.x and 2.0 applications to Access 95 and helps you avoid some of the pitfalls that may occur when you make the conversion.

- Appendix B, "Naming Conventions for Access Objects and Variables," describes the *Leszynski Naming Conventions for Microsoft Access*, on which are based the Access VBA constant and variable prefixes used in the examples of this chapter.

Chapter 33

Migrating Access 2.0 Applications to Access 95

Each version of Access—1.0, 1.1, 2.0, and Access 95—has a different database file structure at the binary (byte) level. The differences between .MDB files created with versions 1.0 and 1.1 were relatively minor; thus, you could use the Compact feature of Access to convert version 1.0 .MDBs to version 1.1, or *vice versa*.

Microsoft made substantial changes to Access 2.0's .MDB file structure. These changes were beyond the capability of the Compact feature, so Microsoft added the File, Convert Database command to re-create version 1.0 and 1.1 .MDB files in 2.0 format. Access 95's 32-bit .mdb file format differs greatly from that of version 2.0, and Access 95 runs only under Windows 95 or Windows NT. Therefore, you're faced with the choice of converting your Access 2.0 files or running your existing Access applications under Access 95.

The Convert Database process is *not reversible*; once you've converted a database to the Access 95 .mdb structure, you can't convert it back to version 2.0. However, you can open and use version 2.0 .MDB and some version 1.x files with Access 95. Consequently, this chapter begins by addressing the ramifications of continuing to use version 1.x or 2.0 .MDB files with Access 95 and then explains how to convert your existing .MDB files to Access 95's 32-bit .mdb structure.

In this chapter, you learn to

- Convert version 2.0 application .MDBs to Access 95 .mdbs

- Use Access 95 application .mdbs with version 2.0 data .MDBs

- Detect and correct import errors

- Eradicate elusive run-time and compile-time errors

VIII

Completing an App

> **Note**
>
> The likelihood of being able to run complex Access 1.x applications under Access 95 is quite small, especially if the applications contain appreciable amounts of Access Basic code. There were substantial changes between Access 1.x and 2.0; for the most part these changes are additive to the changes between Access 2.0 and Access 95. However, you can link Access 1.x tables to Access 95 databases without difficulty.

Using Access 2.0 Application .MDB Files with Access 95

Access 95 is designed to be backward compatible with Access 2.0 .MDB files. Nevertheless, the compatibility is not total. The following list describes the principal limitations of running version 2.0 .MDB files with Access 95:

- You cannot save any changes you make to the design of any object contained in a version 2.0 .MDB file.

- You cannot change ownership of, or permissions for, objects contained in a version 2.0 .MDB file.

> **Caution**
>
> You must use the `Version` argument of the `DoCmd.DoMenuItem` action with the `acMenuVer70` intrinsic constant to specify the new Access 95 menu structure in Access VBA code. The default value of the `Version` argument in Access 95 is `acMenuVer1x` for compatibility with versions 1.x and 2.0.

- `DoMenuItem` macro actions that refer to menu choices that have changed in Access 95 occasionally produce an unexpected result.

- `SendKeys` operations that execute Access 95 menu choices and make selections in dialogs are likely to fail due to changes in the Access 95 menu structure and the design of Access 95 dialogs.

- Access VBA statements that use the dot (`.`) operator to refer to a field of a `Recordset` object or a member of a collection fail. Use the bang (`!`) operator, as in `Orders!OrderID` or `Forms!Orders`.

If you don't need to change the design of your Access 2.0 application and the application does not contain any of the specific problem areas in the preceding list, you probably can continue to use the 2.0 application with Access 95 and share the application with other users of Access 95 and earlier versions of Access. The message shown in figure 33.1 appears when you first open an Access 1.x or 2.0 application in Access 95.

To attempt to run an Access 2.0 application under Access 95, choose the Open option in the dialog of figure 33.1. The status bar displays "Opening...", then "Compiling...", and finally the message shown in figure 33.2 appears advising that you can't change the design of objects in the database. The opening and compiling process, which *enables* Access 1.x and 2.0 applications, makes code in Access Basic modules compatible with Access VBA. Fortunately, the opening and compiling process only occurs once, but the message box of figure 33.2 appears each time you open the database.

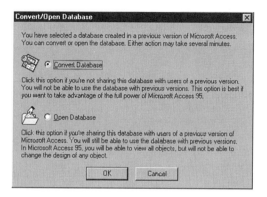

Fig. 33.1   This message is displayed when you first open an Access 1.x or 2.0 .MDB file in Access 95.

> **Note**
>
> If you make changes to a Access 1.x or 2.0 application, the enabling process reoccurs when you first open the application. Make sure you compile all of the modules in your earlier version .MDB file before opening it in Access 95.

Fig. 33.2   This message is displayed every time you open an enabled Access 1.x or 2.0 .MDB file in Access 95.

If your application contains code that Access VBA can't handle, you're likely to receive the message shown in figure 33.3. To find the offending code, open a module and click the Compile All Modules button. As an example, Access 2.0's ORDERS.MDB sample database contains a function call to code in WIZLIB.MDA that is deliberately modified to create an error. (The wlib_GetFileNameInfo user-defined data type is renamed). When you choose Run, Compile All Modules button—with ORDERS.MDB open—compilation may fail at the GetMDBName2() function with a "User-defined type not defined" message (see fig. 33.4). You can't save corrections to Access Basic code in Access 95, so you must make any required changes to the unconverted .MDB file in the appropriate version of Access.

Fig. 33.3   If the Access VBA interpreter can't handle your Access Basic code, this message appears.

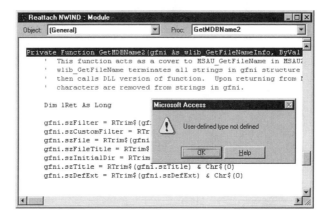

Fig. 33.4   When you click the Compile All Modules button, the interpreter highlights the offending Access Basic code.

Another problem you may encounter is the appearance of the mysterious message box of figure 33.5. Unfortunately, the message box does not tell you *what* function name Microsoft Access can't find. Even if you don't plan to convert your application .MDB file, you'll likely need to convert the .MDB to Access 95 to identify the function call (in a form, report, or macro object) that caused the message. Once you solve the problem in Access 95, you must make the same correction to your Access 1.x or 2.0 .MDB file.

Fig. 33.5   You may receive this message saying that Access can't find a function used in a form, report, or macro object.

Using Access 1.x and 2.0 Data .MDB Files with Access 95

If you use the recommended two-database method (storing application objects and data objects in two separate .MDB files), you can convert your application .MDB file to Access 95, but leave the data .MDB as a version 1.x or 2.0 .MDB file. Users of 16-bit Access,

Access 95, and Visual Basic 3.0 or 4.0 can share the linked data .MDB files. When you attach tables contained in Access 1.x or 2.0 .MDB files, you don't receive a warning message. You cannot use new Access 95 features, such as Briefcase replication, with .MDB files created with prior versions of Access.

> **Note**
>
> It is a relatively easy process to split Access 1.x or 2.0 applications into separate data and application .MDB files. (Access 95 includes the Database Splitter add-in that automates this process; prior versions of Access do not offer this feature.) In your prior version of Access, create a new .MDB file, then import the tables from your existing .MDB file. Verify that the imported tables contain valid data, then delete the tables from your original .MDB file. Move the table to its final location, such as on a network server. Choose File, Attach Table, and attach the tables to the application .MDB file.

If any of the conditions in the following list apply to your Access applications, maintain your files in their earlier Access format.

- Some of the users of your Access applications have not upgraded to Windows 95 or Windows NT, so those users are unable to run the Access 95 retail or run-time versions.

- You are converting a series of different application .MDB files from version 1.x or 2.0 to Access 95 and need to maintain data compatibility with all application .MDBs until the conversion process is complete.

- You are sharing the database .MDB with a Visual Basic 3.0 application.

If you have developed several workgroup applications using earlier versions of Access, you must maintain the shared data .MDB file in its original format until you have converted all of the application databases to Access 95. There is little or no performance penalty for attaching tables and maintaining the original data .MDB file format.

> **Troubleshooting**
>
> Do not convert existing shared Access 2.0 SYSTEM.MDA or *WORKGROUP*.MDA files to Access 95 format. If you do, users of prior versions of Access will not even be able to launch Access. (They receive an "Unable to open '*filename.mda*'. It many not be an Access database or the file may be corrupt.") Access system files are attached, so you can use existing workgroup system files with Access 95.

Converting Access 1.x and 2.0 Files to Access 95

If you elect to convert your earlier versions of Access application .MDB files to Access 95 and all of your users have not converted to Access 95, you need to maintain two versions of the application .MDB file. If the application is mature and does not require significant maintenance, temporarily supplying a 32-bit Access 95 version to users of Windows 95 and Windows NT, and a 16-bit Access 2.0 or earlier version to users of Windows 3.1+ is not likely to present a problem.

If you're in the development or early roll-out phase, however, consider completion of the application in Access 2.0. Make sure to observe the syntax rules for Access VBA while writing your Access Basic code; doing so minimizes the trauma when converting your Access 2.0 application to Access 95.

The sections that follow supplement the content of Appendix A, "Converting or Using Applications Created in Previous Versions," of the manual, *Building Applications with Microsoft Access for Windows 95,* that accompanies the retail version of Access 95.

Converting versus Importing .MDB Files

You have the following options for converting version 1.x or 2.0 application, data, or combined application and data .MDB files to Access 95 format:

    ◀◀ See "Converting Databases to Access 95 Format," p. 105

Tip

If you encounter problems with permissions to modify objects in your converted .mdb file, try the import method so that you become the owner of the objects in the database.

- Open the file in Access 95 and accept the default Convert Database option. Alternatively, close any open database, then choose <u>T</u>ools, Database <u>U</u>tilities, Conver<u>t</u>. This is the fastest method of performing the conversion. The ownership of objects in the converted database does not change. Make sure to specify a different file name or directory for the converted .mdb file so you don't overwrite the existing version. If the conversion process fails, the source database file might become corrupted and irreparable.

- Choose <u>F</u>ile, <u>G</u>et External Data, <u>I</u>mport to import all of the objects from the version 1.x or 2.0 .MDB to a newly created Access 95 .mdb file. When you import the objects, you become the owner (Creator) of the objects.

Note

When importing an entire database you can select all of the objects for import at once by clicking each tab (Tables, Queries, Forms, and so on) and clicking the Select All button for each class of object. Once you've selected all of the objects to be imported click the OK button.

The database object permissions assigned to users and groups are not affected by either converting or importing the objects. Only ownership of the objects is affected.

Handling Conversion and Import Errors. Small Access 1.x and 2.0 applications, especially applications without Access Basic code, are likely to convert to Access 95 without problems. However, large applications that contain substantial amounts of code or use code contained in Access libraries or custom .DLLs, generate errors during the conversion process. The following sections describe the most common conversion errors and how to fix them.

Converting from Win16 to Win32 Function Calls. If your application makes use of calls to the Windows API, you must convert the function declarations from the 16-bit (Win16) to the 32-bit (Win32) version. You cannot call 16-bit functions from 32-bit code and vice-versa. You receive the error message shown in figure 33.6 when Access 95 converts your Access 1.x or 2.0 code containing Windows API function calls.

Fig. 33.6   You receive this message when Access 95 encounters a 16-bit Windows API function call in Access Basic code.

The Win32 API functions with arguments of the **String** data type come in two types: ANSI (suffix A) and Unicode (suffix W, for wide); the ANSI versions are used by Access 95. Most Windows API function arguments that were of the **Integer** data type in the Win16 version must be declared as **Long** in the Win32 version. Examples include all Win32 handles, such as hWnd and hDC, and values of **Integer** fields in structures. To avoid the need to change all function calls to Win32 API functions in your Access VBA code, you alias the function calls, as shown in the following example:

```
Declare Function OriginalName Lib "lib32" _
Alias "OriginalName[A]" ([AgumentList]) As Datatype
```

OriginalName is the name of the Win16 function in your Access VBA function calls. Win32 libraries, for the most part, have a 32 suffix, as in Kernel32.exe and GDI32.exe. In the majority of cases, you need only include the A suffix in the **Alias** name if **As String** appears in Argument List. For most Win32 functions, **Datatype** is **Long**.

The Win API Viewer, which is included with the Access Developer Toolkit (ADT) and Visual Basic 4.0, lets you copy **Declare** statements for Win32 function calls to the clipboard, then paste them into the Declarations section of your modules. If you don't have the ADT or Visual Basic 4.0, you must either have the Win32 Software Development Kit (SDK) or guess the correct Win32 API function name and data types, then try compiling and executing your code.

Converting and Adding References to Libraries and Add-Ins. In addition to converting your application .MDB file to Access 95, you also must convert any Access 2.0 libraries and add-ins used by your application to 32-bit versions. Converting your own libraries and add-ins follows the same process as converting .MDB files. If you use third-party libraries, you'll likely need updated Access 95 versions; the source code of many third-party libraries is password-protected.

> **Note**
>
> If you are using only a few functions in a library, such as the WIZLIB.MDA library included with Access 2.0, consider creating a new library or incorporating the function code in your Access 95 application. Doing so eliminates dealing with problems converting library functions you don't need. Copy the required function(s) to the clipboard and paste the code into an Access 95 module. (You can run prior versions of Access and Access 95 simultaneously.)

Prior versions of Access use the [Libraries] section of MSACC??0.INI to attach libraries to any application opened in Access. Access 95 uses references to 32-bit libraries in place of entries in MSACC??0.INI. To add a reference to a library, such as Access 95's Utility.mda, follow these steps:

1. Open a module and choose Tools, References to open the References dialog.

2. Click the Browse button to open the Add Reference dialog.

3. Select Databases (.mdb, .mda) in the Files of Type drop-down list.

4. Maneuver to the folder that contains your library, select the library file, and click the OK button to add the reference at the bottom of the Available References list.

5. When you close and reopen the References dialog, the new reference appears as the last active reference (see fig. 33.7).

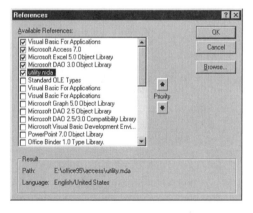

Fig. 33.7 References to Access 95 library databases appear below Access 95's default references and any references you added previously.

Access 95 library references are stored in your .mdb file; thus, you must create a reference to a library in each .mdb file that uses the library. Unlike [Libraries] entries in MSACC??0.INI, the full path to the library is *hard-coded*. You may need to alter the reference for users who don't install your application in the folder specified by the reference in your .mdb file. You cannot modify references with Access VBA; VBA does not expose a References collection.

Hard-coded reference paths are a compelling reason to move library code to your Access application .mdb if you only use a few library functions. If your library code does not contain visible objects, other than message boxes and modal dialogs, an alternative is to convert the library to an in-process Visual Basic 32-bit OLE .DLL that you can access through OLE Automation code.

> **Note**
>
> Access 95, unlike prior versions of Access, allows duplicate function names in libraries. If you have duplicate function names in libraries, your application calls the function in the library with the highest priority in the Available References list of the References dialog.

Access 2.0 uses the [Menu Add-Ins] section of MSACC20.INI to specify the function name of the entry point for an add-in and the [Libraries] section to attach the .MDA file that contains the add-in. These entries are replaced by the Registry entries in Access 95. If your Access 95 application uses add-ins, a record in the USysRegInfo table of the add-in is required to make the add-in visible to the Add-In Manager.

You can import the USysRegInfo table of one of the Access 95 wizards, then modify the entries as required for your add-in. When you use the Add-In Manager to install the add-in, an entry is appended to the MenuAdd-Ins section of the Registry entries for Access 95. Figure 33.8 shows the data for Access 95's Database Splitter add-in. Unlike references to library databases, add-ins are available to all databases you open in Access 95.

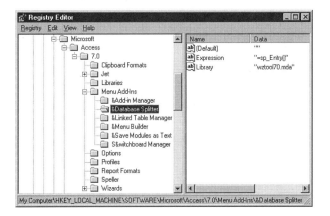

Fig. 33.8 The Add-In Manager appends entries to the MenuAdd-Ins section of the Registry.

The 32-Index Limit on Tables. Access 95 imposes a limit of 32 indexes per table. Each relationship between tables creates an index on the two tables that participate in the relationship, a feature new to Access 95. If you have a very complex database with many relationships between tables, you may exceed the 32-index per table limit.

Although your Access 2.0 table may have less than 32 indexes, when you convert the table to Access 95, the additional indexes for relationships may exceed the limit of 32. In this case, you either cannot convert the database or, if the database converts, you lose indexes. Your only option in this situation is to reduce the number of indexes on your table in your prior version of Access, then try the conversion process again.

 Finding Other Conversion Problems. The Compile All Modules operation finds the majority of the conversion errors, although some of the error messages you receive may be confusing. As an example, the problem with dot (.) operators and fields of Recordset objects described in the "Using Access 2.0 Application .MDB Files with Access 95" section earlier in this chapter produces the error message shown in figure 33.9. Replacing the dot operator in the highlighted line of figure 33.9 with the bang (!) operator solves the problem, which is compounded by the use of a field name (Name) that is also a property name of the object.

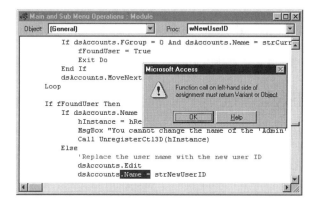

Fig. 33.9 A dot operator and a field name of a Recordset object that is the same as a property name produces this obscure error message.

Note

It's important to compile all of your Access Basic code in prior versions of Access before conversion. As an example, Access 95 may fail to change all Access Basic DoCmd *MacroAction* statements to the Access VBA DoCmd.*MacroAction* syntax if you don't compile your Access Basic code prior to conversion.

From Here...

You're on your own with Access 95.

This book's objective has been to provide you with the information you need to master the development of Access database applications at the beginning and intermediate levels. Access 95 is a very sophisticated application, and publishing limitations preclude complete descriptions of its every function and keyword. Access 95, however, has an exceptionally complete online Help system. Thus any feature or function that you find missing here undoubtedly can be located as a topic or cross-reference entry in Access 95's six fully-indexed and cross-referenced help files.

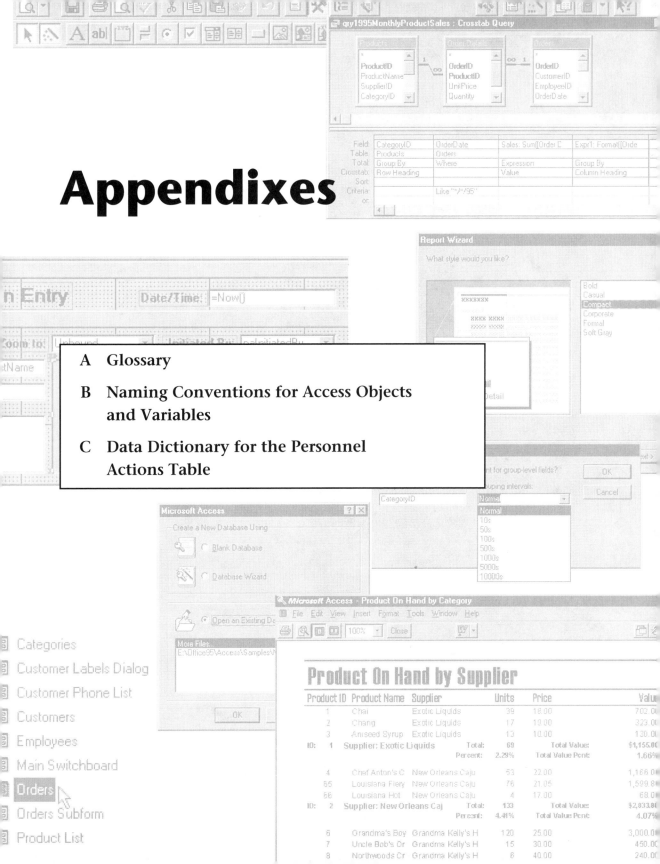

Appendixes

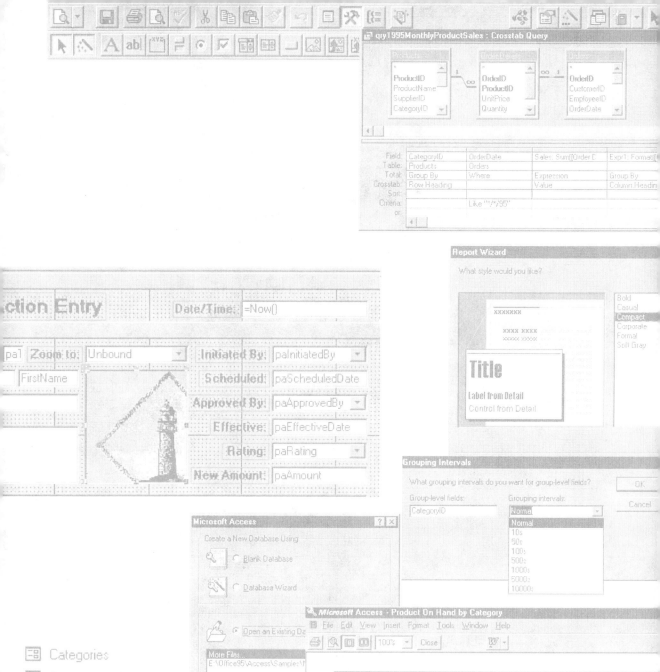

Appendix A

Glossary

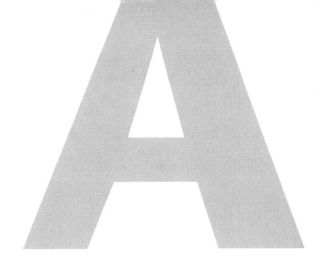

Accelerator key   A key combination that provides access to a menu choice, macro, or other function of the application in lieu of selection with the mouse, usually by combining Alt+*Key*. It is sometimes called a shortcut key, but shortcut keys usually consist of Ctrl+*Key* combinations.

Access Developer's Toolkit   See *ADT*.

Activation   An OLE 2.0 term meaning to place an object in a running state, which includes binding the object, or to invoke a method of the object. See also *Binding*.

Active   In Windows, the currently running application or the window to which user input is directed; the window with the focus. See also *Focus*.

Add-in   A wizard (such as the Query Wizard) or builder (such as the Menu Builder) that helps users of Access create or run database applications. You use Access 7.0's Add-In Manager to install wizards and builders. (Choose Tools, Add-Ins.) See also *Builder*.

Address   The numerical value, usually in hexadecimal format, of a particular location in your computer's random-access memory (RAM).

ADT   Abbreviation for the Access Developer's Toolkit that allows distribution of MSaccess.exe and other files needed to run (but not design) Access 95 applications. The ADT includes a Setup Wizard to create distribution diskettes for Access run-time applications and several 32-bit OLE Controls that also are distributed with Visual Basic 4.0. (Prior versions of the ADT included a run-time Access executable, MSARN??0.EXE. Access 95 uses the retail executable, Msaccess.exe, and an entry in the Registry to disable design-mode features.)

Aggregate functions   These are the ANSI SQL functions AVG(), SUM(), MIN(), MAX(), and COUNT() and Access SQL functions StDev(), Var(), First(), and Last(). Aggregate functions calculate summary values from a group of values in a specified column. They are usually associated with GROUP BY and HAVING clauses. See also *Domain aggregate functions*.

Aggregate object   An OLE 2.0 term that refers to an object class that contains one or more member objects of another class.

Alias   A temporary name assigned to a table in a self join, to a column of a query, or to rename a table, implemented by the AS reserved word in ANSI SQL. **Alias** is also an embedded keyword option for the **Declare** statement. The **Alias** keyword is used to register prototypes of DLL functions so that the function can be called from programs by another name. Aliasing the ANSI versions of 32-bit Windows API functions to function names without the "A" suffix is common when converting Access 1.x and 2.0 applications to Access 95.

ANSI   An abbreviation for the American National Standards Institute. ANSI in the Windows context refers to the ANSI character set that Microsoft decided to use for Windows (rather than the IBM PC character set that includes special characters such as those used for line drawing, called the OEM character set). The most common character set is ASCII (the American Standard Code for Information Interchange), which for English alphabetic and numeric characters, is the same as ANSI. Windows 95 and Windows NT include both ANSI (suffix "A") and Unicode (suffix "W") versions of Windows API functions. See *ASCII* and *Unicode*.

API   An abbreviation for Application Programming Interface. Generically, a method by which a program can obtain access to or modify the operating system. In 32-bit Windows, the 1,000 or so functions provided by Windows 95 and Windows NT DLLs that allow applications to open and close windows, read the keyboard, interpret mouse movements, etc. Programmers call them *hooks*. VBA provides access to these functions with the **Declare** statement. See also *DLL*.

Applet   A Windows application that is supplied as a component of another Windows application, rather than a retail product. The Notepad, Wordpad, and Character Map applications supplied with Windows 95 are examples of applets.

Application   The software product that results from the creation of a program, often used as a synonym for the programming (source) code that creates it. Microsoft Word, Microsoft Excel, WordPerfect for Windows, and Lotus 1-2-3 are called *mainstream* Windows productivity applications in this book. Applications are distinguished by the environment for which they are designed (such as Windows, DOS, Macintosh, UNIX) and their purpose. Windows applications carry the DOS executable file extension, .exe.

Application Close button   The small, square button with an "X" caption at the extreme right of the title bar of an application running in Windows 95. Clicking the Application Close button closes the running application.

Application Control menu box   The small, square button with a miniature application icon at the extreme left of the title bar of an application. Clicking the Application Control menu box displays the Application Control menu. Double-clicking the Application Control-menu box closes the application.

Argument   Arguments are data supplied to a function and upon which the function acts or uses to perform its task. Arguments are enclosed in parentheses. Additional arguments, if any, are separated by commas. Arguments passed to procedures usually are called *parameters*.

Array   An ordered sequence of values (elements) stored within a single named variable, accessed by referring to the variable name with the number of the element (index or subscript) in parentheses, as in `strValue = strArray(3)`. Arrays in VBA may have more than one dimension, in which case, access to the value includes indexes for each dimension, as in `strValue = strArray(3,3)`.

ASCII   Abbreviation for the American Standard Code for Information Interchange. A set of standard numerical values for printable, control, and special characters used by PCs and most other computers. Other commonly used codes for character sets are ANSI (used by Windows 3.1+), Unicode (used by Windows 95 and Windows NT), and EBCDIC (Extended Binary-Coded Decimal Interchange Code, used by IBM for mainframe computers). See *Unicode*.

Assign   To give a value to a named variable.

Asynchronous   A process that can occur at any time, regardless of the status of the operating system or applications that are running.

Attached table   A table that is not stored in the currently open Access database (native or base table), but which you can manipulate as if the table were a native table. In Access 95 terminology, an *attached table* is a *linked table*. See *Linked table*.

Authentication   The process of verifying a user's login ID and password.

Automation   An OLE 2.0 term that refers to a means of manipulating another application's objects. See also *OLE Automation*.

Automation client   An OLE 2-compliant Windows application with an application programming (macro) language, such as VBA, that is capable of referencing and manipulating objects exposed by OLE Automation servers.

Automation server   Technically, any OLE 2-compliant Windows application that supports OLE Automation operations by exposing a set of objects for manipulation by OLE Automation client applications. This book restricts the term automation server to applications that are not OLE 2+ full servers, but expose application objects. Access 95 is an example of an automation server.

AutoNumber   An Access 95 replacement for the Counter field data type of Access 1.x and 2.0. AutoNumber fields may be of the Increment or Random type. Fields of the Increment AutoNumber field data type usually are used to create primary keys in cases where a unique primary key cannot be created from data in the table.

Back up   To create a file (backup file) that duplicates data stored in one or more files on a client or server computer.

Background   In multitasking computer operations, the application or procedure that is not visible on-screen and that does not receive user generated input. In Windows, an application that is minimized and does not have the focus is in the background.

Base date   A date used as a reference from which other date values are calculated. In the case of VBA and SQL Server, the base date is January 1, 1900.

Base tables   The permanent tables from which a query is created. A synonym for underlying tables. Each base table in a database is identified by a name unique to the database. Access also uses the term base table to refer to a table in the current database in contrast to a linked (attached) table. See *Linked table*.

Batch   A group of statements processed as an entity. Execution of DOS batch files, such as AUTOEXEC.BAT, and SQL statements are examples of a batch process.

Binary file   A file whose content does not consist of lines of text. Executable (.exe), dynamic link library (.dll), and most database files are stored in binary format.

Binary string   A string consisting of binary, not text, data that contains bytes outside the range of ANSI or ASCII values for printable characters. Access 95 requires that you store binary strings as arrays of the `Byte` data type to avoid problems with Unicode/ANSI conversion.

Binding   In Access, attaching a `Form` or `Report` object to a table, or a control object to a field of a table or the column of a query result set. The bound `Form` or `Report` object determines the current record of the table or the bound control object reflects the value of the data cell or field of the current record or row.

Bit   The smallest piece of information processed by a computer. A bit, derived from the contraction of BInary digiT (or Binary digIT) has two states, on (1) or off (0). Eight bits make up a *byte*, and 16 bits combined is called a *word*.

Bitmap   The representation of a screen or printed image, usually graphic, as a series of bytes.

Bitwise   A process that evaluates each bit of a combination, such as a byte or word, rather than processing the combination as a single element. Logical operations and masks use bitwise procedures.

Blitting   The process of using the `BitBlt()` function of Windows' Gdi32.exe to modify a bitmap using bit block transfer.

Boolean   A type of arithmetic in which all digits are bits; that is, the numbers may have only two states, on (true or 1) or off (false or 0). Widely used in set theory and computer programming, `Boolean`, named after the mathematician George Boole, also is used to describe a VBA data type that may only have two states, true or false. In VBA, `True` is represented by &HFF (all bits of an 8-bit byte set to 1) and `False` by &H0 (all bits set to 0).

Bound   See *Binding* and *Object frame*.

Break   To cause an interruption in program operation. Ctrl+C is the standard DOS break key combination, but it seldom halts operation of a Windows application. Esc is more commonly used in Windows to cause an operation to terminate prior to completion.

Breakpoint A designated statement that causes program execution to halt after executing the statement preceding it. Breakpoints may be toggled on or off by an Access menu selection, Run, Toggle Breakpoint, or the F9 function key.

Briefcase replication A feature of Access 95 running under Windows 95 that permits the creation of Access replication sets stored in Windows 95 Briefcase folders, which can be updated by mobile users. Subsequently, the briefcase replicates are used to update the design-master replica to synchronize the design-master replica with the contents of the briefcase replicas. See *Design-master replica*.

Buffer An area in memory of a designated size (number of bytes or characters) reserved, typically, to hold a portion of a file or the value of a variable. When string variables are passed as arguments of DLL functions, you must create a buffer of sufficient size to hold the returned string. This is accomplished by creating a fixed-length string variable of the necessary size, using the `String` () function, prior to calling the DLL function.

Builder A component of Access that provides assistance in creating expressions (Expression Builder) or controlling objects (Menu Builder).

Built-in functions Functions that are included in a computer language and need not be created by the programmer as user-defined functions.

Business rules A set of rules for entering data in a database that are specific to an enterprise's method of conducting its operations. Business rules are in addition to rules for maintaining the domain and referential integrity of tables in a database. Business rules most commonly are implemented in a three-tier client-server database environment. See *Three-tier*.

Cache A block of memory reserved for temporary storage. Caches usually store data from disk files in memory to make access to the data faster. By default, Windows 95 caches all disk read and write operations.

Caption The title that appears in the title bar of a window. Access calls the text of a label, check box, frame, and command or option button control object, the `Caption` property.

Caret The term used by Windows to indicate the cursor used when editing a text field, usually shaped as an I-beam. The caret, also called the insertion point, can be positioned independently of the mouse pointer.

Cartesian product Named for René Descartes, a French mathematician. Used in JOIN operations to describe all possible combinations of rows and columns from each table in a database. The number of rows in a Cartesian product is equal to the number of rows in table 1 times that in table 2 times that in table 3, and so on. Cartesian rows that do not satisfy the JOIN condition are disregarded.

Cascading deletion A trigger that deletes data from one table based on a deletion from another table to maintain referential integrity. Usually used to delete detail data (such as invoice items) when the master record (invoice) is deleted. Access 2+ provides cascading deletion as an optional component of its referential integrity features. See *Referential integrity*.

Case sensitivity   A term used to define whether the interpreter or compiler treats lowercase and uppercase letters as the same character. Most are case insensitive. C is an exception; it is case sensitive, and all of its keywords are lowercase. Many interpreters, VBA included, reformat keywords to its standard: a combination of uppercase and lowercase letters. VBA does not distinguish between uppercase and lowercase letters used as names for variables.

Channel   In Windows, channel ordinarily refers to a unique task ID assigned to a dynamic data exchange (DDE) conversation. Channel IDs are **Long** integers under Windows 95 and Windows NT. Channel is also used to identify an I/O port in mini- and mainframe computers

Check box   A windows dialog and Access control object that consists of a square box and an associated caption. A diagonal cross or other mark in the box is created or erased (toggled) by alternate clicks on the box or the label with the mouse or by pressing an assigned hot key.

Child   In Windows, usually an abbreviation for an MDI child window. Child is also used in computer programming in general to describe an object that is related to but lower in hierarchical level than a parent object.

Chunk   A part of either a RIFF or standard MIDI file that is assigned to a particular function and may be treated as a single element by an application. VBA uses the term chunk to refer to a part of any file that you read or write with the GetChunk and AppendChunk methods. See *RIFF*.

Class identifier   See *CLSID*.

Clause   The portion of an SQL statement that begins with a keyword that names a basic operation to be performed.

Client   The device or application that receives data from or manipulates a server device or application. The data may be in the form of a file received from a network file server, an object from an OLE server, or values from a DDE server assigned to client variables. See *Automation client*.

Clipboard   Windows' temporary storage location for text and graphic objects, as well as Access objects, such as control objects, forms, tables, reports, and so on. The Clipboard is the intermediary in all copy, cut, and paste operations. You can view and save the contents of the Clipboard using the Program Manager's Clipboard applet.

CLSID   An identification tag that is associated with an OLE 2.0 object created by a specific server. CLSID values appear in the Registry and must be unique for each OLE 2.0 server and each type of object that the server can create. See *Registry*.

Clustered index   An index in which the physical record order and index order of a table are the same.

Code   Short for source code. The text you enter in your program to create an application. Code consists of instructions and their parameters, functions and their arguments, objects and their events, properties and methods, constants, variable declarations and assignments, and expressions and comments.

Code template   Self-contained groups of modules and resources that perform a group of standard functions and that may be incorporated within other applications requiring these functions, usually with little or no modification.

Code Window   In Access, the window that appears when you select Module from the Database window or click the Ellipsis button of an event property to create or edit an event-handling subprocedure. Also called the code editing window.

Collection   A group of objects of the same class that are contained within another object. Collections are named as the plural of their object class. As an example, the `Forms` and `Reports` collections are groups of `Form` and `Report` objects contained in the `Database` object.

Color palette   A means of establishing a foreground or background color in Windows by selecting a color from those displayed with the mouse. The color palette then converts the selection to the standard Windows RGB (red/green/blue) color format. The color palette provides the set of colors for graphic objects of 256 colors or less. Access 2+ allows you to specify a particular palette for individual forms. Also called *palette* or *Windows palette*.

COM   An acronym for Component Object Model, the name of Microsoft's design strategy to implement OLE 2+. The final COM implementation will allow networked and cross-platform implementation of OLE 2+ operations and OLE Automation.

Combo list   A Windows object that combines text box and list elements into a single object. In Access, combo lists are of the drop-down type by default. The list element of a drop-down combo list appears when a downward-pointing arrow to the right of the text box is clicked.

Command   A synonym for instruction. Specifies an action to be taken by the computer.

Command button   A Windows object that causes an event when clicked. Command buttons are ordinarily a gray rectangle containing a caption and surrounded by a border.

Comment   Explanatory material within source code not designed to be interpreted or compiled into the final application. In VBA, comments are usually preceded by an apostrophe ('), but can also be created by preceding them with the `Rem` keyword.

Common Dialog   A standardized dialog box, provided by Windows 95 and Windows NT, that may be created by a Windows API function call to functions contained in Cmdlg32.dll. Common dialogs include FileOpen, FileSave, Print and Printer Setup, ColorPalette, Font, and Search and Replace. Using the common dialogs in Access applications requires that you use the **Declare** statement to create function prototypes for the functions in Comdlg32.dll that you plan to use. The Comdlg32.ocx OLE Control, included with the Access Developer's Toolkit, lets you implement most of the common dialogs without the necessity of calling Comdlg32.dll functions.

Common User Access   See *CUA*.

Comparison operators   See *Operator*.

Compile   To create an executable or object (machine-language) file from source (readable) code. In Access, compile means to create pseudo-code (tokenized code) from the VBA source code you write in the code editing windows.

Component object model   See *COM*.

Composite key or index   A key or index based on the values in two or more columns. Equivalent to an INDEX ON *field*1 + *field*2 + ... TO *index_filename* statement in xBase. See also *Key* and *Index*.

Composite menu   A menu that includes menu choices from an OLE 2.0 server application that uses in-place (in-situ) activation (editing). Creating a compostite menu also is called *grafting* a menu.

Composite moniker   The location within a container document or object where the compound document is located.

Compound   In computer programming, a set of instructions or statements that requires more than one keyword or group of related keywords to complete. **Select Case...Case...End Select** is an example of a compound statement in VBA.

Compound document   A document that contains OLE objects created by an application other than the application that originally created or is managing the document.

Concatenation   Combining two expressions, usually strings, to form a longer expression. The concatenation operator is **&** in SQL, although VBA also permits the + symbol to be used to concatenate strings.

Concurrency   The condition when more than one user has access to a specific set of records or files at the same time. Concurrency is also used to describe the ability of a database management system to handle simultaneous queries against a single set of tables.

Container   An object or application that can create or manipulate compound documents.

Control   A synonym for a dialog object in Access. Controls include labels, text boxes, lists, combo lists, option buttons, and command buttons. Access 95 also provides compatibility with OLE Custom Controls.

Control array   In Visual Basic, the term given to multiple controls on a single form with the same Name property. (Access does not support control arrays.) Individual controls (elements) of a control array are designated by their index, starting with 0, up to one less than the number of controls with the same name.

Control-menu box See *Application Control-menu box* and *Document Control-menu box*.

Conversation In DDE operations, the collection of Windows messages that are passed between two different applications, the client and server, during an interprocess communication.

Correlated subquery A subquery that cannot be independently evaluated. Subqueries depend on an outer query for their result. See also *Subquery* and *Nested query*.

Counter A special field data type of Access 1.x and 2.0 tables that numbers each new record consecutively; called an AutoNumber field in Access 95. See *AutoNumber*.

CUA An abbreviation for Common User Access, an element of IBM's SAA (Systems Application Architecture) specification, which establishes a set of standards for user interaction with menus, dialogs, and other user-interactive portions of an application. The CUA was first implemented in Windows and OS/2 and has been an integral part of these GUIs since their inception.

Current database The database opened in Access by choosing File, Open Database (or the equivalent) that contains the objects of an Access application.

Current record The record in a Table or Recordset object whose values you modify. The current record supplies values of the current record's data cells to control objects that are bound to the table's fields.

Current statement The statement or instruction being executed at a particular instance in time. In debugging or stepwise operation of interpreted applications such as Access, it is the next statement that will be executed by the interpreter when program operation is resumed.

Custom control A control object not native to the application. Access 95 supports 32-bit OLE Controls (OCXs). Visual Basic 3.0 and Visual C++ 3.0 use 16-bit Visual Basic Extension custom controls (VBXs). Visual Basic 4.0 supports 16-bit VBXs and OCXs, plus 32-bit OCXs. See *OLE Control*.

Data access object The container for all of the objects that can be embodied in an Access application. The top member of the data access object hierarchy of Access is the DBEngine object, which contains Workspace, User, and Group objects in collections. Database objects are contained in Workspace objects.

Data definition The process of describing databases and database objects such as tables, indexes, views, procedures, rules, default values, triggers, and other characteristics.

Data dictionary The result of the data definition process. Also used to describe a set of database system tables that contain the data definitions of database objects.

Data element The value contained in a data cell, also called a data item, or simply an element. A piece of data that describes a single property of a data entity, such as a person's first name, last name, Social Security number, age, sex, or hair color. In this case, the person is the data entity.

Data entity   A distinguishable set of objects that is the subject of a data table and usually has at least one unique data element. A data entity might be a person (unique Social Security number), an invoice (unique invoice number), or a vehicle (unique vehicle ID number; license plates are not necessarily unique across state lines).

Data integrity   The maintenance of rules that prevent inadvertent or intentional modifications to the content of a database that would be deleterious to its accuracy or reliability. See *Domain integrity* and *Referential integrity*.

Data modification   Changing the content of one or more tables in a database. Data modification includes adding, deleting, or changing information with the INSERT, DELETE, and UPDATE SQL statements. Data modification often is called *updating*.

Data sharing   The ability to allow more than one user to access information stored in a database from the same or a different application.

Data type   The description of how the computer is to interpret a particular item of data. Data types are generally divided into two families: strings that usually have text or readable content, and numeric data. The types of numeric data supported vary with the compiler or interpreter used. Most programming languages support a user-defined record or structure data type that can contain multiple data types within it. *Field data types*, which define the data types of database tables, are distinguished from *Access table data types* in this book.

Database   A set of related data tables and other database objects, such as a data dictionary, which are organized as a group.

Database administrator   The individual(s) responsible for the administrative functions of client-server databases. The database administrator (DBA) has privileges (permissions) for all commands that may be executed by the RDBMS and is ordinarily responsible for maintaining system security, including access by users to the RDBMS itself and performing backup and restoration functions.

Database device   A file in which databases and related information, such as transaction logs, are stored. Database devices usually have physical names (such as a DOS or OS/2 file name) and a logical name (the parameter of the USE statement).

Database object   A component of a database. Database objects include tables, views, indexes, procedures, columns, rules, triggers, and defaults. The DBEngine object in Access VBA is the topmost member of the class of Access objects. All objects within a single database are subclasses of the Database object.

Database owner   The user who originally created a database. The database owner has control over all of the objects in the database, but may delegate control to other users. Access calls the database owner the Creator. The database owner is identified by the prefix "dbo" in SQL Server.

Database window   The window that appears when you open an Access database and lists the objects (tables, queries, forms, reports, macros, and modules) that are contained in the Database object.

Date function   A function that provides date and time information or manipulates date and time values.

DDE   An abbreviation for *dynamic data exchange*, DDE is an Interprocess Communication (IPC) method used by Windows and OS/2 to transfer data between different applications.

Deadlock   A condition that occurs when two users with a lock on one data item attempt to lock the other's data item. Most RDBMSs detect this condition, prevent its occurrence, and advise both users of the potential deadlock situation.

Debug   The act of removing errors in the source code for an application.

Debug Window   A non-modal dialog in which you may enter VBA expressions and view results without writing code in a code editing window. You may also direct information to be displayed in the Debug Window by use of the Debug object. The appearance of the Debug Window varies slightly between VBA-enabled applications.

Declaration   A statement that creates a user-defined data type, names a variable, creates a symbolic constant, or registers the prototypes of functions incorporated within dynamic link libraries.

Declaration section   A section of a VBA module reserved for statements containing declarations.

Declare   In text and not as a keyword, to create a user-defined data type, data holder for a variable, or constant. As a VBA keyword, to register a function contained in a dynamic link library in the declarations section of a module.

Default   A value assigned or an option chosen when no value is specified by the user or assigned by a program statement.

Default database   The logical name of the database assigned to a user when he or she logs in to the database application.

Demand lock   Precludes more shared locks from being set on a data resource. Successive requests for shared locks must wait for the demand lock to be cleared.

Dependent   A condition in which master data in a table (such as invoices) is associated with detail data in a subsidiary table (invoice items). In this case, invoice items are dependent upon invoices.

Design-master replica   The member of an Access replica set that allows changes in the design of objects, such as tables. The design-master replica usually (but not necessarily) is the .mdb file that is updated by briefcase replicas of the .mdb. See *Briefcase replication*.

Design mode   One of three modes of operation of Access, also called Design View. Design mode allows you to create and modify tables, queries, forms, reports, and control objects, enter macro actions, and write VBA code. The other two modes are run mode, also called run time (when the application is executing), and startup mode (before you open an Access database).

Destination document   A term used by OLE 1.0 to refer to a compound document.

Detail data   Data in a subsidiary table that depends on data in a master table to have meaning or intrinsic value. If one deletes the master invoice records, the subsidiary table's detail data for items included in the invoice lose their reference in the database—they become "orphan data."

Detail table   A table that depends on a master table. Detail tables usually have a many-to-one relationship with the master table. See also *Detail data.*

Device   A computer system component that is capable of sending or receiving data, such as a keyboard, display, printer, disk drive, or modem. Windows uses device drivers to connect applications to devices.

Device context   A Windows term that describes a record (struct) containing a complete definition of all of the variables required to fully describe a window containing a graphic object. These include the dimensions of the graphic area (viewport), drawing tools (pen, brush) in use, fonts, colors, drawing mode, etc. Windows provides a handle (hDC) for each device context.

Dialog   A popup modal child window, also called a dialog box, that requests information from the user. Dialogs include message boxes, input boxes, and user-defined dialogs for applications, such as choosing files to open.

DIB   An acronym for device-independent bitmap, a Windows-specific bitmap format designed to display graphic information. DIB files take the extension .dib and use a format similar to the .bmp format.

Difference   In data tables, data elements that are contained in one table but not in another.

Directory list   An element of a file selection dialog that selectively lists the subfolders of the designated folder of a specified logical drive.

Distributed database   A database, usually of the client/server type, that is located on more than one database server, often at widely separated locations. Synchronization of data contained in distributed databases is most commonly accomplished by the two-phase commit or replication methods. See *Replication* and *Two-phase commit.*

DLL   An abbreviation for *dynamic link library*, a file containing a collection of Windows functions designed to perform a specific class of operations. Most DLLs carry the .dll extension, but some Windows DLLs, such as Gdi32.exe, use the .exe extension. Functions within DLLs are called (invoked) by applications, as necessary, to perform the desired operation.

Docfile   The file format for creating persistent OLE objects. Docfiles usually have the extension .ole. Applications that are fully OLE 2-compliant create docfiles with specific extensions, such as .doc (Word) and .xls (Excel). Access 95 .mdb files also are OLE 2 docfiles. OLE 2.1 requires that docfiles include file property values derived from choosing File, Properties.

Document   A programming object that contains information that originates with the user of the application, rather than being created by the application itself. The data for documents usually is stored in disk files. Access tables, forms, and reports are documents, as are Excel or Lotus 1-2-3 worksheets. In Windows 95, a document is a file with an association to an application that can display or manipulate the file.

Document Control-menu box   The small, square button at the upper left of the menu bar of an application that uses the multiple document interface (MDI). Clicking the Document Control-menu box displays the Document Control menu. Double-clicking the Document Control-menu box closes the document (but not the application). See also *MDI server*.

Domain   A group of workstations and servers that share a common security account manager (SAM) database and that allow a user to log on to any resource in the domain with a single user ID and password. In Access, a domain is a set of records defined by a table or query.

Domain aggregate functions   A set of functions, identical to the SQL aggregate functions, that you can apply to a specified domain, rather than to one or more `Table` objects. See also *Aggregate functions*.

Domain integrity   The process of assuring that values added to fields of a table comply with a set of rules for reasonableness and other constraints. As an example, domain integrity is violated if you enter a ship date value that is earlier than an order date. In Access, domain integrity is maintained by field-level and table-level validation rules. See *Business rules*.

Drag-and-drop   A Windows process whereby an icon representing an object, such as a file, can be moved (dragged) by the mouse to another location (such as a different directory) and placed (dropped) in it. You can use drag-and-drop techniques in Access 95's design mode. Access does not provide the same drag-and-drop capabilities for control objects that are available with Visual Basic.

Drive   The logical identifier of a disk drive, usually specified as a letter. When used as a component of a path, the drive letter must be followed by a colon and backslash, as in C:\.

Dynamic data exchange   See *DDE*.

Dynamic link library   See *DLL*.

Dynaset   A set of rows and columns in your computer's memory that represent the values in an attached table, a table with a filter applied, or a query result set. You can update the values of the fields of the underlying table(s) by changing the values of the data cells of an updatable `Dynaset` object. In Access 2+, `Dynaset` is a type of `Recordset` object.

Embedded object   A source document stored as an OLE object in a compound or container document.

Empty   A condition of a VBA variable that has been declared but has not been assigned a value. Empty is not the same as the Null value nor is it equal to the empty or zero-length string (" ").

Enabled   The ability of a control object to respond to user actions such as a mouse click, expressed as the **True** or **False** value of the Enabled property of the control.

Environment   A combination of the computer hardware, operating system, and user interface. A complete statement of an environment follows: a 486DX2-66 computer with a VGA display and two-button mouse, using the Windows 95 operating system.

Environmental variable   A DOS term for variables that are declared by PATH and SET statements, usually made in an AUTOEXEC.BAT file, and stored in a reserved memory location by DOS. In Windows 95 and Windows NT, required environmental variables are stored in the Registry, although Windows 95 accepts environmental variables in the AUTOEXEC.BAT file for backward compatibility with 16-bit Windows applications. The environmental variables may be used by applications to adjust their operation for compatibility with user-specific hardware elements or folder structures.

Equi-join   A JOIN where the values in the columns being joined are compared for equality and all columns in both tables are displayed. This results in two identical columns in the result.

Error trapping   A procedure by which errors generated during the execution of an application are rerouted to a designated group of lines of code (called an error handler) that performs a predefined operation, such as ignoring the error. If errors are not trapped in VBA, the standard modal message dialog with the text message for the error that occurred appears.

Event   The occurrence of an action taken by the user and recognized by one of Access's event properties, such as On Click or On DblClick. Events are usually related to mouse movements and keyboard actions; however, events also can be generated by code using the Timer control object, for example.

Event-driven   The property of an operating system or environment, such as Windows, that implies the existence of an idle loop. When an event occurs, the idle loop is exited and event-handler code, specific to the event, is executed. After the event handler has completed its operation, execution returns to the idle loop, awaiting the next event.

Exclusive lock   A lock that prevents others from locking data items until the exclusive lock is cleared. Exclusive locks are placed on data items by update operations, such as SQL's INSERT, UPDATE, and DELETE.

Executable   Code, usually in the form of a disk file, that can be run by the operating system in use to perform a particular set of functions. Executable files in Windows carry the extension .exe and may obtain assistance from dynamic link libraries (DLLs) in performing their tasks.

Exponent   The second element of a number expressed in scientific notation, the power of 10 by which the first element, the mantissa, is multiplied to obtain the actual number.

For +1.23E3, the exponent is 3, so you multiply 1.23 by 1,000 (10 to the third power) to obtain the result, 1,230.

Expression   A combination of variable names, values, functions, and operators that return a result, usually assigned to a variable name. Result = 1 + 1 is an expression that returns 2 to the variable named Result. DiffVar = LargeVar–SmallVar returns the difference between the two variables to DiffVar. Functions may be used in expressions, and the expression may return the value determined by the function to the same variable as that of the argument. strVar = `Mid$`(strVar, 2, 3) replaces the value of strVar with three of its characters, starting at the second character.

Family   In typography, one or more typefaces having a related appearance. Courier roman (standard), italic, and bold constitute the Courier family.

Field   Synonym for a column that contains attribute values. Also, a single item of information in a record or row.

Fifth normal form   The rule for relational databases that requires that a table that has been divided into multiple tables must be capable of being reconstructed to its exact original structure by one or more JOIN statements.

File   The logical equivalent of a table. In dBASE, for instance, each table is a single .dbf file.

File moniker   The location of the well-formed path to a persistent OLE 2+ object.

First normal form   The rule for relational databases that dictates that tables must be flat. Flat tables can contain only one data value set per row. Members of the data value set, called data cells, are contained in one column of the row, and must have only one value.

Flag   A variable, usually `Boolean (True/False)`, that is used to determine the status of a particular condition within an application. The term *set* is often used to indicate turning a flag from `False` to `True`, and *reset* for the reverse.

Flow control   In general usage, conditional expressions that control the sequence of execution of instructions or statements in the source code of an application. `If. . .Then . . .End If` is a flow control statement. The term is also used to describe diagrams that describe the mode of operation of an application.

Focus   A Windows term indicating the currently selected application, or one of its windows, to which all user-generated input (keyboard and mouse operations) is directed. The object with the focus is said to be the *active* object. The title bar of a window with the focus is colored blue for the default Windows color scheme.

Font   A typeface in a single size, usually expressed in points, of a single style or having a common set of attributes. Font often is misused to indicate a typeface family or style.

Foreground   In multitasking operations, the application or procedure that is visible on-screen and to which user-generated input is directed. In Windows, the application that has the focus is in the foreground.

Foreign key   A column or combination of columns whose value must match a primary key in another table when joined with it. Foreign keys need not be unique for each record or row. See also *Primary key*.

Form   A synonym for a user-defined MDI child window in Access. A Form object contains the control objects that appear on its surface and the code associated with the events, methods, and properties applicable to the form and its control objects.

Form-Level   Variables that are declared in the Declarations section of an Access form. These variables are said to have form-level scope, and are not visible to procedures outside the Form object in which the variables are declared, unless declared with the `Public` reserved word.

Fourth normal form   The rule for relational databases that requires that only related data entities be included in a single table and that tables may not contain data related to more than one data entity when many-to-one relationships exist among the entities.

Frame   In Windows, a rectangle, usually with a single-pixel-wide border, that encloses a group of objects, usually of the dialog class. When referring to SMPTE timing with MIDI files, it is one image of a motion picture film (1/24 second) or one complete occurrence of a television image (approximately 1/30 second in NTSC, 1/25 second in PAL).

Front-end   When used in conjunction with database management systems, an application, a window, or a set of windows by which the user may access and view database records, as well as add to or edit them.

Full server   An OLE 2-compliant executable application capable of providing embeddable or linked documents for insertion into OLE 2+ container documents. Excel 95, Word 95, Project 4.1, and Wordpad are examples of OLE 2.1 full server applications. Access 95 is not a full server, because you cannot embed or link an Access .mdb file in an OLE 2.1 container application.

Function   A subprogram called from within an expression in which a value is computed and returned to the program that called it through its name. Functions are classified as internal to the application language when their names are keywords. You may create your own, user-defined functions in VBA by adding code between `Function` *FunctionName*`...End Function` statements.

Global   Pertaining to the program as a whole. Global variables and constants are accessible to, and global variables may be modified by, code at the form, module, and procedure level. VBA uses the reserved word `Public` to create or refer to global variables.

Global module   A code module (container) in which all global variables and constants are declared and in which the prototypes of any external functions contained in DLLs are declared. Use of a global module in Access applications is common, but is not required.

Grid   A preset group of visible or imaginary vertical and horizontal lines used to assist in aligning the position of graphic objects. In Access, the intersection of the imaginary lines is shown as dots on forms and reports in design mode. Control objects automatically align their outlines to these dots if the snap-to-grid option is enabled. In Access Datasheet view, a set of lines that establish the demarcation of columns and rows.

Group   In reports, one or more records that are collected into a single category, usually for the purpose of totaling. Database security systems use the term *group* to identify a collection of database users with common permissions. See also *Permissions*.

Handle   An unsigned `Long` integer assigned by Windows 95 and Windows NT to uniquely identify an instance (occurrence) of a module (application, `hModule`), task (`hTask`), window (`hWnd`), or device context (`hDC`) of a graphic object. Handles in 32-bit Windows applications, including applications for Windows 95 and Windows NT, are 32-bit unsigned integers (`dw` or double-words). Also used to identify the sizing elements of control objects in design mode. See also *Sizing handle*.

Header file   A file type used by C and C++ programs to assign data types and names to variables and to declare prototypes of the functions used in the application. C header files usually carry the extension .H.

Hierarchical menu   A menu with multiple levels, consisting of a main menu bar that leads to one or more levels of submenus from which choices of actions are made. Almost all Windows applications use hierarchical menu structures.

Hot-link   A term used to describe a DDE (dynamic data exchange) operation in which a change in the source of the DDE data (the server) is immediately reflected in the object of the destination application (the client) which has requested it.

Icon   A 32-by-32-pixel graphic image used to identify the application in the program manager window when the application is minimized, and in other locations in the application chosen by the programmer (such as the Help About dialog). Windows 95 also uses 16-by-16-pixel icons to identify the application in the title bar.

Identifier   A synonym for "name" or "symbol," usually applied to variable and constant names.

Idle   In Windows, the condition or state in which both Windows and the application have processed all pending messages in the queue from user- or hardware-initiated events and are waiting for the next to occur. The idle state is entered in VBA when the interpreter reaches the `End Sub` statement of the outermost nesting level of procedures for a form or control object.

Immediate Window   Replaced in Access 95 and other VBA-enabled applications by the Debug Window. See *Debug Window*.

In-place activation   The ability to activate an object (launch another application) and have the container application take on the capabilities of the other application. The primary feature of in-place activation (also called in-situ activation) is that the other application's menu choices merge with or replace the container application's menu choices in the active window.

In-process A term applied to (OLE) Automation servers, also called OLE DLLs, that operate within the same process space (memory allocation) of the OLE Automation client using the server. In-process servers commonly are called *InProc* servers. See *Out-of-process*.

Index For arrays, the position of the particular element with respect to others, usually beginning with 0 as the first element. When used in conjunction with database files or tables, index refers to a lookup table, usually in the form of a file or component of a file, that relates the value of a field in the indexed file to its record or page number and location in the page (if pages are used).

Infinite loop A `Do While...Loop`, `For...Next`, or similar program flow control structure in which the condition to exit the loop and continue with succeeding statements is never fulfilled. In `For...Next` loops, infinite looping occurs when the loop counter is set to a value less than that assigned to the `To` embedded keyword within the structure.

Initialize In programming, setting all variables to their default values and resetting the point of execution to the first executable line of code. Initialization is accomplished automatically in VBA when you start an application.

Inner query Synonym for subquery. See *Subquery*.

Insertion point The position of the cursor within a block of text. When the cursor is in a text field, it is called the caret in Windows.

Instance A term used by Windows to describe the temporal existence of a loaded application or one or more of its windows.

Instantiate The process of creating an instance of an object in memory.

Integer A whole number. In most programming languages, an integer is a data type that occupies two bytes (16 bits). Integers may have signs (as in the VBA `Integer` data type), taking on values from –32,768 to +32,767, or be unsigned. In the latter case, integers can represent numbers up to 65,535.

Interface A noun describing a connection between two dissimilar devices or OLE Automation clients and servers. A common phrase is "user interface," meaning the "connection" between the display-keyboard combination and the user. Adapter cards constitute the interface between the PC data bus and peripheral devices such as displays, modems, CD-ROMs, and the like. Drivers act as a software interface between Windows and the adapter cards. A bridge is an interface between two dissimilar networks. OLE Automation uses Iole... interfaces for inter-process communication. Use of interface as a verb is jargon.

Intersection The group of data elements that are included in both tables that participate in a `JOIN` operation.

Invocation path The route through which an object or routine is invoked. If the routine is deeply nested, the path may be quite circuitous.

Invoke   To cause execution of a block of code, particularly a procedure or subprocedure. Invoke also is used to indicate application of a method to an object.

Item   The name given to the elements contained in a list or the list component of a combo box.

Join   A basic operation, initiated by the SQL JOIN statement, that links the rows or records of two or more tables by one or more columns in each table. Equivalent to the xBase SET RELATION TO. . . command.

Jump   In programming, execution of code in a sequence that is not the same as the sequence in which the code appears in the source code. In most cases, a jump skips over a number of lines of code, the result of evaluation of a conditional expression. In some cases, a jump causes another subroutine to be executed.

Key or key field   A field that identifies a record by its value. Tables are usually indexed on key fields. For a field to be a key field, each data item in the field must possess a unique value. See also *Primary key* and *Foreign key*.

Key value   A value of a key field included in an index.

Keyword   A word that has specific meaning to the interpreter or compiler in use and causes predefined events to occur when encountered in source code. Keywords differ from reserved words because you can use keywords as variable, procedure, or function names. Using keywords for this purpose, however, is not a good programming practice. You cannot use a reserved word as a variable or constant name.

Label   In VBA programming, a name given to a target line in the source code at which execution results upon the prior execution of a GoTo *LabelName* instruction. A label also is an Access control object that displays, but cannot update, text values.

LAN   An acronym for *local area network*. A LAN is a system comprising multiple computers that are physically interconnected through network adapter cards and cabling. LANs allow one computer to share specified resources, such as disk drives, printers, and modems, with other computers on the LAN.

Launch   To start a Windows application.

Leaf level   The lowest level of an index. Indexes are "botmorphic" and derive the names of their elements from the objects found on trees, such as trunks, limbs, and leaves.

Library   A collection of functions, compiled as a group and accessible to applications by calling the function name, together with any required arguments. DLLs are one type of library; those used by compilers to provide built-in functions are another type.

Library database   An Access database that is automatically attached to Access when you launch it. Access library databases usually have the extension .mda. Attachment of library databases to Access is controlled by entries in the Registry.

Linked object A source document in a compound document that is included by reference to a file that contains the object's data, rather than by embedding the source document in the compound document.

Linked table A table that is not stored in the currently open Access database (native or base table), but which you can manipulate as if the table were a native table. Linked tables were called *attached tables* in Access 1.x and 2.0.

List A Windows control object that provides a list of items from which the user may choose with the mouse or the cursor keys.

Livelock A request for an exclusive lock on a data item that is repeatedly denied because of shared locks imposed by other users.

Local The scope of a variable declared within a procedure, rather than at the form, module, or global level. Local variables are visible (defined) only within the procedure in which they were declared. VBA uses the prefix `Private` to define functions, sub-procedures, and variable of local scope.

Local area network See *LAN*.

Lock A restriction of access to a table, portion of a table, or data item imposed to maintain data integrity of a database. Locks may be shared, in which case more than one user can access the locked element(s), or exclusive, where the user with the exclusive lock prevents other users from creating simultaneous shared or exclusive locks on the element(s).

Logical A synonym for Boolean. Logical is a data type that may have true or false values only. Logical is also used to define a class of operators whose result is only `True` or `False`. VBA includes a `Boolean` data type.

Loop A compound program flow control structure that causes statements contained between the instructions that designate the beginning and end of the structure to be repeatedly executed until a given condition is satisfied, at which point program execution continues at the source code line after the loop termination statement.

LRPC An acronym for lightweight remote procedure call used for OLE 2+ operations between OLE clients and OLE full servers on a single computer. LRPC requires that both applications involved in the procedure call be resident on the same computer. See *RPC*.

Machine language Program code in the form of instructions that have meaning to and can be acted upon by the computer hardware and operating system employed. Object files compiled from source code are in machine language, as are executable files that consist of object files linked with library files.

Macro A set of one or more instructions, called actions by Access, that respond to events. Macros and VBA code, which can substitute for Access macros, are used to automate Access applications.

Mantissa The first element of a number expressed in scientific notation that is multiplied by the power of 10 given in the exponent to obtain the actual number.

For +1.23E3, the exponent is 3, so you multiply the mantissa, 1.23, by 1,000 (10 to the third power) to obtain the result, 1,230.

MAPI   Acronym for the Windows Messaging API created by Microsoft for use with Microsoft Mail, which implements Simple MAPI. Microsoft Exchange Server implements MAPI 1.0 (also called Extended MAPI).

Master database   A database that controls user access to other databases, usually in a client-server system.

Master table   A table containing data on which detail data in another table is dependent. Master tables have a primary key that is matched to a foreign key in a detail table. Master tables often have a one-to-many relationship with detail tables. Master tables sometimes are called *base tables*.

MDI server   An OLE 2+ server that supports multiple compound documents within a single running instance of the application.

Memo   An Access field data type that can store text with a length of up to about 64,000 bytes. (The length of the Text field data type is limited to 255 bytes.)

Menu   A set of choices from which the user determines the next set action to take. The design of menus in Windows is governed by the CUA or Common User Access specification developed by IBM.

Metafile   A type of graphics file, used by Windows and other applications, that stores the objects displayed in the form of mathematical descriptions of lines and surfaces. Windows metafiles, which use the extension .wmf, are a special form of metafiles.

Method   One of the characteristics of an object and a classification of keywords in VBA. Methods are the procedures that are applicable to an Access object. Methods that are applicable to a class of objects are inherited by other objects of the same class and may be modified to suit the requirements of the object by a characteristic of an object called polymorphism.

Mini-server   An applet with OLE server capabilities that you cannot run as a stand-alone application.

Mission-critical   A cliché used in software and hardware advertising to describe the necessity of use of the promoted product if one wishes to create a reliable database system.

Modal   A dialog that must be closed before further action can be taken by the user.

Modeless   A window or dialog that may be closed or minimized by the user without taking any other action; the opposite of modal.

Module   A block of code, consisting of one or more procedures, for which the source code is stored in a single location (a `Form` or `Module` object in Access). In a compiled language, a code module is compiled to a single object file.

Module level   Variables and constants that are declared in the Declarations section of a module. These variables have module-level scope and are visible (defined) to all procedures that are contained within the module, unless declared **Public**, in which case the variables are visible to all procedures.

Moniker   A handle to the source of a compound document object.

Monitor   A name often used in place of the more proper terms, display or video display unit (VDU).

Multimedia   The combination of sound and graphic images within a single application for the purpose of selling new computer hardware and software. Related outcomes are the creation of animated presentations that incorporate sound effects and graphics, as well as expansion of the market for PCs in the music industry.

Multiprocessing   The ability of a computer with two or more CPUs to allocate tasks (threads) to a specific CPU. Symmetrical multitasking (SMP), implemented in Windows NT, distributes tasks among CPUs using a load-sharing methodology. Applications must be multithreaded to take advantage of SMP.

Multitasking   The ability of a computer with a single CPU to simulate the processing of more than one task at a time. Multitasking is effective when one or more of the applications spends most of its time in an idle state waiting for a user-initiated event, such as a keystroke or mouse click.

Multithreaded   An application that contains more than one thread of execution; a task or set of tasks that executes semi-independently of other task(s). The Jet 3.0 database engine is multithreaded (three threads); Access 95 and VBA are each singlethreaded.

Multiuser   Concurrent use of a single computer by more than one user, usually through the use of remote terminals. UNIX is inherently a multiuser operating system. Access uses the term multiuser to refer to Access applications that share a common .mdb file on a network file server.

Natural join   A SQL JOIN operation in which the values of the columns engaged in the join are compared, with all columns of each table in the join that do not duplicate other columns being included in the result. Same as an equi-join except that the joined columns are not duplicated in the result.

Nested   An expression applied to procedures that call other procedures within an application. The called procedures are said to be nested within the calling procedure. When many calls to subprocedures and sub-subprocedures are made, the last one in the sequence is said to be deeply nested.

Nested object   An OLE 2+ compound document incorporated in another OLE 2+ compound document. You can nest OLE 2+ documents as deeply as you wish. OLE 1.0 does not supported nested objects.

Nested query   A SQL SELECT statement that contains subqueries. See *Subquery*.

Newline pair   A combination of a carriage return, the Enter key (CR or `Chr$`(13)), and line feed (LF or `Chr$`(10)) used to terminate a line of text on-screen or within a text file. Other characters or combinations may be substituted for the CR/LF pair to indicate the type of newline character (soft, hard, deletable, etc.). The VBA newline constant is `VbCrLf`.

NFS   An abbreviation for Network File Server; a file format and set of drivers, created by Sun Microsystems Incorporated, that allows DOS/Windows and UNIX applications to share a single server disk drive running under UNIX.

Non-clustered index   An index that stores key values and pointers to data based on these values. In this case, the leaf level points to data pages rather than to the data itself, as is the case for a clustered index. Equivalent to `SET INDEX TO` *field_name* in xBase.

Normal forms   A set of five rules, the first three of which originally were defined by Dr. E. F. Cobb, that are used to design relational databases. Five normal forms are generally accepted in the creation of relational databases. See also *First normal form*, *Second normal form*, and so on.

Normalization   Creation of a database according to the five generally accepted rules of normal forms. See also *Normal forms*.

Not-equal join   A `JOIN` statement that specifies that the columns engaged in the join do not equal one another. In Access, you must specify a not-equal join using the SQL `WHERE` *field*1 `<>` *field*2 clause.

NT   An abbreviation for New Technology used by Windows NT.

NTFS   An abbreviation for New Technology File System; Windows NT's replacement for the DOS FAT (file allocation table) and OS/2's HPFS (high-performance file system). NTFS offers many advantages over other file systems, including improved security and the ability to reconstruct files in the event of hardware failures. Windows 3.1+ and Windows 95 can access files stored on NTFS volumes via a network connection, but cannot open NTFS files directly.

Null   A variable of no value or of unknown value. The default values, 0 for numeric variables and an empty string (`""`) for string variables, are not the same as the **Null** value. The `NULL` value in SQL statements specifies a data cell with no value assigned to the cell.

Object   In programming, elements that combine data (properties) and behavior (methods) in a single container of code called an object. An Access `Form` or `Report` object is a member of the class of Access `Database` objects; a particular control object is a subclass of the control objects class. Objects inherit their properties and methods from the classes above them in the hierarchy and can modify the properties and methods to suit their own purposes. The code container may be part of the language itself, or you may define your own objects in source code.

Object code   Code in machine-readable form that can be executed by your computer's CPU and operating system, usually linked with libraries to create an executable file.

Object frame   An Access control object that contains and displays or plays an OLE object. Bound object frames display or play OLE objects contained in OLE Object fields of Access tables. Unbound object frames display or play objects that are either embedded in a Form or Report object or are linked to a file that supplies the object's data. OLE Controls are inserted into bound or unbound object frames, depending upon whether or not the OLE Control is classified as a data-bound control.

Object library   A file with the extension.olb that contains information on the objects, properties, and methods exposed by an .exe or .dll file of the same file name that supports OLE Automation.

Object permissions   Permissions granted by the database administrator for others to view and modify the values of database objects, including data in tables. See also *Statement permissions*.

ODBC   An abbreviation for the Microsoft Open Database Connectivity API, a set of functions that provides access to client-server RDBMSs, desktop database files, text files, and Excel worksheet files through ODBC drivers. Access 95 uses 32-bit ODBC 2.5 and requires 32-bit ODBC drivers. ODBC most commonly is used to connect to client-server databases, such as Microsoft SQL Server, Sybase SQL Server and System 10+, Informix, and Oracle7. Access 95 includes a 32-bit ODBC 2.5 driver for Microsoft SQL Server 4.2+; a similar driver for Oracle RDBMSs is expected to be available shortly after the release of Access 95.

Offset   The number of bytes from a reference point, usually the beginning of a file, to the particular byte of interest. The first byte in a file, when offset is used to specify location, is always 0.

OLE Automation   An extension of OLE 2+ that provides the framework (interfaces) for applications and libraries to expose *programmable objects* that can be manipulated by client applications. Applications that expose programmable objects are called (OLE) Automation servers. See *Programmable object*.

OLE Control   An in-process OLE Automation server with the extension .ocx that exposes a single object, plus the properties, methods, and events of the object. Exposing events differentiates OLE Controls from other types of (OLE) Automation servers. Access refers to OLE Controls (the official Microsoft term) as Custom Controls; the term Custom Control is more commonly used for 16-bit Visual Basic Extensions, VBXs.

OLE DLL   A synonym for an in-process OLE Automation server implemented as a Windows DLL. See *In-process*.

OpenDoc   A standard proposed by Apple Computer, Borland International, Lotus Development, Novell, and other competitors of Microsoft to supplant or replace OLE 2+.

Operand   One of the variables or constants upon which an operator acts. In 1 + 2 = 3, both 1 and 2 are operands; + and = are the operators. See *Operator*.

Operating system   Applications that translate basic instructions, such as keyboard input, to language understood by the computer. The most common operating systems used with personal computers are MS-DOS (Microsoft Disk Operating System), Windows 95, Windows NT, UNIX, and OS/2.

Operator A keyword or reserved symbol that, in its unary form, acts on a single variable, or otherwise acts on two variables, to give a result. Operators may be of the conventional mathematic type such as + (add), - (subtract), / (divide), and * (multiply), as well as logical, such as **And** or **Not**. The unary minus (-), when applied to a single variable in a statement such as intVar = -intVar, inverts the sign of intVar from - to + or from + to -.

Optimistic locking A method of locking a record or page of a table that makes the assumption that the probability of other users locking the same record or page is low. With optimistic locking, the record or page is locked only when the data is updated, not during the editing process (LockEdits property set to **False**).

Option button A synonym for radio button, the original terminology in the CUA specification. Option buttons are circular control objects whose center is filled when selected. If grouped, only one option button of a group may be selected.

Outer join An SQL JOIN operation in which all rows of the joined tables are returned, whether or not a match is made between columns. SQL database managers that do not support the OUTER JOIN reserved words use the *= (LEFT JOIN) operator to specify that all of the rows in the preceding table return, and =* (RIGHT JOIN) to return all of the rows in the succeeding table.

Outer query A synonym for the primary query in a statement that includes a subquery. See also *Subquery*.

Out-of-process An (OLE) Automation server in the form of an executable (.exe) file that operates in its own process space (memory allocation) and uses LRPCs (lightweight remote procedure calls) to communicate with the Automation client. The term *OutOfProc* often is used as shorthand for Out-of-process.

Page In tables of client-server RDBMSs, such as Microsoft SQL Server, and Access databases, a 2K block that contains records of tables. Client-server and Access databases lock pages, while DOS desktop databases usually lock individual records. Page-locking is required by most RDBMSs when variable-length records are used in tables.

Parameter The equivalent of an argument, but associated with the procedure that receives the value of an argument from the calling function. The terms parameter and argument, however, are often used interchangeably.

Parse The process of determining if a particular expression is contained within another expression. Parsing breaks program statements into keywords, operators, operands, arguments, and parameters for subsequent processing of each by the computer. Parsing string variables involves searching for the occurrence of a particular character or set of characters in the string, and then taking a specified set of actions when found or not found.

Permissions Authority given by the system administrator, database administrator, or database owner to perform operations on a network or upon data objects in a database.

Persistent (graphics)   A Windows graphic image that survives movement, resizing, or overwriting of the window in which it appears. Persistent images are stored in global memory blocks and are not released until the window containing them is destroyed.

Persistent (objects)   An object that is stored in the form of a file or an element of a file, rather than only in memory. Table and QueryDef objects are persistent because these objects are stored in .mdb files. Recordset objects, on the other hand, are stored in memory. Such objects are called *temporal* or *impersistent* objects.

Pessimistic locking   A method of locking a record or page of a table that makes the assumption that the probability of other users locking the same record or page is high. With pessimistic locking, the record or page is locked during the editing and updating process (LockEdits property set to **True**).

Point   In typography, the unit of measurement of the vertical dimension of a font, about 1/72 of an inch. The point is also a unit of measurement in Windows, where it represents exactly 1/72 of a logical inch or 20 twips. Unless otherwise specified, all distance measurements in VBA are in twips.

Pointer   A data type that comprises a number representing a memory location. Near pointers are constrained to the 64K default local data segment. Far pointers can access any location in the computer's memory. Pointers are used extensively in C-language applications to access elements of arrays, strings, structures, and the like. VBA has only one pointer data type—to a zero-terminated string when the **ByVal...As String** keywords are applied to a VBA string passed to an external function contained in a dynamic link library.

Poke   In DDE terminology, the transmission of an unrequested data item to a DDE server by the DDE client. In BASIC language terminology, placing a byte of data in a specific memory location. VBA does not support the BASIC POKE keyword and uses the DDEPoke method for DDE operations.

Precedence   The sequence of execution of operators in statements that contain more than one operator.

Primary key   The column or columns whose individual or combined values (in the case of a composite primary key) uniquely identify a row in a table.

Primary verb   The default verb for activating an OLE 2+ object. Edit is the default verb for most OLE objects, except multimedia objects, whose default verb is usually Play.

Print zone   The area of a sheet of paper upon which a printer can create an image. For most laser printers and standard dot-matrix printers, this is 8 inches in width. The vertical dimension is unlimited for dot-matrix printers and usually is 13.5 inches for a laser printer with legal-size paper capabilities.

Printer object   A VBA object representing the printer chosen as the default by the Control Panel Printers function's Set Default choice.

Procedure   A self-contained collection of source code statements, executable as an entity. All VBA procedures begin either with the reserved word **Sub** or **Function**, which may be preceded by the `Public`, `Private`, or `Static` reserved words, and terminate with `End Sub` or `End Function`.

Process server   An "unoffical" term used in this book to specify an (OLE) Automation server, either in-process or out-of-process, that does not provide user-interface components, such as dialogs or windows. Process servers often are used in three-tier client-server applications to implement business rules. See *Business rules* and *Three-tier*.

Program   All of the code required to create an application, consisting basically of declarations, statements, and in Windows, resource definition and help files.

Programmable object   An object exposed by an (OLE) Automation server, together with a set of properties and methods applicable to the object. The exposed object can be manipulated by the application programming language of an (OLE) Automation client application.

Projection   A projection identifies the desired subset of the columns contained in a table. You create a projection with a query that defines the fields of the table you want to display, but without criteria that limit the records that are displayed.

Properties window   A window that displays the names and properties of Access `Table`, `Form`, `Report`, and `Control` objects.

Property   One of the two principal characteristics of objects (the other is methods). Properties define the manifestation of the object, for example, its appearance. Properties may be defined for an object or for the class of objects to which the particular object belongs, in which case they are said to be inherited.

Pseudo-object   Objects that are contained within other OLE 2+ objects, such as the cells of a spreadsheet object.

Qualification   A search condition that data values must meet to be included in the result of the search.

Qualified   To precede the name of a database object with the name of the database and the object's owner, or to precede the name of a file with its drive designator and the path to the directory in which the file is stored. The terms well-qualified path and well-formed path to a file appear often in documentation.

Query   A request to retrieve data from a database with the SQL SELECT instruction or to manipulate data in the database, called an "action query" by Access.

QueryDef   A persistent Access object that stores the Access SQL statements that comprise a query. `QueryDef` objects are optimized, when applicable, by the Jet database engine's query optimizer and stored in a special optimized format.

RDBMS   An abbreviation for relational database management system. An RDBMS is an application that is capable of creating, organizing, and editing databases; displaying data through user-selected views; and printing formatted reports. Most RDBMSs include at least a macro or macro language, and most provide a system programming language. dBASE, Paradox, and FoxPro are desktop RDBMSs.

Record   A synonym for a user-defined data type, called a structure in C and C++. Record also is used in database applications to define a single element of a relational database file that contains each of the fields defined for the file. Records need not contain data to exist—the xBase command, APPEND BLANK, adds a record to a database that contains default data for strings (all spaces), numeric, and date fields (zeroes), but **Null** data (?) for logical fields. A record is the logical equivalent of the row of a table. A set of related fields or columns of information that are treated as a unit by an RDBMS application.

Recursion   A condition in which a procedure or function calls itself. As a general rule, you should avoid recursive procedures and functions in VBA unless you are an experienced programmer.

Reference   In VBA, the incorporation of pointers to specific sets of programmable objects exposed by Automation servers and manipulated by VBA code in the Automation client. You create a VBA reference to a set of objects exposed by an Automation server, such as Microsoft Excel 95, in the References dialog that is accessible from the Tools, References command when a module is the active Access object. Once you declare a reference to the set of objects, the VBA pseudo-compiler checks the syntax of your code against the syntax specified for the referenced object. You also can utilize predefined intrinsic constants for the referenced objects in your VBA code.

Referential integrity   Rules governing the relationships between primary keys and foreign keys of tables within a relational database that determine data consistency. Referential integrity requires that the values of every foreign key in every table be matched by the value of a primary key in another table. Access 2+ includes features for maintaining referential integrity, such as cascading updates and cascading deletions.

Refresh   To redisplay records in Access's datasheet views or in a form or report so as to reflect changes others in a multiuser environment have made to the records.

Registry   A database that contains information required for the operation of Windows 95 and Windows NT, plus applications installed under Windows 95 and Windows NT. The Windows Registry takes the place of Windows 3.1+'s REG.DAT, WIN.INI, and SYSTEM.INI files, plus *PROFILE*.INI files installed by Windows 3.1 applications. The Registry also includes user information, such as user IDs, encrypted passwords, and permissions. Windows 95 and Windows NT include RegEdit.exe for editing the Registry. OLE 2+ servers add entries to the Registry to specify the location of their .exe files. Automation servers add Registry entries for each of the objects they expose.

Relation   Synonym for a table or a data table in an RDBMS.

Relational database   See *RDBMS*.

Relational operators   Relational operators consist of operators such as >, <, <>, and = that compare the values of two operands and return true or false depending on the values compared. They are sometimes called *comparative operators*.

Remote Automation Object   An out-of-process (OLE) Automation server, usually called an RAO, that resides on a server and is accessible to RAO-compliant applications that connect to the server. When this edition was written, only Visual Basic 4.0 was capable of creating RAOs and creating applications to connect to RAOs.

Remote Data Object   A substitute for the Jet 3.0 Data Access Object that provides a more direct connection to the ODBC API. The 32-bit (only) Remote Data Object (RDO) is included in the Enterprise edition of Visual Basic 4.0. You can reference the RDO in Access 95 applications and write VBA code for the RDO to speed queries against client-server databases. RDO also offers additional RDBMS connection management features.

Remote procedure call (RPC)   An interprocess communication method that allows an application to run specific parts of the application on more than one computer in a distributed computing environment. Visual Basic 4.0 is capable of creating Remote Automation Objects (RAOs) that use RPCs for communication over a network.

Replication   The process of duplicating database objects (usually tables) in more than one location, including a method of periodically rationalizing (synchronizing) updates to the objects. Database replication is an alternative to the two-phase commit process. Microsoft SQL Server 6.0 supports replication of databases across multiple Windows NT servers. Access 95 includes a mini-replication feature designed for mobile users of Access databases running Windows 95. See *Briefcase replication* and *Two-phase commit*.

Reserved word   Words that comprise the vocabulary of a programming language and that are reserved for specific use by the programming language. You cannot assign a reserved word as the name of a constant, variable, function, or subprocedure. Although the terms reserved word and keyword often are used interchangeably, they do not describe an identical set of words. See also *Keyword*.

Restriction   A query statement that defines a subset of the rows of a table based on the value of one or more of its columns.

RGB   A method of specifying colors by using numbers to specify the individual intensities of its red, green, and blue components, the colors created by the three "guns" of the cathode-ray tube (CRT) of a color display.

RIFF   An acronym for the Windows Resource Interchange File Format used in conjunction with the Multimedia Extensions to Windows. Depending upon their definition, these files may contain MIDI sequence, sample dump or system exclusive data, waveform files, or data to create graphic images. RIFF is the preferred file format, at least by Microsoft Corporation, for multimedia files.

Rollback   A term used in transaction processing that cancels a proposed transaction that modifies one or more tables and undoes changes, if any, made by the transaction prior to a COMMIT or COMMIT TRANSACTION SQL statement.

Routine   A synonym for procedure.

Row   A set of related columns that describes a specific data entity. A synonym for record.

Row aggregation functions   See *Aggregate functions*.

Rule   A specification that determines the type of data and value of data that may be entered in a column of a table. Rules are classified as validation rules and business rules.

Run mode   The mode of Access operation when Access is executing your database application. Run mode is called run time by Microsoft; however, the term run time normally refers to errors that occur when running the executable version of an application.

Running state   An OLE 2+ object is in the running state when the application that created the object is launched and has control of the object.

Scope   In programming terminology, the extent of visibility (definition) of a variable. VBA has global (`Public`, visible to all objects and procedures in the application), form/report (visible to all objects and procedures within a single form or report), module (visible to all procedures in a single module file), and local (`Private`, visible only within the procedure in which declared) scope. The scope of a variable depends upon where it is declared. See also *Global*, *Form-Level*, *Module Level*, and *Local*.

Screen object   An Access VBA object and object class defined as the entire usable area of the video display unit. All visible form and control objects are members of subclasses of the Screen object.

Scroll bar   Vertical and horizontal bars at the right side and bottom, respectively, of a multiline text box that allow the user to scroll the window to expose otherwise hidden text. Access also provides scroll bars for tables and queries in run mode (datasheet view) and for forms or reports that exceed the limits of the display.

SDI server   An OLE 2+ server that supports only a single compound document (Single Document Interface) within an instance of the application. SDI is the preferred design of applications for Windows 95; however, all Microsoft Office 95 productivity applications are multiple-document interface (MDI) applications. Windows 95's Explorer and Exchange client are examples of SDI applications.

Second normal form   The rule for relational databases requiring columns that are not key fields each be related to the key field. That is, a row may not contain values in data cells that do not pertain to the value of the key field. In an invoice item table, for instance, the columns of each row must pertain solely to the value of the invoice number key field.

Seek   To locate a specific byte, record, or chunk within a disk file. The `Seek` method of Access VBA can only be used in conjunction with `Recordset` objects of the `Table` type and requires that the table be indexed.

Select list   The list of column names, separated by commas, that specify the columns to be included in the result of a `SELECT` statement.

Selection   In Windows, one or more objects that have been chosen by clicking the surface of the object with the mouse or otherwise assigning the focus to the object. When used in conjunction with text, selection means the highlighted text that appears in a text box or window. See also *Restriction*.

Self-join   An SQL JOIN operation used to compare values within the columns of one table. Self-joins join a table with itself, requiring that the table be assigned two different names, one of which must be an alias.

Separator   A reserved symbol used to distinguish one item from another, as exemplified by the use of the exclamation point (!, bang character) in Access to separate the name of an object class from a specific object of the class, and an object contained within a specified object. The period separator (., dot) separates the names of objects and their methods or properties.

Sequential access file   A file in which one record follows another in the sequence applicable to the application. Text files, for the most part, are sequential.

Server   A computer on a LAN that provides services or resources to client computers by sharing its resources. Servers may be dedicated, in which case they share their resources but do not use them themselves except in performing administrative tasks. Servers in client-server databases are ordinarily dedicated to making database resources available to client computers. Servers may also be used to run applications for users, in which case, the server is called an application server. Peer-to-peer or workgroup servers, such as servers created by using Windows 95 and Windows NT to share disk folders, are another class of server.

Session   In Access, an instance of the Jet 3.0 database engine for a single user, represented by the Workspace object. You can establish multiple sessions which become members of the Workspaces collection. In RDBMS terminology, the period between the time that a user opens a connection to a database and the time that the connection to the database is closed.

Shared application memory   Memory that is allocated between processes involved in an LRPC call. See also *LRPC*.

Shared lock   A lock created by read-only operations that does not enable the user who creates the shared lock to modify the data. Other users can place shared locks on data so they can read it, but no user may apply an exclusive lock on the data while any shared locks are in effect.

Shortcut key   A key combination that provides access to a menu choice, macro, or other function of the application in lieu of selection with the mouse.

Single-stepping   A debugging process by which the source code is executed one line at a time to allow you to inspect the value of variables, find infinite loops, or remove other types of bugs.

Sizing handle   The small black rectangles on the perimeter of Access control objects that appear on the surface of the form or report in design mode when the object is selected. You drag the handles of the rectangles to shrink or enlarge the size of control objects.

Source code   The readable form of code that you create in a high-level language. Source code is converted to machine-language object code by a compiler or interpreter.

Source document   A term used by OLE 1.0 to refer to a compound object in a container document.

SQL   An acronym, pronounced either as "sequel" or "seekel," for Structured Query Language, a language developed by IBM Corporation for processing data contained in mainframe computer databases. (Sequel is the name of a language, similar to SQL, developed by IBM but no longer in use.) SQL has now been institutionalized by the creation of an ANSI standard for the language.

SQL aggregate functions   See *Aggregate functions.*

Statement   A syntactically acceptable (to the interpreter or compiler of the chosen language) combination of instructions or keywords and symbols, constants, and variables that must appear on a single line or use the line continuation pair (a space followed by an underscore) to use multiple lines.

Statement permissions   Permissions granted by the owner of a database or the database administrator for other users to execute specified SQL statements that act on the database's objects.

Static   When applied to a variable, a variable that retains its last value until another is assigned, even though the procedure in which it is defined has completed execution. All global variables are static. Variables declared as `Static` are similar to global variables; however, their visibility is limited to their declared scope. Static is also used to distinguish between statically linked (conventional) executable files and those that use DLLs.

Stored procedure   A set of SQL statements (and with those RDBMSs that support them, flow control statements) that are stored under a procedure name so that the statements can be executed as a group by the database server. Some RDBMSs, such as Microsoft and Sybase SQL Server, pre-compile stored procedures so that they execute more rapidly.

String   A data type used to contain textual material, such as alphabetic characters and punctuation symbols. Numbers may be included in or constitute the value of string variables, but cannot be manipulated by mathematical operators.

Structure   Two or more keywords that are used together to create an instruction, which is usually conditional in nature. In C and C++ programming, a user-defined data type. See also *Compound.*

Structured Query Language   See *SQL.*

Stub   A procedure or user-defined function that, in VBA, consists only of `Sub` *SubName*...`End Sub` or `Function` *FnName*...`End Function` lines with no intervening code. Stubs for subprocedures are created automatically by Access for event-handling code stored in Form and Report objects. Stubs are used to block out the procedures required by the application that can be called by the Main program. The intervening code statements are filled in during the programming process.

Style   In typography, a characteristic or set of attributes of a member of a family of typefaces created by an outline or bit map designed specifically to implement it.

Styles include bold, italic, bold-italic, bold-italic-condensed, and so forth. Styles may contain attributes for weight (bold, demi-bold, black), form (italic, roman), and spacing (compressed or extended) in various combinations.

Subform   A form contained within another form.

Submenu   A set of choices presented when a main menu choice is made. In Windows, the first-level submenus are similar to drop-down dialogs. Second-level submenus usually appear horizontally at the point of the first submenu choice.

Subprocedure   A procedure called by another procedure other than the main procedure (`WinMain` in Windows). In Access, all procedures except functions are subprocedures because Msaccess.exe contains the `WinMain` function.

Subquery   A SQL `SELECT` statement that is included (nested) within another `SELECT`, `INSERT`, `UPDATE`, or `DELETE` statement, or nested within another subquery.

Subreport   A report contained within another report.

Syntax   The rules governing the expression of a language. Like English, Spanish, Esperanto, or Swahili, programming languages each have their own syntax. Some languages allow much more latitude (irregular forms) in their syntax. VBA has a relatively rigid syntax, while C provides more flexibility at the expense of complexity.

System administrator   The individual(s) responsible for the administrative functions for all applications on a LAN or users of a UNIX cluster or network, usually including supervision of all databases on servers attached to the LAN. If the system administrator's (SA's) responsibility is limited to databases, the term database administrator (DBA) is ordinarily assigned.

System colors   The 20 standard colors used by Windows for elements of its predefined objects such as backgrounds, scroll bars, borders, and title bars. You may change the system colors from the defaults through Control Panel's Color and Desktop functions.

System databases   Databases that control access to databases on a server or across a LAN. Microsoft SQL Server has three system databases: the master database, which controls user databases; tempdb, which holds temporary tables; and model, which is used as the skeleton to create new user databases. Any database that is not a user database is a system database.

System function   Functions that return data about the database rather than from the content of the database.

System object   An object defined by Access rather than by the user. Examples of system objects are the `Screen` and `Debug` objects.

System table   A data dictionary table that maintains information on users of the database manager and each database under the control by the system. Access system tables carry the prefix `MSys`.

Tab order   The order in which the focus is assigned to multiple control objects within a form or dialog with successive depression of the Tab key.

Table   A database object consisting of a group of rows (records) divided into columns (fields) that contain data or Null values. A table is treated as a database device or object.

Text box   A Windows object designed to receive printable characters typed from the keyboard. Access provides two basic types: single- and multi-line. Entries in single-line text boxes are terminated with an Enter keystroke. Multi-line text boxes accept more than one line of text, either by a self-contained word-wrap feature (if a horizontal scroll bar is not present) or by a Ctrl+Enter key combination.

Text file   A disk file containing characters with values ordinarily ranging from Chr$(1) through Chr$(127) in which lines of text are separated from one another with newline pairs (Chr$(13) & Chr$(10)).

Theta join   A SQL JOIN operation that uses comparison or relational operators in the JOIN statement. See also *Operator*.

Third normal form   The rule for relational databases that imposes the requirement that a column that is not a key column may not be dependent upon another column that is not a key column. The third normal form is generally considered the most important because it is the first in the series that is not intuitive.

Thread   A part of a process, such as an executing application, that can run as an object or an entity.

Three-tier   The architecture of a database application, usually involving a client-server RDBSM, where the front-end application is separated from the back-end RDBMS by a middle tier application. In Access and Visual Basic applications, the middle tier usually is implemented as an OLE Automation process server, which implements the database connection, enforces business rules, and handles transfer of data to and from databases of the RDBMS. See *Business rules* and *Process server*.

Time stamp   The date and time data attributes applied to a disk file when created or edited. Time stamp is a database type for SQL Server and the ODBC API.

Timer   An Access control object that is invisible in run mode and that is used to trigger a Timer event at preselected intervals.

Title bar   The heading area, usually blue, of a window in which the title of the window appears, usually in bright white (reverse).

Toggle   A property of an object, such as a check box, that alternates its state when repeatedly clicked with the mouse or activated by a shortcut key combination.

Toolbar   A group of command button icons, usually arranged horizontally across the top of a window, that perform functions that would ordinarily require one or more menu choices. Floating toolbars can be located anywhere on your display.

Toolbox   A collection of command buttons designated as tools, usually with icons substituted for the default appearance of a command button, that choose a method applicable to an object (usually graphic) until another tool is selected. An example is the Access toolbox.

Topic   In DDE conversations, the name of the file or other identifying title of a collection of data. When used in conjunction with help files, the name of the subject matter of a single help screen display.

TRANSACT-SQL   A superset of ANSI SQL used by Microsoft and Sybase SQL Server. TRANSACT-SQL includes flow control instructions and the capability to define and use stored procedures that include conditional execution and looping.

Transaction   A group of processing steps that are treated as a single activity to perform a desired result. A transaction might entail all of the steps necessary to modify the values in or add records to each table involved when a new invoice is created. RDBMSs that are capable of transaction processing usually include the capability to cancel the transaction by a rollback instruction or to cause it to become a permanent part of the tables with the COMMIT or COMMIT TRANSACTION statement. See *Rollback*.

Trigger   A stored procedure that occurs when a user executes an instruction that may affect the referential integrity of a database. Triggers usually occur prior to the execution of INSERT, DELETE, or UPDATE statements so that the effect of the statement on referential integrity can be examined by a stored procedure prior to execution. See also *Stored procedure*.

Twip   The smallest unit of measurement in Windows and the default unit of measurement of VBA. The twip is 1/20 of a point, or 1/1440 of a logical inch.

Two-phase commit   A process applicable to updates to multiple (distributed) databases that prevents a transaction from completing until all of the distributed databases acknowledge that the transaction can be completed. The replication process has supplanted two-phase commit in most of today's distributed client-server RDBMSs. See *Replication*.

Type   See *Data type*.

Type library   A file with the extension .tlb that provides information about the types of objects exposed by an (OLE) Automation server. The type library for Msaccess.exe is Msaccess.tlb. See *Object library*.

Typeface   Synonym for face. A set of fonts of a single family in any available size possessing an identical style or set of attributes.

Unary   See *Operator*.

UNC   An abbreviation for uniform naming convention, the method of identifying the location of files on a remote server. UNC names begin with \\. Windows 95 and Windows NT support UNC; 32-bit Windows applications must support UNC to qualify for application of Microsoft's "Designed for Windows 95" logo. All Microsoft Office 95 applications support UNC.

Unicode   A replacement for the 7-bit or 8-bit ASCII and ANSI representations of characters with a 16-bit model that allows a wider variety of characters to be used. Windows 95 and Windows NT support unicode. Access 95 automatically converts Unicode to ANSI and vice-versa.

Uniform data transfer (UDT)   The interprocess communication (IPC) method used by OLE 2+. OLE 1.0 uses DDE for IPC.

Unique index   An index in which no two key fields or combinations of key fields upon which the index is created may have the same value.

UNIX   Registered trademark of Novell, Incorporated (formerly of AT&T) for its multiuser operating system, now administered by the Open Systems Foundation (OSF). Extensions and modifications of UNIX include DEC Ultrix, SCO UNIX, IBM AIX, and similar products.

Update   A permanent change to data values in one or more data tables. An update occurs when the INSERT, DELETE, UPDATE, or TRUNCATE TABLE SQL commands are executed.

User-defined   A data type, also called a record, that is specified in your VBA source code by a Type. . .End Type declaration statement in the Declarations Section of a module. The elements of the user-defined record type can be any data type valid for the language and may include other user-defined types.

User-defined transaction   A group of instructions combined under a single name and executed as a block when the name is invoked in a statement executed by the user.

Validation   The process of determining if an update to a value in a table's data cell is within a pre-established range or is a member of a set of allowable values. Validation rules establish the range or set of allowable values. Access 2+ supports validation rules at the field and table levels.

Variable   The name given to a symbol that represents or substitutes for a number (numeric), letter, or combination of letters (string).

VBA   An abbreviation for Visual Basic for Applications, the official name of which is "Visual Basic, Applications Edition." VBA is Microsoft's common application programming (macro) language for Access 95, Excel 5+, Project 4+, and Visual Basic 4.0. Each application has its own "flavor" of VBA as a result of automatically created references to the application's object hierarchy in VBA code. Thus, this book uses the terms *Excel VBA*, and *Project VBA* when referring to a particular flavor of VBA. VBA alone is used when the subject matter is applicable to all current flavors of VBA.

View   The method by which the data is presented for review by the user, usually on the computer display. Views can be created from subsets of columns from one or more tables by implementing the SQL CREATE VIEW instruction.

Visual Basic for Applications   See *VBA*.

WAN   An acronym for *wide area network*. A WAN is a system for connecting multiple computers in different geographical locations through the use of the switched telephone network or leased data lines, by optical or other long-distance cabling, or by infra-red, radio, or satellite links.

WAVE file   A file containing waveform audio data, usually with a .WAV extension.

Waveform audio   A data type standard of the Windows Multimedia Extensions that defines how digitally sampled sounds are stored in files and processed by Windows API functions calls.

Wildcard   A character that substitutes for and allows a match by any character or set of characters in its place. The DOS ? and * wildcards are similarly used in Windows applications.

Win32   An API for creating 32-bit applications that run under Windows 95 and Windows NT. Applications that are written to the Win32 API are purported to provide substantially improved performance when run under Windows 95 and Windows NT.

Win32s   A subset of the Win32 API designed to add limited 32-bit capabilities to Windows 3.1+. Very few applications have been written to the Win32s API, which appears to have become obsolete.

WinHelp32   A contraction used to describe the Windows help engine of Windows 95 and the files that are used in the creation of Windows 95 help systems. WinHelp 32 offers many useful built-in features not available in 16-bit WinHelp, including full-text indexing and search capability.

Workstation   A client computer on a LAN or WAN that is used to run applications and is connected to a server from which it obtains data shared with other computers. It is possible, but not common, for some network servers to be used as both a server and a workstation. Microsoft Windows NT, for instance, permits this. Workstation is also used to describe a high-priced PC that uses a proprietary microprocessor and proprietary architecture to create what some call an "open" system.

WOSA   Acronym for the Windows Open Services Architecture that is the foundation for such APIs as ODBC, MAPI, and TAPI. Microsoft also develops special vertical-market WOSA APIs for the banking, financial, and other industries.

WOW   An acronym for Windows on Win32, a subsystem of Windows NT that allows 16-bit Windows applications to run in protected memory spaces called virtual DOS machines (VDMs).

xBase   Any language interpreter or compiler or a database manager built upon the dBASE III+ model and incorporating all dBASE III+ commands and functions. Microsoft's FoxPro and Computer Associates' Clipper are xBase dialects. Most xBase database managers add a substantial number of commands and functions to the dBASE III+ vocabulary. xBase RDBMSs often do not use the same index file structure as dBASE III+, but all use the same database file (.DBF) structure.

Yes/No field   A term used by Access to describe a field of a table whose allowable values are Yes (**True**) or No (**False**). Yes/No fields are called logical or `Boolean` fields by Access 95.

Appendix B

Naming Conventions for Access Objects and Variables

By: Stan Leszynski, Leszynski Company, Inc. and Kwery Corporation

This appendix describes the Leszynski Naming Conventions (*LNC*), a set of standardized approaches to naming objects during Access development. These naming conventions were born of necessity, since some members of the staff of my firm spend all day in Access development, year after year. They were also born of a different need—a void that existed in the marketplace due to a lack of consensus about development styles among leading Access developers.

I am grateful to Greg Reddick, a former contractor with one of my companies, for jointly authoring the Access 1.x and 2.0 versions of our Access naming conventions with me (referred to as "L/R"). The L/R conventions were distributed broadly, with over 500,000 copies in print, and have become the most widely used such conventions in the Access community. Over the last few years, we have received feedback about L/R from hundreds of developers and companies, and have tried to accommodate some of their input, as well as our ongoing experiences, into *LNC*.

LNC improves upon the previous Access style by considering developers who work with multiple Microsoft development tools. Access, Visual Basic, Excel, and other Microsoft products have more in common in their Windows 95 versions than in any previous iterations. Consequently, this Access style dovetails with the *LNC* development style for all of VBA and FoxPro.

The prefixes, tags, and qualifiers in the naming conventions described in this appendix that are derived from L/R are underlined. If you are a user of the Access 2.x version of L/R, new additions for you to note are those conventions that are not underlined. I use the terms *naming conventions*, *style*, and *LNC* interchangeably throughout this chapter.

> **Note**
>
> Publishing limitations preclude reprinting of the complete text of *LNC* in this appendix. To obtain the unabridged version of the *LNCs*, see the "How to Get the Complete Text of the *LNCs*" section at the end of this appendix.

The Leszynski Naming Conventions for Microsoft Access—A Primer

Naming conventions are one of the foundation elements of your overall development style. The naming conventions were developed primarily to achieve four objectives:

- To enable you to quickly understand an application's structure and code by making object names more informative.

- To simplify team development of applications by creating a standardized vocabulary for all team members.

- To improve your ability to work with Access objects, including enforcing object name sort orders, creating self-documenting program code, and enhancing find and replace capabilities.

- To increase your ability to create tools for our Access development work, and to create code libraries across various VBA platforms.

To meet these objectives, you create and apply consistent naming conventions to the Access objects listed in table B.1.

Table B.1 Target Objects for Naming Conventions		
Tables	Reports	Modules
Table fields	Report controls	Procedures
Queries	Macros	Variables
Forms		Constants
Form controls		User-defined types

Object names are the foundation upon which your entire application is built, so they are almost impossible to change once development has begun in earnest. Therefore, you will probably not find it cost- or time-efficient to retrofit these conventions into your existing applications. For new applications, however, you should apply these naming conventions consistently from the moment you create your first object in a new Access database file.

Your naming conventions rely primarily on leading tags—several characters placed before an object's name (for example, `qryOrderByMonth`). This approach is sometimes referred to as *Hungarian Notation*. Leading tags provide several benefits:

- The first thing you see about an object when you see its name is the leading type tag, which is often more important than the name itself.

- Leading tags drive the ordering of object names in Access lists, sorting by type and then by base name.

- Leading tags are consistently located in the same place in an object's name, making them easier to find by parsers and other tools.

> **Note**
>
> The term Hungarian refers to the nationality of Charles Simonyi, a programmer at Microsoft who wrote a doctoral thesis, titled "Program Identifier Naming Conventions," in the 1980s.

If you are averse to Hungarian Notation for some reason and prefer trailing tags, *LNC* will still work for you. However, *LNC* prescribes no standard for locating and punctuating trailing tags. You will have to decide if they are offset with an underscore (OrderByMonth_qry), or by capitalization (OrderByMonthQry), or by some other technique.

Using trailing tags on database objects is problematic for you when your application also contains Visual Basic for Applications (VBA) code. The primary justification given by developers who prefer trailing tags on database objects is that it allows the objects to sort by base names rather than tags in ordered lists. However, such developers often still use *leading* tags and prefixes in their VBA code, because there seems to be no compelling argument that can be made for trailing tags on VBA objects such as variables. If you mix your styles like this, be prepared to justify your lack of consistency.

Because some developers, especially newer ones, prefer to minimize the complexity of a naming convention, *LNC* provides the following two levels for Access users:

- *Level One* has the minimum realistic subset of tags, but consequently provides lesser detail about the application. It is intended for users whose work is centered around the Database window and who do not develop applications, only database objects.

- *Level Two* provides greater detail and the flexibility to create your own extensions. It is intended for application developers.

Access Object Types

For purposes of this appendix, the standardized terminology in table B.2 for grouping objects was created. These group names are used when discussing naming conventions.

Table B.2 Object Name Groupings		
Database Objects	**Control Objects**	**VBA Objects**
Tables	Form controls	Procedures
Table fields	Report controls	Variables
Queries		Constants
Forms		User-defined types
Reports		
Macros		
Modules		

Structuring Object Names

In *LNC*, object names are constructed using this syntax for Level One:

[*prefix(es)*] [*tag*] *BaseName* [*Qualifier*] [*Suffix*]

For Level Two, the syntax varies slightly:

[*prefix(es)*] *tag* [*BaseName*] [*Qualifier*] [*Suffix*]

The brackets indicate optional syntax elements. Notice that, for Level One, the `BaseName` element is required and the `tag` is optional in some cases. At Level Two, the `tag` element is required even though the `BaseName` is not in some cases. These options are explained in the "What is a Tag?" and "Creating Database Object Base Names" sections later in this appendix.

> **Note**
>
> In the syntax diagrams, the case of each element reflects its case in actual use. The element `tag` is in lower case since the tags themselves are always lower case.

Table B.3 shows sample object names using these constructions.

Table B.3   Object Names Constructed in   Format

Object Name	Prefix	Tag	Base Name	Qualifier	Suffix
`tblCust`		tbl	Cust		
`qsumSalesPerfBest_WA`		qsum	SalesPerf	Best	_WA
`plngRecNumMax`	p	lng	RecNum	Max	
`ialngPartNum`	ia	lng	PartNum		

What Is a Prefix?

A *prefix* is an identifier that precedes a tag and clarifies it narrowly. Prefixes describe one or more important properties of an object. For example, a **Long** variable that is public in scope (declared **Public**) has a prefix *p*, as in `plngRecNumMax`. Prefixes are one or two characters long and in lower case. Multiple prefixes can be used together on one object.

What Is a Tag?

A *tag* is a multi-character phrase placed against an object base name to characterize it. In object-oriented programming terms, the tag is basically an identifier for the *class*. At Level One, you could say that tags define an object's general class; for example, `qry` for a query of any type. At Level Two, the tag defines the specific class; for example, `qdel` defines a delete query. Note that the word *class* here refers to a naming convention construction, not an exact object model construction. For example, there is only one Query (or QueryDef) class object in Access, and the data action (delete, update, etc.) is determined by its SQL statement, not its class. *LNC* prescribes several tags for this one Access class.

Tags are three or four characters long for readability and to allow for the hundreds of combinations necessary as the Office object model grows over time. They are always to the left of the base name and in lower case, so that your eye reads past them to the beginning of the base name.

A tag is created to mnemonically represent the word it abbreviates, such as `frm` for form. However, some tags may not seem fully mnemonic for two reasons. First, the perfect (or obvious) tag for a particular object may already be assigned to another object. Secondly, where common objects (objects with similar properties and usage) exist in multiple Microsoft applications, the tag for one may be used to represent similar objects in other products, even if the names are different. For example, an Access Rectangle object is almost identical in structure and purpose to a Visual Basic Shape object. Since the Visual Basic conventions have existed longer than your Access conventions, you use the Visual Basic Shape object tag you were already using, `shp`, to represent Access Rectangles.

What Is a Base Name?

The *base name* is the starting point when you name a particular object—the name you would use anyway if you had no naming conventions. The *LNC* guidelines for creating base names are driven by a set of rules stated in the following sections.

What Is a Qualifier?

A *qualifier* is an extension following the base name that provides context to the specific use of an object. Unlike prefixes, which detail properties of the object (for example, that the variable has public scope), qualifiers describe how the object is being used in a context. For example, `plngRecNumMax` is obviously the maximum record number, in an application that could also have variables for the minimum (`plngRecNumMin`) and current (`plngRecNumCur`) record numbers. Qualifiers are short and written with mixed upper and lower case, using the list in table B.4.

Table B.4	Standard	Qualifiers		
Qualifier	**Usage**		**Qualifier**	**Usage**
Cur	Current element of a set		Next	Next element of a set
Dest	Destination		New	New instance or value
First	First element of a set		Old	Prior instance or value
Hold	Hold a value for later		Prev	Previous element re-use of a set
Last	Last element of a set		Src	Source
Max	Maximum item in a set		Temp	Temporary value
Min	Minimum item in a set			

What Is a Suffix?

Suffix elements provide specific information about the object and are only used as "tie-breakers" when more detail is required to differentiate one object name from another. These are the only elements in the syntax where your naming conventions do not specify standardized values. You will create suffix items as needed by your company, development team, or application. For example, a series of queries that summarized the best sales performance by state would need the state name in each object name to properly qualify it, as in `qsumSalesPerfBest_AK`. Placing the state name at the very end of the name as a *suffix* item allows the entire collection of related queries to sort together, like this:

```
qsumSalesPerfBest_AK
qsumSalesPerfBest_AL
...
qsumSalesPerfBest_WY
```

Since the suffix is the last piece of information on a name, it can be easier for the eye to find if delimited from the rest of the object name with an underscore, as above. Use of the underscore is optional, not required.

Creating Database Object Base Names

The building blocks of your Access application are its database objects. When creating base names for these objects, you should give careful consideration to the purpose of the object, the approaches used to name associated objects, and the rules of thumb that follow for naming database objects.

Rules for Base Names

Follow these rules when developing a base name for a new database object:

- Spaces are not allowed in any object name. Spaces create a multitude of problems with consistency, readability, and documentation. Where the readability of a space is required, use an underscore instead.

- Object names begin with a letter and should only include letters, digits, and underscores. The use of special characters in object names is disallowed to comply with the naming rules of both VBA and Microsoft SQL Server. This allows your Basic variable names to include database object base names, and your entire Access schema to be easily *upsized* to the more powerful Microsoft SQL Server platform.

- Object names use mixed upper and lower case to add readability to the name. (Previously, some developers used all lower case names to allow for upsizing to Microsoft SQL Server. Starting with SQL Server version 6.0, that product is now installed case-insensitive and allows you to maintain upper and lower case in object names that are moved to the server from Access.)

- The only syntax element that can have multiple capital letters is the base name. A qualifier or suffix begins with a single capital letter and then contains only lower case letters, unless it is an abbreviation, as in `qsumSalesPerfBestUSA`. If you need to clearly see the elements of a name (prefixes, tag, base name, qualifier, and suffix), *LNC* allows for—but does not require—underscores as separators, as in `qsum_SalesPerf_Best_USA`.

- Object names are usually singular (`Widget`) rather than plural (`Widgets`). By implication, tables, queries, forms, and reports are plural, since they usually work with more than one record, so why restate the obvious?

■ An object's base name should include the base names of any table objects it is built on, if practical. This rule is explained later in this section.

Rules 1 and 2 also apply to the other naming convention elements: prefixes, tags, qualifiers, and suffixes. These elements should never include spaces or special characters.

You should abbreviate object base name elements wherever possible using a standardized abbreviation table. You can extend *LNC* with your own standard abbreviations as well. You should create and use standardized terminology in your applications wherever possible.

Base Name Length Limits

LNC includes some constraints and suggestions for object name lengths. You should *target* table name lengths at a 15-character maximum, for two reasons:

■ Short names (15 characters or less) fully display within the default column width of the Access query design grid.

■ Query, form, and report names usually include the base name(s) of the primary table object(s) they relate to, and will be unusably long if the table base names are long.

Beyond the 15-character target, you should *absolutely limit* table name lengths to 30 characters, which maintains compatibility with the table name length limit in SQL Server. For other objects, you should *target* a 30-character limit as well, because Access shows no more than the first 30 characters of object names in the default width of any of its lists or property grids.

Compound Base Names

The name of an object that is driven by a table must include the base name of the table. Thus, for the `tblCust` table, the primary query would be qryCust, the primary form `frmCust`, and so forth. Queries, forms, and reports that are sourced from multiple tables should reflect the base names of all the tables if it is practical. If not, you must decide which tables are the primary tables and list as many as possible in the name. Generally, in a multi-table query, form, or report, the most *important* tables are not necessarily the first and second, but more often the first and last. So, a query joining `tblCust` to `tblAddr` to `tblPhone` to get the phone numbers for customers, would be named `qryCustAddrPhone` if the address information is included in the query result, or simply `qryCustPhone` if the address information is used to join to the phone numbers and is not displayed.

Bound control base names on forms and reports are always equivalent to the base name of the bound field (the ControlSource). For example, a text box tied to the LastName field is named `txtLastName`.

Field Base Names

As a part of standardizing terminology, you should adhere to the concept of a centralized data dictionary. This principal dictates that any fields in the data structure that have the same name must have the same properties and data purpose. For example, if the LastName field in `tblCust` is of type Text 30, and holds the customer last name, any other field named LastName in the same application must have the same type, length, properties, and purpose. If your application needs last name fields for both customers and dealers, this philosophy dictates that you name them differently (such as CustLastName and DlrLastName).

Applying the centralized data dictionary principal also means that table fields do not get leading prefixes or tags, since your data dictionaries should be platform-neutral. That way, a field does not have to be renamed if data is upsized or ported to a platform with different data types. A table is still called a table in SQL Server, so moving `tblCust` there from Access would require no rename. However, if `tblCust` had a field `lngCustID` defined as a Long Integer in Access, moving the database to SQL Server would require a field rename to `intCustID`, since SQL Server uses the data type name Integer to mean the same as Access's Long Integer. Renaming fields affects all dependent objects and code, so should be avoided at all costs. You would call the field simply `CustID`.

Qualifiers and suffixes are acceptable in field names, however, because they describe the object's data purpose and not its type.

Ordering Base Name Elements

Object base name elements should be ordered from left to right with respect to their importance, readability, and desired sort order. In the example from the previous paragraph, CustLastName is a better name than LastNameCust, because the group name portion (Cust or Dlr) carries greater weight in an object's name than the specific item name (LastName or PhoneNum). Think of Cust as the name of a collection of customer-related items and this rule becomes clear—what you are really saying is that CustLastName is analogous to `Cust(LastName)` or `Cust.LastName` in *Collection.Object* terminology.

Some of you will naturally carry this example to its extreme and say that the `Customers` collection really has a `Names` collection with multiple elements, including Last, thus the representation of that idea as `Cust.Name(Last)` would lead to the field name CustNameLast instead. Such a construction model still fits within the rules of *LNC*, and there's no reason not to use it. In practice, however, such names often become fairly unreadable, even if they are accurate.

Naming Conventions for Database Objects

In Level Two of *LNC*, tags are required for all of the Access (and Jet) database objects listed in tables B.1 and B.2. Level One also recommends that you place tags on every object name, but recognizes that non-developers may prefer to save time, effort, and complexity by leaving tags off of objects where the context is obvious while viewing the Database window. Thus, Level One users are required only to place the `qry` tag on queries in order to differentiate them from tables in any combined lists, such as the "Choose the table or query..." combo box on form and report wizards. Placing tags on the other objects listed above is recommended, but optional.

> **Warning**
>
> It can be difficult to propagate name changes throughout a database, so if you are a casual user now but expect to become a developer later—and thus migrate from Level One of *LNC* to Level Two—you would be unwise to leave tags off of any object names. Use the Level One tags now on all objects.

Tags for Database Window Objects

Table B.5 lists the Level One tags for Database window objects. Note that only one tag exists for each object type.

Table B.5	Level One Database Window Object Tags		
Object	**Tag**	**Object**	**Tag**
Form	frm	Report	rpt
Macro	mcr	Subform	fsub
Module	bas	Subreport	rsub
Query	qry	Table	tbl

Though Level One is the simplified naming model, you provide tags to identify subform and subreport objects specifically. The distinction between objects and subobjects is critical for non-developers who navigate using the Database window. Since it is not appropriate to open subforms and subreports directly from the Database window, they must be clearly identified and grouped using tags.

Table B.6 lists the Level Two tags for Database window objects. Numbers in parenthesis refer to table footnotes.

Table B.6	Level Two Database Window Object Tags		
Object	**Tag**	**Object**	**Tag**
Form	frm	Query (select)	qsel
Form (class module)[1]	fcls	Query (SQL pass-through)	qspt
Form (dialog)	fdlg	Query (union)	quni
Form (lookup table)[2]	flkp	Query (update)	qupd
Form (menu/switchboard)	fmnu	Report	rpt
Form (message/alert)	fmsg	Report (detail)	rdet
Form (subform)[3]	fsub	Report (sub)[4]	rsub
Macro	mcr	Report (summary)	rsum
Macro (for form/report)	m[obj]	Table	tbl
Macro (bar menu)	mmbr	Table (attached Btrieve)	tbtv
Macro (general menu)	mmnu	Table (attached dBASE)	tdbf
Macro (shortcut menu)	mmct	Table (attached Excel)	txls
Macro (submenu/drop down)	mmsb	Table (attached Fox)	tfox

(continues)

Table B.6 Continued			
Object	**Tag**	**Object**	**Tag**
Module[4]	bas	Table (attached Lotus)	twks
Query	qry	Table (attached ODBC)	todb
Query (form/report source)	q[*obj*]	Table (attached Paradox)	tpdx
Query (append)	qapp	Table (attached SQL Server)	tsql
Query (crosstab)	qxtb	Table (attached text)	ttxt
Query (data definition)	qddl	Table (audit log)	tlog
Query (delete)	qdel	Table (lookup)[3]	tlkp
Query (form filter)	qflt	Table (many-to-many relation)	trel
Query (lookup table)[2]	qlkp	Table (summary information)	tsum
Query (make table)	quak		

[1]*Access does not implement class modules formally as an object type, as Visual Basic does.*
[2]*A lookup table has records that map short codes to full text values, like state abbreviations to states, and is used to populate combo and list boxes, validate fields, and so forth.*
[3]*A single subform or subreport may be used in several different parent objects, thus naming subobjects is not as simple as just adding _Sub to the end of the parent's base name (or some similar technique).*
[4]*You use the module tag bas to maintain consistency with the file name extension used by Visual Basic modules.*

The tags for Level Two provide rich detail about the objects and sort objects with similar attributes together. For example, lookup tables and their maintenance forms are often used over and over in multiple applications. The tags tlkp, qlkp, and flkp clearly identify these objects, making it easy for you to import them from an existing database into a new one when using the object list in Access's Import dialog. However, if a particular database does not warrant rich detail, you have generic tags to use as well (for example, qry instead of qsel).

In two special cases, the conventions prescribe a single character tag added to the front of the full object name (including the tag) of the related object. This situation occurs where: (a) a macro is created solely for a particular form or report, as in mfrmCust; and (b) a query is created solely to serve as the RecordSource property for one particular form or report, as in qfrmCust.

Tags for Form and Report Control Objects

Table B.7 lists the Level One tags for control objects on forms and reports.

Table B.7 Level One Form and Report Control Object Tags	
Control	**Tag**
Label	lbl
Other types	ctl

These Level One control tags provide no differentiation of control type other than to distinguish labels, which do not interact with the user, from controls that can display or modify data. This level of detail is not adequate for applications where VBA code will be written behind forms or reports, but can be a convenience with macro-centric applications.

Table B.8 lists the Level Two tags for control objects on forms and reports. A different tag is provided for each built-in control type. Tags also can be created for standard OLE controls. VBA code written behind forms and reports using this convention will reflect a control's type in its event procedure names (for example, cboState_AfterUpdate). The automatic sorting provided by this notation in the Access module design window can be very helpful during development. The value returned by the **TypeOf**() function for an Access control is a reflection of its class.

Tip

Make sure all control tags are three characters long so objects sort correctly.

Table B.8   Level Two Form and Report Control Object Tags

Control	Tag	TypeOf
Bound object frame	frb	BoundObjectFrame
Chart (graph)	cht	ObjectFrame
Check Box	chk	CheckBox
Combo box	cbo	ComboBox
Command button	cmd	CommandButton
Custom control	ocx	CustomControl
Image	img	Image
Label	lbl	Label
Line	lin	Line
List box	lst	ListBox
Option button	opt	OptionButton
Option group	grp	OptionGroup
Page break	brk	PageBreak
Rectangle	shp	Rectangle
Subform/Subreport	sub	Subform
Text box	txt	TextBox
Toggle button	tgl	ToggleButton
Unbound object frame	fru	ObjectFrame

Using Menu Macros

Menu macros behave differently than standard macros, thus they fall under separate guidelines when creating their names. Menu macros are either used for bar menus or for shortcut menus.

If you use the Menu Builder add-in, your custom menu macros will be assigned names when the builder saves your menu design. You will have little control over anything but the tag and base name for the primary (bar) menu. If you use the *LNC* convention of mmnu*name* for your menu macro, the builder will create an entire tree of macros beginning with the string you enter, for example:

```
mmnuMain
mmnuMain_File
mmnuMain_File_Print
```

If you prefer to create and name menus yourself, you can use a similar convention, but with more explicit tags. Bar menus should be prefixed with mmbr, sub (drop-down) menus with mmsb, and shortcut menus with mmct. Detailed tags like this help greatly when you are selecting from a list of menus to assign to the MenuBar or ShortcutMenuBar properties of a form. This convention also sorts menus by type in the Database window. The macro listing above, if produced manually rather than with the builder, would look like this:

```
mmbrMain
mmctMain_File
mmsbMain_File
mmsbMain_File_Print
```

Any saved sub menu macro can be selected as the primary object in a shortcut menu, so this convention gives you the flexibility shown here to create *component* sub menus, which can be called from both multiple bar menus and multiple shortcut menus, and thus re-used.

Creating VBA Object Base Names

When creating VBA object base names, remember that the base name must be descriptive even in the absence of its tag. For some programmers, the syntax `Dim I As Integer` for a loop variable is quite acceptable. Within *LNC*, however, the variable named *I* would become iintLoop. Single character variable names, especially without tags, are not allowed. Instead, create a list of short and standardized work variables to handle common daily needs. The following sections describe the *LNC* rules for creating VBA object base names.

Rules for Base Names

Creating VBA object base names involves following the same rules listed above for creating database object base names:

- Spaces are not allowed in any object name.

- Object names begin with a letter and should only include letters, digits, and underscores.

- Object names use mixed upper and lower case to add readability to the name.

- The only non-abbreviated syntax element that can have multiple capital letters is the base name.

- Object names are usually singular rather than plural.

■ An object's base name should include the base names of any objects it is built on, if practical.

Note that the final rule is an expanded version of the corresponding rule for database objects, which stated that table base names should propagate into names of dependent objects. In Visual Basic, that rule expands to require a reference in variable names to objects of any type that they relate to. For example, a Recordset variable created on tblCust should be named rstCust. Also, if a string array variable of part numbers astrPartNum had an Integer index variable, it should include the array's base name in its own: iaintPartNum.

Base Name Lengths

There is no *LNC* rule limiting variable name length, but common sense dictates that variable names longer than 15 or 20 characters waste a lot of keystrokes at each use. For procedure names, the VBA module editor by default shows the first 30 characters of a procedure name, so this number is suggested as the target maximum procedure name length.

Abbreviate VBA object base name elements wherever possible using a standardized abbreviation table. You can extend *LNC* by creating your own standard abbreviations as well. You should create and use standardized terminology in your applications wherever possible.

Compound Base Names

Procedure base names should follow the construction *ObjectVerb*, where the *Object* portion describes the primary object type affected (often the same as the primary argument), and *Verb* describes the action. This style sorts functions and subs by their target object when shown in ordered lists:

```
FormCtlHide
FormCtlShow
FormPropAdd
FormPropGet
FormPropSet
```

This sort order is much more appealing than the more common alternative with *VerbObject* construction:

```
AddFormProp
GetFormProp
HideFormCtl
SetFormProp
ShowFormCtl
```

Naming Conventions for VBA Objects

In Level Two of *LNC*, tags are required for the following VBA objects:

■ Variables

■ Type structures

■ Constants

Optional tags also are available for some types of procedures. By definition, if you are a Level One user, *LNC* assumes that you are not writing VBA code. If you are creating procedures, you are a Level Two user and should always apply Level Two tags and prefixes to database objects as well as VBA objects.

In the syntax diagram earlier you saw that base names are optional in some Level Two constructions. When programming in VBA in Level Two, the *tag* element is always required, but the *base name* is optional for local variables only. For example, a procedure that declared only one form object variable could legitimately use the variable name *frm*, which is a tag without a base name. Type structures, constants, and variables that have module-level or public scope must have both a tag and base name.

Tags for Variables

Visual Basic variable tags are noted in tables B.9 through B.11 below, grouped by type of variable.

Table B.9   Tags for VBA Data Variables

Variable Type	Tag	Variable Type	Tag
Boolean	bln	Integer	int
Byte	byt	Long	lng
Conditional Compilation Constant	ccc	Object	obj
Currency	cur	Single	sng
Date	dtm	String	str
Double	dbl	User-Defined Type	typ
Error	err	Variant	var

Note

Many developers use dat as a tag for date objects, but this conflicts for us with the tag for Visual Basic's Data control.

In the preceding table, note that Conditional Compilation Constant, Error, and User-Defined Type are not true data types (created with **Dim** *Name* **As** *Datatype*), but rather programming concepts. A Conditional Compilation Constant variable is a flag of type **Boolean**, an Error variable is a **Variant** created with the **CVErr()** function, and user-defined types are unique constructs. Table B.10 lists examples of tabs for VBA object variables.

Table B.10 Tags for VBA Object Variables			
Object	**Tag**	**Object**	**Tag**
Access.Application	acca	Graph.Application	gpha
Application	app	Graph.Chart	gphc
Collection	col	GroupLevel	lvl
Control	<u>ctl</u>	MSProject.Application	prja
Controls	ctls	MSProject.Project	prjp
CustomControl	ocx	PowerPoint.Application	ppta
CustomControlInReport	ocx	Report	<u>rpt</u>
Excel.Application	xlsa	Reports	rpts
Excel.Chart	xlsc	SchedulePlus.Application	scda
Excel.Sheet	xlsw	Word.Application	wrda
Form	<u>frm</u>	Word.Basic	wrdb
Forms	frms		

Note

Tags for PowerPoint.Application and Word.Application are reserved for future use.

Table B.10 mixes entry points for OLE automation server objects, like Excel worksheets and Project projects, with objects internal to Access, such as collections. While all of these items are *objects*, the two object types are treated differently in code.

Variables for objects in the Access object hierarchy can be dimensioned directly by class, as in this line:

```
Dim colFrmBldr As Collection
```

OLE Automation variables are created and used with a different syntax, as in this example:

```
Dim oxlsa As Object
Set oxlsa = CreateObject("Excel.Application")
```

The naming convention for entry points into OLE Automation server applications follows this syntax:

```
applicationtag entrypoint
```

where *applicationtag* is three characters and *entrypoint* is a single character. See the section "Creating Your Own Tags" later in this appendix for a complete explanation of this syntax. Note also that OLE Automation object variables are prefixed with o, as described in the "Prefixes for Variables" section that follows. Table B.11 lists the *LNC* tags for Access DAO (data access object) variables.

Table B.11 Tags for Data Access Object Variables

Object	Tag	Object	Tag
Container	con	QueryDef (Paradox)	qpdx
Containers	cons	QueryDef (SQL Server)	qsql
DBEngine	dbe	QueryDef (Text)	qtxt
Database (any type)	dbs	QueryDefs	qdfs
Database (Btrieve)	dbtv	Recordset (any type)	rst
Database (dBASE)	ddbf	Recordset (Btrieve)	rbtv
Database (Excel)	dxls	Recordset (dBASE)	rdbf
Database (FoxPro)	dfox	Recordset (dynaset)	rdyn
Database (Jet)	djet	Recordset (Excel)	rxls
Database (Lotus)	dwks	Recordset (Fox)	rfox
Database (ODBC)	dodb	Recordset (Lotus)	rwks
Database (Paradox)	dpdx	Recordset (ODBC)	rodb
Database (SQL Server)	dsql	Recordset (Paradox)	rpdx
Database (Text)	dtxt	Recordset (snapshot)	rsnp
Databases	dbss	Recordset (SQL Server)	rsql
Document	doc	Recordset (table)	rtbl
Documents	docs	Recordset (text)	rtxt
Dynaset	dyn	Recordsets	rsts
Error	err	Relation	rel
Errors	errs	Relations	rels
Field	fld	Snapshot	snp
Fields	flds	Table	tbl
Group	gru	TableDef (any type)	tdf
Groups	grus	TableDef (Btrieve)	tbtv
Index	idx	TableDef (dBASE)	tdbf
Indexes	idxs	TableDef (Excel)	txls
Parameter	prm	TableDef (FoxPro)	tfox
Parameters	prms	TableDef (Jet)	tjet
Property	prp	TableDef (Lotus)	twks
Properties	prps	TableDef (ODBC)	todb
QueryDef (any type)	qdf	TableDef (Paradox)	tpdx
QueryDef (Btrieve)	qbtv	TableDef (SQL Server)	tsql
QueryDef (dBASE)	qdbf	TableDef (Text)	ttxt
QueryDef (Excel)	qxls	TableDefs	tdfs
QueryDef (FoxPro)	qfox	User	usr
QueryDef (Jet)	qjet	Users	usrs
QueryDef (Lotus)	qwks	Workspace	wsp
QueryDef (ODBC)	qodb	Workspaces	wsps

In tables B.10 and B.11, tags for collection variables are made by adding s after the tag for the object type stored in the collection. The tags dyn, snp, and tbl above for Dynaset, Snapshot, and Table objects are directly relevant to users of Access 1.x and Access 2.0. Starting with Access 95, these object types are allowed only as a subtype of recordset variables, thus the recordset tags rdyn, rsnp, and rtbl.

Note

Although you saw earlier that a tag by itself is a legitimate variable name, a few variable tags shown (such as int) are VBA reserved words and will not compile in your procedures. Such tags require a base name.

Prefixes for Variables

The prefixes for Visual Basic variables can be categorized into two groups: prefixes for scope, and all other prefixes. Since the model for variable scope has changed somewhat in Access 95, you examine scope prefixes first. The prefixes in the following list are ordered by increasing (broader) scope:

- No Prefix. Use no prefix for variables that are local to a procedure.

- s. Place this prefix before variables that are declared locally to a procedure with a Static statement.

- m. Use this prefix for module-level variables that are declared with Dim or Private statements in the Declarations section of a module.

- p. Use this prefix to denote variables declared as Public in the Declarations section of a form or report module. Such variables are publicly available to other procedures in the same database only.

- g. Use this prefix to denote variables declared as Public in the Declarations section of a standard module. Such variables are truly global and may be referenced from procedures in the current or other databases.

When used, scope prefixes always begin a variable name and precede any other prefixes.

In addition to scope, there are other characteristics of variables that can be identified by prefixes, as in the following list:

- a. Use this prefix to denote a variable that is declared as an array, including a ParamArray argument to a function.

- c. This prefix is placed before constants defined by the user.

- e. Use this prefix for a variable that is an element of a collection. Such variables are usually part of a **For Each**... loop structure.

- i. Use this prefix to denote a variable (usually of type **Integer**) that serves as an index into an array or an index counter in a **For**...**Next** loop.

- o. This prefix is placed before object variables that reference OLE Automation servers, where the tag denotes the type of server.

- r. Use this prefix for variables that are arguments (parameters) passed in to a procedure and declared **ByRef**, or not declared as either **ByRef** or **ByVal** (including a ParamArray), which implies **ByRef**.

- t. Use this prefix to describe a variable that is declared as a user-defined **Type** structure.

- v. Use this prefix for variables that are arguments (parameters) passed in to a procedure and declared **ByVal**.

A prefix provides a very detailed description of a variable, so the number of allowable prefix combinations is limited, as shown in table B.12.

Table B.12 Allowable Prefix Combinations	
Any One of These...	**...Can Come Before This**
s, m, p, g, r, v	a
m, p, g	c
s, m, p, g, r, v	e
s, m, p, g, r, v	i
s, m, p, g, r, v	ia
s, m, p, g, r, v	o
m, p, g	t

Variables require a unique prefix when declared **Public** in a widely distributed application to prevent name contentions. See the later "Tags and Prefixes for Procedures" section for more information.

Naming Constants

Access 95 introduces sweeping changes in the area of constants. The changes most relevant to naming conventions include these:

- A constant can now be assigned a data type when it is defined.

- All Access constants have been renamed and carry a tag of ac, db, or vb to identify their primary functional area, Access, Jet, or VBA, respectively.

- Constants can now be created with the **Variant** data type.

When creating constants, use a scope prefix (if appropriate), the prefix c, and the suitable tag for the constant's data type. To properly synchronize the tag and the data type, do not let Access assign the type; always use the full **Const**NameAs**Datatype** syntax.

Constants require a unique prefix when declared **Public** in a widely distributed application to prevent name contention. See the following sections for more information on name contention.

Tags and Prefixes for Procedures

Whether and how to prefix and tag procedure names is a debatable subject. In general, this style neither requires nor encourages placing characters before a procedure name except in the following situations.

Prefixes for Procedures. Procedures can have scope similar to that of variables: s (`Static`), m (`Private`), p (`Public`), or g (global `Public`). *LNC* supports the use of these scope prefixes on function names if they: (a) solve a particular need, and (b) are used consistently throughout an application.

If you are creating software for retail sale, for inclusion in the public domain, or that will be broadly distributed in some other manner, *LNC* requires that you prefix `Public` variables, constants, and procedures with a unique author prefix identifying you or your company. The prefix consists of two or three unique characters and an underscore, and prevents your object names from conflicting with object names in other referenced or referencing databases on a user's machine.

To create an author prefix, use your personal or company initials. For example, author prefixes for my companies are lci for Leszynski Company, Inc., and kwc for Kwery Corporation. Before using your selected prefix, make an effort to determine if the prefix is already widely in use. Kwery Corporation maintains a registry of VBA prefixes for Office add-in vendors.

Tags for Procedures. The *LNC* style prescribes the following naming convention tags for procedures:

- cbf. Use this tag on procedure names for code behind a form or report. This tag clearly differentiates such procedures from **Property** procedures and event procedures.

- prp. Use this tag on **Property** procedure names defined with **Property Get**, **Property Let**, and **Property Set** statements. This tag clearly differentiates such procedures from functions, sub procedures, and event procedures.

LNC does not require or suggest assigning a data type tag to functions to reflect their return value. However, if you have a specific need to tag procedures to reflect their return value type, use the appropriate tags from the preceding "Tags for Variables" section and apply the tags consistently to all procedures in an application.

Using Macros Instead of VBA

Occasionally, you might have a good reason for using macros to create action scripts. If so, apply the rules previously described for VBA procedure base names to your macro base names. Macro groups in the Database window should also utilize the macro prefixes and tags noted above. Individual macros within a macro group do not have prefixes or tags, except for event macros as noted later.

All macros for a specific form or report should be placed into one macro group, with the form or report name as the macro base name. Within the macro group, create standard macros and event macros for the form or report. If a macro is tied to a form or report event, show the event name or an abbreviation in the macro name. For example, you would store macros related to frmCust in macro group mfrmCust. Event macro names in the group might include Form_Current and txtLastName_Change.

Macros that are not specific to a form or report should hold actions that have some common functionality or purpose. Use the same grouping methodology (related items together) that you would apply to locate procedures in standard VBA modules.

VBA Object Name Examples

Table B.13 shows examples of VBA variables applying the various conventions in this section.

Table B.13 VBA Variable Name Examples	
Declaration	**Description**
Dim oxlsaBudget **As Object**	Excel.Application
Function lci_ArraySum (**ParamArray** _ ravarNum() **As Variant**) **As Double**	Company identifier
Public giaintPartNum **As Integer**	Global index into array
Const clngCustNumMax **As Long** = 10000	**Const** for maximum value of CustID
Function FileLock(**ByVal** vstrFile **As** _ **String**) **As Integer**	**ByVal** argument

Creating Your Own Tags

What do you do when *LNC* doesn't address a particular object naming need? First, contact Kwery Corporation with an explanation of your need, so that the *LNC* style can be improved for the benefit of all users. Second, consider if what you are trying to do is covered by the style in some other way. For example, in your development team you call tables that link two other tables in a many-to-many relationship *linking* tables, and you want to create a new table tag *tlnk* as a result. However, on examination of all table tags, you would find trel already exists, defined as "Table (many-to-many relation)," which is the correct tag for what you need. Even though the nomenclature is not exactly what you require, it is better to use an existing tag than create another one.

Finally, when other options are exhausted, you can create a custom tag to address your need. When creating a custom tag, these should be your guidelines:

- ■ Do not redefine an existing tag. No matter how badly you really want the three- or four-character combination for your own purpose, never re-use a defined tag.

- ■ Do not change the rule for tags. Stay within the three- to four-character range followed by *LNC*.

- ■ Use the conventions in existing tags as your guide for the new one. For example, all table tags start with *t*, all query tags with *q*, and so forth. Any new tags you make for these objects should begin with the correct letter. See table B.14 for guidelines on standard tag components. Note that some of the examples are from the

Office version of *LNC*. Tag components that can be easily inferred from the preceeding tags are not listed in the table (for example, the component fox for FoxPro can be inferred from the tags tfox and dfox.)

When creating a new tag, it should be mnemonic enough to uniquely shorten the word it represents, and should only use characters from the root word or a generally accepted shorthand.

Table B.14   Some Standard Tag Components

Item	Segment	Examples	Location
bar	br	mmbr, pbr, tbr	anywhere
data/databound	d	dout	leading
database	db	dbe	leading
form	f	fdlg	leading
macro	m	mmnu	leading
MAPI	mp	mpm	leading
module	b	bas	leading
query	q	qsel	leading
report	r	rdet	leading
set	st	rst	anywhere
table	t	tdf	leading
view	vw	lvw, tvw	anywhere

To create tags for object variables pointing to OLE Automation server applications, start with the three-character DOS file extension for the files created by the server application, if unique and applicable. If not unique, create a meaningful abbreviation of the application name. Add to the three-character abbreviation a single character for the actual object that serves as the entry point for the application, such as Basic in Word.Basic.

For example, to create a tag for OLE Automation with Shapeware's Visio program, which is an OLE server, use either vsd (the data file extension) or vis (a mnemonic for Visio) as the basis for the tag, then add a for Application, because the entry point to Visio's automation engine is a call to Visio.Application. Thus the tag and its use in variable declarations would appear as:

```
Dim ovisa As Object
Dim ovisaDoc As Object
Set ovisa = CreateObject("Visio.Application")
Set ovisaDoc = ovisa.Documents.Open("C:\VISIO\HOUSE.VSD")
```

How to Get the Complete Text of the *LNCs*

The full text of the *Leszynski Naming Conventions for Microsoft Access* and an expanded discussion of the naming convention philosophy appears in *Access Expert Solutions* by Stan Leszynski (Que Books, 1995, ISBN 0-7897-0367-X). You also can obtain the full text of the *Leszynski Naming Conventions for Microsoft Access*, on which this abridged appendix is based, from Kwery Corporation. The following additional information is also available:

the *Leszynski Naming Conventions for Microsoft Solution Developers* paper, the *Leszynski Naming Conventions for Microsoft Visual Basic* paper, Windows Help file versions of each *LNC* document, and *LNC* programmers' tools. Contact Kwery via the order line at 1-800-ATKWERY, or on the product information line at 206-644-7830. Kwery also can be reached on CompuServe at 71573,3261 or by fax at 206-644-8409.

Appendix C

Data Dictionary for the Personnel Actions Table

You use the Personnel Actions table in examples in the following chapters:

The step-by-step procedures for creating the Personnel Actions table and adding the first nine records to the table are included in Chapter 4, "Working with Access Databases and Tables."

Tables C.1 through C.5 provide a tabular data dictionary for the Personnel Actions table.

Table C.1 lists the values of the `FieldName`, `Caption`, `DataType`, `FieldSize`, and `Format` properties of the Personnel Actions table. These values are entered in the Properties text boxes for each field.

Table C.1 Field Properties for the Personnel Actions Table				
Field Name	**Caption**	**Data Type**	**Field Size**	**Format**
paID	ID	Number	Long Integer	General Number
paType	Type	Text	1	@> (all caps)
paInitiatedBy	Initiated By	Number	Integer	General Number
paScheduledDate	Scheduled	Date/Time	N/A	Short Date
paApprovedBy	Approved By	Number	Integer	General Number
paEffectiveDate	Effective	Date/Time	N/A	Short Date
paRating	Rating	Number	Integer	General Number
paAmount	Amount	Currency	N/A	##,##0.00#
paComments	Comments	Memo	N/A	None

Table C.2 lists the entries you make to assign default values to each field for which default values are required. You enter these values in the Default Values text box of the indicated field.

Table C.2 Default Field Values for the Personnel Actions Table		
Field Name	**Default Value**	**Comments**
paType	Q	Quarterly performance reviews are the most common personnel action
paScheduledDate	=Date()	The expression to enter today's (DOS) date
paEffectiveDate	=Date() +28	Four weeks from today's date

Table C.3 lists the values you enter as Validation Rules and the accompanying Validation text that is displayed in the status bar if an entry violates one of the rules. Only those fields with validation rules are shown in table C.3.

Table C.3 Validation Criteria for Fields of the Personnel Actions Table		
Field Name	**Validation Rule**	**Validation Text**
paID	>0	Please enter a valid employee ID number.
paType	"H" Or "S" Or "Q" Or "C" Or "Y" Or "B"	Only H, S, Q, Y, B, and C codes may be entered.
paInitiatedBy	>0	Please enter a valid supervisor ID number.
paScheduledDate	Between Date()-3650 And Date()+365	Scheduled dates cannot be more than 10 years ago nor more than 1 year from now.
paApprovedBy	>0 Or Is Null	Please enter a valid manager ID number or leave blank if not approved.
paRating	Between 0 And 9 Or Is Null	Rating range is 0 for terminated employees, 1 to 9, or blank.

Table C.4 lists the key fields, indexes, and relationships for the Personnel Actions table. A composite key field is used so that duplication of an entry of a record for an employee is precluded. The default index that Access creates on the primary key field is shown for completeness; you do not add this index because Access creates indexes on key fields automatically. You establish the relationship with the Employees table by opening the Database window, choosing Tools, Relationships, and making the selections that are listed for the Relationships property in table C.4 in the Relationships dialog.

Table C.4 Key Fields, Indexes, and Relationships for the Personnel Actions Table	
Property	**Value**
Primary Key Fields	paID;paType;paScheduledDate
Primary Key Index	paID;paType;paScheduledDate
Relationships	Primary table: Employees Related table: Personnel Actions Enforce Referential Integrity: True (checked) Cascade Deletions: True (checked) Cascade Updates: True (checked)

Table C.5 lists the first nine entries in the Personnel Actions table that are used to demonstrate use of the table. The Scheduled and Effective entries are based on the HiredDate information in the Employees table. Enter these values after you have created the composite primary key for the table. Assigning performance ratings (except 0, terminated) to the records is optional.

Table C.5 First Nine Entries for the Personnel Actions Table							
ID	Type	Initiated By	Scheduled	Approved By	Effective Date	New Amount	Comments
1	H	1	01-May-92		01-May-92	2,000	Hired
2	H	1	14-Aug-92		14-Aug-92	3,500	Hired
3	H	1	01-Apr-92		01-Apr-92	2,250	Hired
4	H	2	03-May-93	2	03-May-93	2,250	Hired
5	H	2	17-Oct-93	2	17-Oct-93	2,500	Hired
6	H	5	17-Oct-93	2	17-Oct-93	4,000	Hired
7	H	5	02-Jan-94	2	02-Jan-94	3,000	Hired
8	H	2	05-Mar-94	2	05-Mar-94	2,500	Hired
9	H	5	15-Nov-94	2	15-Nov-94	3,000	Hired

Index

Symbols

, (comma) placeholder, 125
! (exclamation point)
    identifier operator, 289
    separator, 1211
(pound sign) placeholder,
    125
$ (dollar sign) placeholder,
    125
% (percent sign) placeholder,
    125
& (ampersand)
    concatenation operator, 168,
        289, 1188
    placeholder, 125
^ (caret) arithmetic operator,
    287
* (asterisk)
    arithmetic operator, 287
    placeholder, 126
    table records, 62
    wild card character, 290
+ (plus sign)
    arithmetic operator, 287
    concatenation operator,
        1188
- (minus sign) arithmetic
    operator, 287
. (period)
    identifier operator, 289
    placeholder, 125
    separator, 1211
\ (backslash)
    arithmetic operator, 287
    placeholder, 125
: (colon) placeholder, 125
< (less than sign)
    comparison operator, 288
    placeholder, 126

<= (less than or equal to sign)
    comparison operator, 288
<> (not equal sign)
    comparison operator, 288
= (equal sign) comparison
    operator, 288
> (greater than sign)
    comparison operator, 288
    placeholder, 126
>= (greater than or equal to
    sign) comparison operator,
    288
? (question mark) wild card
    character, 290
@ (at sign) placeholder, 125
\ (escape character), 128
    arithmetic operator, 287
0 (zero) placeholder, 125
1 Database command
    (Windows menu), 154
32-bit OLE 2.1, 23, 48-51
    compliant applications,
        707-708
32-bit Windows API Viewer,
    1130-1132

A

Abs( ) function, 302
accelerator key, defined, 1181
Access 1.x files
    converting to Access 95,
        1173-1178
    importing, 1174-1178
    splitting, 1172-1173
Access 2.0 files
    converting to Access 95, 52,
        1173-1178
    importing, 1174-1178

    running, limitations,
        1170-1172
    splitting, 1172-1173
Access 95
    as DDE server, 1108-1113
    as OLE Automation server,
        1098-1100
    comparisons between
        runtime and retail
        versions, 1118-1120
    converting 2.0 applications
        to, 52
    installation, network
        environment, 904-905
    naming conventions
        (Leszynski Naming
        Conventions)
        list, 1239
        objectives, 1220-1221
        objects, 1221-1224
    new features
        32-bit OLE 2.1, 23, 48-51
        briefcase replication, 23,
            47-48
        Database Splitter (add-in),
            23, 31-3
        Database Wizard, 29-31
        Developer's Toolkit, 23,
            52-53
        Filter by Form searches,
            23, 43-46
        Filter by Selection
            searches, 23, 43-46
        Import/Export Wizard, 23
        lookup fields, 23, 42-43
        Macro to VBA Code
            Converter (add-in),
            34-35
        multithreaded
            multitasking, 22

O

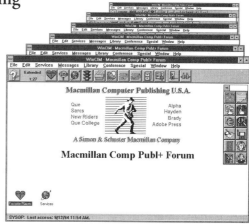

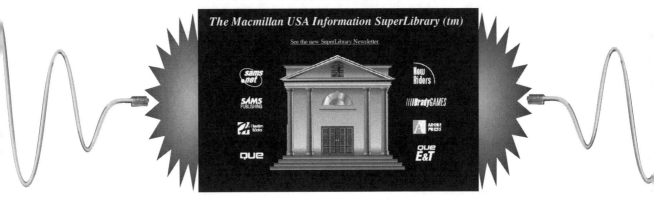

Complete and Return this Card
for a *FREE* Computer Book Catalog

Thank you for purchasing this book! You have purchased a superior computer book written expressly for your needs. To continue to provide the kind of up-to-date, pertinent coverage you've come to expect from us, we need to hear from you. Please take a minute to complete and return this self-addressed, postage-paid form. In return, we'll send you a free catalog of all our computer books on topics ranging from word processing to programming and the internet.

r. ☐   Mrs. ☐   Ms. ☐   Dr. ☐

ame (first) ⬚⬚⬚⬚⬚⬚⬚⬚⬚⬚⬚⬚ (M.I.) ☐ (last) ⬚⬚⬚⬚⬚⬚⬚⬚⬚⬚⬚

ddress ⬚⬚⬚⬚⬚⬚⬚⬚⬚⬚⬚⬚⬚⬚⬚⬚⬚⬚⬚⬚⬚⬚⬚

⬚⬚⬚⬚⬚⬚⬚⬚⬚⬚⬚⬚⬚⬚⬚⬚⬚⬚⬚⬚⬚⬚⬚

ty ⬚⬚⬚⬚⬚⬚⬚⬚⬚⬚ State ☐☐ Zip ⬚⬚⬚⬚ ⬚⬚⬚

one ☐☐☐☐ Fax ☐☐☐ ☐☐☐☐

mpany Name ⬚⬚⬚⬚⬚⬚⬚⬚⬚⬚⬚⬚⬚⬚⬚⬚⬚⬚⬚⬚

mail address ⬚⬚⬚⬚⬚⬚⬚⬚⬚⬚⬚⬚⬚⬚⬚⬚⬚⬚⬚⬚⬚⬚

Please check at least (3) influencing factors for purchasing this book.

ont or back cover information on book .... ☐
ecial approach to the content .... ☐
mpleteness of content .... ☐
thor's reputation .... ☐
blisher's reputation .... ☐
ok cover design or layout .... ☐
lex or table of contents of book .... ☐
ce of book .... ☐
ecial effects, graphics, illustrations .... ☐
her (Please specify): _____ ☐

How did you first learn about this book?

w in Macmillan Computer Publishing catalog .... ☐
commended by store personnel .... ☐
w the book on bookshelf at store .... ☐
commended by a friend .... ☐
ceived advertisement in the mail .... ☐
w an advertisement in: _____ ☐
ad book review in: _____ ☐
her (Please specify): _____ ☐

How many computer books have you purchased in the last six months?

s book only .... ☐   3 to 5 books .... ☐
ooks .... ☐   More than 5 .... ☐

4. Where did you purchase this book?

Bookstore .... ☐
Computer Store .... ☐
Consumer Electronics Store .... ☐
Department Store .... ☐
Office Club .... ☐
Warehouse Club .... ☐
Mail Order .... ☐
Direct from Publisher .... ☐
Internet site .... ☐
Other (Please specify): _____ ☐

5. How long have you been using a computer?

☐ Less than 6 months   ☐ 6 months to a year
☐ 1 to 3 years   ☐ More than 3 years

6. What is your level of experience with personal computers and with the subject of this book?

	With PCs	With subject of book
New	☐	☐
Casual	☐	☐
Accomplished	☐	☐
Expert	☐	☐

Source Code ISBN:0-7897-0184-7

7. Which of the following best describes your job title?

Administrative Assistant .... ☐
Coordinator .... ☐
Manager/Supervisor .... ☐
Director .... ☐
Vice President .... ☐
President/CEO/COO .... ☐
Lawyer/Doctor/Medical Professional .... ☐
Teacher/Educator/Trainer .... ☐
Engineer/Technician .... ☐
Consultant .... ☐
Not employed/Student/Retired .... ☐
Other (Please specify): _____ ☐

8. Which of the following best describes the area of the company your job title falls under?

Accounting .... ☐
Engineering .... ☐
Manufacturing .... ☐
Operations .... ☐
Marketing .... ☐
Sales .... ☐
Other (Please specify): _____ ☐

9. What is your age?

Under 20 .... ☐
21-29 .... ☐
30-39 .... ☐
40-49 .... ☐
50-59 .... ☐
60-over .... ☐

10. Are you:

Male .... ☐
Female .... ☐

11. Which computer publications do you read regularly? (Please list)

_____
_____
_____
_____
_____
_____
_____
_____
_____

Comments: _____
_____
_____

Fold here and scotch-tape to mail.